G000145101

admirador _m_, **~a** _f_ admire...
campeón _m_, **-ona** _f_ cham...
salvapantallas _m inv_ INF ... saver
ronquido _m_ snore; **~s** _pl_ s...
enemigo 1 _adj_ enemy _atr_ **ser ~ de** _fig_ be opposed t...
lleno _adj_ full (**de** of); _pa..._ (**de** with)

debatir <3a> **1** _v/t_ debate, discuss **2** _v/i_ struggle **3** _v/r_ **~se: ~se entre la vida y la muerte** fight for one's life

Division de artículo en categorías gramaticales

Entries divided into grammatical categories

uva _f_ BOT grape; **estar de mala ~** F be in a foul mood; **tener mala ~** F be a nasty piece of work
fiambre _m_ cold cut, _Br_ cold meat; P (_cadáver_) stiff P
profiláctico 1 _adj_ preventive, prophylactic _fml_ **2** _m_ condom

Marcas de registro

Register labels

acomedido _adj_ _L.Am._ obliging, helpful; **acomedirse** <3l> _v/r_ _Méx_ offer to help
residencial 1 _adj_ residential **2** _f_ _Arg_, _Chi_ boarding house
sablear <1a> _v/t_ & _v/i_ _L.Am._ F scrounge (**a** from)

Español latinoamericano

Latin American Spanish

riñonera _f_ fanny pack, _Br_ bum bag
rotonda _f_ traffic circle, _Br_ roundabout

Variantes del inglés británico

British variants

A B C D E F G H I J K L M N Ñ O P Q R S T U V W X Y Z

Spanish
Compact Dictionary

Spanish – English
Inglés – Español

Berlitz Publishing

New York · Munich · Singapore

Original edition edited by the Langenscheidt editorial staff

Compiled by LEXUS Ltd.

Book in cover photo: © Punchstock/Medioimages

Berlitz Publishing
193 Morris Avenue
Springfield, NJ 07081
USA

Printed in Germany
ISBN 978-981-268-648-0

(98273)

13 12 11 10 09

3. 4. 5.

Preface

Here is a new dictionary of English and Spanish, a tool with some 50,000 references for those who work with the English and Spanish languages at beginner's or intermediate level.

Focusing on modern usage, the dictionary offers coverage of everyday language – and this means including vocabulary from areas such as computer use and business. English means both American and British English; Spanish means both Latin American and European Spanish.

The editors have provided a reference tool to enable the user to get straight to the translation that fits a particular context of use. Indicating words are given to identify senses. Is the *mouse* you need for your computer, for example, the same in Spanish as the *mouse* you don't want in the house? Is *flimsy* referring to furniture the same in Spanish as *flimsy* referring to an excuse? This dictionary is rich in sense distinctions like this – and in translation options tied to specific, identified senses.

Vocabulary needs grammar to back it up. So in this dictionary you'll find irregular verb forms, in both English and Spanish, irregular English plural forms, guidance on Spanish feminine endings and on prepositional usage with verbs.

Since some vocabulary items are often only clearly understood when contextualized, a large number of idiomatic phrases are given to show how the two languages correspond in particular contexts.

All in all, this is a book full of information, which will, we hope, become a valuable part of your language toolkit.

Contents

How to use the dictionary

To get the most out of your dictionary you should understand how and where to find the information you need. Whether you are yourself writing text in a foreign language or wanting to understand text that has been written in a foreign language, the following pages should help.

1. How and where do I find a word?

1.1 Spanish and English headwords The word list for each language is arranged in alphabetical order and also gives irregular forms of verbs and nouns in their correct alphabetical order.

Sometimes you might want to look up terms made up of two separate words, for example **shooting star**, or hyphenated words, for example **absent-minded** These words are treated as though they were a single word and their alphabetical ordering reflects this.

The only exception to this strict alphabetical ordering is made for English phrasal verbs - words like **go off, go out, go up** These are positioned in a block directly after their main verb (in this case **go**), rather than being scattered around in alphabetical positions.

Spanish words beginning with **ch** and **ll** are positioned in their alphabetical position in letters C and L. Words beginning with **ñ** are listed after N.

1.2 Spanish feminine headwords are shown as follows:

> **abogado** *m*, **-a** *f* lawyer
> **fumador** *m*, **~a** *f* smoker
> **bailarín** *m*, **-ina** *f* dancer
> **pibe** *m*, **-a** *f Rpl* F kid F
> **edil** *m*, **~a** *f* council(l)or

The feminine forms of these headwords are: **abogada**, **fumadora**, **bailarina**, **piba** and **edila**.

When a Spanish headword has a feminine form which translates differently from the masculine form, the feminine is entered as a separate headword in alphabetical order:

> **empresaria** *f* businesswoman; **empresario** *m* businessman

1.3 Running heads

If you are looking for a Spanish or English word you can use the **running heads** printed in bold in the top corner of each page. The running head on the left tells you the *first* headword (either blue or black) on the left-hand page and the one on the right tells you the *last* headword (either blue or black) on the right-hand page.

1.4 How is the word spelt?

You can look up the spelling of a word in your dictionary in the same way as you would in a spelling dictionary. British spelling variants are marked *Br.* If just a single letter is omitted in the American spelling, this is put between round brackets:

colo(u)r – hono(u)r – travel(l)er

2. How do I split a word?

Spanish speakers find English hyphenation very difficult. All you have to do with this dictionary is look for the bold dots between syllables. These dots show you where you can split a word at the end of a line but you should avoid having just one letter before or after the hyphen as in a•mend or thirst•y. In such cases it is better to take the entire word over to the next line.

3. Swung dashes and long dashes

3.1 A swung dash (~) replaces the entire headword, when the headword is repeated within an entry:

face [feɪs] **1** *n* cara *f*; **~ to ~** cara a cara

Here **~ to ~** means **face to face**.

rencor *m* resentment; **guardar ~ a alguien** bear s.o. a grudge

Here **guardar ~ a alguien** means **guardar rencor a alguien**.

3.2 When a headword changes form in an entry, for example if it is put in the past tense or in the plural, then the past tense or plural ending is added to the swung dash – but only if the rest of the word doesn't change:

flame [fleɪm] *n* llama *f*; **go up in ~s** ser pasto de las llamas
parch [pɑːrtʃ] *v/t* secar; **be ~ed** F *of person* estar muerto de sed F

But:

sur•vive [sərˈvaɪv] **1** *v/i* sobrevivir; **how are you? – I'm surviving** ¿cómo estás? – voy tirando
saltón *adj*: **ojos saltones** bulging eyes

3.3 Double headwords are replaced by a single swung dash:

Pan•a•ma Ca'nal *n*: **the ~** el Canal de Panamá
one-track 'mind *hum*: **have a ~** ser un obseso

3.4 In the Spanish-English part of the dictionary, when a headword is repeated in a phrase or compound with an altered form, a long dash is used:

escaso *adj* ... **-as posibilidades de** not much chance of, little chance of

Here **-as posibilidades** means **escasas posibilidades**.

4. What do the different typefaces mean?

4.1 All Spanish and English headwords and the Arabic numerals differentiating between parts of speech appear in **bold**:

> **neoyorquino 1** *adj* New York *atr* **2** *m*, **-a** New Yorker
> **splin·ter** ['splɪntər] **1** *n* astilla *f* **2** *v/i* astillarse

4.2 *Italics* are used for:

a) abbreviated grammatical labels: *adj, adv, v/i, v/t* etc

b) gender labels: *m, f, mpl* etc

c) all the indicating words which are the signposts pointing to the correct translation for your needs:

> **sport·y** ['spɔːrtɪ] *adj person* deportista; *clothes* deportivo
> ◆ **work out 1** *v/t problem, puzzle* resolver; *solution* encontrar, hallar
>   **2** *v/i at gym* hacer ejercicios; *of relationship etc* funcionar, ir bien
> **completo** *adj* complete; *autobús, teatro* full
> **grano** *m* grain; *de café* bean; *en la piel* pimple, spot

4.3 All phrases (examples and idioms) are given in ***secondary bold italics***:

> **sym·pa·thet·ic** [sɪmpə'θetɪk] *adj* (*showing pity*) compasivo;
>   (*understanding*) comprensivo; ***be ~ toward a person/ an idea***
>   simpatizar con una persona / idea
> **salsa** *f* GASTR sauce; *baile* salsa; ***en su ~*** *fig* in one's element

4.4 The normal typeface is used for the translations.

4.5 If a translation is given in italics, and not in the normal typeface, this means that the translation is more of an *explanation* in the other language and that an explanation has to be given because there just is no real equivalent:

> **'walk-up** *n apartamento en un edificio sin ascensor*
> **adobera** *f Méx type of mature cheese*

5. Stress

To indicate where to put the **stress** in English words, the stress marker ' appears before the syllable on which the main stress falls:

> **mo·tif** [mou'tiːf] motivo *m*
> **rec·ord**[1] ['rekɔːrd] *n* MUS disco *m*; SP etc récord *m*
> **re·cord**[2] [rɪ'kɔːrd] *v/t electronically* grabar; *in writing* anotar

Stress is shown either in the pronunciation or, if there is no pronunciation given, in the actual headword or compound itself:

> **'rec·ord hold·er** plusmarquista *m/f*

6. What do the various symbols and abbreviations tell you?

6.1 A solid blue diamond is used to indicate a phrasal verb:

> ♦ **call off** *v/t* (*cancel*) cancelar; *strike* desconvocar

6.2 A white diamond is used to divide up longer entries into more easily digested chunks of related bits of text:

> **de** *prp* ◊ *origen* from; ~ **Nueva York** from New York; ~ **... a** from ... to ◊ *posesión* of; **el coche ~ mi amigo** my friend's car ◊ *material* (made) of; **un anillo ~ oro** a gold ring ◊ *contenido* of; **un vaso ~ agua** a glass of water ◊ *cualidad*: **una mujer ~ 20 años** a 20 year old woman ◊ *causa* with; **temblaba ~ miedo** she was shaking with fear ...

6.3 The abbreviation F tells you that the word or phrase is used colloquially rather than in formal contexts. The abbreviation V warns you that a word or phrase is vulgar or taboo. Words or phrases labeled P are slang. Be careful how you use these words.

These abbreviations, F, V and P, are used both for headwords and phrases (placed after) and for the translations of headwords and phrases (placed after). If there is no such label given, then the word or phrase is neutral.

6.4 A colon before an English or Spanish word or phrase means that usage is restricted to this specific example (at least as far as this dictionary's translation is concerned):

> **catch-22** [kætʃtwentɪˈtuː]: **it's a ~ situation** es como la pescadilla que se muerde la cola
> **co-au-thor** [ˈkoʊɒːθər] ... **2** *v/t*: **~ a book** escribir un libro conjuntamente
> **decantarse** <1a> *v/r*: **~ por** opt for

7. Does the dictionary deal with grammar too?

7.1 All English headwords are given a part of speech label:

> **tooth·less** [ˈtuːθlɪs] *adj* desdentado
> **top·ple** [ˈtɑːpl] **1** *v/i* derrumbarse **2** *v/t government* derrocar

But if a headword can only be used as a noun (in ordinary English) then no part of speech is given, since none is needed:

> **'tooth·paste** pasta *f* de dientes, dentífrico *m*

7.2 Spanish headwords have part of speech labels. Spanish gender markers are given:

> **barbacoa** *f* barbecue
> **bocazas** *m/f inv* F loudmouth F
> **budista** *m/f & adj* Buddhist

7.3 If an English translation of an Spanish adjective can only be used in front of a noun, and not after it, this is marked with *atr*:

> **bursátil** *adj* stock market *atr*
> **campestre** *adj* rural, country *atr*

7.4 If the Spanish, unlike the English, doesn't change form if used in the plural, this is marked with *inv*:

> **cortacircuitos** *m inv* circuit breaker
> **metrópolis** *f inv* metropolis

7.5 If the English, in spite of appearances, is not a plural form, this is marked with *nsg*:

> **bil·li·ards** ['bɪljərdz] *nsg* billar *m*
> **mea·sles** ['mi:zlz] *nsg* sarampión *m*

English translations are given a *pl* or *sg* label (for plural or singular) in cases where this does not match the Spanish:

> **acciones** *pl* COM stock *sg*, *Br* shares
> **entarimado** *m* (*suelo*) floorboards *pl*

7.6 Irregular English plurals are identified:

> **the·sis** ['θi:sɪs] (*pl* **theses** ['θi:si:z]) tesis *f inv*
> **thief** [θi:f] (*pl* **thieves** [θi:vz]) ladrón(-ona) *m(f)*
> **trout** [traʊt] (*pl* **trout**) trucha *f*

7.7 Words like **physics** or **media studies** have not been given a label to say if they are singular or plural for the simple reason that they can be either, depending on how they are used.

7.8 Irregular and semi-irregular verb forms are identified:

> **sim·pli·fy** ['sɪmplɪfaɪ] *v/t* (*pret & pp* **-ied**) simplificar
> **sing** [sɪŋ] *v/t & v/i* (*pret* **sang**, *pp* **sung**) cantar
> **la·bel** ['leɪbl] **1** *n* etiqueta *f* **2** *v/t* (*pret & pp* **-ed**, *Br* **-led**) bags etiquetar

7.9 Cross-references are given to tables of Spanish conjugations:

> **gemir** <3l> *v/i* moan, groan
> **esconder** <2a> **1** *v/t* hide, conceal ...

7.10 Grammatical information is provided on the prepositions you'll need in order to create complete sentences:

> **'switch·o·ver** *to new system* cambio *m* (**to** a)
> **sneer** [sni:r] **1** *n* mueca *f* desdeñosa **2** *v/i* burlarse (**at** de)
> **escindirse** <3a> *v/r* (*fragmentarse*) split (**en** into); (*segregarse*) break away (**de** from)
> **enviciarse** <1b> *v/r* get addicted (**con** to)

Abbreviations

and	&	y	electronics,	ELEC	electrónica,
see	→	véase	electronic		electrotecnia
registered	®	marca	engineering		
trademark		registrada	Spain	*Esp*	España
abbreviation	*abbr*	abreviatura	especially	*esp*	especialmente
abbreviation	*abr*	abreviatura	euphemistic	*euph*	eufemismo
adjective	*adj*	adjetivo	familiar,	F	familiar
adverb	*adv*	adverbio	colloquial		
agriculture	AGR	agricultura	feminine	*f*	femenino
anatomy	ANAT	anatomía	feminine noun	*f/adj*	sustantivo
architecture	ARCHI	arquitectura	and adjective		femenino y
Argentina	*Arg*	Argentina			adjetivo
architecture	ARQUI	arquitectura	railroad	FERR	ferrocarriles
article	*art*	artículo	figurative	*fig*	figurativo
astronomy	AST	astronomía	financial	FIN	finanzas
astrology	ASTR	astrología	physics	FÍS	física
attributive	*atr*	atributivo	formal	*fml*	formal
motoring	AUTO	automóvil	photography	FOT	fotografía
civil aviation	AVIA	aviación	feminine plural	*fpl*	femenino
biology	BIO	biología			plural
Bolivia	*Bol*	Bolivia	feminine	*fsg*	femenino
botany	BOT	botánica	singular		singular
British English	*Br*	inglés	gastronomy	GASTR	gastronomía
		británico	geography	GEOG	geografía
Central	*C.Am.*	América	geology	GEOL	geología
America		Central	geometry	GEOM	geometría
chemistry	CHEM	química	grammatical	GRAM	gramática
Chile	*Chi*	Chile	historical	HIST	histórico
Colombia	*Col*	Colombia	humorous	*hum*	humorístico
commerce,	COM	comercio	IT term	INFOR	informática
business			interjection	*int*	interjección
comparative	*comp*	comparativo	interrogative	*interr*	interrogativo
computers,	COMPUT	informática	invariable	*inv*	invariable
IT term			ironic	*iron*	irónico
conjunction	*conj*	conjunción	ironic	*irón*	irónico
Southern Cone	*CSur*	Cono Sur	law	JUR	jurisprudencia
sports	DEP	deporte	Latin	*L.Am.*	América
contemptuous	*desp*	despectivo	America		Latina
determiner	*det*	determinante	law	LAW	jurisprudencia
Ecuador	*Ecuad*	Ecuador	linguistics	LING	lingüística
education	EDU	educación,	literary	*lit*	literario
(schools,		enseñanza	masculine	*m*	masculino
universities)		(sistema	masculine	*m/adj*	sustantivo
		escolar y	noun and		masculino y
		universitario)	adjective		adjetivo
electronics,	EL	electrónica,	nautical	MAR	navegación,
electronic		electrotecnia			marina
engineering			mathematics	MAT	matemáticas

mathematics	MATH	matemáticas
medicine	MED	medicina
meteorology	METEO	meteorología
Mexico	*Mex*	México
Mexico	*Méx*	México
masculine and feminine	*m/f*	masculino y femenino
masculine and feminine plural	*m/fpl*	masculino y femenino plural
military	MIL	militar
mineralogy	MIN	mineralogía
motoring	MOT	automóvil
masculine plural	*mpl*	masculino plural
music	MUS	música
music	MÚS	música
mythology	MYTH	mitología
noun	*n*	sustantivo
nautical	NAUT	navegación, náutica
negative	*neg*	negativo
noun plural	*npl*	sustantivo plural
noun singular	*nsg*	sustantivo singular
ornithology	ORN	ornitología
oneself	o.s.	sí mismo
popular, slang	P	popular
painting	PAINT	pintura
Paraguay	*Parag*	Paraguay
past participle	*part*	participio pasado
Peru	*Pe*	Perú
pejorative	*pej*	peyorativo
photography	PHOT	fotografía
physics	PHYS	física
painting	PINT	pintura
plural	*pl*	plural
politics	POL	política
possessive	*pos*	posesivo
possessive	*poss*	posesivo
past participle	*pp*	participio pasado
predicative usage	*pred*	predicativo
prefix	*pref*	prefijo
preposition	*prep*	preposición
preterite (past tense)	*pret*	pretérito
pronoun	*pron*	pronombre
preposition	*prp*	preposición
psychology	PSI	psicología
psychology	PSYCH	psicología
chemistry	QUÍM	química
radio	RAD	radio
railroad	RAIL	ferrocarriles
relative	*rel*	relativo
religion	REL	religión
River Plate	*Rpl*	Río de la Plata
South America	*S.Am.*	América del Sur
singular	*sg*	singular
someone	s.o.	alguien
sports	SP	deporte
Spain	*Span*	España
something	*sth*	algo, alguna cosa
subjunctive	*subj*	subjuntivo
superlative	*sup*	superlativo
bullfighting	TAUR	tauromaquia
also	*tb*	también
theater, theatre	TEA	teatro
technology	TÉC	técnica
technology	TECH	técnica
telecommunications	TELEC	telecomunicaciones
theater	THEA	teatro
typography, typesetting	TIP	tipografía
transportation	TRANSP	transportes
television	TV	televisión
vulgar	V	vulgar
auxiliary verb	*v/aux*	verbo auxiliar
verb	*vb*	verbo
Venezuela	*Ven*	Venezuela
intransitive verb	*v/i*	verbo intransitivo
impersonal verb	*v/impers*	verbo impersonal
reflexive verb	*v/r*	verbo reflexivo
transitive verb	*v/t*	verbo transitivo
West Indies	*W.I.*	Antillas
zoology	ZO	zoología

The pronunciation of Spanish

Stress

1. If a word ends in a vowel, or in *n* or *s*, the penultimate syllable is stressed: **espada, biblioteca, hablan, telefonean, edificios**.

2. If a word ends in a consonant other than *n* or *s*, the last syllable is stressed: **dificultad, hablar, laurel, niñez**.

3. If a word is to be stressed in any way contrary to rules 1 and 2, an acute accent is written over the stressed vowel: **rubí, máquina, crímenes, carácter, continúa, autobús**.

4. **Diphthongs and syllable division.** Of the 5 vowels *a, e, o* are considered "strong" and *i* and *u* "weak":

   a) A combination of weak + strong forms a diphthong, the stress falling on the stronger element: **reina, baile, cosmonauta, tiene, bueno**.

   b) A combination of weak + weak forms a diphthong, the stress falling on the second element: **viuda, ruido**.

   c) Two strong vowels together remain two distinct syllables, the stress falling according to rules 1 and 2: **ma/estro, atra/er**.

   d) Any word having a vowel combination not stressed according to these rules has an accent: **traído, oído, baúl, río**.

Sounds

Since the pronunciation of Spanish is (unlike English) adequately represented by the spelling of words, Spanish headwords have not been given a phonetic transcription. The sounds of Spanish are described below.

The pronunciation described is primarily that of the educated Spaniard. But the main features of Latin American pronunciation are also covered.

Vowels

a   As in English *father*: **paz, pata**.

e   Like *e* in English *they* (but without the following sound of *y*): **grande, pelo**. A shorter sound when followed by a consonant in the same syllable, like *e* in English *get*: **España, renta**.

i   Like *i* in English *machine*, though somewhat shorter: **pila, rubí**.

o   As in English *November, token*: **solo, esposa**. A shorter sound when followed by a consonant in the same syllable, like *au* in English *fault* or the *a* in *fall*: **costra, bomba**.

u   Like *oo* in English *food*: **pura, luna**. Silent after **q** and in **gue, gui**, unless marked with a dieresis (**antigüedad, argüir**).

y   when occurring as a vowel (in the conjunction **y** or at the end of a word), is pronounced like *i*.

Diphthongs

ai   like *i* in English *right*: **baile**, **vaina**.

ei   like *ey* in English *they*: **reina**, **peine**.

oi   like *oy* in English *boy*: **boina**, **oigo**.

au   like *ou* in English *bout*: **causa**, **audacia**.

eu   like the vowel sounds in English *may-you*, without the sound of the *y*: **deuda**, **reuma**.

Semiconsonants

i, y   like *y* in English *yes*: **yerno**, **tiene**; in some cases in *L.Am.* this *y* is pronounced like the *s* in English *measure*: **mayo**, **yo**.

u   like *w* in English *water*: **huevo**, **agua**.

Consonants

b, v   These two letters represent the same value in Spanish. There are two distinct pronunciations:
   1. At the start of a word and after *m* and *n* the sound is like English *b*: **batalla**, **ventaja**; **tromba**, **invierno**.
   2. In all other positions the sound is what is technically a "bilabial fricative". This sound does not exist in English. Go to say a *b* but do not quite bring your lips together: **estaba**, **cueva**, **de Vigo**.

c   1. *c* before *a, o, u* or a consonant is like English *k*: **café**, **cobre**.
   2. *c* before *e, i* is like English *th* in *thin*: **cédula**, **cinco**. In *L.Am.* this is pronounced like an English *s* in *chase* .

ch   like English *ch* in *church*: **mucho**, **chocho**.

d   Three distinct pronunciations:
   1. At the start of a word and after *l* and *n*, the sound is like English *d*: **doy**, **aldea**, **conde**.
   2. Between vowels and after consonants other than *l* and *n* the sound is relaxed and approaches English *th* in *this*: **codo**, **guardar**; in parts of Spain it is further relaxed and even disappears, particularly in the **-ado** ending.
   3. In final position, this type 2 is further relaxed or omitted altogether: **usted**, **Madrid**.

f   like English *f*: **fuero**, **flor**.

g   Three distinct pronunciations:
   1. Before *e* and *i* it is the same as the Spanish j (below): **coger**, **general**.
   2. At the start of a word and after *n*, the sound is that of English *g* in *get*: **granada**, **rango**.
   3. In other positions the sound is like 2 above, but much softer, the *g* almost disappearing: **agua**, **guerra**. N.B. In the group **gue**, **gui** the **u** is silent (**guerra**, **guindar**) unless marked with a dieresis (**antigüedad**, **argüir**). In the group **gua** all letters are sounded.

h   always silent: **honor**, **búho**.

j   A strong guttural sound not found in English, but like the *ch* in Scots *loch*, German *Achtung*: **jota**, **ejercer**.

k   like English *k*: **kilogramo**, **ketchup**.

l   like English *l*: **león**, **pala**.

ll approximating to English *lli* in *million*: **millón**, **calle**. In *L.Am.* like the *s* in English *measure*.

m   like English *m*: **mano**, **como**.

n   like English *n*: **nono**, **pan**; except before **v**, when the group is pronounced like *mb*: **enviar**, **invadir**.

ñ   approximating to English *ni* in *onion*: **paño**, **ñoño**.

p   like English *p*: **Pepe**, **copa**.

q   like English *k*; always in combination with **u**, which is silent: **que**, **quiosco**.

r   a single trill stronger than any *r* in English, but like Scots *r*: **caro**, **querer**. Somewhat relaxed in final position. Pronounced like **rr** at the start of a word and after **l**, **n**, **s**: **rata**.

rr strongly trilled: **carro**, **hierro**.

s   like *s* in English *chase*: **rosa**, **soso**. But before **b**, **d**, hard **g**, **l**, **m** and **n** it is like English *s* in *rose*: **desde**, **mismo**, **asno**. Before "impure **s**" in recent loan-words, an extra *e*-sound is inserted in pronunciation: **e-sprint**, **e-stand**.

t   like English *t*: **patata**, **tope**.

v   see **b**.

w   found in a few recent loan-words only and pronounced pretty much as the English *w*, but sometimes with a very slight *g* sound before it: **whisky**, **windsurf**. In one exceptional case it is pronounced like an English *v* or like Spanish **b** and **v**: **wáter**.

x   like English *gs* in *big sock*: **máximo**, **examen**. Before a consonant like English *s* in *chase*: **extraño**, **mixto**.

z   like English *th* in *thin*: **zote**, **zumbar**. In *L.Am.* like English *s* in *chase*.

The Spanish Alphabet

a [ah]	g [Heh]	m ['emeh]	rr ['erreh]	x ['ekees]
b [beh]	h ['acheh]	n ['eneh]	s ['eseh]	y [eegree-'eh-ga]
c [theh]	i [ee]	ñ ['en-yeh]	t [teh]	z ['theh-ta]
ch[cheh]	j ['Hota]	o [oh]	u [oo]	
d [deh]	k [ka]	p [peh]	v ['ooveh]	*H is pronounced*
e [eh]	l ['eleh]	q [koo]	w ['ooveh	*as in the Scottish*
f ['ef-feh]	ll ['el-yeh]	r ['ereh]	doh-bleh]	*way of saying loch*

Written Spanish

I. Capitalization

The rules for capitalization in Spanish largely correspond to those for the English language. In contrast to English, however, adjectives derived from proper nouns are not capitalized (*americano* American, *español* Spanish).

II. Word division

Spanish words are divided according to the following rules:

1. If there is a **single consonant** between two vowels, the division is made between the first vowel and the consonant (*di-ne-ro, Gra-na-da*).

2. **Two consecutive consonants** may be divided (*miér-co-les, dis-cur-so*). If the second consonant is an *l* or *r*, however, the division comes before the two consonants (*re-gla, nie-bla; po-bre, ca-bra*). This also goes for ch, ll and rr (*te-cho, ca-lle, pe-rro*).

3. In the case of **three consecutive consonants** (usually including an *l* or *r*), the division comes after the first consonant (*ejem-plo, siem-pre*). If the second consonant is an *s*, however, the division comes after the *s* (*cons-tan-te, ins-ti-tu-to*).

4. In the case of **four consecutive consonants** (the second of these is usually an *s*), the division is made between the second and third consonants (*ins-tru-men-to*).

5. **Diphthongs** and **triphthongs** may not be divided (*bien, buey*). Vowels which are part of different syllables, however, may be divided (*frí-o, acre-e-dor*).

6. **Compounds**, including those formed with prefixes, are divided morphologically (*nos-otros, des-ali-ño, dis-cul-pa*).

III. Punctuation

In Spanish a comma is often placed after an adverbial phrase introducing a sentence (*sin embargo, todos los esfuerzos fueron inútiles* however, all efforts were in vain). A subsidiary clause beginning a sentence is also followed by a comma (*si tengo tiempo, lo haré* if I have time, I'll do it, **but**: *lo haré si tengo tiempo* I'll do it if I have time).

Questions and exclamations are introduced by an inverted question mark and exclamation point respectively, which immediately precedes the question or exclamation (*Dispense usted, ¿está en casa el señor Pérez?* Excuse me, is Mr. Pérez at home?; *¡Que lástima!* What a shame!).

English pronunciation

	Vowels		Consonants
[ɑː]	*father* ['fɑːðər]	[b]	*bag* [bæg]
[æ]	*man* [mæn]	[d]	*dear* [dɪr]
[e]	*get* [get]	[f]	*fall* [fɔːl]
[ə]	*about* [ə'baʊt]	[g]	*give* [gɪv]
[ɜː]	*absurd* [əb'sɜːrd]	[h]	*hole* [hoʊl]
[ɪ]	*stick* [stɪk]	[j]	*yes* [jes]
[iː]	*need* [niːd]	[k]	*come* [kʌm]
[ɒː]	*in-laws* ['ɪnlɒːz]	[l]	*land* [lænd]
[ɔː]	*more* [mɔːr]	[m]	*mean* [miːn]
[ʌ]	*mother* ['mʌðər]	[n]	*night* [naɪt]
[ʊ]	*book* [bʊk]	[p]	*pot* [pɑːt]
[uː]	*fruit* [fruːt]	[r]	*right* [raɪt]
		[s]	*sun* [sʌn]
	Diphthongs	[t]	*take* [teɪk]
[aɪ]	*time* [taɪm]	[v]	*vain* [veɪn]
[aʊ]	*cloud* [klaʊd]	[w]	*wait* [weɪt]
[eɪ]	*name* [neɪm]	[z]	*rose* [roʊz]
[ɔɪ]	*point* [pɔɪnt]	[ŋ]	*bring* [brɪŋ]
[oʊ]	*oath* [oʊθ]	[ʃ]	*she* [ʃiː]
		[tʃ]	*chair* [tʃer]
		[dʒ]	*join* [dʒɔɪn]
		[ʒ]	*leisure* ['liːʒər]
		[θ]	*think* [θɪŋk]
		[ð]	*the* [ðə]
		[']	means that the following syllable is stressed: *ability* [ə'bɪlətɪ]

a *prp* ◊ *dirección* to; **al este de** to the east of; **a casa** home; **ir a la cama/ al cine** go to bed / to the movies; **vamos a Bolivia** we're going to Bolivia; **voy a casa de Marta** I'm going to Marta's (house) ◊ *situación* at; **a la mesa** at the table; **al lado de** next to; **a la derecha** on the right; **al sol** in the sun; **a treinta kilómetros de Quito** thirty kilometers (*Br* kilometres) from Quito; **está a cinco kilómetros** it is five kilometers (*Br* kilometres) away ◊ *tiempo:* **¿a qué hora llegas?** what time do you arrive?; **a las tres** at three o'clock; **estamos a quince de febrero** it's February fifteenth; **a los treinta años** at the age of thirty ◊ *modo:* **a la española** the Spanish way; **a mano** by hand; **a pie** on foot; **a 50 kilómetros por hora** at fifty kilometers (*Br* kilometres) an hour ◊ *precio:* **¿a cómo** or **cuánto está?** how much is it? ◊ *objeto indirecto:* **dáselo a tu hermano** give it to your brother ◊ *objeto directo:* **vi a mi padre** I saw my father ◊ *en perífrasis verbal:* **empezar a** begin to; **jugar a las cartas** play cards; **a decir verdad** to tell the truth ◊ *para introducir pregunta:* **¿a que no lo sabes?** I bet you don't know; **a ver ...** OK ..., right ...

ábaco *m* abacus

abadía *f* abbey

abajo 1 *adv situación* below, underneath; *en edificio* downstairs; **ponlo ahí ~** put it down there; **el cajón de ~** *siguiente* the drawer below; *último* the bottom drawer ◊ *dirección* down; *en edificio* downstairs; **cuesta ~** downhill; **empuja hacia** ~ push down ◊ *con cantidades:* **de diez para ~** ten or under, ten or below **2** *int:* **¡~ los traidores!** down with the traitors!

abalanzarse <1f> *v/i* rush *o* surge forward; **~ sobre algo/alguien** leap *o* pounce on sth / s.o.

abalear <1a> *v/t S.Am.* shoot

abandonar <1a> **1** *v/t lugar* leave; *objeto, a alguien* abandon; *a esposa, hijos* desert; *idea* give up, abandon; *actividad* give up **2** *v/r* **~se** let o.s. go; **~se a** abandon o.s. to

abanicar <1g> **1** *v/t* fan **2** *v/r* **~se** *v/r* fan o.s.; **abanico** *m* fan; *fig* range; **~ eléctrico** *Méx* electric fan

abaratar <1a> *v/t* reduce *o* lower the price of; *precio* reduce, lower

abarcar <1g> *v/t territorio* cover; *fig* comprise, cover; *L.Am.* (*acaparar*) hoard, stockpile; **el libro abarca desde ... hasta ...** the book covers the period from ... to ...; **~ con la vista** take in

abarrotado *adj* packed; **abarrotar** <1a> **1** *v/t lugar* pack; *L.Am.* COM buy up, stockpile **2** *v/r* **~se** *L.Am. del mercado* become glutted; **abarrotería** *f Méx, C.Am.* grocery store, *Br* grocer's; **abarrotero** *m,* **-a** *f Méx, C.Am.* storekeeper, shopkeeper; **abarrotes** *mpl L.Am.* (*mercancías*) groceries *pl;* (*tienda de*) ~ grocery store, *Br* grocer's

abastecer <2d> **1** *v/t* supply (**de** with) **2** *v/r* **~se** stock up (**de** on *o* with); **abastecimiento** *m* supply

abasto *m:* **no dan ~** they can't cope (**con** with)

abatí *m Rpl* corn, *Br* maize; *Parag:* fermented maize drink

abatible *adj* collapsible, folding *atr;* **abatido** *adj* depressed; **abatimiento** *m* gloom; **abatir** <3a> *v/t edificio* knock *o* pull down; *árbol* cut down, fell; AVIA shoot *o* bring down; *fig* kill; (*deprimir*) depress

abdicación *f* abdication; **abdicar** <1g> *v/t* abdicate

abdomen *m* abdomen; **abdominal** *adj* abdominal; **abdominales** *mpl* sit-ups

abecedario *m* alphabet

abedul *m* birch

abeja *f* ZO bee; **abejorro** *m* bumble-bee

aberración *f* aberration

abertura *f* opening

abeto *m* fir (tree)

abiertamente *adv* openly; **abierto 1** *part* → **abrir 2** *adj tb persona* open; **está ~ a nuevas ideas** *fig* he's open to new ideas

abigarrado *adj* multicolo(u)red

abismo *m* abyss; *fig* gulf

ablandar <1a> **1** *v/t tb fig* soften **2** *v/r* **~se** soften, get softer; *fig* relent; **ablande** *m Arg* AUTO running in

abnegación *f* self-denial; **abnegado** *adj* selfless

abocado *adj* doomed; **~ al fracaso** doomed to failure, destined to fail

abochornar <1a> **1** *v/t* embarrass **2** *v/r* **~se** feel embarrassed

abogacía *f* law

abogaderas *fpl L.Am.* F (*discusiones*) arguments

abogado *m*, **-a** *f* lawyer; *en tribunal superior* attorney, *Br* barrister; **no le faltaron ~s** *fig* there were plenty of people who defended him; **abogar** <1h> *v/i*: **~ por** *alguien* defend; *algo* advocate

abolición *f* abolition; **abolir** <3a> *v/t* abolish

abollado *adj* dented; **abolladura** *f* dent; **abollar** <1a> *v/t* dent

abombado *adj S.Am.* F *comida* rotten, bad; F (*tonto*) dopey F; **abombarse** *S.Am. de comida* go off, go bad

abominable *adj* abominable; **abominar** <1a> *v/t* detest, loathe

abonado *m*, **-a** *f* subscriber; *a teléfono, gas, electricidad* customer; *a ópera, teatro* season-ticket holder;

abonar <1a> **1** *v/t* COM pay; AGR fertilize; *Méx* pay on account; **~ el terreno** *fig* sow the seeds **2** *v/r* **~se** *a espectáculo* buy a season ticket (*a* for); *a revista* take out a subscription (*a* to); **abono** *m* COM payment; AGR fertilizer; *para espectáculo, transporte* season ticket

abordar <1a> *v/t* MAR board; *tema, asunto* broach, raise; *problema* tackle, deal with; *a una persona* approach

aborigen 1 *adj* native, indigenous **2** *m/f* native

aborrecer <2d> *v/t* loathe, detest

abortar <1a> **1** *v/i* MED *espontáneamente* miscarry; *de forma provocada* have an abortion **2** *v/t* plan foil; **abortivo** *adj* abortion *atr*; **píldora -a** abortion pill; **aborto** *m* espontáneo miscarriage; *provocado* abortion; *fig* F freak F; **tener un ~** have a miscarriage

abotonar <1a> *v/t* button up

abra *f L.Am.* clearing

abrasador *adj* scorching (hot); **abrasar** <1a> **1** *v/t* burn **2** *v/i del sol* burn, scorch; *de bebida, comida* be boiling hot **3** *v/r* **~se**: **~se de sed** F be parched F; **~se de calor** F be sweltering F; **~se de pasión** *lit* be aflame with passion *lit*

abrazar <1f> **1** *v/t* hug **2** *v/r* **~se** embrace; **abrazo** *m* hug; **dar un ~ a alguien** hug s.o., give s.o. a hug; **un ~ en carta** best wishes; **más íntimo** love

abrebotellas *m inv* bottle opener; **abrelatas** *m inv* can opener, *Br tb* tin opener

abreviar <1b> *v/t* shorten; *palabra* abbreviate; *texto* abridge; **abreviatura** *f* abbreviation

abridor *m* bottle opener

abrigado *adj* warmly dressed; **abrigar** <1h> **1** *v/t* wrap up; *esperanzas* hold out; *duda* entertain **2** *v/r* **~se** wrap up warm; **~se del frío** (take) shelter from the cold; **abrigo** *m* coat; (*protección*) shelter; **ropa de ~** warm clothes; **al ~ de** in the shelter of

abril *m* April

abrir <3a; *part* **abierto**> **1** *v/t* open; *túnel* dig; *grifo* turn on; **le abrió el apetito** it gave him an appetite **2** *v/i de persona* open up; *de ventana, puerta* open; **en un ~ y cerrar de ojos** in the twinkling of an eye **3** *v/r* **~se** open; **~se a algo** *fig* open up to sth; **~se paso entre** make one's way through

abrochar <1a> **1** *v/t* do up; *cinturón de seguridad* fasten **2** *v/r* **~se** do up; *cinturón de seguridad* fasten; **tendremos que abrocharnos el cinturón** we'll have to tighten our belts

abrumador *adj* overwhelming; **abrumar** <1a> *v/t* overwhelm (**con** *or* **de** with); **abrumado de** *or* **con trabajo** snowed under with work

abrupto *adj terreno* rough; *pendiente* steep; *tono, respuesta* abrupt; *cambio* sudden

absentismo *m* absenteeism; **~ escolar** truancy

absolución *f* absolution

absolutamente *adv* absolutely; **no entendió ~ nada** he didn't understand a thing; **absolutismo** *m* absolutism; **absoluto** *adj* absolute; **en ~** not at all

absolver <2h; *part* **absuelto**> *v/t* JUR acquit; REL absolve

absorbente *adj* absorbent; **absorber** <2a> *v/t* absorb; (*consumir*) take; (*cautivar*) absorb; **absorto** *adj* absorbed (**en** in), engrossed (**en** in)

abstemio 1 *adj* teetotal **2** *m*, **-a** *f* teetotal(l)er

abstención *f* abstention; **abstenerse** <2l> *v/r* refrain (**de** from); POL abstain; **abstinencia** *f* abstinence; **síndrome de ~** MED withdrawal symptoms *pl*

abstracto *adj* abstract; **abstraerse** <2p; *part* **abstraído**> *v/r* shut o.s. off (**de** from); **abstraído 1** *adj* preocupied; **~ en algo** engrossed in sth **2** *part* → **abstraer**

absuelto *part* → **absolver**

absurdo 1 *adj* absurd **2** *m*: **es un ~ que** it's absurd that

abuchear <1a> *v/t* boo; **abucheo(s)** *m*(*pl*) booing *sg*, boos *pl*

abuela *f* grandmother; F *persona mayor* old lady; **¡cuéntaselo a tu ~!** F don't try to put one over on me! F, Br pull the other one! F; **abuelo** *m* grandfather; F *persona mayor* old man; **~s** grandparents

abultado *adj* bulging; *derrota* heavy; **abultamiento** *m* bulge; **abultar** <1a> *v/i* be bulky; **no abulta casi nada** it takes up almost no room at all

abundancia *f* abundance; **había comida en ~** there was plenty of food; **abundante** *adj* plentiful, abundant; **abundar** <1a> *v/i* be plentiful *o* abundant

aburguesarse <1a> *v/r desp* become bourgeois *o* middle class

aburrido *adj* (*que aburre*) boring; (*que se aburre*) bored; **~ de algo** bored *o* fed up F with sth; **aburrimiento** *m* boredom; **aburrir** <3a> **1** *v/t* bore **2** *v/r* **~se** get bored; **~se de algo** get bored *o* fed up F with sth; **~se como una ostra** F get bored stiff F

abusado *adj Méx* F smart, clever; **¡~!** look out!; **abusar** <1a> *v/i*: **~ de poder, confianza** abuse; *persona* take advantage of; **~ del alcohol** drink too much; **~ sexualmente de alguien** sexually abuse s.o.; **abusivo** *adj* JUR unfair; **abuso** *m* abuse; **~s** *pl* **deshonestos** indecent assault *sg*

A.C. *abr* (= **antes de Cristo**) BC (= before Christ)

acá *adv* here; **de ~ para allá** from here to there; **de entonces para ~** since then

acabado *m* finish

acabar <1a> **1** *v/t* finish **2** *v/i de persona* finish; *de función, acontecimiento* finish, end; **acabé haciéndolo yo** I ended up doing it myself; **~ con** put an end to; *caramelos* finish off; *persona* destroy; **~ de hacer algo** have just done sth; **va a ~ mal** F *persona* he'll come to no good; **esto va a ~ mal** F this is going to end badly **3** *v/r* **~se** *de actividad* finish, end; *de pan, dinero* run out; **se nos ha acabado el azúcar** we've run out of sugar; **¡se acabó!** that's that!

acacia *f* acacia

academia *f* academy; **~ de idiomas** language school; **~ militar** military academy; **académico 1** *adj* academic **2** *m*, **-a** *f* academician

acalenturarse <1a> *v/r* L.Am. (*afiebrarse*) get a temperature *o* fever

acallar <1a> *v/t tb* fig silence

acalorarse <1a> *v/r* (*enfadarse*) get worked up; (*sofocarse*) get embarrassed

acampada *f* camp; **ir de ~** go camping; **acampar** <1a> *v/i* camp

acantilado *m* cliff

acaparar <1a> *v/t* hoard, stockpile; *tiempo* take up; *interés* capture; (*monopolizar*) monopolize

acápite *m* L.Am. section; (*párrafo*) paragraph

acaramelado *adj fig* F lovey-dovey F

acariciar <1b> *v/t* caress; *perro* stroke; **~ una idea** *fig* contemplate an idea

acarrear <1a> *v/t* carry; *fig* give rise to, cause

acaso *adv* perhaps; **por si ~** just in case

acatar <1a> *v/t* comply with, obey

acatarrarse <1a> *v/r* catch a cold

acaudalado *adj* wealthy, well-off

acceder <2a> *v/i* (*ceder*) agree (**a** to), accede (**a** to) *fml*; **~ a lugar** gain access to; *cargo* accede to *fml*

accesible *adj* accessible; **acceso** *m tb* INFOR access; *de fiebre* attack, bout; *de tos* fit; **de difícil ~** inaccessible; **accesorio 1** *adj* incidental **2** *m* accessory

accidentado 1 *adj* terreno, camino rough; *viaje* eventful **2** *m*, **-a** *f* casualty; **accidental** *adj* (*no esencial*)

incidental; (*casual*) chance *atr*; **accidente** *m* accident; (*casualidad*) chance; GEOG feature; **~ de tráfico** *or* **de circulación** road traffic accident, RTA; **~ laboral** industrial accident

acción *f* action; **acciones** *pl* COM stock *sg*, *Br* shares; **poner en ~** put into action; **accionar** <1a> *v/t* activate; **accionista** *m/f* stockholder, *Br* shareholder

acebo *m* holly

acechar <1a> *v/t* lie in wait for; **acecho** *m*: **al ~** lying in wait

aceite *m* oil; **~ de girasol / oliva** sunflower / olive oil; **~ lubricante** lubricating oil; **aceitera** *f* TÉC oilcan; GASTR cruet; **aceitoso** *adj* oily; **aceituna** *f* olive

aceleración *f* acceleration; **acelerador** *m* accelerator; **acelerar** <1a> **1** *v/t motor* rev up; *fig* speed up; **aceleró el coche** she accelerated **2** *v/i* accelerate **3** *v/r* **~se** L.Am. F (*enojarse*) lose one's cool

acelgas *fpl* BOT Swiss chard *sg*

acento *m en ortografía, pronunciación* accent; (*énfasis*) stress, emphasis; **poner el ~ en** fig stress, emphasize; **acentuar** <1e> **1** *v/t* stress; *fig* accentuate, emphasize **2** *v/r* **~se** become more pronounced

acepción *f* sense, meaning

aceptable *adj* acceptable; **aceptación** *f* acceptance; (*éxito*) success; **aceptar** <1a> *v/t* accept

acequia *f* irrigation ditch

acera *f* sidewalk, *Br* pavement; **ser de la otra ~, ser de la ~ de enfrente** F be gay

acerca *adv*: **~ de** about

acercar <1g> **1** *v/t* bring closer; **~ a alguien a un lugar** give s.o. a ride (*Br* lift) somewhere **2** *v/r* **~se** approach; (*ir*) go; *de grupos, países* come closer together; *de fecha* draw near; **se acercó a mí** she came up to me *o* approached me; **acércate** come closer; **no te acerques a la pared** don't get close to the wall

acero *m* steel; **~ inoxidable** stainless steel

acertado *adj comentario* apt; *elección* good, wise; **estar muy ~** be dead right; **acertar** <1k> **1** *v/t respuesta* get right; *al hacer una conjetura* guess *v/i* be right; **~ con algo** get sth right

acertijo *m* riddle, puzzle

achacar <1g> *v/t* attribute (**a** to)

achantarse <1a> *v/r* F keep quiet, keep one's mouth shut F

achaque *m* ailment

achatado *adj* flattened; **achatarse** <1a> *v/r* be flattened

achicharrar <1a> *v/t* **1** burn **2** *v/r* **~se** *fig* F roast F

achinado *adj L.Am.* oriental-looking

achinero *m C.Am. vendedor* peddler

achiquitarse <1a> *v/r L.Am.* become frightened *o* scared

achisparse <1a> *v/r* F get tipsy F

acholar <1a> *v/t S.Am.* embarrass

achuchar <1a> *v/t fig* F pester, nag; **achuchón** *m* F squeeze, hug; (*empujón*) push; **le dio un ~** *desmayo* she felt faint

achuras *fpl S.Am.* variety meat *sg*, *Br* offal *sg*

aciago *adj* fateful

acicalarse <1a> *v/r* get dressed up

acidez *f* acidity; **~ de estómago** heartburn; **ácido 1** *adj tb fig* sour, acid **2** *m* acid

acierto *m idea* good idea; *respuesta* correct answer; *habilidad* skill

aclamación *f* acclaim; **aclamar** <1a> *v/t* acclaim

aclaración *f* clarification; **aclarar** <1a> *v/t duda, problema* clarify, clear up; *ropa, vajilla* rinse **2** *v/i de día* break, dawn; *del tiempo* clear up **3** *v/r* **~se**: **~se la voz** clear one's throat; **no me aclaro** F I don't understand; *por cansancio, ruido etc* I can't think straight

aclimatarse <1a> *v/r* acclimatize, become acclimatized

acné *m* acne

ACNUR *abr* (= **Alto Comisionado de las Naciones Unidas para los Refugiados**) UNHCR (= United Nations High Commission for Refugees)

acobardar <1a> **1** *v/t* daunt **2** *v/r* **~se** get frightened, lose one's nerve

acodarse <1a> *v/r* lean (one's elbows) (**en** on)

acogedor *adj* welcoming; *lugar* cozy, *Br* cosy; **acoger** <2c> **1** *v/t* receive; *en casa* take in; **~ con satisfacción** welcome, greet with satisfaction **2** *v/r* **~se a algo** have recourse to sth; **acogida** *f* reception; **tener buena ~** get a good reception, be well received

acojonar <1a> **1** *v/t* V (*asustar*) scare the shit out of P; (*asombrar*) knock out F, blow away P **2** *v/r* **~se** V be shit scared P

acolchado *adj Rpl* quilted; **acolchonar** <1a> *v/t Rpl* quilt

acomedido *adj L.Am.* obliging, helpful; **acomedirse** <3l> *v/r Méx* offer to help

acometer <2a> **1** *v/t* attack; *tarea, proyecto* undertake, tackle **2** *v/i* attack; **~ contra algo** attack sth

acomodado *adj* well-off; **acomodador** *m* usher; **acomodadora** *f* usherette; **acomodar** <1a> **1** *v/t* (*adaptar*) adapt; *a alguien* accommodate **2** *v/r* **~se** make o.s. comfortable; (*adaptarse*) adapt (**a** to)

acompañamiento *m* accompaniment; **acompañante** *m/f* companion; MÚS accompanist; **acompañar** <1a> *v/t* (*ir con*) go with, accompany *fml*; (*permanecer con*) keep company; MÚS, GASTR accompany; **acompaño** *m C.Am.* (*reunión*) meeting

acomplejar <1a> **1** *v/t*: **~ a alguien** give s.o. a complex **2** *v/r* **~se** get a complex

acondicionar <1a> *v/t un lugar* equip, fit out; *pelo* condition

acongojar <1a> *v/t lit* grieve *lit*, distress

aconsejable *adj* advisable; **aconsejar** <1a> *v/t* advise

acontecer <2d> *v/i* take place, occur; **acontecimiento** *m* event

acopio *m*: **hacer ~** *tb* gather, muster

acoplar <1a> **1** *v/t piezas* fit together **2** *v/r ~se de persona* fit in (*a* with); *de nave espacial* dock (*a* with); *de piezas* fit together

acorazado *adj* armo(u)red

acordar <1m> **1** *v/t* agree **2** *~se* *v/r* remember; **¿te acuerdas de él?** do you remember him?; **acorde 1** *adj*: **~ con** appropriate to, in keeping with **2** *m* MÚS chord

acordeón *m* accordion; **acordeonista** *m/f* accordionist

acordonar <1a> *v/t* cordon off

acorralar <1a> *v/t tb fig* corner

acortar <1a> **1** *v/t* shorten **2** *v/i* take a short cut **3** *v/r ~se* get shorter

acosar <1a> *v/t* hound, pursue; *con preguntas* bombard (*con* with)

acosijar <1a> *v/t Méx* badger, pester

acoso *m fig* hounding, harrassment; **~ sexual** sexual harrassment

acostar <1m> **1** *v/t* put to bed **2** *v/r ~se* go to bed; (*tumbarse*) lie down; **~se con alguien** go to bed with s.o., sleep with s.o.

acostumbrado *adj* (*habitual*) usual; **estar ~ a algo** be used to sth; **acostumbrar** <1a> **1** *v/t* get used (*a* to) **2** *v/i*: **acostumbraba a venir a este café todas las mañanas** he used to come to this café every morning **3** *v/r ~se* get used (*a* to); **se acostumbró a levantarse temprano** he got used to getting up early

ácrata *m/f & adj* anarchist

acre *adj olor* acrid; *crítica* biting

acrecentar <1k> **1** *v/t* increase **2** *v/r ~se* increase, grow

acreditar <1a> **1** *v/t* diplomático *etc* accredit (*como* as); (*avalar*) prove; **un documento que lo acredita como el propietario** a document that is proof of his ownership **2** *v/r ~se* acquire a good reputation

acreedor *m*, **~a** *f* creditor; **acreencia** *f L.Am.* credit

acribillar <1a> *v/t*: **~ a alguien a balazos** riddle s.o. with bullets; **~ a alguien a preguntas** bombard s.o. with questions

acrílico *m/adj* acrylic

acristalar <1a> *v/t* glaze

acróbata *m/f* acrobat; **acrobático** *adj* acrobatic; **vuelo ~** stunt flight

acta(s) *f*(*pl*) minutes *pl*

actitud *f* (*disposición*) attitude; (*posición*) position; **activar** <1a> *v/t* activate; (*estimular*) stimulate; **actividad** *f* activity; **activista** *m/f* POL activist; **activo 1** *adj* active; **en ~** on active service; **población -a** labo(u)r force **2** *m* COM assets *pl*

acto *m* (*acción*), TEA act; *ceremonia* ceremony; **~ sexual** sexual intercourse; **~ seguido** immediately afterward(s); **en el ~** instantly, there and then

actor *m* actor; **actriz** *f* actress

actuación *f* TEA performance; (*intervención*) intervention; **actual** *adj* present, current; **un tema muy ~** a very topical issue; **actualidad** *f* current situation; **en la ~** at present, presently; (*hoy en día*) nowadays; **~es** current affairs; **actualizar** <1f> *v/t* bring up to date, update; **actualmente** *adv* currently

actuar <1e> *v/i* (*obrar, ejercer*), TEA act; MED work, act

acuarela *f* watercolo(u)r

acuario *m* aquarium

Acuario *m/f inv* ASTR Aquarius

acuático *adj* aquatic; **deporte ~** water sport

acuchillar <1a> *v/t* stab

acuciante *adj* pressing, urgent

acudir <3a> *v/i* come; **~ a alguien** turn to s.o.; **~ a las urnas** go to the polls

acueducto *m* aqueduct

acuerdo *m* agreement; **estar de ~ con** agree with; **llegar a un ~, ponerse de ~** come to *o* reach an agreement (*con* with); **de ~ con**

algo in accordance with sth; **¡de ~!** all right!, OK!

acumulación f accumulation; **acumular** <1a> **1** v/t accumulate **2** v/r **~se** accumulate

acunar <1a> v/t rock

acuñar <1a> v/t monedas mint; término, expresión coin

acuoso adj watery

acupuntura f acupuncture

acurrucarse <1g> v/r curl up

acusación f accusation; **acusado** m, **-a** f defendant; **acusar** <1a> v/t accuse (**de** of); JUR charge (**de** with); (manifestar) show; **~ recibo de** acknowledge receipt of; **acuse** m: **~ de recibo** acknowledg(e)ment

acusetas m/f inv S.Am. F tattletale F, Br tell-tale F; **acusica** m/f F tattletale F, Br tell-tale F

acústica f acoustics

adaptable adj adaptable; **adaptación** f adaptation; **~ cinematográfica** screen o movie version; **adaptador** m adaptor; **adaptar** <1a> **1** v/t adapt **2** **~se** v/r adapt (**a** to)

A. de C. abr (= **año de Cristo**) AD (= Anno Domini)

adecentar <1a> v/t straighten up, tidy up

adecuadamente adv properly; **adecuado** adj suitable, appropriate; **adecuar** <1d> **1** v/t adapt (**a** to) **2** v/r **~se** fit in (**a** with)

adefesio m fig F monstrosity F; persona freak F; **estar hecho un ~** look a sight

a. de J.C. abr (= **antes de Jesucristo**) BC (= before Christ)

adelantado adj advanced; **por ~** in advance; **ir ~** de un reloj be fast; **adelantamiento** m AUTO passing maneuver, Br overtaking manoeuvre; **adelantar** <1a> **1** v/t mover move forward; reloj put forward; AUTO overtake, Br overtake; dinero advance; (conseguir) achieve, gain **2** v/i de un reloj be fast; (avanzar) make progress; AUTO pass, Br overtake **3** v/r **~se** mover move forward; (ir delante) go on ahead; de

estación, cosecha be early; de un reloj gain; **se me adelantó** she beat me to it, she got there first; **adelante** adv en espacio forward; **seguir ~** carry on, keep going; **¡~!** come in; **más ~** en tiempo later on; **de ahora** o **de aquí en ~** from now on; **salir ~** fig: de persona succeed; de proyecto go ahead; **adelanto** m tb COM advance

adelfa f BOT oleander

adelgazante adj weight-reducing, slimming atr; **adelgazar** <1f> **1** v/t lose **2** v/i lose weight

ademán m gesture; **hacer ~ de** make as if to

además 1 adv as well, besides **2** prp: **~ de** as well as

adentrarse <1a> v/r: **~ en** territorio penetrate; tema go into; **adentro 1** adv inside; **¡~!** get inside!; **mar ~** out to sea; **~ de** L.Am. inside **2** mpl: **para sus ~s** to oneself

adepto m follower; fig supporter

aderezar <1f> v/t con especias season; ensalada dress; fig liven up

adeudar <1a> v/t owe

adherente adj adhesive; **adherir** <3i> **1** v/i stick, adhere fml **2** v/t stick **3** v/r **~se** a superficie stick (**a** to), adhere (**a** to) fml; **~se a una organización** become a member of o join an organization; **~se a una idea** support an idea; **adhesivo** m/adj adhesive

adicción f addiction; **~ a las drogas** drug addiction

adicional adj additional

adictivo adj addictive; **adicto 1** adj addicted (**a** to); **ser ~ al régimen** be a supporter of the regime **2** m, **-a** f addict

adiestrar <1a> v/t train

adinerado adj wealthy

adiós 1 int goodbye, bye; al cruzarse hello **2** m goodbye; **decir ~** say goodbye (**a** to)

aditivo m additive

adivinanza f riddle; **adivinar** <1a> v/t guess; de adivino foretell

adjetivo m adjective

adjudicar <1g> **1** v/t award **2** v/r **~se** win

adjuntar <1a> v/t enclose

adm. abr (= **administración**) admin (= administration)

administración f administration; de empresa etc management; (gobierno) administration, government; **~ pública** civil service; **administrador** m, **~a** f administrator; de empresa etc manager; **administrar** <1a> v/t medicamento, sacramentos administer, give; empresa run, manage; bienes manage; **administrativo 1** adj administrative **2** m, **-a** f administrative assistant

admirable adj admirable; **admiración** f admiration; **signo de ~** exclamation mark; **admirador** m, **~a** f admirer; **admirar** <1a> **1** v/t admire; (asombrar) amaze **2** v/r **~se** be amazed (**de** at o by)

admisible adj admissible; **admisión** f admission; **derecho de ~** right of admission; **admitir** <3a> v/t (aceptar) accept; (reconocer) admit

admón. abr (= **administración**) admin (= administration)

ADN abr (= **ácido desoxirribonucleico**) DNA (= deoxyribonucleic acid)

adobar <1a> v/t GASTR marinate; **adobera** f Méx type of mature cheese; **adobo** m GASTR marinade

adoctrinar <1a> v/t indoctrinate

adolecer <2d> v/t suffer (**de** from)

adolescencia f adolescence; **adolescente** m/f adolescent

adonde adv where

adónde interr where

adopción f adoption; **adoptar** <1a> v/t adopt; **adoptivo** adj padres adoptive; hijo adopted

adoquín m paving stone

adorable adj lovable, adorable; **adoración** f adoration; **adorar** <1a> v/t love, adore; REL worship

adormecer <2d> **1** v/t make sleepy **2** v/r **~se** doze off; **adormidera** f BOT poppy; **adormilado** adj sleepy; **adormilarse** <1a> v/r doze off

adornar <1a> v/t decorate; **adorno** m ornament; de Navidad decoration

adosar <1a> v/t: **~ algo a algo** put sth (up) against sth

adquirir <3i> v/t acquire; (comprar) buy; **adquisición** f acquisition; **hacer una buena ~** make a good purchase; **adquisitivo** adj: **poder ~** purchasing power

adrede adv on purpose, deliberately

adrenalina f adrenaline

aduana f customs; **aduanero 1** adj customs atr **2** m, **-a** f customs officer

aducir <3o> v/t razones, argumentos give, put forward; (alegar) claim

adueñarse <1a> v/r: **~ de** take possession of

adulación f flattery; **adular** <1a> v/t flatter; **adulón 1** adj S.Am. fawning **2** m, **-ona** f flatterer

adultera f adulteress; **adulterar** <1a> v/t adulterate; **adulterio** m adultery; **cometer ~** commit adultery; **adúltero 1** adj adulterous **2** m adulterer

adultez f adulthood; **adulto 1** adj adult; **edad -a** adulthood **2** m, **-a** f adult

adusto adj paisaje harsh; persona stern, severe; L.Am. (inflexible) stubborn

adverbio m adverb

adversario m, **-a** f adversary, opponent; **adverso** adj adverse

advertencia f warning; **advertir** <3i> v/t warn (**de** about, of); (notar) notice

adyacente adj adjacent

aéreo adj air atr; vista, fotografía aerial; **compañía -a** airline

aerobic, aeróbic m aerobics

aerodinámico adj aerodynamic

aeroespacial adj aerospace atr

aerolínea f airline

aeromozo m, **-a** f L.Am. flight attendant

aeronáutico adj aeronautical

aeropuerto m airport

aerosol m aerosol

afable *adj* pleasant, affable

afamado *adj* famous

afán *m* (*esfuerzo*) effort; (*deseo*) eagerness; **sin ~ de lucro** organización not-for-profit, non-profit (making); **afanar** <1a> **1** *v/i C.Am.* (*ganar dinero*) make money **2** *v/t C.Am. dinero* make; *Rpl* F (*robar*) pinch F **3** *v/r* **~se** make an effort

afección *f* MED complaint, condition; **afectado** *adj* (*afligido*) upset (*por* by); (*amanerado*) affected; **afectar** <1a> *v/t* (*producir efecto en*) affect; (*conmover*) upset, affect; (*fingir*) feign; **afectivo** *adj* emotional; **afecto** *m* affection; **tener ~ a alguien** be fond of s.o.; **afectuoso** *adj* affectionate

afeitada *f* shave; **afeitado** *m* shave; **afeitadora** *f* electric razor; **afeitar** <1a> **1** *v/t* shave; *barba* shave off **2** *v/r* **~se** shave, have a shave

afeminado *adj* effeminate

aferrarse <1k> *v/r fig* cling (**a** to)

Afganistán Afghanistan

afianzar <1f> **1** *v/t fig* strengthen **2** *v/r* **~se** become consolidated

afición *f* love (*por* of); (*pasatiempo*) pastime, hobby; **la ~** DEP the fans; **aficionado 1** *adj*: **ser ~ a** be interested in, *Br tb* be keen on **2** *m*, **-a** *f* enthusiast; *no profesional* amateur; **un partido de ~s** an amateur game; **aficionarse** <1a> *v/r* become interested (**a** in)

afiebrarse <1a> *v/r L.Am.* develop a fever

afilado *adj* sharp; **afilador** *m* sharpener; **afilalápices** *m inv* pencil sharpener; **afilar** <1a> **1** *v/t* sharpen; *L.Am.* F (*halagar*) flatter, butter up F; *S.Am.* (*seducir*) seduce **2** *v/r* **~se** *S.Am.* F (*prepararse*) get ready

afiliarse <1a> *v/r*: **~ a un partido** become a member of a party, join a party

afinar <1a> *v/t* MÚS tune; *punta* sharpen; *fig* perfect, fine-tune

afincarse <1g> *v/r* settle

afinidad *f* affinity

afirmación *f* statement; *declaración positiva* affirmation; **afirmar** <1a> *v/t* state, declare; **afirmativo** *adj* affirmative

afligido *adj* upset, **afligir** <3c> **1** *v/t* afflict; (*apenar*) upset; *L.Am.* F (*golpear*) beat up **2** *v/r* **~se** get upset

aflojar <1a> **1** *v/t nudo, tornillo* loosen; F *dinero* hand over **2** *v/i de tormenta* abate; *de viento, fiebre* drop **3** *v/r* **~se** come *o* work loose

afluente *m* tributary

afmo. *abr* (= **afectísimo**): **su ~** Yours truly

afónico *adj*: **está ~** he has lost his voice

aforo *m* capacity

afortunado *adj* lucky, fortunate

afrecho *f Arg* bran

África Africa; **~ del Sur** South Africa; **africano 1** *adj* African **2** *m*, **-a** *f* African

afrodisíaco *m* aphrodisiac

afrontar <1a> *v/t* face (up to)

afuera *adv* outside; **afueras** *fpl* outskirts

agachar <1a> **1** *v/i* duck **2** *v/r* **~se** bend down; (*acuclillarse*) crouch down; *L.Am.* (*rendirse*) give in

agalla *f* ZO gill; **tener ~s** F have guts F

agarrado *adj fig* F mean, stingy F; **agarrar** <1a> **1** *v/t* (*asir*) grab; *L.Am.* (*tomar*) take; *L.Am.* (*atrapar, pescar*), *resfriado* catch; *L.Am. velocidad* gather, pick up; **~ una calle** *L.Am.* go up *o* along a street **2** *v/i* (*asirse*) hold on; *de planta* take root; *L.Am. por un lugar* go; **agarró y se fue** he upped and went **3** *v/r* **~se** (*asirse*) hold on; *L.Am. a golpes* get into a fight; **agarrón** *m Rpl* P (*pleito*) fight, argument; *L.Am.* (*tirón*) pull, tug

agarrotado *adj* stiff; **agarrotarse** <1a> *v/r de músculo* stiffen up; TÉC seize up

agasajar <1a> *v/t* fête

agazaparse <1a> *v/r* crouch (down); (*ocultarse*) hide

agencia f agency; **~ inmobiliaria** real estate office, Br estate agency; **~ de viajes** travel agency; **agenciarse** <1b> v/r F get hold of

agenda f diario diary; programa schedule; de mitin agenda

agente 1 m agent **2** m/f agent; **~ de cambio y bolsa** stockbroker; **~ de policía** police officer

ágil adj agile; **agilidad** f agility

agilizar <1f> v/t speed up

agitación f POL unrest; **agitar** <1a> **1** v/t shake; brazos, pañuelo wave; fig stir up **2** v/r **~se** become agitated o worked up

aglomeración f de gente crowd; **aglomerar** <1a> v/t pile up

aglutinar <1a> v/t fig bring together

agobiante adj oppressive; **agobiar** <1b> **1** v/t de calor oppress; de problemas get on top of, overwhelm **2** v/r **~se** F feel overwhelmed; **agobio** m: **es un ~** it's unbearable, it's a nightmare F

agolparse <1a> v/r crowd together

agonía f agony; **la espera fue una ~** the wait was unbearable; **agonizante** adj dying; **agonizar** <1f> v/i de persona be dying; de régimen be crumbling

agorero adj ominous

agosto m August; **hacer su ~** F make a fortune

agotado adj (cansado) exhausted, worn out; (terminado) exhausted; (vendido) sold out; **agotador** adj exhausting; **agotar** <1a> **1** v/t (cansar) wear out, exhaust; (terminar) use up, exhaust **2** v/r **~se** (cansarse) get worn out, exhaust o.s.; (terminarse) run out, become exhausted; (venderse) sell out

agraciado adj persona attractive

agradable adj pleasant, nice; **agradar** <1a> v/i: **me agrada la idea** fml I like the idea; **nos ~ía mucho que ...** fml we would be delighted o very pleased if ...

agradecer <2d> v/t: **~ algo a alguien** thank s.o. for sth; **te lo agradezco** I appreciate it; **agradecimiento** m

appreciation; **agrado** m: **ser del ~ de alguien** be to s.o.'s liking

agrandar <1a> **1** v/t make bigger **2** v/r **~se** get bigger

agrario adj land atr, agrarian; política agricultural

agravar <1a> **1** v/t make worse, aggravate **2** v/r **~se** get worse, deteriorate

agravio m offense, Br offence

agredir <3a> v/t attack, assault

agregado m, **~a** f en universidad senior lecturer; en colegio senior teacher; POL attaché; **~ cultural** cultural attaché

agregar <1h> v/t add

agresión f aggression; **agresividad** f aggression; **agresivo** adj aggressive; **agresor** m, **~a** f aggressor

agreste adj terreno rough; paisaje wild

agriarse <1b or 1c> v/r de vino go sour; de carácter become bitter

agrícola adj agricultural, farming atr; **agricultor** m, **~a** f farmer; **agricultura** f agriculture

agridulce adj bittersweet

agriera f L.Am. heartburn

agrietarse <2a> v/r crack; de manos, labios chap

agringarse <1h> v/r L.Am. become Americanized

agrio adj fruta sour; disputa, carácter bitter

agrios mpl BOT citrus fruit sg

agropecuario adj farming atr, agricultural

agrupar <1a> **1** v/t group, put into groups **2** v/r **~se** gather

agua f water; **~ corriente** running water; **~ dulce** fresh water; **~ mineral** mineral water; **~ oxigenada** (hydrogen) peroxide; **~ potable** drinking water; **es ~ pasada** it's water under the bridge; **está con el ~ al cuello** con problemas he's up to his neck in problems F; con deudas he's up to his neck in debt F; **se me hace la boca ~** it makes my mouth water; **aguas** fpl waters; **~ residuales** effluent sg, sewage sg

aguacate *m* BOT avocado

aguacero *m* downpour

aguachento *adj CSur* watery

aguafiestas *m/f inv* partypooper F, killjoy

aguaitar <1a> *v/t S.Am.* spy on

aguamala *f S.Am.* jellyfish

aguamiel *f L.Am.* mixture of water and honey; *Méx* (*jugo de maguey*) agave sap

aguanieve *f* sleet

aguantar <1a> **1** *v/t un peso* bear, support; *respiración* hold; (*soportar*) put up with; *no lo puedo ~* I can't stand *o* bear it **2** *v/i* hang on, hold out **3** *v/r ~se contenerse* keep quiet; *me tuve que ~ conformarme* I had to put up with it; **aguante** *m* patience; *física* stamina, endurance

aguar <1a> *v/t fiesta* spoil

aguardar <1a> **1** *v/t* wait for, await **2** *v/i* wait

aguardiente *m fruit-based alcoholic spirit*

aguarrás *m* turpentine, turps F

aguatero *m*, **-a** *f S.Am.* water-seller

agudeza *f de voz, sonido* high pitch; MED intensity; (*perspicacia*) sharpness; *~ visual* sharp-sightedness

agudizar <1f> **1** *v/t un sentido* sharpen; *~ un problema* make a problem worse **2** *v/r ~se* MED get worse; *de un sentido* become sharper

agudo *adj* acute; (*afilado*) sharp; *sonido* high-pitched; (*perspicaz*) sharp

agüero *m* omen; *ser de mal ~* be an ill omen

aguijón *m* ZO sting; *fig* spur

águila *f* eagle; *¿~ o sol? Méx* heads or tails?; *ser un ~ fig* be very sharp; **aguilucho** *m* eaglet

agüita *f L.Am.* F (*agua*) water; (*infusión*) infusion

aguja *f* needle; *de reloj* hand; *buscar una ~ en un pajar fig* look for a needle in a haystack

agujerear <1a> **1** *v/t* make holes in

2 *v/r ~se* develop holes; **agujero** *m* hole

agujetas *fpl* stiffness *sg*; *tener ~* be stiff

aguzar <1f> *v/t* sharpen; *~ el ingenio* sharpen one's wits; *~ el oído* prick up one's ears

ah *int* ah!

ahí *adv* there; *está por ~* it's (some-where) over there; *dando direcciones* it's that way

ahijada *f* goddaughter; **ahijado** *m* godson

ahínco *m* effort; *trabajar con ~* work hard

ahogado *adj en agua* drowned; **ahogar** <1h> **1** *v/t* (*asfixiar*) suffocate; *en agua* drown; AUTO flood; *protestas* stifle **2** *v/r ~se* choke; (*asfixiarse*) suffocate; *en agua* drown; AUTO flood; *~se en un vaso de agua fig* F get in a state over nothing

ahondar <1a> *v/i*: *~ en algo* go into sth in depth

ahora *adv* (*en este momento*) now; (*pronto*) in a moment; *~ mismo* right now; *por ~* for the present, for the time being; *~ bien* however; *desde ~, de ~ en adelante* from now on; *¡hasta ~!* see you soon

ahorcar <1g> **1** *v/t* hang **2** *v/r ~se* hang o.s.

ahorita *adv L.Am.* (*en este momento*) (right) now; *Méx, C.Am.* (*pronto*) in a moment; *Méx, C.Am.* (*hace poco*) just now

ahorrar <1a> **1** *v/t* save; *~ algo a alguien* save s.o. (from) sth **2** *v/i* save (up) **3** *v/r ~se dinero* save; *fig* spare o.s., save o.s.; **ahorro** *m* saving; *~s pl* savings; *caja de ~s* savings bank

ahulado *m C.Am.*, *Méx* oilskin

ahumar <1a> *v/t* smoke

ahuyentar <1a> **1** *v/t* scare off *o* away **2** *v/r ~se L.Am.* run away

AI *abr* (= *Amnistía Internacional*) AI (= Amnesty International)

airado *adj* angry

airbag *m* AUTO airbag

aire *m* air; **~ acondicionado** air-conditioning; **al ~ libre** in the open air; **a mi ~** in my own way; **estar en el ~** *fig* F be up in the air F; **hace mucho ~** it is very windy; **airear** <1a> *v/t tb* air

airoso *adj*: **salir ~ de algo** do well in sth

aislado *adj* isolated; **aislante 1** *adj* insulating, insulation *atr* **2** *m* insulator; **aislar** <1a> *v/t* isolate; EL insulate **2** *v/r* **~se** cut o.s. off

ajardinado *adj* landscaped; **zona ~a** area with parks and gardens

a. J.C. *abr* (= **antes de Jesucristo**) BC (= before Christ)

ajedrez *m* chess

ajeno *adj propiedad, problemas etc* someone else's; **me era totalmente ~** it was completely alien to me; **estar ~ a** be unaware of, be oblivious to; **por razones ~as a nuestra voluntad** for reasons beyond our control

ajete *m* BOT young garlic

ajetreo *m* bustle

ají *m S.Am.* chili, *Br* chilli; **ajiaco** *m Col* spicy potato stew; **ajillo** *m*: **al ~** with garlic; **ajo** *m* BOT garlic; **estar** *or* **andar en el ~** F be in the know F

ajuar *m de novia* trousseau

ajustar <1a> **1** *v/t máquina etc* adjust; *tornillo* tighten; *precio* set; **~ cuentas** *fig* settle a score **2** *v/i* fit **3** *v/r* **~se** *el cinturón* tighten; **~se a algo** *fig* keep within sth; **~se a la ley** comply with the law; **ajuste** *m*: **~ de cuentas** settling of scores

ajusticiar <1b> *v/t* execute

al *prp* **a** *y art* **el**; **~ entrar** on coming in, when we / they *etc* came in

ala *f* wing; MIL flank; **~ delta** hang glider; **cortar las ~s a alguien** clip s.o.'s wings

alabanza *f* acclaim; **alabar** <1a> *v/t* praise, acclaim

alacena *f* larder

alacrán *m* ZO scorpion

alambrada *f* wire fence; **alambrar** <1a> *v/t* fence; **alambre** *m* wire; **~ de espino** *or* **de púas** barbed wire

álamo *m* BOT poplar; **~ temblón** aspen

alarde *m* show, display; **hacer ~ de** make a show of; **alardear** <1a> *v/i* show off (**de** about)

alargador *m* TÉC extension cord, *Br* extension lead; **alargar** <1h> **1** *v/t* lengthen; *prenda* let down; *en tiempo* prolong; *mano, brazo* stretch out **2** *v/r* **~se** *de sombra, día* get longer, lengthen

alarido *m* shriek; **dar ~s** shriek

alarma *f* (*mecanismo, miedo*) alarm; **dar la voz de ~** raise the alarm; **alarmante** *adj* alarming; **alarmar** <1a> **1** *v/t* alarm **2** *v/r* **~se** become alarmed

alba *f* dawn

albahaca *f* BOT basil

Albania Albania

albañil *m* bricklayer

albaricoque *m* BOT apricot

albatros *m inv* ZO albatross

albedrío *m*: **libre ~** free will

alberca *f* reservoir; *Méx* (swimming) pool

albergar <1h> *v/t* (*hospedar*) put up; (*contener*) house; *esperanzas* hold out

albergue *m* refuge, shelter; **~ juvenil** youth hostel

albino *m*, **-a** *f* albino

albóndiga *f* meatball

albornoz *m* bathrobe

alborotador *m*, **~a** *f* rioter; **alborotar** <1a> **1** *v/t* stir up; (*desordenar*) disturb **2** *v/i* make a racket **3** *v/r* **~se** get excited; (*inquietarse*) get worked up; **alboroto** *m* commotion

álbum *m* album

alcachofa *f* BOT artichoke; *de ducha* shower head

alcalde *m*, **-esa** *f* mayor

alcalino *adj* alkaline

alcance *m* reach; *de arma etc* range; *de medida* scope; *de tragedia* extent, scale; **al ~ de la mano** within reach; **¿está al ~ de tu bolsillo?** can you afford it?; **dar ~ a alguien** catch up with s.o.; **poner al ~ de alguien** put within s.o.'s reach

alcancía f *L.Am.* piggy bank

alcantarilla f sewer; (*sumidero*) drain

alcanzar <1f> **1** v/t *a alguien* catch up with; *lugar* reach, get to; *en nivel* reach; *cantidad* amount to; *objetivo* achieve **2** v/i *en altura* reach; *en cantidad* be enough; **~ a oír/ver** manage to hear/see

alcaparra f BOT caper

alcayata f hook

alcázar m fortress

alce m ZO elk

alcista adj *en bolsa* rising, bull atr; **tendencia ~** upward trend

alcoba f *S.Am.* bedroom

alcohol m alcohol; MED rubbing alcohol, *Br* surgical spirit; **~ de quemar** denatured alcohol, *Br* methylated spirits sg; **alcoholemia** f blood alcohol level; **prueba de ~** drunkometer test, *Br* Breathalyzer® test; **alcohólico 1** adj alcoholic **2** m, -a f alcoholic; **alcoholismo** m alcoholism

alcornoque m BOT cork oak; **pedazo de ~** F blockhead F

alcurnia f ancestry

aldea f (small) village

aleación f alloy

aleatorio adj random

aleccionar <1a> v/t instruct; (*regañar*) lecture

aledaños mpl surrounding area sg; *de ciudad* outskirts

alegador adj *L.Am.* argumentative; **alegar** <1h> **1** v/t *motivo, razón* cite; **~ que** claim o allege that **2** v/i *L.Am.* (*discutir*) argue; (*quejarse*) moan, gripe

alegrar <1a> **1** v/t make happy; (*animar*) cheer up **2** v/r **~se** cheer up; F *bebiendo* get tipsy; **~se por alguien** be pleased for s.o. (*de* about); **alegre** adj (*contento*) happy; *por naturaleza* happy, cheerful; F *bebido* tipsy; **alegría** f happiness

alejar <1a> **1** v/t move away **2** v/r **~se** move away (*de* from); *de situación, ámbito* get away (*de* from); **¡no te alejes mucho!** don't go too far away!

alelar <1a> v/t stupefy

aleluya m & int hallelujah

alemán 1 m/adj German **2** m, -ana f *persona* German; **Alemania** Germany

alentado adj *L.Am.* encouraged; **alentar** <1k> **1** v/t (*animar*) encourage; *esperanzas* cherish **2** v/r **~se** *L.Am.* get better

alergia f allergy; **alérgico** adj allergic (*a* to)

alerta 1 adv: **estar ~** be on the alert **2** f alert; **dar la ~** raise the alarm; **poner en ~** alert; **alertar** <1a> v/t alert (*de* to)

aleta f ZO fin; *de buzo* flipper; *de la nariz* wing

aletargarse <1h> v/r feel lethargic

aletear <1a> v/i flap one's wings

alevosía f treachery

alfabético adj alphabetical; **alfabetizar** <1f> v/t *lista etc* put into alphabetical order; **~ a alguien** teach s.o. to read and write; **alfabeto** m alphabet

alfalfa f BOT alfalfa

alfanumérico adj alphanumeric

alfarero m, -a f potter

alfil m bishop

alfiler m pin; **~ de gancho** *Arg* safety pin; **no cabe un ~** fig F there's no room for anything else; **alfiletero** m (*cojín*) pincushion; (*estuche*) needlecase

alfombra f carpet; *más pequeña* rug; **alfombrado** m *L.Am.* carpeting, carpets pl; **alfombrar** <1a> v/t carpet; **alfombrilla** f mouse mat

alga f BOT alga; *marina* seaweed

álgebra f algebra

álgido adj fig decisive

algo 1 pron *en frases afirmativas* something; *en frases interrogativas o condicionales* anything; **~ es ~** it's something, it's better than nothing **2** adv rather, somewhat

algodón m cotton; **criado entre algodones** F mollycoddled, pampered

alguacil m, **-esa** f bailiff

alguien pron *en frases afirmativas*

somebody, someone; *en frases interrogativas o condicionales* anybody, anyone

algún *adj en frases afirmativas* some; *en frases interrogativas o condicionales* any; ~ *día* some day

alguno 1 *adj en frases afirmativas* some; *en frases interrogativas o condicionales* any; *no la influyó de modo* ~ it didn't influence her in any way; *¿has estado alguna vez en ...?* have you ever been to ...? **2** *pron: persona* someone, somebody; ~*s opinan que ...* some people think that ...; ~ *se podrá usar objeto* we'll be able to use some of them

alhaja *f* piece of jewel(le)ry; *fig* gem; ~*s* jewelry *sg*

alhelí *m* BOT wallflower

aliado *m*, **-a** *f* ally; **alianza** *f* POL alliance; (*anillo*) wedding ring; **aliarse** <1c> *v/r* form an alliance (*con* with)

alias *m inv* alias

alicaído *adj* F down F

alicatar <1a> *v/t* tile

alicates *mpl* pliers

aliciente *m* (*estímulo*) incentive; (*atractivo*) attraction

alienar <1a> *v/t* alienate; **alienígena** *m/f* alien

aliento *m* breath; *fig* encouragement

aligerar <1a> *v/t carga* lighten; ~ *el paso* quicken one's pace

alijo *m* MAR consignment

alimentación *f* (*dieta*) diet; *acción* feeding; EL power supply; **alimentar** <1a> **1** *v/t tb* TÉC, *fig* feed; EL power **2** *v/i* be nourishing **3** *v/r* ~**se** feed o.s.; ~*se de algo de persona*, *animal* live on sth; *de máquina* run on sth; **alimento** *m* (*comida*) food; *tiene poco* ~ it has little nutritional value; ~*s dietéticos* (*de régimen*) slimming aids

alineación *f* DEP line-up; **alinear** <1a> **1** *v/t* align **2** *v/r* ~**se** (*ponerse en fila*) line up; POL align o.s. (*con* with)

aliñar <1a> *v/t* dress; **aliño** *m* dressing

alioli *m* GASTR garlic mayonnaise

alisar <1a> *v/t* smooth

alistarse <1a> *v/r* MIL enlist

aliviar <1b> *v/t* alleviate, relieve; **alivio** *m* relief

allá *adv de lugar* (over) there; ~ *por los años veinte* back in the twenties; *más* ~ further on; *más* ~ *de* beyond; *el más* ~ the hereafter; ~ *él/ella* F that's up to him/her

allanamiento *m*: ~ *de morada* JUR breaking and entering; **allanar** <1a> *v/t* (*alisar*) smooth; (*aplanar*) level (out); *obstáculos* overcome

allegado *m*, **-a** *f* relation, relative

allí *adv* there; *por* ~ over there; *dando direcciones* that way; *¡*~ *está!* there it is!

alma *f* soul; *se me cayó el* ~ *a los pies* F my heart sank; *llegar al* ~ *conmover* move deeply; *herir* ~ hurt deeply; *no se ve un* ~ there isn't a soul to be seen; *lo siento en el* ~ I am truly sorry

almacén *m* warehouse; (*tienda*) store, shop; *grandes almacenes pl* department store *sg*; **almacenamiento** *m* storage; ~ *de datos* data storage; **almacenar** <1a> *v/t tb* INFOR store; **almacenero** *m*, **-a** *f* storekeeper, shopkeeper

almanaque *m* almanac

almeja *f* ZO clam

almenas *fpl* battlements

almendra *f* almond; **almendro** *m* almond tree

almíbar *m* syrup; *en* ~ in syrup; **almibarado** *adj fig* syrupy

almidón *m* starch

almirante *m* admiral

almirez *m* mortar

almohada *f* pillow; *consultarlo con la* ~ sleep on it; **almohadilla** *f* small cushion; TÉC pad; **almohadón** *m* large cushion

almorranas *fpl* piles

almorzada *f Méx* lunch; **almorzar** <1f & 1m> **1** *v/i al mediodía* have lunch; *a media mañana* have a mid-morning snack **2** *v/t*: ~ *algo al* *mediodía* have sth for lunch; *a media mañana* have sth as a mid-morning snack

almuerzo *m al mediodía* lunch; *a media mañana* mid-morning snack; **~ de trabajo** working lunch

¿alo? *L.Am.* hello?

alocado 1 *adj* crazy **2** *m*, **-a** *f* crazy fool

áloe *m* BOT aloe

alojamiento *m* accommodations *pl*, *Br* accommodation; **alojar** <1a> **1** *v/t* accommodate **2** *v/r* **~se** stay (*en* in); **alojo** *m L.Am.* → **alojamiento**

alondra *f* ZO lark

alopecia *f* MED alopecia

alpaca *f animal, lana* alpaca

alpargata *f Esp* espadrille

alpinismo *m* mountaineering; **alpinista** *m/f* mountaineer, climber

alpiste *m* birdseed

alquilar <1a> *v/t de usuario* rent; *de dueño* rent out; **alquiler** *m acción: de coche etc* rental; *de casa* renting; *dinero* rental, *Br tb* rent; **~ de coches** car rental, *Br tb* car hire

alquitrán *m* tar

alrededor 1 *adv* around **2** *prp:* **~ de** around; **alrededores** *mpl* surrounding area *sg*

alta *f* MED discharge; **dar de ~** MED discharge; **darse de ~** *en organismo* register

altanero *adj* arrogant

altar *m* altar; **llevar al ~** marry

altavoz *m* loudspeaker

alteración *f* alteration; **alterar** <1a> **1** *v/t* (*cambiar*) alter; *a alguien* upset; **~ el orden público** cause a breach of the peace **2** *v/r* **~se** get upset (*por* because of)

altercado *m* argument, altercation *fml*

alternar <1a> **1** *v/t* alternate; **~ el trabajo con el descanso** alternate work and study **2** *v/i* mix **3** *v/r* **~se** alternate, take turns; **alternativa** *f* alternative; **alternativo** *adj* alternative; **alterno** *adj* alternate; **corriente -a** EL alternating current;

en días ~s on alternate days

Alteza *f título* Highness

altibajos *mpl* ups and downs

altillo *m* (*desván*) attic; *en armario* top (part of the) closet

altiplano *m* high plateau

altisonante *adj* high-flown

altitud *f* altitude

altivo *adj* haughty

alto[1] **1** *adj persona* tall; *precio, número, montaña* high; **-as presiones** high pressure; **~ horno** blast furnace; **clase -a** high class; **en -a mar** on the high seas; **en voz -a** out loud **2** *adv volar, saltar* high; **hablar ~** speak loudly; **pasar por ~** overlook; **poner más ~** TV, RAD turn up; **por todo lo ~** F lavishly **3** *m* (*altura*) height; *Chi* pile

alto[2] *m* halt; (*pausa*) pause; **hacer un ~** stop; **~ el fuego** ceasefire; **¡~!** halt!

altoparlante *m L.Am.* loudspeaker

altozano *m* hillock

altramuz *m planta* lupin; *semilla* lupin seed

altruismo *m* altruism; **altruista** *adj* altruistic

altura *f* MAT height; MÚS pitch; AVIA altitude, height; GEOG latitude; *a estas ~s* by this time, by now; *estar a la ~ de algo* be up to sth F

alubia *f* BOT kidney bean

alucinación *f* hallucination; **alucinado** *adj* F gobsmacked F; **alucinante** *adj* F incredible

alucinar <1a> **1** *v/i* hallucinate **2** *v/t* F amaze; **alucine** *m: de ~* F amazing; **alucinógeno** *m* hallucinogen

alud *m* avalanche

aludir <3a> *v/i:* **~ a algo** allude to sth; **aludido: darse por ~** take it personally

alumbrar <1a> **1** *v/t* (*dar luz a*) light (up) **2** *v/i* give off light

aluminio *m* aluminum, *Br* aluminium; **papel de ~** aluminum (*Br* aluminium) foil

alumno *m*, **-a** *f* student

alusión *f* allusion (*a* to); **hacer ~ a** refer to, allude to

aluvión *m* barrage

alza *f* rise; **~** *en bolsa* rising; **alzado** *m*, **-a** *f L.Am.* insurgent; **alzar** <1f> **1** *v/t barrera, brazo* lift, raise; *precios* raise **2** *v/r* **~se** rise; *en armas* rise up; **alzo** *m C.Am.* theft

a.m. *abr* (= *ante meridiem*) a.m. (= ante meridiem)

ama *f* (*dueña*) owner; **~** *de casa* housewife, homemaker; **~** *de llaves* housekeeper; **~** *de leche* or *cría L.Am.* wetnurse

amabilidad *f* kindness; **amable** *adj* kind (*con* to)

amaestrar <1a> *v/t* train

amagom threat; *hizo* **~** *de levantarse* she made as if to get up; **~** *de infarto* minor heart attack

amainar <1a> *v/i de lluvia, viento* ease up, slacken off

amalgamar <1a> **1** *v/t fig* combine **2** *v/r* **~se** amalgamate

amamantar <1a> *v/t bebé* breastfeed; *cría* feed

amanecer <2d> *v/i* get light; *de persona* wake up **2** *m* dawn

amanerado *adj* affected

amante 1 *adj* loving; *es* **~** *de la buena vida* he's fond of good living **2** *m/f en una relación* lover; *los* **~s** *de la naturaleza* nature lovers

amañar <1a> *v/t* F rig F; *partido* fix F

amapola *f* BOT poppy

amar <1a> *v/t* love

amargar <1h> **1** *v/t día, ocasión* spoil; **~** *a alguien* make s.o. bitter **2** *v/r* **~se** get bitter; **~se la vida** get upset; **amargo** *adj tb fig* bitter; **amargura** *f tb fig* bitterness

amarillento *adj* yellowish; **amarillo** *m/adj* yellow

amarrar <1a> *v/t L.Am.* (*atar*) tie

amasar <1a> *v/t pan* knead; *fortuna* amass

amatista *f* amethyst

amazona *f* horsewoman; **amazónico** *adj* GEOG Amazonian

Amazonas *el* **~** the Amazon

ambages *mpl*: *decirlo sin* **~** say it straight out

ámbar *m* amber; *el semáforo está*

en **~** the lights are yellow, *Br* the lights are at amber

ambición *f* ambition; **ambicioso** *adj* ambitious

ambidextro, ambidiestro *adj* ambidextrous

ambientador *m* air freshener; **ambiental** *adj* environmental; **ambientar** <1a> **1** *v/t película, novela* set **2** *v/r* **~se** be set; **ambiente 1** *adj*: *medio* **~** environment; *temperatura* **~** room temperature **2** *m* (*entorno*) environment; (*situación*) atmosphere

ambigüedad *f* ambiguity; **ambiguo** *adj* ambiguous

ámbito *m* area; (*límite*) scope

ambom *Arg* two-piece suit

ambos, ambas 1 *adj* both **2** *pron* both (of us / you / them)

ambulancia *f* ambulance; **ambulante 1** *adj* travel(l)ing; *venta* **~** peddling, hawking **2** *m/f L.Am.* (*vendedor*) street seller; **ambulatorio 1** *adj* MED out-patient *atr* **2** *m* out-patient clinic

amedrentar <1a> *v/t* terrify

amén 1 *m* amen **2** *prp*: **~** *de* as well as

amenaza *f* threat; **~** *de bomba* bomb scare; **amenazador** *adj* threatening; **amenazante** *adj* threatening; **amenazar** <1f> **1** *v/t* threaten (*con, de* with) **2** *v/i*: **~** *con* threaten to; *amenaza tempestad* there's a storm brewing

amenizar <1f> *v/t*: **~** *algo* make sth more entertaining *o* enjoyable

ameno *adj* enjoyable

América America; **~** *del Norte* North America; **~** *del Sur* South America; **americana** *f* American (woman); *prenda* jacket; **americano** *m/adj* American

amerizar <1f> *v/i de nave espacial* splash down

ametralladora *f* machine gun

amianto *m* MIN asbestos

amígdala *f* ANAT tonsil; **amigdalitis** *f* MED tonsillitis

amigo 1 *adj* friendly; *ser* **~** *de algo*

be fond of sth **2** *m*, **-a** *f* friend; **hacerse ~s** make friends

aminorar <1a> *v/t* reduce; **~ la marcha** slow down

amistad *f* friendship; **~es** friends; **amistosamente** *adv* amicably; **amistoso** *adj* friendly; **partido ~** DEP friendly (game)

amnesia *f* amnesia

amnistía *f* amnesty

amo *m* (*dueño*) owner; HIST master

amoblado *S.Am.* **1** *adj* furnished **2** *m* furniture

amodorrarse <1a> *v/r* feel sleepy

amoldarse <1a> *v/r* adapt (*a* to)

amonestación *f* warning; DEP caution; **amonestar** <1a> *v/t reñir* reprimand; DEP caution

amoníaco, amoniaco *m* ammonia

amontonar <1a> **1** *v/t* pile up **2** *v/r* **~se** *de objetos, problemas* pile up; *de gente* crowd together

amor *m* love; **~ mío** my love, darling; **~ propio** self-respect; **por ~ al arte** *fig* just for the fun of it; **por ~ de Dios** for God's sake; **hacer el ~** make love; **amoral** *adj* amoral

amoratado *adj* bruised

amordazar <1f> *v/t* gag; *animal, la prensa* muzzle

amorfo *adj* shapeless

amoroso *adj* amorous

amortajar <1a> *v/t* shroud

amortiguador *m* AUTO shock absorber; **amortiguar** <1i> *v/t impacto* cushion; *sonido* muffle

amortizar <1f> *v/t* pay off; COM *bienes* charge off, *Br* write off

amotinarse <1a> *v/r* rebel

amp. *abr* (= **amperios**) amp (= amperes)

amparar <1a> **1** *v/t* protect; (*ayudar*) help **2** *v/r* **~se** seek shelter (*de* from); **~se en algo** seek protection in sth; **amparo** *m* protection; (*cobijo*) shelter; **al ~ de** under the protection of

ampliación *f de casa, carretera* extension; FOT enlargement; **~ de capital** COM increase in capital; **ampliadora** *f* FOT enlarger;

ampliamente *adv* widely; **ampliar** <1c> **1** *v/t plantilla* increase; *negocio* expand; *plazo, edificio* extend; FOT enlarge **2** *v/r* **~se** broaden; **amplificador** *m* amplifier; **amplificar** <1g> *v/t* amplify; **amplio** *adj casa* spacious; *gama, margen* wide; *falda* full; **amplitud** *f* breadth

ampolla *f* MED blister; (*botellita*) vial, *Br* phial; **ampolleta** *f Arg, Chi* light bulb

ampuloso *adj* pompous

amputación *f* amputation; **amputar** <1a> *v/t brazo, pierna* amputate

amueblar <1a> *v/t* furnish

amuermar <1a> *v/t* F bore

amuleto *m* charm

anabolizante *m* anabolic steroid

anacardo *m* BOT cashew

anaconda *f* ZO anaconda

anacoreta *m/f* hermit

anacrónico *adj* anachronistic

ánade *m* ZO duck

anagrama *m* anagram

anal *adj* anal

anales *mpl* annals

analfabeto 1 *adj* illiterate **2** *m*, **-a** *f* illiterate

analgésico 1 *adj* painkilling, analgesic **2** *m* painkiller, analgesic

análisis *m inv* analysis; **~ de mercado** market research; **~ de sangre** blood test; **~ de sistemas** INFOR systems analysis; **analista** *m/f* analyst; **analizar** <1f> *v/t* analyze

analogía *f* analogy; **analógico** *adj* analog, *Br* analogue; **análogo** *adj* analogous

ananá(s) *m S.Am.* BOT pineapple

anarquía *f* anarchy; **anárquico** *adj* anarchic; **anarquista 1** *adj* anarchist *atr* **2** *m/f* anarchist

anatema *m* anathema

anatomía *f* anatomy; **anatómico** *adj* anatomical; **asiento ~** AUTO anatomically designed seat

anca *f* haunch; **~s** *pl de rana* GASTR frogs' legs

ancestral *adj* ancestral

ancho 1 *adj* wide, broad; **a sus -as** at

ease, relaxed; **quedarse tan ~** F carry on as if nothing had happened **2** m width; **~ de vía** FERR gauge; **dos metros de ~** two meters (*Br* metres) wide

anchoa f anchovy

anchura f width

anciana f old woman; **anciano 1** *adj* old **2** m old man

ancla f MAR anchor; **anclar** <1a> *v/i* MAR anchor

andadas *fpl*: **volver a las ~** F fall back into one's old ways

andador m **para bebé** baby walker; **para anciano** walker, Zimmer®

andamio m scaffolding

andanzas *fpl* adventures

andar <1q> **1** *v/i* (*caminar*) walk; (*funcionar*) work; **andando** on foot; **~ bien/mal** *fig* go well/badly; **~ con cuidado** be careful; **~ en algo** (*buscar*) rummage in sth; **~ tras algo** be after sth F; **~ haciendo algo** be doing sth; **¡anda!** come on! **2** *v/t* walk **3** *v/r* **~se**: **~se con bromas** kid around F

andas *fpl*: **llevar en ~** carry on one's shoulders

andén m platform; *L.Am.* sidewalk, *Br* pavement

Andes *mpl* Andes

andinismo m *L.Am.* mountaineering, climbing; **andinista** m/f *L.Am.* mountaineer, climber

andino *adj* Andean

Andorra Andorra

andrajoso *adj* ragged

andurriales *mpl*: **por estos ~** F around here

anécdota f anecdote

anegar <1h> **1** *v/t* flood **2** *v/r* **~se de campo, terreno** be flooded; **~se en llanto** dissolve into tears

anemia f MED an(a)emia; **anémico** *adj* an(a)emic

anestesia f MED an(a)esthesia; **anestesiado** *adj* an(a)esthetized, under F; **anestesiar** <1b> *v/t* an(a)esthetize

anexión f POL annexation; **anexionar** <1a> *v/t* POL annex; **anexo**

1 *adj* attached **2** m *edificio* annex, *Br* annex(e)

anfeta F, **anfetamina** f MED amphetamine

anfibio m/*adj* amphibian

anfiteatro m TEA amphitheater, *Br* amphitheatre; **de teatro** dress circle

anfitrión m host; **anfitriona** f hostess

ánfora f *L.Am.* POL ballot box; HIST amphora

ángel m angel; **~ custodio** or **de la guarda** guardian angel; **angelical** *adj* angelic

angina f MED: **~s** pl sore throat *sg*, strep throat *sg*; **~ de pecho** angina

anglicano 1 *adj* Anglican **2** m, **-a** f Anglican; **anglicismo** m Anglicism; **anglófono** *adj* English-speaking; **anglosajón 1** *adj* Anglo-Saxon **2** m, **-ona** f Anglo-Saxon

angora f angora

angosto *adj* narrow

anguila f ZO eel; **angula** f ZO, GASTR elver

ángulo m MAT, *fig* angle

angustia f anguish; **angustiado** *adj* distraught; **angustiante** *adj* distressing; **angustiar** <1b> **1** *v/t* distress **2** *v/r* **~se** agonize (**por** over); **angustioso** *adj* agonizing

anhelar <1a> *v/t* long for; **anhelo** m longing, desire (**de** for)

anhídrido m QUÍM anhydride; **~ carbónico** carbon dioxide

anidar <1a> *v/i* nest

anilla f ring; **cuaderno de ~s** ring binder; **~s** pl DEP rings

anillo m ring; **te viene como ~ al dedo** F it suits you perfectly

animación f liveliness; *en películas* animation; **hay mucha ~** it's very lively; **animado** *adj* lively; **animador** m host; **~ turístico** events organizer; **animadora** f hostess; DEP cheerleader

animal 1 *adj* animal *atr*; *fig* stupid **2** m *tb fig* animal; **~ doméstico** *mascota* pet; *de granja* domestic animal; **animalada** f: **decir/hacer una ~** F say/do something nasty

animar <1a> **1** v/t cheer up; (*alentar*) encourage **2** v/r **-se** cheer up

anímico adj mental; **estado ~** state of mind

ánimo m spirit; (*coraje*) encouragement; **estado de ~** state of mind; **con ~ de** with the intention of; **¡~!** cheer up!

animosidad f animosity

aniquilar <1a> v/t annihilate

anís m BOT aniseed; *bebida* anisette

aniversario m anniversary

ano m ANAT anus

anoche adv last night; **antes de ~** the night before last; **anochecer** <2d> **1** v/i get dark; **anocheció** night fell, it got dark **2** m dusk

anodino adj anodyne; *fig* bland

anómalo adj anomalous

anonadar <1a> v/t: **~ a alguien** take s.o. aback

anónimo 1 adj anonymous **2** m poison pen letter

anorak m anorak

anorexia f MED anorexia; **anoréxico** adj anorexic

anormal adj abnormal

anotar <1a> v/t note down

anquilosarse <1a> v/r get stiff

ansia f yearning; (*inquietud*) anxiousness; **ansiar** <1b> v/t yearn for, long for; **ansiedad** f anxiety; **ansioso** adj anxious; **está ~ por verlos** he's longing to see them

anta f L.Am. ZO tapir

antagonista m/f antagonist

antaño adv long ago

antártico adj Antarctic; **Antártida** Antarctica

ante[1] m suede; ZO moose; *Méx* (*postre*) egg and coconut dessert

ante[2] prp *posición* before; *dificultad* faced with; **~ todo** above all

anteayer adv the day before yesterday

antebrazo m forearm

antecedente m precedent; **~s penales** previous convictions; **poner a alguien en ~s** put s.o. in the picture; **antecesor** m, **-a** f predecessor

antediluviano adj prehistoric *hum*

antelación f: **con ~** in advance

antemano: **de ~** beforehand

antena f de radio, televisión antenna, *Br* aerial; ZO antenna; **~ parabólica** satellite dish

anteojos mpl binoculars

antepasado m, **-a** f ancestor

antepenúltimo adj third last

anteponer <2r> v/t: **~ algo a algo** put sth before sth

anteproyecto m draft

anterior adj previous, former

antes 1 adv before; **cuanto ~, lo posible** as soon as possible; **poco ~** shortly before; **~ que nada** first of all **2** prp: **~ de** before

antesala f lobby

antiadherente adj non-stick

antiaéreo adj anti-aircraft atr

antibala(s) adj bulletproof

antibelicista adj anti-war

antibiótico m antibiotic

anticiclón m anticyclone

anticipado adj *pago* advance atr; *elecciones* early; **por ~** in advance; **anticipar** <1a> **1** v/t *sueldo* advance; *fecha, viaje* move up, *Br* bring forward; *información, noticias* give a preview of **2** v/r **-se** *de suceso* come early; **-se a alguien** get there ahead of s.o.

anticonceptivo 1 adj contraceptive atr **2** m contraceptive

anticongelante m antifreeze

anticonstitucional adj unconstitutional

anticuado adj antiquated; **anticuario** m antique dealer

anticuerpo m BIO antibody

antideslizante adj non-slip

antidisturbios adj: **policía ~** riot police

antidoping adj: **control ~** dope test, drug test

antídoto m MED antidote; *fig* cure

antifaz m mask

antiguamente adv in the past; **antigüedad** f age; *en el trabajo* length of service; **~es** antiques; **antiguo** adj old; *del pasado remoto* ancient; **su ~ novio** her old *o* former boyfriend

antiinflamatorio *adj* MED anti-inflammatory

Antillas *fpl* West Indies

antílope *m* ZO antelope

antinatural *adj* unnatural

antinuclear *adj* anti-nuclear

antioxidante *m/adj* antioxidant

antipatía *f* antipathy, dislike; **antipático** *adj* disagreeable, unpleasant

antípodas *mpl* antipodes

antirreglamentario *adj* DEP *posición* offside; **una jugada -a** a foul

antirrobo *m* AUTO antitheft device

antisemitismo *m* anti-Semitism

antiséptico *m/adj* antiseptic

antisocial *adj* antisocial

antiterrorista *adj* **brigada** antiterrorist; **la lucha ~** the fight against terrorism

antítesis *f inv* antithesis

antojarse <1a> *v/r:* **se le antojó salir** he felt like going out; **se me antoja que ...** it seems to me that ...; **antojo** *m* whim; *de embarazada* craving; **a mi ~** as I please

antología *f* anthology; **de ~** *fig* F fantastic, incredible F

antonomasia *f:* **por ~** par excellence

antorcha *f* torch

antro *m* F dive F, dump F

antropófago *m*, **-a** *f* cannibal

antropología *f* anthropology

anual *adj* annual; **anualidad** *f* annual payment; **anualmente** *adv* yearly

anudar <1a> *v/t* knot

anular[1] <1a> *v/t* cancel; *matrimonio* annul; *gol* disallow

anular[2] *adj* ring-shaped; **dedo ~** ring finger

anunciante *m* COM advertiser; **anunciar** <1b> *v/t* announce; COM advertise; **anuncio** *m* announcement; (*presagio*) sign; COM advertisement; **~ luminoso** illuminated sign; **~s por palabras, pequeños ~s** classified advertisements

anzuelo *m* (fish) hook; **morder** *or* **tragar el ~** *fig* F take the bait

añadidura *f:* **por ~** in addition; **añadir** <3a> *v/t* add

añejo *adj* mature

añicos *mpl:* **hacer ~** F smash to smithereens F

año *m* year; **~ bisiesto** leap year; **~ fiscal** fiscal year, *Br* financial year; **~ luz** light year; **~ nuevo** New Year; **¿cuándo cumples ~s?** when's your birthday?; **¿cuántos ~s tienes?** how old are you?; **a los diez ~s** at the age of ten; **los ~s veinte** the twenties

añorar <1a> *v/t* miss

aorta *f* ANAT aorta

apabullante *adj* overwhelming; **apabullar** <1a> *v/t* overwhelm

apacible *adj* mild-mannered

apaciguar <1i> **1** *v/t* pacify, calm down **2** *v/r* **~se** calm down

apadrinar <1a> *v/t* be godparent to; *político* support, back; *artista etc* sponsor; **~ a la novia** give the bride away

apagado *adj fuego* out; *luz* off; *persona* dull; *color* subdued; **apagar** <1h> **1** *v/t televisor, luz* turn off; *fuego* put out **2** *v/r* **~se** *de luz* go off; *de fuego* go out; **apagón** *m* blackout

apaisado *adj* landscape *atr*

apalabrar <1a> *v/t* agree (verbally)

apalancar <1g> **1** *v/t* lever **2** *v/r* **~se** F settle

apalear <1a> *v/t* beat

apañar <1a> **1** *v/t* tidy up; *aparato* repair; *resultado* rig F, fix F; **estamos apañados** F we've had it F **2** *v/r* **~se** manage; **apañárselas** manage, get by; **apaño** *m fig* F makeshift repair

aparador *m* sideboard; *Méx* (*escaparate*) shop window

aparato *m* piece of equipment; *doméstico* appliance; BIOL, ANAT system; *de partido político* machine; **~ respiratorio** respiratory system; **al ~** TELEC speaking; **aparatoso** *adj* spectacular

aparcacoches *m inv* valet; **aparcamiento** *m* parking lot, *Br* car park; **~ subterráneo** underground parking garage, *Br* underground car park;

aparcar <1g> **1** v/t park; *tema, proyecto* shelve **2** v/i park

aparearse <1a> v/r ZO mate

aparecer <2d> **1** v/i appear **2** v/r ~se turn up

aparejador m, ~a f architectural technician; *Br* quantity surveyor; **aparejo** m: ~s pl **de pesca** fishing gear sg

aparentar <1a> v/t pretend; *no aparenta la edad que tiene* she doesn't look her age; **aparente** adj (*evidente*) apparent; *L.Am.* (*fingido*) feigned; **aparentemente** adv apparently; **aparición** f appearance; (*fantasma*) apparition; *hacer su* ~ make one's appearance; **apariencia** f appearance; *en* ~ outwardly; *las* ~*s engañan* appearances can be deceptive

apartado m section; ~ *de correos* PO box; **apartamento** m apartment, *Br* flat; **apartamiento** m separation; *L.Am.* (*apartamento*) apartment, *Br* flat; **apartar** <1a> **1** v/t separate; *para después* set o put aside; *de un sitio* move away (*de* from); ~ *a alguien de hacer algo* dissuade s.o. from doing sth **2** v/r ~se move aside (*de* from); ~se del tema stray from the subject; **aparte** adv to one side; (*por separado*) separately; ~ *de* aside from, *Br* apart from; **punto y** ~ new paragraph

apasionado 1 adj passionate **2** m/f enthusiast; **apasionante** adj fascinating; **apasionar** <1a> v/t fascinate

apatía f apathy; **apático** adj apathetic

apdo. abr (= **apartado (de correos**)) PO Box (= Post Office Box)

apearse <1a> v/r get off, alight fml; ~ *de algo* get off sth, alight from sth fml

apechugar <1h> v/i: ~ *con algo* cope with sth

apego m attachment

apelación f JUR appeal; **apelar** <1a> v/t tb JUR appeal (*a* to)

apellidarse <1a> v/r: *¿cómo se apellida?* what's your/his/her surname?; *se apellida Ocaña* his/her surname is Ocaña; **apellido** m surname; ~ *de soltera* maiden name

apelmazarse <1f> v/r *de lana* get matted; *de arroz* stick together

apelotonarse <1a> v/r crowd together

apenado adj sad; *L.Am.* (*avergonzado*) ashamed; *L.Am.* (*incómodo*) embarrassed; *L.Am.* (*tímido*) shy; **apenar** <1a> **1** v/t sadden **2** v/r ~se be upset o distressed; *L.Am.* (*avergonzarse*) be ashamed; *L.Am.* (*sentir incómodo*) be embarrassed; *L.Am.* (*ser tímido*) be shy

apenas 1 adv hardly, scarcely **2** conj as soon as

apéndice m appendix; **apendicitis** f MED appendicitis

apercibirse <3a> v/r: ~ *de algo* notice sth

apergaminado adj fig wrinkled

aperitivo m comida appetizer; bebida aperitif

apero m utensilio implement; *L.Am.* (*arneses*) harness; ~*s de labranza* farming implements

apertura f opening; FOT aperture; POL opening up

apesadumbrado adj heavy-hearted

apestar <1a> **1** v/t stink out F **2** v/i reek (*a* of); *huele que apesta* it reeks of smelly; **apestoso** adj smelly

apetecer <2d> v/i: *me apetece ir a dar un paseo* I feel like going for a walk; *¿qué te apetece?* what do you feel like?; **apetito** m appetite; **apetitoso** adj appetizing

apiadarse <1a> v/r take pity (*de* on)

ápice m: *ni un* ~ not an ounce; *no ceder ni un* ~ fig not give an inch

apicultura f beekeeping

apilar <1a> v/t pile up

apiñarse <1a> v/r crowd together

apio m BOT celery

apisonadora f steamroller

aplacar <1g> v/t *hambre* satisfy; *sed* quench; *a alguien* calm down, placate fml aplanar <1a> **1** v/t level, flatten; **~ las calles** C.Am., Pe hang around the streets **2** v/r **~se** fig (descorazonarse) lose heart

aplastante adj overwhelming; calor suffocating; **aplastar** <1a> v/t tb fig crush

aplaudida f L.Am. applause; **aplaudir** <3a> **1** v/i applaud, clap **2** v/t tb fig applaud; **aplauso** m round of applause

aplazamiento m de visita, viaje postponement; **aplazar** <1f> v/t visita, viaje put off, postpone; Arg fail

aplicación f application; **aplicar** <1g> **1** v/t apply; sanciones impose **2** v/r **~se** apply o.s.

aplomo m composure, aplomb fml

apocalíptico adj apocalyptic

apócrifo adj apocryphal

apodar <1a> v/t nickname, call

apoderado m COM agent; **apoderar** <1a> **1** v/t authorize **2** v/r **~se** take possession o control (**de** of)

apodo m nickname

apogeo m fig height, peak; **estar en su** ~ be at its height

apolillarse <1a> v/r get moth-eaten

apolítico adj apolitical

apología f defense, Br defence

apoltronarse <1a> v/r en asiento settle down; en trabajo, rutina get into a rut

apoplejía f MED apoplexy; **ataque de** ~ MED stroke

aporrear <1a> v/t pound on

aportación f contribution; COM investment; **aportar** <1a> v/t contribute; ~ **pruebas** JUR provide evidence

apósito m dressing

aposta adv on purpose, deliberately; **apostar** <1m> **1** v/t bet (**por** on) **2** v/i bet; ~ **por algo** opt for sth **3** v/r **~se** bet; MIL position o.s.

apóstata m/f apostate

apóstol m apostle

apóstrofe, apóstrofo m apostrophe

apoteosis f fig climax

apoyar <1a> **1** v/t lean (**en** against), rest (**en** against); (respaldar, confir-

mar) support **2** v/r **~se** lean (**en** on; **contra** against); en persona rely (**en** on); **¿en qué te apoyas para decir eso?** what are you basing that comment on?; **apoyo** m fig support

apreciable adj (visible) appreciable, noticeable; (considerable) considerable, substantial; **apreciar** <1b> v/t appreciate; (sentir afecto por) be fond of, think highly of; **aprecio** m respect

apremiar <1b> **1** v/t pressure, put pressure on **2** v/i: **el tiempo apremia** time is pressing

aprender <2a> **1** v/t learn **2** v/r **~se** learn; ~**se algo de memoria** learn sth (off) by heart; **aprendiz** m, ~**a** f apprentice, trainee; **aprendizaje** m apprenticeship

aprensión f (miedo) apprehension; (asco) squeamishness

apresar <1a> v/t nave seize; ladrón, animal catch, capture

aprestarse <1a> v/r: ~ **a** get ready to

apresurar <1a> **1** v/t hurry **2** v/r **~se** hurry up; ~**se a hacer algo** hurry o rush to do sth

apretado adj tight; **iban muy ~s en el coche** they were very cramped o squashed in the car; **apretar** <1k> **1** v/t botón press; (pellizcar, pinzar) squeeze; tuerca tighten; ~ **el paso** quicken one's pace; ~ **los puños** clench one's fists **2** v/i de ropa, zapato be too tight **3** v/r **~se** squeeze o squash together; ~**se el cinturón** fig tighten one's belt; **apretón** m squeeze; ~ **de manos** handshake

apretujar <1a> **1** v/t F squeeze, squash **2** v/r **~se** F squash o squeeze together

aprieto m predicament

aprisa adv quickly

aprisionar <1a> v/t fig trap

aprobación f approval; de ley passing; **aprobado** m EDU pass; **aprobar** <1m> v/t approve; comportamiento, idea approve of; exa-

men pass

apropiado *adj* appropriate, suitable; **apropiarse** <1b> *v/r:* **~ de algo** take sth

aprovechado 1 *adj desp* opportunistic **2** *m*, **-a** *f desp* opportunist; **aprovechar** <1a> **1** *v/t* take advantage of; *tiempo, espacio* make good use of; ***quiero ~ la ocasión para ...*** I would like to take this opportunity to ... **2** *v/i* take the opportunity (**para** to); *¡que aproveche!* enjoy your meal! **3** *v/r* **~se** take advantage (**de** of)

aprovisionarse <1a> *v/r* stock up (**de** on)

aproximadamente *adv* approximately; **aproximado** *adj* approximate; **aproximar** <1a> **1** *v/t* bring closer **2** *v/r* **~se** approach

aptitud *f* aptitude (**para** for), flair (**para** for); **apto** *adj* suitable (**para** for); *para servicio militar* fit; EDU pass

apuesta *f* bet

apuesto *adj* handsome

apunado *adj Pe, Bol* suffering from altitude sickness; **apunarse** <1a> *v/r S.Am.* get altitude sickness

apuntador *m*, **-a** *f* TEA prompter

apuntalar <1a> *v/t edificio* shore up; *fig* prop up

apuntar <1a> **1** *v/t* (*escribir*) note down, make a note of; TEA prompt; *en curso, para viaje etc* put down (**en**, **a** on; *para* for); **~ con el dedo** point at *o* to **2** *v/i con arma* aim **3** *v/r* **~se** put one's name down (**para, en** *o* **a** for); *¡me apunto!* count me in!; **apunte** *m* note

apuñalar <1a> *v/t* stab

apurado *adj L.Am.* (*con prisa*) in a hurry; (*pobre*) short (of cash); **apurar** <1a> **1** *v/t vaso* finish off; *a alguien* pressure, put pressure on **2** *v/t Chi: no me apura* I'm not in a hurry for it **3** *v/r* **~se** worry; *L.Am.* (*darse prisa*) hurry (up); **apuro** *m* predicament, tight spot F; *vergüenza* embarrassment; *L.Am.* rush; *me da* **~** I'm embarrassed

aquejado *adj:* ***estar ~ de*** be suffering from

aquel, aquella, aquellos, aquellas *det singular* that; *plural* those

aquél, aquélla aquéllos, aquéllas *pron singular* that (one); *plural* those (ones)

aquello *pron* that

aquí *adv en el espacio* here; *en el tiempo* now; *desde* **~** from here; *por* **~** here

árabe 1 *m/f & adj* Arab **2** *m idioma* Arabic

Arabia Saudí Saudi Arabia

arado *m* plow, *Br* plough

arancel *m* tariff; **arancelario** *adj* tariff *atr*

arándano *m* blueberry

arandela *f* washer

araña *f* ZO spider; *lámpara* chandelier

arañar <1a> *v/t* scratch; **arañazo** *m* scratch

arar <1a> *v/t* plow, *Br* plough

arbitraje *m* arbitration; **arbitrar** <1a> *v/t en fútbol, boxeo* referee; *en tenis, béisbol* umpire; *en conflicto* arbitrate; **arbitrario** *adj* arbitrary; **árbitro** *m en fútbol, boxeo* referee; *en tenis, béisbol* umpire; *en conflicto* arbitrator

árbol *m* tree; **~ genealógico** family tree; **arboleda** *f* grove

arbusto *m* shrub, bush

arca *f* chest; **~ de Noé** Noah's Ark

arcada *f* MED: *me provocó* **~s** it made me retch *o* heave F

arcaico *adj* archaic

arce *m* BOT maple

arcén *m* shoulder, *Br* hard shoulder

archidiócesis *f inv* archdiocese

archipiélago *m* archipelago

archivador *m* filing cabinet; **archivar** <1a> *v/t papeles, documentos* file; *asunto* shelve; **archivo** *m* archive; INFOR file

arcilla *f* clay

arco *m* ARQUI arch; MÚS bow; *L.Am.* DEP goal; **~ iris** rainbow

arder <2a> *v/i* burn; *estar muy caliente* be exceedingly hot; *la reunión está* *que arde* F the meeting is about to erupt F

ardilla *f* ZO squirrel

ardor *m entusiasmo* fervo(u)r; *~ de estómago* heartburn

arduo *adj* arduous

área *f* area; DEP *~ de castigo or de penalty* penalty area; *~ de descanso* pull-in (at the side of the road); *~ de servicio* service area

arena *f* sand; *~s pl movedizas* quicksand *sg*

arenga *f* morale-boosting speech; (*sermón*) harangue

arenque *m* herring

arepa *f C.Am., Ven* cornmeal roll

aretem *L.Am. joya* earring

Argelia Algeria

Argentina Argentina; **argentino 1** *adj* Argentinian **2** *m*, **-a** *f* Argentinian

argolla *f L.Am.* ring

argot *m* slang

argucia *f* clever argument; **argüir** <3g> *v/t & v/i* argue; **argumentar** <1a> *v/t* argue; **argumento** *m razón* argument; *de libro, película etc* plot

árido *adj* arid, dry; *fig* dry

Aries *m/f inv* ASTR Aries

arisco *adj* unfriendly

aristocracia *f* aristocracy; **aristócrata** *m/f* aristocrat; **aristocrático** *adj* aristocratic

aritmética *f* arithmetic

arma *f* weapon; *~ blanca* knife; *~ de doble filo or de dos filos* fig twoedged sword; *~ de fuego* firearm; *alzarse en ~s* rise up in arms

armada *f* navy

armadillo *m* ZO armadillo

armado *adj* armed; **armadura** *f* armo(u)r; **armamento** *m* armaments *pl*

armar <1a> **1** *v/t* MIL arm; TÉC assemble, put together; *~ un escándalo* F kick up a fuss F, make a scene F **2** *v/r ~se* arm o.s.; *la que se va a armar* F all hell will break loose F; *~se de valor* pluck up courage

armario *m* closet, *Br* wardrobe; *de cocina* cabinet, *Br* cupboard

armazón *f* skeleton, framework

armisticio *m* armistice

armonía *f* harmony; **armónica** *f* harmonica, mouth organ; **armonioso** *adj* harmonious; **armonizar** <1f> **1** *v/t* harmonize; *diferencias* reconcile **2** *v/i de color, estilo* blend (*con* with); *de persona* get on (*con* with)

arnés *m* harness; *para niños* leading strings *pl*, *Br* leading reins *pl*

aro *m* hoop; *L.Am.* (*pendiente*) earring; *entrar or pasar por el ~* fig F bite the bullet, take the plunge

aroma *m* aroma; *de flor* scent

arpa *f* harp

arpía *f* harpy

arpón *m* harpoon

arquear <1a> *v/t espalda* arch; *cejas* raise

arqueología *f* arch(a)eology; **arqueológico** *adj* arch(a)eological; **arqueólogo** *m*, **-a** *f* arch(a)eologist

arquero *m* archer; *L.Am. en fútbol* goalkeeper

arquetipo *m* archetype

arquitectónico *adj* architectural; **arquitecto** *m*, **-a** *f* architect; **arquitectura** *f* architecture

arrabal *m* poor outlying area

arraigado *adj* entrenched; **arraigar** <1h> **1** *v/i* take root **2** *v/r ~se de persona* settle (*en* in); *de costumbre, idea* take root

arramblar <1a> *v/t* (*destruir*) destroy

arrancar <1g> **1** *v/t planta, página* pull out; *vehículo* start (up); (*quitar*) snatch **2** *v/i de vehículo, máquina* start (up); INFOR boot (up); *Chi* (*huir*) run away **3** *v/r ~se Chi* run away; **arranque** *m* AUTO starting mechanism; (*energía*) drive; (*ataque*) fit

arrasar <1a> **1** *v/t* devastate **2** *v/i* F be a big hit

arrastrar <1a> **1** *v/t por el suelo*, INFOR drag (*por* along); *carry away* **2** *v/i por el suelo* trail on the ground **3** *v/r ~se* crawl; *fig* (*humillarse*) grovel (*delante de* to); **arrastre** *m*: **estar para el ~** *fig* F be fit to drop F

arreada *f Rpl* round-up

arrebatar <1a> *v/t* snatch (*a* from); **arrebato** *m* fit

arrebujarse <1a> *v/r* F wrap o.s. up; *en cama* snuggle up

arreciar <1b> *v/i* get worse; *de viento* get stronger

arrecife *m* reef

arredrarse <1a> *v/r* be intimidated (*ante* by)

arreglar <1a> **1** *v/t* (*reparar*) fix, repair; (*ordenar*) tidy (up); (*solucionar*) sort out; MÚS arrange; **~ cuentas** settle up; *fig* settle scores **2** *v/r* **~se** get (o.s.) ready; *de problema* get sorted out; (*apañarse*) manage; **arreglárselas** manage; **arreglo** *m* (*reparación*) repair; (*solución*) solution; (*acuerdo*) arrangement, agreement; MÚS arrangement; **~ de cuentas** settling of scores; **con ~ a** in accordance with; **esto no tiene ~** there's nothing to be done

arrellanarse <1a> *v/r* settle

arremangarse <1h> *v/r* roll up one's sleeves

arremeter <2a> *v/i*: **~ contra** charge (at); *fig* (*criticar*) attack

arremolinarse <1a> *v/r* mill around

arrendamiento *m* renting; **arrendar** <1k> *v/t L.Am.* (*dar en alquiler*) rent (out), let; (*tomar en alquiler*) rent; **se arrenda** for rent

arreo *m Rpl* driving, herding; (*manada*) herd

arrepentimiento *m* repentance; (*cambio de opinión*) change of heart; **arrepentirse** <3i> *v/r* be sorry; (*cambiar de opinión*) change one's mind; **~ de algo** regret sth

arrestar <1a> *v/t* arrest; **arresto** *m* arrest

arriba 1 *adv* ◊ *situación* up; *en edificio* upstairs; **ponlo ahí ~** put it up there; **el cajón de ~** *siguiente* the next drawer up, the drawer above; *último* the top drawer; **~ del todo**

right at the top ◊ *dirección* up; *en edificio* upstairs; **sigan hacia ~** keep going up; **me miró de ~ abajo** *fig* she looked me up and down ◊ *con cantidades*: **de diez para ~** ten or above **2** *int* long live

arribeño *m*, **-a** *f L.Am.* uplander, highlander

arribista *m/f* social climber

arriesgado *adj* adventurous; **arriesgar** <1h> **1** *v/t* risk **2** *v/r* **-se** take a risk; **-se a hacer algo** risk doing sth

arrimar <1a> **1** *v/t* move closer; **~ el hombro** F pull one's weight **2** *v/r* **-se** move closer (*a* to)

arrinconar <1a> *v/t* (*acorralar*) corner; *libros etc* put away; *persona* cold-shoulder

arroba *f* INFOR 'at' symbol, @

arrodillarse <1a> *v/r* kneel (down)

arrogancia *f* arrogance; **arrogante** *adj* arrogant

arrojar <1a> **1** *v/t* (*lanzar*) throw; *resultado* produce; (*vomitar*) throw up **2** *v/r* **-se** throw o.s.

arrollador *adj* overwhelming

arropar <1a> *v/t* wrap up; *fig* protect

arrope *m Rpl, Chi, Pe* fruit syrup

arroyo *m* stream; **sacar a alguien del ~** *fig* lift s.o. out of the gutter

arroz *m* rice; **~ con leche** rice pudding

arruga *f* wrinkle; **arrugar** <1h> **1** *v/t* wrinkle; **2** *v/r* **-se** *de piel, ropa* get wrinkled

arruinado *adj* ruined, broke F; **arruinar** <1a> **1** *v/t* ruin **2** *v/r* **-se** be ruined

arrullo *m de paloma* cooing; *para niño* lullaby

arsenal *m* arsenal

arsénico *m* arsenic

art *abr* (= **artículo**) art. (= article)

art.° *abr* (= **artículo**) art. (= article)

arte *m* (*pl f*) art; **~ dramático** dramatic art; **bellas ~s** *pl* fine art *sg*; **malas ~s** *pl* guile *sg*

artefacto *m* (*dispositivo*) device

arteria *f* artery

arterio(e)sclerosis f arteriosclerosis

artesana f craftswoman; **artesanía** f (handi)crafts pl; **artesano** m craftsman

Ártico zona, océano Arctic

articulación f ANAT, TÉC joint; de sonidos articulation; **artículo** m de periódico, GRAM, JUR article; COM product, item

artificial adj artificial

artillería f artillery; **~ ligera / pesada** light / heavy artillery

artilugio m aparato gadget

artimaña f trick

artista m/f artist; **artístico** adj artistic

artritis f MED arthritis

arveja f Rpl, Chi, Pe BOT pea

arzobispo m archbishop

as m tb fig ace

asa f handle

asado 1 adj roast atr **2** m roast

asalariado m, **-a** f wage earner; de empresa employee

asaltante m/f assailant; **asaltar** <1a> v/t persona attack; banco rob; **asalto** m a persona attack (**a** on); robo robbery, raid; en boxeo round

asamblea f reunión meeting; ente assembly

asar <1a> **1** v/t roast; **~ a la parrilla** broil, Br grill **2** v/r **~se** fig F be roasting F

ascender <2g> **1** v/t a empleado promote **2** v/i de precios, temperatura etc rise; de montañero climb; DEP, en trabajo be promoted (**a** to); **ascensión** f ascent; **ascenso** m de temperatura, precios rise (**de** in); de montaña ascent; DEP, en trabajo promotion; **ascensor** m elevator, Br lift

ascético adj ascetic

asco m disgust; **me da ~** I find it disgusting; **¡qué ~!** how revolting o disgusting!

ascua f ember; **estar en** or **sobre ~s** be on tenterhooks

asearse <1a> v/r wash up, Br have a wash

asediar <1b> v/t tb fig besiege; **asedio** m MIL siege, blockade; **a alguien** hounding

aseguradora f insurance company; **asegurar** <1a> **1** v/t (afianzar) secure; (prometer) assure; (garantizar) guarantee; COM insure **2** v/r **~se** make sure

asentamiento m settlement; **asentarse** <1k> v/r settle

asentir <3i> v/i agree (**a** to), consent (**a** to); con la cabeza nod

aseo m cleanliness; (baño) restroom, toilet

aséptico adj aseptic

asequible adj precio affordable; obra accessible

aserrar <1k> v/t saw; **aserrín** m L.Am. sawdust

asesinar <1a> v/t murder; POL assassinate; **asesinato** m murder; POL assassination; **asesino** m, **-a** f murderer; POL assassin

asesor m, **~a** f consultant, advisor, Br adviser; **~ fiscal** financial advisor (Br adviser); **~ de imagen** public relations consultant; **asesorar** <1a> v/t advise; **asesoría** f consultancy

asestar <1a> v/t golpe deal (**a** to); **me asestó una puñalada** he stabbed me

asfaltar <1a> v/t asphalt; **asfalto** m asphalt

asfixia f asphyxiation; **asfixiante** adj asphyxiating, suffocating; **asfixiar** <1b> **1** v/t asphyxiate, suffocate **2** v/r **~se** asphyxiate, suffocate

así 1 adv (de este modo) like this; (de ese modo) like that; **~ no más** S.Am. just like that; **~ pues** so; **~ que** so; **~ de grande** this big **2** conj: **~ como** al igual que while, whereas

Asia Asia

asiático 1 adj Asian **2** m, **-a** f Asian

asiduidad f frequency; **con ~** con frecuencia regularly; **asiduo** adj regular

asiento m seat; **tomar ~** take a seat

asignación f acción allocation; dinero allowance; **asignar** <1a> v/t allocate; *persona*, *papel* assign; **asignatura** f subject

asilarse <1a> v/r take refuge, seek asylum; **asilo** m home, institution; POL asylum; **~ de ancianos** old people's home

asimétrico adj asymmetrical

asimilar <1a> v/t assimilate

asimismo adv (*también*) also; (*igualmente*) in the same way, likewise

asistencia f (*ayuda*) assistance; *a lugar* attendance (**a** at); **~ en carretera** AUTO roadside assistance; **~ médica** medical care; **asistenta** f cleaner, cleaning woman; **asistente** m/f (*ayudante*) assistant; **~ social** social worker; **los ~s** those present; **asistir** <3a> **1** v/t help, assist **2** v/i be present; **~ a una boda** attend a wedding

asma f asthma; **asmático** adj asthmatic

asno m ZO donkey; *persona* idiot

asociación f association; **asociar** <1b> **1** v/t associate; **~ a alguien con algo** associate s.o. with sth **2** v/r **~se** team up (**con** with), go into partnership (**con** with); **~se a** grupo, club become a member of

asolar <1m> v/t devastate

asoleada f: **pegarse una ~** Bol, Pe sunbathe

asomar <1a> **1** v/t put o stick out **2** v/i show **3** v/r **~se** lean out; **~se a** or **por la ventana** lean out of the window

asombrado adj amazed; **asombrar** <1a> v/t amaze, astonish **2** v/r **~se** be amazed o astonished; **asombro** m amazement, astonishment; **asombroso** adj amazing

asomo m: **ni por ~** no way

asorocharse <1a> v/r Pe, Bol get altitude sickness

aspecto m de persona, cosa look, appearance; (*faceta*) aspect; **tener buen ~** look good

áspero adj superficie rough; sonido harsh; persona abrupt

aspersor m sprinkler

aspiraciones fpl aspirations

aspirador m, **~a** f vacuum cleaner; **aspirante** m/f a cargo candidate (**a** for); a título contender (**a** for); **aspirar** <1a> **1** v/t suck up; al respirar inhale, breathe in **2** v/i: **~ a** aspire to

aspirina f aspirin

asqueado adj disgusted; **asquear** <1a> v/t disgust; **asqueroso 1** adj (*sucio*) filthy; (*repugnante*) revolting, disgusting **2** m, **-a** f creep

asterisco m asterisk

astigmatismo m astigmatism

astilla f splinter; **~s** pl para fuego kindling sg; **hacer ~s algo** fig smash sth to pieces

astillero m shipyard

astral adj astral

astringente m/adj astringent

astro m AST, fig star

astrología f astrology; **astrólogo** m, **-a** f astrologer

astronauta m/f astronaut

astronave f spaceship

astronomía f astronomy; **astronómico** adj astronomical; **astrónomo** m, **-a** f astronomer

astucia f shrewdness, astuteness

astuto adj shrewd, astute

asumir <3a> v/t assume; (*aceptar*) accept, come to terms with

asunto m matter; F (*relación*) affair; **~s exteriores** foreign affairs; **no es ~ tuyo** it's none of your business

asustar <1a> **1** v/t frighten, scare **2** v/r **~se** be frightened o scared

atacar <1g> v/t attack

atajar <1a> **1** v/t check the spread of; contain; L.Am. pelota catch **2** v/i take a short cut; **atajo** m L.Am. short cut

atañer <2f> v/i concern

ataque m (*agresión*) attack; (*acceso*) fit; **~ cardíaco** or **al corazón** MED heart attack; **le dio un ~ de risa** she burst out laughing

atar <1a> v/t tie (up); fig tie down

atardecer <2d> **1** v/i get dark **2** m dusk

atareado adj busy

atascar <1g> **1** v/t block **2** v/r ~**se**
de cañería get blocked; *de mecanismo* jam, stick; *al hablar* dry up; **atasco** m traffic jam
ataúd m coffin, casket
atemorizar <1f> v/t frighten
atención f attention; (*cortesía*) courtesy; *¡~!* your attention, please!; **llamar la ~ a alguien** reñir tell s.o. off; *por ser llamativo* attract s.o.'s attention; **prestar ~** pay attention (**a** to)
atender <2g> **1** v/t *a enfermo* look after; *en tienda* attend to, serve **2** v/i pay attention (**a** to)
atenerse <2l> v/r: ~ **a** *normas* abide by; *consecuencias* face, accept; **saber a qué ~** know where one stands
atentado m attack (**contra, a** on); ~ **terrorista** terrorist attack
atentamente adv attentively; *en carta* sincerely, Br Yours sincerely
atentar <1k> v/i: ~ **contra** *vida* make an attempt on; *moral etc* be contrary to
atento adj attentive; **estar ~ a algo** pay attention to sth
atenuante adj JUR extenuating; **circunstancia ~** JUR extenuating circumstance; **atenuar** <1e> v/t lessen, reduce
ateo **1** adj atheistic **2** m, **-a** f atheist
aterciopelado adj tb fig velvety
aterido adj frozen
aterrador adj frightening; **aterrar** <1a> v/t terrify
aterrizaje m AVIA landing; ~ **forzoso** or **de emergencia** emergency landing; **aterrizar** <1f> v/i land
aterrorizado adj terrified, petrified F; **aterrorizar** <1f> v/t terrify; (*amenazar*) terrorize
atestado adj overcrowded
atestiguar <1i> v/t JUR testify; fig bear witness to
atiborrarse <1a> v/r F stuff o.s. F. (**de** with)
ático m piso top floor; *apartamento* top floor' apartment (*Br* flat); (*desván*) attic
atinar <1a> v/i manage (**a** to); **no**

atinó con la respuesta correcta she couldn't come up with the right answer
atípico adj atypical
atisbo m sign
atizar <1f> v/t *fuego* poke; *pasiones* stir up; **le atizó un golpe** she hit him
Atlántico m/adj: **el** (**océano**) ~ the Atlantic (Ocean)
atlas m inv atlas
atleta m/f athlete; **atlético** adj athletic; **atletismo** m athletics
atmo. abr (= **atentísimo**): **su ~** Yours truly
atmósfera f atmosphere
atole m Méx flavored hot drink with maize flour
atolladero m: **sacar a alguien del ~** fig F get s.o. out of a tight spot
atolondrado adj scatterbrained
atómico adj atomic; **átomo** m atom; **ni un ~ de** fig not an iota of
atónito adj astonished, amazed
atontar <1a> v/t make groggy o dopey; *de golpe* stun, daze; (*volver tonto*) turn into a zombie
atorar <1a> L.Am. **1** v/t cañería etc block (up) **2** v/r ~**se** choke; *de cañería etc* get blocked (up)
atormentar <1a> v/t torment
atornillar <1a> v/t screw on
atorrante m Rpl, Chi F bum F, Br tramp; (*holgazán*) layabout
atosigar <1h> v/t pester
atrabancado adj Méx clumsy
atracar <1g> **1** v/t banco, tienda hold up; *a alguien* mug; Chi F make out with F; neck with Br F **2** v/i MAR dock
atracción f attraction
atraco m de banco, tienda robbery; de persona mugging
atracón m: **darse un ~ de** stuff o.s. with F
atractivo **1** adj attractive **2** m appeal, attraction; **atraer** <2p> v/t attract
atragantarse <1a> v/r choke (**con** on); **se le ha atragantado** fig she can't stand o stomach him
atrancar <1g> **1** v/t puerta barricade

2 v/r ~**se** fig get stuck

atrapar<1a> v/t catch, trap

atrásadv para indicar posición at the back, behind; para indicar movimiento back; **años ~** years ago o back; **hacia ~** back, backwards; **quedarse ~** get left behind; **atrasado** adj en estudios, pago behind (**en** in o with); reloj slow; **pueblo** backward; **ir ~** de un reloj be slow; **atrasar** <1a> **1** v/t reloj put back; fecha postpone, put back **2** v/i de reloj lose time; **atraso** m backwardness; COM ~**s** arrears

atravesar <1k> v/t cross; (perforar) go through, pierce; crisis go through

atrevidoadj daring; **atreverse** <2a> v/r dare

atribuir <3g> **1** v/t attribute (**a** to) **2** v/r ~**se** claim

atrincherarse <1a> v/r MIL dig o.s. in, entrench o.s.; **se atrincheró en su postura** fig he dug his heels in

atrocidadf atrocity

atrofiado adj atrophied; **atrofiarse** <1b> v/r atrophy

atropellar<1a> v/t knock down

atrozadj appalling, atrocious

ATS abr (= **ayudante técnico sanitario**) registered nurse

atte.abr (= **atentamente**) sincerely (yours)

atuendom outfit

atufar<1a> v/t F stink out F

atúnm tuna (fish)

aturdido adj in a daze; **aturdir** <3a> **1** v/t de golpe, noticia stun, daze; (confundir) bewilder, confuse **2** v/r ~**se** be stunned o dazed; (confundirse) be bewildered o confused

aturullar <1a> **1** v/t confuse **2** v/r ~**se** get confused

audaciaf audacity; **audaz** adj daring, bold, audacious

audiciónfTEA audition; JUR hearing

audiencia f audience; JUR court; **índice de ~** TV ratings pl

audífonom para sordos hearing aid

audiovisualadj audiovisual

auditivo adj auditory; problema

hearing atr

auditorm, **~a** f auditor; **auditoría** f audit; **auditorio** m (público) audience; sala auditorium

augem peak; **estar en ~** aumento be enjoying a boom

augurar<1a> v/t de persona predict, foretell; de indicio augur; **augurio** m omen, sign; **un buen/ mal ~** a good / bad omen

aulaf classroom; en universidad lecture hall, Br lecture theatre

aullidom howl

aumentar<1a> **1** v/t increase; precio increase, raise, put up **2** v/i de precio, temperatura rise, increase, go up; **aumento** m de precios, temperaturas etc rise (**de** in), increase (**de** in); de sueldo raise, Br rise; **ir en ~** be increasing

aunadv even; ~ **así** even so

aúnadv en oraciones no negativas still; en oraciones negativas yet; en comparaciones even; ~ **no** not yet

aunar<1a> v/t combine

aunqueconj although, even though; + subj even if

auricularm de teléfono receiver; ~**es** headphones, earphones

aurora f dawn; ~ **boreal** northern lights pl

auscultar<1a> v/t: ~ **a alguien** listen to s.o.'s chest

ausencia f de persona absence; no existencia lack (**de** of); **brillaba por su ~** he was conspicuous by his absence; **ausente** adj absent

auspiciom sponsorship; **bajo los ~s de** under the auspices of.

austeridadf austerity; **austero** adj austere

australadj southern

Australia Australia; **australiano 1** adj Australian **2** m, **-a** f Australian

Austria Austria; **austriano 1** adj Austrian **2** m, **-a** f Austrian

auténtico adj authentic; **autentificar** <1g> v/t authenticate

autismom autism

autom JUR order; L.Am. AUTO car

autoadhesivo *adj* self-adhesive
autoayuda *f* self-help
autobiografía *f* autobiography
autobombo *m* F self-glorification
autobús *m* bus
autocar *m* bus
autocaravana *f* camper van
autocontrol *m* self-control
autocrítica *f* self-criticism
autóctono *adj* indigenous, native
autodefensa *f* self-defense, *Br* self-defence
autodeterminación *f* self-determination
autodidacta **1** *adj* self-taught **2** *m/f* self-taught person
autoedición *f* desktop publishing, DTP
autoescuela *f* driving school
autoestima *f* self-esteem
autoestop *m* hitchhiking; **autoestopista** *m/f* hitchhiker
autógrafo *m* autograph
automático *adj* automatic; **automatizar** <1f> *v/t* automate
automedicación *f* self-medication
automóvil *m* car, automobile; **automovilismo** *m* driving; **automovilista** *m/f* motorist
autonomía *f* autonomy; *en España* automous region; **autónomo** *adj* autonomous
autopista *f* freeway, *Br* motorway; **~ de la información** or **de la comunicación** INFOR information (super)highway
autopsia *f* post mortem, autopsy
autor *m*, **~a** *f* author; *de crimen* perpetrator
autoridad *f* authority; **autoritario** *adj* authoritarian; **autorización** *f* authority; **autorizar** <1f> *v/t* authorize
autorradio *m* car radio
autorretrato *m* self-portrait
autoservicio *m* supermarket; *restaurante* self-service restaurant
autostop *m* hitchhiking; **hacer ~** hitch(hike)
autosuficiencia *f* self-sufficiency; *desp* smugness; **autosuficiente** *adj*

self-sufficient; *desp* smug
autovía *f* divided highway, *Br* dual carriageway
auxiliar **1** *adj* auxiliary; *profesor* assistant **2** *m/f* assistant; **~ f de vuelo** stewardess, flight attendant **3** <1b> *v/t* help; **auxilio** *m* help; **primeros ~s** *pl* first aid *sg*
Av. *abr* (= **Avenida**) Ave (= Avenue)
aval *m* guarantee; **~ bancario** bank guarantee
avalancha *f* avalanche
avalar <1a> *v/t* guarantee; *fig* back
avance *m* advance
avanzado *adj* advanced; **avanzar** <1f> **1** *v/t* move forward, advance **2** *v/i* advance, move forward; MIL advance (**hacia** on); *en trabajo* make progress
avaricia *f* avarice; **avaro 1** *adj* miserly **2** *m*, **-a** *f* miser
avasallar <1a> *v/t* subjugate; **no dejes que te avasallen** *fig* don't let them push you around
Av.^da *abr* (= **Avenida**) Ave (= Avenue)
ave *f* bird; *S.Am.* (*pollo*) chicken; **~ de presa** or **de rapiña** bird of prey
avecinarse <1a> *v/r* approach
avejentar <1a> *v/t* age
avellana *f* BOT hazelnut; **avellano** *m* BOT hazel
avena *f* oats *pl*
avenida *f* avenue
avenirse <3s> *v/r* agree (**a** to)
aventajar <1a> *v/t* be ahead of
aventura *f* adventure; *riesgo* venture; *amorosa* affair; **aventurar** <1a> **1** *v/t* risk; *opinión* venture **2** *v/r* **~se** venture; **~se a hacer algo** dare to do sth; **aventurero** *adj* adventurous
avergonzar <1n & 1f> **1** *v/t* (*abor-chornar*) embarrass; **le avergüenza** *algo reprensible* she's ashamed of it **2** *v/r* **~se** be ashamed (**de** of)
avería *f* TÉC fault; AUTO breakdown; **averiarse** <1c> *v/r* break down
averiguar <1i> *v/t* find out
aversión *f* aversion
avestruz *m* ZO ostrich; **del ~ política**,

táctica head-in-the-sand

aviación *f* aviation; MIL air force

avicultor *m*, **~a** *f* poultry farmer

avidez *f* eagerness; **ávido** *adj* eager (**de** for), avid (**de** for)

avinagrarse <1a> *v/r de vino* turn vinegary; *fig* become bitter *o* sour

avión *m* plane; **por ~** *mandar una carta* (by) airmail; **avioneta** *f* light aircraft

avisar <1a> *v/t notificar* let know, tell; (*llamar*) call, send for; **aviso** *m comunicación* notice; (*advertencia*) warning; *L.Am.* (*anuncio*) advertisement; **hasta nuevo ~** until further notice; **sin previo ~** unexpectedly, without any warning

avispa *f* ZO wasp

avivar <1a> *v/t fuego* revive; *interés* arouse

avizor *adj*: **estar ojo ~** be alert

axila *f* armpit

axioma *m* axiom

ay *int de dolor* ow!, ouch!; *de susto* oh!

ayer *adv* yesterday; **~ por la mañana** yesterday morning

ayuda *f* help; **~ al desarrollo** development aid *o* assistance; **ayudante** *m/f* assistant; **ayudar** <1a> *v/t* help

ayunas: **estoy en ~** I haven't eaten

anything; **ayuno** *m* fast

ayuntamiento *m* city council, town council; *edificio* city hall

azabache *m* MIN jet

azadón *m* mattock

azafata *f* flight attendant; **~ de congresos** hostess

azafrán *m* BOT saffron

azalea *f* BOT azalea

azar *m* fate, chance; **al ~** at random

azorarse <1a> *v/r* be embarrassed

azotar <1a> *v/t con látigo* whip, flog; *con mano* smack; *de enfermedad, hambre* grip; *Méx puerta* slam; **azote** *m con látigo* lash; *con mano* smack; *fig* scourge; **dar un ~ a alguien** F smack s.o.

azotea *f* flat roof; **estar mal de la ~** *fig* F be crazy F

azteca *m/f* & *adj* Aztec

azúcar *m* (*also f*) sugar; **~ glas** confectioner's sugar, *Br* icing sugar; **~ moreno** brown sugar; **azucarero** *m* sugar bowl

azucena *f* BOT Madonna lily

azufre *m* sulfur, *Br* sulphur

azul 1 *adj* blue; **~ celeste** sky-blue; **~ marino** navy(-blue) **2** *m* blue

azulejo *m* tile

azuzar <1f> *v/t*: **~ los perros a alguien** set the dogs on s.o.; *fig* egg s.o. on

B.A. *abr* (= **Buenos Aires**) Buenos Aires

baba *f* drool, dribble; **se le caía la ~** F he was drooling F (**con** over); **babear** <1a> *v/i* dribble; **babero** *m* bib

Babia *f*: **estar en ~** be miles away

babor *m* MAR port

babosa *f* ZO slug

babosada *f L.Am.* F stupid thing to

do / say; **baboso** *adj L.Am.* F stupid

baca *f* AUTO roof rack

bacalao *m* cod; **cortar el ~** F call the shots F

bache *m* pothole; *fig* rough patch

bachicha 1 *m/f Rpl*, *Chi desp* wop *desp* **2** *f Méx* cigarette stub

bachillerato *m Esp* high school leaver's certificate

bacón *m* bacon

bacteriaf bacteria

bádmintonm badminton

baflem loudspeaker

bahíaf bay

bailaor m, ~**a** f flamenco dancer; **bailar** <1a> **1** v/i dance; *de zapato* be loose **2** v/t dance; *se lo bailó Méx* F he pinched F *o* swiped F it; **bailarín** m, -**ina** f dancer; **baile** m dance; *fiesta formal* ball; ~ **de salón** ballroom dancing; ~ **de San Vito** *fig* St. Vitus's dance

bajaf *descenso* fall, drop; *estar de* ~ (*por enfermedad*) be off sick; ~**s** MIL casualties; **bajada** f fall; **bajar** <1a> **1** v/t *voz, precio* lower; *escalera* go down; ~ **algo** *de arriba* get sth down **2** v/i go down; *de intereses* fall, drop **3** v/r ~**se** get down; *de automóvil* get out (*de* of); *de tren, autobús* get off (*de* sth)

bajíom *L.Am.* lowland

bajo1 *adj* low; *persona* short; *por lo* ~ at least **2** m MÚS bass; *piso* first floor, *Br* ground floor **3** *adv* *cantar, hablar* quietly,softly; *volar* low **4** *prp* under; *tres grados* ~ *cero* three degrees below zero

bajónm sharp decline; *dar un* ~ decline sharply, slump

bala f bullet; *como una* ~ like lightning; *ni a* ~ *L.Am.* F no way; **balaceo** m *L.Am.*, **balacera** f *L.Am.* shooting

baladaf ballad

balancem COM balance; **balancearse** <1a> v/r swing, sway

balanzaf scales pl; ~ **comercial** balance of trade; ~ **de pagos** balance of payments

balaustradaf balustrade

balazom shot

balbucear<1a>, **balbucir** <3f; *defective*> **1** v/i stammer; *de niño* babble **2** v/t stammer

Balcanes mpl Balkans; **balcánico** *adj* Balkan

balcónm balcony

baldado*adj* *fig* F bushed F

balde*adv*: *de* ~ for nothing; *en* ~ in vain

baldosaf floor tile

balear<1a> v/t *L.Am.* shoot

Baleares *fpl* Balearic Islands; **baleárico** *adj* Balearic

baleom *L.Am.* shooting

balizaf MAR buoy

ballenaf ZO whale

balletm ballet

balneariom spa

balónm ball; **baloncesto** m basketball; **balonmano** m handball; **balonvolea** m volleyball

balsaf raft; *como una* ~ *de aceite* *fig* like a mill pond

bálsamom balsam

baluartem stronghold; *persona* pillar, stalwart

balumbaf *L.Am.* F heap, pile; F (*ruido*) noise, racket F

bambolearse<1a> v/r sway

bambollaf *L.Am.* F fuss

bambúm BOT bamboo

banaladj banal

bananaf *L.Am.*, *Rpl*, *Pe*, *Bol* banana

bancaf *actividad* banking; *conjunto de bancos* banks pl; *en juego* bank; DEP, *Méx* (*asiento*) bench

bancalm terrace; *división de terreno* plot

bancario*adj* bank *atr*; **bancarrota** f bankruptcy; *estar en* ~ be bankrupt

banco m COM bank; *para sentarse* bench; ~ **de arena** sand bank; ~ **de datos** data bank

bandaf MÚS, (*grupo*) band; *de delincuentes* gang; (*cinta*) sash; *en fútbol* touchline; ~ **sonora** soundtrack; **bandada**f *de pájaros* flock

bandazom: *dar* ~**s** *de coche* swerve

bandejaf tray; *servir en* ~ hand on a plate

bandera f flag; (*lleno*) *hasta la* ~ packed (out); *bajar la* ~ *de taxi* start the meter running; **banderilla** f TAUR banderilla (*dart stuck into bull's neck during bullfight*)

bandidom, -**a** f bandit

bandom edict; *en disputa* side

bandolerom, -**a** f bandit

banjom MÚS banjo

banquerom, -**a** f banker

banqueta f L.Am. stool; L.Am. (acera) sidewalk, Br pavement; ~ **trasera** AUTO back seat
banquete m banquet; ~ **de bodas** wedding reception
banquillo m JUR dock; DEP bench
bañadera f Rpl (baño) bath; **bañador** m swimsuit; **bañar** <1a> 1 v/t de sol, mar bathe; a un niño, un enfermo bathe, Br bath; GASTR coat (**con** with, **en** in) 2 v/r ~**se** have a bath; en el mar go for a swim; **bañera** f (bath)tub, bath; **bañista** m/f swimmer; **baño** m bath; en el mar swim; esp L.Am. bathroom; TÉC plating; ~ **de sangre** blood bath; ~ **María** bain-marie
baptisterio m baptistry
baquiano L.Am. 1 adj expert atr 2 m, **-a** f guide
bar m bar
baraja f deck of cards
barandilla f handrail, banister
barata f Méx bargain counter; (saldo) sale; **baratero** m, **-a** f Chi tendero junk-shop owner; **baratija** f trinket; **barato** adj cheap
barba f tb BOT beard; **por** ~ F a head, per person
barbacoa f barbecue
barbaridad f barbarity; **costar una** ~ cost a fortune; **decir** ~**es** say outrageous things; **¡qué** ~! what a thing to say/do!; **bárbaro 1** adj F tremendous, awesome F; **¡qué** ~! amazing!, wicked! F **2** m, **-a** f F punk F
barbería f barber's shop; **barbero** m barber
barbilla f chin
barbitúrico m barbiturate
barbo m pescado barbel
barca f boat; **barcaza** f MAR barge; **barco** m boat; más grande ship; ~ **de vela** sailing ship
baremo m scale
barniz m para madera varnish; **barnizar** <1f> v/t varnish
barómetro m barometer
barquero m boatman
barquillo m wafer; Méx, C.Am. ice-cream cone

barra f de metal, en bar bar; de cortinas rod; ~ **de labios** lipstick; ~ **de pan** baguette; ~ **espaciadora** space-bar; ~ **de herramientas** INFOR tool bar; ~ **invertida** backslash
barraca f (chabola) shack; de tiro stand; de feria stall; L.Am. (deposito) shed; ~**s** pl L.Am. shanty town sg
barracón f MIL barrack room
barranco m ravine
barrenar <1a> v/t drill
barrendero m, **-a** f street sweeper
barreno m drill hole
barreño m washing up bowl
barrer <2a> v/t sweep
barrera f barrier; ~ **del sonido** sound barrier
barriada f C.Am. (barrio marginal) slum, shanty town
barrial m L.Am. bog
barricada f barricade
barrida f L.Am. sweep; L.Am. (redada) police raid
barriga f belly; **rascarse la** ~ fig F sit on one's butt F; **barrigón** adj F pudgy F
barril m barrel
barrio m neighbo(u)rhood, area; ~ **de chabolas** Esp shanty town; **irse al otro** ~ F kick the bucket P
barro m mud
barroco m/adj baroque
barrote m bar
bártulos mpl F things, gear sg F
barullo m uproar, racket
basar <1a> 1 v/t base (**en** on) 2 v/r ~**se** be based (**en** on)
báscula f scales
base f QUÍM, MAT, MIL base; ~ **de datos** INFOR database; ~**s de concurso** rules; conditions; **a** ~ **de** by dint of; **básico** adj basic
basílica f basilica
básquetbol m L.Am. basketball
bastante 1 adj enough; número o cantidad considerable plenty of; **quedan** ~**s plazas** there are plenty of seats left **2** adv quite, fairly; **bebe** ~ she drinks quite a lot;

bastar <1a> *v/i* be enough; **basta con uno** one is enough; **¡basta!** that's enough!

bastardo 1 *adj* bastard *atr* **2** *m* bastard

bastidor *m*: **entre ~es** F behind the scenes

bastión *m* bastion

basto 1 *adj* rough, coarse **2** *mpl*: **~s** (*en naipes*) suit in Spanish deck of cards

bastón *m* stick

basura *f* tb *fig* trash, *Br* rubbish; **cubo de la ~** trash can, *Br* rubbish bin; **basural** *m L.Am.* dump, *Br* tip; **basurero** *m* garbage collector, *Br* dustman

bata *f* robe, *Br* dressing gown; MED (white) coat; TÉC lab coat

batacazo *m* F bump

batalla *f* battle; **batallón** *m* battalion

batata *f* BOT sweet potato

bate *m* DEP bat

batería *f* MIL, EL, AUTO battery; MÚS drums, drum kit; **~ de cocina** set of pans; **aparcar en ~** AUTO parallel park

batido 1 *adj camino* well-trodden **2** *m* GASTR milkshake; **batidora** *f* mixer

batir <3a> *v/t* beat; *nata* whip; *récord* break

baúl *m* chest, trunk; *L.Am.* AUTO trunk, *Br* boot

bautismo *m* baptism, christening; **~ de fuego** baptism of fire; **bautizar** <1f> *v/t* baptize, christen; *barco* name; *vino* F water down; **bautizo** *m* baptism, christening

baya *f* berry

bayeta *f* cloth

bayoneta *f* bayonet

bayunco *adj C.Am.* P silly, stupid

baza *f en naipes* trick; *fig* trump card; **meter ~** F interfere

bazar *m* hardware and fancy goods store; *mercado* bazaar

bazo *m* ANAT spleen

bazofia *f fig* F load of trash F

beatífico *adj* beatific; **beatitud** *f* beatitude; **beato 1** *adj desp* over-

pious **2** *m*, **-a** *f desp* over-pious person

bebé *m* baby

bebedor *m*, **~a** *f* drinker; **beber** <2a> **1** *v/i* & *v/t* drink **2** *v/r* **~se** drink up; **bebida** *f* drink

beca *f* scholarship; (*del estado*) grant

becerro *m* calf

béchamel *f* GASTR béchamel (sauce)

bedel *m* porter

beige *adj* beige

béisbol *m* baseball

belén *m* nativity scene

belga *m/f* & *adj* Belgian; **Bélgica** Belgium

Belice Belize

belicista *m/f* warmonger; **bélico** *adj* war *atr*; **beligerante** *adj* belligerent

bellaco *m*, **-a** *f Arg* rascal

belleza *f* beauty; **bello** *adj* beautiful

bellota *f* BOT acorn

bemol *m* MÚS flat; **mi ~** E flat; **tener ~es** *fig* F be tricky F

bencina *f* benzine; *Pe, Bol* (*gasolina*) gas, *Br* petrol

bendecir <3p> *v/t* bless; **bendición** *f* blessing; **bendito** *adj* blessed

benefactor *adj* charitable; **beneficencia** *f* charity; **beneficiar** <1b> **1** *v/t* benefit; *Rpl ganado* slaughter **2** *v/r* **~se** benefit (**de, con** from); **beneficio** *m* benefit; COM profit; *Rpl* slaughterhouse; *C.Am.* coffee-processing plant; **en ~ de** in aid of; **beneficioso** *adj* beneficial; **benéfico** *adj* charity *atr*; **función -a** charity function *o* event

beneplácito *m* approval

benévolo *adj* benevolent, kind; (*indulgente*) lenient

bengala *f* flare

benigno *adj* MED benign

benjamín *m* youngest son; **benjamina** *f* youngest daughter

beodo *adj* drunk

berberecho *m* ZO cockle

berenjena *f* BOT egg plant, *Br* aubergine; **berenjenal** *m*: **meterse en un ~** *fig* F get o.s. into a jam F

bermudas *mpl, fpl* Bermuda shorts

berrear <1a> *v/i* bellow; *de niño* bawl, yell; **berrido** *m* bellow; *de niño* yell

berrinche *m* F tantrum; *coger un ~* F throw a tantrum

berro *m* BOT watercress

berza *f* BOT cabbage

besamel *f* GASTR béchamel (sauce)

besar <1a> **1** *v/t* kiss **2** *v/r* **~se** kiss; **beso** *m* kiss

bestia 1 *f* beast **2** *m/f fig* F brute F, swine F; *mujer* bitch F; *conducir a lo ~* F drive like a madman

besugo *m* ZO bream; *fig* F idiot

betún *m* shoe polish

biberón *m* baby's bottle

Biblia *f* Bible

bibliografía *f* bibliography; **biblioteca** *f* library; *mueble* bookcase; **bibliotecario** *m*, *-a* *f* librarian

bicarbonato *m:* *~ (de sodio)* bicarbonate of soda, bicarb F

bíceps *mpl* biceps

bicho *m* bug, *Br tb* creepy-crawly; (*animal*) creature; *fig* F *persona* nasty piece of work; *¿qué ~ te ha picado?* what's eating you?

bici *f* F bike; **bicicleta** *f* bicycle; *ir o montar en ~* go cycling; *~ de montaña* mountain bike

BID *abr* (= *Banco Interamericano de Desarollo*) IADB (= Inter-American Development Bank)

bidé *m* bidet

bidón *m* drum

bien 1 *m* good; *por tu ~* for your own good; *~es pl* goods, property *sg*; *~es de consumo* consumer goods *o* durables; *~es inmuebles* real estate *sg* **2** *adv* well; (*muy*) very; *más ~* rather; *o ... o ...* either ... or ...; *¡está ~!* it's OK!, it's alright!; *estoy ~* I'm fine, I'm OK; *¿estás ~ aquí?* are you comfortable here?; *¡~ hecho!* well done!

bienestar *m* well-being

bienvenida *f* welcome; *dar la ~ a alguien* welcome s.o.; **bienvenido** *adj* welcome

bife *m* Rpl steak

bifocal *adj* bifocal

bifurcación *f* fork; *de línea férrea* junction; **bifurcarse** <1g> *v/r* fork

bigamia *f* bigamy

bigote *m* m(o)ustache; *~s de gato etc* whiskers

bikini *m* bikini

bilateral *adj* bilateral

bilingüe *adj* bilingual

bilis *f* bile; *fig* F bad mood

billar *m* billiards; *~ americano* pool

billete *m* ticket; *~ abierto* open ticket; *~ de autobús* bus ticket; *~ de banco* bill, *Br* banknote; *~ de ida, ~ sencillo* one-way ticket, *Br* single (ticket); *~ de ida y vuelta* round-trip ticket, *Br* return (ticket); **billetera** *f L.Am.*, **billetero** *m* billfold, *Br* wallet

billón *m* trillion

binario *adj* binary

bingo *m* bingo; *lugar* bingo hall

biodegradable *adj* biodegradable

biodiversidad *f* biodiversity

biografía *f* biography

biología *f* biology; **biológico** *adj* biological; AGR organic; **biólogo** *m*, *-a* *f* biologist

biombo *m* folding screen

biopsia *f* MED biopsy

bioquímica *f* biochemistry

bipartidismo *m* POL two-party system

biquini *m* bikini

birlar <1a> *v/t* F lift F, swipe F

birome *m* Rpl ballpoint (pen)

birria *f* F piece of junk F; *va hecha una ~* F she looks a real mess

bis *m* encore; *9 ~* 9A

bisabuela *f* great-grandmother; **bisabuelo** *m* great-grandfather

bisagra *f* hinge

biscote *m* rusk

bisexual *adj* bisexual

bisiesto *adj: año ~* leap year

bisnieta *f* great-granddaughter; **bisnieto** *m* great-grandson

bisonte *m* ZO bison

bisoñé *m* hairpiece, toupee

bisté, bistec *m* steak

bisturí *m* MED scalpel

B

bisutería f costume jewel(le)ry

bit m INFOR bit

bizco adj cross-eyed

bizcocho m sponge (cake)

blanca f persona white; MÚS half-note, Br minim; **estar sin ~** fig F be broke F; **blanco 1** adj white; (sin escrito) blank; **arma -a** knife **2** m persona white; (diana), fig target; **dar en el ~** hit the nail on the head; **ser el ~ de todas las miradas** be the center (Br centre) of attention

blando adj soft

blanquear <1a> v/t whiten; pared whitewash; dinero launder; **blanqueo** m whitewashing; **~ de dinero** money laundering; **blanquillo** m Méx egg

blasfemar <1a> v/i curse, swear; REL blaspheme; **blasfemia** f REL blasphemy

blindado adj armo(u)red; puerta reinforced; EL shielded

bloc m pad

blof m L.Am. bluff

bloque m block; POL bloc; **~ de apartamentos** apartment building, Br block of flats; **en ~** en masse; **bloquear** <1a> v/t block; DEP obstruct; (atascar) jam; MIL blockade; COM freeze; **bloqueo** m blockade

blusa f blouse

boa f ZO boa constrictor

bobada f piece of nonsense

bobina f bobbin; FOT reel, spool; EL coil

bobo 1 adj silly, foolish **2** m, **-a** f fool

boca f mouth; **~ a ~** mouth to mouth; **~ de metro** subway entrance; **~ abajo** face down; **~ arriba** face up; **dejar con la ~ abierta** leave open-mouthed; **se me hace la ~ agua** my mouth is watering; **bocacalle** f side street; **bocadillo** m sandwich; **bocado** m mouthful, bite; **bocana** f river mouth; **bocanada** f mouthful; de viento gust; **bocata** m F → **bocadillo**; **bocazas** m/f inv F loudmouth F

boceto m sketch

bochar <1a> v/t Rpl F en examen fail,

flunk F; Méx cold-shoulder, rebuff

bochinche m Méx uproar

bochorno m sultry weather; fig embarrassment

bocina f MAR, AUTO horn

bocio m MED goiter, Br goitre

boda f wedding

bodega f wine cellar; MAR, AVIA hold; L.Am. bar; C.Am., Pe, Bol grocery store

bodeguero m, **-a** f C.Am., Pe, Ven storekeeper

body m prenda body

bofetada f slap; **bofetear** <1a> v/t L.Am. slap

bofia f F cops pl F

boga f: **estar en ~** fig be in fashion

bogavante m ZO lobster

bohemio 1 adj bohemian **2** m, **-a** f bohemian

bohío m Cuba, Ven hut

boicot m boycott; **boicotear** <1a> v/t boycott; **boicoteo** m boycotting

boina f beret

bojote m L.Am. fig bundle

bol m bowl

bola f ball; TÉC ball bearing; de helado scoop; F (mentira) fib F; **~ de nieve** snowball; **no dar pie con ~** get everything wrong; **bolada** f L.Am. throw; (suerte) piece of luck; **bolado** m S.Am. deal; L.Am. F (mentira) fib F

boleada f Arg hunt; **boleador** m, **~a** f Méx bootblack; **boleadoras** fpl L.Am. bolas; **bolear** <1a> **1** v/i L.Am. DEP have a knockabout **2** v/t L.Am. DEP bowl; Rpl con boleadoras bring down; Méx zapatos shine **3** v/r **~se** Rpl fall; (aperarse) get embarrassed; **bolera** f bowling alley

bolero 1 m MÚS bolero **2** m/f Méx F bootblack

boleta f L.Am. ticket; L.Am. (pase) pass, permit; L.Am. (voto) ballot paper; **boletería** f L.Am. ticket office; en cine, teatro box office; **boletero** m, **-a** f L.Am. ticket clerk; en cine, teatro box office employee; **boletín** m bulletin, report; **~ de**

evaluación report card; *~ meteorológico* weather report; **boleto** *m* *L.Am.* ticket; *~ de autobús L.Am.* bus ticket; *~ de ida y vuelta L.Am.*, *~ redondo Méx* round-trip ticket, *Br* return

boliche *m* AUTO jack; *CSur* grocery store, *Br* grocer's

bólido *m fig* racing car

bolígrafo *m* ball-point pen

bolillo *m* bobbin; *Méx* bread roll; *encaje de ~s* handmade lace

Bolivia Bolivia; **boliviano 1** *adj* Bolivian **2** *m*, *-a f* Bolivian

bollo *m* bun; *(abolladura)* bump

bolo *m* pin; *C.Am.*, *Méx* christening present; **bolos** *mpl* bowling *sg*

bolsa *f* bag; COM stock exchange; *L.Am.* *(bolsillo)* pocket; *~ de agua caliente* hot-water bottle; **bolsero** *m*, *-a f Méx* F scrounger

bolsillo *m* pocket; *meterse a alguien en el ~* F win s.o. over; **bolso** *m* purse, *Br* handbag; **bolsón** *m Arg*, *Pe* traveling bag, *Br* holdall

bomba *f* bomb; TÉC pump; *S.Am.* gas station; *~ de relojería* time bomb; *caer como una ~ fig* F come as a bombshell; *pasarlo ~* F have a great time

bombacha *f Arg* panties *pl*, *Br tb* knickers *pl*; **bombacho** *m*: *~s pl*, *pantalón ~* baggy pants *pl*

bombardear <1a> *v/t* bomb

bombero *m*, *-a f* firefighter; *llamar a los ~* call the fire department

bombilla *f* light bulb; *Rpl* metal straw for the mate gourd; **bombillo** *m C.Am.*, *Pe*, *Bol* light bulb; **bombita** *f Arg* light bulb

bombo *m* MÚS bass drum; TÉC drum

bombón *m* chocolate; *fig* F babe F

bombona *f* cylinder

bonaerense 1 *adj* of Buenos Aires, Buenos Aires *atr* **2** *m/f* native of Buenos Aires

bonanza *f fig* boom, bonanza

bondad *f* goodness, kindness; *tenga la ~ de* please be so kind as to; **bondadoso** *adj* caring

bongo *m L.Am.* bongo

boniato *m* BOT sweet potato

bonito 1 *adj* pretty **2** *m* ZO tuna

bono *m* voucher; COM bond

bonsái *m* bonsai

boñiga *f* dung

boom *m* boom

boquerón *m* ZO anchovy

boquete *m* hole

boquiabierto *adj fig* F speechless

borbotón *m*: *salir a borbotones de agua* gush out; *hablaba a borbotones fig* it all came out in a rush; *hablar ~* burble, splutter

borda *f* MAR gunwale; *echar or tirar por la ~* throw overboard

bordado 1 *adj* embroidered **2** *m* embroidery; **bordar** <1a> *v/t* embroider; *~ algo fig* do sth brilliantly

borde[1] *adj* rude, uncouth

borde[2] *m* edge; *al ~ de fig* on the verge *o* brink of

bordear <1a> *v/t* border; **bordillo** *m* curb, *Br* kerb

bordo *m*: *a ~ MAR*, AVIA on board

borona *f* corn, *Br* maize

borrachera *f* drunkenness; *agarrar una ~* get drunk; **borrachería** *f Méx*, *Rpl* → **borrachera**; **borracho 1** *adj* drunk **2** *m*, *-a f* drunk

borrador *m* eraser; *de texto* draft; *(boceto)* sketch; **borrar** <1a> *v/t* erase; INFOR delete; *pizarra* clean; *recuerdo* blot out

borrasca *f* area of low pressure

borrego *m* ZO lamb; *fig*: *persona* sheep

borrico *m*, *-a f* donkey; *fig* dummy

borrón *m* blot; *mancha extendida* smudge; *hacer ~ y cuenta nueva fig* wipe the slate clean; **borroso** *adj* blurred, fuzzy

Bosnia Bosnia

bosque *m* wood; *grande* forest

bosquejo *m* sketch; *fig* outline

bostezar <1f> *v/i* yawn; **bostezo** *m* yawn

bota *f* boot; *~ de montar* riding boot; *ponerse las ~s fig* F coin it F, rake it in F; *(comer mucho)* make a pig of o.s. F

botado *L.Am.* F **1** *adj (barato)* dirt

cheap **2** *m*, **-a** *f* abandoned child

botana *f Méx* snack

botánica *f* botany

botar <1a> **1** *v/t* MAR launch; *pelota* bounce; *L.Am.* (*echar*) throw; *L.Am.* (*desechar*) throw out; *L.Am.* (*despedir*) fire **2** *v/i de pelota* bounce

bote *m* (*barco*) boat; *L.Am.* (*lata*) can, *Br tb* tin; (*tarro*) jar; *pegar un ~* jump; *~ de la basura Méx* trash can, *Br* rubbish bin; *~ salvavidas* lifeboat; *chupar del ~ fig* F line one's pockets F; *tener a alguien en el ~* have s.o. in one's pocket F; *de ~ en ~* packed out

botella *f* bottle

botijo *m* container with a spout for drinking from

botín *m* loot; *calzado* ankle boot

botiquín *m* medicine chest; *estuche* first-aid kit

botón *m en prenda*, TÉC button; BOT bud; **botones** *m inv en hotel* bellhop, bellboy

boutique *f* boutique

bóveda *f* vault

bovino *adj* bovine

boxeador *m*, **~a** *f* boxer; **boxear** <1a> *v/i* box; **boxeo** *m* boxing

boya *f* buoy; *de caña* float; **boyante** *adj fig* buoyant

bragas *fpl* panties, *Br tb* knickers

bragueta *f* fly

bramido *m* roar, bellow

brandy *m* brandy

branquia *f* ZO gill

brasa *f* ember; *a la ~* GASTR char-broiled, *Br* char-grilled; **brasero** *m* brazier; *eléctrico* electric heater

Brasil Brazil; **brasileño 1** *adj* Brazilian **2** *m*, **-a** *f* Brazilian

bravata *f* boast; (*amenaza*) threat

bravo *adj animal* fierce; *mar* rough, choppy; *persona* brave; *L.Am.* (*furioso*) angry; *¡~!* well done!; *en concierto etc* bravo!

bravucón *m*, **-ona** *f* F boaster, blowhard F

braza *f* breaststroke; **brazalete** *m* bracelet; (*banda*) armband; **brazo**

m arm; *~ de gitano* GASTR jelly roll, *Br* Swiss roll; *con los ~s abiertos* with open arms; *dar su ~ a torcer* give in

brebaje *m desp* concoction

brecha *f* breach; *fig* F gap; MED gash; *seguir en la ~* F hang on in there F

brécol *m* broccoli

breva *f* BOT early fig; *no caerá esa ~ fig* F no such luck!

breve *adj* brief; *en ~* shortly; **brevedad** *f* briefness, shortness; **brevemente** *adv* briefly

brezo *m* BOT heather

bribón *m*, **-ona** *f* rascal

bricolaje *m* do-it-yourself, DIY

brigada *f* MIL brigade; *en policía* squad

brillante 1 *adj* bright; *fig* brilliant **2** *m* diamond; **brillar** <1a> *v/i fig* shine; **brillo** *m* shine; *de estrella, luz* brightness; *dar or sacar ~ a algo* polish sth

brincar <1g> *v/i* jump up and down; **brinco** *m* F leap, bound; *dar ~s* jump

brindar <1a> **1** *v/t* offer **2** *v/i* drink a toast (*por* to); **brindis** *m inv* toast

brío *m fig* F verve, spirit

brisa *f* MAR breeze; **brisera** *f L.Am.* windshield, *Br* windscreen

británico 1 *adj* British **2** *m*, **-a** *f* Briton, Brit F

broca *f* TÉC drill bit

brocha *f* brush

broche *m* brooch; (*cierre*) fastener; *L.Am.* (*pinza*) clothes pin; **brocheta** *f* skewer

brócoli *m* broccoli

broma *f* joke; *en ~* as a joke; *gastar ~s* play jokes; *tomar algo a ~* take sth as a joke; **bromear** <1a> *v/i* joke; **bromista** *m/f* joker

bronca *f* F telling off F; *Méx* P fight; *armar una ~ Méx* get into a fight; *echar ~ a alguien* F give s.o. a telling off, tell s.o. off

bronce *m* bronze; **bronceado 1** *adj* tanned **2** *m* suntan; **bronceador** *m* suntan lotion; **broncearse** <1a> *v/r* get a tan

bronquitis *f* MED bronchitis

brotar <1a> *v/i* BOT sprout, bud; *fig* appear, arise; **brote** *m* BOT shoot; MED, *fig* outbreak; **~s de bambú** bamboo shoots; **~s de soja** beansprouts

bruces: *caer de ~* F fall flat on one's face

bruja *f* witch; **brujo** *m* wizard

brújula *f* compass

bruma *f* mist

bruñir <3h> *v/t* burnish, polish; *C.Am.* F (*molestar*) annoy

brusco *adj* sharp, abrupt; *respuesta, tono* brusque, curt

Bruselas Brussels

brutalidad *f* brutality; **bruto 1** *adj* brutish; (*inculto*) ignorant; (*torpe*) clumsy; COM gross **2** *m*, **-a** *f* brute, animal

buceador *m*, **~a** *f* diver; **bucear** <1a> *v/i* dive; *fig* delve (*en* into)

bucólico *adj* bucolic

budista *m/f* & *adj* Buddhist

buen *adj* → **bueno**

buenaventura *f* fortune

bueno *adj* good; (*bondadoso*) kind; (*sabroso*) nice; *por las -as* willingly; *de -as a primeras* without warning; *ponerse* ~ get well; *¡~!* well!; *¿~?* *Méx* hello; *-a voluntad* goodwill; *¡-as!* hello!; *~s días* good morning; *-as noches* good evening; *-as tardes* good evening

buey *m* ZO ox

búfalo *m* ZO buffalo

bufanda *f* scarf; *fig* F perk

bufete *m* lawyer's office

buffet *m* GASTR buffet

bufón *m* buffoon, fool

buganvilla *f* BOT bougainvillea

buhardilla *f* attic, loft

búho *m* ZO owl

buitre *m* ZO vulture

bulbo *m* BOT bulb

bulevar *m* boulevard

Bulgaria Bulgaria

bulimia *f* MED bulimia

bulla *f* din, racket; **bullicio** *m* hubbub, din; (*actividad*) bustle;

bullir <3h> *v/i fig*: *de sangre* boil; *de lugar* swarm, teem (*de* with)

bulo *m* F rumo(u)r

bulto *m* package; MED lump; *en superficie* bulge; (*silueta*) vague shape; (*pieza de equipaje*) piece of baggage

bumerán *m* boomerang

buque *m* ship; *~ de guerra* warship

burbuja *f* bubble

burdel *m* brothel

burdo *adj* rough

burgués 1 *adj* middle-class, bourgeois **2** *m*, **-esa** *f* middle-class person, member of the bourgeoisie; **burguesía** *f* middle class, bourgeoisie

burla *f* joke; (*engaño*) trick; *hacer ~ de alguien* F make fun of s.o.; **burlar** <1a> **1** *v/t* get round **2** *v/r* **~se** make fun (*de* of)

burlete *m* L.Am. draft excluder, *Br* draught excluder

buró *m* bureau

burocracia *f* bureaucracy; **burócrata** *m/f* bureaucrat; **burocrático** *adj* bureaucratic

burrada *f fig* F piece of nonsense; *hay una ~* there's loads F; *costar una ~* cost a packet F

burro *m* ZO donkey; *no ver tres en un ~* be as blind as a bat

bursátil *adj* stock market *atr*

bus *m* bus

busca 1 *f* search; *en ~ de* in search of **2** *m* F pager; **buscador** *m* searcher; INFOR search engine; **buscapersonas** *m inv* pager; **buscapleitos** *m/f inv* F troublemaker; **buscar** <1a> *v/t* search for, look for

búsqueda *f* search

busto *m* bust

butaca *f* armchair; TEA seat

butano *m* butane

butifarra *f* type of sausage

buzo *m* diver

buzón *m* mailbox, *Br* postbox; *~ de voz* TELEC voicemail

byte *m* INFOR byte

C *abr* (= *Centígrado*) C (= Centigrade); (= *compañía*) Co. (= Company); c (= *calle*) St. (= Street); (= *capítulo*) ch. (= chapter)

cabal *adj*: *no estar en sus ~es* not be in one's right mind

cabalgar <1h> *v/i* ride

cabalgata *f* procession

caballa *f* ZO mackerel

caballada *f Rpl*: *decir / hacer una ~* say / do sth stupid

caballería *f* MIL cavalry; (*caballo*) horse

caballero 1 *adj* gentlemanly, chivalrous **2** *m hombre* gentleman, man; *hombre educado* gentleman; HIST knight; *trato* sir; (*servicio de*) *~s pl* men's room, gents; *en tienda de ropa* menswear; **caballeroso** *adj* gentlemanly, chivalrous

caballito *m*: *~ del diablo* ZO dragonfly; *~ de mar* ZO seahorse; *~s pl* carousel *sg*, merry-go-round *sg*

caballo *m* horse; *en ajedrez* knight; *~ balancín* rocking horse; *a ~ entre* halfway between; *montar* or *andar Rpl a ~* ride (a horse); *me gusta montar a ~* I like riding; *ir a ~* go on horseback

cabaña *f* cabin

cabaret *m* cabaret

cabecear <1a> **1** *v/i* nod **2** *v/t el balón* head; **cabecera** *f de mesa, cama* head; *de periódico* masthead; *de texto* top; **cabecero** *m de cama* headboard

cabecilla *m/f* ringleader

cabello *m* hair

caber <2m> *v/i* fit; *caben tres litros* it holds three liters *o Br* litres; *cabemos todos* there's room for all of us; *no cabe duda fig* there's no doubt; *no me cabe en la cabeza* I just don't understand

cabestrillo *m* MED sling

cabeza *f* ANAT head; *~ de ajo* bulb of garlic; *~* (*de ganado*) head (of cattle); *~ nuclear* nuclear warhead; *el equipo a la ~* or *en ~* the team at the top; *por ~* per head, per person; *estar mal* or *no estar bien de la ~* F not be right in the head F **2** *m/f*: *~ de familia* head of the family; *~ de turco* scapegoat; *~ rapada* skinhead

cabezada *f*: *echar una ~* have a nap

cabezonería *f* pigheadedness; **cabezota 1** *adj* pig-headed **2** *m/f* pigheaded person

cabida *f* capacity; *dar ~ a* hold

cabildo *m* POL council

cabina *f* cabin; *~ telefónica* phone booth

cabizbajo *adj* dejected, downhearted

cable *m* EL cable; MAR line, rope; *echar un ~ a alguien* give s.o. a hand

cabo *m* end; GEOG cape; MAR rope; MIL corporal; *de ~ a rabo* F from start to finish; *atar ~s* F put two and two together F; *llevar a ~* carry out

cabra *f* ZO goat; *estar como una ~* F be nuts F

cabrear <1a> **1** *v/t* P bug F **2** *v/r -se* P get mad F

cabriola *f*: *hacer ~s de niño* jump around

cabro *m Chi* boy; *~ chico Chi* baby

cabrón *m* V bastard P, son of a bitch V

caca *f* F poop F, *Br* pooh F; *cosa mala* piece of trash F; *hacer ~* poop F, *Br* do a pooh F

cacahuate *m Méx* peanut

cacahuete *m* peanut

cacalote *m C.Am., Cuba, Méx* crow

cacao *m* cocoa; *de labios* lip salve; *no*

valer un ~ *L.Am. fig* F not be worth a bean F

cacatúa *f* ZO cockatoo

cacería *f* hunt

cacerola *f* pan

cachar <1a> *v/t L.Am.* (*engañar*) trick; *L.Am.* (*sorprender*) catch out; **¿me cachas?** *Chi* get it?

cacharro *m* pot; *Méx, C.Am.* F (*trasto*) piece of junk; *Méx, C.Am.* F *coche* junkheap; **lavar los ~s** *Méx, C.Am.* wash the dishes

cachas *adj*: **estar ~** F be a real hunk F

cachear <1a> *v/t* frisk

cachemira *f* cashmere

cachetada *f L.Am.* slap; **cachete** *m* cheek; **cachetear** <1a> *v/t L.Am.* slap

cachimba *f* pipe

cachivache *m* thing; **~s** *pl* (*cosas*) things, stuff *sg* F; (*basura*) junk *sg*

cacho *m* F bit; *Rpl* (*cuerno*) horn; *Ven, Col* F (*marijuana*) joint F; **jugar al ~** *Bol, Pe* play dice; **ponerle ~s a alguien** cheat on sb

cachondeo *m*: **estar de ~** F be joking; **tomar a ~** F take as a joke; **¡vaya ~!** F what a laugh! F

cachondo *adj* ~ (*caliente*) horny F; (*gracioso*) funny

cachorro *m* ZO pup

cacique *m* chief; POL *local political boss*; *fig* F tyrant

cacle *m Méx* shoe

caco *m* F thief

cactus *m inv* BOT cactus

cada *adj considerado por separado* each; *con énfasis en la totalidad* every; **~ cosa en su sitio** everything in its place; **~ uno, ~ cual** each one; **~ vez** every time, each time; **~ vez más** more and more, increasingly; **~ tres días** every three days; **uno de ~ tres** one out of every three

cadáver *m* (dead) body, corpse

cadena *f* chain; *de perro* leash, *Br* lead; TV channel; **~ perpetua** life sentence

cadencia *f* MÚS rhythm, cadence

cadera *f* hip

caducado *adj* out of date; **caducar** <1g> *v/i* expire; **caducidad** *f*: **fecha de ~** expiry date; *de alimentos, medicinas* use-by date

caer <2o> **1** *v/i* fall; **me cae bien / mal** *fig* I like / don't like him; **dejar ~ algo** drop sth; **estar al ~** be about to arrive; **~ enfermo** fall ill; **~ en lunes** fall on a Monday; **¡ahora caigo!** *fig* now I get it! **2** *v/r* **~se** fall (down)

café *m* coffee; (*bar*) café; **~ con leche** white coffee; **~ descafeinado** decaffeinated coffee; **~ instantáneo** instant coffee; **~ solo** black coffee; **cafeína** *f* caffeine; **cafetera** *f* coffee maker; *para servir* coffee pot; **cafetería** *f* coffee shop

cagar <1h> V **1** *v/i* have a shit P **2** *v/r* **~se** shit o.s. P; **~se de miedo** shit o.s. P

caguama *f Méx* (*tortuga*) turtle

caída *f* fall

caigo *vb* → **caer**

caimán *m* ZO alligator; *Méx, C.Am. útil* monkey wrench

Cairo: **El ~** Cairo

caja *f* box; *de reloj, ordenador* case, casing; COM cash desk; *en supermercado* checkout; **~ de ahorros** savings bank; **~ de cambios** gearbox; **~ de caudales, ~ fuerte** safe, strongbox; **~ de cerillas** matchbox; **~ de música** music box; **~ postal** post office savings bank; **~ registradora** cash register; **echar a alguien con ~s destempladas** send s.o. packing; **cajero** *m*, **-a** *f* cashier; *de banco* teller; **~ automático** ATM, *Br tb* cash point

cajeta *f Méx* caramel spread

cajón *m* drawer; *L.Am.* casket, coffin

cajuela *f Méx* AUTO trunk, *Br* boot

cal *f* lime

cala *f* cove

calabacín *m* BOT zucchini, *Br* courgette; **calabaza** *f* pumpkin; **dar ~s a alguien** F *en examen* fail s.o., flunk s.o. F; *en relación* give s.o. the brush off F

calabozo *m* cell

calada f puff

calado adj soaked; ~ **hasta los huesos** soaked to the skin

calamar m ZO squid

calambre m EL shock; MED cramp

calamidad f calamity

calaña f desp sort, type

calar <1a> **1** v/t (mojar) soak; techo, tela soak through; persona, conjura see through **2** v/i de zapato leak; de ideas, costumbres take root; ~ **hondo en** make a big impression on **3** v/r ~**se de motor** stall; ~**se hasta los huesos** get soaked to the skin

calato adj Chi, Pe naked

calavera f skull

calcar <1g> v/t trace

calceta f: **hacer** ~ knit; **calcetín** m sock

calcinado adj burnt

calcio m calcium

calcomanía f decal, Br transfer

calculador adj fig calculating; **calculadora** f calculator; **calcular** <1a> v/t tb fig calculate; **cálculo** m calculation; MED stone; ~ **biliar** gallstone; ~ **renal** kidney stone

caldear <1a> v/t warm up; ánimos inflame

caldera f boiler; Rpl, Chi kettle; **calderilla** f small change; **caldero** m (small) boiler; **caldillo** m Méx GASTR stock

caldo m GASTR stock; ~ **de cultivo** fig breeding ground

caldoso adj watery

calefacción f heating; ~ **central** central heating; **calefactor** m heater

calendario m calendar; (programa) schedule

caléndula f BOT marigold

calentador m heater; ~ **de agua** water heater; **calentamiento** m: ~ **global** global warming; **calentar** <1k> **1** v/t heat (up); ~ **a alguien** fig provoke s.o. **2** v/i DEP warm up **3** v/r ~**se** warm up; fig: de discusión, disputa become heated; **calentura** f fever

calibrar <1a> v/t gauge; fig weigh up;

calibre m tb fig caliber, Br calibre

calidad f quality; ~ **de vida** quality of life; **en** ~ **de médico** as a doctor

cálido adj tb fig warm

caliente adj hot; F (cachondo) horny F; **en** ~ in the heat of the moment

calificable adj gradable; **calificación** f description; EDU grade, Br mark; **calificar** <1g> v/t describe, label (**de** as); EDU grade, Br mark

caligrafía f calligraphy

caliza f limestone

callado adj quiet; **callar** <1a> **1** v/i (dejar de hablar) go quiet; (guardar silencio) be quiet, keep quiet; **¡calla!** be quiet!, shut up! **2** v/t silence **3** v/r ~**se** (dejar de hablar) go quiet; (guardar silencio) be quiet, keep quiet; ~**se algo** keep sth quiet

calle f street; DEP lane; **echar a alguien a la** ~ fig throw s.o out onto the street; **callejón** m alley; ~ **sin salida** blind alley; fig dead end

callo m callus; ~**s** pl GASTR tripe sg

calma f calm; **calmante 1** adj soothing **2** m MED sedative; **calmar** <1a> **1** v/t calm (down) **2** v/r ~**se** calm down

calor m heat; fig warmth; **hace mucho** ~ it's very hot; **tengo** ~ I'm hot; **caloría** f calorie

calumnia f oral slander; por escrito libel; **calumniar** <1b> v/t oralmente slander; por escrito libel

caluroso adj hot; fig warm

calva f bald patch

calvario m fig calvary

calvicie f baldness; **calvo 1** adj bald **2** m bald man

calzada f road (surface); **calzado** m footwear; **calzador** m shoe horn; **calzar** <1f> **1** v/t zapato, bota etc put on; mueble, rueda wedge **2** v/r ~**se** zapato, bota etc put on

calzón m DEP shorts pl; L.Am. de hombre shorts pl, Br (under)pants pl; L.Am. de mujer panties pl, Br tb knickers pl; **calzones** L.Am. shorts, Br (under)pants

calzoncillos mpl shorts, Br (under)pants

cama *f* bed; **~ de matrimonio** double bed; **hacer la ~** make the bed; **irse a la ~** go to bed

camaleón *m* chameleon

cámara *f* FOT, TV camera; (*sala*) chamber; **~ de comercio e industria** chamber of commerce and industry; **a ~ lenta** in slow motion; **~ de vídeo** video camera

camarada *m/f* comrade; *de trabajo* colleague, co-worker; **camaradería** *f* camaraderie, comradeship

camarera *f* waitress; **camarero** *m* waiter

camarógrafo *m*, **-a** *f L.Am.* camera operator

camarón *m L.Am.* ZO shrimp, *Br* prawn

camarote *m* MAR cabin; **camarotero** *m L.Am.* steward

cambalache *m Arg* F second-hand shop

cambiar <1b> **1** *v/t* change (**por** for); *compra exchange* (**por** for) **2** *v/i* change; **~ de lugar** change places; **~ de marcha** AUTO shift gear, *Br* change gear **3** *v/r* **~se** change; **~se de ropa** change (one's clothes); **cambio** *m* change; COM exchange rate; **~ climático** climate change; **~ de marchas** AUTO gear shift, *Br* gear change; **~ de sentido** U-turn; *a ~ de* in exchange for; **en ~** on the other hand

camelia *f* BOT camellia

camello **1** *m* ZO camel **2** *m/f* F (*vendedor de drogas*) pusher F, dealer

camelo *m* F con F; (*broma*) joke

camilla *f* stretcher

caminar <1a> **1** *v/i* walk; *fig* move; **caminando** on foot **2** *v/t* walk; **camino** *m* (*senda*) path; (*ruta*) way; *a medio ~* halfway; *de ~ a* on the way to; **por el ~** on the way; **abrirse ~** *fig* make one's way; *ir por buen/mal ~* *fig* be on the right/wrong track; **ponerse en ~** set out

camión *m* truck, *Br tb* lorry; *Méx* bus; **camionero** *m*, **-a** *f* truck driver, *Br tb* lorry driver; *Méx* bus driver;

camioneta *f* van

camisa *f* shirt; **camiseta** *f* T-shirt; **camisón** *m* nightdress

camorra *f* F fight; **armar ~** F cause trouble

campal *adj*: **batalla ~** pitched battle

campamento *m* camp

campana *f* bell; **~ extractora** extractor hood; **campanada** *f* chime; **dar la ~** cause a stir; **campanario** *m* bell tower

campanazo *m L.Am.* warning

campanilla *f* small bell; ANAT uvula

campante *adj*: **tan ~** F as calm as anything F

campaña *f* campaign; **~ electoral** election campaign

campechano *adj* down-to-earth

campeón *m*, **-ona** *f* champion; **campeonato** *m* championship; **de ~** F terrific F

campesino **1** *adj* peasant *atr* **2** *m*, **-a** *f* peasant; **campestre** *adj* rural, country *atr*

camping *m* campground, *Br tb* campsite

campo *m* field; DEP field, *Br tb* pitch; (*estadio*) stadium, *Br tb* ground; **el ~** (*área rural*) the country; **~ de batalla** battlefield; **~ de concentración** concentration camp; **~ de golf** golf course; **~ visual** MED field of vision; **a ~ traviesa**, **~ a través** cross-country

campus *m inv*: **~ universitario** university campus

Canadá Canada; **canadiense** *m/f &* *adj* Canadian

canal *m* channel; TRANSP canal; **canalete** *m* paddle; **canalizar** <1f> *v/t* channel

canalla *m* swine F, rat F

canalón *m* gutter

canapé *m* (*sofá*) couch; *para cama* base; GASTR canapé

Canarias *fpl* Canaries; **canario 1** *adj* Canary *atr* **2** *m* ZO canary

canasta f basket; *juego* canasta

cancela f (wrought-iron) gate

cancelación f cancellation; **cancelar** <1a> v/t cancel; *deuda, cuenta* settle, pay

cáncer m MED, fig cancer; **Cáncer** m/f inv ASTR Cancer; **cancerígeno** adj carcinogenic; **canceroso** adj cancerous

cancha f DEP court; *L.Am. de fútbol* field, *Br tb* pitch; **~ de tenis** tennis court; **¡~!** *Rpl* F gangway! F; **abrir** or **hacer ~** *Rpl* make room; **canchear** <1a> v/i *L.Am.* climb

canciller m Chancellor; *S.Am. de asuntos exteriores* Secretary of State, *Br* Foreign Minister

canción f song; **siempre la misma ~** F the same old story F

candado m padlock

candela f *L.Am.* fire; **¿me das ~?** have you got a light?

candelabro m candelabra; **candelero** m: **estar en el ~ de persona** be in the limelight

candente adj red-hot; *tema* topical

candidato m, -a f candidate; **candidatura** f candidacy

cándido adj naive; **candor** m innocence; (*franqueza*) cando(u)r

canela f cinnamon

canelones mpl GASTR cannelloni sg

cangrejo m ZO crab

canguro 1 m ZO kangaroo **2** m/f F baby-sitter

caníbal 1 adj cannibal atr **2** m/f cannibal

canica f marble

caniche m poodle

canícula f dog days pl

canijo adj F puny

canilla f *L.Am.* faucet, *Br* tap

canillita m/f *Arg* newspaper vendor

canjear <1a> v/t exchange (**por** for)

canoa f canoe

canónico adj canonical; **canónigo** m canon; **canonizar** <1f> v/t canonize

cansado adj tired; **cansancio** m tiredness; **cansar** <1a> **1** v/t tire; (*aburrir*) bore **2** v/r **~se** get tired;

(*aburrirse*) get bored; **~se de algo** get tired of sth

cantante m/f singer; **cantar** <1a> **1** v/i sing; *de delincuente* squeal P **2** v/t sing **3** m: **ése es otro ~** fig F that's a different story

cántaro m pitcher; **llover a ~s** F pour (down)

cantautor m, ~a f singer-songwriter

cante m: **~ hondo** or **jondo** flamenco singing

cantera f quarry

cantidad f quantity, amount; **había ~ de** there was (pl were) a lot of

cantimplora f water bottle

cantina f canteen

canto[1] m singing; *de pájaro* song

canto[2] m edge; (*roca*) stone; **~ rodado** boulder; **darse con un ~ en los dientes** count o.s. lucky

canturrear <1a> v/t sing softly

canutas: las pasé ~ F it was really tough F

caña f BOT reed; (*tallo*) stalk; *cerveza* small glass of beer; *L.Am.* straw; **muebles de ~** cane furniture; **~ de azúcar** sugar cane; **~ de pescar** fishing rod; **dar** or **meter ~ a alguien** F wind s.o. up F; **¡dale ~!** get off your butt! F

cañada f ravine; *L.Am.* (*arroyo*) stream

cáñamo m hemp; *L.Am.* marijuana plant

cañería f pipe

cañero adj *L.Am.* sugar-cane atr

caño m pipe; *de fuente* spout; **cañón 1** m HIST cannon; *antiaéreo, antitanque etc* gun; *de fusil* barrel; GEOG canyon **2** adj F great, fantastic F; **cañonazo** m gunshot

caoba f mahogany

caos m chaos; **caótico** adj chaotic

cap abr (= **capítulo**) ch. (= chapter)

capa f layer; *prenda* cloak; **~ de ozono** ozone layer; **~ de pintura** coat of paint

capacidad f capacity; (*aptitud*) competence; **~ de memoria / de almacenamiento** INFOR memory / storage capacity; **capacitar** <1a>

v/t prepare; ~ *alguien para hacer* *algo* qualify s.o. to do sth

capar <1a> *v/t* castrate

caparazón *m* ZO shell

capataz *m* foreman; **capataza** *f* forewoman

capaz *adj* able (*de* to); **ser ~ de** be capable of

capcioso *adj*: **pregunta -a** trick question

capear <1a> *v/t temporal* weather

capellán *m* chaplain

capicúa *adj*: **número ~** reversible number

capilar 1 *adj* capillary *atr*; *loción* hair *atr* **2** *m* capillary

capilla *f* chapel; ~ *ardiente* chapel of rest

capirotada *f Méx* type of French toast with honey, cheese, raisins etc

capital 1 *adj importancia* prime; **pena ~** capital punishment **2** *f de país* capital **3** *m* COM capital; **capitalismo** *m* capitalism; **capitalista 1** *adj* capitalist *atr* **2** *m/f* capitalist

capitán *m* captain; **capitanear** <1a> *v/t* captain

capitel *m* ARQUI capital

Capitolio *m* Capitol

capitulación *f* capitulation, surrender; (*pacto*) agreement; **capitular** <1a> *v/i* surrender, capitulate

capítulo *m* chapter

capó *m* AUTO hood, *Br* bonnet

capón *m Rpl* mutton

capota *f* AUTO top, *Br* hood

capote *m* cloak; MIL greatcoat; **capotera** *f L.Am.* coat stand

capricho *m* whim; **caprichoso** *adj* capricious

Capricornio *m/f inv* ASTR Capricorn

cápsula *f* capsule; ~ *espacial* space capsule

captar <1a> *v/t* understand; RAD pick up; *negocio* take

capturar <1a> *v/t* capture

capucha *f* hood

capuchino *m* cappuccino

capullo *m* ZO cocoon; BOT bud

caqui 1 *adj* khaki **2** *m* BOT persimmon

cara *f* face; (*expresión*) look; *fig* nerve; ~ *a algo* facing sth; ~ *a* ~ face to face; *de* ~ *a fig* with regard to; *dar la* ~ face the consequences; *echar algo en* ~ *a alguien* remind s.o. of sth; *tener* ~ *dura* have a nerve; *tener buena/mala* ~ *de persona* look good/bad; *de persona* look well/sick; ~ *o cruz* heads or tails

carabinero *m* GASTR (large) shrimp, *Br* prawn; (*agente de aduana*) border guard

caracol *m* snail; *¡~es!* wow! F; *enfado* damn! F; **caracola** *f* ZO conch

carácter *m* character; (*naturaleza*) nature; **característica** *f* characteristic; **característico** *adj* characteristic (*de* of); **caracterizar** <1f> **1** *v/t* characterize; TEA play (the part of) **2** *v/r* -**se** be characterized (*por* by)

caradura *m/f* F guy/woman with a nerve, *Br* cheeky devil F

carajillo *m* coffee with a shot of liquor

carajo *m*: **irse al** ~ F go down the tubes F

caramba *int* wow!; *enfado* damn! F

carambola *f billar* carom, *Br* cannon; **por** *or* **de** ~ F by sheer chance

caramelo *m dulce* candy, *Br* sweet; (*azúcar derretida*) caramel

carantoña *f* caress

caraqueño 1 *adj* of/from Caracas, Caracas *atr* **2** *m*, **-a** *f* native of Caracas

carátula *f de disco* jacket, *Br tb* sleeve; *L.Am. de reloj* face

caravana *f* (*remolque*) trailer, *Br* caravan; *de tráfico* queue of traffic, traffic jam; *Méx* (*reverencia*) bow

caray *int* F wow! F; *enfado* damn! F

carbón *m* coal; **carboncillo** *m* charcoal; **carbonizar** <1f> *v/t* char; **carbono** *m* QUÍM carbon

carburador *m* AUTO carburet(t)or; **carburante** *m* fuel

carca *m/f & adj* F reactionary

carcajada *f* laugh, guffaw; *reír a* ~*s* roar with laughter; **carcajearse** <1a> *v/r* have a good laugh (*de* at)

cárcel *f* prison; **carcelero** *m*, -**a** *f*

warder, jailer

carcinoma *f* MED carcinoma

carcoma *f* ZO woodworm; **carcomer** <2a> **1** *v/t* eat away; *fig: de envidia* eat away at, consume **2** *v/r* **~se** be eaten away; **~se de** *fig* be consumed with

cardamomo *m* BOT cardamom

cardenal *m* REL cardinal; (*hematoma*) bruise

cardíaco, cardiaco *adj* cardiac

cardinal *adj* cardinal; **número ~** cardinal number; **puntos ~es** points of the compass, cardinal points

cardiólogo *m*, **-a** *f* cardiologist

cardo *m* BOT thistle

carecer <2d> *v/i*: **~ de algo** lack sth; **carencia** *f* lack (**de** of); **carente** *adj*: **~ de** lacking in

careta *f* mask

carga *f* load; *de buque* cargo; MIL, EL charge; (*responsabilidad*) burden; **~ explosiva** explosive charge; **~ fiscal** *or* **impositiva** tax burden; **ser una ~ para alguien** be a burden to s.o.; **volver a la ~** return to the attack; **cargado** *adj* loaded (**de** with); *aire* stuffy; *ambiente* tense; *café* strong; **cargamento** *m* load; **cargante** *adj* F annoying

cargar <1h> **1** *v/t arma, camión* load; *batería, acusado* charge; COM charge (**en** to); *L.Am.* (*traer*) carry; **esto me carga** *L.Am.* P I can't stand this **2** *v/i* (*apoyarse*) rest (**sobre** on); (*fastidiar*) be annoying; **~ con algo** carry sth; **~ con la culpa** *fig* shoulder the blame; **~ contra alguien** MIL, DEP charge (at) s.o. **3** *v/r* **~se** *con peso, responsabilidad* weigh o.s. down; F (*matar*) bump off F; F (*romper*) wreck F

cargo *m* position; JUR charge; **alto ~** high-ranking position; *persona* high-ranking official; **a ~ de la madre** in the mother's care; **está a ~ de Gómez** Gómez is in charge of it; **hacerse ~ de algo** take charge of sth

cariarse <1b> *v/r* decay

Caribe *m* Caribbean; **caribeño** *adj* Caribbean

caricatura *f* caricature; **caricaturizar** <1f> *v/t* caricature

caricia *f* caress

caridad *f* charity

caries *f* MED caries

cariño *m* affection, fondness; **hacer ~ a alguien** *L.Am.* (*acariciar*) caress s.o.; (*abrazar*) hug s.o.; **¡~!** darling!; **con ~** with love; **cariñoso** *adj* affectionate

carisma *m* charisma; **carismático** *adj* charismatic

caritativo *adj* charitable

cariz *m* look; **tomar mal ~** start to look bad

carmín *m de labios* lipstick

carnaval *m* carnival

carne *f* meat; *de persona* flesh; **~ de gallina** *fig* goose bumps *pl*, *Br* gooseflesh; **~ picada** ground meat, *Br* mince; **de ~ y hueso** flesh and blood; **sufrir algo en sus propias ~s** *fig* go through sth oneself

carné *m* → **carnet**

carnear <1a> *v/t L.Am.* slaughter

carnero *m* ram

carnet *m* card; **~ de conducir** driver's license, *Br* driving licence; **~ de identidad** identity card

carnicería *f* butcher's; *fig* carnage; **carnicero** *m*, **-a** *f* butcher

carnívoro *adj* carnivorous

carnoso *adj* fleshy

caro *adj* expensive, dear; **costar ~** *fig* cost dear

carozo *m Chi, Rpl* pit

carpa *f de circo* big top; ZO carp; *L.Am. para acampar* tent; *L.Am. de mercado* stall

carpeta *f* file

carpintero *m* carpenter; *de obra* joiner; **pájaro ~** woodpecker

carpir <3a> *v/t L.Am.* hoe

carraspear <1a> *v/i* clear one's throat; **carraspera** *f* hoarseness

carrera *f* race; EDU degree course; *profesional* career; **~ de armamento** arms race; **a las ~s** at top speed; **con prisas** in a rush; **hacer la ~** F *de* *prostituta* turn tricks F; **~s** *pl de coches* motor racing *sg*; **carrerilla** *f*: *tomar* **~** take a run up; *decir algo de* **~** reel sth off

carreta *f* cart; **carrete** *m* FOT (roll of) film; **~** *de hilo* reel of thread

carretera *f* highway, (main) road; **~** *de circunvalación* ring road; **carretilla** *f* wheelbarrow

carril *m* lane; **~-bici** cycle lane; **~-bus** bus lane

carrillo *m* cheek; *comer a dos* **~s** F stuff oneself F

carrito *m* cart, *Br* trolley; **~** *de bebé* buggy, *Br* pushchair; **carro** *m* cart; *L.Am.* car; *L.Am.* (*taxi*) taxi, cab; **~** *de combate* tank; **~-patrulla** *L.Am.* F patrol car

carrocería *f* AUTO bodywork

carroña *f* carrion

carruaje *m* carriage

carta *f* letter; GASTR menu; (*naipe*) playing card; (*mapa*) chart; **~** *certificada or registrada* registered letter; **~** *urgente* special-delivery letter; *a la* **~** a la carte; *dar* **~** *blanca a alguien* give s.o. carte blanche *o* a free hand; *poner las* **~s** *boca arriba fig* put one's cards on the table; *tomar* **~s** *en el asunto* intervene in the matter; **cartearse** <1a> *v/r* write to each other

cartel *m* poster; *estar en* **~** *de película, espectáculo* be on

cártel *m* cartel

cartelera *f* billboard; *de periódico* listings, entertainments section

cartera *f* wallet; (*maletín*) briefcase; COM, POL portfolio; *de colegio* knapsack, *Br* satchel; *L.Am.* purse, *Br* handbag; *mujer* mailwoman, *Br* postwoman; **carterista** *m/f* pickpocket; **cartero** *m* mailman, *Br* postman

cartílago *m* cartilage

cartilla *f* reader; *Méx* identity card; **~** *de ahorros* savings book; *leerle a alguien la* **~** F give s.o. a telling off F

cartógrafo *m*, **-a** *f* cartographer

cartón *m* cardboard; *de tabaco* car-

ton; **~** *piedra* pap(i)er-mâché

cartuchera *f* cartridge belt; **cartucho** *m* *de arma* cartridge

cartulina *f* sheet of card; **~** *roja* DEP red card

casa *f* house; (*hogar*) home; *en* **~** at home; *como una* **~** huge F; **~** *cuna* children's home; **~** *de huéspedes* rooming house, *Br* boarding house; **~** *matriz* head office; **~** *de socorro* first aid post; **~** *adosada*, **~** *pareada* → **chalet**

casaca *f* cassock

casado *adj* married; *recién* **~** newlywed; **casamentero** *m*, **-a** *f* matchmaker; **casar** <1a> **1** *v/i fig* match (up); **~** *con* go with **2** *v/r* **~se** get married; **~se** *con alguien* marry s.o.; *no* **~se** *con nadie fig* refuse to compromise

cascabel *m* small bell

cascada *f* waterfall

cascado *adj voz* hoarse; F *persona* worn out F

cascanueces *m inv* nutcracker

cascar <1g> *v/t* crack; *algo quebradizo* break; *fig* F whack F; **~la** peg out F

cáscara *f de huevo* shell; *de naranja, limón* peel

cascarón *m* shell; *salir del* **~** hatch (out)

cascarrabias *m inv* F grouch F

casco *m* helmet; *de barco* hull; (*botella vacía*) empty (bottle); *edificio* empty building; *de caballo* hoof; *de vasija* fragment; **~** *urbano* urban area; **~s** *azules* MIL blue berets, UN peace-keeping troops

cascote *m* piece of rubble

casera *f* landlady; **casero 1** *adj* home-made; *comida* **-a** home cooking **2** *m* landlord

caseta *f* hut; *de feria* stall

casete *m* (*also f*) cassette

casi *adv* almost, nearly; *en frases negativas* hardly

casilla *f en formulario* box; *en tablero* square; *de correspondencia* pigeon hole; *S.Am.* post office box; *sacar a alguien de sus* **~s** drive s.o. crazy

casino *m* casino

caso *m* case; **en ~ de que**, **~ de** in the event that, in case of; **hacer ~** take notice; **ser un ~** F be a real case F; **no venir al ~** be irrelevant; **en todo ~** in any case, in any event; **en el peor de los ~s** if the worst comes to the worst; **en último ~** as a last resort

caspa *f* dandruff

caspiroleta *f S.Am.* eggnog

casquillo *m de cartucho* case; EL bulb holder; *L.Am.* horseshoe

cassette *m* (*also f*) cassette; **~ virgen** blank cassette

casta *f* caste

castaña *f* chestnut; **sacar las ~s del fuego a alguien** *fig* F pull s.o.'s chestnuts out of the fire F; **castaño 1** *adj color* chestnut, brown **2** *m* chestnut (tree); *color* chestnut, brown; **ya pasa de ~ oscuro** F it's gone too far, it's beyond a joke; **castañuela** *f* castanet; **estar como unas ~s** F be over the moon F

castellano *m* (Castilian) Spanish

castidad *f* chastity

castigar <1h> *v/t* punish; **castigo** *m* punishment

castillo *m* castle; **~ de fuegos artificiales** firework display

castizo *adj* pure

casto *adj* chaste

castor *m* ZO beaver

castrar <1a> *v/t* castrate; *fig* emasculate

castrense *adj* army *atr*

casual *adj* chance *atr*; **casualidad** *f* chance, coincidence; **por** *or* **de ~** by chance

cataclismo *m* cataclysm, catastrophe

catalán 1 *adj* Catalan **2** *m*, **-ana** *f* Catalan

catalejo *m* telescope

catalizador *m* catalyst; AUTO catalytic converter; **catalizar** <1f> *v/t* catalyze

catalogar <1h> *v/t* catalog(ue); *fig* class; **catálogo** *m* catalog(ue)

catamarán *m* MAR catamaran

cataplasma *f* MED poultice; *fig: persona* bore

catapulta *f* slingshot, *Br* catapult; **catapultar** <1a> *v/t* catapult

catar <1a> *v/t* taste

catarata *f* GEOG waterfall; MED cataract

catarro *m* cold; *inflamación* catarrh

catástrofe *f* catastrophe; **catastrófico** *adj* catastrophic

cate *m* EDU F fail; **catear** <1a> *v/t* F flunk F

catecismo *m* catechism

catedral *f* cathedral; **una mentira como una ~** F a whopping great lie F

catedrático *m*, **-a** *f* EDU head of department

categoría *f* category; *social* class; *fig: de local, restaurante* class; (*estatus*) standing; **actor de primera ~** first-rate actor; **categórico** *adj* categorical

catequesis *f* catechism

catéter *m* MED catheter

catolicismo *m* (Roman) Catholicism; **católico 1** *adj* (Roman) Catholic **2** *m*, **-a** *f* (Roman) Catholic

catorce *adj* fourteen

catre *m* bed

cauce *m* riverbed; *fig* channel; **volver a su ~** *fig* get back to normal

caucho *m* rubber; *L.Am.* (*neumático*) tire, *Br* tyre

caudal *m de río* volume of flow; *fig* wealth

caudillo *m* leader

causa *f* cause; (*motivo*) reason; JUR lawsuit; **a ~ de** because of; **causante** *m* cause; **causar** <1a> *v/t* cause

cáustico *adj tb fig* caustic

cautela *f* caution; **cauteloso** *adj* cautious

cauterizar <1f> *v/t* cauterize

cautivar <1a> *v/t fig* captivate; **cautiverio** *m*, **cautividad** *f* captivity; **cautivo 1** *adj* captive **2** *m*, **-a** *f* captive

cauto *adj* cautious

cava *m* cava, sparkling wine

cavar <1a> v/t dig

caverna f cavern; **cavernícola** m/f caveman; *mujer* cavewoman

caviar m caviar

cavidad f cavity

cavilar <1a> v/t meditate on

cayó vb → **caer**

caza **1** f hunt; *actividad* hunting; **~ mayor/menor** big/small game; **andar a la ~ de algo/alguien** be after sth/s.o. **2** m AVIA fighter; **cazador** m hunter; **cazadora** f hunter; *prenda* jacket; **cazar** <1f> **1** v/t *animal* hunt; *fig: información* track down; *(pillar, captar)* catch; **~ un buen trabajo** get o.s. a good job **2** v/i hunt; **ir a ~** go hunting

cazo m saucepan; **cazuela** f pan; *de barro, vidrio* casserole

cazurro adj stubborn; *(basto)* coarse; *(lento de entender)* dense F, thick F

c.c. abr (= **centímetro cúbico**) c.c. (= cubic centimeter)

c/c abr (= **cuenta corriente**) C/A (= checking account)

CD m (= **disco compacto**) CD (= compact disc); *reproductor* CD-player; **CD-ROM** m CD-ROM

cebada f barley

cebar <1a> **1** v/t fatten; *anzuelo* bait; TÉC prime; *L.Am. mate* prepare **2** v/r **~se** feed (**en** on); **~ con alguien** vent one's fury on s.o.; **cebo** m bait

cebolla f onion

cebra f zebra; **paso de ~** crosswalk, Br zebra crossing

ceceo m pronunciation of 's' with 'th' sound

cecina f cured meat

cedazo m sieve

ceder <2a> **1** v/t give up; *(traspasar)* transfer, cede; **~ el paso** AUTO yield, Br give way **2** v/i give way, yield; *de viento, lluvia* ease off

cedro m BOT cedar

cédula f L.Am. identity document

cegar <1h & 1k> v/t blind; *tubería* block; **ceguera** f tb fig blindness

ceja f eyebrow; **lo tiene entre ~ y ~** F she can't stand him F

cejar <1a> v/i give up; **no ~ en** not let up in

celador m, **~a** f orderly; *de cárcel* guard; *de museo* attendant

celda f cell

celebración f celebration; **celebrar** <1a> v/t *misa* celebrate; *reunión, acto oficial* hold; *fiesta* have, hold; **célebre** adj famous

celeste adj light blue, sky blue; **celestial** adj celestial; *fig* heavenly

celibato m celibacy

celo m zeal; *(cinta adhesiva)* Scotch® tape, Br Sellotape®; **en ~** ZO in heat; **~s** pl jealousy sg; **tener ~s de** be jealous of

celofán m cellophane

celoso adj jealous (**de** of)

célula f cell; **celular** adj cellular; **celulitis** f cellulite; **celulosa** f cellulose

cementerio m cemetery

cemento m cement

cena f dinner; *más tarde* supper

cenagoso adj boggy

cenar <1a> **1** v/t: **~ algo** have sth for dinner **2** v/i have dinner

cencerro m cowbell

cenicero m ashtray

ceniza f ash; **~s** ashes

censo m census; **~ electoral** voting register, electoral roll

censura f censorship; **censurar** <1a> v/t censor; *tratamiento* condemn

cent abr (= **céntimo**) cent

centavo m cent

centellear <1a> v/i sparkle; *de estrella* twinkle

centena f hundred; **centenar** m hundred; **regalos a ~es** hundreds of gifts; **centenario 1** adj hundred-year-old atr **2** m centennial, Br centenary

centeno m BOT rye

centígrado adj centigrade; **dos grados ~s** two degrees centigrade; **centímetro** m centimeter, Br centimetre; **céntimo** m cent; **estar** *sin un* ~ not have a red cent F

centinela *m/f* sentry; *de banda criminal* lookout

central 1 *adj* central; (*principal*) main, central 2 *f* head office; ~ **atómica** or **nuclear** nuclear power station; ~ **eléctrica** power station; ~ **telefónica** telephone exchange; ~ **térmica** thermal power station; **centralismo** *m* POL centralism; **centralita** *f* TELEC switchboard; **centralizar** <1f> *v/t* centralize; **centrar** <1a> 1 *v/t tb* DEP center, *Br* centre; *esfuerzos* focus (*en* on) 2 *v/r* ~**se** concentrate (*en* on); **céntrico** *adj* central

centrifugar <1h> *v/t* spin

centro *m* center, *Br* centre; ~ **comercial** (shopping) mall, *Br* shopping centre; ~ **urbano** *en señal* town center (*Br* centre)

Centroamérica Central America; **centroamericano** *adj* Central American

ceñido *adj* tight; **ceñirse** <3h & 3l> *v/r*: ~ **a algo** *fig* stick to sth

ceño *m*: **fruncir el** ~ frown

cepa *f de vid* stock

cepillar <1a> 1 *v/t* brush 2 *v/r* ~**se** brush; F (*comerse*) polish off F; F (*matar*) kill, knock off F; **cepillo** *m* brush; ~ **de dientes** toothbrush

cera *f* wax

cerámica *f* ceramics

cerca[1] *f* fence

cerca[2] *adv* near, close; **de** ~ close up; ~ **de** near, close to; (*casi*) nearly

cercanía *f*: **tren de** ~**s** suburban train; **cercano** *adj* nearby; ~ **a** close to, near to; **cercar** <1g> *v/t* surround; *con valla* fence in

cerciorarse <1a> *v/r* make sure (*de* of)

cerco *m* ring; *de puerta* frame; *L.Am.* fence; **poner** ~ **a** lay siege to

cerda *f animal* sow; *fig* F *persona* pig F; *de brocha* bristle; **cerdo** *m* hog, *Br* pig; *fig* F *persona* pig F

cereal *m* cereal; ~**es** *pl* (breakfast) cereal *sg*

cerebro *m* ANAT brain; *fig: persona* brains *sg*

ceremonia *f* ceremony

cereza *f* cherry; **cerezo** *m* cherry (tree)

cerilla *f* match

cernerse <2g> *v/r*: ~ **sobre** *fig* hang over

cernícalo *m* ZO kestrel

cero *m* EDU zero, *Br tb* nought; *en fútbol etc* zero, *Br* nil; *en tenis* love; **bajo/sobre** ~ below/above zero; **empezar desde** ~ *fig* start from scratch; **vencer por tres a** ~ win three-zero (*Br* nil)

cerrado *adj* closed; *persona* narrow-minded; (*tímido*) introverted; *cielo* overcast; *curva* -*a* tight curve

cerradura *f* lock; *ojo de la* ~ keyhole; **cerrajero** *m*, -**a** *f* locksmith

cerrar <1k> 1 *v/t* close; *para siempre* close down; *tubería* block; *grifo* turn off; ~ **con llave** lock 2 *v/i* close; *para siempre* close down 3 *v/r* ~**se** close; *de cielo* cloud over; *de persona* shut o.s. off (*a* from); ~**se de golpe** slam shut

cerrazón *f fig* narrow-mindedness

cerrero *adj L.Am. persona* rough

cerril *adj animal* wild; (*terco*) stubborn, pig-headed F; (*torpe*) F dense F

cerro *m* hill

cerrojo *m* bolt; **echar el** ~ bolt the door

certamen *m* competition

certeza *f* certainty; **certidumbre** *f* certainty

certificado 1 *adj carta* registered 2 *m* certificate; **certificar** <1g> *v/t* certify; *carta* register

cerval *adj*: **miedo** ~ terrible fear

cervecería *f* bar

cerveza *f* beer; ~ **de barril** or **de presión** draft, *Br* draught (beer); ~ **negra** stout; ~ **rubia** lager; **fábrica de** ~ brewery

cesante *adj Chi* unemployed, jobless; **dejar** ~ **a alguien** let s.o. go; **cesar** <1a> *v/i* stop; **no** ~ **de hacer algo** keep on doing sth; **sin** ~ nonstop

cesárea f MED C(a)esarean

cese m cessation

cesión f transfer

césped m lawn

cesta f basket; **~ de la compra** shopping basket; **cesto** m large basket

C.F. abr (= **Club de Fútbol**) FC (= Football Club)

cfc abr (= **clorofluorocarbono**) CFC (= chlorofluorocarbon)

cg. abr (= **centigramo**) centigram

ch/ abr (= **cheque**) check

chabacano adj vulgar, tacky F

chabola f shack; **barrio de ~s** shanty town

chacal m ZO jackal

chacarero m, **-a** f Rpl, Chi smallholder, farmer

chacha f F maid

cháchara fpl L.Am. junk sg, bits and pieces

chachi adj F great F

chacra f L.Am. AGR smallholding

chafar <1a> v/t squash; **cosa erguida** flatten; F **planes etc** ruin F

chaflán m corner

chal m shawl

chalado adj F crazy (**por** about)

chalé m → **chalet**

chaleco m de traje waistcoat; de sport gilet, bodywarmer; **~ salvavidas** life vest; **~ antibalas** bulletproof vest

chalet m chalet; **~ adosado** house sharing one or more walls with other houses; **~ pareado** semi-detached house

chalupa f MAR small boat; Méx stuffed tortilla

chamaca f C.Am., Méx girl; **chamaco** m C.Am., Méx boy

chamarra f Méx (saco) (short) jacket

chamba f Méx F job

chambón m, **-ona** f Méx F clumsy idiot F

champán m, **champaña** m champagne

champiñón m BOT mushroom

champú m shampoo

chamuscar <1g> v/t scorch; **pelo** singe

chamusquina f: **oler a ~** F smell fishy F

chance **1** m L.Am. chance; **dame ~** let me have a go **2** conj Méx perhaps, maybe

chanchería f L.Am. pork butcher's shop; **chancho** m L.Am. hog, Br pig; **carne** pork

chanchullo m F trick, scam F

chancla f thong, Br flip-flop; Méx, C.Am. (zapato) slipper; **chancleta** f thong, Br flip-flop; S.Am. F baby girl

chándal m tracksuit

changa f Rpl odd job

chango **1** adj Méx F sharp, smart **2** m, **-a** f Méx monkey

chanquetes mpl GASTR whitebait sg

chantaje m blackmail; **hacer ~ a alguien** blackmail s.o.; **chantajear** <1a> v/t blackmail; **chantajista** m/f blackmailer

chanza f wisecrack

chao int bye

chapa f (tapón) cap; (plancha) sheet (of metal); (insignia) badge; AUTO bodywork; **chapado** adj plated; **~ a la antigua** old-fashioned; **~ en oro** gold-plated; **chapar** <1a> v/t plate; Arg, Pe catch

chaparro adj Méx small

chaparrón m downpour; fig F de insultos barrage

chapotear <1a> v/i splash

chapucero **1** adj shoddy, slapdash **2** m, **-a** f shoddy worker

chapurrear <1a> v/t: **~ el francés** speak poor French

chapuza f (trabajo mal hecho) shoddy piece of work; (trabajo menor) odd job

chapuzón m dip; **darse un ~** go for a dip

chaqué m morning coat; **chaqueta** f jacket; **~ de punto** cardigan; **chaquetero** m, **-a** f F turncoat; **chaquetón** m three-quarter length coat

charango m Pe, Bol five string guitar

charca f pond; **charco** m puddle

charcutería f delicatessen

charla f chat; *organizada* talk; **charlar** <1a> v/i chat; **charlatán 1** adj talkative **2** m, **-ana** f chatterbox

charol m patent leather; *zapatos de* ~ patent leather shoes

charqui m L.Am. beef jerky

charro 1 adj desp garish, gaudy **2** m Méx (Mexican) cowboy

chasco m joke; *llevarse un* ~ be disappointed

chasis m inv AUTO chassis

chasquear <1a> v/t click; *látigo* crack; **chasquido** m click; *de látigo* crack

chatarra f scrap

chato adj nariz snub; L.Am. nivel low

chau int Rpl bye

chaucha f Rpl French bean

chaval m F kid F, boy; **chavala** f F kid F, girl; **chavalo** m C.Am. F kid F, boy

che int Rpl hey!, look!

checar <1g> v/t Méx check

checo 1 adj Czech **2** m, **-a** f Czech

chef m chef

chelo m MÚS cello

chepa f F hump; *subírsele a la* ~ get too familiar

cheque m check, Br cheque; ~ *cruzado* crossed check (Br cheque); ~ *sin fondos* bad check (Br cheque); ~ *de viaje* traveler's check, Br traveller's cheque; **chequear** <1a> v/t check; C.Am. equipaje check (in); **chequeo** m MED check-up; **chequera** f checkbook, Br chequebook

chica f girl

chicha f L.Am. corn liquor; *no ser ni* ~ *ni limonada* F be neither one thing nor the other

chícharo m Méx pea

chiche 1 adj C.Am. F (fácil) easy **2** m S.Am. (juguete) toy; (adorno) trinket

chichera f C.Am. jail

chichería f L.Am. bar selling corn liquor

chichón m bump

chicle m chewing gum

chico 1 adj small, little **2** m boy

chifa m Pe Chinese restaurant; (comida china) Chinese food

chifla f Méx whistling; **chiflado** adj F crazy F (por about), nuts F (por about); **chiflar** <1a> **1** v/t boo **2** v/i whistle; *me chifla ...* F I'm crazy about ... F

chile m chilli (pepper)

Chile Chile; **chileno 1** adj Chilean **2** m, **-a** f Chilean

chillar <1a> v/i scream, shriek; *de cerdo* squeal; **chillido** m scream, shriek; *de cerdo* squeal; **chillón 1** adj voz shrill; *color* loud **2** m, **-ona** f loudmouth

chilote m C.Am. baby corn

chimenea f chimney; *de salón* fireplace

chimichurri m Rpl hot sauce

chimpancé m ZO chimpanzee

China China

china[1] f Chinese woman

china[2] f piedra small stone

chincheta f thumbtack, Br drawing pin

chinchorro m hammock

chinear <1a> v/t C.Am. niños look after

chingar <1h> v/t Méx V screw V, fuck V; *¡chinga tu madre!* screw you! V, fuck you! V; *no chingues* don't screw me around V

chino 1 adj Chinese **2** m Chinese man; *idioma* Chinese; L.Am. desp half-breed desp; *trabajo de* ~s F hard work; *me suena a* ~ F it's all Chinese o double Dutch to me F

chip m INFOR chip

chipirón m baby squid

chiquilla f girl, kid; **chiquillo** m boy, kid

chirimoya f BOT custard apple

chiringuito m beach bar

chiripa f: *de* ~ F by sheer luck

chirona f: *en* ~ F in the can F, inside F

chirriar <1c> v/i squeak; **chirrido** m squeak

chisme m F bit of gossip; *objeto* doodad F, Br doodah F; **chismografía** f F gossip; **chismorrear** <1a> v/i F gossip; **chismoso 1** adj gossipy **2** *m*, **-a** *f* F gossip

chispa *f* spark; (*cantidad pequeña*) spot; *fig* F wit; **chispear** <1a> *v/i* spark; *fig* sparkle; *de lluvia* spit

chistar <1a> *v/i*: **sin ~** without saying a word

chiste *m* joke

chiva *f* *L.Am.* goat; *C.Am.*, *Col* bus

chivarse <1a> *v/r* F rat F (**a** to);

chivato *m*, **-a** *f* F stool pigeon F;

chivo *m* ZO kid; *C.Am.*, *Méx* wages *pl*

chocante *adj* (*sorprendente*) startling; (*que ofende*) shocking; (*extraño*) odd; *L.Am.* (*antipático*) unpleasant;

chocar <1g> **1** *v/t*: **¡choca esos cinco!** P give me five! P, put it there! P **2** *v/i* crash (**con, contra** into), collide (**con** with); **~le a alguien** (*sorprender*) surprise s.o.; (*ofender*) shock s.o.; **me choca ese hombre** F that guy disgusts me; **~ con un problema** come up against a problem

chocho *adj* F senile; **estar ~ con** dote on

choclo *m* *Rpl* corn, *Br* corn on the cob

chocolate *m* chocolate; F (*hachís*) hashish, hash F; **chocolatina** *f* chocolate bar

chófer, *L.Am.* **chofer** *m* driver

chollo *m* F bargain

cholo *m* *L.Am.* half-caste *desp*

chompa *f* *S.Am.* jumper, sweater

chop *m* *L.Am.* large beer

chopo *m* BOT poplar

choque *m* collision, crash; DEP, MIL clash; MED shock

chorizo *m* chorizo (*spicy cured sausage*); F thief; *Rpl* (*filete*) rump steak

chorlito *m*: **cabeza de ~** F featherbrain F

chorrada *f* F piece of junk; **decir ~s** F talk garbage, *Br* talk rubbish

chorrear <1a> *v/i* gush out, stream; (*gotear*) drip; **chorro** *m* líquido jet, stream; *fig* stream; *C.Am.* faucet, *Br* tap

chovinista *m/f* chauvinist

choza *f* hut

chubasco *m* shower; **chubasquero** *m* raincoat

chuchería *f* knick-knack; (*golosina*) candy, *Br* sweet

chucho 1 *adj* *C.Am.* mean **2** *m* F (*perro*) mutt F, mongrel; *Chi* (*cárcel*) can F, prison

chueco *adj* *L.Am.* (*torcido*) twisted

chulería *f* bragging

chuleta *f* GASTR chop

chulo F **1** *adj* fantastic F, great F; *Méx* (*guapo*) attractive; (*presuntuoso*) cocky F **2** *m* pimp F

chumbera *f* *C.Am.* prickly pear

chumpipe *m* *C.Am.* turkey

chupa *f* jacket

chupado *adj* F (*delgado*) skinny F; F (*fácil*) dead easy F; *L.Am.* F drunk; **chupar** <1a> **1** *v/t* suck; (*absorber*) soak up **2** *v/r* ~**se**: **~se algo** suck sth; *fig* F put up with sth; **~se los dedos** F lick one's fingers; **chupete** *m* *de bebé* pacifier, *Br* dummy; (*sorbete*) Popsicle®, *Br* ice lolly

chupi *adj* F great F, fantastic F

churrasco *m* *Rpl* steak

churro *m* fritter; (*chapuza*) botched job

chusma *f* *desp* rabble *desp*

chutar <1a> *v/i* DEP shoot; **esto va que chuta** F this is working out fine; **y vas que chutas** F and that's your lot! F

chuzo *m* *Chi* F persona dead loss F; **caer ~s de punta** F pelt down F

Cía. *abr* (= **Compañía**) Co. (= Company)

ciberespacio *m* cyberspace; **cibernauta** *m/f* Internet surfer; **cibernética** *f* cybernetics

cicatriz *f* scar; **cicatrizar** <1f> scar

cíclico *adj* cyclical; **ciclismo** *m* cycling; **ciclista** *m/f* cyclist; **ciclo** *m* cycle; *de cine* season; **ciclomotor** *m* moped; **ciclón** *m* cyclone; **cicloturismo** *m* bicycle touring

ciega *f* blind woman; **ciego 1** *adj* blind; **a ~as** blindly **2** *m* blind man

cielito *m* *Rpl* folk dance

cielo *m* sky; REL heaven; **ser un ~** F be an angel F; **~ raso** ceiling

ciempiés *m inv* ZO centipede

cien *adj* a o one hundred

ciencia *f* science; **~ ficción** science fiction; **a ~ cierta** for certain, for sure; **científico 1** *adj* scientific **2** *m*, **-a** *f* scientist

ciento *pron* a o one hundred; **~s de** hundreds of; **el cinco por ~** five per cent

ciernes: en ~ *fig* potential, in the making

cierre *m* fastener; **de negocio** closure; **~ centralizado** AUTO central locking; **~ relámpago** *L.Am.* zipper, *Br* zip

cierto *adj* certain; **hasta ~ punto** up to a point; **un ~ encanto** a certain charm; **es ~** it's true; **~ día** one day; **por ~** incidentally; **estar en lo ~** be right

ciervo *m* ZO deer; **~ volante** ZO stag beetle

c.i.f. *abr* (= **costo, seguro y flete**) cif (= cost, insurance, freight)

cifra *f* figure

cigala *f* ZO crayfish

cigarra *f* ZO cicada

cigarrería *f* *L.Am.* shop selling cigarettes *etc*; **cigarrillo** *m* cigarette; **cigarro** *m* cigar; *L.Am.* cigarette

cigüeña *f* ZO stork

cigüeñal *m* AUTO crankshaft

cilantro *m* BOT coriander

cilindrada *f* AUTO cubic capacity; **cilíndrico** *adj* cylindrical; **cilindro** *m* cylinder

cima *f* summit; *fig* peak

cimarrón *adj* *L.Am. animal* wild; *esclavo* runaway; **mate ~** *Arg* unsweetened maté

cimentar <1k> *v/t* lay the foundations of; *fig* base (**en** on); **cimientos** *mpl* foundations

cinc *m* zinc

cincel *m* chisel

cinco 1 *adj* five **2** *m* five; **no tener ni ~** F not have a red cent F

cincuenta *adj* fifty; **cincuentón** *m* man in his fifties; **cincuentona** *f* woman in her fifties

cine *m* movies *pl*, cinema; **cineasta**

m/f film-maker; **cinéfilo** *m*, **-a** *f* movie buff; **cinematográfico** *adj* movie *atr*

cinético *adj* kinetic

cínico 1 *adj* cynical **2** *m*, **-a** *f* cynic; **cinismo** *m* cynicism

cinta *f* ribbon; **de música, vídeo** tape; **~ adhesiva** adhesive tape; **~ aislante** electrical tape, friction tape, *Br* insulating tape; **~ métrica** tape measure; **~ de vídeo** video tape

cintura *f* waist; **cinturón** *m* belt; **~ de seguridad** AUTO seatbelt

cíper *m* *Méx* zipper, *Br* zip

ciprés *m* BOT cypress

circo *m* circus

circuito *m* circuit; **corto ~** EL short circuit; **circulación** *f* movement; FIN, MED circulation; AUTO traffic; **poner en ~** put into circulation; **circular 1** *adj* circular **2** <1a> *v/i* circulate; AUTO drive, travel; *de persona* move (along); **círculo** *m* circle; **~ vicioso** vicious circle

circuncisión *f* circumcision

circundante *adj* surrounding

circunferencia *f* circumference

circunscribir <3a; *part* **circunscrito**> *v/t* limit (**a** to); **circunscripción** *f* POL electoral district, *Br* constituency

circunspecto *adj* circumspect, cautious

circunstancia *f* circumstance; **circunstancial** *adj* circumstantial

circunvalación *f*: (**carretera de**) **~** beltway, *Br* ring-road

cirio *m* candle; **armar** or **montar un ~** F kick up a fuss F

ciruela *f* plum; **~ pasa** prune

cirugía *f* surgery; **~ estética** cosmetic surgery; **cirujano** *m*, **-a** *f* surgeon

cisco *m*: **hacer ~** smash

cisne *m* ZO swan

cisterna *f* de WC cistern

cistitis *f* MED cystitis

cita *f* appointment; *de texto* quote, quotation; **citar** <1a> **1** *v/t* a reunión arrange to meet; *a juicio* summon; (*mencionar*) mention; *de texto* quote **2** v/r **~se** arrange to meet

citología f smear test

cítrico m citrus fruit

ciudad f town; **más grande** city; **~ universitaria** university campus; **ciudadano** m, **-a** f citizen

cívico adj civic; **civil** adj civil; **casarse por lo ~** have a civil wedding; **civilización** f civilization; **civismo** m civility

cizaña f: **sembrar** or **meter ~** cause trouble

cl. abr (= **centilitro**) cl. (= centiliter)

clamar <1a> v/i: **~ por algo** clamo(u)r for sth, cry out for sth; **clamor** m roar; fig clamo(u)r

clan m clan

clandestino adj POL clandestine, underground

claqué m tap-dancing

clara f de huevo white; bebida beer with lemonade, Br shandy

claraboya f skylight

claridad f light; fig clarity; **clarificar** <1g> v/t clarify

clarinete m clarinet

clarividente m/f clairvoyant

claro adj tb fig clear; color light; (luminoso) bright; salsa thin; **¡~!** of course!; **hablar ~** speak plainly

clase f class; (variedad) kind, sort; **~ particular** private class; **dar ~(s)** teach

clásico adj classical

clasificación f DEP league table; **clasificar** <1g> **1** v/t classify **2** v/r **~se** DEP qualify

claudicar <1g> v/i give in

claustro m ARQUI cloister

claustrofobia f claustrophobia

cláusula f clause

clausurar <1a> v/t acto oficial close; por orden oficial close down

clavadista m/f Méx diver

clavado adj: **ser ~ a alguien** be the spitting image of s.o. F; **clavar** <1a> **1** v/t stick (**en** into); clavos, estaca drive (**en** into); uñas sink (**en** into); **~ los ojos en alguien** fix one's eyes on s.o.; **~ a alguien por algo** F overcharge s.o. for sth **2** v/r **~se**: **~se un**

cuchillo en la mano stick a knife into one's hand

clave 1 f key; **en ~** in code **2** adj (importante) key

clavel m BOT carnation

clavícula f ANAT collarbone

clavija f EL pin

clavo m de metal nail; GASTR clove; CSur F persona dead loss F; **dar en el ~** hit the nail on the head

claxon m AUTO horn

clemencia f clemency, mercy

clementina f BOT clementine

clérigo m priest, clergyman; **clero** m clergy

clic m INFOR click; **hacer ~ en** click on

cliché m cliché

clienta, **cliente** m/f de tienda customer; de empresa client; **clientela** f clientele, customers pl

clima m climate; **climatizado** adj air-conditioned; **climatizar** <1f> v/t air-condition

clímax m fig climax

clínica f clinic; **clínico** adj clinical

clip m para papeles paperclip; para el pelo bobby pin, Br hairgrip

cloaca f tb fig sewer

clon m BIO clone; **clonación** f BIO cloning; **clonar** <1a> v/t clone

cloro m QUÍM chlorine

clóset m L.Am. closet, Br wardrobe

club m club; **~ náutico** yacht club

cm abr (= **centímetro**) cm (= centimeter)

coacción f coercion; **coaccionar** <1a> v/t coerce

coagular <1a> **1** v/t coagulate; sangre clot **2** v/r **~se** coagulate; de sangre clot; **coágulo** m clot

coala m ZO koala

coalición f coalition; **coaligarse** <1h> v/r tb POL work together, join forces

coartada f JUR alibi

coba f: **dar ~ a alguien** F soft-soap s.o. F

cobarde 1 adj cowardly **2** m/f coward

cobaya m/f guinea pig

cobertizo *m* shed; **cobertor** *m* (*manta*) blanket; **cobertura** *f* cover; TV *etc* coverage

cobija *f L.Am.* blanket; **cobijar** <1a> **1** *v/t* give shelter to; (*acoger*) take in **2** *v/r* **~se** take shelter; **cobijo** *m* shelter, refuge

cobra *f* ZO cobra

cobrador *m*, **~a** *f* a domicilio collector; **cobrar** <1a> **1** *v/t* charge; *subsidio, pensión* receive; *deuda* collect; *cheque* cash; *salud, fuerzas* recover; *importancia* acquire **2** *v/i* be paid, get paid; **vas a ~** F (*recibir un palo*) you're going to get it! F

cobre *m* copper

cobro *m* charging; *de subsidio* receipt; *de deuda* collection; *de cheque* cashing

coca *f* F *droga* coke F; **de ~** *Méx* free

cocacho *m S.Am.* F whack on the head F

cocada *f L.Am.* coconut cookie

cocaína *f* cocaine; **cocainómano** *m*, **~a** *f* cocaine addict

cocción *f* cooking; *en agua* boiling; *al horno* baking; **cocer** <2b & 2h> **1** *v/t* cook; *en agua* boil; *al horno* bake **2** *v/r* **~se** cook; *en agua* boil; *al horno* bake; *fig* F *de persona* roasting F

cochambroso *adj* F filthy

coche *m* car; *Méx* (*taxi*) cab, taxi; **~ de caballos** horse-drawn carriage; **~ cama** sleeping car; **~ comedor** *L.Am.* dining car; **~ de línea** (long-distance) bus; **cochecito** *m*: **~ de niño** stroller, *Br* pushchair; **cochera** *f* garage; *de trenes* locomotive shed

cochina *f* sow; F *persona* pig F; **cochino 1** *adj fig* filthy, dirty; (*asqueroso*) disgusting **2** *m* hog, *Br* pig; F *persona* pig F

cocido 1 *adj* boiled **2** *m* stew

cociente *m* quotient

cocina *f habitación* kitchen; *aparato* cooker, stove; *actividad* cooking; **~ de gas** gas cooker *o* stove; **cocinar** <1a> **1** *v/t* cook; *fig* F plot **2** *v/i* cook; **cocinero** *m*, **~a** *f* cook

coco *m* BOT coconut; *monstruo* bogeyman F; **comer el ~ a alguien** F softsoap s.o.; **más fuerte** brainwash s.o.

cocodrilo *m* crocodile

cocoliche *m Arg* pidgin Spanish

cocotazo *m L.Am.* F whack on the head F

cocotero *m* coconut palm

cóctel *m* cocktail; **~ Molotov** Molotov cocktail

cód *abr* (= **código**) code

codazo *m*: **darle a alguien un ~** elbow s.o.

codearse <1a> *v/r*: **~ con alguien** rub shoulders with s.o.

codicia *f* greed; **codiciar** <1b> *v/t* covet; **codicioso** *adj* greedy

codificado *adj* TV encrypted; **código** *m* code; **~ de barras** COM barcode; **~ postal** zip code, *Br* postcode

codo *m* ANAT elbow; **~ con ~** *fig* F side by side; **hablar por los ~s** F talk nineteen to the dozen F

codorniz *f* ZO quail

coeficiente *m* coefficient

coetáneo *m*, **-a** *f* contemporary

coexistir <3a> *v/i* coexist (**con** with)

cofradía *f* fraternity; (*gremio*) guild

cofre *m de tesoro* chest; *para alhajas* jewel(le)ry box

coger <2c> **1** *v/t* (*asir*) take (hold of); *del suelo* pick up; *ladrón, enfermedad* catch; TRANSP catch, take; (*entender*) get; *L.Am.* V screw V **2** *v/i en un espacio* fit; *L.Am.* V screw V; **~ por la primera a la derecha** take the first right **3** *v/r* **~se** hold on (tight); **~se de algo** hold on to sth

cogorza *f*: **agarrar una ~** F get plastered F

cogote *m* F nape of the neck

cohabitar <1a> *v/i* live together, cohabit

cohecho *m* JUR bribery

coherencia *f* coherence; **coherente** *adj* coherent; **ser ~ con** be consistent with; **cohesión** *f* cohesion

cohete *m* rocket

cohibir <3a> *v/t* inhibit

COI *abr* (= **Comité Olímpico Internacional**) IOC (= International Olympic Committee)

coima *f L.Am.* bribe

coincidencia *f* coincidence; **coincidir** <3a> *v/i* coincide

coito *m* intercourse

cojear <1a> *v/i de persona* limp, hobble; *de mesa, silla* wobble; **cojera** *f* limp

cojín *m* cushion

cojo *adj persona* lame; *mesa, silla* wobbly

cojón *m* V ball V

cojonudo *adj* P awesome F, brilliant

col. *abr* (= **columna**) col. (= column)

col *f* cabbage; **~ de Bruselas** Brussels sprout

cola¹ *f* (*pegamento*) glue

cola² *f* (*de animal*) tail; *de gente* line, *Br* queue; *L.Am. F de persona* butt F, *Br* bum F; **hacer ~** stand in line, *Br* queue; **estar a la ~** be in last place

colaboración *f* collaboration; **colaborador** *m*, **~a** *f* collaborator; *en periódico* contributor; **colaborar** <1a> *v/i* collaborate

colación *f*: **traer** *o* **sacar a ~** bring up

colada *f*: **hacer la ~** do the laundry *o* washing; **colado** *adj*: **estar ~ por alguien** F be nuts about s.o. F; **colador** *m* colander; *para té etc* strainer

colapsar <1a> **1** *v/t* paralyze; **~ el tráfico** bring traffic to a standstill **2** *v/r* **~se** grind to a halt; **colapso** *m* collapse; **provocar un ~ en la ciudad** bring the city to a standstill

colar <1m> **1** *v/t líquido* strain; *billete falso* pass; **~ algo por la aduana** F smuggle sth through customs **2** *v/i fig*: **no cuela** I'm not buying it F **3** *v/r* **~se** F *en un lugar* get in; *en una fiesta* gatecrash; *en una cola* cut in line, *Br* push in

colcha *f L.Am.* bedspread; **colchón** *m* mattress; *fig* buffer; **colchoneta** *f* DEP mat; *hinchable* air bed

cole *m* F school

colección *f* collection; **coleccionar** <1a> *v/t* collect; **coleccionista** *m/f* collector; **colecta** *f* collection; **colectivero** *m*, **-a** *f Arg* bus driver; **colectivo 1** *adj* collective **2** *m L.Am.* bus; *Méx, C.Am.* taxi

colega *m/f* colleague; F pal

colegiado *m*, **-a** *f* DEP referee

colegial *m* student, schoolboy; **colegiala** *f* student, schoolgirl; **colegio** *m* school; **~ electoral** electoral college; **~ profesional** professional institute

cólera 1 *f* anger; **montar en ~** get in a rage **2** *m* MED cholera

colesterol *m* cholesterol

coleta *f* ponytail; **~s de pelo** bunches

colgado *adj*: **dejar ~ a alguien** F let s.o. down; **colgador** *m L.Am.* hanger; **colgante 1** *adj* hanging **2** *m* pendant; **colgar** <1h & 1m> **1** *v/t* hang; TELEC put down **2** *v/i* hang (**de** from); TELEC hang up **3** *v/r* **~se** hang o.s.; INFOR F lock up; **~se de algo** hang from sth; **~se de alguien** hang onto s.o.

colibrí *m* ZO hummingbird

cólico *m* MED colic

coliflor *f* cauliflower

colilla *f* cigarette end

colina *f* hill

colindante *adj* adjoining

colirio *m* MED eye drops *pl*

colisión *f* collision; *fig* clash; **colisionar** <1a> *v/i* collide (**con** with)

colitis *f* MED colitis

collar *m* necklace; *para animal* collar

colleras *fpl Chi* cuff links

colmar <1a> *v/t deseos, ambición etc* fulfill; **~ un vaso** fill a glass to the brim; **~ a alguien de elogios** heap praise on s.o.

colmena *f* beehive

colmillo *m* ANAT eye tooth; *de perro* fang; *de elefante, rinoceronte* tusk

colmo *m*: **¡es el ~!** this is the last straw!; **para ~** to cap it all

colocación *f* positioning, placing; (*trabajo*) position; **colocar** <1g> **1** *v/t* put, place; **~ a alguien en un trabajo** get s.o. a job **2** *v/r* **~se de**

persona position o.s.; **se colocó a mi lado** he stood next to me; **se colocaron en primer lugar** they moved into first place
colofón *m fig* culmination
Colombia Colombia; **colombiano 1** *adj* Colombian **2** *m*, **-a** *f* Colombian
Colón Columbus
colonia *f* colony; *de viviendas* subdivision, *Br* estate; *perfume* cologne; ~ **de verano** summer camp; **colonial** *adj* colonial; **colonización** *f* colonization; **colonizar** <1f> *v/t* colonize
coloquial *adj* colloquial; **coloquio** *m* talk
color *m* colo(u)r; ~ **café** coffee-colo(u)red; *L.Am.* brown; **colorado** *adj* red; **colorante** *m* colo(u)ring; **colorear** <1a> *v/t* colo(u)r; **colorete** *m* blusher; **colorido** *m* colo(u)rs *pl*
colosal *adj* colossal
columna *f* column; ~ **vertebral** ANAT spinal column; **columnista** *m/f* columnist
columpiar <1b> **1** *v/t* swing **2** *v/r* ~**se** swing; **columpio** *m* swing
colza *f* BOT rape
coma **1** *f* GRAM comma **2** *m* MED coma
comadre *f* *L.Am.* godmother
comadrear <1a> *v/i* F gossip
comadrona *f* midwife
comandante *m* MIL commander; *rango* major; AVIA captain
comarca *f* area
comba *f* jump rope, *Br* skipping rope; *jugar or* **saltar a la** ~ jump rope, *Br* skip
combate *m* *acción* combat; MIL engagement; DEP fight; *fuera de* ~ out of action; **combatir** <3a> *v/t* & *v/i* fight
combi *m* *Méx* minibus
combinación *f* combination; *prenda* slip; *hacer* ~ TRANSP change; **combinar** <1a> *v/t* combine
combustible *m* fuel; **combustión** *f* combustion
comedia *f* comedy; **comedianta** *f*

actress; **comediante** *m* actor
comedido *adj* moderate
comedor *m* dining room
comején *m* termite
comensal *m/f* diner
comentar <1a> *v/t* comment on; **comentario** *m* comment; ~ **de texto** textual analysis; ~**s** *pl* gossip *sg*; **comentarista** *m/f* commentator
comenzar <1f & 1k> *v/t* begin
comer <2a> **1** *v/t* eat; *a mediodía* have for lunch **2** *v/i* eat; *a mediodía* have lunch **3** *v/r* ~**se** *tb fig* eat up; *se comió una palabra* she missed out a word; *está para comértela* F she's really tasty F
comercial **1** *adj* commercial; *de negocios* business *atr*; *el déficit* ~ the trade deficit **2** *m/f* representative; **comercializar** <1f> *v/t* market, sell; *desp* commercialize; **comerciante** *m/f* trader; ~ **al por menor** retailer; **comercio** *m* *actividad* trade; *local* store, shop; ~ **exterior** foreign trade
comestible **1** *adj* eatable, edible **2** *m* foodstuff; ~**s** *pl* food *sg*
cometa **1** *m* comet **2** *f* kite
cometer <2a> *v/t* commit; *error* make; **cometido** *m* task
comezón *f* itch
cómic *m* comic
comicios *mpl* elections *pl*
cómico **1** *adj* comical **2** *m*, **-a** *f* comedian
comida *f* (*comestibles*) food; *ocasión* meal
comienzo *m* beginning
comillas *fpl* quotation marks, inverted commas
comino *m* BOT cumin; *me importa un* ~ F I don't give a damn F
comisaría *f* precinct, *Br* police station; **comisario** *m* commissioner; *de policía* captain, *Br* superintendent; **comisión** *f* committee; *de gobierno* commission; (*recompensa*) commission
comité *m* committee
comitiva *f* retinue

como 1 *adv* as; **así ~** as well as; **había ~ cincuenta** there were about fifty **2** *conj* if; **~ si** as if; **~ no bebas vas a enfermar** if you don't drink you'll get sick; **~ no llegó, me fui solo** as *o* since she didn't arrive, I went by myself

cómo *adv* how; **¿~ estás?** how are you?; **¡~ me gusta!** I really like it; **me gusta ~ habla** I like the way he talks; **¿~ dice?** what did you say?; **¡~ no!** *Méx* of course!

cómoda *f* chest of drawers

comodidad *f* comfort

comodín *m en naipes* joker

cómodo *adj* comfortable

comp. *abr* (= **compárese**) cf (= confer)

compacto *adj* compact

compadecer <2d> **1** *v/t* feel sorry for **2** *v/r* **-se** feel sorry (**de** for)

compadre *m L.Am.* F buddy F; **compadrear** <1a> *v/i Arg* F brag; **compadrito** *m Arg* F show-off

compaginar <1a> *v/t fig* combine

compañero *m*, **-a** *f* companion; *en una relación, un juego* partner; **~ de trabajo** coworker, colleague; **~ de clase** classmate; **compañía** *f* company; **hacer ~ a alguien** keep s.o. company

comparación *f* comparison; **en ~ con** in comparison with; **comparado** *adj*: **~ con** compared with; **comparar** <1a> *v/t* compare

comparecencia *f* JUR appearance; **comparecer** <2d> *v/i* appear

compartir <3a> *v/t* share (**con** with)

compás *m* MAT compass; MÚS rhythm; **al ~** to the beat

compasión *f* compassion

compatibilidad *f* compatibility; **compatible** *adj* INFOR compatible

compatriota *m/f* compatriot

compendio *m* summary

compenetrado *adj*: **están muy ~s** they are very much in tune with each other; **compenetrarse** <1a> *v/r*: **~ con alguien** reach a good understanding with s.o.

compensación *f* compensation;

compensar <1a> **1** *v/t* compensate (**por** for) **2** *v/i fig* be worthwhile

competencia *f* (**habilidad**) competence; *entre rivales* competition; (*incumbencia*) area of responsibility, competency; **~ desleal** unfair competition; **competente** *adj* competent

competición *f* DEP competition; **competir** <3l> *v/i* compete (**con** with); **competitivo** *adj* competitive

compilar <1a> *v/t* compile

compinche *m/f* F buddy F; *desp* crony F

complacencia *f* (*placer*) pleasure; (*tolerancia*) indulgence; **complacer** <2x> *v/t* please; **complaciente** *adj* obliging, helpful

complejidad *f* complexity

complejo 1 *adj* complex **2** *m* PSI complex; **~ de inferioridad** inferiority complex

complementar <1a> *v/t* complement; **complemento** *m* complement; GRAM complement, object; **~s de moda** fashion accessories

completar <1a> *v/t* complete; **completo** *adj* complete; *autobús, teatro* full; **por ~** completely

complicación *f* complication; **complicado** *adj* complicated; **complicar** <1g> **1** *v/t* complicate **2** *v/r* **~se** get complicated; **~se la vida** make things difficult for o.s.

cómplice *m/f* accomplice

complot *m* plot

componente *m* component; **componer** <2r; *part* **compuesto**> **1** *v/t* make up, comprise; *sinfonía, poema etc* compose; *algo roto* fix, mend **2** *v/r* **~se** be made up (**de** of); *L.Am.* MED get better

comportamiento *m* behavio(u)r; **comportarse** <1a> *v/r* behave

composición *f* composition; **compositor** *m*, **~a** *f* composer

compostura *f fig* composure

compota *f* compote

compra *f acción* purchase; (*cosa comprada*) purchase, buy; **ir de ~s** go shopping; **comprar** <1a> *v/t* buy, purchase; **compraventa** f buying and selling

comprender <2a> v/t understand; (abarcar) include; **comprensión** f understanding; de texto, auditiva comprehension; **comprensivo** adj understanding

compresa f sanitary napkin, Br sanitary towel; **compresión** f tb INFOR compression; **comprimido** m MED pill; **comprimir** <3a> v/t compress

comprobación f check; **comprobar** <1m> v/t check; (darse cuenta de) realize

comprometer <2a> **1** v/t compromise; (obligar) commit **2** v/r ~**se** promise (a to); a una causa commit o.s.; de novios get engaged; **comprometido** adj committed; **estar ~ en algo** be implicated in sth; **estar ~ de novios** be engaged; **compromiso** m commitment; (obligación) obligation; (acuerdo) agreement; (apuro) awkward situation; **sin ~** COM without commitment; **soltero y sin ~** F footloose and fancy-free

compuesto 1 part → **componer 2** adj composed; **estar ~ de** be composed of

compulsar <1a> v/t certify; **compulsivo** adj PSI compulsive

computación f L.Am. computer science

computadora f L.Am. computer; ~ **de escritorio** desktop (computer); ~ **personal** personal computer; ~ **portátil** laptop; **computarizar** <1f> v/t computerize

comulgar <1h> v/i take communion; ~ **con alguien (en algo)** fig F think the same way as s.o. (on sth)

común adj common; **por lo ~** generally; **comuna** f commune; L.Am. (población) town

comunicación f communication; TRANSP link; **comunicado 1** adj connected; **el lugar está bien ~** the place has good transport links **2** m POL press release, communiqué;

comunicar <1g> **1** v/t TRANSP connect, link; ~ **algo a alguien** inform s.o. of sth **2** v/i communicate; TELEC be busy, Br tb be engaged **3** v/r ~**se** communicate

comunidad f community; ~ **autónoma** autonomous region

comunión f REL communion

comunismo m Communism; **comunista** m/f & adj Communist

comunitario adj POL EU atr, Community atr

con prp with; **voy ~ ellos** I'm going with them; **pan ~ mantequilla** bread and butter; ~ **todo eso** in spite of all that; ~ **tal de que** provided that, as long as; ~ **hacer eso** by doing that

conato m: ~ **de violencia** minor outbreak of violence; ~ **de incendio** small fire

cóncavo adj concave

concebir <3l> v/t conceive

conceder <2a> v/t concede; entrevista, permiso give; premio award

concejal m, ~**a** f council(l)or

concentración f concentration; de personas gathering; **concentrar** <1a> **1** v/t concentrate **2** v/r ~**se** concentrate (en on); de gente gather

concepto m concept; **en ~ de algo** COM (in payment) for sth; **bajo ningún ~** on no account

concernir <3i> v/i concern; **en lo que concierne a X** as far as X is concerned

concertar <1k> v/t cita arrange; precio agree; esfuerzos coordinate

concesión f concession; COM dealership; **hacer concesiones** make concessions; **concesionario** m dealer

concha f ZO shell

conchabar <1a> **1** v/t L.Am. trabajador hire **2** v/r ~**se** F plot

conciencia f conscience; **a ~** conscientiously; **con plena ~ de** fully conscious of; **concienciar** <1b> **1** v/t: ~ **a alguien de algo** make s.o. aware of sth **2** v/r ~**se** realize (de sth); **concienzudo** adj conscientious

concierto *m* MÚS concert; *fig* agreement

conciliador *adj* conciliatory; **conciliar** <1b> *v/t* reconcile; **~ el sueño** get to sleep

conciso *adj* concise

concluir <3g> *v/t & v/i* conclude; **conclusión** *f* conclusion; **en ~** in short

concretar <1a> **1** *v/t* specify; (*hacer concreto*) realize **2** *v/r* **~se** materialize; *de esperanzas* be fulfilled; **concreto 1** *adj* specific; (*no abstracto*) concrete; **en ~** specifically **2** *m* L.Am. concrete

concurrencia *f* audience; *de circunstancias* combination; **concurrido** *adj* crowded; **concursante** *m/f* competitor; **concursar** <1a> *v/i* compete; **concurso** *m* competition; COM tender

conde *m* count

condecoración *f* decoration; **condecorar** <1a> decorate

condena *f* JUR sentence; (*desaprobación*) condemnation; **condenar** <1a> *v/t* JUR sentence (*a* to); (*desaprobar*) condemn

condensación *f* condensation; **condensado** *adj* condensed; **condensar** <1a> **1** *v/t* condense; *libro* abridge **2** *v/r* **~se** condense

condesa *f* countess

condescendiente *adj* *actitud* accommodating; *desp* condescending

condición *f* condition; **a ~ de que** on condition that; **estar en condiciones de** be in a position to

condimentar <1a> flavo(u)r; **condimento** *m* seasoning

condón *m* condom

cóndor *m* ZO condor

conducir <3o> **1** *v/t vehículo* drive; (*dirigir*) lead (*a* to); EL, TÉC conduct **2** *v/i* drive; *de camino* lead (*a* to); **conducta** *f* conduct, behavio(u)r; **conducto** *m* pipe; *fig* channel; **por ~ de** through; **conductor** *m*, **~a** *f* driver; **~ de orquesta** L.Am. conductor

condujo *vb* → **conducir**

conectar <1a> *v/t* connect, link; EL connect

conejillo *m*: **~ de Indias** *tb fig* guinea pig; **conejo** *m* rabbit

conexión *f tb* EL connection

confabularse <1a> *v/r* plot

confección *f* making; *de vestidos* dressmaking; *de trajes* tailoring; **confeccionar** <1a> *v/t* make

confederación *f* confederation

conferencia *f* lecture; (*reunión*) conference; TELEC long-distance call; **conferenciante** *m/f* lecturer; **conferencista** *m/f* L.Am. lecturer; **conferir** <3i> *v/t* award

confesar <1k> **1** *v/t* REL confess; *delito* confess to, admit **2** *v/i* JUR confess **3** *v/r* **~se** confess; (*declararse*) admit to being; **confesión** *f* confession

confeti *m* confetti

confiado *adj* trusting; **confianza** *f* confidence; **~ en sí mismo** self-confidence; **de ~** *persona* trustworthy; **amigo de ~** good friend; **confiar** <1c> **1** *v/t secreto* confide (*a* to); **~ algo a alguien** entrust s.o. with sth, entrust sth to s.o. **2** *v/i* trust (*en* in); (*estar seguro*) be confident (*en* of); **confidencia** *f* confidence; **confidencial** *adj* confidential

configuración *f* configuration; INFOR set-up, configuration; **configurar** <1a> *v/t* shape; INFOR set up, configure

confinar <1a> *v/t* confine

confirmación *f* confirmation; **confirmar** <1a> *v/t* confirm

confiscar <1g> *v/t* confiscate

confitería *f* confectioner's

confitura *f* preserve

conflagración *f* conflagration; (*guerra*) war

conflicto *m* conflict

conformarse <1a> *v/r* make do (*con* with); **conforme 1** *adj* satisfied (*con* with) **2** *prp*: **~ a** in accordance with

confortable *adj* comfortable

confrontación *f* confrontation

confundir <3a> **1** v/t confuse; (*equivocar*) mistake (**con** for) **2** v/r **~se** make a mistake; **~se de calle** get the wrong street; **confusión** f confusion; **confuso** adj confused

congelación f freezing; **~ de precios / de salarios** price / wage freeze; **congelado** adj frozen; **congelador** m freezer; **congelar** <1a> **1** v/t freeze **2** v/r **~se** freeze

congeniar <1b> v/i get on well (**con** with)

congénito adj congenital

congestión f MED congestion; **~ del tráfico** traffic congestion; **congestionar** <1a> v/t congest

congoja f anguish

congregar <1h> v/t bring together; **congresal** m/f L.Am., **congresista** m/f conference o convention delegate, conventioneer; **congreso** m conference, convention; **Congreso en EE.UU** Congress; **~ de los diputados** lower house of Spanish parliament

congrio m ZO conger eel

conjetura f conjecture

conjugar <1h> v/t GRAM conjugate; *fig* combine

conjunción f GRAM conjunction; **conjuntivitis** f MED conjunctivitis; **conjunto 1** adj joint **2** m de personas, objetos collection; de prendas outfit; MAT set; **en ~** as a whole

conllevar <1a> v/t entail

conmemorar <1a> v/t commemorate

conmigo pron with me

conmoción f shock; (*agitación*) upheaval; **conmocionar** <1a> v/t shock; **conmovedor** adj moving; **conmover** <2h> **1** v/t move **2** v/r **~se** be moved

conmutador m EL switch; L.Am. TELEC switchboard

connotación f connotation

cono m cone

conocer <2d> **1** v/t know; por primera vez meet; tristeza, amor etc experience, know; (*reconocer*) recognize; **dar a ~** make known **2** v/r **~se** know one another; por primera vez meet one another; a sí mismo know o.s.; **se conoce que** it seems that; **conocido 1** adj well-known **2** m, **-a** f acquaintance; **conocimiento** m knowledge; MED consciousness; **perder el ~** lose consciousness

conquista f conquest; **conquistar** <1a> v/t conquer; persona win over

consabido adj usual

consagrar <1a> **1** v/t REL consecrate; (*hacer famoso*) make famous; vida devote **2** v/r **~se** devote o.s. (**a** to)

consciente adj MED conscious; **~ de** aware of, conscious of

consecuencia f consequence; **a ~ de** as a result of; **en ~** consequently; **consecuente** adj consistent; **consecutivo** adj consecutive; **tres años ~s** three years in a row; **conseguir** <3l & 3d> v/t get; objetivo achieve

consejero m, **-a** f adviser; COM director; **consejo** m piece of advice; **~ de administración** board of directors; **~ de ministros** grupo cabinet; reunión cabinet meeting

consenso m consensus; **consentido** adj spoilt; **consentimiento** m consent; **consentir** <3i> **1** v/t allow; a niño indulge **2** v/i: **~ en algo** agree to sth

conserje m/f superintendent, Br caretaker

conserva f: **en ~** canned, Br tinned; **~s** pl canned (Br tinned) food sg; **conservación** f de alimentos preservation; de edificios, especies conservation; **conservador** adj conservative; **conservante** m preservative; **conservar** <1a> **1** v/t conserve; alimento preserve **2** v/r **~se** survive; **conservatorio** m conservatory

considerable adj considerable; **consideración** f consideration; **considerar** <1a> v/t consider

consigna f order; de equipaje baggage room, Br left-luggage

consigo *pron* with him / her; (*con usted, con ustedes*) with you; (*con uno*) with you, with one *fml*

consiguiente *adj* consequent; *por ~ and so*, therefore

consistencia *f* consistency; **consistente** *adj* consistent; (*sólido*) solid; **consistir** <3a> *v/i* consist (*en* of)

consola *f* INFOR console

consolar <1m> *v/t* console

consolidar <1a> **1** *v/t* consolidate **2** *v/r ~se* strengthen

consomé *m* GASTR consommé

consonancia *f*: *en ~ con* in keeping with; **consonante** *f* consonant

consorte *m/f* spouse

conspiración *f* conspiracy; **conspirar** <1a> *v/i* conspire

constancia *f* constancy; *dejar ~ de* leave a record of; **constante** *adj* constant; **constar** <1a> *v/i* be recorded; *~ de* consist of

constatación *f* verification; **constatar** <1a> *v/t* verify

constelación *f* AST constellation

consternar <1a> *v/t* dismay

constipado 1 *adj*: *estar ~* have a cold **2** *m* cold; **constiparse** <1a> *v/r* get a cold

constitución *f* constitution; **constituir** <3g> *v/t* constitute, make up; *empresa, organismo* set up

construcción *f* construction; (*edificio*) building; **construir** <3g> *v/t* build, construct

consuelo *m* consolation

cónsul *m/f* consul; **consulado** *m* consulate

consulta *f* consultation; MED *local office*, *Br* surgery; **consultar** <1a> *v/t* consult; **consultor** *m*, *~a f* consultant; **consultoría** *f* consultancy; **consultorio** *m* MED office, *Br* surgery

consumidor *m*, *~a f* COM consumer; **consumir** <3a> **1** *v/t* consume **2** *v/i ~se* waste away; **consumo** *m* consumption; *de bajo ~* economical

contabilidad *f* accountancy; *llevar la ~* do the accounts; **contable** *m/f* accountant

contactar <1a> *v/i*: *~ con alguien* contact s.o.; **contacto** *m* contact; AUTO ignition; *ponerse en ~* get in touch (*con* with)

contado *adj*: *al ~* in cash; **contador 1** *m* meter **2** *m*, *~a f L.Am.* accountant

contagiar <1b> **1** *v/t*: *~ la gripe a alguien* give s.o. the flu; *nos contagió su entusiasmo* he infected us with his enthusiasm **2** *v/r ~se* become infected; **contagioso** *adj* contagious

contaminación *f de agua etc* contamination; *de río, medio ambiente* pollution; **contaminar** <1a> *v/t* contaminate; *río, medio ambiente* pollute

contar <1m> **1** *v/t* count; (*narrar*) tell **2** *v/i* count; *~ con* count on

contemplación *f*: *sin contemplaciones* without ceremony; **contemplar** <1a> *v/t* (*mirar*) look at, contemplate; *posibilidad* consider

contemporáneo 1 *adj* contemporary **2** *m*, *~a f* contemporary

contenedor *m* TRANSP container; *~ de basura* dumpster, *Br* skip; *~ de vidrio* bottle bank; **contener** <2l> **1** *v/t* contain; *respiración* hold; *muchedumbre* hold back **2** *v/r ~se* control o.s.; **contenido** *m* content

contentarse <1a> *v/r* be satisfied (*con* with); **contento** *adj* (*satisfecho*) pleased; (*feliz*) happy

contestación *f* answer; **contestador** *m*: *~ automático* TELEC answer machine; **contestar** <1a> **1** *v/t* answer, reply to **2** *v/i* reply (*a* to), answer (*a* sth); *de forma insolente* answer back

contexto *m* context

contigo *pron* with you

contiguo *adj* adjoining, adjacent

continental *adj* continental; **continente** *m* continent

continuación *f* continuation; *a ~* (*ahora*) now; (*después*) then; **continuar** <1e> **1** *v/t* continue **2** *v/i* continue; *~ haciendo algo* continue *o* carry on doing sth; **continuidad** *f* continuity; **continuo** *adj* (*sin parar*) continuous; (*frecuente*) continual

contorno *m* outline

contra *prp* against; **en ~ de** against

contraataque *m* counterattack

contrabajo *m* double bass

contrabandista *m/f* smuggler; **contrabando** *m* contraband, smuggled goods *pl*; **acción** smuggling; **hacer ~** smuggle; **pasar algo de ~** smuggle sth in

contracción *f* contraction

contraceptivo *m/adj* contraceptive

contradecir <3p> *v/t* contradict; **contradicción** *f* contradiction; **contradictorio** *adj* contradictory

contraer <2p> *part* **contraído** 1 *v/t* contract; *músculo* tighten; **~ matrimonio** marry 2 *v/r* **~se** contract

contraindicación *f* MED contraindication

contraluz *f*: **a ~** against the light

contrapartida *f* COM balancing entry; **como ~** *fig* in contrast

contrapeso *m* counterweight

contraposición *f*: **en ~ a** in comparison to

contraproducente *adj* counterproductive

contrariedad *f* setback; (*disgusto*) annoyance

contrario 1 *adj* contrary; *sentido* opposite; *equipo* opposing; **al ~**, **por el ~** on the contrary; **de lo ~** otherwise; **ser ~ a algo** be opposed to sth; **llevar la ~a a alguien** contradict s.o. 2 *m*, **-a** *f* adversary, opponent

contrarreloj *f* DEP time trial

contrarrestar <1a> *v/t* counteract

contraseña *f* password

contrastar <1a> *v/t & v/i* contrast (*con* with); **contraste** *m* contrast

contratar <1a> *v/t* contract; *trabajadores* hire

contratiempo *m* setback

contrato *m* contract

contravenir <3s> *v/i* contravene

contribución *f* contribution; (*impuesto*) tax; **contribuir** <3g> *v/t*

contribute (*a* to); **contribuyente** *m/f* taxpayer

contrincante *m/f* opponent

control *m* control; (*inspección*) check; **~ remoto** remote control; **controlador** *m*, **~a** *f*: **~ aéreo** air traffic controller; **controlar** <1a> 1 *v/t* control; (*vigilar*) check 2 *v/r* **~se** control o.s.

controversia *f* controversy

contundente *adj arma* blunt; *fig: derrota* overwhelming; **contusión** *f* MED bruise

convalecencia *f* convalescence; **convaleciente** *m/f* convalescent

convalidar <1a> *v/t* recognize

convencer <2b> *v/t* convince

convención *f* convention; **convencional** *adj* conventional

conveniencia *f* de hacer algo advisability; **hacer algo por ~** do sth in one's own interest; **conveniente** *adj* convenient; (*útil*) useful; (*aconsejable*) advisable; **convenio** *m* agreement; **convenir** <3s> 1 *v/t* agree 2 *v/i* be advisable; **no te conviene** it's not in your interest; **~ a alguien hacer algo** be in s.o.'s interests to do sth

conventillo *m* CSur tenement

convento *m* de monjes monastery; *de monjas* convent

converger <2c> *v/i* converge

conversación *f* conversation; **conversar** <1a> *v/i* make conversation

conversión *f* conversion; **convertible** 1 *adj* COM convertible 2 *m* L.Am. convertible; **convertir** <3i> 1 *v/t* convert 2 *v/r* **~se**: **~se en algo** turn into sth

convexo *adj* convex

convicción *f* conviction

convidar <1a> *v/t* invite (*a* to)

convincente *adj* convincing

convivencia *f* living together; **convivir** <3a> *v/i* live together

convocar <1g> *v/t* summon; *huelga* call; *oposiciones* organize; **convocatoria** *f* announcement; *de huelga* call

convoy *m* convoy

convulsión f convulsion; *fig* upheaval

conyugal *adj* conjugal; **cónyuge** *m/f* spouse

coña f: **decir algo de ~** F say sth as a joke; **darle la ~ a alguien** F bug s.o. F; **¡ni de ~!** F no way! F

coñac m (pl ~s) brandy, cognac

coño m V cunt V

cooperación f cooperation; **cooperar** <1a> v/i cooperate; **cooperativa** f cooperative

coordinación f coordination; **coordinar** <1a> v/t coordinate

copa f de vino etc glass; DEP cup; **tomar una ~** have a drink; **~s** pl (en naipes) suit in Spanish deck of cards

copia f copy; **~ pirata** pirate copy; **copiar** <1b> v/t copy

copiloto m/f copilot

copioso adj copious

copla f verse; (canción) popular song

copo m flake; **~ de nieve** snowflake; **~s de maíz** cornflakes

copropietario m, **-a** f co-owner, joint owner

coquetear <1a> v/i flirt; **coquetería** f flirtatiousness; **coqueto** adj flirtatious; lugar pretty

coraje m courage; **me da ~** fig F it makes me mad F; **corajudo** adj L.Am. brave

coral[1] m ZO coral

coral[2] f MÚS choir

Corán m Koran

coraza f cuirasse; ZO shell; fig shield

corazón m heart; de fruta core; **corazonada** f hunch

corbata f tie

corcho m cork

cordel m string

cordero m lamb

cordial adj cordial

cordillera f mountain range

cordón m cord; de zapato shoelace; **~ umbilical** ANAT umbilical cord

cordura f sanity; (prudencia) good sense

Corea Korea; **coreano 1** adj Korean **2** m, **-a** f Korean

coreografía f choreography

cormorán m ZO cormorant

cornada f TAUR goring

corneja f ZO crow

córner m en fútbol corner (kick)

corneta f MIL bugle

cornisa f ARQUI cornice

cornudo 1 adj horned **2** m cuckold

coro m MÚS choir; de espectáculo, pieza musical chorus; **a ~** together, in chorus

corona f crown; **~ de flores** garland; **coronar** <1a> v/t crown; **coronario** adj MED coronary

coronel m MIL colonel

coronilla f ANAT crown; **estoy hasta la ~** F I've had it up to here F

corotos mpl L.Am. F bits and pieces

corporación f corporation; **corporal** adj placer, estética physical; fluido body atr; **corpulento** adj solidly built

corral m farmyard

correa f lead; de reloj strap

corrección f correction; en el trato correctness; **correcto** adj correct; (educado) polite

corredizo adj sliding; **corredor 1** m, **-a** f DEP runner; COM agent; **~ de bolsa** stockbroker **2** m ARQUI corridor

corregir <3c & 3l> v/t correct

correlación f correlation

correligionario m, **-a** f: **sus ~s republicanos** his fellow republicans

correntada f L.Am. current; **correntoso** adj L.Am. fast-flowing

correo m mail, Br tb post; **~s** pl post office sg; **~ aéreo** airmail; **~ electrónico** e-mail; **por ~** by mail; **echar al ~** mail, Br tb post

correr <2a> **1** v/i run; (apresurarse) rush; de tiempo pass; de agua run, flow; **~ con los gastos** pay the expenses; **a todo ~** at top speed **2** v/t run; cortinas draw; mueble slide, move; **~ la misma suerte** suffer the same fate **3** v/r **~se** move; de tinta run

correspondencia *f* correspondence; FERR connection (*con* with); **corresponder** <2a> *v/i:* ~ *a alguien* de bienes be for s.o., be due to s.o.; *de responsabilidad* be up to s.o.; *de asunto* concern s.o.; *a un favor* repay s.o. (*con* with); *actuar como corresponde* do the right thing; **correspondiente** *adj* corresponding; **corresponsal** *m/f* correspondent

corretear <1a> *v/i* run around

corrida *f:* ~ *de toros* bullfight; **corrido** *adj: decir algo de* ~ *fig* say sth parrot-fashion

corriente 1 *adj* (*actual*) current; (*común*) ordinary; ~ *y moliente* run-of-the-mill; *estar al* ~ be up to date **2** *f* EL, *de agua* current; ~ *de aire* draft, *Br* draught

corro *m* ring

corroborar <1a> *v/t* corroborate

corroer <2za> *v/t* corrode; *fig* eat up

corromper <2a> **1** *v/t* corrupt **2** *v/r* ~*se* become corrupted

corrosión *f* corrosion; **corrosivo** *adj* corrosive; *fig* caustic

corrupción *f* decay; *fig* corruption; ~ *de menores* corruption of minors; **corrupto** *adj* corrupt

corsetería *f* lingerie store

cortacésped *m* lawnmower

cortacircuitos *m inv* circuit breaker

cortada *f L.Am.* cut; **cortado 1** *adj* cut; *calle* closed; *leche* curdled; *persona* shy; *quedarse* ~ be embarrassed **2** *m* coffee with a dash of milk; **cortar** <1a> **1** *v/t* cut; *electricidad* cut off; *calle* close **2** *v/i* cut **3** *v/r* ~*se* cut o.s.; *fig* F get embarrassed; ~*se el pelo* have one's hair cut; **cortaúñas** *m inv* nail clippers *pl*

corte[1] *m* cut; ~ *de luz* power outage; ~ *de pelo* haircut; ~ *de tráfico* F road closure; *me da* ~ F I'm embarrassed

corte[2] *f* court; *L.Am.* JUR (law) court; *las Cortes* Spanish parliament

cortejar <1a> *v/t* court

cortés *adj* courteous; **cortesía** *f* courtesy

corteza *f de árbol* bark; *de pan* crust; *de queso* rind

cortina *f* curtain

corto *adj* short; ~ *de vista* near-sighted; *ni* ~ *ni perezoso* as bold as brass; *quedarse* ~ fall short; **cortocircuito** *m* EL short circuit

corzo *m* ZO roe deer

cosa *f* thing; *como si tal* ~ as if nothing had happened; *decir a alguien cuatro* ~*s* give s.o. a piece of one's mind; *eso es otra* ~ that's another matter; *¿qué pasa? – poca* ~ what's new? – nothing much

coscorrón *m* bump on the head

cosecha *f* harvest; **cosechar** <1a> *v/t* harvest; *fig* gain, win

coser <2a> *v/t* sew; *ser* ~ *y cantar* F be dead easy F

cosmético *m/adj* cosmetic

cósmico *adj* cosmic; **cosmonauta** *m/f* cosmonaut; **cosmopolita** *adj* cosmopolitan; **cosmos** *m* cosmos; **cosmovisión** *f L.Am.* world view

cosquillas *fpl: hacer* ~ *a alguien* tickle s.o.; *tener* ~ be ticklish; **cosquilleo** *m* tickle

costa[1] *f:* *a* ~ *de* at the expense of; *a toda* ~ at all costs

costa[2] *f* GEOG coast

costado *m* side; *por los cuatro* ~*s fig* throughout, through and through

costar <1m> **1** *v/t en dinero* cost; *trabajo, esfuerzo etc* take; *¿cuánto cuesta?* how much does it cost? **2** *v/i en dinero* cost; *me costó* it was hard work; *cueste lo que cueste* at all costs; ~ *caro* fig cost dear

Costa Rica Costa Rica; **costarricense** *m/f & adj* Costa Rican

coste *m* → *costo*

costear <1a> *v/t* pay for

costero *adj* coastal

costilla *f* ANAT rib; GASTR sparerib

costo *m* cost; ~ *de la vida* cost of living; **costoso** *adj* costly

costra *f* MED scab

costumbre *f* custom; *de una persona* habit; *de* ~ usual

costura f sewing; **costurear** <1a> v/t L.Am. sew

cotarro m: **manejar el ~** F be the boss F

cotejar <1a> v/t compare

cotidiano adj daily

cotilla m/f F gossip; **cotillear** <1a> v/i F gossip

cotizado adj COM quoted; fig sought-after; **cotizar** <1f> v/i de trabajador pay social security, Br pay National Insurance; de acciones, bonos be listed (**a** at); **~ en bolsa** be listed on the stock exchange

coto[1] m: **~ de caza** hunting reserve; **poner ~ a algo** fig put a stop to sth

coto[2] m S.Am. MED goiter, Br goitre

cotorra f ZO parrot; F persona motormouth F

coyote m ZO coyote

coyuntura f situation; ANAT joint

C.P. abr (= **código postal**) zip code, Br post code

cráneo m ANAT skull, cranium

cráter m crater

creación f creation; **creador** m, ~a f creator; **crear** <1a> v/t create; empresa set up; **creativo** adj creative

crecer <2d> v/i grow; **creces** fpl: **con ~** superar by a comfortable margin; pagar by interest; **creciente** adj growing; luna waxing; **crecimiento** m growth

credencial f document

credibilidad f credibility; **crédito** m COM credit; **a ~** on credit; **no dar ~ a sus oídos / ojos** F not believe one's ears / eyes

credo m REL, fig creed; **crédulo** adj credulous; **creencia** f belief; **creer** <2e> 1 v/i believe (**en** in) 2 v/t think; (dar por cierto) believe; **no creo que esté aquí** I don't think he's here; **¡ya lo creo!** F you bet! F 3 v/r ~se: **~se que ...** believe that ...; **se cree muy lista** she thinks she's very clever

crema f GASTR cream

cremallera f zipper, Br zip; TÉC rack

crematorio m crematorium

cremoso adj creamy

crepe f GASTR crêpe, pancake

crepitar <1a> v/i crackle

crepúsculo m tb fig twilight

cresta f crest

cretino m, -a f F cretin F, moron F

creyente 1 adj: **ser ~** REL believe in God 2 m REL believer

creyó vb → **creer**

cría f acción breeding; de zorro, león cub; de perro puppy; de gato kitten; de oveja lamb; **sus ~s** her young; **criada** f maid; **criado** m servant; **criar** <1c> 1 v/t niños raise, bring up; animales breed 2 v/r ~se grow up; **criatura** f creature; F (niño) baby, child

crimen m crime; **criminal** m/f & adj criminal

crío m, -a f F kid F

criollo 1 adj Creole 2 m, -a f Creole

cripta f crypt

crisantemo m BOT chrysanthemum

crisis f inv crisis

crismas m inv Christmas card

crispar <1a> v/t irritate; **~le a alguien los nervios** get on s.o.'s nerves

cristal m crystal; (vidrio) glass; (lente) lens; de ventana pane; **~ líquido** liquid crystal; **cristalizar** <1f> v/i crystallize; de idea, proyecto jell

cristianismo m Christianity; **cristiano** 1 adj Christian 2 m, -a f Christian

Cristo Christ

criterio m criterion; (juicio) judg(e)-ment

crítica f criticism; **muchas ~s** a lot of criticism; **criticar** <1g> v/t criticize; **crítico** 1 adj critical 2 m, -a f critic

Croacia Croatia

crol m crawl

cromo m QUÍM chrome; (estampa) picture card, trading card

crónica f chronicle; en periódico report

crónico adj MED chronic

cronológico adj chronological

cronometrar <1a> v/t DEP time; **cronómetro** m stopwatch

croqueta f GASTR croquette

croquis m inv sketch

cross m DEP cross-country (running); con motocicletas motocross

cruce m cross; de carreteras crossroads sg; ~ en las líneas TELEC crossed line

crucero m cruise

crucial adj crucial

crucificar <1g> v/t crucify; **crucifijo** m crucifix; **crucigrama** m crossword

crudo 1 adj alimento raw; fig harsh **2** m crude (oil)

cruel adj cruel

cruento adj bloody

crujiente adj GASTR crunchy; **crujir** <3a> v/i creak; al arder crackle; de grava crunch

cruz f cross; **Cruz Roja** Red Cross; **cruzar** <1f> **1** v/t cross **2** v/r ~se pass one another; ~se de brazos cross one's arms; ~se con alguien pass s.o.

c.s.f. abr (= costo, seguro, flete) cif (= cost, insurance, freight)

cta, c.ta abr (= cuenta) A/C (= account)

cuaderno m notebook; EDU exercise book

cuadra f stable; L.Am. (manzana) block; **cuadrado 1** adj square **2** m square; al ~ squared

cuadrilla f squad, team

cuadro m painting; (grabado) picture; (tabla) table; DEP team; ~ de mandos or de instrumentos AUTO dashboard; de or a ~s checked; **cuádruple, cuadruplo** m cuadruple

cuajada f GASTR curd; **cuajar** <1a> v/i de nieve settle; fig: de idea, proyecto etc come together, jell F

cuajo m: de ~ by the roots

cual 1 pron rel: el ~, la ~ etc cosa which; persona who; por lo ~ (and) so **2** adv like

cuál interr which (one)

cualidad f quality

cualificar <1g> v/t qualify

cualquier adj any; ~ día any day; ~

cosa anything; **de ~ modo** or **forma** anyway; **cualquiera** pron persona anyone, anybody; cosa any (one); **un ~** a nobody; **¡~ lo comprende!** nobody can understand it!

cuando 1 conj when; condicional if; ~ **quieras** whenever you want **2** adv when; **de ~ en ~** from time to time; ~ **menos** at least

cuándo interr when

cuantía f amount, quantity; fig importance; **cuantificar** <1g> v/t quantify; **cuantioso** adj substantial

cuanto 1 adj: ~ **dinero quieras** as much money as you want; **unos ~s chavales** a few boys **2** pron all, everything; **se llevó ~ podía** she took all o everything she could; **le dio ~ necesitaba** he gave her everything she needed; **unas -as** a few; **todo ~** everything **3** adv: ~ **antes, mejor** the sooner the better; **en ~** as soon as; **en ~ a** as for

cuánto 1 interr adj how much; pl how many; **¿~ café?** how much coffee?; **¿~s huevos?** how many eggs? **2** pron how much; pl how many; **¿~ necesita Vd.?** how much do you need?; **¿~s ha dicho?** how many did you say?; **¿a ~ están?** how much are they?; what's the date today? **3** exclamaciones: **¡cuánta gente había!** there were so many people!; **¡~ me alegro!** I'm so pleased!

cuarenta adj forty

Cuaresma f Lent

cuartear <1a> **1** v/t cut up, quarter **2** v/r ~se crack

cuartel m barracks pl; ~ **general** headquarters pl; **cuartelazo** m L.Am. military uprising; **cuartilla** f sheet of paper

cuarto 1 adj fourth **2** m (habitación) room; (parte) quarter; ~ **de baño** bathroom; ~ **de estar** living room; ~ **de hora** quarter of an hour; ~ **de kilo** quarter of a kilo; **de tres al** ~ F third-rate; **las diez y** ~ quarter past ten, quarter after ten; **las tres menos** ~ a quarter to o of three

cuarzo *m* quartz

cuatro *adj* four; **~ gotas** F a few drops; **cuatrocientos** *adj* four hundred

cuba *f*: **estar como una ~** F be plastered F

Cuba Cuba; **cubano 1** *adj* Cuban **2** *m*, **-a** *f* Cuban

cubierta *f* MAR deck; AUTO tire, *Br* tyre; **cubierto 1** *part* → **cubrir 2** *m* piece of cutlery; **en la mesa** place setting; **~s** *pl* cutlery *sg*

cubito *m*: **~ de hielo** ice cube; **cubo** *m* cube; *recipiente* bucket; **~ de la basura** *dentro* garbage can, *Br* rubbish bin; *fuera* garbage can, *Br* dustbin

cubrir <3a; *part* **cubierto**> **1** *v/t* cover (**de** with) **2** *v/r* **~se** cover o.s.

cucaracha *f* ZO cockroach

cuchara *f* spoon; **meter su ~** *L.Am.* F stick one's oar in F; **cucharada** *f* spoonful; **cucharilla** *f* teaspoon; **cucharón** *m* ladle

cuchichear <1a> *v/i* whisper

cuchilla *f* razor blade; **cuchillo** *m* knife

cuclillas: **en ~** squatting

cuco 1 *m* ZO cuckoo; **reloj de ~** cuckoo clock **2** *adj* (*astuto*) sharp

cucurucho *m* *de papel etc* cone; *sombrero* pointed hat

cuece *vb* → **cocer**

cuelgo *vb* → **colgar**

cuello *m* ANAT neck; *de camisa etc* collar

cuelo *vb* → **colar**

cuenca *f* GEOG basin; **cuenco** *m* bowl

cuenta *f* (*cálculo*) sum; *de restaurante* check, *Br* bill; COM account; **~ atrás** countdown; **~ bancaria** bank account; **~ corriente** checking account, *Br* current account; **más de la ~** too much; **caer en la ~** realize; **darse ~ de algo** realize sth; **pedir ~s a alguien** ask s.o. for an explanation; **perder la ~** lose count; **tener** *or* **tomar en ~** take into account; **corre por mi/su ~** I'll/he'll pay for it

cuentagotas *m inv* dropper

cuentakilómetros *m inv* odometer, *Br* mileometer

cuentista *m/f* story-teller; F (*mentiroso*) fibber F

cuento *m* (short) story; (*pretexto*) excuse; **~ chino** F tall story F; **venir a ~** be relevant

cuerda *f* rope; *de guitarra, violín* string; **dar ~ al reloj** wind the clock up; **dar ~ a algo** *fig* F string sth out F; **~s vocales** ANAT vocal chords

cuerdo *adj* sane; (*sensato*) sensible

cuerno *m* horn; *de caracol* feeler; **irse al ~** F fall through, be wrecked; **poner los ~s a alguien** F be unfaithful to s.o.

cuero *m* leather; *Rpl* (*fuete*) whip; **en ~s** F naked

cuerpo *m* body; *de policía* force; **~ diplomático** diplomatic corps *sg*; **a ~ de rey** like a king; **en ~ y alma** body and soul

cuervo *m* ZO raven, crow

cuesta *f* slope; **~ abajo** downhill; **~ arriba** uphill; **a ~s** on one's back

cuestión *f* question; (*asunto*) matter, question; **en ~ de ...** in a matter of ...; **cuestionar** <1a> *v/t* question; **cuestionario** *m* questionnaire

cueva *f* cave

cuidado *m* care; **¡~!** look out!; **andar con ~** tread carefully; **me tiene sin ~** I couldn't care less; *o Br* couldn't care less; **tener ~** be careful; **cuidadora** *f* *Méx* nursemaid; **cuidadoso** *adj* careful

cuidar <1a> **1** *v/t* look after, take care of **2** *v/i*: **~ de** look after, take care of **3** *v/r* **~se** look after o.s., take care of o.s.; **~se de hacer algo** take care to do sth

culebra *f* ZO snake

culebrón *m* TV soap

culinario *adj* cooking *atr*, culinary

culminación *f* culmination; **culminante** *adj*: **punto ~** peak, climax; **culminar** <1a> *v/i* culminate (**en** in); *fig* reach a peak *o* climax **2** *v/t* finish

culo *m* V ass V, *Br* arse V; F butt F, *Br* bum F; **ser ~ de mal asiento** *fig* F be restless, have ants in one's pants F

culpa f fault; **echar la ~ de algo a alguien** blame s.o. for sth; **ser por ~ de alguien** be s.o.'s fault; **tener la ~** be to blame (**de** for); **culpabilidad** f guilt; **culpable 1** adj guilty **2** m/f culprit; **culpar** <1a> v/t: **~ a alguien de algo** blame s.o. for sth

cultivar <1a> v/t AGR grow; tierra farm; fig cultivate; **cultivo** m AGR crop; BIO culture; **culto 1** adj educated **2** m worship; **cultura** f culture; **cultural** adj cultural; **un nivel ~ muy pobre** a very poor standard of education

cumbre f tb POL summit

cumpleaños m inv birthday

cumplido m compliment; **no andarse con ~s** not stand on ceremony

cumplimentar <1k> v/t trámite carry out

cumplir <3a> **1** v/t orden carry out; promesa fulfill; condena serve; **~ diez años** reach the age of ten, turn ten **2** v/i: **~ con algo** carry sth out; **~ con su deber** do one's duty; **te invita sólo por ~** he's only inviting you out of politeness **3** v/r **~se de plazo** expire

cúmulo m (montón) pile, heap

cuna f tb fig cradle

cundir <3a> v/i spread; (dar mucho de sí) go a long way

cuneta f ditch

cuñada f sister-in-law; **cuñado** m brother-in-law

cuota f share; de club, asociación fee

cupón m coupon

cúpula f dome; esp POL leadership

cura 1 m priest **2** f cure; (tratamiento) treatment; Méx, C.Am. F hangover; **tener ~** be curable; **curado** adj Méx, C.Am. F drunk; **curandero** m, **-a** f faith healer; **curar** <1a> **1** v/t tb GASTR cure; (tratar) treat; herida dress; pieles tan **2** v/i MED recover (**de** from) **3** v/r **~se** MED recover; Méx, C.Am. F get drunk

curda f: **agarrarse una ~** F get plastered F

curiosidad f curiosity; **curioso 1** adj curious; (raro) curious, odd, strange **2** m, **-a** f onlooker

curita f L.Am. Band-Aid®, Br Elastoplast®

currar <1a> v/i F work

currículum vitae m résumé, Br CV, Br curriculum vitae

curry m GASTR curry

cursi adj F persona affected

cursillo m short course

cursiva f italics pl

curso m course; **~ a distancia** or **por correspondencia** correspondence course; **en el ~ de** in the course of

cursor m INFOR cursor

curtir <3a> v/t tan; fig harden

curva f curve; **curvo** adj curved

cúspide f de montaña summit; de fama etc height

custodia f JUR custody; **custodiar** <1b> v/t guard

cususa f C.Am. corn liquor

cutre adj F shabby, dingy

cuyo, -a adj whose

CV m resumé, Br CV

D

D. abr (= **Don**) Mr

Dª. abr (= **Doña**) Mrs

dactilar adj finger atr

dadivoso adj generous

dado[1] m dice

dado[2] **1** part → **dar 2** adj given; **ser ~**

a algo be given to sth **3** *conj*: **~ que** since, given that

dalia *f* BOT dahlia

daltónico *adj* colo(u)r-blind; **daltonismo** *m* colo(u)r-blindness

dama *f* lady; **~ de honor** bridesmaid; (**juego de**) **~s** checkers *sg*, *Br* draughts *sg*

damasco *m* damask; *L.Am. fruta* apricot

damnificado 1 *adj* affected **2** *m*, **-a** *f* victim

danés 1 *adj* Danish **2** *m*, **-esa** *f* Dane

danza *f* dance; **danzar** <1f> *v/i* dance

dañar <1a> **1** *v/t* harm; *cosa* damage **2** *v/r* **~se** harm o.s.; *de un objeto* get damaged; **dañino** *adj* harmful; *fig* malicious; **daño** *m* harm; *a un objeto* damage; **hacer ~** hurt; **~s** *pl* damage *sg*; **~s y perjuicios** damages

dar <1r; *part* **dado**> **1** *v/t* give; *beneficio* yield; *luz* give off; *fiesta* give, have; **~ un golpe** a hit; **~ un salto/una patada/miedo** jump/kick/frighten; **el jamón me dió sed** the ham made me thirsty **2** *v/i*: **dame** give it to me, give me it; **~ a de ventana** look onto; **~ con algo** come across sth; **~ de comer a alguien** feed s.o.; **~ de beber a alguien** give s.o. something to drink; **~ de sí** *de material* stretch, give; **le dio por insultar a su madre** F she started insulting her mother; **¡qué más da!** what does it matter!; **da igual** it doesn't matter **3** *v/r* **~se** *de una situación* arise; **~se a algo** take to sth; **esto se me da bien** I'm good at this; **dárselas de algo** make o.s. out to be sth, claim to be sth

dardo *m* dart

datar <1a> *v/i*: **~ de** date from

dátil *m* BOT date

dato *m* piece of information; **~s** *pl* information *sg*, data *sg*; **~s personales** personal details

D.C. *abr* (= **después de Cristo**) AD (= Anno Domini)

dcho., dcha *abr* (= **derecho, derecha**) r (= right)

d. de J.C. *abr* (= **después de**

Jesucristo) AD (= Anno Domini)

de *prp* ◊ *origen* from; **~ Nueva York** from New York; **~ ... a** from ... to ◊ *posesión* of; **el coche ~ mi amigo** my friend's car ◊ *material* (made) of; **un anillo ~ oro** a gold ring ◊ *contenido* of; **un vaso ~ agua** a glass of water ◊ *cualidad*: **una mujer ~ 20 años** a 20 year old woman ◊ *causa* with; **temblaba ~ miedo** she was shaking with fear ◊ *hora*: **~ noche** at night, by night; **~ día** by day ◊ *en calidad de* as; **trabajar ~ albañil** work as a bricklayer ◊ *agente* by; **~ Goya** by Goya ◊ *condición* if; **~ haberlo sabido** if I'd known

dé *vb* → **dar**

deambular <1a> *v/i* wander around

debajo 1 *adv* underneath **2** *prp*: (**por**) **~ de** under; **un grado por ~ de lo normal** one degree below normal

debate *m* debate, discussion; **debatir** <3a> **1** *v/t* debate, discuss **2** *v/i* struggle **3** *v/r* **~se**: **~se entre la vida y la muerte** fight for one's life

deber **1** *m* duty; **~es** *pl* homework *sg* **2** <2a> *v/t* owe **3** *v/i* **en presente** must, have to; **en pretérito** should have; **en futuro** (will) have to; **en condicional** should; **debe de tener quince años** he must be about 15 **4** *v/r* **~se**: **~se a** be due to, be caused by; **debido 1** *part* → **deber 2** *adj*: **como es** ~ properly; **~ a** owing to, on account of

débil *adj* weak; **debilitar** <1a> **1** *v/t* weaken **2** *v/r* **~se** weaken, become weak; *de salud* deteriorate

debut *m* debut

década *f* decade

decadencia *f* decadence; *de un imperio* decline; **decaer** <2o; *part* **decaído**> *v/i* tb *fig* decline; *de rendimiento* fall off, decline; *de salud* deteriorate; **decaído 1** *part* → **decaer 2** *adj* *fig* depressed, down F

decantarse <1a> *v/r*: **~ por** opt for

decapitar <1a> *v/t* behead, decapitate

decenio *m* decade

decente *adj* decent

decepción *f* disappointment; **decepcionado** *adj* disappointed; **decepcionante** *adj* disappointing; **decepcionar** <1a> *v/t* disappoint

decidido 1 *part* → **decidir 2** *adj* decisive; **estar ~** be determined (**a** to); **decidir** <3a> **1** *v/t* decide **2** *v/r* **~se** make up one's mind, decide

decimal *adj* decimal *atr*; **décimo 1** *adj* tenth **2** *m de lotería* share of a lottery ticket

decir <3p; *part* **dicho**> **1** *v/t* say; (*contar*) tell; **querer ~** mean; **~ que sí** say yes; **~ que no** say no; **es ~** in other words; **no es rico, que digamos** let's say he's not rich; **¡no me digas!** you're kidding!; **¡quién lo diría!** who would believe it!; **se dice que ...** they say that ..., it's said that ... **2** *v/i*: **¡diga!, ¡dígame!** *Esp* TELEC hello

decisión *f* decision; *fig* decisiveness; **decisivo** *adj* critical, decisive

declaración *f* declaration; **~ de la renta** *or* **de impuestos** tax return; **prestar ~** JUR testify, give evidence; **declarar** <1a> **1** *v/t* state; *bienes* declare; **~ culpable** find guilty **2** *v/i* JUR give evidence **3** *v/r* **~se** declare o.s.; *de incendio* break out; **~se a alguien** declare one's love for s.o.

declinar <1a> *v/t* & *v/i* decline

declive *m fig* decline; **en ~** in decline

decodificador *m* → **descodificador**, **decodificar** <1g> *v/t* → **descodificar**

decolaje *m L.Am.* takeoff; **decolar** <1a> *v/i L.Am.* take off

decolorar <1a> *v/t* bleach

decoración *f* decoration; **decorado** *m* TEA set; **decorador** *m*, **~a** *f*: **~ (de interiores)** interior decorator; **decorar** <1a> *v/t* decorate; **decorativo** *adj* decorative

decreciente *adj* decreasing, diminishing

decrépito *adj* decrepit

decretar <1a> *v/t* order, decree; **decreto** *m* decree

dedicación *f* dedication; **dedicar** <1g> **1** *v/t* dedicate; *esfuerzo* devote **2** *v/r* **~se** devote o.s. (**a** to); **¿a qué se dedica?** what do you do (for a living)?; **dedicatoria** *f* dedication

dedillo *m*: **conocer algo al ~** F know sth like the back of one's hand; **saber algo al ~** F know sth off by heart

dedo *m* finger; **~ del pie** toe; **~ gordo** thumb; **~ índice** forefinger; **no tiene dos ~s de frente** F he doesn't have much commonsense

deducción *f* deduction; **deducir** <3o> *v/t* deduce; COM deduct

defecar <1g> *v/i* defecate

defecto *m* defect; *moral* fault; INFOR default; **defectuoso** *adj* defective, faulty

defender <2g> **1** *v/t* defend **2** *v/r* **~se** defend o.s. (**de** against); *fig* F manage, get by; **~se del frío** ward off the cold

defenestrar <1a> *v/t fig* F oust

defensa 1 *f* JUR, DEP defense, *Br* defence; *L.Am.* AUTO fender, *Br* bumper; **~s** MED defenses, *Br* defences **2** *m/f* DEP defender; **defensivo** *adj* defensive; **defensor** *m*, **~a** *f* defender, champion; JUR defense counsel, *Br* defending counsel; **~ del pueblo** *en España* ombudsman

deficiente 1 *adj* deficient; (*insatisfactorio*) inadequate **2** *m/f* handicapped person; **déficit** *m* deficit

definición *f* definition; **de alta ~** TV high definition; **definir** <3a> **1** *v/t* define **2** *v/r* **~se** come down (**por** in favor of); **definitivo** *adj* definitive; *respuesta* definite; **en -a** all in all

deforestación *f* deforestation

deformar <1a> *v/t* distort; MED deform; **deforme** *adj* deformed

defraudar <1a> *v/t* disappoint; (*estafar*) defraud; **~ a Hacienda** evade taxes

defunción *f* death, demise *fml*

degenerar <1a> *v/i* degenerate (**en** into)

degollar <1n> *v/t* cut the throat of

degradante *adj* degrading; **degra-**

dar <1a> **1** *v/t* degrade; MIL demote; PINT gradate **2** *v/r* **~se** demean o.s.

degustar <1a> *v/t* taste

dejadez *f* slovenliness; (*negligencia*) neglect

dejar <1a> **1** *v/t* leave; (*permitir*) let, allow; (*prestar*) lend; *beneficios* yield; *déjame en la esquina* drop me at the corner; **~** *para mañana* leave until tomorrow; **~** *caer algo* drop sth **2** *v/i*: **~** *de hacer algo* (*parar*) stop doing sth; *no deja de fastidiarme* he keeps (on) annoying me **3** *v/r* **~se** let o.s. go; **~se llevar** let o.s. be carried along

del *prp* **de** *y art* **el**

delantal *m* apron

delante *adv* in front; (*más avanzado*) ahead; (*enfrente*) opposite; *por* **~** ahead; *se abrocha por* **~** it does up at the front; *tener algo por* **~** have sth ahead of *o* in front of one; **~** *de* in front of; *el asiento de* **~** the front seat; **delantera** *f* DEP forward line; *llevar la* **~** be ahead of, lead; **delantero** *m*, **-a** *f* DEP forward

delatar <1a> *v/t*: **~** *a alguien* inform on s.o.; *fig* give s.o. away

delegación *f* delegation; (*oficina*) local office; **~** *de Hacienda* tax office; **delegado** *m*, **-a** *f* delegate; COM representative; **delegar** <1h> *v/t* delegate

deleitar <1a> **1** *v/t* delight **2** *v/r* **~se** take delight

deletrear <1a> *v/t* spell

delfín *m* ZO dolphin

delgado *adj* slim; *lámina, placa* thin

deliberado *adj* deliberate; **deliberar** <1a> *v/i* deliberate (*sobre* on)

delicadeza *f* gentleness; *de acabado, tallado* delicacy; (*tacto*) tact; **delicado** *adj* delicate

delicia *f* delight; *hacer las* **~s de alguien** delight s.o.; **delicioso** *adj* delightful; *comida* delicious

delimitar <1a> *v/t* delimit

delincuente *m/f* criminal

delineante *m/f* draftsman, *Br* draughtsman; *mujer* draftswoman,

Br draughtswoman; **delinear** <1a> *v/t* draft; *fig* draw up

delirar <1a> *v/i* be delirious; *¡tú deliras!* *fig* you must be crazy!; **delirio** *m* MED delirium; *fig* madness; *tener* **~** *por el fútbol* *fig* be mad about soccer; **~s** *de grandeza* delusions of grandeur

delito *m* offense, *Br* offence

demacrado *adj* haggard

demagógico *adj* demagogic

demanda *f* demand (*de* for); JUR lawsuit, claim; **demandar** <1a> *v/t* JUR sue

demás 1 *adj* remaining **2** *adv*: *lo* **~** the rest; *los* **~** the rest, the others; *por lo* **~** apart from that; **demasiado 1** *adj* too much; *antes de pl* too many; **-a** *gente* too many people; *hace* **~** *calor* it's too hot **2** *adv antes de adj, adv* too; *con verbo* too much

demencia *f* MED dementia; *fig* madness; **~** *senil* MED senile dementia; **demencial** *adj* *fig* crazy, mad; **demente 1** *adj* demented, crazy **2** *m/f* mad person

democracia *f* democracy; **demócrata 1** *adj* democratic **2** *m/f* democrat; **democrático** *adj* democratic

demografía *f* demographics

demoler <2h> *v/t* demolish

demoniaco, **demoníaco** *adj* demonic; **demonio** *m* demon; *¡~s!* F hell! F, damn! F

demora *f* delay; *sin* **~** without delay; **demorar** <1a> **1** *v/i* stay on; *L.Am.* (*tardar*) be late; *no demores* don't be long **2** *v/t* delay **3** *v/r* **~se** be delayed; *¿cuánto se demora de Concepción a Santiago?* how long does it take to get from Concepción to Santiago?

demostración *f* proof; *de método* demonstration; *de fuerza, sentimiento* show; **demostrar** <1m> *v/t* prove; (*enseñar*) demonstrate; (*mostrar*) show

denegar <1h & 1k> *v/t* refuse

denigrante *adj* degrading; *artículo* denigrating; **denigrar** <1a> *v/t* degrade; (*criticar*) denigrate

denominación f name; ~ **de origen** guarantee of quality of a wine; **denominador** m: ~ **común** fig common denominator; **denominar** <1a> **1** v/t designate **2** v/r ~**se** be called

denotar <1a> v/t show, indicate

densidad f density; **denso** adj bosque dense; fig weighty

dentadura f: ~ **postiza** false teeth pl, dentures pl; **dental** adj dental; **dentera** f: **darle** ~ **a alguien** set s.o.'s teeth on edge; **dentífrico** m toothpaste; **dentista** m/f dentist

dentro 1 adv inside; **por** ~ inside; **de** ~ from inside **2** ~ **de** en espacio in, inside; en tiempo in, within

denuncia f report; **poner una** ~ make a formal complaint; **denunciar** <1b> v/t report; fig condemn, denounce

departamento m department; L.Am. (apartamento) apartment, Br flat

depender <2a> v/i depend (**de** on); ~ **de alguien** en una jerarquía report to s.o.; **eso depende** that all depends; **dependiente 1** adj dependent **2** m, -a f sales clerk, Br shop assistant

depilación f hair removal; con cera waxing; con pinzas plucking; **depilar** <1a> v/t con cera wax; con pinzas pluck

deplorar <1a> v/t deplore

deportar <1a> v/t deport

deporte m sport; **deportista** m/f sportsman; mujer sportswoman

depositar <1a> v/t tb fig put, place; dinero deposit (**en** in); **depósito** m COM deposit; (almacén) store; de agua, AUTO tank; ~ **de cadáveres** morgue, Br mortuary

depravado adj depraved; **depravar** <1a> v/t deprave

depreciación f depreciation; **depreciar** <1b> **1** v/t lower the value of **2** v/r ~**se** depreciate, lose value

depredador 1 adj predatory **2** m ZO predator

depresión f MED depression; **deprimente** adj depressing; **deprimir**

<3a> **1** v/t depress **2** v/r ~**se** get depressed

depuradora f purifier; **depurar** <1a> v/t purify; agua treat; POL purge

derecha f tb POL right; **la** ~ the right(-hand); **a la** ~ posición on the right; dirección to the right

derecho 1 adj lado right; (recto) straight; C.Am. fig straight, honest **2** adv straight **3** m (privilegio) right; JUR law; **del** ~ on the right side; ~ **de asilo** right to asylum; ~**s de autor** royalties; ~**s humanos** human rights; ~ **de voto** right to vote; **no hay** ~ it's not fair, it's not right; **tener** ~ **a** have a right to **4** mpl: ~**s** fees; ~**s de inscripción** registration fee sg

derechura f straightness; C.Am., Pe (suerte) luck; **en** ~ straight away

deriva f: **ir a la** ~ MAR, fig drift; **derivar** <1a> **1** v/i derive (**de** from); de barco drift **2** v/r ~**se** be derived (**de** from)

dermatólogo m, -a f dermatologist

derogar <1h> v/t repeal

derramar <1a> **1** v/t spill; luz, sangre shed; (esparcir) scatter **2** v/r ~**se** spill; de gente scatter; **derrame** m MED: ~ **cerebral** stroke

derrapar <1a> v/i AUTO skid

derrengado adj exhausted

derretir <3l> **1** v/t melt **2** v/r ~**se** melt; fig be besotted (**por** with)

derribar <1a> v/t edificio, persona knock down; avión shoot down; POL bring down

derrocar <1g> v/t POL overthrow

derrochador m, ~**a** f spendthrift; **derrochar** <1a> v/t waste; salud, felicidad exude, burst with; **derroche** m waste

derrota f defeat; **derrotar** <1a> v/t MIL defeat; DEP beat, defeat

derruir <3g> v/t edificio demolish

derrumbar <1a> **1** v/t knock down **2** v/r ~**se** collapse, fall down; de una persona go to pieces

desabrido adj (soso) tasteless; persona surly; tiempo unpleasant

desabrochar <1a> v/t undo, unfasten

desacato m JUR contempt

desaceleración f deceleration

desacertado adj misguided

desaconsejar <1a> v/t advise against

desacreditado adj discredited; **desacreditar** <1a> v/t discredit

desactivar <1a> v/t bomba etc deactivate

desacuerdo m disagreement; **estar en ~ con** disagree with

desafiar <1c> v/t challenge; peligro defy

desafinar <1a> v/i MÚS be out of tune

desafío m challenge; al peligro defiance

desafortunado adj unfortunate, unlucky

desagradable adj unpleasant, disagreeable; **desagradar** <1a> v/i: me desagrada tener que ... I dislike having to ...; **desagradecido** adj ungrateful; una tarea -a a thankless task; **desagrado** m displeasure

desagravio m apology

desagüe m drain; acción drainage; (cañería) drainpipe

desahogar <1h> 1 v/t sentimiento vent 2 v/r ~se fig F let off steam F, get it out of one's system F; **desahogo** m comfort; con ~ comfortably

desahuciar <1b> v/t: ~ a alguien declare s.o. terminally ill; (inquilino) evict s.o.

desairar <1a> v/t snub

desajustar <1a> v/t tornillo, pieza loosen; mecanismo, instrumento affect, throw out of balance; **desajuste** m disruption; COM imbalance

desalentar <1k> v/t discourage; **desaliento** m discouragement

desalinización f desalination

desaliñado adj slovenly

desalojar <1a> v/t ante peligro evacuate; (desahuciar) evict; (vaciar) vacate

desamparar <1a> v/t: ~ a alguien abandon s.o.

desangelado adj lugar soulless

desangrarse <1a> v/r bleed to death

desanimar <1a> 1 v/t discourage, dishearten 2 v/r ~se become discouraged o disheartened; **desánimo** m discouragement

desapacible adj nasty, unpleasant

desaparecer <2d> 1 v/i disappear, vanish 2 v/t L.Am. disappear F; **desaparecido** m, -a f L.Am.: un ~ one of the disappeared; **desaparición** f disappearance

desapego m indifference; (distancia) distance, coolness

desapercibido adj unnoticed; pasar ~ go unnoticed

desaprensivo adj unscrupulous

desaprobar <1m> v/t disapprove of

desaprovechar <1a> v/t oportunidad waste

desarmado adj unarmed; **desarmar** <1a> v/t MIL disarm; TÉC take to pieces, dismantle; **desarme** m MIL disarmament

desarraigo m fig rootlessness

desarreglar <1a> v/t make untidy; horario disrupt

desarrollar <1a> 1 v/t develop; tema explain; trabajo carry out 2 v/r ~se develop, evolve; (ocurrir) take place; **desarrollo** m development

desarticular <1a> v/t banda criminal break up; MED dislocate

desaseado adj F scruffy

desasirse <3a> v/r get free, free o.s.

desasosiego m disquiet, unease

desastre m tb fig disaster; **desastroso** adj disastrous

desatar <1a> 1 v/t untie; fig unleash 2 v/r ~se de animal, persona get free; de cordón come undone; fig be unleashed, break out

desatascar <1g> v/t unblock

desatender <2g> v/t neglect; (ignorar) ignore

desatino m mistake

desatornillador m esp L.Am. screwdriver; **desatornillar** <1a> v/t unscrew

desatrancar <1g> *v/t cañería* un-block

desavenencia *f* disagreement

desaventajado *adj* unfavo(u)rable

desayunar <1a> **1** *v/i* have breakfast **2** *v/t*: ~ *algo* have sth for breakfast; **desayuno** *m* breakfast

desazón *f* (*ansiedad*) uneasiness, anxiety; **desazonar** <1a> *v/t* worry, make anxious

desbancar <1g> *v/t fig* displace, take the place of

desbandarse <1a> *v/r* disband; *de un grupo de personas* scatter

desbarajuste *m* mess

desbaratar <1a> *planes* ruin; *organización* disrupt

desbarrancar <1g> *L.Am.* **1** *v/t* push over the edge of a cliff **2** *v/r* ~*se* go over the edge of a cliff

desbocarse <1g> *v/r de un caballo* bolt

desbordante *adj energía, entusiasmo etc* boundless; ~ *de* bursting with, overflowing with; **desbordar** <1a> **1** *v/t de un río* overflow, burst; *de un multitud* break through; *de un acontecimiento* overwhelm; *fig* exceed **2** *v/i* overflow **3** *v/r* ~*se de un río* burst its banks, overflow; *fig* get out of control

descabellado *adj*: *idea -a* F harebrained idea F; **descabellar** <1a> *v/t* TAUR kill with a knife-thrust in the neck; **descabello** *m* fatal knife thrust

descafeinado *adj* decaffeinated; *fig* watered-down

descalabro *m* calamity, disaster

descalificar <1g> *v/t* disqualify

descalzarse <1f> *v/r* take one's shoes off; **descalzo** *adj* barefoot

descaminado *adj fig* misguided; *andar or ir* ~ be on the wrong track

descamisado *adj* shirtless; *fig* ragged

descampado *m* open ground

descansar <1a> *v/i* rest, have a rest; ¡*que descanses!* sleep well; **descansillo** *m* landing; **descanso** *m* rest; DEP half-time; TEA interval;

sin ~ without a break

descapotable *m* AUTO convertible

descarado *adj* rude, impertinent

descarga *f* EL, MIL discharge; *de mercancías* unloading; **descargar** <1h> *v/t arma*, EL discharge; *fig*: *ira etc* take out (*en, sobre* on); *mercancías* unload; *de responsabilidad, culpa* clear (*de* of)

descaro *m* nerve

descarriado *adj*: *ir* ~ go astray

descarrilar <1a> *v/t* derail

descartar <1a> *v/t* rule out

descastado *adj* cold, uncaring

descender <2g> **1** *v/i para indicar alejamiento* go down, descend; *para indicar acercamiento* come down, descend; *fig* go down, decrease, diminish; ~ *de* descend from **2** *v/t escalera* go down; *para indicar acercamiento* come down; **descendiente 1** *adj* descended **2** *m/f* descendant; **descenso** *m de precio etc* drop; *de montaña*, AVIA descent; DEP relegation; *la prueba de* ~ *en esquí* the downhill (race *o* competition)

descentralizar <1f> *v/t* decentralize

descentrar <1a> *v/t fig* shake

descifrar <1a> *v/t* decipher; *fig* work out

descodificación *f* decoding; **descodificador** *m* decoder; **descodificar** <1g> *v/t* decode

descolgar <1h & 1m> **1** *v/t* take down; *teléfono* pick up **2** *v/r* ~*se por una cuerda* lower o.s.; *de un grupo* break away

descollar <1m> *v/i* stand out (*sobre* among)

descolonización *f* decolonization

descolorido *adj* faded; *fig* colo(u)rless

descomponer <2r; *part* **descompuesto**> **1** *v/t* (*dividir*) break down; (*pudrir*) cause to decompose; *L.Am.* (*romper*) break **2** *v/r* ~*se* (*pudrirse*) decompose, rot; TÉC break down; *Rpl* (*emocionarse*) break down (in tears); *se le descompuso la cara* he turned pale;

descomposición f breaking down; *putrefacción* decomposition; (*diarrea*) diarrh(o)ea; **descompuesto 1** *part* → **descomponer 2** *adj alimento* rotten; *cadáver* decomposed; *persona* upset; *L.Am.* tipsy; *L.Am.* *máquina* broken down

descomunal *adj* huge, enormous

desconcertar <1k> *v/t a persona* disconcert

desconchado, desconchón m place where the paint is peeling; *en porcelana* chip

desconcierto m uncertainty

desconectar <1a> **1** *v/t* EL disconnect **2** *v/i* fig switch off **3** *v/r* ~**se** fig lose touch (**de** with)

desconfiar <1c> *v/i* be mistrustful (**de** of), be suspicious (**de** of)

descongelar <1a> *v/t comida* thaw, defrost; *refrigerador* defrost; *precios* unfreeze

descongestionar <1a> *v/t* MED clear; ~ **el tráfico** relieve traffic congestion

desconocer <2d> *v/t* not know; **desconocido 1** *adj* unknown **2** *m*, **-a** f stranger

desconsiderado *adj* inconsiderate

desconsolado *adj* inconsolable; **desconsuelo** m grief

descontado 1 *part* → **descontar 2** *adj:* **dar por ~** take for granted; **por ~** certainly

descontaminar <1a> *v/t* decontaminate

descontar <1m> *v/t* COM deduct, take off; *fig* exclude

descontento 1 *adj* dissatisfied **2** m dissatisfaction

descontrol m chaos; **descontrolarse** <1a> *v/r* get out of control

desconvocar <1g> *v/t* call off

descorazonar <1a> **1** *v/t* discourage **2** *v/r* ~**se** get discouraged

descorchar <1a> *v/t botella* uncork

descortés *adj* impolite, rude

descoserse <2a> *v/r de costura, dobladillo etc* come unstitched; *de prenda* come apart at the seams; **descosido** m: **como un ~** F like

mad F

descoyuntar <1a> *v/t* dislocate

descremado *adj* skimmed

describir <3a; *part* descrito> *v/t* describe; **descripción** f description; **descrito** *part* → **describir**

descuajaringarse <1h> *v/r* F fall apart, fall to bits

descuartizar <1f> *v/t* quarter

descubierto 1 *part* → **descubrir 2** *adj* uncovered; *persona* bareheaded; *cielos* clear; *piscina* open-air; **al ~** in the open; **quedar al ~** be exposed **3** m COM overdraft; **descubrimiento** m discovery; (*revelación*) revelation; **descubrir** <3a; *part* descubierto> **1** *v/t* discover; *poner de manifiesto* uncover, reveal; *estatua* unveil **2** *v/r* ~**se** take one's hat off; *fig* give o.s. away

descuento m discount; DEP stoppage time

descuerar <1a> *v/t L.Am.* skin; ~ **a alguien** fig tear s.o. to pieces

descuidado *adj* careless; **descuidar** <1a> **1** *v/t* neglect **2** *v/i:* **¡descuida!** don't worry! **3** *v/r* ~**se** get careless; *en cuanto al aseo* let o.s. go; (*despistarse*) let one's concentration drop; **descuido** m carelessness; (*error*) mistake; (*omisión*) oversight; **en un ~** *L.Am.* in a moment of carelessness

desde 1 *prp en el tiempo* since; *en el espacio* from; *en escala* from; ~ **1993** since 1993; ~ **hace tres días** for three days; ~ **... hasta ...** from ... to ... **2** *adv:* ~ **luego** of course; ~ **ya** *Rpl* right away

desdén m disdain, contempt; **desdeñable** *adj* contemptible; **nada ~** far from insignificant; **desdeñar** <1a> *v/t* scorn

desdibujado *adj* blurred

desdichado 1 *adj* unhappy; (*sin suerte*) unlucky **2** m, -a f poor soul

desdoblar <1a> *v/t* unfold; (*dividir*) split

desear <1a> *v/t* wish for; *suerte etc* wish; **¿qué desea?** what would you like?

desecar <1g> v/t dry

desechable adj disposable; **desechar** <1a> v/t (tirar) throw away; (rechazar) reject; **desechos** mpl waste sg

desembalar <1a> v/t unpack

desembarazarse <1f> v/r: ~ **de** get rid of; **desembarazo** m ease

desembarcadero m MAR landing stage; **desembarcar** <1g> v/i disembark

desembocadura f mouth; **desembocar** <1g> v/i flow (**en** into); de calle come out (**en** into); de situación end (**en** in)

desembolsar <1a> v/t pay out

desembuchar <1a> v/i fig F spill the beans F, come out with it F

desempacar <1g> v/t unpack

desempaquetar <1a> v/t unwrap

desempatar <1a> v/i DEP, POL decide the winner

desempeñar <1a> v/t deber, tarea carry out; cargo hold; papel play

desempleado **1** adj unemployed **2** m, **-a** f unemployed person; **desempleo** m unemployment

desencadenar <1a> **1** v/t fig trigger **2** v/r ~**se** fig be triggered

desencajarse <1a> v/r de una pieza come out; **se me ha desencajado la mandíbula** I dislocated my jaw

desencantado adj fig disenchanted (**con** with); **desencanto** m fig disillusion

desenchufar <1a> v/t EL unplug

desenfadado adj self-assured; programa light, undemanding

desenfocado adj FOT out of focus

desenfrenado adj frenzied, hectic; **desenfreno** m frenzy

desenfundar <1a> v/t arma take out, draw

desengañarse <1a> v/r become disillusioned (**de** with); (dejar de engañarse) stop kidding o.s.; **desengaño** m disappointment

desenlace m outcome, ending

desenmascarar <1a> v/t fig unmask, expose

desenredar <1a> v/t untangle; situación confusa straighten out, sort out

desenrollar <1a> v/t unroll

desenroscar <1g> v/t unscrew

desentenderse <2g> v/r not want to know (**de** about); **desentendido** adj: **hacerse el ~** F pretend not to notice

desentonar <1a> v/i MÚS go off key; ~ **con** fig clash with; **decir algo que desentona** say sth out of place

desentrañar <1a> v/t fig unravel

desenvoltura f ease; **desenvolverse** <2h; part **desenvuelto**> v/r fig cope; **desenvuelto 1** part → **desenvolver 2** adj self-confident

deseo m wish

desequilibrar <1a> v/t unbalance; ~ **a alguien** throw s.o. off balance; **desequilibrio** m imbalance; ~ **mental** mental instability

desertar <1a> v/i MIL desert

desértico adj desert atr; **desertización** f desertification

desertor m, **~a** f deserter

desesperación f despair; **desesperado** adj in despair; **desesperante** adj infuriating, exasperating; **desesperar** <1a> **1** v/t infuriate, exasperate **2** v/i give up hope (**de** of), despair (**de** of) **3** v/r ~**se** get exasperated

desestabilizar <1f> v/t POL destabilize

desfachatez f impertinence

desfalco m embezzlement

desfallecer <2d> v/i faint

desfase m fig gap

desfavorable adj unfavo(u)rable; **desfavorecer** <2d> v/t (no ser favorable) not favo(u)r, be disadvantageous to; de ropa etc not suit

desfigurar <1a> v/t disfigure

desfiladero m ravine; **desfilar** <1a> v/i parade; **desfile** m parade; ~ **de modelos** or **de modas** fashion show

desfogarse <1h> v/r fig vent one's emotions

desforestación f deforestation

desgana *f* loss of appetite; **con ~** *fig* reluctantly, half-heartedly

desgañitarse <1a> *v/r* F shout one's head off F

desgarbado *adj* F ungainly

desgarrador *adj* heartrending; **desgarrar** <1a> *v/t* tear up; *fig: corazón* break

desgastar <1a> *v/t* wear out; *defensas* wear down; **desgaste** *m* wear (and tear)

desglose *m* breakdown, itemization

desgracia *f* misfortune; *suceso* accident; **por ~** unfortunately; **desgraciadamente** *adv* unfortunately; **desgraciado 1** *adj* unfortunate; (*miserable*) wretched **2** *m*, **-a** *f* wretch; (*sinvergüenza*) swine F

desgravar <1a> *v/t* deduct **2** *v/i* be tax-deductible

desguazar <1f> *v/t* scrap

deshabitado *adj* uninhabited

deshacer <2s; *part* **deshecho**> **1** *v/t* undo; *maleta* unpack; *planes* wreck, ruin; *eso los obligó a ~ todos sus planes* this forced them to cancel their plans **2** *v/r* **~se** *de nudo de corbata, lazo etc* come undone; *de hielo* melt; **~se de** get rid of; **deshecho 1** *part* → **deshacer 2** *adj* F *anímicamente* devastated F; *de cansancio* beat F, exhausted

desheredar <1a> *v/t* disinherit

deshice *vb* → **deshacer**

deshidratar <1a> *v/t* dehydrate

deshielo *m* thaw

deshinchar <1a> **1** *v/t globo* deflate, let down **2** *v/r* **~se** deflate, go down; *fig* lose heart

deshonesto *adj* dishonest

deshonra *f* dishono(u)r; **deshonroso** *adj* dishono(u)rable

deshora *f*: **a ~(s)** at the wrong time

desidia *f* apathy, lethargy

desierto 1 *adj lugar* empty, deserted; *isla -a* desert island **2** *m* desert

designar <1a> *v/t* appoint, name; *lugar* select; **designio** *m* plan

desigual *adj* unequal; *terreno* uneven, irregular; **desigualdad** *f* inequality

desilusión *f* disappointment; **desilusionado** *adj* disappointed; **desilusionar** <1a> **1** *v/t* disappoint; (*quitar la ilusión*) disillusion **2** *v/r* **~se** be disappointed; (*perder la ilusión*) become disillusioned

desinfectante *m* disinfectant; **desinfectar** <1a> *v/t* disinfect

desinflar <1a> **1** *v/t globo, neumático* let the air out of, deflate **2** *v/r* **~se** *de neumático* deflate; *fig* lose heart

desinformación *f* disinformation

desinhibir <3a> **1** *v/t*: **~ alguien** get rid of s.o.'s inhibitions **2** *v/r* **~se** lose one's inhibitions

desintegrar <1a> **1** *v/t* cause to disintegrate; *grupo de gente* break up **2** *v/r* **~se** disintegrate; *de grupo de gente* break up

desinterés *m* lack of interest; (*generosidad*) unselfishness; **desinteresado** *adj* unselfish

desintoxicación *f* detoxification; *hacer una cura de ~* go into detox F, have treatment for drug/alcohol abuse

desistir <3a> *v/i* give up; *tuvo que ~ de hacerlo* I had to stop doing it

deslealtad *f* disloyalty

desligar <1h> **1** *v/t* separate (*de* from); *fig persona* cut off (*de* from) **2** *v/r* **~se** *fig* cut o.s. off (*de* from)

desliz *m fig* F slip-up F; **deslizar** <1f> **1** *v/t* slide, run (*por* along); *idea, frase* slip in **2** *v/i* slide **3** *v/r* **~se** slide

deslomarse <1a> *v/r fig* kill o.s.

deslucido *adj* tarnished; *colores* dull, drab; **deslucir** <3f> *v/t* tarnish; *fig* spoil

deslumbrante *adj* dazzling; **deslumbrar** <1a> **1** *v/t fig* dazzle **2** *v/r* **~se** *fig* be dazzled

desmadre *m* F chaos

desmandarse <1a> *v/r de animal* break loose

desmantelar <1a> *v/t fortificación, organización* dismantle

desmañado *adj* clumsy

desmaquillar <1a> **1** v/t remove makeup from **2** v/r **~se** remove one's makeup

desmarcarse <1g> v/r DEP lose one's marker; **~ de** distance o.s. from

desmayarse <1a> v/r faint; **desmayo** m fainting fit; **sin ~** without flagging

desmedido adj excessive

desmelenarse <1a> v/r fig F let one's hair down F; (enfurecerse) hit the roof F

desmembrar <1k> v/t dismember

desmemoriado adj forgetful

desmentido m denial; **desmentir** <3i> v/t deny; a alguien contradict

desmenuzar <1f> v/t crumble up; fig break down

desmerecer <2d> **1** v/t not do justice to **2** v/i be unworthy (**con** of); **~ de** not stand comparison with; **no ~ de** be in no way inferior to

desmesurado adj excessive

desmilitarización f demilitarization

desmitificar <1g> v/t demystify, demythologize

desmontar <1a> **1** v/t dismantle, take apart; tienda de campaña take down **2** v/i dismount

desmoralizado adj demoralized; **desmoralizar** <1f> v/t demoralize

desmoronamiento m tb fig collapse; **desmoronarse** <1a> v/r tb fig collapse

desnatado adj skimmed

desnaturalizado adj QUÍM denatured

desnivel m unevenness; entre personas disparity; **desnivelar** <1a> v/t upset the balance of

desnucarse <1g> v/r break one's neck

desnudar <1a> **1** v/t undress; fig fleece **2** v/r **~se** undress; **desnudo 1** adj naked; (sin decoración) bare **2** m PINT nude

desnutrición f undernourishment

desobedecer <2d> v/t disobey; **desobediencia** f disobedience; **desobediente** adj disobedient

desocupación f L.Am. unemployment; **desocupado 1** adj apartamento vacant, empty; L.Am. sin trabajo unemployed **2** mpl: **los ~s** the unemployed; **desocupar** <1a> v/t vacate

desodorante m deodorant

desoído part → **desoír**; **desoír** <3q; part **desoído**> v/t ignore, turn a deaf ear to

desolado adj desolate; fig griefstricken, devastated; **desolar** <1m> v/t tb fig devastate

desollar <1m> v/t skin

desorbitado adj astronomical; **con ojos ~s** pop-eyed

desorden m disorder; **desordenado** adj untidy, messy F; fig disorganized; **desordenar** <1a> v/t make untidy

desorganización f lack of organization; **desorganizado** adj disorganized

desorientar <1a> **1** v/t disorient; (confundir) confuse **2** v/r **~se** get disoriented, lose one's bearings; fig get confused

despabilado adj fig bright; **despabilar** <1a> **1** v/t wake up; **¡despabila!** get your act together! **2** v/r **~se** fig get one's act together

despachar <1a> **1** v/t a persona, cliente attend to; problema sort out; (vender) sell; (enviar) send, dispatch **2** v/i meet (**con** with) **3** v/r **~se** F polish off F; **~se a su gusto** speak one's mind; **despacho** m office; diplomático dispatch; **~ de billetes** ticket office

despacio adv slowly; L.Am. (en voz baja) in a low voice

desparpajo m self-confidence

desparramar <1a> **1** v/t scatter; líquido spill; dinero squander **2** v/r **~se** spill; fig scatter

despavorido adj terrified

despecho m spite; **a ~ de** in spite of

despectivo adj contemptuous; GRAM pejorative

despedazar <1f> v/t tear apart

despedida f farewell; **~ de soltero**

stag party; **~ de soltera** hen party;
despedir <3l> **1** *v/t* see off; *emplea-do* dismiss; *perfume* give off; *de jinete* throw **2** *v/r* **~se** say goodbye (*de* to)

despegar <1h> **1** *v/t* remove, peel off **2** *v/i* AVIA, *fig* take off **3** *v/r* **~se** come unstuck (*de* from), come off (*de* sth); *de persona* distance o.s. (*de* from); **despegue** *m* AVIA, *fig* take-off

despeinar <1a> *v/t:* **~ a alguien** muss s.o.'s hair

despejado *adj cielo, cabeza* clear; **despejar** <1a> **1** *v/t* clear; *persona* wake up **2** *v/r* **~se** *de cielo* clear up; *fig* wake o.s. up

despellejar <1a> *v/t* skin; **~ a alguien** tear s.o. to pieces

despenalizar <1f> *v/t* decriminalize

despensa *f* larder

despeñarse <1a> *v/r* throw o.s. off a cliff

desperdiciar <1b> *v/t oportunidad* waste; **desperdicio** *m* waste; **~s** *pl* waste *sg*; **no tener ~** be worthwhile

desperdigar <1h> *v/t* scatter

despertador *m* alarm (clock); **despertar** <1k> **1** *v/t* wake, waken; *apetito* whet; *sospecha* arouse; *recuerdo* reawaken, trigger **2** *v/i* wake up **3** *v/r* **~se** wake (up)

despiadado *adj* ruthless

despido *m* dismissal

despierto *adj* awake; *fig* bright

despilfarrar <1a> *v/t* squander

despistado *adj* scatterbrained; **despistarse** <1a> *v/r* get distracted; **despiste** *m* distraction; **tener un ~** become distracted

desplante *m:* **hacer un ~ a alguien** *fig* be rude to s.o.

desplazar <1f> **1** *v/t* move; (*suplantar*) take over from **2** *v/r* **~se** travel

desplegar <1h & 1k> *v/t* unfold, open out; MIL deploy; **despliegue** *m* MIL deployment; **con gran ~ de** *fig* with a great show of

desplomarse <1a> *v/r* collapse; **desplome** *m* collapse

despojar <1a> **1** *v/t* strip (*de* of)

2 *v/r* **~se:** **~se de** *prenda* take off ; **despojos** *mpl* (*restos*) left-overs; (*desperdicios*) waste *sg*; *fig* spoils; *de animal* offal *sg*

desposeídos *mpl:* **los ~** the dispossessed

déspota *m/f* despot

despotricar <1g> *v/i* F rant and rave F (*contra* about)

despreciar <1b> *v/t* look down on; *propuesta* reject; **desprecio** *m* contempt; (*indiferencia*) disregard; *acto* slight

desprender <2a> **1** *v/t* detach, separate; *olor* give off **2** *v/r* **~se** come off; **~se de** *fig* part with; **de este estudio se desprende que ...** what emerges from the study is that ...

despreocupación *f* indifference; **despreocuparse** <1a> *v/r* not worry (*de* about)

desprestigio *m* loss of prestige

desprevenido *adj* unprepared; **pillar** *or L.Am.* **agarrar ~** catch unawares

desproporcionado *adj* disproportionate

despropósito *m* stupid thing

desprotegido *adj* unprotected

desprovisto *adj:* **~ de** lacking in

después *adv* (*más tarde*) afterward, later; *seguido en orden* next; *en el espacio* after; **yo voy ~** I'm next; **~ de** after; **~ de todo** after all; **~ de que se vaya** after he's gone

desquiciar <1b> **1** *v/t fig* drive crazy **2** *v/r* **~se** *fig* lose one's mind

desquitarse <1a> *v/r* get one's own back (*de* for)

desrielar <1a> *v/t Chi* derail

destacado *adj* outstanding; **destacar** <1g> **1** *v/i* stand out **2** *v/r* **~se** stand out (*por* because of); (*ser excelente*) be outstanding (*por* because of)

destajo *m:* **a ~** piecework

destapar <1a> **1** *v/t* open, take the lid off; *fig* uncover **2** *v/r* **~se** take one's coat off; *en cama* kick off the bedcovers; *fig* strip (off)

destartalado *adj vehículo, casa*

dilapidated

destello *m de estrella* twinkling; *de faros* gleam; *fig* brief period, moment

destemplarse <1a> *v/r fig* become unwell

desteñir <3h & 3l> **1** *v/t* discolo(u)r, fade **2** *v/r* **~se** fade

desternillante *adj* F hilarious

desterrar <1k> *v/t* exile

destiempo *m*: **a ~** at the wrong moment

destierro *m* exile

destilar <1a> *v/t* distill; *fig* exude

destinar <1a> *v/t fondos* allocate (**para** for); *a persona* post (**a** to); **destino** *m* fate; *de viaje etc* destination; *en el ejército etc* posting

destituir <3g> *v/t* dismiss

destornillador *m* screwdriver; **destornillar** <1a> *v/t* unscrew

destreza *f* skill

destrozar <1f> *v/t* destroy; *emocionalmente* shatter, devastate; **destrozos** *mpl* damage *sg*

destrucción *f* destruction; **destruir** <3g> *v/t* destroy; (*estropear*) ruin, wreck

desunir <3a> *v/t* divide

desuso *m* disuse; **caer en ~** fall into disuse

desvaído *adj color, pintura* faded

desvalido *adj* helpless; **desvalijar** <1a> *v/t* rob; *apartamento* burglarize, burgle

desván *m* attic

desvanecimiento *m* MED fainting fit

desvarío *m* delirium; **~s** ravings

desvelar <1a> **1** *v/t* keep awake; *secreto* reveal **2** *v/r* **~se** stay awake; *fig* do one's best (**por** for); **desvelo** *m* sleeplessness; **~s** efforts

desventaja *f* disadvantage

desventura *f* misfortune

desvergonzado *adj* shameless; **desvergüenza** *f* shamelessness

desvestir <3l> **1** *v/t* undress **2** *v/r* **~se** get undressed, undress

desviar <1c> **1** *v/t golpe* deflect, parry; *tráfico* divert; *río* alter the

course of; **~ la conversación** change the subject; **~ la mirada** look away; **~ a alguien del buen camino** lead s.o. astray **2** *v/r* **~se** (*girar*) turn off; (*bifurcarse*) branch off; (*apartarse*) stray (**de** from)

desvincular <1a> **1** *v/t* dissociate (**de** from) **2** *v/r* **~se** dissociate o.s. (**de** from)

desvío *m* diversion

detallar <1a> *v/t* explain in detail, give details of; COM itemize; **detalle** *m* detail; *fig* thoughtful gesture; **al ~** retail

detección *f* detection; **detectar** <1a> *v/t* detect; **detective** *m/f* detective; **~ privado** private detective; **detector** *m* detector; **~ de mentiras** lie detector

detención *f* detention; **orden de ~** arrest warrant; **detener** <2l> **1** *v/t* stop; *de policía* arrest, detain **2** *v/r* **~se** stop; **detenido 1** *adj* held up; (*minucioso*) detailed **2** *m*, **-a** *f* person under arrest; **detenimiento** *m*: **con ~** thoroughly

detentar <1a> *v/t* hold

detergente *m* detergent

deteriorar <1a> **1** *v/t* damage **2** *v/r* **~se** deteriorate; **deterioro** *m* deterioration

determinado *adj* certain; **determinar** <1a> **1** *v/t* determine **2** *v/r* **~se** decide (**a** to)

detestar <1a> *v/t* detest

detonación *f* detonation; **detonante** *m* explosive; *fig* trigger; **detonar** <1a> **1** *v/i* detonate, go off **2** *v/t* detonate, set off

detractor *m*, **~a** *f* detractor, critic

detrás *adv* behind; **por ~** at the back; *fig* behind your / his etc back; **~ de** behind; **uno ~ de otro** one after the other; **estar ~ de algo** *fig* be behind sth

detrimento *m*: **en ~ de** to the detriment of

detritus *m* detritus

detuvo *vb* → **detener**

deuda *f* debt; **estar en ~ con alguien** *fig* be in s.o.'s debt, be indebted to s.o.; **deudor** *m*, **~a** *f* debtor

devaluación *f* devaluation; **devaluar** <1e> *v/t* devalue

devanarse <1a> *v/r:* **~ los sesos** F rack one's brains F

devaneo *m* affair

devastar <1a> *v/t* devastate

devoción *f tb fig* devotion

devolver <2h; *part* **devuelto**> **1** *v/t* give back, return; *fig:* **visita, saludo** return; F (*vomitar*) throw up F **2** *v/r* **~se** *L.Am.* go back, return

devorar <1a> *v/t* devour

devuelto *part* → **devolver**

D.F. *abr Méx* (= **Distrito Federal**) Mexico City

dg. *abr* (= **decigramo**) decigram

di *vb* → **dar**

día *m* day; **~ de fiesta** holiday; **~ festivo** holiday; **~ hábil** *or* **laborable** work day; **poner al ~** update, bring up to date; **a los pocos ~s** a few days later; **algún ~, un ~** some day, one day; **de ~** by day, during the day; **de un ~ a** *or* **para otro** from one day to the next; **el ~ menos pensado** when you least expect it; **hace mal ~ tiempo** it's a nasty day; **hoy en ~** nowadays; **todo el ~** all day long; **todos los ~s** every day; **un ~ sí y otro no** every other day; **ya es de ~** it's light already; **¡buenos ~s!** good morning

diabetes *f* diabetes; **diabético 1** *adj* diabetic **2** *m*, **-a** *f* diabetic

diablesa *f* F she-devil; **diablo** *m* devil; **un pobre ~** *fig* a poor devil; **mandar a alguien al ~** tell s.o. to go to hell; **diablura** *f* prank, lark; **diabólico** *adj* diabolical

diadema *f* tiara; *para el pelo* hairband

diáfano *adj* clear

diafragma *m* diaphragm

diagnosticar <1g> *v/t* diagnose; **diagnóstico 1** *adj* diagnostic **2** *m* diagnosis

diagonal 1 *adj* diagonal **2** *f* diagonal (line)

diagrama *m* diagram

dialecto *m* dialect

dialogar <1h> *v/i* talk (**sobre** about), discuss (**sobre** sth); (*negociar*) hold talks (**con** with); **diálogo** *m* dialog(ue)

diamante *m* diamond

diametralmente *adv:* **~ opuesto** diametrically opposed; **diámetro** *m* diameter

diana *f* MIL reveille; (*blanco*) target; *para jugar a los dardos* dartboard; (*centro de blanco*) bull's eye; **dar en la ~** *fig* hit the nail on the head

diantre *int* F hell! F

diapositiva *f* FOT slide, transparency

diariero *m*, **-a** *f Arg* newspaper vendor; **diario 1** *adj* daily **2** *m* diary; (*periódico*) newspaper; **a ~** daily

diarrea *f* MED diarr(h)ea

dibujante *m/f* draftsman, *Br* draughtsman; *mujer* draftswoman, *Br* draughtswoman; *de viñetas* cartoonist; **dibujar** <1a> **1** *v/t* draw; *fig* describe **2** *v/r* **~se** *fig* appear; **dibujo** *m arte* drawing; *ilustración* drawing, sketch; *estampado* pattern; **~s animados** cartoons; **película de ~s animados** animation

diccionario *m* dictionary

dic.° *abr* (= **diciembre**) Dec. (= December)

dice *vb* → **decir**

díceres *mpl L.Am.* sayings

dicharachero *adj* chatty; (*gracioso*) witty

dicho 1 *part* → **decir 2** *adj* said; **~ y hecho** no sooner said than done; **mejor ~** or rather **3** *m* saying

dichoso *adj* happy; F (*maldito*) damn F

diciembre *m* December

diciendo *vb* → **decir**

dictado *m* dictation; **dictador** *m*, **~a** *f* dictator; **dictadura** *f* dictatorship

dictaminar <1a> *v/t* state

dictar <1a> *v/t* lección, *texto* dictate; *ley* announce; **~ sentencia** JUR pass sentence

didáctico *adj* educational

diecinueve *adj* nineteen; **dieciocho** *adj* eighteen; **dieciséis** *adj* sixteen;

adj eighteen; **dieciséis** *adj* sixteen; **diecisiete** *adj* seventeen

diente *m* tooth; **~ de ajo** clove of garlic; **~ de león** BOT dandelion; **poner los ~s largos a alguien** make s.o. jealous

diesel *m* diesel

diestro 1 *adj:* **a ~ y siniestro** *fig* F left and right **2** *m* TAUR bullfighter

dieta *f* diet; **estar a ~** be on a diet; **~s** travel(l)ing expenses; **dietético** *adj* dietary

diez *adj* ten

diezmar <1a> *v/t* decimate

difamar <1a> *v/t* slander, defame; **por escrito** libel, defame; **difamatorio** *adj* defamatory

diferencia *f* difference; **a ~ de** unlike; **con ~** *fig* by a long way; **diferenciar** <1b> **1** *v/t* differentiate **2** *v/r* **~se** differ (**de** from); **no se diferencian en nada** there's no difference at all between them; **diferente** *adj* different

diferido *adj* TV: **en ~** prerecorded

difícil *adj* difficult; **dificultad** *f* difficulty; **poner ~es** make it difficult

dificultar <1a> *v/t* hinder

difundir <3a> **1** *v/t* spread; (*programa*) broadcast **2** *v/r* **~se** spread

difunto 1 *adj* late **2** *m*, **-a** *f* deceased

difuso *adj idea, conocimientos* vague, sketchy

digerir <3i> *v/t* digest; F *noticia* take in; **digestión** *f* digestion

digital *adj* digital; **digitalizar** <1f> *v/t* INFOR digitalize; **dígito** *m* digit

dignarse <1a> *v/r* deign; **dignidad** *f* dignity; **digno** *adj* worthy; *trabajo* decent; **~ de mención** worth mentioning

digo *vb* → **decir**

digresión *f* digression

dije *vb* → **decir**

dilación *f:* **sin ~** without delay

dilapidar <1a> *v/t* waste

dilatar <1a> **1** *v/t* dilate; (*prolongar*) prolong; (*aplazar*) postpone **2** *v/i Méx* (*tardar*) be late; **no me dilato** I won't be long

dilema *m* dilemma

diligencia *f* diligence; *vehículo* stagecoach; **~s** JUR procedures, formalities; **diligente** *adj* diligent

dilucidar <1a> *v/t* clarify

diluir <3g> *v/t* dilute

diluviar <1b> *v/i* pour down; **diluvio** *m* downpour; *fig* deluge

dimensión *f* dimension; *fig* size, scale; **dimensiones** measurements

diminutivo *m* diminutive; **diminuto** *adj* tiny, diminutive

dimisión *f* resignation; **dimitir** <3a> *v/i* resign

Dinamarca Denmark

dinámico *adj fig* dynamic

dinamita *f* dynamite

dinastía *f* dynasty

dinero *m* money; **~ en efectivo**, **~ en metálico** cash

dinosaurio *m* dinosaur

dio *vb* → **dar**

Dios *m* God; **hazlo como ~ manda** do it properly; **¡~ mío!** my God!; **¡por ~!** for God's sake!; **sabe ~ lo que dijo** God knows what he said

dios *m tb fig* god; **diosa** *f* goddess

diploma *m* diploma; **diplomacia** *f* diplomacy; **diplomático 1** *adj* diplomatic **2** *m*, **-a** *f* diplomat

diputado *m*, **-a** *f* representative, *Br* Member of Parliament

dique *m* dike, *Br* dyke

dirá *vb* → **decir**

diré *vb* → **decir**

dirección *f tb* TEA, *de película* direction; COM management; POL leadership; *de coche* steering; *en carta* address; **en aquella ~** that way; **~ asistida** AUTO power steering; **~ de correo electrónico** e-mail address; **directiva** *f* board of directors; POL executive committee; **directivo 1** *adj* governing; COM managing **2** *m*, **-a** *f* COM manager; **directo** *adj* direct; **en ~** TV, RAD live; **director 1** *adj* leading **2** *m*, **-a** *f* manager; EDU principal, *Br* head (teacher); TEA, *de película* director; **~ de orquesta** conductor; **directriz** *f* guideline

dirigir <3c> **1** *v/t* TEA, *película* direct;

COM manage, run; MÚS conduct; ~ **una carta a** address a letter to; ~ **una pregunta a** direct a question to 2 v/r ~**se** make, head (**a, hacia** for)

discapacidad f disability; **discapacitado 1** adj disabled 2 m, -a f disabled person

discar <1g> v/t L.Am. TELEC dial

discernir <3i> v/t distinguish, discern

disciplina f discipline; **disciplinar** <1a> v/t discipline; **discípulo** m, -a f REL, fig disciple

disco m disk, Br disc; MÚS record; (discoteca) disco; DEP discus; ~ **compacto** compact disc; ~ **duro**, L.Am. ~ **rígido** INFOR hard disk

discordante adj discordant; **discordia** f discord; (colección de discos) record collection

discreción f discretion; **a** ~ disparar at will; **a** ~ **de** at the discretion of

discrepancia f discrepancy; (desacuerdo) disagreement; **discrepar** <1a> v/i disagree

discreto adj discreet

discriminación f discrimination; **discriminar** <1a> v/t discriminate against; (diferenciar) differentiate

disculpa f apology; **disculpar** <1a> 1 v/t excuse 2 v/r ~**se** apologize

discurrir <3a> v/i de tiempo pass; de acontecimiento pass off; (reflexionar) reflect (**sobre** on); **discurso** m speech; de tiempo passage, passing

discusión f discussion; (disputa) argument; **discutir** <3a> 1 v/t discuss 2 v/i argue (**sobre** about)

diseminar <1a> v/t scatter; fig spread

disentir <3i> v/i disagree (**de** with)

diseñador m, -a f designer; **diseñar** <1a> v/t design; **diseño** m design; ~ **gráfico** graphic design

disfraz m para ocultar disguise; para fiestas costume, fancy dress; **disfrazarse** <1f> v/r para ocultarse disguise o.s. (**de** as); para divertirse dress up (**de** as)

disfrutar <1a> 1 v/t enjoy 2 v/i have fun, enjoy o.s.; ~ **de buena salud** be in o enjoy good health

disgregarse <1h> v/r disintegrate

disgustar <1a> 1 v/t upset 2 v/r ~**se** get upset; **disgusto** m: **me causó un gran** ~ I was very upset; **llevarse un** ~ get upset; **a** ~ unwillingly

disidente m/f dissident

disimular <1a> 1 v/t disguise 2 v/i pretend; **disimulo** m: **con** ~ unobtrusively

disipar <1a> 1 v/t duda dispel 2 v/r ~**se** de niebla clear; de duda vanish

diskette m diskette, floppy (disk)

dislexia f dyslexia

dislocar <1g> v/t dislocate

disminución f decrease; **disminuido 1** adj handicapped 2 m, -a f handicapped person; ~ **físico** physically handicapped person; **disminuir** <3g> 1 v/t gastos, costos reduce, cut; velocidad reduce 2 v/i decrease, diminish

disociar <1b> v/t separate

disolvente m solvent; **disolver** <1h; part **disuelto**> v/t dissolve; manifestación break up

disparada f L.Am.: **a la** ~ in a rush; **disparar** <1a> v/t tiro, arma fire; foto take; precios send up 2 v/i shoot, fire 3 v/r ~**se** de arma, alarma go off; de precios rise dramatically, rocket F

disparatado adj absurd; **disparate** m F piece of nonsense; **es un** ~ **hacer eso** it's crazy to do that

disparo m shot

dispendio m waste

dispensar <1a> v/t dispense; recibimiento give; (eximir) excuse (**de** from); **dispensario** m MED clinic

dispersar <1a> 1 v/t disperse 2 v/r ~**se** disperse; **disperso** adj scattered

displicente adj disdainful

disponer <2r; part **dispuesto**> 1 v/t (arreglar) arrange; (preparar) prepare; (ordenar) stipulate 2 v/i: ~ **de algo** have sth at one's disposal 3 v/r ~**se** get ready (**a** to); **disponibilidad** f COM availability; **disponible** adj available; **disposición** f disposition; *de objetos* arrangement; **~ de ánimo** state of mind; **estar a ~ de alguien** be at s.o.'s disposal

dispositivo *m* device

dispuesto 1 *part* → **disponer 2** *adj* ready (**a** to)

disputa *f* dispute; **disputar** <1a> **1** *v/t* dispute; *partido* play **2** *v/i* argue (**sobre** about) **3** *v/r* **~se** compete for

disquería *f L.Am.* record store

disquete *m* INFOR diskette, floppy (disk); **disquetera** *f* disk drive

distancia *f tb fig* distance; **distanciarse** <1b> *v/r* distance o.s. (**de** from); **distante** *adj tb fig* distant; **distar** <1a> *v/i* be far (**de** from)

distinción *f* distinction; **a ~ de** unlike; **distinguido** *adj* distinguished; **distinguir** <3d> *v/t* distinguish (**de** from); (*divisar*) make out; **con un premio** hono(u)r; **distintivo** *m* emblem; MIL insignia; **distinto** *adj* different; **~s** (*varios*) several

distorsión *f* distortion

distracción *f* distraction; (*descuido*) absent-mindedness; (*diversión*) entertainment; (*pasatiempo*) pastime; **por ~** out of absent-mindedness; **distraer** <2p> *part* **distraído**> **1** *v/t* distract; **la radio la distrae** she enjoys listening to the radio **2** *v/r* **~se** get distracted; (*disfrutar*) enjoy o.s.; **distraído 1** *part* → **distraer 2** *adj* absent-minded; *temporalmente* distracted

distribución *f* COM, *de película* distribution; **distribuir** <3g> *v/t* distribute; *beneficio* share out

distrito *m* district

disturbio *m* disturbance

disuadir <3a> *v/t* dissuade; POL deter; **~ a alguien de hacer algo** dissuade s.o. from doing sth

disuelto *part* → **disolver**

disyuntiva *f* dilemma

diurético *adj* diuretic

diurno *adj* day *atr*

divagar <1h> *v/i* digress

diván *m* couch

diversidad *f* diversity

diversión *f* fun; (*pasatiempo*) pastime; **aquí no hay muchas diversiones** there's not much to do around here; **diverso** *adj* diverse; **~s** several, various

divertido *adj* funny; (*entretenido*) entertaining; **divertir** <3i> **1** *v/t* entertain **2** *v/r* **~se** have fun, enjoy o.s.

dividendo *m* dividend; **dividir** <3a> *v/t* divide

divinamente *adv fig* wonderfully; **divinidad** *f* divinity; **divino** *adj tb fig* divine

divisa *f* currency; **~s** *pl* foreign currency *sg*

divisar <1a> *v/t* make out

división *f* MAT, DEP division; **hubo ~ de opiniones** there were differences of opinion

divorciado 1 *adj* divorced **2** *m*, **-a** *f* divorcee; **divorciarse** <1b> *v/r* get divorced; **divorcio** *m* divorce

divulgación *f* spread; **divulgar** <1h> **1** *v/t* spread **2** *v/r* **~se** spread

d.J.C. *abr* (= **después de Jesucristo**) A.D. (= Anno Domini)

dl. *abr* (= **decilitro**) deciliter

dm. *abr* (= **decímetro**) decimeter

dobladillo *m* hem; **doblado** *adj* *película* dubbed; **doblaje** *m de película* dubbing; **doblar** <1a> **1** *v/t* fold; *cantidad* double; *película* dub; MAR round; *pierna, brazo* bend; *en una carrera* pass, *Br* overtake; **~ la esquina** go round *o* turn the corner **2** *v/i* turn; **~ a la derecha** turn right **3** *v/r* **~se** bend; *fig* give in; **doble 1** *adj* double; *nacionalidad* dual; **~ clic** *m* double click **2** *m*: **el ~** twice as much (**de** as); **el ~ de gente** twice as many people; **~s** *tenis* doubles **3** *m/f en película* double

doblegar <1h> *v/t fig*: *voluntad* break; *orgullo* humble

doblez 1 *m* fold **2** *f fig* deceit

doce *adj* twelve; **docena** *f* dozen

docente *adj* teaching *atr*

dócil *adj* docile

doctor *m*, **~a** *f* doctor; **~ honoris**

causa honorary doctor; **doctora-do** *m* doctorate

doctrina *f* doctrine

documentación *f* documentation; *de una persona* papers; **documental** *m* documentary; **documento** *m* document; ~ *nacional de identidad* national identity card

dogma *m* dogma

dogo *m* ZO mastiff

dólar *m* dollar

dolencia *f* ailment; **doler** <2h> *v/t tb* *fig* hurt; *me duele el brazo* my arm hurts; *le dolió que le mintieran fig* she was hurt that they had lied to her

dolor *m tb fig* pain; ~ *de cabeza* headache; ~ *de estómago* stomach-ache; ~ *de muelas* toothache; **dolorido** *adj* sore, aching; *fig* hurt; **doloroso** *adj tb fig* painful

domador *m*, ~a *f* tamer

domesticar <1g> *v/t* domesticate; **doméstico 1** *adj* domestic, household *atr* **2** *m*, ~a *f* servant

domiciliación *f* *de sueldo* credit transfer; *de pagos* direct billing, *Br* direct debit; *repartir a* ~ do home deliveries

dominante *adj* dominant; *desp* domineering; **dominar** <1a> *v/t* dominate; *idioma* have a good command of **2** *v/i* dominate **3** *v/r* ~*se* control o.s.

domingo *m* Sunday; ~ *de Ramos* Palm Sunday; **dominguero** *m*, -a *f* F weekender, Sunday tripper; **dominical** *adj* Sunday *atr*

dominicano GEOG **1** *adj* Dominican **2** *m*, -a *f* Dominican

dominio *m* control; *fig* command; *ser del* ~ *público* be in the public domain

dominó *m* dominoes *pl*

don[1] *m* gift; ~ *de gentes* way with people

don[2] *m* Mr; ~ *Enrique* Mr Sanchez *English uses the surname while Spanish uses the first name*

donación *f* donation; ~ *de sangre* blood donation; ~ *de órganos* organ donation; **donante** *m/f* donor; ~ *de sangre* blood donor; **donar** <1a> *v/t sangre, órgano, dinero* donate; **donativo** *m* donation

doncella *f* maid

donde 1 *adv* where **2** *prp esp L.Am.:* *fui* ~ *el médico* I went to the doctor's

dónde *interr* where; *¿de* ~ *eres?* where are you from?; *¿hacia* ~ *vas?* where are you going?

dondequiera *adv* wherever

doña *f* Mrs; ~ *Estela* Mrs Sanchez *English uses the surname while Spanish uses the first name*

dopaje, doping *m* doping

dorada *f* ZO gilthead

dorado *adj* gold; *montura* gilt

dormido *adj* asleep; *quedarse* ~ fall asleep; **dormir** <3k> **1** *v/i* sleep; *(estar dormido)* be asleep **2** *v/t* put to sleep; ~ *a alguien* MED give s.o. a general an(a)esthetic **3** *v/r* ~*se* go to sleep; *(quedarse dormido)* fall asleep; *(no despertarse)* oversleep; *no podía dormirme* I couldn't get to sleep; **dormitorio** *m* bedroom

dorso *m* back

dos *adj* two; *de* ~ *en* ~ in twos; *los* ~ both; *anda con ojo con los* ~ watch out for the pair of them; *cada* ~ *por tres* all the time, continually

doscientos *adj* two hundred

dosificar <1g> *v/t* cut down on; **dosis** *f inv* dose

dotar <1a> *v/t* equip (*de* with); *fondos* provide (*de* with); *cualidades* endow (*de* with); **dote** *f a novia* dowry; *tener* ~*s para algo* have a gift for sth

doy *vb* → *dar*

dpto. *abr* (= *departamento*) dept (= department)

Dr. *abr* (= *Doctor*) Dr (= Doctor)

Dra. *abr* (= *Doctora*) Dr (= Doctor)

dragar <1h> *v/t* dredge

dragón *m* dragon; MIL dragoon

drama *m* drama; **dramático** *adj* dramatic; *arte* ~ dramatic art;

dramatizar <1f> v/t dramatize
drástico adj drastic
drenaje m drainage
droga f drug; **~ de diseño** designer drug; **drogadicto 1** adj: **una mujer -a** a woman addicted to drugs **2** m, **-a** f drug addict; **drogarse** <1h> v/r take drugs; **drogodependencia** f drug dependency; **droguería** f store selling cleaning and household products
dromedario m ZO dromedary
d.to abr (= **descuento**) discount
ducha f shower; **ser una ~ de agua fría** fig come as a shock; **ducharse** <1a> v/r have a shower, shower
duda f doubt; **sin ~** without doubt; **poner en ~** call into question; **dudar** <1a> **1** v/t doubt **2** v/i hesitate (**en** to); **dudoso** adj doubtful; (indeciso) hesitant
duele vb → **doler**
duelo m grief; (combate) duel
duende m imp
dueño m, **-a** f owner
duermo vb → **dormir**
dulce 1 adj sweet; fig gentle **2** m candy, Br sweet; **dulzura** f tb fig sweetness

dumping m dumping
duna f dune
duo m MÚS duo
duodécimo adj twelfth
dúplex m duplex (apartment)
duplicado 1 adj duplicate; **por ~** in duplicate **2** m duplicate; **duplicar** <1g> v/t duplicate
duque m duke; **duquesa** f duchess
duración f duration; **duradero** adj lasting; ropa, calzado hard-wearing
durante prp indicando duración during; indicando período for; **~ seis meses** for six months
durar <1a> v/i last
duraznero m L.Am. BOT peach (tree); **durazno** m L.Am. BOT peach
Durex® m Méx Scotch tape®, Br Sellotape®
duro 1 adj hard; carne tough; clima, fig harsh; **~ de oído** F hard of hearing; **ser ~ de pelar** be a tough nut to crack **2** adv hard **3** m five peseta coin
DVD abr (= **Disco de Vídeo Digital**) DVD (= Digital Versatile o Video Disc)

E

E abr (= **este**) E (= East(ern))
e conj (instead of **y** before words starting with **i, hi**) and
ebanista m cabinetmaker; **ébano** m ebony
ebrio adj drunk
ebullición f: **punto de ~** boiling point
eccema m eczema
echar <1a> **1** v/t (lanzar) throw; (poner) put; de un lugar throw out; humo give off; carta mail, Br tb post; **lo han echado del trabajo** he's been fired; **~ abajo** pull down, destroy; **~ la culpa a alguien** blame s.o., put the blame on s.o.; **me echó 40 años** he thought I was 40 **2** v/i: **~ a** start to, begin to; **~ a correr** start o begin to run, start running **3** v/r **~se** (tirarse) throw o.s.; (tumbarse) lie down; (ponerse) put on; **~se a llorar** start o begin to cry, start crying
eclesiástico adj ecclesiastical, church atr
eclipsar <1a> v/t eclipse; **eclipse** m eclipse

eco *m* echo; **tener ~** *fig* make an impact

ecografía *f* (ultrasound) scan

ecología *f* ecology; **ecológico** *adj* ecological; *alimentos* organic; **ecologista** *m/f* ecologist

economato *m* co-operative store

economía *f* economy; *ciencia* economics; **~ de mercado** market economy; **~ sumergida** black economy; **económico** *adj* economic; (*barato*) economical; **economista** *m/f* economist; **economizar** <1f> *v/t* economize on, save

ecosistema *m* ecosystem

ecoturismo *m* ecotourism

ecuación *f* equation

ecuador *m* equator

Ecuador *m* Ecuador

ecuánime *adj* (*sereno*) even-tempered; (*imparcial*) impartial

ecuatorial *adj* equatorial

ecuatoriano **1** *adj* Ecuadorean **2** *m*, **-a** *f* Ecuadorean

eczema *m* eczema

ed. *abr* (= **edición**) ed (= edition)

edad *f* age; **la Edad Media** the Middle Ages *pl*; **la tercera ~** the over 60s; **estar en la ~ del pavo** be at that awkward age; **a la ~ de** at the age of; **¿qué ~ tienes?** how old are you?

edición *f* edition

edificar <1g> *v/t* construct, build; **edificio** *m* building

edil *m*, **-a** *f* council(l)or

editar <1a> *v/t* edit; (*publicar*) publish; **editor** *m*, **~a** *f* editor; **editorial 1** *m* editorial, leading article **2** *f* publishing company *o* house, publisher

edredón *m* eiderdown

educación *f* (*crianza*) upbringing; (*modales*) manners; **~ física** physical education, PE; **educado** *adj* polite, well-mannered; **mal ~** rude, ill-mannered; **educar** <1g> *v/t* educate; (*criar*) bring up; *voz* train; **educativo** *adj* educational

edulcorante *m* sweetener

EE. UU. *abr* (= **Estados Unidos**) US(A) (= United States (of America))

efectista *adj* theatrical, dramatic; **efectivamente** *adv* indeed; **efectivo 1** *adj* effective; **hacer ~** COM cash **2** *m*: **en ~** (in) cash; **efecto** *m* effect; **~ invernadero** greenhouse effect; **~s secundarios** side effects; **en ~** indeed; **surtir ~** take effect, work

efectuar <1e> *v/t* carry out

efervescente *adj* effervescent; *bebida* carbonated, sparkling

eficacia *f* efficiency; **eficaz** *adj* (*efectivo*) effective; (*eficiente*) efficient; **eficiencia** *f* efficiency; **eficiente** *adj* efficient

efímero *adj* ephemeral, short-lived

efusivo *adj* effusive

egipcio **1** *adj* Egyptian **2** *m*, **-a** *f* Egyptian; **Egipto** Egypt

ego *m* ego; **egocéntrico** *adj* egocentric, self-centered (*Br* -centred); **egoísmo** *m* selfishness, egoism; **egoísta 1** *adj* selfish, egoistic **2** *m/f* egoist

egresar <1a> *v/i* L.Am. *de universidad* graduate; *de colegio* graduate from high school, *Br* leave school; **egreso** *m* L.Am. graduation

eh *int para llamar atención* hey!; **¿~?** eh?

eje *m* axis; *de auto* axle; *fig* linchpin

ejecución *f* (*realización*) implementation, carrying out; *de condenado* execution; MÚS performance; **ejecutar** <1a> *v/t* (*realizar*) carry out, implement; *condenado* execute; INFOR run, execute; MÚS play, perform; **ejecutiva** *f* executive; **ejecutivo 1** *adj* executive; **el poder ~** POL the executive **2** *m* executive; **el Ejecutivo** the government

ejemplar **1** *adj* *alumno, padre etc* model *atr*, exemplary **2** *m* *de libro* copy; *de revista* issue; *animal, planta* specimen; **ejemplo** *m* example; **dar buen ~** set a good example; **por ~** for example

ejercer <2b> **1** *v/t cargo* practice, *Br* practise; *influencia* exert **2** *v/i* de *profesional* practice, *Br* practise; **ejerce de médico** he's a practicing (*Br* practising) doctor; **ejercicio** *m* exercise; COM fiscal year, *Br* financial year; **hacer ~** exercise; **ejercitar** <1a> **1** *v/t músculo, derecho* exercise **2** *v/r* **~se** train; **~se en** practice, *Br* practise; **ejército** *m* army

ejido *m Méx* traditional rural communal farming unit

ejote *m L.Am.* green bean

el 1 *art* the **2** *pron:* **~ de ...** that of ...; **~ de Juan** Juan's; **~ más grande** the biggest (one); **~ que está ...** the one who is ...

él *pron sujeto* he; *cosa* it; *complemento* him; *cosa* it; **de ~** his

elaborar <1a> *v/t* produce, make; *metal etc* work; *plan* devise, draw up

elasticidad *f* elasticity; **elástico 1** *adj* elastic **2** *m* elastic; (*goma*) elastic band, *Br* rubber band

elección *f* choice; **eleccionario** *adj L.Am.* election atr, electoral; **elecciones** *fpl* election *sg*; **elector** *m* voter; **electorado** *m* electorate; **electoral** *adj* election atr, electoral

electricidad *f* electricity; **electricista** *m/f* electrician; **eléctrico** *adj luz, motor* electric; *aparato* electrical; **electrocutar** <1a> **1** *v/t* electrocute **2** *v/r* **~se** be electrocuted, electrocute o.s.

electrodo *m* electrode

electrodoméstico *m* electrical appliance

electrón *m* electron; **electrónica** *f* electronics; **electrónico** *adj* electronic

elefante *m* ZO elephant; **~ marino** elephant seal, sea elephant

elegancia *f* elegance, stylishness; **elegante** *adj* elegant, stylish; **elegantoso** *adj L.Am.* F stylish, classy

elegía *f* elegy

elegible *adj* eligible; **elegir** <3c & 3l> *v/t* choose; *por votación* elect

elemental *adj* (*esencial*) fundamental, essential; (*básico*) elementary,

basic; **elemento** *m* element

elevado *adj* high; *fig* elevated; **elevador** *m* hoist; *L.Am.* elevator, *Br* lift; **elevar** <1a> **1** *v/t* raise **2** *v/r* **~se** rise; *de monumento* stand

eliminación *f* elimination; *de desperdicios* disposal; **eliminar** <1a> *v/t* eliminate; *desperdicios* dispose of; **eliminatoria** *f* DEP qualifying round, heat

élite *f* elite; **elitista** *adj* elitist

elixir *m* elixir; **~ bucal** mouthwash

ella *pron sujeto* she; *cosa* it; *complemento* her; *cosa* it; **de ~** her; **es de ~** it's hers

ellas *pron sujeto* they; *complemento* them; **de ~** their; **es de ~** it's theirs

ello *pron* it

ellos *pron sujeto* they; *complemento* them; **de ~** their; **es de ~** it's theirs

elocuente *adj* eloquent

elogiar <1b> *v/t* praise; **elogio** *m* praise

elote *m L.Am.* corncob; *granos* corn, *Br* sweetcorn

El Salvador El Salvador

eludir <3a> *v/t* evade, avoid

emanar <1a> **1** *v/i fml* emanate (**de** from); *fml; fig* stem (**de** from), derive (**de** from) **2** *v/t* exude, emit

emancipación *f* emancipation; **emanciparse** <1a> *v/r* become emancipated

embadurnar <1a> *v/t* smear (**de** with)

embajada *f* embassy; **embajador** *m*, **~a** *f* ambassador

embalaje *m* packing; **embalar** <1a> **1** *v/t* pack **2** *v/r* **~se** *de persona* get excited; **el coche se embaló** the car went faster and faster; **no te embales** don't go so fast

embalse *m* reservoir

embarazada 1 *adj* pregnant **2** *f* pregnant woman; **embarazo** *m* pregnancy; **interrupción del ~** termination, abortion; **embarazoso** *adj* awkward, embarrassing

embarcación *f* vessel, craft; **embarcadero** *m* wharf; **embarcar** <1g> **1** *v/t pasajeros* board, embark; *mer-*

cancías load **2** *v/i* board, embark **3** *v/r* **~se** *en barco* board, embark; *en avión* board; **~se en** *fig* embark on

embargo *m* embargo; JUR seizure; **sin ~** however

embarque *m* boarding; *de mercancías* loading

embarrancar <1g> **1** *v/i* MAR run aground **2** *v/r* **~se** MAR run aground

embaucador 1 *adj* deceitful **2** *m*, **~a** *f* trickster

embeberse <2a> *v/r* get absorbed *o* engrossed (*en* in)

embelesar <1a> *v/t* captivate

embestir <3l> **1** *v/t* charge **2** *v/i* charge (*contra* at)

emblema *m* emblem

embobar <1a> *v/t* fascinate

embolarse <1a> *v/r* C.Am., Méx F get plastered F

émbolo *m* TÉC piston

embolsar <1a> **1** *v/t* pocket **2** *v/r* **~se** pocket

emborrachar <1a> **1** *v/t* make drunk, get drunk **2** *v/r* **~se** get drunk

emborronar <1a> *v/t* blot, smudge

emboscada *f* ambush

embotar <1a> *v/t* blunt

embotellamiento *m* traffic jam; **embotellar** <1a> *v/t* bottle

embrague *m* AUTO clutch

embriagar <1h> *v/t fig* intoxicate; **embriaguez** *f* intoxication

embrión *m* embryo; **en ~** in an embryonic state, in embryo

embrollo *m* tangle; *fig* mess, muddle

embromar <1a> *v/t Rpl* F (*molestar*) annoy

embrujar <1a> *v/t tb fig* bewitch

embrutecer <2d> **1** *v/t* brutalize **2** *v/r* **~se** become brutalized

embudo *m* funnel

embustero 1 *adj* deceitful **2** *m*, **-a** *f* liar

embutido *m* GASTR *type of dried sausage*

emergencia *f* emergency

emerger <2c> *v/i* emerge

emigración *f* emigration; **emigrante** *m* emigrant; **emigrar** <1a> *v/i* emigrate; ZO migrate

eminente *adj* eminent

emirato *m* emirate

emisario *m* emissary; **emisión** *f* emission; COM issue; RAD, TV broadcast; **emisora** *f* radio station; **emitir** <3a> *v/t calor, sonido* give out, emit; *moneda* issue; *opinión* express, give; *veredicto* deliver; RAD, TV broadcast; *voto* cast

emoción *f* emotion; **¡qué ~!** how exciting!; **emocionado** *adj* excited; **emocionante** *adj* (*excitante*) exciting; (*conmovedor*) moving; **emocionarse** <1a> *v/r* get excited; (*conmoverse*) be moved

emotivo *adj* emotional; (*conmovedor*) moving

empacar <1g> **1** *v/t* & *v/i* L.Am. pack **2** *v/r* **~se** L.Am. (*ponerse tozudo*) dig one's heels in; *tragar* devour

empacharse <1a> *v/r* F get an upset stomach (*de* from); **~ de** *fig* overdose on; **empacho** *m* F upset stomach; *fig* bellyful F; **sin ~** unashamedly

empadronar <1a> **1** *v/t* register **2** *v/r* **~se** register

empalagoso *adj* sickly; *fig* sickly sweet, cloying

empalizada *f* palisade

empalmar <1a> **1** *v/t* connect, join **2** *v/i* connect (*con* with), join up (*con* with); *de idea, conversación* run *o* follow on (*con* from)

empanada *f* pie; **empanadilla** *f* pasty; **empanar** <1a> *v/t* coat in breadcrumbs

empantanarse <1a> *v/r* become swamped *o* waterlogged; *fig* get bogged down

empañado *adj* misty; **empañar** <1a> **1** *v/t* steam up, mist up; *fig* tarnish, sully **2** *v/r* **~se** *de vidrio* steam up, mist up

empapado *adj* soaked, dripping wet; **empapar** <1a> **1** *v/t* soak; (*absorber*) soak up; **2** *v/r* **~se** get soaked *o* drenched; **~se de algo** immerse o.s. in sth

empapelar <1a> *v/t* wallpaper

empaque *m* presence; (*seriedad*) solemnity; **empaquetar** <1a> *v/t* pack

emparedado *m* sandwich

emparejar <1a> *v/t personas* pair off; *calcetines* match up

emparentado *adj* related

empastador *m*, **~a** *f L.Am.* bookbinder; **empastar** <1a> *v/t muela* fill; *libro* bind; **empaste** *m* filling

empatar <1a> *v/i* tie, *Br* draw; (*igualar*) tie the game, *Br* equalize; **empate** *m* tie, draw; **gol del ~** *en fútbol* equalizer

empecinarse <1a> *v/r* get an idea into one's head; **~ en algo** insist on sth

empedernido *adj* inveterate, confirmed

empedrado *m* paving

empeine *m* instep

empellón *m* shove; **entró a empellones** he shoved his way in

empelotarse <1a> *v/r L.Am.* P one's clothes off, strip off

empeñado *adj* (*endeudado*) in debt; **estar ~ en hacer algo** be determined to do sth; **empeñar** <1a> **1** *v/t* pawn **2** *v/r* **~se** (*endeudarse*) get into debt; (*esforzarse*) strive (**en** to), make an effort (**en** to); **~se en hacer** *obstinarse* insist on doing, be determined to do

empeñero *Méx* **1** *adj* determined **2** *m*, **~a** *f* determined person; **empeño** *m* (*obstinación*) determination; (*esfuerzo*) effort; *Méx fig* pawn shop; **empeñoso** *adj L.Am.* hardworking

empeorar <1a> **1** *v/t* make worse **2** *v/i* deteriorate, get worse

empequeñecer <2d> *v/t fig* diminish

emperador *m* emperor; *pez* swordfish; **emperatriz** *f* empress

emperrarse <1a> *v/r* F: **~ en hacer algo** have one's heart set on doing sth; **~ con algo** set one's heart on sth

empezar <1f & 1k> **1** *v/t* start, begin **2** *v/i* start, begin; **~ a hacer algo** start to do sth, start doing sth; **~ por hacer algo** start *o* begin by doing sth; **empiezo** *m S.Am.* start, beginning

empinado *adj* steep; **empinar** <1a> *v/t* raise; **~ el codo** F raise one's elbow F

empírico *adj* empirical

emplazamiento *m* site, location; *JUR* subpœna, summons

empleado **1** *adj*: **le está bien ~** it serves him right **2** *m*, **~a** *f* employee; **~a de hogar** maid; **emplear** <1a> *v/t* (*usar*) use; *persona* employ; **empleo** *m* employment; (*puesto*) job; (*uso*) use; **modo de ~** instructions for use *pl*, directions *pl*

emplomar <1a> *v/t S.Am.* fill

empobrecer <2d> **1** *v/t* impoverish, make poor **2** *v/i* become impoverished, become poor **3** *v/r* **~se** become impoverished, become poor; **empobrecimiento** *m* impoverishment

empollar <1a> *v/i* F cram F, *Br* swot F; **empollón** *m* F grind F, *Br* swot F

emporio *m L.Am. almacén* department store

empotrado *adj* built-in, fitted; **empotrarse** <1a> *v/r* crash (**contra** into)

emprendedor *adj* enterprising; **emprender** <2a> *v/t* embark on, undertake; **~la con alguien** F take it out on s.o.

empresa *f* company; *fig* venture, undertaking; **~ de trabajo temporal** temping agency; **empresaria** *f* businesswoman; **empresarial** *adj* business *atr*; **ciencias ~es** business studies; **empresario** *m* businessman

empujar <1a> *v/t* push; *fig* urge on, spur on; **empujón** *m* push, shove; **salían a empujones** F they were pushing and shoving their way out

empuñar <1a> *v/t* grasp

emular <1a> *v/t* emulate

emulsión *f* emulsion

en *prp* (*dentro de*) in; (*sobre*) on; **~ un mes** in a month; **~ la mesa** on the table; **~ inglés** in English; **~ la calle** on the street, *Br tb* in the street; **~ casa** at home; **~ coche/tren** by car/train

enajenación *f* JUR transfer; **~ mental** insanity; **enajenar** <1a> *v/t* JUR transfer; (*trastornar*) drive insane

enamorado *adj* in love (**de** with); **enamorar** <1a> *v/t*: **lo enamoró** she captivated him **2** *v/r* **~se** fall in love (**de** with)

enano 1 *adj* tiny; *perro, árbol, árbol* miniature, dwarf *atr* **2** *m* dwarf; **trabajar como un ~** *fig* F work like a dog F

enarbolar <1a> *v/t* hoist, raise

encabezamiento *m* heading; **encabezar** <1f> *v/t* head; *movimiento, revolución* lead

encabritarse <1a> *v/r de caballo* rear up

encadenar <1a> **1** *v/t* chain (up); *fig* link *o* put together **2** *v/r* **~se** chain oneself (**a** to)

encajar <1a> **1** *v/t piezas* fit; *golpe* take <1a> *v/i* fit (**en** in; **con** with); **encaje** *m* lace

encalado *m* whitewashing; **encalar** <1a> *v/t* whitewash

encallar <1a> *v/i* MAR run aground

encaminarse <1a> *v/r* set off (**a** for), head (**a** for); *fig* be aimed *o* directed (**a** at)

encandilar <1a> *v/t* dazzle

encantado *adj* (*contento*) delighted; *castillo* enchanted; **¡~!** nice to meet you; **encantador** *adj* charming; **encantar** <1a> *v/t*: **me/le encanta** I love/he loves it; **encanto** *m* (*atractivo*) charm; **como por ~** as if by magic; **eres un ~** you're an angel

encapricharse <1a> *v/r* fall in love (**de** with)

encapuchado *adj* hooded

encaramarse <1a> *v/r* climb

encarar <1a> *v/t* approach; *desgracia etc* face up to

encarcelar <1a> *v/t* put in prison, imprison

encarecer <2d> **1** *v/t* put up the price of, make more expensive **2** *v/r* **~se** become more expensive; *de*

precios increase, rise; **encarecidamente** *adv*: **le ruego ~ que ...** I beg *o* urge you to ...

encargado *m*, **-a** *f* person in charge; *de un negocio* manager; **encargar** <1h> **1** *v/t* (*pedir*) order; **le encargué que me trajera ...** I asked him to bring me ... **2** *v/r* **~se** (*tener responsabilidad*) be in charge; **yo me encargo de la comida** I'll take care of *o* see to the food; **encargo** *m* job, errand; COM order; **¿te puedo hacer un ~?** can I ask you to do something for me?; **hecho por ~** made to order

encariñarse <1a> *v/r*: **~ con alguien/algo** grow fond of s.o/sth, become attached to s.o/sth

encarnado *adj* red; **encarnar** <1a> *v/t cualidad etc* embody; TEA play; **encarnizado** *adj* bitter, fierce

encarrilar <1a> *v/t fig* direct, guide

encasillar <1a> *v/t* class, classify; (*estereotipar*) pigeonhole

encasquetar <1a> *v/t gorro etc* pull down; **me lo encasquetó** F he landed me with it F

encasquillarse <1a> *v/r de arma* jam

encauzar <1f> *v/t tb fig* channel

encefalopatía *f*: **~ espongiforme bovina** bovine spongiform encephalitis, BSE

encendedor *m* lighter; **encender** <2g> **1** *v/t fuego* light; *luz, televisión* switch on, turn on; *fig* inflame, arouse, stir up **2** *v/r* **~se de luz, televisión** come on; **encendido 1** *adj luz, televisión* (switched) on; *fuego* lit; *cara* red **2** *m* AUTO ignition

encerado *m* blackboard

encerar <1a> *v/t* polish, wax

encerrar <1k> **1** *v/t* lock up, shut up; (*contener*) contain **2** *v/r* **~se** shut o.s. up; **encerrona** *f tb fig* trap

encestar <1a> *v/i* score

encharcado *adj* flooded, waterlogged

enchicharse <1a> *v/r L.Am.* (*emborracharse*) get drunk; *Rpl* P (*enojarse*) get angry, get mad F

enchilada f *Méx* GASTR enchilada (*tortilla with a meat or cheese filling*)

enchiloso adj *C.Am.*, *Méx* hot

enchufado m: **es un ~** F he has connections, he has friends in high places; **enchufar** <1a> v/t EL plug in; **enchufe** m EL *macho* plug; *hembra* socket; **tener ~** fig F have pull F, have connections F; **enchufismo** m string-pulling

encía f gum

enciclopedia f encyclop(a)edia

encierro m *protesta* sit-in; *de toros* bull running

encima adv on top; **~ de** on top of, on; **por ~ de** over, above; **por ~ de todo** above all; **lo ayudo, y ~ se queja** I help him and then he goes and complains; **hacer algo muy por ~** do sth very quickly; **no lo llevo ~** I haven't got it on me; **ponerse algo ~** put sth on; **encimera** f *sábana* top sheet; *Esp mostrador* worktop

encina f BOT holm oak

encinta adj pregnant

enclaustrarse <1a> v/r fig shut o.s. away

enclave m enclave

enclenque 1 adj sickly, weak **2** m/f weakling

encoger <2c> **1** v/t shrink; *las piernas* tuck in **2** v/i *de material* shrink **3** v/r **~se** *de material* shrink; fig: *de persona* be intimidated, cower; **~se de hombros** shrug (one's shoulders)

encolar <1a> v/t glue, stick

encolerizarse <1f> v/r get angry

encomienda f *L.Am.* HIST grant of land and labor by colonial authorities after the Conquest

enconado adj fierce, heated

encontrar <1m> **1** v/t find **2** v/r **~se** (*reunirse*) meet; (*estar*) be; **~se con alguien** meet s.o., run into s.o.; **me encuentro bien** I'm fine, I feel fine; **encontronazo** m smash, crash

encorvar <1a> v/t hunch; *estantería* cause to buckle

encrespar <1a> **1** v/t *pelo* curl; *mar* make rough o choppy; fig arouse, inflame **2** v/r **~se** *del mar* turn choppy; fig become inflamed

encrucijada f crossroads; fig dilemma

encuadernar <1a> v/t bind

encuadrar <1a> v/t *en marco* frame; *en grupo* include, place

encuartelar <1a> v/t *L.Am.* billet

encubierto part → **encubrir**; **encubrir** <3a; part **encubierto**> v/t *delincuente* harbo(u)r; *delito* cover up, conceal

encuentro m meeting, encounter; DEP game; **salir** o **ir al ~ de alguien** meet s.o., greet s.o.

encuerado adj *L.Am.* naked

encuesta f survey; (*sondeo*) (opinion) poll; **encuestar** <1a> v/t poll

encumbrarse <1a> v/r fig rise to the top

encurtidos mpl pickles

ende adv: **por ~** therefore, consequently

endeble adj weak, feeble

endémico adj endemic

endemoniado adj possessed; fig F terrible, awful

enderezar <1f> **1** v/t straighten out **2** v/r **~se** straighten up, stand up straight; fig straighten o.s. out, sort o.s out

endeudarse <1a> v/r get (o.s.) into debt

endiablado adj fig (*malo*) terrible, awful; (*difícil*) tough

endibia f BOT endive

endilgar <1h> v/t: **me lo endilgó a mí** F he landed me with it F; **~ un sermón a alguien** F lecture s.o., give s.o. a lecture

endosar <1a> v/t COM endorse; **me lo endosó a mí** F she landed me with it F

endrina f BOT sloe

endrogarse <1h> v/r *Méx*, *C.Am.* get into debt

endulzar <1f> v/t sweeten; (*suavizar*) soften

endurecer <2d> **1** v/t harden; fig toughen up **2** v/r **~se** harden, become harder; *fig* become harder, toughen up

enebro *m* BOT juniper

enema *m* MED enema

enemigo 1 *adj* enemy *atr* **2** *m* enemy; **ser ~ de** *fig* be opposed to, be against; **enemistarse** <1a> *v/r* fall out

energético *adj crisis* energy *atr*; *alimento* energy-giving; **energía** *f* energy; **~ eólica** wind power; **~ nuclear** nuclear power, nuclear energy; **~ solar** solar power, solar energy; **enérgico** *adj* energetic; *fig* forceful, strong

energúmeno *m* lunatic; **ponerse hecho un ~** go crazy F, blow a fuse F

ene. *abr* (= *enero*) Jan. (= January)

enero *m* January

enervar <1a> *v/t* irritate, get on the nerves of

enésimo *adj* nth; **por -a vez** for the umpteenth time

enfadado *adj* annoyed (**con** with); (*encolerizado*) angry (**con** with); **enfadar** <1a> **1** *v/t* (*molestar*) annoy; (*encolerizar*) make angry, anger **2** *v/r* **~se** (*molestarse*) get annoyed (**con** with); (*encolerizarse*) get angry (**con** with); **enfado** *m* (*molestia*) annoyance; (*cólera*) anger

enfangarse <1h> *v/r* get muddy; **~ en** *fig* get (o.s.) mixed up in

énfasis *m* emphasis; **poner ~ en** emphasize, stress; **enfático** *adj* emphatic

enfermar <1a> **1** *v/t* drive crazy **2** *v/i* get sick, *Br tb* get ill; **enfermedad** *f* illness, disease; **enfermería** *f sala* infirmary, sickbay; *carrera* nursing; **enfermero** *m*, **-a** *f* nurse; **enfermizo** *adj* unhealthy; **enfermo 1** *adj* sick, ill **2** *m*, **-a** *f* sick person; **enfermoso** *adj L.Am.* sickly, unhealthy

enfiestarse <1a> *v/r L.Am.* F party F, live it up F

enfocar <1g> *v/t cámara* focus; *imagen* get in focus; *fig: asunto* look at, consider

enfoque *m fig* approach

enfrentamiento *m* clash, confrontation; **enfrentar** <1a> **1** *v/t* confront, face up to **2** *v/r* **~se** DEP meet; **~se con alguien** confront s.o.; **~se a algo** face (up to) sth

enfrente *adv* opposite; **~ del colegio** opposite the school, across (the street) from the school

enfriar <1c> **1** *v/t vino* chill; *algo caliente* cool (down); *fig* cool **2** *v/r* **~se** (*perder calor*) cool down; (*perder demasiado calor*) get cold, go cold; *fig* cool, cool off; MED catch a cold, catch a chill

enfurecer <2d> **1** *v/t* infuriate, make furious **2** *v/r* **~se** get furious, get into a rage **enfurecido** *adj* furious, enraged

enfurruñado *adj* F sulky; **enfurruñarse** <1a> *v/r* F go into a huff F

engalanar <1a> *v/t* decorate, deck

enganchar <1a> **1** *v/t* hook; F *novia, trabajo* land F **2** *v/r* **~se** get caught (**en** on); MIL sign up, enlist; **~se a la droga** F get hooked on drugs F

engañar <1a> **1** *v/t* deceive, cheat; (*ser infiel a*) cheat on, be unfaithful to; **te han engañado** you've been had **2** *v/r* **~se** (*mentirse*) deceive o.s., kid o.s. F; (*equivocarse*) be wrong; **engaño** *m* (*mentira*) deception, deceit; (*ardid*) trick

engarzar <1f> *v/t joya* set

engatusar <1a> *v/t* F sweet-talk

engendrar <1a> *v/t* father; *fig* breed, engender *fml*; **engendro** *m fig* eyesore

englobar <1a> *v/t* include, embrace *fml*

engordar <1a> **1** *v/t* put on, gain **2** *v/i de persona* put on weight, gain weight; *de comida* be fattening

engorrar <1a> *v/t Méx, W.I.* F annoy

engorroso *adj* tricky

engranaje *m* TÉC gears *pl*; *fig* machinery

engrasar <1a> *v/t* grease, lubricate; **engrase** *m* greasing, lubrication

engreído *adj* conceited

engrosar <1m> **1** *v/t* swell, increase

2 v/i put on weight, gain weight

engrudo m (flour and water) paste

engullir <3h> v/t bolt (down)

enhebrar <1a> v/t thread, string

enhiesto adj lit persona erect, upright; torre, árbol lofty

enhorabuena f congratulations pl; **dar la ~** congratulate (por on)

enigma m enigma; **enigmático** adj enigmatic

enjabonar <1a> v/t soap

enjambre m tb fig swarm

enjoyado adj bejewel(l)ed

enjuagar <1h> v/t rinse

enjugar <1h> v/t deuda etc wipe out; líquido mop up; lágrimas wipe away

enjuiciar <1b> v/t JUR institute proceedings against; fig judge

enlace m link, connection; **~ matrimonial** marriage

enlatar <1a> v/t can, Br tb tin

enlazar <1f> **1** v/t link (up), connect; L.Am. con cuerda rope, lasso **2** v/i de carretera link up (con with); AVIA, FERR connect (con with)

enloquecer <2d> **1** v/t drive crazy o mad **2** v/i go crazy o mad

enmarañar <1a> **1** v/t pelo tangle; asunto complicate, muddle **2** v/r **~se** de pelo get tangled; **~se en algo** get entangled o embroiled in sth

enmarcar <1g> v/t frame

enmascarar <1a> v/t hide, disguise

enmendar <1k> **1** v/t asunto rectify, put right; JUR, POL amend; **~le la plana a alguien** find fault with what s.o. has done **2** v/r **~se** mend one's ways; **enmienda** f POL amendment

enmicar <1g> v/t L.Am. laminate

enmudecer <2d> **1** v/t silence **2** v/i fall silent

ennoblecer <2d> v/t ennoble

enojado adj L.Am. angry; **enojar** <1a> **1** v/t (molestar) annoy; L.Am. (encolerizar) make angry **2** v/r **~se** L.Am. (molestarse) get annoyed; (encolerizarse) get angry; **enojo** m L.Am. anger; **enojón** adj L.Am. F irritable, touchy; **enojoso** adj (delicado) awkward; (aburrido) tedious,

tiresome

enorgullecer <2d> **1** v/t make proud, fill with pride **2** v/r **~se** be proud (de of)

enorme adj enormous, huge

enrarecido adj aire rarefied; relaciones strained

enredadera f BOT creeper, climbing plant

enredar <1a> **1** v/t tangle, get tangled; fig complicate, make complicated **2** v/i make trouble **3** v/r **~se** get tangled; fig get complicated; **~se en algo** get mixed up o involved in sth; **enredo** m tangle; (confusión) mess, confusion; (intriga) intrigue; amoroso affair

enrevesado adj complicated, involved

enriquecer <2d> **1** v/t make rich; fig enrich **2** v/r **~se** get rich; fig be enriched

enrojecer <2d> **1** v/t turn red **2** v/i blush, go red

enrolarse <1a> v/r MIL enlist

enrollar <1a> **1** v/t roll up; cable coil; hilo wind; **me enrolla** F I like it, I think it's great **2** v/r **~se** F hablar go on and on F; **se enrolló mucho con nosotros** (se portó bien) he was great to us; **¡no te enrolles!** F get to the point!; **~se con alguien** fig F neck with s.o.

enroscar <1g> **1** v/t tornillo screw in; cable, cuerda coil **2** v/r **~se** coil up

ensaimada f GASTR pastry in the form of a spiral

ensalada f GASTR salad; **ensaladera** f salad bowl; **ensaladilla** f: **~ rusa** GASTR Russian salad

ensalmo m: **como por ~** as if by magic

ensalzar <1f> v/t extol, praise

ensamblar <1a> v/t assemble

ensanchar <1a> **1** v/t widen; prenda let out **2** v/r **~se** widen, get wider; de prenda stretch

ensangrentar <1k> v/t stain with blood, cover with blood

ensañarse <1a> v/r show no mercy

(*con* to)

ensartar <1a> **1** *v/t* **en** *hilo* string; *aguja* (*engañar*) trick, trap **2** *v/r* **~se** *L.Am.* **en** *discusión* get involved, get caught up

ensayar <1a> *v/t* test, try (out); TEA rehearse; **ensayo** *m* TEA rehearsal; *escrito* essay; **~ general** dress rehearsal

enseguida *adv* immediately, right away

ensenada *f* inlet, cove

enseñanza *f* teaching; **~ primaria** elementary education, *Br* primary education; **~ secundaria** *or* **media** secondary education; **~ superior** higher education; **enseñar** <1a> *v/t* (*dar clases*) teach; (*mostrar*) show

ensillar <1a> *v/t* saddle

ensimismarse <1a> *v/r* become lost in thought; *L.Am.* F get conceited *o* big-headed F

ensombrecer <2d> *v/t* cast a shadow over

ensordecedor *adj* deafening

ensuciar <1b> **1** *v/t* (get) dirty; *fig* sully, tarnish **2** *v/r* **~se** get dirty; *fig* get one's hands dirty

ensueño *m*: **de ~** *fig* fairy-tale *atr*, dream *atr*

entablar <1a> *v/t* strike up, start

entablillar <1a> *v/t* splint, put in a splint

entarimado *m* (*suelo*) floorboards *pl*; (*plataforma*) stage, platform

ente *m* (*ser*) being, entity; F (*persona rara*) oddball F; (*organización*) body

entejar <1a> *v/t L.Am.* tile

entender <2g> **1** *v/t* understand; **dar a ~ a alguien** give s.o. to understand **2** *v/i* understand; **~ de algo** know about sth **3** *v/r* **~se** communicate; **a ver si nos entendemos** let's have this straight; **yo me entiendo** I know what I'm doing; **~se con alguien** get along with s.o., get on with s.o. **4** *m*: **a mi ~** in my opinion, to my mind; **entendido 1** *adj* understood; **¿~?** do you

understand?, understood?; **tengo ~ que** I gather *o* understand that **2** *m*, **-a** *f* expert, authority; **entendimiento** *m* understanding; (*inteligencia*) mind

enterado *adj* knowledgeable, well-informed; **estar ~ de** know about, have heard about; **darse por ~** get the message, take the hint; **enterarse** <1a> *v/r* find out, hear (**de** about); **¡para que te enteres!** F so there! F; **¡se va a enterar!** F he's in for it! F

entereza *f* fortitude

enternecer <2d> *v/t* move, touch

entero 1 *adj* (*completo*) whole, entire; (*no roto*) intact, undamaged; **por ~** completely, entirely **2** *m* (*punto*) point

enterrar <1k> *v/t* bury; **~ a todos** *fig* outlive everybody

entidad *f* entity, body

entierro *m* burial; (*funeral*) funeral

entonar <1a> **1** *v/t* intone, sing; *fig* F perk up **2** *v/i* sing in tune **3** *v/r* **~se con bebida** get tipsy

entonces *adv* then; **desde ~** since, since then; **por ~, en aquel ~** in those days, at that time

entornar <1a> *v/t puerta* leave ajar; *ojos* half close; **entorno** *m* environment

entorpecer <2d> *v/t* hold up, hinder; *paso* obstruct; *entendimiento* dull

entrada *f acción* entry; *lugar* entrance; *localidad* ticket; *pago* deposit, down payment; **de comida** starter; **de ~** from the outset, from the start

entrañable *adj amistad* close, deep; *amigo* close, dear; *recuerdo* fond; **entrañar** <1a> *v/t* entail, involve; **entrañas** *fpl* entrails

entrar <1a> **1** *v/i para indicar acercamiento* come in, enter; *para indicar alejamiento* go in, enter; *caber* fit; **me entró frío/sueño** I got cold/sleepy, I began to feel cold/sleepy; **no me entra en la cabeza** I can't understand it **2** *v/t para indicar acercamiento* bring in; *para indicar* *alejamiento* take in

entre *prp dos cosas, personas* between; *más de dos* among(st); *expresando cooperación* between; **la relación ~ ellos** the relationship between them; **~ nosotros** among us; **lo pagamos ~ todos** we paid for it among *o* between us

entreabierto 1 *part →* **entreabrir 2** *adj* half-open; *puerta* ajar; **entreabrir** <3a; *part* **entreabierto**> *v/t* half-open

entreacto *m* TEA interval

entrecejo *m:* **fruncir el ~** frown

entrecomillar <1a> *v/t* put in quotation marks

entrecortado *adj habla* halting; *respiración* difficult, labo(u)red

entrecot *m* entrecote

entredicho *m:* **poner en ~** call into question, question

entrega *f handing over; de mercancías* delivery; *(dedicación)* dedication, devotion; **~ a domicilio** (home) delivery; **~ de premios** prize-giving, presentation; **hacer ~ de algo a alguien** present s.o. with sth; **entregar** <1h> **1** *v/t* give, hand over; *trabajo, deberes* hand in; *mercancías* deliver; *premio* present **2** *v/r* **~se** give o.s. up; **~se a** *fig* devote o.s. to, dedicate o.s. to

entrelazar <1f> *v/t* interweave, intertwine

entremeses *mpl* GASTR appetizers, hors d'œuvres

entremezclar <1a> **1** *v/t* intermingle, mix **2** *v/r* **~se** intermingle, mix

entrenador *m*, **~a** *f* coach; **entrenamiento** *m* coaching; **entrenar** <1a> **1** *v/t* train **2** *v/r* **~se** train

entrepierna *f* ANAT crotch

entresacar <1g> *v/t* extract, select

entresijos *mpl fig* details, ins and outs F

entresuelo *m* mezzanine; TEA dress circle

entretanto *adv* meanwhile, in the meantime

entretecho *m Arg, Chi* attic

entretener <2l> **1** *v/t (divertir)* entertain, amuse; *(retrasar)* keep, detain; *(distraer)* distract **2** *v/i* be entertaining **3** *v/r* **~se** *(divertirse)* amuse o.s.; *(distraerse)* keep o.s. busy; *(retrasarse)* linger; **entretenido** *adj (divertido)* entertaining, enjoyable; **estar ~** *ocupado* be busy; **entretenimiento** *m* entertainment, amusement

entrevero *m S.Am. (lío)* mix-up, mess; *Chi (discusión)* argument

entrevista *f* interview; **entrevistar** <1a> **1** *v/t* interview **2** *v/r* **~se: ~se con alguien** meet (with) s.o.

entristecer <2d> **1** *v/t* sadden **2** *v/r* **~se** grow sad

entrometerse <2a> *v/r* meddle *(en* in); **entrometido 1** *part →* **entrometerse 2** *adj* meddling *atr*, interfering **3** *m* meddler, busybody

entronizar <1f> *v/t fig* instal(l)

entumecer <2d> **1** *v/t* numb **2** *v/r* **~se** go numb, get stiff

enturbiar <1b> *v/t tb fig* cloud

entusiasmado *adj* excited, delirious; **entusiasmar** <1a> *v/t* excite, make enthusiastic; **entusiasmo** *m* enthusiasm; **entusiasta 1** *adj* enthusiastic **2** *m/f* enthusiast

enumerar <1a> *v/t* list, enumerate

enunciar <1b> *v/t* state

envalentonarse <1a> *v/r* become bolder *o* more daring; *(insolentarse)* become defiant

envanecerse <2d> *v/r* become conceited *o* vain

envasar <1a> *v/t en botella* bottle; *en lata* can; *en paquete* pack; **envase** *m* container; *botella* (empty) bottle; **~ de cartón** carton; **~ no retornable** nonreturnable bottle

envejecer <2d> **1** *v/t* age, make look older **2** *v/i* age, grow old; **envejecimiento** *m* aging, ageing

envenenar <1a> *v/t tb fig* poison

envergadura *f* AVIA wingspan; MAR breadth; *fig* magnitude, importance; **de gran** *or* **mucha ~** *fig* of great importance

enviado *m*, **-a** *f* POL envoy; *de un*

periódico reporter, correspondent; **~ especial** POL special envoy; *de un periódico* special correspondent; **enviar** <1c> *v/t* send

enviciarse <1b> *v/r* get addicted (**con** to)

envidia *f* envy, jealousy; **me da ~** I'm envious *o* jealous; **tener ~ a alguien de algo** envy s.o. sth; **envidiar** <1b> *v/t* envy; **~ a alguien por algo** envy s.o. sth; **envidioso** *adj* envious, jealous

envilecer <2d> **1** *v/t* degrade, debase **2** *v/r* **~se** degrade o.s., debase o.s.

envío *m* shipment

enviudar <1a> *v/i* be widowed

envoltorio *m* wrapper; **envoltura** *f* cover, covering; *de regalo* wrapping; *de caramelo* wrapper

envolver <2h; *part* **envuelto**> **1** *v/t* wrap (up); (*rodear*) surround, envelop; (*involucrar*) involve; **~ a alguien en algo** involve s.o. in sth **2** *v/r* **~se** wrap o.s. up; **~se en** *fig* become involved in; **envuelto** *part* → **envolver**

enyesado *m* plastering

enzarzarse <1f> *v/r* get involved (**en** in)

eólico *adj* wind *atr*

épico *adj* epic

epidemia *f* epidemic

epilepsia *f* MED epilepsy

epílogo *m* epilog(ue)

episcopal *adj* episcopal

episodio *m* episode

epistolar *adj* epistolary

epitafio *m* epitaph

época *f* time, period; *parte del año* time of year; GEOL epoch; **hacer ~** be epoch-making

epopeya *f* epic, epic poem

equidad *f* fairness

equidistante *adj* equidistant

equilibrado *adj* well-balanced; **equilibrar** <1a> *v/t* balance; **equilibrio** *m* balance; FÍS equilibrium

equino *adj* equine

equinoccio *m* equinox

equipaje *m* baggage; **~ de mano** hand baggage

equipamiento *m*: **~ de serie** AUTO standard features *pl*; **equipar** <1a> *v/t* equip (**con** with)

equiparar <1a> *v/t* put on a level (**a** *o* **con** with); **~ algo con algo** *fig* compare *o* liken sth to sth

equipo *m* DEP team; *accesorios* equipment; **~ de música** *or* **de sonido** sound system

equitación *f* riding

equitativo *adj* fair, equitable

equivalente *m/adj* equivalent; **equivaler** <2q> *v/i* be equivalent (**a** to)

equivocación *f* mistake; **por ~** by mistake; **equivocado** *adj* wrong; **estar ~** be wrong, be mistaken; **equivocar** <1g> **1** *v/t*: **~ a alguien** make s.o. make a mistake **2** *v/r* **~se** make a mistake; **te has equivocado** you are wrong *o* mistaken; **~se de número** TELEC get the wrong number; **equívoco 1** *adj* ambiguous, equivocal **2** *m* misunderstanding; (*error*) mistake

era *f* era

erección *f* erection

eres *vb* → **ser**

ergonómico *adj* ergonomic

erguir <3n> **1** *v/t* raise, lift; (*poner derecho*) straighten **2** *v/r* **~se** *de persona* stand up, rise; *de edificio* rise

erial *m* uncultivated land

erigir <3c> **1** *v/t* erect **2** *v/r* **~se**: **~se en** set o.s. up as

erizarse <1f> *v/r de pelo* stand on end; **erizo** *m* ZO hedgehog; **~ de mar** ZO sea urchin

ermita *f* chapel; **ermitaño 1** *m* ZO hermit crab **2** *m*, **-a** *f* hermit

erogación *f Méx, S.Am.* expenditure, outlay

erógeno *adj* erogenous

erosión *f* erosion; **erosionar** <1a> *v/t* GEOL erode

erótico *adj* erotic; **erotismo** *m* eroticism

erradicar <1g> *v/t* eradicate, wipe out

errante *adj* wandering; **errar** <1l>

1 v/t miss; ~ **el tiro** miss **2** v/i miss; ~ **es humano** to err is human

equivocarse be wrong, be mistaken

errata f mistake, error; *de imprenta* misprint

erre f: ~ **que ~** F doggedly, stubbornly

erróneo adj wrong, erroneous fml; **error** m mistake, error; ~ **de cálculo** error of judg(e)ment

eructar <1a> v/i belch F, burp F; **eructo** m belch F, burp F

erudito 1 adj learned, erudite **2** m scholar

erupción f GEOL eruption; MED rash

esbelto adj slim, slender

esbozar <1f> v/t sketch; *idea, proyecto etc* outline; **esbozo** m sketch; *de idea, proyecto etc* outline

escabeche m type of marinade

escabroso adj rough; *problema* tricky; *relato* indecent

escabullirse <3h> v/r escape, slip away

escala f tb MÚS scale; AVIA stopover; ~ **de cuerda** rope ladder; ~ **de valores** scale of values; **a ~** to scale, life-sized

escalada f DEP climb, ascent; ~ **de los precios** increase in prices, escalation of prices; **escalador** m, **~a** f climber; **escalafón** m fig ladder; **escalar** <1a> **1** v/t climb, scale **2** v/i climb

escaldar <1a> v/t GASTR blanch; *manos* scald

escalera f stairs pl, staircase; ~ **de caracol** spiral staircase; ~ **de incendios** fire escape; ~ **de mano** ladder; ~ **mecánica** escalator

escalfar <1a> v/t poach

escalofriante adj horrifying; **escalofrío** m shiver

escalón m step; *de escalera de mano* rung; **escalonar** <1a> v/t *en tiempo* stagger; *terreno* terrace

escalope m escalope

escama f ZO scale; *de jabón, piel* flake; **escamar** <1a> **1** v/t scale, remove the scales from; *fig* make suspicious **2** v/r **~se** become suspicious

escamotear <1a> v/t *(ocultar)* hide, conceal; *(negar)* withhold

escampar <1a> v/i clear up, stop raining

escanciar <1b> v/t fml pour

escandalizar <1f> v/t **1** v/t shock, scandalize **2** v/r **~se** be shocked; **escándalo** m *(asunto vergonzoso)* scandal; *(jaleo)* racket, ruckus; **armar un ~** make a scene; **escandaloso** adj *(vergonzoso)* scandalous, shocking; *(ruidoso)* noisy, rowdy

Escandinavia Scandinavia

escanear <1a> v/t scan; **escáner** m scanner

escaño m POL seat

escapar <1a> **1** v/t escape *(de* from); **dejar** ~ *oportunidad* pass up, let slip; *suspiro* let out, give **2** v/r **~se** *(huir)* escape *(de* from); *de casa* run away *(de* from); **~se de** *situación* get out of

escaparate m store window

escapatoria f: **no tener ~** have no way out

escape m *de gas* leak; AUTO exhaust; **salir a ~** rush out

escarabajo m ZO beetle

escaramuza f skirmish

escarbadientes m inv toothpick; **escarbar** <1a> **1** v/i tb fig dig around *(en* in) **2** v/t dig around in

escarceos mpl forays, dabbling sg; ~ **amorosos** romantic o amorous adventures

escarcha f frost

escardar <1a> v/t hoe

escarmentar <1k> **1** v/t teach a lesson to **2** v/i learn one's lesson; ~ **en cabeza ajena** learn from other people's mistakes; **escarmiento** m lesson; **le sirvió de ~** it taught him a lesson

escarnio m ridicule, derision

escarola f endive, escarole

escarpado adj sheer, steep

escarpia f hook

escasear <1a> v/i be scarce, be in short supply; **escasez** f shortage, scarcity; **escaso** adj *recursos* limited; **andar ~ de algo** *falto* be short of sth; *-as posibilidades de* not much chance of, little chance of; *falta un mes ~* it's barely a month away

escatimar <1a> *v/t* be mean with, be very sparing with; *no ~ esfuerzos* be unstinting in one's efforts, spare no effort

escayola *f* (plaster) cast; **escayolar** <1a> *v/t* put in a (plaster) cast

escena *f* scene; *escenario* stage; *entrar en ~* come on stage; *hacer una ~ fig* make a scene; **escenario** *m* stage; *fig* scene; **escénico** *adj* stage *atr*; **escenificar** <1g> *v/t* stage

escepticismo *m* skepticism, *Br* scepticism; **escéptico 1** *adj* skeptical, *Br* sceptical **2** *m*, **-a** *f* skeptic, *Br* sceptic

escindirse <3a> *v/r* (*fragmentarse*) split (*en* into); (*segregarse*) break away (*de* from); **escisión** *f* (*fragmentación*) split; (*segregación*) break

esclarecer <2d> *v/t* throw *o* shed light on; *misterio* clear up; **esclarecimiento** *m* clarification; *de misterio* solving

esclavitud *f* slavery; **esclavizar** <1f> *v/t* enslave; *fig* tie down; **esclavo** *m* slave

esclerosis *f* MED: *~ múltiple* multiple sclerosis

escoba *f* broom; **escobilla** *f* small brush; AUTO wiper blade

escocer <2b & 2h> *v/i* sting, smart; *todavía escuece la derrota* he's still smarting from the defeat

escocés 1 *adj* Scottish **2** *m* Scot, Scotsman; **escocesa** *f* Scot, Scotswoman; **Escocia** Scotland

escoger <2c> *v/t* choose, select; **escogido** *adj* select

escolar 1 *adj* school *atr* **2** *m/f* student; **escolarización** *f* education, schooling; *~ obligatoria* compulsory education; **escolarizar** <1f> *v/t* educate, provide schooling for; **escolástico** *adj* scholarly

escollera *f* breakwater; **escollo** *m*

MAR reef; (*obstáculo*) hurdle, obstacle

escolta 1 *f* escort **2** *m/f motorista* outrider; (*guardaespaldas*) bodyguard; **escoltar** <1a> *v/t* escort

escombros *mpl* rubble *sg*

esconder <2a> **1** *v/t* hide, conceal **2** *v/r* *~se* hide; **escondidas** *fpl* *S.Am.* hide-and-seek; *a ~* in secret, secretly; **escondite** *m lugar* hiding place; *juego* hide-and-seek; **escondrijo** *m* hiding place

escopeta *f* shotgun; *~ de aire comprimido* air gun, air rifle; **escopetado** *adj: salir ~* F shoot *o* dash off F; **escopetazo** *m* gunshot

escorbuto *m* scurvy

escoria *f* slag; *desp* dregs *pl*

Escorpio *m/f inv* ASTR Scorpio; **escorpión** *m* ZO scorpion

escotado *adj* low-cut; **escote** *m* neckline; *de mujer* cleavage

escotilla *f* MAR hatch

escozor *m* burning sensation, stinging; *fig* bitterness

escribir <3a; *part escrito*> *v/t* write; (*deletrear*) spell; *~ a mano* handwrite, write by hand; *~ a máquina* type; **escrito 1** *part* → **escribir** **2** *adj* written; *por ~* in writing **3** *m* document; *~s* writings; **escritor** *m*, *~a* *f* writer, author; **escritorio** *m* desk; *artículos de ~* stationery; **escritura** *f* writing; JUR deed; *Sagradas Escrituras* Holy Scripture

escrúpulo *m* scruple; *sin ~s* unscrupulous; **escrupuloso** *adj* (*cuidadoso*) meticulous; (*honrado*) scrupulous; (*aprensivo*) fastidious

escrutar <1a> *v/t* scrutinize; *votos* count; **escrutinio** *m de votos* count; (*inspección*) scrutiny

escuadrón *m* squadron

escuálido *adj* skinny, emaciated

escucha *f: estar a la ~* be listening out; *~s pl telefónicas* wiretapping *sg*, *Br tb* phone-tapping *sg*; **escuchar** <1a> **1** *v/t* listen to; *L.Am.* (*oír*) hear **2** *v/i* listen

escuchimizado *adj* F puny F, scrawny F

escudarse <1a> *v/r fig* hide (*en* behind)

escudilla *f* bowl

escudo *m arma* shield; *insignia* badge; *moneda* escudo; **~ de armas** coat of arms

escudriñar <1a> *v/t* (*mirar de lejos*) scan; (*examinar*) scrutinize

escuela *f* school; **~ de comercio** business school; **~ de idiomas** language school; **~ primaria** elementary school, *Br* primary school

escuelero 1 *adj L.Am.* school *atr* **2** *m*, **-a** *f L.Am.* (*maestro*) teacher; *Pe, Bol* (*alumno*) student

escueto *adj* succinct, concise

escuincle *m/f Méx, C.Am.* F kid

esculpir <3a> *v/t* sculpt; **escultor** *m*, **-a** *f* sculptor; **escultura** *f* sculpture

escupidera *f* spitoon; *L.Am.* chamber pot; **escupir** <3a> **1** *v/i* spit **2** *v/t* spit out; **escupitajo** *m* F gob of spit F

escurreplatos *m inv* plate rack

escurridizo *adj* slippery; *fig* evasive; **escurridor** *m* (*colador*) colander; (*escurreplatos*) plate rack; **escurrir** <3a> **1** *v/t ropa* wring out; *platos, verduras* drain **2** *v/i* de *platos* drain; *de ropa* drip-dry **3** *v/r* **-se** de *líquido* drain away; (*deslizarse*) slip; (*escaparse*) slip away

escusado *m* bathroom

ese, esa, esos, esas *det singular* that; *plural* those

ése, ésa, ésos, ésas *pron singular* that (one); *plural* those (ones); **le ofrecí dinero pero ni por ésas** I offered him money but even that wasn't enough; **no soy de ésos que** I'm not one of those who

esencia *f* essence; **esencial** *adj* essential

esfera *f* sphere; **~ de actividad** *fig* field *o* sphere (of activity); **esférico 1** *adj* spherical **2** *m* DEP F ball

esfinge *f* sphinx

esforzarse <1f & 1m> *v/r* make an effort, try hard; **esfuerzo** *m* effort; **hacer un ~** make an effort; **sin ~** effortlessly

esfumarse <1a> *v/r* F *tb fig* disappear

esgrima *f* fencing; **esgrimir** <3a> *v/t arma* wield; *fig: argumento* put forward, use

esguince *m* sprain

eslabón *m* link; **el ~ perdido** the missing link

eslavo 1 *adj* Slavic, Slavonic **2** *m*, **-a** *f* Slav

eslogan *m* slogan

eslora *f* length

Eslovaquia Slovakia

Eslovenia Slovenia

esmalte *m* enamel; **~ de uñas** nail polish, nail varnish

esmerado *adj* meticulous

esmeralda *f* emerald

esmerarse <1a> *v/r* take great care (*en* over)

esmerilado *adj*: **cristal ~** frosted glass

esmero *m* care; **con ~** carefully

esmirriado *adj* F skinny F, scrawny F

esmoquin *m* tuxedo, *Br* dinner jacket

esnifar <1a> *v/t* F *pegamento* sniff F; *cocaína* snort F

esnob 1 *adj* snobbish **2** *m* snob; **esnobismo** *m* snobbishness

eso *pron* that; **en ~** just then, just at that moment; **~ mismo, ~ es** that's it, that's the way; **a ~ de las dos** at around two; **por ~** that's why; **¿y ~?** why's that?; **y ~ que le dije que no se lo contara** and after I told him not to tell her

esotérico *adj* esoteric

espabilado *adj* (*listo*) bright, smart; (*vivo*) sharp, on the ball F; **espabilar** <1a> **1** *v/t* (*quitar el sueño*) wake up, revive; **lo ha espabilado** (*avivado*) she's got him to wise up **2** *v/i* (*darse prisa*) hurry up, get a move on; (*avivarse*) wise up **3** *v/r* **-se** del *sueño* wake oneself up; (*darse prisa*) hurry up, get a move on; (*avivarse*) wise up

espacial adj cohete, viaje space atr; FÍS, MAT spatial; **espaciarse** <1a> v/r become more (and more) infrequent; **espacio** m space; TV program, Br programme; **~s verdes** green spaces; **~ de tiempo** space of time; **~ vital** living space; **espacioso** adj spacious, roomy

espada f sword; **~s** pl (en naipes) suit in Spanish deck of cards; **estar entre la ~ y la pared** be between a rock and a hard place; **espadachín** m skilled swordsman

espaguetis mpl spaghetti sg

espalda f back; **a ~s de alguien** behind s.o.'s back; **de ~s a** with one's back to; **por la ~** from behind; **caerse de ~s** fall flat on one's back; **no me des la ~** don't sit with your back to me; **nadar a ~** swim backstroke; **tener cubiertas las ~s** fig keep one's back covered; **volver la ~ a alguien** fig turn one's back on s.o.; **espaldarazo** m slap on the back; (reconocimiento) recognition; **espalderas** fpl wall bars

espantajo m scarecrow; fig sight; **espantapájaros** m inv scarecrow; **espantar** <1a> **1** v/t (asustar) frighten, scare; (ahuyentar) frighten away, shoo away; F (horrorizar) horrify, appal(l) **2** v/r **~se** get frightened, get scared; F (horrorizarse) be horrified, appal(l)ed; **espanto** m (susto) fright; L.Am. (fantasma) ghost; **nos llenó de ~** desagrado we were horrified; **¡qué ~!** how awful!; **de ~** terrible; **espantoso** adj horrific, appalling; para enfatizar terrible, dreadful; **hace un calor ~** it's terribly hot, it's incredibly hot

España Spain; **español 1** adj Spanish **2** m idioma Spanish **3** m, **-a** f Spaniard; **los ~es** the Spanish

esparadrapo m Band-Aid®, Br plaster

esparcimiento m relaxation; **esparcir** <3b> **1** v/t papeles scatter; rumor spread **2** v/r **~se** de papeles be

scattered; de rumor spread

espárrago m BOT asparagus; **~ triguero** wild asparagus; **¡vete a freír ~s!** F get lost! F

espartano adj spartan

esparto m BOT esparto grass

espasmo m spasm

espátula f spatula; en pintura palette knife

especia f spice

especial adj special; (difícil) fussy; **en ~** especially; **especialidad** f specialty, Br speciality; **especialista** m/f specialist, expert; en cine stuntman; mujer stuntwoman; **especializarse** <1f> v/r specialize (**en** in)

especie f BIO species; (tipo) kind, sort

especiero m spice rack

especificar <1g> v/t specify; **específico** adj specific

espectacular adj spectacular; **espectáculo** m TEA show; (escena) sight; **dar el ~** fig make a spectacle of o.s.; **espectador** m, **~a** f en cine etc member of the audience; DEP spectator; (observador) on-looker, observer

espectro m FÍS spectrum; (fantasma) ghost

especulación f speculation; **especular** <1a> v/i speculate; **especulativo** adj speculative

espejismo m mirage; **espejo** m mirror; **~ retrovisor** rear-view mirror

espeleólogo m spelunker, Br potholer

espeluznante adj horrific, horrifying

espera f wait; **sala de ~** waiting room; **en ~ de** pending; **estar a la ~ de** be waiting for; **esperanza** f hope; **~ de vida** life expectancy; **esperar** <1a> **1** v/t (aguardar) wait for; con esperanza hope; (suponer, confiar en) expect **2** v/i (aguardar) wait

esperma f sperm

espesar <1a> **1** v/t thicken **2** v/r **~se** thicken, become thick; **espeso** adj thick; *vegetación*, *niebla* thick, dense; **espesor** *m* thickness; **espesura** *f* dense vegetation

espía *m/f* spy; **espiar** <1c> **1** *v/t* spy on **2** *v/i* spy

espiga *f* BOT ear, spike

espina *f de planta* thorn; *de pez* bone; ~ **dorsal** spine, backbone; *dar mala* ~ *a alguien* F make s.o. feel uneasy

espinacas *fpl* BOT spinach *sg*

espinazo *m* spine, backbone; *doblar el* ~ *fig* (*trabajar mucho*) work o.s. into the ground; (*humillarse*) kowtow (*ante* to)

espinilla *f de la pierna* shin; *en la piel* pimple, spot

espinoso *adj* thorny, prickly; *fig* thorny, knotty

espionaje *m* spying, espionage

espiral 1 *adj* spiral *atr* **2** *f* spiral

espirar <1a> *v/t* & *v/i* exhale

espiritismo *m* spiritualism; **espíritu** *m* spirit; **espiritual** *adj* spiritual

espléndido *adj* splendid, magnificent; (*generoso*) generous; **esplendor** *m* splendo(u)r

espliego *m* lavender

espolear <1a> *v/t tb fig* spur on

espolvorear <1a> *v/t* sprinkle

esponja *f* sponge; **esponjoso** *adj bizcocho* spongy; *toalla* soft, fluffy

espónsor *m/f* sponsor; **esponsorizar** <1f> *v/t* sponsor

espontáneo *adj* spontaneous

esporádico *adj* sporadic

esposa *f* wife; **esposas** *fpl* (*manillas*) handcuffs *pl*; **esposar** <1a> *v/t* handcuff; **esposo** *m* husband

esprint *m* sprint

espuela *f* spur

espuerta *f*: *ganar dinero a* ~*s* F make money hand over fist F

espuma *f* foam; *de jabón* lather; *de cerveza* froth; ~ *de afeitar* shaving foam; ~ *moldeadora* styling mousse; **espumadera** *f* slotted spoon, skimmer; **espumarajo** *m* froth, foam

espumilla *f C.Am.* GASTR meringue

espumoso *adj* frothy, foamy; *caldo* sparkling

esqueje *m* cutting

esquela *f aviso* death notice, obituary

esquelético *adj* skeletal; **esqueleto** *m* skeleton; *Méx*, *C.Am.*, *Pe*, *Bol fig* blank form; *mover or menear el* ~ F dance

esquema *m* (*croquis*) sketch, diagram; (*sinopsis*) outline, summary; **esquemático** *adj dibujo* schematic, diagrammatic; *resumen* simplified

esquí *m tabla* ski; *deporte* skiing; ~ *de fondo* cross-country skiing; ~ *náutico* o *acuático* waterskiing; **esquiador** *m*, ~**a** *f* skier; **esquiar** <1a> *v/i* ski

esquilar <1a> *v/t* shear

esquilmar <1a> *v/t* overexploit; *a alguien* suck dry

esquina *f* corner; **esquinazo** *m Arg*, *Chi* serenade; *dar* ~ *a alguien* F give s.o. the slip F

esquirol *m/f* strikebreaker, scab F

esquite *m C.Am.*, *Méx* popcorn

esquivar <1a> *v/t* avoid, dodge F; **esquivo** *adj* (*huraño*) unsociable; (*evasivo*) shifty, evasive

esquizofrenia *f* schizophrenia; **esquizofrénico** *adj* schizophrenic

esta *det* this

está *vb* → *estar*

estabilidad *f* stability; **estabilizante** *m* stabilizer; **estabilizar** <1f> *v/t* stabilize; **estable** *adj* stable

establecer <2d> **1** *v/t* establish; *negocio* set up **2** *v/r* ~*se en lugar* settle; *en profesión* set up; **establecimiento** *m* establishment

establo *m* stable

estaca *f* stake; **estacada** *f*: *dejar a alguien en la* ~ F leave s.o. in the lurch

estación *f* station; *del año* season; ~ *espacial* or *orbital* space station; ~ *de invierno* or *invernal* winter resort; ~ *de servicio* service station; ~ *de trabajo* INFOR work station; **estacional** *adj* seasonal; **estacionamiento** *m* AUTO parking; *L.Am.* parking lot, *Br* car park; **estacionar** <1a> **1** *v/t* AUTO park **2** *v/r* ~*se* stabilize; **estacionómetro** *m Méx* parking meter

estadio *m* DEP stadium

estadística *f cifra* statistic; *ciencia* statistics

estado *m* state; MED condition; ~ **civil** marital status; ~ **de guerra** state of war; **en buen** ~ in good condition; **el Estado** the State; ~ **del bienestar** welfare state; **los Estados Unidos (de América)** the United States (of America)

estadounidense 1 *adj* American, US *atr* **2** *m/f* American

estafa *f* swindle, cheat; **estafador** *m*, ~**a** *f* con artist F, fraudster; **estafar** <1a> *v/t* swindle, cheat (**a** out of), defraud (**a** of)

estalactita *f* stalactite; **estalagmita** *f* stalagmite

estallar <1a> *v/i* explode; *de guerra* break out; *de escándalo* break; **estalló en llanto** she burst into tears; **estallido** *m* explosion; *de guerra* outbreak

estamento *m* stratum, class

estampa *f de libro* illustration; *(aspecto)* appearance; REL prayer card; **estampado** *adj tejido* patterned; **estampar** <1a> *v/t sello* put; *tejido* print; *pasaporte* stamp; **le estampó una bofetada en la cara** F she smacked him one F

estampido *m* bang

estampilla *f L.Am.* stamp

estancado *adj agua* stagnant; *fig* at a standstill; **estancar** <1g> **1** *v/t río* dam up, block; *fig* bring to a standstill **2** *v/r* ~**se** stagnate; *fig* come to a standstill

estancia *f* stay; *Rpl* farm, ranch; **estanciero** *m*, ~**a** *f Rpl* farmer, rancher

estanco 1 *adj* watertight **2** *m shop selling cigarettes etc*

estándar *m* standard; **estandarizar** <1f> *v/t* standardize

estandarte *m* standard, banner

estanque *m* pond

estante *m* shelf; **estantería** *f* shelves *pl*; *para libros* bookcase

estaño *m* tin

estar <1p> **1** *v/i* be; **¿está Javier?** is Javier in?; ~ **haciendo algo** be doing sth; **estamos a 3 de enero** it's January 3rd; **el kilo está a cien pesetas** they're a hundred pesetas a kilo; **te está grande** it's too big for you; ~ **con alguien** agree with s.o.; *(apoyar)* support s.o.; **ahora estoy con Vd.** I'll be with you in just a moment; ~ **a bien/mal con alguien** be on good/bad terms with s.o.; ~ **de ocupación** work as, be; ~ **en algo** be working on sth; ~ **para hacer algo** be about to do sth; **no** ~ **para algo** not be in a mood for sth; ~ **por algo** be in favo(u)r of sth; **está por hacer** it hasn't been done yet; ~ **sin dinero** have no money; **¿cómo está Vd.?** how are you?; **estoy mejor** I'm (feeling) better; **¡ya estoy!** I'm ready!; **¡ya está!** that's it! **2** *v/r* ~**se** stay; ~**se quieto** keep still

estárter *m* choke

estatal *adj* state *atr*

estático *adj* static

estatua *f* statue; **estatura** *f* height; **estatutario** *adj* statutory; **estatuto** *m* statute; ~**s** articles of association; **estatus** *m* status

este[1] *m* east

este[2], **esta**, **estos**, **estas** *det singular* this; *plural* these

éste, **ésta**, **éstos**, **éstas** *pron singular* this (one); *plural* these (ones)

estela *f* MAR wake; AVIA, *fig* trail; **estelar** *adj* star *atr*

estepa *f* steppe

estera *f* mat

estercolero *m* dunghill, dung heap

estéreo *adj* stereo; **estereofónico** *adj* stereophonic; **estereotipo** *m* stereotype

estéril *adj* MED sterile; *trabajo, esfuerzo etc* futile; **esterilidad** *f* sterility; **esterilizar** <1f> *v/t tb persona* sterilize

esterilla *f* mat

esterlina *adj*: **libra** ~ pound sterling

esternón *m* breast bone, sternum

estero *m Rpl* marsh

estertor *m* death rattle

esteticista *m/f* beautician; **estético** *adj* esthetic, *Br* aesthetic

estetoscopio *m* MED stethoscope

estibador *m* stevedore

estiércol *m* dung; (*abono*) manure

estilarse <1a> *v/r* be fashionable; **estilista** *m/f* stylist; *de modas* designer; **estilo** *m* style; **al ~ de** in the style of; **algo por el ~** something like that; **son todos por el ~** they're all the same

estilográfica *f* fountain pen

estima *f* esteem, respect; **tener a alguien en mucha ~** hold s.o. in high regard *o* esteem; **estimación** *f* (*cálculo*) estimate; (*estima*) esteem, respect; **estimar** <1a> *v/t* respect, hold in high regard; **estimo conveniente que** I consider it advisable to

estimulante 1 *adj* stimulating **2** *m* stimulant; **estimular** <1a> *v/t* stimulate; (*animar*) encourage; **estímulo** *m* stimulus; (*incentivo*) incentive

estío *m lit* summertime

estipular <1a> *v/t* stipulate

estirado *adj* snooty F, stuck-up F

estirar <1a> *v/t* stretch; (*alisar*) smooth out; *dinero* stretch, make go further; **~ la pata** F kick the bucket F; **~ las piernas** stretch one's legs

estirpe *f* stock

estival *adj* summer *atr*

esto *pron* this; **~ es** that is to say; **por ~** this is why; **a todo ~** (*mientras tanto*) meanwhile; (*a propósito*) incidentally

estofa *f*: **de baja ~** *desp* low-class *desp*

estofado *adj* stewed; **estofar** <1a> *v/t* stew

estoico 1 *adj* stoic(al) **2** *m*, **-a** *f* stoic

estómago *m* stomach

estor *m* blind

estorbar <1a> *v/t* (*dificultar*) hinder; **nos estorbaba** he was in our way **2** *v/i* get in the way; **estorbo** *m* hindrance, nuisance

estornino *m* ZO starling

estornudar <1a> *v/i* sneeze; **estornudo** *m* sneeze

estoy *vb* → **estar**

estrado *m* platform

estrafalario *adj* F eccentric; *ropa* outlandish

estragón *m* BOT tarragon

estragos *mpl* devastation *sg*; **causar ~ entre** wreak havoc among

estrambótico *adj* F eccentric; *ropa* outlandish

estrangular <1a> *v/t* strangle

estraperlo *m* black market; **de ~** on the black market

estratagema *f* stratagem; **estrategia** *f* strategy; **estratégico** *adj* strategic

estrato *m fig* stratum

estrechar <1a> **1** *v/t ropa* take in; *mano* shake; **~ entre los brazos** hug, embrace **2** *v/r* **~se** narrow, get narrower; **estrechez** *f fig* hardship; **~ de miras** narrow-mindedness; **pasar ~es** suffer hardship; **estrecho 1** *adj* narrow; (*apretado*) tight; *amistad* close; **~ de miras** narrow-minded **2** *m* strait, straits *pl*

estrella *f tb de cine etc* star; **~ fugaz** falling star, shooting star; **~ de mar** ZO starfish; **~ polar** Pole star; **estrellar** <1a> **1** *v/t* smash; **~ algo contra algo** smash sth against sth; **estrelló el coche contra un muro** he smashed the car into a wall **2** *v/r* **~se** crash (*contra* into); **estrellón** *m Pe, Bol* crash

estremecer <2d> **1** *v/t* shock, shake F **2** *v/r* **~se** shake, tremble; *de frío* shiver; *de horror* shudder

estrenar <1a> **1** *v/t ropa* wear for the first time, christen F; *objeto* try out, christen F; TEA, *película* premiere; **a ~** brand new **2** *v/r* **~se** make one's debut; **estreno** *m* TEA, *de película* premiere; *de persona* debut; **estar de ~** be wearing new clothes

estreñimiento *m* constipation

estrépito *m* noise, racket

estrés *m* stress; **estresar** <1a> *v/t*: **~**

alguien cause s.o. stress, subject s.o. to stress

estría *f en piel* stretch mark

estribar <1a> *v/i:* ~ **en** stem from, lie in

estribillo *m* chorus, refrain

estribo *m* stirrup; **perder los ~s** *fig* fly off the handle F

estrictez *f S.Am.* strictness; **estricto** *adj* strict

estridente *adj* shrill, strident

estrofa *f* stanza, verse

estropajo *m* scourer; **estropajoso** *adj persona* wiry; *boca* dry; *camisa* scruffy

estropeado *adj* (*averiado*) broken; **estropear** <1a> **1** *v/t aparato* break; *plan* ruin, spoil **2** *v/r* ~**se** break down; *de comida* go off, go bad; *de plan* go wrong

estructura *f* structure; **estructurar** <1a> *v/t* structure, organize

estruendo *m* racket, din

estrujar <1a> *v/t* F crumple up, scrunch up F; *trapo* wring out; *persona* squeeze, hold tightly

estuario *m* estuary

estuche *m* case, box

estuco *m* stuccowork

estudiante *m/f* student; **estudiantil** *adj* student *atr*; **estudiar** <1b> *v/t & v/i* study; **estudio** *m disciplina* study; *apartamento* studio, *Br* studio flat; *de cine, música* studio; **estudioso** *adj* studious

estufa *f* heater

estupefaciente *m* narcotic (drug); **estupefacto** *adj* stupefied, speechless

estupendo *adj* fantastic, wonderful

estupidez *f cualidad* stupidity; *acción* stupid thing; **estúpido 1** *adj* stupid **2** *m,* **-a** *f* idiot

estupor *m* astonishment, amazement; MED stupor

esturión *m* ZO sturgeon

estuve *vb* → **estar**

estuvo *vb* → **estar**

etapa *f* stage; *por* ~*s* in stages

etarra *m/f* member of ETA

etc *abr* (= **etcétera**) etc (= etcetera)

etcétera *m* etcetera, and so on; *y un largo* ~ *de ...* and a long list of ..., and many other ...

etéreo *adj* ethereal

eternidad *f* eternity; **eterno** *adj* eternal; *la película se me hizo -a* the movie seemed to go on for ever

ética *f en filosofía* ethics; *comportamiento* principles *pl*; **ético** *adj* ethical

etimología *f* etymology

Etiopía Ethiopia

etiqueta *f* label; (*protocolo*) etiquette; **etiquetar** <1a> *v/t tb fig* label

étnico *adj* ethnic

eucalipto *m* BOT eucalyptus

eucaristía *f* Eucharist

eufemismo *m* euphemism

euforia *f* euphoria; **eufórico** *adj* euphoric

euro *m* euro

eurodiputado *m,* **-a** *f* MEP, member of the European Parliament

Europa Europe

europeísta *m/f* pro-European

europeo 1 *adj* European **2** *m,* **-a** *f* European

eusquera *m/adj* Basque

eutanasia *f* euthanasia

evacuación *f* evacuation; **evacuar** <1d> *v/t* evacuate

evadir <3a> **1** *v/t* avoid; *impuestos* evade **2** *v/r* ~**se** *tb fig* escape

evaluación *f* evaluation, assessment; (*prueba*) test; **evaluar** <1e> *v/t* assess, evaluate

evangelio *m* gospel; **evangelizar** <1f> *v/t* evangelize

evaporación *f* evaporation; **evaporarse** <1a> *v/r* evaporate; *fig* F vanish into thin air

evasión *f tb fig* escape; ~ *de capitales* flight of capital; ~ *fiscal* tax evasion; **evasiva** *f* evasive reply

evento *m* event; **eventual** *adj* possible; *trabajo* casual, temporary; *en el caso* ~ *de* in the event of; **eventualidad** *f* eventuality

evidencia *f* evidence, proof; *poner*

en ~ demonstrate; **poner a alguien en** ~ show s.o. up; **evidente** *adj* evident, clear

evitar <1a> *v/t* avoid; (*impedir*) prevent; *molestias* save; **no puedo ~lo** I can't help it

evocar <1g> *v/t* evoke

evolución *f* BIO evolution; (*desarrollo*) development; **evolucionar** <1a> *v/i* BIO evolve; (*desarrollar*) develop

ex 1 *pref* ex- **2** *m/f* F ex F

exabrupto *m* sharp remark

exacerbar <1a> *v/t* exacerbate, make worse; (*irritar*) exasperate

exacto *adj medida* exact, precise; *informe* accurate; **¡~!** exactly!, precisely!

exageración *f* exaggeration; **exagerado** *adj* exaggerated; **exagerar** <1a> *v/t* exaggerate

exaltación *f* (*alabanza*) exaltation; (*entusiasmo*) agitation, excitement; **exaltar** <1a> *v/t* excite, get worked up

examen *m* test, exam; MED examination; (*análisis*) study; **~ de conducir** driving test; **examinar** <1a> **1** *v/t* examine **2** *v/r* **~se** take an exam

exasperar <1a> **1** *v/t* exasperate **2** *v/r* **~se** get exasperated

excarcelar <1a> *v/t* release (from prison)

excavación *f* excavation; **excavadora** *f* digger; **excavar** <1a> *v/t* excavate; *túnel* dig

excedencia *f* extended leave of absence; **excedente 1** *adj* surplus; *empleado* on extended leave of absence **2** *m* surplus; **exceder** <2a> **1** *v/t* exceed **2** *v/r* **~se** go too far, get carried away

excelencia *f* excellence; **Su Excelencia la señora embajadora** Her Excellency the Ambassador; **por** ~ par excellence; **excelente** *adj* excellent

excéntrico 1 *adj* eccentric **2** *m*, **-a** *f* eccentric

excepción *f* exception; **a** ~ **de** ex-

cept for; **sin** ~ without exception; **excepcional** *adj* exceptional; **excepto** *prp* except; **exceptuar** <1e> *v/t* except; **exceptuando** with the exception of, except for

excesivo *adj* excessive; **exceso** *m* excess; ~ **de equipaje** excess baggage; ~ **de velocidad** speeding; **en** ~ in excess, too much

excitación *f* excitement, agitation; **excitante 1** *adj* exciting; **una bebida** ~ a stimulant **2** *m* stimulant; **excitar** <1a> **1** *v/t* excite; *sentimientos, sexualmente* arouse **2** *v/r* **~se** get excited; *sexualmente* become aroused

exclamación *f* exclamation; **exclamar** <1a> *v/t* exclaim

excluir <3g> *v/t* leave out (**de** of), exclude (**de** from); *posibilidad* rule out; **exclusiva** *f privilegio* exclusive rights *pl* (**de** to); *reportaje* exclusive; **exclusivo** *adj* exclusive

excomunión *f* excommunication

excremento *m* excrement

exculpar <1a> *v/t* exonerate

excursión *f* trip, excursion; **excursionista** *m/f* excursionist

excusa *f* excuse; **~s** apologies

excusado *m* bathroom; **excusar** <1a> *v/t* excuse

execrable *adj* abominable, execrable *fml*

exención *f* exemption; ~ **fiscal** tax exemption; **exento** *adj* exempt (**de** from); ~ **de impuestos** tax-exempt, tax-free

exhalación *f*: **salir como una** ~ *fig* rush *o* dash out

exhaustivo *adj* exhaustive; **exhausto** *adj* exhausted

exhibición *f* display, demonstration; *de película* screening, showing; **exhibicionista** *m/f* exhibitionist; **exhibir** <3a> **1** *v/t* show, display; *película* screen, show; *cuadro* exhibit **2** *v/r* **~se** show o.s., be seen

exhumar <1a> *v/t* exhume

exigencia *f* demand; **exigente** *adj* demanding; **exigir** <3c> *v/t* demand; (*requerir*) call for, demand;

le exigen mucho they ask a lot of him

exiguo *adj* meager, *Br* meagre

exiliado 1 *adj* exiled, in exile *pred* **2** *m*, **-a** *f* exile; **exiliar** <1a> **1** *v/t* exile **2** *v/r* **~se** go into exile; **exilio** *m* exile; **en el ~** in exile

eximir <3a> *v/t* exempt (**de** from)

existencia *f* existence; (*vida*) life; **~s** COM supplies, stocks; **existencialista** *m/f* & *adj* existentialist; **existir** <3a> *v/i* exist; **existen muchos problemas** there are a lot of problems

éxito *m* success; **~ de taquilla** box office hit; **tener ~** be successful, be a success; **exitoso** *adj* successful

Exmo. *abr* (= **Excelentísimo**) Your / His Excellency

exonerar <1a> *v/t* exonerate; **~ a alguien de algo** exempt s.o. from sth

exorbitante *adj* exorbitant

exorcista *m/f* exorcist

exótico *adj* exotic

expandir <3a> **1** *v/t* expand **2** *v/r* **~se** expand; *de noticia* spread; **expansión** *f* expansion; (*recreo*) recreation

expatriarse <1b> *v/r* leave one's country

expectación *f* sense of anticipation; **expectativa** *f* (*esperanza*) expectation; **estar a la ~ de algo** be waiting for sth; **~s** (*perspectivas*) prospects

expedición *f* expedition

expediente *m* file, dossier; (*investigación*) investigation, inquiry; **~ académico** student record; **~ disciplinario** disciplinary proceedings *pl*; **abrir un ~ a alguien** take disciplinary action against s.o.

expedir <3l> *v/t documento* issue; *mercancías* send, dispatch

expeditar <1a> *v/t L.Am.* (*apresurar*) hurry; (*concluir*) finish, conclude

expeditivo *adj* expeditious

expendedor *adj*: **máquina ~a** vend-

ing machine

expendio *m L.Am.* store, shop

expensas *fpl*: **a ~ de** at the expense of

experiencia *f* experience

experimentado *adj* experienced; **experimentar** <1a> **1** *v/t* try out, experiment with **2** *v/i* experiment (**con** on); **experimento** *m* experiment

experto 1 *adj* expert; **~ en hacer algo** expert *o* very good at doing sth **2** *m* expert (**en** on)

expiar <1c> *v/t* expiate, atone for

expirar <1a> *v/i* expire

explanada *f* open area; *junto al mar* esplanade

explayarse <1a> *v/r* speak at length; (*desahogarse*) unburden o.s.; (*distraerse*) relax, unwind; **~ sobre algo** expound on sth

explicación *f* explanation; **explicar** <1g> **1** *v/t* explain **2** *v/r* **~se** (*comprender*) understand; (*hacerse comprender*) express o.s.; **no me lo explico** I can't understand it, I don't get it F

explícito *adj* explicit

explorador *m*, **-a** *f* explorer; MIL scout; **explorar** <1a> *v/t* explore

explosión *f* explosion; **~ demográfica** population explosion; **hacer ~** go off, explode; **explosionar** <1a> *v/t* & *v/i* explode; **explosivo** *m/adj* explosive

explotación *f de mina, tierra* exploitation, working; *de negocio* running, operation; *de trabajador* exploitation; **explotar** <1a> **1** *v/t tierra, mina* work, exploit; *situación* take advantage of, exploit; *trabajador* exploit **2** *v/i* go off, explode; *fig* explode, blow a fuse F

expoliar <1b> *v/t* plunder, pillage

exponente *m* exponent; **exponer** <2r; *part* **expuesto**> **1** *v/t idea, teoría* set out, put forward; (*revelar*) expose; *pintura, escultura* exhibit, show; (*arriesgar*) risk **2** *v/r* **~se**: **~se a algo** (*arriesgarse*) lay o.s. open to sth

exportación *f* export; **exportar** <1a> *v/t* export

exposición *f* exhibition

expresar <1a> **1** *v/t* express **2** *v/r* ~**se** express o.s.; **expresión** *f* expression; **expresivo** *adj* expressive

expreso 1 *adj* express *atr*; **tren** ~ express (train) **2** *m* **tren** express (train); *café* espresso

exprimidor *m* lemon squeezer; *eléctrico* juicer; **exprimir** <3a> *v/t* squeeze; *(explotar)* exploit

ex profeso *adv (especialmente)* expressly; *(a propósito)* deliberately

expropiar <1b> *v/t* expropriate

expuesto *part* → **exponer**

expugnar <1a> *v/t* take by storm

expulsar <1a> *v/t* expel, throw out F; DEP expel from the game, *Br* send off; **expulsión** *f* expulsion; DEP sending off

exquisito *adj comida* delicious; *(bello)* exquisite; *(refinado)* refined

extasiarse <1c> *v/r* be enraptured, go into raptures; **éxtasis** *m tb droga* ecstasy

extender <2g> **1** *v/t brazos* stretch out; *(untar)* spread; *tela, papel* spread out; *(ampliar)* extend; **me extendió la mano** she held out her hand to me **2** *v/r* ~**se** *de campos* stretch; *de influencia* extend; *(difundirse)* spread; *(durar)* last; *explayarse* go into detail; **extendido 1** *part* → **extender 2** *adj costumbre* widespread; *brazos* outstretched; *mapa* spread out; **extensión** *f tb* TELEC extension; *superficie* expanse, area; **por** ~ by extension; **extenso** *adj* extensive, vast; *informe* lengthy, long

extenuar <1e> **1** *v/t* exhaust, tire out **2** *v/r* ~**se** exhaust o.s., tire o.s. out

exterior 1 *adj aspecto* external, outward; *capa* outer; *apartamento* overlooking the street; POL foreign; **la parte ~ del edificio** the exterior *o* the outside of the building **2** *m* *(fachada)* exterior, outside; *aspecto* exterior, outward appearance; **viajar al** ~ *(al extranjero)* travel abroad; **exteriorizar** <1f> *v/t* externalize

exterminar <1a> *v/t* exterminate, wipe out

externo 1 *adj aspecto* external, outward; *influencia* external, outside; *capa* outer; *deuda* foreign **2** *m*, **-a** *f* EDU student who attends a boarding school but returns home each evening, *Br* day boy / girl

extinción *f*: **en peligro de** ~ in danger of extinction; **extinguidor** *m* *L.Am.*: ~ **(de incendios)** (fire) extinguisher; **extinguir** <3d> **1** *v/t* BIO, ZO wipe out; *fuego* extinguish, put out **2** *v/r* ~**se** BIO, ZO become extinct, die out; *de fuego* go out; *de plazo* expire; **extintor** *m* fire extinguisher

extirpar <1a> *v/t* MED remove; *vicio* eradicate, stamp out

extorsión *f* extortion; **extorsionar** <1a> *v/t* extort money from

extra 1 *adj excelente* top quality; *adicional* extra; **horas** ~ overtime; **paga** ~ extra month's pay **2** *m/f de cine* extra **3** *m gasto* additional expense

extracto *m* extract; *(resumen)* summary; GASTR, QUÍM extract, essence; ~ **de cuenta** bank statement; **extractor** *m* extractor; ~ **de humos** extractor fan

extradición *f* extradition; **extraditar** <1a> *v/t* extradite

extraer <2p> *v/t* extract, pull out; *conclusión* draw

extrajudicial *adj* out-of-court

extralimitarse <1a> *v/r* go too far, exceed one's authority

extramatrimonial *adj* extramarital

extranjería *f*: **ley de** ~ immigration laws *pl*; **extranjero 1** *adj* foreign **2** *m*, **-a** *f* foreigner; **en el** ~ abroad

extranjis: **de** ~ F on the quiet F, on the sly F

extrañar <1a> **1** *v/t L.Am.* miss **2** *v/r* ~**se** be surprised (**de** at); **extraño 1** *adj* strange, odd **2** *m*, **-a** *f* stranger

extraordinario *adj* extraordinary
extrapolar <1a> *v/t* extrapolate
extrarradio *m* outlying districts *pl*, outskirts *pl*
extraterrestre *adj* extraterrestial, alien
extravagante *adj* outrageous
extravertido *adj* extrovert
extraviar <1c> **1** *v/t* lose, mislay **2** *v/r* **~se** get lost, lose one's way
extremadamente *adv* extremely; **extremado** *adj* extreme; **extremar** <1a> *v/t* maximize

extremidad *f* end; **~es** extremities; **extremista 1** *adj* extreme **2** *m/f* POL extremist; **extremo 1** *adj* extreme **2** *m* extreme; *parte primera o última* end; *punto* point; ***llegar al ~ de*** reach the point of **3** *m/f*: **~ derecho/izquierdo** DEP right/left wing; ***en ~*** in the extreme
extrovertido *adj* extrovert
exuberante *adj* exuberant; *vegetación* lush
exultante *adj* elated
eyacular <1a> *v/t* ejaculate

F

F

fabada *f* GASTR *Asturian stew with pork sausage, bacon and beans*
fábrica *f* plant, factory; **fabricación** *f* manufacturing; **fabricante** *m* manufacturer, maker; **fabricar** <1g> *v/t* manufacture
fábula *f* fable; *(mentira)* lie; **fabuloso** *adj* fabulous, marvel(l)ous
facción *f* POL faction; **facciones** *pl (rasgos)* features
faceta *f fig* facet
facha 1 *f* look; *(cara)* face **2** *m/f desp* fascist
fachada *f tb fig* façade
facial *adj* facial
fácil *adj* easy; **es ~ que** it's likely that; **facilidad** *f* ease; **con ~** easily; **tener ~ para algo** have a gift for sth; **~es de pago** credit facilities, credit terms; **facilitar** <1a> *v/t* facilitate, make easier; *(hacer factible)* make possible; *medios, dinero etc* provide
factible *adj* feasible
factor *m* factor
factoría *f esp L.Am.* plant, factory
factura *f* COM invoice; *de luz, gas etc* bill; **facturación** *f* COM invoicing; *(volumen de negocio)* turnover;

AVIA check-in; **facturar** <1a> *v/t* COM invoice, bill; *volumen de negocio* turn over; AVIA check in
facultad *f* faculty; *(autoridad)* authority
faena *f* task, job; **hacer una ~ a alguien** play a dirty trick on s.o.
fagot *m* MÚS bassoon
faisán *m* ZO pheasant
faja *f prenda interior* girdle
fajarse <1a> *v/r Méx, Ven F* get into a fight
fajo *m* wad; *de periódicos* bundle
falacia *f* fallacy; *(engaño)* fraud
falange *f* ANAT phalange; MIL phalanx
falda *f* skirt; *de montaña* side
faldero *adj*: **perro ~** lap dog
falla *f* fault; *de fabricación* flaw; **fallar** <1a> **1** *v/i* fail; *(no acertar)* miss; *de sistema etc* go wrong; JUR find *(en favor de* for; *en contra de* against); **~ a alguien** let s.o. down **2** *v/t* JUR pronounce judg(e)ment in; *pregunta* get wrong; **~ el tiro** miss
fallecer <2d> *v/i* pass away; **fallecimiento** *m* demise
fallo *m* mistake; TÉC fault; JUR

F

judg(e)ment; **~ cardíaco** heart failure

falsedad f falseness; (*mentira*) lie; **falsificación** f de moneda counterfeiting; de documentos, firma forgery; (**falsificar** <1g> v/t moneda counterfeit; documento, firma forge, falsify; **falso** adj false; joyas fake; documento, firma forged; **jurar en ~** commit perjury

falta f (*escasez*) lack, want; (*error*) mistake; (*ausencia*) absence; **en tenis** fault; **en fútbol** foul; (*tiro libre*) free kick; **hacerle ~ a alguien** foul s.o.; **~ de** lack of, shortage of; **sin ~** without fail; **buena ~ le hace** it's about time; **echar en ~ a alguien** miss s.o.; **hacer ~** be necessary

faltar <1a> v/i be missing; **falta una hora** there's an hour to go; **faltan 10 kilómetros** there are 10 kilometers to go; **sólo falta hacer la salsa** there's only the sauce to do; **~ a** absent from; **~ a clase** miss class, be absent from class; **~ a alguien** be disrespectful to s.o.; **~ a su palabra** not keep one's word; **falto** adj: **~ de** lacking in, devoid of; **~ de recursos** short of resources

fama f fame; (*reputación*) reputation; **tener mala ~** have a bad reputation

familia f family; **sentirse como en ~** feel at home; **familiar 1** adj family atr; (*conocido*) familiar; LING colloquial **2** m/f relation, relative; **familiaridad** f familiarity; **familiarizarse** <1f> v/r familiarize o.s. (**con** with)

famoso 1 adj famous **2** m, **-a** f celebrity

fan m/f fan

fanático 1 adj fanatical **2** m, **-a** f fanatic; **fanatismo** m fanaticism

fanfarrón 1 adj boastful **2** m, **-ona** f boaster; **fanfarronear** <1a> v/i boast, brag

fango m tb fig mud

fantasear <1a> v/i fantasize; **fantasía** f fantasy; (*imaginación*) imagination; **joyas de ~** costume

jewel(l)ery; **fantasma** m ghost; **fantástico** adj fantastic

farándula f show business

fardar <1a> v/i: **~ de algo** F boast about sth, show off about sth

fardo m bundle

faringitis f MED inflammation of the pharynx, pharyngitis

fariña f S.Am. manioc flour, cassava

farmacéutico 1 adj pharmaceutical **2** m, **-a** f pharmacist, Br chemist; **farmacia** f pharmacy, Br chemist's; estudios pharmacy; **~ de guardia** 24-hour pharmacist, Br emergency chemist; **fármaco** m medicine; **farmacología** f pharmacology

faro m MAR lighthouse; AUTO headlight, headlamp; **~ antiniebla** fog light; **farol** m lantern; (*farola*) streetlight, streetlamp; en juegos de cartas bluff; **farola** f streetlight, streetlamp; **farolillo** m: **ser el ~ rojo** fig F be bottom of the league

farragoso adj texto dense

farrear <1a> v/i L.Am. F go out on the town F

farrista adj L.Am. F hard-drinking

farsa f tb fig farce; **farsante** m/f fraud, fake

fascículo m TIP instal(l)ment

fascinación f fascination; **fascinante** adj fascinating; **fascinar** <1a> v/t fascinate

fascismo m fascism; **fascista** m/f & adj fascist

fase f phase

fastidiar <1b> **1** v/t annoy; F (*estropear*) spoil **2** v/r **~se** grin and bear it; **fastidio** m annoyance; **¡qué ~!** what a nuisance!

fastuoso adj lavish

fatal 1 adj fatal; (*muy malo*) dreadful, awful **2** adv very badly

fatídico adj fateful

fatiga f tiredness, fatigue; **fatigar** <1h> **1** v/t tire **2** v/r **~se** get tired

fatuo adj conceited; (*necio*) fatuous

fauces fpl ZO jaws

fauna f fauna

favor m favo(u)r; **a ~ de** in favo(u)r of; **por ~** please; **hacer un ~** do

a favo(u)r; **favorecer** <2d> v/t
favo(u)r; *de ropa*, *color* suit;
favoritismo m favo(u)ritism; **favorito 1** adj favo(u)rite **2** m, **-a** f
favo(u)rite

fax m fax; *enviar un ~ a alguien* send
s.o. a fax, fax s.o.

fayuca f Méx smuggling; **fayuquero**
m, **-a** f Méx dealer in smuggled
goods

F.C. abr (= **Fútbol Club**) FC (= Football Club)

fdo. abr (= **firmado**) signed

fe f faith (*en* in); *~ de erratas* errata

fealdad f ugliness

feb. abr (= **febrero**) Feb. (= February)

febrero m February

fecal adj f(a)ecal

fecha f date; *~ límite de consumo*
best before date; *~ de nacimiento*
date of birth; **fechador** m Chi, Méx
postmark

fécula f starch

fecundación f fertilization; *~ in vitro*
MED in vitro fertilization; **fecundar**
<1a> v/t fertilize; **fecundo** adj fer-
tile

federación f federation; **federal** adj
federal

felicidad f happiness; *¡~es!* congratulations!; **felicitación** f letter
of congratulations; *¡felicitaciones!*
congratulations!; **felicitar** <1a> v/t
congratulate (*por* on)

felino adj tb fig feline

feliz adj happy; *¡~ Navidad!* Merry
Christmas!

felpa f towel(l)ing; **felpudo** m door-
mat

femenino 1 adj feminine; *moda,
equipo* women's **2** GRAM feminine;
femin(e)idad f femininity; **feminismo** m feminism; **feminista** m/f
& adj feminist

fenomenal 1 adj F fantastic F, phe-
nomenal F **2** adv: *lo pasé ~* F I had a
fantastic time F; **fenómeno 1** m
phenomenon; *persona* genius **2** adj
F fantastic F, great F

feo 1 adj ugly; *fig* nasty **2** m: *hacer*

un ~ a alguien F snub s.o.

féretro m casket, coffin

feria f COM fair; *L.Am.* (*mercado*)
market; *Méx* (*calderilla*) small
change; *~ de muestras* trade fair;
feriado 1 adj L.Am.: *día ~* (public)
holiday **2** m L.Am. (public) holiday;
abierto ~s open on public holidays;
ferial 1 adj: *recinto ~* fairground
2 m fair

fermentación f fermentation; **fermentar** <1a> v/t ferment; **fermen-
to** m ferment

ferocidad f ferocity; **feroz** adj fierce;
(*cruel*) cruel

férreo adj tb fig iron atr; del ferrocarril
rail atr; **ferretería** f hardware store;
ferrocarril m railroad, Br railway;
ferrocarrilero m L.Am. railroad o
Br railway worker; **ferroviario** adj
rail atr

ferry m ferry

fértil adj fertile; **fertilidad** f fertility;
fertilizante m fertilizer

ferviente adj fig fervent; **fervor** m
fervo(u)r

festejar <1a> v/t persona wine and
dine; *L.Am.* celebrate; **festejo** m
celebration; *~s* festivities; **festín** m
banquet; **festival** m festival; *~
cinematográfico* film festival;
festividad f feast; *~es* festivities;
festivo adj festive

fetal adj fetal

fetiche m fetish

fétido adj fetid

feto m fetus

feudal adj feudal; **feudo** m fig domain

FF. AA. abr (= **fuerzas armadas**)
armed forces

FF. CC. abr (= **ferrocarriles**) rail-
roads

fiable adj trustworthy; datos, máquina
etc reliable

fiambre m cold cut, Br cold meat; P
(*cadáver*) stiff P; **fiambrera** f lunch
pail, Br lunch box; **fiambrería** f
L.Am. delicatessen

fianza f deposit; JUR bail; *bajo ~* on
bail

F

fiar <1c> **1** v/i give credit **2** v/r ~**se**: ~**se de alguien** trust s.o.; **no me fío** I don't trust him / them *etc*

fiasco *m* fiasco

fibra *f en tejido, alimento* fiber, *Br* fibre; ~ **óptica** optical fiber (*Br* fibre); ~ **de vidrio** fiberglass, *Br* fibreglass; **fibroso** *adj* fibrous

ficción *f* fiction

ficha *f* file card, index card; *en juegos de mesa* counter; *en un casino* chip; *en damas* checker, *Br* draught; *en ajedrez* man, piece; TELEC token; **fichar** <1a> **1** v/t DEP sign; JUR open a file on **2** v/i DEP sign (*por* for); **fichero** *m* file cabinet, *Br* filing cabinet; INFOR file

ficticio *adj* fictitious

fidedigno *adj* reliable

fidelidad *f* fidelity

fideo *m* noodle

fiebre *f* fever; (*temperatura*) temperature; ~ **del heno** hay fever

fiel 1 *adj* faithful; (*leal*) loyal **2** *mpl*: *los* ~**es** REL the faithful *pl*

fieltro *m* felt

fiera *f* wild animal; **ponerse hecho una** ~ F go wild F; **fiero** *adj* fierce

fierro *m* L.Am. iron

fiesta *f* festival; (*reunión social*) party; (*día festivo*) public holiday; **estar de** ~ be in a party mood

fifí *m* L.Am. P *afeminado* sissy F

figura *f* figure; (*estatuilla*) figurine; (*forma*) shape; *naipes* face card, *Br* picture card; **tener buena** ~ have a good figure; **figurado** *adj* figurative; **sentido** ~ figurative sense; **figurar** <1a> **1** v/i appear (*en* in); **aquí figura como** … she appears *o* is down here as … **2** v/r ~**se** imagine; **¡figúrate!** just imagine!

fijar <1a> **1** v/t fix; *cartel* stick; *fecha, objetivo* set; *residencia* establish; *atención* focus **2** v/r ~**se** (*establecerse*) settle; (*prestar atención*) pay attention (*en* to); ~**se en algo** (*darse cuenta*) notice sth; **fijo** *adj* fixed; *trabajo* permanent; *fecha* definite

fila *f* line, *Br* queue; *de asientos* row; *en* ~ *india* in single file; ~**s** MIL ranks

filatelia *f* philately, stamp collecting

filete *m* GASTR fillet

filial 1 *adj* filial **2** *f* COM subsidiary

Filipinas *fpl* Philippines

film(e) *m* movie, film; **filmación** *f* filming, shooting; **filmar** <1a> v/t film, shoot

filo *m* edge; *de navaja* cutting edge; **al** ~ **de las siete** *fig* around 7 o'clock

filología *f* philology; ~ **hispánica** EDU Spanish language and literature; **filólogo** *m*, **-a** *f* philologist

filón *m* vein, seam; *fig* goldmine

filoso *adj* L.Am. sharp

filosofía *f* philosophy; **filosófico** *adj* philosophical; **filósofo** *m*, **-a** *f* philosopher

filtración *f* leak; **filtrar** <1a> **1** v/t filter; *información* leak **2** v/r ~**se** filter (*por* through); *de agua, información* leak; **filtro** *m* filter

fin *m* end; (*objetivo*) aim, purpose; ~ **de semana** weekend; **a** ~**es de mayo** at the end of May; **al** ~ **y al cabo** at the end of the day, after all; **en** ~ anyway

final *f/adj* final; **finalidad** *f* purpose, aim; **finalista 1** *adj*: *las dos selecciones* ~**s** the two teams that reached the final **2** *m/f* finalist; **finalización** *f* completion; **finalizado** *adj* complete; **finalizar** <1f> v/t & v/i end, finish; **finalmente** *adv* eventually

financiación *f* funding; **financiar** <1b> v/t finance, fund; **financista** *m/f* L.Am. financier; **finanzas** *fpl* finances

finca *f* (*bien inmueble*) property; L.Am. (*granja*) farm

fingido *adj* false; **fingir** <3c> **1** v/t feign *fml*; **fingió no haberlo oído** I pretended I hadn't heard **2** v/r ~**se**: ~**se enfermo** pretend to be ill, feign illness *fml*

finlandés 1 *adj* Finnish **2** *m*, **-esa** *f* Finn; **Finlandia** Finland

fino *adj* *calidad* fine; *libro, tela* thin;

(*esbelto*) slim; *modales, gusto* refined; *sentido de humor* subtle

firma f signature; *acto* signing; COM firm

firmamento m firmament

firmar <1a> v/t sign

firme adj firm; (*estable*) steady; **en ~** COM firm

fiscal 1 adj tax atr, fiscal **2** m/f district attorney, Br public prosecutor

fisgar <1h> v/i F snoop F; **~ en algo** snoop around in sth; **fisgón** m, **-ona** f snoop; **fisgonear** <1a> v/i F snoop around F (**en** in)

física f physics; **físico 1** adj physical **2** m, **-a** f crack; **3** m de una persona physique

fisiología f physiology

fisión f fission

fisioterapeuta m/f physical therapist, Br physiotherapist; **fisioterapia** f physical therapy, Br physiotherapy

fisonomía f features pl

fisura f crack; MED fracture

flác(c)ido adj flabby

flaco adj thin; **punto ~** weak point

flacuchento adj L.Am. F skinny

flagelar <1a> v/t flagellate

flagrante adj flagrant; **en ~ delito** red-handed, in flagrante delicto

flamante adj (*nuevo*) brand-new

flamenco 1 adj MÚS flamenco **2** m MÚS flamenco; ZO flamingo

flan m crème caramel

flanco m flank

flaquear <1a> v/i weaken; *de entusiasmo* flag; **flaqueza** f fig weakness

flash m FOT flash

flato m MED stitch

flatulencia f MED flatulence

flauta f flute; *Méx* fried taco; **~ dulce** recorder; **~ travesera** (transverse) flute; **flautista** m/f flautist

flecha f arrow; **flechazo** m fig love at first sight

flecos mpl fringe sg

flema f fig phlegm; **flemático** adj phlegmatic

flemón m MED gumboil

flequillo m del pelo fringe

fletar <1a> v/t charter; (*embarcar*) load; **flete** m L.Am. freight, cost of transport; **fletero** adj L.Am. hire atr, charter atr

flexibilidad f flexibility; **flexible** adj flexible

flexión f en gimnasia push-up, Br press-up; *de piernas* squat; *de la voz* inflection; **flexionar** <1a> **1** v/t flex **2** v/r **~se** bend

flexo m desk lamp

flipar <1a> v/i: **le flipa el cine** P he's mad about the movies F

flirtear <1a> v/i flirt (**con** with)

flojera f L.Am. laziness; **me da ~** I can't be bothered; **flojo** adj loose; *café, argumento* weak; COM *actividad* slack; *novela, redacción* poor; L.Am. lazy

flor f flower; **flora** f flora; **florear** <1a> **1** v/t decorate with flowers; *Méx* (*halagar*) flatter, compliment **2** v/i flower, bloom; **florecer** <2d> v/i BOT flower. bloom; *de negocio, civilización* etc flourish; **floreciente** adj flourishing; **florero** m vase; **florista** m/f florist; **floristería** f florist's, flower shop

flota f fleet; **flotación** f flotation; **flotador** m float; **flotar** <1a> v/i float; **flote** MAR: **a ~** afloat

fluctuación f fluctuation; **fluctuar** <1e> v/i fluctuate

fluidez f fluidity; **fluido 1** adj fluid; *tráfico* free-flowing; *lenguaje* fluent **2** m fluid; **fluir** <3g> v/i flow

flujo m flow

fluorescente 1 adj fluorescent **2** m strip light

fluvial adj river atr

FM abr (= **frecuencia modulada**) FM (= frequency modulation)

FMI abr (= **Fondo Monetario Internacional**) IMF (= International Monetary Fund)

fobia f phobia

foca f ZO seal

foco m focus; TEA, TV spotlight; *de infección* center, Br centre; *de incendio* seat; L.Am. (*bombilla*) lightbulb; *de auto* headlight; *de calle* streetlight

fofo *adj* flabby

fogata *f* bonfire; **fogoso** *adj* fiery, ardent

foie-gras *m* foie gras

folclore *m* folklore

fólico *adj*: **ácido ~** folic acid

folio *m* sheet (of paper)

folklore *m* folklore

follaje *m* foliage

folleto *m* pamphlet

follón *m* argument; (*lío*) mess; **armar un ~** kick up a fuss

fomentar <1a> *v/t* foster; COM promote; *rebelión* foment, incite; **fomento** *m* COM promotion

fonda *f* L.Am. cheap restaurant; (*pensión*) boarding house

fondear <1a> **1** *v/t* MAR anchor **2** *v/r* **~se** L.Am. get rich

fondero *m*, **-a** *f* L.Am. restaurant owner

fondista *m/f* DEP long-distance runner

fondo *m* bottom; *de sala, cuarto etc* back; *de pasillo* end; (*profundidad*) depth; PINT, FOT background; *de un museo etc* collection; COM fund; **~ de inversión** investment fund; **~ de pensiones** pension fund; **Fondo Monetario Internacional** International Monetary Fund; **~s** *pl* money *sg*, funds; **tiene buen ~** he's got a good heart; **en el ~** deep down; **tocar ~** *fig* reach bottom

fonética *f* phonetics

fontanería *f* plumbing; **fontanero** *m* plumber

footing *m* DEP jogging; **hacer ~** go jogging, jog

forastero 1 *adj* foreign **2** *m*, **-a** *f* outsider, stranger

forcejear <1a> *v/i* struggle; **forcejeo** *m* struggle

forense 1 *adj* forensic **2** *m/f* forensic scientist

forestación *f* afforestation; **forestal** *adj* forest *atr*; **forestar** <1a> *v/t* L.Am. afforest

forjar <1a> *v/t* metal forge

forma *f* form; (*apariencia*) shape; (*manera*) way; **de todas ~s** in any case, anyway; **estar en ~** be fit; **formación** *f* formation; (*entrenamiento*) training; **~ profesional** vocational training; **formal** *adj* formal; *niño* well-behaved; (*responsable*) responsible; **formalizar** <1f> *v/t* formalize; *relación* make official; **formar** <1a> **1** *v/t* form; (*educar*) educate **2** *v/r* **~se** form

formatear <1a> *v/t* INFOR format; **formato** *m* format

formidable *adj* huge; (*estupendo*) tremendous

fórmula *f* formula; **formular** <1a> *v/t* *teoría* formulate; *queja* make, lodge; **formulario** *m* form

fornicar <1g> *v/i* fornicate

fornido *adj* well-built

foro *m* forum

forofo *m*, **-a** *f* F fan

forrado *adj* *prenda* lined; *libro* covered; *fig* F loaded F

forraje *m* fodder

forrar <1a> **1** *v/t* *prenda* line; *libro, silla* cover **2** *v/r* **~se** F make a fortune F; **forro** *m* *de prenda* lining; *de libro* cover

fortalecer <2d> **1** *v/t tb fig* strengthen **2** *v/r* **~se** strengthen; **fortaleza** *f* strength of character; MIL fortress; **fortificar** <1g> *v/t* MIL fortify

fortuito *adj* chance *atr*, accidental

fortuna *f* fortune; (*suerte*) luck; **por ~** fortunately, luckily

forzar <1f & 1m> *v/t* force; (*violar*) rape; **forzoso** *adj* *aterrizaje* forced; **forzudo** *adj* brawny

fosa *f* pit; (*tumba*) grave; **~ común** common grave; **~s nasales** nostrils

fósforo *m* QUÍM phosphorus; L.Am. (*cerilla*) match

fósil 1 *adj* fossilized **2** *m* fossil

foso *m* ditch; TEA, MÚS pit; *de castillo* moat

foto *f* photo

fotocopia *f* photocopy; **fotocopiadora** *f* photocopier; **fotocopiar** <1a> *v/t* photocopy

fotogénico *adj* photogenic

fotografía *f* photography; **fotografiar** <1c> *v/t* photograph; **fotógrafo** *m*, **-a** *f* photographer

FP *f* (= *formación profesional*) vocational training

frac *m* tail coat

fracasado 1 *adj* unsuccessful **2** *m*, **-a** *f* loser; **fracasar** <1a> *v/i* fail; **fracaso** *m* failure

fracción *f* fraction; POL faction; **fraccionamiento** *m L.Am.* (housing) project, *Br* estate; **fraccionar** <1a> *v/t* break up; FIN pay in instal(l)ments

fractura *f* MED fracture; **fracturar** <1a> *v/t* MED fracture

fragancia *f* fragrance

frágil *adj* fragile

fragmentar <1a> *v/t* fragment; **fragmento** *m* fragment; *de novela, poema* excerpt, extract

fraguar <1i> *v/t* forge; *plan* devise; *complot* hatch

fraile *m* friar, monk

frambuesa *f* raspberry

francés 1 *adj* French **2** *m* Frenchman; *idioma* French; **francesa** *f* Frenchwoman; **Francia** France

franco *adj* (*sincero*) frank; (*evidente*) distinct, marked; COM free

francotirador *m* sniper

franela *f* flannel

franja *f* fringe; *de tierra* strip

franquear <1a> *v/t carta* pay the postage on; *camino, obstáculo* clear; **franqueo** *m* postage; **franqueza** *f* frankness; **franquicia** *f* (*exención*) exemption; COM franchise

frasco *m* bottle

frase *f* phrase; (*oración*) sentence; **~ hecha** set phrase

fraternal *adj* brotherly; **fraternidad** *f* brotherhood, fraternity; **fraternizar** <1f> *v/i* POL fraternize

fraude *m* fraud; **fraudulento** *adj* fraudulent

frazada *f L.Am.* blanket

frecuencia *f* frequency; **~ modulada** RAD frequency modulation; **con ~** frequently; **frecuentar** <1a> *v/t* frequent; **frecuente** *adj* frequent; (*común*) common; **frecuentemente** *adv* often, frequently

fregadero *m* sink; **fregar** <1h & 1k> *v/t platos* wash; *el suelo* mop; *L.Am.* F bug F; **fregón 1** *adj* annoying **2** *m L.Am.* F nuisance, pain in the neck F; **fregona** *f* mop; *L.Am.* F nuisance, pain in the neck F

freidora *f* deep fryer; **freidura** *f* frying; **freír** <3m; *part* **frito**> *v/t* fry; F (*matar*) waste P

frenada *f esp L.Am.*: **dar una ~** slam the brakes on, hit the brakes F; **frenar** <1a> **1** *v/i* AUTO brake **2** *v/t fig* slow down; *impulsos* check; **frenazo** *m*: **pegar** *or* **dar un ~** F slam the brakes on, hit the brakes F

frenesí *m* frenzy; **frenético** *adj* frenetic

freno *m* brake; **~ de mano** parking brake, *Br* handbrake

frente 1 *f* forehead **2** *m* MIL, METEO front; **de ~ colisión** head-on; **de ~ al grupo** *L.Am.* facing the group; **hacer ~ a** face up to **3** *prp*: **~ a** opposite

fresa *f* strawberry

fresco 1 *adj* cool; *pescado etc* fresh; *persona* F fresh F, *Br* cheeky F **2** *m*, **-a** *f*: **¡eres un ~!** F you've got nerve! F, *Br* you've got a cheek! F **3** *m* fresh air; *C.Am.* fruit drink; **frescor** *m* freshness; **frescura** *f* freshness; (*frío*) coolness; *fig* nerve

fresno *m* BOT ash tree

fresón *m* strawberry

frialdad *f tb fig* coldness

fricción *f* TÉC, *fig* friction; **friccionar** <1a> *v/t* rub

friega *f L.Am.* F hassle F, drag F

frígido *adj* MED frigid; **frigorífico 1** *adj* refrigerated **2** *m* fridge

fríjol *m*, **frijol** *m L.Am.* bean

frío 1 *adj tb fig* cold **2** *m* cold; **tener ~** be cold; **friolento** *L.Am.*, **friolero** *adj*: **es ~** he feels the cold

fritar <1a> *v/t L.Am.* fry; **frito 1** *part* → **freír 2** *adj* fried **3** *mpl*: **~s** fried

F

food *sg*; **fritura** *f* fried food
frívolo *adj* frivolous
frondoso *adj* leafy
frontal *adj* frontal; *ataque etc* head-on; (*delantero*) front *atr*
frontera *f* border; **fronterizo** *adj* border *atr*
frontón *m* DEP pelota; *cancha* pelota court
frotar <1a> *v/t* rub
fructífero *adj* fruitful, productive
frugal *adj persona* frugal
fruncir <3b> *v/t material* gather; **~ el ceño** frown
frustración *f* frustration; **frustrante** *adj* frustrating; **frustrar** <1a> **1** *v/t* frustrate; *plan* thwart **2** *v/r* **~se** fail
fruta *f* fruit; **frutal 1** *adj* fruit *atr* **2** *m* fruit tree; **frutería** *f* fruit store, *Br* greengrocer's
frutilla *f S.Am.* strawberry
fruto *m tb fig* fruit; *nuez, almendra etc* nut; **~s secos** nuts
fucsia *adj* fuchsia
fue *vb* → *ir, ser*
fuego *m* fire; **¿tienes ~?** do you have a light?; **~s artificiales** fireworks; **pegar** *o* **prender ~ a** set fire to
fuel(-oil) *m* fuel oil
fuelle *m* bellows *pl*
fuente *f* fountain; *recipiente* dish; *fig* source
fuera 1 *vb* → *ir, ser* **2** *adv* outside; (*en otro lugar*) away; (*en otro país*) abroad; **por ~** on the outside; **¡~!** get out! **3** *prp:* **~ de** outside; **¡sal ~ de aquí!** get out of here!; **está ~ del país** he's abroad, he's out of the country
fuero *m:* **en el ~ interno** deep down
fuerte 1 *adj* strong; *dolor* intense; *lluvia* heavy; *aumento* sharp; *ruido* loud; *fig* P incredible F **2** *adv* hard **3** *m* MIL fort; **fuerza** *f* strength; (*violencia*) force; EL power; **~ aérea** air force; **~ de voluntad** willpower; **~s armadas** armed forces; **~s de seguridad** security forces; **a ~ de ...** by (dint of)
fuese *vb* → *ir, ser*
fuete *m L.Am.* whip

fuga *f* escape; *de gas, agua* leak; **darse a la ~** flee; **fugarse** <1h> *v/r* run away; *de la cárcel* escape; **fugaz** *adj fig* fleeting; **fugitivo 1** *adj* run-away *atr* **2** *m*, **-a** *f* fugitive
fui *vb* → *ir, ser*
fuimos *vb* → *ir, ser*
fulano *m* so-and-so
fulgor *m* brightness; **fulgurante** *adj fig* dazzling
fulminante *adj* sudden; **fulminar** <1a> *v/t:* **lo fulminó un rayo** he was killed by lightning; **~ a alguien con la mirada** look daggers at s.o. F
fumador *m*, **~a** *f* smoker; **fumar** <1a> **1** *v/t* smoke **2** *v/i* smoke; **prohibido ~** no smoking **3** *v/r* **~se una clase** F skip a class F
fumigar <1h> *v/t* fumigate
función *f* purpose, function; *en el trabajo* duty; TEA performance; **en ~ de** according to; **funcional** *adj* functional; **funcionamiento** *m* working; **funcionar** <1a> *v/i* work; **no funciona** out of order; **funcionario** *m*, **-a** *f* government employee, civil servant
funda *f* cover; *de gafas* case; *de almohada* pillowcase
fundación *f* foundation; **fundador** *m*, **~a** *f* founder
fundamental *adj* fundamental; **fundamentalismo** *m* fundamentalism; **fundamentalista** *m/f* fundamentalist; **fundamentalmente** *adv* essentially; **fundamento** *m* foundation; **~s** (*nociones*) fundamentals; **fundar** <1a> **1** *v/t fig* base (**en** on) **2** *v/r* **~se** be based (**en** on)
fundición *f* smelting; (*fábrica*) foundry; **fundir** <3a> **1** *v/t hielo* melt; *metal* smelt; COM merge **2** *v/r* **~se** melt; *de bombilla* fuse; *de plomos* blow; COM merge; *L.Am. fig: de empresa* go under
fúnebre *adj* funeral *atr*; *fig: ambiente* gloomy; **funeral** *m* funeral; **funeraria** *f* funeral parlo(u)r, *Br* undertaker's
funesto *adj* disastrous

135   **ganado**

funicular *m* funicular; (*teleférico*)
cable car
furcia *f* P whore P
furgón *m* van; FERR boxcar, *Br* goods
van; ~ *de equipajes* baggage car, *Br*
luggage van; **furgoneta** *f* van
furia *f* fury; *ponerse hecho una ~* go
into a fury *o* rage; **furibundo** *adj* furious; **furioso** *adj* furious; **furor** *m*:
hacer ~ *fig* be all the rage F
furtivo *adj* furtive
fuselaje *m* fuselage
fusible *m* EL fuse
fusil *m* rifle; **fusilar** <1a> *v/t* shoot; *fig*
F (*plagiar*) lift F

fusión *f* FÍS fusion; COM merger; **fu-
sionar** <1a> **1** *v/t* COM merge **2** *v/r*
~*se* merge
fusta *f* riding crop
fútbol *m* soccer, *Br* football; ~ *americano* football, *Br* American football; ~ *sala* five-a-side soccer (*Br*
football); **futbolín** *m* Foosball®,
table football; **futbolista** *m/f* soccer
player, *Br* footballer, *Br* football
player
fútil *adj* trivial
futre *m* Chi dandy
futuro **1** *adj* future *atr* **2** *m* future;
futurólogo *m*, **-a** *f* futurologist

G

g. *abr* (= *gramo*(*s*)) gr(s) (= gram(s))
gabardina *f prenda* raincoat; *material*
gabardine
gabinete *m* (*despacho*) office; *en una
casa* study; POL cabinet; *L.Am. de
médico* office, *Br* surgery
gacela *f* ZO gazelle
gaceta *f* gazette
gachas *fpl* porridge *sg*
gachupín *m* Méx desp Spaniard
gacilla *f* C.Am. safety pin
gafas *fpl* glasses; ~ *de sol* sun-
glasses
gafe **1** *adj* jinxed **2** *m* jinx **3** *m/f*: *es
un ~* he's jinxed
gaita *f* MÚS bagpipes *pl*
gajes *mpl*: ~ *del oficio irón* occupa-
tional hazard
gajo *m* segment
gala *f* gala; *traje de ~* formal dress
galante *adj* gallant
galápago *m* ZO turtle
galardonar <1a> *v/t*: *fue galardo-
nado con ...* he was awarded ...
galaxia *f* galaxy
galería *f* gallery; ~ *de arte* art
gallery

Gales Wales; **galés** Welsh
galgo *m* greyhound
gallera *f* L.Am. cockpit
galleta *f* cookie, *Br* biscuit
gallina **1** *f* hen **2** *m* F chicken
gallinazo *m* L.Am. turkey buzzard
gallo *m* rooster, *Br* cock
galón *m* *adorno* braid; MIL stripe;
medida gallon
galope *m* gallop
galpón *m* L.Am. large shed; *W.I.* HIST
slave quarters *pl*
gama *f* range
gamba *f* ZO GASTR shrimp, *Br* prawn
gamberro *m*, **-a** *f* troublemaker
gamín *m*, **-ina** *f* Col street kid
gamo *m* ZO fallow deer
gamonal *m* Pe, Bol desp chief
gamuza *f* chamois
gana *f*: *de mala ~* unwillingly, grudg-
ingly; *no me da la ~* I don't want to;
... me da ~s de ... makes me want
to; *tener ~s de* (*hacer*) *algo* feel
like (doing) sth
ganadería *f* stockbreeding; **gana-
dero** *m*, **-a** *f* stockbreeder; **ganado**
m cattle *pl*

ganador *m* winner; **ganancia** *f*
profit; **ganar** <1a> **1** win; *mediante
el trabajo* earn **2** *v/i mediante el
trabajo* earn; (*vencer*) win; (*mejorar*)
improve **3** *v/r* **~se** earn; *a alguien*
win over; **~se la vida** earn one's living

ganchillo *m* crochet; **gancho** *m*
hook; *L.Am., Arg fig* F sex-appeal;
hacer ~ *L.Am.* (*ayudar*) lend a
hand; **tener ~** F *de un grupo, una
campaña* be popular; *de una persona*
have that certain something

gandul *m* lazybones *sg*; **gandulear**
<1a> *v/i* F loaf around F

ganga *f* bargain

gangrena *f* MED gangrene

gángster *m* gangster

ganso *m* goose; *macho* gander

garabatear <1a> *v/i & v/t* doodle;
garabato *m* doodle

garaje *m* garage

garantía *f* guarantee; **garantizar**
<1f> *v/t* guarantee

garapiña *f Cuba, Méx* pineapple
squash

garbanzo *m* BOT chickpea

garbo *m al moverse* grace

gardenia *f* BOT gardenia

garete *m*: **irse al ~** *fig* F go to pot F

garfio *m* hook

gargajo *m* piece of phlegm

garganta *f* ANAT throat; GEOG gorge;
gargantilla *f* choker

gárgaras *fpl*: **hacer ~** gargle

garito *m* gambling den

garra *f* claw; *de ave* talon; **caer en las
~s de alguien** fig fall into s.o.'s
clutches; **tener ~** F be compelling

garrafa *f* carafe

garrafal *adj error etc* terrible

garrapata *f* ZO tick

garrote *m palo* club, stick; *tipo de
ejecución* garrotte

garúa *f L.Am.* drizzle; **garuar** <1e>
v/i L.Am. drizzle

garzón *m Rpl* (*mesero*) waiter

garza *f* ZO heron

gas *m* gas; **~ natural** natural gas; **~es**
pl MED gas *sg*, wind *sg*; **con ~** sparkling, carbonated; **sin ~** still

gasa *f* gauze

gaseosa *f* lemonade; **gasfitero** *m
Pe, Bol* plumber; **gasoducto** *m* gas
pipeline; **gasoil, gasóleo** *m* oil;
para motores diesel; **gasolina** *f* gas,
Br petrol; **gasolinera** *f* gas station,
Br petrol station

gastar <1a> **1** *v/t dinero* spend; *energía, electricidad etc* use; (*llevar*) wear;
(*desperdiciar*) waste; (*desgastar*)
wear out; **¿qué número gastas?**
what size do you take?, what size
are you? **2** *v/r* **~se** *dinero* spend; *gasolina, agua* run out of; *pila* run
down; *ropa, zapatos* wear out; **gasto**
m expense

gastronomía *f* gastronomy

gata *f* (female) cat; *Méx* servant,
maid; **a ~s** F on all fours; **andar a ~s**
F crawl; **gatear** <1a> *v/i* crawl

gatillo *m* trigger

gato *m* cat; AUTO jack; **aquí hay ~
encerrado** F there's something
fishy going on here F; **cuatro ~s** a
handful of people

gaucho *m Rpl* gaucho

gaviota *f* (sea)gull

gay **1** *adj* gay **2** *m* gay (man)

gazpacho *m* gazpacho (*cold soup
made with tomatoes, peppers, garlic
etc*)

gel *m* gel

gelatina *f* gelatin(e); GASTR Jell-O®,
Br jelly

gélido *adj* icy

gema *f* gem

gemelo **1** *adj* twin *atr*; **hermano ~**
twin brother **2** *mpl*: **~s** twins; *de
camisa* cuff links; (*prismáticos*) binoculars

gemido *m* moan, groan

Géminis *m/f inv* ASTR Gemini

gemir <3l> *v/i* moan, groan

gen *m* gene

genealógico *adj*: **árbol ~** family tree

generación *f* generation; **generador** *m* EL generator

general **1** *adj* general; **en ~** in general; **por lo ~** usually, generally **2** *m*
general; **generalización** *f* generali-
zation; **generalizar** <1f> **1** *v/t*

spread **2** v/i generalize **3** v/r **~se** spread; **generalmente** adv generally

generar <1a> v/t generate

género m (tipo) type; de literatura genre; GRAM gender; COM goods pl, merchandise

generosidad f generosity; **generoso** adj generous

genética f genetics; **genético** adj genetic

genial adj brilliant; F (estupendo) fantastic F, great F; **genialidad** f brilliance; **genio** m talento, persona genius; (carácter) temper; **tener mal ~** be bad-tempered

genital adj genital; **genitales** mpl genitals

genocidio m genocide

gente f people pl; L.Am. (persona) person

gentileza f kindness; **por ~ de** by courtesy of

gentío m crowd

genuino adj genuine, real

geografía f geography; **geográfico** adj geographical

geología f geology; **geológico** adj geological; **geólogo** m, **-a** f geologist

geometría f geometry; **geométrico** adj geometric(al)

geranio m BOT geranium

gerente m/f manager

geriatría f geriatrics sg

germen m germ

germinar <1a> v/i tb fig germinate

gerundio m GRAM gerund

gestación f gestation

gesticular <1a> v/i gesticulate

gestión f management; **gestiones** pl (trámites) formalities, procedure sg; **gestionar** <1a> v/t trámites take care of; negocio manage

gesto m movimiento gesture; (expresión) expression

gestoría f Esp agency offering clients help with official documents

gigante 1 adj giant atr **2** m giant

gilipollas m/f inv P jerk P

gilipollez f Esp V bullshit V

gimnasia f gymnastics; **hacer ~** do exercises; **gimnasio** m gym; **gimnasta** m/f gymnast

gimotear <1a> v/i whine, whimper

ginebra f gin

ginecólogo m, **-a** f gyn(a)ecologist

gin-tonic m gin and tonic, G and T F

gira f tour; **girar** <1a> **1** v/i (dar vueltas, torcer) turn; alrededor de algo revolve; fig (tratar) revolve (**en torno a** around) **2** v/t COM transfer

girasol m BOT sunflower

giro m turn; GRAM idiom; **~ postal** COM money order

gis m L.Am. chalk

gitano 1 adj gypsy atr **2** m, **-a** f gypsy

glacial adj icy; **glaciar** m glacier

glándula f ANAT gland

global adj (de todo el mundo) global; visión, resultado overall; cantidad total; **globo** m aerostático, de niño balloon; terrestre globe; **~ terráqueo** globe

gloria f glory; (delicia) delight; **estar en la ~** F be in seventh heaven; **gloriado** m Pe, Bol, Ecuad type of punch; **glorieta** f traffic circle, Br roundabout; **glorioso** adj glorious

glosario m glossary

glotón 1 adj greedy **2** m, **-ona** f glutton

glucosa f glucose

gnomo m gnome

gobernador m governor; **gobernante** m leader; **gobernar** <1k> v/t & v/i rule, govern; **gobierno** m government

goce m pleasure, enjoyment

gofre m waffle

gol m DEP goal; **goleador** m DEP (goal-)scorer

golf m DEP golf; **golfista** m/f golfer

golfo 1 m GEOG gulf **2** m, **-a** f good-for-nothing; niño little devil

Golfo de México m Gulf of Mexico

golondrina f ZO swallow

golosina f candy, Br sweet; **goloso** adj sweet-toothed

golpe m knock, blow; **~ de Estado** coup d'état; **de ~** suddenly; **no da ~** F she doesn't do a thing; **golpear**

<1a> v/t *cosa* bang, hit; *persona* hit

goma f (*caucho*) rubber; (*pegamento*) glue; (*banda elástica*) rubber band; F (*preservativo*) condom, rubber P; *C.Am.* F (*resaca*) hangover; **~ (de borrar)** eraser; **~ espuma** foam rubber; **gomina** f hair gel; **gominola** f jelly bean

góndola f *Chi* bus

gong m gong

gordinflón m, **-ona** f F fatso F; **gordo 1** adj fat; **me cae ~** F I can't stand him; **se va a armar la -a** all hell will break loose F **2** m, **-a** f fat person **3** m *premio* jackpot

gorila m zo gorilla

gorjeo m *de pájaro* chirping, warbling; *de niño* gurgling

gorra f cap; **de ~** F for free F

gorrino m *fig* pig

gorrión m zo sparrow

gorro m cap; **estar hasta el ~ de algo** F be fed up to the back teeth with sth F

gorrón m, **-ona** f F scrounger; **gorronear** <1a> v/t & v/i F scrounge F

gota f drop; **ni ~** F *de cerveza, leche etc* not a drop; *de pan* not a scrap; **gotear** <1a> v/i drip; *filtrarse* leak; **gotera** f leak; (*mancha*) stain; **gotero** m MED drip; *L.Am.* (eye)-dropper

gozar <1f> v/i (*disfrutar*) enjoy o.s.; **~ de** (*disfrutar de*) enjoy; (*poseer*) have, enjoy; **gozo** m (*alegría*) joy; (*placer*) pleasure

grabación f recording; **grabado** m engraving; **grabadora** f tape recorder; **grabar** <1a> v/t *en vídeo, cinta etc* record; PINT, *fig* engrave

gracia f: *tener* ~ (*ser divertido*) be funny; (*tener encanto*) be graceful; **me hace ~** I think it's funny, it makes me laugh; **no le veo la ~** I don't think it's funny; **dar las ~s a alguien** thank s.o.; **~s** thank you

grácil adj dainty

gracioso adj funny

gradas fpl DEP stands, grandstand *sg*; **graderío** m stands *pl*

grado m degree; **de buen ~** with

good grace, readily

graduación f TÉC etc adjustment; *de alcohol* alcohol content; EDU graduation; MIL rank; **gradual** adj gradual; **gradualmente** adv gradually

graduarse <1e> v/r graduate, get one's degree

gráfica f graph; **gráfico 1** adj graphic; *artes* **-as** graphic arts **2** m MAT graph; INFOR graphic

gragea f tablet, pill

grajo m zo rook

Gral. abr (= **General**) Gen (= General)

gramática f grammar; **gramatical** adj grammatical

gramo m gram

gran *short form of* **grande** *before a noun*

granada f BOT pomegranate; **~ de mano** MIL hand grenade

granangular m wide-angle lens

granate adj dark crimson

Gran Bretaña Great Britain

grande 1 adj big; **a lo ~** in style **2** m/f L.Am. (*adulto*) grown-up, adult; (*mayor*) eldest; **pasarlo en ~** F have a great time; **grandeza** f greatness; **grandiosidad** f grandeur; **grandioso** adj impressive, magnificent

granel m: **vender a ~** COM sell in bulk; **había comida a ~** F there was loads of food F

granero m granary

granito m granite

granizada f hailstorm; **granizado** m *type of soft drink made with crushed ice*; **granizar** <1f> v/i hail; **granizo** m hail

granja f farm

granjearse <1a> v/r win, earn

granjero m, **-a** f farmer

grano m grain; *de café* bean; *en la piel* pimple, spot; **ir al ~** get (straight) to the point

granuja m rascal

grapa f staple; **grapadora** f stapler; **grapar** <1a> staple

grasa f BIO, GASTR fat; *lubricante, suciedad* grease; **grasiento** adj greasy, oily; **graso** *adj* greasy; *carne* fatty

gratificación *f* gratification; **gratificar** <1g> *v/t* reward

gratinar <1a> *v/t* cook au gratin

gratis *adj & adv* free; **gratitud** *f* gratitude; **gratuito** *adj* free

grava *f* gravel

gravar <1a> *v/t* tax

grave *adj* serious; *tono* grave, solemn; *nota* low; *voz* deep; **estar ~** be seriously ill; **gravedad** *f* seriousness, gravity; FÍS gravity; **gravemente** *adv* seriously

gravilla *f* grave

Grecia Greece

gremio *m* HIST guild; *fig* F (*oficio manual*) trade; (*profesión*) profession

griego 1 *adj* Greek **2** *m*, **-a** *f* Greek

grieta *f* crack

grifo 1 *adj Méx* F high **2** *m* faucet, *Br* tap; *Pe* (*gasolinera*) gas station, *Br* petrol station

grillo *m* ZO cricket

grima *f*: **me da ~** *Esp* de ruido, material etc it sets my teeth on edge; *de algo asqueroso* it gives me the creeps F; **en ~** *Pe* alone

gringo *m L.Am. desp* gringo *desp*, foreigner

gripe *f* flu, influenza; **~ aviar** bird flu

gris *adj* gray, *Br* grey

gritar <1a> *v/t & v/i* shout, yell; **griterío** *m* shouting; **grito** *m* cry, shout; **a ~ pelado** at the top of one's voice; **pedir algo a ~s** F be crying out for sth

grosella *f* redcurrant

grosero 1 *adj* rude **2** *m*, **-a** *f* rude person; **grosor** *m* thickness

grotesco *adj* grotesque

grúa *f* crane; AUTO wrecker, *Br* breakdown truck

grueso *adj* thick; *persona* stout

grulla *f* ZO crane

grumo *m* lump

gruñido *m* grunt; *de perro* growl; **gruñir** <3h> *v/i* (*quejarse*) grumble, moan F; *de perro* growl; *de cerdo* grunt; **gruñón 1** *adj* F grumpy

2 *m*, **-ona** *f* F grouch F

grupo *m* group

gruta *f* cave; *artificial* grotto

guacamol, guacamole *m* guacamole

guachimán *m Chi* watchman

guacho 1 *adj S.Am.* (*sin casa*) homeless; (*huérfano*) orphaned **2** *m*, **-a** *f S.Am. sin casa* homeless person; (*huérfano*) orphan

guadaño *m Cuba, Méx* small boat

guagua *f W.I., Ven, Canaries* bus; *Pe, Bol, Chi* (*niño*) baby

guajolote *m Méx, C.Am.* turkey

guanaco 1 *adj L.Am.* F dumb F, stupid **2** *m* ZO guanaco **3** *m*, **-a** *f persona* idiot

guantazo *m* slap

guante *m* glove; **guantera** *f* AUTO glove compartment

guapo *adj hombre* handsome, good-looking; *mujer* beautiful; *S.Am.* gutsy

guaracha *f W.I.* street band

guarache → **huarache**

guarapo *m L.Am.* alcoholic drink made from sugar cane and herbs

guarda *m/f* keeper; **~ jurado** security guard

guardabosques *m/f inv* forest ranger

guardacostas *m inv* coastguard vessel

guardaespaldas *m/f inv* bodyguard

guardameta *m/f* DEP goalkeeper

guardar <1a> **1** *v/t* keep; *poner en un lugar* put (away); *recuerdo* have; *apariencias* keep up; INFOR save; **~ silencio** remain silent, keep silent **2** *v/r* **~se** keep; **~se de** refrain from

guardarropa *m* checkroom, *Br* cloakroom; (*ropa, armario*) wardrobe

guardería *f* nursery

guardia 1 *f* guard; **de ~** on duty; **bajar la ~** *fig* lower one's guard **2** *m/f* MIL guard; (*policía*) police officer; **~ civil** *Esp* civil guard; **~ de seguridad** security guard; **~ de tráfico** traffic warden

guardián 1 *adj*: **perro ~** guard dog

2 *m*, **-ana** *f* guard; *fig* guardian

guarecer <2d> **1** *v/t* shelter **2** *v/r* **~se** shelter, take shelter (**de** from)

guarida *f* ZO den; *de personas* hide-out

guarnición *f* GASTR accompaniment; MIL garrison

guaro *m* C.Am. sugar-cane liquor

guarro 1 *adj* F *sucio* filthy **2** *m tb fig* F pig

guarura *m* Méx (*guardaespaldas*) bodyguard; F (*gamberro*) thug

guasa *f* L.Am. joke; **de ~** as a joke

guaso 1 *adj* S.Am. rude **2** *m* Chi peasant

guata *f* L.Am. F paunch

Guatemala Guatemala

guatemalteco 1 *adj* Guatemalan **2** *m*, **-a** *f* Guatemalan

guatón *adj* L.Am. F pot-bellied, big-bellied

guay *int* Esp F cool F, neat F

guayaba *f* L.Am. BOT guava

guayabera *f* Méx, C.Am., W.I. loose embroidered shirt

gubernamental *adj* governmental, government *atr*

guepardo *m* ZO cheetah

güero 1 *adj* Méx, C.Am. fair, light-skinned **2** *m*, **-a** *f* Méx, C.Am. blond(e)

guerra *f* war; **~ civil** civil war; **~ fría** cold war; **~ mundial** world war; **dar ~ a alguien** F give s.o. trouble; **guerrero 1** *adj* warlike **2** *m* warrior; **guerrilla** *f* guerillas *pl*; **guerrillero** *m* guerilla

gueto *m* ghetto

guevear *v/i* → **huevear**

guevón → **huevón**

guía 1 *m/f* guide; **~ turístico** tourist guide **2** *f libro* guide (book); **~ telefónica** *or* **de teléfonos** phone book; **guiar** <1c> **1** *v/t* guide **2** *v/r* **~se**: **~se por** follow

guijarro *m* pebble

guillotina *f* guillotine

güinche *m* L.Am. winch, pulley

guinda 1 *adj* L.Am. purple **2** *f fresca* morello cherry; **en dulce** glacé cherry

guindilla *f* GASTR chil(l)i

guiñar <1a> *v/t*: **le guiñó un ojo** she winked at him; **guiño** *m* wink

guión *m* de película script; GRAM *corto* hyphen; *largo* dash; **guionista** *m/f* scriptwriter

guiri *m* Esp P (light-skinned) foreigner

guirnalda *f* garland

guisante *m* pea; **guisar** <1a> *v/t* GASTR stew, casserole; **guiso** *m* GASTR stew, casserole

guitarra *f* guitar; **guitarrista** *m/f* guitarist

gula *f* gluttony

gusano *m* worm

gustar <1a> *v/i*: **me gusta viajar** I like to travel, I like travelling; **¿te gusta el ajo?** do you like garlic?; **no me gusta** I don't like it; **gusto** *m* taste; (*placer*) pleasure; **a ~** at ease; **con mucho ~** with pleasure; **de buen ~** in good taste, tasteful; **de mal ~** in bad taste, tasteless; **da ~ ...** it's a pleasure ...; **mucho** *or* **tanto ~** how do you do

gutural *adj* guttural

H

ha *vb* → **haber**

haba *f* broad bean; **en todas partes se cuecen ~s** it's the same the world over

Habana: La ~ Havana; **habanero** *m*, **-a** *f* citizen of Havana; **habano** *m*

Havana (cigar)

haber <2k> **1** *v/aux* have; *hemos llegado* we've arrived; *he de levantarme pronto* I have to *o* I've got to get up early; *de ~lo sabido* if I'd known; *has de ver Méx* you ought to see it **2** *v/impers*: *hay* there is *sg*, there are *pl*; *hubo un incendio* there was a fire; *¿qué hay?, Méx ¿qué hubo?* how's it going?, what's happening?; *hay que hacerlo* it has to be done; *no hay de qué* not at all, don't mention it; *no hay más que decir* there's nothing more to be said **3** *m* asset; *pago* fee; *tiene en su ~ 5.000 ptas* she's 5,000 pesetas in credit

habichuela *f* kidney bean

hábil *adj* skilled; (*capaz*) capable; (*astuto*) clever, smart; **habilidad** *f* skill; (*capacidad*) ability; (*astucia*) cleverness; **habilitar** <1a> *v/t lugar* fit out; *persona* authorize

habitación *f* room; (*dormitorio*) bedroom; ~ *doble / individual* double / single room; **habitante** *m/f* inhabitant; **habitar** <1a> *v/i* live (*en* in); **hábitat** *m* habitat

hábito *m tb* REL habit; (*práctica*) knack; *colgar los ~s fig de sacerdote* give up the priesthood; **habitual 1** *adj* usual, regular **2** *m/f* regular; **habituar** <1e> **1** *v/t*: ~ *a alguien a algo* get s.o. used to sth **2** *v/r ~se*: *~se a algo* get used to sth

habla *f* speech; *¡al ~!* TELEC speaking; *quedarse sin ~ fig* be speechless; **hablada** *f L.Am.* piece of gossip; *~s pl* gossip *sg*; **hablador** *adj* talkative; *Méx* boastful; **habladurías** *fpl* gossip *sg*

hablante *m/f* speaker

hablar <1a> **1** *v/i* speak; (*conversar*) talk; *~ claro fig* say what one means; *~ con alguien* talk to s.o., talk with s.o.; *~ de libro etc* be about, deal with; *~ por ~* talk for the sake of it; *¡ni ~!* no way! **2** *v/r ~se* speak to one another; *no se hablan* they're not speaking (to each other)

hacendado 1 *adj* land-owning **2** *m*, **-a** *f* land-owner; **hacendoso** *adj* hardworking

hacer <2s; *part hecho*> **1** *v/t* (*realizar*) do; (*elaborar, crear*) make; *¡haz algo!* do something!; *~ una pregunta* ask a question; *¡qué le vamos a ~!* that's life; *no hace más que quejarse* all he does is complain; *le hicieron ir* they made him go; *tengo que ~ los deberes* I have to do my homework **2** *v/i*: *haces bien / mal en ir* you are doing the right / wrong thing by going; *me hace mal* it's making me ill; *esto hará de mesa de objeto* this will do as a table; *~ como que* or *como si* act as if; *no le hace L.Am.* it doesn't matter; *se me hace qué L.Am.* it seems to me that **3** *v/impers*: *hace calor / frío* it's hot / cold; *hace tres días* three days ago; *hace mucho (tiempo)* a long time ago; *desde hace un año* for a year **4** *v/r ~se* make; *casa* build o.s.; (*cocinarse*) cook; (*convertirse, volverse*) get, become; *~se viejo* get old; *~se de noche* get dark; *se hace tarde* it's getting late; *~se el sordo / el tonto* pretend to be deaf / stupid; *~se a algo* get used to sth; *~se con algo* get hold of sth

hacha *f* ax, *Br* axe; *ser un ~ para algo* F be brilliant at sth

hachís *m* hashish

hacia *prp* toward; *~ adelante* forward; *~ abajo* down; *~ arriba* up; *~ atrás* back(ward); *~ las cuatro* about four (o'clock)

Hacienda *f ministerio* Treasury Department, *Br* Treasury; *oficina* Internal Revenue Service, *Br* Inland Revenue

hacienda *f L.Am.* (*granja*) ranch, estate

hacinar <1a> *v/t* stack

hada *f* fairy

haga *vb* → **hacer**

hago *vb* → **hacer**

Haití Haiti

hala *int* come on!; *sorpresa* wow!

halagar <1h> *v/t* flatter; **halago** *m* flattery

halar <1a> *v/t L.Am.* haul, pull

halcón *m* ZO falcon

halitosis *f* MED halitosis, bad breath

hall *m* hall

hallar <1a> **1** *v/t* find; (*descubrir*) discover; *muerte, destino* meet **2** *v/r* **~se** be; (*sentirse*) feel; **hallazgo** *m* find; (*descubrimiento*) discovery

halógeno *adj* halogen

halterofilia *f* DEP weight-lifting

hamaca *f* hammock; (*tumbona*) deck chair; *L.Am.* (*mecedora*) rocking chair; **hamacar** <1g> *v/t L.Am.* swing; **hamaquear** <1a> *v/t L.Am.* swing

hambre *f* hunger; *morirse de* ~ *fig* be starving; *pasar* ~ be starving; **hambriento** *adj tb fig* hungry (*de* for); **hambruna** *f* famine

hamburguesa *f* GASTR hamburger; **hamburguesería** *f* hamburger bar

hampa *f* underworld

hámster *m* ZO hamster

hangar *m* hangar

haragán *m*, **-ana** *f* shirker

harapo *m* rag

hardware *m* INFOR hardware

haré *vb* → *hacer*

harina *f* flour; **harinoso** *adj* floury

hartar <1a> **1** *v/t*: ~ *a alguien con algo* tire s.o. with sth; ~ *a alguien de algo* give s.o. too much of sth **2** *v/r* ~**se** get sick (*de* of) F, get tired (*de* of); (*llenarse*) stuff o.s. (*de* with); **harto 1** *adj* fed up F; (*lleno*) full (up); *había* ~*s pasteles* there were cakes in abundance; *hace* ~ *frío L.Am.* it's very cold; *estar* ~ *de algo* be sick of sth F, be fed up with sth F **2** *adv* very much; *delante del adjetivo* extremely; *me gusta* ~ *L.Am.* F I like it a lot; **hartón 1** *adj L.Am.* greedy **2** *m*: *darse un* ~ *de algo* overdose on sth

has *vb* → *haber*

hasta 1 *prp* until, till; *llegó* ~ *Bilbao* he went as far as Bilbao; ~ *ahora* so far; ~ *aquí* up to here; *¿* ~ *cuándo?* how long?; ~ *que* until; *¡* ~ *luego!*

see you (later); *¡* ~ *la vista!* see you (later) **2** *adv* even

hastiar <1c> *v/t* tire; (*aburrir*) bore; **hastío** *m* boredom

hatajo *m* bunch; **hato** *m L.Am.* bundle

hay *vb* → *haber*

haya 1 *vb* → *haber* **2** *f* BOT beech

haz 1 *m* bundle; *de luz* beam **2** *vb* → *hacer*

hazaña *f* achievement

hazmerreír *m fig* F laughing stock

he *vb* → *haber*

hebilla *f* buckle

hechicero 1 *adj* bewitching, captivating **2** *m* sorcerer; *de tribu* witch-doctor; **hechizado** *adj* spellbound; **hechizar** <1f> *v/t fig* bewitch, captivate; **hechizo** *m* spell, charm

hecho 1 *part* → *hacer*, ~ *a mano* hand-made; *¡bien* ~*!* well done!; *muy* ~ *carne* well-done **2** *adj* finished; *un hombre* ~ *y derecho* a fully grown man **3** *m* fact; *de* ~ in fact

hectárea *f* hectare (*10,000 sq m*)

hedor *m* stink, stench

helada *f* frost; **heladera** *f Rpl* fridge; **heladería** *f* ice-cream parlo(u)r; **helado 1** *adj* frozen; *fig* icy; *quedarse* ~ be stunned **2** *m* ice cream; **helar** <1k> **1** *v/t* freeze **2** *v/i* freeze; *anoche heló* there was a frost last night **3** *v/r* ~**se** *tb fig* freeze

helecho *m* BOT fern

hélice *f* propeller

helicóptero *m* helicopter

hematoma *m* bruise

hembra *f* ZO, TÉC female

hemiplejía *f* MED hemiplegia; **hemisferio** *m* hemisphere

hemofilia *f* MED h(a)emophilia; **hemorragia** *f* MED h(a)emorrhage, bleeding; **hemorroides** *fpl* MED h(a)emorrhoids, piles

hendidura *f* crack

heno *m* hay

hepatitis *f* MED hepatitis

herbicida *m* herbicide, weed-killer; **herboristería** *f* herbalist

hercúleo *adj* Herculean

heredar <1a> *v/t* inherit (*de* from); **heredera** *f* heiress; **heredero** *m* heir; **hereditario** *adj* hereditary

hereje *m* heretic

herencia *f* inheritance

herida *f de arma* wound; (*lesión*) injury; *mujer* wounded woman; *mujer lesionada* injured woman; **herido 1** *adj de arma* wounded; (*lesionado*) injured **2** *m de bala* wounded man; (*lesionado*) injured man; **herir** <3i> *v/t con arma* wound; (*lesionar*) injure; *fig* (*ofender*) hurt

hermana *f* sister; **hermanastra** *f* stepsister; **hermanastro** *m* stepbrother; **hermano** *m* brother

hermético *adj* airtight, hermetic; *fig*: *persona* inscrutable

hermoso *adj* beautiful

hernia *f* MED hernia

héroe *m* hero; **heroico** *adj* heroic; **heroína** *f mujer* heroine; *droga* heroin

heroinómano *m*, **-a** *f* heroin addict

herpes *m* MED herpes

herradura *f* horseshoe

herramienta *f* tool

hervidero *m fig* hotbed; **hervido** *m* *S.Am.* stew; **hervir** <3i> **1** *v/i* boil; *fig* swarm, seethe (*de* with) **2** *v/t* boil

heterodoxo *adj* unorthodox

heterogéneo *adj* heterogeneous

hez *f* scum, dregs *pl*

hibernar <1a> *v/i* hibernate

híbrido 1 *adj* hybrid *atr* **2** *m* hybrid

hice *vb* → **hacer**

hicimos *vb* → **hacer**

hidratante *adj* moisturizing; *crema* ~ moisturizing cream; **hidratar** <1a> *v/t* hydrate; *piel* moisturize; **hidrato** *m*: ~ *de carbono* carbohydrate

hidráulico *adj* hydraulic

hidroavión *m* seaplane

hidroeléctrico *adj* hydroelectric

hidrógeno *m* hydrogen

hiedra *f* BOT ivy

hielo *m* ice; *romper el* ~ *fig* break the ice

hiena *f* ZO hyena

hierba *f* grass; *mala* ~ weed

hiere *vb* → **herir**

hierro *m* iron

hierve *vb* → **hervir**

hígado *m* liver; *ser un* ~ *C.Am.*, *Méx* F be a pain in the butt F

higiene *f* hygiene; **higiénico** *adj* hygienic

higo *m* BOT fig; **higuera** *f* BOT fig tree

hija *f* daughter; **hijastra** *f* stepdaughter; **hijastro** *m* stepson; **hijo** *m* son; ~**s** children *pl*; ~ *de puta* P son of a bitch V, bastard P; ~ *único* only child

hilachos *mpl* Méx rags

hilera *f* row, line

hilo *m* thread; ~ *dental* dental floss; *sin* ~**s** TELEC cordless; *colgar* or *pender de un* ~ *fig* hang by a thread; *perder el* ~ *fig* lose the thread

himno *m* hymn; ~ *nacional* national anthem

hincapié *m*: *hacer* ~ put special emphasis (*en* on)

hincar <1g> **1** *v/t* thrust, stick (*en* into); ~ *el diente* F sink one's teeth (*en* into) **2** *v/r* ~**se**: ~*se de rodillas* kneel down

hincha *m* F fan, supporter; **hinchado** *adj* swollen; **hinchar** <1a> **1** *v/t* inflate, blow up; *Rpl* P annoy **2** *v/r* ~**se** MED swell; *fig* stuff o.s (*de* with); (*mostrarse orgulloso*) swell with pride; **hinchazón** *f* swelling

hiperactivo *adj* hyperactive

hipermercado *m* hypermarket

hipertensión *f* MED high blood pressure, hypertension

hipertexto *m* hypertext

hípico *adj* equestrian; *concurso* ~ show-jumping event; *carrera -a* horse race

hipnosis *f* hypnosis; **hipnotizar** <1f> *v/t* hypnotize

hipo *m* hiccups *pl*, hiccoughs *pl*; *quitar el* ~ F take one's breath away

hipocondríaco 1 *adj* hypochondriac **2** *m*, **-a** *f* hypochondriac

hipocresía *f* hypocrisy; **hipócrita 1** *adj* hypocritical **2** *m/f* hypocrite

H

hipódromo *m* racetrack

hipopótamo *m* zo hippopotamus

hipoteca *f* COM mortgage; **hipotecar** <1g> *v/t* COM mortgage; *fig* compromise

hipótesis *f* hypothesis; **hipotético** *adj* hypothetical

hispánico *adj* Hispanic; **hispano 1** *adj* (*español*) Spanish; (*hispanohablante*) Spanish-speaking; *en EE.UU.* Hispanic **2** *m*, **-a** *f* (*español*) Spaniard; (*hispanohablante*) Spanish speaker; *en EE.UU.* Hispanic; **hispanohablante** *adj* Spanish-speaking

histeria *f* COM hysteria; **histérico** *adj* hysterical

historia *f* history; (*cuento*) story; *una ~ de drogas* F some drugs business; *déjate de ~s* F stop making excuses; **historiador** *m*, **~a** *f* historian; **historial** *m* record; **histórico** *adj* historical; (*importante*) historic; **historieta** *f* anecdote; (*viñetas*) comic strip

hito *m tb fig* milestone

hizo *vb* → **hacer**

Hnos. *abr* (= **Hermanos**) Bros (= Brothers)

hobby *m* hobby

hocico *m* snout; *de perro* muzzle

hockey *m* field hockey, *Br* hockey; *~ sobre hielo* hockey, *Br* ice hockey

hogar *m fig* home; **hogareño** *adj* home *atr*; *persona* home-loving

hoguera *f* bonfire

hoja *f* BOT leaf; *de papel* sheet; *de libro* page; *de cuchillo* blade; *~ de afeitar* razor blade; *~ de cálculo* INFOR spreadsheet

hojalata *f* tin

hojaldre *m* GASTR puff pastry

hojear <1a> *v/t* leaf through, flip through

hola *int* hello, hi F

Holanda Holland

holandés **1** *adj* Dutch **2** *m* Dutchman; **holandesa** *f* Dutchwoman

holding *m* holding company

holgado *adj* loose, comfortable; *estar ~ de tiempo* have time to spare

holgazán *m* idler; **holgazanear** <1a> *v/i* laze around

holgura *f* ease; *de ropa* looseness; TÉC play; *vivir con ~* live comfortably

hollín *m* soot

holocausto *m* holocaust

hombre *m* man; *el ~* (*la humanidad*) man, mankind; *~ lobo* werewolf; *~ de negocios* businessman; *~ rana* frogman; *¡claro, ~!* you bet!, sure thing!; *¡~, qué alegría!* that's great!

hombro *m* shoulder; *~ con ~* shoulder to shoulder; *encogerse de ~s* shrug (one's shoulders)

homenaje *m* homage; *rendir ~ a alguien* pay tribute to s.o.

homeopatía *f* hom(o)eopathy

homicidio *m* homicide

homogéneo *adj* homogenous

homologación *f* approval; *de título*, *diploma* official recognition

homólogo *m*, **-a** *f* counterpart, opposite number

homosexual *m/f & adj* homosexual

hondo *adj* deep

Honduras Honduras; **hondureño 1** *adj* Honduran **2** *m*, **-a** *f* Honduran

honesto *adj* hono(u)rable, decent

hongo *m* fungus

honor *m* hono(u)r; *en ~ a* in hono(u)r of; *hacer ~ a* live up to; *palabra de ~* word of hono(u)r

honorarios *mpl* fees

honra *f* hono(u)r; *¡a mucha ~!* I'm hono(u)red; **honradez** *f* honesty; **honrado** *adj* honest

hora *f* hour; *~s pl extraordinarias* overtime *sg*; *~ local* local time; *~ punta* rush hour; *a la ~ de ...* fig when it comes to ...; *a última ~* at the last minute; *¡ya era ~!* about time too!; *tengo ~ con el dentista* I have an appointment with the dentist; *¿qué ~ es?* what time is it?; **horario** *m* schedule, *Br* timetable; *~ comercial* business hours *pl*; *~ flexible* flextime, *Br* flexitime; *~ de trabajo* (working) hours *pl*

horca *f* gallows *pl*; **horcajadas** *fpl*: *a*

~ astride

horchata *f drink made from tiger-nuts*

horda *f* horde

horizontal *adj* horizontal; **horizonte** *m* horizon

hormiga *f* ant

hormigón *m* concrete; **~ armado** reinforced concrete

hormigueo *m* pins and needles *pl*; **hormiguero** *m* ant hill; *la sala era un ~ de gente* the hall was swarming with people

hormona *f* hormone

hornilla *f* ring; **horno** *m* oven; *de cerámica* kiln; *alto ~* blast furnace

horóscopo *m* horoscope

horqueta *f L.Am. de camino* fork

horquilla *f para pelo* hairpin

horrendo *adj* horrendous

horrible *adj* horrible, dreadful; **horripilante** *adj* horrible; **horror** *m* horror (*a* of); *tener ~ a* be terrified of; *me gusta ~es* F I like it a lot; *¡qué ~!* how awful!; **horrorizar** <1f> *v/t* horrify; **horroroso** *adj* terrible; (*de mala calidad*) dreadful; (*feo*) hideous

hortaliza *f* vegetable

hortensia *f* BOT hydrangea

hortera 1 *f* F *adj* tacky F **2** *m/f* F tacky person F; **horterada** *f* F tacky thing F; *es una ~* it's tacky F

horticultor *m*, **~a** *f* horticulturist; **horticultura** *f* horticulture

hosco *adj* sullen

hospedaje *m* accommodations *pl*, *Br* accommodation; *dar ~ a alguien* put s.o. up; **hospedarse** <1a> *v/r* stay (*en* at); **hospital** *m* hospital; **hospitalario** *adj* hospitable; MED hospital *atr*; **hospitalidad** *f* hospitality; **hospitalizar** <1f> *v/t* hospitalize

hostal *m* hostel

hostelera *f* landlady; **hostelería** *f* hotel industry; **hostelero 1** *adj* hotel *atr* **2** *m* landlord

hostia *f* REL host; P (*golpe*) sock F, wallop F; *¡~s!* P Christ! P

hostigar <1h> *v/t* pester; MIL harass; *caballo* whip

hostil *adj* hostile; **hostilidad** *f* hostility

hotel *m* hotel; **hotelero** *m*, **-a** *f* hotelier

hoy *adv* today; *de ~* of today; *los padres de ~* today's parents, parents today; *de ~ en adelante* from now on; *por ~* for today; *~ por ~* at the present time; *~ en día* nowadays

hoya *f* hole; *de tumba* grave; GEOG plain; *S.Am.* river basin; **hoyo** *m* hole; (*depresión*) hollow; **hoyuelo** *m* dimple

hoz *f* sickle

huachafo *adj Pe* (*cursi*) affected, pretentious

huarache *m Méx* rough sandal

huayno *m Pe, Bol* Andean dance rhythm

hubo *vb* → **haber**

hucha *f* money box

hueco 1 *adj* hollow; (*vacío*) empty; *fig: persona* shallow **2** *m* gap; (*agujero*) hole; *de ascensor* shaft

huele *vb* → **oler**

huelga *f* strike; *~ de celo* work-to-rule; *~ general* general strike; *~ de hambre* hunger strike; *declararse en ~, ir a la ~* go on strike; **huelguista** *m/f* striker

huella *f* mark; *de animal* track; *~s dactilares* finger prints

huelo *vb* → **oler**

huérfano 1 *adj* orphan *atr* **2** *m*, **-a** *f* orphan

huero *adj fig* empty; *L.Am.* blond

huerta *f* truck farm, *Br* market garden; **huerto** *m* kitchen garden; *llevar a alguien al ~* F put one over on s.o. F

huesear <1a> *v/t C.Am.* beg

huesillo *m S.Am.* sun-dried peach

hueso *m* bone; *de fruta* pit, stone; *persona* tough nut; *Méx* F cushy number F; *Méx* F (*influencia*) influence, pull F; *~ duro de roer fig* F hard nut to crack F; *estar en los ~s* be all skin and bone

huésped *m/f* guest

huesudo *adj* bony

huevas *fpl* roe *sg*; **huevear** <1a> *v/i Chi* P mess around F; **huevo** *m* egg; P (*testículo*) ball V; **~ duro** hard-boiled egg; **~ escalfado** poached egg; **~ frito** fried egg; **~ pasado por agua** soft-boiled egg; **~s revueltos** scrambled eggs; **un ~ de** P a load of F; **huevón** *m*, **-ona** *f Chi* P idiot; *L.Am.* F (*flojo*) idler F

huida *f* flight, escape; **huir** <3g> *v/i* flee, escape (**de** from); **~ de algo** avoid sth

hulado *m C.Am.*, *Méx* rubberized cloth; **hule** *m* oilcloth; *L.Am.* (*caucho*) rubber

humanidad *f* humanity; **~es** humanities; **humanismo** *m* humanism; **humanitario** *adj* humanitarian; **humanizar** <1f> *v/t* humanize; **humano** *adj* human

humareda *f* cloud of smoke; **humear** <1a> *v/i con humo* smoke; *con vapor* steam

humedad *f* humidity; *de una casa* damp(ness); **humedecer** <2d> *v/t* dampen; **húmedo** *adj* humid; *toalla* damp

humildad *f* humility; **humilde** *adj* humble; (*sin orgullo*) modest; *clase social* lowly; **humillación** *f* humiliation; **humillante** *adj* humiliating;

humillar <1a> *v/t* humiliate

humita *f S.Am.* meat and corn paste wrapped in leaves

humo *m* smoke; (*vapor*) steam; **tener muchos ~s** F be a real big-head F

humor *m* humo(u)r; **estar de buen/mal ~** be in a good/bad mood; **sentido del ~** sense of humo(u)r; **humorista** *m/f* humo(u)rist; (*cómico*) comedian

humus *m* GASTR hummus

hundido *adj fig: persona* depressed; **hundir** <3a> **1** *v/t* sink; *fig: empresa* ruin, bring down; *persona* devastate **2** *v/r* **~se** sink; *fig: de empresa* collapse; *de persona* go to pieces

húngaro 1 *adj* Hungarian **2** *m*, **-a** *f* Hungarian

Hungría Hungary

huracán *m* hurricane

huraño *adj* unsociable

hurgar <1h> **1** *v/i* rummage (**en** in) **2** *v/r* **~se**: **~se la nariz** pick one's nose

hurón *m* ZO ferret

hurtadillas *fpl*: **a ~** furtively

hurtar <1a> *v/t* steal; **hurto** *m* theft

husmear <1a> *v/i* F nose around F (**en** in)

huy *int sorpresa* wow!; *dolor* ouch!

huyo *vb* → **huir**

I

I+D *abr* (= *investigación y desarrollo*) R&D (= research and development)

iba *vb* → **ir**

ibérico *adj* Iberian; **iberoamericano** *adj* Latin American

iceberg *m* iceberg

icono *m tb* INFOR icon

ida *f* outward journey; (*billete de*) **~ y vuelta** round trip (ticket), *Br* re-

turn (ticket)

idea *f* idea; **hacerse a la ~ de que ...** get used to the idea that ...; **no tener ni ~** not have a clue; **ideal** *m/adj* ideal; **idealista 1** *adj* idealistic **2** *m/f* idealist; **idear** *v/t* <1a> think up, come up with

idéntico *adj* identical

identidad *f* identity; **identificación** *f* identification; **identificar** <1g>

1 *v/t* identify **2** *v/r* ~**se** identify o.s.

ideología *f* ideology

idílico *adj* idyllic; **idilio** *m* idyll; (*relación amorosa*) romance

idioma *m* language

idiota 1 *adj* idiotic **2** *m/f* idiot; **idiotez** *f* stupid thing to say / do

ido 1 *part* → **ir 2** *adj* (*chiflado*) nuts F; **estar** ~ be miles away F

idolatrar <1a> *v/t tb fig* worship; **ídolo** *m tb fig* idol

idóneo *adj* suitable

iglesia *f* church

ignominioso *adj* ignominious

ignorancia *f* ignorance; **ignorante** *adj* ignorant; **ignorar** <1a> *v/t* not know, not be aware of; **ignoro cómo sucedió** I don't know how it happened

igual 1 *adj* (*idéntico*) same (**a, que** as); (*proporcionado*) equal (**a** to); (*constante*) constant; **al** ~ **que** like, the same as; **me da** ~ I don't mind **2** *m/f* equal; **no tener** ~ have no equal; **igualado** *adj* even; **igualar** <1a> *v/t precio, marca* equal, match; (*nivelar*) level off; ~ **algo** MAT make sth equal (**con, a** to) **2** *v/i* DEP tie the game, *Br* equalize; **igualdad** *f* equality; ~ **de oportunidades** equal opportunities; **igualitario** *adj* egalitarian; **igualmente** *adv* equally

iguana *f* ZO iguana

ilegal *adj* illegal

ilegible *adj* illegible

ilegítimo *adj* unlawful; *hijo* illegitimate

ileso *adj* unhurt

ilícito *adj* illicit

ilimitado *adj* unlimited

Ilmo. *abr* (= **ilustrísimo**) His / Your Excellency

ilógico *adj* illogical

iluminación *f* illumination; **iluminar** <1a> *v/t edificio, calle etc* light, illuminate; *monumento* light up, illuminate; *fig* light up

ilusión *f* illusion; (*deseo, esperanza*) hope; **ilusionarse** <1a> *v/r* get one's hopes up; (*entusiasmarse*) get

excited (**con** about)

ilustración *f* illustration; **ilustrar** <1a> *v/t* illustrate; (*aclarar*) explain; **ilustre** *adj* illustrious

imagen *f tb fig* image; **ser la viva** ~ **de** be the spitting image of; **imaginable** *adj* imaginable; **imaginación** *f* imagination; **imaginar** <1a> **1** *v/t* imagine **2** *v/r* ~**se** imagine; **¡ya me lo imagino!** I can just imagine it!; **imaginativo** *adj* imaginative

imán *m* magnet

imbatible *adj* unbeatable

imbécil 1 *adj* stupid **2** *m/f* idiot, imbecile; **imbecilidad** *f* stupidity; **¡qué** ~ **decir eso!** what a stupid thing to say!

imitación *f* imitation; **imitar** <1a> *v/t* imitate

impaciencia *f* impatience; **impacientar** <1a> **1** *v/t* make impatient **2** *v/r* ~**se** lose (one's) patience; **impaciente** *adj* impatient

impactar <1a> *v/t* hit; (*impresionar*) have an impact on; **impacto** *m tb fig* impact; ~ **de bala** bullet wound; ~ **ecológico** ecological

impar *adj número* odd

imparcial *adj* impartial; **imparcialidad** *f* impartiality

impasible *adj* impassive

impávido *adj* fearless, undaunted

impecable *adj* impeccable

impedimento *m* impediment; **impedir** <3l> *v/t* prevent; (*estorbar*) impede

imperante *adj* ruling; *fig* prevailing; **imperar** <1a> *v/i* rule; *fig* prevail; **imperativo 1** *adj* GRAM imperative; *obligación* pressing **2** *m* GRAM imperative

imperdible *m* safety pin

imperdonable *adj* unpardonable, unforgivable

imperfecto *m/adj* imperfect

imperial *adj* imperial; **imperio** *m* empire; **imperioso** *adj necesidad* pressing; *persona* imperious

impermeable 1 *adj* waterproof **2** *m* raincoat

impersonal *adj* impersonal

impertérrito *adj* unperturbed, unmoved

impertinente 1 *adj* impertinent **2** *m/f*: **¡eres un ~!** you've got nerve! F, *Br* you've got a cheek! F

ímpetu *m* impetus; **impetuoso** *adj* impetuous

implacable *adj* implacable

implemento *m* implement

implicar <1g> *v/t* mean, imply; (*involucrar*) involve; *en un delito* implicate (*en* in)

implícito *adj* implicit

implorar <1a> *v/t* beg for

imponente *adj* impressive, imposing; F terrific; **imponer** <2r> **1** *v/t* impose; *miedo, respeto* inspire; *impuesto* impose, levy **2** *v/i* be imposing *o* impressive **3** *v/r* **~se** (*hacerse respetar*) assert o.s.; DEP win; (*prevalecer*) prevail; (*ser necesario*) be imperative; **~se una tarea** set o.s. a task

importación *f* import, importation; *artículo* import

importancia *f* importance; **dar ~ a** attach importance to; **darse ~** give o.s. airs; **tener ~** be important; **importante** *adj* important; **importar** <1a> *v/i* matter; *no importa* it doesn't matter; *eso a ti no te importa* that's none of your business; *¿qué importa?* what does it matter?; *¿le importa ...?* do you mind ...?; **importe** *m* amount; (*coste*) cost

importuno *adj* inopportune

imposibilitar <1a> *v/t*: **~ algo** make sth impossible, prevent sth; **imposible** *adj* impossible

impostor *m*, **~a** *f* impostor

impotencia *f* impotence, helplessness; MED impotence; **impotente** *adj* helpless, powerless, impotent; MED impotent

impreciso *adj* imprecise

impredecible *adj* unpredictable

impregnar <1a> *v/t* saturate (*de* with); TÉC impregnate (*de* with)

imprenta *f taller* printer's; *arte, técnica* printing; *máquina* printing press

imprescindible *adj* essential; *persona* indispensable

impresión *f* impression; *acto* printing; (*tirada*) print run; *la sangre le da ~* he can't stand the sight of blood; **impresionante** *adj* impressive; **impresionar** <1a> *v/t*: **~le a alguien** impress s.o.; (*conmover*) move s.o.; (*alterar*) shock s.o.; **impresionismo** *m* impressionism; **impreso** *m* form; **~s** *pl* printed matter *sg*; **impresora** *f* INFOR printer; **~ de chorro de tinta** inkjet (printer); **~ de inyección de tinta** inkjet (printer); **~ láser** laser (printer)

imprevisible *adj* unpredictable; **imprevisto 1** *adj* unforeseen, unexpected **2** *m* unexpected event

imprimir <3a> *v/t tb* INFOR print; *fig* transmit

improbable *adj* unlikely, improbable

improcedente *adj* improper

improductivo *adj* unproductive

impropio *adj* inappropriate

improvisar <1a> *v/t* improvise; **improviso** *adj*: **de ~** unexpectedly

imprudencia *f* recklessness, rashness; **imprudente** *adj* reckless, rash

impuesto *m* tax; **~ sobre el valor añadido** sales tax, *Br* value-added tax; **~ sobre la renta** income tax

impugnar <1a> *v/t* challenge

impulsar <1a> *v/t* TÉC propel; COM boost

impulsivo *adj* impulsive; **impulso** *m* impulse; (*empuje*) impetus; COM boost; *fig* urge, impulse; **tomar ~** take a run up

impunidad *f* impunity

impureza *f* impurity

imputar <1a> *v/t* attribute

inacabable *adj* endless, never-ending

inaccesible *adj* inaccessible

inaceptable *adj* unacceptable

inactivo *adj* inactive

inadaptado *adj* maladjusted

inadecuado *adj* inadequate

inadmisible *adj* inadmissible

inadvertido *adj*: **pasar ~** go unnoticed

inagotable *adj* inexhaustible

inaguantable *adj* unbearable

inalámbrico 1 *adj* TELEC cordless **2** *m* TELEC cordless telephone

inamovible *adj* immovable

inanición *f* starvation

inapreciable *adj* (*valioso*) priceless; (*insignificante*) negligible

inasequible *adj objetivo* unattainable; *precio* prohibitive

inaudito *adj* unprecedented

inauguración *f* official opening, inauguration; **inaugurar** <1a> *v/t* (officially) open, inaugurate

inca *m/f & adj* HIST Inca

incalculable *adj* incalculable

incalificable *adj* indescribable

incandescente *adj* incandescent

incansable *adj* tireless

incapacidad *f* disability; (*falta de capacidad*) inability; (*ineptitud*) incompetence; **incapacitar** <1a> *v/t* JUR disqualify; **incapaz** *adj* incapable (**de** of)

incautarse <1a> *v/r*: **~ de** seize

incauto *adj* unwary

incendiar <1b> **1** *v/t* set fire to **2** *v/r* **~se** burn; **incendio** *m* fire; **~ forestal** forest fire

incentivo *m* incentive

incertidumbre *f* uncertainty

incesante *adj* incessant

incesto *m* incest

incidencia *f* (*efecto*) effect; (*frecuencia*) incidence; (*incidente*) incident; **incidente** *m* incident; **incidir** <3a> *v/i*: **~ en** (*afectar*) have an effect on, affect; (*recalcar*) stress; **~ en un error** make a mistake

incienso *m* incense

incierto *adj* uncertain

incineración *f de cadáver* cremation; **incinerador** *adj* incinerator; **incinerar** <1a> *v/t* incinerate; *cadáver* cremate

incipiente *adj* incipient

incitante *adj* provocative; **incitar** <1a> *v/t* incite

inclemencia *f del tiempo* inclemency

inclinación *f* inclination; *de un terreno* slope; *muestra de respeto* bow; *fig* tendency; **inclinar** <1a> **1** *v/t* tilt; **~ la cabeza** nod (one's head); **me inclina a creer que ...** it makes me think that ... **2** *v/r* **~se** bend (down); *de un terreno* slope; *desde la vertical* lean; *en señal de respeto* bow; **~se a** *fig* tend to, be inclined to

incluido *prp* inclusive; **incluir** <3g> *v/t* include; **inclusive** *adv* inclusive; **incluso** *adv, prp & conj* even

incógnita *f* unknown factor; MAT unknown (quantity); **incógnito** *adj*: **de ~** incógnito

incoherente *adj* incoherent

incombustible *adj* fireproof

incomodidad *f* uncomfortableness; (*fastidio*) inconvenience; **incómodo** *adj* uncomfortable; (*fastidioso*) inconvenient

incomparable *adj* incomparable

incompatibilidad *f* incompatibility; **incompatible** *adj tb* INFOR incompatible

incompetencia *f* incompetence; **incompetente** *adj* incompetent

incompleto *adj* incomplete

incomprendido *adj* misunderstood; **incomprensible** *adj* incomprehensible

incomunicado *adj* isolated, cut off; JUR in solitary confinement

inconcebible *adj* inconceivable

incondicional *adj* unconditional;

inconexo *adj* unconnected

inconfesable *adj* shameful

inconformista *m/f* nonconformist

inconfundible *adj* unmistakable

incongruente *adj* incongruous

inconsciencia *f* MED unconsciousness; (*desconocimiento*) lack of awareness, unawareness; (*irreflexión*) thoughtlessness; **inconsciente** *adj* MED unconscious; (*ignorante*) unaware; (*irreflexivo*) thoughtless

inconsecuente *adj* inconsistent

inconsistente *adj* flimsy, weak

inconsolable *adj* inconsolable

inconstante *adj* fickle

incontable *adj* uncountable

incontinencia *f* MED incontinence

incontrolable *adj* uncontrollable

inconveniente **1** *adj* (*inoportuno*) inconvenient; (*impropio*) inappropriate **2** *m* (*desventaja*) drawback, disadvantage; (*estorbo*) problem; **no tengo ~** I don't mind

incordiar <1b> *v/t* annoy; **incordio** *m* nuisance

incorporar <1a> **1** *v/t* incorporate **2** *v/r* **~se** sit up; **~se a** MIL join

incorrecto *adj* incorrect, wrong; *comportamiento* impolite; **incorregible** *adj* incorrigible

incorruptible *adj* incorruptible

incredulidad *f* disbelief, incredulity; **incrédulo** *adj* incredulous; **increíble** *adj* incredible

incrementar <1a> **1** *v/t* increase **2** *v/r* **~se** increase; **incremento** *m* growth

incriminar <1a> *v/t* incriminate

incruento *adj* bloodless

incrustar <1a> **1** *v/t* incrust (*de* with) **2** *v/r* **~se** *de la suciedad* become ingrained

incubación *f* incubation; **incubadora** *f* incubator; **incubar** <1a> *v/t* incubate

incuestionable *adj* unquestionable

inculcar <1g> *v/t* instil(l) (*en* in)

inculpar <1a> *v/t* JUR accuse;

inculto *adj* ignorant, uneducated; **incultura** *f* ignorance, lack of education

incumbencia *f* responsibility, duty; **no es de mi ~** it's not my responsibility

incumplimiento *m* non-fulfillment (*de* of), non-compliance (*de* with); **incumplir** <3a> *v/t* break

incurable *adj* incurable

incurrir <3a> *v/i*: **~ en un error** make a mistake; **~ en gastos** incur costs; **incursión** *f* MIL raid; *fig* foray

indagar <1h> *v/i* investigate

indecente *adj* indecent; *película* obscene

indecisión *f* indecisiveness; **indeci-**

so *adj* undecided; *por naturaleza* indecisive

indefenso *adj* defenseless, *Br* defenceless

indefinidamente *adv* indefinitely; **indefinido** *adj* (*impreciso*) vague; (*ilimitado*) indefinite

indemnización *f* compensation; **indemnizar** <1f> *v/t* compensate (*por* for)

independencia *f* independence; **independentismo** *m* POL pro-independence movement; **independiente** *adj* independent; **independizarse** <1f> *v/r* become independent

indescriptible *adj* indescribable

indeseable *adj* undesirable

indestructible *adj* indestructible

indeterminado *adj* indeterminate; (*indefinido*) indefinite

India: **la ~** India; **indiada** *f L.Am.* group of Indians

indicación *f* indication; (*señal*) sign; **indicaciones para llegar** directions; (*instrucciones*) instructions; **indicado** *adj* (*adecuado*) suitable; **lo más/menos ~** the best/worst thing; **hora -a** specified time; **indicador** *m* indicator; **indicar** <1g> *v/t* show, indicate; (*señalar*) point out; (*sugerir*) suggest; **índice** *m* index; **dedo ~** index finger; **~ de precios al consumo** consumer price index, *Br* retail price index; **indicio** *m* indication, sign; (*vestigio*) trace

indiferencia *f* indifference; **indiferente** *adj* indifferent; (*irrelevante*) immaterial

indígena **1** *adj* indigenous, native **2** *m/f* native

indigente *adj* destitute

indigestión *f* indigestion; **indigesto** *adj* indigestible

indignación *f* indignation; **indignado** *adj* indignant; **indignar** <1a> **1** *v/t*: **~ a alguien** make s.o. indignant **2** *v/r* **~se** become indignant

indigno *adj* unworthy (*de* of)

indio **1** *adj* Indian **2** *m*, **-a** *f* Indian; **hacer el ~** F clown around F, play the fool F

indirecta f insinuation; (*sugerencia*) hint

indirecto adj indirect

indiscreción f indiscretion, lack of discretion; (*declaración*) indiscreet remark; **indiscreto** adj indiscreet

indiscriminado adj indiscriminate

indiscutible adj indisputable

indispensable adj indispensable

indisponerse <2r> v/r become unwell; **~ con alguien** fall out with s.o.; **indisposición** f indisposition; **indispuesto** adj indisposed, unwell

indistinto adj forma indistinct, vague; *noción* vague; *sonido* faint

individual adj individual; *cama, habitación* single; **individualismo** m individualism; **individualista** m/f individualist; **individuo** m individual

indivisible adj indivisible

indocumentado adj: **un hombre ~** a man with no identity papers

índole f nature

indolente adj lazy

indoloro adj painless

indómito adj indomitable

Indonesia Indonesia

inducir <3o> v/t (*persuadir*) lead, induce (**a** to); EL induce

indudable adj undoubted; **indudablemente** adv undoubtedly

indulgente adj indulgent

indultar <1a> v/t pardon; **indulto** m pardon

indumentaria f clothing

industria f industry; (*esfuerzo*) industriousness, industry; **industrial** **1** adj industrial **2** m/f industrialist; **industrializar** <1f> **1** v/t industrialize **2** v/r **~se** industrialize

inédito adj unpublished; *fig* unprecedented

ineficacia f inefficiency; *de un procedimiento* ineffectiveness; **ineficaz** adj inefficient; *procedimiento* ineffective; **ineficiencia** f inefficiency; **ineficiente** adj inefficient

ineludible adj unavoidable

inepto 1 adj inept, incompetent **2** m, **-a** f incompetent fool

inequívoco adj unequivocal

inercia f inertia; **inerte** adj fig lifeless; FÍS inert

inesperado adj unexpected

inestabilidad f instability; **inestable** adj unstable; *tiempo* unsettled

inestimable adj invaluable

inevitable adj inevitable

inexacto adj inaccurate

inexcusable adj inexcusable

inexistente adj non-existent

inexperto adj inexperienced

inexplicable adj inexplicable

infalible adj infallible

infame adj vile, loathsome; (*terrible*) dreadful

infancia f infancy

infantería f MIL infantry

infantil adj children's *atr*; *naturaleza* childlike; *desp* infantile, childish

infarto m MED heart attack

infección f MED infection; **infeccioso** adj infectious; **infectar** <1a> **1** v/t infect **2** v/r **~se** become infected

infecundo adj infertile

infeliz 1 adj unhappy, miserable **2** m/f poor devil

inferior 1 adj inferior (**a** to); *en el espacio* lower (**a** than) **2** m/f inferior; **inferioridad** f inferiority

inferir <3i> v/t infer (**de** from); *daño* do, cause (**a** to)

infernal adj *ruido* infernal; (*muy malo*) diabolical

infertilidad f infertility

infestar <1a> v/t infest; (*invadir*) overrun

infidelidad f infidelity; **infiel 1** adj unfaithful **2** m/f unbeliever

infierno m hell

infiltrarse <1a> v/r: **~ en** infiltrate; *de agua* seep into

infinidad f: **~ de** countless; **infinitivo** m GRAM infinitive; **infinito 1** adj infinite **2** m infinity

inflación f COM inflation; **tasa de ~** inflation rate; **inflacionista** adj inflationary

inflamable *adj* flammable; **inflamación** *f* MED inflammation; **inflamar** <1a> **1** *v/t tb fig* inflame **2** *v/r* **~se** MED become inflamed

inflar <1a> **1** *v/t* inflate **2** *v/r* **~se** swell (up); *fig* F get conceited

infligir <3c> *v/t* inflict

inflexible *adj fig* inflexible

influencia *f* influence; **tener ~s** have contacts; **influenciar** <1b> *v/t* influence; **influir** <3g> *v/i*: **~ en alguien/algo** influence s.o./sth, have an influence on s.o./sth; **influjo** *m* influence; **influyente** *adj* influential

infografía *f* computer graphics *pl*

información *f* information; (*noticias*) news *sg*; **informal** *adj* informal; (*irresponsable*) unreliable; **informar** <1a> **1** *v/t* inform (*de, sobre* about) **2** *v/r* **~se** find out (*de, sobre* about); **informática** *f* information technology; **informático 1** *adj* computer *atr* **2** *m*, **-a** *f* IT specialist; **informativo 1** *adj* informative; *programa* news *atr* **2** *m* TV, RAD news *sg*; **informatizar** <1f> *v/t* computerize

informe **1** *adj* shapeless **2** *m* report; **~s** (*referencias*) references

infracción *f* offense, *Br* offence

infraestructura *f* infrastructure

in fraganti *adv* F in the act F

infrahumano *adj* subhuman

infrarrojo *adj* infra-red

infravalorar <1a> *v/t* undervalue

infrecuente *adj* infrequent

infringir <3c> *v/t* JUR infringe, violate

infructuoso *adj* fruitless

infundado *adj* unfounded, groundless

infundir <3a> *v/t* inspire; *terror* instil(l); *sospechas* arouse

infusión *f* infusion; *de tila, manzanilla* tea

ingeniarse <1b> *v/r*: **ingeniárselas para** manage to; **ingeniería** *f* engineering; **ingeniero** *m*, **-a** *f* engineer; **ingenio** *m* ingenuity; (*aparato*) device; **~ azucarero** *L.Am.* sugar

refinery; **ingenioso** *adj* ingenious

ingenuidad *f* naivety; **ingenuo 1** *adj* naive **2** *m*, **-a** *f* naive person, sucker F

ingerir <3i> *v/t* swallow

Inglaterra England

ingle *f* groin

inglés **1** *adj* English **2** *m* Englishman; *idioma* English; **inglesa** *f* Englishwoman

ingrato *adj* ungrateful; *tarea* thankless

ingrediente *m* ingredient

ingresar <1a> **1** *v/i*: **~ en** *en universidad* go to; *en asociación, cuerpo* join; *en hospital* be admitted to **2** *v/t cheque* pay in, deposit; **ingreso** *m* entry; *en una asociación* joining; *en hospital* admission; COM deposit; **~s** *pl* income *sg*; **examen de ~** entrance exam

inhabitable *adj* uninhabitable

inhalar <1a> *v/t* inhale

inherente *adj* inherent

inhibición *f* inhibition; JUR disqualification; **inhibir** <3a> *v/t* inhibit

inhóspito *adj* inhospitable

inhumano *adj* inhuman

iniciación *f* initiation; **inicial** *f/adj* initial; **iniciar** <1b> *v/t* initiate; *curso* start, begin; **iniciativa** *f* initiative; **tomar la ~** take the initiative; **inicio** *m* start, beginning

inigualable *adj* incomparable; *precio* unbeatable

inimaginable *adj* unimaginable

inimitable *adj* inimitable

ininteligible *adj* unintelligible

ininterrumpido *adj* uninterrupted

injerencia *f* interference

injertar <1a> *v/t* graft; **injerto** *m* graft

injuriar <1b> *v/t* insult

injusticia *f* injustice; **injustificado** *adj* unjustified; **injusto** *adj* unjust

inmaculado *adj* immaculate

inmaduro *adj* immature

inmediaciones *fpl* immediate area *sg* (*de* of), vicinity *sg* (*de* of); **inmediatamente** *adv* immediately; **inmediato** *adj* immediate; **de ~**

immediately

inmejorable *adj* unbeatable

inmenso *adj* immense

inmersión *f* immersion; *de submarino* dive; **inmerso** *adj fig* immersed (**en** in)

inmigración *f* immigration; **inmigrante** *m/f* immigrant; **inmigrar** <1a> *v/i* immigrate

inminente *adj* imminent

inmiscuirse <3g> *v/r* meddle

inmobiliaria *f* realtor's office, *Br* estate agency

inmoderado *adj* excessive, immoderate

inmoral *adj* immoral; **inmoralidad** *f* immorality

inmortal *adj* immortal

inmóvil *adj persona* motionless; *vehículo* stationary; **inmovilizar** <1f> *v/t* immobilize

inmueble *m* building

inmundo *adj* filthy

inmune *adj* immune; **inmunidad** *f* MED, POL immunity; **inmunizar** <1f> *v/t* immunize

inmutarse <1a> *v/r*: **no** ~ not bat an eyelid; **sin** ~ without batting an eyelid

innato *adj* innate, inborn

innecesario *adj* unnecessary

innegable *adj* undeniable

innovación *f* innovation

innumerable *adj* innumerable, countless

inocencia *f* innocence; **inocente** *adj* innocent

inocuo *adj* harmless, innocuous; *película* bland

inodoro *m* toilet

inofensivo *adj* inoffensive, harmless

inoficioso *adj L.Am. (inútil)* useless

inolvidable *adj* unforgettable

inopia *f*: **estar en la** ~ F *(distraído)* be miles away F; *(alejado de la realidad)* be on another planet F

inoportuno *adj* inopportune; *(molesto)* inconvenient

inorgánico *adj* inorganic

inoxidable *adj*: **acero** ~ stainless steel

inquietar <1a> **1** *v/t* worry **2** *v/r* ~**se** worry, get worried *o* anxious; **inquietud** *f* worry, anxiety; *intelectual* interest

inquilino *m* tenant

inquisitivo *adj* inquisitive

insaciable *adj* insatiable

insatisfacción *f* dissatisfaction; **insatisfactorio** *adj* unsatisfactory; **insatisfecho** *adj* dissatisfied

inscribir <3a> **1** *v/t (grabar)* inscribe; *en lista, registro* register, enter; *en curso, concurso* enrol(l), register **2** *v/r* ~**se** *en un curso* enrol(l), register; *en un concurso* enter; **inscripción** *f* inscription; *en lista, registro* registration, entry; *en curso, concurso* enrol(l)ment, registration;

insecticida *m* insecticide; **insecto** *m* insect

inseguro *adj* insecure; *estructura* unsteady; *(peligroso)* dangerous, unsafe

inseminación *f* insemination; ~ **artificial** artificial insemination

insensato *adj* foolish

insensible *adj* insensitive (**a** to)

inseparable *adj* inseparable

insertar <1a> *v/t* insert

inservible *adj* useless

insidia *f* treachery; **actuar con** ~ act treacherously

insignia *f* insignia

insignificante *adj* insignificant

insinuante *adj* suggestive

insinuar <1e> **1** *v/t* insinuate **2** *v/r* ~**se**: ~**se a alguien** make advances to s.o.

insípido *adj* insipid

insistencia *f* insistence; **insistir** <3a> *v/i* insist; ~ **en hacer algo** insist on doing sth; ~ **en algo** stress sth

insociable *adj* unsociable

insolación *f* MED sunstroke

insolente *adj* insolent

insólito *adj* unusual

insolvente *adj* insolvent

insomnio *m* insomnia

insondable *adj* unfathomable

insonorizar <1f> *v/t* soundproof

insoportable *adj* unbearable, intolerable

insospechado *adj* unexpected

inspección *f* inspection; **inspeccionar** <1a> *v/t* inspect; **inspector** *m*, **~a** *f* inspector

inspiración *f* inspiration; MED inhalation; **inspirar** <1a> *v/t* inspire; MED inhale

instalación *f acto* installation; ***instalaciones deportivas*** sports facilities; **instalar** <1a>**1** *v/t* instal(l); (*colocar*) put; *un negocio* set up **2** *v/r* **~se** *en un sitio* instal(l) o.s.

instancia *f* JUR petition; (*petición por escrito*) application; ***a ~s de*** at the request of

instantáneo *adj* immediate, instantaneous; **instante** *m* moment, instant; ***al ~*** right away, immediately; **instar** <1a> *v/t* urge, press

instaurar <1a> *v/t* establish

instigar <1h> *v/t* incite (***a*** to)

instinto *m* instinct

institución *f* institution; **instituto** *m* institute; *Esp* high school, *Br* secondary school; ***~ de belleza*** beauty salon; ***~ de educación secundaria*** high school, *Br* secondary school

instrucción *f* education; (*formación*) training; MIL drill; INFOR instruction, statement; JUR hearing; ***instrucciones de uso*** instructions, directions (for use); **instructor** *m*, **~a** *f* instructor; **instruido** *adj* educated; **instruir** <3g> *v/t* educate; (*formar*) train; JUR *pleito* hear

instrumental 1 *adj* instrumental **2** *m* MED instruments *pl*; **instrumento** *m* instrument; (*herramienta*) tool, instrument; *fig* tool; ***~ musical*** musical instrument

insubordinación *f* insubordination; **insubordinarse** <1a> *v/r con un superior* be insubordinate; (*rebelarse*) rebel

insuficiente 1 *adj* insufficient, inadequate **2** *m* EDU *nota* fail

insufrible *adj* insufferable

insulina *f* insulin

insulso *adj* bland, insipid

insultada *f L.Am.* (*insultos*) string of insults; **insultar** <1a> *v/t* insult; **insulto** *m* insult

insumiso *m* person who refuses to do military service

insuperable *adj* insurmountable

insurrección *f* insurrection

insustancial *adj conferencia* lightweight; *estructura* flimsy

intachable *adj* faultless

intacto *adj* intact; (*sin tocar*) untouched

integración *f* integration; **integral** *adj* complete; *alimento* whole; **integrar** <1a> *v/t* integrate; *equipo* make up; **íntegro** *adj* whole, entire; ***un hombre ~*** *fig* a man of integrity

intelectual *m/f & adj* intellectual

inteligencia *f* intelligence; **inteligente** *adj* intelligent; **inteligible** *adj* intelligible

intemperie *f*: ***a la ~*** in the open air

intempestivo *adj* untimely

intención *f* intention; ***doble*** or ***segunda ~*** ulterior motive; **intencionado** *adj* deliberate

intendente *m Rpl* military governor; (*alcalde*) mayor

intensidad *f* intensity; (*fuerza*) strength; **intensificar** <1g> **1** *v/t* intensify **2** *v/r* **~se** intensify; **intensivo** *adj* intensive; **intenso** *adj* intense; (*fuerte*) strong

intentar <1a> *v/t* try, attempt; **intento** *m* attempt, try; *Méx* (*intención*) aim

interacción *f* interaction; **interactivo** *adj* interactive

intercalar <1a> *v/t* insert

intercambiar <1a> *v/t* exchange, swap; **intercambio** *m* exchange, swap

interceder <2a> *v/i* intercede (***por*** for)

interceptar <1a> *v/t tb* DEP intercept

intercesión *f* intercession

interés *m tb* COM interest; *desp* self-interest; ***sin ~*** interest free; ***intereses*** (*bienes*) interests; **interesante** *adj* interesting; **interesar** <1a> **1** *v/t* interest **2** v/r ~se: ~se por take an interest in

interface m, **interfaz** f INFOR interface

interferencia f interference; **interferir** <3i> **1** v/t interfere with **2** v/i interfere (**en** in)

interino adj substitute atr, replacement atr; (provisional) provisional, acting atr

interior 1 adj interior; bolsillo inside atr; COM, POL domestic **2** m interior; DEP inside-forward; **en su** ~ fig inwardly; **interiorista** m/f interior designer

interjección f GRAM interjection

interlocutor m, ~a f speaker; **mi** ~ the person I was talking to

intermediario m COM intermediary, middle-man; **intermedio 1** adj nivel intermediate; tamaño medium; calidad average, medium **2** m intermission

interminable adj interminable, endless

intermitente 1 adj intermittent **2** m AUTO turn signal, Br indicator

internacional adj international

internado m boarding school; **internarse** <1a> v/r: ~ **en** go into

internauta m/f INFOR Internet user, Net surfer

Internet f INFOR Internet

interno 1 adj internal; POL domestic, internal **2** m, -**a** f EDU boarder; (preso) inmate; MED intern, Br houseman

interpelar <1a> v/t question

interplanetario adj interplanetary

interpolar <1a> v/t insert, interpolate fml

interponerse <2r> v/r intervene

interpretación f interpretation; TEA performance (**de** as); **interpretar** <1a> v/t interpret; TEA play; **intérprete** m/f interpreter

interrogación f interrogation; **signo de** ~ question mark; **interrogante 1** adj questioning **2** m (also f) question; fig question mark, doubt; **interrogar** <1h> v/t question; de po-

licía interrogate, question; **interrogatorio** m questioning, interrogation

interrumpir <3a> **1** v/t interrupt; servicio suspend; reunión, vacaciones cut short, curtail **2** v/i interrupt; **interrupción** f interruption; de servicio suspension; de reunión, vacaciones curtailment; **sin** ~ non-stop; **interruptor** m EL switch

intersección f intersection

intervalo m tb MÚS interval; (espacio) gap

intervención f intervention; en debate, congreso participation; en película, espectáculo appearance; MED operation; **intervenir** <3s> **1** v/i intervene; en debate, congreso take part, participate; en película, espectáculo appear **2** v/t TELEC tap; contrabando seize; MED operate on

intestino m intestine

intimar <1a> v/i (hacerse amigos) become friendly (**con** with); (tratar) mix (**con** with); **intimidad** f intimacy; (lo privado) privacy; **en la** ~ in private

intimidar <1a> v/t intimidate

íntimo adj intimate; (privado) private; **somos** ~**s amigos** we're close friends

intolerable adj intolerable, unbearable; **intolerante** adj intolerant

intoxicación f poisoning

intranquilidad f unease; (nerviosismo) restlessness; **intranquilo** adj uneasy; (nervioso) restless

intransferible adj non-transferable

intransigente adj intransigent

intransitable adj impassable

intransitivo adj GRAM intransitive

intrascendente adj unimportant

intravenoso adj MED intravenous

intrépido adj intrepid

intriga f intrigue; de novela plot; **intrigante 1** adj scheming; (curioso) intriguing **2** m/f schemer; **intrigar** <1h> **1** v/t (interesar) intrigue **2** v/i plot, scheme

intrincado adj intricate

intrínseco adj intrinsic

introducción *f* introduction; *acción de meter* insertion; INFOR input; **introducir** <3o> **1** *v/t* introduce; (*meter*) insert; INFOR input **2** *v/r*: **~se**: **~se en** get into; **~se en un mercado** gain access to *o* break into a market

intromisión *f* interference

introvertido *adj* introverted

intruso *m* intruder

intuición *f* intuition; **intuir** <3g> *v/t* sense; **intuitivo** *adj* intuitive

inundación *f* flood; **inundadizo** *adj* L.Am. prone to flooding; **inundar** <1a> *v/t* flood

inusitado *adj* unusual, uncommon; **inusual** *adj* UNUSUAL

inútil 1 *adj* useless; MIL unfit **2** *m/f*: **es un ~** he's useless; **inutilidad** *f* uselessness; **inutilizar** <1f> *v/t*: **~ algo** render sth useless; **inútilmente** *adv* uselessly

invadir <3a> *v/t* invade; *de un sentimiento* overcome

invalidar <1a> *v/t* invalidate; **invalidez** *f* disability; **inválido 1** *adj persona* disabled; *documento, billete* invalid **2** *m*, **-a** *f* disabled person

invasión *f* MIL invasion; **invasor** *m*, **~a** *f* invader

invencible *adj* invincible; *miedo* insurmountable

invención *f* invention; **inventar** <1a> *v/t* invent; **inventario** *m* inventory; **invento** *m* invention; **inventor** *m* inventor

invernada *f* Rpl winter pasture; **invernadero** *m* greenhouse; **invernal** *adj* winter *atr*

inverosímil *adj* unlikely

inversión *f* reversal; COM investment; **inverso** *adj* opposite; *orden* reverse; *a la -a* the other way round; **inversor** *m*, **~a** *f* investor; **invertir** <3i> *v/t* reverse; COM invest (**en** in)

invertebrado *m* invertebrate

investigación *f* research; EDU, TÉC research and development; **investigador** *m*, **~a** *f* researcher; **investi-**

-gar <1h> *v/t* investigate; EDU, TÉC research

inviable *adj* nonviable

invidente *m/f* blind person

invierno *m* winter

inviolable *adj* inviolable

invisible *adj* invisible

invitación *f* invitation; **invitado** *m*, **-a** *f* guest; **invitar** <1a> *v/t* invite (**a** to); (*convidar*) treat (**a** to)

invocar <1g> *v/t* invoke

involucrar <1a> *v/t* involve (**en** in)

involuntario *adj* involuntary

invulnerable *adj* invulnerable

inyección *f* MED, AUTO injection; **inyectar** <1a> *v/t tb* TÉC inject

IPC *abr* (= **índice de precios al consumo**) CPI (= consumer price index), Br RPI (= retail price index)

ir <3t> **1** *v/i* go (**a** to); **~ a pie** walk, go on foot; **~ en avión** fly; *¡ya voy!* I'm coming!; **~ a por algo** go and fetch sth; **~ bien / mal** go well / badly; *iba de amarillo / de uniforme* she was wearing yellow / a uniform; *van dos a dos* DEP the score is two all; *¿de qué va la película?* what's the movie about?; *¡qué va!* you must be joking! F; *¡vamos!* come on!; *¡vaya!* well! **2** *v/aux*: *va a llover* it's going to rain; *ya voy comprendiendo* I'm beginning to understand; **~ para viejo** be getting old **3** *v/r* **~se** go (away), leave; *¡vete!* go away!; *¡vámonos!* let's go

ira *f* anger

Irak Iraq, Irak

Irán Iran; **iraní** *m/f & adj* Iranian

iraquí *m/f & adj* Iraqi, Iraki

iris *m inv* ANAT iris; *arco ~* rainbow

Irlanda Ireland; **irlandés 1** *adj* Irish **2** *m* Irishman; **irlandesa** *f* Irishwoman

ironía *f* irony; **irónico** *adj* ironic

irracional *adj tb* MAT irrational

irradiar <1b> *v/t* radiate; MED irradiate

irreal *adj* unreal; **irrealizable** *adj* unattainable; *proyecto* unfeasible

irreconciliable *adj* irreconcilable
irrecuperable *adj* irretrievable
irrefutable *adj* irrefutable
irregular *adj* irregular; *superficie* uneven; **irregularidad** *f* irregularity; *de superficie* unevenness
irrelevante *adj* irrelevant
irremediable *adj fig* irremediable
irreparable *adj* irreparable
irreprochable *adj* irreproachable
irresistible *adj* irresistible
irrespetuoso *adj* disrespectful
irresponsable *adj* irresponsible
irreverente *adj* irreverent
irreversible *adj* irreversible
irrevocable *adj* irrevocable
irrigar <1h> *v/t* MED, AGR irrigate
irrisorio *adj* laughable, derisory
irritación *f tb* MED irritation; **irritante** *adj tb* MED irritating; **irritar** <1a> **1** *v/t tb* MED irritate **2** *v/r* ~**se** get irritated
irrompible *adj* unbreakable

irrumpir <3a> *v/i* burst in; **irrupción** *f*: **hacer ~ en** burst into
isla *f* island
islám *m* Islam; **islámico** *adj* Islamic; **islamismo** *m* Islam
isleño 1 *adj* island *atr* **2** *m*, **-a** *f* islander
Israel Israel; **israelí** *m/f & adj* Israeli
Italia Italy; **italiano 1** *adj* Italian **2** *m*, **-a** *f* Italian
itinerario *m* itinerary
ITV *abr Esp* (= **inspección técnica de vehículos**) *compulsory annual test of motor vehicles of a certain age*, *Br* MOT
IVA *abr* (= **impuesto sobre el valor añadido**) *sales tax*, *Br* VAT (= value-added tax)
izar <1f> *v/t* hoist
izdo., izda. *abr* (= **izquierdo, izquierda**) l (= left)
izquierda *f tb* POL left; *por la* ~ on the left; **izquierdo** *adj* left

J

jabalí *m* ZO wild boar
jabalina *f* javelin
jabón *m* soap; ~ **de afeitar** shaving soap; **jabonera** *f* soap dish; **jabonoso** *adj* soapy
jacinto *m* hyacinth
jactancia *f* boasting; **jactancioso** *adj* boastful; **jactarse** <1a> *v/r* boast (**de** about), brag (**de** about)
jacuzzi *m* jacuzzi®
jade *m* MIN jade
jadear <1a> *v/i* pant; **jadeo** *m* panting
jaguar *m* ZO jaguar
jalar <1a> **1** *v/t* L.Am. pull; *con esfuerza* haul; *(atraer)* attract; *Méx* F *(dar aventón)* give a ride *o Br* a lift to; *¿te jala el arte? Méx* do you feel drawn to art? **2** *v/i* L.Am. pull; *(trabajar*

mucho) work hard; *Méx* F *(tener influencia)* have pull F; ~ **hacia** F head toward; ~ **para la casa** F clear off home F **3** *v/r* ~**se** *Méx* (*irse*) go, leave; F (*emborracharse*) get plastered F
jalea *f* jelly; ~ **real** royal jelly
jaleo *m* (*ruido*) racket, uproar; (*lío*) mess, muddle; **armar** ~ F kick up a fuss F
jalón *m* pull; **dar un ~ a algo** pull sth; **de un** ~ *Méx fig* in one go
jalonar <1a> *v/t fig* mark out
Jamaica Jamaica
jamás *adv* never; ~ **te olvidaré** I'll never forget you; *¿viste ~ algo así?* did you ever see anything like it?; *nunca* ~ never ever; *por siempre* ~ for ever and ever

jamón *m* ham; **~ de York** cooked ham; **~ serrano** cured ham; **¡y un ~!** F *(¡no!)* no way! F; *(¡bromeas!)* come off it! F

jangada *f S.Am.* F dirty trick

Japón Japan; **japonés 1** *adj* Japanese **2** *m*, **-esa** *f* Japanese

jaque *m* check; **~ mate** checkmate; **dar ~ a** checkmate

jaqueca *f* MED migraine

jarabe *m* syrup; *Méx type of folk dance*

jardín *m* garden; **~ botánico** botanic(al) gardens; **~ de infancia** kindergarten; **jardinería** *f* gardening; **jardinero** *m*, **-a** *f* gardener

jarra *f* pitcher, *Br* jug; **en ~s** with hands on hips; **jarro** *m* pitcher, *Br* jug; **un ~ de agua fría** *fig* a total shock, a bombshell; **jarrón** *m* vase

jauja *f*: **¡esto es ~!** this is the life!

jaula *f* cage

jauría *f* pack

jazmín *m* BOT jasmine

J.C. *abr* (= **Jesucristo**) J.C. (= Jesus Christ)

jefatura *f* headquarters; *(dirección)* leadership; **~ de policía** police headquarters; **jefe** *m*, **-a** *f* de departamento, organización head; *(superior)* boss; POL leader; *de tribu* chief; **~ de cocina** (head) chef; **~ de estado** head of state

jengibre *m* BOT ginger

jeque *m* sheik

jerarquía *f* hierarchy

jerez *m* sherry

jerga *f* jargon; *(argot)* slang

jeringa *f* MED syringe; **jeringuilla** *f* MED syringe; **~ desechable** or **de un solo uso** disposable syringe

jeroglífico *m* hieroglyphic; *rompecabezas* puzzle

jersey *m* sweater

Jesucristo *m* Jesus Christ; **Jesús** *m* Jesus; **¡~!** good grief!; *por estornudo* bless you!

jet 1 *m* AVIA jet **2** *f*: **~** (**set**) jet set

jeta *f* F face, mug F; **¡qué ~ tiene!** F he's got nerve! F, *Br* what a cheek! F

jibia *f* ZO cuttlefish

jícara *f Méx* drinking bowl; **jícaro** *m* L.Am. BOT calabash

jilguero *m* ZO goldfinch

jilote *m* C.Am., *Méx* young corn

jineta *f* ZO civet

jinete *m* rider; *en carrera* jockey

jirafa *f* ZO giraffe

jitomate *m Méx* tomato

JJ.OO. *abr* (= **Juegos Olímpicos**) Olympic Games

jocoso *adj* humorous, joking

joder <2a> **1** *v/i* V screw V, fuck V **2** *v/t* V *(follar)* screw V, fuck V; *(estropear)* screw up V, fuck up V; *L.Am.* F *(fastidiar)* annoy, irritate; **¡~!** V fuck! V; **me jode un montón** V it really pisses me off P

jolgorio *m* F partying F

jolín *int* wow! F, jeez! F

jornada *f* (working) day; *distancia* day's journey; **media ~** half-day; **~ laboral** work day; **~ partida** split shift; **jornal** *m* day's wage; **jornalero** *m*, **-a** *f* day labo(u)rer

joroba *f* hump; *fig* pain F, drag F; **jorobado** *adj* hump-backed; *fig* F in a bad way F; **jorobar** <1a> *v/t* F *(molestar)* bug F; *planes* ruin

jorongo *m Méx* poncho

jota *f* letter 'j'; **no saber ni ~** F not have a clue F

joven 1 *adj* young **2** *m/f* young man; *mujer* young woman; **los jóvenes** young people

jovial *adj* cheerful

joya *f* jewel; *persona* gem; **~s** *pl* jewelry *sg*, *Br* jewellery *sg*; **joyería** *f* jewelry store, *Br* jeweller's; **joyero 1** *m*, **-a** *f* jewel(l)er **2** *m* jewelry (*Br* jewellery) box

juanete *m* MED bunion

jubilación *f* retirement; **~ anticipada** early retirement; **jubilado 1** *adj* retired **2** *m*, **-a** *f* retiree, *Br* pensioner; **jubilar** <1a> **1** *v/t* retire; *(desechar)* get rid of **2** *v/r* **~se** retire; *C.Am.* play hooky F, play truant; **júbilo** *m* jubilation; **jubiloso** *adj* jubilant

judaísmo *m* Judaism

judía f BOT bean; **~ verde** green bean, runner bean

judicial adj judicial

judío 1 adj Jewish **2** m, **-a** f Jew

judo m DEP judo

juego m game; *acción* play; *por dinero* gambling; (*conjunto de objetos*) set; **~ de azar** game of chance; **~ de café** coffee set; **~ de manos** conjuring trick; **~ de mesa** board game; **~ de rol** role-playing game; **~ de sociedad** game; **Juegos Olímpicos** Olympic Games; *estar en ~ fig* be at stake; *fuera de ~* DEP offside; *hacer ~ con* go with, match

juerga f F partying F; *irse de ~* F go out on the town F, go out partying F

juergista m/f F party animal F

jueves m inv Thursday

juez m/f judge; **~ de línea** en fútbol assistant referee; *en fútbol americano* line judge; **jueza** f → **juez**

jugada f play, Br move; *en ajedrez* move; *hacerle una mala ~ a alguien* play a dirty trick on s.o.; **jugador** m, **-a** f player; **jugar** <1o> **1** v/t play **2** v/i play; *con dinero* gamble; **~ al baloncesto** play basketball **3** v/r **~se la vida** risk one's life; *jugársela a alguien* do the dirty on s.o. F; **jugarreta** f F dirty trick F

jugo m juice; *sacar ~ a algo* get the most out of sth; **jugoso** adj tb fig juicy

juguete m toy; **juguetear** <1a> v/i play; **juguetería** f toy store, Br toy shop

juicio m judg(e)ment; (*sensatez*) sense; (*cordura*) sanity; *a mi ~* in my opinion; *estar en su ~* be in one's right mind; *perder el ~* lose one's mind

julio m July

junco m BOT reed

jungla f jungle

junio m June

júnior adj tb DEP junior

junta f POL (regional) government; *militar* junta; COM board; (*sesión*) meeting; TÉC joint; **~ directiva** board of directors; **~ general anual** annual general meeting; **juntar** <1a> **1** v/t put together; *gente* gather together; *bienes* collect, accumulate **2** v/r **~se** (*reunirse*) meet, assemble; *de pareja: empezar a salir* start going out; *empezar a vivir juntos* move in together; *de caminos, ríos* meet, join; **~se con alguien** *socialmente* mix with s.o.; **junto 1** adj together **2** prp: **~ a** next to, near; **~ con** together with

juntura f TÉC joint

jupa f C.Am., Méx fig F head, nut F

jura f (*promesa*) oath; *ceremonia* swearing (on oath); **jurado** m JUR jury; **juramento** m oath; *bajo ~* under oath; **jurar** <1a> v/i swear; **jurídico** adj legal; **jurisdicción** f jurisdiction; **jurisprudencia** f jurisprudence

justamente adv fairly; (*precisamente*) precisely

justicia f justice; *la ~* (*la ley*) the law; *hacer ~ a* do justice to; **justificable** adj justifiable; **justificación** f tb TIP justification; **justificante** m de pago receipt; *de ausencia, propiedad* certificate; **justificar** <1g> v/t tb TIP justify; *mala conducta* justify, excuse; **justo** adj just, fair; (*exacto*) right, exact; *lo ~* just enough; *¡~!* right!, exactly!

juvenil adj youthful; **juventud** f youth

juzgado 1 part → **juzgar 2** m court; **juzgar** <1h> v/t JUR try; (*valorar*) judge; *considerar* consider, judge; **a ~ por** to judge by, judging by

J

K

kárate *m* DEP karate
kayak *m* DEP kayak
ketchup *m* ketchup
kg. *abr* (= **kilogramo**) kg (= kilogram)
kilo *m* kilo; *fig* F million
kilogramo *m* kilogram, *Br* kilogramme
kilómetro *m* kilometer, *Br* kilometre

kiosco *m* kiosk
kiwi *m* BOT kiwi (fruit)
kleenex® *m* kleenex, tissue
km. *abr* (= **kilómetro**) km (= kilometer)
km./h. *abr* (= **kilómetros por hora**) kph (= kilometers per hour)
kv. *abr* (= **kilovatio**) kw (= kilowatt)

L

la 1 *art* the **2** *pron complemento directo sg* her; *a usted* you; *algo it*; **~ que está embarazada** the one who is pregnant; **~ más grande** the biggest (one); **dame ~ roja** give me the red one
laberinto *m* labyrinth, maze
labia *f*: **tener mucha ~** have the gift of the gab; **labio** *m* lip
labor *f* work; (*tarea*) task, job; **hacer ~es** do needlework; **no estar por la ~** F not be enthusiastic about the idea; **laborable** *adj*: **día ~** workday; **laboral** *adj* labo(u)r *atr*; **laboratorio** *m* laboratory, lab F; **laborioso** *adj* laborious; *persona* hardworking; **labrador** *m* farm labo(u)rer, farm worker; **labranza** *f de la tierra* cultivation; **labrar** <1a> *v/t tierra* work; *piedra* carve; **labriego** *m* farm labo(u)rer, farm worker
laca *f* lacquer; *para el cabello* hairspray; **~ de uñas** nail varnish o

polish
lacear <1a> *v/t Rpl* lasso
lacio *adj* limp; *pelo* lank
lacónico *adj* laconic
lacra *f* scar; *L.Am.* (*llaga*) sore; **la corrupción es una ~ social** corruption is a blot on society
lacre *m* sealing wax
lacrimógeno *adj fig* tear-jerking
lactancia *f* lactation; **lácteo** *adj*: **Vía Láctea** Milky Way; **productos ~s** dairy products
ladear <1a> *v/t* tilt; **ladera** *f* slope
ladino 1 *adj* cunning, sly **2** *m C.Am.* Indian who has become absorbed into white culture
lado *m* side; (*lugar*) place; **al ~** nearby; **al ~ de** beside, next to; **de ~** sideways; **ir por otro ~** go another way; **por un ~ ... por otro ~** on the one hand ... on the other hand; **hacerse a un ~** tb *fig* stand aside
ladrar <1a> *v/i* bark

ladrillo *m* brick
ladrón *m* thief
lagartija *f* ZO small lizard; **lagarto** *m* ZO lizard
lago *m* lake
lágrima *f* tear
laguna *f* lagoon; *fig* gap
laico *adj* lay
lamentable *adj* deplorable; **lamentablemente** *adv* regretfully; **lamentar** <1a> 1 *v/t* regret, be sorry about; *muerte* mourn 2 *v/r* ~*se* complain (*de* about); **lamento** *m* whimper; *por dolor* groan
lamer <2a> *v/t* lick
lámina *f* sheet
lámpara *f* lamp; ~ *halógena* halogen lamp; ~ *de pie* floor lamp, *Br* standard lamp; **lamparón** *m* F grease mark
lana *f* wool; *Méx* P dough F; *pura ~ virgen* pure new wool
lancha *f* launch; ~ *fueraborda* outboard
langosta *f* ZO *insecto* locust; *crustáceo* spiny lobster; **langostino** *m* ZO king prawn
languidecer <2d> *v/i* languish; **lánguido** *adj* languid
lanza *f* lance; **lanzadera** *f* shuttle; ~ *espacial* space shuttle; **lanzado** 1 *adj fig* go-ahead; *es muy ~ con las chicas* he's not shy with girls 2 *part* → **lanzar**; **lanzamiento** *m* MIL, COM launch; ~ *de disco/de martillo* discus/hammer (throw); ~ *de peso* shot put; **lanzar** <1f> 1 *v/t* throw; *cohete, producto* launch; *bomba* drop 2 *v/r* ~*se* throw o.s. (*en* into); (*precipitarse*) pounce (*sobre* on); ~*se a hacer algo* rush into doing sth
lapa *f* ZO limpet
lapicera *f* Rpl, Chi (ballpoint) pen; ~ *fuente* L.Am. fountain pen; **lapicero** *m* automatic pencil, *Br* propelling pencil
lápida *f* memorial stone; **lapidario** *adj* memorable
lápiz *m* pencil; ~ *de ojos* eyeliner; ~ *labial or de labios* lipstick; ~ *óptico* light pen
lapso *m de tiempo* space, period; **lapsus** *m inv* slip; *tener un* ~ have a momentary lapse
larga *f*: *poner la(s)* ~(*s*) put the headlights on full beam; *dar* ~*s a alguien* F put s.o. off; **largar** <1h> 1 *v/t* drive away 2 *v/r* ~*se* F clear off *o* out F; **largo** 1 *adj* long; *persona* tall; *a la -a* in the long run; *a lo ~ del día* throughout the day; *a lo ~ de la calle* along the street; *¡~!* F scram! F; *esto va para* ~ this will take some time; *pasar de* ~ go (straight) past 2 *m* length; **largometraje** *m* feature film; **larguero** *m* DEP crossbar
laringe *f* larynx; **laringitis** *f* MED laryngitis
larva *f* ZO larva
las 1 *art fpl* the 2 *pron complemento directo pl* them; *a ustedes* you; *llévate ~ que quieras* take whichever ones you want; ~ *de ...* those of ...; ~ *de Juan* Juan's; ~ *que llevan falda* the ones *o* those that are wearing dresses
lasaña *f* GASTR lasagne
lascivo *adj* lewd
láser *m* laser; *rayo* ~ laser beam
lástima *f* pity, shame; *me da* ~ *no usarlo* it's a shame *o* pity not to use it; *¡qué* ~! what a pity *o* shame!; **lastimar** <1a> 1 *v/t* (*herir*) hurt 2 *v/r* ~*se* hurt o.s.; **lastimoso** *adj* pitiful; (*deplorable*) shameful
lastre *m* ballast; *fig* burden
lata *f* can, *Br tb* tin; *fig* F drag F, pain F; *dar la* ~ F be a drag F *o* a pain F
latente *adj* latent
lateral 1 *adj* side *atr*; *cuestiones* ~*es* side issues 2 *m* DEP: ~ *derecho/izquierdo* right/left back
latería *f* L.Am. tin works; **latero**, *-a* *f* L.Am. tinsmith
latido *m* beat
latifundio *m* large estate
latigazo *m* lash; (*chasquido*) crack; **látigo** *m* whip
latín *m* Latin; **latino** *adj* Latin; **Latinoamérica** Latin America;

L

latinoamericano 1 *adj* Latin American **2** *m*, **-a** *f* Latin American

latir <3a> *v/i* beat

latitud *f* GEOG latitude

latón *m* brass

laucha *f S.Am.* mouse

laurel *m* BOT laurel; *dormirse en los ~es fig* rest on one's laurels

lava *f* lava

lavable *adj* washable; **lavabo** *m* washbowl; **lavada** *f L.Am.* wash; **lavado** *m* washing; *~ de cerebro fig* brainwashing; **lavadora** *f* washing machine; **lavamanos** *m inv L.Am.* → **lavabo**

lavanda *f* BOT lavender

lavandería *f* laundry

lavaplatos *m inv* dishwasher; *L.Am.* sink

lavar <1a> **1** *v/t* wash; *~ los platos* wash the dishes; *~ la ropa* do the laundry, *Br tb* do the washing; *~ en seco* dry-clean **2** *v/i* (*lavar los platos*) do the dishes; *de detergente* clean **3** *v/r* *~se* wash up, *Br* have a wash; *~se los dientes* brush one's teeth; *~se las manos* wash one's hands; *yo me lavo las manos fig* I wash my hands of it

lavarropas *m inv L.Am.* washing machine

lavavajillas *m inv líquido* dishwashing liquid, *Br* washing-up liquid; *electrodoméstico* dishwasher

laxante *m/adj* MED laxative; **laxo** *adj* relaxed; (*poco estricto*) lax

lazada *f* bow

lazarillo *m* guide; *perro ~* seeing eye dog, *Br* guide dog

lazo *m* knot; *de adorno* bow; *para atrapar animales* lasso

le *pron sg complemento indirecto* (to) him; (*a ella*) (to) her; (*a usted*) (to) you; (*a algo*) (to) it; *complemento directo* him; (*a usted*) you

leal *adj* loyal; **lealtad** *f* loyalty

lección *f* lesson; *esto le servirá de ~* that will teach him a lesson

lechar <1a> *v/t L.Am.* (*ordeñar*) milk; **leche** *f* milk; *~ condensada* condensed milk; *~ entera* whole milk; *~ en polvo* powdered milk; *estar de mala ~* P be in a foul mood; *tener mala ~* P be out to make trouble; **lechería** *f* dairy; **lechero 1** *adj* dairy *atr* **2** *m* milkman

lecho *m tb de río* bed

lechón *m* suckling pig

lechuga *f* lettuce; *ser más fresco que una ~* F have a lot of nerve

lechuza *f* ZO barn-owl; *Cuba, Méx* P hooker F

lectivo *adj*: *día ~* school day; **lector** *m*, *~a* *f* reader; **lectura** *f* reading

leer <2e> *v/t* read

legado *m* legacy; *persona* legate

legal *adj* legal; *fig* F *persona* great F, terrific F; **legalidad** *f* legality; **legalizar** <1f> *v/t* legalize

legaña *f*: *tener ~s en los ojos* have sleep in one's eyes

legar <1h> *v/t* leave

legendario *adj* legendary

legible *adj* legible

legión *f* legion

legislación *f* legislation; **legislar** <1a> *v/i* legislate; **legislativo** *adj* legislative; **legislatura** *f cuerpo* legislature; *periodo* term of office

legitimar <1a> *v/t* justify; *documento* authenticate; **legítimo** *adj* legitimate; (*verdadero*) authentic

lego *adj* lay *atr*; *fig* ignorant

legua *f*: *se ve a la ~ fig* F you can see it a mile off F; *hecho* it's blindingly obvious F

legumbre *f* BOT pulse

leída *f L.Am.* reading

lejanía *f* distance; *en la ~* in the distance; **lejano** *adj* distant

lejía *f* bleach

lejos 1 *adv* far, far away; *Navidad queda ~* Christmas is a long way off; *a lo ~* in the distance; *ir demasiado ~ fig* go too far, overstep the mark; *llegar ~ fig* go far **2** *prp*: *~ de* far from

lele *adj C.Am.* stupid

lema *m* slogan

lencería *f* lingerie

lengua f tongue; **~ materna** mother tongue; **con la ~ fuera** fig with one's tongue hanging out; **irse de la ~** let the cat out of the bag; **sacar la ~ a alguien** stick one's tongue out at s.o.; **lo tengo en la punta de la ~** it's on the tip of my tongue

lenguado m ZO sole

lenguaje m language; **~ de programación** INFOR programming language; **lenguaraz** adj foulmouthed; **lengüeta 1** f de zapato tongue **2** adj: **ser ~** S.Am. F be a gossip

lenitivo m balm

lente f lens; **~s de contacto** contact lenses, contacts; **lentes** mpl L.Am. glasses

lenteja f BOT lentil

lentejuela f sequin

lentillas fpl contact lenses

lentitud f slowness; **lento** adj slow; **a fuego ~** on a low heat

leña f (fire)wood; **echar ~ al fuego** fig add fuel to the fire; **leñador** m woodcutter; **leño** m log

Leo m/f inv ASTR Leo

león m ZO lion; L.Am. puma; **~ marino** sealion; **leona** f lioness; **leonera** f lion's den; jaula lion's cage; Rpl, Chi fig F habitación desordenada etc pigsty F; L.Am. F para prisioneros bullpen F, Br communal cell for holding prisoners temporarily

leopardo m ZO leopard

leotardo m de gimnasta leotard; **~s** tights, Br heavy tights

lépero adj C.Am., Méx coarse

lerdo adj (torpe) slow(-witted)

les pron pl complemento indirecto (to) them; (a ustedes) (to) you; complemento directo them; (a ustedes) you

lesbiana f lesbian

lesión f injury; **lesionado** adj injured; **lesionar** <1a> v/t injure

letal adj lethal

letanía f litany

letárgico adj lethargic

letra f letter; de canción lyrics pl; **~ de cambio** COM bill of exchange; **~ de imprenta** block capital; **~ mayúscula** capital letter; **al pie de la ~** word for word

letrero m sign

letrina f latrine

leucemia f MED leuk(a)emia

levadura f yeast

levantamiento m raising; (rebelión) rising; de embargo lifting; **levantar** <1a> **1** v/t raise; bulto lift (up); del suelo pick up; edificio, estatua put up, erect; embargo lift; **~ sospechas** arouse suspicion; **¡levanta los ánimos!** cheer up!; **~ la voz** raise one's voice **2** v/r **~se** get up; (ponerse de pie) stand up; de un edificio, una montaña rise; en rebelión rise up

levante m east

levar <1a> v/t: **~ anclas** weigh anchor

leve adj slight; sonrisa faint; **levedad** f lightness

levitar <1a> v/i levitate

léxico m lexicon

ley f law; **con todas las de la ~** fairly and squarely

leyenda f legend

leyendo vb → **leer**

leyó vb → **leer**

liana f BOT liana, creeper

liar <1c> **1** v/t tie (up); en papel wrap (up); cigarillo roll; persona confuse **2** v/r **~se** de una persona get confused; **~se a hacer algo** get tied up doing sth; **~se con alguien** F get involved with s.o.

Líbano Lebanon

libélula f ZO dragonfly

liberación f release; de un país liberation; **liberal** adj liberal; **liberalización** f liberalization; **liberalizar** <1f> v/t liberalize; **liberar** <1a> **1** v/t (set) free, release; país liberate; energía release **2** v/r **~se**: **~se de algo** free o.s. of sth; **libertad** f freedom, liberty; **~ bajo fianza** JUR bail; **~ condicional** JUR probation; **dejar a alguien en ~** release s.o., let s.o. go

libertinaje m licentiousness

Libia Libya

líbido f libido

libio(-a) m/f & adj Libyan

libra f pound; **~ esterlina** pound (sterling)

Libra m/f inv ASTR Libra

librar <1a> **1** v/t free (**de** from); *cheque* draw; *batalla* fight **2** v/i: *libro los lunes* I have Mondays off **3** v/r **~se**: **~se de algo** get out of sth; *de buena nos hemos librado* F that was lucky

libre adj free; *tiempo* spare, free; *eres ~ de* you're free to; **librecambio** m free trade

librera f bookseller; **librería** f book store; **librero** m bookseller; *L.Am. mueble* bookcase; **libreta** f notebook; **~ de ahorros** bankbook, passbook; **libro** m book; **~ de bolsillo** paperback (book); **~ de cocina** cookbook, cookery book; **~ de familia** booklet recording family births, marriages and deaths; **~ de reclamaciones** complaints book

licencia f permit, license, Br licence; (*permiso*) permission; MIL leave; **~** (**de manejar** or **conducir**) L.Am. driver's license, Br driving licence; *tomarse demasiadas ~s* take liberties; **licenciado** m, **-a** f graduate; **licenciar** <1b> **1** v/t MIL discharge **2** v/r **~se** graduate; MIL be discharged; **licenciatura** f EDU degree

liceo m L.Am. high school, Br secondary school

licitación f L.Am. bidding; **licitador** m, **~a** f L.Am. bidder; **licitar** <1a> v/t L.Am. en subasta bid for

lícito adj legal; (*razonable*) fair, reasonable

licor m liquor, Br spirits pl

licuado m Méx fruit milkshake; **licuadora** f blender; **licuar** <1d> v/t blend, liquidize

líder **1** m/f leader **2** adj leading; **liderar** <1a> v/t lead; **liderazgo** m leadership

lidia f bullfighting; **lidiar** <1b> **1** v/i fig do battle, struggle **2** v/t toro fight

liebre f ZO hare

lienzo m canvas

liga f POL, DEP league; *de medias* garter; **ligamento** m ANAT ligament; **ligar** <1h> **1** v/t bind; (*atar*) tie **2** v/i: **~ con** F pick up F

ligereza f lightness; (*rapidez*) speed; *de movimiento* agility; *de carácter* shallowness, superficiality; **ligero** **1** adj (*de poco peso*) light; (*rápido*) rapid, quick; *movimiento* agile, nimble; (*leve*) slight; **~ de ropa** scantily clad; **a la -a** (*sin pensar*) lightly, casually; *tomar algo a la -a* not take sth seriously **2** adv quickly

ligón m F: *es un ~* he's a real Don Juan F

ligue m F: *estar de ~* be on the pick-up F, Br be on the pull F

liguero m garter belt, Br suspender belt

lija f: *papel de ~* sandpaper; **lijar** <1a> v/t sand

lila f BOT lilac

lima f file; BOT lime; **~ de uñas** nail file; **limar** <1a> v/t file; fig polish

limitado **1** adj limited **2** part → **limitar**; **limitar** <1a> **1** v/t limit **2** v/i: **~ con** border on **3** v/r **~se** limit o restrict o.s. (**a** to); **límite** **1** m limit; (*línea de separación*) boundary; **~ de velocidad** speed limit **2** adj: *situación* ~ life-threatening situation; **limítrofe** adj neighbo(u)ring

limón m lemon; **limonada** f lemonade

limosna f: *una ~, por favor* can you spare some change?

limpiabotas m/f inv bootblack

limpiacristales m inv window cleaner

limpiada f L.Am. clean

limpiamanos m inv L.Am. hand towel

limpiaparabrisas m inv AUTO windshield wiper, Br windscreen wiper

limpiar <1b> v/t clean; *con un trapo* wipe; fig clean up; **~ a alguien** F clean s.o. out F; **limpieza** f *estado* cleanliness; *acto* cleaning; **~ general**

spring cleaning; **~ en seco** dry-cleaning; **hacer la ~** do the cleaning; **limpio** *adj* clean; *(ordenado)* neat, tidy; *político* honest; **gana $5.000 ~s al mes** he takes home $5,000 a month; **quedarse ~** *S.Am.* F be broke F; **sacar algo en ~** *fig* make sense of sth

limusina *f* limousine

linaje *m* lineage

lince *m* ZO lynx; **ojos** *or* **vista de ~** *fig* eyes like a hawk

linchar <1a> *v/t* lynch

lindar <1a> *v/i:* **~ con algo** adjoin sth; *fig* border on sth

lindo *adj* lovely; **de lo ~** a lot, a great deal

línea *f* line; **~ aérea** airline; **mantener la ~** watch one's figure; **de primera ~** *fig* first-rate; **tecnología de primera ~** state-of-the art technology; **entre ~s** *fig* between the lines; **lineal** *adj* linear

linfático *adj* lymphatic

lingote *m* ingot; **~ de oro** gold bar

lingüista *m/f* linguist; **lingüística** *f* linguistics; **lingüístico** *adj* linguistic

linier *m* DEP assistant referee, linesman

lino *m* linen; BOT flax

linterna *f* flashlight, *Br* torch

lío *m* bundle; F *(desorden)* mess; F *(jaleo)* fuss; **~ amoroso** F affair; **estar hecho un ~** be all confused; **hacerse un ~** get into a muddle; **meterse en ~s** get into trouble

liposucción *f* MED liposuction

lipotimia *f* MED blackout

liquen *m* BOT lichen

liquidación *f* COM *de cuenta, deuda* settlement; *de negocio* liquidation; **~ total** clearance sale; **liquidar** <1a> *v/t cuenta, deuda* settle; COM *negocio* wind up, liquidate; *existencias* sell off; F *(matar)* liquidate, bump off F; **liquidez** *f* COM liquidity; **líquido 1** *adj* liquid; COM net **2** *m* liquid

lira *f* lira

lírico *adj* lyrical

lirio *m* BOT lily

lirón *m* ZO dormouse; **dormir como un ~** *fig* F sleep like a log

lisiado 1 *adj* crippled **2** *m* cripple

liso *adj* smooth; *terreno* flat; *pelo* straight; *(sin adornos)* plain; **-a y llanamente** plainly and simply

lisonja *f* flattery

lista *f* list; **~ de boda** wedding list; **~ de espera** waiting list; **pasar ~** take the roll call, *Br* call the register; **listado** *m* INFOR printout; **listín** *m:* **~ (telefónico)** phone book

listo *adj (inteligente)* clever; *(preparado)* ready; **pasarse de ~** F try to be too smart F

listón *m de madera* strip; DEP bar; **poner el ~ muy alto** *fig* set very high standards

lisura *f Rpl, Pe* curse, swearword

litera *f* bunk; *de tren* couchette

literal *adj* literal; **literario** *adj* literary; **literatura** *f* literature

litigante *m/f & adj* JUR litigant; **litigar** <1h> *v/i* JUR go to litigation; **litigio** *m* lawsuit

litografía *f* lithography

litoral 1 *adj* coastal **2** *m* coast

litro *m* liter, *Br* litre

liturgia *f* REL liturgy

liviano *adj* light; *(de poca importancia)* trivial

lívido *adj* pale

llaga *f* ulcer; **poner** *or* **meter el dedo en la ~** *fig* put one's finger on it

llama *f* flame; ZO llama

llamada *f* call; *en una puerta* knock; *en timbre* ring; **~ a cobro revertido** collect call; **~ de auxilio** distress call; **llamado** *m L.Am.* call; **llamador** *m* (door) knocker; **llamamiento** *m* call; **hacer un ~ a algo** call for sth; **llamar** <1a> **1** *v/t* call; TELEC call, *Br tb* ring **2** *v/i* TELEC call, *Br tb* ring; **~ a la puerta** knock at the door; *con timbre* ring the bell; **el fútbol no me llama nada** football doesn't appeal to me in the slightest **3** *v/r* **~se** be called; **¿cómo te llamas?** what's your name?

llamarada *f* flare-up

llamativo *adj* eyecatching; *color* loud

llamón *adj Méx* moaning

llano 1 *adj terreno* level; *trato* natural; *persona* unassuming **2** *m* flat ground

llanta *f* wheel rim; *C.Am.*, *Méx* (*neumático*) tire, *Br* tyre

llanto *m* sobbing

llanura *f* plain

llave *f* key; *para tuerca* wrench, *Br tb* spanner; **~ de contacto** AUTO ignition key; **~ inglesa** TÉC monkey wrench; **~ de paso** stop cock; **~ en mano** available for immediate occupancy; *bajo* ~ under lock and key; *cerrar con* ~ lock; **llavero** *m* key ring

llegada *f* arrival; **llegar** <1h> **1** *v/i* arrive; (*alcanzar*) reach; *la comida no llegó para todos* there wasn't enough food for everyone; *me llega hasta las rodillas* it comes down to my knees; *el agua me llegaba a la cintura* the water came up to my waist; **~ a saber** find out; **~ a ser** get to be; **~ a viejo** live to a ripe old age **2** *v/r* ~**se**: *llégate al vecino* F run over to the neighbo(u)r's

llenar <1a> **1** *v/t* fill; *impreso* fill out *o* in **2** *v/i* be filling **3** *v/r* ~**se** fill up; *me he llenado* I have had enough (to eat); **lleno** *adj* full (*de* of); *pared* covered (*de* with); *de* ~ fully

llevadero *adj* bearable

llevar <1a> **1** *v/t* take; *ropa, gafas* wear; *ritmo* keep up; **~ a alguien en coche** drive s.o., take s.o. in the car; **~ dinero encima** carry money; **~ las de perder** be likely to lose; *me lleva dos años* he's two years older than me; *llevo ocho días aquí* I've been here a week; *llevo una hora esperando* I've been waiting for an hour **2** *v/i* lead (*a* to) **3** *v/r* ~**se** take; *susto, sorpresa* get; **~se bien/mal** get on well/badly; *se lleva el color rojo* red is fashionable

llorar <1a> *v/i* cry, weep; **lloriquear** <1a> *v/i* snivel, whine; **lloro** *m* weeping, crying; **llorón 1** *adj*: *ser* ~ be a crybaby F **2** *m* F crybaby F

llovedera *f L.Am.*, **llovedero** *m L.Am.* rainy season

llover <2h> *v/i* rain; *llueve* it is raining

llovizna *f* drizzle; **lloviznar** <1a> *v/i* drizzle

llueve *vb* → **llover**

lluvia *f* rain; *Rpl* (*ducha*) shower; **~ ácida** acid rain; **lluvioso** *adj* rainy

lo 1 *art sg* the; **~ bueno** the good thing; *no sabes* **~ difícil que es** you don't know how difficult it is **2** *pron sg*: *a él* him; *a usted* you; *algo* it; **~ sé** I know **3** *pron rel sg*: **~ que** what; **~ cual** which

loable *adj* praiseworthy, laudable

lobo *m* wolf; **~ marino** seal; **~ de mar** *fig* sea dog

lóbrego *adj* gloomy

lóbulo *m* lobe; **~ de la oreja** earlobe

loca *f* madwoman

locador *m S.Am.* landlord

local 1 *adj* local **2** *m* premises *pl*; **~ comercial** commercial premises *pl*; **localidad** *f* town; TEA seat; **localización** *f* location; **localizar** <1f> *v/t* locate; *incendio* contain, bring under control

loción *f* lotion

loco 1 *adj* mad, crazy; *a lo* ~ F (*sin pensar*) hastily; *es para volverse* ~ it's enough to drive you mad *o* crazy **2** *m* madman

locomoción *f* locomotion; *medio de* ~ means of transport; **locomotora** *f* locomotive

locro *m S.Am.* stew of meat, corn and potatoes

locuaz *adj* talkative, loquacious *fml*; **locución** *f* phrase

locura *f* madness; *es una* ~ it's madness

locutor *m*, **~a** *f* RAD, TV presenter; **locutorio** *m* TELEC phone booth

lodazal *m* quagmire; **lodo** *m* mud

lógica *f* logic; **lógico** *adj* logical; **logística** *f* logistics

logopeda *m/f* speech therapist

logotipo *m* logo

logrado *adj* excellent; **lograr** <1a> *v/t* achieve; (*obtener*) obtain; ~ **hacer algo** manage to do sth; ~ **que alguien haga algo** (manage to) get s.o. to do sth; **logrero** *m L.Am.* F profiteer; **logro** *m* achievement

loma *f L.Am.* small hill

lombriz *f*: ~ **de tierra** earthworm

lomo *m* back; GASTR loin; **a ~s de burro** on a donkey

lona *f* canvas

loncha *f* slice

lonche *m L.Am.* afternoon snack; **lonchería** *f L.Am.* diner, luncheonette

londinense 1 *adj* London *atr* **2** *m/f* Londoner; **Londres** London

longaniza *f* type of dried sausage

longevidad *f* longevity; **longevo** *adj* long-lived

longitud *f* longitude; (*largo*) length; **longitudinal** *adj* longitudinal

lonja *f de pescado* fish market; (*loncha*) slice

loquera *f L.Am.* F shrink F; *enfermera* psychiatric nurse; **loquero** *m L.Am.* F *persona* shrink F; *enfermero* psychiatric nurse; (*manicomio*) mental hospital, funny farm F

loro *m* parrot; **estar al** ~ F (*enterado*) be clued up F, be on the ball F

los *mpl* **1** *art* the **2** *pron complemento directo pl* them; *a ustedes* you; **llévate** ~ **que quieras** take whichever ones you want; ~ **de ...** those of ...; ~ **de Juan** Juan's; ~ **que juegan** the ones *o* those that are playing

losa *f* flagstone

lote *m en reparto* share, part; *L.Am.* (*solar*) lot; **lotería** *f* lottery; **loto 1** *m* BOT lotus **2** *f* F lottery

loza *f* china

lozano *adj* healthy-looking

lubina *f* ZO sea bass

lubri(fi)cación *f* lubrication; **lubri(fi)cante 1** *adj* lubricating **2** *m* lubricant; **lubri(fi)car** <1g> *v/t* lubricate

lucero *m* bright star; (*Venus*) Venus

lucha *f* fight, struggle; DEP wrestling;

~ **libre** DEP all-in wrestling; **luchador 1** *adj espíritu* fighting **2** *m*, ~**a** *f* fighter; **luchar** <1a> *v/i* fight (*por* for)

lúcido *adj* lucid, clear

luciérnaga *f* ZO glow-worm

lucimiento *m* (*brillo*) splendo(u)r; **le ofrece oportunidades de** ~ it gives him a chance to shine

lucio *m* ZO pike

lucir <3f> **1** *v/i* shine; *L.Am.* (*verse bien*) look good **2** *v/t ropa, joya* wear **3** *v/r* ~**se** *tb irón* excel o.s., surpass o.s.

lucrativo *adj* lucrative; **lucro** *m* profit; **afán de** ~ profit-making; **sin ánimo de** ~ non-profit (making), not-for-profit

ludopatía *f* compulsive gambling

luego 1 *adv* (*después*) later; *en orden, espacio* then; *L.Am.* (*en seguida*) right now; ~ ~ *Méx* straight away; **¡desde ~!** of course!; **¡hasta ~!** see you (later) **2** *conj* therefore; ~ **que** *L.Am.* after

lugar *m* place; ~ **común** cliché; **en ~ de** instead of; **en primer** ~ in the first place, first(ly); **fuera de** ~ out of place; **yo en tu** ~ if I were you, (if I were) in your place; **dar** ~ **a** give rise to; **tener** ~ take place

lúgubre *adj* gloomy

lujo *m* luxury; **lujoso** *adj* luxurious; **lujuria** *f* lust; **lujurioso** *adj* lecherous

lumbago *m* MED lumbago

lumbre *f* fire; **lumbrera** *f* genius; **luminoso** *adj* luminous; *lámpara, habitación* bright

luna *f* moon; *de tienda* window; *de vehículo* windshield, *Br* windscreen; ~ **de miel** honeymoon; ~ **llena/nueva** full/new moon; **media** ~ *L.Am.* GASTR croissant; **estar en la** ~ F have one's head in the clouds F; **lunar 1** *adj* lunar **2** *m en la piel* mole; **de ~es** spotted, polka-dot; **lunático** *adj* lunatic

lunes *m inv* Monday

luneta *f*: ~ **térmica** AUTO heated windshield, *Br* heated windscreen

L

lunfardo *m Arg slang used in Buenos Aires*

lupa *f* magnifying glass; **mirar algo con ~** *fig* go through sth with a fine toothcomb

lustrabotas *m/f inv L.Am.* bootblack; **lustrador** *m*, **~a** *f L.Am.* bootblack; **lustrar** <1a> *v/t* polish; **lustre** *m* shine; *fig* luster, *Br* lustre; **dar ~ a** *fig* give added luster (*Br* lustre) to; **lustro** *m* period of five years; **lustroso** *adj* shiny

luto *m* mourning; **estar de ~ por alguien** be in mourning for s.o.

luxación *f MED* dislocation

luz *f* light; **~ trasera** AUTO rear light; **luces de carretera** *or* **largas** AUTO full *o* main beam headlights; **luces de cruce** *or* **cortas** AUTO dipped headlights; **~ verde** *tb fig* green light; **arrojar ~ sobre algo** *fig* shed light on s.th.; **dar a ~** give birth to; **salir a la ~** *fig* come to light; **a todas luces** evidently, clearly; **de pocas luces** *fig* F dim F, not very bright

M

m *abr* (= **metro**) m (= meter); (= **minuto**) m (= minute)

macabro **1** *adj* macabre **2** *m*, **-a** *f* ghoul

macaco *m* ZO macaque

macana *f L.Am.* billyclub, *Br* truncheon; F (*mentira*) lie, fib F; **hizo/dijo una ~** he did/said something stupid; **¡qué ~!** *Rpl* P what a drag!; **macanear** <1a> *v/t L.Am.* (*aporrear*) beat; **macanudo** *S.Am.* F great F, fantastic F

macarra **1** *m* P pimp **2** *adj* F: **ser ~** be a bastard P

macarrones *mpl* macaroni *sg*

macedonia *f*: **~ de frutas** fruit salad

macerar <1a> *v/t* GASTR soak

maceta *f* flowerpot; **macetero** *m* flowerpot holder; *L.Am.* flowerpot

machacar <1g> *v/t* crush; *fig* thrash

machete *m* machete

machismo *m* male chauvinism; **machista** **1** *adj* sexist **2** *m* sexist, male chauvinist; **macho** **1** *adj* male; (*varonil*) tough; *desp* macho **2** *m* male; *apelativo* F man F, *Br* mate F; *L.Am.* (*plátano*) banana

macizo **1** *adj* solid; **estar ~** F be a

dish F **2** *m* GEOG massif; **~ de flores** flower bed

macuto *m* backpack

madeja *f* hank

madera *f* wood; **tener ~ de** have the makings of; **maderera** *f* timber merchant; **madero** *m* P cop P

madrastra *f* step-mother

madre **1** *f* mother; **~ soltera** single mother; **dar en la ~ a alguien** F hit s..o. where it hurts ; **¡me vale ~!** *Méx* V I don't give a fuck! V **2** *adj Méx*, *C.Am.* F great F, fantastic F; **madreselva** *f* BOT honeysuckle

Madrid Madrid

madriguera *f* (*agujero*) burrow; (*guarida*) *tb fig* den

madrileño **1** *adj* of/from Madrid, Madrid *atr* **2** *m*, **-a** *f* native of Madrid

madrina *f* godmother

madrugada *f* early morning; (*amanecer*) dawn; **de ~** in the small hours; **madrugador** *m*, **~a** *f* early riser; **madrugar** <1h> *v/i L.Am.* (*quedar despierto*) stay up till the small hours; (*levantarse temprano*) get up early

madurar <1a> **1** *v/t fig*: *idea* think

through **2** v/i *de persona* mature; *de fruta* ripen; **madurez** f *mental* maturity; *edad* middle age; *de fruta* ripeness; **maduro** *adj mentalmente* mature; *de edad* middle-aged; *fruta* ripe

maestría f mastery; *Méx* EDU master's (degree); **maestro 1** *adj* master *atr* **2** *m*, **-a** f EDU teacher; MÚS maestro

mafia f mafia; **mafioso 1** *adj* mafia *atr* **2** *m* mafioso, gangster

magdalena f cupcake, *Br tb* fairy cake

magia f *tb fig* magic; **mágico** *adj* magic

magisterio *m* teaching profession; **magistrado** *m* judge; **magistral** *adj* masterly

magnanimidad f magnanimity; **magnánimo** *adj* magnanimous

magnate *m* magnate, tycoon

magnesio *m* magnesium

magnético *adj* magnetic

magnetofón *m* tape recorder

magnífico *adj* wonderful, magnificent

magnitud f magnitude

magnolia f BOT magnolia

mago *m tb fig* magician; **los Reyes Magos** the Three Wise Men, the Three Kings

magrear <1a> v/t F feel up F

Magreb Maghreb

magro *adj carne* lean

magulladura f bruise; **magullar** <1a> v/t bruise; **magullón** *m L.Am.* bruise

mahometano 1 *adj* Muslim **2** *m*, **-a** f Muslim

mahonesa f mayonnaise

maillot *m* DEP jersey

maíz *m* corn

majada f *CSur* flock of sheep

majaderear <1a> *L.Am.* F **1** v/t bug F **2** v/i keep going on F

majadería f: *decir / hacer una ~* say / do something stupid

majadero 1 *adj* idiotic, stupid **2** *m*, **-a** f idiot

majareta *adj* F nutty F, screwy F

majestad f majesty; **majestuoso** *adj* majestic

majo *adj* F nice; (*bonito*) pretty

mal 1 *adj* → **malo 2** *adv* badly; **~ que bien** one way or the other; **¡menos ~!** thank goodness!; **ponerse a ~ con alguien** fall out with s.o.; **tomarse algo a ~** take sth badly **3** *m* MED illness; **el ~ menor** the lesser of two evils

malabar *m/adj*: (*juegos*) **-es** *pl* juggling *sg*; **malabarista** *m/f* juggler

malacrianza f *L.Am.* rudeness

malaria f MED malaria

malcriadez f *L.Am.* bad upbringing; **malcriado** *adj* spoilt; **malcrianza** f *L.Am.* rudeness; **malcriar** <1c> v/t spoil

maldad f evil; *es una ~ hacer eso* it's a wicked thing to do

maldecir <3p> **1** v/i curse; **~ de alguien** speak ill of s.o. **2** v/t curse; **maldición** f curse; **maldito** *adj* F damn F; **¡-a sea!** (god)damn it!

maleante *m/f & adj* criminal

malecón *m* breakwater

maleducado *adj* rude, bad-mannered

maleficio *m* curse; **maléfico** *adj* evil

malentendido *m* misunderstanding

malestar *m* MED discomfort; *social* unrest

maleta f bag, suitcase; *L.Am.* AUTO trunk, *Br* boot; *hacer la ~* pack one's bags; **maletero** *m* trunk, *Br* boot; **maletín** *m* briefcase

malévolo *adj* malevolent

maleza f undergrowth

malformación f MED malformation

malgastar <1a> v/t waste

malgenioso *adj Méx* bad-tempered

malhablado *adj* foul-mouthed

malhechor *m*, **~a** f criminal

malherir <3i> v/t hurt badly

malhumorado *adj* bad-tempered

malicia f (*mala intención*) malice; (*astucia*) cunning, slyness; *no tener ~* F be very naive; **malicioso** *adj* (*malintencionado*) malicious; (*astuto*) cunning, sly

maligno *adj* harmful; MED malignant

M

malinchismo *m Méx* treason

malla *f* mesh; *Rpl* swimsuit

malo 1 *adj* bad; *calidad* poor; *(enfermo)* sick, ill; **por las buenas o por las -as** whether he/she etc likes it or not; **por las -as** by force; **lo ~ es que** unfortunately; **ponerse ~** fall ill **2** *m hum* bad guy, baddy F

malogrado *adj muerto* dead before one's time; **malograr** <1a> **1** *v/t* waste; *trabajo* spoil, ruin **2** *v/r* **~se** fail; *de plan* come to nothing; *fallecer* die before one's time; *S.Am. (descomponerse)* break down; *(funcionar mal)* go wrong

maloliente *adj* stinking

malparado *adj:* **quedar** *or* **salir ~ de algo** come out badly from sth

malpensado *adj:* **ser ~** have a nasty mind

malsano *adj* unhealthy

malsonante *adj* rude

malta *f* malt

maltratar <1a> *v/t* mistreat; **maltrato** *m* abuse, harsh words *pl*

maltrecho *adj* weakened, diminished; *cosa* damaged

malva *adj* mauve

malvado *adj* evil

malversación *f:* **~ de fondos** embezzlement; **malversar** <1a> *v/t* embezzle

Malvinas: **las ~** the Falklands, the Falkland Islands

malvivir <3a> *v/i* scrape by

mamá *f* mom, *Br* mum

mama *f* breast; **mamadera** *f L.Am.* feeding bottle

mamar <1a> *v/i* suck; **dar de ~** (breast)feed

mamarracho *m:* **vas hecho un ~** F you look a mess F

mamífero *m* mammal

mamila *f Méx* feeding bottle

mamografía *f MED* mammography

mamón 1 *adj Méx* P cocky **2** *m* P bastard P; **mamona** *f* P bitch P

mamotreto *m F libro* hefty tome

mampara *f* screen

mamporro *m* F punch

mampostería *f* masonry

maná *m fig* manna

manada *f* herd; *de lobos* pack

manantial *m* spring

manar <1a> *v/i* flow

manatí *m* ZO manatee

manaza *f:* **ser un ~s** F be ham-handed F

mancebo *m* youth

Mancha: **Canal de la ~** English Channel

mancha *f* (dirty) mark; *de grasa, sangre etc* stain; **manchar** <1a> **1** *v/t* get dirty; *de grasa, sangre etc* stain **2** *v/r* **~se** get dirty

mancillar <1a> *v/t fig* sully

manco *adj de mano* one-handed; *de brazo* one-armed

mancornas *fpl Pe, Bol* cufflinks

mancuernas *fpl C.Am.* cufflinks

mandamás *m inv* F big shot F

mandado *m Méx, C.Am.:* **los ~s** *pl* the shopping *sg*; **mandamiento** *m* order; JUR warrant; REL commandment

mandar <1a> **1** *v/t* order; *(enviar)* send; **a mí no me manda nadie** nobody tells me what to do; **~ hacer algo** have sth done **2** *v/i* be in charge; **¿mande?** *Méx* can I help you?; *Méx* TELEC hallo?; *(¿cómo?)* what did you say?, excuse me?

mandarina *f* mandarin (orange)

mandatario *m* leader; **primer ~** *Méx* President; **mandato** *m* order; POL mandate

mandíbula *f* ANAT jaw; **reírse a ~ batiente** F laugh one's head off F

mandioca *f* cassava

mando *m* command; **alto ~** high command; **~ a distancia** TV remote control; **tablero de ~s** AUTO dashboard

mandolina *f* MÚS mandolin

mandón *adj* F bossy F

manecilla *f* hand

manejable *adj* easy to handle; *automovil* maneuverable, *Br* manoeuvrable; **manejar** <1a> **1** *v/t* handle; *máquina* operate; *L.Am.* AUTO drive **2** *v/i L.Am.* AUTO drive

3 v/r **~se** manage, get by; **manejo** m handling; **de una máquina** operation

manera f way; **esa es su ~ de ser** that's the way he is; **~s** manners; **lo hace a su ~** he does it his way; **de ~ que** so (that); **de ninguna ~** certainly not; **no hay ~ de** it is impossible to; **de todas ~s** anyway, in any case

manga f sleeve; **~ de riego** hosepipe; **en ~s de camisa** in shirtsleeves; **sin ~s** sleeveless; **sacarse algo de la ~** fig make sth up; **traer algo en la ~** F have sth up one's sleeve

manganeso m manganese

mangar <1h> v/t P swipe F, pinch F

mangle m BOT mangrove

mango m BOT mango; **CSur** (dinero) dough F, cash; **estoy sin un ~ CSur** F I'm broke F, I don't have a bean F

mangonear <1a> **1** v/i F boss people around; (entrometerse) meddle **2** v/t F: **~ a alguien** boss s.o. around

manguera f hose(pipe)

maní m S.Am. peanut

manía f (costumbre) habit, mania; (antipatía) dislike; (obsesión) obsession; **~ persecutoria** persecution complex; **tiene sus ~s** she has her little ways; **tener ~ a alguien** F have it in for s.o. F; **maniaco** m maniac

maniatar <1a> v/t: **~ a alguien** tie s.o.'s hands

maniático adj F fussy

manicomio m lunatic asylum

manicura f manicure; **hacerse la ~** have a manicure

manido adj fig clichéd, done to death F

manifestación f de gente demonstration; (muestra) show; (declaración) statement; **manifestante** m/f demonstrator; **manifestar** <1k> **1** v/t (demostrar) show; (declarar) declare, state **2** v/r **~se** demonstrate; **manifiesto 1** adj clear, manifest; **poner de ~** make clear **2** m manifesto

manigua f W.I. thicket, bush

manija f L.Am. (asa) handle

manillar m handlebars pl

maniobra f maneuver, Br manoeuvre; **hacer ~s** maneuver, Br manoeuvre; **maniobrar** <1a> v/i maneuver, Br manoeuvre

manipulación f manipulation; (manejo) handling; **manipular** <1a> v/t manipulate; (manejar) handle

maniquí 1 m dummy **2** m/f model

manirroto 1 adj extravagant **2** m, **-a** f spendthrift

manisero m, **-a** f W.I., S.Am. peanut seller

manitas fpl: **ser un ~** be handy

manito m Méx pal, buddy

manivela f handle

manjar m delicacy

mano f **1** hand; **~ de obra** labo(u)r, manpower; **~ de pintura** coat of paint; **¡~s arriba!** hands up!; **a ~ derecha / izquierda** on the right / left; **atar las ~s a alguien** fig tie s.o.'s hands; **de segunda ~** secondhand; **echar una ~ a alguien** give s.o. a hand; **estar a ~s** L.Am. F be even, be quits; **hecho a ~** handmade; **poner la ~ en el fuego** fig swear to it; **poner ~s a la obra** get down to work; **se le fue la ~ con** fig he overdid it with; **tener a ~** have to hand; **traerse algo entre ~s** be plotting sth **2** m Méx F pal F, buddy F

manojo m handful; **~ de llaves** bunch of keys; **~ de nervios** fig bundle of nerves

manopla f mitten

manosear <1a> v/t fruta handle; persona F grope F

manotazo m slap; **manotear** <1a> **1** v/t Arg, Méx grab **2** v/i Arg, Méx wave one's hands around

mansalva f: **a ~** in vast numbers; bebida, comida in vast amounts

mansedumbre f docility; de persona mildness

mansión f mansion

manso adj docile; persona mild

manta f blanket; **tirar de la ~ fig**

uncover the truth

manteca *f* fat; *Rpl* butter; **~ de cacao** cocoa butter; **~ de cerdo** lard

mantel *m* tablecloth; **~ individual** table mat; **mantelería** *f* table linen; **una ~** a set of table linen

mantención *f L.Am.* → **manutención**

mantener <2l> **1** *v/t* (*sujetar*) hold; *techo etc* hold up; (*preservar*) keep; *conversación, relación* have; *económicamente* support; (*afirmar*) maintain **2** *v/r* **~se** (*sujetarse*) be held; *económicamente* support o.s.; *en forma* keep; **mantenimiento** *m* maintenance; *económico* support; **gimnasia de ~** gym

mantequilla *f* butter; **mantequillera** *f L.Am.* butter dish

mantilla *f de bebé* shawl; *estar en* **~s** *fig F* be in its infancy

mantuvo *vb* → **mantener**

manual *m/adj* manual; **manualidades** *fpl* handicrafts; **manubrio** *m* handle; *S.Am.* handlebars *pl*

manufacturar <1a> *v/t* manufacture

manuscrito 1 *adj* handwritten **2** *m* manuscript

manutención *f* maintenance

manzana *f* apple; *de casas* block; **~ de la discordia** *fig* bone of contention; **manzanilla** *f* camomile tea; **manzano** *m* apple tree

maña *f* skill; *darse or tener ~ para* be good at; *tiene muchas ~s L.Am.* she's got lots of tricks up her sleeve F

mañana 1 *f* morning; *por la ~* in the morning; *~ por la ~* tomorrow morning; *de la ~ a la noche* from morning until night; *de la noche a la ~ fig* overnight; *esta ~* this morning; *muy de ~* very early (in the morning) **2** *adv* tomorrow; *pasado ~* the day after tomorrow

mañanita *f* shawl

mañero *adj Rpl* (*animal: terco*) stubborn; (*nervioso*) skittish, nervous

mañoso *adj* skil(l)ful; *L.Am. animal* stubborn

mapa *m* map; **~ de carreteras** road map

mapache *m* raccoon

mapamundi *m* map of the world

maqueta *f* model

maquillador *m*, **~a** *f* make-up artist; **maquillaje** *m* make-up; **maquillar** <1a> **1** *v/t* make up **2** *v/r* **~se** put on one's make-up

máquina *f* machine; *FERR* locomotive; *C.Am., W.I.* car; **~ de afeitar** (electric) shaver; **~ de coser** sewing machine; **~ de fotos** camera; **~ recreativa** arcade game; *pasar algo a ~* type sth; *a toda ~* at top speed; **maquinaciones** *fpl* scheming *sg*; **maquinador 1** *adj* scheming **2** *m*, **~a** *f* schemer; **maquinal** *adj fig* mechanical; **maquinar** <1a> *v/t* plot; **maquinaria** *f* machinery; **maquinilla** *f*: **~ de afeitar** razor; **~ eléctrica** electric razor; **maquinista** *m/f FERR* engineer, *Br* train driver

mar *m* (*also f*) *GEOG* sea; *sudaba a* **~es** *fig* F the sweat was pouring off him F; *llover a ~es fig* F pour, bucket down F; *alta ~* high seas *pl*; *la ~ de bien* (*muy bien*) really well

maraca *f MÚS* maraca

maraña *f de hilos* tangle; (*lío*) jumble

marasmo *m fig* stagnation

maratón *m* (*also f*) marathon; **maratoniano** *adj* marathon *atr*

maravilla *f* marvel, wonder; *BOT* marigold; *de ~* marvellously, wonderfully; *a las mil ~s* marvellously, wonderfully; **maravillar** <1a> **1** *v/t* amaze, astonish **2** *v/r* **~se** be amazed *o* astonished (*de* at); **maravilloso** *adj* marvellous, wonderful

marca *f* mark; *COM* brand; **~ registrada** registered trademark; *de* **~** brand-name *atr*; **marcador** *m DEP* scoreboard; **marcaje** *m DEP* marking; **marcapasos** *m inv MED* pacemaker; **marcar** <1g> *v/t* mark; *número de teléfono* dial; *gol* score; *res* brand; *de termómetro, contador etc* read, register

marcha *f* (*salida*) departure;

(*velocidad*) speed; (*avance*) progress; MIL march; AUTO gear; DEP walk; **~ atrás** AUTO reverse (gear); *a ~s forzadas* fig flat out; *a toda ~* at top speed; *hacer algo sobre la ~* do sth as one goes along; *ponerse en ~* get started, get going; *tener mucha ~* F be very lively

marchante *m* L.Am. regular customer

marchar <1a> **1** *v/i* (*progresar*) go; (*funcionar*) work; (*caminar*) walk; MIL march **2** *v/r* **~se** leave, go

marchitarse <1a> *v/r* wilt

marcial *adj* martial; *artes ~es* martial arts

marciano *m* Martian

marco *m* *moneda* mark; *de cuadro, puerta* frame; fig framework

marea *f* tide; **~ alta** high tide; **~ baja** low tide; **~ negra** oil slick

mareado *adj* dizzy; **marear** <1a> **1** *v/t* make feel nauseous, *Br* make feel sick; fig (*confundir*) confuse **2** *v/r* **~se** feel nauseous, *Br* feel sick

marejada *f* heavy sea; **maremoto** *m* tidal wave; **mareo** *m* seasickness

marfil *m* ivory

margarina *f* margarine

margarita *f* BOT daisy

margen *m tb* fig margin; **al ~ de eso** apart from that; **mantenerse al ~** keep out; **marginación** *f* marginalization; **marginal** *adj* marginal; **marginar** <1a> *v/t* marginalize

mariachi 1 *m* mariachi band **2** *m/f* mariachi player

marica *m* F fag P, *Br* poof P

maricón *m* P fag P, *Br* poof P

marido *m* husband

marihuana *f* marijuana

marimacho *m* F butch woman

marimba *f* Rpl MÚS marimba

marina *f* navy; **~ mercante** merchant navy

marinar <1a> *v/t* GASTR marinade

marinero 1 *adj* sea *atr* **2** *m* sailor; **marino 1** *adj* *brisa* sea *atr*; *planta, animal* marine; *azul ~* navy blue **2** *m* sailor

marioneta *f tb* fig puppet

mariposa *f* butterfly

mariquita *f* ladybug, *Br* ladybird

marisco *m* seafood

marisma *f* salt marsh

marítimo *adj* maritime

marketing *m* marketing

marmita *f* pot, pan

mármol *m* marble

marmota *f*: *dormir como una ~* F sleep like a log

marqués *m* marquis; **marquesa** *f* marchioness

marquesina *f* marquee, *Br* canopy

marranada *f* F dirty trick; **marrano 1** *adj* filthy **2** *m* hog, *Br* pig; F *persona* pig F

marras *adv*: *el ordenador de ~* the darned computer F

marrón *m/adj* brown

marroquinería *f* leather goods

Marruecos Morocco

marta *f* ZO marten

Marte *m* AST Mars

martes *m inv* Tuesday

martillero *m* S.Am. auctioneer; **martillo** *m* hammer; **~ neumático** pneumatic drill

martín *m*: **~ pescador** ZO kingfisher

mártir *m/f* martyr; **martirio** *m tb* fig martyrdom; **martirizar** <1f> *v/t tb* fig martyr

marzo *m* March

mas *conj* but

más 1 *adj* more **2** *adv comp* more; *sup* most; MAT plus; **~ grande/pequeño** bigger/smaller; *el ~ grande/pequeño* the largest/smallest; *trabajar ~* work harder; **~ bien** rather; **~ que, ~ de lo que** more than; **~ o menos** more or less; *¿qué ~?* what else?; *no ~* L.Am. → **nomás**; *por ~ que* however much; *sin ~* without more ado; *~ lejos* further

masa *f* mass; GASTR dough; *pillar a alguien con las manos en la ~* F catch s.o. red-handed

masacrar <1a> *v/t* massacre; **masacre** *f* massacre

masaje *m* massage; **masajista** *m/f*

masseur; *mujer* masseuse

mascar <1g> **1** *v/t* chew **2** *v/i L.Am.* chew tobacco

máscara *f* mask; **mascarilla** *f* mask; *cosmética* face pack

mascota *f* mascot; *animal doméstico* pet

masculino *adj* masculine

mascullar <1a> *v/t* mutter

masificación *f* overcrowding

masilla *f* putty

masita *f L.Am. small sweet cake or bun*

masivo *adj* massive

masón *m* mason

masoquismo *m* masochism; **masoquista 1** *adj* masochistic **2** *m/f* masochist

máster *m* master's (degree)

masticación *f* chewing; **masticar** <1g> *v/t* chew

mástil *m* mast; *de tienda* pole

mastín *m* ZO mastiff

mastodóntico *adj* colossal, enormous

mastuerzo *m* BOT cress

masturbarse <1a> *v/r* masturbate

mata *f* bush

matadero *m* slaughterhouse; **matador** *m* TAUR matador; **matanza** *f de animales* slaughter; *de gente* slaughter, massacre; **matar** <1a> **1** *v/t* kill; *ganado* slaughter **2** *v/r* **~se** kill o.s.; *morir* be killed; **~se a trabajar** work o.s. to death; **matarratas** *m* rat poison; **matasanos** *m/f inv* F quack F

matasellos *m inv* postmark

mate 1 *adj* matt **2** *m en ajedrez* mate; *L.Am. (infusión)* maté

matear <1a> **1** *v/t CSur* checkmate **2** *v/i L.Am.* drink maté

matemáticas *fpl* mathematics; **matemático 1** *adj* mathematical **2** *m*, **-a** *f* mathematician

materia *f* matter; *(material)* material; *(tema)* subject; **~ prima** raw material; **en ~ de** as regards; **material** *m/adj* material; **materialismo** *m* materialism; **materializar** <1f> *v/t*: **~ algo** make sth a reality

maternal *adj* maternal

matero *m*, **-a** *f L.Am.* maté drinker

matinal *adj* morning *atr*

matiz *m de ironía* touch; *de color* shade; **matizar** <1f> *v/t comentarios* qualify

matón *m* bully; *(criminal)* thug

matorral *m* thicket

matrícula *f* AUTO license plate, *Br* numberplate; EDU enrol(l)ment, registration; **matricular** <1a> **1** *v/t* register **2** *v/r* **-se** EDU enrol(l), register

matrimonial *adj* marriage *atr*, marital; **matrimonio** *m* marriage; *boda* wedding

matriz *f* matrix; ANAT womb

matrona *f (comadrona)* midwife

matutino *adj* morning *atr*

maullar <1a> *v/i* miaow; **maullido** *m* miaow

mausoleo *m* mausoleum

máxima *f* maxim; **máxime** *adv* especially; **máximo** *adj* maximum

mayo *m* May

mayonesa *f* GASTR mayonnaise

mayor 1 *adj comp*: *en tamaño* larger, bigger; *en edad* older; *en importancia* greater; *ser ~ de edad* be an adult; *al por ~* COM wholesale **2** *adj sup*: *el ~ en edad* the oldest *o* eldest; *en tamaño* the largest *o* biggest; *en importancia* the greatest; *los ~es* adults; *la ~ parte* the majority

mayordomo *m* butler

mayoreo *m*: *vender al ~ Méx* sell wholesale

mayoría *f* majority; *alcanzar la ~ de edad* come of age; *la ~ de* the majority of, most (of); *en la ~ de los casos* in the majority of cases, in most cases; **mayorista** *m/f* wholesaler; **mayoritario** *adj* majority *atr*

mayúscula *f* capital (letter), upper case letter

mazamorra *f S.Am. kind of porridge made from corn*

mazapán *m* marzipan

mazmorra *f* dungeon

mazo *m* mallet

mazorca *f* cob

me *pron pers complemento directo* me; *complemento indirecto* (to) me; *reflexivo* myself; **~ dio el libro** he gave me the book, he gave the book to me

mear <1a> F **1** *v/i* pee F **2** *v/r* ~se pee o.s. F; **~se de risa** wet o.s. (laughing) F

meca *f fig* mecca

mecachis *int* F blast! F

mecánica *f* mechanics; **mecánico 1** *adj* mechanical **2** *m*, **-a** *f* mechanic; **mecanismo** *m* mechanism; **mecanizar** <1f> *v/t* mechanize; **mecanografiar** <1c> *v/t* type; **mecanógrafo** *m*, **-a** *f* typist

mecate *m Méx* string, cord

mecedora *f* rocking chair

mecenas *m inv* patron, sponsor

mecer <2b> **1** *v/t* rock **2** *v/r* ~se rock

mecha *f* wick; *de explosivo* fuse; *del pelo* highlight; *Méx* F fear; **mechero** *m* cigarette lighter; **mechón** *m de pelo* lock

medalla *f* medal; **medallista** *m/f* medal(l)ist

media *f* stocking; **~s** *pl* pantyhose *pl*, *Br* tights *pl*

mediación *f* mediation; **mediado** *adj*: **a ~s de junio** in mid-June, halfway through June; **mediador** *m*, **~a** *f* mediator; **mediana** *f* AUTO median strip, *Br* central reservation; **mediano** *adj* medium, average; **medianoche** *f* midnight; **mediante** *prp* by means of; **mediar** <1b> *v/i* mediate

mediático *adj* media *atr*

medicación *f* medication; **medicamento** *m* medicine, drug; **medicina** *f* medicine; **medicinal** *adj* medicinal; **médico 1** *adj* medical **2** *m/f* doctor; **~ de cabecera** or **de familia** family physician, *Br* GP, *Br* general practitioner; **~ de urgencia** emergency doctor

medida *f* measure; *acto* measurement; *(grado)* extent; **hecho a ~** made to measure; **a ~ que** as; **tomar ~s** *fig* take measures *o* steps

medidor *m S.Am.* meter

medieval *adj* medi(a)eval

medio **1** *adj* half; *tamaño* medium; *(de promedio)* average; **las tres y -a** half past three, three-thirty **2** *m* environment; *(centro)* middle; *(manera)* means; **~ ambiente** environment; **por ~ de** by means of; **en ~ de** in the middle of; **~s dinero** means, resources; **~s de comunicación** or **de información** (mass) media; **~s de transporte** means of transport **3** *adv* half; **hacer algo a -as** half do sth; **ir a -as** go halves; **día por ~** *L.Am.* every other day; **quitar de en ~ algo** F move sth out of the way

medioambiental *adj* environmental

mediocre *adj* mediocre

mediodía *m* midday; **a ~** *(a las doce)* at noon, at twelve o'clock; *(a la hora de comer)* at lunchtime

medir <3l> **1** *v/t* measure **2** *v/i*: **mide 2 metros de ancho / largo / alto** it's 2 meters *(o Br* metres*)* wide / long / tall

meditación *f* meditation; **meditar** <1a> **1** *v/t* ponder **2** *v/i* meditate

Mediterráneo *m/adj*: *(mar)* ~ Mediterranean (Sea)

médium *m/f* medium

médula *f* marrow; **~ espinal** spinal cord; **hasta la ~** *fig* through and through, to the core

medusa *f* ZO jellyfish

megafonía *f* public-address *o* PA system; **megáfono** *m* bullhorn, *Br* loud-hailer

megalomanía *f* megalomania

mejicano **1** *adj* Mexican **2** *m*, **-a** *f* Mexican; **Méjico** Mexico; *Méx DF* Mexico City

mejilla *f* cheek

mejillón *m* ZO mussel

mejor *adj comp* better; **el ~** *sup* the best; **lo ~** the best thing; **lo ~ posible** as well as possible; **a lo ~** perhaps, maybe; **tanto ~** all the better; **mejora** *f* improvement

mejorana *f* BOT marjoram

mejorar <1a> **1** *v/t* improve **2** *v/i*

M

improve; **¡que te mejores!** get well soon!; **mejoría** *f* improvement

mejunje *m desp* concoction

melancolía *f* melancholy; **melancólico** *adj* gloomy, melancholic

melena *f* long hair; **de león** mane

melindroso *adj* affected

mella *f*: **hacer ~ en alguien** have an effect on s.o., affect s.o.; **mellado** *adj* gap-toothed

mellizo 1 *adj* twin *atr* **2** *m*, **-a** *f* twin

melocotón *m* peach; **melocotonero** *m* peach tree

melodía *f* melody

melodrama *m* melodrama

melón *m* melon

membrana *f* membrane

membrillo *m* quince; **dulce de ~** quince jelly

memela *f Méx* corn tortilla

memo 1 *adj* F dumb **F 2** *m*, **-a** *f* F idiot

memorable *adj* memorable

memoria *f tb* INFOR memory; (*informe*) report; **de ~** by heart; **~s** (*biografía*) memoirs

memorizar <1f> *v/t* memorize

mención *f*: **hacer ~ de** mention; **mencionar** <1a> *v/t* mention

mendigar <1h> *v/t* beg for; **mendigo** *m* beggar

menear <1a> **1** *v/t* shake; **las caderas** sway; **~ la cola** wag its tail **2** *v/r* **~se** fidget

menestra *f* vegetable stew

mengano *m*, **-a** *f* F so-and-so F

menguante *adj* decreasing, diminishing; *luna* waning; **menguar** <1i> *v/i* decrease, diminish; **de la luna** wane

meningitis *f* MED meningitis

menopausia *f* MED menopause

menor *adj comp* less; *en tamaño* smaller; *en edad* younger; **ser ~ de edad** be a minor; **al por ~** COM retail; **el ~** *sup*: *en tamaño* the smallest; *en edad* the youngest; **el número ~** the lowest number

menos 1 *adj en cantidad* less; *en número* fewer **2** *adv comp en cantidad* less; *sup en cantidad* least; MAT minus; **es ~ guapa que Ana** she is not as pretty as Ana; **tres ~ dos** three minus two; **a ~ que** unless; **al ~, por lo ~** at least; **echar de ~** miss; **eso es lo de ~** that's the least of it; **ni mucho ~** far from it; **son las dos ~ diez** it's ten to two, it's ten to two

menoscabar <1a> *v/t autoridad* diminish; (*dañar*) harm

menospreciar <1b> *v/t* underestimate; (*desdeñar*) look down on

mensaje *m* message; **mensajero** *m* courier

menstruación *f* menstruation; **menstruar** <1h> *v/i* menstruate

mensual *adj* monthly; **mensualidad** *f* monthly instal(l)ment, monthly payment; **mensualmente** *adv* monthly

menta *f* BOT mint

mental *adj* mental; **mentalidad** *f* mentality; **mentalizar** <1f> **1** *v/t*: **~ a alguien** make s.o. aware **2** *v/r* **~se** mentally prepare o.s.; **mente** *f* mind

mentecato 1 *adj* F dim **F 2** *m* F fool

mentir <3i> *v/i* lie; **mentira** *f* lie; **mentiroso 1** *adj*: **ser muy ~** tell a lot of lies **2** *m*, **-a** *f* liar

mentón *m* chin

mentor *m* mentor

menú *m tb* INFOR menu; **~ de ayuda** help menu

menudencias *fpl Méx* giblets; **menudeo** *m L.Am.* retail trade; **menudo 1** *adj* small; **¡-a suerte!** *fig* F lucky devil!; **¡-as vacaciones!** *irón* F some vacation!; **a ~** often **2** *m L.Am.* small change; **~s** GASTR giblets

meñique *m/adj*: (*dedo*) **~** little finger

meollo *m fig* heart

mercader *m* trader; **mercadería** *f L.Am.* merchandise; **mercadillo** *m* street market; **mercado** *m* market; **Mercado Común** Common Market; **~ negro** black market; **mercadotecnia** *f* marketing; **mercancía** *f* merchandise; **mercantil** *adj* commercial

merced *f*: **estar a ~ de alguien** be at

s.o.'s mercy

mercenario *m/adj* mercenary

mercería *f* notions *pl, Br* haberdashery

MERCOSUR *abr* (= *Mercado Común del Sur*) Common Market including Argentina, Brazil, Paraguay and Uruguay

mercurio *m* mercury

merecer <2d> *v/t* deserve; **no ~ la pena** it's not worth it; **merecido** *m* just deserts *pl*

merendar <1k> **1** *v/t*: **~ algo** have sth as an afternoon snack **2** *v/i* have an afternoon snack

merengue *m* GASTR meringue

meridiano *m/f* meridian; **meridional 1** *adj* southern **2** *m* southerner

merienda *f* afternoon snack

mérito *m* merit

merluza *f* ZO hake; *agarrar una ~ fig* F get plastered F

mermar <1a> **1** *v/t* reduce **2** *v/i* diminish

mermelada *f* jam

mero **1** *adj* mere; **el ~ jefe** *Méx* F the big boss **2** *m* ZO grouper

merodear <1a> *v/i* loiter

mes *m* month

mesa *f* table; **~ de centro** coffee table; **~ redonda** *fig* round table; **poner/quitar la ~** set/clear the table; **mesera** *f L.Am.* waitress; **mesero** *m L.Am.* waiter; **meseta** *f* plateau; **mesilla, mesita** *f*: **~ (de noche)** night stand, *Br* bedside table

mesón *m* traditional restaurant decorated in rustic style

mestizo *m* person of mixed race

mesura *f*: **con ~** in moderation

meta *f en fútbol* goal; *en carrera* finishing line; *fig (objetivo)* goal, objective

metabolismo *m* metabolism

metafísica *f* metaphysics

metáfora *f* metaphor

metal *m* metal; **metálico 1** *adj* metallic **2** *m*: **en ~** (in) cash; **metalúrgico** *adj* metallurgical

metamorfosis *f inv* transformation, metamorphosis

metedura *f*: **~ de pata** F blunder

meteorito *m* meteorite; **meteorológico** *adj* weather *atr*, meteorological; **pronóstico ~** weather forecast; **meteorólogo** *m*, **-a** *f* meteorologist

meter <2a> **1** *v/t gen* put (**en** in, into); *(involucrar)* involve (**en** in); **~ a alguien en un lío** get s.o. into a mess **2** *v/r* **~se**: **~se en algo** get into sth; *(involucrarse)* get involved in sth, get mixed up in sth; **~se con alguien** pick on s.o.; **~se de administrativo** get a job in admin; **¿dónde se ha metido?** where has he got to?

meticuloso *adj* meticulous

metido *adj* involved; *L.Am.* F nosy F; **estar muy ~ en algo** be very involved in sth

metódico *adj* methodical; **método** *m* method

metomentodo *m/f* F busybody F

metralleta *f* sub-machine gun

métrico *adj* metric; **metro** *m medida* meter, *Br* metre; *para medir* rule; *transporte* subway, *Br* underground

metrópolis *f inv* metropolis; **metropolitano** *adj* metropolitan

mexicano 1 *adj* Mexican **2** *m*, **-a** Mexican; **México** Mexico; *Méx DF* Mexico City

mezcal *m Méx* mescal

mezcla *f sustancia* mixture; *de tabaco, café etc* blend; *acto* mixing; *de tabaco, café etc* blending; **mezclar** <1a> **1** *v/t* mix; *tabaco, café etc* blend; **~ a alguien en algo** get s.o. mixed up *o* involved in sth **2** *v/r* **~se** mix; **~se en algo** get mixed up *o* involved in sth

mezquinar <1a> *v/t L.Am.* skimp on; **mezquino** *adj* mean

mezquita *f* mosque

mg. *abr* (= **miligramo**) mg (= milligram)

mi, mis *adj pos* my

mí *pron* me; *reflexivo* myself; **¿y a ~ qué?** so what?, what's it to me?

michelín *m* F spare tire, *Br* spare tyre

mico *m* ZO monkey

micro *m or f Chi* bus

microbio *m* microbe

microbús *m* minibus

microchip *m* (micro)chip

microfilm(e) *m* microfilm

micrófono *m* microphone; **~ oculto** bug

microondas *m inv* microwave

microordenador *m* microcomputer

microprocesador *m* microprocessor

microscópico *adj* microscopic; **microscopio** *m* microscope

mide *vb* → **medir**

miedo *m* fear (**a** of); **dar ~** be frightening; **me da ~ la oscuridad** I'm frightened of the dark; **tener ~ de que** be afraid that; **por ~ a** for fear of; **de ~** F great F, awesome F; **miedoso** *adj* timid; **¡no seas tan ~!** don't be scared!

miel *f* honey

miembro *m* member; (*extremidad*) limb, member *fml*

mientras 1 *conj* while; **~ que** whereas **2** *adv*: **~ tanto** in the meantime, meanwhile

miércoles *m inv* Wednesday

mierda *f* P shit P, crap P; **una ~ de película** a crap movie P; **¡una ~!** no way! F

miga *f de pan* crumb; **~s** crumbs; **hacer buenas/malas ~s** *fig* F get on well/badly

migraña *f* MED migraine

migratorio *adj* migratory

mijo *m* BOT millet

mil *adj* thousand

milagro *m* miracle; **de ~** miraculously, by a miracle; **milagroso** *adj* miraculous

milano *m* ZO kite

milenio *m* millennium

mili *f* F military service

milicia *f* militia

milico *m S.Am. desp* soldier

milímetro *m* millimeter, *Br* millimetre

militante *m/f & adj* militant; **militar 1** *adj* military **2** *m* soldier; **los ~es** the military **3** <1a> *v/i* POL: **~ en** be a member of

milla *f* mile

millar *m* thousand

millón *m* million; (*mil millones*) billion; **millonario** *m* millionaire

milpa *f Méx, C.Am.* corn, *Br* maize; **terreno** cornfield, *Br* field of maize

mimar <1a> *v/t* spoil, pamper

mimbre *m* BOT willow; **muebles** *pl* **de ~** wicker furniture *sg*

mímica *f* mime; **mimo** *m* TEA mime

mimosa *f* BOT mimosa

mimoso *adj*: **ser ~** be cuddly

mina *f* MIN mine; *Rpl* F broad F, *Br* bird F; **~ antipersonal** MIL antipersonnel mine; **minar** <1a> *v/t* mine; *fig* undermine

mineral *m/adj* mineral; **minería** *f* mining; **minero 1** *adj* mining **2** *m* miner

miniatura *f* miniature

minifalda *f* miniskirt

minimizar <1f> *v/t* minimize; **mínimo 1** *adj* minimum; **como ~** at the very least **2** *m* minimum

minino *m* F puss F, pussy (cat) F

ministerio *m* POL department; **~ de Asuntos Exteriores**, *L.Am.* **~ de Relaciones Exteriores** State Department, *Br* Foreign Office; **~ de Hacienda** Treasury Department, *Br* Treasury; **~ del Interior** Department of the Interior, *Br* Home Office; **ministro** *m*, **-a** *f* minister; **~ del Interior** Secretary of the Interior, *Br* Home Secretary; **primer ~** Prime Minister

minoría *f* minority

minorista COM **1** *adj* retail *atr* **2** *m/f* retailer

minoritario *adj* minority *atr*

mintió *vb* → **mentir**

minucia *f* minor detail; **minucioso** *adj* meticulous, thorough

minúscula *f* small letter, lower case letter; **minúsculo** *adj* tiny, minute

minusvalía *f* disability; **minusválido 1** *adj* disabled **2** *m*, **-a** *f* disabled person; **los ~s** the disabled

minutero *m* minute hand

minuto *m* minute

mío, **mía** *pron* mine; **el ~ / la -a** mine

miope *adj* near-sighted, short-sighted; **miopía** *f* near-sightedness, short-sightedness

mira *f*: **con ~s a** with a view to; **mirada** *f* look; **echar una ~** take a look (*a* at); **mirador** *m* viewpoint; **mirar** <1a> **1** *v/t* look at; (*observar*) watch; *L.Am.* (*ver*) see; **¿qué miras desde aquí?** what can you see from here? **2** *v/i* look; **~ al norte** *de una ventana etc* face north; **~ por la ventana** look out of the window; **mirilla** *f* spyhole

mirlo *m* ZO blackbird

misa *f* REL mass

misántropo *m* misanthrope

miserable *adj* wretched; **miseria** *f* poverty; *fig* misery; **misericordia** *f* mercy, compassion; **mísero** *adj* wretched; *sueldo* miserable

misil *m* missile

misión *f* mission; **misionero** *m*, **-a** *f* missionary

mismo 1 *adj* same; **lo ~ que** the same as; **yo ~** I myself; **da lo ~** it doesn't matter, it's all the same; **me da lo ~** I don't care, it's all the same to me **2** *adv*: **aquí ~** right here; **ahora ~** right now, this very minute

misógino *adj* misogynistic

misterio *m* mystery; **misterioso** *adj* mysterious; **místico** *adj* mystic(al)

mitad *f* half; **a ~ del camino** halfway; **a ~ de la película** halfway through the movie; **a ~ de precio** half-price

mítico *adj* mythical

mitigar <1h> *v/t* mitigate; *ansiedad, dolor etc* ease

mitin *m* POL meeting

mito *m* myth; **mitología** *f* mythology

mixto *adj* mixed; *comisión* joint

mm. *abr* (= **milímetro**) mm (= millimeter)

mobiliario *m* furniture

mochila *f* backpack; **mochilero** *m*, **-a** *f* backpacker

mochuelo *m* ZO little owl

moción *f* POL motion; **~ de confianza / censura** vote of confidence / no confidence

moco *m*: **tener ~s** have a runny nose; **mocoso** *m*, **-a** *f* F snotty-nosed kid F

moda *f* fashion; **de ~** fashionable, in fashion; **estar pasado de ~** be out of fashion

modales *mpl* manners

modalidad *f* form; DEP discipline; **~ de pago** method of payment

modelar <1a> *v/t* model; **modelismo** *m* model making; **modelo 1** *m* model **2** *m/f persona* model

módem *m* INFOR modem

moderado 1 *adj* moderate **2** *m*, **-a** *f* moderate; **moderador** *m*, **-a** *f* TV presenter; **moderar** <1a> **1** *v/t* moderate; *impulsos* control, restrain; *velocidad, gastos* reduce; *debate* chair **2** *v/r* **~se** control o.s., restrain o.s.

modernización *f* modernization; **modernizar** <1f> *v/t* modernize; **moderno** *adj* modern

modestia *f* modesty; **~ aparte** though I say so myself; **modesto** *adj* modest

módico *adj precio* reasonable

modificación *f* modification; **modificar** <1g> *v/t* modify

modista *m/f* dressmaker; *diseñador* fashion designer

modo *m* way; **a ~ de** as; **de ~ que** so that; **de ningún ~** not at all; **en cierto ~** in a way *o* sense; **de todos ~s** anyway

modorra *f* drowsiness

módulo *m* module

mofarse <1a> *v/r*: **~ de** make fun of

mofeta *f* ZO skunk

mofletes *mpl* chubby cheeks

mogollón *m* F (*discusión*) argument; **~ de** F loads of F

moho *m* mo(u)ld

moisés *m inv* Moses basket

mojado *adj* (*húmedo*) damp, moist; (*empapado*) wet; **mojar** <1a> **1** *v/t* (*humedecer*) dampen, moisten; (*empapar*) wet; *galleta* dunk, dip **2** *v/r* **~se** get wet

mojigato 1 *adj* prudish **2** *m*, **-a** *f* prude

M

mojón *m tb fig* milestone

molar <2h> **1** *v/t*: **me mola ese tío** P I like the guy a lot **2** *v/i* P be cool F

molcajete *m Méx, C.Am. (mortero)* grinding stone

molde *m* mo(u)ld; *para bizcocho (cake)* tin; **romper ~s** *fig* break the mo(u)ld; **moldear** <1a> *v/t* mo(u)ld; **moldura** *f* ARQUI mo(u)lding

mole 1 *f* mass **2** *m Méx* mole *(spicy sauce made with chilies and tomatoes)*

molécula *f* molecule

moler <2h> *v/t* grind; *fruta* mash; **carne molida** ground meat, *Br* mince; **~ a alguien a palos** *fig* beat s.o. to a pulp

molestar <1a> **1** *v/t* bother, annoy; *(doler)* trouble; **no ~** do not disturb **2** *v/r* **~se** get upset; *(ofenderse)* take offense *(Br* offence); *(enojarse)* get annoyed; **~ en hacer algo** take the trouble to do sth; **molestia** *f* nuisance; **~s** *pl* MED discomfort *sg;* **molesto** *adj* annoying; *(incómodo)* inconvenient; **molestoso** *adj L.Am.* annoying

molido *adj* F bushed F

molinillo *m*: **~ de café** coffee grinder *o* mill; **molino** *m* mill; **~ de viento** windmill

mollera *f* F head; **duro de ~** F pigheaded F

molusco *m* ZO mollusk, *Br* mollusc

momento *m* moment; **al ~** at once; **por el ~, de ~** for the moment

momia *f* mummy; **momificar** <1g> *v/t* mummify

monada *f*: **su hija es una ~** her daughter is lovely; **¡qué ~!** how lovely!

monaguillo *m* altar boy

monarca *m* monarch; **monarquía** *f* monarchy

monasterio *m* monastery

mondadientes *m inv* toothpick

mondar <1a> **1** *v/t* peel; *árbol* prune **2** *v/r* **~se**: **~se de risa** F split one's sides laughing

mondongo *m* tripe

moneda *f* coin; *(divisa)* currency; **monedero** *m* change purse, *Br* purse; **monetario** *adj* monetary

monigote *m* rag doll; F *(tonto)* idiot

monitor¹ *m* TV, INFOR monitor

monitor² *m*, **~a** *f (profesor)* instructor

monja *f* nun; **monje** *m* monk

mono 1 *m* ZO monkey; *prenda* coveralls *pl, Br* boilersuit **2** *adj* pretty, cute

monógamo *adj* monogamous

monólogo *m* monolog(ue)

monopatín *m* skateboard

monopolio *m* monopoly; **monopolizar** <1f> *v/t tb fig* monopolize

monosílabo *adj* monosyllabic

monotonía *f* monotony; **monótono** *adj* monotonous

monovolumen *m* AUTO minivan, *Br* people carrier, MPV

monsergas *fpl*: **déjate de ~** F stop going on F

monstruo *m* monster; *(fenómeno)* phenomenon; **monstruosidad** *f* eyesore, monstrosity; **monstruoso** *adj* monstrous

monta *f*: **de poca ~** unimportant

montacargas *m inv* hoist

montada *f L.Am.* mounted police

montaje *m* TÉC assembly; *de película* editing; TEA staging; *fig* F con F

montante *m* COM total

montaña *f* mountain; **~ rusa** roller coaster; **montañero** *m*, **-a** *f* mountaineer; **montañismo** *m* mountaineering; **montañoso** *adj* mountainous

montaplatos *m inv* dumb waiter

montar <1a> **1** *v/t* TÉC assemble; *tienda* put up; *negocio* set up; *película* edit; *caballo* mount; **~ la guardia** mount guard **2** *v/i*: **~ en bicicleta** ride a bicycle; **~ a caballo** ride a horse

monte *m* mountain; *(bosque)* woodland

montículo *m* mound

montón *m* pile, heap; **ser del ~** *fig* be average, not stand out; **montones de** F piles of F, loads of F

montura *f de gafas* frame
monumento *m* monument
moño *m* bun
moqueta *f* (wall-to-wall) carpet
mora *f* BOT *de zarza* blackberry; *de morera* mulberry
morada *f* dwelling
morado *adj* purple; ***pasarlas -as*** F have a rough time
moral **1** *adj* moral **2** *f* (*moralidad*) morals *pl*; (*ánimo*) morale; **moraleja** *f* moral; **moralidad** *f* morality; **moralista** *m/f* moralist
moratón *m* bruise
moratoria *f* moratorium
morbo *m* F perverted kind of pleasure; **morboso** *adj* perverted
morcilla *f* blood sausage, *Br* black pudding
mordaz *adj* biting; **mordaza** *f* gag; **morder** <2h> *v/t* bite; **mordida** *f* *Méx* F bribe; **mordisco** *m* bite; **mordisquear** <1a> *v/t* nibble
morena *f* ZO moray eel
moreno *adj pelo, piel* dark; (*bronceado*) tanned
morera *f* BOT white mulberry tree
moretón *m* *L.Am.* bruise
morfina *f* morphine
morfología *f* morphology
moribundo *adj* dying
morir <3k; *part* **muerto**> **1** *v/i* die (*de* of); ~ *de hambre* die of hunger, starve to death **2** *v/r* ~**se** die; ~**se de** *fig* die of; ~**se por** *fig* be dying for
morisco *adj* Moorish
mormón *m* Mormon
moro **1** *adj* North African **2** *m* North African; *no hay* ~*s en la costa* F the coast is clear
morocho *adj S.Am. persona* dark
moronga *f C.Am., Méx* blood sausage, *Br* black pudding
morralla *f Méx* small change
morriña *f* homesickness
morro *m* ZO snout; *tener mucho* ~ F have a real nerve
morrongo *m* F pussycat F
morsa *f* ZO walrus
mortaja *f* shroud; *L.Am.* cigarette paper
mortal **1** *adj* mortal; *accidente, herida* fatal; *dosis* lethal **2** *m/f* mortal; **mortalidad** *f* mortality; **mortalmente** *adv* fatally
mortero *m tb* MIL mortar
mortífero *adj* lethal; **mortificar** <1g> **1** *v/t* torment **2** *v/r* ~**se** *fig* distress o.s.; *Méx* (*apenarse*) be embarrassed *o* ashamed
mosaico *m* mosaic
mosca *f* fly; *por si las* ~*s* F just to be on the safe side
moscardón *m* hornet
Moscú Moscow
mosquear <1a> **1** *v/t Esp* F rile **2** *v/r* ~**se** F get hot under the collar F; (*sentir recelo*) smell a rat F
mosquitero *m* mosquito net; **mosquito** *m* mosquito
mostaza *f* mustard
mosto *m* grape juice
mostrador *m* counter; *en bar* bar; ~ *de facturación* check-in desk; **mostrar** <1m> **1** *v/t* show **2** *v/r* ~**se** *contento* seem happy
mota *f* speck; *en diseño* dot
mote *m* nickname; *S.Am.* boiled corn *o Br* maize
motel *m* motel
motín *m* mutiny; *en una cárcel* riot
motivación *f* motivation; **motivar** <1a> *v/t* motivate; **motivo** *m* motive, reason; MÚS, PINT motif; *con* ~ *de* because of
moto *f* motorcycle, motorbike; ~ *acuática or de agua* jet ski
motocicleta *f* motorcycle; **motociclismo** *m* motorcycle racing; **motociclista** *m/f* motorcyclist
motocross *m* motocross
motor *m* engine; *eléctrico* motor; **motora** *f* motorboat; **motorista** *m/f* motorcyclist
motosierra *f* chain saw
motriz *adj* motor
mover <2h> **1** *v/t* move; (*agitar*) shake; (*impulsar, incitar*) drive **2** *v/r* ~**se** move; *¡muévete!* get a move on! F, hurry up!

M

movida f F scene

móvil 1 adj mobile **2** m TELEC cellphone, Br mobile (phone); **movilidad** f mobility; **movilizar** <1f> v/t mobilize; **movimiento** m movement; COM, fig activity

moza f girl; camarera waitress; **mozo 1** adj: **en mis años ~s** in my youth **2** m boy; camarero waiter

mucama f Rpl maid; **mucamo** m Rpl servant

muchacha f girl; **muchachada** f Arg group of youngsters; **muchacho** m boy

muchedumbre f crowd

mucho 1 adj cantidad a lot of, lots of; esp neg much; **no tengo ~ dinero** I don't have much money; **~s** a lot of, lots of; many; esp neg many; **no tengo ~s amigos** I don't have many friends; **tengo ~ frío** I am very cold; **es ~ coche para mí** it's too big a car for me **2** adv a lot; esp neg much; **no me gustó ~** I didn't like it very much; **¿dura/tarda ~?** does it last/take long?; **como ~** at the most; **ni ~ menos** far from it; **por ~ que** however much **3** pron a lot, much; **~s** a lot of people, many people

muda f de ropa change of clothes; **mudanza** f de casa move; **mudarse** <1a> v/r: **~ de casa** move house; **~ de ropa** change (one's clothes)

mudo adj mute; letra silent

mueble m piece of furniture

mueca f de dolor grimace; **hacer ~s** make faces

muela f tooth; ANAT molar; **~ del juicio** wisdom tooth

muelle m TÉC spring; MAR wharf

muérdago m BOT mistletoe

muerde vb → **morder**

muere vb → **morir**

muermo m fig F boredom; **ser un ~** fig F be a drag F

muerte f death; **de mala ~** fig F lousy F, awful F; **muerto 1** part → **morir 2** adj dead **3** m, -a f dead person

muestra f sample; (señal) sign; (exposición) show; **muestrario** m collection of samples

mueve vb → **mover**

mugir <3c> v/i moo

mugre f filth; **mugriento** adj filthy; **mugroso** adj dirty

mujer f woman; (esposa) wife; **mujeriego** m womanizer

mújol m ZO gray o Br grey mullet

mula f mule; Méx trash, Br rubbish

mulato m mulatto

muleta f crutch; TAUR cape

mullido adj soft

mullir <3h> v/t almohada plump up

multa f fine; **multar** <1a> v/t fine

multicine m multiscreen

multicolor adj multicolo(u)red

multilateral adj multilateral

multimedia f/adj multimedia

multimillonario m multimillionaire

multinacional f multinational

múltiple adj multiple; **multiplicación** f multiplication; **multiplicar** <1g> **1** v/t multiply **2** v/r **~se** multiply; **múltiplo** m MAT multiple

multipropiedad f timeshare

multitud f crowd; **~ de** thousands of; **multitudinario** adj mass atr

multiuso adj multipurpose

mundano adj society atr; REL wordly; **mundial 1** adj world atr **2** m: **el ~ de fútbol** the World Cup; **mundo** m world; **el otro ~** the next world; **nada del otro ~** nothing out of the ordinary; **todo el ~** everybody, everyone

munición f ammunition

municipal adj municipal; **municipio** m municipality

muñeca f doll; ANAT wrist; **muñeco** m doll; fig puppet; **~ de nieve** snowman

muñón m MED stump

mural 1 adj wall atr **2** m mural; **muralla** f de ciudad wall

murciélago m ZO bat

murga f: **dar la ~ a alguien** F bug s.o. F

murió vb → **morir**

murmullo m murmur; **murmurar** <1a> v/i hablar murmur; criticar gossip

muro m wall

musa *f* muse

musaraña *f* ZO shrew; *pensar en las ~s* F daydream

muscular *adj* muscular; **músculo** *m* muscle; **musculoso** *adj* muscular

museo *m* museum; *de pintura* art gallery

musgo *m* BOT moss

música *f* music; **musical** *m/adj* musical; **músico** *m*, **-a** *f* musician

musitar <1a> *v/i* mumble

muslo *m* thigh

mustio *adj* withered; *fig* down F

musulmán 1 *adj* Muslim **2** *m*, **-ana** *f* Muslim

mutilado *m*, **-a** *f* disabled person; **mutilar** <1a> *v/t* mutilate

mutualidad *f* benefit society, *Br* friendly society; **mutuo** *adj* mutual

muy *adv* very; (*demasiado*) too; *~ valorado* highly valued

N

N *abr* (= *norte*) N (North(ern))

nabo *m* **1** *adj Arg* F dumb F **2** *m* turnip

nácar *m* mother-of-pearl

nacatamal *m C.Am., Méx* meat, rice and corn in a banana leaf

nacer <2d> *v/i* be born; *de un huevo* hatch; *de una planta* sprout; *de un río, del sol* rise; (*surgir*) arise (*de* from); **naciente** *adj país, gobierno* newly formed; *sol* rising; **nacimiento** *m* birth; *de Navidad* crèche, nativity scene

nación *f* nation; **nacional** *adj* national; **nacionalidad** *f* nationality; **nacionalismo** *m* nationalism; **nacionalización** *f* COM nationalization; **nacionalizar** <1f> **1** *v/t* COM nationalize; *persona* naturalize **2** *v/r ~se* become naturalized

naco *m Col* purée

nada 1 *pron* nothing; *no hay ~* there isn't anything; *¡~ de eso!* F you can put that idea out of your head; *~ más* nothing else; *~ menos que* no less than; *lo dices como si ~* you talk about it as if it was nothing; *¡de ~!* you're welcome, not at all; *no es ~* it's nothing **2** *adv* not at all; *no ha llovido ~* it hasn't rained **3** *f* nothingness

nadador *m*, **~a** *f* swimmer; **nadar** <1a> *v/i* swim

nadería *f* trifle

nadie *pron* nobody, no-one; *no había ~* there was nobody there, there wasn't anyone there

nado: *atravesar a ~* swim across

nafta *f Arg* gas(oline), *Br* petrol; **naftalina** *f* naphthalene

nailon *m* nylon

naipe *m* (playing) card

nalga *f* buttock

nana *f* lullaby; *Rpl* F (*abuela*) grandma

napias *fpl* F schnozzle *sg* F, *Br* hooter *sg* F

naranja 1 *f* orange; *media ~* F (*pareja*) other half **2** *adj* orange; **naranjada** *f* orangeade; **naranjo** *m* orange tree

narciso *m* BOT daffodil

narcótico *m/adj* narcotic; **narcotráfico** *m* drug trafficking

nariz *f* nose; *¡narices!* F nonsense!; *estar hasta las narices de algo* F be sick of sth F, be up to here with sth F; *meter las narices en algo* F stick one's nose in sth F

narración *f* narration; **narrador** *m*, **~a** *f* narrator; **narrar** <1a> *v/t: ~ algo* tell the story of sth nasal *adj* nasal

nata *f* cream; **~ montada** whipped cream

natación *f* swimming

natal *adj* native; **ciudad ~** city of one's birth, home town; **natalidad** *f* birthrate

natillas *fpl* custard *sg*

nativo *m*, **-a** *f* native; **nato** *adj* born

natural 1 *adj* natural; **ser ~ de** come from; **es ~** it's only natural 2 *m*: **fruta al ~** fruit in its own juice; **naturaleza** *f* nature; **naturalidad** *f* naturalness; **naturalmente** *adv* naturally; **naturista** 1 *adj* nudist, naturist; **medicina natural** 2 *m/f* nudist, naturist

naufragar <1h> *v/i* be shipwrecked; *fig* fail; **naufragio** *m* shipwreck; **náufrago** 1 *adj* shipwrecked 2 *m*, **-a** *f* shipwrecked person

náuseas *fpl* nausea *sg*; **nauseabundo** *adj* nauseating

náutico *adj* nautical

navaja *f* knife; **navajazo** *m* knife wound, slash; **navajero** *m*: **le asaltó un ~** he was attacked by a man with a knife

naval *adj* naval; **nave** *f* ship; *de iglesia* nave; **~ espacial** spacecraft; **navegación** *f* navigation; **~ a vela** sailing; **navegador** *m* INFOR browser; **navegante** *m/f* navigator; **navegar** <1h> 1 *v/i* sail; *por el aire, espacio* fly; **~ por la red** *o por Internet* INFOR surf the Net 2 *v/t* sail

Navidad *f* Christmas; **navideño** *adj* Christmas *atr*

navío *m* ship

nazi *m/f* & *adj* Nazi; **nazismo** *m* Nazi(i)sm

N.B. *abr* (= *nótese bien*) NB (= *nota bene*)

neblina *f* mist; **nebuloso** *adj fig* hazy, nebulous

necesario *adj* necessary; **neceser** *m* toilet kit, *Br* toilet bag; **necesidad** *f* need; (*cosa esencial*) necessity; **de primera ~** essential; **en caso de ~** if necessary; **hacer sus -es** F relieve o.s.; **necesitado** *adj* needy; **necesitar** <1a> *v/t* need

necio *adj* brainless

necrológica *f* obituary

nefasto *adj* harmful

negación *f* negation; *de acusación* denial; **negar** <1h & 1k> *v/t* acusación deny; (*no conceder*) refuse 2 *v/r* **~se** refuse (*a* to); **negativa** *f* refusal; *de acusación* denial; **negativo** 1 *adj* negative 2 *m* FOT negative

negligencia *f* JUR negligence

negociable *adj* negotiable; **negociación** *f* negotiation; **negociaciones** talks; **negociador** *m*, **-a** *f* negotiator; **negociante** *m/f* businessman; *mujer* businesswoman; *desp* money-grubber; **negociar** <1b> *v/t* negotiate; **negocio** *m* business; (*trato*) deal

negra *f* black woman; MÚS quarter note, *Br* crotchet; *L.Am.* (*querida*) honey, dear; **negrita** *f* bold; **negro** 1 *adj* black; **estar ~** F be furious 2 *m* black man; *L.Am.* (*querido*) honey, dear

nena *f* F little girl, kid F; **nene** *m* F little boy, kid F

nenúfar *m* BOT water lily

neocelandés *m*, **-esa** *f* New Zealander

neón *m* neon

neoyorquino 1 *adj* New York *atr* 2 *m*, **-a** *f* New Yorker

nepotismo *m* nepotism

nervio *m* ANAT nerve; **nerviosismo** *m* nervousness; **nervioso** *adj* nervous; **ponerse ~** get nervous; (*agitado*) get agitated; **poner a alguien ~** get on s.o.'s nerves

neto *adj* COM net

neumático 1 *adj* pneumatic 2 *m* AUTO tire, *Br* tyre

neumonía *f* MED pneumonia

neurocirujano *m*, **-a** *f* brain surgeon

neurólogo *m*, **-a** *f* neurologist

neurosis *f inv* neurosis; **neurótico** *adj* neurotic

neutral *adj* neutral; **neutralidad** *f* neutrality; **neutralizar** <1f> *v/t* neutralize; **neutro** *adj* neutral

nevada *f* snowfall; **nevar** <1k> *v/i* snow; **nevazón** *f Arg, Chi* snowstorm; **nevera** *f* refrigerator, fridge; **~ portátil** cooler; **nevería** *f Méx, C.Am.* ice-cream parlo(u)r; **nevero** *m* snowdrift

nexo *m* link; GRAM connective

ni *conj* neither; **~ ... ~** neither ... nor; **~ siquiera** not even; **no di ~ una** I made a real mess of things

Nicaragua Nicaragua; **nicaragüense** *m/f & adj* Nicaraguan

nicho *m* niche

nicotina *f* nicotine; **bajo en ~** low in nicotine

nido *m* nest

niebla *f* fog

nieta *f* granddaughter; **nieto** *m* grandson; **~s** grandchildren

nieva *vb* → **nevar**

nieve *f* snow; *Méx* water ice, sorbet

nihilismo *m* nihilism

nimiedad *f* triviality; **nimio** *adj* trivial

ningún *adj* → **ninguno**

ninguno *adj* no; **no hay ~a razón** there's no reason why, there isn't any reason why

niña *f* girl; *forma de cortesía* young lady; **niñato** *m*, **-a** *f* brat; **niñera** *f* nanny; **niñería** *f*: **una ~** a childish thing; **niñez** *f* childhood; **niño 1** *adj* young; *desp* childish **2** *m* boy; *forma de cortesía* young man; **~s** children *pl*; **~ de pecho** infant

níquel *m* nickel

níspero *m* BOT loquat

nítido *adj* clear; *imagen* sharp

nitrógeno *m* nitrogen; **nitroglicerina** *f* nitroglycerin

nivel *m* level; *(altura)* height; **~ del mar** sea level; **~ de vida** standard of living; **nivelar** <1a> *v/t* level

nixtamal *m Méx, C.Am.* dough from which corn tortillas are made

n.º *abr* (= **número**) No. (= number)

no *adv* no; *para negar verbo* not; **no entiendo** I don't understand, I do not understand; **~ te vayas** don't go; **~ bien** as soon as; **~ del todo** not

entirely; **ya ~** not any more; **~ más** *L.Am.* → **nomás**; **así ~ más** just like that; **te gusta, ¿~?** you like it, don't you?; **te ha llamado, ¿~?** he called you, didn't he?; **¿a que ~?** I bet you don't / can't etc

nobiliario *adj* noble; **noble** *m/f & adj* noble; **nobleza** *f* nobility

noche *f* night; **de ~, por la ~** at night; **de la ~ a la mañana** *fig* overnight; **¡buenas ~s!** *saludo* good evening; *despedida* good night; **Nochebuena** *f* Christmas Eve; **nochecita** *f L.Am.* evening; **nochero** *m L.Am.* night watchman; **Nochevieja** *f* New Year's Eve

noción *f* notion

nocivo *adj* harmful

noctámbulo *m*, **-a** *f* sleepwalker; **nocturno** *adj* night *atr*; ZO nocturnal; **clase -a** evening class

nogal *m* BOT walnut

nómada 1 *adj* nomadic **2** *m/f* nomad

nomás *adv L.Am.* just, only; **llévaselo ~** just take it away; **~ llegue, te avisaré** as soon as he arrives, I'll let you know; **siga ~** just carry on; **~ lo vio, echó a llorar** as soon as she saw him she started to cry

nombramiento *m* appointment; **nombrar** <1a> *v/t* mention; *para un cargo* appoint; **nombre** *m* name; GRAM noun; **~ de pila** first name; **no tener ~** *fig* be inexcusable

nomenclatura *f* nomenclature

nomeolvides *f inv* BOT forget-me-not

nómina *f* pay slip; **nominal** *adj* nominal; **nominar** <1a> *v/t* nominate

non *adj* odd

nono *adj* ninth

nopal *m L.Am.* BOT prickly pear

nor(d)este *m* northeast

noria *f de agua* waterwheel; *en feria* ferris wheel

norma *f* standard; *(regla)* rule, regulation; **normal** *adj* normal; **normalidad** *f* normality; **normalizar** <1f> *v/t* standardize; **normativa** *f* rules *pl*, regulations *pl*

noroeste *m* northwest

N

norte *m* north

Norteamérica North America; **norteamericano 1** *adj* North American **2** *m*, **-a** *f* North American

norteño 1 *adj* northern **2** *m*, **-a** *f* northerner

Noruega Norway; **noruego 1** *adj* Norwegian **2** *m*, **-a** *f* Norwegian

nos *pron complemento directo* us; *complemento indirecto* (to) us; *reflexivo* ourselves; **~ dio el dinero** he gave us the money, he gave the money to us

nosotros, **nosotras** *pron* we; *complemento* us; **ven con ~** come with us; **somos ~** it's us

nostalgia *f* nostalgia; **por la patria** homesickness; **nostálgico** *adj* nostalgic

nota *f tb* MÚS note; EDU grade, mark; **a pie de página** footnote; **tomar ~ de algo** make a note of sth; **notable** *adj* remarkable, notable; **notar** <1a> *v/t* notice; (*sentir*) feel; **hacer ~ algo a alguien** point sth out to s.o.; **se nota que** you can tell that; **hacerse ~** draw attention to o.s.

notaría *f* notary's office; **notario** *m*, **-a** *f* notary

noticia *f* piece of news; *en noticiario* news story, item of news; **~s** *pl* news *sg*; **noticiario** *m* RAD, TV news *sg*

notificación *f* notification; **notificar** <1g> *v/t* notify

notorio *adj* famous, well-known

novatada *f* practical joke

novato *m*, **-a** *f* beginner, rookie F

novecientos *adj* nine hundred

novedad *f* novelty; *cosa* new thing; (*noticia*) piece of news; *acontecimiento* new development; **llegar sin ~** arrive safely; **novedoso** *adj* novel, new; *invento* innovative; **novela** *f* novel; **~ negra** crime novel; **~ rosa** romantic novel; **novelista** *m/f* novelist

noveno *adj* ninth; **noventa** *adj* ninety

novia *f* girlfriend; *el día de la boda* bride; **noviazgo** *m* engagement

noviembre *m* November

novilla *f vaca* heifer; **novillada** *f* bullfight featuring novice bulls; **novillero** *m* novice (bullfighter); **novillo** *m* ZO young bull; **hacer ~s** F play hooky F, play truant

novio *m* boyfriend; *el día de la boda* bridegroom; **los ~s** the bride and groom; (*recién casados*) the newlyweds

nube *f* cloud; **estar en las ~s** *fig* be miles away; **estar por las ~s** *fig* F be incredibly expensive; **nublado 1** *adj* cloudy, overcast **2** *m* storm cloud; **nublarse** <1a> *v/r* cloud over; **nuboso** *adj* cloudy

nuca *f* nape of the neck

nuclear *adj* nuclear; **núcleo** *m* nucleus; *de problema* heart

nudillo *m* knuckle

nudista *m/f* nudist; **playa ~** nudist beach

nudo *m* knot; **se me hace un ~ en la garganta** F I get a lump in my throat

nuera *f* daughter-in-law

nuestro 1 *adj pos* our **2** *pron* ours

nueva *f lit* piece of news; **nuevamente** *adv* again

Nueva York New York

Nueva Zelanda New Zealand

nueve *adj* nine

nuevo *adj* new; (*otro*) another; **de ~** again

nuez *f* BOT walnut; ANAT Adam's apple

nulidad *f* nullity; *fig* F dead loss F; **nulo** *adj* null and void; F *persona* hopeless; (*inexistente*) nonexistent, zero

núm. *abr* (= **número**) No. (= number)

numerar <1a> *v/t* number; **numérico** *adj* numerical; **teclado ~** numeric keypad, number pad; **número** *m* number; *de publicación* issue; *de zapato* size; **~ complementario** *en lotería* bonus number; **~ secreto** PIN (number); **en ~s rojos** *fig* in the red; **montar un ~** F make a scene; **numeroso** *adj* numerous

numismática *f* numismatics

nunca *adv* never; **~ jamás** *or* **más**

never again; **más que** ~ more than
ever
nupcial *adj* wedding *atr*
nutria *f* ZO otter
nutrición *f* nutrition; **nutrido** *adj* fig

large; **nutriente** *m* nutrient; **nutrir**
<3a> *v/t* nourish; *fig: esperanzas*
cherish; **nutritivo** *adj* nutritious,
nourishing
nylon *m* nylon

Ñ

ñandú *m* ZO rhea
ñandutí *m Parag* type of lace
ñapa *f S.Am.* extra, bonus; **le di dos
de** ~ I threw in an extra two
ñato *adj Rpl* snub-nosed
ñeque *m S.Am.* strength; **de** ~ F gutsy

F; **tener mucho** ~ F have a lot of
guts F
ñoñería *f* feebleness F, wimpish
behavio(u)r F; **ñoño 1** *adj* feeble F,
wimpish F **2** *m,* -**a** *f* drip F, wimp F
ñu *m* ZO gnu

O

O *abr* (= **oeste**) W (= West(ern))
o *conj* or; ~ ... ~ either ... or; ~ **sea** in
other words
oasis *m inv* oasis
obcecación *f* obstinacy; **obcecarse**
<1g> *v/r* stubbornly insist
obedecer <2d> **1** *v/t* obey **2** *v/i* obey;
de una máquina respond; ~ **a** *fig* be
due to; **obediencia** *f* obedience;
obediente *adj* obedient
obelisco *m* obelisk
obesidad *f* obesity; **obeso** *adj* obese
obispo *m* bishop
objeción *f* objection; ~ **de conciencia** conscientious objection; **obje-
tar** <1a> *v/t* object; **tener algo
que** ~ have any objection **2** *v/i*
become a conscientious objector
objetividad *f* objectivity; **objetivo
1** *adj* objective **2** *m* objective; MIL
target; FOT lens
objeto *m* object; **con** ~ **de** with the

aim of
objetor *m,* ~**a** *f* objector; ~ **de
conciencia** conscientious objector
oblicuo *adj* oblique, slanted
obligación *f* obligation, duty; COM
bond; **obligar** <1h> *v/t:* ~ **a alguien**
oblige *o* force s.o. (**a** to); *de una ley*
apply to s.o.; **obligatorio** *adj* obliga-
tory, compulsory
obnubilar <1a> *v/t* cloud
oboe *m* MÚS oboe
obra *f* work; ~**s** *pl de construcción*
building work *sg; en la vía pública*
road works; ~ **de arte** work of art; ~
maestra masterpiece; ~ **de teatro**
play; **obraje** *m Méx* butcher's;
obrar <1a> *v/i* act; **obrero 1** *adj*
working **2** *m,* -**a** *f* worker
obsceno *adj* obscene
obsequiar <1b> *v/t:* ~ **a alguien con
algo** present s.o. with sth; **obsequio**
m gift; **obsequioso** *adj* attentive

O

observación f observation; JUR observance; **observador_1** adj observant **2** m, **~a** f observer; **observar** <1a> v/t observe; (*advertir*) notice, observe; (*comentar*) remark, observe; **observatorio** m observatory

obsesión f obsession; **obsesionar** <1a> **1** v/t obsess **2** v/r **~se** become obsessed (*con* with); **obsesivo** adj obsessive

obsoleto adj obsolete

obstaculizar <1f> v/t hinder, hamper; **obstáculo** m obstacle

obstante: *no* ~ nevertheless

obstetra m/f obstetrician; **obstetricia** f obstetrics

obstinación f obstinacy; **obstinado** adj obstinate; **obstinarse** <1a> v/r insist (*en* on)

obstrucción f obstruction, blockage; **obstruir** <3g> v/t obstruct, block

obtener <2l; *part* **obtuvo**> v/t get, obtain *fml*

obturador m shutter

obtuvo vb → **obtener**

obvio adj obvious

oca f goose

ocasión f occasion; (*oportunidad*) chance, opportunity; *con* ~ *de* on the occasion of; *de* ~ COM cut-price, bargain *atr*; *de segunda mano* second-hand, used; **ocasional** adj occasional; **ocasionar** <1a> v/t cause

ocaso m *del sol* setting; *de un imperio, un poder* decline

occidental 1 adj western **2** m/f Westerner; **occidente** m west

OCDE abr (= *Organización de Cooperación y Desarrollo Económico*) OECD (= Organization for Economic Cooperation and Development)

océano m ocean; **oceanógrafo** m, **-a** f oceanographer

ocelote m ZO ocelot

ochenta adj eighty; **ocho** adj eight; **ochocientos** adj eight hundred

ocio m leisure time, free time; *desp* idleness; **ociosear** <1a> v/i *S.Am.* laze around; **ocioso** adj idle

ocre m/adj ocher, *Br* ochre

oct.ᵉ abr (= *octubre*) Oct. (= October)

octavilla f leaflet; **octavo 1** adj eighth **2** m eighth; DEP **~s de final** last 16

octógono m octagon

octubre m October

ocular adj eye atr; **oculista** m/f ophthalmologist

ocultación f concealment; **ocultar** <1a> v/t hide, conceal; **ocultismo** m occult; **oculto** adj hidden; (*sobrenatural*) occult

ocupación f tb MIL occupation; (*actividad*) activity; **ocupado** adj busy; *asiento* taken; **ocupante** m/f occupant; **ocupar** <1a> **1** v/t *espacio* take up, occupy; (*habitar*) live in, occupy; *obreros* employ; *periodo de tiempo* spend, occupy; MIL occupy **2** v/r **~se**: **~se de** deal with; (*cuidar de*) look after

ocurrencia f occurrence; (*chiste*) quip, funny remark; **ocurrir** <3a> v/i happen, occur; *se me ocurrió* it occurred to me, it struck me

odiar <1b> v/t hate; **odio** m hatred, hate; **odioso** adj odious, hateful

odisea f *fig* odyssey

odontólogo m odontologist

OEA abr (= *Organización de los Estados Americanos*) OAS (= Organization of American States)

oeste m west

ofender <2a> **1** v/t offend **2** v/r **~se** take offense (*por* at); **ofensa** f insult; **ofensiva** f offensive; **ofensivo** adj offensive

oferta f offer; ~ *pública de adquisición* takeover bid

oficial 1 adj official **2** m/f MIL officer; **oficialista** adj *L.Am.* pro-government; **oficina** f office; ~ *de correos* post office; ~ *de empleo* employment office; ~ *de turismo* tourist office; **oficinista** m/f office worker; **oficio** m *trabajo* trade; **oficioso** adj unofficial

ofimática f INFOR office automation

ofrecer <2d> **1** v/t offer **2** v/r **~se**

volunteer, offer one's services (*de* as); (*presentarse*) appear; **¿qué se le ofrece?** what can I do for you?; **ofrecimiento** *m* offer; **ofrenda** *f* offering

oftalmólogo *m*, **-a** *f* ophthalmologist

ofuscar <1g> *v/t tb fig* blind

ogro *m tb fig* ogre

oída *f*: **conocer algo de ~s** have heard of sth; **oído** *m* hearing; **hacer ~s sordos** turn a deaf ear; **ser todo ~s** *fig* be all ears

oigo *vb* → **oír**

oír <3q> *v/t tb* JUR hear; (*escuchar*) listen to; **¡oye!** listen!, hey! F; **como quien oye llover, salió sin él** F he turned a deaf ear and went off without it

OIT *abr* (= **Organización Internacional de Trabajo**) ILO (= International Labor Organization)

ojal *m* buttonhole

ojalá *int*: **¡~!** let's hope so; **¡~ venga!** I hope he comes; **¡~ tuvieras razón!** I only hope you're right

ojeada *f* glance; **echar una ~ a alguien** glance at s.o.; **ojeras** *fpl* bags under the eyes; **ojo** *m* ANAT eye; **¡~!** F watch out!, mind! F; **~ de la cerradura** keyhole; **a ~** roughly; **andar con ~** F keep one's eyes open F; **costar un ~ de la cara** F cost an arm and a leg F; **no pegar ~** F not sleep a wink F

ojota *f* C.Am., Méx sandal

okupa *m/f* Esp F squatter

ola *f* wave; **~ de calor** heat wave; **~ de frío** cold spell; **oleada** *f fig* wave, flood; **oleaje** *m* swell

óleo *m* oil; **oleoducto** *m* (oil) pipeline

oler <2i> **1** *v/i* smell (**a** of) **2** *v/t* smell **3** *v/r*: **me huelo algo** *fig* there's something fishy going on, I smell a rat; **olfatear** <1a> *v/t* sniff; **olfato** *m* sense of smell; *fig* nose

olimpíada, olimpiada *f* Olympics *pl*; **olímpico** *adj* Olympic

olisquear <1a> *v/t* sniff

oliva *f* BOT olive; **olivo** *m* olive tree

olla *f* pot; **~ exprés** *or* **a presión** pressure cooker

olmo *m* BOT elm

olor *m* smell; *agradable* scent; **~ corporal** body odo(u)r, BO; **oloroso** *adj* scented

OLP *abr* (= **Organización para la Liberación de Palestina**) PLO (= Palestine Liberation Organization)

olvidadizo *adj* forgetful; **olvidar** <1a> **1** *v/t* forget **2** *v/r* **-se**: **~se de algo** forget sth; **olvido** *m* oblivion

ombligo *m* ANAT navel

OMC *abr* (= **Organización Mundial de Comercio**) WTO (= World Trade Organization)

omisión *f* omission; **omiso** *adj*: **hacer caso ~ de algo** ignore sth; **omitir** <3a> *v/t* omit, leave out

omnipotente *adj* omnipotent

omóplato, omoplato *m* ANAT shoulder blade

OMS *abr* (= **Organización Mundial de la Salud**) WHO (= World Health Organization)

once *adj* eleven

oncología *f* MED oncology

onda *f* wave; **estar en la ~** F be with it F; **¿qué ~?** Méx F what's happening? F; **ondulado** *adj* wavy; **cartón** corrugated

ONG *abr* (= **Organización no Gubernamental**) NGO (= non-governmental organization)

onomatopeya *f* onomatopœia

ONU *abr* (= **Organización de las Naciones Unidas**) UN (= United Nations)

onza *f* ounce

OPA *abr* (= **oferta pública de adquisición**) takeover bid

opaco *adj* opaque

opción *f* option, choice; (*posibilidad*) chance; **opcional** *adj* optional

OPEP *abr* (= **Organización de Países Exportadores de Petróleo**) OPEC (= Organization of Petroleum Exporting Countries)

ópera *f* MÚS opera; **~ prima** first work

operación *f* operation; **operador** *m*,

O

~a f TELEC, INFOR operator; **~ turístico** tour operator; **operar** <1a> **1** v/t MED operate on; *cambio* bring about **2** v/i operate; COM do business (**con** with) **3** v/r **~se** MED have an operation (**de** on); *de un cambio* occur; **operario** m, **-a** f operator, operative; **operativo 1** adj operational; *sistema ~* INFOR operating system **2** m L.Am. operation

opereta f MÚS operetta

opinar <1a> **1** v/t think (**de** about) **2** v/i express an opinion; **opinión** f opinion; **la ~ pública** public opinion; **en mi ~** in my opinion

opio m opium

opíparo adj sumptuous

oponente m/f opponent; **oponer** <2r; part **opuesto**> **1** v/t resistance put up (**a** to), offer (**a** to); *razón, argumento* put forward (**a** against) **2** v/r **~se** be opposed (**a** to); (*manifestar oposición*) object (**a** to)

oporto m port

oportunidad f opportunity; **oportunista 1** adj opportunistic **2** m/f opportunist; **oportuno** adj timely; *momento* opportune; *respuesta, medida* suitable, appropriate

oposición f POL opposition; **oposiciones** official entrance exams

opresión f oppression; **opresor 1** adj oppressive **2** m, **-a** f oppressor; **oprimir** <3a> v/t oppress; *botón* press; *de zapatos* be too tight for

optar <1a> v/i (*elegir*) opt (**por** for); **~** be in the running for; **~ por hacer algo** opt to do sth; **optativo** adj optional

óptica f optician's; FÍS optics; *fig* point of view; **óptico 1** adj optical **2** m, **-a** f optician

optimismo m optimism; **optimista 1** adj optimistic **2** m/f optimist

optimizar <1f> v/t optimize; **óptimo** adj ideal

opuesto 1 part → **oponer 2** adj opposite; *opinión* contrary

opulencia f opulence

opuso vb → **oponer**

oquedad f cavity

oración f REL prayer; GRAM sentence

orador m, **-a** f orator; **oral** adj oral; **prueba de inglés ~** English oral (exam)

orangután m ZO orangutan

orar <1a> v/i pray (**por** for); **oratoria** f oratory

órbita f orbit; **colocar** or **poner en ~** put into orbit

orca m ZO killer whale

órdago m: **de ~** F terrific F

orden 1 m order; **~ del día** agenda; **por ~ alfabético** in alphabetical order; **poner en ~** tidy up **2** f (*mandamiento*) order; **¡a la ~!** yes, sir; **por ~ de** by order of, on the orders of; **ordenado** adj tidy; **ordenador** m INFOR computer; **~ de escritorio** desktop (computer); **~ personal** personal computer; **~ portátil** portable (computer); laptop; **asistido por ~** computer aided; **ordenanza 1** f by-law **2** m office junior, gofer F; MIL orderly; **ordenar** <1a> v/t *habitación* tidy up; *alfabéticamente* arrange; (*mandar*) order

ordeñar <1a> v/t milk

ordinario adj ordinary; *desp* vulgar; **de ~** usually, ordinarily

orégano m BOT oregano

oreja f ear; **aguzar las ~s** L.Am. prick one's ears up; **ver las ~s al lobo** fig F wake up to the danger; **orejeras** fpl earmuffs

orfanato m orphanage

orfebrería f goldsmith / silversmith work

orfelinato m orphanage

orgánico adj organic

organigrama m flow chart; *de empresa* organization chart, tree diagram

organillo m barrel organ

organismo m organism; POL agency, organization; **~ modificado genéticamente** genetically modified organism

organización f organization; **Or-**

ganización de Cooperación y Desarrollo Económico Organization for Economic Cooperation and Development; **Organización de las Naciones Unidas** United Nations; **Organización de los Estados Americanos** Organization of American States; **Organización del Tratado del Atlántico Norte** North Atlantic Treaty Organization; **Organización de Países Exportadores de Petróleo** Organization of Petroleum Exporting Countries; **Organización Internacional de Trabajo** International Labor Organization; **Organización Mundial de Comercio** World Trade Organization; **Organización Mundial de la Salud** World Health Organization; **Organización para la Liberación de Palestina** Palestine Liberation Organization; **organizador 1** *adj* organizing **2** *m*, **-a** *f* organizer; **~ personal** personal organizer; **organizar** <1f> **1** *v/t* organize **2** *v/r* **-se** *de persona* organize one's time

órgano *m* MÚS, ANAT, *fig* organ

orgasmo *m* orgasm

orgía *f* orgy

orgullo *m* pride; **orgulloso** *adj* proud (**de** of)

orientación *f* orientation; (*ayuda*) guidance; **sentido de la ~** sense of direction; **orientador** *m*, **~a** *f* counsel(l)or

oriental 1 *adj* oriental, eastern **2** *m/f* Oriental

orientar <1a> **1** *v/t* (*aconsejar*) advise; **~ algo hacia algo** turn sth toward sth **2** *v/r* **-se** get one's bearings; *de una planta* turn (**hacia** toward)

oriente *m* east; **Oriente** Orient; **Oriente Medio** Middle East; **Extremo** *or* **Lejano Oriente** Far East

orificio *m* hole; *en cuerpo* orifice

origen *m* origin; **dar ~ a** give rise to; **original** *m/adj* original; **originalidad** *f* originality; **originar** <1a> **1** *v/t* give rise to **2** *v/r* **-se**

originate; *de un incendio* start; **originario** *adj* original; (*nativo*) native (**de** of)

orilla *f* shore; *de un río* bank

orina *f* urine; **orinal** *m* urinal; **orinar** <1a> *v/i* urinate

oriundo *adj* native (**de** to)

ornamental *adj* ornamental

ornitología *f* ornithology; **ornitólogo** *m*, **-a** *f* ornithologist

oro *m* gold; **guardar como ~ en paño** *con mucho cariño* treasure sth; *con mucho cuidado* guard sth with one's life; **prometer el ~ y el moro** promise the earth; **~s** (*en naipes*) suit in Spanish deck of cards

orondo *adj* fat; *fig* smug

oropéndola *f* ZO golden oriole

orquesta *f* orchestra; **orquestar** <1a> *v/t fig* orchestrate

orquídea *f* BOT orchid

ortiga *f* BOT nettle

ortodoncia *f* MED orthodontics

ortodoxo *adj* orthodox

ortografía *f* spelling

ortopédico 1 *adj* orthop(a)edic **2** *m*, **-a** *f* orthop(a)edist

oruga *f* ZO caterpillar; TÉC (caterpillar) track

orujo *m liquor made from the remains of grapes*

orzuelo *m* MED stye

os *pron complemento directo* you; *complemento indirecto* (to) you; *reflexivo* yourselves; **~ lo devolveré** I'll give you it back, I'll give it back to you

osa *f* AST: **Osa Mayor** Great Bear; **Osa Menor** Little Bear

osadía *f* daring; (*descaro*) audacity

osamenta *f* bones *pl*

osar <1a> *v/i* dare

oscilación *f* oscillation; *de precios* fluctuation; **oscilar** <1a> *v/i* oscillate; *de precios* fluctuate

oscurecer <2d> **1** *v/t* darken; *logro, triunfo* overshadow **2** *v/i* get dark **3** *v/r* **-se** darken; **oscuridad** *f* darkness; **oscuro** *adj* dark; *fig* obscure; **a -as** in the dark

óseo *adj* bone *atr*

osezno *m* cub

osito *m*: **~ de peluche** teddy bear; **oso** *m* bear; **~ hormiguero** anteater; **~ panda** panda; **~ polar** polar bear

ostensible *adj* obvious

ostentación *f* ostentation; **hacer ~ de** flaunt; **ostentar** <1a> *v/t* flaunt; *cargo* hold; **ostentoso** *adj* ostentatious

osteoporosis *f* MED osteoporosis

ostra *f* ZO oyster; **¡~s!** F hell! F

ostrero *m* ZO oyster-catcher

OTAN *abr* (= **Organización del Tratado del Atlántico Norte**) NATO (= North Atlantic Treaty Organization)

otitis *f* MED earache

otoño *m* fall, *Br* autumn

otorgar <1h> *v/t* award; *favor* grant

otorrino F, **otorrinolaringólogo** *m* MED ear, nose and throat *o* ENT specialist

otro **1** *adj* (*diferente*) another; *con el, la* other; **~s** other; **~s dos libros** another two books **2** *pron* (*adicional*) another (one); (*persona distinta*) someone *o* somebody else; (*cosa distinta*) another one, a different one; **~s** others; **entre ~s** among

others **3** *siguiente*: **¡hasta -a!** see you soon **4** *pron recíproco*: **amar el uno al ~** love one another

ovación *f* ovation; **ovacionar** <1a> *v/t* cheer, give an ovation to

ovalado *adj* oval; **óvalo** *m* oval

ovario *m* ANAT ovary

oveja *f* sheep; **~ negra** *fig* black sheep

overol *m* Méx overalls *pl*, *Br* dungarees *pl*

ovillo *m* ball; **hacerse un ~** *fig* curl up (into a ball)

ovino **1** *adj* sheep *atr* **2** *m* sheep; **~s** sheep *pl*

OVNI *abr* (= **objeto volante no identificado**) UFO (= unidentified flying object)

ovulación *f* ovulation; **óvulo** *m* egg

oxidado *adj* rusty; **oxidar** <1a> **1** *v/t* rust **2** *v/r* **~se** rust, go rusty; **óxido** *m* QUÍM oxide; (*herrumbre*) rust; **oxigenarse** <1a> *v/r* *fig* get some fresh air; **oxígeno** *m* oxygen

oye *vb* → **oír**

oyendo *vb* → **oír**

oyente *m/f* listener

oyó *vb* → **oír**

ozono *m* ozone; **capa de ~** ozone layer

P

pabellón *m* pavilion; *edificio* block; MÚS bell; MAR flag

pachanga *f*: **ir de ~** Méx, W.I., C.Am. F go on a spree F

pachocha L.Am., **pachorra** *f* F slowness

pachucho *adj* MED F poorly

paciencia *f* patience; **paciente** *m/f* & *adj* patient

pacificador *m*, **~a** *f* peace-maker; **pacificar** <1g> *v/t* pacify; **pacífico 1** *adj* peaceful; *persona* peaceable;

el océano Pacífico the Pacific Ocean **2** *m*: **el Pacífico** the Pacific; **pacifista 1** *adj* pacifist *atr* **2** *m/f* pacifist

paco *m*, **-a** *f* L.Am. F (*policía*) cop F

pacotilla *f*: **de ~** third-rate, lousy F; **pacotillero** *m*, **-a** *f* L.Am. street vendor

pactar <1a> **1** *v/t* agree; **~ un acuerdo** reach (an) agreement **2** *v/i* reach (an) agreement; **pacto** *m* agreement, pact

padecer <2d> **1** v/t suffer **2** v/i suffer; **~ de** have trouble with

padrastro m step-father; **padre** m father; REL Father; **de ~ y muy señor mío** terrible; **~s** parents; **¡qué ~!** Méx F brilliant!; **padrenuestro** m Lord's Prayer; **padrillo** m Rpl stallion; **padrino** m en bautizo godfather; (en boda) man who gives away the bride

padrón m register of local inhabitants

paella f GASTR paella

pág. abr (= **página**) p. (= page)

paga f pay; de niño allowance, Br pocket money; **pagado** adj paid

pagano adj pagan

pagar <1h> **1** v/t pay; compra, gastos, crimen pay for; favor repay; **¡me las pagarás!** you'll pay for this! **2** v/i pay; **~ a escote** F go Dutch F; **pagaré** m IOU

página f page; **~ web** web page; **~s amarillas** yellow pages

pago m payment; Rpl (quinta) piece of land; **~ al contado** or **en efectivo** payment in cash; **en ~ de** in payment for; **por estos ~s** F in this neck of the woods F

país m country; **~ en vías de desarrollo** developing country; **los Países Bajos** the Netherlands; **paisaje** m landscape; **paisano** m: **de ~** MIL in civilian clothes; policía in plain clothes

paja f straw; **hacerse una ~** V jerk off V; **pajar** m hayloft

pajarería f pet shop; **pajarita** f corbata bow tie; de papel paper bird; **pájaro** m bird; fig ugly customer F, nasty piece of work F; **~ carpintero** woodpecker; **matar dos ~s de un tiro** kill two birds with one stone

Pakistán Pakistan; **pakistaní** m/f & adj Pakistani

pala f spade; raqueta paddle; para servir slice; para recoger dustpan

palabra f tb fig word; **~ de honor** word of hono(u)r; **bajo ~** on parole; **en una ~** in a word; **tomar la ~** speak; **palabrota** f swearword

palacete m small palace; **palaciego** adj palace atr; **palacio** m palace; **~ de deportes** sports center (Br centre); **~ de justicia** law courts

paladar m palate

palanca f lever; **~ de cambios** AUTO gearshift, Br gear lever; **tener ~** Méx fig F have pull F o clout F

palangana f plastic bowl for washing dishes, Br washing-up bowl

palanganear <1a> v/i S.Am. show off

palanqueta f crowbar

palco m TEA box

palenque m L.Am. cockpit (in cock fighting)

Palestina Palestine; **palestino 1** adj Palestinian **2** m, **-a** f Palestinian

palestra f arena; **salir** or **saltar a la ~** fig hit the headlines

paleta f PINT palette; TÉC trowel; **paletilla** f GASTR shoulder

paleto 1 adj hick atr F, provincial **2** m, **-a** f hick F, Br yokel*

paliar <1b> v/t alleviate; dolor relieve; **paliativo** m/adj palliative

palidecer <2d> v/i de persona turn pale; **palidez** f paleness; **pálido** adj pale

palillo m para dientes toothpick; para comer chopstick

palique m: **estar de ~** F have a chat

paliza 1 f beating; (derrota) thrashing F, drubbing F; (pesadez) drag F **2** m/f F drag F

palma f palm; **dar ~s** clap (one's hands); **palmada** f pat; (manotazo) slap

palmar <1a> v/t: **~la** P kick the bucket F

palmera f BOT palm tree; (dulce) heart-shaped pastry; **palmito** m BOT palmetto; GASTR palm heart; fig F attractiveness

palmo m hand's breadth; **~ a ~** inch by inch

palo m de madera etc stick; MAR mast; de portería post, upright; **~ de golf** golf club; **~ mayor** MAR mainmast; **a medio ~** L.Am. F half-drunk; **a ~ seco** whisky straight up; **ser un ~**

L.Am. F be fantastic; *de tal ~ tal astilla* a chip off the old block F

paloma *f* pigeon; *blanca* dove; *~ mensajera* carrier pigeon; **palomar** *m* pigeon loft

palometa *f* ZO *pez* pompano

palomilla *f C.Am.*, *Méx* F gang

palomita *f Méx* checkmark, *Br* tick; *~s pl de maíz* popcorn *sg*

palpable *adj fig* palpable; **palpar** <1a> *v/t con las manos* feel, touch; *fig* feel

palpitación *f* palpitation; **palpitante** *adj corazón* pounding; *cuestión* burning; **palpitar** <1a> *v/i del corazón* pound; *Rpl fig* have a hunch F, have a feeling

palta *f S.Am.* BOT avocado

palto *m S.Am.* jacket

paludismo *m* MED malaria

palurdo 1 *adj* hick *atr* F, provincial **2** *m*, *-a f* F hick F, *Br* yokel F

pamela *f* picture hat

pampa *f* GEOG pampa, prairie; *a la ~ Rpl* in the open

pamplinas *fpl* nonsense *sg*

pan *m* bread; *un ~* a loaf; *~ francés L.Am.* French bread; *~ integral* wholemeal bread; *~ de molde* sliced bread; *~ de barra* French bread; *~ rallado* breadcrumbs *pl*; *~ tostado* toast; *ser ~ comido* F be easy as pie F

pana *f* corduroy

panacea *f* panacea

panadería *f* baker's shop; **panadero** *m*, *-a f* baker

panal *m* honeycomb

Panamá Panama; *el Canal de ~* the Panama Canal; *Ciudad de ~* Panama city; **panameño 1** *adj* Panamanian **2** *m*, *-a f* Panamanian

pancarta *f* placard

panceta *f* belly pork

páncreas *m inv* ANAT

panda *m* ZO panda

pandereta *f* tambourine

pandilla *f* group; *de delincuentes* gang

panecillo *m* (bread) roll

panel *m tb grupo de personas* panel; *~ solar* solar panel

panela *f L.Am.* brown sugar loaf

panera *f* bread basket

panfleto *m* pamphlet

pánico *m* panic; *sembrar el ~* spread panic

panocha, panoja *f* ear

panoli *adj* F dopey

panorama *m* panorama; **panorámico** *adj*: *vista -a* panoramic view

panqueque *m L.Am.* pancake

pantalla *f* TV, INFOR screen; *de lámpara* shade; *pequeña ~ fig* small screen

pantalón *m*, **pantalones** *mpl* pants *pl*, *Br* trousers *pl*; *llevar los pantalones fig* F wear the pants (*Br* trousers) F

pantano *m* reservoir

panteón *m* pantheon

pantera *f* ZO panther

pantomima *f* pantomime

pantorrilla *f* ANAT calf

pantufla *f* slipper

panty *m* pantyhose *pl*, *Br* tights *pl*

panza *f de persona* belly

pañal *m* diaper, *Br* nappy

paño *m* cloth; *~ de cocina* dishtowel; **pañuelo** *m* handkerchief; *el mundo es un ~ fig* it's a small world

papa 1 *m* Pope **2** *f L.Am.* potato

papá *m* F pop F, dad F; *~s L.Am.* parents; *Papá Noel* Santa Claus

papada *f* double chin

papagayo *m* ZO parrot

papal 1 *adj* papal **2** *m L.Am.* potato field

papalote *m Méx* kite

papanatas *m/f inv* F dope F, dimwit F

paparruchas *fpl* F baloney *sg* F

papaya *f* BOT papaya

papel *m* paper; *trozo* piece of paper; TEA, *fig* role; *~ de aluminio* foil; *~ de envolver* wrapping paper; *~ de regalo* giftwrap; *~ higiénico* toilet paper *o* tissue; *~ reciclado* recycled paper; *perder los ~es* lose control; *ser ~ mojado fig* not be worth the paper it's written on; **papelada** *f L.Am.* farce; **papeleo** *m* paperwork; **papelera** *f* wastepaper basket; **papelería** *f* stationer's shop; **papelerío** *m L.Am.* F muddle, mess; **papeleta** *f de rifa* raffle ticket; *fig* chore; **~ de voto** ballot paper

paperas *fpl* MED mumps

papilla *f para bebés* baby food; *para enfermos* puree; **hacer ~ a alguien** F beat s.o. to a pulp F

papista *adj*: **ser más ~ que el papa** hold extreme views

paquete *m* package, parcel; *de cigarrillos* packet; F *en moto* (pillion) passenger

Paquistán Pakistan; **paquistaní** *m/f & adj* Pakistani

par 1 *f* par; **es bella a la ~ que inteligente** she is beautiful as well as intelligent, she is both beautiful and intelligent 2 *m* pair; **abierto de ~ en ~** wide open; **un ~ de** a pair of

para *prp* ◊ *dirección* toward(s); *ir ~* head for; *va ~ directora* she's going to end up as manager ◊ *tiempo* for; *listo ~ mañana* ready for tomorrow; **~ siempre** forever; **diez ~ las ocho** *L.Am.* ten of eight, ten to eight ◊ *finalidad*: **lo hace ~ ayudarte** he does it (in order) to help you; **~ que** so that; **¿~ qué te marchas?** what are you leaving for?; **~ mí** for me; **lo heredó todo ~ morir a los 30** he inherited it all, only to die at 30

parabólica *f* satellite dish

parabrisas *m inv* AUTO windshield, *Br* windscreen; **paracaídas** *m inv* parachute; **paracaidista** *m/f* parachutist; MIL paratrooper; **parachoques** *m inv* AUTO fender, *Br* bumper

parada *f* stop; **~ de autobús** bus stop; **~ de taxis** taxi rank

paradero *m* whereabouts *sg*; *L.Am.* → *parada*

parado 1 *adj* unemployed; *L.Am.* (*de pie*) standing (up); **salir bien/mal ~** come off well/badly 2 *m*, **-a** *f* unemployed person

paradoja *f* paradox; **paradójico** *adj* paradoxical

parador *m Esp* parador (*state-run luxury hotel*)

parafernalia *f* F paraphernalia

parafina *f* kerosene, *Br* paraffin

paraguas *m inv* umbrella

Paraguay Paraguay; **paraguayo** 1 *adj* Paraguayan 2 *m*, **-a** *f* Paraguayan

paraíso *m* paradise; **~ fiscal** tax haven

paralelismo *m* parallel; **paralelo** *m/adj* parallel

parálisis *f tb fig* paralysis; **paralítico** 1 *adj* paralytic 2 *m*, **-a** *f* person who is paralyzed; **paralización** *f tb fig* paralysis; **paralizar** <1f> *v/t* MED paralyze; *actividad* bring to a halt; *país, economía* paralyze, bring to a standstill

parámetro *m* parameter

paramilitar *adj* paramilitary

parangón *m*: **sin ~** incomparable

paranoia *f* paranoia; **paranoico** 1 *adj* MED paranoid 2 *m*, **-a** *f* MED person suffering from paranoia

paranormal *adj* paranormal

parapente *m* hang glider; *actividad* hang gliding

parapeto *m* parapet

parapléjico 1 *adj* MED paraplegic 2 *m*, **-a** *f* paraplegic

parar <1a> 1 *v/t* stop; *L.Am.* (*poner de pie*) stand up 2 *v/i* stop; *en alojamiento* stay; **~ de llover** stop raining; *ir a* **~** end up 3 *v/r* **~se** stop; *L.Am.* (*ponerse de pie*) stand up

pararrayos *m inv* lightning rod

parásito *m* parasite

parcela *f* lot, *Br* plot

parchar <1a> *v/t L.Am.* patch; (*arreglar*) repair; **parche** *m* patch

parcial *adj* (*partidario*) bias(s)ed

pardo 1 *adj* color dun; *L.Am. desp* half-breed *desp*, *Br tb* half-caste *desp* 2 *m color* dun; *L.Am. desp* half-breed *desp*

parecer 1 *m* opinion, view; **al ~** apparently 2 <2d> *v/i* seem, look; *me parece que* I think (that), it seems to me that; *me parece bien* it seems fine to me; *¿qué te parece?* what do you think? 3 *v/r* **~se** resemble

each other; **~se a alguien** resemble
s.o.; **parecido 1** *adj* similar **2** *m*
similarity
pared *f* wall; **subirse por las ~es** F
hit the roof F
pareja *f* (*conjunto de dos*) pair; *en una
relación* couple; *de una persona* partner; *de un objeto* other one
parejo *adj L.Am. suelo* level, even;
andar ~s be neck and neck; **llega-
ron ~s** they arrived at the same
time
paréntesis *m inv* parenthesis; *fig*
break; **entre ~** *fig* by the way
pareo *m* wrap-around skirt
parida *f* P stupid thing to say / do
pariente *m/f* relative
paripé *m*: **hacer el ~** F put on an act F
parir <3a> **1** *v/i* give birth **2** *v/t* give
birth to
París Paris; **parisino 1** *adj* Parisian
2 *m*, **-a** *f* Parisian
parka *f* parka
parking *m* parking lot, *Br* car park
parlamentario 1 *adj* parliamentary
2 *m*, **-a** *f* member of parliament;
parlamento *m* parliament
parlanchín *adj* chatty; **parlante** *m*
L.Am. loudspeaker
parlotear <1a> *v/i* chatter
parmesano *m/adj* Parmesan
paro *m* unemployment; **estar en ~**
be unemployed; **~ cardíaco** cardiac
arrest
parodia *f* parody
parpadear <1a> *v/i* blink; **parpa-
deo** *m* blinking; **párpado** *m* eye lid
parque *m* park; *para bebé* playpen; **~
de atracciones** amusement park; **~
de bomberos** fire station; **~
nacional** national park; **~ natural**
nature reserve; **~ temático** theme
park
parqué *m* → **parquet**
parquear <1a> *v/t L.Am.* park
parquet *m* parquet
parquímetro *m* parking meter
parra *f* (*grape*) vine
párrafo *m* paragraph
parranda *f*: **andar** *or* **irse de ~** F go
out on the town F

parricidio *m* parricide
parrilla *f* broiler, *Br* grill; **a la ~**
broiled, *Br* grilled; **parrillada** *f*
L.Am. barbecue
párroco *m* parish priest; **parroquia** *f*
REL parish; COM clientele, custom-
ers *pl*
parsimonia *f* calm
parte 1 *m* report; **~ meteorológico**
weather report; **dar ~ a alguien** inform s.o. **2** *f trozo* part; JUR party;
alguna ~ somewhere; **ninguna ~**
nowhere; **otra ~** somewhere else;
de ~ de on behalf of; **en ~** partly; **en**
or **por todas ~s** everywhere; **la
mayor ~ de** the majority of, most of;
por otra ~ moreover; **estar de ~ de
alguien** be on s.o.'s side; **formar ~
de** form part of; **tomar ~ en** take
part in
participación *f* participation; **participante** *m/f* participant; **participar**
<1a> **1** *v/t una noticia* announce
2 *v/i* take part (**en** in), participate
(**en** in); **participio** *m* GRAM participle
partícula *f* particle
particular 1 *adj clase, propiedad* private; *asunto* personal; (*específico*)
particular; (*especial*) peculiar; **en ~**
in particular **2** *m* (*persona*) individual; **~es** particulars; **particu-
laridad** *f* peculiarity
partida *f* en *juego* game; (*remesa*)
consignment; *documento* certificate;
~ de nacimiento birth certificate;
partidario 1 *adj*: **ser ~ de** be in
favo(u)r of **2** *m*, **-a** *f* supporter; **par-
tidismo** *m* partisanship; **partido** *m*
POL party; DEP game; **sacar ~ de**
take advantage of; **tomar ~** take
sides
partir <3a> **1** *v/t* (*dividir, repartir*)
split; (*romper*) break open, split
open; (*cortar*) cut **2** *v/i* (*irse*) leave; **a
~ de hoy** (starting) from today; **a ~
de ahora** from now on; **~ de** *fig* start
from **3** *v/r* **~se** (*romperse*) break;
~se de risa F split one's sides laughing F
partitura *f* MÚS score

parto *m* birth; *fig* creation

parvulario *m* kindergarten

pasa *f* raisin

pasable *adj* passable

pasada *f con trapo* wipe; *de pintura* coat; *de ~* in passing; *¡qué ~!* F that's incredible! F; **pasadizo** *m* passage; **pasado 1** *adj tiempo* last; *el lunes ~* last Monday; *~ de moda* old-fashioned **2** *m* past

pasaje *m* (*billete*) ticket; MÚS, *de texto* passage; **pasajero 1** *adj* temporary; *relación* brief **2** *m*, *-a f* passenger

pasamano(s) *m* handrail

pasamontañas *m inv* balaclava (helmet)

pasaporte *m* passport

pasar <1a> **1** *v/t* pass; *el tiempo* spend; *un lugar* go past; *frontera* cross; *problemas, dificultades* experience; AUTO (*adelantar*) pass, *Br* overtake; *una película* show; *para ~ el tiempo* (in order) to pass the time; *~ la mano por* run one's hand through; *~lo bien* have a good time **2** *v/i* (*suceder*) happen; *en juegos* pass; *~ de alguien* F not want anything to do with s.o.; *paso de coger el teléfono* F I can't be bothered to pick up the phone; *pasé a visitarla* I dropped by to see her; *~ de moda* go out of fashion; *~ por* go by; *pasé por la tienda* I stopped off at the shop; *pasa por aquí* come this way; *dejar ~ oportunidad* miss; *hacerse ~ por* pass o.s. off as; *pasaré por tu casa* I'll drop by your house; *¡pasa!* come in; *¿qué pasa?* what's happening?, what's going on?; *¿qué te pasa?* what's the matter?; *pase lo que pase* whatever happens, come what may **3** *v/r* *~se tb fig* go too far; *del tiempo* pass, go by; (*usar el tiempo*) spend; *de molestia, dolor* go away; *~se al enemigo* go over to the enemy; *se le pasó llamar* he forgot to call

pasarela *f* catwalk

pasatiempo *m* pastime

Pascua *f* Easter; *¡felices ~s!* Merry Christmas!

pase *m tb* DEP, TAUR pass; *en el cine* showing; *~ de modelos* fashion show

pasear <1a> **1** *v/t* take for a walk; (*exhibir*) show off **2** *v/i* walk **3** *v/r* *~se* walk; *paseo m* walk; *~ marítimo* seafront; *dar un ~* go for a walk; *mandar a alguien a ~ fig* F tell s.o. to get lost

pasillo *m* corridor; *en avión, cine* aisle

pasión *f* passion

pasividad *f* passivity; **pasivo** *adj* passive

pasmar <1a> *v/t* amaze, astonish

paso *m* step; (*manera de andar*) walk; (*ritmo*) pace, rate; *de agua* flow; *de tráfico* movement; (*cruce*) crossing; *de tiempo* passing; (*huella*) footprint; *~ a nivel* grade crossing, *Br* level crossing; *~ de peatones* crosswalk, pedestrian crossing; *a este ~ fig* at this rate; *de ~* on the way; *estar de ~* be passing through

pasta *f sustancia* paste; GASTR pasta; P (*dinero*) dough P; *~ de dientes* toothpaste; *~s de té* type of cookie (*Br* biscuit)

pastel *m* GASTR cake; *pintura, color* pastel; **pastelería** *f* cake shop; **pastelero** *m*, *-a f* pastry cook

paste(u)rizar <1f> *v/t* pasteurize

pastilla *f* tablet; *de jabón* bar; *a toda ~* F at top speed F, flat out F

pasto *m* (*hierba*) grass; *a todo ~* F for all one is worth F; **pastor** *m* shepherd; REL pastor; *~ alemán* German shepherd

pata¹ *m/f Pe* F pal F, buddy F

pata² *f* leg; *a cuatro ~s* on all fours; *meter la ~* F put one's foot in it F; *tener mala ~* F be unlucky; **patada** *f* kick; *dar una ~* kick; **patalear** <1a> *v/i* stamp one's feet; *fig* kick and scream

patata *f* potato; *~s fritas de sartén* French fries, *Br* chips; *de bolsa* chips, *Br* crisps

patatús m: *le dio un* ~ F he had a fit F

paté m paté

patear <1a> v/t & v/i *L.Am. de animal* kick

patentar <1a> v/t patent; **patente 1** adj clear, obvious **2** f patent; *L.Am.* AUTO license plate, *Br* numberplate

paternidad f paternity, fatherhood; **paterno** adj paternal

patético adj pitiful

patíbulo m scaffold

patilla f de gafas arm; ~s *barba* sideburns

patín m skate; ~ (*de ruedas*) *en línea* rollerblade®; **patinador** m, ~a f skater; **patinaje** m skating; ~ *artístico* figure skating; ~ *sobre hielo* ice-skating; ~ *sobre ruedas* roller-skating; **patinar** <1a> v/i skate; **patinazo** m skid; *fig* F blunder; *dar un* ~ skid; **patinete** m scooter

patio m courtyard, patio; ~ *de butacas* TEA orchestra, *Br* stalls pl

pato m ZO duck; *pagar el* ~ F take the rap F, *Br* carry the can F

patojo adj *Chi* F squat

patológico adj pathological

patoso adj clumsy

patraña f tall story

patria f homeland

patriarca m patriarch

patrimonio m heritage; ~ *artístico* artistic heritage

patriota m/f patriot; **patriótico** adj patriotic; **patriotismo** m patriotism

patrocinador m, ~a f sponsor; **patrocinar** <1a> v/t sponsor; **patrocinio** m sponsorship

patrón m (*jefe*) boss; REL patron saint; *para costura* pattern; (*modelo*) standard; MAR skipper; **patrona** f (*jefa*) boss; REL patron saint; **patronal** f employers pl

patrulla f patrol; **patrullar** <1a> v/t patrol; **patrullero** m patrolman

paulatino adj gradual

pausa f pause; *en una actividad* break; MÚS rest; ~ *publicitaria* commercial break; **pausado** adj slow, deliberate

pauta f guideline; *marcar la* ~ set the guidelines

pavimento m pavement, *Br* road surface

pavo 1 adj *L.Am.* F stupid **2** m ZO turkey; ~ *real* peacock

pavonearse <1a> v/r boast (*de* about)

pavor m terror; *me da* ~ it terrifies me

payada f *Rpl* improvized ballad

payador m *Rpl* gaucho singer

payasadas fpl antics; *hacer* ~ fool o clown around; **payaso** m clown

paz f peace; *dejar en* ~ leave alone

PC abr (= *Partido Comunista*) CP (= Communist Party)

P.D. abr (= *posdata*) PS (= postscript)

pe: *de* ~ *a pa* F from start to finish

peaje m *dinero, lugar* toll

peatón m pedestrian; **peatonal** adj pedestrian atr

pebete m, ~a f *Rpl* F kid F

peca f freckle

pecado m sin; **pecador** m, ~a f sinner; **pecaminoso** adj sinful

pecar <1g> v/i sin; ~ *de ingenuo* / *generoso* be very naive / generous

pecera f fish tank, aquarium

pecho m (*caja torácica*) chest; (*mama*) breast; *tomar algo a* ~ take sth to heart; **pechuga** f GASTR breast; *L.Am. fig* F (*caradura*) nerve F

pecoso adj freckled

pectoral adj ANAT pectoral

peculiar adj peculiar, odd; (*característico*) typical; **peculiaridad** f (*característica*) peculiarity

pedagogía f education; **pedagogo** m, ~a f teacher

pedal m pedal; **pedalear** <1a> v/i pedal

pedante 1 adj pedantic; (*presuntuoso*) pretentious **2** m/f pedant; (*presuntuoso*) pretentious individual; **pedantería** f pedantry; (*presunción*) pretentiousness

pedazo m piece, bit; ~ *de bruto* F

blockhead F; *hacer ~s* F smash to bits F

pederasta *m* pederast

pedestal *m* pedestal

pediatra *m/f* p(a)ediatrician

pedicura *f* pedicure; **pedicuro** *m*, **-a** *f* pedicurist, *Br* chiropodist

pedido *m* order

pedigrí *m* pedigree

pedigüeño *m*, **-a** *f* person who is always asking to borrow things, moocher F

pedir <3l> **1** *v/t* ask for; (*necesitar*) need; *en bar, restaurante* order; *me pidió que no fuera* he asked me not to go **2** *v/i mendigar* beg; *en bar, restaurante* order

pedo 1 *adj* drunk **2** *m* F fart F; *agarrarse un ~* F get plastered F; *tirarse o echar un ~* F fart F; **pedorreta** *f* F Bronx cheer F, *Br* raspberry F

pedrada *f* blow with a stone; *me dio una ~ en la cabeza* he hit me over the head with a stone; **pedregal** *m* stony ground; **pedregoso** *adj* stony

Pedro *m*: *como ~ por su casa fig* F as if he/she owned the place

pega *f* snag F, hitch F; **poner ~s** raise objections; **pegadizo** *adj* catchy; **pegado** *adj* (*adherido*) stuck (*a* to); *estar ~ a* (*cerca de*) be right up against; *estar ~ a alguien fig* follow s.o. around, be s.o.'s shadow; **pegajoso** *adj* sticky; *fig: persona* clingy; **pegamento** *m* glue

pegar <1h> **1** *v/t* (*golpear*) hit; (*adherir*) stick, glue; *bofetada, susto, resfriado* give; *~ un grito* shout; *no me pega la gana Méx* F I don't feel like it **2** *v/i* (*golpear*) hit; (*adherir*) stick; *del sol* beat down; (*armonizar*) go (together) **3** *v/r* **~se** *resfriado* catch; *acento* pick up; *susto* give o.s.; *~se un golpe/un tiro* hit/shoot o.s.; *pegársela a alguien* F con s.o. F

pegatina *f* sticker

pegote *m* F (*cosa fea*) eyesore

peinado *m* hairstyle; **peinador** *m*, **~a** *f L.Am.* hairdresser; **peinar** <1a>

1 *v/t tb fig* comb; *~ a alguien* comb s.o.'s hair **2** *v/r* **~se** comb one's hair; **peine** *m* comb

p. ej. *abr* (= *por ejemplo*) e.g. (= exempli gratia, for example)

Pekín Beijing

pela *f* F peseta

peladero *m L.Am.* vacant lot

peladilla *f* sugared almond

pelado *adj* peeled; *fig* bare; F (*sin dinero*) broke F; **pelar** <1a> **1** *v/t manzana, patata etc* peel; *hace un frío que pela* F it's freezing **2** *v/r* **~se** (*cortarse el pelo*) have a haircut; *Rpl* F (*chismear*) gossip

pelazón *f C.Am.* backbiting

peldaño *m* step

pelea *f* fight; **pelear** <1a> **1** *v/i* fight **2** *v/r* **~se** fight

pelele *m* puppet

peleón *adj* argumentative; *vino ~* F jug wine, *Br* plonk F

peletería *f* furrier's

peliagudo *adj* tricky

pelícano *m* ZO pelican

película *f* movie, film; FOT film; *~ del Oeste* Western; *de ~* F awesome F, fantastic F

peligrar <1a> *v/i* be at risk; **peligro** *m* danger; *correr ~* be in danger; *poner en ~* endanger, put at risk; **peligroso** *adj* dangerous

pelillo *m*: *¡~s a la mar fig* F let's bury the hatchet

pelín: *un ~* F a (little) bit

pelirrojo *adj* red-haired, red-headed

pellejo *m de animal* skin, hide; *salvar el ~ fig* F save one's (own) skin F

pellizcar <1g> *v/t* pinch; **pellizco** *m* pinch; *un buen ~* F a tidy sum F

pelma *f adj* annoying **2** *m/f* pain F; **pelmazo** *m*, **-a** *f* F pain F

pelo *m de persona, de perro* hair; *de animal* fur; *tiene el ~ muy largo* he has very long hair; *a ~* F (*sin preparación*) unprepared; *montar a ~* ride bareback; *por los ~s* F by a whisker F, by the skin of one's teeth F; *tomar el ~ a alguien* pull s.o.'s leg F

P

pelota 1 *f* ball; **~s** F nuts F, balls F; **en ~s** P stark naked; **hacer la ~ a alguien** suck up to s.o. F **2** *m/f* F creep F; **pelotazo** *m*: **rompió el cristal de un ~** he smashed the window with a ball; **pelotero** *m*, **-a** *f* L.Am. (base)ball player

pelotón *m* MIL squad; DEP bunch, pack

peluca *f* wig

peluche *m* soft toy; **oso de ~** teddy bear

peludo *adj persona* hairy; *animal* furry

peluquearse <1a> *v/r* L.Am. get one's hair cut; **peluquería** *f* hairdresser's; **peluquero** *m*, **-a** *f* hairdresser; **peluquín** *m* toupee, hairpiece

pelusa *f* fluff

pelvis *f inv* ANAT pelvis

pena *f* (*tristeza*) sadness, sorrow; (*congoja*) grief, distress; (*lástima*) pity; JUR sentence; **~ capital** death penalty, capital punishment; **~ de muerte** death penalty; **no vale** or **no merece la ~** it's not worth it; **¡qué ~!** what a shame *o* pity!; **a duras ~s** with great difficulty; **me da ~** L.Am. I'm ashamed; **penal** *adj* penal; **derecho ~** criminal law; **penalidad** *f fig* hardship; **penalización** *f acción* penalization; DEP penalty; **penalizar** <1f> *v/t* penalize; **penalty** *m* DEP penalty

penca 1 *adj Chi* soft, weak **2** *f* L.Am. (*nopal*) leaf of the prickly pear plant

pendejada *f* L.Am. stupid thing to do

pendejo 1 *m* (*pelea*) fight **2** *m*, **-a** *f* L.Am. F dummy F

pendenciero *adj* troublemaker

pendiente 1 *adj* unresolved, unfinished; *cuenta* unpaid **2** *m* earring **3** *f* slope

pendón 1 *adj* swinging F **2** *m*, **-ona** *f* F swinger F

péndulo *m* pendulum

pene *m* ANAT penis

penetración *f* penetration; **penetrante** *adj mirada* penetrating; *soni-*

do piercing; *frío* bitter; *herida* deep; *análisis* incisive; **penetrar** <1a> *v/i* penetrate; (*entrar*) enter; *de un líquido* seep in

penicilina *f* penicillin

península *f* peninsula; **~ Ibérica** Iberian Peninsula

penique *m* penny

penitencia *f* penitence; **penitenciado** *m* L.Am. prisoner, convict; **penitenciario** *adj* penitentiary *atr*, prison *atr*

penoso *adj* distressing; *trabajo* laborious

pensamiento *m* thought; BOT pansy; **pensar** <1k> **1** *v/t* think about; (*opinar*) think; **¡ni ~lo!** don't even think about it **2** *v/i* think (**en** about); **pensativo** *adj* thoughtful

pensión *f hotel* rooming house, *Br* guesthouse; *dinero* pension; **~ alimenticia** child support, *Br* maintenance; **~ completa** American plan, *Br* full board; **pensionista** *m/f* pensioner

pentagrama *m* MÚS stave

pentatlón *m* DEP pentathlon

penúltimo *adj* penultimate

penumbra *f* half-light

penuria *f* shortage (**de** of); (*pobreza*) poverty

peña *f* crag, cliff; (*roca*) rock; F *de amigos* group, circle; **peñasco** *m* boulder; **peñón** *m*: **el Peñón de Gibraltar** the Rock of Gibraltar

peón *m en ajedrez* pawn; *trabajador* labo(u)rer

peor *adj comp* worse; **de mal en ~** from bad to worse

pepa *f* L.Am. (*semilla*) seed; **soltar la ~** F spill the beans

pepinillo *m* gherkin; **pepino** *m* cucumber; **me importa un ~** F I don't give a damn F

pepita *f* pip

pequeño 1 *adj* small, little; **de ~** when I was small *o* little **2** *m*, **-a** *f* little one

pequinés *m* ZO Pekinese, Peke F

pera *f* pear; **peral** *m* pear tree

perca *f pez* perch

percance *m* mishap

percatarse <1a> *v/r* notice; **~ de algo** notice sth

percebe *m* ZO barnacle

percepción *f* perception; COM *acto* receipt

percha *f* coat hanger; *gancho* coat hook; **perchero** *m* coat rack

percibir <3a> *v/t* perceive; COM *sueldo* receive

percusión *f* MÚS percussion

perdedor *m*, **~a** *f* loser; **perder** <2g> **1** *v/t objeto* lose; *tren, avión* etc miss; *el tiempo* waste **2** *v/i* lose; **echar a ~** ruin; **echarse a ~ de alimento** go bad **3** *v/r* **~se** get lost; **perdición** *f* downfall; **pérdida** *f* loss; **perdido** *adj* lost; **ponerse ~** get filthy

perdigón *m* pellet

perdiz *f* ZO partridge

perdón *m* pardon; REL forgiveness; *pedir* ~ say sorry, apologize; **¡~!** sorry; **perdonar** <1a> *v/t* forgive; JUR pardon; **~ algo a alguien** forgive s.o. sth; **¡perdone!** sorry; **perdone, ¿tiene hora?** excuse me, do you have the time?

perdurar <1a> *v/i* endure

perecedero *adj* perishable; **perecer** <2d> *v/i* perish

peregrinación *f* pilgrimage; **peregrinar** <1a> *v/i* go on a pilgrimage; **peregrino** *m*, **-a** *f* pilgrim

perejil *m* BOT parsley

perenne *adj* BOT perennial

perentorio *adj* (*urgente*) urgent, pressing; (*apremiante*) peremptory

pereza *f* laziness; **perezoso 1** *adj* lazy **2** *m* ZO sloth

perfección *f* perfection; **a la ~** perfectly, to perfection; **perfeccionamiento** *m* perfecting; **perfeccionar** <1a> *v/t* perfect; **perfeccionista** *m/f* perfectionist; **perfecto** *adj* perfect

pérfido *adj* treacherous

perfil *m* profile; **de ~** in profile, from the side

perforación *f* puncture; **perforadora** *f* punch; **perforar** <1a> *v/t* pierce;

calle dig up

perfumar <1a> *v/t* perfume; **perfume** *m* perfume; **perfumería** *f* perfume shop

pergamino *m* parchment

pergenio *m*, **-a** *f* Rpl F kid F

pericia *f* expertise

pericote *m* Chi, Pe ZO large rat

periferia *f* periphery; *de ciudad* outskirts *pl*

perilla *f* goatee; **me viene de ~** F that'll be very useful; **tu visita me viene de ~** F you've come at just the right time

perímetro *m* perimeter

periódico 1 *adj* periodic **2** *m* newspaper; **periodismo** *m* journalism; **periodista** *m/f* journalist; **período**, **periodo** *m* period

peripecia *f* adventure

periquete *m*: **en un ~** F in a second, in no time F

periquito *m* ZO budgerigar

periscopio *m* periscope

perito 1 *adj* expert **2** *m*, **-a** *f* expert; COM *en seguros* loss adjuster

perjudicar <1g> *v/t* harm, damage; **perjudicial** *adj* harmful, damaging; **perjuicio** *m* harm, damage; **sin ~ de** without affecting

perjurio *m* perjury

perla *f* pearl; **nos vino de ~s** F it suited us fine F

permanecer <2d> *v/i* remain, stay; **permanente 1** *adj* permanent **2** *f* perm

permeable *adj* permeable

permisible *adj* permissible; **permisivo** *adj* permissive; **permiso** *m* permission; *documento* permit; **~ de conducir** driver's license, *Br* driving licence; **~ de residencia** residence permit; **con ~** excuse me; **estar de ~** be on leave; **permitir** <3a> **1** *v/t* permit, allow **2** *v/r* **~se** afford; **~se el lujo de** permit o.s. the luxury of

pernicioso *adj* harmful

pernoctar <1a> *v/i* spend the night

pero 1 *conj* but **2** *m* flaw, defect; **no hay ~s que valgan** no excuses

perogrullada f platitude

peronismo m Peronism; **peronista** m/f Peronist

perorata f F lecture

perpendicular adj perpendicular

perpetrar <1a> v/t crimen perpetrate, commit

perpetuar <1e> v/t perpetuate; **perpetuidad** f: **a** ~ in perpetuity; **perpetuo** adj fig perpetual

perplejidad f perplexity; **perplejo** adj puzzled, perplexed

perra f dog; **el perro y la** ~ the dog and the bitch; ~**s** F pesetas; **perrera** f kennels pl; **perrería** f F dirty trick; **perrito** m: ~ **caliente** GASTR hot dog; **perro** m dog; ~ **callejero** stray; ~ **guardián** guard dog; ~ **lazarillo** seeing eye dog, Br guide dog; ~ **pastor** sheepdog; **llevarse como el** ~ **y el gato** fig fight like cat and dog; **hace un tiempo de** ~**s** F the weather is lousy F

persecución f pursuit; (acoso) persecution; **perseguidor** m, -a f persecutor; **perseguir** <3l & 3d> v/t pursue; delincuente look for; (molestar) pester; (acosar) persecute

perseverancia f perseverance; **perseverar** <1a> v/i persevere (**en** with)

persiana f blind

pérsico adj Persian

persignarse <1a> v/r cross o.s.

persistente adj persistent; **persistir** <3a> v/i persist

persona f person; **quince** ~**s** fifteen people; **personaje** m TEA character; famoso celebrity; **personal 1** adj personal **2** m personnel, staff; **personalidad** f personality; **personalizar** <1f> v/t personalize; **personificar** <1g> v/t personify, embody

perspectiva f perspective; fig point of view; ~**s** pl outlook sg, prospects

perspicacia f shrewdness, perspicacity

persuadir <3a> v/t persuade; **persuasión** f persuasion; **persuasivo** adj persuasive

pertenecer <2d> v/i belong (**a** to); **pertenencias** fpl belongings

pértiga f pole; **salto con** ~ DEP pole vault

pertinaz adj persistent; (terco) obstinate

pertinente adj relevant, pertinent

pertrechos mpl MIL equipment sg

perturbar <1a> v/t disturb; reunión disrupt

Perú Peru; **peruano 1** adj Peruvian **2** m, -a f Peruvian

perversión f perversion; **perverso** adj perverted; **pervertido** m, -a f pervert; **pervertir** <3i> v/t pervert

pesa f para balanza weight; DEP shot; C.Am., W.I. butcher's shop

pesadez f fig drag F

pesadilla f nightmare

pesado 1 adj objeto heavy; libro, clase etc tedious, boring; trabajo tough **2** m, -a f bore; **¡qué** ~ **es!** F he's a real pain F

pésame m condolences pl

pesar <1a> **1** v/t weigh **2** v/i be heavy; (influir) carry weight; fig weigh heavily (**sobre** on); **me pesa tener que informarle ...** I regret to have to inform you ... **3** m sorrow; **a** ~ **de** in spite of, despite

pesca f actividad fishing; (peces) fish pl; **pescadería** f fish shop; **pescadero** m, -a f fishmonger; **pescadilla** f pez whiting; **pescado** m GASTR fish; **pescador** m fisherman; **pescar** <1g> **1** v/t un pez, resfriado etc catch; (intentar tomar) fish for; trabajo, marido etc land **2** v/i fish

pescuezo m neck

pese: ~ **a** despite

pesero m L.Am. minibus; Méx (collective) taxi

peseta f peseta; **pesetero** adj F money-grubbing F

pesimismo m pessimism; **pesimista 1** adj pessimistic **2** m/f pessimist

pésimo adj sup awful, terrible

peso m weight; moneda peso; **de** ~ fig weighty

pesquero 1 *adj* fishing *atr* **2** *m* fishing boat

pesquisa *f* investigation

pestaña *f* eyelash; **pestañear** <1a> *v/i* flutter one's eyelashes; **sin ~** *fig* without batting an eyelid

peste *f* MED plague; F *olor* stink F; **echar ~s** F curse and swear

pesticida *m* pesticide

pestilente *adj* foul-smelling

pestillo *m* (*picaporte*) door handle; (*cerradura*) bolt

petaca *f para tabaco* tobacco pouch; *para bebida* hip flask; *C.Am.* F *insecto* ladybug, *Br* ladybird

pétalo *m* petal

petanca *f type of bowls*

petardo 1 *m* firecracker **2** *m*, **-a** *f* F nerd F

petate *m* kit bag; *L.Am.* F *en el suelo* mat

petición *f* request; **a ~ de** at the request of

petirrojo *m* ZO robin

petiso *L.Am.* **1** *m*, **-a** *f* F shorty F **2** *m* pony

peto *m* bib; **pantalón de ~** overalls *pl*, *Br* dungarees *pl*

petrificado *adj* petrified

petróleo *m* oil, petroleum; **petrolero 1** *adj* oil *atr* **2** *m* MAR oil tanker; **petrolífero** *adj* oil *atr*; **petroquímica** *f* petrochemical

petulante *adj* smug

peyorativo *adj* pejorative

pez *m* ZO fish; **~ espada** swordfish; **~ gordo** F big shot F; **estar ~ en algo** F be clueless about sth F

pezón *m* nipple

pezuña *f* ZO hoof

piadoso *adj* pious

pianista *m/f* pianist; **piano** *m* piano; **~ de cola** grand piano

piar <1c> *v/i* tweet, chirrup

PIB *abr* (= **producto interior bruto**) GDP (= gross domestic product)

pibe *m*, **-a** *f Rpl* F kid F

picada *f de serpiente* bite; *de abeja* sting; *L.Am. para comer* snacks *pl*, nibbles *pl*; *Rpl* (*camino*) path; **picadero** *m escuela* riding school;

picado 1 *adj diente* decayed; *mar* rough, choppy; *carne* ground, *Br* minced; *verdura* minced, *Br* finely chopped; *fig* offended **2** *m L.Am.* dive; **caer en ~ de precios** nosedive, plummet; **picadora** *f en cocina* mincer; **picadura** *f de reptil, mosquito* bite; *de avispa* sting; *tabaco* cut tobacco

picaflor *m L.Am.* ZO hummingbird; *fig* womanizer

picante 1 *adj* hot, spicy; *chiste* risqué **2** *m* hot spice

picaporte *m* door handle

picar <1g> **1** *v/t de mosquito, serpiente* bite; *de avispa* sting; *de ave* peck; *carne* grind, *Br* mince; *verdura* mince, *Br* finely chop; TAUR jab with a lance; (*molestar*) annoy; *la curiosidad* pique **2** *v/i* tb *fig* take the bait; *L.Am. de la comida* be hot; (*producir picor*) itch; *del sol* burn

picardía *f* (*astucia*) craftiness, slyness; (*travesura*) mischievousness; *Méx* (*taco, palabrota*) swearing, swearwords *pl*

pícaro *adj persona* crafty, sly; *comentario* mischievous

picarón *m Méx, Chi, Pe* (*buñuelo*) fritter

picatoste *m* piece of fried bread

picha *f* V prick V

pichicato *m Pe, Bol* P coke P

pichincha *f L.Am.* bargain

pichón *m L.Am.* ORN chick; F (*novato*) rookie F

Picio: más feo que ~ F as ugly as sin F

picnic *m* (*pl* ~s) picnic

pico *m* ZO beak; F (*boca*) mouth; *de montaña* peak; *herramienta* pickax(e); **a las tres y ~** some time after three o'clock; **cerrar el ~** F shut one's mouth F

picor *m* itch

picota *f* bigarreau (*type of sweet cherry*)

picotazo *m* peck; **picotear** <1a> *v/t* peck

pido *vb* → **pedir**

pie *m* foot; *de estatua, lámpara* base; **a**

~ on foot; **de** ~ standing; **no tiene ni ~s ni cabeza** it doesn't make any sense at all, I can't make head nor tail of it

piedad f pity; (*clemencia*) mercy

piedra f tb MED stone; ~ **preciosa** precious stone; **quedarse de** ~ fig F be stunned

piel f *de persona, fruta* skin; *de animal* hide, skin; (*cuero*) leather; **abrigo de** ~**es** fur coat

pienso¹ vb → **pensar**

pienso² m animal feed

pierdo vb → **perder**

pierna f leg; **dormir a** ~ **suelta** sleep like a log

pieza f *de un conjunto*, MÚS piece; *de aparato* part; TEA play; (*habitación*) room; ~ **de recambio** spare (part); **quedarse de una** ~ F be amazed

pifia f F (*error*) booboo F; *Chi, Pe, Rpl* defect

pigmento m pigment

pigmeo m, **-a** f pigmy

pijama m pajamas pl, Br pyjamas pl

pijo 1 adj posh **2** m V (*pene*) prick V **3** m, **-a** f F *persona* rich kid F

pila f EL battery; (*montón*) pile; (*fregadero*) sink

pilar m tb fig pillar

píldora f pill

pileta f Rpl sink; (*alberca*) swimming pool

pillaje m pillage; **pillar** <1a> v/t (*tomar*) seize; (*atrapar*) catch; (*atropellar*) hit; *chiste* get

pillo 1 adj mischievous **2** m, **-a** f rascal

pilón m Méx: **me dio dos de** ~ he gave me two extra

pilotar <1a> v/t AVIA fly, pilot; AUTO drive; MAR steer; **piloto** m AVIA, MAR pilot; AUTO driver; EL pilot light; ~ **automático** autopilot

piltrafa f: ~**s** rags; **estar hecho una** ~ fig be a total wreck F

pimentón m paprika; **pimienta** f pepper; **pimiento** m pepper; **me importa un** ~ F I couldn't care less F

pimpón m ping-pong

PIN m PIN

pinar m pine forest

pincel m paintbrush

pinchadiscos m/f F disc jockey, DJ

pinchar <1a> **1** v/t prick; AUTO puncture; TELEC tap; F (*molestar*) bug F, needle F; ~ **le a alguien** MED give s.o. a shot **2** v/i prick; AUTO get a flat tire, Br get a puncture **3** v/r ~**se con aguja etc** prick o.s.; F (*inyectarse*) shoot up P; **se nos pinchó una rueda** we got a flat (tire) o Br a puncture; **pinchazo** m *herida* prick; *dolor* sharp pain; AUTO flat (tire), Br puncture; F flop F

pinche¹ m cook's assistant

pinche² adj Méx F rotten F; C.Am., Méx (*tacaño*) tight-fisted

pincho m GASTR bar snack

pingajo m F rag

ping-pong m ping-pong

pingüino m ZO penguin

pino m BOT pine; **hacer el** ~ do a handstand

pinol(e) m C.Am., Méx cornstarch, Br cornflour; L.Am. roasted corn

pinta f pint; *aspecto* looks pl; **tener buena** ~ fig look inviting

pintalabios m lipstick

pintar <1a> **1** v/t paint; **no** ~ **nada** fig F not count **2** v/r ~**se** put on one's makeup

pintor m, ~**a** f painter; ~ (**de brocha gorda**) (house) painter; **pintoresco** adj picturesque; **pintura** f *sustancia* paint; *obra* painting

pinza f clothes pin, Br clothes peg; ZO claw; ~**s** tweezers; L.Am. (*alicates*) pliers

piña f *del pino* pine cone; *fruta* pineapple; **piñón** m BOT pine nut; TÉC pinion

piojo m ZO louse; ~**s** pl lice pl

piola f L.Am. cord, twine; **piolín** m Arg cord, twine

pionero 1 adj pioneering **2** m, **-a** f tb fig pioneer

pipa f pipe; ~**s semillas** sunflower seeds; **pasarlo** ~ F have a great time

pipí *m* F pee F; *hacer ~* F pee F

pipiolo *m* *C.Am.*, *Méx* F kid F; *~s pl* *C.Am.* F (*dinero*) cash *sg*

pique *m* resentment; (*rivalidad*) rivalry; *irse a ~* *fig* go under, go to the wall

piqueta *f herramienta* pickax(e); *en cámping* tentpeg

piquete *m* POL picket

pirado *adj* F crazy F

piragua *f* canoe; **piragüista** *m/f* DEP canoeist

pirámide *f* pyramid

piraña *f* ZO piranha

pirarse <1a> *v/r* F (*marcharse*) clear off F; *~ por alguien* F lose one's head over s.o.

pirata *m/f* pirate; *~ informático* hacker; **piratear** <1a> *v/t* INFOR pirate

pirenaico *adj* Pyrenean; **Pirineos** *mpl* Pyrenees

pirómano *m*, *-a f* pyromaniac; JUR arsonist

piropo *m* compliment

pirotécnico *adj* fireworks *atr*

piruleta *f*, **pirulí** *m* lollipop

pis *m* F pee F; *hacer ~* F have a pee F

pisada *f* footstep; *huella* footprint; **pisapapeles** *m* paperweight; **pisar** <1a> *v/t* step on; *uvas* tread; *fig* (*maltratar*) walk all over; *idea* steal; *~ a alguien* step on s.o.'s foot

piscifactoría *f* fish farm

piscina *f* swimming pool

Piscis *m/f inv* ASTR Pisces

piso *m* apartment, *Br* flat; (*planta*) floor

pisotear <1a> *v/t* trample

pista *f* track, trail; (*indicio*) clue; *de atletismo* track; *~ de aterrizaje* AVIA runway; *~ de baile* dance floor; *~ de tenis / squash* tennis / squash court; *seguir la ~ a alguien* be on the trail of s.o.

pistacho *m* BOT pistachio

pisto *m* GASTR mixture of tomatoes, peppers etc cooked in oil; *C.Am.*, *Méx* F (*dinero*) cash, dough F

pistola *f* pistol

pistón *m* piston

pitada *f* (*abucheo*) whistle; *S.Am. de cigarillo* puff; **pitar** <1a> **1** *v/i* whistle; *con bocina* beep, hoot; *L.Am.* (*fumar*) smoke; *salir pitando* F dash off F **2** *v/t* (*abuchear*) whistle at; *penalti*, *falta etc* call, *Br* blow for; *silbato* blow; **pitazo** *m* *L.Am.* whistle; **pitear** <1a> *v/i* *L.Am.* blow a whistle; **pitido** *m* whistle; *con bocina* beep, hoot

pitillo *m* cigarette; *hecho a mano* roll-up

pito *m* whistle; (*bocina*) horn; *me importa un ~* F I don't give a hoot F

pitón *m* ZO python; **pitonisa** *f* fortune-teller

pitorrearse <1a> *v/r*: *~ de alguien* F make fun of s.o.

pívot *m en baloncesto* center, *Br* centre

piyama *m* *L.Am.* pajamas *pl*, *Br* pyjamas *pl*

pizarra *f* blackboard; *piedra* slate

pizca *f* pinch; *Méx* AGR harvest; *ni ~ de* not a bit of

pizza *f* pizza

placa *f* (*lámina*) sheet; (*plancha*) plate; (*letrero*) plaque; *Méx* AUTO license plate, *Br* number plate; *~ madre* INFOR motherboard; *~ (dental)* plaque; *~ de matrícula* AUTO license plate, *Br* number plate

placer <2x> **1** *v/i* please; *siempre hace lo que le place* he always does as he pleases **2** *m* pleasure

plácido *adj* placid

plaga *f* AGR pest; MED plague; *fig* scourge; (*abundancia*) glut; **plagado** *adj* infested; (*lleno*) full; *~ de gente* swarming with people

plagiar <1b> *v/t* plagiarize; *L.Am.* (*secuestrar*) kidnap; **plagio** *m* plagiarism

plan *m* plan

plana *f*: *primera ~* front page

plancha *f para planchar* iron; *en cocina* broiler, *Br* grill; *de metal* sheet; F (*metedura de pata*) goof F; *a la ~* GASTR broiled, *Br* grilled; **planchar** <1a> *v/t* iron; *Méx* F (*dar* *plantón*) stand up F; *L.Am.* (*lisonjear*) flatter

planeador *m* glider; **planear** <1a> **1** *v/t* plan **2** *v/i* AVIA glide

planeta *m* planet; **planetario** *m* planetarium

planificación *f* planning; **~ familiar** family planning; **planificar** <1g> *v/t* plan

plano 1 *adj* flat **2** *m* ARQUI plan; *de ciudad* map; *en cine* shot; MAT plane; *fig* level

planta *f* BOT plant; (*piso*) floor; **~ del pie** sole of the foot; **plantación** *f* plantation

plantado *adj*: **dejar a alguien ~** F stand s.o. up F; **plantar** <1a> **1** *v/t árbol etc* plant; *tienda de campaña* put up; **~ a alguien** F stand s.o. up F **2** *v/r* **~se** put one's foot down

planteamiento *m de problema* posing; (*perspectiva*) approach; **plantear** <1a> *v/t dificultad, problema* pose, create; *cuestión* raise

plantel *m* (*equipo*) team; *L.Am.* staff

plantilla *f para zapato* insole; (*personal*) staff; DEP squad; *para cortar*, INFOR template

plantón *m*: **dar un ~ a alguien** F stand s.o. up F

plasma *m* plasma

plasmar <1a> *v/t* (*modelar*) shape; *fig* (*representar*) express

plasta 1 *m/f* F pain F, drag F **2** *adj*: **ser ~** F be a pain *o* drag F

plástica *f* EDU *handicrafts*; **plástico** *m* plastic

plastificado *adj* laminated; **plastificar** <1g> *v/t documento* laminate

plastilina *f* Plasticine®

plata *f* silver; *L.Am.* F (*dinero*) cash, dough F

plataforma *f tb* POL platform; **~ petrolífera** oil rig

platal *m L.Am.* fortune

plátano *m* banana

plateado *adj Méx* wealthy

plática *f Méx* chat, talk; **platicar** <1g> **1** *v/t L.Am.* tell **2** *v/i Méx* chat, talk

platillo *m*: **~ volante** flying saucer; **~s**

MÚS cymbals

platino *m* platinum

plato *m* plate; GASTR dish; **~ principal** main course; **~ preparado/ precocinado** ready meal; **~ sopero/ hondo** soup dish; **pagar los ~s rotos** F carry the can F

plató *m de película* set; TV studio

platónico *adj* platonic

platudo *adj Chi* rich

plausible *adj* plausible

playa *f* beach; **~ de estacionamiento** *L.Am.* parking lot, *Br* car park; **playeras** *fpl* canvas shoes

playo *adj Rpl* shallow

plaza *f* square; (*vacante*) job opening, *Br* vacancy; *en vehículo* seat; *de trabajo* position; **~ de toros** bull ring

plazo *f* period; (*pago*) instal(l)ment; **a corto/largo ~** in the short/long term; **a ~s** in instal(l)ments

plebiscito *m* plebiscite

plegable *adj* collapsible, folding; **plegar** <1h & 1k> **1** *v/t* fold (up) **2** *v/r* **~se** *fig* submit (**a** to)

plegaria *f* prayer

pleito *m* JUR lawsuit; *fig* dispute; **poner un ~ a alguien** sue s.o.

pleno 1 *adj* full; **en ~ día** in broad daylight **2** *m* plenary session

pliego 1 *vb* → **plegar 2** *m* (*hoja de papel*) sheet (of paper); (*carta*) sealed letter *o* document; **pliegue** *m* fold, crease

plomería *f Méx* plumbing; **plomero** *m Méx* plumber; **plomo** *m* lead; EL fuse; *fig* F drag F; **sin ~** AUTO unleaded

pluma *f* feather; *para escribir* fountain pen; **plumaje** *m* plumage; **plumero** *m para limpiar* feather duster; *CSur para maquillaje* powder puff; **vérsele el ~ a alguien** *fig* F see what s.o. is up to F; **plumífero** *m* F down jacket

plural 1 *adj* plural **2** *m* GRAM plural; **pluralismo** *m* POL pluralism; **pluriempleo** *m* having more than one job

plus *m* bonus

plusmarquista *m/f* record holder

plusvalía f COM capital gain
plutonio m QUÍM plutonium
pluviosidad f rainfall
PNB abr (= **producto nacional bruto**) GNP (= gross national product)
P.° abr (= **Paseo**) Ave (= Avenue)
p.o. abr (= **por orden**) p.p. (per procurationem, by proxy)
población f gente population; (ciudad) city, town; (pueblo) village; Chi shanty town; **poblado 1** adj populated; barba bushy; **~ de** fig full of **2** m (pueblo) settlement; **poblador** m, **-a** f Chi shanty town dweller; **poblar** <1m> v/t populate
pobre 1 adj económicamente, en calidad poor **2** m/f poor person; los **~s** the poor; **pobreza** f poverty
pocilga f pigpen
pócima f concoction
poción f potion
poco 1 adj sg little, not much; pl few, not many; **un ~ de** a little; **unos ~s** a few **2** adv little; **trabaja ~** he doesn't work much; **ahora se ve muy ~** it's seldom seen now; **estuvo ~ por aquí** he wasn't around much; **~ conocido** little known; **~ a ~** little by little; **dentro de ~** soon, shortly; **hace ~** a short time ago, not long ago; **por ~** nearly, almost; **¡a ~ no lo hacemos!** Méx don't tell me we're not doing it; **de a ~ me fui tranquilizando** Rpl little by little I calmed down **3** m: **un ~** a little, a bit
podar <1a> v/t AGR prune
poder <2t> **1** v/aux capacidad can, be able to; permiso can, be allowed to; posibilidad may, might; **no pude hablar con ella** I wasn't able to talk to her; **¿puedo ir contigo?** can o may I come with you?; **¡podías habérselo dicho!** you could have o you might have told him **2** v/i: **~ con** (sobreponerse a) manage, cope with; **me puede** he can beat me; **es franco a más no ~** F he's as frank as they come F; **comimos a más no ~** F we ate to bursting point F; **no puedo más** I can't take any more,

I've had enough; **puede ser** perhaps, maybe; **puede que** perhaps, maybe; **¿se puede?** can I come in?, do you mind if I come in? **3** m tb POL power; **en ~ de alguien** in s.o.'s hands; **poderoso** adj powerful
podio m podium
podólogo m, **-a** f MED podiatrist, Br chiropodist
podrido adj tb fig rotten
poema m poem; **poesía** f género poetry; (poema) poem; **poeta** m/f poet; **poético** adj poetic; **poetisa** f poet
polaco 1 adj Polish **2** m, **-a** f Pole
polar adj polar
polea f TÉC pulley
polémica f controversy; **polémico** adj controversial
polen m BOT pollen
poleo m BOT pennyroyal
polera f Chi turtle neck (sweater)
poli m/f F cop F; **la ~** F the cops pl F
policía 1 f police **2** m/f police officer, policeman; mujer police officer, policewoman; **policíaco**, **policiaco** adj detective atr; **policial** adj police atr
polideportivo m sports center, Br sports centre
poliéster m polyester
polifacético adj versatile, multifaceted
poligamia f polygamy
políglota m/f polyglot
polígono m MAT polygon; **~ industrial** industrial zone, Br industrial estate
polilla f ZO moth
polio f MED polio; **poliomielitis** f MED poliomyelitis
política f politics; **políticamente** adv: **~ correcto** politically correct; **político 1** adj political **2** m, **-a** f politician
póliza f policy; **~ de seguros** insurance policy
polizón m stowaway
polla f V prick V, cock V
pollera f L.Am. skirt
pollería f poulterer's; **pollito** m

chick; **pollo** *m* ZO, GASTR chicken; **polluelo** *m* ZO chick

polo *m* GEOG, EL pole; *prenda* polo shirt; DEP polo; **Polo Norte** North Pole; **Polo Sur** South Pole

polola *f Chi* girlfriend; **pololear** <1a> *v/i Chi* be going steady; **pololo** *m Chi* boyfriend

Polonia Poland

poltrona *f* easy chair

polución *f* pollution; ~ **atmosférica** air pollution, atmospheric pollution; **polucionar** <1a> *v/t* pollute

polvo *m* dust; *en química, medicina etc* powder; **~s** *pl* **de talco** talcum powder *sg*; **echar un** ~ ∨ have a screw ∨; **estar hecho** ~ F be all in F; **pólvora** *f* gunpowder; **polvorín** *m almacén* magazine; *fig* powder keg; **polvorón** *m* GASTR *type of small cake*

pomada *f* cream

pomelo *m* BOT grapefruit

pómez *f*: **piedra** ~ pumice stone

pomo *m* doorknob

pompa *f* pomp; ~ **de jabón** bubble; **~s** *pl* **fúnebres** *ceremonia* funeral ceremony *sg*; *establecimiento* funeral parlo(u)r *sg*; **pomposo** *adj* pompous

pómulo *m* ANAT cheekbone

pon *vb* → **poner**

ponchadura *f Méx* flat, *Br* puncture; **ponchar** <1a> **1** *v/t L.Am.* puncture **2** *v/r* **~se** *Méx* get a flat *o Br* puncture

ponche *m* punch

poncho *m* poncho; **pisarse el** ~ *S.Am.* be mistaken

ponderación *f* *mesura* deliberation; *en estadísticas* weighting

ponencia *f* presentation; EDU paper

poner <2r; *part* **puesto**> **1** *v/t* put; *(añadir)* put in; RAD, TV turn on, switch on; *la mesa* set; *ropa* put on; *telegrama* send; *(escribir)* put down; *en periódico, libro etc* say; *negocio* set up; *huevos* lay; ~ **a alguien furioso** make s.o. angry; **~le a alguien con alguien** TELEC put s.o. through to s.o.; **~le una multa a alguien** fine

s.o.; **pongamos que** let's suppose *o* assume that **2** *v/r* **~se** *ropa* put on; **ponte en el banco** go and sit on the bench; **se puso ahí** she stood over there; **dile que se ponga** TELEC tell her to come to the phone; **~se pálido** turn pale; **~se furioso** get angry; **~se enfermo** become *o* fall ill; **~se a** start to

pongo[1] *vb* → **poner**

pongo[2] *m Pe* indentured Indian laborer

poni *m* ZO pony

poniente *m* west

pontífice *m* pontiff; **sumo** ~ Pope

ponzoñoso *adj* poisonous

pop 1 *adj* pop; **música** ~ pop music **2** *m* pop

popa *f* MAR stern

popular *adj* popular; *(del pueblo)* folk *atr*; *barrio* lower-class; **popularidad** *f* popularity; **popularizar** <1f> *v/t* popularize

póquer *m* poker

por *prp* ◊ *motivo* for, because of; **lo hizo** ~ **amor** she did it out of love; **luchó** ~ **sus ideales** he fought for his ideals ◊ *medio* by; ~ **avión** by air; ~ **correo** by mail, *Br tb* by post ◊ *tiempo:* ~ **un segundo** *L.Am.* for a second; ~ **la mañana** in the morning ◊ *movimiento:* ~ **la calle** down the street; ~ **un tunel** through a tunnel; ~ **aquí** this way ◊ *posición aproximada* around, about; **está** ~ **aquí** it's around here (somewhere) ◊ *cambio:* ~ **cincuenta pesos** for fifty pesos ◊ *otros usos:* ~ **hora** an *o* per hour; **dos** ~ **dos** two times two; **¿**~ **qué?** why?; **el motivo** ~ **el cual** *or* ~ **el que ...** the reason why ...

porcelana *f* porcelain, china; **de** ~ porcelain *atr*, china *atr*

porcentaje *m* percentage

porche *m* porch

porción *f* portion

pordiosero *m*, **-a** *f* beggar

porfiar <1c> *v/i* insist (**en** on)

pormenor *m* detail

porno 1 *adj* porn *atr* **2** *m* porn; **pornografía** *f* pornography; **porno-**

gráfico *adj* pornographic

poro *m* pore; **poroso** *adj* porous

poroto *m Rpl*, *Chi* bean; **~s verdes** *L.Am.* green beans

porque *conj* because; **~ sí** just because

porqué *m* reason

porquería *f* (*suciedad*) filth; F *cosa de poca calidad* piece of trash F

porra *f* baton; (*palo*) club; **¡vete a la ~!** F go to hell! F; **porrazo** *m*: **darle un ~ a alguien** F hit s.o.; **darse** or **pegarse un ~** F crash (*contra* into)

porro *m* F joint F

porrón *m container from which wine is poured straight into the mouth*

portaaviones *m inv* aircraft carrier

portada *f* TIP front page; *de revista* cover; ARQUI front

portafolios *m inv* briefcase

portal *m* foyer; (*entrada*) doorway

portaligas *m inv Arg*, *Chi* garter belt, *Br* suspender belt

portarse <1a> *v/r* behave

portátil *adj* portable

portavoz *m/f* spokesman; *mujer* spokeswoman

portazo *m*: **dar un ~** F slam the door

porte *m* (*aspecto*) appearance, air; (*gasto de correo*) postage

portento *m* wonder; *persona* genius

porteño *Arg* **1** *adj* of Buenos Aires, Buenos Aires *atr* **2** *m*, **-a** *f* native of Buenos Aires

portería *f* reception; *casa* superintendent's apartment, *Br* caretaker's flat; DEP goal; **portero** *m* doorman; *de edificio* superintendent, *Br* caretaker; DEP goalkeeper; **~ automático** intercom, *Br* entryphone

portón *m* large door

Portugal Portugal; **portugués 1** *m/adj* Portuguese **2** *m*, **-esa** *f persona* Portuguese

porvenir *m* future

posada *f C.Am.*, *Méx* Christmas party; (*fonda*) inn

posar <1a> **1** *v/t mano* lay, place (*sobre* on); **~ la mirada en** gaze at **2** *v/r* **-se** *de ave, insecto*, AVIA land

posavasos *m inv* coaster

posdata *f* postscript

poseer <2e> *v/t* possess; (*ser dueño de*) own, possess; **posesión** *f* possession; **tomar ~** (*de un cargo*) POL take up office

posguerra *f* postwar period

posibilidad *f* possibility; **posibilitar** <1a> *v/t* make possible; **posible** *adj* possible; **en lo ~** as far as possible; **hacer todo lo ~** do everything possible; **es ~ que ...** perhaps ...

posición *f tb* MIL, *fig* position; *social* standing, status

positivo *adj* positive

posmoderno *adj* postmodern

poso *m* dregs *pl*

posología *f* dosage

posponer <2r; *part* **pospuesto**> *v/t* postpone; **pospuesto** *part* → **posponer**

posta *f*: **a ~** on purpose

postal 1 *adj* mail *atr*, postal **2** *f* postcard

poste *m* post

póster *m* poster

postergar <1a> *v/t* postpone

posteridad *f* posterity; **posterior** *adj* later, subsequent; (*trasero*) rear *atr*, back *atr*

postizo 1 *adj* false **2** *m* hairpiece

postor *m* bidder; **al mejor ~** to the highest bidder

postrar <1a> **1** *v/t*: **la gripe lo postró** he was laid up with flu **2** *v/r* **~se** prostrate o.s.

postre *m* dessert; **a la ~** in the end

postular <1a> *v/t hipótesis* put forward, advance

póstumo *adj* posthumous

postura *f tb fig* position

pos(t)venta *adj inv* after-sales *atr*

potable *adj* drinkable; *fig* F passable; **agua ~** drinking water

potaje *m* GASTR stew

potasio *m* potassium

potencia *f* power; **en ~** potential; **potencial** *m/adj* potential; **potenciar** <1b> *v/t fig* foster, promote

potentado *m*, **-a** *f* tycoon

potente *adj* powerful

potestad *f* authority; **patria ~** parental authority

potingue *m* F *desp* lotion, cream

potro *m* ZO colt

pozo *m* well; MIN shaft; *Rpl* pothole; **un ~ sin fondo** *fig* a bottomless pit

pozol *m* C.Am. corn liquor

pozole *m* Méx corn stew

práctica *f* practice; **practicar** <1g> *v/t* practice, *Br* practise; *deporte* play; **~ la equitación / la esgrima** ride / fence; **práctico** *adj* practical

pradera *f* prairie, grassland; **prado** *m* meadow

pragmático *adj* pragmatic; **pragmatismo** *m* pragmatism

pral. *abr* (= **principal**) first

preámbulo *m* preamble

prebenda *f* sinecure

precalentamiento *m* DEP warm-up

precario *adj* precarious

precaución *f* precaution; **tomar precauciones** take precautions

precavido *adj* cautious

precedente 1 *adj* previous **2** *m* precedent; **preceder** <2a> *v/t* precede

preceptivo *adj* compulsory, mandatory

preciado *adj* precious; **preciarse** <1b> *v/r*: **cualquier fontanero que se precie ...** any self-respecting plumber ...

precinto *m* seal

precio *m* price; **~ de venta al público** recommended retail price; **preciosidad** *f*: **esa casa / chica es una ~** that house / girl is gorgeous *o* beautiful; **precioso** *adj* (*de valor*) precious; (*hermoso*) beautiful; **preciosura** *f* L.Am. F → **preciosidad**

precipicio *m* precipice

precipitación *f* (*prisa*) hurry, haste; **precipitaciones** rain *sg*; **precipitado** *adj* hasty, sudden; **precipitarse** <1a> *v/r* rush; *fig* be hasty

precisamente *adv* precisely; **precisión** *f* precision; **preciso** *adj* precise, accurate; **ser ~** be necessary

preconcebido *adj* preconceived

precoz *adj* early; **niño** precocious

precursor *m*, **~a** *f* precursor, forerunner

predecesor *m*, **~a** *f* predecessor

predecir <3p; *part* **predicho**> *v/t* predict

predestinar <1a> *v/t* predestine

predicado *m* predicate; **predicador** *m*, **~a** *f* preacher; **predicar** <1g> *v/t* preach; **~ con el ejemplo** F practice (*Br* practise) what one preaches

predicción *f* prediction, forecast

predicho *part* → **predecir**

predilecto *adj* favo(u)rite

predisponer <2r> *v/t* prejudice; **predisposición** *f tb* MED predisposition; (*tendencia*) tendency; **una ~ en contra de** a prejudice against; **predispuesto** *adj* predisposed (*a* to)

predominante *adj* predominant; **predominar** <1a> *v/t* predominate

preeminente *adj* preeminent

preescolar *adj* preschool

preestreno *m* preview

preexistente *adj* pre-existing

prefabricado *adj* prefabricated

prefacio *m* preface, foreword

preferencia *f* preference; **preferente** *adj* preferential; **preferible** *adj* preferable (*a* to); **es ~ que ...** it's better if ...; **preferido 1** *part* → **preferir 2** *adj* favo(u)rite; **preferir** <3i> *v/t* prefer

prefijo *m* prefix; TELEC area code, *Br* dialling code

pregonar <1a> *v/t* proclaim, make public

pregunta *f* question; **preguntar** <1a> **1** *v/t* ask **2** *v/i* ask; **~ por algo** ask about sth; **~ por alguien** *paradero* ask for s.o.; *salud etc* ask about s.o. **3** *v/r* **~se** wonder

prehistoria *f* prehistory; **prehistórico** *adj* prehistoric

prejuicio *m* prejudice

prelado *m* prelate

prelavado *m* prewash

preliminar 1 *adj* preliminary; DEP qualifying **2** *m* L.Am. qualifier

preludio *m* prelude

premamá *adj* maternity *atr*

prematrimonial *adj* premarital

prematuro 1 *adj* premature **2** *m*, **-a** *f* premature baby

premeditado *adj* premeditated; **premeditación** *f* premeditation; **con** ~ deliberately

premiado 1 *adj* prizewinning **2** *m*, **-a** *f* prizewinner; **premiar** <1b> *v/t* award a prize to; **premio** *m* prize

premisa *f* premise

premonición *f* premonition

premura *f* haste

prenatal *adj* prenatal

prenda *f* item of clothing, garment; *garantía* security; *en juegos* forfeit; **no soltar** ~ not say a word (*sobre* about)

prender <2a; *part* **preso**> **1** *v/t a fugitivo* capture; *sujetar* pin up; *L.Am. fuego* light; *L.Am. luz* switch on, turn on; ~ **fuego a** set fire to **2** *v/i de planta* take; (*empezar a arder*) catch; *de moda* catch on

prendería *f Esp* pawnbroker's, pawn shop

prensa *f* press; ~ **amarilla** gutter press; **prensar** <1a> *v/t* press

preñado *adj* pregnant

preocupación *f* worry, concern; **preocupado** *adj* worried (*por* about), concerned (*por* about); **preocupante** *adj* worrying; **preocupar** <1a> **1** *v/t* worry, concern **2** *v/r* ~**se** worry (*por* about); ~**se de** (*encargarse*) look after, take care of

preparación *f* preparation; (*educación*) education; *para trabajo* training; **preparado** *adj* ready, prepared; **preparador** *m*, **-a** *f*: *físico* trainer; **preparar** <1a> **1** *v/t* prepare, get ready **2** *v/r* ~**se** get ready (*para* for), prepare o.s. (*para* for); *de tormenta, crisis* is brewing; **preparativos** *mpl* preparations

preponderante *adj* predominant

preposición *f* preposition

prepotente *adj* arrogant

prerrogativa *f* prerogative

presa *f* (*dique*) dam; (*embalse*) reservoir; (*víctima*) prey; *L.Am. para comer* bite to eat

presagio *m* omen, sign; (*premonición*) premonition

prescindir <3a> *v/i*: ~ **de** (*privarse de*) do without; (*omitir*) leave out, dispense with; (*no tener en cuenta*) disregard

prescribir <3a; *part* **prescrito**> *v/i* JUR prescribe; **prescrito** *part* → **prescribir**

presencia *f* presence; **buena** ~ smart appearance; **presenciar** <1b> *v/t* witness; (*estar presente a*) attend, be present at

presentación *f* presentation; COM launch; *entre personas* introduction; **presentador** *m*, **-a** *f* TV presenter; **presentar** <1a> **1** *v/t* present; *a alguien* introduce; *producto* launch; *solicitud* submit **2** *v/r* ~**se en sitio** show up; (*darse a conocer*) introduce o.s.; *a examen* take; *de problema, dificultad* arise; *a elecciones* run

presente 1 *adj* present; **tener algo** ~ bear sth in mind; **¡~!** here! **2** *m tiempo* present **3** *m/fpl*: **los** ~**s** those present

presentimiento *m* premonition; **presentir** <3i> *v/t* foresee; **presiento que vendrá** I have a feeling he'll come

preservar <1a> *v/t* protect; **preservativo** *m* condom

presidencia *f* presidency; *de compañía* presidency, *Br* chairmanship; *de comité* chairmanship; **presidencial** *adj* presidential; **presidente** *m*, **-a** *f* president; *de gobierno* premier, prime minister; *de compañía* president, *Br* chairman, *Br mujer* chairwoman; *de comité* chair

presidiario *m*, **-a** *f* prisoner

presidir <3a> *v/t* be president of; *reunión* chair, preside over

presión *f* pressure; ~ **sanguínea** blood pressure; **presionar** <1a> *v/t botón* press; *fig* put pressure on, pressure

preso 1 *part* → **prender 2** *m*, **-a** *f* prisoner

prestación *f* provision; ~ **social sustitutoria** MIL community service in lieu of military service; **prestado** *adj*: *dejar ~ algo* lend sth; *pedir ~ algo* borrow sth; **prestamista** *m/f* moneylender; **préstamo** *m* loan; *~ bancario* bank loan; **prestar** <1a> *v/t dinero* lend; *ayuda* give; *L.Am.* borrow; *~ atención* pay attention

prestidigitador *m*, *~a f* conjurer

prestigio *m* prestige; **prestigioso** *adj* prestigious

presumido *adj* conceited; (*coqueto*) vain; **presumir** <3a> *v/t* presume **2** *v/i* show off; *~ de algo* boast *o* brag about sth; *presume de listo* he thinks he's very clever; **presuntamente** *adv* allegedly; **presunto** *adj* alleged, suspected; **presuntuoso** *adj* conceited

presuponer <2r>; *part presupuesto*> *v/t* assume; **presupuesto 1** *part* → *presuponer* **2** *m* POL budget

presuroso *adj* hurried

pretencioso *adj* pretentious

pretender <2a> *v/t*: *pretendía convencerlos* he was trying to persuade them; **pretendiente** *m de mujer* suitor

pretensión *f L.Am.* (*arrogancia*) vanity; *sin pretensiones* unpretentious

pretérito *m* GRAM preterite

pretextar <1a> *v/t* claim; **pretexto** *m* pretext

prevalecer <2d> *v/i* prevail (*sobre* over)

prevaricación *f* corruption

prevención *f* prevention

prevenido 1 *part* → *prevenir* **2** *adj* well-prepared; **prevenir** <3s> *v/t* prevent; (*avisar*) warn (*contra* against); **preventivo** *adj* preventive, preventative

prever <2v; *part previsto*> *v/t* foresee

previo *adj* previous; *sin ~ aviso* without (prior) warning

previsible *adj* foreseeable; **previsión** *f* (*predicción*) forecast; (*preparación*) foresight; **previsor** *adj*

farsighted; **previsto 1** *part* → *prever* **2** *adj* foreseen, expected; *tener ~* have planned

prieto *adj L.Am.* dark-skinned

prima *f de seguro* premium; (*pago extra*) bonus

primacía *f* supremacy, primacy; (*prioridad*) priority; **primario** *adj* primary

primavera *f* spring; BOT primrose

primer *adj* first

primera *f* first class; AUTO first gear; *a la ~* first-time; *de ~* F first-class, first-rate; **primerizo** *adj* inexperienced, green F; *madre* new, first-time; **primero 1** *adj* first; *~s auxilios pl* first aid *sg* **2** *m*, *~a f* first (one) **3** *adv* first

primitivo *adj* primitive; (*original*) original

primo *m*, *~a f* cousin

primogénito 1 *adj* first **2** *m*, *~a f* first child

primordial *adj* fundamental

primoroso *adj* exquisite

princesa *f* princess

principal *adj* main, principal; *lo ~* the main *o* most important thing

príncipe *m* prince

principiante 1 *adj* inexperienced **2** *m/f* beginner; **principio** *m* principle; *en tiempo* beginning; *a ~s de abril* at the beginning of April; *en ~* in principle

pringar <1h> **1** *v/t ensuciar* get greasy; *fig* F get involved (*en* in) **2** *v/r ~se* get greasy; *fig* F get mixed up (*en* in); **pringoso** *adj* greasy

prioridad *f* priority; **prioritario** *adj* priority *atr*

prisa *f* hurry, rush; *darse ~* hurry (up); *tener ~* be in a hurry *o* rush

prisión *f* prison, jail; **prisionero 1** *adj* captive **2** *m*, *~a f* prisoner

prismáticos *mpl* binoculars

priva *f Esp* F booze F

privacidad *f* privacy

privación *f acción* deprivation; *sufrir privaciones* suffer privation(s) *o* hardship

privado 1 *part* → *privar* **2** *adj*

private; **privar** <1a> **1** v/t: ~ *a alguien de algo* deprive s.o. of sth **2** v/r ~**se** deprive o.s.; ~**se de algo** deprive o.s. of sth, go without sth; **privatización** f privatization; **privatizar** <1f> v/t privatize

privilegiado adj privileged; (*excelente*) exceptional; **privilegio** m privilege

pro 1 prp for, in aid of; *en ~ de* for **2** m pro; *los ~s y los contras* the pros and cons

proa f MAR bow

probabilidad f probability; **probable** adj probable, likely; *es ~ que venga* she'll probably come

probador m fitting room; **probar** <1m> **1** v/t *teoría* test, try out; (*comer un poco de*) taste, try; (*comer por primera vez*) try **2** v/i try; ~ *a hacer* try doing **3** v/r ~**se** try on; **probeta** f test tube

problema m problem; **problemático** adj problematic

procedencia f origin, provenance; **proceder** <2a> **1** v/i come (*de* from); (*actuar*) proceed; (*ser conveniente*) be fitting; ~ *a* proceed to; ~ *contra alguien* initiate proceedings against s.o. **2** m conduct; **procedimiento** m procedure, method; JUR proceedings pl

procesado m, **-a** f accused, defendant

procesador m INFOR processor; ~ *de textos* word processor

procesamiento m: ~ *de textos* word processing

procesar <1a> v/t INFOR process; JUR prosecute

procesión f procession

proceso m process; JUR trial; ~ *de datos / textos* INFOR data / word processing

proclamar <1a> v/t proclaim

proclive adj given (*a* to)

procrear <1a> v/i breed, procreate fml

procurar <1a> v/t try; *procura no llegar tarde* try not to be late

prodigar <1h> **1** v/t be generous

with **2** v/r ~**se** (*aparecer*) be seen in public

prodigio m wonder, miracle; *persona* prodigy; **prodigioso** adj prodigious

pródigo adj (*generoso*) generous; (*derrochador*) extravagant

producción f production; **producir** <3o> **1** v/t produce; (*causar*) cause **2** v/r ~**se** happen, occur; *se produjo un ruido tremendo* there was a tremendous noise

productividad f productivity; **productivo** adj productive; *empresa* profitable; **producto** m product; ~ *interior bruto* gross domestic product; ~ *nacional bruto* gross national product; **productor** m, **-a** f producer

produjo vb → **producir**

produzco vb → **producir**

proeza f feat, exploit

profana f laywoman; **profanar** <1a> v/t defile, desecrate; **profano 1** adj fig lay atr **2** m layman

profecía f prophecy

profesar <1a> v/t REL profess; fig feel, have; **profesión** f profession; **profesional** m/f & adj professional; **profesor** m, **-a** f teacher; *de universidad* professor, Br lecturer; **profesorado** m faculty, Br staff pl

profeta m prophet; **profetizar** <1f> v/t prophesy

profiláctico 1 adj preventive, prophylactic fml **2** m condom

prófugo m, **-a** f JUR fugitive

profundidad f depth; **profundizar** <1f> v/i: ~ *en algo* go into sth in depth; **profundo** adj deep; *pensamiento, persona* profound

profuso adj abundant, plentiful

programa m program, Br programme; INFOR program; EDU syllabus; ~ *de estudios* curriculum; **programación** f RAD, TV programs pl, Br programmes; INFOR programming; **programador** m, **-a** f programmer; **programar** <1a> v/t *aparato* program, Br programme; INFOR program; (*planear*) schedule

P

progresar <1a> v/i progress, make progress; **progresista** m/f & adj progressive; **progresivo** adj progressive; **progreso** m progress

prohibición f ban (**de** on); **prohibido** adj forbidden; **prohibir** <3a> v/t forbid; *oficialmente* ban; **prohibitivo** adj *precio* prohibitive

prójimo m fellow human being

prole f offspring

proletario 1 adj proletarian **2** m, **-a** f proletarian

proliferación f proliferation; **proliferar** <1a> v/t proliferate; **prolífico** adj prolific

prolijo adj long-winded; (*minucioso*) detailed

prólogo m preface

prolongado adj prolonged, lengthy; **prolongar** <1h> **1** v/t extend, prolong **2** v/r **~se** go o carry on; *en espacio* extend

promedio m average

promesa f promise; **prometedor** adj bright, promising; **prometer** <2a> **1** v/t promise **2** v/r **~se** get engaged; **prometida** f fiancée; **prometido 1** part → **prometer 2** adj engaged **3** m fiancé

prominente adj prominent

promiscuidad f promiscuity; **promiscuo** adj promiscuous

promoción f promotion; EDU year; **promocionar** <1a> v/t promote; **promotor** m, **~a** f promoter; **~ inmobiliario** developer; **promover** <2h> v/t promote; (*causar*) provoke, cause

promulgar <1h> v/t *ley* promulgate

pronombre m GRAM pronoun

pronosticar <1g> v/t forecast; **pronóstico** m MED prognosis; **~ del tiempo** weather forecast

pronto 1 adj prompt **2** adv (*dentro de poco*) soon; (*temprano*) early; **de ~** suddenly; **tan ~ como** as soon as

pronunciación f pronunciation; **pronunciar** <1b> v/t pronounce; (*decir*) say; **~ un discurso** give a speech

propaganda f advertising; POL propaganda; **propagar** <1h> **1** v/t spread **2** v/r **~se** spread

propano m propane

propasarse <1a> v/r go too far

propenso adj prone (**a** to); **ser ~ a hacer** be prone to do, have a tendency to do

propiciar <1b> v/t (*favorecer*) promote; (*causar*) bring about; **propicio** adj favo(u)rable

propiedad f property; **propietario** m, **-a** f owner

propina f tip; **propinar** <1a> v/t *golpe, paliza* give

propio adj own; (*característico*) characteristic (**de** of), typical (**de** of); (*adecuado*) suitable (**para** for); **la -a directora** the director herself

proponer <2r; part propuesto> v/t propose, suggest

proporción f proportion; **proporcional** adj proportional; **proporcionar** <1a> v/t provide, supply; *satisfacción* give

proposición f proposal, suggestion

propósito m (*intención*) intention; (*objetivo*) purpose; **a ~** on purpose; (*por cierto*) by the way

propuesta f proposal

propuesto part → **proponer**

propugnar <1a> v/t advocate

propulsar <1a> v/t TÉC propel; *fig* promote; **propulsor** m (*motor*) engine

prórroga f DEP overtime, Br extra time; **prorrogar** <1h> v/t *plazo* extend

prorrumpir <3a> v/i burst (**en** into)

prosa f prose; **prosaico** adj mundane, prosaic

proseguir <3d & 3l> **1** v/t carry on, continue **2** v/i continue (**con** with)

proselitismo m proselytism

prospecto m directions for use pl; *de propaganda* leaflet

prosperar <1a> v/i prosper, thrive; **prosperidad** f prosperity; **próspero** adj prosperous, thriving

próstata f prostate

prostíbulo m brothel

prostitución f prostitution; **prostituirse** <3g> v/r prostitute o.s.; **prostituta** f prostitute; **prostituto** m male prostitute

protagonista m/f *personaje* main character; *actor, actriz* star; *de una hazaña* hero; *mujer* heroine; **protagonizar** <1f> v/t star in, play the lead in; *incidente* play a leading role in

protección f protection; **proteger** <2c> v/t protect (*de* from)

proteína f protein

protésico m, **-a** f: ~ **dental** dental technician; **prótesis** f prosthesis

protesta f protest; **protestante** m/f Protestant; **protestar** <1a> **1** v/t protest **2** v/i (*quejarse*) complain (*por, de* about); (*expresar oposición*) protest (*contra, por* about, against)

protocolo m protocol

prototipo m TÉC prototype

protuberancia f protuberance

prov. abr (= **provincia**) province

provecho m benefit; *¡buen* ~! enjoy (your meal); *sacar* ~ *de* benefit from

proveedor m, **-a** f supplier; ~ *de* (*acceso a*) *Internet* Internet Service Provider, ISP; **proveer** <2e; *part* **provisto**> v/t supply; ~ *a alguien de algo* supply s.o. with sth

provenir <3s> v/i come (*de* from)

proverbio m proverb

providencia f providence

provincia f province; **provincial** adj provincial; **provinciano 1** adj provincial **2** m, **-a** f provincial

provisional adj provisional; **provisiones** fpl provisions

provisto 1 part → **proveer 2** adj: ~ *de* equipped with

provocación f provocation; **provocador** adj provocative; **provocar** <1g> v/t cause; *al enfado* provoke; *sexualmente* lead on; *¿te provoca un café? S.Am.* how about a coffee?; **provocativo** adj provocative

proxeneta m pimp; **proxenetismo** m procuring

proximidad f proximity; **próximo** adj (*siguiente*) next; (*cercano*) near, close

proyección f MAT, PSI projection; *de película* showing; **proyectar** <1a> v/t project; (*planear*) plan; *película* show; *sombra* cast; **proyectil** m missile; **proyecto** m plan; *trabajo* project; ~ *de ley* bill; *tener en* ~ *hacer algo* plan to do sth; **proyector** m projector

prudencia f caution, prudence; **prudente** adj careful, cautious

prueba f tb TIP proof; JUR piece of evidence; DEP event; EDU test; *a* ~ *de bala* bulletproof; *poner algo a* ~ put sth to the test

P.S. abr (= **postscriptum** (**posdata**)) PS (= postscript)

pseudo... pref pseudo-

pseudónimo m pseudonym

psicoanálisis f (psycho)analysis; **psicoanalista** m/f (psycho)analyst

psicodélico adj psychedelic

psicología f psychology; **psicológico** adj psychological; **psicólogo** m, **-a** f psychologist

psicópata m/f psychopath

psicosis f inv psychosis

psicoterapia f psychotherapy

psiquiatra m/f psychiatrist; **psiquiatría** f psychiatry; **psiquiátrico** adj psychiatric

psíquico adj psychic

pta abr (= **peseta**) peseta

ptas abr (= **pesetas**) pesetas

púa f ZO spine, quill; MÚS plectrum, pick

pub m bar

pubertad f puberty

publicación f publication; **publicar** <1g> v/t publish **2** v/r ~se come out, be published; **publicidad** f (*divulgación*) publicity; COM advertising; (*anuncios*) advertisements pl; **publicista** m/f advertising executive; **publicitario 1** adj advertising atr **2** m, **-a** f advertising executive; **público 1** adj public; *escuela* public, Br state **2** m public; TEA audience; DEP spectators pl,

P

crowd

pucho *m S.Am.* P cigarette butt, *Br* fag end F; *no valer un* ~ be completely worthless

pude *vb* → *poder*

púdico *adj* modest

pudín *m* pudding

pudo *vb* → *poder*

pudor *m* modesty

pudrir <3a> **1** *v/t* rot **2** *v/r* ~**se** rot; ~*se de envidia* be green with envy

pueblerino *m*, **-a** *f* hick *desp*; **pueblero** *m*, **-a** *f L.Am.* villager; *de pueblo más grande* townsman; *mujer* townswoman; **pueblo** *m* village; *más grande* town

puedo *vb* → *poder*

puente *m* bridge; *hacer* ~ have a day off between a weekend and a public holiday

puenting *m* bungee jumping

puerco 1 *adj* dirty; *fig* filthy F **2** *m* ZO pig; ~ *espín* porcupine

puericultura *f* childcare

puerro *m* BOT leek

puerta *f* door; *en valla* gate; DEP goal; ~ *de embarque* gate

puerto *m* MAR port; GEOG pass

Puerto Rico Puerto Rico; **puertorriqueño 1** *adj* Puerto Rican **2** *m*, **-a** *f* Puerto Rican

pues *conj* well; *fml (porque)* as, since; ~ *bien* well; *¡~ sí!* of course!

puesta *f*: ~ *a punto* tune-up; ~ *de sol* sunset

puestero *m*, **-a** *f L.Am.* stall holder

puesto 1 *part* → *poner* **2** *m lugar* place; *en mercado* stand, stall; MIL post; ~ *(de trabajo)* job **3** *conj*: ~ *que* since, given that

pugnar <1a> *v/i* fight *(por* for; *por hacer* to do)

puja *f (lucha)* struggle; *en subasta* bid; **pujar** <1a> *v/i (luchar)* struggle; *en subasta* bid

pulcro *adj* immaculate

pulga *f* ZO flea; *tener malas* ~*s fig* F be bad-tempered

pulgada *f* inch

pulgar *m* thumb

pulimentar <1a> *v/t* polish; **pulir**

<3a> *v/t* polish

pulla *f* gibe

pulmón *m* lung; **pulmonía** *f* MED pneumonia

pulpa *f* pulp

pulpería *f L.Am.* mom-and-pop store, *Br* corner shop; **pulpero** *m*, **-a** *f S.Am.* storekeeper, shopkeeper

púlpito *m* pulpit

pulpo *m* ZO octopus

pulque *m Méx* pulque *(alcoholic drink made from cactus)*; **pulquería** *f Méx* pulque bar

pulsación *f* beat; *al escribir a máquina* key stroke; **pulsar** <1a> *v/t botón, tecla* press

pulsera *f* bracelet

pulso *m* pulse; *fig* steady hand; *tomar el* ~ *a alguien* take s.o.'s pulse; *tomar el* ~ *a algo fig* take the pulse of sth

pulular <1a> *v/i* mill around

pulverizador *m* spray; **pulverizar** <1f> *v/t* spray; *(convertir en polvo)* pulverize, crush

puma *m* ZO puma, mountain lion

puna *f L.Am.* GEOG high Andean plateau; MED altitude sickness

pundonor *m* pride

punitivo *adj* punitive

punta *f* tip; *(extremo)* end; *de lápiz,* GEOG point; *L.Am. (grupo)* group; *sacar* ~ *a* sharpen

puntada *f* stitch

puntapié *m* kick

puntera *f* toe

puntería *f* aim

puntero 1 *adj* leading **2** *m* pointer

puntiagudo *adj* pointed, sharp

puntilla *f*: *de* ~*s* on tippy-toe, *Br* on tiptoe

puntilloso *adj* particular, punctilious *fml*

punto *m* point; *señal* dot; *signo de puntuación* period, *Br* full stop; *en costura, sutura* stitch; *dos* ~*s* colon; ~ *muerto* AUTO neutral; ~ *de vista* point of view; ~ *y coma* semicolon; *a* ~ *(listo)* ready; *(a tiempo)* in time; *de* ~ knitted; *en* ~ on the dot; *estar a* ~ *de* be about to; *hacer* ~ knit;

hasta cierto ~ up to a point; *empresa f* ~.com dot.com (company))

puntuación *f* punctuation; DEP score; EDU grade, mark; **puntual** *adj* punctual; **puntualidad** *f* punctuality; **puntualizar** <1f> *v/t (señalar)* point out; *(aclarar)* clarify

punzada *f* sharp *o* stabbing pain; **punzante** *adj* stinging

puñado *m* handful

puñal *m* dagger; **puñalada** *f* stab wound

puñeta *f*: *¡~(s)!* F for heaven's sake! F; **hacer la ~ a alguien** F give s.o. a hard time F

puñetazo *m* punch; *dar un* ~ punch

puño *m* fist; *de camisa* cuff; *de bastón, paraguas* handle

pupa *f en labio* cold sore; **hacerse ~** *lenguaje infantil* hurt o.s.

pupila *f* pupil

pupitre *m* desk

pupusa *f L.Am.* filled dumpling

purasangre *m* thoroughbred

puré *m* purée; *sopa* cream; **~ de patatas** *or* **papas** *L.Am.* mashed potatoes

pureza *f* purity

purga *f* POL purge; **purgante** *m/adj* laxative, purgative; **purgatorio** *m* REL purgatory

purificación *f* purification; **purificar** <1g> *v/t* purify

purista *m/f* purist

puritano 1 *adj* puritanical **2** *m*, *-a f* puritan

puro 1 *adj* pure; *casualidad, coincidencia* sheer; *Méx (único)* sole, only; *la -a verdad* the honest truth; *te sirven la -a comida Méx* they just serve food **2** *m* cigar

púrpura *f* purple

pus *m* pus

puse *vb* → *poder*

pusilánime *adj* fainthearted

puso *vb* → *poder*

puta *f* P whore P; **putada** *f* P dirty trick; *¡qué ~!* shit! P; **putear** <1a> *v/t L.Am.* P swear at; *~ alguien Esp* give s.o. a hard time, make life difficult for s.o.

puto *adj* P goddamn F, *Br* bloody F; *de puta madre* P great F, fantastic F

putrefacción *f* putrefaction

puzzle *m* jigsaw (puzzle)

PVC *abr (= cloruro de polivinilo)* PVC (= polyvinyl chloride)

P.V.P. *abr (= precio de venta al público)* RRP (= recommended retail price)

pza. *abr (= plaza)* sq (= square)

Q

q.e.p.d. *abr (= que en paz descanse)* RIP (= requiescat in pace)

que 1 *pron rel sujeto*: *persona* who, that; *cosa* which, that; *complemento*: *persona* that, whom *fml*; *cosa* that, which; *el coche ~ ves* the car you can see, the car that *o* which you can see; *el* ~ the one that **2** *conj* that; *lo mismo ~ tú* the same as you; *¡~ entre!* tell him to come in; *¡~ descanses!* sleep well; *¡~ sí!* I said

yes; *¡~ no!* I said no; *es ~ ...* the thing is ...; *yo ~ tú* if I were you

qué 1 *adj & pron interr* what; *¿~ pasó?* what happened?; *¿~ día es?* what day is it?; *¿~ vestido prefieres?* which dress do you prefer? **2** *adj & pron int*: *¡~ moto!* what a motorbike!; *¡~ de flores!* what a lot of flowers! **3** *adv*: *¡~ alto es!* he's so tall!; *¡~ bien!* great!

quebrada *f L.Am.* stream

quebradero *m:* **~s de cabeza** F headaches; **quebradizo** *adj* brittle; **quebrado 1** *adj* broken **2** *m* MAT fraction; **quebrantahuesos** *m inv* ZO lammergeier; **quebrantar** <1a> *v/t ley, contrato* break; **quebrar** <1k> **1** *v/t* break **2** *v/i* COM go bankrupt **3** *v/r* **~se** break

quedar <1a> **1** *v/i (permanecer)* stay; *en un estado* be; *(sobrar)* be left; *quedó sin resolver* it remained unresolved, it wasn't sorted out; *te queda bien/mal de estilo* it suits you/doesn't suit you; *de talla* it fits you/doesn't fit you; **~ cerca** be nearby; **~ con alguien** F arrange to meet (with) s.o.; **~ en algo** agree to sth; *¿queda mucho tiempo?* is there much time left? **2** *v/r* **~se** stay; **~se ciego** go blind; **~se con algo** keep sth; *me quedé sin comer* I ended up not eating

quehaceres *mpl* tasks

queja *f* complaint; **quejarse** <1a> *v/r* complain (*a* to; *de* about); **quejica** *adj* F whining F; **quejido** *m* moan, groan; **quejumbroso** *adj* moaning

quemado *adj* burnt; *Méx (desvirtuado)* discredited; **~ por el sol** sunburnt; *oler a* **~** smell of burning; **quemadura** *f* burn; **quemar** <1a> **1** *v/t* burn; *con agua* scald; F *recursos* use up; F *dinero* blow F **2** *v/i* be very hot **3** *v/r* **~se** burn o.s.; *de tostada, papeles* burn; *fig* burn o.s. out; *Méx (desvirtuarse)* become discredited

quena *f S.Am.* Indian flute

quepo *vb* → **caber**

queque *m L.Am.* cake

querella *f* JUR lawsuit; **querellarse** <1a> *v/r* JUR bring a lawsuit (*contra* against)

querer <2u> *v/t (desear)* want; *(amar)* love; **~ decir** mean; *sin* **~** unintentionally; *quisiera ...* I would like ...; **querido 1** *part* → **querer** **2** *adj* dear **3** *m,* **-a** *f* darling

queroseno *m* kerosene

querrá *vb* → **querer**

querría *vb* → **querer**

quesadilla *f* quesadilla (*folded tortilla*)

queso *m* cheese; **~ para untar** cheese spread; **~ rallado** grated cheese

quicio *m:* **sacar de ~ a alguien** F drive s.o. crazy F

quid *m:* **el ~ de la cuestión** the nub of the question

quiebra *f* COM bankruptcy

quien *pron rel sujeto* who, that; *objeto* who, whom *fml,* that; *no soy* **~** *para hacerlo* I'm not the right person to do it

quién *pron* who; *¿~ es?* who is it?; *¿de ~ es este libro?* whose is this book?, who does this book belong to?

quienquiera *pron* whoever

quiero *vb* → **querer**

quieto *adj* still; *¡estáte ~!* keep still!

quijotesco *adj* quixotic

quilate *m* carat

quilla *f* keel

quimera *f* pipe dream

química *f* chemistry; **químico 1** *adj* chemical **2** *m,* **-a** *f* chemist

quimioterapia *f* MED chemotherapy

quimono *m* kimono

quincalla *f* junk

quince *adj* fifteen; **quincena** *f* two weeks, *Br* fortnight

quiniela *f* lottery where the winners are decided by soccer results

quinientos *adj* five hundred

quinina *f* quinine

quinquenio *m* five-year period

quinta *f* MIL draft, *Br* call-up; *es de mi* **~** he's my age

quinteto *m* MÚS quintet

quinto 1 *adj* fifth **2** *m* MIL conscript

quiosco *m* kiosk; **~ de prensa** newsstand, *Br* newsagent's; **quiosquero** *m,* **-a** *f* newspaper vendor

quirófano *m* operating room, *Br* operating theatre

quiromancia, quiromancía *f* palmistry

quirúrgico *adj* surgical

quise *vb* → **querer**

quisiera *vb* → **querer**

quiso *vb* → **querer**

quisque F: *todo* ~ everyone and his brother F, *Br* the world and his wife F

quisquilla *f* ZO shrimp

quisquilloso *adj* touchy

quiste *m* MED cyst

quitaesmalte *m* nail varnish remover

quitamanchas *m inv* stain remover

quitar <1a> **1** *v/t ropa* take off, remove; *obstáculos* remove; ~ *algo a alguien* take (away) from s.o.; ~ *la mesa* clear the table **2** *v/i:* ¡*quita!* get out of the way! **3** *v/r* ~*se ropa, gafas* take off; (*apartarse*) get out of the way; ~*se algo/a alguien de encima* get rid of s.o./sth; ¡*quítate de en medio!* F get out of the way!

quizá(s) *adv* perhaps, maybe

quórum *m* quorum

R

rabadilla *f* ANAT coccyx

rábano *m* BOT radish; *me importa un* ~ F I don't give a damn F

rabia *f* MED rabies *sg*; *dar* ~ *a alguien* make s.o. mad; *tener* ~ *a alguien* have it in for s.o.; **rabiar** <1b> *v/i:* ~ *de dolor* be in agony; *hacer* ~ *a alguien fig* F jerk s.o.'s chain F, pull s.o.'s leg F; ~ *por* be dying for

rabieta *f* tantrum

rabino *m* rabbi

rabioso *adj* MED rabid; *fig* furious

rabo *m* tail

rabón *adj L.Am. animal* short-tailed

rácano *adj* F stingy F, mean

racha *f* spell

racial *adj* racial

racimo *m* bunch

ración *f* share; (*porción*) serving, portion; **racional** *adj* rational; **racionalizar** <1f> *v/t* rationalize; **racionamiento** *m* rationing; **racionar** <1a> *v/t* ration

racismo *m* racism; **racista** *m/f & adj* racist

radar *m* radar

radiación *f* radiation; **radiactividad** *f* radioactivity; **radiactivo** *adj* radioactive; **radiador** *m* radiator; **radiante** *adj* radiant; **radiar** <1b> *v/t* radiate

radical *m/f & adj* radical; **radicalismo** *m* radicalism; **radicar** <1g> *v/i* stem (*en* from), lie (*en* in)

radio 1 *m* MAT radius; QUÍM radium; *L.Am.* radio; *en un* ~ *de* within a radius of; ~ *de acción* range **2** *f* radio; ~ *despertador* clock radio

radioaficionado *m* radio ham

radiocasete *m* radio cassette player

radiodifusión *f* broadcasting

radiofónico *adj* radio *atr*

radiografía *f* X-ray; **radiografiar** <1c> *v/t* X-ray

radiología *f* radiology; **radiólogo** *m*, **-a** *f* radiologist

radiotaxi *m* radio taxi

radiotelegrafista *m/f* radio operator

radioyente *m/f* listener

ráfaga *f* gust; *de balas* burst

rafia *f* raffia

rafting *m* rafting

ragú *m* GASTR ragout

raído *adj* threadbare

rail, **raíl** *m* rail

raíz *f* root; ~ *cuadrada/cúbica* MAT square/cube root; *a* ~ *de* as a result of; *echar raíces de persona* put down roots

raja *f* (*rodaja*) slice; (*corte*) cut; (*grieta*) crack; **rajar** <1a> **1** *v/t fruta* cut, slice; *cerámica* crack; *neumático* slash 2 *v/i* F gossip 3 *v/r* **~se** *fig* F back out F

rajatabla: a ~ strictly, to the letter

ralentí *m*: **al ~** AUTO idling; FOT in slow motion; **ralentizar** <1f> *v/t* slow down

rallador *m* grater; **rallar** <1a> *v/t* GASTR grate

rally(e) *m* rally

rama *f* branch; POL wing; **andarse por las ~s** beat about the bush; **ramificación** *f* ramification

ramo *m* COM sector; **~ de flores** bunch of flowers

rampa *f* ramp; **~ de lanzamiento** launch pad

ramplón *adj* vulgar

rana *f* ZO frog

ranchera *f typical Mexican song*

ranchero 1 *adj*: **canción -a** romantic ballad; **música -a** *music of northern Mexico* **2** *m L.Am.* rancher; **rancho** *m Méx* small farm; *L.Am.* (*barrio de chabolas*) shanty town

rancio *adj* rancid; *fig* ancient

rango *m* rank; **de alto ~** high-ranking

ranking *m* ranking

ranura *f* slot

rapapolvo *m* F telling-off F

rapar <1a> *v/t pelo* crop

rapaz 1 *adj* predatory; **ave ~** bird of prey **2** *m*, **-a** *f* F kid F

rape *m pescado* anglerfish; **al ~ pelo** cropped

rapidez *f* speed, rapidity; **rápido 1** *adj* quick, fast **2** *m* rapids *pl*

rapiña *f* pillage

raptar <1a> *v/t* kidnap; **rapto** *m* kidnap; **raptor** *m*, **~a** *f* kidnapper

raqueta *f* racket

raquítico *adj fig* rickety

rareza *f* scarcity, rarity; **raro** *adj* rare

ras *m*: **a ~ de tierra** at ground level; **rasante** *adj vuelo* low

rasca *f L.Am.*: **pegarse una ~** F get plastered F; **rascacielos** *m inv* skyscraper; **rascado** *adj L.Am.* F plastered F; **rascar** <1g> *v/t* scratch;

superficie scrape, scratch

rasero *m*: **medir por el mismo ~** treat equally

rasgado *adj boca* wide; **ojos ~s** almond-shaped eyes; **rasgar** <1h> *v/t* tear (up); **rasgo** *m* feature; **a grandes ~s** broadly speaking; **rasguño** *m* MED scratch

raso 1 *adj* flat, level; **soldado ~** private **2** *m material* satin; **al ~** in the open air

raspa *f* fishbone; *L.Am.* F (*reprimanda*) telling-off; **raspado** *m Méx* water ice; **raspadura** *f* scrape; **raspar** <1a> **1** *v/t* scrape; *con lija* sand **2** *v/i* be rough

rastra *f*: **entrar a ~s** drag o.s. in, crawl in; **rastreador** *adj*: **perro ~** tracker dog; **rastrear** <1a> **1** *v/t persona* track; *bosque, zona comb* **2** *v/i* rake; **rastrero** *adj* mean, low; **rastrillo** *m* rake; **rastro** *m* flea market; (*huella*) trace; **desaparecer sin dejar ~** vanish without trace; **rastrojo** *m* stubble

rasurar <1a> *v/t* shave

rata *f* ZO rat

ratero *m*, **-a** *f* petty thief

raticida *m* rat poison

ratificar <1g> *v/t* POL ratify

rato *m* time, while; **~s libres** spare time *sg*; **al poco ~** after a short time *o* while; **todo el ~** all the time; **un buen ~** a good while, a pretty long time; **pasar el ~** pass the time; **he pasado un buen/mal ~** I've had a great/an awful time

ratón *m* ZO, INFOR mouse; **ratonera** *f* mouse trap

raudal *m*: **tienen dinero a ~es** they've got loads of money F; **raudo** *adj* swift

raya *f* GRAM dash; ZO ray; **de pelo** part, *Br* parting; **a or de ~s** striped; **pasarse de la ~** overstep the mark, go too far; **rayado** *adj disco*, *superficie* scratched

rayano *adj* bordering (**en** on)

rayar <1a> **1** *v/t* scratch; (*tachar*) cross out **2** *v/i* border (**en** on), verge (**en** on)

R

rayo m FÍS ray; METEO (bolt of) lightning; **~ láser** laser beam; **~ X** X-ray; **~s ultravioleta** ultraviolet rays

raza f race; *de animal* breed

razón f reason; **a ~ de** *precio* at; **dar la ~ a alguien** admit that s.o. is right; **entrar en ~** see sense; **perder la ~** lose one's mind; **tener ~** be right; **razonable** *adj precio* reasonable; **razonamiento** m reasoning; **razonar** <1a> v/i reason

RDSI *abr* (= **Red Digital de Servicios Integrados**) ISDN (= Integrated Services Digital Network)

reacción f reaction (**a** to); **avión a ~** jet (aircraft); **reaccionar** <1a> v/i react (**a** to); **reaccionario 1** *adj* reactionary **2** m, **-a** f reactionary

reacio *adj* reluctant (**a** to)

reactivación f COM revival, upturn; **reactivar** <1a> v/t COM revive

reactor m reactor; (*motor*) jet engine

reafirmar <1a> **1** v/t reaffirm **2** v/r **~se**: **~se en** *idea* reassert

reajuste m adjustment; **~ ministerial** POL cabinet reshuffle

real *adj* (*regio*) royal; (*verdadero*) real

realeza f royalty

realidad f reality; **en ~** in fact, in reality; **realismo** m realism; **realista 1** *adj* realistic **2** m/f realist

realización f fulfil(l)ment; RAD, TV production; **realizador** m, **-a** f *de película* director; RAD, TV producer; **realizar** <1f> **1** v/t *tarea* carry out; RAD, TV produce; COM realize **2** v/r **~se** *de persona* fulfil(l) o.s.

realquilar <1a> v/t sublet

realzar <1f> v/t highlight

reanimación f revival; **reanimar** <1a> v/t revive

reanudación f resumption; **reanudar** <1a> v/t resume

reaparecer <2d> v/i reappear; **reaparición** f reappearance

reaseguro m reinsurance

rebaja f reduction; **~s de verano /**

invierno summer / winter sale; **rebajar** <1a> **1** v/t *precio* lower, reduce; *mercancías* reduce **2** v/r **~se** lower o.s., humble o.s.

rebanada f slice; **rebanar** <1a> v/t slice

rebañar <1a> v/t: **~ algo** wipe sth clean

rebaño m flock

rebasar <1a> v/t *Méx* AUTO pass, *Br* overtake

rebatir <3a> v/t *razones* rebut, refute

rebeca f cardigan

rebeco m ZO chamois

rebelarse <1a> v/r rebel; **rebelde 1** *adj* rebel *atr* **2** m/f rebel; **rebeldía** f rebelliousness; **rebelión** f rebellion

reblandecer <2d> v/t soften

rebobinar <1a> v/t rewind

rebosar <1a> v/i overflow

rebotar <1a> **1** v/t bounce; (*disgustar*) annoy **2** v/i bounce, rebound; **rebote** m bounce; **de ~** on the rebound

rebozar <1f> v/t GASTR coat

rebuscado *adj* over-elaborate

rebuznar <1a> v/i bray

recado m errand; *Rpl* (*arnés*) harness; **dejar un ~** leave a message

recaída f MED relapse

recalar <1a> v/i MAR put in (**en** at), call (**en** at)

recalcar <1g> v/t stress, emphasize

recalcitrante *adj* recalcitrant

recalentar <1k> v/t *comida* warm o heat up

recámara f *de arma de fuego* chamber; *L.Am.* (*dormitorio*) bedroom

recambio m COM spare part

recapacitar <1a> v/t think over, reflect on

recapitular <1a> v/t recap

recargar <1h> v/t *batería* recharge; *recipiente* refill; **~ un 5%** charge 5% extra; **recargo** m surcharge

recatado *adj* modest; (*cauto*) cautious; **recato** m modesty; (*prudencia*) caution

recauchutar <1a> v/t *neumáticos* retread

recaudación f *acción* collection; *cantidad* takings pl; **recaudar** <1a> v/t *impuestos, dinero* collect; **recaudo** m: **poner a buen ~** put in a safe place

recelo m mistrust

recepción f *en hotel* reception; **recepcionista** m/f receptionist; **receptivo** adj receptive; **receptor** m receiver

recesión f recession

receta f GASTR recipe; **~ médica** prescription; **recetar** <1a> v/t MED prescribe; **recetario** m recipe book

rechazar <1f> v/t reject; MIL repel; **rechazo** m rejection

rechinar <1a> v/i creak, squeak

rechistar <1a> v/i protest; **sin ~** F without a murmur, without complaining

rechoncho adj F dumpy F

rechupete: **de ~** F delicious

recibidor m entrance hall; **recibimiento** m reception; **recibir** <3a> v/t receive; **recibo** m (sales) receipt

reciclable adj recyclable; **reciclado, reciclaje** m recycling; **reciclar** <1a> v/t recycle

recién adv newly; L.Am. (hace poco) just; **~ casados** newly-weds; **~ nacido** newborn; **~ pintado** wet paint; **~ llegamos** we've only just arrived; **reciente** adj recent

recinto m premises pl; *área* grounds pl

recio adj sturdy, tough

recipiente m container

recíproco adj reciprocal

recital m recital; **recitar** <1a> v/t recite

reclamación f complaint; POL claim, demand; **reclamar** <1a> **1** v/t claim, demand **2** v/i complain; **reclame** m L.Am. advertisement

reclamo m lure

reclinable adj: **asiento ~** reclining seat; **reclinar** <1a> **1** v/t rest **2** v/r **~se** lean, recline (*contra* against)

recluir <3g> v/t imprison, confine;

reclusión f JUR imprisonment, confinement; **recluso** m, **-a** f prisoner

recluta m/f recruit; **reclutar** <1a> v/t tb COM recruit

recobrar <1a> **1** v/t recover **2** v/r **~se** recover (*de* from)

recogedor m dustpan

recogepelotas m/f inv ball boy; *niña* ball girl

recoger <2c> **1** v/t pick up, collect; *habitación* tidy up; AGR harvest; (*mostrar*) show **2** v/r **~se** go home; **recogida** f collection; **~ de basuras** garbage collection, Br refuse collection; **~ de equipajes** baggage reclaim

recolectar <1a> v/t AGR harvest, bring in

recomendación f recommendation; **recomendar** <1k> v/t recommend

recompensa f reward; **recompensar** <1a> v/t reward

recomponer <2r; part **recompuesto**> v/t mend

reconciliación f reconciliation; **reconciliar** <1b> **1** v/t reconcile **2** v/r **~se** make up (*con* with), be reconciled (*con* with)

recóndito adj remote

reconfortar <1a> v/t comfort

reconocer <2d> v/t recognize; *errores* admit, acknowledge; *area* reconnoiter, Br reconnoitre; MED examine; **reconocimiento** m recognition; *de error* acknowledge(e)ment; MED examination, check-up; MIL reconnaissance

reconquista f reconquest; **reconquistar** <1a> v/t reconquer

reconsiderar <1a> v/t reconsider

reconstrucción f reconstruction; **reconstruir** <3g> v/t fig reconstruct

reconvenir <3s> v/i JUR counterclaim

reconversión f COM restructuring

recopilación f compilation; **recopilar** <1a> v/t compile

récord 1 adj record(-breaking) **2** m record

recordar <1m> v/t remember, recall; **~ algo a alguien** remind s.o. of sth;

recordatorio m reminder

recorrer <2a> v/t *distancia* cover, do; *a pie* walk; *territorio, país* go around, travel around; *camino* go along, travel along; **recorrido** m route; DEP round

recortar <1a> v/t cut out; *fig* cut; **recorte** m *fig* cutback; **~** *de periódico* cutting, clipping; **~** *salarial* salary cut

recostarse <1m> v/r lie down

recoveco m nook, cranny; *en camino* bend

recrearse <1a> v/r amuse o.s.; **recreativo** adj recreational; *juegos* **~s** amusements; **recreo** m recreation; EDU recess, Br break

recriminar <1a> v/t reproach

recrudecerse <2d> v/r intensify

recta f DEP straight; **~** *final tb fig* home straight

rectángulo m rectangle

rectificar <1g> v/t correct, rectify; *camino* straighten

rectitud f rectitude, probity; **recto** adj straight; *(honesto)* honest

rector m rector, Br vice-chancellor; **rectorado** m rector's office, Br vice-chancellor's office

recuadro m TIP inset, box

recubierto part → **recubrir**; **recubrir** <3a; part *recubierto*> v/t cover *(de* with)

recuento m count; **~** *de votos* recount

recuerdo m memory; *da* **~s** *a Luís* give my regards to Luís

recuperación f tb fig recovery; **recuperar** <1a> 1 v/t *tiempo* make up; *algo perdido* recover 2 v/r **~se** recover *(de* from)

recurrir <3a> 1 v/t JUR appeal against 2 v/i: **~** *a* resort to, turn to; **recurso** m JUR appeal; *material* resource; **~s** *humanos* human resources; **~s** *naturales* natural resources

red f net; INFOR, *fig* network; *caer en las* **~es** *de fig* fall into the clutches of; *Red Digital de Servicios Integrados* Integrated Services Digital Network

redacción f writing; *de editorial* editorial department; EDU essay; **redactar** <1a> v/t write, compose; **redactor** m, **~a** f editor

redada f raid

redentor m, **~a** f COM redeemer; *el Redentor* REL the Savio(u)r

redoble m MÚS (drum)roll

redomado adj F total, out-and-out

redonda f: *a la* **~** around, round about; **redondear** <1a> v/t *para más* round up; *para menos* round down; *(rematar)* round off; **redondo** adj round; *negocio* excellent; *caer* **~** flop down

reducción f reduction; MED setting; **reducido** adj *precio* reduced; *espacio* small, confined; **reducir** <3o> 1 v/t reduce *(a* to); MIL overcome 2 v/r **~se** come down *(a* to)

reducto m redoubt

redujo vb → **reducir**

redundancia f tautology

redundar <1a> v/i have an impact *(en* on)

reeditar <1a> v/t republish, reissue

reelegir <3c & 3l> v/t re-elect

reembolsar <1a> v/t refund; **reembolso** m refund; *contra* **~** collect on delivery, Br cash on delivery, COD

reemplazar <1f> v/t replace

reencarnación f REL reincarnation

reestructurar <1a> v/t restructure

refacción f *L.Am. de edificio* refurbishment; AUTO spare part

referencia f reference; *hacer* **~** *a* refer to, make reference to; **~s** COM references; **referéndum** m referendum; **referente** adj: **~** *a* referring to, relating to; **referirse** <3i> v/r refer *(a* to)

refilón m: *mirar de* **~** glance at

refinado adj tb fig refined; **refinar** <1a> v/t TÉC refine; **refinería** f TÉC refinery

reflector m reflector; EL spotlight; **reflejar** <1a> 1 v/t tb fig reflect 2 v/r **~se** be reflected; **reflejo** m reflex; *imagen* reflection; **reflexión** f fig reflection, thought; **reflexionar** <1a>

v/t reflect on, ponder; **reflexivo** *adj* GRAM reflexive

reflotar <1a> *v/t* COM refloat

reforestar <1a> *v/t* reforest

reforma *f* reform; **~s** *pl* (*obras*) refurbishment *sg*; (*reparaciones*) repairs; **reformador** *m*, **~a** *f* reformer; **reformar** <1a> **1** *v/t* reform; *edificio* refurbish; (*reparar*) repair **2** *v/r* **~se** mend one's ways, reform; **reformatorio** *m* reform school, reformatory; **reformista 1** *adj* reformist, reform *atr* **2** *m/f* reformer

reforzar <1f & 1m> *v/t* reinforce; *vigilancia* increase, step up

refrán *m* saying

refrenar <1a> *v/t* restrain, contain

refrescante *adj* refreshing; **refrescar** <1g> **1** *v/t* BOT fig refresh; *conocimientos* brush up **2** *v/i* cool down **3** *v/r* **~se** cool down; **refresco** *m* soda, *Br* soft drink

refriega *f* MIL clash, skirmish

refrigerador *m* refrigerator; **refrigerar** <1a> *v/t* refrigerate; **refrigerio** *m* snack

refuerzo *m* reinforcement; **~s** MIL reinforcements

refugiado *m*, **-a** *f* refugee; **refugiarse** <1b> *v/r* take refuge; **refugio** *m* refuge

refulgente *adj* dazzling

refunfuñar <1a> *v/i* grumble

refutar <1a> *v/t* refute

regadera *f* watering can; *Méx* (*ducha*) shower; *estar como una ~* F be nuts F; **regadío** *m*: *tierra de ~* irrigated land

regalar <1a> *v/t*: *~ algo a alguien* give sth to s.o., give s.o. sth

regaliz *m* BOT licorice, *Br* liquorice

regalo *m* gift, present

regañadientes: *a ~* reluctantly

regañar <1a> **1** *v/t* tell off **2** *v/i* quarrel; **regañina** *f* F telling off

regar <1h & 1k> *v/t* water; AGR irrigate

regata *f* regatta

regatear <1a> *v/t* DEP get past, dodge; *no ~ esfuerzos* spare no effort

regazo *m* lap

regenerar <1a> *v/t* regenerate

regente *m/f* regent

regidor 1 *adj* governing, ruling **2** *m*, **~a** *f* TEA stage manager

régimen *m* POL regime; MED diet; *estar a ~* be on a diet; **regimiento** *m* MIL regiment

regio *adj* regal, majestic; *S.Am.* F (*estupendo*) great F, fantastic F

región *f* region; **regional** *adj* regional; **regionalismo** *m* regionalism

regir <3l & 3c> **1** *v/t* rule, govern **2** *v/i* apply, be in force **3** *v/r* **~se** be guided (*por* by)

registrar <1a> **1** *v/t* register; *casa* search **2** *v/r* **~se** be recorded; *se registró un máximo de 45°C* a high of 45°C was recorded; **registro** *m* register; *de casa* search; *~ civil* register of births, marriages and deaths

regla *f* (*norma*) rule; *para medir* ruler; MED period; *por ~ general* as a rule

reglamentar <1a> *v/t* regulate; **reglamentario** *adj* regulation *atr*; **reglamento** *m* regulation

regocijarse <1a> *v/r* rejoice (*de* at), take delight (*de* in); **regocijo** *m* delight

regodearse <1a> *v/r* gloat (*con* over), delight (*en* in)

regresar <1a> **1** *v/i* return **2** *v/t Méx* return, give back **3** *v/r* **~se** *L.Am.* return; **regreso** *m* return

regüeldo *m* F belch

reguero *m* trail; *como un ~ de pólvora* fig like wildfire

regulación *f* regulation; *de temperatura* control; **regular 1** *adj sin variar* regular; (*común*) ordinary; (*habitual*) regular, normal; (*no muy bien*) so-so **2** *v/t* TÉC regulate; *temperatura* control; **regularidad** *f* regularity; **regularizar** <1f> *v/t* regularize

regusto *m* aftertaste

rehabilitación *f* MED, fig rehabilitation; ARQUI restoration; **rehabilitar**

<1a> v/t ARQUI restore

rehacer <2s; *part* **rehecho**> v/t *película, ropa, cama* remake; *trabajo, ejercicio* redo; *casa, vida* rebuild

rehén *m* hostage

rehice *vb* → **rehacer**

rehizo *vb* → **rehacer**

rehogar <1h> v/t GASTR fry

rehuir <3g> v/t shy away from

rehusar <1a> v/t refuse, decline

reimprimir <3a> v/t reprint

reina *f* queen; **reinado** *m* reign; **reinante** *adj tb fig* reigning; **reinar** <1a> v/i tb fig reign

reincidente 1 *adj* repeat **2** *m/f* repeat offender; **reincidir** <3a> v/i reoffend

reincorporarse <1a> v/r return (*a* to)

reino *m tb fig* kingdom; **el Reino Unido** the United Kingdom

reinserción *f*: ~ **social** social rehabilitation; **reinsertar** <1a> v/t rehabilitate

reinstaurar <1a> v/t bring back

reintegrarse <1a> v/r return (*a* to); **reintegro** *m* (*en lotería*) prize in the form of a refund of the stake money

reír <3m> **1** v/i laugh **2** v/r ~**se** laugh (*de* at)

reiterar <1a> v/t repeat, reiterate

reivindicación *f* claim; **reivindicar** <1g> v/t claim; ~ **un atentado** claim responsibility for an attack

reja *f* AGR ploughshare, *Br* ploughshare; (*barrote*) bar, railing; **meter entre ~s** *fig* F put behind bars; **rejilla** *f* FERR luggage rack

rejuvenecer <2d> v/t rejuvenate

relación *f* relationship; **relaciones públicas** *pl* public relations, PR *sg*; **relacionado** *adj* related (*con* to); **relacionarse** <1a> v/r be connected (*con* to), be related (*con* to)

relajación *f* relaxation; **relajante** *adj* relaxing; **relajar** <1a> **1** v/t relax **2** v/r ~**se** relax; **relajo** *m* C.Am., Méx uproar

relamerse <2a> v/r lick one's lips

relámpago *m* flash of lightning; **viaje** ~ flying visit

<1a> v/t ARQUI restore

relatar <1a> v/t tell, relate

relatividad *f* relativity

relativo *adj* relative; ~ **a** regarding, about

relato *m* short story

relax *m* relaxation

releer <2e> v/t reread

relegar <1h> v/t relegate

relevante *adj* relevant

relevar <1a> v/t MIL relieve; ~ **a alguien de algo** relieve s.o. of sth; **relevo** *m* MIL change; (*sustituto*) relief, replacement; **carrera de ~s** relay (race); **tomar el ~ de alguien** take over from s.o., relieve s.o.

relicario *m* shrine

relieve *m* relief; **poner de ~** highlight

religión *f* religion; **religiosa** *f* nun; **religioso 1** *adj* religious **2** *m* monk

relinchar <1a> v/i neigh

reliquia *f* relic

rellano *m* landing

rellenar <1a> v/t fill; GASTR *pollo, pimientos* stuff; *formulario* fill out, fill in; **relleno 1** *adj* GASTR *pollo, pimientos* stuffed; *pastel* filled **2** *m tb en cojín* stuffing; *en pastel* filling

reloj *m* clock; *de pulsera* watch, wristwatch; ~ **de pared** wall clock; ~ **de sol** sundial; **relojería** *f* watchmaker's; **relojero** *m*, **-a** *f* watchmaker

reluciente *adj* sparkling, glittering

remanso *m* backwater; ~ **de paz** *fig* haven of peace

remar <1a> v/i row

remarcar <1g> v/t stress, emphasize

rematar <1a> **1** v/t finish off; L.Am. COM auction **2** v/i *en fútbol* shoot; **remate** *m* L.Am. COM auction, sale; *en fútbol* shot; **ser tonto de ~** be a complete idiot

remediar <1b> v/t remedy; **no puedo ~lo** I can't do anything about it; **remedio** *m* remedy; **sin ~** hopeless; **no hay más ~ que ...** there's no alternative but to ...

rememorar <1a> v/t remember

remendar <1k> v/t con parche patch;

R

(zurcir) darn

remesa f *(envío)* shipment, consignment; *L.Am. dinero* remittance

remezón m *L.Am.* earth tremor

remiendo m *(parche)* patch; *(zurcido)* darn

remilgado adj fussy, finicky

reminiscencia f reminiscence

remiso adj reluctant (**a** to)

remite m *en carta* return address; **remitente** m/f sender; **remitir** <3a> **1** v/t send, ship; *en texto* refer (**a** to) **2** v/i MED go into remission; *de crisis* ease (**de** off)

remo m *pala* oar; *deporte* rowing

remodelar <1a> v/t redesign, remodel

remojar <1a> v/t soak; *L.Am.* F *acontecimiento* celebrate

remojo m: **poner a** o **en ~** leave to soak; **remojón** m drenching, soaking; **darse un ~** go for a dip

remolacha f beet, *Br* beetroot; **~ azucarera** sugar beet

remolcador m tug; **remolcar** <1g> v/t AUTO, MAR tow

remolino m *de aire* eddy; *de agua* whirlpool

remolón m, **-ona** f F slacker; **hacerse el ~** slack (off)

remolque m AUTO trailer

remontarse <1a> v/r *en el tiempo* go back (**a** to)

remonte m ski lift

remorder <2h> v/t: **me remuerde la conciencia** I have a guilty conscience; **remordimiento** m remorse

remoto adj remote; **no tengo ni la más -a idea** I haven't the faintest idea

remover <2h> v/t *(agitar)* stir; *L.Am. (destituir)* dismiss; *C.Am., Méx (quitar)* remove

remplazar v/t → **reemplazar**

remuneración f remuneration; **remunerar** <1a> v/t pay

renacentista adj Renaissance *atr*; **renacer** <2d> v/i *fig* be reborn; **Renacimiento** m Renaissance

renacuajo m ZO tadpole; F *persona* shrimp F

renal adj ANAT renal, kidney *atr*

rencilla f fight, argument

rencor m resentment; **guardar ~ a alguien** bear s.o. a grudge; **rencoroso** adj resentful

rendición f surrender

rendija f *crack; (hueco)* gap

rendimiento m performance; FIN yield; *(producción)* output; **rendir** <3l> **1** v/t *honores* pay, do; *beneficio* produce, yield **2** v/i perform **3** v/r **~se** surrender

renegado 1 adj renegade *atr* **2** m renegade; **renegar** <1h & 1k> v/i: **~ de alguien** disown s.o.; **~ de algo** renounce sth

renegrido adj blackened

RENFE abr (= **Red Nacional de Ferrocarriles Españoles**) *Spanish rail operator*

renglón m line; **a ~ seguido** immediately after

rengo adj *CSur* lame; **renguear** <1a> v/i *CSur* limp, walk with a limp

reno m ZO reindeer

renombre m: **de ~** famous, renowned

renovación f renewal; **renovador** adj: **las fuerzas ~es** the forces of renewal; **renovar** <1m> v/t renew

renta f income; *de casa* rent; **~ per cápita** income per capita; **rentabilidad** f profitability; **rentable** adj profitable; **rentar** <1a> v/t *(arrendar)* rent out; *(alquiler)* rent; *carro* hire

renuente adj reluctant, unwilling

renunciar <1b> v/i: **~ a tabaco, alcohol** etc give up; *puesto* resign; *demanda* drop

reñir <3h & 3l> **1** v/t tell off **2** v/i quarrel, fight

reo m, **-a** f accused

reojo: **de ~** out of the corner of one's eye

repantigarse <1h> v/r lounge, sprawl

reparación f repair; *fig* reparation; **reparar** <1a> **1** v/t repair **2** v/i: **~ en algo** notice sth; **reparo** m: **poner ~s a** find problems with; **no tener ~s**

en have no reservations about

repartición *f S.Am.* department; **repartidor** *m* delivery man; **repartir** <3a> *v/t* (*dividir*) share out, divide up; *productos* deliver; **reparto** *m* (*división*) share-out, distribution; TEA cast; **~ a domicilio** home delivery

repasar <1a> *v/t trabajo* go over again; EDU revise

repecho *m* steep slope

repelente 1 *adj fig* repellent, repulsive; F *niño* horrible **2** *m* repellent

repelús *m*: **dar ~ a alguien** F give s.o. the creeps F

repente: **de ~** suddenly; **repentino** *adj* sudden

repercusión *f fig* repercussion; **repercutir** <3a> *v/i* have repercussions (**en** on)

repertorio *m* TEA, MÚS repertoire

repetición *f* repetition; **repetido** *adj* repeated; **repetir** <3l> **1** *v/t* repeat **2** *v/i de comida* repeat **3** *v/r* **~se** happen again; **repetitivo** *adj* repetitive

repipi *adj* F (*afectado*) affected; **es tan ~ niño** he's such a know-it-all F

repisa *f* shelf

replantear <1a> *v/t pregunta*, *problema* bring up again

replegarse <1h & 1k> *v/r* MIL withdraw

repleto *adj* full (**de** of)

réplica *f* replica

replicar <1g> *v/t* reply

repoblar <1m> *v/t* repopulate

repollo *m* BOT cabbage

reponerse <2r; *part* **repuesto**> *v/r* recover (**de** from)

reportaje *m* story, report; **reportero** *m*, **-a** *f* reporter; **~ gráfico** press photographer

reposacabezas *m inv* AUTO headrest

reposar <1a> *v/i* rest; *de vino* settle

reposera *f L.Am.* lounger

reposición *f* TEA revival; TV repeat

reposo *m* rest

repostar <1a> *v/i* refuel

repostería *f* pastries *pl*

reprender <2a> *v/t* scold, tell off

represa *f* dam; (*embalse*) reservoir

represalia *f* reprisal

representación *f* representation; TEA performance; **en ~ de** on behalf of; **representante** *m/f tb* COM representative; **representar** <1a> *v/t* represent; *obra* put on, perform; *papel* play; **~ menos años** look younger

represión *f* repression

reprimenda *f* reprimand

reprimir <3a> *v/t tb* PSI repress

reprobar <1m> *v/t* condemn; *L.Am.* EDU fail

reprochar <1a> *v/t* reproach; **reproche** *m* reproach

reproducción *f* BIO reproduction; **reproducir** <3o> **1** *v/t* reproduce **2** *v/r* **~se** BIO reproduce, breed

reptil *m* ZO reptile

república *f* republic; **republicano 1** *adj* republican **2** *m*, **-a** *f* republican

repudiar <1b> *v/t fml* repudiate; *herencia* renounce

repuesto 1 *part* → **reponer 2** *m* spare part, replacement; **de ~** spare

repugnancia *f* disgust, repugnance; **repugnante** *adj* disgusting, repugnant; **repugnar** <1a> *v/t* disgust, repel

repulsión *f* repulsion; **repulsivo** *adj* repulsive

repuse *vb* → **reponerse**

reputación *f* reputation

requerir <3i> *v/t* require; JUR summons

requesón *m* cottage cheese

requetebién *adv* F really well, brilliantly F

réquiem *m* requiem

requisar <1a> *v/t Arg, Chi* MIL requisition; **requisito** *m* requirement

res *f L.Am.* bull; **carne f de ~** beef; **~es** *pl* cattle *pl*

resaca *f* MAR undertow, undercurrent; *de beber* hangover

resaltar <1a> **1** *v/t* highlight, stress **2** *v/i* ARQUI jut out; *fig* stand out

resarcirse <3b> *v/r* make up (**de**

R

for)

resbaladizo *adj* slippery; *fig* tricky; **resbalar** <1a> *v/i* slide; *fig* slip (up); **resbalón** *m* slip; *fig* F slip-up; **resbaloso** *adj* L.Am. slippery

rescatar <1a> *v/t persona, animal* rescue, save; *bienes* save; **rescate** *m de peligro* rescue; *en secuestro* ransom

rescindir <3a> *v/t* cancel; *contrato* terminate; **rescisión** *f* cancellation; *de contrato* termination

reseco *adj* (*seco*) parched; (*flaco*) skinny

resentimiento *m* resentment; **resentirse** <3i> *v/r* get upset; *de rendimiento, calidad* suffer; **~ de algo** suffer from the effects of sth

reseña *f de libro etc* review; **reseñar** <1a> *v/t* review

reserva 1 *f* reservation; **~ natural** nature reserve; **sin ~s** without reservation; 2 *m/f* DEP reserve; **reservar** <1a> 1 *v/t* (*guardar*) set aside, put by; *billete* reserve 2 *v/r* **~se** save o.s. (*para* for)

resfriado 1 *adj*: **estar ~** have a cold 2 *m* cold; **resfriarse** <1c> *v/r* catch cold; **resfrío** *m* L.Am. cold

resguardar <1a> 1 *v/t* protect (*de* from) 2 *v/r* **~se** protect o.s. (*de* from); **resguardo** *m* COM counterfoil

residencia *f* residence; **~ de ancianos** or **para la tercera edad** retirement home; **residencial** 1 *adj* residential 2 *f Arg, Chi* boarding house; **residente** 1 *adj* resident 2 *m/f* resident; **residir** <3a> *v/i* reside; **~ en** *fig* lie in; **residual** *adj* residual; (*de desecho*) waste *atr*; **residuo** *m* residue; **~s** waste *sg*

resignación *f actitud* resignation; **resignarse** <1a> *v/r* resign o.s. (*a* to)

resina *f* resin

resistencia *f* resistance; EL, TÉC resistor; **resistir** <3a> 1 *v/i* resist; (*aguantar*) hold out 2 *v/t tentación* resist; *frío, dolor etc* stand, bear 3 *v/r* **~se** be reluctant (*a* to)

resolución *f actitud* determination, decisiveness; *de problema* solution (*de* to); JUR ruling; **resolver** <2h; *part* **resuelto**) solve 2 *v/r* **~se** decide (*a* to; *por* on)

resonar <1m> *v/i* echo

resoplar <1a> *v/i* snort

resorte *m* spring

respaldar <1a> *v/t* back, support; **respaldo** *m de silla* back; *fig* backing, support

respectar <1a> *v/i*: **por lo que respecta a ...** as regards ..., as far as ... is concerned; **respectivo** *adj* respective; **respecto** *m*: **al ~** on the matter; **con ~ a** regarding, as regards

respetable *adj* respectable; **respetar** <1a> *v/t* respect; **respeto** *m* respect; **respetuoso** *adj* respectful

respiración *f* breathing; **estar con ~ asistida** MED on a respirator; **respirar** <1a> *v/t & v/i* breathe; **respiratorio** *adj* respiratory; **respiro** *m fig* breather, break

resplandeciente *adj* shining; **resplandor** *m* shine, gleam

responder <2a> 1 *v/t* answer 2 *v/i*: **~ a** answer, reply to; MED respond to; *descripción* fit, match; (*ser debido a*) be due to

responsabilidad *f* responsibility; **responsabilizarse** <1f> *v/r* take responsibility (*de* for); **responsable** 1 *adj* responsible (*de* for) 2 *m/f* person responsible (*de* for); **los ~s del crimen** those responsible for the crime

respuesta *f* (*contestación*) reply, answer; *fig* response

resquebrajar <1a> 1 *v/t* crack 2 *v/r* **~se** crack

resquicio *m* gap

resta *f* MAT subtraction

restablecer <2d> 1 *v/t* re-establish 2 *v/r* **~se** recover; **restablecimiento** *m* re-establishment; *de enfermo* recovery

restante 1 *adj* remaining 2 *m/fpl*: **los/las ~s** *pl* the rest *pl*, the remainder *pl*; **restar** <1a> 1 *v/t* subtract; **~ importancia a** play down the importance of **2** *v/i* remain, be left

restauración *f* restoration

restaurante *m* restaurant

restaurar <1a> *v/t* restore

restituir <3g> *v/t* restore; **en cargo** re-instate

resto *m* rest, remainder; **los ~s mortales** the (mortal) remains

restregar <1h & 1k> *v/t* scrub

restricción *f* restriction; **restringir** <3c> *v/t* restrict, limit

resucitar <1a> **1** *v/t* resuscitate; *fig* revive **2** *v/i de persona* rise from *o* come back from the dead

resuello *m* puffing, heavy breathing

resuelto 1 *part* → **resolver 2** *adj* decisive, resolute

resultado *m* result; **sin ~** without success; **resultar** <1a> *v/i* turn out; **~ caro** prove expensive, turn out to be expensive; **resulta que ...** it turns out that ...

resumen *m* summary; **en ~** in short; **resumir** <3a> *v/t* summarize

resurgir <3c> *v/i* reappear, come back; **resurrección** *f* REL resurrection

retaguardia *f* MIL rearguard

retahíla *f* string

retar <1a> *v/t* challenge; *Rpl* (*regañar*) scold, tell off

retardar <1a> *v/t* delay

retazo *m fig* snippet, fragment

retención *f* MED retention; *de persona* detention; **~ fiscal** tax deduction; **retener** <2l> *v/t dinero etc* withhold, deduct; *persona* detain, hold

reticencia *f* reticence; **reticente** *adj* reticent

retintín *m*: **con ~** F sarcastically

retirada *f* MIL retreat, withdrawal; **retirado** *adj* (*jubilado*) retired; (*alejado*) remote, out-of-the-way; **retirar** <1a> **1** *v/t* take away, remove; *acusación, dinero* withdraw **2** *v/r* **~se** MIL withdraw; **retiro** *m lugar* retreat

reto *m* challenge; *Rpl* (*regaña*)

scolding, telling-off

retobado *adj L.Am.* unruly

retocar <1g> *v/t* FOT retouch, touch up; (*acabar*) put the finishing touches to

retomar <1a> *v/t*: **~ algo** *fig* take sth up again

retoque *m* FOT touching-up; (*acabado*) finishing touch

retorcer <2b & 2h> *v/t* twist; **retorcido** *adj fig* twisted; **retorcijón** *m* stomach cramp

retórica *f* rhetoric

retornar <1a> *v/i* return; **retorno** *m* return

retortijón *m* cramps *pl*, *Br* stomach cramp

retractar <1a> *v/t* retract, withdraw

retraer <2p; *part* retraído> **1** *v/t* retract **2** *v/r* **~se** withdraw; **retraído 1** *part* → **retraer 2** *adj* withdrawn

retransmisión *f* RAD, TV transmission, broadcast; **retransmitir** <3a> *v/t* transmit, broadcast

retrasado 1 *part* → **retrasar 2** *adj tren, entrega* late; *con trabajo, pagos* behind; **está ~ en clase** he's lagging behind in class; **~ mental** mentally handicapped; **retrasar** <1a> **1** *v/t* hold up; *reloj* put back; *reunión* postpone, put back **2** *v/i de reloj* lose time; *en los estudios* be behind **3** *v/r* **~se** (*atrasarse*) be late; *de reloj* lose time; *con trabajo, pagos* get behind; **retraso** *m* delay; **ir con ~** be late

retratar <1a> *v/t* FOT take a picture of; *fig* depict; **retrato** *m* picture; **~-robot** composite photo, E-Fit®

retrete *m* bathroom

retribución *f* salary

retroactivo *adj* retroactive; **retroceder** <2a> *v/i* go back, move back; *fig* back down; **retroceso** *m fig* backward step; **retrógrado** *adj* retrograde; **retroproyector** *m* overhead projector; **retrospectiva** *f* retrospective; **retrovisor** *m* AUTO rearview mirror; **~ exterior** wing mirror

retumbar <1a> *v/i* boom

retuve *vb* → **retener**

reuma, reúma *m* MED rheumatism

reunificación *f* POL reunification

reunión *f* meeting; *de amigos* get-together; **reunir** <3a> **1** *v/t personas* bring together; *requisitos* meet, fulfil(l); *datos* gather (together) **2** *v/r* **~se** meet up, get together; COM meet

reutilizar <1f> *v/t* re-use

revalorizar <1f> **1** *v/t* revalue **2** *v/r* **~se** appreciate (*en* by), increase in value (*en* by)

revaluar <1e> *v/t idea* re-evaluate

revancha *f* revenge

revelación *f* revelation; **revelado** *m* development; **revelar** <1a> *v/t* FOT develop

reventa *f* resale

reventar <1k> **1** *v/i* burst; *lleno a* **~** full to bursting **2** *v/t puerta etc* break down **3** *v/r* **~se** burst; *se reventó a trabajar* fig he worked his butt off F; **reventón** *m* AUTO blowout

reverberar <1a> *v/i de sonido* reverberate

reverencia *f* reverence; *saludo: de hombre* bow; *de mujer* curtsy; **reverendo** *m* REL reverend

reversible *adj ropa* reversible; **reverso** *m* reverse, back

revés *m* setback; *tenis* backhand; *al* or *del* **~** back to front; *con el interior fuera* inside out

revestir <3l> *v/t* TÉC cover (*de* with); **~ gravedad** be serious

revisación *f L.Am.* check-up

revisada *f L.Am.* → **revisión**; **revisar** <1a> *v/t* check, inspect; **revisión** *f* check, inspection; AUTO service; *técnica* roadworthiness test, *Br* MOT (test); **~ médica** check-up; **revisor** *m*, **-a** *f* FERR (ticket) inspector

revista *f* magazine; *pasar* **~ a** MIL inspect, review; *fig* review

revivir <3a> **1** *v/i* revive **2** *v/t* relive

revocar <1g & 1m> *v/t pared* render; JUR revoke

revolcarse <1g & 1m> *v/r* roll around; **revolcón** *m* tumble; F *de amantes* roll in the hay F

revolotear <1a> *v/i* flutter

revoltijo, revoltillo *m* mess, jumble

revoltoso *adj niño* naughty

revolución *f* revolution; **revolucionario** **1** *adj* revolutionary **2** *m*, **-a** *f* revolutionary

revólver *m* revolver

revolver <2h; *part* **revuelto**> **1** *v/t* GASTR stir; *estómago* turn; (*desordenar*) mess up **2** *v/i* rummage (*en* in) **3** *v/r* **~se** *del tiempo* worsen

revuelo *m* stir

revuelto **1** *part* → **revolver** **2** *adj mar* rough; *gente* restless

rey *m* king

reyerta *f* fight

rezagarse <1h> *v/r* drop back, fall behind

rezar <1f> **1** *v/t oración* say **2** *v/i* pray; *de texto* say; **rezo** *m* prayer

rezongar <1h> *v/i* grumble

rezumar <1a> *v/t & v/i* ooze

ría 1 *vb* → **reír 2** *f* estuary

riachuelo *m* stream

riada *f* flood

ribera *f* shore, bank; **riberano** *L.Am.* **1** *adj L.Am.* coastal; *de río* riverside *atr* **2** *m*, **-a** *f* person who lives by the sea / river; **ribereño**: **~ de** bordering (on)

rica *f* rich woman; **rico 1** *adj* rich; *comida* delicious; F *niño* cute, sweet; **~ en vitaminas** rich in vitamins **2** *m* rich man; *nuevo* **~** nouveau riche

ridiculizar <1f> *v/t* ridicule; **ridículo 1** *adj* ridiculous **2** *m* ridicule; *hacer el* **~**, *quedar en* **~** make a fool of o.s.

ríe *vb* → **reír**

riego 1 *vb* → **regar 2** *m* AGR irrigation; **~ sanguíneo** blood flow

ríen *vb* → **reír**

rienda *f* rein; *dar* **~ suelta a** give free rein to

riesgo *m* risk; *a* **~ de** at the risk of; *correr el* **~** run the risk (*de* of); **riesgoso** *adj L.Am.* risky

rifa *f* raffle; **rifar** <1a> **1** *v/t* raffle **2** *v/r* **~se** *fig* fight over

rifle *m* rifle
rige *vb* → **regir**
rigidez *f* rigidity; *de carácter* inflexibility; *fig* strictness; **rígido** *adj* rigid; *carácter* inflexible; *fig* strict; **rigor** *m* rigo(u)r; **riguroso** *adj* rigorous, harsh
rima *f* rhyme; **rimar** <1a> *v/i* rhyme (**con** with)
rimbombante *adj* ostentatious
rímel *m* mascara
rincón *m* corner
rinde *vb* → **rendir**
rinoceronte *m* ZO rhino, rhinoceros
riña *f* quarrel, fight
riñe *vb* → **reñir**
riñón *m* ANAT kidney; **costar un ~** F cost an arm and a leg F
riñonera *f* fanny pack, *Br* bum bag
río 1 *m* river; **~ abajo / arriba** up / down river; **el Río de la Plata** the River Plate **2** *vb* → **reír**
rioplatense *adj* of the River Plate area, River Plate *atr*
riqueza *f* wealth
risa *f* laugh; **~s** *pl* laughter *sg*; **dar ~** be funny; **morirse de ~** kill o.s. laughing; **tomar algo a ~** treat sth as a joke
ristra *f* string
risueño *adj* cheerful
rítmico *adj* rhythmic(al); **ritmo** *m* rhythm; *de desarrollo* rate, pace
rito *m* rite; **ritual** *m/adj* ritual
rival *m/f* rival; **rivalidad** *f* rivalry; **rivalizar** <1f> *v/i*: **~ con** rival
rizado *adj* curly; **rizar** <1f> **1** *v/t* curl **2 ~se** *v/r* curl; **rizo** *m* curl
robar <1a> *v/t persona, banco* rob; *objeto* steal; *naipe* take, pick up
roble *m* BOT oak
robo *m* robbery; *en casa* burglary
robot *m* robot; **~ de cocina** food processor; **robótica** *f* robotics
robustecer <2d> **1** *v/t* strengthen **2** *v/r* **~se** become stronger; **robusto** *adj* robust, sturdy
roca *f* rock
roce *m fig* friction; **tener ~s con** come into conflict with
rociar <1c> *v/t* spray

rocín *m* F nag
rocío *m* dew
rock *m* MÚS rock
rococó *adj* rococo
rocódromo *m* climbing wall
rocoto *m S.Am.* hot red pepper
rodaballo *m* ZO turbot
rodaja *f* slice
rodaje *m de película* shooting, filming; AUTO breaking in, *Br* running in
rodapié *m* baseboard, *Br* skirting board
rodar <1m> **1** *v/i* roll; *de coche* go, travel (**a** at); *sin rumbo fijo* wander **2** *v/t película* shoot; AUTO break in, *Br* run in
rodear <1a> **1** *v/t* surround **2** *v/r* **~se** surround o.s. (**de** with); **rodeo** *m* detour; *con caballos y vaqueros etc* rodeo; **andarse con ~s** beat about the bush; **hablar sin ~s** speak plainly, not beat about the bush
rodilla *f* knee; **de ~s** kneeling, on one's knees; **hincarse** or **ponerse de ~s** kneel (down)
rodillo *m* rolling pin; TÉC roller
rododendro *m* BOT rhododendron
roedor *m* rodent; **roer** <2za> *v/t* gnaw; *fig* eat into
rogar <1h & 1m> *v/t* ask for; *(implorar)* beg for, plead for; **hacerse de ~** play hard to get
rojizo *adj* reddish; **rojo 1** *adj* red; **al ~ vivo** red hot **2** *m* color red **3** *m*, **-a** *f* POL red, commie F
rol *m* role
rollizo *adj* F chubby
rollo *m* FOT roll; *fig* F drag F; **buen / mal ~** F good / bad atmosphere; **¡qué ~!** F what a drag! F
Roma Rome
romance *m* romance; **románico** *m/adj* Romanesque; **romano 1** *adj* Roman **2** *m*, **-a** *f* Roman; **romántico 1** *adj* romantic **2** *m*, **-a** *f* romantic
rombo *m* rhombus
romero *m* BOT rosemary
rompecabezas *m* puzzle; **rompehielos** *m inv* icebreaker**

R

romper <2a; *part roto*> **1** v/t break; (*hacer añicos*) smash; *tela*, *papel* tear **2** v/i break; ~ *a* start to; ~ *con alguien* break up with s.o. **3** v/r ~**se** break

rompopo *m* C.Am., Méx bebida eggnog

ron *m* rum

roncar <1g> v/i snore

roncha *f* MED bump, swelling

ronco *adj* hoarse; *quedarse* ~ go hoarse

ronda *f* round; **rondar** <1a> v/t patrol; *me ronda una idea* I have an idea going around in my head **2** v/i F hang around

ronquido *m* snore; ~*s pl* snoring *sg*

ronronear <1a> v/i *de gato* purr

roña *f* grime; **roñoso** *adj* grimy, grubby

ropa *f* clothes *pl*; ~ *de cama* bedclothes *pl*; ~ *interior* underwear; ~ *íntima* L.Am. underwear; **ropero** *m* closet, Br wardrobe

rosa 1 *adj* pink **2** *f* BOT rose; *fresco como una* ~ fresh as a daisy; *ver algo de color de* ~ see sth through rose-colo(u)red glasses; **rosado 1** *adj* pink; *vino* rosé **2** *m* rosé; **rosal** *m* rosebush

rosario *m* REL rosary; *fig* string

rosbif *m* GASTR roast beef

rosca *f* TÉC thread; GASTR F *pastry similar to a donut*

rosco *m* GASTR *pastry similar to a donut*; *no comerse un* ~ P not get anywhere

roscón *m* GASTR *large ring-shaped cake*

rosquilla *f pastry similar to a donut*

rosticería *f* L.Am. *type of deli that sells roast chicken*

rostro *m* face

rotación *f* rotation

rotisería *f* L.Am. deli, delicatessen

roto 1 *part* → **romper 2** *adj* pierna etc broken; (*hecho añicos*) smashed; *tela*, *papel* torn **3** *m*, -**a** *f* Chi one of the urban poor

rotonda *f* traffic circle, Br roundabout

rotoso *adj* Rpl F scruffy

rotulador *m* fiber-tip, Br fibre-tip, felt-tip; **rótulo** *m* sign

rotundo *adj fig* categorical

rotura *f* breakage; *una* ~ *de cadera* MED a broken hip

rozadura *f* chafing, rubbing; **rozagante** *adj* healthy; **rozar** <1f> **1** v/t rub; (*tocar ligeramente*) brush; *fig* touch on **2** v/i rub **3** v/r ~**se** rub; (*desgastarse*) wear

rte. *abr* (= **remitente**) sender

ruana *f* Ecuad poncho

rubeola, **rubéola** *f* MED German measles *sg*

rubí *m* ruby

rubicundo *adj* ruddy; **rubio** *adj* blond; *tabaco* ~ Virginia tobacco

ruborizarse <1f> v/r go red, blush

rúbrica *f* heading; *de firma* flourish

rubro *m* L.Am. category, heading

rudeza *f* roughness

rudimentario *adj* rudimentary

rudo *adj* rough

rueda *f* wheel; ~ *dentada* cogwheel; ~ *de prensa* press conference; ~ *de recambio* spare wheel

ruedo *m* TAUR bullring

ruego 1 *vb* → **rogar 2** *m* request

rufián *m* rogue

rugby *m* rugby

rugido *m* roar; **rugir** <3c> v/i roar

rugoso *adj superficie* rough

ruido *m* noise; *hacer* ~ make a noise; *mucho* ~ *y pocas nueces* all talk and no action; **ruidoso** *adj* noisy

ruin *adj* despicable, mean; (*tacaño*) mean, miserly

ruina *f* ruin; *llevar a alguien a la* ~ *fig* bankrupt s.o.

ruiseñor *m* ZO nightingale

ruleta *f* roulette

ruletero *m* Méx cab o taxi driver

rulo *m* roller

rumbeador *m* Rpl tracker; **rumbear** <1a> v/i L.Am. head (*para* for)

rumbo *m* course; *tomar* ~ *a* head for; *perder el* ~ *fig* lose one's way

rumboso *adj* lavish

rumiar <1b> v/t *fig* ponder

rumor *m* rumo(u)r; **rumorearse** <1a> *v/r* be rumo(u)red

rupestre *adj*: *pintura* ~ cave painting

ruptura *f de relaciones* breaking off; *de pareja* break-up

rural 1 *adj* rural **2** *m Rpl* station wagon, *Br* estate car; *~es Méx* (rural) police

Rusia Russia; **ruso 1** *adj* Russian **2** *m*, **-a** *f* Russian

rústico *adj* rustic

ruta *f* route

rutina *f* routine; **rutinario** *adj* routine atr

S

S *abr* (= *sur*) S (= South(ern))

S.A. *abr* (= *sociedad anónima*) inc (= incorporated), *Br* plc (= public limited company)

sábado *m* Saturday

sábana *f* sheet; ~ *ajustable* fitted sheet

sabana *f* savanna(h)

sabandija *f* bug, creepy-crawly

sabañón *m* chilblain

sabelotodo *m* F know-it-all F, *Br* know-all F

saber <2n> **1** *v/t* know (*de* about); ~ *hacer algo* know how to do sth, be able to do sth; *no lo supe hasta más tarde* I didn't find out till later; *hacer* ~ *algo a alguien* let s.o. know sth; *¡qué sé yo!* who knows?; *que yo sepa* as far as I know; *sabérselas todas* F know every trick in the book **2** *v/i* taste (*a* of); *me sabe a quemado* it tastes burnt to me; *me sabe mal fig* it upsets me **3** *m* knowledge, learning

sabiduría *f* wisdom; (*conocimientos*) knowledge; **sabiendas** *fpl*: *a* ~ knowingly; *a* ~ *que* knowing full well that; **sabio 1** *adj* wise; (*sensato*) sensible **2** *m*, **-a** *f* wise person; (*experto*) expert; **sabiondo**, **-a** *f* know-it-all F, *Br* know-all F

sablazo *m*: *dar un* ~ *a alguien* F scrounge money off s.o.

sable *m* saber, *Br* sabre

sablear <1a> *v/t* & *v/i L.Am.* F scrounge (*a* from)

sabor *m* flavo(u)r, taste; *dejar mal* ~ *de boca fig* leave a bad taste in the mouth; **saborear** <1a> *v/t* savo(u)r; *fig* relish

sabotaje *m* sabotage; **saboteador** *m*, **-a** *f* saboteur; **sabotear** <1a> *v/t* sabotage

sabroso *adj* tasty; *fig* juicy; *L.Am.* (*agradable*) nice, pleasant; **sabrosura** *f L.Am.* tasty dish

sabueso *m fig* sleuth

sacacorchos *m inv* corkscrew; **sacamuelas** *m inv desp* F dentist; **sacapuntas** *m inv* pencil sharpener

sacar <1g> **1** *v/t* take out; *mancha* take out, remove; *información* get; *disco, libro* bring out; *fotocopias* make; ~ *a alguien a bailar* ask s.o. to dance; ~ *algo en claro* (*entender*) make sense of sth; ~ *de paseo* take for a walk **2** *v/r* ~*se L.Am. ropa* take off

sacarina *f* saccharin(e)

sacerdote *m* priest; **sacerdotisa** *f* priestess

saciar <1b> *v/t fig* satisfy, fulfill; **saciedad** *f*: *repetir algo hasta la* ~ *fig* repeat sth time and again, repeat sth ad nauseam

saco *m* sack; *L.Am.* jacket; ~ *de dormir* sleeping bag; *entrar a* ~ *en* F burst into, barge into F

sacramento *m* sacrament

sacrificar <1g> **1** *v/t* sacrifice;

(*matar*) slaughter **2** *v/r* **~se** make sacrifices (*por* for); **sacrificio** *m* sacrifice; **sacrilegio** *m* sacrilege; **sacristán** *m* sexton; **sacristía** *f* vestry

sacudida *f* shake, jolt; EL shock; **sacudir** <3a> **1** *v/t tb fig* shake; F *niño* beat, wallop F **2** *v/r* **~se** shake off, shrug off; **~se alguien** (*de encima*) get rid of s.o.

sádico 1 *adj* sadistic **2** *m*, **-a** *f* sadist; **sadismo** *m* sadism

safari *m* safari; **~ fotográfico** photographic safari

sagaz *adj* shrewd, sharp

Sagitario *m/f inv* ASTR Sagittarius

sagrado *adj* sacred, holy; **sagrario** *m* tabernacle

Sahara Sahara

sainete *m* TEA short farce, one-act play

sal 1 *f* salt; **~ común** cooking salt; **~ marina** sea salt **2** *vb* → **salir**

sala *f* room, hall; *de cine* screen; JUR court room; **~ de embarque** AVIA departure lounge; **~ de espera** waiting room; **~ de estar** living room; **~ de fiestas** night club; **~ de sesiones** *or* **de juntas** boardroom

saladero *m L.Am.* meat / fish salting factory; **salado** *adj* salted; (*con demasiada sal*) salty; (*no dulce*) *fig* funny, witty; *C.Am.*, *Chi*, *Rpl* F pric(e)y F

salamandra *f* ZO salamander

salamanquesa *f* ZO gecko

salami *m* salami

salar <1a> **1** *v/t* add salt to, salt; *para conservar* salt **2** *m Arg* salt mine

salarial *adj* salary *atr*; **salario** *m* salary; **~ base** basic wage; **~ mínimo** minimum wage

salazón *f* salted fish / meat; **en ~** salt *atr*

salchicha *f* sausage; **salchichón** *m* type of spiced sausage

saldar <1a> *v/t disputa* settle; *deuda* settle, pay; *géneros* sell off; **saldo** *m* COM balance; (*resultado*) result; **~ acreedor** credit balance; **~ deudor** debit balance; **de ~** reduced, on

sale

saldré *vb* → **salir**

salero *m* salt cellar; *fig* wit; **saleroso** *adj* funny, witty

salga *vb* → **salir**

salgo *vb* → **salir**

salida *f* exit, way out; TRANSP departure; *de carrera* start; **~ de emergencia** emergency exit; **~ de tono** ill-judged remark

saliente *adj* projecting, protruding; *presidente* retiring, outgoing

salir <3r> **1** *v/i* leave, go out; (*aparecer*) appear, come out; **~ de** (*ir fuera de*) leave, go out of; (*venir fuera de*) leave, come out of; **~ a alguien** take after s.o.; **~ a 1000 pesetas** cost 1000 pesetas; **~ bien / mal** turn out well / badly; **el dibujo no me sale** F I can't get this drawing right; **no me salió el trabajo** I didn't get the job; **~ con alguien** date s.o., go out with s.o.; **~ perdiendo** end up losing **2** *v/r* **~se** *de líquido* overflow; (*dejar*) leave; **~se de la carretera** leave the road, go off the road; **~se con la suya** get what one wants

salitre *m* saltpeter, *Br* saltpetre

saliva *f* saliva; **tragar ~** hold one's tongue

salmo *m* psalm

salmón *m* ZO salmon; **color ~** salmon; **salmonete** *m* ZO red mullet

salmuera *f* pickle, brine

salobre *adj* salt; (*con demasiada sal*) salty

salomónico *adj* just, fair

salón *m* living room; **~ de actos** auditorium, hall; **~ de baile** dance hall; **~ de belleza** beauty parlo(u)r, beautician's

salpicadera *f Méx* AUTO fender, *Br* mudguard; **salpicadero** *m* AUTO dash(board); **salpicadura** *f* stain; **salpicar** <1g> *v/t* splash, spatter (*con* with); *fig* sprinkle, pepper; **salpicón** *m* GASTR *vegetable salad with chopped meat or fish*

salpimentar <1k> *v/t* season (with

salt and pepper)

salsa f GASTR sauce; *baile* salsa; *en su ~* fig in one's element; **salsera** f sauce boat

saltamontes m inv ZO grasshopper

saltar <1a> **1** v/i jump, leap; *~ a la vista* fig be obvious, be clear; *~ sobre* pounce on; *~ a la comba* jump rope, Br skip **2** v/t valla jump **3** v/t *~se* (omitir) miss, skip

saltear <1a> v/t GASTR sauté

saltimbanqui m acrobat

salto m leap, jump; *~ de agua* waterfall; *~ de altura* high jump; *~ de longitud* long jump; *~ mortal* somersault; **saltón** adj: *ojos saltones* bulging eyes

salubridad f L.Am. health; *Salubridad* L.Am. Department of Health; **salud** f health; *¡(a tu) ~!* cheers!; **saludable** adj healthy; **saludar** <1a> v/t say hello to, greet; MIL salute; **saludo** m greeting; MIL salute; *~s en carta* best wishes

salva f: *~ de aplausos* round of applause

salvación f REL salvation

salvado m bran

salvador m REL savio(u)r

salvadoreño **1** adj Salvador(e)an **2** m, *-a* f Salvador(e)an

salvaguardar <1a> v/t safeguard, protect

salvajada f atrocity, act of savagery; *decir una ~* say something outrageous; **salvaje** **1** adj wild; (bruto) brutal **2** m/f savage; **salvajismo** m savagery

salvamanteles m inv table mat

salvamento m rescue; *buque de ~* life boat

salvapantallas m inv INFOR screensaver

salvar <1a> **1** v/t save; obstáculo get round, get over **2** v/r *~se* escape, get out; **salvavidas** m inv life belt; **salvedad** f (excepción) exception

salvo **1** adj: *estar a ~* be safe (and sound); *ponerse a ~* reach safety **2** adv & prp except, save; *~ error u omisión* errors and omissions ex-

cepted

sambenito m: *le han colgado el ~ de vago* F they've got him down as idle F

sambumbia f L.Am. watery drink

San adj Saint

sanar <1a> **1** v/t cure **2** v/i de persona get well, recover; de herida heal; **sanatorio** m sanitarium, clinic

sanción f JUR penalty, sanction; **sancionar** <1a> v/t penalize; (multar) fine

sancocho m W.I. type of stew

sandalia f sandal

sándalo m BOT sandalwood

sandez f nonsense; *decir sandeces* talk nonsense

sandía f watermelon

sandunga f F wit; **sandunguero** adj L.Am. F witty

sandwich m tostado toasted sandwich; L.Am. sin tostar sandwich

saneamiento m cleaning up; COM restructuring, rationalization; **sanear** <1a> v/t clean up; COM restructure, rationalize

sangrar <1a> **1** v/t *~ a alguien* fig F sponge off s.o. **2** v/i bleed; **sangre** f blood; *~ fría* fig calmness, coolness; *a ~ fría* fig in cold blood; *no llegará la ~ al río* it won't come to that, it won't be that bad; **sangría** f GASTR sangria; **sangriento** adj bloody; **sangrigordo** adj Méx tedious, boring; **sanguijuela** f ZO, fig leech; **sanguinario** adj bloodthirsty

sanidad f health; **sanitario** adj (public) health atr; **sanitarios** mpl bathroom fittings; **sano** adj healthy; *~ y salvo* safe and well; *cortar por lo ~* take drastic measures

sanseacabó: *y ~* F and that's that F

santa f Saint

santiamén m: *en un ~* F in an instant

santidad f: *Su Santidad* His Holiness

santiguarse <1i> v/r cross o.s., make the sign of the cross

santo **1** adj holy **2** m saint; *~ y seña* F password; *¿a ~ de qué?* F what on earth for? F; *no es ~ de mi*

devoción F I don't like him very much; **santuario** m fig sanctuary; **santurrón** m, **-ona** f sanctimonious person

saña f viciousness

sapo m ZO toad; **echar ~s y culebras** fig curse and swear

saque m en tenis serve; **~ de banda** en fútbol throw-in; **~ de esquina** corner (kick); **tener buen ~** F have a big appetite

saquear <1a> v/t sack, ransack

sarampión m MED measles

sarao m party

sarape m Méx poncho, blanket

sarcasmo m sarcasm; **sarcástico** adj sarcastic

sarcófago m sarcophagus

sardina f sardine; **como ~s en lata** like sardines

sargento m sergeant

sarna f MED scabies; **sarnoso** adj scabby

sarpullido m MED rash

sarro m tartar

sarta f string, series

sartén f frying pan; **tener la ~ por el mango** fig be the boss, be in the driving seat

sastra f tailor(ess); **sastre** m tailor

satán, **satanás** m Satan; **satánico** adj satanic

satélite m satellite; **ciudad ~** satellite town

satén, **satín** m satin

sátira f satire; **satírico** adj satirical; **satirizar** <1f> v/t satirize

satisfacción f satisfaction; **satisfacer** <2s; part **satisfecho**> v/t satisfy; requisito, exigencia meet, fulfil(l); deuda settle, pay off; **satisfactorio** adj satisfactory; **satisfecho 1** part → **satisfacer 2** adj satisfied; (lleno) full; **darse por ~** be satisfied (con with)

saturar <1a> v/t saturate

sauce m BOT willow; **~ llorón** weeping willow

saúco m BOT elder

saudí m/f & adj Saudi

saudita m/f Saudi

sauna f sauna

savia f sap

saxofón, **saxófono** m saxophone, sax F

sazón f: **a la ~** at that time; **sazonar** <1a> v/t GASTR season

scooter m motor scooter

se ◊ pron complemento indirecto: a él (to) him; a ella (to) her; a usted, ustedes (to) you; a ellos (to) them; **~ lo daré** I will give it to him/ her/you/them ◊ reflexivo: con él himself; con ella herself; cosa itself; con usted yourself; con ustedes yourselves; con ellos themselves; **~ vistió** he got dressed, he dressed himself; **se lavó las manos** she washed her hands; **~ abrazaron** they hugged each other ◊ oración impersonal: **~ cree** it is thought; **~ habla español** Spanish spoken

sé vb → **saber**

sea vb → **ser**

sebo m grease, fat

secador m: **~ (de pelo)** hair dryer; **secadora** f dryer; **secar** <1g> **1** v/t dry **2** v/r **~se** dry

sección f section

secesión f POL secession

seco adj dry; fig persona curt, brusque; **parar en ~** stop dead

secreción f secretion

secretaria f secretary; **~ de dirección** executive secretary; **secretaría** f secretary's office; de organización secretariat; **secretario** m tb POL secretary; **secreter** m mueble writing desk; **secretismo** m secrecy; **secreto 1** adj secret **2** m secret; **un ~ a voces** an open secret; **en ~** in secret

secta f sect; **sectario** adj sectarian; **sectarismo** m sectarianism

sector m sector

secuaz m/f follower

secuela f MED after-effect

secuencia f sequence; **secuencial** adj INFOR sequential

secuestrador m, **~a** f kidnapper; **secuestrar** <1a> v/t barco, avión hijack; persona abduct, kidnap;

secuestro *m de barco, avión* hijacking; *de persona* abduction, kidnapping; **~ aéreo** hijacking

secundar <1a> *v/t* support, back; **secundario** *adj* secondary

sed *f tb fig* thirst; **tener ~** be thirsty

seda *f* silk; **como una ~** F as smooth as silk

sedal *m* fishing line

sedante *m* sedative

sede *f de organización* headquarters; *de acontecimiento* site; **~ social** head office

sedentario *adj* sedentary

sedición *f* sedition

sediento *adj* thirsty; **estar ~ de** *fig* thirst for

sedimentar <1a> *v/t* deposit; **sedimento** *m* sediment

sedoso *adj* silky

seducción *f* seduction; *(atracción)* attraction; **seducir** <3o> *v/t* seduce; *(atraer)* attract; *(cautivar)* captivate, charm; **seductor 1** *adj* seductive; *(atractivo)* attractive; *oferta* tempting **2** *m* seducer; **seductora** *f* seductress

segadora *f* reaper, harvester; **segar** <1h & 1k> *v/t* reap, harvest

seglar *adj* secular, lay *atr*

segmento *m* segment

segregación *f* segregation; **~ racial** racial segregation; **segregar** <1h> *v/t* segregate

seguida *f*: **en ~** at once, immediately; **seguido 1** *adj* consecutive, successive; **ir todo ~** go straight on **2** *adv* L.Am. often, frequently; **seguidor** *m*, **~a** *f* follower, supporter; **seguimiento** *m* monitoring; **seguir** <3l & 3d> **1** *v/t* follow; **~ a alguien** follow s.o. **2** *v/i* continue, carry on; **sigue enfadado conmigo** he's still angry with me; **~ haciendo algo** go on doing sth, continue to do sth

según 1 *prp* according to; **~ él** according to him **2** *adv* it depends

segunda *f*: **de ~** *fig* second-rate; **segundero** *m* second hand; **segundo** *m/adj* second

seguridad *f* safety; *contra crimen* security; *(certeza)* certainty; **Seguridad Social** *Esp* Social Security; **seguro 1** *adj* safe; *(estable)* steady; *(cierto)* sure; **es ~** *(cierto)* it's a certainty; **~ de sí mismo** self-confident, sure of o.s. **2** *adv* for sure **3** *m* COM insurance; *de puerta, coche* lock; *L.Am. (imperdible)* safety pin; **poner el ~** lock the door; **ir sobre ~** be on the safe side

seis *adj* six; **seiscientos** *adj* six hundred

seísmo *m* earthquake

selección *f* selection; **~ nacional** DEP national team; **seleccionador** *m*, **~a** *f* DEP: **~ nacional** national team manager; **seleccionar** <1a> *v/t* choose, select; **selectividad** *f en España* university entrance exam; **selecto** *adj* select, exclusive

sellar <1a> *v/t* seal; **sello** *m* stamp; *fig* hallmark; **~ discográfico** record label

selva *f (bosque)* forest; *(jungla)* jungle

semáforo *m* traffic light

semana *f* week; **Semana Santa** Holy Week, Easter; **semanal** *adj* weekly; **semanario** *m* weekly

semblante *m* face

sembrado *m* sown field; **sembrar** <1k> *v/t* sow; *fig: pánico, inquietud etc* spread

semejante 1 *adj* similar; **jamás he oído ~ tontería** I've never heard such nonsense **2** *m* fellow human being, fellow creature; **semejanza** *f* similarity; **semejarse** <1a> *v/r* look alike, resemble each other

semen *m* BIO semen; **semental** *m toro* stud bull; *caballo* stallion

semestre *m* six-month period; EDU semester

semicírculo *m* semicircle; **semiconductor** *m* EL semiconductor; **semifinal** *f* DEP semifinal

semilla *f* seed

seminario *m* seminary; **seminarista** *m* seminarian

semítico *adj* Semitic

sémola *f* semolina

senado *m* senate; **senador** *m*, **~a** *f* senator

sencillez *f* simplicity; **sencillo 1** *adj* simple **2** *m L.Am.* small change

senda *f* path, track; **senderismo** *m* trekking, hiking; **senderista** *m/f* walker, hiker; **sendero** *m* path, track

sendos, -as *adj pl*: **les entregó ~ diplomas** he presented each of them with a diploma

senil *adj* senile

seno *m tb fig* bosom; **~s** breasts

sensación *f* feeling, sensation; **causar ~** *fig* cause a sensation; **sensacional** *adj* sensational; **sensacionalista** *adj* sensationalist

sensatez *f* good sense; **sensato** *adj* sensible

sensibilidad *f* feeling, (*emotividad*) sensitivity; **sensibilizar** <1f> *v/t* make aware (**sobre** of); **sensible** *adj* sensitive; (*apreciable*) appreciable, noticeable; **sensiblero** *adj* sentimental, schmaltzy F; **sensor** *m* sensor; **sensorial** *adj* sensory; **sensual** *adj* sensual; **sensualidad** *f* sensuality

sentada *f* sit-down; **sentado** *adj* sitting, seated; **dar por ~** *fig* take for granted, assume; **sentar** <1k> **1** *v/t fig* establish, create; **~ las bases** lay the foundations, pave the way **2** *v/i*: **~ bien a alguien** *de comida* agree with s.o.; **le sienta bien esa chaqueta** that jacket suits her, she looks good in that jacket **3** *v/r* **~se** sit down

sentencia *f* JUR sentence; **sentenciar** <1b> *v/t* JUR sentence

sentido *m* sense; (*significado*) meaning; **~ común** common sense; **~ del humor** sense of humo(u)r; **perder / recobrar el ~** lose / regain consciousness

sentimental *adj* emotional; **ser ~** be sentimental; **sentimentalismo** *m* sentiment; **sentimiento** *m* feeling; **lo acompaño en el ~** my condolences

sentir 1 *m* feeling, opinion **2** <3i> *v/t*

feel; (*percibir*) sense; **lo siento** I'm sorry **3** *v/r* **~se** feel; (*ofenderse*) take offense, *Br* take offence

seña *f* gesture, sign; **me hizo una ~ para que entrara** he gestured to me to go in; **~s** *pl* address *sg*; **hacer ~s** wave

señal *f* signal; *fig* sign, trace; COM deposit, down payment; **en ~ de** as a token of, as a mark of; **señalado** *adj* special; **señalar** <1a> *v/t* indicate, point out; **señalizar** <1f> *v/t* signpost

Señor *m* Lord

señor 1 *m* gentleman, man; *trato* sir; *escrito* Mr; **el ~ López** Mr López; **los ~es López** Mr and Mrs López; **señora** *f* lady, woman; *trato* ma'am, *Br* madam; *escrito* Mrs, Ms; **la ~ López** Mrs Lopez; **mi ~** my wife; **~s y señores** ladies and gentlemen; **señoría** *f*: **su ~** your Hono(u)r; **señorial** *adj* lordly, noble; **señorita** *f* young lady, young woman; *tratamiento* miss; *escrito* Miss; **la ~ López** Ms López, Miss López

señuelo *m* decoy

sepa *vb* → **saber**

separación *f* separation; **~ de bienes** JUR division of property; **separado** *adj* separated; **por ~** separately; **separar** <1a> **1** *v/t* separate **2** *v/r* **~se** separate, split up F; **separatismo** *m* separatism; **separatista** *m/f & adj* separatist

sepia *f* ZO cuttlefish

sept.* *abr* (= **septiembre**) Sept. (= September)

septentrional *adj* northern

septiembre *m* September

séptimo *adj* seventh

sepulcro *m* tomb; **sepultar** <1a> *v/t* bury; **sepultura** *f* burial; (*tumba*) tomb; **dar ~ a alguien** bury s.o.

sequedad *f fig* curtness

sequía *f* drought

séquito *m* retinue, entourage

ser <2w; *part* **sido**> **1** *v/i* be; **~ de Sevilla** be from Seville; **~ de madera / plata** be made of wood /

silver; *es de Juan* it's Juan's, it belongs to Juan; *~ para* be for; *a no ~ que* unless; *¡eso es!* exactly!, that's right!; *es que ...* the thing is ...; *es de esperar* it's to be hoped; *¿cuánto es?* how much is it?; *¿qué es de ti?* how's life?, how're things?; *o sea* in other words **2** *m* being

Serbia Serbia

serenarse <1a> *v/r* calm down; *del tiempo* clear up

serenata *f* MÚS serenade

serenidad *f* calmness, serenity; **sereno 1** *m*: *dormir al ~* sleep outdoors **2** *adj* calm, serene

serial *m* TV, RAD series; **serie** *f* series; *fuera de ~* out of this world, extraordinary

seriedad *f* seriousness; **serio** *adj* serious; (*responsable*) reliable; *en ~* seriously

sermón *m* sermon; **sermonear** <1a> *v/i* preach

seropositivo *adj* MED HIV positive

serpentina *f* streamer; **serpiente** *f* ZO snake; *~ de cascabel* rattlesnake

serranía *f* mountainous region

serrar <1k> *v/t* saw; **serrín** *m* sawdust; **serrucho** *m* handsaw

servicial *adj* obliging, helpful; **servicio** *m* service; *~s* *pl* restroom *sg*, *Br* toilets; *~ doméstico* domestic service; *~ militar* military service; *~ pos(t)venta* after-sales service; *~ de atención al cliente* customer service; *estar de ~* be on duty

servidor *m* INFOR server

servil *adj* servile; **servilismo** *m* servility

servilleta *f* napkin, serviette; **servilletero** *m* napkin ring

servir <3l> **1** *v/t* serve **2** *v/i* be of use; *¿para qué sirve esto?* what is this (used) for?; *no ~ de nada* be no use at all **3** *v/r ~se* help o.s.; *comida* help oneself to

servodirección *f* power steering

sésamo *m* sesame

sesenta *adj* sixty

sesgar <1h> *v/t* slant, skew

sesión *f* session; *en cine, teatro* show, performance; **sesionar** <1a> *v/i* L.Am. be in session

seso *m* ANAT brain; *fig* brains *pl*, sense; *~s* GASTR brains

set *m tenis* set

seta *f* BOT mushroom; *venenosa* toadstool

setecientos *adj* seven hundred; **setenta** *adj* seventy

seto *m* hedge

s.e.u.o. *abr* (= *salvo error u omisión*) E & OE (= errors and omissions excepted)

seudónimo *m* pseudonym

severo *adj* severe

sevillanas *fpl* folk dance from Seville

sexismo *m* sexism; **sexista** *m/f & adj* sexist; **sexo** *m* sex

sexto *adj* sixth

sexual *adj* sexual; **sexualidad** *f* sexuality

sexy *adj inv* sexy

shock *m* MED shock

si *conj* if; *~ no* if not; *como ~* as if; *por ~* in case; *me pregunto si vendrá* I wonder whether he'll come

sí 1 *adv* yes **2** *pron tercera persona*: *singular masculino* himself; *femenino* herself; *cosa, animal* itself; *plural* themselves; *usted* yourself; *ustedes* yourselves; *por ~ solo* by himself / itself, on his / its own

siamés *adj* Siamese

sibarita *m* bon vivant, epicure

Siberia Siberia

sicario *m* hired assassin

Sicilia Sicily

SIDA *abr* (= *síndrome de inmunidad deficiente adquirida*) Aids (= acquired immune-deficiency syndrome)

sidecar *m* sidecar

sideral *adj viajes* space *atr*; *espacio ~* outer space

siderurgia *f* iron and steel making

sido *part → ser*

sidra *f* cider

siembra *f* sowing

siempre *adv* always; **~ que** providing that, as long as; **lo de ~** the same old story; **para ~** for ever

sien *f* ANAT temple

siendo *vb* → **ser**

siento *vb* → **sentir**

sierra *f* saw; GEOG mountain range

siesta *f* siesta, nap; **dormir la ~** have a siesta *o* nap

siete *adj* seven

sífilis *f* MED syphilis

siga *vb* → **seguir**

sigilo *m* (*secreto*) secrecy; (*disimulo*) stealth; **sigiloso** *adj* stealthy

sigla *f* abbreviation, acronym

siglo *m* century; **hace ~s o un ~ que no le veo** *fig* I haven't seen him in a long long time

signatario *m*, **-a** *f* signatory

significado *m* meaning; **significar** <1g> *v/t* mean, signify; **significativo** *adj* meaningful, significant

signo *m* sign; **~ de admiración** exclamation mark; **~ de interrogación** question mark; **~ de puntuación** punctuation mark

sigo *vb* → **seguir**

siguiente **1** *adj* next, following **2** *pron* next (one)

sílaba *f* syllable

silbar <1a> *v/i & v/t* whistle; **silbato** *m* whistle; **silbido** *m* whistle

silenciador *m* AUTO muffler, *Br* silencer; **silencio** *m* silence; **en ~** in silence, silently; **silencioso** *adj* silent

silicio *m* QUÍM silicon; **silicona** *f* silicone

silla *f* chair; **~ de montar** saddle; **~ de ruedas** wheelchair

sillín *m* saddle

sillón *m* armchair, easy chair

silueta *f* silhouette

silvestre *adj* wild; **silvicultura** *f* forestry

simbiosis *f* symbiosis

simbolismo *m* symbolism; **simbolizar** <1f> *v/t* symbolize; **símbolo** *m* symbol

simétrico *adj* symmetrical

similar *adj* similar; **similitud** *f* similarity

simio *m* ZO ape

simpatía *f* warmth, friendliness; **simpático** *adj* nice, lik(e)able; **simpatizante** *m/f* sympathizer, supporter; **simpatizar** <1f> *v/i* sympathize

simple 1 *adj* simple; (*mero*) ordinary **2** *m/f* simpleton; **simplicidad** *f* simplicity; **simplificar** <1g> *v/t* simplify; **simplista** *adj* simplistic

simposio *m* symposium

simulación *f* simulation; **simulacro** *m* (*cosa falsa*) pretense, *Br* pretence, sham; (*simulación*) simulation; **~ de incendio** fire drill; **simulador** *m* simulator; **simular** <1a> *v/t* simulate

simultanear <1a> *v/t*: **~ dos cargos** hold two positions at the same time; **simultáneo** *adj* simultaneous

sin *prp* without; **~ que** without; **~ preguntar** without asking

sinagoga *f* synagogue

sinceridad *f* sincerity; **sincero** *adj* sincere

síncope *m* MED blackout

sincronizar <1f> *v/t* synchronize

sindical *adj* (labor, *Br* trade) union *atr*; **sindicalismo** *m* (labor, *Br* trade) union movement; **sindicalista** *m/f* (labor, *Br* trade) union member; **sindicato** *m* (labor, *Br* trade) union

síndrome *m* syndrome

sinfín *m*: **un ~ de ...** no end of ...

sinfonía *f* MÚS symphony

singular 1 *adj* singular; *fig* outstanding, extraordinary **2** *m* GRAM singular

siniestro 1 *adj* sinister **2** *m* accident; (*catástrofe*) disaster

sinnúmero *m*: **un ~ de** no end of

sino 1 *m* fate **2** *conj* but; (*salvo*) except; **no cena en casa, ~ en el bar** he doesn't have dinner at home, he has it in the bar

sinónimo 1 *adj* synonymous **2** *m* synonym

sinopsis *f inv* synopsis

sinsentido *m* nonsense

sintaxis *f* syntax

síntesis *f inv* synthesis; (*resumen*) summary; **sintético** *adj* synthetic; **sintetizador** *m* MÚS synthesizer

síntoma *m* symptom

sintonía *f melodía* theme tune, signature tune; RAD tuning, reception; **estar en la ~ de** RAD be tuned to; **sintonizar** <1f> **1** *v/t radio* tune in **2** *v/i fig* be in tune (**con** with)

sinuoso *adj* winding

sinusitis *f* MED sinusitis

sinvergüenza *m/f* swine; **¡qué ~!** (*descarado*) what a nerve!

siquiera *adv*: **ni ~** not even; **~ bebe algo** L.Am. at least have a drink

sirena *f* siren; MYTH mermaid

Siria Syria

sirve *vb* → **servir**

sirvienta *f* maid; **sirviente** *m* servant

sisar <1a> *v/t* F pilfer

sísmico *adj* seismic

sistema *m* system; **~ operativo** operating system; **sistemático** *adj* systematic

sitiar <1b> *v/t* surround, lay siege to; **sitio** *m* place; (*espacio*) room; **hacer ~** make room; **en ningún ~** nowhere; **~ web** web site; **situación** *f* situation; **situar** <1e> **1** *v/t* place, put **2** *v/r* **~se** be

S.L. *abr* (= **sociedad limitada**) Ltd (= limited)

slip *m* underpants *pl*

s/n *abr* (= **sin número**) not numbered

sobaco *m* armpit

sobar <1a> *v/t* handle, finger; F *sexualmente* grope F

soberanía *f* sovereignty; **soberano** *m*, **-a** *f* sovereign

soberbia *f* pride, arrogance; **soberbio** *adj* proud, arrogant; *fig* superb

sobornar <1a> *v/t* bribe; **soborno** *m* bribe

sobra *f* surplus, excess; **hay de ~** there's more than enough; **~s** leftovers; **sobradamente** *adv conocido* well; **sobrar** <1a> *v/t*: **sobra comida** there's food left over; **me sobró pintura** I had some paint

left over; **sobraba uno** there was one left

sobre **1** *m* envelope **2** *prp* on; **~ esto** about this; **~ las tres** about three o'clock; **~ todo** above all, especially

sobrecargar <1h> *v/t* overload; **sobrecargo** *m* AVIA chief flight attendant; MAR purser

sobrecoger <2c> *v/t* (*asustar*) strike fear into; (*impresionar*) have an effect on

sobredosis *f inv* overdose

sobrehumano *adj* superhuman

sobremesa *f*: **de ~** afternoon *atr*

sobrenatural *adj* supernatural

sobrenombre *m* nickname

sobrentenderse <2g> *v/r*: **se sobrentiende que ...** needless to say, ...

sobrepasar <1a> **1** *v/t* exceed, surpass; **me sobrepasa en altura** he is taller than me **2** *v/r* **~se** go too far; **sobrepeso** *m* excess weight

sobreponerse <2r; *part* **sobrepuesto**> *v/r*: **~ a** overcome, get over

sobrepuesto *part* → **sobreponerse**

sobresaliente *adj* outstanding, excellent; **sobresalir** <3r> *v/t* stick out, protrude; *fig* excel; **~ entre** stand out among

sobresaltar <1a> **1** *v/t* startle **2** *v/r* **~se** jump, start; **sobresalto** *m* jump, start

sobreseer <2e> *v/t* JUR dismiss

sobrestimar <1a> *v/t* overestimate

sobresueldo *m* bonus

sobrevalorar <1a> *v/t* overrate

sobrevalorar <1a> *v/t* overrate

sobrevenir <3s> *v/i* happen; *de guerra* break out

sobrevivir <3a> *v/i* survive

sobrevolar <1m> *v/t* fly over

sobriedad *f* soberness; *de comida, decoración* simplicity; (*moderación*) restraint

sobrina *f* niece; **sobrino** *m* nephew

sobrio *adj* sober; *comida, decoración* simple; (*moderado*) restrained

socarrón *adj* sarcastic, snide F

socavar <1a> *v/t tb fig* undermine

S

socavón *m* hollow

sociable *adj* sociable; **social** *adj* social; **socialismo** *m* socialism; **socialista** *m/f & adj* socialist

sociedad *f* society; **~ anónima** public corporation, *Br* public limited company; **~ de consumo** consumer society

socio *m*, **-a** *f* de club, asociación etc member; COM partner; **sociología** *f* sociology

socorrer <2a> *v/t* help, assist; **socorrista** *m/f* life guard; **socorro** *m* help, assistance; **¡~!** help!

soda *f* soda (water)

sodio *m* sodium

sofá *m* sofa

sofisticación *f* sophistication; **sofisticado** *adj* sophisticated

sofocante *adj* suffocating; **sofocar** <1g> **1** *v/t* suffocate; *incendio* put out **2** *v/r* **~se** *fig* get embarrassed; (*irritarse*) get angry; **sofoco** *m* fig embarrassment

sofreír <3m> *v/t* sauté; **sofrito** *m* GASTR mixture of fried onions, peppers etc

software *m* INFOR software

soga *f* rope; **estar con la ~ al cuello** F be in big trouble F

sois *vb* → **ser**

soja *f* soy, *Br* soya

sol *m* sun; **hace ~** it's sunny; **tomar el ~** sunbathe

solamente *adv* only

solapa *f* lapel

solar *m* vacant lot

solariego *adj:* **casa -a** family seat

solario, **solárium** *m* solarium

soldado *m/f* soldier

soldador *m* welder; **soldadura** *f* welding, soldering; **soldar** <1m> *v/t* weld, solder

soleado *adj* sunny

soledad *f* solitude, loneliness

solemne *adj* solemn

soler <2h> *v/i:* **~ hacer algo** usually do sth; **suele venir temprano** he usually comes early; **solía visitarme** he used to visit me

solera *f* traditional character

solfeo *m* (tonic) sol-fa

solicitante *m/f* applicant; **solicitar** <1a> *v/t* request; *empleo, beca* apply for; **solícito** *adj* attentive; **solicitud** *f* application, request

solidaridad *f* solidarity; **solidario** *adj* supportive, understanding; **solidarizarse** <1f> *v/r:* **~ con alguien** support s.o., back s.o.; **solidez** *f* solidity; *fig* strength; **sólido** *adj* solid; *fig* sound

solista *m/f* soloist

solitaria *f* ZO tapeworm; **solitario 1** *adj* solitary; *lugar* lonely **2** *m* solitaire, *Br* patience; **actuó en ~** he acted alone

soliviantar <1a> **1** *v/t* incite, stir up **2** *v/r* **~se** *v/r* rise up, rebel

sollozar <1f> *v/i* sob; **sollozo** *m* sob

solo *adj* single; **estar ~** be alone; **sentirse ~** feel lonely; **un ~ día** a single day; **a solas** alone, by o.s.; **por sí ~** by o.s.

sólo *adv* only, just

solomillo *m* GASTR sirloin

solsticio *m* solstice

soltar <1m> **1** *v/t* let go of; (*librar*) release, let go; *olor* give off **2** *v/r* **~se** free o.s.; **~se a andar/hablar** begin *o* start to walk / talk

soltera *f* single *o* unmarried woman; **soltero 1** *adj* single, not married **2** *m* bachelor, unmarried man; **solterona** *f desp* old maid

soltura *f* fluency, ease

soluble *adj* soluble; **solución** *f* solution; **solucionar** <1a> *v/t* solve

solventar <1a> *v/t* resolve, settle; **solvente** *adj* solvent

somanta *f* F beating

sombra *f* shadow; **a la ~ de un árbol** in the shade of a tree; **a la ~ de** *fig* under the protection of; **~ de ojos** eye shadow

sombrero *m* hat; **~ de copa** top hat

sombrilla *f* sunshade, beach umbrella

sombrío *adj fig* somber, *Br* sombre

someter <2a> **1** *v/t* subject; **~ algo a votación** put sth to the vote **2** *v/r* **~se** yield (**a** to); **al ley** comply (**a**

with); (*rendirse*) give in (*a* to); **~se a tratamiento** undergo treatment

somier *m* bed base

somnífero *m* sleeping pill

somnolencia *f* sleepiness, drowsiness; **somnoliento** *adj* sleepy, drowsy

somos *vb* → **ser**

son[1] *m* sound; **al ~ de** to the sound of; **en ~ de paz** in peace

son[2] *vb* → **ser**

sonado *adj* F famous, well-known

sonajero *m* rattle

sonámbulo *m* sleep-walker

sonar <1m> **1** *v/i* ring out; **~ a** sound like; **me suena esa voz** I know that voice, that voice sounds familiar **2** *v/r* **~se**: **~se** (*la nariz*) blow one's nose

sonata *f* MÚS sonata

sonda *f* MED catheter; **~ espacial** space probe; **sondaje** *m L.Am.* poll, survey; **sondear** <1a> *v/t fig* survey, poll; **sondeo** *m*: **~** (*de opinión*) survey, (opinion) poll

soneto *m* sonnet

sonido *m* sound

soniquete *m* droning

sonreír <3m> *v/i* smile; **sonriente** *adj* smiling; **sonrisa** *f* smile

sonrojar <1a> **1** *v/t*: **~ a alguien** make s.o. blush **2** *v/r* **~se** blush; **sonrojo** *m* blush

sonsacar <1g> *v/t*: **~ algo** worm sth out (*a* of), wheedle sth out (*a* of)

sonso *adj L.Am.* silly

soñador 1 *adj* dreamy **2** *m* dreamer; **soñar** <1m> **1** *v/t* dream (*con* about); **2** *v/i* dream; **¡ni ~lo!** dream on! F

soñolencia *f* → **somnolencia**; **soñoliento** *adj* → **somnoliento**

sopa *f* soup; **estar hecho una ~** F be sopping wet; **hasta en la ~** F all over the place F

sopapo *m* F smack, slap

sopera *f* soup tureen

sopesar <1a> *v/t fig* weigh up

sopetón *m*: **de ~** unexpectedly

soplar <1a> **1** *v/i del viento* blow **2** *v/t vela* blow out; *polvo* blow away;

~ algo a la policía tip the police off about sth; **soplete** *m* welding torch; **soplo** *m*: **en un ~** F in an instant; **soplón** *m* F informer, stool pigeon F

soponcio *m*: **le dio un ~** F he passed out

sopor *m* drowsiness, sleepiness; **soporífero** *adj* soporific

soportal *m* porch

soportar <1a> *v/t fig* put up with, bear; **no puedo ~ a José** I can't stand José; **soporte** *m* support, stand; **~ lógico** INFOR software; **~ físico** INFOR hardware

soprano MÚS **1** *m* soprano **2** *m/f* soprano

sorber <2a> *v/t* sip

sorbete *m* sorbet; *C.Am.* ice cream; **sorbetería** *f C.Am.* ice-cream parlo(u)r

sorbo *m* sip

sordera *f* deafness

sórdido *adj* sordid

sordo 1 *adj* deaf **2** *m*, **-a** *f* deaf person; **hacerse el ~** turn a deaf ear; **sordomudo 1** *adj* deaf and dumb **2** *m*, **-a** *f* deaf-mute

sorna *f* sarcasm; **con ~** sarcastically, mockingly

sorocharse <1a> *v/r Pe, Bol* get altitude sickness; **soroche** *m Pe, Bol* altitude sickness

sorprendente *adj* surprising; **sorprender** <2a> *v/t* surprise; **sorpresa** *f* surprise; **de** or **por ~** by surprise

sortear <1a> *v/t* draw lots for; *obstáculo* get round; **sorteo** *m* (*lotería*) lottery, (prize) draw

sortija *f* ring

sortilegio *m* spell, charm

SOS *m* SOS

sosa *f* QUÍM: **~ cáustica** caustic soda

sosegado *adj* calm; **sosegarse** <1h & 1k> *v/r* calm down

sosería *f* insipidness, dullness

sosiego *m* calm, quiet

soslayo *adj*: **de ~** sideways

soso 1 *adj* tasteless, insipid; *fig* dull **2** *m*, **-a** *f* stick-in-the-mud F

S

sospecha f suspicion; **sospechar** <1a> **1** v/t suspect **2** v/i be suspicious; ~ *de alguien* suspect someone; **sospechoso 1** adj suspicious **2** m, **-a** f suspect

sostén m brassiere, bra; fig pillar, mainstay; **sostener** <2l> **1** v/t familia support; opinión hold **2** v/r ~**se** support o.s.; de pie stand up; en el poder stay, remain

sota f naipes jack

sotana f REL cassock

sótano m basement, Br cellar

soterrar <1k> v/t bury

soviético adj Soviet

soy vb → **ser**

soya f L.Am. soy, Br soya

spot m TV commercial

spray m spray

sprint m sprint

squash m DEP squash

Sr. abr (= **señor**) Mr

Sra. abr (= **señora**) Mrs

Sres. abr (= **Señores**) Messrs (= Messieurs)

Srta. abr (= **Señorita**) Miss

stand m COM stand

stock m stock; **tener en** ~ have in stock

su, sus adj pos: de él his; de ella her; de cosa its; de usted, ustedes your; de ellos their; de uno one's

suave adj soft, smooth; sabor, licor mild; **suavidad** f softness, smoothness; de sabor, licor mildness; **suavizante** m de pelo, ropa conditioner; **suavizar** <1f> v/t tb fig soften

subacuático adj underwater

subalterno 1 adj subordinate **2** m, **-a** f subordinate

subasta f auction; **sacar a** ~ put up for auction; **subastar** <1a> v/t auction (off)

subcampeón m DEP runner-up

subconsciente m/adj subconscious

subcontrata(ción) f subcontracting

subdesarrollado adj underdeveloped; **subdesarrollo** m underdevelopment

subdirector m, ~**a** f deputy manager

súbdito m subject

subestimar <1a> v/t underestimate

subida f rise, ascent; ~ *de los precios* rise in prices; **subido 1** part → **subir** **2** adj: ~ *de tono* fig risqué, racy; **subir** <3a> **1** v/t cuesta, escalera go up, climb; montaña climb; objeto raise, lift; intereses, precio raise **2** v/i para indicar acercamiento come up; para indicar alejamiento go up; de precio rise, go up; a un tren, autobús get on; a un coche get in **3** v/r ~**se** go up; a un árbol climb

súbito adj: **de** ~ suddenly, all of a sudden

subjetivo adj subjective

subjuntivo m GRAM subjunctive

sublevar <1a> **1** v/t incite to revolt; fig infuriate, get angry **2** v/r ~**se** rise up, revolt

sublimación f fig sublimation; **sublime** adj sublime, lofty; **subliminal** adj subliminal

submarinismo m scuba diving; **submarinista** m/f scuba diver; **submarino 1** adj underwater **2** m submarine

subnormal adj subnormal

subordinado 1 adj subordinate **2** m, **-a** f subordinate

subproducto m by-product

subrayar <1a> v/t underline; fig underline, emphasize

subrepticio adj surreptitious

subsanar <1a> v/t put right, rectify

subsidiario adj subsidiary

subsidio m welfare, Br benefit; ~ *de paro* or *desempleo* unemployment compensation (Br benefit)

subsistencia f subsistence, survival; de pobreza, tradición persistence; **subsistir** <3a> v/i live, survive; de pobreza, tradición live on, persist

subte m Rpl subway, Br underground

subterfugio m subterfuge

subterráneo 1 adj underground **2** m L.Am. subway, Br underground

subtítulo m subtitle

suburbio m slum area

subvención f subsidy; **subvencio-**

nar <1a> v/t subsidize

subversivo adj subversive

subyacente adj underlying

subyugar <1h> v/t subjugate

succionar <1a> v/t suck

sucedáneo m substitute

suceder <2a> v/i happen, occur; ~ **a** follow; **¿qué sucede?** what's going on?; **sucesión** f succession; ~ **al trono** succession to the throne; **sucesivo** adj successive; **en lo ~** from now on; **suceso** m event; **sucesor** m, **-a** f successor

suciedad f dirt; **sucio** adj tb fig dirty

suculento adj succulent

sucumbir <3a> v/i succumb, give in

sucursal f COM branch

sudaca m/f desp South American

sudadera f sweatshirt

Sudáfrica South Africa; **sudafricano 1** adj South African **2** m, **-a** f South African

Sudamérica South America; **sudamericano 1** adj South American **2** m, **-a** f South American

sudar <1a> v/i sweat

sudario m REL shroud

sudeste m southeast; **sudoeste** m southwest

sudor m sweat; **sudoración** f perspiration; **sudoroso** adj sweaty

Suecia Sweden; **sueco 1** adj Swedish **2** m, **-a** f Swede; **hacerse el ~** F pretend not to hear, act dumb F

suegra f mother-in-law; **suegro** m father-in-law

suela f de zapato sole

sueldo m salary

suelo m en casa floor; en el exterior earth, ground; AGR soil; **estar por los ~s** F be at rock bottom F

suelto 1 adj loose, free; **un pendiente ~** a single earring; **andar ~** be at large **2** m loose change

sueño m (estado de dormir) sleep; (fantasía, imagen mental) dream; **tener ~** be sleepy

suero m MED saline solution; ~ sanguíneo blood serum

suerte f luck; **por ~** luckily; **echar a**

~s toss for, draw lots for; **probar ~** try one's luck; **suertero** m, **-a** f L.Am. F, **suertudo** m, **-a** f L.Am. F lucky devil F

suéter m sweater

suficiente 1 adj enough, sufficient **2** m EDU pass

sufragar <1h> v/t COM meet, pay; **sufragio** m: ~ **universal** universal suffrage

sufrimiento m suffering; **sufrir** <3a> **1** v/t fig suffer, put up with **2** v/i suffer (**de** from)

sugerencia f suggestion; **sugerir** <3i> v/t suggest; **sugestionar** <1a> v/t influence; **sugestivo** adj suggestive

suicida 1 adj suicidal **2** m/f suicide victim; **suicidarse** <1a> v/r commit suicide; **suicidio** m suicide

suite f suite

Suiza Switzerland; **suizo 1** adj Swiss **2** m, **-a** f Swiss **3** m GASTR sugar topped bun

sujetador m brassiere, bra; **sujetapapeles** m inv paperclip; **sujetar** <1a> v/t hold (down), keep in place; (sostener) hold; **sujeto 1** adj secure **2** m individual; GRAM subject

sulfurarse <1a> v/r fig F blow one's top F

suma f sum; **en ~** in short; **sumamente** adv extremely, highly; **sumar** <1a> **1** v/t add; **5 y 6 suman 11** 5 and 6 make 11 **2** v/i add up **3** v/r **~se:** **~se a** join; **sumario** m summary; JUR indictment

sumergir <3c> **1** v/t submerge, immerse **2** v/r **~se** fig immerse o.s. (**en** in), throw o.s. (**en** into)

sumidero m drain

suministrar <1a> v/t supply, provide; **suministro** m supply

sumir <3a> **1** v/t fig plunge, throw (**en** into) **2** v/r **~se** fig sink (**en** into); **sumisión** f submission; **sumiso** adj submissive

sumo adj supreme; **con ~ cuidado** with the utmost care; **a lo ~** at the most

S

suntuoso adj sumptuous

supe vb → **saber**

supeditar <1a> v/t make conditional (**a** upon)

súper adj F super F, great F

superable adj surmountable; **superación** f overcoming, surmounting; **superar** <1a> 1 v/t persona beat; límite go beyond, exceed; obstáculo overcome, surmount 2 v/r ~**se** surpass o.s., excel o.s.

superávit m surplus

superchería f trick, swindle

superdotado adj gifted

superficial adj superficial, shallow; **superficialidad** f superficiality, shallowness; **superficie** f surface

superfluo adj superfluous

superior 1 adj upper; en jerarquía superior; **ser ~ a** be superior to **2** m superior; **superiora** f REL Mother Superior; **superioridad** f superiority

superlativo adj superlative

supermercado m supermarket

superpoblación f overpopulation

superponer <2r> v/t superimpose

superpotencia f POL superpower

superpuesto adj superimposed

supersónico adj supersonic

superstición f superstition; **supersticioso** adj superstitious

supervisar <1a> v/t supervise; **supervisor** m, ~**a** f supervisor

supervivencia f survival; **superviviente 1** adj surviving **2** m/f survivor

suplantar <1a> v/t replace, take the place of

suplementario adj supplementary; **suplemento** m supplement

suplente m/f substitute, stand-in

súplica f plea; **suplicar** <1g> v/t cosa plead for, beg for; persona beg

suplicio m fig torment, ordeal

suplir <3a> v/t carencia make up for; (sustituir) substitute

supo vb → **saber**

suponer <2r; part **supuesto**> v/t suppose, assume; **suposición** f supposition

supositorio m MED suppository

supremacía f supremacy; **supremo** adj supreme

supresión f suppression; de impuesto, ley abolition; de restricción lifting; de servicio withdrawal; **suprimir** <3a> v/t suppress; ley, impuesto abolish; restricción lift; servicio withdraw; puesto de trabajo cut

supuesto 1 part → **suponer 2** adj supposed, alleged; **por ~** of course **3** m assumption

sur m south

surco m AGR furrow

sureño adj southern

surf(ing) m surfing; **surfista** m/f surfer

surgir <3c> v/i fig emerge; de problema come up; de agua spout

surrealismo m surrealism

surtido 1 adj assorted; **bien ~** COM well stocked **2** m assortment, range; **surtidor** m: ~ **de gasolina** or **de nafta** gas pump, Br petrol pump; **surtir** <3a> 1 v/t supply; ~ **efecto** have the desired effect **2** v/i spout **3** v/r ~**se** stock up (**de** with)

susceptible adj touchy; **ser ~ de mejora** leave room for improvement

suscitar <1a> v/t arouse; polémica generate; escándalo provoke

suscribir <3a; part **suscrito**> 1 v/t subscribe to **2** v/r ~**se** subscribe; **suscripción** f subscription; **suscriptor** m, ~**a** f subscriber; **suscrito** part → **suscribir**

suspender <2a> 1 v/t empleado, alumno suspend; objeto hang; reunión adjourn; examen fail **2** v/i EDU fail; **suspense** m fig suspense; **suspensión** f suspension; **suspenso 1** adj alumnos ~**s** students who have failed; **en ~** suspended **2** m fail; **suspensores** mpl L.Am. suspenders, Br braces

suspicacia f suspicion; **suspicaz** adj suspicious

suspirar <1a> v/i sigh; ~ **por algo** yearn for sth, long for sth; **suspiro**

m sigh

sustancia *f* substance; **sustancial** *adj* substantial; **sustantivo** *m* GRAM noun

sustentar <1a> *v/t* sustain; *familia* support; *opinión* maintain; **sustento** *m* means of support

sustitución *f* substitution; **sustituir** <3g> *v/t*: ~ **X por Y** replace X with Y, substitute Y for X; **sustituto** *m* substitute

susto *m* fright, scare; *dar* or *pegar un ~ a alguien* give s.o. a fright

sustraer <2p; *part* **sustraido**> *v/t* subtract, take away; (*robar*) steal; **sustraido** *part* → **sustraer**

susurrar <1a> *v/t* whisper; **susurro** *m* whisper

sutil *adj fig* subtle; **sutileza** *f fig* subtlety

suyo, suya *pron pos*: *de él* his; *de ella* hers; *de usted, ustedes* yours; *de ellos* theirs; *los ~* his / her etc folks, his / her etc family; *hacer de las -as* get up to one's old tricks; *salirse con la -a* get one's own way

T

tabaco *m* tobacco

tábano *m* ZO horsefly

tabarra *f*: *dar la ~ a alguien* F bug s.o. F

taberna *f* bar; **tabernero** *m* bar owner, *Br* landlord; (*camarero*) bartender

tabique *m* partition, partition wall

tabla *f de madera* board, plank; PINT panel; (*cuadro*) table; ~ *de multiplicar* multiplication table; ~ *de planchar* ironing board; ~ *de surf* surf board; *acabar* or *quedar en ~s* end in a tie; **tablero** *m* board, plank; *de juego* board; ~ *de mandos* or *de instrumentos* AUTO dashboard; **tableta** *f*: ~ *de chocolate* chocolate bar; **tablón** *m* plank; ~ *de anuncios* bulletin board, *Br* notice board

tabú *m* taboo

tabulador *m tb* INFOR tab key

taburete *m* stool

tacañería *f* F miserliness, stinginess F; **tacaño 1** *adj* F miserly, stingy F **2** *m*, **-a** *f* F miser F, tightwad F

tacha *f* flaw, blemish; *sin ~* beyond reproach

tachadura *f* crossing-out

tachar <1a> *v/t* cross out

tacho *m Rpl* (*papelera*) wastepaper basket; *en la calle* garbage can, *Br* litter basket

tachón *m* crossing-out

tachuela *f* thumbtack, *Br* drawing pin

tácito *adj* tacit; **taciturno** *adj* taciturn

taco *m* F (*palabrota*) swear word; *L.Am.* heel; GASTR taco (*filled tortilla*)

tacón *m de zapato* heel; *zapatos de ~* high-heeled shoes

táctica *f* tactics *pl*; **táctico** *adj* tactical

tacto *m* (sense of) touch; *fig* tact, discretion

TAE *abr* (= *tasa anual efectiva*) APR (= annual percentage rate)

tahona *f* bakery

tahúr *m* gambler, card-sharp F

taita *m S.Am.* F dad, pop F; *S.Am.* (*abuelo*) grandfather

tajada *f* GASTR slice; *agarrar una ~* F get drunk; *sacar ~* take a cut F; **tajamar** *m S.Am.* (*dique*) dike; **tajante** *adj* categorical; **tajo** *m* cut

tal 1 *adj* such; *no dije ~ cosa* I said no such thing; *el gerente era un ~*

Lucas the manager was someone called Lucas **2** *adv:* ~ *como* such as; *dejó la habitación ~ cual la encontró* she left the room just as she found it; ~ *para cual* two of a kind; ~ *vez* maybe, perhaps; *¿qué ~?* how's it going?; *¿que ~ la película?* what was the movie like?; *con ~ de que* + *subj* as long as, provided that

tala *f de árboles* felling

taladrar <1a> *v/t* drill; **taladro** *m* drill

talante *m* (*genio, humor*) mood; *un ~ bonachón* a kindly nature; *de mal* ~ in a bad mood

talar <1a> *v/t árbol* fell, cut down

talco *m* talc, talcum; *polvos de ~* talcum powder

talego *m* P 1000 pesetas

talento *m* talent

talismán *m* talisman

talla *f* size; (*estatura*) height; *C.Am.* (*mentira*) lie; *dar la ~ fig* make the grade; **tallar** <1a> *v/t* carve; *piedra preciosa* cut

tallarín *m* noodle

taller *m* workshop; ~ *mecánico* auto repair shop; ~ *de reparaciones* repair shop

tallo *m* BOT stalk, stem

talón *m* ANAT heel; (*calcular a ojo*) *~ de Aquiles fig* Achilles' heel; *pisar los talones a alguien* be hot on s.o.'s heels; **talonario** *m:* ~ *de cheques* check book, *Br* cheque book

tamal *m Méx, C.Am.* tamale (*meat wrapped in a leaf and steamed*)

tamaño 1 *adj:* ~ *fallo/problema* such a great mistake / problem **2** *m* size

tambalearse <1a> *v/r* stagger, lurch; *de coche* sway

tambarria *f C.Am., Pe, Bol* F party

también *adv* also, too, as well; *yo ~* me too; *él ~ dice que ...* he also says that ...

tambo *m Rpl* dairy farm; *Méx* type of large container

tambor *m* drum; *persona* drummer; **tamborilear** <1a> *v/i* drum with

one's fingers

tamiz *m* sieve

tampoco *adv* neither; *él ~ va* he's not going either

tampón *m* tampon; *de tinta* ink-pad

tan *adv* so; ~ *... como ...* as ... as ...; ~ *sólo* merely

tanatorio *m* funeral parlo(u)r

tanda *f* series, batch; (*turno*) shift; *L.Am.* (*commercial*) break; ~ *de penaltis* DEP penalty shootout

tanga *m* tanga

tangente *f* MAT tangent; *salir or irse por la ~* F sidestep the issue, duck the question F

tangible *adj fig* tangible

tango *m* tango

tanque *m tb* MIL tank

tantear <1a> *v/t* feel; (*calcular a ojo*) work out roughly; *situación* size up; *persona* sound out; (*probar*) try out; ~ *el terreno fig* see how the land lies

tantito *adv Méx* a little

tanto 1 *pron* so much; *igual cantidad* as much; *un* ~ a little; *~s* pl so many pl; *igual número* as many; *tienes* ~ you have so much; *no hay ~s como ayer* there aren't as many as yesterday; *a las -as de la noche* in the small hours **2** *adv* so much; *igual cantidad* as much; *periodo* so long; *tardó ~ como él* she took as long as him; ~ *mejor* so much the better; *no es para* ~ it's not such a big deal; *estar al* ~ be informed (*de* about); *por lo* ~ therefore, so **3** *m* point; ~ *por ciento* percentage

tapa *f* lid; ~ *dura* hardback

tapacubos *m inv* AUTO hub cap

tapadera *f* lid; *fig* front; **tapadillo** *m:* *de* ~ on the sly; **tapado** *m Arg, Chi* coat; **tapar** <1a> **1** *v/t* cover; *recipiente* put the lid on **2** *v/r ~se* wrap up; *~se los ojos* cover one's eyes

taparrabo *m* loincloth

tapete *m* tablecloth; *poner algo sobre el* ~ bring sth up for discussion

tapia *f* wall; *más sordo que una ~* as

deaf as a post

tapicería f upholstery; **tapicero** m, **-a** f upholsterer

tapioca f tapioca

tapir m tapir

tapiz m tapestry; **tapizar** <1f> v/t upholster

tapón m top, cap; *de baño* plug; *de tráfico* traffic jam; **taponar** <1a> v/t block; *herida* swab

tapujo m: *sin ~s* openly

taquicardia f MED tachycardia

taquigrafía f shorthand

taquilla f ticket office; TEA box-office; *C.Am.* (*bar*) small bar

taquillero 1 adj cantante popular; *una película -a* a hit movie, a box-office hit **2** m, **-a** f ticket clerk

tara f defect

tarado adj F stupid, dumb F

tarántula f ZO tarantula

tararear <1a> v/t hum

tardar <1a> v/i take a long time; *tardamos dos horas* we were two hours overdue *o* late; *¡no tardes!* don't be late; *a más ~* at the latest; *¿cuánto se tarda ...?* how long does it take to ...?; **tarde 1** adv late; *~ o temprano* sooner or later **2** f hasta *las 5 ó 6* afternoon; *desde las 5 ó 6* evening; *¡buenas ~s!* good afternoon / evening; *por la ~* in the afternoon / evening; *de ~ en ~* from time to time; **tardón** adj F slow; (*impuntual*) late

tarea f task, job; *~s pl domésticas* housework *sg*

tarifa f rate; *de tren* fare; *~ plana* flat rate

tarima f platform; *suelo de ~* wooden floor

tarjeta f card; *~ amarilla* DEP yellow card; *~ de crédito* credit card; *~ de embarque* AVIA boarding card; *~ de sonido* INFOR sound card; *~ de visita* (business) card; *~ gráfica* INFOR graphics card; *~ inteligente* smart card; *~ monedero* electronic purse; *~ postal* postcard; *~ roja* DEP red card; *~ telefónica* phone card

tarro m jar; P (*cabeza*) head

tarta f cake; *plana* tart; *~ helada* ice-cream cake

tartamudear <1a> v/i stutter, stammer; **tartamudez** f stuttering, stammering; **tartamudo 1** adj stuttering, stammering; *ser ~* stutter, stammer **2** m, **-a** f stutterer, stammerer

tartera f lunch box

tarugo m F blockhead

tarumba F crazy F; *volverse ~* go crazy

tasa f rate; (*impuesto*) tax; *~ de desempleo or paro* unemployment rate; **tasar** <1a> v/t fix a price for; (*valorar*) assess

tasca f F bar

tata m L.Am. F (*abuelo*) grandpa F

tatarabuela f great-great-grand-mother; **tatarabuelo** m great-great-grandfather; **tataranieta** f great-great-granddaughter; **tataranieto** m great-great-grandson

tate int F (*ahora caigo*) oh I see; (*cuidado*) look out!

tatuaje m tattoo

taurino adj bullfighting atr

Tauro m/f inv ASTR Taurus

tauromaquia f bullfighting

taxi m cab, taxi; **taxista** m/f cab o taxi driver

taza f cup; *del wáter* bowl; **tazón** m bowl

te pron directo you; *indirecto* (to) you; *reflexivo* yourself

té m tea

teatral adj fig theatrical; **teatro** m tb fig theater, Br theatre

tebeo m children's comic

techar <1a> v/t roof; **techo** m ceiling; (*tejado*) roof; *~ solar* AUTO sunroof; *los sin ~* the homeless; *tocar* fig peak

tecla f key; **teclado** m MÚS, INFOR keyboard; **teclear** <1a> v/t key

técnica f technique; **técnico 1** adj technical **2** m/f technician; *de televisor, lavadora etc* repairman; **tecnología** f technology; *alta ~* hi-tech; *~ punta* state-of-the-art technology, leading-edge technology

T

tecolote *m Méx, C.Am. (búho)* owl

tedio *m* tedium; **tedioso** *adj* tedious

teja *f* roof tile; ***a toca ~*** in hard cash; **tejado** *m* roof

tejanos *mpl* jeans

tejemanejes *mpl* F scheming *sg*, plotting *sg*; **tejer** <2a> *v/t* weave; *(hacer punto)* knit; F *intriga* devise **2** *v/i L.Am.* F plot, scheme; **tejido** *m* fabric; ANAT tissue

tejo *m* BOT yew; ***tirar a alguien los ~s*** F hit on s.o. F, come on to s.o. F

tejón *m* ZO badger

Tel. *abr* (= *teléfono*) Tel. (= telephone)

tela *f* fabric, material; ***~ de araña*** spiderweb; ***poner en ~ de juicio*** call into question; ***hay ~ para rato*** F there's a lot to be done

telar *m* loom

telaraña *f* spiderweb

tele *f* F TV, *Br* telly F

telebanca *f* telephone banking

telecabina *f* cable car

telecomedia *f* sitcom

telecompra *f* home shopping

telecomunicaciones *fpl* telecommunications

teleconferencia *f* conference call

telediario *m* TV (television) news *sg*

teledirigido *adj* remote-controlled

teléf. *abr* (= *teléfono*) tel. (= telephone)

teleférico *m* cable car

telefilm(e) *m* TV movie

telefonear <1a> *v/t & v/i* call, phone; **telefonema** *m L.Am.* (phone) message; **telefónico** *adj* (tele)phone *atr*; **teléfono** *m* (tele)phone; ***~ inalámbrico*** cordless (phone); ***~ móvil*** cellphone, *Br* mobile (phone); ***~ con cámara*** camera phone

telégrafo *m* telegraph

telegrama *m* telegram

telemando *m* remote control

telemática *f* data comms

telenovela *f* soap (opera)

teleobjetivo *m* FOT telephoto lens

telepatía *f* telepathy

telescópico *adj* telescopic; **telescopio** *m* telescope

teleserie *f* (television) series

telesilla *f* chair lift

telespectador *m*, **~a** *f* (television) viewer

telesquí *m* drag lift

teletexto *m* teletext

teletienda *f* home shopping

teletrabajo *m* teleworking; **teletrabajador** *m*, **~a** *f* teleworker

televidente *m/f* (television) viewer; **televisar** <1a> *v/t* televise; **televisión** *f* television; ***~ por cable*** cable (television); ***~ digital*** digital television; ***~ de pago*** pay-per-view television; ***~ vía satélite*** satellite television; **televisivo** *adj* television *atr*; **televisor** *m* TV, television (set); ***~ en color*** color TV

télex *m* telex

telón *m* TEA curtain; ***el ~ de acero*** POL the Iron Curtain; ***~ de fondo*** *fig* backdrop, background

telonero *m*, **-a** *f* supporting artist

tema *m* subject, topic; MÚS, *de novela* theme; **temario** *m* syllabus; **temático** *adj* thematic

temblar <1k> *v/i* tremble, shake; *de frío* shiver; **temblor** *m* trembling, shaking; *de frío* shivering; *L.Am.* *(terremoto)* earthquake; ***~ de tierra*** earth tremor; **tembloroso** *adj* trembling, shaking; *de frío* shivering

temer <2a> **1** *v/t* be afraid of **2** *v/r* ***~se*** be afraid; ***me temo que no podrá venir*** I'm afraid he won't be able to come; ***~se lo peor*** fear the worst

temerario *adj* rash, reckless; **temeridad** *f* rashness, recklessness

temor *m* fear

témpano *m* ice floe

temperamento *m* temperament; **temperante** *adj Méx* teetotal

temperatura *f* temperature

tempestad *f* storm; **tempestuoso** *adj tb fig* stormy

templado *adj* warm; *clima* temperate; *fig* moderate, restrained; **templanza** *f* restraint; **templar**

<1a> v/t *ira, nervios etc* calm

templo *m* temple

temporada *f* season; *una ~* a time, some time; **temporal 1** *adj* temporary **2** *m* storm; **temporizador** *m* timer; **temporanear** <1a> v/i *L.Am.* get up early; **temprano** *adj & adv* early

ten *vb* → **tener**

tenacidad *f* tenacity; **tenaz** *adj* determined, tenacious; **tenaza** *f* pincer, claw; **~s** pincers; *para las uñas* pliers

tendedero *m* clotheshorse, airer

tendencia *f* tendency; *(corriente)* trend

tendencioso *adj* tendentious

tender <2g> **1** v/t *ropa* hang out; *cable* lay; *le tendió la mano* he held out his hand to her **2** v/i: *~ a* tend to **3** v/r *~se* lie down

tenderete *m* stall

tendero *m*, *-a* *f* storekeeper, shopkeeper

tendido *m* EL: *~ eléctrico* power lines *pl*

tendón *m* ANAT tendon; *~ de Aquiles* Achilles' tendon

tenebroso *adj* dark, gloomy

tenedor *m* fork

tener <2l> **1** v/t have; *~ 10 años* be 10 (years old); *~ un metro de ancho/largo* be one metre *(Br meter)* wide/long; *~ por* consider to be; *tengo que madrugar* I must get up early, I have to *o* I've got to get up early; *conque ¿esas tenemos?* so that's how it is, eh? **2** v/r *~se* stand up; *fig* stand firm; *se tiene por atractivo* he thinks he's attractive

tenga *vb* → **tener**

tengo *vb* → **tener**

tenia *f* ZO tapeworm

teniente *m/f* MIL lieutenant

tenis *m* tennis; *~ de mesa* table tennis; **tenista** *m/f* tennis player

tenor *m* MÚS tenor; *a ~ de* along the lines of

tenorio *m* lady-killer

tensar <1a> v/t tighten; *músculo*

tense, tighten; **tensión** *f* tension; EL voltage; MED blood pressure; **tenso** *adj* tense; *cuerda, cable* taut

tentación *f* temptation

tentáculo *m* ZO, *fig* tentacle

tentador *adj* tempting; **tentar** <1k> v/t tempt, entice; **tentativa** *f* attempt

tentempié *m* F snack

tenue *adj* faint

teñir <3h & 3l> v/t dye; *fig* tinge

teología *f* theology

teorema *m* theorem; **teoría** *f* theory; *en ~* in theory

tequila *m* tequila

terapeuta *m/f* therapist; **terapéutico** *adj* therapeutic; **terapia** *f* therapy

tercer *adj* third; *Tercer Mundo* Third World; **tercermundista** *adj* Third-World *atr*; **tercero** *m/adj* third; **terciarse** <1b> v/r *si de oportunidad* come up; **tercio** *m* third

terciopelo *m* velvet

terco *adj* stubborn

tergiversar <1a> v/t distort, twist

termas *fpl* hot springs; **térmico** *adj* heat *atr*

terminación *f* GRAM ending; **terminal 1** *m* INFOR terminal **2** *f* AVIA terminal; *~ de autobuses* bus station; **terminante** *adj* categorical; **terminar** <1a> **1** v/t end, finish **2** v/i end, finish; *(parar)* stop **3** v/r *~se* run out; *(finalizar)* come to an end; *se ha terminado la leche* we've run out of milk, the milk's all gone; **término** *m* end, conclusion; *(palabra)* term; *~ municipal* municipal area; *por ~ medio* on average; *poner ~ a algo* put an end to sth

terminología *f* terminology

termita *f* ZO termite

termo *m* thermos® (flask)

termómetro *m* thermometer; **termostato** *m* thermostat

ternera *f* calf; GASTR veal; **ternero** *m* calf

terno *m* CSur suit

ternura *f* tenderness

T

terracota f terracotta

terraplén m embankment

terrateniente m/f landowner

terraza f terrace; (balcón) balcony; (café) sidewalk café

terremoto m earthquake

terrenal adj earthly, worldly

terreno m land; fig field; un ~ a plot o piece of land; ~ de juego DEP field

terrestre adj animal land atr; transporte surface atr; la atmósfera ~ the earth's atmosphere

terrible adj terrible, awful

territorial adj territorial; **territorio** m territory

terrón m lump, clod; ~ de azúcar sugar lump

terror m terror; **terrorífico** adj terrifying; **terrorismo** m terrorism; **terrorista 1** adj terrorist atr **2** m/f terrorist

terso adj smooth

tertulia f TV debate, round table discussion; **tertuliar** <1b> v/i L.Am. get together for a discussion

tesina f dissertation

tesis f inv thesis

tesitura f situation

tesón m tenacity, determination

tesorero m, **-a** f treasurer; **tesoro** m treasure; ~ público treasury

test m test

testa f head

testaferro m front man

testamento m JUR will

testarudez f stubbornness; **testarudo** adj stubborn

testículo m ANAT testicle

testificar <1g> **1** v/t (probar, mostrar) be proof of; ~ que JUR testify that, give evidence that **2** v/i testify, give evidence; **testigo 1** m/f JUR witness; ~ de cargo witness for the prosecution; ~ ocular or presencial eye witness **2** m DEP baton; **testimonio** m testimony, evidence

teta f F boob F; ZO teat, nipple

tétanos m MED tetanus

tetera f teapot

tetilla f de hombre nipple

tetina f de biberón teat

tetrabrik® m carton

tétrico adj gloomy

textil 1 adj textile atr **2** mpl: ~es textiles

texto m text; **textual** adj textual

textura f texture

tez f complexion

ti pron you; reflexivo yourself; ¿y a ~ qué te importa? so what?, what's it to you?

tía f aunt; F (chica) girl, chick F; ¡~ buena! F hey gorgeous! F

tianguis m Méx, C.Am. market

tibio adj tb fig lukewarm

tiburón m ZO, fig F shark

tic m MED tic

ticket m (sales) receipt

tictac m tick-tock

tiempo m time; (clima) weather; GRAM tense; ~ libre spare time, free time; ~ real INFOR real time; a ~ in time; a un ~, al mismo ~ at the same time; antes de ~ llegar ahead of time, early; celebrar victoria too soon; con ~ in good time, early; desde hace mucho ~ for a long time; hace buen/mal ~ the weather's fine/bad; hace mucho ~ a long time ago

tienda f store, shop; ~ de campaña tent; ir de ~s go shopping

tiene vb → tener

tientas fpl: andar a ~ fig feel one's way; **tiento** m: con ~ fig carefully

tierno adj soft; carne tender; pan fresh; persona tender-hearted

tierra f land; materia soil, earth; (patria) native land, homeland; la Tierra the earth; ~ firme dry land, terra firma; echar por ~ ruin, wreck

tieso adj stiff, rigid

tiesto m flower pot

tifón m typhoon

tifus m MED typhus

tigre m ZO tiger; L.Am. puma; L.Am. (leopardo) jaguar; **tigresa** f tigress

tijeras fpl scissors

tila f lime blossom tea

tildar <1a> v/t: ~ a alguien de fig brand s.o. as

T

tilde *f* accent; *en* *ñ* tilde

tilín *m*: **me hizo ~ F** I took an immediate liking to her

timador *m*, **~a** *f* cheat; **timar** <1a> *v/t* cheat

timba *f* F gambling den

timbal *m* MÚS kettle drum

timbre *m* de puerta bell; *Méx* (postage) stamp

timidez *f* shyness, timidity; **tímido** *adj* shy, timid

timo *m* confidence trick, swindle

timón *m* MAR, AVIA rudder

tímpano *m* ANAT eardrum

tina *f* large jar; *L.Am.* (*bañera*) (bath)tub

tinglado *m* *fig* F mess

tinieblas *fpl* darkness *sg*

tino *m* aim, marksmanship; (*sensatez*) judg(e)ment; **con mucho ~** wisely, sensibly

tinta *f* ink; **de buena ~** *fig* on good authority; **medias ~s** *fig* half measures; **tinte** *m* dye; *fig* veneer, gloss

tinterillo *m* *L.Am.* F shyster F

tintero *m* inkwell; **dejarse algo en el ~** leave sth unsaid

tintin(e)ar <1a> *v/t* jingle

tinto *adj*: **vino ~** red wine

tintorería *f* dry cleaner's

tío *m* uncle; F (*tipo*) guy F; F *apelativo* pal F

tiovivo *m* carousel, merry-go-round

típico *adj* typical (**de** of); **tipo** *m* type, kind; F *persona* guy F; COM rate; **~ de cambio** exchange rate; **~ de interés** interest rate; **tener buen ~** be well built; **de mujer** have a good figure

tipográfico *adj* typographic(al)

tiquet, **tiquete** *m* *L.Am.* receipt

tiquismiquis *m/f* F fuss-budget F, *Br* fusspot F

tira *f* strip; **la ~ de** F loads of F, masses of F; **~ y afloja** *fig* give and take

tirabuzón *m* curl; (*sacacorchos*) corkscrew

tirachinas *m* *inv* slingshot, *Br* catapult

tirada *f* TIP print run; **de una ~** in one

go; **tiradero** *m* *Méx* dump; **tirado** *adj* P (*barato*) dirt-cheap F; **estar ~** F (*fácil*) be a walkover F *o* a piece of cake F; **tiradores** *mpl* *Arg* suspenders, *Br* braces

tiranía *f* tyranny; **tirano 1** *adj* tyrannical **2** *m*, **-a** *f* tyrant

tirante 1 *adj* taut; *fig* tense **2** *m* strap; **~s** suspenders, *Br* braces; **tirantez** *f* *fig* tension

tirar <1a> **1** *v/t* throw; *edificio, persona* knock down; (*volcar*) knock over; *basura* throw away; *dinero* waste, throw away F; TIP print; F *en examen* fail **2** *v/i* pull, attract; (*disparar*) shoot; **~ a** tend toward; **~ a conservador** have conservative tendencies; **~ de algo** pull sth; **ir tirando** F get by, manage **3** *v/r* **~se** throw o.s.; F *tiempo* spend; **~se a alguien** P screw s.o. P

tirita *f* MED Bandaid®, *Br* plaster

tiritar <1a> *v/i* shiver

tiro *m* shot; **~ al blanco** target practice; **al ~** *CSur* F at once, right away; **de ~s largos** F dressed up; **ni a ~s** F for love nor money; **le salió el ~ por la culata** F it backfired on him; **le sentó como un ~** F he needed it like a hole in the head F

tirón *m* tug, jerk; **de un ~** at a stretch, without a break

tiroteo *m* shooting

tirria *f*: **tener ~ a alguien** F have it in for s.o. F

tisana *f* herbal tea

títere *m* *tb* *fig* puppet; **no dejar ~ con cabeza** F spare no-one; **titiritero** *m*, **-a** *f* acrobat

titubear <1a> *v/i* waver, hesitate; **titubeo** *m* wavering, hesitation

titular *m* de periódico headline; **titularse** <1a> *v/r* be entitled; **título** *m* title; *universitario* degree; JUR title; COM bond; **tener muchos ~s** be highly qualified; **a ~ de** as; **~s de crédito** credits

tiza *f* chalk

tiznar <1a> *v/t* blacken; **tizón** *m* ember

tlapalería *f* *Méx* hardware store

TLC *abr* (= *Tratado de Libre Comercio*) NAFTA (= North American Free Trade Agreement)

toalla *f* towel; **tirar** or **arrojar la ~** *fig* throw in the towel; **tollero** *m* towel rail

tobillo *m* ankle

tobogán *m* slide

tocadiscos *m inv* record player

tocado *adj*: **estar ~** *fig* F be crazy F

tocador *m* dressing-table

tocante: **en lo ~ a ...** with regard to ...

tocar <1g> **1** *v/t* touch; MÚS play **2** *v/i L.Am.* **a la puerta** knock (on the door); *L.Am.* (*sonar la campanita*) ring the doorbell; **te toca jugar** it's your turn **3** *v/r* **~se** touch

tocateja: **a ~** in hard cash

tocayo *m*, **-a** *f* namesake

tocino *m* bacon

tocólogo *m*, **-a** *f* obstetrician

todavía *adv* still, yet; **~ no ha llegado** he still hasn't come, he hasn't come yet; **~ no** not yet

todo 1 *adj* all; **~s los domingos** every Sunday; **-a la clase** the whole o the entire class **2** *adv* all; **estaba ~ sucio** it was all dirty; **con ~** all the same; **del ~** entirely, absolutely **3** *pron* all, everything; *pl* everybody, everyone; **ir a por -as** go all out

todoterreno *m* AUTO off-road o all-terrain vehicle

toldo *m* awning; *L.Am.* Indian hut

tolerancia *f* tolerance; **tolerar** <1a> *v/t* tolerate

toma *f* FOT shot, take; **~ de conciencia** realization; **~ de corriente** outlet, socket; **~ de posesión** POL taking office; **tomado** *adj Méx* F (*borracho*) drunk; **tomadura** *f*: **~ de pelo** F joke

tomar <1a> **1** *v/t* take; *decisión* make, take; *bebida, comida* have; **~la con alguien** F have it in for s.o. F; **~ el sol** sunbathe; **¡toma!** here (you are); **toma y daca** give and take **2** *v/i L.Am.* drink; **~ por la derecha** turn right **3** *v/r* **~se** take; *comida, bebida* have; **se lo tomó a pecho**

he took it to heart

tomate *m* tomato

tomavistas *m inv* movie camera, cine camera

tomillo *m* BOT thyme

tomo *m* volume, tome; **un timador de ~ y lomo** F an out-and-out con-man

ton *m*: **sin ~ ni son** for no particular reason

tonada *f* song

tonalidad *f* tonality

tonel *m* barrel, cask; **tonelada** *f peso* ton

tónica *f* tonic; **tónico** *m* MED tonic; **tonificar** <1g> *v/t* tone up; **tono** *m* MÚS, MED, PINT tone

tontería *f fig* stupid o dumb F thing; **~s** *pl* nonsense *sg*

tonto 1 *adj* silly, foolish **2** *m*, **-a** *f* fool, idiot; **hacer el ~** play the fool; **hacerse el ~** act dumb F

top *m prenda* top

topacio *m* MIN topaz

toparse <1a> *v/r*: **~ con alguien** bump into s.o., run into s.o.

tope *m* limit; *pieza* stop; *Méx* **en la calle** speed bump; **pasarlo a ~** F have a great time; **estar hasta los ~s** F be bursting at the seams F

tópico *m* cliché, platitude

topo *m* ZO mole

toque *m*: **~ de queda** MIL, *fig* curfew; **dar los últimos ~s** put the finishing touches (**a** to)

toquilla *f* shawl

tórax *m* ANAT thorax

torbellino *m* whirlwind

torcer <2b & 2h> **1** *v/t* twist; (*doblar*) bend; (*girar*) turn **2** *v/i* turn; **~ a la derecha** turn right **3** *v/r* **~se** twist, bend; *fig* go wrong; **~se un pie** sprain one's ankle; **torcido** *adj* twisted, bent

toreador *m esp L.Am.* bullfighter; **torear** <1a> **1** *v/i* fight bulls **2** *v/t* fight; *fig* dodge, sidestep; **toreo** *m* bullfighting

torera *f*: **saltarse algo a la ~** F flout sth, disregard sth

torero *m* bullfighter

tormenta f storm; **tormento** m torture

tornado m tornado, twister F

tornarse <1a> v/r triste, difícil etc become

torneo m competition, tournament

tornillo m screw; con tuerca bolt; **le falta un ~** F he's got a screw loose F

torniquete m turnstile; MED tourniquet

torno m de alfarería wheel; **en ~ a** around, about

toro m bull; **ir a los ~s** go to a bullfight; **coger al ~ por los cuernos** take the bull by the horns

toronja f L.Am. grapefruit

torpe adj clumsy; (tonto) dense, dim

torpedo m MIL torpedo

torpeza f clumsiness; (necedad) stupidity

torre f tower; **~ de control** AVIA control tower

torrencial adj torrential; **torrente** m fig avalanche, flood

torrezno m GASTR fried rasher of bacon

tórrido adj torrid

torrija f GASTR French toast

torta f cake; plana tart; F slap; **tortazo** m F crash; (bofetada) punch

tortícolis m MED crick in the neck

tortilla f omelette; L.Am. tortilla

tortillera f V dyke F, lesbian

tortuga f ZO tortoise; marina turtle; **a paso de ~** fig at a snail's pace

tortuoso adj fig tortuous

tortura f tb fig torture; **torturar** <1a> v/t torture

tos f cough

tosco adj fig rough, coarse

toser <2a> v/i cough

tostada f piece of toast; **tostado** adj (moreno) brown, tanned; **tostador** m toaster; **tostar** <1m> 1 v/t toast; café roast; al sol tan 2 v/r **~se** tan, get brown; **tostón** m F bore

total 1 adj total, complete; **en ~** altogether, in total 2 m total; **un ~ de 50 personas** a total of 50 people; **totalidad** f totality; **totalitario** adj totalitarian

tóxico adj toxic; **toxicómano** m, **-a** f drug addict; **toxina** f toxin

tozudo adj obstinate

trabajador 1 adj hard-working 2 m, **~a** f worker; **~ eventual** casual worker; **trabajar** <1a> v/i work 2 v/t work; tema, músculos work on; **trabajo** m work; **~ en equipo** team work; **~ temporal** temporary work; **~ a tiempo parcial** part-time work; **trabajoso** adj hard, laborious

trabalenguas m inv tongue twister

trabar <1a> 1 v/t conversación, amistad strike up 2 v/r **~se** get tangled up

trabucarse <1g> v/r get all mixed up

tracción f TÉC traction; **~ delantera / trasera** front / rear-wheel drive

tractor m tractor

tradición f tradition; **tradicional** adj traditional

traducción f translation; **traducir** <3o> v/t translate; **traductor** m, **~a** f translator

traer <2p; part traído> 1 v/t bring; **~ consigo** involve, entail; **este periódico lo trae en portada** this newspaper carries it on the front page 2 v/r **~se**: **este asunto se las trae** F it's a very tricky matter

traficante m dealer; **traficar** <1g> v/i deal (en in); **tráfico** m traffic; **~ de drogas** drug trafficking, drug dealing

tragaperras f inv slot machine

tragar <1h> 1 v/t swallow; **no lo trago** I can't stand him o bear him 2 v/r **~se** tb fig F swallow

tragedia f tragedy; **trágico** adj tragic

tragicomedia f tragicomedy

trago m mouthful; F bebida drink; **de un ~** in one gulp; **pasar un mal ~** fig have a hard time; **tragón** adj greedy

traición f treachery, betrayal; **traicionar** <1a> v/t betray; **traidor** 1 adj treacherous 2 m, **~a** f traitor

traído part → **traer**

traigo vb → **traer**

tráiler m trailer

T

traje 1 *m* suit; **~ de baño** swimsuit **2** *vb* → **traer**

trajín *m* hustle and bustle

trajo *vb* → **traer**

trama *f* (*tema*) plot; **tramar** <1a> *v/t complot* hatch

tramitar <1a> *v/t documento: de persona* apply for; *de banco etc* process; **trámite** *m* formality

tramo *m* section, stretch; *de escaleras* flight

trampa *f* trap; (*truco*) scam F, trick; **hacer ~s** cheat

trampilla *f* trapdoor

trampolín *m* diving board

tramposo *m*, **-a** *f* cheat, crook

tranca *f*: **llevaba una ~ increíble** F he was wasted F *o* smashed F; **a ~s y barrancas** with great difficulty

trancazo *m* F dose of flu

trance *m* (*momento difícil*) tough time; **en ~** in a trance

tranquilidad *f* calm, quietness; **tranquilizante** *m* tranquil(l)izer; **tranquilizar** <1f> *v/t*: **~ a alguien** calm s.o. down

tranquillo *m*: **coger el ~ de algo** F get the hang of sth F

tranquilo *adj* calm, quiet; **¡~!** don't worry; **déjame ~** leave me alone

transacción *f* COM deal, transaction;

transar <1a> *v/i L.Am.* (*ser vendido*) sell out

transatlántico 1 *adj* transatlantic **2** *m* liner

transbordador *m* ferry; **~ espacial** space shuttle; **transbordo** *m*: **hacer ~** TRANSP transfer, change

transcendental *adj fig* momentous

transcurrir <3a> *v/i de tiempo* pass, go by; **transcurso** *m* course; *de tiempo* passing

transeúnte *m/f* passer-by

transexual *m/f* transsexual

transferencia *f* COM transfer

transformación *f* transformation; **transformador** *m* EL transformer; **transformar** <1a> *v/t* transform

transfronterizo *adj* cross-border

tránsfuga *m/f* POL defector

transfusión *f*: **~ de sangre** blood transfusion; **transgénico** *adj* genetically modified; **transgredir** <3a> *v/t* infringe

transición *f* transition

transigir <3c> *v/i* compromise, make concessions

transistor *m* transistor

transitivo *adj* GRAM transitive; **tránsito** *m* COM transit; *L.Am.* (*circulación*) traffic

translúcido *adj* translucent

transmisión *f* transmission; **~ de datos** data transmission; **enfermedad de ~ sexual** sexually transmitted disease; **transmitir** <3a> *v/t* spread, RAD, TV broadcast, transmit

transparencia *f* *para proyectar* transparency, slide; **transparente** *adj* transparent

transpiración *f* perspiration; **transpirar** <1a> *v/i* perspire

transplantar <1a> *v/t* transplant

transportar <1a> *v/t* transport; **transporte** *m* transport

tranvía *m* streetcar, *Br* tram

trapecio *m* trapeze; **trapecista** *m/f* trapeze artist(e)

trapiche *m CSur* sugar mill *o* press

trapicheo *m* F shady deal F

trapo *m viejo* rag; *para limpiar* cloth; **~s** F clothes

trapujear <1a> *v/t & v/i C.Am.* smuggle

tráquea *f* windpipe, trachea

traqueteo *m* rattle, clatter

tras *prp en el espacio* behind; *en el tiempo* after

trasero 1 *adj* rear *atr*, back *atr* **2** *m* F butt F, *Br* rear end F

trasiego *m fig* bustle

trasladar <1a> **1** *v/t* move; *trabajador* transfer; **2** *v/r* **~se** move (**a** to); **se traslada** *Méx: en negocio* under new management; **traslado** *m* move; *de trabajador* transfer; **~ al aeropuerto** airport transfer

trasluz *m*: **al ~** against the light; **trasnochar** <1a> *v/i* (*acostarse tarde*) go to bed late, stay up late; (*no dormir*) stay up all night; *L.Am.* stay overnight, spend the night;

traspapelar <1a> v/t mislay; **traspasar** <1a> v/t (*atravesar*) go through; COM transfer

traspié m trip, stumble; *dar un ~ fig* slip up, blunder

trasplantar <1a> v/t AGR, MED transplant; **trasplante** m AGR, MED transplant

trastada f F prank, trick; *hacer ~s* get up to mischief; **traste** m: *irse al ~* F fall through, go down the tubes F; **trastero** m lumber room; **trasto** m desp piece of junk; *persona* good-for-nothing

trastornar <1a> v/t upset; (*molestar*) inconvenience; **trastorno** m inconvenience; MED disorder

tratado m esp POL treaty; *Tratado de Libre Comercio* North American Free Trade Agreement

tratamiento m treatment; *~ de datos / textos* INFOR data / word processing; **tratar** <1a> **1** v/t treat; (*manejar*) handle; (*dirigirse a*) address (*de* as); *gente* come into contact with; *tema* deal with **2** v/i: *~ con alguien* deal with s.o.; *~ de* (*intentar*) try to **3** v/r *~se: ¿de qué se trata?* what's it about?; *trato m de prisionero, animal* treatment; COM deal; *malos ~s pl* ill treatment sg, abuse sg.; *tener ~ con alguien* have dealings with s.o.; *¡~ hecho!* it's a deal

trauma m trauma; **traumatizar** <1f> v/t traumatize; **traumatólogo** m, **-a** f trauma specialist, traumatologist

través m: *a ~ de* through; **travesaño** m en fútbol crossbar; **travesía** f crossing

travesti m transvestite, drag artist

travesura f bit of mischief, prank; **travieso** adj niño mischievous

trayecto m journey; *10 dólares por ~* 10 dollars each way; **trayectoria** f fig course, path

trazar <1f> v/t (*dibujar*) draw; *ruta* plot, trace; (*describir*) outline, describe; **trazo** m line

trébol m BOT clover

trece adj thirteen; *mantenerse or seguir en sus ~* stand firm, not budge

trecho m stretch, distance

tregua f truce, cease-fire; *sin ~* relentlessly

treinta adj thirty

tremebundo adj horrendous, frightening

tremendo adj awful, dreadful; *éxito, alegría* tremendous

tren m FERR train; *~ de alta velocidad* high speed train; *~ de lavado* car wash; *vivir a todo ~* F live in style; *estar como un ~* F be absolutely gorgeous

trenca f duffel coat

trenza f plait

trepa m F socialmente social climber; *en el trabajo* careerist; **trepar** <1a> v/i climb (*a* up), scale (*a* sth)

trepidante adj fig frenetic

tres adj three; **trescientos** adj three hundred

tresillo m living-room suite, Br three-piece suite

treta f trick, ploy

triángulo m triangle

tribu f tribe

tribuna f grandstand

tribunal m court; *Tribunal Supremo* Supreme Court

tributo m tribute; (*impuesto*) tax

triciclo m tricycle

tricotar <1a> v/i knit

trifulca f F brawl, punch-up F

trigo m wheat

trillado adj fig hackneyed, clichéd; **trillar** <1a> v/t AGR thresh

trillizos mpl triplets

trillón m quintillion, Br trillion

trimestral adj quarterly; **trimestre** m quarter; *escolar* semester, Br term

trinar <1a> v/i trill, warble; *está que trina fig* F he's fuming F, he's hopping mad F

trincar <1g> v/t F criminal catch

trinchera f MIL trench

trineo m sled, sleigh

trino m trill, warble

trío *m* trio

tripa *f* F belly F, gut F; **hacer de ~s corazón** *fig* pluck up courage

triple *m*: **el ~ que el año pasado** three times as much as last year; **triplicar** <1g> *v/t* triple, treble

trípode *m* tripod

tripulación *f* AVIA, MAR crew; **tripular** <1a> *v/t* man

triquiñuela *f* F dodge F, trick

tris *m*: **estuvo en un ~ de caerse** F she came within an inch of falling

triste *adj* sad; **tristeza** *f* sadness

triturar <1a> *v/t* grind

triunfador 1 *adj* winning **2** *m*, **~a** *f* winner, victor; **triunfar** <1a> *v/i* triumph, win; **triunfo** *m* triumph, victory; **en naipes** trump

trivial *adj* trivial

triza *f*: **hacer ~s** F *jarrón* smash to bits; *papel, vestido* tear to shreds

trocear <1a> *v/t* cut into pieces, cut up

troche: **había errores a ~ y moche** F there were mistakes galore F

trofeo *m* trophy

troglodita *m/f* cave-dweller

troj(e) *f Arg* granary

trola *f* F fib

trolebús *m* trolley bus

tromba *f*: **~ de agua** downpour

trombón *m* MÚS trombone

trombosis *f* MED thrombosis

trompa 1 *adj* F wasted F **2** *f* MÚS horn; ZO trunk

trompazo *m L.Am.* F whack F; **darse un ~ con algo** F bang into sth; **trompearse** <1a> *L.Am.* F fight, lay into each other F

trompeta *f* MÚS trumpet; **trompetista** *m/f* MÚS trumpeter

trompicón *m*: **a trompicones** in fits and starts

trompo *m* spinning top

trona *f* high chair

tronar <1m> *v/i* thunder

troncha *f S.Am.* slice, piece; **tronchante** *adj* F sidesplitting; **troncharse** <1a> *v/r*: **~ de risa** F split one's sides laughing

tronco *m* trunk; *cortado* log; **dormir como un ~** sleep like a log

trono *m* throne

tropa *f* MIL (*soldado raso*) ordinary soldier; **~s** troops

tropel *m*: **en ~** in a mad rush; **salir en ~** pour out

tropezar <1f & 1k> *v/i* trip, stumble

tropical *adj* tropical; **trópico** *m* tropic

tropiezo *m fig* setback

tropilla *f L.Am.* herd

trotar <1a> *v/i fig* gad around; **trote** *m* trot; **ya no estoy para esos ~s** I'm not up to it any more

trozo *m* piece

trucha *f* ZO trout

truco *m* trick; **coger el ~ a algo** F get the hang of sth F

truculento *adj* horrifying

trueno *m* thunder

trueque *m* barter

trufa *f* BOT truffle

truhán *m* rogue

Tte. *abr* (= **Teniente**) Lieut. (= Lieutenant)

tú *pron sg* you; **tratar de ~** address as 'tu'

tu, tus *adj pos* your

tuberculosis *f* MED TB, tuberculosis

tubería *f* pipe; **tubo** *m* tube; **~ de escape** AUTO exhaust (pipe); **por un ~** F an enormous amount

tucán *m* ZO toucan

tuerca *f* TÉC nut

tulipán *m* BOT tulip

tullido *m* cripple

tumba *f* tomb, grave

tumbar <1a> **1** *v/t* knock down **2** *v/r* **~se** lie down; **tumbo** *m* tumble; **ir dando ~s** stagger along; **tumbona** *f* (sun) lounger

tumor *m* MED tumo(u)r

tumulto *m* uproar

tuna *f Méx fruta* prickly pear

tunda *f* F beating

tundra *f* GEOG tundra

túnel *m* tunnel; **~ de lavado** car wash

Túnez Tunisia

túnica *f* tunic

tuntún: **decir algo al buen ~** say sth off the top of one's head

tupé *m* F quiff

tupido *adj pelo* thick; *vegetación* dense, thick

turbante *m* turban

turbar <1a> **1** *v/t* (*emocionar*) upset; *paz, tranquilidad* disturb; (*avergonzar*) embarrass **2** *v/r* **~se** (*emocionarse*) get upset; *de paz, tranquilidad* be disturbed; (*avergonzarse*) get embarrassed

turbina *f* turbine

turbio *adj* cloudy, murky; *fig* shady, murky

turbo *m* turbo

turbulencia *f* turbulence; **turbulento** *adj* turbulent

turco 1 *adj* Turkish **2** *m*, **-a** *f* Turk

turismo *m* tourism; *automóvil* sedan, *Br* saloon (car); **~ rural** tourism in rural areas; **turista** *m/f* tourist; **turístico** *adj* tourist *atr*

turnarse <1a> *v/r* take it in turns; **turno** *m* turn; **~ de noche** night shift; **por ~s** in turns

turquesa *f piedra preciosa* turquoise; **azul ~** turquoise

Turquía Turkey

turrón *m* nougat

turulato *adj* F stunned, dazed

tute *m*: **darse un ~** F work like a dog F, slave F

tutear <1a> *v/t* address as 'tu'

tutiplén: **había comida a ~** F there was loads *o* masses to eat F

tutor *m*, **~a** *f* EDU tutor

tuve *vb* → **tener**

tuvo *vb* → **tener**

tuyo, tuya *pron pos* yours; **los tuyos** your folks, your family

TV *abr* (= **televisión**) TV (= television)

U

u *conj* (*instead of* **o** *before words starting with o*) or

ubicación *f L.Am.* location; (*localización*) finding; **ubicado** *adj* located, situated; **ubicar** <1g> **1** *v/t L.Am.* place, put; (*localizar*) locate **2** *v/r* **~se** be located, be situated; *en un empleo* get a job; **ubicuo** *adj* ubiquitous

ubre *f* udder

UCI *abr* (= **Unidad de Cuidados Intensivos**) ICU (= Intensive Care Unit)

Ud. *pron* → **usted**

Uds. *pron* → **ustedes**

UE *abr* (= **Unión Europea**) EU (= European Union)

ufano *adj* conceited; (*contento*) proud

ujier *m* usher

úlcera *f* MED ulcer; **ulcerarse** <1a> *v/r* MED become ulcerous, ulcerate

ulterior *adj* subsequent

últimamente *adv* lately; **ultimar** <1a> *v/t* finalize; *L.Am.* (*rematar*) finish off; **ultimátum** *m* ultimatum; **último** *adj* last; (*más reciente*) latest; *piso* top *atr*; **-as noticias** latest news *sg*; **por ~** finally; **está en las -as** he doesn't have long (to live)

ultra *m* POL right-wing extremist; **ultraderecha** *f* POL extreme right

ultrajante *adj* outrageous; *palabras* insulting; **ultrajar** <1a> *v/t* outrage; (*insultar*) insult; **ultraje** *m* outrage; (*insulto*) insult

ultraligero *m* AVIA microlight

ultramarinos *mpl* groceries; **tienda de ~** grocery store, *Br* grocer's (shop)

ultramoderno *adj* ultramodern

ultranza: **a ~** for all one is worth; **un defensor a ~ de algo** an ardent defender of sth

U

ultrasónico *adj* ultrasonic; **ultrasonido** *m* ultrasound

ultratumba *f*: *la vida de* ~ life beyond the grave

ultravioleta *adj* ultraviolet

ulular <1a> *v/i de viento* howl; *de búho* hoot

umbilical *adj* ANAT umbilical

umbral *m fig* threshold; *en el* ~ *de fig* on the threshold of

umbrío *adj* shady

un, una *art* a; *antes de vocal y h muda* an; *~os coches/pájaros* some cars/birds

unánime *adj* unanimous; **unanimidad** *f* unanimity; *por* ~ unanimously

unción *f fig* unction

undécimo *adj* eleventh

ungir <3c> *v/t* REL anoint; **ungüento** *m* ointment

únicamente *adv* only; **único** *adj* only; (*sin par*) unique; *es* ~ it's unique; *hijo* ~ only child; *lo* ~ *que ...* the only thing that ...

unicornio *m* MYTH unicorn

unidad *f* MIL, MAT unit; (*cohesión*) unity; ~ *de cuidados intensivos*, ~ *de vigilancia intensiva* MED intensive care unit; ~ *de disco* INFOR disk drive; ~ *monetaria* monetary unity; **unido** *adj* united; *una familia -a* a close-knit family; **unificación** *f* unification; **unificar** <1g> *v/t* unify

uniformar <1a> *v/t fig* standardize; **uniforme 1** *adj* uniform; *superficie* even **2** *m* uniform

unilateral *adj* unilateral

unión *f* union; *Unión Europea* European Union

unir <3a> **1** *v/t* join; *personas* unite; *características* combine (*con* with); *ciudades* link **2** *v/r* ~*se* join together; ~*se a* join

unisex *adj* unisex

unísono *adj*: *al* ~ in unison

unitario *adj* unitary; *precio* ~ unit price

universal *adj* universal

universidad *f* university; ~ *a distancia* university correspondence school, *Br* Open University; **universitario 1** *adj* university *atr* **2** *m*, -a *f* (*estudiante*) university student

universo *m* universe

uno 1 *pron* one; *es la -a* it's one o'clock; *me lo dijo* ~ someone *o* somebody told me; ~ *a* ~, ~ *por* ~, *de* ~ *en* ~ one by one; *no dar ni -a* F not get anything right; ~*s cuantos* a few, some; ~*s niños* some children; *-as mil pesetas* about a thousand pesetas **2** *m* one; *el* ~ *de enero* January first, the first of January

untar <1a> *v/t* spread; ~ *a alguien* F (*sobornar*) grease s.o.'s palm; **untuoso** *adj fig* oily

uña *f* ANAT nail; ZO claw; *defenderse con* ~*s y dientes fig* F fight tooth and nail; *ser* ~ *y carne personas* be extremely close

uperisado *adj*: *leche -a* UHT milk

uranio *m* uranium

urbanidad *f* civility; **urbanismo** *m* city planning, *Br* town planning; **urbanización** *f* (urban) development; (*colonia*) housing development, *Br* housing estate; **urbanizar** <1f> *v/t terreno* develop; **urbano** *adj* urban; (*cortés*) courteous; *guardia* ~ local police officer; **urbe** *f* city

urdir <3a> *v/t complot* hatch

urea *f* urea

uretra *f* ANAT urethra

urgencia *f* urgency; (*prisa*) haste; MED emergency; ~*s pl* emergency room *sg*, *Br* casualty *sg*; **urgente** *adj* urgent; **urgir** <3c> *v/i* be urgent

urinario *m* urinal

urna *f* urn; ~ *electoral* ballot box

urólogo *m* MED urologist

urraca *f* ZO magpie

URSS *abr* (= *Unión de las Repúblicas Socialistas Soviéticas*) HIST USSR (= Union of Soviet Socialist Republics)

urticaria *f* MED hives

Uruguay Uruguay; **uruguayo 1** *adj* Uruguayan **2** *m*, -a *f* Uruguayan

usado *adj* (*gastado*) worn; (*de segunda mano*) second hand; **usar** <1a> **1** *v/t* use; *ropa, gafas* wear **2** *v/i*: **listo para ~** ready to use **3** *v/r* **~se** be used; **uso** *m* use; (*costumbre*) custom; *obligatorio el ~ de casco* helmets must be worn; *en buen ~* still in use

usted *pron* you; *tratar de ~* address as 'usted'; *~es pl* you; *de ~ / ~es* your; *es de ~ / ~es* it's yours

usual *adj* common, usual

usuario *m*, **-a** *f* INFOR user

usufructo *m* JUR usufruct

usura *f* usury; **usurero** *m*, **-a** *f* usurer

usurpar <1a> *v/t* usurp

utensilio *m* tool; *de cocina* utensil; *~s*

pl equipment *sg*; *~s pl de pesca* fishing tackle *sg*

útero *m* ANAT uterus

útil **1** *adj* useful **2** *m* tool; *~es pl de pesca* fishing tackle *sg*; **utilidad** *f* usefulness; **utilitario 1** *adj* functional, utilitarian **2** *m* AUTO compact; **utilitarismo** *m* utilitarianism; **utilización** *f* use; **utilizar** <1f> *v/t* use

utopía *f* utopia; **utópico** *adj* utopian

uva *f* BOT grape; *estar de mala ~* F be in a foul mood; *tener mala ~* F be a nasty piece of work F

UVI *abr* (= **Unidad de Vigilancia Intensiva**) ICU (= Intensive Care Unit)

úvula *f* ANAT uvula

V

va *vb* → *ir*

vaca *f* cow; GASTR beef; *~ lechera* dairy cow; *~ marina* manatee, sea cow; *mal or enfermedad de las ~s locas* F mad cow disease F

vacaciones *fpl* vacation *sg*, *Br* holiday *sg*; *de ~* on vacation, *Br* on holiday

vacante **1** *adj* vacant, empty **2** *f* job opening, position, *Br* vacancy; *cubrir una ~* fill a position; **vaciar** <1b> **1** *v/t* empty **2** *v/r* **~se** empty

vacilación *f* hesitation; **vacilante** *adj* unsteady; (*dubitativo*) hesitant; **vacilar** <1a> **1** *v/i* hesitate; *de fe, resolución* waver; *de objeto* wobble, rock; *de persona* stagger; *Méx* F (*divertirse*) have fun **2** *v/t* F make fun of

vacío **1** *adj* empty **2** *m* FÍS vacuum; *fig espacio* void; *~ de poder* power vacuum; *~ legal* loophole; *dejar un ~ fig* leave a gap; *envasado al ~* vacuum packed; *hacer el ~ a*

alguien fig ostracize s.o.

vacuna *f* vaccine; **vacunación** *f* vaccination; **vacunar** <1a> *v/t* vaccinate

vacuno *adj* bovine; *ganado ~* cattle *pl*

vacuo *adj fig* vacuous

vadear <1a> *v/t río* ford; *dificultad* get around; **vado** *m* ford; *en la calle* entrance ramp; *~ permanente letrero* keep clear

vagabundear <1a> *v/i* drift around; **vagabundo 1** *adj perro* stray **2** *m*, **-a** *f* hobo, *Br* tramp; **vagancia** *f* laziness, idleness; **vagar** <1h> *v/i* wander

vagido *m de bebe* cry

vagina *f* ANAT vagina

vago *adj* (*holgazán*) lazy; (*indefinido*) vague; *hacer el ~* laze around

vagón *m de carga* wagon; *de pasajeros* car, *Br* coach; *~ restaurante* dining car, *Br tb* restaurant car

vaguear <1a> *v/i* laze around

vaguedad f vagueness

vahido m MED dizzy spell; **vaho** m (*aliento*) breath; (*vapor*) steam

vaina f BOT pod; *S.Am.* F drag F

vainilla f vanilla

vais vb → **ir**

vaivén m to-and-fro, swinging; **vaivenes** fig ups and downs

vajilla f dishes pl; *juego* dinner service, set of dishes

vale m voucher, coupon

valedero adj valid

valentía f bravery

valer <2q> **1** v/t be worth; (*costar*) cost **2** v/i *de billete, carné* be valid; (*estar permitido*) be allowed; (*tener valor*) be worth; (*servir*) be of use; **no ~ para algo** be no good at sth; **vale más caro** it's more expensive; **sus consejos me valieron de mucho** his advice was very useful to me; **más vale …** it's better to …; **más te vale …** you'd better …; **¡vale!** okay, sure **3** v/r **~se** manage (by o.s.); **~se de** make use of

valeriana f BOT valerian

valeroso adj valiant

valga vb → **valer**

valgo vb → **valer**

valía f worth

validar <1a> v/t validate; **validez** f validity; **válido** adj valid

valiente adj brave; *irón* fine

valija f (*maleta*) bag, suitcase, *Br* tb case; **~ diplomática** diplomatic bag

valioso adj valuable

valla f fence; DEP, fig hurdle; **~ publicitaria** billboard, *Br* hoarding; **carrera de ~s** DEP hurdles; **vallado** m fence; **vallar** <1a> v/t fence in

valle m valley

valor m value; (*valentía*) courage; **~ añadido**, *L.Am.* **~ agregado** value added; **~ nominal** de acción nominal value; *de título* par value; **objetos de ~** valuables; **~es** COM securities

valoración f (*tasación*) valuation; **valorar** <1a> v/t value (*en* at); (*estimar*) appreciate, value

vals m waltz

valuar <1e> v/t value

válvula f ANAT, EL valve; **~ de escape** fig safety valve

vampiro m fig vampire

van vb → **ir**

vanagloriarse <1b> v/r boast (*de* about), brag (*de* about)

vandálico adj destructive; **vandalismo** m vandalism; **vándalo** m, **-a** f vandal

vanguardia f MIL vanguard; *de ~* fig avant-garde

vanidad f vanity; **vanidoso** adj conceited, vain; **vano** adj futile, vain; *en ~* in vain

vapor m vapo(u)r; *de agua* steam; **cocinar al ~** steam; **vaporizar** <1f> **1** v/t vaporize **2** v/r **~se** vaporize; **vaporoso** adj vaporous; *fig: vestido* gauzy, filmy

vapulear <1a> v/t beat up; **vapuleo** m beating

vaquería f dairy; **vaquero 1** adj *tela* denim; *pantalones* **~s** jeans **2** m cowboy, cowhand; **vaquilla** f heifer

vara f stick; TÉC rod; (*bastón de mando*) staff

varapalo m F (*contratiempo*) hitch F, setback

variable adj variable; *tiempo* changeable; **variación** f variation; **variado** adj varied; **variar** <1c> **1** v/t vary; (*cambiar*) change **2** v/i vary; (*cambiar*) change; *para ~* for a change

varice f MED varicose vein

varicela f MED chickenpox

variedad f variety; **~es** pl vaudeville sg, *Br* variety sg

variopinto adj varied, diverse

varios adj several

varita f: **~ mágica** magic wand

variz f varicose vein

varón m man, male; **varonil** adj manly, virile

vas vb → **ir**

vasallo m vassal

vasco 1 adj Basque; *País Vasco* Basque country **2** m *idioma* Basque **3** m, **-a** f Basque; **Vascongadas** fpl

Basque country *sg*; **vascuence** *m* Basque

vascular *adj* ANAT vascular

vasectomía *f* MED vasectomy

vaselina *f* Vaseline®

vasija *f* container, vessel; **vaso** *m* glass; ANAT vessel

vasto *adj* vast

Vaticano *m* Vatican

vaticinar <1a> *v/t* predict, forecast; **vaticinio** *m* prediction, forecast

vatio *m* EL watt

vaya 1 *vb* → **ir 2** *int* well!

V.° B.° *abr* (= **visto bueno**) approved, OK

Vd. *pron* → **usted**

Vds. *pron* → **usted**

ve *vb* → **ir, ver**

vea *vb* → **ver**

vecindad *f* *Méx* poor area; **vecindario** *m* neighbo(u)rhood; **vecino 1** *adj* neighbo(u)ring **2** *m*, **-a** *f* neighbo(u)r

vedado *m*: **~ de caza** game reserve

vedar <1a> *v/t* ban, prohibit

vedette *f* star

vegetación *f* vegetation; **vegetal 1** *adj* vegetable, plant *atr* **2** *m* vegetable; **vegetar** <1a> *v/i* *fig* vegetate; **vegetariano 1** *adj* vegetarian **2** *m*, **-a** *f* vegetarian

vehemente *adj* vehement

vehículo *m* *tb* *fig* vehicle; MED carrier

veinte *m/adj* twenty; **veintena** *f* twenty; *aproximadamente* about twenty

vejación *f* humiliation; **vejar** <1a> *v/t* humiliate

vejestorio *m* F old fossil F, old relic F

vejez *f* old age

vejiga *f* ANAT bladder

vela *f* *para alumbrar* candle; DEP sailing; *de barco* sail; **a toda ~** F flat out F, all out F; *estar a dos ~s* F be broke F; *pasar la noche en ~* stay up all night; **velada** *f* evening; **velador** *m* *L.Am. lámpara* bedlamp, *Br* bedside light; *Chi mueble* nightstand, *Br* bedside table; **velar** <1a> *v/i*: **~ por algo** look after sth;

velatorio *m* wake

velcro® *m* Velcro

veleidad *f* fickleness

velero *m* MAR sailing ship

veleta 1 *f* weathervane **2** *m/f* *fig* weathercock

vello *m* (body) hair

velo *m* veil

velocidad *f* speed; (*marcha*) gear

velódromo *m* velodrome

veloz *adj* fast, speedy

ven *vb* → **venir**

vena *f* ANAT vein; *le dio la ~ y lo hizo* F she just upped and did it F; *estar en ~* F be on form

venado *m* ZO deer

vencedor 1 *adj* winning **2** *m*, **~a** *f* winner

vencejo *m* ZO swift

vencer <2b> **1** *v/t* defeat; *fig* (*superar*) overcome **2** *v/i* win; COM *de plazo etc* expire; **vencido** *adj*: *darse por ~* admit defeat, give in; *a la tercera va la -a* third time lucky; **vencimiento** *m* expiration, *Br* expiry; *de bono* maturity

venda *f* bandage; **vendaje** *m* MED dressing; **vendar** <1a> *v/t* MED bandage, dress; *~ los ojos a alguien* blindfold s.o.

vendaval *m* gale

vendedor *m*, **~a** *f* seller; **vender** <2a> **1** *v/t* sell; *fig* (*traicionar*) betray **2** *v/r* **~se** sell o.s.; *~se al enemigo* sell out to the enemy

vendimia *f* grape harvest; **vendimiar** <1b> *v/t uvas* harvest, pick

vendré *vb* → **venir**

veneno *m* poison; **venenoso** *adj* poisonous

venerable *adj* venerable; **venerar** <1a> *v/t* venerate, worship

venéreo *adj* MED venereal

venezolano 1 *adj* Venezuelan **2** *m*, **-a** *f* Venezuelan; **Venezuela** Venezuela

venga *vb* → **venir**

venganza *f* vengeance, revenge; **vengar** <1h> **1** *v/t* avenge **2** *v/r* **~se** take revenge (*de* on; *por* for); **vengativo** *adj* vengeful

V

vengo *vb* → **venir**

venir <3s> **1** *v/i* come; **~ de España** come from Spain; **~ bien** be convenient; **~ mal** be inconvenient; **le vino una idea** an idea occurred to him; **viene a ser lo mismo** it comes down to the same thing; **el año que viene** next year; **¡venga!** come on; **¿a qué viene eso?** why do you say that? **2** *v/r* **~se**: **~se abajo** collapse; *fig: de persona* fall apart, go to pieces

venta *f* sale; **~ por correo o por catálogo** mail order; **~ al detalle** *o* **al por menor** retail; **en ~** for sale

ventaja *f* advantage; DEP *en carrera, partido* lead; **~ fiscal** tax advantage; **ventajoso** *adj* advantageous

ventana *f* window; **~ de la nariz** nostril; **ventanilla** *f* AVIA, AUTO, FERR window; MAR porthole

ventilación *f* ventilation; **ventilador** *m* fan; **ventilar** <1a> *v/t* air; *fig: problema* talk over; *opiniones* air

ventisca *f* blizzard

ventosa *f* ZO sucker

ventosidad *f* wind, flatulence

ventrílocuo *m* ventriloquist

veo *vb* → **ver**

ver <2v; *part* visto> **1** *v/t* see; *televisión* watch; JUR *pleito* hear; *L.Am.* (*mirar*) look at; **está por ~** it remains to be seen; **no puede verla** *fig* he can't stand the sight of her; **no tiene nada que ~ con** it doesn't have anything to do with; **¡a ~!** let's see; **¡hay que ~!** would you believe it!; **ya veremos** we'll see **2** *v/i* L.Am. (*mirar*) look; **ve aquí dentro** L.Am. look in here **3** *v/r* **~se** see o.s.; (*encontrarse*) see one another; **¡habráse visto!** would you believe it!; **¡se las verá conmigo!** F he'll have me to deal with!

veranear <1a> *v/i* spend the summer vacation *o* Br holidays; **veraniego** *adj* summer *atr*; **verano** *m* summer

veras *f*: **de ~** really, truly

verbal *adj* GRAM verbal

verbena *f* (*fiesta*) party

verbo *m* GRAM verb; **verborrea** *f*

desp verbosity

verdad *f* truth; **a decir ~** to tell the truth; **de ~** real, proper; **no te gusta, ¿~?** you don't like it, do you?; **vas a venir, ¿~?** you're coming, aren't you?; **es ~** it's true, it's the truth; **verdadero** *adj* true; (*cierto*) real

verde 1 *adj* green; *fruta* unripe; F *chiste* blue, dirty; **viejo ~** dirty old man; **poner ~ a alguien** F criticize s.o. **2** *m* green; **los ~s** POL the Greens; **verdoso** *adj* greenish

verdugo *m* executioner

verdulería *f* fruit and vegetable store, Br greengrocer's; **verdura** *f*: **~(s)** (*hortalizas*) greens *pl*, (green) vegetables *pl*

vereda *f* S.Am. sidewalk, Br pavement; **meter alguien en ~** *fig* put s.o. back on the straight and narrow, bring s.o. into line

veredicto *m* JUR, *fig* verdict

verga *f* rod

vergel *m* orchard

vergonzoso *adj* disgraceful, shameful; (*tímido*) shy; **vergüenza** *f* shame; (*escándalo*) disgrace; **me da ~** I'm embarrassed; **es una ~** it's a disgrace; **no sé cómo no se te cae la cara de ~** you should be ashamed (of yourself)

vericuetos *mpl fig* twists and turns

verídico *adj* true

verificar <1g> *v/t* verify

verja *f* railing; (*puerta*) iron gate

vermú, vermut *m* vermouth

verosímil *adj* realistic; (*creíble*) plausible

verruga *f* wart

versado *adj* well-versed (**en** in)

versar <1a> *v/i*: **~ sobre** deal with, be about

versátil *adj* fickle; *artista* versatile

versículo *m* verse

versión *f* version; **en ~ original** *película* original language version

verso *m* verse

vértebra *f* ANAT vertebra

vertedero *m* dump, tip; **verter** <2g> *v/t* dump; (*derramar*) spill; *fig:*

opinión voice

vertical *adj* vertical

vertido *m* dumping; **~s** *pl* waste *sg*

vertiente *f L.Am.* (*cuesta*) slope; (*lado*) side

vertiginoso *adj* dizzy; (*rápido*) frantic; **vértigo** *m* MED vertigo; **darle a alguien** ~ make s.o. dizzy

vesícula *f* blister; **~ biliar** ANAT gallbladder

vespa® *f* motorscooter

vestíbulo *m de casa* hall; *de edifico público* lobby

vestido *m* dress; *L.Am. de hombre* suit

vestigio *m* vestige, trace

vestir <3l> **1** *v/t* dress; (*llevar puesto*) wear **2** *v/i* dress; **~ de negro** wear black, dress in black; **~ de uniforme** wear a uniform **3** *v/r* **~se** get dressed; (*disfrazarse*) dress up; **~se de algo** wear sth

vestuario *m* DEP locker room; TEA wardrobe

veta *f* MIN vein

vetar <1a> *v/t* POL veto

veterano 1 *adj* veteran; (*experimentado*) experienced **2** *m*, **-a** *f* veteran

veterinario 1 *adj* veterinary **2** *m*, **-a** *f* veterinarian, vet

veto *m* veto

vetusto *adj* ancient

vez *f* time; **a la** ~ at the same time; **a su** ~ for his / her part; **cada** ~ **que** every time that; **de** ~ **en cuando** from time to time; **en** ~ **de** instead of; **érase una** ~ once upon a time, there was; **otra** ~ again; **tal** ~ perhaps, maybe; **una** ~ once; **a veces** sometimes; **muchas veces** (*con frecuencia*) often; **hacer las veces de** *de objeto* serve as; *de persona* act as

vi *vb* → **ver**

vía 1 *f* FERR track; **~ estrecha** FERR narrow gauge; **darle ~ libre a alguien** give s.o. a free hand; **por ~ aérea** by air; **en ~s de** *fig* in the process of **2** *prp* via

viable *adj plan, solución* viable, feasible

viaducto *m* viaduct

viajante *m/f* sales rep; **viajar** <1a> *v/i* travel; **viaje** *m* trip, journey; **~ organizado** package tour; **~ de ida** outward journey; **~ de ida y vuelta** round trip; **~ de novios** honeymoon; **~ de vuelta** return journey; **viajero** *m*, **-a** *f* travel(l)er

viario *adj* road *atr*; **educación -a** instruction in road safety

víbora *f tb fig* viper

vibración *f* vibration; **vibrante** *adj fig* exciting; **vibrar** <1a> *v/i* vibrate

vicaría *f* pastor's house, vicarage; **pasar por la** ~ F get married in church

vicecónsul *m* vice-consul

vicepresidente *m*, **-a** *f* POL vice-president; COM vice-president, *Br* deputy chairman

vicerrector *m* vice-rector

viceversa *adv*: **y** ~ and vice versa

viciado *adj aire* stuffy; **viciarse** <1b> *v/r* fall into bad habits; **vicio** *m* vice; **pasarlo de** ~ F have a great time F; **vicioso** *adj* vicious; (*corrompido*) depraved

vicisitudes *fpl* ups and downs

víctima *f* victim; **victimar** <1a> *v/t L.Am.* kill

victoria *f* victory; **cantar** ~ claim victory; **victorioso** *adj* victorious

vicuña *f* ZO vicuna

vid *f* vine

vida *f* life; *esp* TÉC life span; **de por** ~ for life; **en mi** ~ never (in my life); **ganarse la** ~ earn a living; **hacer la ~ imposible a alguien** make s.o.'s life impossible; **~ mía** my love

vidente *m/f* seer, clairvoyant

vídeo *m* video

videocámara *f* video camera

videocas(s)et(t)e *m* video cassette

videoclip *m* pop video

videoconferencia *f* video conference

videojuego *m* video game

videotex(to) *m* videotext

vidriera *f L.Am.* shop window; **vidrio** *m L.Am.* glass; (*ventana*) window

V

vieira f ZO scallop

vieja f old woman; **viejo 1** adj old **2** m old man; **mis ~s** F my folks F

viendo vb → **ver**

viene vb → **venir**

viento m wind; **~ en popa** fig F splendidly; **contra ~ y marea** fig come what may; **hacer ~** be windy; **proclamar a los cuatro ~s** fig shout from the rooftops

vientre m belly

viernes m inv Friday; **Viernes Santo** Good Friday

Vietnam Vietnam; **vietnamita** adj & m/f Vietnamese

viga f beam, girder

vigente adj legislación in force

vigésimo adj twentieth

vigilante 1 adj watchful, vigilant **2** m L.Am. policeman; **~ nocturno** night watchman; **~ jurado** security guard; **vigilar** <1a> v/t keep watch **2** v/t watch; a un preso guard

vigor m vigo(u)r; **en ~** in force; **vigoroso** adj vigorous

vil adj vile, despicable

vilipendiar <1b> v/t insult, vilify fml; (despreciar) revile

villa f town

villancico m Christmas carol

villano 1 adj villainous **2** m, **-a** f villain

vilo en ~ in the air; fig in suspense, on tenterhooks; **levantar en ~** lift off the ground; **tener a alguien en ~** fig keep s.o. in suspense o on tenterhooks

vinagre m vinegar; **vinagrera** f vinegar bottle; S.Am. (indigestión) indigestion; **~s** pl cruet sg; **vinagreta** f vinaigrette

vincha f S.Am. hairband

vinculante adj binding; **vincular** <1a> v/t link (**a** to); (comprometer) bind; **vínculo** m link; fig (relación) tie, bond

vindicar <1g> v/t vindicate

vine vb → **venir**

vinícola adj región, país wine-growing atr; industria wine-making atr

viniendo vb → **venir**

vinicultura f wine-growing

vino 1 m wine; **~ blanco** white wine; **~ de mesa** table wine; **~ tinto** red wine **2** vb → **venir**

viña f vineyard; **viñatero** m, **-a** f S.Am. wine grower; **viñedo** m vineyard

viñeta f TIP vignette

vio vb → **ver**

viola f MÚS viola

violación f rape; de derechos violation; **violador** m, **-a** f rapist; **violar** <1a> v/t rape

violencia f violence; **violentar** <1a> v/t puerta force; (incomodar) embarrass; **violento** adj violent; (embarazoso) embarrassing; persona embarrassed

violeta 1 f BOT violet **2** m/adj violet

violín m violin; **violinista** m/f violinist; **violonc(h)elo** m cello

VIP m VIP

viperino adj malicious; **lengua -a** sharp tongue

viral adj viral

virar <1a> v/t MAR, AVIA turn

virgen 1 adj virgin; cinta blank; **lana ~** pure new wool **2** f virgin; **virginidad** f virginity

Virgo m/f inv ASTR Virgo

virguería f: **hace ~s** P he's a whizz F

vírico adj viral

viril adj virile, manly

virtual adj virtual

virtud f virtue; **en ~ de** by virtue of; **virtuoso 1** adj virtuous **2** m, **-a** f virtuoso

viruela f MED smallpox

virulento adj MED, fig virulent

virus m inv MED virus; **~ informático** computer virus

viruta f shaving

visa f L.Am. visa

visado m visa

vísceras fpl guts, entrails; **visceral** adj fig gut atr, visceral

viscoso adj viscous

visera f de gorra peak; de casco visor

visibilidad f visibility; **visible** adj visible; fig evident, obvious

visillo m sheer, Br net curtain

visión f vision, sight; fig vision; (*opinión*) view; **tener ~ de futuro** be forward looking

visita f visit; **~ a domicilio** house call; **~ guiada** guided tour; **hacer una ~ a alguien** visit s.o.; **visitante 1** adj visiting; DEP away **2** m/f visitor; **visitar** <1a> v/t visit

vislumbrar <1a> v/t glimpse

visos mpl: **tener ~ de** show signs of

visón m ZO mink

víspera f eve; **en ~s de** on the eve of

vista f (eye)sight; JUR hearing; **~ cansada** MED tired eyes; **a la ~** COM at sight, on demand; **a primera ~** at first sight; **con ~s a** with a view to; **en ~ de** in view of; **hasta la ~** bye!, see you!; **hacer la ~ gorda** fig F turn a blind eye; **tener ~ para algo** fig have a good eye for sth; **volver la ~ atrás** tb fig look back; **vistazo** m look; **echar un ~ a** take a (quick) look at

viste vb → **ver**, **vestir**

visto 1 part → **ver 2** adj: **está bien ~** it's the done thing; **está mal ~** it's not done, it's not the done thing; **está ~ que** it's obvious that; **estar muy ~** be old hat, not be original; **por lo ~** apparently **3** m check(mark), Br tick; **dar el ~ bueno** give one's approval; **vistoso** adj eye-catching

visual adj visual; **visualizar** <1f> v/t visualize; **en pantalla** display

vital adj vital; **persona** lively; **vitalicio** adj life atr, for life; **renta -a** life annuity; **vitalidad** f vitality, liveliness

vitamina f vitamin

viticultor m, **~a** f wine grower

vitores mpl cheers, acclaim sg; **vitorear** <1a> v/t cheer

vítreo adj vitreous; **vitrificar** <1g> v/t vitrify

vitrina f display cabinet; L.Am. shop window

vitrocerámica f ceramic hob

vituperar <1a> v/t condemn

viuda f widow; **viudedad** f widowhood; **pensión de ~** widow's pen-

sion; **viudo 1** adj widowed **2** m widower; **quedarse ~** be widowed

viva int hurrah!; **¡~ el rey!** long live the king!

vivaz adj bright, sharp

vivencia f experience

víveres mpl provisions

vívido adj vivid

vivienda f housing; (*casa*) house

vivir <3a> **1** v/t live through, experience **2** v/i live; **~ de algo** live on sth; **vivo** adj alive; color bright; ritmo lively; fig F sharp, smart

vocabulario m vocabulary

vocación f vocation

vocal 1 m/f member **2** f vowel; **vocalista** m/f vocalist; **vocalizar** <1f> v/i vocalize

voceador m, **~a** f Méx newspaper vendor

vocerío m uproar; **vocero** m, **-a** f esp L.Am. spokesperson; **vociferar** <1a> v/i shout

vodka m vodka

volador adj flying

volandas: **en ~** fig in the air

volante 1 adj flying **2** m AUTO steering wheel; de vestido flounce; MED referral (slip)

volar <1m> **1** v/i fly; fig vanish **2** v/t fly; edificio blow up

volátil adj tb fig volatile; **volatilizarse** <1f> v/r fig vanish into thin air

volcán m volcano; **volcánico** adj volcanic

volcar <1g & 1m> **1** v/t knock over; (vaciar) empty; barco, coche overturn **2** v/i de coche, barco overturn **3** v/r **~se** tip over; **~se por alguien** F bend over backwards for s.o., go out of one's way for s.o.; **~se en algo** throw o.s. into sth

volea f tenis volley

voleibol m volleyball

voleo m: **a ~** at random

voley-playa m beach volleyball

voltaje m EL voltage

voltear <1a> **1** v/t L.Am. (invertir) turn over; Rpl (tumbar) knock over; **~ el jersey** turn the sweater inside out; **~ la cabeza** turn one's head

2 *v/i* roll over; *de campanas* ring out;
voltereta *f* somersault
voltio *m* EL volt
voluble *adj* erratic, unpredictable
volumen *m* TIP, MÚS, RAD volume; **~
de negocios** COM turnover
voluntad *f* will; **buena / mala ~**
good / ill will; **voluntario 1** *adj*
volunteer **2** *m*, **-a** *f* volunteer; **vo-
luntarioso** *adj* willing, enthusiastic
voluptuoso *adj* voluptuous
volver <2h; *part* **vuelto**> **1** *v/t* página,
mirada *etc* turn (*a* to; *hacia* toward);
~ loco drive crazy **2** *v/i* return; **~ a
hacer algo** do sth again **3** *v/r* **~se**
turn round; **~se loco** go crazy
vomitar <1a> **1** *v/t* throw up; *lava*
hurl, throw out **2** *v/i* throw up, be
sick; **tengo ganas de ~** I feel nauseous, *Br* I feel sick; **vómito** *m* MED
vomit
vorágine *f* (*remolino*) whirlpool; *fig*
whirl
voraz *adj* voracious; *incendio* fierce
vos *pron pers sg Rpl, C.Am., Ven* you
vosotros, vosotras *pron pers pl* you
votación *f* vote, ballot; **votar** <1a>
1 *v/t* (*aprobar*) vote **2** *v/i* vote; **voto**
m POL vote; **~ en blanco** spoiled
ballot paper
voy *vb* → *ir*
voz *f* voice; *fig* rumo(u)r; **~ activa /
pasiva** GRAM active / passive voice;

a media ~ in a hushed voice, in a
low voice; **a ~ en grito** at the top of
one's voice; **en ~ alta** aloud; **en ~
baja** in a low voice; **correr la ~**
spread the word; **llevar la ~
cantante** *fig* call the tune, call the
shots; **no tener ~ ni voto** *fig* not
have a say; **~ en off** voice-over
vuelco 1 *vb* → *volcar* **2** *m*: **dar un ~**
fig F take a dramatic turn; **me dio
un ~ el corazón** my heart missed a
beat
vuelo 1 *vb* → *volar* **2** *m* flight; **~
chárter** charter flight; **~ nacional**
domestic flight; **al ~ coger, cazar** in
mid-air; **una falda con ~** a full skirt
vuelta *f* return; *en carrera* lap; **~ de
carnero** *L.Am.* half-somersault; **~
al mundo** round-the- world trip; **a
la ~** on the way back; **a la ~ de la
esquina** *fig* just around the corner;
dar la ~ llave etc turn; **dar media ~**
turn round; **dar una ~** go for a walk;
dar cien ~s a alguien F be a hundred times better than s.o. F
vuelto 1 *part* → *volver* **2** *m L.Am.*
change
vuelvo *vb* → *volver*
vuestro 1 *adj pos* your **2** *pron* yours
vulgar *adj* vulgar, common; *abundante* common; **vulgaridad** *f* vul-
garity; **vulgo** *m* lower classes *pl*
vulnerable *adj* vulnerable

W

w. *abr* (= **watio**) w (= watt)
walkman *m* personal stereo
wáter *m* bathroom, toilet
waterpolo *m* DEP water polo

WC *abr* WC
whisky *m* whiskey, *Br* whisky
windsurf(ing) *m* wind-surfing;
windsurfista *m/f* windsurfer

X

xenofobia *f* xenophobia

xilófono *m* MÚS xylophone

Y

y *conj* and
ya *adv* already; (*ahora mismo*) now;
¡**~!** *incredulidad* oh, yeah!, sure!;
comprensión I know, I understand;
asenso OK, sure; *al terminar* finished!, done!; **~ no vive aquí** he
doesn't live here any more, he no
longer lives here; **~ que** since, as; **~
lo sé** I know; **~ viene** she's coming
now; ¿**lo puede hacer? – ¡~ lo creo!**
can she do it? – you bet!; **~ ... ~ ...**
either ... or ...
yacaré *m L.Am.* ZO cayman
yacer <2y> *v/i* lie; **yacimiento** *m* MIN
deposit
yanqui *m/f* Yankee
yapa *f L.Am.* bit extra (for free); *Pe,
Bol* (*propina*) tip
yate *m* yacht
yaya *f* grandma
yayo *m* grandpa
yedra *f* BOT ivy

yegua *f* ZO mare
yema *f* yolk; **~ del dedo** fingertip
yendo *vb* → **ir**
yerba *f L.Am.* grass; **~ mate** maté;
yerbatero *m*, **-a** *f Rpl* herbalist
yerno *m* son-in-law
yeso *m* plaster
yo *pron* I; **soy ~** it's me; **~ que tú** if I
were you
yodo *m* iodine
yoga *m* yoga
yogur *m* yog(h)urt
yonqui *m/f* F junkie
yuca *f* BOT yucca
yugo *m* yoke
Yugoslavia Yugoslavia; **yugoslavo
1** *adj* Yugoslav(ian) **2** *m*, **-a** *f*
Yugoslav(ian)
yugular *adj* ANAT jugular
yute *m* jute
yuxtaposición *f* juxtaposition
yuyo *m L.Am.* weed

Z

zacatal *m C.Am.*, *Méx* pasture;
zacate *m C.Am.*, *Méx* fodder
zafarse <1a> *v/r* get away (**de** from);
(*soltarse*) come undone; **~ de algo**

(*evitar*) get out of sth
zafio *adj* coarse
zafiro *m* sapphire
zaga *f*: **ir a la ~** bring up the rear

Z

zalamero 1 *adj* flattering; *empalago-so* syrupy, sugary **2** *m*, **-a** *f* flatterer, sweet talker

zamba *f Arg* (*baile*) Argentinian folkdance

zambomba *f* MÚS *type of drum*

zambullirse <3h> *v/r* dive (*en* into); *fig* throw o.s. (*en* into), immerse o.s. (*en* in)

zamparse <1a> *v/r* F wolf down F

zanahoria *f* carrot

zancada *f* stride

zancadilla *f fig* obstacle; *poner or echar la ~ a alguien* trip s.o. up

zancudo *m L.Am.* mosquito

zángano *m* ZO drone; *fig* F lazybones *sg*

zanja *f* ditch; **zanjar** <1a> *v/t fig problemas* settle; *dificultades* overcome

zapatería *f* shoe store, shoe shop; **zapatero** *m*, **-a** *f* shoemaker; *~ remendón* shoe mender; **zapatilla** *f* slipper; *de deporte* sneaker, *Br* trainer

Zapatista *m/f Méx* member or supporter of the Zapatista National Liberation Army

zapato *m* shoe

zapear <1a> *v/i* TV F channel hop; **zapeo, zapping** *m* TV F channel hopping

zarandear <1a> *v/t* shake violently, buffet; *~ a alguien fig* give s.o. a hard time

zarpa *f* paw

zarpar <1a> *v/i* MAR set sail (*para* for)

zarza *f* BOT bramble; **zarzamora** *f* BOT blackberry

zarzuela *f* MÚS *type of operetta*

zascandilear <1a> *v/i* mess around

zigzaguear <1a> *v/i* zigzag

zinc *m* zinc

zócalo *m* baseboard, *Br* skirting board

zodíaco, zodiaco *m* AST zodiac

zona *f* area, zone

zoncería *f L.Am.* F stupid thing; **zonzo** *adj L.Am.* F stupid

zoo *m* zoo; **zoológico 1** *adj* zoological **2** *m* zoo

zoom *m* FOT zoom

zopilote *m L.Am.* ZO turkey buzzard

zorra *f* ZO vixen; P whore P; **zorro 1** *adj* sly, crafty **2** *m* ZO fox; *fig* old fox

zozobrar <1a> *v/i* MAR overturn; *fig* go under

zueco *m* clog

zulo *m* hiding place

zumba *f L.Am., Méx* (*paliza*) beating; **zumbar** <1a> **1** *v/i* buzz; *me zumban los oídos* my ears are ringing *o* buzzing **2** *v/t golpe, bofetada* give; **zumbido** *m* buzzing

zumo *m* juice

zurcir <3b> *v/t calcetines* darn; *chaqueta, pantalones* patch

zurdo 1 *adj* left-handed **2** *m*, **-a** *f* lefthander

zurrar <1a> *v/t* TÉC tan; *~ a alguien* F tan s.o.'s hide F

A

a [ə] *stressed* [eɪ] *art* un(a); ***an island*** una isla; ***$5 a ride*** 5 dólares por vuelta

a·back [ə'bæk] *adv*: ***taken ~*** desconcertado (***by*** por)

a·ban·don [ə'bændən] *v/t* abandonar

a·bashed [ə'bæʃt] *adj* avergonzado

a·bate [ə'beɪt] *v/i of storm, flood* amainar

ab·at·toir ['æbətwɑːr] matadero *m*

ab·bey ['æbɪ] abadía *f*

ab·bre·vi·ate [ə'briːvɪeɪt] *v/t* abreviar

ab·bre·vi·a·tion [əbriːvɪ'eɪʃn] abreviatura *f*

ab·di·cate ['æbdɪkeɪt] *v/i* abdicar

ab·di·ca·tion [æbdɪ'keɪʃn] abdicación *f*

ab·do·men ['æbdəmən] abdomen *m*

ab·dom·i·nal [æb'dɑːmɪnl] *adj* abdominal

ab·duct [əb'dʌkt] *v/t* raptar, secuestrar

ab·duc·tion [əb'dʌkʃn] rapto *m*, secuestro *m*

♦ **a·bide by** [ə'baɪd] *v/t* atenerse a

a·bil·i·ty [ə'bɪlətɪ] capacidad *f*, habilidad *f*

a·blaze [ə'bleɪz] *adj* en llamas

a·ble ['eɪbl] *adj (skillful)* capaz, hábil; ***be ~ to*** poder; ***I wasn't ~ to see/hear*** no conseguí *or* pude ver/escuchar

a·ble-bod·ied [eɪbl'bɑːdiːd] *adj* sano

ab·nor·mal [æb'nɔːrml] *adj* anormal

ab·nor·mal·ly [æb'nɔːrməlɪ] *adv* anormalmente; *behave* de manera anormal

a·board [ə'bɔːrd] **1** *prep* a bordo de **2** *adv* a bordo; ***be ~*** estar a bordo; ***go ~*** subir a bordo

a·bol·ish [ə'bɑːlɪʃ] *v/t* abolir

ab·o·li·tion [æbə'lɪʃn] abolición *f*

a·bort [ə'bɔːrt] *v/t mission, launch* suspender, cancelar; COMPUT cancelar

a·bor·tion [ə'bɔːrʃn] aborto *m* (*provocado*); ***have an ~*** abortar

a·bor·tive [ə'bɔːrtɪv] *adj* fallido

a·bout [ə'baʊt] **1** *prep (concerning)* acerca de, sobre; ***what's it ~?*** *of book, movie* ¿de qué trata? **2** *adv (roughly)* más o menos; ***be ~ to ...*** *(be going to)* estar a punto de ...

a·bove [ə'bʌv] **1** *prep* por encima de; ***500 m ~ sea level*** 500 m sobre el nivel del mar; ***~ all*** por encima de todo, sobre todo **2** *adv*: ***on the floor ~*** en el piso de arriba

a·bove-men·tioned [əbʌv'menʃnd] *adj* arriba mencionado

ab·ra·sion [ə'breɪʒn] abrasión *f*

ab·ra·sive [ə'breɪsɪv] *adj personality* abrasivo

a·breast [ə'brest] *adv* de frente, en fondo; ***keep ~ of*** mantenerse al tanto de

a·bridge [ə'brɪdʒ] *v/t* abreviar, condensar

a·broad [ə'brɔːd] *adv live* en el extranjero; *go al* extranjero

a·brupt [ə'brʌpt] *adj departure* brusco, repentino; *manner* brusco, rudo

a·brupt·ly [ə'brʌptlɪ] *adv (suddenly)* repentinamente; *(curtly)* bruscamente

ab·scess ['æbsɪs] absceso *m*

ab·sence ['æbsəns] *of person* ausencia *f*; *(lack)* falta *f*

ab·sent ['æbsənt] *adj* ausente

ab·sen·tee [æbsən'tiː] *n* ausente *m/f*

ab·sen·tee·ism [æbsən'tiːɪzm] absentismo *m*

ab·sent-mind·ed [æbsənt'maɪndɪd] *adj* despistado, distraído

ab·sent-mind·ed·ly [æbsənt'maɪndɪdlɪ] *adv* distraídamente

ab·so·lute ['æbsəlu:t] *adj power* absoluto; *idiot* completo; *mess* total

ab·so·lute·ly ['æbsəlu:tlɪ] *adv* (*completely*) absolutamente, completamente; ~ **not!** ¡en absoluto!; *do you agree?* – ~ ¿estás de acuerdo? – ¡completamente!

ab·so·lu·tion [æbsə'lu:ʃn] REL absolución *f*

ab·solve [əb'zɑ:lv] *v/t* absolver

ab·sorb [əb'sɔ:rb] *v/t* absorber; ~*ed in* absorto en

ab·sorb·en·cy [əb'sɔ:rbənsɪ] absorbencia *f*

ab·sorb·ent [əb'sɔ:rbənt] *adj* absorbente

ab·sorb·ent 'cot·ton algodón *m* hidrófilo

ab·sorb·ing [əb'sɔ:rbɪŋ] *adj* absorbente

ab·stain [əb'steɪn] *v/i from voting* abstenerse

ab·sten·tion [əb'stenʃn] *in voting* abstención *f*

ab·stract ['æbstrækt] *adj* abstracto

ab·struse [əb'stru:s] *adj* abstruso

ab·surd [əb'sɜ:rd] *adj* absurdo

ab·surd·i·ty [əb'sɜ:rdətɪ] lo absurdo

a·bun·dance [ə'bʌndəns] abundancia *f*

a·bun·dant [ə'bʌndənt] *adj* abundante

a·buse¹ [ə'bju:s] *n* (*insults*) insultos *mpl*; *of thing* maltrato *m*; (*child*) ~ *physical* malos tratos *mpl* a menores; *sexual* agresión *f* sexual a menores

a·buse² [ə'bju:z] *v/t physically* abusar de; *verbally* insultar

a·bu·sive [ə'bju:sɪv] *adj language* insultante, injurioso; *become* ~ ponerse a insultar

a·bys·mal [ə'bɪʒml] *adj* F (*very bad*) desastroso F

a·byss [ə'bɪs] abismo *m*

AC ['eɪsi:] *abbr* (= *alternating current*) CA (= corriente *f* alterna)

ac·a·dem·ic [ækə'demɪk] **1** *n* académico(-a) *m(f)*, profesor(a) *m(f)* **2** *adj* académico

a·cad·e·my [ə'kædəmɪ] academia *f*

ac·cel·e·rate [ək'seləreɪt] *v/t & v/i* acelerar

ac·cel·e·ra·tion [əkselə'reɪʃn] aceleración *f*

ac·cel·e·ra·tor [ək'seləreɪtər] *of car* acelerador *m*

ac·cent ['æksənt] *when speaking* acento *m*; (*emphasis*) énfasis *m*

ac·cen·tu·ate [ək'sentʊeɪt] *v/t* acentuar

ac·cept [ək'sept] *v/t & v/i* aceptar

ac·cep·ta·ble [ək'septəbl] *adj* aceptable

ac·cep·tance [ək'septəns] aceptación *f*

ac·cess ['ækses] **1** *n* acceso *m*; *have* ~ *to computer* tener acceso a; *child* tener derecho a visitar **2** *v/t also* COMPUT acceder a

'ac·cess code COMPUT código *m* de acceso

ac·ces·si·ble [ək'sesəbl] *adj* accesible

ac·ces·sion [ək'seʃn] acceso *m*

ac·ces·so·ry [ək'sesərɪ] *for wearing* accesorio *m*, complemento *m*; LAW cómplice *m/f*

'ac·cess road carretera *f* de acceso

'ac·cess time COMPUT tiempo *m* de acceso

ac·ci·dent ['æksɪdənt] accidente *m*; *by* ~ por casualidad

ac·ci·den·tal [æksɪ'dentl] *adj* accidental

ac·ci·den·tal·ly [æksɪ'dentlɪ] *adv* sin querer

ac·claim [ə'kleɪm] **1** *n* alabanza *f*, aclamación *f*; *meet with* ~ ser alabado *or* aclamado **2** *v/t* alabar, aclamar

ac·cla·ma·tion [æklə'meɪʃn] aclamación *f*

ac·cli·mate, ac·cli·ma·tize [ə'klaɪmət, ə'klaɪmətaɪz] *v/t* aclimatarse

ac·com·mo·date [ə'kɑ:mədeɪt] *v/t* alojar; *requirements* satisfacer, hacer frente a

ac·com·mo·da·tions [əkɑ:mə'deɪʃnz] *npl* alojamiento *m*

ac·com·pa·ni·ment [ə'kʌmpənɪmənt] MUS acompañamiento *m* ac·com·pa·nist [əˈkʌmpənɪst] MUS acompañante m/f

ac·com·pa·ny [əˈkʌmpənɪ] v/t (pret & pp -ied) also MUS acompañar

ac·com·plice [əˈkʌmplɪs] cómplice m/f

ac·com·plish [əˈkʌmplɪʃ] v/t task realizar; goal conseguir, lograr

ac·com·plished [əˈkʌmplɪʃt] adj consumado

ac·com·plish·ment [əˈkʌmplɪʃmənt] of a task realización f; (talent) habilidad f; (achievement) logro m

ac·cord [əˈkɔːrd] acuerdo m; of one's own ~ de motu propio

ac·cord·ance [əˈkɔːrdəns]: in ~ with de acuerdo con

ac·cord·ing [əˈkɔːrdɪŋ] adv: ~ to según

ac·cord·ing·ly [əˈkɔːrdɪŋlɪ] adv (consequently) por consiguiente; (appropriately) como corresponde

ac·cor·di·on [əˈkɔːrdɪən] acordeón m

ac·cor·di·on·ist [əˈkɔːrdɪənɪst] acordeonista m/f

ac·count [əˈkaʊnt] financial cuenta f; (report, description) relato m, descripción f; give an ~ of relatar, describir; on no ~ de ninguna manera, bajo ningún concepto; on ~ of a causa de; take sth into ~, take ~ of sth tener algo en cuenta, tener en cuenta algo

♦ account for v/t (explain) explicar; (make up, constitute) suponer, constituir

ac·count·a·bil·i·ty [əkaʊntəˈbɪlətɪ] responsabilidad f

ac·count·a·ble [əˈkaʊntəbl] adj responsable (to ante); be held ~ ser considerado responsable

ac·count·ant [əˈkaʊntənt] contable m/f, L.Am. contador(a) m(f)

ac'count hold·er titular m/f de una cuenta

ac'count num·ber número m de cuenta

ac·counts [əˈkaʊnts] npl contabilidad f

ac·cu·mu·late [əˈkjuːmjʊleɪt] 1 v/t acumular 2 v/i acumularse

ac·cu·mu·la·tion [əkjuːmjʊˈleɪʃn] acumulación f

ac·cu·ra·cy [ˈækjʊrəsɪ] precisión f

ac·cu·rate [ˈækjʊrət] adj preciso

ac·cu·rate·ly [ˈækjʊrətlɪ] adv con precisión

ac·cu·sa·tion [ækjuːˈzeɪʃn] acusación f

ac·cuse [əˈkjuːz] v/t: ~ s.o. of sth acusar a alguien de algo; be ~d of LAW ser acusado de

ac·cused [əˈkjuːzd] n LAW acusado(-a) m(f)

ac·cus·ing [əˈkjuːzɪŋ] adj acusador

ac·cus·ing·ly [əˈkjuːzɪŋlɪ] adv say en tono acusador; he looked at me ~ me lanzó una mirada acusadora

ac·cus·tom [əˈkʌstəm] v/t acostumbrar; get ~ed to acostumbrarse a; be ~ed to estar acostumbrado a

ace [eɪs] in cards as m; (in tennis: shot) ace m

ache [eɪk] 1 n dolor m 2 v/i doler

a·chieve [əˈtʃiːv] v/t conseguir, lograr

a·chieve·ment [əˈtʃiːvmənt] of ambition consecución f, logro m; (thing achieved) logro m

ac·id [ˈæsɪd] n ácido m

a·cid·i·ty [əˈsɪdətɪ] acidez f; fig sarcasmo m

ac·id 'rain lluvia f ácida

'ac·id test fig prueba f de fuego

ac·knowl·edge [əkˈnɒːlɪdʒ] v/t reconocer; ~ receipt of a letter acusar recibo de una carta

ac·knowl·edg(e)·ment [əkˈnɒːlɪdʒmənt] reconocimiento m; of a letter acuse m de recibo

ac·ne [ˈæknɪ] MED acné m, acne m

a·corn [ˈeɪkɔːrn] BOT bellota f

a·cous·tics [əˈkuːstɪks] acústica f

ac·quaint [əˈkweɪnt] v/t fml: be ~ed with conocer

ac·quaint·ance [əˈkweɪntəns] person conocido(-a) m(f)

ac·qui·esce [ækwɪˈes] v/i fml acceder

ac·qui·es·cence [ækwɪˈesns] fml aquiescencia f

ac·quire [əˈkwaɪr] v/t adquirir

ac·qui·si·tion [ækwı'zıʃn] adquisición f

ac·quis·i·tive [æ'kwızətıv] *adj* consumista

ac·quit [ə'kwıt] *v/t* LAW absolver

ac·quit·tal [ə'kwıtl] LAW absolución f

a·cre ['eıkər] acre m *(4.047m2)*

ac·ri·mo·ni·ous [ækrı'mounıəs] *adj* áspero, agrio

ac·ro·bat ['ækrəbæt] acróbata m/f

ac·ro·bat·ic [ækrə'bætık] *adj* acrobático

ac·ro·bat·ics [ækrə'bætıks] *npl* acrobacias *fpl*

ac·ro·nym ['ækrənım] acrónimo m

a·cross [ə'krɑːs] **1** *prep* al otro lado de; *she lives ~ the street* vive al otro lado de la calle; *sail ~ the Atlantic* cruzar el Atlántico navegando **2** *adv* de un lado a otro; *it's too far to swim ~* está demasiado lejos como para cruzar a nado; *once you're ~* cuando hayas llegado al otro lado; *10 m ~* 10 m de ancho

a·cryl·ic [ə'krılık] *adj* acrílico

act [ækt] **1** *v/i* THEA actuar; *(pretend)* hacer teatro; *~ as* actuar or hacer de **2** *n (deed)*, *of play* acto m; *in vaudeville* número m; *(law)* ley f; *it's just an ~ (pretense)* es puro teatro; *~ of God* caso m fortuito

act·ing ['æktıŋ] **1** *n* *in a play* interpretación f; *as profession* teatro m **2** *adj (temporary)* en funciones

ac·tion ['ækʃn] acción f; *out of ~ machine* sin funcionar; *person* fuera de combate; *take ~* actuar; *bring an ~ against* LAW demandar a

ac·tion 're·play TV repetición f *(de la jugada)*

ac·tive ['æktıv] *adj also* GRAM activo; *party member* en activo

ac·tiv·ist ['æktıvıst] POL activista m/f

ac·tiv·i·ty [æk'tıvətı] actividad f

ac·tor ['æktər] actor m

ac·tress ['æktrıs] actriz f

ac·tu·al ['æktʃuəl] *adj* verdadero, real

ac·tu·al·ly ['æktʃuəlı] *adv (in fact, to tell the truth)* en realidad; *did you ~ see her?* ¿de verdad llegaste a verla?; *he ~ did it!* ¡aunque parezca mentira lo hizo!; *~, I do know him (stressing converse)* pues sí, de hecho lo conozco; *~, it's not finished yet* el caso es que todavía no está terminado

ac·u·punc·ture ['ækjəpʌŋktʃər] acupuntura f

a·cute [ə'kjuːt] *adj pain* agudo; *sense* muy fino

a·cute·ly [ə'kjuːtlı] *adv (extremely)* extremadamente; *~ aware* plenamente consciente

AD [eı'diː] *abbr (= anno Domini)* D.C. (= después de Cristo)

ad [æd] → *advertisement*

ad·a·mant ['ædəmənt] *adj* firme

Ad·am's ap·ple [ædəmz'æpəl] nuez f

a·dapt [ə'dæpt] **1** *v/t* adaptar **2** *v/i of person* adaptarse

a·dapt·a·bil·i·ty [ədæptə'bılətı] adaptabilidad f

a·dap·ta·ble [ə'dæptəbl] *adj* adaptable

a·dap·ta·tion [ædæp'teıʃn] *of play etc* adaptación f

a·dapt·er [ə'dæptər] *electrical* adaptador m

add [æd] **1** *v/t* añadir; MATH sumar **2** *v/i of person* sumar
♦ **add on** *v/t 15% etc* sumar
♦ **add up 1** *v/t* sumar **2** *v/i fig* cuadrar

ad·der ['ædər] víbora f

ad·dict ['ædıkt] adicto(-a) m(f); *drug ~* drogadicto(-a) m(f)

ad·dict·ed [ə'dıktıd] *adj* adicto; *be ~ to* ser adicto a

ad·dic·tion [ə'dıkʃn] adicción f

ad·dic·tive [ə'dıktıv] *adj* adictivo

ad·di·tion [ə'dıʃn] MATH suma f; *to list, company etc* incorporación f; *of new drive etc* instalación f; *in ~* además; *in ~ to* además de

ad·di·tion·al [ə'dıʃnl] *adj* adicional

ad·di·tive ['ædıtıv] aditivo m

add-on ['ædɑːn] extra m, accesorio m

ad·dress [əˈdres] **1** n dirección f; **form of ~** tratamiento m **2** v/t letter dirigir; audience dirigirse a; **how do you ~ the judge?** ¿qué tratamiento se le da al juez?

ad'dress book agenda f de direcciones

ad·dress·ee [ædreˈsiː] destinatario(-a) m(f)

ad·ept [ˈædept] adj experto; **be ~ at** ser un experto en

ad·e·quate [ˈædɪkwət] adj suficiente; (satisfactory) aceptable

ad·e·quate·ly [ˈædɪkwətlɪ] adv suficientemente; (satisfactorily) aceptablemente

ad·here [ədˈhɪr] v/i adherirse

♦ **adhere to** v/t surface adherirse a; rules cumplir

ad·he·sive [ədˈhiːsɪv] n adhesivo m

ad·he·sive 'plas·ter esparadrapo m

ad·he·sive 'tape cinta f adhesiva

ad·ja·cent [əˈdʒeɪsnt] adj adyacente

ad·jec·tive [ˈædʒɪktɪv] adjetivo m

ad·join [əˈdʒɔɪn] v/t lindar con

ad·join·ing [əˈdʒɔɪnɪŋ] adj contiguo

ad·journ [əˈdʒɜːrn] v/i of court, meeting aplazar

ad·journ·ment [əˈdʒɜːrnmənt] aplazamiento m

ad·just [əˈdʒʌst] v/t ajustar, regular

ad·just·a·ble [əˈdʒʌstəbl] adj ajustable, regulable

ad·just·ment [əˈdʒʌstmənt] ajuste m; psychological adaptación f

ad lib [ædˈlɪb] **1** adj improvisado **2** adv improvisadamente **3** v/i (pret & pp **-bed**) improvisar

ad·min·is·ter [ədˈmɪnɪstər] v/t administrar

ad·min·is·tra·tion [ədmɪnɪˈstreɪʃn] administración f

ad·min·is·tra·tive [ədmɪnɪˈstrɑtɪv] adj administrativo

ad·min·is·tra·tor [ədˈmɪnɪstreɪtər] administrador(a) m(f)

ad·mi·ra·ble [ˈædmərəbl] adj admirable

ad·mi·ra·bly [ˈædmərəblɪ] adv admirablemente

ad·mi·ral [ˈædmərəl] almirante m

ad·mi·ra·tion [ædməˈreɪʃn] admiración f

ad·mire [ədˈmaɪr] v/t admirar

ad·mir·er [ədˈmaɪrər] admirador(a) m(f)

ad·mir·ing [ədˈmaɪrɪŋ] adj de admiración

ad·mir·ing·ly [ədˈmaɪrɪŋlɪ] adv con admiración

ad·mis·si·ble [ədˈmɪsəbl] adj admisible

ad·mis·sion [ədˈmɪʃn] (confession) confesión f; **~ free** entrada gratis

ad·mit [ədˈmɪt] v/t (pret & pp **-ted**) to a place dejar entrar; to school, organization admitir; to hospital ingresar; (confess) confesar; (accept) admitir

ad·mit·tance [ədˈmɪtəns] admisión f; **no ~** prohibido el paso

ad·mit·ted·ly [ədˈmɪtedlɪ] adv: **he didn't use those exact words, ~** es verdad que no utilizó exactamente esas palabras

ad·mon·ish [ədˈmɑːnɪʃ] v/t fml reprender

a·do [əˈduː]: **without further ~** sin más dilación

ad·o·les·cence [ædəˈlesns] adolescencia f

ad·o·les·cent [ædəˈlesnt] **1** n adolescente m/f **2** adj de adolescente

a·dopt [əˈdɑːpt] v/t child, plan adoptar

a·dop·tion [əˈdɑːpʃn] of child adopción f

a·dop·tive 'par·ents [əˈdɑːptɪv] npl padres mpl adoptivos

a·dor·a·ble [əˈdɔːrəbl] adj encantador

ad·o·ra·tion [ædəˈreɪʃn] adoración f

a·dore [əˈdɔːr] v/t adorar; **I ~ choco·late** me encanta el chocolate

a·dor·ing [əˈdɔːrɪŋ] adj expression lleno de adoración; **his ~ fans** sus entregados fans

ad·ren·al·in [əˈdrenəlɪn] adrenalina f

a·drift [əˈdrɪft] adj a la deriva; fig perdido

ad·u·la·tion [ædʊˈleɪʃn] adulación f

a·dult ['ædʌlt] **1** *n* adulto(-a) *m(f)* **2** *adj* adulto

a·dult ed·u·ca·tion educación *f* para adultos

a·dul·ter·ous [ə'dʌltərəs] *adj* relationship adúltero

a·dul·ter·y [ə'dʌltərɪ] adulterio *m*

'a·dult film *euph* película *f* para adultos

ad·vance [əd'væns] **1** *n money* adelanto *m; in science,* MIL avance *m;* **in ~** con antelación; *get money* por adelantado; *48 hours in ~* con 48 horas de antelación; *make ~s* (*progress*) avanzar, progresar; *sexually* insinuarse **2** *v/i* MIL avanzar; (*make progress*) avanzar, progresar **3** *v/t theory* presentar; *sum of money* adelantar; *human knowledge, a cause* hacer avanzar

ad·vance 'book·ing reserva *f* (anticipada)

ad·vanced [əd'vænst] *adj country, level, learner* avanzado

ad·vance 'no·tice aviso *m* previo

ad·vance 'pay·ment pago *m* por adelantado

ad·van·tage [əd'væntɪdʒ] ventaja *f; there's no ~ to be gained* no se gana nada; *it's to your ~* te conviene; *take ~ of* aprovecharse de

ad·van·ta·geous [ædvən'teɪdʒəs] *adj* ventajoso

ad·vent ['ædvent] *fig* llegada *f*

'ad·vent cal·en·dar calendario *m* de Adviento

ad·ven·ture [əd'ventʃər] aventura *f*

ad·ven·tur·ous [əd'ventʃərəs] *adj person* aventurero; *investment* arriesgado

ad·verb ['ædvɜːrb] adverbio *m*

ad·ver·sa·ry ['ædvərserɪ] adversario(-a) *m(f)*

ad·verse ['ædvɜːrs] *adj* adverso

ad·vert ['ædvɜːrt] → *advertisement*

ad·ver·tise ['ædvərtaɪz] **1** *v/t* anunciar **2** *v/i* anunciarse, poner un anuncio

ad·ver·tise·ment [ədvɜːr'taɪsmənt] anuncio *m*

ad·ver·tis·er ['ædvərtaɪzər] anun-

ciante *m/f*

ad·ver·tis·ing ['ædvərtaɪzɪŋ] publicidad *f*

'ad·ver·tis·ing a·gen·cy agencia *f* de publicidad; **'ad·ver·tis·ing budg·et** presupuesto *m* para publicidad; **'ad·ver·tis·ing cam·paign** campaña *f* publicitaria; **'ad·ver·tis·ing rev·e·nue** ingresos *mpl* por publicidad

ad·vice [əd'vaɪs] consejo *m; he gave me some ~* me dio un consejo; *take s.o.'s ~* seguir el consejo de alguien

ad·vis·a·ble [əd'vaɪzəbl] *adj* aconsejable

ad·vise [əd'vaɪz] *v/t person, caution* aconsejar; *government* asesorar; *I ~ you to leave* te aconsejo que te vayas

ad·vis·er [əd'vaɪzər] asesor(a) *m(f)*

ad·vo·cate ['ædvəkeɪt] *v/t* abogar por

aer·i·al ['erɪəl] *n* antena *f*

aer·i·al 'pho·to·graph fotografía *f* aérea

aer·o·bics [e'roʊbɪks] *nsg* aerobic *m*

aer·o·dy·nam·ic [eroʊdaɪ'næmɪk] *adj* aerodinámico

aer·o·nau·ti·cal [eroʊ'nɒːtɪkl] *adj* aeronáutico

aer·o·plane ['eroʊpleɪn] *Br* avión *m*

aer·o·sol ['erəsɒːl] aerosol *m*

aer·o·space in·dus·try ['erəspeɪs] industria *f* aeroespacial

aes·thet·ic *etc Br* → *esthetic etc*

af·fa·ble ['æfəbl] *adj* afable

af·fair [ə'fer] (*matter, business*) asunto *m;* (*love ~*) aventura *f,* lío *m; foreign ~s* asuntos *mpl* exteriores; *have an ~ with* tener una aventura *or* lío con

af·fect [ə'fekt] *v/t also* MED afectar

af·fec·tion [ə'fekʃn] afecto *m,* cariño

af·fec·tion·ate [ə'fekʃnət] *adj* afectuoso, cariñoso

af·fec·tion·ate·ly [ə'fekʃnətlɪ] *adv* con afecto, cariñosamente

af·fin·i·ty [ə'fɪnətɪ] afinidad *f*

af·firm·a·tive [ə'fɜːrmətɪv] *adj* afirmativo; *answer in the ~* responder afirmativamente

af·flu·ence [ˈæfluəns] prosperidad *f*, riqueza *f*

af·flu·ent [ˈæfluənt] *adj* próspero, acomodado; **~ society** sociedad *f* opulenta

af·ford [əˈfɔːrd] *v/t* permitirse; **be able to ~ sth** *financially* poder permitirse algo; **I can't ~ the time** no tengo tiempo

af·ford·a·ble [əˈfɔːrdəbl] *adj* asequible

a·float [əˈfloʊt] *adj boat* a flote; **keep the company ~** mantener la compañía a flote

a·fraid [əˈfreɪd] *adj*: **be ~** tener miedo; **be ~ of** tener miedo de; **I'm ~ of cats** tengo miedo a los gatos; **he's ~ of the dark** le da miedo la oscuridad; **I'm ~ of annoying him** me da miedo enfadarle; **I'm ~** *expressing regret* me temo; **he's very ill, I'm ~** me temo que está muy enfermo; **I'm ~ so** (me) temo que sí; **I'm ~ not** (me) temo que no

a·fresh [əˈfreʃ] *adv* de nuevo

Af·ri·ca [ˈæfrɪkə] África

Af·ri·can [ˈæfrɪkən] **1** *adj* africano **2** *n* africano(-a) *m(f)*

af·ter [ˈæftər] **1** *prep* después de; **~ all** después de todo; **~ that** después de eso; **it's ten ~ two** son las dos y diez **2** *adv* (*afterward*) después; **the day ~** el día siguiente

af·ter·math [ˈæftərmæθ] *time* periodo *m* posterior (*of* a); *state of affairs* repercusiones *fpl*

af·ter·noon [æftərˈnuːn] tarde *f*; **in the ~** por la tarde; **this ~** esta tarde; **good ~** buenas tardes

'af·ter sales serv·ice servicio *m* posventa; **'af·ter·shave** loción *f* para después del afeitado, after shave *m*; **'af·ter·taste** regusto *m*

af·ter·ward [ˈæftərwərd] *adv* después

a·gain [əˈgeɪn] *adv* otra vez; **I never saw him ~** no lo volví a ver

a·gainst [əˈgenst] *prep lean* contra; **the USA ~ Brazil** SP Estados Unidos contra Brasil; **I'm ~ the idea** es-

toy en contra de la idea; **what do you have ~ her?** ¿que tienes en contra de ella?; **~ the law** ilegal

age [eɪdʒ] **1** *n of person, object* edad *f*; (*era*) era *f*; **at the ~ of ten** a los diez años; **under ~** menor de edad; **she's five years of ~** tiene cinco años **2** *v/i* envejecer

aged¹ [eɪdʒd] *adj*: **~ 16** con 16 años de edad

a·ged² [ˈeɪdʒɪd] **1** *adj*: **her ~ parents** sus ancianos padres **2** *n*: **the ~** los ancianos

'age group grupo *m* de edades

'age lim·it límite *m* de edad

a·gen·cy [ˈeɪdʒənsɪ] agencia *f*

a·gen·da [əˈdʒendə] orden *m* del día; **on the ~** en el orden del día

a·gent [ˈeɪdʒənt] agente *m/f*, representante *m/f*

ag·gra·vate [ˈægrəveɪt] *v/t* agravar; (*annoy*) molestar

ag·gre·gate [ˈægrɪgət] *n* SP: **win on ~** ganar en el total de la eliminatoria

ag·gres·sion [əˈgreʃn] agresividad *f*

ag·gres·sive [əˈgresɪv] *adj* agresivo; (*dynamic*) agresivo, enérgico

ag·gres·sive·ly [əˈgresɪvlɪ] *adv* agresivamente

a·ghast [əˈgæst] *adj* horrorizado

ag·ile [ˈædʒəl] *adj* ágil

a·gil·i·ty [əˈdʒɪlətɪ] agilidad *f*

ag·i·tate [ˈædʒɪteɪt] *v/i*: **~ for** hacer campaña a favor de

ag·i·tat·ed [ˈædʒɪteɪtɪd] *adj* agitado

ag·i·ta·tion [ædʒɪˈteɪʃn] agitación *f*

ag·i·ta·tor [ˈædʒɪteɪtər] agitador(a) *m(f)*

ag·nos·tic [ægˈnɑːstɪk] *n* agnóstico(-a) *m(f)*

a·go [əˈgoʊ] *adv*: **2 days ~** hace dos días; **long ~** hace mucho tiempo; **how long ~?** ¿hace cuánto tiempo?; **how long ~ did he leave?** ¿hace cuánto se marchó?

a·gog [əˈgɑːg] *adj*: **be ~ at sth** estar emocionado con algo

ag·o·nize [ˈægənaɪz] *v/i* atormentarse (*over* por), angustiarse (*over* por)

ag·o·niz·ing [ˈægənaɪzɪŋ] *adj* pain

atroz; *wait* angustioso

ag·o·ny ['ægənɪ] agonía *f*

a·gree [ə'griː] **1** *v/i* estar de acuerdo; *of figures* coincidir; (*reach agreement*) ponerse de acuerdo; *I* ~ estoy de acuerdo; *it doesn't* ~ *with me of food* no me sienta bien **2** *v/t price* acordar; ~ *that sth should be done* acordar que hay que hacer algo

a·gree·a·ble [ə'griːəbl] *adj* (*pleasant*) agradable; *be* ~ *fml* (*in agreement*) estar de acuerdo

a·gree·ment [ə'griːmənt] (*consent, contract*) acuerdo *m*; *reach* ~ *on* llegar a un acuerdo sobre

ag·ri·cul·tur·al [ægrɪ'kʌltʃərəl] *adj* agrícola

ag·ri·cul·ture ['ægrɪkʌltʃər] agricultura *f*

a·head [ə'hed] *adv position* delante; *movement* adelante; *in race* por delante, en cabeza; *be* ~ *of* estar por delante de; *plan / think* ~ planear con antelación / pensar con anticipación

aid [eɪd] **1** *n* ayuda *f*; *come to s.o.'s* ~ acudir a ayudar a alguien **2** *v/t* ayudar

aide [eɪd] asistente *m/f*

Aids [eɪdz] *nsg* sida *m*

ail·ing ['eɪlɪŋ] *economy* débil, frágil

ail·ment ['eɪlmənt] achaque *m*

aim [eɪm] **1** *n in shooting* puntería *f*; (*objective*) objetivo *m* **2** *v/i in shooting* apuntar; ~ *at doing sth*, ~ *to do sth* tener como intención hacer algo **3** *v/t remark* dirigir; *he* ~*ed the gun at me* me apuntó con la pistola; *be* ~*ed at of remark etc* estar dirigido a; *of gun* estar apuntando a

aim·less ['eɪmlɪs] *adj* sin objetivos

air [er] **1** *n* aire *m*; *by* ~ *travel* en avión; *send mail* por correo aéreo; *in the open* ~ al aire libre; *on the* ~ RAD, TV en el aire **2** *v/t room* airear; *fig: views* airear, ventilar

'**air·bag** airbag *m*, bolsa *f* de aire; '**air·base** base *f* aérea; '**air·con·di-**

tioned *adj* con aire acondicionado, climatizado; '**air·con·di·tion·ing** aire *m* acondicionado; '**air·craft** avión *m*, aeronave *f*; '**air·craft car·ri·er** portaaviones *m inv*; '**air cy·in·der** (*for diver*) escafandra *f* autónoma; '**air fare** (precio *m* del) *Span* billete *m or L.Am.* boleto *m* de avión; '**air·field** aeródromo *m*, campo *m* de aviación; '**air force** fuerza *f* aérea; '**air host·ess** azafata *f*, *L.Am.* aeromoza *f*; '**air let·ter** aerograma *m*; '**air·lift 1** *n* puente *m* aéreo **2** *v/t* transportar mediante puente aéreo; '**air·line** línea *f* aérea; '**air·lin·er** avión *m* de pasajeros; '**air·mail**: *by* ~ por correo aéreo; '**air·plane** avión *m*; '**air·pock·et** bolsa *f* de aire; '**air pol·lu·tion** contaminación *f* del aire; '**air·port** aeropuerto *m*; '**air·sick**: *get* ~ marearse (*en avión*); '**air·space** espacio *m* aéreo; '**air ter·mi·nal** terminal *f* aérea; '**air·tight** *adj container* hermético; '**air traf·fic** tráfico *m* aéreo; '**air-traf·fic con·trol** control *m* del tráfico aéreo; **air-traf·fic con·trol·ler** controlador(a) *m(f)* del tráfico aéreo

air·y ['erɪ] *adj room* aireado

aisle [aɪl] pasillo *m*

'**aisle seat** asiento *m* de pasillo

a·jar [ə'dʒɑːr] *adj*: *be* ~ estar entreabierto

a·lac·ri·ty [ə'lækrɪtɪ] presteza *f*

a·larm [ə'lɑːrm] **1** *n* alarma *f*; *raise the* ~ dar la alarma **2** *v/t* alarmar

a'larm clock reloj *m* despertador

a·larm·ing [ə'lɑːrmɪŋ] *adj* alarmante

a·larm·ing·ly [ə'lɑːrmɪŋlɪ] *adv* de forma alarmante

al·bum ['ælbəm] *for photographs*, (*record*) álbum *m*

al·co·hol ['ælkəhɑːl] alcohol *m*

al·co·hol·ic [ælkə'hɑːlɪk] **1** *n* alcohólico(-a) *m(f)* **2** *adj* alcohólico

a·lert [ə'lɜːrt] **1** *n signal* alerta *f*; *be on the* ~ estar alerta **2** *v/t* alertar **3** *adj* alerta

al·ge·bra ['ældʒɪbrə] álgebra *f*

al·i·bi ['ælɪbaɪ] coartada *f*

a·li·en ['eɪlɪən] **1** *n* (*foreigner*) extranjero(-a) *m(f)*; *from space* extraterrestre *m/f* **2** *adj* extraño; **be ~ to s.o.** ser ajeno a alguien

a·li·en·ate ['eɪlɪəneɪt] *v/t* alienar, provocar el distanciamiento de

a·light [ə'laɪt] *adj* en llamas

a·lign [ə'laɪn] *v/t* alinear

a·like [ə'laɪk] **1** *adj*: **be ~** parecerse **2** *adv* igual; *old and young ~* viejos y jóvenes sin distinción

al·i·mo·ny ['ælɪmənɪ] pensión *f* alimenticia

a·live [ə'laɪv] *adj*: **be ~** estar vivo

all [ɔːl] **1** *adj* todo(s) **2** *pron* todo; **~ of us/them** todos nosotros/ellos; **he ate ~ of it** se lo comió todo; **that's ~, thanks** eso es todo, gracias; **for ~ I care** para lo que me importa; **for ~ I know** por lo que sé **3** *adv*: **~ at once** (*suddenly*) de repente; (*at the same time*) a la vez; **~ but** (*except*) todos menos; (*nearly*) casi; **~ the better** mucho mejor; **~ the time** desde el principio; **they're not at ~ alike** no se parecen en nada; **not at ~!** ¡en absoluto!; **two ~** SP empate a dos; **~ right → alright**

al·lay [ə'leɪ] *v/t* apaciguar

al·le·ga·tion [ælɪ'geɪʃn] acusación *f*

al·lege [ə'ledʒ] *v/t* alegar

al·leged [ə'ledʒd] *adj* presunto

al·leg·ed·ly [ə'ledʒɪdlɪ] *adv* presuntamente, supuestamente

al·le·giance [ə'liːdʒəns] lealtad *f*

al·ler·gic [ə'lɜːrdʒɪk] *adj* alérgico; **be ~ to** ser alérgico a

al·ler·gy ['ælərdʒɪ] alergia *f*

al·le·vi·ate [ə'liːvɪeɪt] *v/t* aliviar

al·ley ['ælɪ] callejón *m*

al·li·ance [ə'laɪəns] alianza *f*

al·lo·cate ['æləkeɪt] *v/t* asignar

al·lo·ca·tion [ælə'keɪʃn] asignación *f*

al·lot [ə'lɑːt] *v/t* (*pret & pp* **-ted**) asignar

al·low [ə'laʊ] *v/t* (*permit*) permitir; (*calculate for*) calcular; **it's not ~ed** no está permitido; **he ~ed us to leave** nos permitió salir

♦ **allow for** *v/t* tener en cuenta

al·low·ance [ə'laʊəns] (*money*) asig-

nación *f*; (*pocket money*) paga *f*; **make ~s for weather etc** tener en cuenta; *for person* disculpar

al·loy ['ælɔɪ] aleación *f*

'all-pur·pose *adj* multiuso; **'all-round** *adj* completo; **'all-time**: **be at an ~ low** haber alcanzado un mínimo histórico

♦ **al·lude to** [ə'luːd] *v/t* aludir a

al·lur·ing [ə'luːrɪŋ] *adj* atractivo, seductor

all-wheel 'drive *adj* con tracción a las cuatro ruedas

al·ly ['ælaɪ] *n* aliado(-a) *m(f)*

al·mond ['ɑːmənd] almendra *f*

al·most ['ɔːlmoʊst] *adv* casi

a·lone [ə'loʊn] *adj* solo

a·long [ə'lɒːŋ] **1** *prep* (*situated beside*) a lo largo de; **walk ~ this path** sigue por esta calle **2** *adv*: **would you like to come ~?** ¿te gustaría venir con nosotros?; **he always brings the dog ~** siempre trae al perro; **~ with** junto con; **all ~** (*all the time*) todo el tiempo, desde el principio

a·long·side [əlɒːŋ'saɪd] *prep* (*in cooperation with*) junto a; (*parallel to*) al lado de

a·loof [ə'luːf] *adj* distante, reservado

a·loud [ə'laʊd] *adv* en voz alta

al·pha·bet ['ælfəbet] alfabeto *m*

al·pha·bet·i·cal [ælfə'betɪkl] *adj* alfabético

al·read·y [ɔːl'redɪ] *adv* ya

al·right [ɔːl'raɪt] *adj* (*not hurt, in working order*) bien; **is it ~ to leave now?** (*permitted*) ¿puedo irme ahora?; **is it ~ to take these out of the country?** ¿se pueden sacar éstos del país?; **is it ~ with you if I ...?** ¿te importa si ...?; **~, you can have one!** de acuerdo, ¡puedes tomar uno!; **~, I heard you!** vale, ¡te he oído!; **everything is ~ now between them** vuelven a estar bien; **that's ~** (*don't mention it*) de nada; (*I don't mind*) no importa

al·so ['ɔːlsoʊ] *adv* también

al·tar ['ɔːltər] altar *m*

al·ter ['ɔːltər] *v/t* alterar

al·ter·a·tion [ɒːltə'reɪʃn] alteración f

al·ter·nate 1 v/i ['ɒːltərneɪt] alternar 2 adj ['ɒːltərnət] alterno

al·ter·nat·ing cur·rent ['ɒːltərneɪtɪŋ] corriente f alterna

al·ter·na·tive [ɒːlt'ɜːrnətɪv] 1 n alternativa f 2 adj alternativo

al·ter·na·tive·ly [ɒːlt'ɜːrnətɪvlɪ] adv si no

al·though [ɒːl'ðou] conj aunque, si bien

al·ti·tude ['æltɪtuːd] of plane, city altitud f; of mountain altura f

al·to·geth·er [ɒːltə'geðər] adv (completely) completamente; (in all) en total

al·tru·ism ['æltruːɪzm] altruismo m

al·tru·is·tic [æltruːˈɪstɪk] adj altruista

a·lu·min·i·um [æljuːˈmɪnɪəm] Br, a·lu·mi·num [ə'luːmənəm] aluminio m

al·ways ['ɒːlweɪz] adv siempre

a.m. ['eɪem] abbr (= ante meridiem) a.m.; at 11 ~ a las 11 de la mañana

a·mal·gam·ate [ə'mælgəmeɪt] v/i of companies fusionarse

a·mass [ə'mæs] v/t acumular

am·a·teur ['æmətʃʊr] n unskilled aficionado(-a) m(f); SP amateur m/f

am·a·teur·ish ['æmətʃʊrɪʃ] adj pej chapucero

a·maze [ə'meɪz] v/t asombrar

a·mazed [ə'meɪzd] adj asombrado; we were ~ to hear ... nos asombró oír ...

a·maze·ment [ə'meɪzmənt] asombro m

a·maz·ing [ə'meɪzɪŋ] adj (surprising) asombroso; F (very good) alucinante F

a·maz·ing·ly [ə'meɪzɪŋlɪ] adv increíblemente

Am·a·zon ['æməzən] n: the ~ el Amazonas

Am·a·zo·ni·an [æmə'zounɪən] adj amazónico

am·bas·sa·dor [æm'bæsədər] embajador(a) m(f)

am·ber ['æmbər] adj ámbar; at ~ en

ámbar

am·bi·dex·trous [æmbɪ'dekstrəs] adj ambidiestro

am·bi·ence ['æmbɪəns] ambiente m

am·bi·gu·i·ty [æmbɪ'gjuːətɪ] ambigüedad f

am·big·u·ous [æm'bɪgjʊəs] adj ambiguo

am·bi·tion [æm'bɪʃn] also pej ambición f

am·bi·tious [æm'bɪʃəs] adj ambicioso

am·biv·a·lent [æm'bɪvələnt] adj ambivalente

am·ble ['æmbl] v/i deambular

am·bu·lance ['æmbjʊləns] ambulancia f

am·bush ['æmbʊʃ] 1 n emboscada f 2 v/t tender una emboscada a

a·mend [ə'mend] v/t enmendar

a·mend·ment [ə'mendmənt] enmienda f

a·mends [ə'mendz] npl: make ~ for compensar

a·men·i·ties [ə'miːnətɪz] npl servicios mpl

A·mer·i·ca [ə'merɪkə] continent América; USA Estados mpl Unidos

A·mer·i·can [ə'merɪkən] 1 adj North American estadounidense 2 n North American estadounidense m/f

A·mer·i·can plan pensión f completa

a·mi·a·ble ['eɪmɪəbl] adj afable, amable

a·mi·ca·ble ['æmɪkəbl] adj amistoso

a·mi·ca·bly ['æmɪkəblɪ] adv amistosamente

am·mu·ni·tion [æmjʊ'nɪʃn] munición f; fig argumentos mpl

am·ne·sia [æm'niːzɪə] amnesia f

am·nes·ty ['æmnəstɪ] amnistía f

a·mong(st) [ə'mʌŋ(st)] prep entre

a·mor·al [eɪ'mɒːrəl] adj amoral

a·mount [ə'maunt] cantidad f; (sum of money) cantidad f, suma f

♦ amount to v/t ascender a; his contribution didn't amount to much su contribución no fue gran cosa

am·phib·i·an [æm'fɪbɪən] anfibio m

am·phib·i·ous [æmˈfɪbɪəs] adj animal, vehicle anfibio

am·phi·the·a·ter, Br **am·phi·the·a·tre** [ˈæmfɪθɪətər] anfiteatro m

am·ple [ˈæmpl] adj abundante; **$4 will be ~** 4 dólares serán más que suficientes

am·pli·fi·er [ˈæmplɪfaɪr] amplificador m

am·pli·fy [ˈæmplɪfaɪ] v/t (pret & pp **-ied**) sound amplificar

am·pu·tate [ˈæmpjʊteɪt] v/t amputar

am·pu·ta·tion [æmpjʊˈteɪʃn] amputación f

a·muse [əˈmjuːz] v/t (make laugh etc) divertir; (entertain) entretener

a·muse·ment [əˈmjuːzmənt] (merriment) diversión f; (entertainment) entretenimiento m; **~s** (games) juegos mpl; **what do you do for ~?** ¿qué haces para entretenerte?; **to our great ~** para nuestro regocijo

a·muse·ment ar·cade [ɑːrˈkeɪd] salón m de juegos recreativos

a·muse·ment park parque m de atracciones

a·mus·ing [əˈmjuːzɪŋ] adj divertido

an [æn] unstressed [ən] → **a**

an·a·bol·ic ster·oid [ænəˈbɑːlɪk] esteroide m anabolizante

a·nae·mi·a etc Br → **anemia** etc

an·aes·thet·ic etc Br → **anesthetic** etc

an·a·log [ˈænəlɑːg] adj analógico

a·nal·o·gy [əˈnælədʒɪ] analogía f

a·nal·y·sis [əˈnæləsɪs] (pl **analyses** [əˈnæləsiːz]) análisis m inv; (psychoanalysis) psicoanálisis m inv

an·a·lyst [ˈænəlɪst] analista m/f; PSYCH psicoanalista m/f

an·a·lyt·i·cal [ænəˈlɪtɪkl] adj analítico

an·a·lyze [ˈænəlaɪz] v/t analizar; (psychoanalyse) psicoanalizar

an·arch·y [ˈænərkɪ] anarquía f

a·nat·o·my [əˈnætəmɪ] anatomía f

an·ces·tor [ˈænsestər] antepasado(-a) m(f)

an·chor [ˈæŋkər] **1** n NAUT ancla f; TV presentador(a) m(f) **2** v/i NAUT anclar

an·cient [ˈeɪnʃənt] adj antiguo

an·cil·lar·y [ænˈsɪlərɪ] adj staff auxiliar

and [ənd] stressed [ænd] conj y

An·de·an [ˈændɪən] adj andino

An·des [ˈændiːz] npl: **the ~** los Andes

an·ec·dote [ˈænɪkdoʊt] anécdota f

a·ne·mia [əˈniːmɪə] anemia f

a·ne·mic [əˈniːmɪk] adj anémico

an·es·thet·ic [ænəsˈθetɪk] n anestesia f

an·es·the·tist [əˈniːsθətɪst] anestesista m/f

an·gel [ˈeɪndʒl] REL ángel m; fig ángel m, cielo m

an·ger [ˈæŋgər] **1** n enfado m, enojo m **2** v/t enfadar, enojar

an·gi·na [ænˈdʒaɪnə] angina f (de pecho)

an·gle [ˈæŋgl] n ángulo m

an·gry [ˈæŋgrɪ] adj enfadado, enojado; **be ~ with s.o.** estar enfadado or enojado con alguien

an·guish [ˈæŋgwɪʃ] angustia f

an·gu·lar [ˈæŋgjʊlər] adj anguloso

an·i·mal [ˈænɪml] animal m

an·i·ma·ted [ˈænɪmeɪtɪd] adj animado

an·i·ma·ted car·toon dibujos mpl animados

an·i·ma·tion [ænɪˈmeɪʃn] (liveliness), of cartoon animación f

an·i·mos·i·ty [ænɪˈmɑːsətɪ] animosidad f

an·kle [ˈæŋkl] tobillo m

an·nex [ˈæneks] **1** n building edificio m anexo **2** v/t state anexionar

an·nexe [ˈæneks] n Br edificio m anexo

an·ni·hi·late [əˈnaɪəleɪt] v/t aniquilar

an·ni·hi·la·tion [ənaɪəˈleɪʃn] aniquilación f

an·ni·ver·sa·ry [ænɪˈvɜːrsərɪ] (wedding ~) aniversario m

an·no·tate [ˈænəteɪt] v/t report anotar

an·nounce [əˈnaʊns] v/t anunciar

an·nounce·ment [əˈnaʊnsmənt] anuncio m

an·nounc·er [əˈnaʊnsər] TV, RAD

an·noy[ə'nɔɪ] v/t molestar, irritar; **be ~ed** estar molesto or irritado

an·noy·ance [ə'nɔɪəns] (*anger*) irritación f; (*nuisance*) molestia f

an·noy·ing [ə'nɔɪɪŋ] adj molesto, irritante

an·nu·al ['ænʊəl] adj anual

an·nu·i·ty[ə'nuːətɪ] anualidad f

an·nul [ə'nʌl] v/t (*pret & pp* -**led**) *marriage* anular

an·nul·ment[ə'nʌlmənt] anulación f

a·non·y·mous[ə'nɑːnɪməs] adj anónimo

an·o·rak ['ænəræk] Br anorak m

an·o·rex·i·a [ænə'reksɪə] anorexia f

an·o·rex·ic [ænə'reksɪk] adj anoréxico

an·oth·er [ə'nʌðər] **1** adj otro **2** pron otro(-a) m(f); **they helped one ~** se ayudaron (el uno al otro); **do they know one ~?** ¿se conocen?

ans·wer['ænsər] **1** n to letter, person, question respuesta f, contestación f; to problem solución f **2** v/t letter, person, question responder, contestar; **~ the door**abrir la puerta; **~ the telephone** responder or Span coger al teléfono

♦**answer back** v/t & v/i contestar, replicar

♦**answer for**v/t responder de

ans·wer·phone ['ænsərfoʊn] TELEC contestador m (automático)

ant[ænt] hormiga f

an·tag·o·nism [æn'tægənɪzm] antagonismo m

an·tag·o·nis·tic [æntægə'nɪstɪk] adj hostil

an·tag·o·nize [æn'tægənaɪz] v/t antagonizar, enfadar

Ant·arc·tic [ænt'ɑːrktɪk] n: **the ~** el Antártico

an·te·na·tal[æntɪ'neɪtl] adj prenatal

an·ten·na [æn'tenə] of insect, for TV antena f

an·thol·o·gy[æn'θɑːlədʒɪ] antología f

an·thro·pol·o·gy [ænθrə'pɑːlədʒɪ] antropología f

an·ti·bi·ot·ic [æntɪbaɪ'ɑːtɪk] n antibiótico m

an·ti·bod·y ['æntɪbɑːdɪ] anticuerpo m

an·tic·i·pate [æn'tɪsɪpeɪt] v/t esperar, prever

an·tic·i·pa·tion [æntɪsɪ'peɪʃn] expectativa f, previsión f

an·ti·clock·wise ['æntɪklɑːkwaɪz] adv Br en dirección contraria a las agujas del reloj

an·tics['æntɪks] npl payasadas fpl

an·ti·dote['æntɪdoʊt] antídoto m

an·ti·freeze ['æntɪfriːz] anticongelante m

an·tip·a·thy [æn'tɪpəθɪ] antipatía f

an·ti·quat·ed ['æntɪkweɪtɪd] adj anticuado

an·tique [æn'tiːk] n antigüedad f

an'tique deal·eranticuario(-a) m(f)

an·tiq·ui·ty [æn'tɪkwətɪ] antigüedad f

an·ti·sep·tic[æntɪ'septɪk] **1** adj antiséptico **2** n antiséptico m

an·ti·so·cial [æntɪ'soʊʃl] adj antisocial, poco sociable

an·ti·vi·rus pro·gram [æntɪ'vaɪrəs] COMPUT (programa m) antivirus m inv

anx·i·e·ty[æŋ'zaɪətɪ] ansiedad f

anx·ious ['æŋkʃəs] adj preocupado; (*eager*) ansioso; **be ~ for** for news etc esperar ansiosamente

an·y ['enɪ] **1** adj: **are there ~ dis·kettes/ glasses?** ¿hay disquetes/ vasos?; **is there ~ bread/im·provement?** ¿hay algo de pan/alguna mejora?; **there aren't ~ dis·kettes/ glasses** no hay disquetes/ vasos; **there isn't ~ bread/ improvement** no hay pan/ninguna mejora; **have you ~ idea at all?** ¿tienes alguna idea?; **~ one of them could win** cualquiera de ellos podría ganar **2** pron alguno(-a); **do you have ~?** ¿tienes alguno(s)?; **there aren't ~ left** no queda ninguno; **there isn't ~ left** no queda; **~ of them could be guilty** cualquiera de ellos podría ser culpable **3** adv: **is that ~ better/ easier?** ¿es mejor/más fácil así?; **I**

don't like it ~ more ya no me gusta

an·y·bod·y ['enɪbɒdɪ] *pron* alguien; **there wasn't ~ there** no había nadie allí

an·y·how ['enɪhaʊ] *adv* en todo caso, de todos modos; **if I can help you ~, please let me know** si puedo ayudarte de alguna manera, por favor dímelo

an·y·one ['enɪwʌn] → **anybody**

an·y·thing ['enɪθɪŋ] *pron* algo; **with negatives** nada; **I didn't hear ~** no oí nada; **~ but** todo menos; **~ else?** ¿algo más?

an·y·way ['enɪweɪ] → **anyhow**

an·y·where ['enɪweə] *adv* en alguna parte; **is Peter ~ around?** ¿está Peter por ahí?; **he never goes ~** nunca va a ninguna parte; **I can't find it ~** no lo encuentro por ninguna parte

a·part [ə'pɑːrt] *adv* aparte; **the two cities are 250 miles ~** las dos ciudades están a 250 millas la una de la otra; **live ~ of people** vivir separado; **~ from** aparte de

a·part·ment [ə'pɑːrtmənt] apartamento *m*, *Span* piso *m*

a'part·ment block bloque *m* de apartamentos *or Span* pisos

ap·a·thet·ic [æpə'θetɪk] *adj* apático

ap·a·thy ['æpəθɪ] apatía *f*

ape [eɪp] simio *m*

a·per·i·tif [ə'perɪtiːf] aperitivo *m*

ap·er·ture ['æpərtʃər] PHOT apertura *f*

a·piece [ə'piːs] *adv* cada uno

a·pol·o·get·ic [əpɑːlə'dʒetɪk] *adj letter* de disculpa; **he was very ~ about ...** pedía constantes disculpas por ...

a·pol·o·gize [ə'pɑːlədʒaɪz] *v/i* disculparse, pedir perdón

a·pol·o·gy [ə'pɑːlədʒɪ] disculpa *f*; **owe s.o. an ~** deber disculpas a alguien

a·pos·tle [ə'pɑːsl] REL apóstol *m*

a·pos·tro·phe [ə'pɑːstrəfɪ] GRAM apóstrofo *m*

ap·pall [ə'pɒːl] *v/t* horrorizar, espantar

ap·pal·ling [ə'pɒːlɪŋ] *adj* horroroso

ap·pa·ra·tus [æpə'reɪtəs] aparatos *mpl*

ap·par·ent [ə'pærənt] *adj* aparente, evidente; **become ~ that** hacerse evidente que

ap·par·ent·ly [ə'pærəntlɪ] *adv* al parecer, por lo visto

ap·pa·ri·tion [æpə'rɪʃn] *(ghost)* aparición *f*

ap·peal [ə'piːl] **1** *n (charm)* atractivo *m*; *for funds etc* llamamiento *m*; LAW apelación *f* **2** *v/i* LAW apelar

♦ **appeal for** *v/t* solicitar

♦ **appeal to** *v/t (be attractive to)* atraer a

ap·peal·ing [ə'piːlɪŋ] *adj idea, offer* atractivo; *glance* suplicante

ap·pear [ə'pɪr] *v/i* aparecer; *in court* comparecer; *(look, seem)* parecer; *it ~s that ...* parece que ...

ap·pear·ance [ə'pɪrəns] aparición *f*; *in court* comparecencia *f*; *(look)* apariencia *f*, aspecto *m*; **put in an ~** hacer acto de presencia

ap·pease [ə'piːz] *v/t* apaciguar

ap·pen·di·ci·tis [əpendɪ'saɪtɪs] apendicitis *m*

ap·pen·dix [ə'pendɪks] MED, *of book* apéndice *m*

ap·pe·tite ['æpɪtaɪt] *also fig* apetito *m*

ap·pe·tiz·er ['æpɪtaɪzər] aperitivo *m*

ap·pe·tiz·ing ['æpɪtaɪzɪŋ] *adj* apetitoso

ap·plaud [ə'plɒːd] **1** *v/i* aplaudir **2** *v/t also fig* aplaudir

ap·plause [ə'plɒːz] aplauso *m*

ap·ple ['æpl] manzana *f*

ap·ple 'pie tarta *f* de manzana

ap·ple 'sauce compota *f* de manzana

ap·pli·ance [ə'plaɪəns] aparato *m*; *household* electrodoméstico *m*

ap·plic·a·ble [ə'plɪkəbl] *adj* aplicable; **it's not ~ to foreigners** no se aplica a extranjeros

ap·pli·cant ['æplɪkənt] solicitante *m/f*

ap·pli·ca·tion [æplɪ'keɪʃn] *for job, passport etc* solicitud *f*; *for university* solicitud *f* (de admisión)

ap·pli'ca·tion form *for passport etc* impreso *m* de solicitud; *for university* impreso *m* de solicitud de admisión

ap·ply [ə'plaɪ] **1** *v/t* (*pret & pp* **-ied**) *rules, solution, ointment* aplicar **2** *v/i* (*pret & pp* **-ied**) *of rule, law* aplicarse

♦ **apply for** *v/t job, passport* solicitar; *university* solicitar el ingreso en

♦ **apply to** *v/t* (*contact*) dirigirse a; (*affect*) aplicarse a

ap·point [ə'pɔɪnt] *v/t to position* nombrar, designar

ap·point·ment [ə'pɔɪntmənt] *to position* nombramiento *m*, designación *f*; *meeting* cita *f*; **make an ~ with the doctor** pedir hora con el doctor

ap·point·ments di·a·ry agenda *f* de citas

ap·prais·al [ə'preɪz(ə)l] evaluación *f*

ap·pre·cia·ble [ə'priːʃəbl] *adj* apreciable

ap·pre·ci·ate [ə'priːʃɪeɪt] **1** *v/t* (*value*) apreciar; (*be grateful for*) agradecer; (*acknowledge*) ser consciente de; *thanks, I ~ it* te lo agradezco **2** *v/i* FIN revalorizarse

ap·pre·ci·a·tion [əpriːʃɪ'eɪʃn] *of kindness etc* agradecimiento *m*; *of music etc* aprecio *m*

ap·pre·ci·a·tive [ə'priːʃətɪv] *adj* agradecido

ap·pre·hen·sive [æprɪ'hensɪv] *adj* aprensivo, temeroso

ap·pren·tice [ə'prentɪs] aprendiz(a) *m(f)*

ap·proach [ə'prəʊtʃ] **1** *n* aproximación *f*; (*proposal*) propuesta *f*; *to problem* enfoque *m* **2** *v/t* (*get near to*) aproximarse a; (*contact*) ponerse en contacto con; *problem* enfocar

ap·proach·a·ble [ə'prəʊtʃəbl] *adj person* accesible

ap·pro·pri·ate¹ [ə'prəʊprɪət] *adj* apropiado, adecuado

ap·pro·pri·ate² [ə'prəʊprɪeɪt] *v/t also euph* apropiarse de

ap·prov·al [ə'pruːvl] aprobación *f*

ap·prove [ə'pruːv] **1** *v/i: my parents don't* ~ a mis padres no les parece bien **2** *v/t* aprobar

♦ **approve of** *v/t* aprobar; *her parents don't approve of me* no les gusto a sus padres

ap·prox·i·mate [ə'prɑːksɪmət] *adj* aproximado

ap·prox·i·mate·ly [ə'prɑːksɪmətlɪ] *adv* aproximadamente

ap·prox·i·ma·tion [əprɑːksɪ'meɪʃn] aproximación *f*

APR [eɪpiː'ɑː] *abbr* (= **annual percentage rate**) TAE *f* (= tasa *f* anual equivalente)

a·pri·cot ['eɪprɪkɑːt] albaricoque *m*, *L.Am.* damasco *m*

A·pril ['eɪprəl] abril *m*

apt [æpt] *adj remark* oportuno; *be ~ to ...* ser propenso a ...

ap·ti·tude ['æptɪtuːd] aptitud *f*; *he has a natural ~ for ...* tiene aptitudes naturales para ...

'ap·ti·tude test prueba *f* de aptitud

a·quar·i·um [ə'kweərɪəm] acuario *m*

A·quar·i·us [ə'kweərɪəs] ASTR Acuario *m/f inv*

a·quat·ic [ə'kwætɪk] *adj* acuático

Ar·ab ['ærəb] **1** *adj* árabe **2** *n* árabe *m/f*

Ar·a·bic ['ærəbɪk] **1** *adj* árabe **2** *n* árabe *m*

ar·a·ble ['ærəbl] *adj* arable, cultivable

ar·bi·tra·ry ['ɑːrbɪtrerɪ] *adj* arbitrario

ar·bi·trate ['ɑːrbɪtreɪt] *v/i* arbitrar

ar·bi·tra·tion [ɑːrbɪ'treɪʃn] arbitraje *m*

ar·bi·tra·tor ['ɑːrbɪ'treɪtər] árbitro(-a) *m(f)*

arch [ɑːrtʃ] *n* arco *m*

ar·chae·ol·o·gy *etc Br* → **archeology** *etc*

ar·cha·ic [ɑːr'keɪɪk] *adj* arcaico

ar·che·o·log·i·cal [ɑːrkɪə'lɑːdʒɪkl] *adj* arqueológico

ar·che·ol·o·gist [ɑːrkɪ'ɑːlədʒɪst] arqueólogo(-a) *m(f)*

ar·che·ol·o·gy [ɑːrkɪ'ɑːlədʒɪ] arqueología *f*

ar·cher ['ɑːrtʃər] arquero(-a) *m(f)*

ar·chi·tect ['ɑːrkɪtekt] arquitecto(-a) *m(f)*

ar·chi·tec·tur·al [ɑːrkɪ'tektʃərəl] *adj* arquitectónico

ar·chi·tec·ture ['ɑːrkɪtektʃər] arquitectura *f*

ar·chives ['ɑːrkaɪvz] *npl* archivos *mpl*

arch·way ['ɑːrtʃweɪ] arco *m*

Arc·tic ['ɑːrktɪk] *n*: **the ~** el Ártico

ar·dent ['ɑːrdənt] *adj* ardiente, ferviente

ar·du·ous ['ɑːrdjʊəs] *adj* arduo

ar·e·a ['erɪə] área *f*, zona *f*; *of activity, study etc* área *f*, ámbito *m*

'ar·e·a code TELEC prefijo *m*

a·re·na [ə'riːnə] SP estadio *m*

Ar·gen·ti·na [ɑːrdʒən'tiːnə] Argentina

Ar·gen·tin·i·an [ɑːrdʒən'tɪnɪən] **1** *adj* argentino **2** *n* argentino(-a) *m(f)*

ar·gu·a·bly ['ɑːrgjʊəblɪ] *adv* posiblemente

ar·gue ['ɑːrgjuː] **1** *v/i (quarrel)* discutir; *(reason)* argumentar **2** *v/t*: **~ that ...** argumentar que ...

ar·gu·ment ['ɑːrgjʊmənt] *(quarrel)* discusión *f*; *(reasoning)* argumento *m*

ar·gu·ment·a·tive [ɑːrgjʊ'mentətɪv] *adj* discutidor

a·ri·a ['ɑːrɪə] MUS aria *f*

ar·id ['ærɪd] *adj land* árido

Ar·i·es ['eriːz] ASTR Aries *m/f inv*

a·rise [ə'raɪz] *v/i (pret* **arose**, *pp* **arisen**) *of situation, problem* surgir

a·ris·en [ə'rɪzn] *pp →* **arise**

ar·is·toc·ra·cy [ærɪ'stɑːkrəsɪ] aristocracia *f*

ar·is·to·crat [ə'rɪstəkræt] aristócrata *m/f*

a·ris·to·crat·ic [ærɪstə'krætɪk] *adj* aristocrático

a·rith·me·tic [ə'rɪθmətɪk] aritmética *f*

arm[1] [ɑːrm] *n of person, chair* brazo *m*

arm[2] [ɑːrm] *v/t* armar

ar·ma·ments ['ɑːrməmənts] *npl* armamento *m*

arm·chair ['ɑːrmtʃer] sillón *m*

armed [ɑːrmd] *adj* armado

armed 'forc·es *npl* fuerzas *fpl* armadas

armed 'rob·ber·y atraco *m* a mano armada

ar·mor, *Br* **ar·mour** ['ɑːrmər] armadura *f*

ar·mored 've·hi·cle, *Br* **ar·moured 've·hi·cle** ['ɑːrmərd] vehículo *m* blindado

arm·pit ['ɑːrmpɪt] sobaco *m*

arms [ɑːrmz] *npl (weapons)* armas *fpl*

ar·my ['ɑːrmɪ] ejército *m*

a·ro·ma [ə'roumə] aroma *m*

a·rose [ə'rouz] *pret →* **arise**

a·round [ə'raund] **1** *prep (enclosing)* alrededor de; **it's ~ the corner** está a la vuelta de la esquina; **he lives ~ here** vive por aquí **2** *adv (in the area)* por ahí; *(encircling)* alrededor; *(roughly)* alrededor de, aproximadamente; *(with expressions of time)* en torno a; **walk ~** pasear; **she has been ~** *(has traveled, is experienced)* tiene mucho mundo; **he's still ~** F *(alive)* todavía está rondando por ahí F

a·rouse [ə'rauz] *v/t* despertar; *sexually* excitar

ar·range [ə'reɪndʒ] *v/t (put in order)* ordenar; *furniture* ordenar, disponer; *flowers, music* arreglar; *meeting, party etc* organizar; *time and place* acordar; **I've ~d to meet her** he quedado con ella

♦ **arrange for** *v/t*: **I arranged for Jack to collect it** quedé para que Jack lo recogiera

ar·range·ment [ə'reɪndʒmənt] *(plan)* plan *m*, preparativo *m*; *(agreement)* acuerdo *m*; *(layout: of furniture etc)* orden *m*, disposición *f*; *of flowers, music* arreglo *m*; **I've made ~s for the neighbors to water my plants** he quedado con los vecinos para que rieguen mis plantas

ar·rears [ə'rɪərz] *npl* atrasos *mpl*; **be in ~** *of person* ir atrasado

ar·rest [əˈrest] **1** n detención f, arresto m; **be under** ~ estar detenido or arrestado **2** v/t detener, arrestar

ar·riv·al [əˈraɪvl] llegada f; **on your** ~ al llegar; **~s at airport** llegadas fsg

ar·rive [əˈraɪv] v/i llegar

♦ **arrive at** v/t place, decision etc llegar a

ar·ro·gance [ˈærəgəns] arrogancia f

ar·ro·gant [ˈærəgənt] adj arrogante

ar·ro·gant·ly [ˈærəgəntlɪ] adv con arrogancia

ar·row [ˈærou] flecha f

arse [ɑːrs] Br P culo m P

ar·se·nic [ˈɑːrsənɪk] arsénico m

ar·son [ˈɑːrsn] incendio m provocado

ar·son·ist [ˈɑːrsənɪst] pirómano(-a) m(f)

art [ɑːrt] arte m; **the ~s** las artes

ar·te·ry [ˈɑːrtərɪ] MED arteria f

'art gal·ler·y public museo m; private galería f de arte

ar·thri·tis [ɑːrˈθraɪtɪs] artritis f

ar·ti·choke [ˈɑːrtɪtʃouk] alcachofa f, L.Am. alcaucil m

ar·ti·cle [ˈɑːrtɪkl] artículo m

ar·tic·u·late [ɑːrˈtɪkjulət] adj person elocuente

ar·ti·fi·cial [ɑːrtɪˈfɪʃl] adj artificial

ar·ti·fi·cial in·tel·li·gence inteligencia f artificial

ar·til·le·ry [ɑːrˈtɪlərɪ] artillería f

ar·ti·san [ˈɑːrtɪzæn] artesano(-a) m(f)

ar·tist [ˈɑːrtɪst] (painter, artistic person) artista m/f

ar·tis·tic [ɑːrˈtɪstɪk] adj artístico

'arts de·gree licenciatura f en letras

as [æz] **1** conj (while, when) cuando; (because, like) como; ~ **if** como si; ~ **usual** como de costumbre; ~ **necessary** como sea necesario **2** adv como; ~ **high / pretty / ...** tan alto / guapa como ...; ~ **much that?** ¿tanto? **3** prep como; **work ~ a team** trabajar en equipo; ~ **a child / schoolgirl** cuando era un niño / una colegiala; **work ~ a teacher / translator** trabajar como profesor / traductor; ~ **for** por lo

que respecta a; ~ **Hamlet** en el papel del Hamlet

asap [ˈeɪzæp] abbr (= **as soon as possible**) cuanto antes

as·bes·tos [æzˈbestɑːs] amianto m, asbesto m

As·cen·sion [əˈsenʃn] REL Ascensión f

ash [æʃ] ceniza f; **~es of person** cenizas fpl

a·shamed [əˈʃeɪmd] adj avergonzado, L.Am. apenado; **be ~ of** estar avergonzado or L.Am. apenado de; **you should be ~ of yourself** debería darte vergüenza or L.Am. pena; **it's nothing to be ~ of** no tienes por qué avergonzarte or L.Am. apenarte

'ash can cubo m de la basura

a·shore [əˈʃɔːr] adv en tierra; **go ~** desembarcar

ash·tray [ˈæʃtreɪ] cenicero m

A·sia [ˈeɪʒə] Asia

A·sian [ˈeɪʒn] **1** adj asiático **2** n asiático(-a) m(f)

a·side [əˈsaɪd] adv a un lado; **move ~ please** apártense, por favor; **he took me ~** me llevó aparte; ~ **from** aparte de

ask [æsk] **1** v/t person preguntar; question hacer; (invite) invitar; favor pedir; **can I ~ you something?** ¿puedo hacerte una pregunta?; ~ **s.o. for sth** pedir algo a alguien; **he ~ed me to leave** me pidió que me fuera; ~ **s.o. about sth** preguntar por algo a alguien **2** v/i: **all you need to do is ~** no tienes más que pedirlo

♦ **ask after** v/t person preguntar por

♦ **ask for** v/t pedir; person preguntar por

♦ **ask out** v/t invitar a salir

ask·ing price [ˈæskɪŋ] precio m de salida

a·sleep [əˈsliːp] adj dormido; **be (fast) ~** estar (profundamente) dormido; **fall ~** dormirse, quedarse dormido

as·par·a·gus [əˈspærəgəs] espárragos mpl

as·pect ['æspekt] aspecto *m*

as·phalt ['æsfælt] *n* asfalto *m*

as·phyx·i·ate [æ'sfıksıeıt] *v/t* asfixiar

as·phyx·i·a·tion [əsfıksı'eıʃn] asfixia *f*

as·pi·ra·tion [æspə'reıʃn] aspiración *f*

as·pi·rin ['æsprın] aspirina *f*

ass[1] [æs] (*idiot*) burro(-a) *m(f)*

ass[2] [æs] P (*backside*) culo P; (*sex*) sexo *m*

as·sai·lant [ə'seılənt] asaltante *m/f*

as·sas·sin [ə'sæsın] asesino(-a) *m(f)*

as·sas·sin·ate [ə'sæsıneıt] *v/t* asesinar

as·sas·sin·a·tion [əsæsı'neıʃn] asesinato *m*

as·sault [ə'sɒːlt] **1** *n* agresión *f*; (*attack*) ataque *m* **2** *v/t* atacar, agredir

as·sem·ble [ə'sembl] **1** *v/t parts* montar **2** *v/i of people* reunirse

as·sem·bly [ə'semblı] *of parts* montaje *m*; POL asamblea *f*

as'sem·bly line cadena *f* de montaje

as'sem·bly plant planta *f* de montaje

as·sent [ə'sent] *v/i* asentir, dar el consentimiento

as·sert [ə'sɜːrt] *v/t* afirmar, hacer valer; **~ o.s.** mostrarse firme

as·ser·tive [ə'sɜːrtıv] *adj person* seguro y firme

as·sess [ə'ses] *v/t situation* evaluar; *value* valorar

as·sess·ment [ə'sesmənt] evaluación *f*

as·set ['æset] FIN activo *m*; *fig* ventaja *f*; **she's an ~ to the company** es un gran valor para la compañía

ass·hole ['æʃhoul] V ojete *m* V; (*idiot*) *Span* gilipollas *m/f inv* V, *L.Am.* pendejo(-a) *m(f)* V

as·sign [ə'saın] *v/t* asignar

as·sign·ment [ə'saınmənt] (*task, study*) trabajo *m*

as·sim·i·late [ə'sımıleıt] *v/t information* asimilar; *person into group* integrar

as·sist [ə'sıst] *v/t* ayudar

as·sist·ance [ə'sıstəns] ayuda *f*, asistencia *f*

as·sis·tant [ə'sıstənt] ayudante *m/f*; *Br in store* dependiente(-a) *m(f)*

as·sis·tant di'rec·tor director(a) *m(f)* adjunto

as·sis·tant 'man·ag·er *of business* subdirector(a) *m(f)*; *of hotel, restaurant, store* subdirector(a) *m(f)*, subgerente *m/f*

as·so·ci·ate 1 *v/t* [ə'souʃıeıt] asociar; **he has long been ~d with the Ballet** ha estado vinculado al Ballet durante mucho tiempo **2** *v/i* [ə'souʃıeıt]: **~ with** relacionarse con **3** *n* [ə'souʃıət] colega *m/f*

as·so·ci·ate pro'fes·sor profesor(a) *m(f)* adjunto(a)

as·so·ci·a·tion [əsousı'eıʃn] asociación *f*; **in ~ with** conjuntamente con

as·sort·ed [ə'sɒːrtıd] *adj* surtido, diverso

as·sort·ment [ə'sɒːrtmənt] *of food* surtido *m*; *of people* diversidad *f*

as·sume [ə'suːm] *v/t* (*suppose*) suponer

as·sump·tion [ə'sʌmpʃn] suposición *f*

as·sur·ance [ə'ʃurəns] garantía *f*; (*confidence*) seguridad *f*

as·sure [ə'ʃur] *v/t* (*reassure*) asegurar

as·sured [ə'ʃurd] *adj* (*confident*) seguro

as·ter·isk ['æstərısk] asterisco *m*

asth·ma ['æsmə] asma *f*

asth·mat·ic [æs'mætık] *adj* asmático

as·ton·ish [ə'stɒːnıʃ] *v/t* asombrar, sorprender; **be ~ed** estar asombrado *or* sorprendido

as·ton·ish·ing [ə'stɒːnıʃıŋ] *adj* asombroso, sorprendente

as·ton·ish·ing·ly [ə'stɒːnıʃıŋlı] *adv* asombrosamente

as·ton·ish·ment [ə'stɒːnıʃmənt] asombro *m*, sorpresa *f*

as·tound [ə'staund] *v/t* pasmar

as·tound·ing [ə'staundıŋ] *adj* pasmoso

a·stray [ə'streı] *adv*: **go ~** extraviarse; *morally* descarriarse

a·stride [əˈstraɪd] **1** *adv* a horcajadas **2** *prep* a horcajadas sobre

as·trol·o·ger [əˈstrɑːlədʒər] astrólogo(-a) *m(f)*

as·trol·o·gy [əˈstrɑːlədʒɪ] astrología *f*

as·tro·naut [ˈæstrənɔːt] astronauta *m/f*

as·tron·o·mer [əˈstrɑːnəmər] astrónomo(-a) *m(f)*

as·tro·nom·i·cal [æstrəˈnɑːmɪkl] *adj price etc* astronómico

as·tron·o·my [əˈstrɑːnəmɪ] astronomía *f*

as·tute [əˈstuːt] *adj* astuto, sagaz

a·sy·lum [əˈsaɪləm] (*mental* ~) manicomio *m*; *political* asilo *m*

at [ət] *stressed* [æt] *prep with places* en; ~ *Joe's house* en casa de Joe; *bar* en el bar de Joe; ~ *the door* a la puerta; ~ *10 dollars* a 10 dólares; ~ *the age of 18* a los 18 años; ~ *5 o'clock* a las 5; ~ *150 km/h* a 150 km./h.; *be good/bad* ~ *sth* ser bueno/malo haciendo algo

ate [eɪt] *pret* → *eat*

a·the·ism [ˈeɪθɪɪzm] ateísmo *m*

a·the·ist [ˈeɪθɪɪst] ateo(-a) *m(f)*

ath·lete [ˈæθliːt] atleta *m/f*

ath·let·ic [æθˈletɪk] *adj* atlético

ath·let·ics [æθˈletɪks] atletismo *m*

At·lan·tic [ətˈlæntɪk] *n*: *the* ~ el Atlántico

at·las [ˈætləs] atlas *m inv*

ATM [etiːˈem] *abbr* (= *automatic teller machine*) cajero *m* automático

at·mos·phere [ˈætməsfɪr] *of earth* atmósfera *f*; (*ambience*) ambiente *m*

at·mos·pher·ic pol·lu·tion [ætməsˈferɪk] contaminación *f* atmosférica

at·om [ˈætəm] átomo *m*

'at·om bomb bomba *f* atómica

a·tom·ic [əˈtɑːmɪk] *adj* atómico

a·tom·ic 'en·er·gy energía *f* atómica *or* nuclear

a·tom·ic 'waste desechos *mpl* radiactivos

a·tom·iz·er [ˈætəmaɪzər] atomiza-

dor *m*

a·tone [əˈtoʊn] *v/i*: ~ *for* expiar

a·tro·cious [əˈtroʊʃəs] *adj* atroz, terrible

a·troc·i·ty [əˈtrɑːsətɪ] atrocidad *f*

at·tach [əˈtætʃ] *v/t* sujetar, fijar; *importance* atribuir; *be ~ed to* (*fond of*) tener cariño a

at·tach·ment [əˈtætʃmənt] (*fondness*) cariño *m* (*to* por); *to e-mail* archivo *m* adjunto

at·tack [əˈtæk] **1** *n* ataque *m* **2** *v/t* atacar

at·tempt [əˈtempt] **1** *n* intento *m*; *an* ~ *on the world record* un intento de batir el récord del mundo **2** *v/t* intentar

at·tend [əˈtend] *v/t* acudir a

♦ **attend to** *v/t* ocuparse de; *customer* atender

at·tend·ance [əˈtendəns] asistencia *f*

at·tend·ant [əˈtendənt] *in museum etc* vigilante *m/f*

at·ten·tion [əˈtenʃn] atención *f*; *bring sth to s.o.'s* ~ informar a alguien de algo; *your* ~ *please* atención, por favor; *pay* ~ prestar atención

at·ten·tive [əˈtentɪv] *adj listener* atento

at·tic [ˈætɪk] ático *m*

at·ti·tude [ˈætɪtuːd] actitud *f*

attn *abbr* (= *for the attention of*) atn (= a la atención de)

at·tor·ney [əˈtɜːrnɪ] abogado(-a) *m(f)*; *power of* ~ poder *m* (notarial)

at·tract [əˈtrækt] *v/t* atraer; ~ *attention* llamar la atención; ~ *s.o.'s attention* atraer la atención de alguien; *be ~ed to s.o.* sentirse atraído por alguien

at·trac·tion [əˈtrækʃn] atracción *f*, atractivo *m*; *romantic* atracción *f*

at·trac·tive [əˈtræktɪv] *adj* atractivo

at·trib·ute[1] [əˈtrɪbjuːt] *v/t* atribuir; ~ *sth to ...* atribuir algo a ...

at·trib·ute[2] [ˈætrɪbjuːt] *n* atributo *m*

au·ber·gine [ˈoʊbərʒiːn] *Br* berenjena *f*

auc·tion [ˈɒːkʃn] **1** n subasta f, L.Am. remate m **2** v/t subastar, L.Am. rematar

♦ **auction off** v/t subastar, L.Am. rematar

auc·tio·neer [ɒːkʃəˈnɪr] subastador(a) m(f), L.Am. rematador(a) m(f)

au·da·cious [ɒːˈdeɪʃəs] adj plan audaz

au·dac·i·ty [ɒːˈdæsətɪ] audacia f

au·di·ble [ˈɒːdəbl] adj audible

au·di·ence [ˈɒːdɪəns] in theater, at show público m, espectadores mpl; TV audiencia f

au·di·o [ˈɒːdɪoʊ] adj de audio

au·di·o·vi·su·al [ɒːdɪoʊˈvɪʒʊəl] adj audiovisual

au·dit [ˈɒːdɪt] **1** n auditoría f **2** v/t auditar; course asistir de oyente a

au·di·tion [ɒːˈdɪʃn] **1** n audición f **2** v/i hacer una prueba

au·di·tor [ˈɒːdɪtər] auditor(a) m(f)

au·di·to·ri·um [ɒːdɪˈtɔːrɪəm] of theater etc auditorio m

Au·gust [ˈɒːgəst] agosto m

aunt [ænt] tía f

au pair [oʊˈper] au pair m/f

au·ra [ˈɒːrə] aura f

aus·pic·es [ˈɒːspɪsɪz] npl auspicios mpl; **under the ~ of** bajo los auspicios de

aus·pi·cious [ɒːˈspɪʃəs] adj propicio

aus·tere [ɒːˈstiːr] adj interior austero

aus·ter·i·ty [ɒːsˈterətɪ] economic austeridad f

Aus·tra·li·a [ɒːˈstreɪlɪə] Australia

Aus·tra·li·an [ɒːˈstreɪlɪən] **1** adj australiano **2** n australiano(-a) m(f)

Aus·tri·a [ˈɒːstrɪə] Austria

Aus·tri·an [ˈɒːstrɪən] **1** adj austriaco **2** n austriaco(-a) m(f)

au·then·tic [ɒːˈθentɪk] adj auténtico

au·then·tic·i·ty [ɒːθenˈtɪsətɪ] autenticidad f

au·thor [ˈɒːθər] of story, novel escritor(a) m(f); of text autor(a) m(f)

au·thor·i·tar·i·an [əθɑːrɪˈterɪən] adj autoritario

au·thor·i·ta·tive [əˈθɑːrɪtətɪv] adj autorizado

au·thor·i·ty [əˈθɑːrətɪ] autoridad f; (permission) autorización f; **be an ~ on** ser una autoridad en; **the authorities** las autoridades

au·thor·i·za·tion [ɒːθəraɪˈzeɪʃn] autorización f

au·thor·ize [ˈɒːθəraɪz] v/t autorizar; **be ~d to ...** estar autorizado para ...

au·tis·tic [ɒːˈtɪstɪk] adj autista

au·to·bi·og·ra·phy [ɒːtəbaɪˈɑːgrəfɪ] autobiografía f

au·to·crat·ic [ɒːtəˈkrætɪk] adj autocrático

au·to·graph [ˈɒːtəgræf] autógrafo m

au·to·mate [ˈɒːtəmeɪt] v/t automatizar

au·to·mat·ic [ɒːtəˈmætɪk] **1** adj automático **2** n car (coche m) automático m; gun pistola f automática; washing machine lavadora f automática

au·to·mat·i·cal·ly [ɒːtəˈmætɪklɪ] adv automáticamente

au·to·ma·tion [ɒːtəˈmeɪʃn] automatización f

au·to·mo·bile [ˈɒːtəmoʊbiːl] automóvil m, coche m, L.Am. carro m, Rpl auto m

'au·to·mo·bile in·dus·try industria f automovilística

au·ton·o·mous [ɒːˈtɑːnəməs] adj autónomo

au·ton·o·my [ɒːˈtɑːnəmɪ] autonomía f

au·to·pi·lot [ˈɒːtoʊpaɪlət] piloto m automático

au·top·sy [ˈɒːtɑːpsɪ] autopsia f

au·tumn [ˈɒːtəm] Br otoño m

aux·il·ia·ry [ɒːgˈzɪljərɪ] adj auxiliar

a·vail [əˈveɪl] **1** n: **to no ~** en vano **2** v/t: **~ o.s. of** aprovechar

a·vail·a·ble [əˈveɪləbl] adj disponible

av·a·lanche [ˈævəlænʃ] avalancha f, alud m

av·a·rice [ˈævərɪs] avaricia f

av·e·nue [ˈævənuː] avenida f; fig camino m

av·e·rage [ˈævərɪdʒ] **1** adj medio; (of mediocre quality) regular **2** n promedio m, media f; **above / below ~**

por encima / por debajo del promedio; **on ~** como promedio, de media **3** v/t: **I ~ six hours of sleep a night** duermo seis horas cada noche como promedio *or* de media
♦ **average out** v/t calcular el promedio *or* la media de
♦ **average out at** v/t salir a
a·verse [ə'vɜːrs] *adj*: **not be ~ to** no ser reacio a
a·ver·sion [ə'vɜːrʃn] aversión *f*; **have an ~ to** tener aversión a
a·vert [ə'vɜːrt] v/t one's eyes apartar; *crisis* evitar
a·vi·a·tion [eɪvi'eɪʃn] aviación *f*
av·id ['ævɪd] *adj* ávido
av·o·ca·do [ævə'kɑːdoʊ] aguacate *m, S.Am.* palta *f*
a·void [ə'vɔɪd] v/t evitar; **you've been ~ing me** has estado huyendo de mí
a·wait [ə'weɪt] v/t aguardar, esperar
a·wake [ə'weɪk] *adj* despierto; **it kept me ~** no me dejó dormir
a·ward [ə'wɔːrd] **1** n (prize) premio *m* **2** v/t prize, damages conceder
a·ware [ə'wer] *adj*: **be ~ of sth** ser consciente de algo; **become ~ of**

sth darse cuenta de algo
a·ware·ness [ə'wernɪs] conciencia *f*
a·way [ə'weɪ] *adv*: **look ~** mirar hacia otra parte; **I'll be ~ until ...** voy a estar fuera hasta ...; *sick* no voy a ir hasta ...; **it's 2 miles ~** está a 2 millas; **Christmas is still six weeks ~** todavía quedan seis semanas para Navidad; **take sth ~ from s.o.** quitar algo a alguien; **put sth ~** guardar algo
a'way game SP partido *m* fuera de casa
awe·some ['ɒːsəm] *adj* F (terrific) alucinante F
aw·ful ['ɒːfəl] *adj* horrible, espantoso; **I feel ~** me siento fatal
aw·ful·ly ['ɒːfəlɪ] *adv* F (very) tremendamente; **~ bad** malísimo
awk·ward ['ɔːkwərd] *adj* (clumsy) torpe; (difficult) difícil; (embarrassing) embarazoso; **feel ~** sentirse incómodo
awn·ing ['ɒːnɪŋ] toldo *m*
ax, Br axe [æks] **1** n hacha *f* **2** v/t project etc suprimir; budget, job recortar
ax·le ['æksl] eje *m*

BA [biː'eɪ] *abbr* (= **Bachelor of Arts**) Licenciatura *f* en Filosofía y Letras
ba·by ['beɪbɪ] n bebé *m*
'ba·by boom explosión *f* demográfica
'ba·by car·riage ['kærɪdʒ] cochecito *m* de bebé
ba·by·ish ['beɪbɪɪʃ] *adj* infantil
'ba·by-sit v/i (pret & pp **-sat**) hacer de Span canguro *or* L.Am. babysitter
'ba·by-sit·ter ['sɪtər] Span canguro *m/f, L.Am.* babysitter *m/f*
bach·e·lor ['bætʃələr] soltero *m*

back [bæk] **1** n of person, clothes espalda *f*; of car, bus, house parte *f* trasera *or* de atrás; of paper, book dorso *m*; of drawer fondo *m*; of chair respaldo *m*; SP defensa *m/f*; **in ~ in** store en la trastienda; **in the ~ (of the car)** atrás (del coche); **at the ~ of the bus** en la parte trasera *or* de atrás del autobús; **~ to front** del revés; **at the ~ of beyond** en el quinto pino **2** *adj* trasero; **~ road** carretera *f* secundaria **3** *adv* atrás; **please stand ~** póngase más para atrás; **2 meters ~ from the edge** a 2 metros del borde; **~ in 1935** allá por el año 1935; **give sth ~ to s.o.** devolver algo a alguien; **she'll be ~ tomorrow** volverá mañana; **when are you coming ~?** ¿cuándo volverás?; **take sth ~ to the store** *because unsatisfactory* devolver algo a la tienda; **they wrote / phoned ~** contestaron a la carta / a la llamada; **he hit me ~** me devolvió el golpe **4** *v/t* (*support*) apoyar, respaldar; *horse* apostar por **5** *v/i* **he ~ed into the garage** entró en el garaje marcha atrás

◆**back away** *v/i* alejarse (hacia atrás)

◆**back down** *v/i* echarse atrás

◆**back off** *v/i* echarse atrás

◆**back onto** *v/t* dar por la parte de atrás a

◆**back out** *v/i of commitment* echarse atrás

◆**back up 1** *v/t* (*support*) respaldar; *file* hacer una copia de seguridad de; **traffic was backed up all the way to …** el atasco llegaba hasta … **2** *v/i in car* dar marcha atrás; *of drains* atascarse

'**back·ache** dolor *m* de espalda; '**back·bit·ing** cotilleo *m*, chismorreo *m*; '**back·bone** ANAT columna *f* vertebral, espina *f* dorsal; *fig* (*courage*) agallas *fpl*; *fig* (*mainstay*) columna *f* vertebral; '**back·break·ing** *adj* extenuante, deslomador; **back 'burn·er: put sth on the ~** aparcar algo; '**back·date** *v/t:* **a salary increase ~d to 1st January** una subida salarial con efecto retroactivo a partir del 1 de enero; '**back·door** puerta *f* trasera

back·er ['bækər]: **the ~s of the movie** *financially* las personas que financiaron la película

back'fire *v/i fig:* **it ~d on us** nos salió el tiro por la culata; '**back·ground** *n* fondo *m*; *of person* origen *m*, historia *f* personal; *of situation* contexto *m*; **she prefers to stay in the ~** prefiere permanecer en un segundo plano; '**back·hand** *n in tennis*

revés *m*

back·ing ['bækıŋ] *n* (*support*) apoyo *m*, respaldo *m*; MUS acompañamiento *m*

'**back·ing group** MUS grupo *m* de acompañamiento

'**back·lash** reacción *f* violenta; '**back·log** acumulación *f*; '**back·pack 1** *n* mochila *f* **2** *v/i* viajar con la mochila a cuestas; '**backpack·er** mochilero(-a) *m(f)*; '**back·pack·ing** viajes *mpl* con la mochila a cuestas; '**back·ped·al** *v/i fig* echarse atrás, dar marcha atrás; '**back seat** *of car* asiento *m* trasero *or* de atrás; **back-seat 'driv·er: he's a terrible ~** va siempre incordiando al conductor con sus comentarios; '**back·space (key)** (tecla *f* de) retroceso *m*; '**back·stairs** *npl* escalera *f* de servicio; '**back street** callejuela *f*; '**back streets** *npl* callejuelas *fpl*; *poorer, dirtier part of a city* zonas *fpl* deprimidas; '**back·stroke** SP espalda *f*; '**back·track** *v/i* volver atrás, retroceder; '**back·up** (*support*) apoyo *m*, respaldo *m*; *for police* refuerzos *mpl*; COMPUT copia *f* de seguridad; **take a ~** COMPUT hacer una copia de seguridad; '**back·up disk** COMPUT disquete *m* con la copia de seguridad

back·ward ['bækwərd] **1** *adj child* retrasado; *society* atrasado; *glance* hacia atrás **2** *adv* hacia atrás

back'yard jardín *m* trasero; **in s.o.'s ~** *fig* en la misma puerta de alguien

ba·con ['beɪkn] tocino *m*, *Span* bacon *m*

bac·te·ri·a [bæk'tɪrɪə] *npl* bacterias *fpl*

bad [bæd] *adj* malo; *before singular masculine noun* mal; *cold, headache etc* fuerte; *mistake, accident* grave; **I've had a ~ day** he tenido un mal día; **smoking is ~ for you** fumar es malo; **it's not ~** no está mal; **that's really too ~** (*shame*) es una verdadera pena; **feel ~ about** (*guilty*) sentirse mal por; **I'm ~ at math** se me dan mal las matemáticas;

B

Friday's ~, how about Thursday? el viernes me viene mal, ¿qué tal el jueves?

bad 'debt deuda *f* incobrable

badge [bædʒ] insignia *f*, chapa *f*; *of policeman* placa *f*

bad·ger ['bædʒər] *v/t* acosar, importunar

bad 'lan·guage palabrotas *fpl*

bad·ly ['bædlɪ] *adv* injured gravemente; *damaged* seriamente; *work* mal; *I did really ~ in the exam* el examen me salió fatal; *he hasn't done ~ in life, business etc* no le ha ido mal; *you're ~ in need of a haircut* necesitas urgentemente un corte de pelo; *he is ~ off* poor anda mal de dinero

bad-man·nered [bæd'mænərd] *adj: be ~* tener malos modales

bad·min·ton ['bædmɪntən] bádminton *m*

bad-tem·pered [bæd'tempərd] *adj* malhumorado

baf·fle ['bæfl] *v/t* confundir, desconcertar; *be ~d* estar confundido *or* desconcertado; *I'm ~d why she left* no consigo entender por qué se fue

baf·fling ['bæflɪŋ] *adj* mystery, software desconcertante, incomprensible

bag [bæg] bolsa *f*, *for school* cartera *f*, (*purse*) bolso *m*, *S.Am.* cartera *f*, *Mex* bolsa *f*

bag·gage ['bægɪdʒ] equipaje *m*

'bag·gage car RAIL vagón *m* de equipajes; **'bag·gage check** consigna *f*; **'bag·gage re·claim** ['riːkleɪm] recogida *f* de equipajes

bag·gy ['bægɪ] *adj* ancho, holgado

'bag·pipes *npl* gaita *f*

bail [beɪl] *n* LAW libertad *f* bajo fianza; (*money*) fianza *f*; *on ~* bajo fianza

◆**bail out 1** *v/t* LAW pagar la fianza de **2** *v/i of airplane* tirarse en paracaídas

bait [beɪt] *n* cebo *m*

bake [beɪk] *v/t* hornear, cocer al horno

baked po'ta·to *Span* patata *f* or

L.Am. papa *f* asada (*con piel*)

bak·er ['beɪkər] panadero(-a) *m(f)*

bak·er·y ['beɪkərɪ] panadería *f*

bak·ing pow·der ['beɪkɪŋ] levadura *f*

bal·ance ['bæləns] **1** *n* equilibrio *m*; (*remainder*) resto *m*; *of bank account* saldo *m* **2** *v/t* poner en equilibrio; **~ the books** cuadrar las cuentas **3** *v/i* mantenerse en equilibrio; *of accounts* cuadrar

bal·anced ['bælənst] *adj* (*fair*) objetivo; *diet, personality* equilibrado

bal·ance of 'pay·ments balanza *f* de pagos; **bal·ance of 'trade** balanza *f* comercial; **'bal·ance sheet** balance *m*

bal·co·ny ['bælkənɪ] *of house* balcón *m*; *in theater* anfiteatro *m*

bald [bɔːld] *adj* calvo; *he's going ~* se está quedando calvo; *~ spot* calva *f*

bald·ing ['bɔːldɪŋ] *adj* medio calvo

Bal·kan ['bɔːlkən] *adj* balcánico

Bal·kans ['bɔːlkənz] *npl: the ~* los Balcanes

ball [bɔːl] *tennis-ball size* pelota *f*; *football size* balón *m*, pelota *f*; *billiard-ball size* bola *f*; *on the ~ fig* despierto; *play ~ fig* cooperar; *the ~'s in his court* le toca actuar a él, la pelota está en su tejado

bal·lad ['bæləd] balada *f*

ball 'bear·ing rodamiento *m* de bolas

bal·le·ri·na [bælə'riːnə] bailarina *f*

bal·let ['bæleɪ] ballet *m*

'bal·let danc·er bailarín (-ina) *m(f)*

'ball game (*baseball game*) partido *m* de béisbol; *that's a different ~* F esa es otra cuestión F

bal·lis·tic mis·sile [bə'lɪstɪk] misil *m* balístico

bal·loon [bə'luːn] globo *m*

bal·loon·ist [bə'luːnɪst] piloto *m* de globo aerostático

bal·lot ['bælət] **1** *n* voto *m* **2** *v/t members* consultar por votación

'bal·lot box urna *f*

'bal·lot pa·per papeleta *f*

'ball·park (*baseball*) campo *m* de

béisbol; *you're in the right* ~ F no vas descaminado; '**ball·park fig·ure** F cifra f aproximada; '**ball·point (pen)** bolígrafo *m*, *Mex* pluma f, *Rpl* birome *m*

balls [bɔːlz] *npl* ∨ huevos *mpl* ∨; (*courage*) huevos *mpl* ∨

bam·boo [bæm'buː] *n* bambú *m*

ban [bæn] **1** *n* prohibición f **2** *v/t* (*pret & pp -ned*) prohibir; ~ *s.o. from doing sth* prohibir a alguien que haga algo

ba·nal [bə'næl] *adj* banal

ba·na·na [bə'nænə] plátano *m*, *Rpl* banana f

band [bænd] banda f; *pop* grupo *m*

ban·dage ['bændɪdʒ] **1** *n* vendaje *m* **2** *v/t* vendar

'**Band-Aid**® *Span* tirita f, *L.Am.* curita f

B&B [biːn'biː] *abbr* (= *bed and breakfast*) hostal *m* familiar

ban·dit ['bændɪt] bandido *m*

'**band·wag·on**: *jump on the* ~ subirse al carro

ban·dy ['bændɪ] *adj legs* arqueado

bang [bæŋ] **1** *n noise* estruendo *m*, estrépito *m*; (*blow*) golpe *m*; *the door closed with a* ~ la puerta se cerró de un portazo **2** *v/t door* cerrar de un portazo; (*hit*) golpear; ~ *o.s. on the head* golpearse la cabeza **3** *v/i* dar golpes; *the door ~ed shut* la puerta se cerró de un portazo

ban·gle ['bæŋgl] brazalete *m*, pulsera f

bangs [bæŋz] *npl* flequillo *m*

ban·is·ters ['bænɪstərz] *npl* barandilla f

ban·jo ['bændʒoʊ] banjo *m*

bank[1] [bæŋk] *of river* orilla f

bank[2] [bæŋk] **1** *n* FIN banco *m* **2** *v/i*: *I* ~ *with ...* mi banco es el ... **3** *v/t money* ingresar, depositar

♦ **bank on** *v/t* contar con; *don't bank on it* no cuentes con ello

'**bank ac·count** cuenta f (bancaria); '**bank bal·ance** saldo *m* bancario; '**bank bill** billete *m*

bank·er ['bæŋkər] banquero *m*

'**bank·er's card** tarjeta f bancaria

bank·ing ['bæŋkɪŋ] banca f

'**bank loan** préstamo *m* bancario; '**bank man·ag·er** director(a) *m(f)* de banco; '**bank rate** tipo *m* de interés bancario; '**bank·roll** *v/t* financiar

bank·rupt ['bæŋkrʌpt] **1** *adj* en bancarrota *or* quiebra; *go* ~ quebrar, ir a la quiebra; *of person* arruinarse **2** *v/t* llevar a la quiebra

bank·rupt·cy ['bæŋkrʌpsɪ] *of person, company* quiebra f, bancarrota f

'**bank state·ment** extracto *m* bancario

ban·ner ['bænər] pancarta f

banns [bænz] *npl* amonestaciones *fpl*

ban·quet ['bæŋkwɪt] *n* banquete *m*

ban·ter ['bæntər] *n* bromas *fpl*

bap·tism ['bæptɪzm] bautismo *m*

bap·tize [bæp'taɪz] *v/t* bautizar

bar[1] [bɑːr] *n of iron* barra f; *of chocolate* tableta f; *for drinks* bar *m*; (*counter*) barra f; *a* ~ *of soap* una pastilla de jabón; *be behind* ~*s* (*in prison*) estar entre barrotes

bar[2] [bɑːr] *v/t* (*pret & pp -red*) *from premises* prohibir la entrada a; ~ *s.o. from doing sth* prohibir a alguien que haga algo

bar[3] [bɑːr] *prep* (*except*) excepto

bar·bar·i·an [bɑːr'berɪən] bárbaro(-a) *m(f)*

bar·bar·ic [bɑːr'bærɪk] *adj* brutal, inhumano

bar·be·cue ['bɑːrbɪkjuː] **1** *n* barbacoa f **2** *v/t* cocinar en la barbacoa

barbed 'wire [bɑːrbd] alambre f de espino

bar·ber ['bɑːrbər] barbero *m*

bar·bi·tu·rate [bɑːr'bɪtʃərət] barbitúrico *m*

'**bar code** código *m* de barras

bare [ber] *adj* (*naked*) desnudo; (*empty: room*) vacío; *mountainside* pelado, raso; *floor* descubierto; *in one's* ~ *feet* descalzo

'**bare·foot** *adj* descalzo

bare-head·ed [ber'hedɪd] *adj* sin sombrero

B

'**bare·ly** ['berlɪ] *adv* apenas; *he's ~ five* acaba de cumplir cinco años

bar·gain ['bɑːrgɪn] **1** *n* (*deal*) trato *m*; (*good buy*) ganga *f*; *into the ~* además **2** *v/i* regatear, negociar
♦ **bargain for** *v/t* (*expect*) imaginarse, esperar

barge [bɑːrdʒ] *n* NAUT barcaza *f*
♦ **barge into** *v/t person* tropezarse con; *room* irrumpir en

bar·i·tone ['bærɪtoun] *n* barítono *m*

bark[1] [bɑːrk] **1** *n of dog* ladrido *m* **2** *v/i* ladrar

bark[2] [bɑːrk] *of tree* corteza *f*

bar·ley ['bɑːrlɪ] cebada *f*

barn [bɑːrn] granero *m*

ba·rom·e·ter [bə'rɑːmɪtər] *also fig* barómetro *m*

Ba·roque [bə'rɑːk] *adj* barroco

bar·racks ['bærəks] *npl* MIL cuartel *m*

bar·rage [bə'rɑːʒ] MIL barrera *f* (de fuego); *fig* aluvión *m*

bar·rel ['bærəl] (*container*) tonel *m*, barril *m*

bar·ren ['bærən] *adj land* yermo, árido

bar·rette [bə'ret] pasador *m*

bar·ri·cade [bærɪ'keɪd] *n* barricada *f*

bar·ri·er ['bærɪər] *also fig* barrera *f*; *language ~* barrera *f* lingüística

bar·ring ['bærɪŋ] *prep* salvo, excepto; *~ accidents* salvo imprevistos

bar·ris·ter ['bærɪstər] *Br* abogado(-a) *m(f)* (*que aparece en tribunales*)

bar·row ['bærou] carretilla *f*

'**bar ten·der** camarero(-a) *m(f)*, *L.Am.* mesero(-a) *m(f)*, *Rpl* mozo(-a) *m(f)*

bar·ter ['bɑːrtər] **1** *n* trueque *m* **2** *v/t* cambiar, trocar (*for* por)

base [beɪs] **1** *n bottom, center* base *f*; *~ camp* campamento *m* base **2** *v/t* basar (*on* en); *be ~d in of soldier* estar destinado en; *of company* tener su sede en

'**base·ball** *ball* pelota *f* de béisbol; *game* béisbol *m*; '**base·ball bat** bate *m* de béisbol; '**base·ball cap** gorra *f* de béisbol; '**base·ball**

'**play·er** jugador(a) *m(f)* de béisbol, *L.Am.* pelotero(-a) *m(f)*

'**base·board** rodapié *m*

base·less ['beɪslɪs] *adj* infundado

base·ment ['beɪsmənt] *of house, store* sótano *m*

'**base rate** FIN tipo *m* de interés básico

bash [bæʃ] **1** *n* F porrazo *m* F **2** *v/t* F dar un porrazo a F

ba·sic ['beɪsɪk] *adj* (*rudimentary*) básico; *room* modesto, sencillo; *language skills* elemental; (*fundamental*) fundamental; *~ salary* sueldo *m* base

ba·sic·al·ly ['beɪsɪklɪ] *adv* básicamente

ba·sics ['beɪsɪks] *npl*: *the ~* lo básico, los fundamentos; *get down to ~* centrarse en lo esencial

bas·il ['bæzɪl] albahaca *f*

ba·sin ['beɪsn] *for washing* barreño *m*; *in bathroom* lavabo *m*

ba·sis ['beɪsɪs] (*pl bases* ['beɪsiːz]) base *f*; *on the ~ of what you've told me* de acuerdo con lo que me has dicho

bask [bæsk] *v/i* tomar el sol

bas·ket ['bæskɪt] cesta *f*; *in basketball* canasta *f*

bas·ket·ball *game* baloncesto *m*, *L.Am.* básquetbol *m*; *ball* balón *m* or pelota *f* de baloncesto; *~ player* baloncestista *m/f*, *L.Am.* basquebolista *m/f*

Basque [bæsk] **1** *adj* vasco **2** *n person* vasco(-a) *m(f)*; *language* vasco *m*

bass [beɪs] **1** *n part, singer* bajo *m*; *instrument* contrabajo *m* **2** *adj* bajo

bas·tard ['bæstərd] *m(f)*, bastardo(-a) *m(f)*; P cabrón(-ona) *m(f)* P; *poor ~* pobre desgraciado; *stupid ~* desgraciado

bat[1] [bæt] **1** *n for baseball* bate *m*; *for table tennis* pala *f* **2** *v/i* (*pret & pp -ted*) *in baseball* batear

bat[2] [bæt] *v/t* (*pret & pp -ted*): *he didn't ~ an eyelid* no se inmutó

bat[3] [bæt] (*animal*) murciélago *m*

batch [bætʃ] *n of students* tanda *f*; *of*

data conjunto *m*; *of bread* hornada *f*; *of products* lote *m*

ba·ted ['beɪtɪd] *adj*: **with ~ breath** con la respiración contenida

bath [bɑːθ] baño *m*; **have a ~, take a ~** darse *or* tomar un baño

bathe [beɪð] *v/i* (*swim, have a bath*) bañarse

'bath mat alfombra *f* de baño; **'bath·robe** albornoz *m*; **'bath·room** *for bath, washing hands*, cuarto *m* de baño; (*toilet*) servicio *m*, *L.Am.* baño *m*; **'bath tow·el** toalla *f* de baño; **'bath·tub** bañera *f*

bat·on [bəˈtɑːn] *of conductor* batuta *f*

bat·tal·i·on [bəˈtælɪən] MIL batallón *m*

bat·ter ['bætər] *n* masa *f*; *in baseball* bateador(a) *m(f)*

bat·tered ['bætərd] *adj* maltratado

bat·ter·y ['bætərɪ] *in watch, flashlight* pila *f*; *in computer, car* batería *f*

'bat·ter·y charg·er ['tʃɑːrdʒər] cargador *m* de pilas/baterías

bat·ter·y-op·er·at·ed ['ɑːpəreɪtɪd] *adj* que funciona con pilas

bat·tle ['bætl] **1** *n also fig* batalla *f* **2** *v/i against illness etc* luchar

'bat·tle·field, **'bat·tle·ground** campo *m* de batalla

'bat·tle·ship acorazado *m*

bawd·y ['bɔːdɪ] *adj* picante, subido de tono

bawl [bɔːl] *v/i* (*shout*) gritar, vociferar; (*weep*) berrear

♦ bawl out *v/t* F echar la bronca a F

bay [beɪ] (*inlet*) bahía *f*

bay·o·net [ˈbeɪənet] *n* bayoneta *f*

bay 'win·dow ventana *f* en saliente

BC [biːˈsiː] *abbr* (= **before Christ**) A.C. (= antes de Cristo)

be [biː] ◊ *v/i* (*pret was/were*, *pp been*) *permanent characteristics, profession, nationality* ser; *position, temporary condition* estar; **was she there?** ¿estaba allí?; **it's me** soy yo; **how much is/are …?** ¿cuánto es/son …?; **there is, there are** hay; **~ careful** ten cuidado; **don't ~ sad** no estés triste ◊ **has the mailman been?** ¿ha venido el cartero?; **I've**

never been to Japan no he estado en Japón; **I've been here for hours** he estado aquí horas ◊ *tags*: **that's right, isn't it?** eso es, ¿no?; **she's Chinese, isn't she?** es china, ¿verdad? ◊ *v/aux*: **I am thinking** estoy pensando; **he was running** corría; **you're ~ing stupid** estás siendo un estúpido ◊ *obligation*: **you are to do what I tell you** harás lo que yo te diga; **I was to help him escape** se suponía que le iba a ayudar a escaparse; **you are not to tell anyone** no debes decírselo a nadie ◊ *passive*: **he was arrested** fue detenido, lo detuvieron; **they have been sold** se han vendido

♦ be in for *v/t*: **he's in for a big disappointment** se va a llevar una gran desilusión

beach [biːtʃ] *n* playa *f*

'beach ball pelota *f* de playa

'beach·wear ropa *f* playera

beads [biːdz] *npl* cuentas *fpl*

beak [biːk] pico *m*

'be-all: **the ~ and end-all** lo más importante del mundo

beam [biːm] **1** *n in ceiling etc* viga *f* **2** *v/i* (*smile*) sonreír de oreja a oreja **3** *v/t* (*transmit*) emitir

bean [biːn] judía *f*, alubia *f*, *L.Am.* frijol *m*, *S.Am.* poroto *m*; **green ~s** judías *fpl* verdes, *Mex* ejotes *mpl*, *S.Am.* porotos *mpl* verdes; **coffee ~s** granos *mpl* de café; **be full of ~s** F estar lleno de vitalidad

'bean·bag *cojín relleno de bolitas*

bear¹ [ber] *animal* oso(-a) *m(f)*

bear² [ber] **1** *v/t* (*pret bore*, *pp borne*) *weight* resistir; *costs* correr con; (*tolerate*) aguantar, soportar; *child* dar a luz; **she bore him six children** le dio seis hijos **2** *v/i* (*pret bore*, *pp borne*): **bring pressure to ~ on** ejercer presión sobre

♦ bear out *v/t* (*confirm*) confirmar

bear·a·ble ['berəbl] *adj* soportable

beard [bɪrd] barba *f*

beard·ed ['bɪrdɪd] *adj* con barba

bear·ing ['berɪŋ] *in machine* rodamiento *m*, cojinete *m*; **that has no ~**

B

on the case eso no tiene nada que ver con el caso

'bear mar·ket FIN mercado *m* a la baja

beast [biːst] *animal* bestia *f*; *person* bestia *m/f*

beat [biːt] **1** *n of heart* latido *m*; *of music* ritmo *m* **2** *v/i* (*pret* beat, *pp* beaten) *of heart* latir; *of rain* golpear; ~ about the bush andarse por las ramas **3** *v/t* (*pret* beat, *pp* beaten) *in competition* derrotar, ganar a; (*hit*) pegar a; (*pound*) golpear; ~ it! F ¡lárgate! F; *it ~s me* no logro entender

♦ beat up *v/t* dar una paliza a

beat·en ['biːtən] **1** *adj*: off the ~ track retirado **2** *pp* → beat

beat·ing ['biːtɪŋ] (*physical*) paliza *f*

beat-up *adj* F destartalado F

beau·ti·cian [bjuː'tɪʃn] esteticista *m/f*

beau·ti·ful ['bjuːtəfəl] *adj woman, house, day, story, movie* bonito, precioso, *L.Am.* lindo; *smell, taste, meal* delicioso, *L.Am.* rico; *vacation* estupendo; *thanks, that's just ~!* ¡muchísimas gracias, está maravilloso!

beau·ti·ful·ly ['bjuːtɪfəlɪ] *adv cooked, done* perfectamente, maravillosamente

beau·ty ['bjuːtɪ] belleza *f*

'beau·ty par·lor, *Br* 'beau·ty par·lour ['pɑːrlər] salón *m* de belleza

bea·ver ['biːvər] castor *m*

♦ beaver away *v/i* F trabajar como un burro F

be·came [bɪ'keɪm] *pret* → become

be·cause [bɪ'kɑːz] *conj* porque; ~ *it was too expensive* porque era demasiado caro; ~ *of* debido a, a causa de; ~ *of you, we can't go* gracias a ti, no podemos ir

beck·on ['bekn] *v/i* hacer señas

be·come [bɪ'kʌm] *v/i* (*pret* became, *pp* become) hacerse, volverse; *it became clear that ...* quedó claro que ...; *he became a priest* se hizo sacerdote; *she's becoming very forgetful* cada vez es más olvidadiza; *what's ~ of her?* ¿qué fue de ella?

be·com·ing [bɪ'kʌmɪŋ] *adj* favorecedor, apropiado

bed [bed] *n* cama *f*; *of flowers* macizo; *of sea* fondo *m*; *of river* cauce *m*, lecho *m*; *go to* ~ ir a la cama; *he's still in* ~ aún está en la cama; *go to* ~ *with s.o.* irse a la cama *or* acostarse con alguien

'bed·clothes *npl* ropa *f* de cama

bed·ding ['bedɪŋ] ropa *f* de cama

bed·lam ['bedləm] F locura *f*, jaleo *m*

bed·rid·den ['bedrɪdən] *adj*: *be* ~ estar postrado en cama; 'bed·room dormitorio *m*, *L.Am.* cuarto *m*; 'bed·side: *be at the* ~ *of* estar junto a la cama de; 'bed·spread colcha *f*; 'bed·time hora *f* de irse a la cama

bee [biː] abeja *f*

beech [biːtʃ] haya *f*

beef [biːf] **1** *n* carne *f* de vaca *or* vacuna; F (*complaint*) queja *f* **2** *v/i* F (*complain*) quejarse

♦ beef up *v/t* reforzar, fortalecer

'beef·bur·ger hamburguesa *f*

'bee·hive colmena *f*

'bee·line: *make a* ~ *for* ir directamente a

been [bɪn] *pp* → be

beep [biːp] **1** *n* pitido *m* **2** *v/i* pitar **3** *v/t* (*call on pager*) llamar con el buscapersonas

beep·er ['biːpər] buscapersonas *m inv*, *Span* busca *m*

beer [bɪr] cerveza *f*

beet [biːt] remolacha *f*

bee·tle ['biːtl] escarabajo *m*

be·fore [bɪ'fɔːr] **1** *prep* (*time*) antes de; (*space, order*) antes de, delante de **2** *adv* antes; *I've seen this movie* ~ ya he visto esta película; *have you been to Japan* ~? ¿habías estado antes *or* ya en Japón?; *the week/day* ~ la semana/el día anterior **3** *conj* antes de que

be·fore·hand *adv* de antemano

be·friend [bɪ'frend] *v/t* hacerse amigo de

beg [beg] **1** *v/i* (*pret & pp* -ged) mendigar, pedir **2** *v/t* (*pret & pp*

-ged): ~ **s.o. to do sth** rogar or suplicar a alguien que haga algo

be·gan [bɪˈgæn] *pret* → **begin**

beg·gar [ˈbegər] *n* mendigo(-a) *m(f)*

be·gin [bɪˈgɪn] **1** *v/i* (*pret* **began**, *pp* **begun**) empezar, comenzar; **to** ~ **with** (*at first*) en un primer momento, al principio; (*in the first place*) para empezar **2** *v/t* (*pret* **began**, *pp* **begun**) empezar, comenzar; ~ **to do sth**, ~ **doing sth** empezar or comenzar a hacer algo

be·gin·ner [bɪˈgɪnər] principiante *m/f*

be·gin·ning [bɪˈgɪnɪŋ] principio *m*, comienzo *m*; (*origin*) origen *m*

be·grudge [bɪˈgrʌdʒ] *v/t* (*envy*) envidiar; (*give reluctantly*) dar a regañadientes

be·gun [bɪˈgʌn] *pp* → **begin**

be·half [bɪˈhɑːf]: **on ~ of**, **in ~ of** en nombre de; **on my/his** ~ en nombre mío/suyo

be·have [bɪˈheɪv] *v/i* comportarse, portarse; ~ (*o.s.*) comportarse or portarse bien; ~ (*yourself*)! ¡pórtate bien!

be·hav·ior, *Br* **be·hav·iour** [bɪˈheɪvɪər] comportamiento *m*, conducta *f*

be·hind [bɪˈhaɪnd] **1** *prep in position, order* detrás de; *in progress* por detrás de; **be** ~ **...** (*responsible for*) estar detrás de ...; (*support*) respaldar ... **2** *adv* (*at the back*) detrás; **be** ~ **with sth** estar atrasado con algo; **leave sth** ~ dejarse algo

beige [beɪʒ] *adj* beige, *Span* beis

be·ing [ˈbiːɪŋ] *existence, creature* ser *m*

be·lat·ed [bɪˈleɪtɪd] *adj* tardío

belch [beltʃ] **1** *n* eructo *m* **2** *v/i* eructar

Bel·gian [ˈbeldʒən] **1** *adj* belga **2** *n* belga *m/f*

Bel·gium [ˈbeldʒəm] Bélgica

be·lief [bɪˈliːf] creencia *f*; **it's my** ~ **that** creo que

be·lieve [bɪˈliːv] *v/t* creer

♦ **believe in** *v/t* creer en

be·liev·er [bɪˈliːvər] REL creyente

m/f; *fig* partidario(a) *m(f)* (**in** de)

be·lit·tle [bɪˈlɪtl] *v/t* menospreciar

Be·lize [beˈliːz] *n* Belice

bell [bel] *of bike, door, school* timbre *m*; *of church* campana *f*

'bell·hop botones *m inv*

bel·lig·er·ent [bɪˈlɪdʒərənt] *adj* beligerante

bel·low [ˈbeloʊ] **1** *n* bramido *m* **2** *v/i* bramar

bel·ly [ˈbeli] *of person* estómago *m*, barriga *f*; (*fat stomach*) barriga *f*, tripa *f*; *of animal* panza *f*

'bel·ly·ache *v/i* F refunfuñar

be·long [bɪˈlɒŋ] *v/i*: **where does this** ~? ¿dónde va esto?; **I don't** ~ **here** no encajo aquí

♦ **belong to** *v/t of object, money* pertenecer a; *club* pertenecer a, ser socio de

be·long·ings [bɪˈlɒŋɪŋz] *npl* pertenencias *fpl*

be·loved [bɪˈlʌvɪd] *adj* querido

be·low [bɪˈloʊ] **1** *prep* debajo de; *in amount, rate, level* por debajo de **2** *adv* abajo; *in text* más abajo; *see* ~ véase más abajo; **10 degrees** ~ 10 grados bajo cero

belt [belt] *n* cinturón *m*; **tighten one's** ~ *fig* apretarse el cinturón

bench [bentʃ] *seat* banco *m*; (*work~*) mesa *f* de trabajo

'bench·mark punto *m* de referencia

bend [bend] **1** *n* curva *f* **2** *v/t* (*pret & pp* **bent**) doblar **3** *v/i* (*pret & pp* **bent**) torcer, girar; *of person* flexionarse

♦ **bend down** *v/i* agacharse

bend·er [ˈbendər] F parranda *f* F

be·neath [bɪˈniːθ] **1** *prep* debajo de; **she thinks a job like that is** ~ **her** cree que un trabajo como ése le supondría rebajarse **2** *adv* abajo

ben·e·fac·tor [ˈbenɪfæktər] benefactor(a) *m(f)*

ben·e·fi·cial [benɪˈfɪʃl] *adj* beneficioso

ben·e·fi·ci·a·ry [benɪˈfɪʃəri] beneficiario(-a) *m(f)*

ben·e·fit [ˈbenɪfɪt] **1** *n* beneficio *m*, ventaja *f* **2** *v/t* beneficiar **3** *v/i* beneficiarse

be·nev·o·lence [bɪˈnevələns] benevolencia f

be·nev·o·lent [bɪˈnevələnt] adj benevolente

be·nign [bɪˈnaɪn] adj agradable; MED benigno

bent [bent] pret & pp → **bend**

be·queath [bɪˈkwiːð] v/t also fig legar

be·quest [bɪˈkwest] legado m

be·reaved [bɪˈriːvd] npl: **the ~** los familiares del difunto

be·ret [bəˈreɪ] boina f

ber·ry [ˈberɪ] baya f

ber·serk [bərˈzɜːrk] adv: **go ~** F volverse loco

berth [bɜːrθ] on ship litera f; on train camarote m; for ship amarradero m; **give s.o. a wide ~** evitar a alguien

be·seech [bɪˈsiːtʃ] v/t: **~ s.o. to do sth** suplicar a alguien que haga algo

be·side [bɪˈsaɪd] prep al lado de, junto a; **be ~ o.s.** estar fuera de sí; **that's ~ the point** eso no tiene nada que ver

be·sides [bɪˈsaɪdz] **1** adv además **2** prep (apart from) aparte de, además de

be·siege [bɪˈsiːdʒ] v/t also fig asediar

best [best] **1** adj mejor; **which did you like ~?** ¿cuál te gustó más?; **it would be ~ if ...** sería mejor si ...; **I like her ~** ella es la que más me gusta **3** n: **do one's ~** hacer todo lo posible; **the ~** person, thing el / la mejor; **we insist on the ~** insistimos en lo mejor; **we'll just have to make the ~ of it** tendremos que arreglárnoslas; **all the ~!** ¡buena suerte!, ¡que te vaya bien!

best be'fore date fecha f de caducidad; **best 'man** at wedding padrino m; **'best-sell·er** éxito m de ventas, best-seller m

bet [bet] **1** n apuesta f; **place a ~** hacer una apuesta **2** v/t & v/i also fig apostar; **I ~ he doesn't come** apuesto a que no viene; **you ~!** ¡ya lo creo!

be·tray [bɪˈtreɪ] v/t traicionar; husband, wife engañar

be·tray·al [bɪˈtreɪəl] traición f; of husband, wife engaño m

bet·ter [ˈbetər] **1** adj mejor; **get ~ in** skills, health mejorar; **he's ~ in** health está mejor **2** adv mejor; **you'd ~ ask permission** sería mejor que pidieras permiso; **I'd really ~ not** mejor no; **all the ~ for us** tanto mejor para nosotros; **I like her ~** me gusta más ella

bet·ter·'off adj (wealthier) más rico

be·tween [bɪˈtwiːn] prep entre; **~ you and me** entre tú y yo

bev·er·age [ˈbevərɪdʒ] fml bebida f

be·ware [bɪˈwer] v/t: **~ of** tener cuidado con

be·wil·der [bɪˈwɪldər] v/t desconcertar

be·wil·der·ment [bɪˈwɪldərmənt] desconcierto m

be·yond [bɪˈjɑːnd] **1** prep in space más allá de; **she has changed ~ recognition** ha cambiado tanto que es difícil reconocerla; **it's ~ me** (don't understand) no logro entender; (can't do it) me es imposible **2** adv más allá

bi·as [ˈbaɪəs] n against prejuicio m; in favor of favoritismo m

bi·as(s)ed [ˈbaɪəst] adj parcial

bib [bɪb] for baby babero m

Bi·ble [ˈbaɪbl] Biblia f

bib·li·cal [ˈbɪblɪkl] adj bíblico

bib·li·og·ra·phy [bɪblɪˈɑːɡrəfɪ] bibliografía f

bi·car·bon·ate of so·da [baɪˈkɑːrbəneɪt] bicarbonato m sódico

bi·cen·ten·ni·al [baɪsenˈtenɪəl] bicentenario m

bi·ceps [ˈbaɪseps] npl bíceps mpl

bick·er [ˈbɪkər] v/i reñir, discutir

bi·cy·cle [ˈbaɪsɪkl] bicicleta f

bid [bɪd] **1** n at auction puja f; (attempt) intento m **2** v/i (pret & pp **bid**) at auction pujar

bid·der [ˈbɪdər] postor(a) m(f); **the highest ~** el mejor postor

bi·en·ni·al [baɪˈenɪəl] adj bienal

bi·fo·cals [baɪˈfoʊkəlz] npl gafas fpl

or L.Am. lentes *mpl* bifocales

big [bɪg] **1** *adj* grande; *before singular nouns* gran; *my ~ brother/ sister* mi hermano/hermana mayor; *~ name* nombre *m* importante **2** *adv*: *talk* ~ alardear, fanfarronear

big·a·mist ['bɪgəmɪst] bígamo(-a) *m(f)*

big·a·mous ['bɪgəməs] *adj* bígamo

big·a·my ['bɪgəmi] bigamia *f*

'big·head F creído(-a) *m(f)* F

big-head·ed [bɪg'hedɪd] *adj* F creído F

big·ot ['bɪgət] fanático(-a) *m(f)*, intolerante *m/f*

bike [baɪk] **1** *n* F bici *f* F; *motorbike* moto *f* F **2** *v/i* ir en bici

bik·er ['baɪkər] motero(-a) *m(f)*

bi·ki·ni [bɪ'kiːni] biquini *m*

bi·lat·er·al [baɪ'lætərəl] *adj* bilateral

bi·lin·gual [baɪ'lɪŋgwəl] *adj* bilingüe

bill [bɪl] **1** *n for gas, electricity* factura *f*, recibo *m*; *Br in hotel, restaurant* cuenta *f*; *(money)* billete *m*; POL proyecto *m* de ley; *(poster)* cartel *m* **2** *v/t (invoice)* enviar la factura a

'bill·board valla *f* publicitaria

'bill·fold cartera *f*, billetera *f*

bil·liards ['bɪljərdz] *nsg* billar *m*

bil·lion ['bɪljən] mil millones *mpl*, millardo *m*

bill of ex·change FIN letra *f* de cambio

bill of 'sale escritura *f* de compraventa

bin [bɪn] *n* cubo *m*

bi·na·ry ['baɪnəri] *adj* binario

bind [baɪnd] *v/t (pret & pp* **bound***) (connect)* unir; *(tie)* atar; *(LAW: oblige)* obligar

bind·ing ['baɪndɪŋ] **1** *adj agreement, promise* vinculante **2** *n of book* tapa *f*

bi·noc·u·lars [bɪ'nɑːkjələrz] *npl* prismáticos *mpl*

bi·o·chem·ist [baɪoʊ'kemɪst] bioquímico(-a) *m(f)*

bi·o·chem·is·try [baɪoʊ'kemɪstri] bioquímica *f*

bi·o·de·gra·da·ble [baɪoʊdɪ'greɪdəbl] *adj* biodegradable

bi·og·ra·pher [baɪ'ɑːgrəfər] biógrafo(-a) *m(f)*

bi·og·ra·phy [baɪ'ɑːgrəfi] biografía *f*

bi·o·log·i·cal [baɪoʊ'lɑːdʒɪkl] *adj* biológico; *~ parents* padres *mpl* biológicos; *~ detergent* detergente *m* biológico

bi·ol·o·gist [baɪ'ɑːlədʒɪst] biólogo(-a) *m(f)*

bi·ol·o·gy [baɪ'ɑːlədʒi] biología *f*

bi·o·tech·nol·o·gy [baɪoʊtek'nɑːlədʒi] biotecnología *f*

bird [bɜːrd] ave *f*, pájaro *m*

'bird·cage jaula *f* para pájaros; **bird of 'prey** ave *f* rapaz; **'bird sanc·tu·a·ry** reserva *f* de aves; **bird's eye 'view** vista *f* panorámica; *get a ~'s eye view of sth* ver algo a vista de pájaro

bi·ro® ['baɪroʊ] *Br* bolígrafo *m*, *Mex* pluma *f*, *Rpl* birome *m*

birth [bɜːrθ] *also fig* nacimiento *m*; *(labor)* parto *m*; *give ~ to child* dar a luz; *of animal* parir; *date of ~* fecha *f* de nacimiento; *the land of my ~* mi tierra natal

'birth cer·tif·i·cate partida *f* de nacimiento; **'birth con·trol** control *m* de natalidad; **'birth·day** cumpleaños *m inv*; *happy ~!* ¡feliz cumpleaños!; **'birth·day cake** tarta *f* de cumpleaños; **'birth·mark** marca *f* de nacimiento, antojo *m*; **'birth·place** lugar *m* de nacimiento; **'birth·rate** tasa *f* de natalidad

bis·cuit ['bɪskɪt] bollo *m*, panecillo *m*; *Br* galleta *f*

bi·sex·u·al ['baɪsekʃʊəl] **1** *adj* bisexual **2** *n* bisexual *m/f*

bish·op ['bɪʃəp] obispo *m*

bit¹ [bɪt] *n (piece)* trozo *m*; *(part)* parte *f*; *of puzzle* pieza *f*; COMPUT bit *m*; *a ~ (a little)* un poco; *let's sit down for a ~* sentémonos un rato; *you haven't changed a ~* no has cambiado nada; *a ~ of (a little)* un poco de; *a ~ of news* una noticia; *a ~ of advice* un consejo; *~ by ~* poco a poco; *I'll be there in a ~* estaré allí dentro de un rato

bit² [bɪt] *pret* → **bite**

B

bitch [bɪtʃ] **1** *n dog* perra *f*; F *woman* zorra *f* F **2** *v/i* F (*complain*) quejarse

bitch·y ['bɪtʃɪ] *adj person* malicioso; *remark* a mala leche F

bite [baɪt] **1** *n of dog* mordisco *m*; *of spider, mosquito* picadura *f*; *of snake* mordedura *f*, picadura *f*; *of food* bocado *m*; **let's have a ~ (to eat)** vamos a comer algo **2** *v/t* (*pret* **bit**, *pp* **bitten**) *of dog* morder; *of mosquito, flea* picar; *of snake* picar, morder; **~ one's nails** morderse las uñas **3** *v/i* (*pret* **bit**, *pp* **bitten**) *of dog* morder; *of mosquito, flea* picar; *of snake* morder, picar; *of fish* picar

bit·ten ['bɪtn] *pp* → **bite**

bit·ter ['bɪtər] *adj taste* amargo; *person* resentido; *weather* helador; *argument* agrio

bit·ter·ly ['bɪtərlɪ] *adv resent* amargamente; **it's ~ cold** hace un frío helador

bi·zarre [bɪ'zɑːr] *adj* extraño, peculiar

blab [blæb] *v/i* (*pret & pp* **-bed**) F irse de la lengua F

blab·ber·mouth ['blæbərmaʊθ] F bocazas *m/f inv* F

black [blæk] **1** *adj* negro; *coffee* solo; *tea* sin leche; *fig* negro, aciago **2** *n* (*color*) negro *m*; (*person*) negro(-a) *m*(*f*); **be in the ~** FIN no estar en números rojos; **in ~ and white** en blanco y negro; **in writing** por escrito

♦ **black out** *v/i* perder el conocimiento

black·ber·ry mora *f*; **black·bird** mirlo *m*; **black·board** pizarra *f*, encerado *m*; **black 'box** caja *f* negra; **black 'cof·fee** café *m* solo; **black e'con·o·my** economía *f* sumergida

black·en ['blækn] *v/t fig: person's name* manchar

black 'eye ojo *m* morado; **black·head** espinilla *f*, punto *m* negro; **black·list 1** *n* lista *f* negra **2** *v/t* poner en la lista negra; **black·mail 1** *n* chantaje *m*; **emotional ~** chantaje *m* emocional **2** *v/t* chantajear; **black·mail·er**

chantajista *m/f*; **black 'mar·ket** mercado *m* negro

black·ness ['blæknɪs] oscuridad *f*

black·out ELEC apagón *m*; MED desmayo *m*; **have a ~** desmayarse

black·smith herrero *m*

blad·der ['blædər] vejiga *f*

blade [bleɪd] *of knife, sword* hoja *f*; *of propeller* pala *f*; *of grass* brizna *f*

blame [bleɪm] **1** *n* culpa *f*; **I got the ~ for it** me echaron la culpa **2** *v/t* culpar; **~ s.o. for sth** culpar a alguien de algo

bland [blænd] *adj smile* insulso; *food* insípido, soso

blank [blæŋk] **1** *adj* (*not written on*) en blanco; *tape* virgen; *look* inexpresivo **2** *n* (*empty space*) espacio *m* en blanco; **my mind's a ~** tengo la mente en blanco

blank 'check, *Br* **blank 'cheque** cheque *m* en blanco

blan·ket ['blæŋkɪt] *n* manta *f*, *L.Am.* frazada *f*; **a ~ of snow** un manto de nieve

blare [bler] *v/i* retumbar

♦ **blare out 1** *v/i* retumbar **2** *v/t* emitir a todo volumen

blas·pheme [blæs'fiːm] *v/i* blasfemar

blas·phe·my ['blæsfəmɪ] blasfemia *f*

blast [blæst] **1** *n* (*explosion*) explosión *f*; (*gust*) ráfaga *f* **2** *v/t tunnel* abrir (con explosivos); *rock* volar; **~!** F ¡mecachis! F

♦ **blast off** *v/i of rocket* despegar

blast fur·nace alto horno *m*

blast-off despegue *m*

bla·tant ['bleɪtənt] *adj* descarado

blaze [bleɪz] **1** *n* (*fire*) incendio *m*; **a ~ of color** una explosión de color **2** *v/i of fire* arder

♦ **blaze away** *v/i with gun* disparar sin parar

blaz·er ['bleɪzər] americana *f*

bleach [bliːtʃ] **1** *n for clothes* lejía *f*; *for hair* decolorante *m* **2** *v/t hair* aclarar, desteñir

bleak [bliːk] *adj countryside* inhóspito; *weather* desapacible; *future* desolador

B

blear·y-eyed ['blɪrɪaɪd] *adj* con ojos
de sueño

bleat [bliːt] *v/i of sheep* balar

bled [bled] *pret & pp* → **bleed**

bleed [bliːd] **1** *v/i* (*pret & pp* **bled**)
sangrar; *he's ~ing internally* tiene
una hemorragia interna; *~ to death*
desangrarse **2** *v/t* (*pret & pp* **bled**)
fig sangrar

bleed·ing ['bliːdɪŋ] *n* hemorragia *f*

bleep [bliːp] **1** *n* pitido *m* **2** *v/i* pitar
3 *v/t* (*call on pager*) llamar con el
buscapersonas

bleep·er ['bliːpər] buscapersonas *m
inv*, *Span* busca *m*

blem·ish ['blemɪʃ] **1** *n* imperfección
f **2** *v/t reputation* manchar

blend [blend] **1** *n of coffee etc* mezcla
f; *fig* combinación *f* **2** *v/t* mezclar

♦ blend in 1 *v/i of person in
environment* pasar desapercibido;
of animal with surroundings etc confundirse; *of furniture etc* combinar
2 *v/t in cooking* añadir

blend·er ['blendər] *machine* licuadora *f*

bless [bles] *v/t* bendecir; (*God*) *~
you!* ¡que Dios te bendiga!; *in
response to sneeze* ¡Jesús!; *be ~ed
with* tener la suerte de tener

bless·ing ['blesɪŋ] *also fig* bendición
f

blew [bluː] *pret* → **blow**

blind [blaɪnd] **1** *adj* ciego; *corner* sin
visibilidad; *be ~ to sth fig* no ver
algo **2** *npl:* *the ~* los ciegos, los
invidentes **3** *v/t of sun* cegar; *she
was ~ed in an accident* se quedó
ciega a raíz de un accidente

blind 'al·ley callejón *m* sin salida;
blind 'date cita *f* a ciegas;
'blind·fold 1 *n* venda *f* **2** *v/t* vendar
los ojos a **3** *adv* con los ojos cerra-
dos

blind·ing ['blaɪndɪŋ] *adj light* cega-
dor; *headache* terrible

blind·ly ['blaɪndlɪ] *adv* a ciegas; *fig*
ciegamente

'blind spot *in road* punto *m* sin visibilidad; *in driving mirror* ángulo *m*
muerto; (*ability that is lacking*) pun-

to *m* flaco

blink [blɪŋk] *v/i* parpadear

blink·ered ['blɪŋkərd] *adj fig* cerrado

blip [blɪp] *on radar screen* señal *f*, luz *f*;
it's just a ~ fig es algo momentáneo

bliss [blɪs] felicidad *f*; *it was ~* fue
fantástico

blis·ter ['blɪstər] **1** *n* ampolla *f* **2** *v/i*
ampollarse; *of paint* hacer burbujas

bliz·zard ['blɪzərd] ventisca *f*

bloat·ed ['bloʊtɪd] *adj* hinchado

blob [blɑːb] *of liquid* goterón *m*

bloc [blɑːk] POL bloque *m*

block [blɑːk] **1** *n* bloque *m*; *buildings*
manzana *f*, *L.Am.* cuadra *f*; *of shares*
paquete *m*; (*blockage*) bloqueo *m*
2 *v/t* bloquear; *sink* atascar

♦ block in *v/t with vehicle* bloquear el paso a

♦ block out *v/t light* impedir el paso
de

♦ block up *v/t sink etc* atascar

block·ade [blɑːˈkeɪd] **1** *n* bloqueo *m*
2 *v/t* bloquear

block·age [blɑːˈkɪdʒ] obstrucción *f*

block·bust·er ['blɑːkbʌstər] gran
éxito *m*

block 'let·ters *npl* letras *fpl* mayúsculas

blond [blɑːnd] *adj* rubio

blonde [blɑːnd] *n woman* rubia *f*

blood [blʌd] sangre *f*; *in cold ~* a sangre fría

'blood al·co·hol lev·el nivel *m* de
alcohol en sangre; **'blood bank**
banco *m* de sangre; **'blood bath**
baño *m* de sangre; **'blood do·nor**
donante *m/f* de sangre; **'blood
group** grupo *m* sanguíneo

blood·less ['blʌdlɪs] *adj coup* incruento, pacífico

'blood poi·son·ing septicemia *f*;
'blood pres·sure tensión *f* (arte-
rial), presión *f* sanguínea; **'blood
re·la·tion: she's not a ~ of mine**
no nos unen lazos de sangre; **'blood
sam·ple** muestra *f* de sangre;
'blood·shed derramamiento *m* de
sangre; **'blood·shot** *adj* enrojecido;
'blood·stain mancha *f* de sangre;
'blood·stained *adj* ensangrentado,

manchado de sangre; '**blood-stream** flujo *m* sanguíneo; '**blood test** análisis *m inv* de sangre; '**blood-thirst-y** *adj* sanguinario; *movie* macabro; '**blood trans-fu-sion** transfusión *f* sanguínea; '**blood ves-sel** vaso *m* sanguíneo

blood-y ['blʌdɪ] *adj hands etc* ensangrentado; *battle* sangriento

bloom [bluːm] **1** *n* flor *f*; **in ~** en flor **2** *v/i also fig* florecer

blos-som ['blɑːsəm] **1** *n* flores *fpl* **2** *v/i also fig* florecer

blot [blɑːt] **1** *n* mancha *f*, borrón *m*; *be a ~ on the landscape* estropear el paisaje **2** *v/t* (*pret & pp **-ted***) (*dry*) secar

♦ **blot out** *v/t* borrar; *sun, view* ocultar

blotch [blɑːtʃ] *on skin* erupción *f*, mancha *f*

blotch-y ['blɑːtʃɪ] *adj*: *~ skin* piel con erupciones

blouse [blaʊz] blusa *f*

blow[1] [bloʊ] *n* golpe *m*

blow[2] [bloʊ] **1** *v/t* (*pret **blew***, *pp **blown***) *smoke* exhalar; *whistle* tocar; F (*spend*) fundir F; F *opportunity* perder, desaprovechar; *~ one's nose* sonarse (la nariz) **2** *v/i* (*pret **blew***, *pp **blown***) *of wind, person* soplar; *of whistle* sonar; *of fuse* fundirse; *of tire* reventarse

♦ **blow off 1** *v/t* llevarse **2** *v/i* salir volando

♦ **blow out 1** *v/t candle* apagar **2** *v/i of candle* apagarse

♦ **blow over 1** *v/t* derribar, hacer caer **2** *v/i* caerse, derrumbarse; *of storm* amainar; *of argument* calmarse

♦ **blow up 1** *v/t with explosives* volar; *balloon* hinchar; *photograph* ampliar **2** *v/i* F (*become angry*) ponerse furioso

'**blow-dry** *v/t* (*pret & pp **-ied***) secar (*con secador*)

'**blow-job** V mamada *f* V

blown [bloʊn] *pp* → **blow**

'**blow-out** *of tire* reventón *m*; F (*big meal*) comilona *f* F

'**blow-up** *of photo* ampliación *f*

blue [bluː] **1** *adj* azul; F *movie* porno *inv* F **2** *n* azul *m*

'**blue-ber-ry** arándano *m*; **blue 'chip** *adj* puntero, de primera fila; **blue-'col-lar work-er** trabajador(a) *m(f)* manual; '**blue-print** plano *m*; *fig* proyecto *m*, plan *m*

blues [bluːz] *npl* MUS blues *m inv*; *have the ~* estar deprimido

'**blues sing-er** cantante *m/f* de blues

bluff [blʌf] **1** *n* (*deception*) farol *m* **2** *v/i* ir de farol

blun-der ['blʌndər] **1** *n* error *m* de bulto, metedura *f* de pata **2** *v/i* cometer un error de bulto, meter la pata

blunt [blʌnt] *adj pencil* sin punta; *knife* desafilado; *person* franco

blunt-ly ['blʌntlɪ] *adv speak* francamente

blur [blɜːr] **1** *n* imagen *f* desenfocada; *everything is a ~* todo está desenfocado **2** *v/t* (*pret & pp **-red***) desdibujar

blurb [blɜːrb] *on book* nota *f* promocional

♦ **blurt out** [blɜːrt] *v/t* soltar

blush [blʌʃ] **1** *n* rubor *m*, sonrojo *m* **2** *v/i* ruborizarse, sonrojarse

blush-er ['blʌʃər] *cosmetic* colorete *m*

blus-ter ['blʌstər] *v/i* protestar encolerizadamente

blus-ter-y ['blʌstərɪ] *adj* tempestuoso

BO [biː'oʊ] *abbr* (= *body odor*) olor *m* corporal

board [bɔːrd] **1** *n* tablón *m*, tabla *f*; *for game* tablero *m*; *for notices* tablón *m*; *~* (*of directors*) consejo *m* de administración; *on ~ on plane, boat, train* a bordo; *take on ~ comments etc* aceptar, tener en cuenta; (*fully realize truth of*) asumir; *across the ~* de forma general **2** *v/t airplane etc* embarcar; *train* subir a **3** *v/i of passengers* embarcar; *~ with as lodger* hospedarse con

♦ **board up** *v/t* cubrir con tablas

board-er ['bɔːrdər] huésped *m/f*

'**board game** juego *m* de mesa; '**board·ing card** tarjeta *f* de embarque; '**board·ing house** hostal *m*, pensión *f*; '**board·ing pass** tarjeta *f* de embarque; '**board·ing school** internado *m*

'**board meet·ing** reunión *f* del consejo de administración; '**board room** sala *f* de reuniones *or* juntas; '**board·walk** paseo marítimo con tablas

boast [bəʊst] **1** *n* presunción *f*, jactancia *f* **2** *v/i* presumir, alardear (*about* de)

boat [bəʊt] barco *m*; *small, for leisure* barca *f*; *go by* ~ ir en barco

bob¹ [bɑːb] *haircut* corte *m* a lo chico

bob² [bɑːb] *v/i* (*pret & pp* -*bed*) *of boat etc* mecerse

♦ **bob up** *v/i* aparecer

'**bob·sled**, '**bob·sleigh** bobsleigh *m*

bod·ice ['bɑːdɪs] cuerpo *m*

bod·i·ly ['bɑːdɪlɪ] **1** *adj* corporal; *needs* físico; *function* fisiológico **2** *adv* eject en volandas

bod·y ['bɑːdɪ] cuerpo *m*; *dead* cadáver *m*; ~ *of water* masa *f* de agua

'**bod·y·guard** guardaespaldas *m/f inv*; '**bod·y lan·guage** lenguaje *m* corporal; '**bod·y o·dor**, *Br* '**bod·y o·dour** olor *m* corporal; '**bod·y pierc·ing** piercing *m*, perforaciones *fpl* corporales; '**bod·y·shop** MOT taller *m* de carrocería; '**bod·y stock·ing** malla *f*; '**bod·y suit** body *m*; '**bod·y·work** MOT carrocería *f*

bog·gle ['bɑːgl] *v/i*: *it* ~*s the mind!* ¡no quiero ni pensarlo!

bo·gus ['bəʊgəs] *adj* falso

boil¹ [bɔɪl] *n* (*swelling*) forúnculo

boil² [bɔɪl] **1** *v/t liquid* hervir; *egg, vegetables* cocer **2** *v/i* hervir

♦ **boil down to** *v/t* reducirse a

♦ **boil over** *v/i of milk etc* salirse

boil·er ['bɔɪlər] caldera *f*

boil·ing point ['bɔɪlɪŋ] *of liquid* punto *m* de ebullición; *reach* ~ *fig* perder la paciencia

bois·ter·ous ['bɔɪstərəs] *adj* escandaloso

bold [bəʊld] **1** *adj* valiente, audaz;

text en negrita **2** *n print* negrita *f*; *in* ~ en negrita

Bo·liv·i·a [bə'lɪvɪə] *n* Bolivia

Bo·liv·i·an [bə'lɪvɪən] **1** *adj* boliviano **2** *n* boliviano(-a) *m(f)*

bol·ster ['bəʊlstər] *v/t confidence* reforzar

bolt [bəʊlt] **1** *n on door* cerrojo *m*, pestillo *m*; *with nut* perno *m*; *of lightning* rayo *m*; *like a* ~ *from the blue* de forma inesperada **2** *adv*: ~ *upright* erguido **3** *v/t* (*fix with bolts*) atornillar; *close* cerrar con cerrojo *or* pestillo **4** *v/i* (*run off*) fugarse, escaparse

bomb [bɑːm] **1** *n* bomba *f* **2** *v/t* MIL bombardear; *of terrorist* poner una bomba en

bom·bard [bɑːm'bɑːrd] *v/t also fig* bombardear

'**bomb at·tack** atentado *m* con bomba

bomb·er ['bɑːmər] *airplane* bombardero *m*; *terrorist* terrorista *m/f* (*que pone bombas*)

'**bomb·er jack·et** cazadora *f* de aviador

'**bomb·proof** *adj* a prueba de bombas; '**bomb scare** amenaza *f* de bomba; '**bomb·shell** *fig: news* bomba *f*

bond [bɑːnd] **1** *n* (*tie*) unión *f*; FIN bono *m* **2** *v/i of glue* adherirse

bone [bəʊn] **1** *n* hueso *m*; *of fish* espina *f* **2** *v/t meat* deshuesar; *fish* quitar las espinas a

bon·fire ['bɑːnfaɪr] hoguera *f*

bon·net *Br of car* capó *m*

bo·nus ['bəʊnəs] *money* plus *m*, bonificación *f*; (*something extra*) ventaja *f* adicional; *a Christmas* ~ un plus por Navidad

boo [buː] **1** *n* abucheo *m* **2** *v/t & v/i* abuchear

boob [buːb] *n* P (*breast*) teta *f* P

boo·boo ['buːbuː] *n* F metedura *f* de pata

book [bʊk] **1** *n* libro *m*; *of matches* caja *f* (*de solapa*) **2** *v/t* (*reserve*) reservar; *of policeman* multar **3** *v/i* (*reserve*) reservar, hacer una reserva

B

'**book·case** estantería f, librería f

booked up [bʊkt'ʌp] adj lleno, completo; person ocupado

book·ie ['bʊkɪ] F corredor(a) m(f) de apuestas

book·ing ['bʊkɪŋ] (reservation) reserva f

'**book·ing clerk** taquillero(-a) m(f)

'**book·keep·er** tenedor(a) m(f) de libros

'**book·keep·ing** contabilidad f

book·let ['bʊklɪt] folleto m

'**book·mak·er** corredor(a) m(f) de apuestas

books [bʊks] npl (accounts) contabilidad f; **do the ~** llevar la contabilidad

'**book·sell·er** librero(-a) m(f); '**book·shelf** (pl -shelves) estante m; '**book·stall** puesto m de venta de libros; '**book·store** librería f; '**book to·ken** vale m para comprar libros

boom¹ [buːm] **1** n boom m **2** v/i of business desarrollarse, experimentar un boom

boom² [buːm] n noise estruendo m

boon·ies ['buːnɪz] npl F: **they live out in the ~** viven en el quinto pino F

boor [bʊr] basto m, grosero m

boor·ish ['bʊrɪʃ] adj basto, grosero

boost [buːst] **1** n to sales, economy impulso m; **your confidence needs a ~** necesitas algo que te dé más confianza **2** v/t production, prices estimular; morale levantar

boot [buːt] n bota f; Br of car maletero m, C.Am., Mex cajuela f, Rpl baúl m

♦**boot out** v/t F echar

♦**boot up** v/t & v/i COMPUT arrancar

booth [buːð] at market, fair cabina f; at exhibition puesto m, stand m; (in restaurant) mesa rodeada por bancos fijos

booze [buːz] n F bebida f, Span priva f F

bor·der ['bɔːrdər] **1** n between countries frontera f; (edge) borde m; on clothing ribete m **2** v/t country limitar con; river bordear

♦**border on** limitar con; (be almost) rayar en

'**bor·der·line** adj: **a ~ case** un caso dudoso

bore¹ [bɔːr] **1** v/t hole taladrar; **~ a hole in sth** taladrar algo

bore² [bɔːr] **1** n (person) pesado(-a) m(f), pelma m/f inv F **2** v/t aburrir

bore³ [bɔːr] pret → **bear**²

bored [bɔːrd] adj aburrido; **I'm ~** me aburro, estoy aburrido

bore·dom ['bɔːrdəm] aburrimiento m

bor·ing ['bɔːrɪŋ] adj aburrido; **be ~** ser aburrido

born [bɔːrn] adj: **be ~** nacer; **where were you ~?** ¿dónde naciste?; **be a ~ teacher** haber nacido para ser profesor

borne [bɔːrn] pp → **bear**²

bor·row ['baːroʊ] v/t tomar prestado

bos·om ['bʊzm] of woman pecho m

boss [baːs] jefe(-a) m(f)

♦**boss around** v/t dar órdenes a

boss·y ['baːsɪ] adj mandón

bo·tan·i·cal [bəˈtænɪkl] adj botánico

bo·tan·ic(·al) 'gar·dens npl jardín m botánico

bot·a·nist ['baːtənɪst] botánico(-a) m(f)

bot·a·ny ['baːtənɪ] botánica f

botch [baːtʃ] v/t arruinar, estropear

both [boʊθ] **1** adj & pron ambos, los dos; **I know ~ (of the) brothers** conozco a ambos hermanos, conozco a los dos hermanos; **~ of them** ambos, los dos **2** adv: **~ my mother and I** tanto mi madre como yo; **he's ~ handsome and intelligent** es guapo y además inteligente; **is it business or pleasure?** – ¿es de negocios o de placer? – las dos cosas

both·er ['baːðər] **1** n molestias fpl; **it's no ~** no es ninguna molestia **2** v/t (disturb) molestar; (worry) preocupar **3** v/i preocuparse; **don't ~!** (you needn't do it) ¡no te preocupes!; **you needn't have ~ed** no deberías haberte molestado

bot·tle ['baːtl] **1** n botella f; for baby

biberón *m* **2** *v/t* embotellar

◆**bottle up** *v/t* feelings reprimir, contener

'**bot·tle bank** contenedor *m* de vidrio

bot·tled wa·ter ['bɑːtld] agua *f* embotellada

'**bot·tle·neck** *n in road* embotellamiento *m*, atasco *m*; *in production* cuello *m* de botella

'**bot·tle-o·pen·er** abrebotellas *m inv*

bot·tom ['bɑːtəm] **1** *adj* inferior, de abajo **2** *n of drawer, case, pan, garden* fondo *m*; *of hill, page* pie *m*; *of pile* parte *f* inferior; (*underside*) parte *f* de abajo; *of street* final *m*; (*buttocks*) trasero *m*; **at the ~ of the screen** en la parte inferior de la pantalla

◆**bottom out** *v/i* tocar fondo

bot·tom 'line (*financial outcome*) saldo *m* final; (*real issue*) realidad *f*

bought [bɔːt] *pret & pp* → **buy**

boul·der ['bouldər] roca *f* redondeada

bounce [bauns] **1** *v/t ball* botar **2** *v/i of ball* botar, rebotar; *on sofa etc* saltar; *of rain* rebotar; *of check* ser rechazado

bounc·er ['baunsər] portero *m*, gorila *m*

bounc·y ['baunsɪ] *adj ball* que bota bien; *cushion, chair* mullido

bound[1] [baund] *adj*: **be ~ to do sth** (*obliged to*) estar obligado a hacer algo; **she's ~ to call an election soon** (*sure to*) seguro que convoca elecciones pronto

bound[2] [baund] *adj*: **be ~ for** *of ship* llevar destino a

bound[3] [baund] **1** *n* (*jump*) salto *m* **2** *v/i* saltar

bound[4] [baund] *pret & pp* → **bind**

bound·a·ry ['baundərɪ] límite *m*; *between countries* frontera *f*

bound·less ['baundlɪs] *adj* ilimitado, infinito

bou·quet [boˈkeɪ] *flowers* ramo *m*

bour·bon ['bɜːrbən] bourbon *m*

bout [baut] MED ataque *m*; *in boxing* combate *m*

bou·tique [buːˈtiːk] boutique *f*

bow[1] [bau] **1** *n as greeting* reverencia *f* **2** *v/i* saludar con la cabeza **3** *v/t head* inclinar

bow[2] [bou] (*knot*) lazo *m*; MUS, *for archery* arco *m*

bow[3] [bau] *of ship* proa *f*

bow·els ['bauəlz] *npl* entrañas *fpl*

bowl[1] [boul] *for rice, cereals etc* cuenco *m*; *for soup* plato *m* sopero; *for salad* ensaladera *f*; *for washing* barreño *m*, palangana *f*

bowl[2] [boul] **1** *n* (*ball*) bola *f* **2** *v/i in bowling* lanzar la bola

◆**bowl over** *v/t fig* (*astonish*) impresionar, maravillar

bowl·ing ['boulɪŋ] bolos *mpl*

'**bowl·ing al·ley** bolera *f*

bow 'tie [bou] pajarita *f*

box[1] [bɑːks] *n container* caja *f*; *on form* casilla *f*

box[2] [bɑːks] *v/i* boxear

box·er ['bɑːksər] boxeador(a) *m(f)*

'**box·er shorts** *npl* calzoncillos *mpl*, boxers *mpl*

box·ing ['bɑːksɪŋ] boxeo *m*

'**box·ing glove** guante *m* de boxeo; '**box·ing match** combate *m* de boxeo; '**box·ing ring** cuadrilátero *m*, ring *m*

'**box num·ber** *at post office* apartado *m* de correos

'**box of·fice** taquilla *f*, *L.Am.* boletería *f*

boy [bɔɪ] niño *m*, chico *m*; (*son*) hijo *m*

boy·cott ['bɔɪkɑːt] **1** *n* boicot *m* **2** *v/t* boicotear

'**boy·friend** novio *m*

boy·ish ['bɔɪɪʃ] *adj* varonil

boy'scout boy scout *m*

bra [brɑː] sujetador *m*, sostén *m*

brace [breɪs] *on teeth* aparato *m*

brace·let ['breɪslɪt] pulsera *f*

brack·et ['brækɪt] *for shelf* escuadra *f*; (*square*) ~ *in text* corchete *m*

brag [bræg] *v/i* (*pret & pp* **-ged**) presumir, fanfarronear

braid [breɪd] *n in hair* trenza *f*; *trimming* trenzado *m*

braille [breɪl] braille *m*

brain [breɪn] cerebro *m*; **use your ~**

utiliza la cabeza

'**brain dead** *adj* MED clínicamente muerto

brain·less ['breɪnlɪs] *adj* F estúpido

brains [breɪnz] *npl* (*intelligence*) inteligencia *f*; **the ~ of the operation** el cerebro de la operación

'**brain·storm** idea *f* genial; **brain·storm·ing** ['breɪnstɔːrmɪŋ] tormenta *f* de ideas; '**brain sur·geon** neurocirujano(-a) *m(f)*; '**brain sur·ger·y** neurocirugía *f*; '**brain tu·mor**, *Br* '**brain tu·mour** tumor *m* cerebral; '**brain·wash** *v/t* lavar el cerebro a; '**brain·wave** (*brilliant idea*) idea *f* genial

brain·y ['breɪnɪ] *adj* F: **be ~** tener mucho coco F, ser una lumbrera

brake [breɪk] **1** *n* freno *m* **2** *v/i* frenar

'**brake flu·id** MOT líquido *m* de frenos; '**brake light** MOT luz *f* de frenado; '**brake ped·al** MOT pedal *m* del freno

branch [bræntʃ] *n* of tree rama *f*; of bank, company sucursal *f*

♦ **branch off** *v/i* of road bifurcarse

♦ **branch out** *v/i* diversificarse; **they've branched out into furniture** han empezado a trabajar también con muebles

brand [brænd] **1** *n* marca *f* **2** *v/t*: **be ~ed a liar** ser tildado de mentiroso

brand 'im·age imagen *f* de marca

bran·dish ['brændɪʃ] *v/t* blandir

brand 'lead·er marca *f* líder del mercado; **brand 'loy·al·ty** lealtad *f* a una marca; '**brand name** nombre *m* comercial; **brand-'new** *adj* nuevo, flamante

bran·dy ['brændɪ] brandy *m*, coñac *m*

brass [bræs] *alloy* latón *m*; **the ~** MUS los metales

brass 'band banda *f* de música

bras·sière [brə'zɪr] sujetador *m*, sostén *m*

brat [bræt] *pej* niñato(-a) *m(f)*

bra·va·do [brə'vɑːdoʊ] bravuconería *f*

brave [breɪv] *adj* valiente, valeroso

brave·ly ['breɪvlɪ] *adv* valientemente, valerosamente

brav·er·y ['breɪvərɪ] valentía *f*, valor *m*

brawl [brɔːl] **1** *n* pelea *f* **2** *v/i* pelearse

brawn·y ['brɔːnɪ] *adj* fuerte, musculoso

Bra·zil [brə'zɪl] Brasil

Bra·zil·ian [brə'zɪlɪən] **1** *adj* brasileño **2** *n* brasileño(-a) *m(f)*

breach [briːtʃ] *n* (*violation*) infracción *f*, incumplimiento *m*; *in party* ruptura *f*

breach of 'con·tract LAW incumplimiento *m* de contrato

bread [bred] *n* pan *m*

'**bread·crumbs** *npl for cooking* pan *m* rallado; *for birds* migas *fpl*

'**bread knife** cuchillo *m* del pan

breadth [bredθ] *of road* ancho *m*; *of knowledge* amplitud *f*

'**bread·win·ner**: **be the ~** ser el que gana el pan

break [breɪk] **1** *n* *in bone etc* fractura *f*, rotura *f*; (*rest*) descanso *m*; *in relationship* separación *f* temporal; **give s.o. a ~** F (*opportunity*) ofrecer una oportunidad a alguien; **take a ~** descansar; **without a ~** *travel* sin descanso **2** *v/t* (*pret* **broke**, *pp* **broken**) *device* romper, estropear; *stick* romper, partir; *arm, leg* fracturar; *glass, egg* romper; *rules, law* violar, incumplir; *promise* romper; *news* dar; *record* batir **3** *v/i* (*pret* **broke**, *pp* **broken**) *of device* romperse, estropearse; *of glass, egg* romperse; *of stick* partirse, romperse; *of news* saltar; *of storm* estallar, comenzar; *of boy's voice* cambiar

♦ **break away** *v/i* (*escape*) escaparse; *from family* separarse; *from organization* escindirse; *from tradition* romper (**from** con)

♦ **break down** **1** *v/i* *of vehicle* averiarse, estropearse; *of machine* estropearse; *of talks* romperse; *in tears* romper a llorar; *mentally* venirse abajo **2** *v/t door* derribar; *figures* detallar, desglosar

♦ **break even** *v/i* COM cubrir gastos

♦ **break in** *v/i* (*interrupt*) interrumpir;

of burglar entrar

♦**break off 1** v/t partir; *relationship* romper; *they've broken it off* han roto **2** v/i (*stop talking*) interrumpirse

♦**break out** v/i (*start up*) comenzar; *of fighting* estallar; *of disease* desatarse; *of prisoners* escaparse, darse a la fuga; *he broke out in a rash* le salió un sarpullido

♦**break up 1** v/t *into component parts* descomponer; *fight* poner fin a **2** v/i *of ice* romperse; *of couple* terminar, separarse; *of band* separarse; *of meeting* terminar

break·a·ble ['breɪkəbl] adj rompible, frágil

break·age ['breɪkɪdʒ] rotura f

'**break·down** *of vehicle, machine* avería f; *of talks* ruptura f; (*nervous ~*) crisis f inv nerviosa; *of figures* desglose m

break-'e·ven point punto m de equilibrio

'**break·fast** ['brekfəst] n desayuno m; *have ~* desayunar

'**break·fast tel·e·vi·sion** televisión f matinal

'**break-in** entrada f (*mediante la fuerza*); *robbery* robo m; *we've had a ~* han entrado a robar; '**break·through** *in plan, negotiations* paso m adelante; *of science, technology* avance m; '**break·up** *of marriage, partnership* ruptura f, separación f

breast [brest] *of woman* pecho m

'**breast·feed** v/t (*pret & pp breastfed*) amamantar

'**breast·stroke** braza f

breath [breθ] respiración f; *get your ~ back* recobrar el aliento; *be out of ~* estar sin respiración; *take a deep ~* respira hondo

Breath·a·lyz·er® ['breθəlaɪzər] alcoholímetro m

breathe [briːð] **1** v/i respirar **2** v/t (*inhale*) aspirar, respirar; (*exhale*) exhalar, espirar

♦**breathe in** v/t & v/i aspirar, inspirar

♦**breathe out** v/i espirar

breath·ing ['briːðɪŋ] n respiración f

breath·less ['breθlɪs] adj: *arrive ~* llegar sin respiración, llegar jadeando

breath·less·ness ['breθlɪsnɪs] dificultad f para respirar

breath·tak·ing ['breθteɪkɪŋ] adj impresionante, sorprendente

bred [bred] pret & pp → **breed**

breed [briːd] **1** n raza f **2** v/t (pret & pp **bred**) criar; *plants* cultivar; *fig* causar, generar **3** v/i (pret & pp **bred**) *of animals* reproducirse

breed·er ['briːdər] *of animals* criador(a) m(f); *of plants* cultivador(a) m(f)

breed·ing ['briːdɪŋ] *of animals* cría f; *of plants* cultivo m; *of person* educación f

breed·ing ground fig caldo m de cultivo

breeze [briːz] brisa f

breez·i·ly ['briːzɪlɪ] adv fig jovialmente, tranquilamente

breez·y ['briːzɪ] adj ventoso; fig jovial, tranquilo

brew [bruː] **1** v/t *beer* elaborar; *tea* preparar, hacer **2** v/i *of storm* avecinarse; *of trouble* fraguarse

brew·er ['bruːər] fabricante m/f de cerveza

brew·er·y ['bruːərɪ] fábrica f de cerveza

bribe [braɪb] **1** n soborno m, Mex mordida f, S.Am. coima f **2** v/t sobornar

brib·er·y ['braɪbərɪ] soborno m, Mex mordida f, S.Am. coima f

brick [brɪk] ladrillo m

'**brick·lay·er** albañil m/f

brid·al suite ['braɪdl] suite f nupcial

bride [braɪd] novia f (*en boda*)

'**bride·groom** novio m (*en boda*)

'**brides·maid** dama f de honor

bridge¹ [brɪdʒ] n *also* NAUT puente m; *of nose* caballete m **2** v/t *gap* superar, salvar

bridge² [brɪdʒ] *card game* bridge m

bri·dle ['braɪdl] n brida f

brief¹ ['briːf] adj breve, corto

brief² [briːf] **1** n (*mission*) misión f **2** v/t: *~ s.o. on sth* informar a al-

B

guien de algo

'brief·case maletín m

brief·ing ['briːfɪŋ] reunión f informativa

brief·ly ['briːflɪ] adv (for a short period of time) brevemente; (in a few words) en pocas palabras; (to sum up) en resumen

briefs [briːfs] npl for women bragas fpl; for men calzoncillos mpl

bright [braɪt] adj color vivo; smile radiante; future brillante, prometedor; (sunny) soleado, luminoso; (intelligent) inteligente

♦bright·en up ['braɪtn] 1 v/t alegrar 2 v/i of weather aclararse; of face, person alegrarse, animarse

bright·ly ['braɪtlɪ] adv shine intensamente, fuerte; smile alegremente

bright·ness ['braɪtnɪs] of light brillo m; of weather luminosidad f; of smile alegría f; (intelligence) inteligencia f

bril·liance ['brɪljəns] of person genialidad f; of color resplandor m

bril·liant ['brɪljənt] adj sunshine etc resplandeciente, radiante; (very good) genial; (very intelligent) brillante

brim [brɪm] of container borde m; of hat ala f

brim·ful ['brɪmfəl] adj rebosante

bring [brɪŋ] v/t (pret & pp brought) traer; ~ it here, will you tráelo aquí, por favor; can I ~ a friend? ¿puedo traer a un amigo?, ¿puedo venir con un amigo?

♦bring about v/t ocasionar; bring about peace traer la paz

♦bring around v/t from a faint hacer volver en sí; (persuade) convencer, persuadir

♦bring back v/t (return) devolver; (re-introduce) reinstaurar; memories traer

♦bring down v/t fence, tree tirar, echar abajo; government derrocar; bird, airplane derribar; rates, inflation, price reducir

♦bring in v/t interest, income generar; legislation introducir; verdict pronunciar

♦bring on v/t illness provocar

♦bring out v/t book, video, new product sacar

♦bring to v/t from a faint hacer volver en sí

♦bring up v/t child criar, educar; subject mencionar, sacar a colación; (vomit) vomitar

brink [brɪŋk] borde m; be on the ~ of (doing) sth fig estar a punto de (hacer) algo

brisk [brɪsk] adj person, voice enérgico; walk rápido; trade animado

bris·tle ['brɪsl] v/i: the streets are bristling with policemen las calles están atestadas de policías

brist·les ['brɪslz] npl on chin pelos mpl; of brush cerdas fpl

Brit [brɪt] F británico(-a) m(f)

Brit·ain ['brɪtn] Gran Bretaña

Brit·ish ['brɪtɪʃ] 1 adj británico 2 npl: the ~ los británicos

Brit·on ['brɪtn] británico(-a) m(f)

brit·tle ['brɪtl] adj frágil, quebradizo

broach [brəʊtʃ] v/t subject sacar a colación

broad [brɔːd] 1 adj ancho; smile amplio; (general) general; in ~ daylight a plena luz del día 2 n F (woman) tía f F

'broad·cast 1 n emisión f; a live ~ una retransmisión en directo 2 v/t emitir, retransmitir

'broad·cast·er presentador(a) m(f)

'broad·cast·ing televisión f

broad·en ['brɔːdn] 1 v/i ensancharse, ampliarse 2 v/t ensanchar; ~ one's horizons ampliar los horizontes

'broad·jump salto m de longitud

broad·ly ['brɔːdlɪ] adv en general; ~ speaking en términos generales

broad·mind·ed [brɔːd'maɪndɪd] adj tolerante, abierto

broad·mind·ed·ness [brɔːd'maɪndɪdnɪs] mentalidad f abierta

broc·co·li ['brɑːkəlɪ] brécol m, brócoli m

bro·chure ['brəʊʃər] folleto m

broil [brɔɪl] v/t asar a la parrilla

broil·er ['brɔɪlər] on stove parrilla f;

chicken pollo *m* (para asar)

broke [broʊk] **1** *adj* F: **be ~** *temporarily* estar sin blanca F; *long term* estar arruinado; **go ~** (*go bankrupt*) arruinarse **2** *pret* → **break**

bro·ken ['broʊkn] **1** *adj* roto; *home* deshecho; **they talk in ~ English** chapurrean el inglés **2** *pp* → **break**

bro·ken-heart·ed [broʊkn'hɑːrtɪd] *adj* desconsolado, destrozado

bro·ker ['broʊkər] corredor(a) *m(f)*, agente *m/f*

bron·chi·tis [brɑːŋ'kaɪtɪs] bronquitis *f*

bronze [brɑːnz] *n* bronce *m*

'**bronze med·al** medalla *f* de bronce

brooch [broʊtʃ] broche *m*

brood [bruːd] *v/i of person* darle vueltas a las cosas; **~ about sth** darle vueltas a algo

broom [bruːm] escoba *f*

broth [brɑːθ] *soup* sopa *f*; *stock* caldo *m*

broth·el ['brɑːθl] burdel *m*

broth·er ['brʌðər] hermano *m*

'**broth·er-in-law** (*pl* **brothers-in-law**) cuñado *m*

broth·er·ly ['brʌðərlɪ] *adj* fraternal

brought [brɔːt] *pret & pp* → **bring**

brow [braʊ] (*forehead*) frente *f*; *of hill* cima *f*

brown [braʊn] **1** *n* marrón *m*, *L.Am.* color *m* café **2** *adj* marrón; *eyes, hair* castaño; (*tanned*) moreno **3** *v/t in cooking* dorar **4** *v/i in cooking* dorarse

'**brown·bag** *v/t* (*pret & pp* **-ged**) F: **~ it** llevar la comida al trabajo

Brown·ie ['braʊnɪ] escultista *f*

'**Brown·ie points** *npl* tantos *mpl*; **earn ~** anotarse tantos

brown·ie ['braʊnɪ] (*cake*) pastel *m* de chocolate y nueces

'**brown-nose** *v/t* P lamer el culo a P; **brown 'pa·per** papel *m* de estraza; **brown pa·per 'bag** bolsa *f* de cartón; **brown 'sug·ar** azúcar *m or f* moreno(-a)

browse [braʊz] **1** *v/i in store* echar una ojeada; **~ through a book** hojear un libro **2** *v/t the Web* navegar por

brows·er ['braʊzər] COMPUT navegador *m*

bruise [bruːz] **1** *n* magulladura *f*, cardenal *f*; *on fruit* maca *f* **2** *v/t arm, fruit* magullar; (*emotionally*) herir **3** *v/i of person* hacerse cardenales; *of fruit* macarse

bruis·ing ['bruːzɪŋ] *adj fig* doloroso

brunch [brʌntʃ] combinación *f* de desayuno y almuerzo

bru·nette [bruː'net] *n* morena *f*

brunt [brʌnt]: **this area bore the ~ of the flooding** esta zona fue la más castigada por la inundación; **we bore the ~ of the layoffs** fuimos los más perjudicados por los despidos

brush [brʌʃ] **1** *n* cepillo *m*; *conflict* roce *m* **2** *v/t cepillar*; (*touch lightly*) rozar; (*move away*) quitar

♦**brush against** *v/t* rozar

♦**brush aside** *v/t* hacer caso omiso a, no hacer caso a

♦**brush off** *v/t* sacudir; *criticism* no hacer caso a

♦**brush up** *v/t* repasar

'**brush·work** PAINT pincelada *f*

brusque [brʊsk] *adj* brusco

Brus·sels ['brʌslz] Bruselas

Brus·sels 'sprouts *npl* coles *fpl* de Bruselas

bru·tal ['bruːtl] *adj* brutal

bru·tal·i·ty [bruː'tælətɪ] brutalidad *f*

bru·tal·ly ['bruːtəlɪ] *adv* brutalmente; **be ~ frank** ser de una sinceridad aplastante

brute [bruːt] bestia *m/f*

brute 'force fuerza *f* bruta

bub·ble ['bʌbl] *n* burbuja *f*

'**bub·ble bath** baño *m* de espuma; '**bub·ble gum** chicle *m*; '**bub·ble wrap** *n* plástico *m* para embalar (*con burbujas*)

bub·bly ['bʌblɪ] *n* F (*champagne*) champán *m*

buck[1] [bʌk] *n* F (*dollar*) dólar *m*

buck[2] [bʌk] *v/i of horse* corcovear

buck[3] [bʌk] *n*: **pass the ~** escurrir el bulto

buck·et ['bʌkɪt] *n* cubo *m*

buck·le[1] ['bʌkl] **1** *n* hebilla *f* **2** *v/t belt* abrochar

buck·le² ['bʌkl] v/i of metal combarse

♦ **buckle down** v/i ponerse a trabajar

bud [bʌd] n BOT capullo m, brote m

bud·dy ['bʌdɪ] F amigo(-a) m(f), Span colega m/f F; form of address Span colega m/f F, L.Am. compadre m/f F

budge [bʌdʒ] **1** v/t mover; (make reconsider) hacer cambiar de opinión **2** v/i moverse; (change one's mind) cambiar de opinión

bud·ger·i·gar ['bʌdʒərɪɡɑːr] periquito m

bud·get ['bʌdʒɪt] **1** n presupuesto m; **be on a ~** tener un presupuesto limitado **2** v/i administrarse

♦ **budget for** v/t contemplar en el presupuesto

bud·gie ['bʌdʒɪ] F periquito m

buff¹ [bʌf] adj color marrón claro

buff² [bʌf] n aficionado(-a) m(f); **a movie ~** un cinéfilo

buf·fa·lo ['bʌfələu] búfalo m

buff·er ['bʌfər] RAIL tope m; COMPUT búfer m; fig barrera f

buf·fet¹ ['bʌfɪt] n (meal) bufé m

buf·fet² ['bʌfɪt] v/t of wind sacudir

bug [bʌɡ] **1** n insect bicho m; virus virus m inv; (spying device) micrófono m oculto; COMPUT error m **2** v/t (pret & pp **-ged**) room colocar un micrófono en; F (annoy) fastidiar F, jorobar F

bug·gy ['bʌɡɪ] for baby silla f de paseo

bu·gle [bjuːɡl] corneta f, clarín m

build [bɪld] **1** n of person constitución f, complexión f **2** v/t (pret & pp **built**) construir, edificar

♦ **build up 1** v/t strength aumentar; relationship fortalecer; collection acumular **2** v/i of dirt acumularse; of pressure, excitement aumentar

build·er ['bɪldər] albañil m/f; company constructora f

build·ing ['bɪldɪŋ] edificio m; activity construcción f

build·ing blocks npl for child piezas fpl de construcción; **build·ing site**

obra f; **build·ing so·ci·e·ty** Br caja f de ahorros; **build·ing trade** industria f de la construcción

build-up (accumulation) accumulación f; **after all the ~** publicity después de tantas expectativas

built [bɪlt] pret & pp → **build**

built-in ['bɪltɪn] adj cupboard empotrado; flash incorporado

built-up 'ar·e·a zona f urbanizada

bulb [bʌlb] BOT bulbo m; (light ~) bombilla f, L.Am. foco m

bulge [bʌldʒ] **1** n bulto m, abultamiento m **2** v/i of eyes salirse de las órbitas; of wall abombarse

bu·lim·i·a [buˈlɪmɪə] bulimia f

bulk [bʌlk]: **the ~ of** el grueso or la mayor parte de; **in ~** a granel

bulk·y ['bʌlkɪ] adj voluminoso

bull [bul] animal toro m

bull·doze ['buldəuz] v/t (demolish) demoler, derribar; **~ s.o. into sth** fig obligar a alguien a hacer algo

bull·doz·er ['buldəuzər] bulldozer m

bul·let ['bulɪt] bala f

bul·le·tin ['bulɪtɪn] boletín m

bul·le·tin board on wall tablón m de anuncios; COMPUT tablón m de anuncios, BBS f

bul·let-proof adj antibalas inv

bull fight corrida f de toros; **bull fight·er** torero(-a) m(f); **bull fight·ing** tauromaquia f, los toros; **bull mar·ket** FIN mercado m al alza; **bull ring** plaza f de toros; **bull's-eye** diana f, blanco m; **hit the ~** dar en el blanco; **bull·shit 1** n V Span gilipollez f V, L.Am. pendejada f V **2** v/i (pret & pp **-ted**) V decir Span gilipolleces V or L.Am. pendejadas V

bul·ly ['bulɪ] **1** n matón(-ona) m(f); child abusón(-ona) m(f) **2** v/t (pret & pp **-ied**) intimidar

bul·ly·ing ['bulɪɪŋ] n intimidación f

bum [bʌm] F **1** n (tramp) vagabundo(-a) m(f); (worthless person) inútil m/f **2** adj (useless) inútil **3** v/t (pret & pp **-med**) cigarette etc gorronear

♦ **bum around** v/i F travel vaga-

bundear (*in* por); (*be lazy*) vaguear
bum·ble·bee ['bʌmblbiː] abejorro *m*
bump [bʌmp] **1** *n* (*swelling*) chichón *m*; *on road* bache *m*; **get a ~ on the head** darse un golpe en la cabeza **2** *v/t* golpear
♦ **bump into** *v/t table* chocar con; (*meet*) encontrarse con
♦ **bump off** *v/t* F (*murder*) cargarse a F
♦ **bump up** *v/t* F *prices* aumentar
bump·er ['bʌmpər] **1** *n* MOT parachoques *m inv*; **the traffic was ~ to ~** el tráfico estaba colapsado **2** *adj* (*extremely good*) excepcional, extraordinario
'**bump-start** *v/t car* arrancar un coche empujándolo; *fig: economy* reanimar
bump·y ['bʌmpɪ] *adj* con baches; *flight* movido
bun [bʌn] *hairstyle* moño *m*; *for eating* bollo *m*
bunch [bʌntʃ] *of people* grupo *m*; *of keys* manojo *m*; *of flowers* ramo *m*; *of grapes* racimo *m*; **thanks a ~** *iron* no sabes lo que te lo agradezco
bun·dle ['bʌndl] *of clothes* fardo *m*; *of wood* haz *m*
♦ **bundle up** *v/t* liar; (*dress warmly*) abrigar
bun·gee jump·ing ['bʌndʒɪdʒʌmpɪŋ] puenting *m*
bun·gle ['bʌŋgl] *v/t* echar a perder
bunk [bʌŋk] litera *f*
bunk beds *npl* literas *fpl*
buoy [bɔɪ] *n* NAUT boya *f*
buoy·ant ['bɔɪənt] *adj* animado, optimista; *economy* boyante
bur·den ['bɜːrdn] **1** *n also fig* carga *f* **2** *v/t*: **~ s.o. with sth** *fig* cargar a alguien con algo
bu·reau ['bjʊrou] (*chest of drawers*) cómoda *f*; (*office*) departamento *m*, oficina *f*; *a translation ~* una agencia de traducción
bu·reauc·ra·cy [bjʊˈrɑːkrəsɪ] burocracia *f*
bu·reau·crat ['bjʊrəkræt] burócrata *m/f*
bu·reau·crat·ic [bjʊrəˈkrætɪk] *adj*

burocrático
burg·er ['bɜːrgər] hamburguesa *f*
bur·glar ['bɜːrglər] ladrón(-ona) *m(f)*
'**bur·glar a·larm** alarma *f* antirrobo
bur·glar·ize ['bɜːrglərɑɪz] *v/t* robar
bur·glar·y ['bɜːrglərɪ] robo *m*
bur·i·al ['berɪəl] entierro *m*
bur·ly ['bɜːrlɪ] *adj* corpulento, fornido
burn [bɜːrn] **1** *n* quemadura *f* **2** *v/t* (*pret & pp* **burnt**) quemar; **be ~t to death** morir abrasado **3** *v/i* (*pret & pp* **burnt**) *of wood, meat, in sun* quemarse
♦ **burn down 1** *v/t* incendiar **2** *v/i* incendiarse
♦ **burn out** *v/t*: **burn o.s. out** quemarse; *a burned-out car* un coche carbonizado
burn·er ['bɜːrnər] *on cooker* placa *f*
'**burn·out** F (*exhaustion*) agotamiento *m*
burnt [bɜːrnt] *pret & pp* → **burn**
burp [bɜːrp] **1** *n* eructo *m* **2** *v/i* eructar **3** *v/t baby* hacer eructar a
burst [bɜːrst] **1** *n in water pipe* rotura *f*; *of gunfire* ráfaga *f*; *in a ~ of energy* en un arrebato de energía **2** *adj tire* reventado **3** *v/t* (*pret & pp* **burst**) *balloon* reventar **4** *v/i* (*pret & pp* **burst**) *of balloon, tire* reventar; **~ into a room** irrumpir en una habitación; **~ into tears** echarse a llorar; **~ out laughing** echarse a reír
bur·y ['berɪ] *v/t* (*pret & pp* **-ied**) enterrar; **be buried under** (*covered by*) estar sepultado por; **~ o.s. in work** meterse de lleno en el trabajo
bus [bʌs] **1** *n local* autobús *m*, *Mex* camión *m*, *Arg* colectivo *m*, *C.Am.* guagua *f*; *long distance* autobús *m*, *Span* autocar *m*; *school ~* autobús *m* escolar **2** *v/t* (*pret & pp* **-sed**) llevar en autobús
'**bus·boy** ayudante *m* de camarero
'**bus driv·er** conductor(a) *m(f)* de autobús
bush [bʊʃ] *plant* arbusto *m*; *type of countryside* monte *m*

B

bushed [buʃt] *adj* F (*tired*) molido F

bush·y ['buʃɪ] *adj beard* espeso

busi·ness ['bɪznɪs] negocios *mpl*; (*company*) empresa *f*; (*sector*) sector *m*; (*affair, matter*) asunto *m*; *as subject of study* empresariales *fpl*; **on ~** de negocios; *that's none of your ~!* ¡no es asunto tuyo!; *mind your own ~!* ¡no te metas en lo que no te importa!

'**busi·ness card** tarjeta *f* de visita; '**busi·ness class** clase *f* ejecutiva; '**busi·ness hours** *npl* horario *m* de oficina; **busi·ness·like** ['bɪznɪslaɪk] *adj* eficiente; '**busi·ness lunch** almuerzo *m* de negocios; '**busi·ness·man** hombre *m* de negocios, ejecutivo *m*; '**busi·ness meet·ing** reunión *f* de negocios; '**busi·ness school** escuela *f* de negocios; '**busi·ness stud·ies** *nsg course* empresariales *mpl*; '**busi·ness trip** viaje *m* de negocios; '**busi·ness·wom·an** mujer *f* de negocios, ejecutiva *f*

'**bus lane** carril *m* bus; '**bus shel·ter** marquesina *f*; '**bus sta·tion** estación *f* de autobuses; '**bus stop** parada *f* de autobús

bust¹ [bʌst] *n of woman* busto *m*

bust² [bʌst] **1** *adj* F (*broken*) escacharrado F; **go ~** quebrar **2** *v/t* F escacharrar F

'**bus tick·et** billete *m or L.Am.* boleto *m* de autobús

◆ **bus·tle around** ['bʌsl] *v/i* trajinar

'**bust-up** F corte *m* F

bust·y ['bʌstɪ] *adj* pechugona

bus·y ['bɪzɪ] **1** *adj also* TELEC ocupado; *full of people* abarrotado; *of restaurant etc*: *making money* ajetreado; *the line was ~* estaba ocupado, *Span* comunicaba; *she leads a very ~ life* lleva una vida muy ajetreada; *be ~ doing sth* estar ocupado *or* atareado haciendo algo **2** *v/t* (*pret & pp -ied*): *~ o.s. with sth* entretenerse con algo

'**bus·y·bod·y** metomentodo *m/f*, entrometido(-a) *m(f)*

'**bus·y sig·nal** señal *f* de ocupado *or Span* comunicando

but [bʌt] *unstressed* [bət] **1** *conj* pero; *it's not me ~ my father you want* no me quieres a mí sino a mi padre; *~ then* (*again*) pero **2** *prep*: *all ~ him* todos excepto él; *the last ~ one* el penúltimo; *the next ~ one* el próximo no, el otro; *the next page ~ one* la página siguiente a la próxima; *~ for you* si no hubiera sido por ti; *nothing ~ the best* sólo lo mejor

butch·er ['butʃər] carnicero(-a) *m(f)*; *murderer* asesino(-a) *m(f)*

butt [bʌt] **1** *n of cigarette* colilla *f*; *of joke* blanco *m*; F (*buttocks*) trasero *m* F **2** *v/t* dar un cabezazo a; *of goat, bull* embestir

◆ **butt in** *v/i* inmiscuirse, entrometerse

but·ter ['bʌtər] **1** *n* mantequilla *f* **2** *v/t* untar de mantequilla

◆ **butter up** *v/t* F hacer la pelota a F

'**but·ter·fly** *insect* mariposa *f*

but·tocks ['bʌtəks] *npl* nalgas *fpl*

but·ton ['bʌtn] **1** *n on shirt, machine* botón *m*; (*badge*) chapa *f* **2** *v/t* abotonar

◆ **button up** *v/t* abotonar

'**but·ton·hole 1** *n in suit* ojal *m* **2** *v/t* acorralar

bux·om ['bʌksəm] *adj* de amplios senos

buy [baɪ] **1** *n* compra *f*, adquisición *f* **2** *v/t* (*pret & pp bought*) comprar; *can I ~ you a drink?* ¿quieres tomar algo?; *$5 doesn't ~ much* con 5 dólares no se puede hacer gran cosa

◆ **buy off** *v/t* (*bribe*) sobornar

◆ **buy out** *v/t* COM comprar la parte de

◆ **buy up** *v/t* acaparar

buy·er ['baɪr] comprador(a) *m(f)*

buzz [bʌz] **1** *n* zumbido *m*; *she gets a real ~ out of it* F (*thrill*) le vuelve loca, le entusiasma **2** *v/i of insect* zumbar; *with buzzer* llamar por el interfono **3** *v/t with buzzer* llamar por el interfono a

◆ **buzz off** *v/i* F largarse F, *Span* pirarse F

buz·zard ['bʌzərd] ratonero *m*
buzz·er ['bʌzər] timbre *m*
'buzz·word palabra *f* de moda
by [baɪ] **1** *prep to show agent* por;
(*near, next to*) al lado de, junto a; (*no
later than*) no más tarde de; *mode of
transport* en; *she rushed ~ me* pasó
rápidamente por mi lado; *as we
drove ~ the church* cuando pasábamos por la iglesia; *side ~ side*
uno junto al otro; *~ day / night* de
día/noche; *~ bus / train* en autobús/tren; *~ the dozen* por docenas;
~ the hour / ton por hora / por tonelada; *~ my watch* en mi reloj; *~
nature* por naturaleza; *a play ~ ...*
una obra de ...; *~ o.s. without
company* solo; *I did it ~ myself* lo

hice yo solito; *~ a couple of
minutes* por un par de minutos; **2 ~
4** *measurement* 2 por 4; *~ this time
tomorrow* mañana a esta hora; *~
this time next year* el año que viene por estas fechas; *go ~, pass ~*
pasar **2** *adv*: *~ and ~* (*soon*) dentro
de poco
bye(-bye) [baɪ] adiós
by·gones ['baɪgɑːnz]: *let ~ be ~* lo
pasado, pasado está; **'by·pass 1** *n
road* circunvalación *f*; MED bypass
m **2** *v/t* sortear; **'by·prod·uct**
subproducto *m*; **by·stand·er**
['baɪstændər] transeúnte *m/f*
byte [baɪt] byte *m*
'by·word: *be a ~ for sth* ser sinónimo de algo

C

cab [kæb] (*taxi*) taxi *m*; *of truck* cabina *f*
cab·a·ret ['kæbəreɪ] cabaret *m*
cab·bage ['kæbɪdʒ] col *f*, repollo *m*
'cab driv·er taxista *m/f*
cab·in ['kæbɪn] *of plane* cabina *f*; *of
ship* camarote *m*
'cab·in at·tend·ant auxiliar *m/f* de
vuelo
'cab·in crew personal *m* de a bordo
cab·i·net ['kæbɪnɪt] armario *m*; POL
gabinete *m*; *drinks ~* mueble *m* bar;
medicine ~ botiquín *m*; *display ~*
vitrina *f*
'cab·i·net mak·er ebanista *m/f*
ca·ble ['keɪbl] cable *m*; *~ (TV)* televisión *f* por cable
'ca·ble car teleférico *m*
'ca·ble tel·e·vi·sion televisión *f* por
cable
'cab stand parada *f* de taxis
cac·tus ['kæktəs] cactus *m inv*
CAD [kæd] *abbr* (= *computer
assisted design*) CAD *m* (= dise-

ño asistido por *Span* ordenador *or
L.Am.* computadora)
ca·dav·er [kə'dævər] cadáver *m*
cad·die ['kædɪ] **1** *n in golf* caddie *m/f*
2 *v/i* hacer de caddie
ca·det [kə'det] cadete *m*
cadge [kædʒ] *v/t* F: *~ sth from s.o.*
gorronear algo a alguien
Cae·sar·e·an *Br* → *Cesarean*
caf·é ['kæfeɪ] café *m*, cafetería *f*
caf·e·te·ri·a [kæfɪ'tɪrɪə] cafetería *f*,
cantina *f*
caf·feine ['kæfiːn] cafeína *f*
cage [keɪdʒ] jaula *f*
ca·gey ['keɪdʒɪ] *adj* cauteloso, reservado; *he's ~ about how old he is*
es muy reservado con respecto a su
edad
ca·hoots [kə'huːts] *npl* F: *be in ~
with s.o.* estar conchabado con
alguien
ca·jole [kə'dʒoʊl] *v/t* engatusar, persuadir
cake [keɪk] **1** *n big* tarta *f*; *small* pas-

tel *m*; **be a piece of ~** F estar chupado F **2** v/i endurecerse

ca·lam·i·ty [kəˈlæmətɪ] calamidad *f*

cal·ci·um [ˈkælsɪəm] calcio *m*

cal·cu·late [ˈkælkjʊleɪt] v/t calcular

cal·cu·lat·ing [ˈkælkjʊleɪtɪŋ] *adj* calculador

cal·cu·la·tion [kælkjʊˈleɪʃn] cálculo *m*

cal·cu·la·tor [ˈkælkjʊleɪtər] calculadora *f*

cal·en·dar [ˈkælɪndər] calendario *m*

calf¹ [kæf] (*pl* **calves** [kævz]) (*young cow*) ternero(-a) *m(f)*, becerro(-a) *m(f)*

calf² [kæf] (*pl* **calves** [kævz]) *of leg* pantorrilla *f*

'calf·skin *n* piel *f* de becerro

cal·i·ber, *Br* **cal·i·bre** [ˈkælɪbər] *of gun* calibre *m*; **a man of his ~** un hombre de su calibre

Cal·i·for·ni·an [kælɪˈfɔːnɪən] **1** *adj* californiano **2** *n* californiano(-a) *m(f)*

call [kɔːl] **1** *n* llamada *f*, (*demand*) llamamiento *m*; **there's a ~ for you** tienes una llamada, te llaman; **I'll give you a ~ tomorrow** te llamaré mañana; **make a ~** hacer una llamada; **a ~ for help** una llamada de socorro; **be on ~** estar de guardia **2** v/t *also* TELEC llamar; *meeting* convocar; **he ~ed him a liar** le llamó mentiroso; **what have they ~ed the baby?** ¿qué nombre le han puesto al bebé?; **but we ~ him Tom** pero le llamamos Tom; **~ s.o. names** insultar a alguien; **I ~ed his name** lo llamé **3** v/i *also* TELEC llamar; (*visit*) pasarse; **can I tell him who's ~ing?** ¿quién le llama?; **~ for help** pedir ayuda a gritos

♦ **call at** v/t (*stop at*) pasarse por; *of train* hacer parada en

♦ **call back 1** v/t (*phone again*) volver a llamar; (*return call*) devolver la llamada; (*summon*) hacer volver **2** v/i *on phone* volver a llamar; (*make another visit*) volver a pasar

♦ **call for** v/t (*collect*) pasar a recoger; (*demand*) pedir, exigir; (*require*) re-

querir

♦ **call in 1** v/t (*summon*) llamar **2** v/i (*phone*) llamar

♦ **call off** v/t (*cancel*) cancelar; *strike* desconvocar

♦ **call on** v/t (*urge*) instar; (*visit*) visitar

♦ **call out** v/t (*shout*) gritar; (*summon*) llamar

♦ **call up** v/t (*on phone*) llamar; COMPUT abrir, visualizar

'call cen·ter, *Br* **'call cen·tre** centro *m* de atención telefónica

call·er [ˈkɔːlər] *on phone* persona *f* que llama; (*visitor*) visitante *m/f*

'call girl prostituta *f* (*que concierta sus citas por teléfono*)

cal·lous [ˈkæləs] *adj* cruel, desalmado

cal·lous·ly [ˈkæləslɪ] *adv* cruelmente

cal·lous·ness [ˈkæləsnɪs] crueldad *f*

calm [kɑːm] **1** *adj sea* tranquilo; *weather* apacible; *person* tranquilo, sosegado; **please keep ~** por favor mantengan la calma **2** *n* calma *f*

♦ **calm down 1** v/t calmar, tranquilizar **2** v/i *of sea, weather* calmarse; *of person* calmarse, tranquilizarse

calm·ly [ˈkɑːmlɪ] *adv* con calma, tranquilamente

cal·o·rie [ˈkælərɪ] caloría *f*

cam·cor·der [ˈkæmkɔːrdər] videocámara *f*

came [keɪm] *pret* → **come**

cam·e·ra [ˈkæmərə] cámara *f*

'cam·e·ra·man cámara *m*, camarógrafo *m*

'camera phone teléfono *m* con cámara

cam·i·sole [ˈkæmɪsoʊl] camisola *f*

cam·ou·flage [ˈkæməflɑːʒ] **1** *n* camuflaje *m* **2** v/t camuflar

camp [kæmp] **1** *n* campamento *m*; **make ~** acampar; **refugee ~** campo *m* de refugiados **2** v/i acampar

cam·paign [kæmˈpeɪn] **1** *n* campaña *f* **2** v/i hacer campaña (**for** a favor de)

cam·paign·er [kæmˈpeɪnər] defensor(a) *m(f)* (**for** de); **a ~ against racism** una persona que hace campaña contra el racismo

camp·er ['kæmpər] *person* campista *m/f*; *vehicle* autocaravana *f*

camp·ing ['kæmpɪŋ] acampada *f*; *on campsite* camping *m*; **go ~** ir de acampada *or* camping

'camp·site camping *m*

cam·pus ['kæmpəs] campus *m*

can¹ [kæn] *unstressed* [kən] *v/aux* (*pret* **could**) ◊ (*ability*) poder; **~ you swim?** ¿sabes nadar?; **~ you hear me?** ¿me oyes?; **I can't see** no veo; **~ you speak French?** ¿hablas francés?; **~ he call me back?** ¿me podría devolver la llamada?; *as fast/well as you* **~** tan rápido/bien como puedas ◊ (*permission*) poder; **~ I help you?** ¿te puedo ayudar?; **~ I have a beer/coffee?** ¿me pones una cerveza/un café?; *that can't be right* debe haber un error

can² [kæn] **1** *n for drinks etc* lata *f* **2** *v/t* (*pret & pp* **-ned**) enlatar

Can·a·da ['kænədə] Canadá

Ca·na·di·an [kə'neɪdɪən] **1** *adj* canadiense **2** *n* canadiense *m/f*

ca·nal [kə'næl] *waterway* canal *m*

ca·nar·y [kə'nerɪ] canario *m*

can·cel ['kænsl] *v/t* (*pret & pp* **-ed**, *Br* **-led**) cancelar

can·cel·la·tion [kænsə'leɪʃn] cancelación *f*

can·cel·la·tion fee tarifa *f* de cancelación de reserva

can·cer ['kænsər] cáncer *m*

Can·cer ['kænsər] ASTR Cáncer *m/f inv*

can·cer·ous ['kænsərəs] *adj* canceroso

c & f *abbr* (= **cost and freight**) C&F (= costo y flete)

can·did ['kændɪd] *adj* sincero, franco

can·di·da·cy ['kændɪdəsɪ] candidatura *f*

can·di·date ['kændɪdət] *for position* candidato(-a) *m(f)*; *in exam* candidato(-a) *m(f)*, examinando(-a) *m(f)*

can·did·ly ['kændɪdlɪ] *adv* sinceramente, francamente

can·died ['kændɪd] *adj* confitado

can·dle ['kændl] vela *f*

'can·dle·stick candelero *m*; *short* palmatoria *f*

can·dor, *Br* **can·dour** ['kændər] sinceridad *f*, franqueza *f*

can·dy ['kændɪ] (*sweet*) caramelo *m*; (*sweets*) dulces *mpl*; *a box of* **~** una caja de caramelos *or* dulces

cane [keɪn] *f*; *for walking* bastón *m*

can·is·ter ['kænɪstər] bote *m*

can·na·bis ['kænəbɪs] cannabis *m*, hachís *m*

canned [kænd] *adj fruit, tomatoes* enlatado, en lata; (*recorded*) grabado

can·ni·bal·ize ['kænɪbəlaɪz] *v/t* canibalizar

can·not ['kænɑːt] → **can¹**

can·ny ['kænɪ] *adj* (*astute*) astuto

ca·noe [kə'nuː] canoa *f*, piragua *f*

'can o·pen·er abrelatas *m inv*

can't [kænt] → **can**

can·tan·ker·ous [kæn'tæŋkərəs] *adj* arisco, cascarrabias

can·teen [kæn'tiːn] *in plant* cantina *f*, cafetería *f*

can·vas ['kænvəs] *for painting* lienzo *m*; *material* lona *f*

can·vass ['kænvəs] **1** *v/t* (*seek opinion of*) preguntar **2** *v/i* POL hacer campaña (*for* en favor de)

can·yon ['kænjən] cañón *m*

cap [kæp] *n hat* gorro *m*; *with peak* gorra *f*; *of bottle, jar* tapón *m*; *of pen, lens* tapa *f*

ca·pa·bil·i·ty [keɪpə'bɪlətɪ] capacidad *f*; *it's beyond my capabilities* no entra dentro de mis posibilidades

ca·pa·ble ['keɪpəbl] *adj* (*efficient*) capaz, competente; *be* **~** *of* ser capaz de

ca·pac·i·ty [kə'pæsətɪ] capacidad *f*; *of car engine* cilindrada *f*; *a* **~** *crowd* un lleno absoluto; *in my* **~** *as ...* en mi calidad de ...

cap·i·tal ['kæpɪtl] *n city* capital *f*; *letter* mayúscula *f*; *money* capital *m*

cap·i·tal ex'pend·i·ture inversión *f* en activo fijo; **cap·i·tal 'gains tax**

impuesto *m* sobre las plusvalías;
cap·i·tal 'growth crecimiento *m*
del capital

cap·i·tal·ism ['kæpɪtəlɪzm] capitalismo *m*

'**cap·i·tal·ist** ['kæpɪtəlɪst] **1** *adj* capitalista **2** *n* capitalista *m/f*

♦ **cap·i·tal·ize on** ['kæpɪtəlaɪz] *v/t* aprovecharse de

cap·i·tal 'let·ter letra *f* mayúscula

cap·i·tal 'pun·ish·ment pena *f* capital, pena *f* de muerte

ca·pit·u·late [kə'pɪtʊleɪt] *v/i* capitular

ca·pit·u·la·tion [kæpɪtʊ'leɪʃn] capitulación *f*

Cap·ri·corn ['kæprɪkɔːrn] ASTR Capricornio *m/f inv*

cap·size [kæp'saɪz] **1** *v/i* volcar **2** *v/t* hacer volcar

cap·sule ['kæpsʊl] *of medicine* cápsula *f*; (*space ~*) cápsula *f* espacial

cap·tain ['kæptɪn] *n of ship, team*, MIL capitán(-ana) *m(f)*; *of aircraft* comandante *m/f*

cap·tion ['kæpʃn] *n* pie *m* de foto

cap·ti·vate ['kæptɪveɪt] *v/t* cautivar, fascinar

cap·tive ['kæptɪv] **1** *adj* prisionero **2** *n* prisionero(-a) *m(f)*

cap·tive 'mar·ket mercado *m* cautivo

cap·tiv·i·ty [kæp'tɪvətɪ] cautividad *f*

cap·ture ['kæptʃər] **1** *n of city* toma *f*; *of criminal, animal* captura *f* **2** *v/t person, animal* capturar; *city, building* tomar; *market share* ganar; (*portray*) captar

car [kɑːr] coche *m*, *L.Am.* carro *m*, *Rpl* auto *m*; *of train* vagón *m*; **by ~** en coche

ca·rafe [kə'ræf] garrafa *f*, jarra *f*

car·at ['kærət] quilate *m*

car·bo·hy·drate [kɑːrboʊ'haɪdreɪt] carbohidrato *m*

'**car bomb** coche *m* bomba

car·bon·at·ed ['kɑːrbəneɪtɪd] *adj drink* con gas

car·bon mon·ox·ide [kɑːrbənmən-'aːksaɪd] monóxido *m* de carbono

car·bu·ret·er, car·bu·ret·or [kɑːr-bʊ'retər] carburador *m*

car·cass ['kɑːrkəs] cadáver *m*

car·cin·o·gen [kɑːr'sɪnədʒen] agente *m* cancerígeno *or* carcinógeno

car·cin·o·gen·ic [kɑːrsɪnə'dʒenɪk] *adj* cancerígeno, carcinógeno

card [kɑːrd] *to mark occasion*, COMPUT, *business* tarjeta *f*; (*post~*) (tarjeta *f*) postal *f*; (*playing ~*) carta *f*, naipe *m*; **game of ~s** partida *f* de cartas

'**card·board** cartón *m*

card·board 'box caja *f* de cartón

car·di·ac ['kɑːrdɪæk] *adj* cardíaco

car·di·ac ar'rest paro *m* cardíaco

car·di·gan ['kɑːrdɪgən] cárdigan *m*

car·di·nal ['kɑːrdɪnl] *n* REL cardenal *m*

'**card in·dex** fichero *m*; '**card key** llave *f* tarjeta; '**card phone** teléfono *m* de tarjeta

care [ker] **1** *n* cuidado *m*; (*medical ~*) asistencia *f* médica; (*worry*) preocupación *f*; **care of →** *c/o*; **take ~** (*be cautious*) tener cuidado; **take ~ (of yourself)!** (*goodbye*) ¡cuídate!; *baby* cuidar (de); (*deal with*) ocuparse de; **I'll take ~ of the bill** yo pago la cuenta; (*handle*) **with ~!** *on label* frágil **2** *v/i* preocuparse; **I don't ~!** ¡me da igual!; **I couldn't ~ less** ¡me importa un pimiento!; **if you really ~d ...** si de verdad te importara ...

♦ **care about** *v/t* preocuparse por

♦ **care for** *v/t* (*look after: person*) cuidar (de); (*look after: plant*) cuidar; **he doesn't care for me the way he used to** ya no le gusto como antes; **would you care for a drink?** ¿le apetece tomar algo?

ca·reer [kə'rɪr] carrera *f*; **~ prospects** perspectivas *fpl* profesionales

ca·reers of·fi·cer asesor(a) *m(f)* de orientación profesional

'**care·free** *adj* despreocupado

care·ful ['kerfl] *adj* (*cautious, thorough*) cuidadoso; **be ~** tener cuidado; (**be**) **~!** ¡(ten) cuidado!

care·ful·ly ['kerfəlɪ] *adv* (*with caution*) con cuidado; *worded etc* cuidadosamente

care·less ['kerlɪs] *adj* descuidado; *you are so ~!* ¡qué descuidado eres!

care·less·ly ['kerlɪslɪ] *adv* descuidadamente

car·er ['kerər] *persona que cuida de un familiar o enfermo*

ca·ress [kə'res] **1** *n* caricia *f* **2** *v/t* acariciar

care·tak·er ['kerteɪkər] conserje *m*

'care·worn *adj* agobiado

'car fer·ry ferry *m*, transbordador *m*

car·go ['kɑːrgoʊ] cargamento *m*

car·i·ca·ture ['kærɪkətʃər] *n* caricatura *f*

car·ing ['kerɪŋ] *adj person* afectuoso, bondadoso; *society* solidario

'car me·chan·ic mecánico(-a) *m(f)* de coches *or* automóviles

car·nage ['kɑːrnɪdʒ] matanza *f*, carnicería *f*

car·na·tion [kɑːr'neɪʃn] clavel *m*

car·ni·val ['kɑːrnɪvl] feria *f*

car·ol ['kærəl] *n* villancico *m*

car·ou·sel [kærə'sel] *at airport* cinta *f* transportadora de equipajes; *for slide projector* carro *m*; (*merry-go-round*) tiovivo *m*

'car park *Br* estacionamiento *m*, *Span* aparcamiento *m*

car·pen·ter ['kɑːrpɪntər] carpintero(-a) *m(f)*

car·pet ['kɑːrpɪt] alfombra *f*

'car phone teléfono *m* de coche; **'car·pool** *n acuerdo para compartir el vehículo entre varias personas que trabajan en el mismo sitio*; **'car port** estacionamiento *m* con techo; **'car ra·di·o** autorradio *m*; **'car ren·tal** alquiler *m* de coches *or* automóviles

car·ri·er ['kærɪər] *company* transportista *m*; *airline* línea *f* aérea; *of disease* portador(a) *m(f)*

car·rot ['kærət] zanahoria *f*

car·ry ['kærɪ] **1** *v/t* (*pret & pp* **-ied**) *of person* llevar; *disease* ser portador de; *of ship, plane, bus etc* transportar;

proposal aprobar; *be ~ing a child of pregnant woman* estar embarazada; *get carried away* dejarse llevar por la emoción, emocionarse **2** *v/i* (*pret & pp* **-ied**) *of sound* oírse

♦ **carry on 1** *v/i* (*continue*) seguir, continuar; (*make a fuss*) organizar un escándalo; (*have an affair*) tener un lío **2** *v/t* (*conduct*) mantener; *business* efectuar

♦ **carry out** *survey etc* llevar a cabo

'car seat *for child* asiento *m* para niño

cart [kɑːrt] carro *m*; *for shopping* carrito *m*

car·tel [kɑːr'tel] cartel *m*

car·ton ['kɑːrtn] *for storage, transport* caja *f* de cartón; *for milk etc* cartón *m*, tetrabrik *m* ®; *for eggs, of cigarettes* cartón *m*

car·toon [kɑːr'tuːn] *in newspaper, magazine* tira *f* cómica; *on TV, movie* dibujos *mpl* animados

car·toon·ist [kɑːr'tuːnɪst] dibujante *m/f* de chistes

car·tridge ['kɑːrtrɪdʒ] *for gun* cartucho *m*

carve [kɑːrv] *v/t meat* trinchar; *wood* tallar

carv·ing ['kɑːrvɪŋ] *figure* talla *f*

'car wash lavado *m* de automóviles

case[1] [keɪs] *container* funda *f*; *of scotch, wine etc* caja *f*; *Br* (*suitcase*) maleta *f*

case[2] [keɪs] *n instance, criminal*, MED caso *m*; LAW causa *f*; *I think there's a ~ for dismissing him* creo que hay razones fundadas para despedirlo; *the ~ for the prosecution* (los argumentos jurídicos de) la acusación; *make a ~ for sth* defender algo; *in ~ ...* por si ...; *in ~ of emergency* en caso de emergencia; *in any ~* en cualquier caso; *in that ~* en ese caso

'case his·to·ry MED historial *m* médico

'case·load número *m* de casos

cash [kæʃ] **1** *n* (dinero *m* en) efectivo *m*; *I'm a bit short of ~* no tengo mucho dinero; *~ down* al contado;

pay (in) ~ pagar en efectivo **2** v/t *check* hacer efectivo

♦ **cash in on** v/t sacar provecho de
'**cash cow** fuente f de ingresos;
'**cash desk** caja f; **cash 'dis·count** descuento m por pago al contado;
'**cash flow** flujo m de caja, cash-flow m; ~ **problems** problemas mpl de liquidez

cash·ier [kæ'ʃɪr] n *in store etc* cajero(-a) m(f)

cash·mere ['kæʃmɪr] adj cachemir m

'**cash·point** cajero m automático
'**cash re·gis·ter** caja f registradora

ca·si·no [kə'si:nou] casino m

cas·ket ['kæskɪt] (*coffin*) ataúd m

cas·se·role ['kæsəroul] n *meal* guiso m; *container* cacerola f, cazuela f

cas·sette [kə'set] cinta f, casete f

cas·sette play·er, **cas·sette re·cord·er** casete m

cast [kæst] **1** n *of play* reparto m; (*mold*) molde m **2** v/t (*pret & pp* **cast**) *doubt, suspicion* proyectar; *metal* fundir; *play* seleccionar el reparto de; *they* ~ *Alan as ...* le dieron a Alan el papel de ...

♦ **cast off** v/i *of ship* soltar amarras

caste [kæst] casta f

cast·er ['kæstər] *on chair etc* ruedecita f

Cas·til·ian [kæs'tɪlɪən] **1** adj castellano **2** n *person* castellano(-a) m(f); *language* castellano m

cast 'i·ron n hierro m fundido

cast-'i·ron adj de hierro fundido

cas·tle ['kæsl] castillo m

'**cast·or** ['kæstər] → **caster**

cas·trate [kæ'streɪt] v/t castrar

cas·tra·tion [kæ'streɪʃn] castración f

cas·u·al ['kæʒuəl] adj (*chance*) casual; (*offhand*) despreocupado; (*not formal*) informal; (*not permanent*) eventual; *it was just a ~ remark* no era más que un comentario hecho de pasada; *he was very ~ about the whole thing* parecía no darle mucha importancia al asunto; ~ *sex* relaciones fpl sexuales (con parejas) ocasionales

cas·u·al·ly ['kæʒuəlɪ] adv *dressed* de manera informal; *say* a la ligera

cas·u·al·ty ['kæʒuəltɪ] víctima f

cas·u·al wear ropa f informal

cat [kæt] gato m

Cat·a·lan ['kætəlæn] **1** adj catalán **2** n *person* catalán(-ana) m(f); *language* catalán m

cat·a·log, *Br* **cat·a·logue** ['kætəlɑːg] n catálogo m

cat·a·lyst ['kætəlɪst] catalizador m

cat·a·lyt·ic con'vert·er [kætə'lɪtɪk] catalizador m

cat·a·pult ['kætəpʌlt] **1** v/t fig *to fame, stardom* catapultar, lanzar **2** n catapulta f; *toy* tirachinas m inv

cat·a·ract ['kætərækt] MED catarata f

ca·tas·tro·phe [kə'tæstrəfɪ] catástrofe f

cat·a·stroph·ic [kætə'strɑːfɪk] adj catastrófico

catch [kætʃ] **1** n parada f (*sin que la pelota toque el suelo*); *of fish* captura f, pesca f; (*locking device*) cierre m; (*problem*) pega f; *there has to be a* ~ tiene que haber una trampa **2** v/t (*pret & pp* **caught**) *ball* agarrar, *Span* coger; *animal* atrapar; *escaped prisoner* capturar; (*get on: bus, train*) tomar, *Span* coger; (*not miss: bus, train*) alcanzar, *Span* coger; *fish* pescar; *in order to speak to* alcanzar, pillar; (*hear*) oír; *illness* agarrar, *Span* coger; ~ (**a**) *cold* agarrar or *Span* coger un resfriado, resfriarse; ~ *s.o.'s eye of person, object* llamar la atención de alguien; ~ *sight of*, ~ *a glimpse of* ver; ~ *s.o. doing sth* atrapar or *Span* coger a alguien haciendo algo

♦ **catch on** v/i (*become popular*) cuajar, ponerse de moda; (*understand*) darse cuenta

♦ **catch up** v/i: *catch up with s.o.* alcanzar a alguien; *he's having to work hard to catch up* tiene que trabajar muy duro para ponerse al día

♦ **catch up on** v/t: *catch up on one's sleep* recuperar sueño;

there's a lot of work to catch up on hay mucho trabajo atrasado

catch-22 [kætʃtwenti'tu:]: *it's a ~ situation* es como la pescadilla que se muerde la cola

catch-er ['kætʃər] *in baseball* cácher *m*, cátcher *m*

catch-ing ['kætʃɪŋ] *adj also fig* contagioso

catch-y ['kætʃɪ] *adj tune* pegadizo

cat-e-go-ric [kætə'gɑːrɪk] *adj* categórico

cat-e-gor-i-cal-ly [kætə'gɑːrɪklɪ] *adv* categóricamente

cat-e-go-ry ['kætəgəːrɪ] categoría *f*

♦ ca-ter for ['keɪtər] *v/t (meet the needs of)* cubrir las necesidades de; *(provide food for)* organizar la comida para

ca-ter-er ['keɪtərər] hostelero(-a) *m(f)*

ca-ter-pil-lar ['kætərpɪlər] oruga *f*

ca-the-dral [kə'θiːdrəl] catedral *f*

Cath-o-lic ['kæθəlɪk] **1** *adj* católico **2** *n* católico(-a) *m(f)*

Ca-thol-i-cism [kə'θɑːlɪsɪzm] catolicismo *m*

'cat's eyes *on road* captafaros *mpl* (en el centro de la calzada)

cat-sup ['kætsʌp] ketchup *m*, catchup *m*

cat-tle ['kætl] *npl* ganado *m*

cat-ty ['kætɪ] *adj* malintencionado

'cat-walk pasarela *f*

caught [kɔːt] *pret & pp* → **catch**

cau-li-flow-er ['kɔːlɪflaʊər] coliflor *f*

cause [kɔːz] **1** *n* causa *f*; *(grounds)* motivo *m*, razón *f* **2** *v/t* causar, provocar

caus-tic ['kɔːstɪk] *adj fig* cáustico

cau-tion ['kɔːʃn] **1** *n (carefulness)* precaución *f*, prudencia *f* **2** *v/t (warn)* prevenir (*against* contra)

cau-tious ['kɔːʃəs] *adj* cauto, prudente

cau-tious-ly ['kɔːʃəslɪ] *adv* cautelosamente, con prudencia

cav-al-ry ['kævəlrɪ] caballería *f*

cave [keɪv] cueva *f*

♦ cave in *v/i of roof* hundirse

cav-i-ar ['kævɪɑːr] caviar *m*

cav-i-ty ['kævətɪ] caries *f inv*

cc[1] [siː'siː] **1** *abbr (= carbon copy)* copia *f* **2** *v/t memo* enviar una copia de; *person* enviar una copia a

cc[2] [siː'siː] *abbr (= cubic centimeters)* cc (centímetros *mpl* cúbicos); MOT cilindrada *f*

CD [siː'diː] *abbr (= compact disc)* CD *m (= disco m compacto)*

CD play-er (reproductor *m* de) CD *m*; **CD-ROM** [siːdiː'rɑːm] CD-ROM *m*; **CD-ROM drive** lector *m* de CD-ROM

cease [siːs] **1** *v/i* cesar **2** *v/t* suspender; *~ doing sth* dejar de hacer algo

'cease-fire alto *m* el fuego

ceil-ing ['siːlɪŋ] *of room* techo *m*; *(limit)* tope *m*, límite *m*

cel-e-brate ['selɪbreɪt] **1** *v/i: let's ~ with a bottle of champagne* celebrémoslo con una botella de champán **2** *v/t* celebrar, festejar; *(observe)* celebrar

cel-e-brat-ed ['selɪbreɪtɪd] *adj* célebre; *be ~ for* ser célebre por

cel-e-bra-tion [selɪ'breɪʃn] celebración *f*

ce-leb-ri-ty [sɪ'lebrətɪ] celebridad *f*

cel-e-ry ['selərɪ] apio *m*

cel-i-ba-cy ['selɪbəsɪ] celibato *m*

cel-i-bate ['selɪbət] *adj* célibe

cell [sel] *for prisoner, in spreadsheet* celda *f*; BIO célula *f*

cel-lar ['selər] sótano *m*; *for wine* bodega *f*

cel-list ['tʃelɪst] violonchelista *m/f*

cel-lo ['tʃeloʊ] violonchelo *m*

cel-lo-phane ['seləfeɪn] celofán *m*

'cell phone, **cel-lu-lar phone** ['seljələr] (teléfono *m*) móvil *m*, *L.Am.* (teléfono *m*) celular *m*

ce-ment [sɪ'ment] **1** *n* cemento *m* **2** *v/t* colocar con cemento; *friendship* consolidar

cem-e-ter-y ['semətərɪ] cementerio *m*

cen-sor ['sensər] *v/t* censor(a) *m(f)*

cen-sus ['sensəs] censo *m*

cent [sent] céntimo *m*

cen·te·na·ry [sen'ti:nərɪ] centenario *m*

cen·ter ['sentər] **1** *n* centro *m*; **in the ~ of** en el centro de **2** *v/t* centrar
♦ **center on** *v/t* centrarse en

cen·ter of 'grav·i·ty centro *m* de gravedad

cen·ti·grade ['sentɪgreɪd] *adj* centígrado; **10 degrees ~** 10 grados centígrados

cen·ti·me·ter *Br* **cen·ti·me·tre** ['sentɪmiːtər] centímetro *m*

cen·tral ['sentrəl] *adj* central; *location, apartment* céntrico; **~ Chicago** el centro de Chicago; **be ~ to sth** ser el eje de algo

Cen·tral A'mer·i·ca *n* Centroamérica, América Central; **Cen·tral A'mer·i·can 1** *adj* centroamericano, de (la) América f Central **2** *n* centroamericano(-a) *m(f)*; **central 'heat·ing** calefacción *f* central

cen·tral·ize ['sentrəlaɪz] *v/t* centralizar

cen·tral 'lock·ing MOT cierre *m* centralizado

cen·tral 'pro·ces·sing u·nit unidad *f* central de proceso

cen·tre *Br* → **center**

cen·tu·ry ['sentʃərɪ] siglo *m*

CEO [siːiː'oʊ] *abbr* (= *Chief Executive Officer*) consejero(-a) *m(f)* delegado

ce·ram·ic [sɪ'ræmɪk] *adj* de cerámica

ce·ram·ics [sɪ'ræmɪks] (*pl: objects*) objetos *mpl* de cerámica; (*sing: art*) cerámica *f*

ce·re·al ['sɪrɪəl] (*grain*) cereal *m*; (*breakfast ~*) cereales *mpl*

cer·e·mo·ni·al [serɪ'moʊnɪəl] **1** *adj* ceremonial **2** *n* ceremonial *m*

cer·e·mo·ny ['serɪmənɪ] (*event, ritual*) ceremonia *f*

cer·tain ['sɜːrtn] *adj* (*sure*) seguro; (*particular*) cierto; **I'm ~** estoy seguro; **a ~ Mr S.** un cierto Sr. S.; **make ~** asegurarse; **know / say for ~** saber / decir con certeza

cer·tain·ly ['sɜːrtnlɪ] *adv* (*definitely*) claramente; (*of course*) por supues-

to; **~ not!** ¡por supuesto que no!

cer·tain·ty ['sɜːrtntɪ] (*confidence*) certeza *f*, certidumbre *f*; (*inevitability*) seguridad *f*; **it's a ~** es seguro; **he's a ~ for the gold medal** va a ganar seguro la medalla de oro

cer·tif·i·cate [sər'tɪfɪkət] (*qualification*) título *m*; (*official paper*) certificado *m*

cer·ti·fied pub·lic ac·count·ant ['sɜːrtɪfaɪd] censor(a) *m(f)* jurado de cuentas

cer·ti·fy ['sɜːrtɪfaɪ] *v/t* (*pret & pp -ied*) certificar

Ce·sar·e·an [sɪ'zerɪən] *n* cesárea *f*

ces·sa·tion [se'seɪʃn] cese *m*

c/f *abbr* (= *cost and freight*) CF (= costo y flete)

CFC [siːef'siː] *abbr* (= *chlorofluorocarbon*) CFC *m* (= clorofluorocarbono *m*)

chain [tʃeɪn] **1** *n also of hotels etc* cadena *f* **2** *v/t* encadenar; **~ sth / s.o. to sth** encadenar algo / a alguien a algo

chain re'ac·tion reacción *f* en cadena; **'chain-smoke** *v/i* fumar un cigarrillo tras otro, fumar como un carretero; **'chain-smok·er** *persona que fuma un cigarrillo tras otro*; **'chain store** *store* tienda *f* (de una cadena); *company* cadena *f* de tiendas

chair [tʃer] **1** *n* silla *f*; (*arm~*) sillón *m*; *at university* cátedra *f*; **the ~** (*electric ~*) la silla eléctrica; *at meeting* la presidencia; **take the ~** ocupar la presidencia **2** *v/t meeting* presidir

'chair lift telesilla *f*;

'chair·man presidente *m*

chair·man·ship ['tʃermənʃɪp] presidencia *f*

'chair·per·son presidente(-a) *m(f)*

'chair·wom·an presidenta *f*

cha·let ['ʃæleɪ] chalet *m*, chalé *f*

chal·ice ['tʃælɪs] REL cáliz *m*

chalk [tʃɔːk] *for writing* tiza *f*; *in soil* creta *f*

chal·lenge ['tʃælɪndʒ] **1** *n* (*difficulty*) desafío *m*, reto *m*; *in race, competition* ataque *m* **2** *v/t* desafiar, retar; (*call into question*) cuestionar

chal·len·ger ['tʃælɪndʒər] aspirante *m/f*

chal·len·ging ['tʃælɪndʒɪŋ] *adj job, undertaking* estimulante

cham·ber·maid ['tʃeɪmbərmeɪd] camarera *f* (de hotel); '**cham·ber mu·sic** música *f* de cámara; **Cham·ber of 'Com·merce** Cámara *f* de Comercio

cham·ois (leath·er) ['ʃæmɪ] ante *m*

cham·pagne [ʃæm'peɪn] champán *m*

cham·pi·on ['tʃæmpɪən] **1** *n* SP campeón(-ona) *m(f)*; *of cause* abanderado (-a) *m(f)* **2** *v/t* (*cause*) abanderar

cham·pi·on·ship ['tʃæmpɪənʃɪp] campeonato *m*

chance [tʃæns] (*possibility*) posibilidad *f*; (*opportunity*) oportunidad *f*; (*risk*) riesgo *m*; (*luck*) casualidad *f*, suerte *f*; *there's not much ~ of that happening* no es probable que ocurra; *leave nothing to ~* no dejar nada a la improvisación; *by ~* por casualidad; *take a ~* correr el riesgo; *I'm not taking any ~s* no voy a correr ningún riesgo

chan·de·lier [ʃændə'lɪr] araña *f* (de luces)

change [tʃeɪndʒ] **1** *n* cambio *m*; (*small coins*) suelto *m*; *from purchase* cambio *m*, *Span* vuelta *f*, *L.Am.* vuelto *m*; *a ~ is as good as a rest* a veces cambiar es lo mejor; *that makes a nice ~* eso es una novedad bienvenida; *for a ~* para variar; *a ~ of clothes* una muda **2** *v/t* cambiar; *~ trains* hacer transbordo; *~ one's clothes* cambiarse de ropa **3** *v/i* cambiar; (*put on different clothes*) cambiarse; (*take different train/bus*) hacer transbordo; *the lights ~d to green* el semáforo se puso verde

change·a·ble ['tʃeɪndʒəbl] *adj* variable, cambiante

'**change·o·ver** transición *f* (*to* a); *in relay race* relevo *m*

chang·ing room ['tʃeɪndʒɪŋ] SP vestuario *m*; *in shop* probador *m*

chan·nel ['tʃænl] *on TV, at sea* canal *m*

chant [tʃænt] **1** *n* REL canto *m*; *of fans* cántico *m*; *of demonstrators* consigna *f* **2** *v/i* gritar **3** *v/t* corear

cha·os ['keɪɑːs] caos *m*; *it was ~ at the airport* la situación en el aeropuerto era caótica

cha·ot·ic [keɪ'ɑːtɪk] *adj* caótico

chap [tʃæp] *n Br* F tipo *m* F, *Span* tío *m* F

chap·el ['tʃæpl] capilla *f*

chapped [tʃæpt] *adj lips* cortado; *hands* agrietado

chap·ter ['tʃæptər] capítulo *m*; *of organization* sección *f*

char·ac·ter ['kærɪktər] *nature, personality, in printing* carácter *m*; *person, in book, play* personaje *m*; *he's a real ~* es todo un personaje

char·ac·ter·is·tic [kærɪktə'rɪstɪk] **1** *n* característica *f* **2** *adj* característico

char·ac·ter·is·ti·cal·ly [kærɪktə'rɪstɪklɪ] *adv* de modo característico; *he was ~ rude* fue grosero como de costumbre

char·ac·ter·ize ['kærɪktəraɪz] *v/t* (*be typical of*) caracterizar; (*describe*) describir, clasificar

cha·rade [ʃə'rɑːd] *fig* farsa *f*

char·broiled ['tʃɑːrbrɔɪld] *adj* a la brasa

char·coal ['tʃɑːrkoʊl] *for barbecue* carbón *m* vegetal; *for drawing* carboncillo *m*

charge [tʃɑːrdʒ] **1** *n* (*fee*) tarifa *f*; LAW cargo *m*, acusación *f*; *free of ~* gratis; *bank ~s* comisiones *fpl* bancarias; *will that be cash or ~?* ¿pagará en efectivo o con tarjeta?; *be in ~* estar a cargo; *take ~* hacerse cargo **2** *v/t sum of money* cobrar; (*put on account*) pagar con tarjeta; LAW acusar (*with* de); *battery* cargar; *please ~ it to my account* cárguelo a mi cuenta **3** *v/i* (*attack*) cargar

'**charge ac·count** cuenta *f* de crédito

'**charge card** tarjeta *f* de compra

cha·ris·ma [kə'rɪzmə] carisma *m*

char·is·ma·tic [kærɪz'mætɪk] *adj* carismático

char·i·ta·ble ['tʃærɪtəbl] *adj institution, donation* de caridad; *person* caritativo

char·i·ty ['tʃærətɪ] *assistance* caridad *f*; *organization* entidad *f* benéfica

char·la·tan ['ʃɑːrlətən] charlatán (-ana) *m(f)*

charm [tʃɑːrm] **1** *n (appealing quality)* encanto *m*; *on bracelet etc* colgante *m* **2** *v/t (delight)* encantar

charm·ing ['tʃɑːrmɪŋ] *adj* encantador

charred [tʃɑːrd] *adj* carbonizado

chart [tʃɑːrt] *(diagram)* gráfico *m*; *(map)* carta *f* de navegación; **the ~s** MUS las listas de éxitos

'**char·ter flight** vuelo *m* chárter

chase [tʃeɪs] **1** *n* persecución *f* **2** *v/t* perseguir

♦ **chase away** *v/t* ahuyentar

chas·sis ['ʃæsɪ] *of car* chasis *m inv*

chat [tʃæt] **1** *n* charla *f*, *Mex* plática *f* **2** *v/i (pret & pp -ted)* charlar, *Mex* platicar

chat·ter ['tʃætər] **1** *n* cháchara *f* **2** *v/i talk* parlotear; *of teeth* castañetear

'**chat·ter·box** charlatán(-ana) *m(f)*

chat·ty ['tʃætɪ] *adj person* hablador

chauf·feur ['ʃoʊfər] *n* chófer *m*, *L.Am.* chofer *m*

'**chauf·feur-driv·en** *adj* con chófer *or L.Am.* chofer

chau·vin·ist ['ʃoʊvɪnɪst] *n (male ~)* machista *m*

chau·vin·ist·ic [ʃoʊvɪ'nɪstɪk] *adj* chovinista; *(sexist)* machista

cheap [tʃiːp] *adj (inexpensive)* barato; *(nasty)* chabacano; *(mean)* tacaño

cheat [tʃiːt] **1** *n (person)* tramposo(-a) *m(f)* **2** *v/t* engañar; **~ s.o. out of sth** estafar algo a alguien **3** *v/i in exam* copiar; *in cards etc* hacer trampa; **~ on one's wife** engañar a la esposa

check¹ [tʃek] **1** *adj shirt* a cuadros **2** *n* cuadro *m*

check² [tʃek] FIN cheque *m*; *in restaurant etc* cuenta *f*; **~ please** la cuenta, por favor

check³ [tʃek] **1** *n to verify sth* comprobación *f*; **keep in ~, hold in ~** mantener bajo control; **keep a ~ on** llevar el control de **2** *v/t (verify)* comprobar; *machinery* inspeccionar; *(restrain, stop)* contener, controlar; *with a ~mark* poner un tic en; *coat* dejar en el guardarropa; *package* dejar en consigna **3** *v/i* comprobar; **~ for** comprobar

♦ **check in** *v/i at airport* facturar; *at hotel* registrarse

♦ **check off** *v/t* marcar *(como comprobada)*

♦ **check on** *v/t* vigilar

♦ **check out 1** *v/i of hotel* dejar el hotel **2** *v/t (look into)* investigar; *club, restaurant etc* probar

♦ **check up on** *v/t* hacer averiguaciones sobre, investigar

♦ **check with** *v/t of person* hablar con; *(tally: of information)* concordar con

'**check·book** talonario *m* de cheques, *L.Am.* chequera *f*

checked [tʃekt] *adj material* a cuadros

check·er·board ['tʃekərbɔːrd] tablero *m* de ajedrez

check·ered ['tʃekərd] *adj pattern* a cuadros; *career* accidentado

check·ers ['tʃekərz] *nsg* damas *fpl*

'**check-in (coun·ter)** mostrador *m* de facturación

check·ing ac·count ['tʃekɪŋ] cuenta *f* corriente

'**check-in time** hora *f* de facturación; '**check·list** lista *f* de verificación; '**check mark** tic *m*; '**check·mate** *n* jaque *m* mate; '**check-out** caja *f*; '**check-out time** *from hotel* hora *f* de salida; '**check·point** control *m*; '**check·room** *for coats* guardarropa *m*; *for baggage* consigna *f*; '**check·up** *medical* chequeo *m* (médico), revisión *f* (médica); *dental* revisión *f* (en el dentista)

cheek [ʧiːk] ANAT mejilla f

'cheek·bone pómulo m

cheer [ʧɪr] **1** n ovación f; **~s!** toast ¡salud!; **the ~s of the fans** los vítores de los aficionados **2** v/t ovacionar, vitorear **3** v/i lanzar vítores

◆ cheer on v/t animar

◆ cheer up **1** v/i animarse **2** v/t animar

cheer·ful ['ʧɪrfəl] adj alegre, contento

cheer·ing ['ʧɪrɪŋ] n vítores mpl

cheer·i·o [ʧɪri'ou] Br F ¡chao! F

'cheer·lead·er animadora f

cheese [ʧiːz] queso m

'cheese·burg·er hamburguesa f de queso

'cheese·cake tarta f de queso

chef [ʃef] chef m, jefe m de cocina

chem·i·cal ['kemɪkl] **1** adj químico **2** n producto m químico

chem·i·cal 'war·fare guerra f química

chem·ist ['kemɪst] in laboratory químico(-a) m(f); Br dispensing farmacéutico(-a) m(f)

chem·is·try ['kemɪstri] química f; fig sintonía f, química f

chem·o·ther·a·py [kiːmou'θerəpi] quimioterapia f

cheque [ʧek] Br → **check²**

cher·ish ['ʧerɪʃ] v/t photo etc apreciar mucho, tener mucho cariño a; person querer mucho; hope albergar

cher·ry ['ʧeri] fruit cereza f; tree cerezo m

cher·ub ['ʧerəb] in painting, sculpture querubín m

chess [ʧes] ajedrez m

'chess·board tablero m de ajedrez

'chess·man, 'chess·piece pieza f de ajedrez

chest [ʧest] of person pecho m; box cofre m; **get sth off one's ~** desahogarse

chest·nut ['ʧesnʌt] castaña f; tree castaño m

chest of 'draw·ers cómoda f

chew [ʧuː] v/t mascar, masticar; of dog, rats mordisquear

◆ chew out v/t F echar una bronca a F

chew·ing gum ['ʧuːɪŋ] chicle m

chic [ʃiːk] adj chic, elegante

chick [ʧɪk] young chicken pollito m; young bird polluelo m; F girl nena f F

chick·en ['ʧɪkɪn] **1** n gallina f; food pollo m; F (coward) gallina f F **2** adj F (cowardly) cobarde; **be ~** ser un(a) gallina F

◆ chicken out v/i F acobardarse

'chick·en·feed F calderilla f

chief [ʧiːf] **1** n jefe(-a) m(f) **2** adj principal

chief ex·ec·u·tive 'of·fi·cer consejero(-a) m(f) delegado

chief·ly ['ʧiːfli] adv principalmente

chil·blain ['ʧɪlbleɪn] sabañón m

child [ʧaɪld] (pl **children** ['ʧɪldrən]) niño(-a) m(f); son hijo m; daughter hija f; pej niño(-a) m(f), crío(-a) m(f)

'child a·buse malos tratos mpl a menores; 'child·birth parto m; 'child·hood ['ʧaɪldhud] infancia f

child·ish ['ʧaɪldɪʃ] adj pej infantil

child·ish·ly ['ʧaɪldɪʃli] adv pej de manera infantil

child·ish·ness ['ʧaɪldɪʃnɪs] pej infantilismo m

child·less ['ʧaɪldlɪs] adj sin hijos

child·like ['ʧaɪldlaɪk] adj infantil

'child·mind·er niñero(-a) m(f)

'child·ren ['ʧɪldrən] pl → **child**

Chil·e ['ʧɪli] n Chile

Chil·e·an ['ʧɪliən] **1** adj chileno **2** n chileno(-a) m(f)

chill [ʧɪl] **1** n illness resfriado m; **there's a ~ in the air** hace bastante fresco **2** v/t wine poner a enfriar

◆ chill out v/i F tranquilizarse

chil·(l)i (pep·per) ['ʧɪli] chile m, Span guindilla f

chill·y ['ʧɪli] adj weather, welcome fresco; **I'm feeling a bit ~** tengo fresco

chime [ʧaɪm] v/i campanada f

chim·ney ['ʧɪmni] chimenea f

chim·pan·zee [ʧɪmpænziː] chimpancé m

chin [ʧɪn] barbilla f

Chi·na ['tʃaɪnə] China

chi·na ['tʃaɪnə] porcelana f

Chi·nese [tʃaɪ'niːz] **1** adj chino **2** n (language) chino m; (person) chino(-a) m(f)

chink [tʃɪŋk] gap resquicio m; sound tintineo m

chip [tʃɪp] **1** n of wood viruta f; of stone lasca f; damage mella f; in gambling ficha f; **~s** patatas fpl fritas **2** v/t (pret & pp **-ped**) (damage) mellar

♦ **chip in** v/i (interrupt) interrumpir; with money poner dinero

chip·munk ['tʃɪpmʌŋk] ardilla f listada

chirp [tʃɜːrp] v/i piar

chis·el ['tʃɪzl] n for stone cincel m; for wood formón m

chit·chat ['tʃɪtʃæt] charla f

chiv·al·rous ['ʃɪvlrəs] adj caballeroso

chive [tʃaɪv] cebollino m

chlo·rine ['klɔːriːn] cloro m

chlor·o·form ['klɔːrəfɔːrm] n cloroformo m

choc·a·hol·ic [tʃɑːkə'hɑːlɪk] n F adicto(-a) al chocolate

chock-full [tʃɑːk'fʊl] adj F de bote en bote F

choc·o·late ['tʃɑːkələt] chocolate m; **a box of ~s** una caja de bombones; **hot ~** chocolate m caliente

'choc·o·late cake pastel m de chocolate

choice [tʃɔɪs] **1** n elección f; (selection) selección f; **you have a ~ of rice or potatoes** puedes elegir entre arroz y patatas; **the ~ is yours** tú eliges; **I had no ~** no tuve alternativa **2** adj (top quality) selecto

choir [kwaɪr] coro m

'choir·boy niño m de coro

choke [tʃoʊk] **1** n MOT estárter m **2** v/i ahogarse; **~ on sth** atragantarse con algo **3** v/t estrangular; screams ahogar

cho·les·te·rol [kə'lestəroʊl] colesterol m

choose [tʃuːz] v/t & v/i (pret **chose**, pp **chosen**) elegir, escoger

choos·ey ['tʃuːzɪ] adj F exigente

chop [tʃɑːp] **1** n meat chuleta f; **with one ~ of the ax** con un hachazo **2** v/t (pret & pp **-ped**) wood cortar; meat trocear; vegetables picar

♦ **chop down** v/t tree talar

chop·per ['tʃɑːpər] F (helicopter) helicóptero m

'chop·sticks npl palillos mpl (chinos)

cho·ral ['kɔːrəl] adj coral

chord [kɔːrd] MUS acorde m

chore [tʃɔːr] tarea f

chor·e·o·graph ['kɔːrɪəgræf] v/t coreografiar

chor·e·og·ra·pher [kɔːrɪ'ɑːgrəfər] coreógrafo(-a) m(f)

chor·e·og·ra·phy [kɔːrɪ'ɑːgrəfɪ] coreografía f

cho·rus ['kɔːrəs] singers coro m; of song estribillo m

chose [tʃoʊz] pret → **choose**

cho·sen ['tʃoʊzn] pp → **choose**

Christ [kraɪst] Cristo!; **~!** ¡Dios mío!

chris·ten ['krɪsn] v/t bautizar

chris·ten·ing ['krɪsnɪŋ] bautizo m

Chris·tian ['krɪstʃən] **1** n cristiano(-a) m(f) **2** adj cristiano

Chris·ti·an·i·ty [krɪstɪ'ænətɪ] cristianismo m

'Chris·tian name nombre m de pila

Christ·mas ['krɪsməs] Navidad(es) f(pl); **at ~** en Navidad(es); **Merry ~!** ¡Feliz Navidad!

'Christ·mas card crismas m inv, tarjeta f de Navidad; **Christ·mas 'Day** día f de Navidad; **Christ·mas 'Eve** Nochebuena f; **'Christ·mas pres·ent** regalo m de Navidad; **'Christ·mas tree** árbol m de Navidad

chrome, chro·mi·um [kroʊm, 'kroʊmɪəm] cromo m

chro·mo·some ['kroʊməsoʊm] cromosoma m

chron·ic ['krɑːnɪk] adj crónico

chron·o·log·i·cal [krɑːnə'lɑːdʒɪkl] adj cronológico; **in ~ order** en orden cronológico

chrys·an·the·mum [krɪˈsænθəməm]
crisantemo *m*

chub·by [ˈtʃʌbɪ] *adj* rechoncho

chuck [tʃʌk] *v/t* F tirar
♦ **chuck out** *v/t* F *object* tirar; *person* echar

chuck·le [ˈtʃʌkl] **1** *n* risita *f* **2** *v/i* reírse por lo bajo

chum [tʃʌm] amigo(-a) *m(f)*

chum·my [ˈtʃʌmɪ] *adj* F: **be ~ with** ser amiguete de F

chunk [tʃʌŋk] trozo *m*

chunk·y [ˈtʃʌŋkɪ] *adj sweater* grueso; *person, build* cuadrado, fornido

church [tʃɜːrtʃ] iglesia *f*

church ˈhall sala parroquial *empleada para diferentes actividades*; **church ˈserv·ice** oficio *m* religioso; **ˈchurch·yard** cementerio *m* (al lado de iglesia)

churl·ish [ˈtʃɜːrlɪʃ] *adj* maleducado, grosero

chute [ʃuːt] rampa *f*; *for garbage* colector *m* de basura

CIA [siːaɪˈeɪ] *abbr* (= *Central Intelligence Agency*) CIA *f* (= Agencia *f* Central de Inteligencia)

ci·der [ˈsaɪdər] sidra *f*

CIF [siːaɪˈef] *abbr* (= *cost, insurance, freight*) CIF (= costo, seguro y flete)

ci·gar [sɪˈɡɑːr] (cigarro *m*) puro *m*

cig·a·rette [sɪɡəˈret] cigarrillo *m*

cig·a·rette end colilla *f*; **cig·a·rette ˈlight·er** encendedor *m*, mechero *m*; **cig·a·rette ˈpa·per** papel *m* de fumar

cin·e·ma [ˈsɪnɪmə] cine *m*

cin·na·mon [ˈsɪnəmən] canela *f*

cir·cle [ˈsɜːrkl] **1** *n* círculo *m* **2** *v/t* (*draw ~ around*) poner un círculo alrededor de; *his name was ~d in red* su nombre tenía un círculo rojo alrededor **3** *v/i of plane, bird* volar en círculo

cir·cuit [ˈsɜːrkɪt] circuito *m*; (*lap*) vuelta *f*

ˈcir·cuit board COMPUT placa *f* or tarjeta *f* de circuitos; **ˈcir·cuit break·er** ELEC cortacircuitos *m inv*; **ˈcir·cuit train·ing** SP: *do* ~ hacer circuitos de entrenamiento

cir·cu·lar [ˈsɜːrkjʊlər] **1** *n giving information* circular *f* **2** *adj* circular

cir·cu·late [ˈsɜːrkjʊleɪt] **1** *v/i* circular **2** *v/t memo* hacer circular

cir·cu·la·tion [sɜːrkjʊˈleɪʃn] circulación *f*; *of newspaper, magazine* tirada *f*

cir·cum·fer·ence [sərˈkʌmfərəns] circunferencia *f*

cir·cum·stan·ces [ˈsɜːrkəmstənsɪs] *npl* circunstancias *fpl*; *financial situation* situación *f* económica; *under no ~* en ningún caso, de ninguna manera; *under the ~* dadas las circunstancias

cir·cus [ˈsɜːrkəs] circo *m*

cir·rho·sis (of the liv·er) [sɪˈroʊsɪs] cirrosis *f* (hepática)

cis·tern [ˈsɪstɜːrn] cisterna *f*

cite [saɪt] *v/t* citar

cit·i·zen [ˈsɪtɪzn] ciudadano(-a) *m(f)*

cit·i·zen·ship [ˈsɪtɪznʃɪp] ciudadanía *f*

cit·rus [ˈsɪtrəs] *adj* cítrico; ~ *fruit* cítrico *m*

cit·y [ˈsɪtɪ] ciudad *f*

cit·y ˈcen·ter, *Br* **cit·y ˈcen·tre** centro *m* de la ciudad

cit·y ˈhall ayuntamiento *m*

civ·ic [ˈsɪvɪk] *adj* cívico

civ·il [ˈsɪvl] *adj* civil; (*polite*) cortés

civ·il en·gi·neer ingeniero(-a) *m(f)* civil

ci·vil·ian [sɪˈvɪljən] **1** *n* civil *m/f* **2** *adj clothes* de civil

ci·vil·i·ty [sɪˈvɪlɪtɪ] cortesía *f*

civ·i·li·za·tion [sɪvəlaɪˈzeɪʃn] civilización *f*

civ·i·lize [ˈsɪvəlaɪz] *v/t* civilizar

civ·il ˈrights *npl* derechos *mpl* civiles; **civ·il ˈser·vant** funcionario(-a) *m(f)*; **civ·il ˈser·vice** administración *f* pública; **civ·il ˈwar** guerra *f* civil

claim [kleɪm] **1** *n* (*request*) reclamación *f* (*for* de); (*right*) derecho *m*; (*assertion*) afirmación *f* **2** *v/t* (*ask for as a right*) reclamar; (*assert*) afirmar; *lost property* reclamar; *they have*

~ed responsibility for the attack se han atribuido la responsabilidad del ataque

claim·ant ['kleɪmənt] reclamante *m/f*

clair·voy·ant [kler'vɔɪənt] *n* clarividente *m/f*, vidente *m/f*

clam [klæm] almeja *f*

♦ **clam up** *v/i* (*pret & pp* **-med**) F cerrarse, callarse

clam·ber ['klæmbər] *v/i* trepar (**over** por)

clam·my ['klæmɪ] *adj* húmedo

clam·or, *Br* **clam·our** ['klæmər] *noise* griterío *m*; *outcry* clamor *m*

♦ **clamor for** *v/t justice* clamar por; *ice cream* pedir a gritos

clamp [klæmp] **1** *n fastener* abrazadera *f*, mordaza *f* **2** *v/t fasten* sujetar con abrazadera; *car* poner un cepo a

♦ **clamp down** *v/i* actuar contundentemente

♦ **clamp down on** *v/t* actuar contundentemente contra

clan [klæn] clan *m*

clan·des·tine [klæn'destɪn] *adj* clandestino

clang [klæŋ] **1** *n* sonido *m* metálico **2** *v/i* resonar; *the metal door ~ed shut* la puerta metálica se cerró con gran estrépito

clap [klæp] *v/t & v/i* (*pret & pp* **-ped**) (*applaud*) aplaudir

clar·et ['klærɪt] *wine* burdeos *m inv*

clar·i·fi·ca·tion [klærɪfɪ'keɪʃn] aclaración *f*

clar·i·fy ['klærɪfaɪ] *v/t* (*pret & pp* **-ied**) aclarar

clar·i·net [klærɪ'net] clarinete *m*

clar·i·ty ['klærətɪ] claridad *f*

clash [klæʃ] **1** *n* choque *m*, enfrentamiento *m*; *of personalities* choque *m* **2** *v/i* chocar, enfrentarse; *of colors* desentonar; *of events* coincidir

clasp [klæsp] **1** *n* broche *m*, cierre *m* **2** *v/t in hand* estrechar

class [klæs] **1** *n lesson, students* clase *f*; *social ~* clase *f* social **2** *v/t* clasificar (**as** como)

clas·sic ['klæsɪk] **1** *adj* clásico **2** *n*

clásico *m*

clas·si·cal ['klæsɪkl] *adj music* clásico

clas·si·fi·ca·tion [klæsɪfɪ'keɪʃn] clasificación *f*

clas·si·fied ['klæsɪfaɪd] *adj information* reservado

'**clas·si·fied ad**(**ver·tise·ment**) anuncio *m* por palabras

clas·si·fy ['klæsɪfaɪ] *v/t* (*pret & pp* **-ied**) clasificar

'**class·mate** compañero(-a) *m(f)* de clase; '**class·room** clase *f*, aula *f*; '**class war·fare** lucha *f* de clases

class·y ['klæsɪ] *adj* F con clase

clat·ter ['klætər] **1** *n* estrépito *m* **2** *v/i* hacer ruido

clause [klɔːz] *in agreement* cláusula *f*; GRAM cláusula *f*, oración *f*

claus·tro·pho·bi·a [klɔːstrə'fəʊbɪə] claustrofobia *f*

claw [klɔː] **1** *n also fig* garra *f*; *of lobster* pinza *f* **2** *v/t* (*scratch*) arañar

clay [kleɪ] arcilla *f*

clean [kliːn] **1** *adj* limpio **2** *adv* F (*completely*) completamente **3** *v/t* limpiar; *~ one's teeth* limpiarse los dientes; *I must have my coat ~ed* tengo que llevar el abrigo a la tintorería

♦ **clean out** *v/t room, closet* limpiar por completo; *fig* desplumar

♦ **clean up 1** *v/t also fig* limpiar; *papers* recoger **2** *v/i* limpiar; (*wash*) lavarse; *on stock market etc* ganar mucho dinero

clean·er ['kliːnər] *person* limpiador(a) *m(f)*; (*dry*) ~ tintorería *f*

clean·ing wom·an ['kliːnɪŋ] señora *f* de la limpieza

cleanse [klenz] *v/t skin* limpiar

cleans·er ['klenzər] *for skin* loción *f* limpiadora

cleans·ing cream ['klenzɪŋ] crema *f* limpiadora

clear [klɪr] **1** *adj* claro; *weather, sky* despejado; *water* transparente; *conscience* limpio; *I'm not ~ about it* no lo tengo claro; *I didn't make myself ~* no me expliqué claramente **2** *adv stand ~ of the doors* apartarse de las puertas; **steer ~ of** evitar **3** *v/t roads etc* despejar; (*acquit*) absolver; (*authorize*) autorizar; (*earn*) ganar, sacar; **the guards ~ed everybody out of the room** los guardias sacaron a todo el mundo de la habitación; **you're ~ed for takeoff** tiene autorización *or* permiso para despegar; **~ one's throat** carraspear **4** *v/i of sky, mist* despejarse; *of face* alegrarse

♦ **clear away** *v/t* quitar

♦ **clear off** *v/i* F largarse F

♦ **clear out 1** *v/t closet* ordenar, limpiar **2** *v/i* marcharse

♦ **clear up 1** *v/i* ordenar; *of weather* despejarse; *of illness, rash* desaparecer **2** *v/t* (*tidy*) ordenar; *mystery, problem* aclarar

clear·ance ['klırəns] *space* espacio *m*; (*authorization*) autorización *f*

clear·ance sale liquidación *f*

clear·ing ['klırıŋ] claro *m*

clear·ly ['klırlı] *adv* claramente; **she is ~ upset** está claro que está disgustada

cleav·age ['kli:vıdʒ] escote *m*

cleav·er ['kli:vər] cuchillo *m* de carnicero

clem·en·cy ['klemənsı] clemencia *f*

clench [klentʃ] *v/t teeth, fist* apretar

cler·gy ['klɜ:rdʒı] clero *m*

cler·gy·man ['klɜ:rdʒımæn] clérigo *m*

clerk [klɜ:rk] *administrative* oficinista *m/f*; *in store* dependiente(-a) *m/f*

clev·er ['klevər] *adj person, animal* listo; *idea, gadget* ingenioso

clev·er·ly ['klevərlı] *adv designed* ingeniosamente

cli·ché ['kli:ʃeı] tópico *m*, cliché *m*

cli·chéd ['kli:ʃeıd] *adj* estereotipado

click [klık] **1** *n* COMPUT clic *m* **2** *v/i* hacer clic

♦ **click on** *v/t* COMPUT hacer clic en

cli·ent ['klaıənt] cliente *m/f*

cli·en·tele [klaıən'tel] clientela *f*

cli·mate ['klaımət] *also fig* clima *m*

'cli·mate change cambio *m* climático

cli·mat·ic [klaı'mætık] *adj* climático

cli·max ['klaımæks] *n* clímax *m*, punto *m* culminante

climb [klaım] **1** *n up mountain* ascensión *f*, escalada *f* **2** *v/t hill, ladder* subir; *mountain* subir, escalar; *tree* trepar a **3** *v/i* subir (**into** a); *up mountain* subir, escalar; *of inflation etc* subir

♦ **climb down** *v/i from ladder etc* bajar

climb·er ['klaımər] *person* escalador(a) *m(f)*, alpinista *m/f*, *L.Am.* andinista *m/f*

climb·ing ['klaımıŋ] escalada *f*, alpinismo *m*, *L.Am.* andinismo *m*

climb·ing wall rocódromo *m*

clinch [klıntʃ] *v/t deal* cerrar; **that ~es it** ¡ahora sí que está claro!

cling [klıŋ] *v/i* (*pret & pp* **clung**) *of clothes* pegarse al cuerpo

♦ **cling to** *v/t person, idea* aferrarse a

'cling·film plástico *m* transparente (para alimentos)

cling·y ['klıŋı] *adj child, boyfriend* pegajoso

clin·ic ['klınık] clínica *f*

clin·i·cal ['klınıkl] *adj* clínico

clink [klıŋk] **1** *n noise* tintineo *m* **2** *v/i* tintinear

clip[1] [klıp] **1** *n fastener* clip *m* **2** *v/t* (*pret & pp* **-ped**): **~ sth to sth** sujetar algo a algo

clip[2] [klıp] **1** *n extract* fragmento *m* **2** *v/t* (*pret & pp* **-ped**) *hair, grass* cortar; *hedge* podar

clip·pers ['klıpərz] *npl for hair* maquinilla *f*; *for nails* cortaúñas *m inv*; *for gardening* tijeras *fpl* de podar

clip·ping ['klıpıŋ] *from newspaper* recorte *m*

clique [kli:k] camarilla *f*

cloak *n* capa *f*

'cloak·room *Br* guardarropa *m*

clock [klɑ:k] reloj *m*

'clock ra·di·o radio *m* despertador; **'clock·wise** *adv* en el sentido de las agujas del reloj; **'clock·work: it went like ~** salió a la perfección

♦ **clog up** [klɑ:g] **1** *v/i* (*pret & pp* **-ged**) bloquearse **2** *v/t* (*pret & pp* **-ged**) bloquear

clone [kloʊn] **1** *n* clon *m* **2** *v/t* clonar
close¹ [kloʊs] **1** *adj family* cercano;
friend íntimo; **bear a ~ resemblance to** parecerse mucho a; **the ~st town** la ciudad más cercana; **be ~ to s.o.** *emotionally* estar muy unido a alguien **2** *adv* cerca; **~ to the school** cerca del colegio; **~ at hand** a mano; **~ by** cerca
close² [kloʊz] **1** *v/t* cerrar **2** *v/i* of *door, shop* cerrar; *of eyes* cerrarse
♦ **close down** *v/t* & *v/i* cerrar
♦ **close in** *v/i of fog* echarse encima; *of troops* aproximarse, acercarse
♦ **close up 1** *v/t building* cerrar **2** *v/i* (*move closer*) juntarse
closed [kloʊzd] *adj store, eyes* cerrado
closed-cir·cuit 'tel·e·vi·sion circuito *m* cerrado de televisión
'close-knit *adj* muy unido
close·ly ['kloʊslɪ] *adv listen, watch* atentamente; *cooperate* de cerca
clos·et ['klɑːzɪt] armario *m*
close-up ['kloʊsʌp] primer plano *m*
clos·ing date ['kloʊzɪŋ] fecha *f* límite
'clos·ing time hora *f* de cierre
clo·sure ['kloʊʒər] cierre *m*
clot [klɑːt] **1** *n of blood* coágulo *m* **2** *v/i* (*pret & pp* **-ted**) *of blood* coagular
cloth [klɑːθ] (*fabric*) tela *f*, tejido *m*; *for cleaning* trapo *m*
clothes [kloʊðz] *npl* ropa *f*
'clothes brush cepillo *m* para la ropa; **'clothes hang·er** percha *f*; **'clothes·horse** tendedero *m* plegable; **'clothes·line** cuerda *f* de tender la ropa; **'clothes peg**, **'clothes·pin** pinza *f* (de la ropa)
cloth·ing ['kloʊðɪŋ] ropa *f*
cloud [klaʊd] *n* nube *f*; **a ~ of dust** una nube de polvo
♦ **cloud over** *v/i of sky* nublarse
'cloud·burst chaparrón *m*
cloud·less ['klaʊdlɪs] *adj sky* despejado
cloud·y ['klaʊdɪ] *adj* nublado
clout [klaʊt] *fig* (*influence*) influencia *f*

clove of 'gar·lic [kloʊv] diente *m* de ajo
clown [klaʊn] *also fig* payaso *m*
club [klʌb] *n weapon* palo *m*, garrote *m*; *in golf* palo *m*; *organization* club *m*; *~s in cards* tréboles
clue [kluː] pista *f*; **I haven't a ~** F (*don't know*) no tengo idea F; **he hasn't a ~** F (*is useless*) no tiene ni idea F
clued-up [kluːd'ʌp] *adj* F puesto F; **be ~ on sth** F estar puesto sobre algo F
clump [klʌmp] *n of earth* terrón *m*; *of flowers etc* grupo *m*
clum·si·ness ['klʌmzɪnɪs] torpeza *f*
clum·sy ['klʌmzɪ] *adj person* torpe
clung [klʌŋ] *pret & pp* → **cling**
clus·ter ['klʌstər] **1** *n* grupo *m* **2** *v/i of people* apiñarse; *of houses* agruparse
clutch [klʌtʃ] **1** *n* MOT embrague *m* **2** *v/t* agarrar
♦ **clutch at** *v/t* agarrarse a
clut·ter ['klʌtər] **1** *n* desorden *m*; **all the ~ on my desk** la cantidad de cosas que hay encima de mi mesa **2** *v/t* (*also: ~ up*) abarrotar
Co. *abbr* (= **Company**) Cía. (= Compañía *f*)
c/o *abbr* (= **care of**) en el domicilio de
coach [koʊtʃ] **1** *n* (*trainer*) entrenador(a) *m(f)*; *of singer, actor* profesor(a) *m(f)*; *Br* (*bus*) autobús *m* **2** *v/t footballer* entrenar; *singer* preparar
coach·ing ['koʊtʃɪŋ] entrenamiento *m*
co·ag·u·late [koʊ'ægjʊleɪt] *v/i of blood* coagularse
coal [koʊl] carbón *m*
co·a·li·tion [koʊə'lɪʃn] coalición *f*
'coal·mine mina *f* de carbón
coarse [kɔːrs] *adj* áspero; *hair* basto; (*vulgar*) basto, grosero
coarse·ly ['kɔːrslɪ] *adv* (*vulgarly*) de manera grosera; **~ ground coffee** café molido grueso
coast [koʊst] *n* costa *f*; **at the ~** en la costa

coast·al ['koustl] *adj* costero

coast·er ['koustər] posavasos *m inv*

'coast·guard *organization* servicio *m* de guardacostas; *person* guardacostas *m/f inv*

'coast·line litoral *m*, costa *f*

coat [kout] **1** *n* chaqueta *f*, *L.Am.* saco *m*; (*over~*) abrigo *m*; *of animal* pelaje *m*; *of paint etc* capa *f*, mano *f* **2** *v/t* (*cover*) cubrir (**with** de)

'coat·hang·er percha *f*

coat·ing ['koutɪŋ] capa *f*

co·au·thor ['koʊɒːθər] **1** *n* coautor(a) *m(f)* **2** *v/t*: ~ *a book* escribir un libro conjuntamente

coax [kouks] *v/t* persuadir; ~ *sth out of s.o.* sonsacar algo a alguien

cob·bled ['kɑːbld] *adj* adoquinado

cob·ble·stone ['kɑːblstoun] adoquín *m*

cob·web ['kɑːbweb] telaraña *f*

co·caine [kəˈkeɪn] cocaína *f*

cock [kɑːk] *n* (*chicken*) gallo *m*; (*any male bird*) macho *m*

cock·eyed [kɑːkˈaɪd] *adj* F *idea etc* ridículo

'cock·pit *of plane* cabina *f*

cock·roach ['kɑːkroutʃ] cucaracha *f*

'cock·tail cóctel *m* (*bebida*)

'cock·tail par·ty cóctel *m* (*fiesta*)

'cock·tail shak·er coctelera *f*

cock·y ['kɑːkɪ] *adj* F creído, chulo

co·coa ['koukou] *drink* cacao *m*

co·co·nut ['koukənʌt] coco *m*

'co·co·nut palm cocotero *m*

COD [siːouˈdiː] *abbr* (= *collect on delivery*) entrega *f* contra reembolso

cod·dle ['kɑːdl] *v/t sick person* cuidar; *pej: child* mimar

code [koud] *n* código *m*; *in ~* cifrado

co·ed·u·ca·tion·al [kouedu'keɪʃnl] *adj* mixto

co·erce [kouˈɜːrs] *v/t* coaccionar

co·ex·ist [kouɪgˈzɪst] *v/i* coexistir

co·ex·ist·ence [kouɪgˈzɪstəns] coexistencia *f*

cof·fee ['kɑːfɪ] café *m*; *a cup of ~* un café

'cof·fee bean grano *m* de café;

'cof·fee break pausa *f* para el café;

'cof·fee cup taza *f* de café;

'cof·fee grind·er ['graɪndər] molinillo *m* de café; **'cof·fee mak·er** cafetera *f* (para preparar); **'cof·fee pot** cafetera *f* (para servir); **'cof·fee shop** café *m*, cafetería *f*; **'cof·fee ta·ble** mesa *f* de centro

cof·fin ['kɑːfɪn] féretro *m*, ataúd *m*

cog [kɑːg] diente *m*

co·gnac [ˈkɑːnjæk] coñac *m*

'cog·wheel rueda *f* dentada

co·hab·it [kouˈhæbɪt] *v/i* cohabitar

co·her·ent [kouˈhɪrənt] *adj* coherente

coil [kɔɪl] **1** *n of rope* rollo *m*; *of smoke* espiral *f*; *of snake* anillo *m* **2** *v/t*: ~ (*up*) enrollar

coin [kɔɪn] *n* moneda *f*

co·in·cide [kouɪnˈsaɪd] *v/i* coincidir

co·in·ci·dence [kouˈɪnsɪdəns] coincidencia *f*

coke [kouk] P (*cocaine*) coca *f*

Coke® [kouk] Coca-Cola® *f*

cold [kould] **1** *adj also fig* frío; *I'm* (*feeling*) ~ tengo frío; *it's* ~ *of weather* hace frío; *in* ~ *blood* a sangre fría; *get* ~ *feet* F ponerse nervioso **2** *n* frío *m*; MED resfriado *m*; *I have a* ~ estoy resfriado, tengo un resfriado

cold-blood·ed [kould'blʌdɪd] *adj* de sangre fría; *fig: murder* a sangre fría

cold call·ing ['kɔːlɪŋ] COM *visitas o llamadas comerciales hechas sin cita previa*

'cold cuts *npl* fiambres *mpl*

cold·ly ['kouldlɪ] *adv* fríamente, con frialdad

cold·ness ['kouldnɪs] frialdad *f*

'cold sore calentura *f*

cole·slaw ['koulslɔː] *ensalada de col, cebolla, zanahoria y mayonesa*

col·ic ['kɑːlɪk] cólico *m*

col·lab·o·rate [kə'læbəreɪt] *v/i* colaborar (**on** en)

col·lab·o·ra·tion [kəlæbə'reɪʃn] colaboración *f*

col·lab·o·ra·tor [kə'læbəreɪtər] colaborador(a) *m(f)*; *with enemy* colaboracionista *m/f*

col·lapse [kə'læps] *v/i of roof, buil-*

C

ding hundirse, desplomarse; *of person* desplomarse

col·lap·si·ble [kə'læpsəbl] *adj* plegable

col·lar ['kɑːlər] cuello *m*; *for dog* collar *m*

'col·lar-bone clavícula *f*

col·league ['kɑːliːg] colega *m/f*

col·lect [kə'lekt] **1** *v/t* recoger; *as hobby* coleccionar **2** *v/i* (*gather together*) reunirse **3** *adv*: **call ~** llamar a cobro revertido

col·lect call llamada *f* a cobro revertido

col·lect·ed [kə'lektɪd] *adj works, poems etc* completo; *person* sereno

col·lec·tion [kə'lekʃn] colección *f*; *in church* colecta *f*

col·lec·tive [kə'lektɪv] *adj* colectivo

col·lec·tive 'bar·gain·ing negociación *f* colectiva

col·lec·tor [kə'lektər] coleccionista *m/f*

col·lege ['kɑːlɪdʒ] universidad *f*

col·lide [kə'laɪd] *v/i* chocar, colisionar (**with** con *or* contra)

col·li·sion [kə'lɪʒn] choque *m*, colisión *f*

col·lo·qui·al [kə'loʊkwɪəl] *adj* coloquial

Co·lom·bi·a [kə'lɑːmbɪə] Colombia

Co·lom·bi·an [kə'lɑːmbɪən] **1** *adj* colombiano **2** *n* colombiano(-a) *m(f)*

co·lon ['koʊlən] *punctuation* dos puntos *mpl*; ANAT colon *m*

colo·nel ['kɜːrnl] coronel *m*

co·lo·ni·al [kə'loʊnɪəl] *adj* colonial

co·lo·nize ['kɑːlənaɪz] *v/t country* colonizar

co·lo·ny ['kɑːlənɪ] colonia *f*

col·or ['kʌlər] **1** *n* color *m*; **in ~** *movie etc* en color; **~s** MIL bandera *f* **2** *v/t one's hair* teñir **3** *v/i* (*blush*) ruborizarse

'col·or-blind *adj* daltónico

col·ored ['kʌlərd] *adj person* de color

'col·or fast *adj* que no destiñe

col·or·ful ['kʌlərfəl] *adj* lleno de colores; *account* colorido

col·or·ing ['kʌlərɪŋ] color *m*

'col·or pho·to·graph fotografía *f* en color; 'col·or scheme combinación *f* de colores; 'col·or TV televisión *f* en color

co·los·sal [kə'lɑːsl] *adj* colosal

col·our *etc Br* → color *etc*

colt [koʊlt] potro *m*

Co·lum·bus [kə'lʌmbəs] Colón *m*

col·umn ['kɑːləm] *architectural, of text* columna *f*

col·umn·ist ['kɑːləmɪst] columnista *m/f*

co·ma ['koʊmə] coma *m*; **be in a ~** estar en coma

comb [koʊm] **1** *n* peine *m* **2** *v/t hair, area* peinar; **~ one's hair** peinarse

com·bat ['kɑːmbæt] **1** *n* combate *m* **2** *v/t* combatir

com·bi·na·tion [kɑːmbɪ'neɪʃn] combinación *f*

com·bine [kəm'baɪn] **1** *v/t* combinar; *ingredients* mezclar **2** *v/i* combinarse

com·bine har·vest·er [kɑːmbaɪn-'hɑːrvɪstər] cosechadora *f*

com·bus·ti·ble [kəm'bʌstɪbl] *adj* combustible

com·bus·tion [kəm'bʌstʃn] combustión *f*

come [kʌm] *v/i* (*pret* **came**, *pp* **come**) *toward speaker* venir; *toward listener* ir; *of train, bus* llegar, venir; **don't ~ too close** no te acerques demasiado; **you'll ~ to like it** llegará a gustarte; **how ~?** F ¿y eso?; **how ~ you've stopped going to the club?** ¿cómo es que has dejado de ir al club?

◆**come about** *v/i* (*happen*) pasar, suceder

◆**come across 1** *v/t* (*find*) encontrar **2** *v/i*: **his humor comes across as ...** su humor da la impresión de ser ...; **she comes across as ...** da la impresión de ser ...

◆**come along** *v/i* (*come too*) venir; (*turn up*) aparecer; (*progress*) marchar; **why don't you come along?** ¿por qué no te vienes con nosotros ...

◆**come apart** *v/i* desmontarse;

(*break*) romperse

♦**come around** *v/i* to *s.o.'s home* venir, pasarse; (*regain consciousness*) volver en sí

♦**come away** *v/i* (*leave*) salir; *of button etc* caerse

♦**come back** *v/i* volver; *it came back to me* lo recordé

♦**come by 1** *v/i* pasarse **2** *v/t* (*acquire*) conseguir; *how did you come by that bruise?* ¿cómo te has dado ese golpe?

♦**come down 1** *v/i* bajar; *of rain, snow* caer **2** *v/t:* *he came down the stairs* bajó las escaleras

♦**come for** *v/t* (*attack*) atacar; (*collect: thing*) venir a por; (*collect: person*) venir a buscar a

♦**come forward** *v/i* (*present o.s.*) presentarse

♦**come from** *v/t* (*travel from*) venir de; (*originate from*) ser de

♦**come in** *v/i* entrar; *of train* llegar; *of tide* subir; *come in!* ¡entre!, ¡adelante!

♦**come in for** *v/t* recibir; *come in for criticism* recibir críticas

♦**come in on** *v/t:* *come in on a deal* participar en un negocio

♦**come off** *v/i of handle etc* soltarse, caerse; *of paint etc* quitarse

♦**come on** *v/i* (*progress*) marchar, progresar; *come on!* ¡vamos!; *oh come on, you're exaggerating* ¡vamos, hombre!, estás exagerando

♦**come out** *v/i* salir; *of book* publicarse; *of stain* irse, quitarse; *of gay* declararse homosexual públicamente

♦**come to 1** *v/t place* llegar a; *of hair, dress, water* llegar hasta; *that comes to $70* suma 70 dólares **2** *v/i* (*regain consciousness*) volver en sí

♦**come up** *v/i* subir; *of sun* salir; *something has come up* ha surgido algo

♦**come up with** *v/t solution* encontrar; *John came up with a great idea* a John se le ocurrió una idea estupenda

'**come·back** regreso *m*; *make a ~* regresar

co·me·di·an [kəˈmiːdɪən] humorista *m/f*, *pej* payaso(-a) *m(f)*

'**come·down** gran decepción *f*

com·e·dy [ˈkɑːmədɪ] comedia *f*

com·et [ˈkɑːmɪt] cometa *m*

come·up·pance [kʌmˈʌpəns] *n* F: *he'll get his ~* tendrá su merecido

com·fort [ˈkʌmfərt] **1** *n* comodidad *f*, confort *m*; (*consolation*) consuelo *m* **2** *v/t* consolar

com·for·ta·ble [ˈkʌmfərtəbl] *adj chair* cómodo; *house, room* cómodo, confortable; *be ~ of person* estar cómodo; *financially* estar en una situación holgada

com·ic [ˈkɑːmɪk] **1** *n to read* cómic *m*; (*comedian*) cómico(-a) *m(f)* **2** *adj* cómico

com·i·cal [ˈkɑːmɪkl] *adj* cómico

'**com·ic book** cómic *m*

'**com·ics** [ˈkɑːmɪks] *npl* tiras *fpl* cómicas

'**com·ic strip** tira *f* cómica

com·ma [ˈkɑːmə] coma *f*

com·mand [kəˈmænd] **1** *n* orden *f* **2** *v/t* ordenar, mandar

com·man·deer [kɑːmənˈdɪr] *v/t* requisar

com·mand·er [kəˈmændər] comandante *m/f*

com·mand·er-in-ˈchief comandante *m/f* en jefe

com·mand·ing of·fi·cer [kəˈmændɪŋ] oficial *m/f* al mando

com·mand·ment [kəˈmændmənt] mandamiento *m*: *the Ten Commandments* REL los Diez Mandamientos

com·mem·o·rate [kəˈmeməreɪt] *v/t* conmemorar

com·mem·o·ra·tion [kəmeməˈreɪʃn]: *in ~ of* en conmemoración de

com·mence [kəˈmens] *v/t* & *v/i* comenzar

com·mend [kəˈmend] *v/t* encomiar, elogiar

com·mend·a·ble [kəˈmendəbl] *adj* encomiable

com·men·da·tion [kəmenˈdeɪʃn] *for bravery* mención *f*

com·men·su·rate [kə'menʃərət] *adj:* ~ **with** acorde con

com·ment ['kɑ:ment] **1** *n* comentario *m*; **no ~!** ¡sin comentarios! **2** *v/i* hacer comentarios (**on** sobre)

com·men·ta·ry ['kɑ:mənterɪ] comentarios *mpl*

com·men·tate ['kɑ:mənteɪt] *v/i* hacer de comentarista

com·men·ta·tor ['kɑ:mənteɪtər] comentarista *m/f*

com·merce ['kɑ:mɜ:rs] comercio *m*

com·mer·cial [kə'mɜ:rʃl] **1** *adj* comercial **2** *n* (*advert*) anuncio *m* (publicitario)

com·mer·cial 'break pausa *f* publicitaria

com·mer·cial·ize [kə'mɜ:rʃlaɪz] *v/t Christmas* comercializar

com·mer·cial 'trav·el·er, *Br* **com·mer·cial 'trav·el·ler** viajante *m/f* de comercio

com·mis·e·rate [kə'mɪzəreɪt] *v/i:* **he ~d with me on my failure to get the job** me dijo cuánto sentía que no hubiera conseguido el trabajo

com·mis·sion [kə'mɪʃn] **1** *n* (*payment, committee*) comisión *f*; (*job*) encargo *m* **2** *v/t:* **she has been commissioned ...** se le ha encargado ...

com·mit [kə'mɪt] *v/t* (*pret & pp* -**ted**) *crime* cometer; *money* comprometer; ~ **o.s.** comprometerse

com·mit·ment [kə'mɪtmənt] compromiso *m* (**to** con); **he's afraid of ~** tiene miedo de comprometerse

com·mit·tee [kə'mɪtɪ] comité *m*

com·mod·i·ty [kə'mɑ:dətɪ] *raw material* producto *m* básico; *product* bien *m* de consumo

com·mon ['kɑ:mən] *adj* común; **in ~** al igual (**with** que); **have sth in ~ with s.o.** tener algo en común con alguien

com·mon·er ['kɑ:mənər] plebeyo(-a) *m(f)*

com·mon 'law wife esposa *f* de hecho

com·mon·ly ['kɑ:mənlɪ] *adv* comúnmente

'com·mon·place *adj* común

com·mon 'sense sentido *m* común

com·mo·tion [kə'moʊʃn] alboroto *m*

com·mu·nal [kə'mju:nl] *adj* comunal

com·mu·nal·ly [kəm'ju:nəlɪ] *adv* en comunidad

com·mu·ni·cate [kə'mju:nɪkeɪt] **1** *v/i* comunicarse **2** *v/t* comunicar

com·mu·ni·ca·tion [kəmju:nɪ'keɪʃn] comunicación *f*

com·mu·ni·ca·tions *npl* comunicaciones *fpl*

com·mu·ni·ca·tions sat·el·lite satélite *m* de telecomunicaciones

com·mu·ni·ca·tive [kə'mju:nɪkətɪv] *adj person* comunicativo

Com·mu·nion [kə'mju:njən] REL comunión *f*

com·mu·ni·qué [kə'mju:nɪkeɪ] comunicado *m*

Com·mu·nism ['kɑ:mjʊnɪzəm] comunismo *m*

Com·mu·nist ['kɑ:mjʊnɪst] **1** *adj* comunista **2** *n* comunista *m/f*

com·mu·ni·ty [kə'mju:nətɪ] comunidad *f*

com'mu·ni·ty cen·ter, *Br* **com'mu·ni·ty cen·tre** centro *m* comunitario

com'mu·ni·ty serv·ice servicios *mpl* a la comunidad (como pena)

com·mute [kə'mju:t] **1** *v/i* viajar al trabajo; ~ **to work** viajar al trabajo **2** *v/t* LAW conmutar

com·mut·er [kə'mju:tər] *persona que viaja al trabajo*

com'mut·er traf·fic *tráfico generado por los que se desplazan al trabajo*

com'mut·er train *tren de cercanías que utilizan los que se desplazan al trabajo*

com·pact 1 *adj* [kəm'pækt] compacto **2** *n* ['kɑ:mpækt] MOT utilitario *m*

com·pact 'disc (disco *m*) compacto *m*

com·pan·ion [kəm'pænjən] compañero(-a) *m(f)*

com·pan·ion·ship [kəm'pænjənʃɪp] compañía *f*

com·pa·ny ['kʌmpənɪ] COM empresa f, compañía f; (*companionship, guests*) compañía f; **keep s.o. ~** hacer compañía a alguien

com·pa·ny 'car coche m de empresa

com·pa·ny 'law derecho m de sociedades

com·pa·ra·ble ['kɑ:mpərəbl] *adj* comparable

com·par·a·tive [kəm'pærətɪv] **1** *adj* (*relative*) relativo; *study* comparado; GRAM comparativo; **~ form** GRAM comparativo m **2** n GRAM comparativo m

com·par·a·tive·ly [kəm'pærətɪvlɪ] *adv* relativamente

com·pare [kəm'per] **1** *v/t* comparar; **~d with ...** comparado con ...; **you can't ~ them** no se pueden comparar **2** *v/i* compararse

com·pa·ri·son [kəm'pærɪsn] comparación f; **there's no ~** no hay punto de comparación

com·part·ment [kəm'pɑ:rtmənt] compartimento m

com·pass ['kʌmpəs] brújula f; (*a pair of*) **~es** GEOM un compás

com·pas·sion [kəm'pæʃn] compasión f

com·pas·sion·ate [kəm'pæʃənət] *adj* compasivo

com·pas·sion·ate 'leave permiso laboral por muerte o enfermedad grave de un familiar

com·pat·i·bil·i·ty [kəmpætə'bɪlɪtɪ] compatibilidad f

com·pat·i·ble [kəm'pætəbl] *adj* compatible; **we're not ~** no somos compatibles

com·pel [kəm'pel] *v/t* (*pret & pp* **-led**) obligar

com·pel·ling [kəm'pelɪŋ] *adj* *argument* poderoso; *movie, book* fascinante

com·pen·sate ['kɑ:mpənseɪt] **1** *v/t* *with money* compensar **2** *v/i* **~ for** compensar

com·pen·sa·tion [kɑ:mpən'seɪʃn] (*money*) indemnización f; (*reward, comfort*) compensación f

com·pete [kəm'pi:t] *v/i* competir

(*for* por)

com·pe·tence ['kɑ:mpɪtəns] competencia f

com·pe·tent ['kɑ:mpɪtənt] *adj* competente; **I'm not ~ to judge** no estoy capacitado para juzgar

com·pe·tent·ly ['kɑ:mpɪtəntlɪ] *adv* competentemente

com·pe·ti·tion [kɑ:mpə'tɪʃn] (*contest*) concurso m; SP competición f; (*competitors*) competencia f; **the government wants to encourage ~** el gobierno quiere fomentar la competencia

com·pet·i·tive [kəm'petətɪv] *adj* competitivo

com·pet·i·tive·ly [kəm'petətɪvlɪ] *adv* competitivamente: **~ priced** con un precio muy competitivo

com·pet·i·tive·ness [kəm'petɪtɪvnɪs] COM competitividad f; *of person* espíritu m competitivo

com·pet·i·tor [kəm'petɪtər] *in contest* concursante m/f; SP competidor(a) m(f), contrincante m/f; COM competidor(a) m(f)

com·pile [kəm'paɪl] *v/t* compilar

com·pla·cen·cy [kəm'pleɪsənsɪ] complacencia f

com·pla·cent [kəm'pleɪsənt] *adj* complaciente

com·plain [kəm'pleɪn] *v/i* quejarse, protestar; *to shop, manager* quejarse; **~ of** MED estar aquejado de

com·plaint [kəm'pleɪnt] queja f, protesta f; MED dolencia f

com·ple·ment ['kɑ:mplɪmənt] *v/t* complementar; **they ~ each other** se complementan

com·ple·men·ta·ry [kɑ:mplɪ'mentərɪ] *adj* complementario; **the two are ~** los dos se complementan

com·plete [kəm'pli:t] **1** *adj* (*total*) absoluto, total; (*full*) completo; (*finished*) finalizado, terminado **2** *v/t* *task, building etc* finalizar, terminar; *course* completar; *form* rellenar

com·plete·ly [kəm'pli:tlɪ] *adv* completamente

com·ple·tion [kəm'pli:ʃn] finalización f, terminación f

com·plex ['kɑːmpleks] **1** adj complejo **2** n also PSYCH complejo m

com·plex·ion [kəm'plekʃn] facial tez f

com·plex·i·ty [kəm'pleksɪtɪ] complejidad f

com·pli·ance [kəm'plaɪəns] cumplimiento (**with** de)

com·pli·cate ['kɑːmplɪkeɪt] v/t complicar

com·pli·cat·ed ['kɑːmplɪkeɪtɪd] adj complicado

com·pli·ca·tion [kɑːmplɪ'keɪʃn] complicación f; **~s** MED complicaciones fpl

com·pli·ment ['kɑːmplɪmənt] **1** n cumplido m **2** v/t hacer un cumplido a (**on** por)

com·pli·men·ta·ry [kɑːmplɪ'mentərɪ] adj elogioso; (free) de regalo, gratis

'**com·pli·ments slip** nota f de cortesía

com·ply [kəm'plaɪ] v/i (pret & pp **-ied**) cumplir; **~ with** cumplir

com·po·nent [kəm'pounənt] pieza f, componente m

com·pose [kəm'pouz] v/t also MUS componer; **be ~d of** estar compuesto de; **~ o.s.** serenarse

com·posed [kəm'pouzd] adj (calm) sereno

com·pos·er [kəm'pouzər] MUS compositor(a) m(f)

com·po·si·tion [kɑːmpə'zɪʃn] also MUS composición f; (essay) redacción f

com·po·sure [kəm'pouʒər] compostura f

com·pound ['kɑːmpaund] n CHEM compuesto m

com·pound 'in·ter·est interés m compuesto o combinado

com·pre·hend [kɑːmprɪ'hend] v/t (understand) comprender

com·pre·hen·sion [kɑːmprɪ'henʃn] comprensión f

com·pre·hen·sive [kɑːmprɪ'hensɪv] adj detallado

com·pre·hen·sive in'sur·ance seguro m a todo riesgo

com·pre·hen·sive·ly [kɑːmprɪ'hensɪvlɪ] adv detalladamente

com·press 1 n ['kɑːmpres] MED compresa f **2** v/t [kəm'pres] air, gas comprimir; information condensar

com·prise [kəm'praɪz] v/t comprender; **be ~d of** constar de

com·pro·mise ['kɑːmprəmaɪz] **1** n solución f negociada; **I've had to make ~s all my life** toda mi vida he tenido que hacer concesiones **2** v/i transigir, efectuar concesiones **3** v/t principles traicionar; (jeopardize) poner en peligro; **~ o.s.** ponerse en un compromiso

com·pul·sion [kəm'pʌlʃn] PSYCH compulsión f

com·pul·sive [kəm'pʌlsɪv] adj behavior compulsivo; reading absorbente

com·pul·so·ry [kəm'pʌlsərɪ] adj obligatorio

com·put·er [kəm'pjuːtər] Span ordenador m, L.Am. computadora f; **have sth on ~** tener algo en el Span ordenador or L.Am. computadora

com·put·er·aid·ed de'sign [kəmpjuːtər'eɪdɪd] diseño m asistido por Span ordenador or L.Am. computadora; **com·put·er·aid·ed man·u·'fac·ture** fabricación f asistida por Span ordenador or L.Am. computadora; **com·put·er·con'trolled** adj controlado por Span ordenador or L.Am. computadora; **com'puter game** juego m de Span ordenador or L.Am. computadora

com·put·er·ize [kəm'pjuːtəraɪz] v/t informatizar, L.Am. computarizar

com·put·er 'lit·er·ate adj con conocimientos de informática or L.Am. computación; **com·put·er 'sci·ence** informática f, L.Am. computación f; **com·put·er 'sci·en·tist** informático(-a) m(f)

com·put·ing [kəm'pjuːtɪŋ] n informática f, L.Am. computación f

com·rade ['kɑːmreɪd] (friend) compañero(-a) m(f); POL camarada m/f com·rade·ship ['kɑːmreɪdʃɪp] camaradería f

con [kɑːn] **1** n F timo m F **2** v/t (pret & pp **-ned**) F timar F

con·ceal [kən'siːl] v/t ocultar

con·ceal·ment [kən'siːlmənt] ocultación f

con·cede [kən'siːd] v/t (admit) admitir, reconocer

con·ceit [kən'siːt] engreimiento m, presunción f

con·ceit·ed [kən'siːtɪd] adj engreído, presuntuoso

con·cei·va·ble [kən'siːvəbl] adj concebible

con·ceive [kən'siːv] v/i of woman concebir; ~ of (imagine) imaginar

con·cen·trate ['kɑːnsəntreɪt] **1** v/i concentrarse **2** v/t one's attention, energies concentrar

con·cen·trat·ed ['kɑːnsəntreɪtɪd] adj juice etc concentrado

con·cen·tra·tion [kɑːnsən'treɪʃn] concentración f

con·cept ['kɑːnsept] concepto m

con·cep·tion [kən'sepʃn] of child concepción f

con·cern [kən'sɜːrn] **1** n (anxiety, care) preocupación f; (business) asunto m; (company) empresa f; **it's none of your ~** no es asunto tuyo; **cause ~** preocupar, inquietar **2** v/t (involve) concernir, incumbir; (worry) preocupar, inquietar; **~ o.s. with** preocuparse de

con·cerned [kən'sɜːrnd] adj (anxious) preocupado, inquieto (about por); (caring) preocupado (about por); (involved) en cuestión; **as far as I'm ~** por lo que a mí respecta

con·cern·ing [kən'sɜːrnɪŋ] prep en relación con, sobre

con·cert ['kɑːnsərt] concierto m

con·cert·ed [kən'sɜːrtɪd] adj (joint) concertado, conjunto

'con·cert·mas·ter primer violín m/f

con·cer·to [kən'ʃertoʊ] concierto m

con·ces·sion [kən'seʃn] (compromise) concesión f

con·cil·i·a·to·ry [kənsɪlɪ'eɪtərɪ] adj conciliador

con·cise [kən'saɪs] adj conciso

con·clude [kən'kluːd] v/t & v/i (deduce, end) concluir (**from** de)

con·clu·sion [kən'kluːʒn] (deduction, end) conclusión f; **in ~** en conclusión

con·clu·sive [kən'kluːsɪv] adj concluyente

con·coct [kən'kɑːkt] v/t meal, drink preparar; excuse, story urdir

con·coc·tion [kən'kɑːkʃn] food menjunje m; drink brebaje m, pócima f

con·crete ['kɑːŋkriːt] **1** adj concreto; **~ jungle** jungla f de asfalto **2** n hormigón m, L.Am. concreto m

con·cur [kən'kɜːr] v/i (pret & pp **-red**) coincidir

con·cus·sion [kən'kʌʃn] conmoción f cerebral

con·demn [kən'dem] v/t condenar; building declarar en ruina

con·dem·na·tion [kɑːndəm'neɪʃn] of action condena f

con·den·sa·tion [kɑːnden'seɪʃn] on walls, windows condensación f

con·dense [kən'dens] **1** v/t (make shorter) condensar **2** v/i of steam condensarse

con·densed 'milk [kən'densd] leche f condensada

con·de·scend [kɑːndɪ'send] v/i: **he ~ed to speak to me** se dignó a hablarme

con·de·scend·ing [kɑːndɪ'sendɪŋ] adj (patronizing) condescendiente

con·di·tion [kən'dɪʃn] **1** n (state) condiciones fpl; of health estado m; illness enfermedad f; (requirement, term) condición f; **~s** (circumstances) condiciones fpl; **on ~ that ...** a condición de que ...; **you're in no ~ to drive** no estás en condiciones de conducir **2** v/t PSYCH condicionar

con·di·tion·al [kən'dɪʃnl] **1** adj acceptance condicional **2** n GRAM condicional m

con·di·tion·er [kən'dɪʃnər] for hair suavizante m, acondicionador m; for fabric suavizante m con·di·tion·ing [kən'dɪʃnɪŋ] PSYCH condicionamiento *m*

con·do ['kɑːndoʊ] F *apartment* apartamento *m, Span* piso *m; building* bloque de apartamentos

con·do·len·ces [kən'doʊlənsɪz] *npl* condolencias *fpl*

con·dom ['kɑːndəm] condón *m*, preservativo *m*

con·do·min·i·um [kɑːndə'mɪniəm] → **condo**

con·done [kən'doʊn] *v/t actions* justificar

con·du·cive [kən'duːsɪv] *adj*: ~ **to** propicio para

con·duct **1** *n* ['kɑːndʌkt] *(behavior)* conducta *f* **2** *v/t* [kən'dʌkt] *(carry out)* realizar, hacer; ELEC conducir; MUS dirigir; ~ **o.s.** comportarse

con·duct·ed 'tour [kən'dʌktɪd] visita *f* guiada

con·duc·tor [kən'dʌktər] MUS director(a) *m(f)* de orquesta; *on train* revisor(-a) *m(f)*; PHYS conductor *m*

cone [koʊn] GEOM, *on highway* cono *m; for ice cream* cucurucho *m; of pine tree* piña *f*

con·fec·tion·er [kən'fekʃənər] pastelero(-a) *m(f)*

con·fec·tion·ers' sug·ar azúcar *m or f* glas

con·fec·tion·e·ry [kən'fekʃənərɪ] *(candy)* dulces *mpl*

con·fed·e·ra·tion [kənfedə'reɪʃn] confederación *f*

con·fer [kən'fɜːr] **1** *v/t* (*pret & pp* **-red**): ~ **sth on s.o.** *(bestow)* conferir *or* otorgar algo a alguien **2** *v/i* (*pret & pp* **-red**) *(discuss)* deliberar

con·fe·rence ['kɑːnfərəns] congreso *m; discussion* conferencia *f*

'con·fe·rence room sala *f* de conferencias

con·fess [kən'fes] **1** *v/t* confesar **2** *v/i* confesar; REL confesarse; ~ **to a weakness for sth** confesar una debilidad por algo

con·fes·sion [kən'feʃn] confesión *f; I've a ~ to make* tengo algo que confesar

con·fes·sion·al [kən'feʃnl] REL confesionario *m*

con·fes·sor [kən'fesər] REL confesor *m*

con·fide [kən'faɪd] **1** *v/t* confiar **2** *v/i*: ~ **in s.o.** confiarse a alguien

con·fi·dence ['kɑːnfɪdəns] confianza *f; (secret)* confidencia *f; in ~* en confianza, confidencialmente

con·fi·dent ['kɑːnfɪdənt] *adj (self-assured)* seguro de sí mismo; *(convinced)* seguro

con·fi·den·tial [kɑːnfɪ'denʃl] *adj* confidencial, secreto

con·fi·den·tial·ly [kɑːnfɪ'denʃlɪ] *adv* confidencialmente

con·fi·dent·ly ['kɑːnfɪdəntlɪ] *adv* con seguridad

con·fine [kən'faɪn] *v/t (imprison)* confinar, recluir; *(restrict)* limitar; *be ~d to one's bed* tener que guardar cama

con·fined [kən'faɪnd] *adj space* limitado

con·fine·ment [kən'faɪnmənt] *(imprisonment)* reclusión *f*; MED parto *m*

con·firm [kən'fɜːrm] *v/t* confirmar

con·fir·ma·tion [kɑːnfər'meɪʃn] confirmación *f*

con·firmed [kɑːn'fɜːrmd] *adj (inveterate)* empedernido; *I'm a ~ believer in ...* creo firmemente en ...

con·fis·cate ['kɑːnfɪskeɪt] *v/t* confiscar

con·flict **1** *n* ['kɑːnflɪkt] conflicto *m* **2** *v/i* [kən'flɪkt] *(clash)* chocar; *~ing loyalties* lealtades *fpl* encontradas

con·form [kən'fɔːrm] *v/i* ser conformista; ~ **to** *to standards etc* ajustarse a

con·form·ist [kən'fɔːrmɪst] *n* conformista *m/f*

con·front [kən'frʌnt] *v/t (face)* hacer frente a, enfrentarse a; *(tackle)* hacer frente a

con·fron·ta·tion [kɑːnfrən'teɪʃn] confrontación *f*, enfrentamiento *m*

con·fuse [kən'fjuːz] *v/t* confundir; ~ **s.o. with s.o.** confundir a alguien con alguien

con·fused [kən'fjuːzd] *adj person*

confundido; *situation, piece of writing* confuso

con·fus·ing [kən'fjuːzɪŋ] *adj* confuso

con·fu·sion [kən'fjuːʒn] (*muddle, chaos*) confusión *f*

con·geal [kən'dʒiːl] *v/i of blood* coagularse; *of fat* solidificarse

con·gen·ial [kən'dʒiːnɪəl] *adj person* simpático, agradable; *occasion, place* agradable

con·gen·i·tal [kən'dʒenɪtl] *adj* MED congénito

con·gest·ed [kən'dʒestɪd] *adj roads* congestionado

con·ges·tion [kən'dʒestʃn] *also* MED congestión *f*; **traffic ~** congestión *f* circulatoria

con·grat·u·late [kən'grætʃʊleɪt] *v/t* felicitar

con·grat·u·la·tions [kəngrætʃʊ'leɪʃnz] *npl* felicitaciones *fpl*; **~ on ...** felicidades por ...; **let me offer my ~** permita que le dé la enhorabuena

con·grat·u·la·to·ry [kəngrætʃʊ'leɪtərɪ] *adj* de felicitación

con·gre·gate ['kɑːŋgrɪgeɪt] *v/i* (*gather*) congregarse

con·gre·ga·tion [kɑːŋgrɪ'geɪʃn] REL congregación *f*

con·gress ['kɑːŋgres] (*conference*) congreso *m*; **Congress** *in US* Congreso *m*

Con·gres·sion·al [kən'greʃnl] *adj* del Congreso

Con·gress·man ['kɑːŋgresmən] congresista *m*

Con·gress·wo·man ['kɑːŋgreswʊmən] congresista *f*

co·ni·fer ['kɑːnɪfər] conífera *f*

con·jec·ture [kən'dʒektʃər] *n* (*speculation*) conjetura *f*

con·ju·gate ['kɑːndʒʊgeɪt] *v/t* GRAM conjugar

con·junc·tion [kən'dʒʌŋkʃn] GRAM conjunción *f*; **in ~ with** junto con

con·junc·ti·vi·tis [kəndʒʌŋktɪ'vaɪtɪs] conjuntivitis *f*

♦ con·jure up ['kʌndʒər] *v/t* (*produce*) hacer aparecer; (*evoke*) evocar

con·jur·er, con·jur·or ['kʌndʒərər]

(*magician*) prestidigitador(a) *m(f)*

con·jur·ing tricks ['kʌndʒərɪŋ] *npl* juegos *mpl* de manos

con man ['kɑːnmæn] F timador *m* F

con·nect [kə'nekt] *v/t* conectar; (*link*) relacionar, vincular; *to power supply* enchufar

con·nect·ed [kə'nektɪd] *adj*: **be well-~** estar bien relacionado; **be ~ with** estar relacionado con

con·nect·ing flight [kə'nektɪŋ] vuelo *m* de conexión

con·nec·tion [kə'nekʃn] conexión *f*; *when traveling* conexión *f*, enlace; (*personal contact*) contacto *m*; **in ~ with** en relación con

con·nois·seur [kɑːnə'sɜːr] entendido(-a) *m(f)*

con·quer ['kɑːŋkər] *v/t* conquistar; *fig: fear etc* vencer

con·quer·or ['kɑːŋkərər] conquistador(a) *m(f)*

con·quest ['kɑːŋkwest] *of territory* conquista *f*

con·science ['kɑːnʃəns] conciencia *f*; **a guilty ~** un sentimiento de culpa; **it was on my ~** me remordía la conciencia

con·sci·en·tious [kɑːnʃɪ'enʃəs] *adj* concienzudo

con·sci·en·tious·ness [kɑːnʃɪ'enʃənəs] aplicación *f*

con·sci·en·tious ob·ject·or objetor(a) *m(f)* de conciencia

con·scious ['kɑːnʃəs] *adj* consciente; **be ~ of** ser consciente de

con·scious·ly ['kɑːnʃəslɪ] *adv* conscientemente

con·scious·ness ['kɑːnʃəsnɪs] (*awareness*) conciencia *f*; MED con(s)ciencia *f*; **lose/regain ~** quedar inconsciente/volver en sí

con·sec·u·tive [kən'sekjʊtɪv] *adj* consecutivo

con·sen·sus [kən'sensəs] consenso *m*

con·sent [kən'sent] **1** *n* consentimiento *m* **2** *v/i* consentir (**to** en)

con·se·quence ['kɑːnsɪkwəns] (*result*) consecuencia *f*; **as a ~ of** como consecuencia de

con·se·quent·ly ['kɑːnsɪkwəntlɪ] *adv* (*therefore*) por consiguiente

con·ser·va·tion [kɑːnsər'veɪʃn] (*preservation*) conservación *f*, protección *f*

con·ser·va·tion·ist [kɑːnsər'veɪʃn-ɪst] ecologista *m/f*

con·ser·va·tive [kən'sɜːrvətɪv] *adj* (*conventional*) conservador; *estimate* prudente

con·ser·va·to·ry [kən'sɜːrvətɔːrɪ] MUS conservatorio *m*

con·serve 1 *n* ['kɑːnsɜːrv] (*jam*) compota *f* **2** *v/t* [kən'sɜːrv] conservar

con·sid·er [kən'sɪdər] *v/t* (*regard*) considerar; (*show regard for*) mostrar consideración por; (*think about*) considerar; *it is ~ed to be ...* se considera que es ...

con·sid·er·a·ble [kən'sɪdrəbl] *adj* considerable

con·sid·er·a·bly [kən'sɪdrəblɪ] *adv* considerablemente

con·sid·er·ate [kən'sɪdərət] *adj* considerado

con·sid·er·ate·ly [kən'sɪdərətlɪ] *adv* con consideración

con·sid·er·a·tion [kənsɪdə'reɪʃn] (*thoughtfulness*, *concern*) consideración *f*; (*factor*) factor *m*; *take sth into ~* tomar algo en consideración; *after much ~* tras muchas deliberaciones; *your proposal is under ~* su propuesta está siendo estudiada

con·sign·ment [kən'saɪnmənt] COM envío *m*

♦ **con·sist of** [kən'sɪst] *v/t* consistir en

con·sis·ten·cy [kən'sɪstənsɪ] (*texture*) consistencia *f*; (*unchangingness*) coherencia *f*, consecuencia *f*; *of player* regularidad *f*, constancia *f*

con·sis·tent [kən'sɪstənt] *adj person* coherente, consecuente; *improvement*, *change* constante

con·sis·tent·ly [kən'sɪstəntlɪ] *adv perform* con regularidad *or* constancia; *improve* continuamente; *he's ~ late* llega tarde sistemáticamente

con·so·la·tion [kɑːnsə'leɪʃn] consuelo *m*; *if it's any ~* si te sirve de consuelo

con·sole [kən'soul] *v/t* consolar

con·sol·i·date [kən'sɑːlɪdeɪt] *v/t* consolidar

con·so·nant ['kɑːnsənənt] *n* GRAM consonante *f*

con·sor·ti·um [kən'sɔːrtɪəm] consorcio *m*

con·spic·u·ous [kən'spɪkjuəs] *adj* llamativo; *he felt very ~* sentía que estaba llamando la atención

con·spir·a·cy [kən'spɪrəsɪ] conspiración *f*

con·spir·a·tor [kən'spɪrətər] conspirador(a) *m(f)*

con·spire [kən'spaɪr] *v/i* conspirar

con·stant ['kɑːnstənt] *adj* (*continuous*) constante

con·stant·ly ['kɑːnstəntlɪ] *adv* constantemente

con·ster·na·tion [kɑːnstər'neɪʃn] consternación *f*

con·sti·pat·ed ['kɑːnstɪpeɪtɪd] *adj* estreñido

con·sti·pa·tion [kɑːnstɪ'peɪʃn] estreñimiento *m*

con·stit·u·ent [kən'stɪtjuənt] *n* (*component*) elemento *m* constitutivo, componente *m*

con·sti·tute ['kɑːnstɪtuːt] *v/t* constituir

con·sti·tu·tion [kɑːnstɪ'tuːʃn] constitución *f*

con·sti·tu·tion·al [kɑːnstɪ'tuːʃənl] *adj* POL constitucional

con·straint [kən'streɪnt] (*restriction*) restricción *f*, límite *m*

con·struct [kən'strʌkt] *v/t building etc* construir

con·struc·tion [kən'strʌkʃn] construcción *f*; *under ~* en construcción

con·struc·tion in·dus·try sector *m* de la construcción; **con'struc·tion site** obra *f*; **con'struc·tion work·er** obrero(-a) *m(f)* de la construcción

con·struc·tive [kən'strʌktɪv] *adj* constructivo

con·sul ['kɑːnsl] cónsul *m/f*

con·su·late ['kɑːnsʊlət] consulado *m*

con·sult [kən'sʌlt] *v/t* (*seek the advice of*) consultar

con·sul·tan·cy [kən'sʌltənsɪ] *company* consultoría *f*, asesoría *f*; (*advice*) asesoramiento *m*

con·sul·tant [kən'sʌltənt] *n* (*adviser*) asesor(a) *m(f)*, consultor(a) *m(f)*

con·sul·ta·tion [kɑːnsl'teɪʃn] consulta *f*; **have a ~ with** consultar con

con·sume [kən'suːm] *v/t* consumir

con·sum·er [kən'suːmər] (*purchaser*) consumidor(a) *m(f)*

con·sum·er 'con·fi·dence confianza *f* de los consumidores; **con·'sum·er goods** *npl* bienes *mpl* de consumo; **con·'sum·er so·ci·e·ty** sociedad *f* de consumo

con·sump·tion [kən'sʌmpʃn] consumo *m*

con·tact ['kɑːntækt] **1** *n* contacto; **keep in ~ with s.o.** mantenerse en contacto con alguien; **come into ~ with s.o.** entrar en contacto con alguien **2** *v/t* contactar con, ponerse en contacto con

'con·tact lens lentes *fpl* de contacto, *Span* lentillas *fpl*

'con·tact num·ber número *m* de contacto

con·ta·gious [kən'teɪdʒəs] *adj also fig* contagioso

con·tain [kən'teɪn] *v/t* (*hold, hold back*) contener; **~ o.s.** contenerse

con·tain·er [kən'teɪnər] (*recipient*) recipiente *m*; COM contenedor *m*

con·tain·er ship buque *m* de transporte de contenedores

con·tam·i·nate [kən'tæmɪneɪt] *v/t* contaminar

con·tam·i·na·tion [kəntæmɪ'neɪʃn] contaminación *f*

con·tem·plate ['kɑːntəmpleɪt] *v/t* contemplar

con·tem·po·ra·ry [kən'tempərerɪ] **1** *adj* contemporáneo **2** *n* contemporáneo(-a) *m(f)*

con·tempt [kən'tempt] desprecio *m*, desdén *m*; **be beneath ~** ser despreciable

con·temp·ti·ble [kən'temptəbl] *adj* despreciable

con·temp·tu·ous [kən'temptʃʊəs] *adj* despectivo

con·tend [kən'tend] *v/i*: **~ for ...** competir por ...; **~ with** enfrentarse a

con·tend·er [kən'tendər] SP, POL contendiente *m/f*; *against champion* aspirante *m/f*

con·tent¹ ['kɑːntent] *n* contenido *m*

con·tent² [kən'tent] **1** *adj* satisfecho; **I'm quite ~ to sit here** me contento con sentarme aquí **2** *v/t*: **~ o.s. with** contentarse con

con·tent·ed [kən'tentɪd] *adj* satisfecho

con·ten·tion [kən'tenʃn] (*assertion*) argumento *m*; **be in ~ for** tener posibilidades de ganar

con·ten·tious [kən'tenʃəs] *adj* polémico

con·tent·ment [kən'tentmənt] satisfacción *f*

con·tents ['kɑːntents] *npl of house, letter, bag etc* contenido *m*; *list: in book* tabla *f* de contenidos

con·test¹ ['kɑːntest] *n* (*competition*) concurso *m*; (*struggle, for power*) lucha *f*

con·test² [kən'test] *v/t leadership etc* presentarse como candidato a; *decision, will* impugnar

con·tes·tant [kən'testənt] concursante *m/f*; *in competition* competidor(a) *m(f)*

con·text ['kɑːntekst] contexto *m*; *look at sth in ~/out of ~* examinar algo en contexto / fuera de contexto

con·ti·nent ['kɑːntɪnənt] *n* continente *m*

con·ti·nen·tal [kɑːntɪ'nentl] *adj* continental

con·tin·gen·cy [kən'tɪndʒənsɪ] contingencia *f*, eventualidad *f*

con·tin·u·al [kən'tɪnjʊəl] *adj* continuo

con·tin·u·al·ly [kən'tɪnjʊəlɪ] *adv* continuamente

con·tin·u·a·tion [kəntɪnjʊ'eɪʃn]

continuación *f*

con·tin·ue [kən'tɪnjuː] **1** *v/t* continuar; **to be ~d** continuará; **he ~d to drink** continuó bebiendo **2** *v/i* continuar

con·ti·nu·i·ty [kɑːntɪ'njuːətɪ] continuidad *f*

con·tin·u·ous [kən'tɪnjʊəs] *adj* continuo

con·tin·u·ous·ly [kən'tɪnjʊəslɪ] *adv* continuamente, ininterrumpidamente

con·tort [kən'tɔːrt] *v/t face* contraer; *body* contorsionar

con·tour [kɑːntʊr] contorno *m*

con·tra·cep·tion [kɑːntrə'sepʃn] anticoncepción *f*

con·tra·cep·tive [kɑːntrə'septɪv] *n* (*device, pill*) anticonceptivo *m*

con·tract¹ [kɑːntrækt] *n* contrato *m*

con·tract² [kən'trækt] **1** *v/i* (*shrink*) contraerse **2** *v/t illness* contraer

con·trac·tor [kən'træktər] contratista *m/f*; **building ~** constructora *f*

con·trac·tu·al [kən'træktʊəl] *adj* contractual

con·tra·dict [kɑːntrə'dɪkt] *v/t statement* desmentir; *person* contradecir

con·tra·dic·tion [kɑːntrə'dɪkʃn] contradicción *f*

con·tra·dic·to·ry [kɑːntrə'dɪktərɪ] *adj account* contradictorio

con·trap·tion [kən'træpʃn] F artilugio *m* F

con·trar·y¹ [kɑːntrərɪ] **1** *adj* contrario; **~ to** al contrario de **2** *n*: **on the ~** al contrario

con·tra·ry² [kən'trerɪ] *adj* (*perverse*) difícil

con·trast 1 *n* [kɑːntræst] contraste *m*; **by ~** por contraste **2** *v/t & v/i* [kən'træst] contrastar

con·trast·ing [kən'træstɪŋ] *adj* opuesto

con·tra·vene [kɑːntrə'viːn] *v/t* contravenir

con·trib·ute [kən'trɪbjuːt] **1** *v/i* contribuir (**to** a) **2** *v/t money, time, suggestion* contribuir con, aportar

con·tri·bu·tion [kɑːntrɪ'bjuːʃn] *money* contribución *f*; *to political party, church* donación *f*; *of time, effort, to debate* contribución *f*, aportación *f*; *to magazine* colaboración *f*

con·trib·u·tor [kən'trɪbjʊtər] *of money* donante *m/f*; *to magazine* colaborador(a) *m(f)*

con·trol [kən'troʊl] **1** *n* control *m*; **take / lose ~ of** tomar / perder el control de; **lose ~ of o.s.** perder el control; **circumstances beyond our ~** circunstancias ajenas a nuestra voluntad; **be in ~ of** controlar; **we're in ~ of the situation** tenemos la situación controlada *or* bajo control; **get out of ~** descontrolarse; **under ~** bajo control; **~s** *of aircraft, vehicle* controles *mpl*; (*restrictions*) controles *mpl* **2** *v/t* (*pret & pp* **-led**) (*govern*) controlar, dominar; (*restrict, regulate*) controlar; **~ o.s.** controlarse

con'trol cen·ter, *Br* **con'trol cen·tre** centro *m* de control

con'trol freak F persona *obsesionada con controlar todo*

con'trolled 'sub·stance [kən'troʊld] estupefaciente *m*

con'trol·ling 'in·ter·est [kən'troʊlɪŋ] FIN participación *f* mayoritaria, interés *m* mayoritario

con'trol pan·el panel *m* de control

con'trol tow·er torre *f* de control

con·tro·ver·sial [kɑːntrə'vɜːrʃl] *adj* polémico, controvertido

con·tro·ver·sy [kɑːntrəvɜːrsɪ] polémica *f*, controversia *f*

con·va·lesce [kɑːnvə'les] *v/i* convalecer

con·va·les·cence [kɑːnvə'lesns] convalecencia *f*

con·vene [kən'viːn] *v/t* convocar

con·ve·ni·ence [kən'viːnɪəns] conveniencia *f*; **at your / my ~** a su / mi conveniencia; **all (modern) ~s** todas las comodidades

con've·ni·ence food comida *f* preparada

con've·ni·ence store tienda *f* de barrio

con·ve·ni·ent [kən'viːnɪənt] *adj location, device* conveniente; *time,* *arrangement* oportuno; ***it's very ~ living so near the office*** vivir cerca de la oficina es muy cómodo; ***the apartment is ~ for the station*** el apartamento está muy cerca de la estación; ***I'm afraid Monday isn't ~*** me temo que el lunes no me va bien

con·ve·ni·ent·ly [kən'vi:nɪəntlɪ] *adv* convenientemente; **~** *located for theaters* situado cerca de los teatros

con·vent ['kɑːnvənt] convento *m*

con·ven·tion [kən'venʃn] (*tradition*) convención *f*; (*meeting*) congreso *m*

con·ven·tion·al [kən'venʃnl] *adj* convencional

con·ven·tion cen·ter, *Br* **con·ven·tion cen·tre** palacio *m* de congresos

con·ven·tion·eer [kən'venʃnɪr] congresista *m/f*

♦ **con·verge on** [kən'vɜːrdʒ] *v/t* converger en

con·ver·sant [kən'vɜːrsənt] *adj*: *be ~ with* estar familiarizado con

con·ver·sa·tion [kɑːnvər'seɪʃn] conversación *f*; *make ~* conversar; *have a ~* mantener una conversación

con·ver·sa·tion·al [kɑːnvər'seɪʃnl] *adj* coloquial

con·verse ['kɑːnvɜːrs] *n* (*opposite*): *the ~* lo opuesto

con·verse·ly [kən'vɜːrslɪ] *adv* por el contrario

con·ver·sion [kən'vɜːrʃn] conversión *f*

con·ver·sion ta·ble tabla *f* de conversión

con·vert 1 *n* ['kɑːnvɜːrt] converso(-a) *m(f)* (*to* a) **2** *v/t* [kən'vɜːrt] convertir

con·ver·ti·ble [kən'vɜːrtəbl] *n car* descapotable *m*

con·vey [kən'veɪ] *v/t* (*transmit*) transmitir; (*carry*) transportar

con·vey·or belt [kən'veɪər] cinta *f* transportadora

con·vict 1 *n* ['kɑːnvɪkt] convicto(-a) *m(f)* **2** *v/t* [kən'vɪkt] LAW: **~** *s.o. of sth* declarar a alguien culpable de

algo

con·vic·tion [kən'vɪkʃn] LAW condena *f*; (*belief*) convicción *f*

con·vince [kən'vɪns] *v/t* convencer: *I'm ~d he's lying* estoy convencido de que miente

con·vinc·ing [kən'vɪnsɪŋ] *adj* convincente

con·viv·i·al [kən'vɪvɪəl] *adj* (*friendly*) agradable

con·voy ['kɑːnvɔɪ] *of ships, vehicles* convoy *m*

con·vul·sion [kən'vʌlʃn] MED convulsión *f*

cook [kʊk] **1** *n* cocinero(-a) *m(f)*; *I'm a good ~* soy un buen cocinero, cocino bien **2** *v/t* cocinar; *a ~ed meal* una comida caliente **3** *v/i* cocinar

'**cook·book** libro *m* de cocina

cook·e·ry ['kʊkərɪ] cocina *f*

cook·ie ['kʊkɪ] galleta *f*

cook·ing ['kʊkɪŋ] *food* cocina *f*

cool [kuːl] **1** *n*: *keep one's ~* F mantener la calma; *lose one's ~* F perder la calma **2** *adj weather, breeze* fresco; *drink* frío; (*calm*) tranquilo, sereno; (*unfriendly*) frío; P (*great*) *Span* guay P, *L.Am.* chévere P, *Mex* padre P, *Rpl* copante P **3** *v/i of food, interest* enfriarse; *of tempers* calmarse **4** *v/t*: **~** *it* F cálmate

♦ **cool down 1** *v/i* enfriarse; *of weather* refrescar; *fig: of tempers* calmarse, tranquilizarse **2** *v/t food* enfriar; *fig* calmar, tranquilizar

cool·ing-'off pe·ri·od fase *f* de reflexión

co·op·e·rate [koʊ'ɑːpəreɪt] *v/i* cooperar

co·op·e·ra·tion [koʊɑːpə'reɪʃn] cooperación *f*

co·op·e·ra·tive [koʊ'ɑːpərətɪv] **1** *n* COM cooperativa *f* **2** *adj* COM conjunto; (*helpful*) cooperativo

co·or·di·nate [koʊ'ɔːrdɪneɪt] *v/t activities* coordinar

co·or·di·na·tion [koʊɔːrdɪ'neɪʃn] coordinación *f*

cop [kɑːp] *n* F poli *m/f* F

cope [koʊp] *v/i* arreglárselas; **~** *with*

poder con

cop·i·er ['kɑːpɪər] *machine* foto-copiadora *f*

co·pi·lot ['koupaɪlət] copiloto *m/f*

co·pi·ous ['koupɪəs] *adj* copioso

cop·per ['kɑːpər] *n metal* cobre *m*

cop·y ['kɑːpɪ] **1** *n* copia *f*; *of book* ejemplar *m*; *of record, CD* copia *f*; *(written material)* texto *m*; **make a ~ of a file** COMPUT hacer una copia de un archivo **2** *v/t (pret & pp* **-ied)** copiar

'cop·y·cat F copión (-ona) *m(f)* F, copiota *m/f* F; **'cop·y·cat crime** delito inspirado en otro; **'cop·y·right** *n* copyright *m*, derechos *mpl* de reproducción; **'cop·y·writ·er** *in advertising* creativo(-a) *m(f) (de publicidad)*

cor·al ['kɑːrəl] coral *m*

cord [kɔːrd] *(string)* cuerda *f*, cordel *m*; *(cable)* cable *m*

cor·di·al ['kɔːrdʒəl] *adj* cordial

cord·less 'phone ['kɔːrdlɪs] teléfono *m* inalámbrico

cor·don ['kɔːrdn] cordón *m*

♦ **cordon off** *v/t* acordonar

cords [kɔːrdz] *npl pants* pantalones *mpl* de pana

cor·du·roy ['kɔːrdərɔɪ] pana *f*

core [kɔːr] **1** *n of fruit* corazón *m*; *of problem* meollo *m*; *of organization, party* núcleo *m* **2** *v/t fruit* sacar el corazón a **3** *adj issue, meaning* central

co·ri·an·der ['kɑːrɪændər] cilantro *m*

cork [kɔːrk] *in bottle* (tapón *m* de) corcho *m*; *material* corcho *m*

'cork·screw *n* sacacorchos *m inv*

corn [kɔːrn] *grain* maíz *m*

cor·ner ['kɔːrnər] **1** *n of page, street* esquina *f*; *of room* rincón *m*; *(bend: on road)* curva *f*; *in soccer* córner *m*, saque *m* de esquina; **in the ~** en el rincón; **I'll meet you on the ~** te veré en la esquina **2** *v/t person* arrinconar; **~ a market** monopolizar un mercado **3** *v/i of driver, car* girar

'cor·ner kick *in soccer* saque *m* de esquina, córner *m*

'corn·flakes *npl* copos *mpl* de maíz

'corn·starch harina *f* de maíz

corn·y ['kɔːrnɪ] *adj* F *(sentimental)* cursi F; *joke* manido

cor·o·na·ry ['kɑːrənerɪ] **1** *adj* coronario **2** *n* infarto *m* de miocardio

cor·o·ner ['kɑːrənər] oficial encargado de investigar muertes sospechosas

cor·po·ral ['kɔːrpərəl] *n* cabo *m/f*

cor·po·ral 'pun·ish·ment castigo *m* corporal

cor·po·rate ['kɔːrpərət] *adj* COM corporativo, de empresa; **~ image** imagen *f* corporativa; **~ loyalty** lealtad *f* a la empresa

cor·po·ra·tion [kɔːrpə'reɪʃn] *(business)* sociedad *f* anónima

corps [kɔːr] *nsg* cuerpo *m*

corpse [kɔːrps] cadáver *m*

cor·pu·lent ['kɔːrpjʊlənt] *adj* corpulento

cor·pus·cle ['kɔːrpʌsl] corpúsculo *m*

cor·ral [kə'ræl] *n* corral *m*

cor·rect [kə'rekt] **1** *adj* correcto; *time* exacto; **you are ~** tiene razón **2** *v/t* corregir

cor·rec·tion [kə'rekʃn] corrección *f*

cor·rect·ly [kə'rektlɪ] *adv* correctamente

cor·re·spond [kɑːrɪ'spɑːnd] *v/i (match)* corresponderse; **~ to** corresponder a; **~ with** corresponderse con; *(write letters)* mantener correspondencia con

cor·re·spon·dence [kɑːrɪ'spɑːndəns] *(matching)* correspondencia *f*, relación *f*; *(letters)* correspondencia *f*

cor·re·spon·dent [kɑːrɪ'spɑːndənt] *(letter writer)* correspondiente *m/f*; *(reporter)* corresponsal *m/f*

cor·re·spon·ding [kɑːrɪ'spɑːndɪŋ] *adj (equivalent)* correspondiente

cor·ri·dor ['kɔːrɪdər] *in building* pasillo *m*

cor·rob·o·rate [kə'rɑːbəreɪt] *v/t* corroborar

cor·rode [kə'roud] **1** *v/t* corroer **2** *v/i* corroerse

cor·ro·sion [kə'rouʒn] corrosión *f*

cor·ru·gat·ed 'card·board ['kɑːrə-geɪtɪd] cartón *m* ondulado

cor·ru·gat·ed 'i·ron chapa *f* ondula-da

cor·rupt [kə'rʌpt] **1** *adj* corrupto; COMPUT corrompido **2** *v/t* corrom-per; (*bribe*) sobornar

cor·rup·tion [kə'rʌpʃn] corrupción *f*

cos·met·ic [kɑː'zmetɪk] *adj* cosmé-tico; *fig* superficial

cos·met·ics [kɑː'zmetɪks] *npl* cos-méticos *mpl*

cos·met·ic 'sur·geon especialista *m/f* en cirugía estética

cos·met·ic 'sur·ger·y cirugía *f* esté-tica

cos·mo·naut ['kɑːzmənɔːt] cosmo-nauta *m/f*

cos·mo·pol·i·tan [kɑːzmə'pɑːlɪtən] *adj city* cosmopolitano

cost¹ [kɑːst] **1** *n also fig* costo *m*, *Span* coste *m*; **at all ~s** cueste lo que cueste; **I've learnt to my ~** por des-gracia he aprendido **2** *v/t* (*pret & pp* **cost**) *money*, *time* costar; **how much does it ~?** ¿cuánto cuesta?

cost² [kɑːst] *v/t* (*pret & pp* **-ed**) FIN *proposal*, *project* estimar el costo de

cost and 'freight COM costo *or Span* coste y flete

Cos·ta Ri·ca ['kɑːstə'riːkə] *n* Costa Rica

Cos·ta Ri·can ['kɑːstə'riːkən] **1** *adj* costarricense **2** *n* costarricense *m/f*

'cost-con·scious *adj* consciente del costo *or Span* coste; **'cost-ef·fec·tive** *adj* rentable; **'cost, in·sur·ance, freight** COM costo *or Span* coste, seguro *or* flete

cost·ly ['kɑːstlɪ] *adj mistake* caro

cost of 'liv·ing costo *m or Span* coste *m* de la vida

cost 'price precio *m* de costo *or Span* coste

cos·tume ['kɑːstuːm] *for actor* traje *m*

cos·tume 'jew·el·lery *Br*, **cos·tume 'jew·el·ry** bisutería *f*

'cos·y *Br* → **cozy**

cot [kɑːt] (*camp-bed*) catre *m*

cot·tage ['kɑːtɪdʒ] casa *f* de campo,

casita *f*

cot·tage 'cheese queso *m* fresco

cot·ton ['kɑːtn] **1** *n* algodón *m* **2** *adj* de algodón

◆**cotton on** *v/i* F darse cuenta

◆**cotton on to** *v/t* F darse cuenta de

◆**cotton to** *v/t* F: **I never cottoned to her** nunca me cayó bien

cot·ton 'can·dy algodón *m* dulce

cot·ton 'wool *Br* algodón *m* (hidrófilo)

couch [kaʊtʃ] *n* sofá *m*

'couch po·ta·to F teleadicto(-a) *m(f)* F

cou·chette [kuː'ʃet] litera *f*

cough [kɑːf] **1** *n* tos *f*; *to get attention* carraspeo *m* **2** *v/i* toser; *to get attention* carraspear

◆**cough up 1** *v/t blood etc* toser; F *money* soltar, *Span* apoquinar F **2** *v/i* F (*pay*) soltar dinero, *Span* apoquinar F

'cough med·i·cine, **'cough syr·up** jarabe *m* para la tos

could [kʊd] **1** *v/aux*: **~ I have my key?** ¿me podría dar la llave?; **~ you help me?** ¿me podrías ayu-dar?; **this ~ be our bus** puede que éste sea nuestro autobús; **you ~ be right** puede que tengas razón; **I ~n't say for sure** no sabría decirlo con seguridad; **he ~ have got lost** a lo mejor se ha perdido; **you ~ have warned me!** ¡me podías haber avi-sado! **2** *pret* → **can**

coun·cil ['kaʊnsl] *n* (*assembly*) con-sejo *m*

'coun·cil·man concejal *m*

coun·cil·or ['kaʊnsələr] concejal(a) *m(f)*

coun·sel ['kaʊnsl] **1** *n* (*advice*) con-sejo *m*; (*lawyer*) abogado(-a) *m(f)* **2** *v/t course of action* aconsejar; *person* ofrecer apoyo psicológico a

coun·sel·ing, *Br* **coun·sel·ling** ['kaʊnslɪŋ] apoyo *m* psicológico

coun·sel·or, *Br* **coun·sel·lor** ['kaʊnslər] (*adviser*) consejero(-a) *m(f)*; *of student* orientador(a) *m(f)*; LAW abogado(-a) *m(f)*

count¹ [kaʊnt] **1** *n* (*number arrived*

C

at) cuenta *f*; *(action of ~ing)* recuento *m*; *in baseball, boxing* cuenta *f*; **what is your ~?** ¿cuántos has contado?; **keep ~ of** llevar la cuenta de; **lose ~ of** perder la cuenta de; **at the last ~** en el último recuento **2** *v/i to ten etc* contar; *(be important)* contar; *(qualify)* contar, valer **3** *v/t* contar
♦ **count on** *v/t* contar con

count² [kaʊnt] *nobleman* conde *m*

'**count·down** cuenta *f* atrás

coun·te·nance ['kaʊntənəns] *v/t* tolerar

coun·ter¹ ['kaʊntər] *n in shop* mostrador *m*; *in café* barra *f*; *in game* ficha *f*

coun·ter² ['kaʊntər] **1** *v/t* contrarrestar **2** *v/i* (*retaliate*) responder

coun·ter³ ['kaʊntər] *adv*: **run ~ to** estar en contra de

'**coun·ter·act** *v/t* contrarrestar

coun·ter·at'tack 1 *n* contraataque *m* **2** *v/i* contraatacar

'**coun·ter·bal·ance 1** *n* contrapeso *m* **2** *v/t* contrarrestar, contrapesar

coun·ter'clock·wise *adv* en sentido contrario al de las agujas del reloj

coun·ter·es·pi·o·nage contraespionaje *m*

coun·ter·feit ['kaʊntərfɪt] **1** *v/t* falsificar **2** *adj* falso

'**coun·ter·part** (*person*) homólogo(-a) *m(f)*

coun·ter·pro'duc·tive *adj* contraproducente

'**coun·ter·sign** *v/t* refrendar

coun·tess ['kaʊntes] condesa *f*

count·less ['kaʊntlɪs] *adj* incontables

coun·try ['kʌntrɪ] *n* (*nation*) país *m*; *as opposed to town* campo *m*; **in the ~** en el campo

coun·try and 'west·ern MUS música *f* country; '**coun·try·man** (*fellow ~*) compatriota *m*; '**coun·try·side** campo *m*

coun·ty ['kaʊntɪ] condado *m*

coup [kuː] POL golpe *m* (de Estado); *fig* golpe *m* de efecto

cou·ple ['kʌpl] *n* pareja *f*; **just a ~** un par; **a ~ of** un par de

cou·pon ['kuːpɒn] cupón *m*

cour·age ['kʌrɪdʒ] valor *m*, coraje *m*

cou·ra·geous [kə'reɪdʒəs] *adj* valiente

cou·ra·geous·ly [kə'reɪdʒəslɪ] *adv* valientemente

cou·ri·er ['kʊrɪr] (*messenger*) mensajero(-a) *m(f)*; *with tourist party* guía *m/f*

course [kɔːrs] *n* (*series of lessons*) curso *m*; (*part of meal*) plato *m*; *of ship, plane* rumbo *m*; *for horse race* circuito *m*; *for golf* campo *m*; *for skiing, marathon* recorrido *m*; **change ~** *of ship, plane* cambiar de rumbo; **of ~** (*certainly*) claro, por supuesto; (*naturally*) por supuesto; **of ~ not** claro que no; **~ of action** táctica *f*; **~ of treatment** tratamiento *m*; **in the ~ of ...** durante ...

court [kɔːrt] *n* LAW tribunal *m*; (*courthouse*) palacio *m* de justicia; SP pista *f*, cancha *f*; **take s.o. to ~** llevar a alguien a juicio

'**court case** proceso *m*, causa *f*

cour·te·ous ['kɜːrtɪəs] *adj* cortés

cour·te·sy ['kɜːrtəsɪ] cortesía *f*

'**court·house** palacio *m* de justicia; **court 'mar·tial 1** *n* consejo *m* de guerra **2** *v/t* formar un consejo de guerra a; '**court or·der** orden *f* judicial; '**court·room** sala *f* de juicios; '**court·yard** patio *m*

cous·in ['kʌzn] primo(-a) *m(f)*

cove [koʊv] (*small bay*) cala *f*

cov·er ['kʌvər] **1** *n protective* funda *f*; *of book, magazine* portada *f*; (*shelter*) protección *f*; (*insurance*) cobertura *f*; **~s** *for bed* manta y sábanas *fpl*; **we took ~ from the rain** nos pusimos a cubierto de la lluvia **2** *v/t* cubrir
♦ **cover up 1** *v/t* cubrir; *scandal* encubrir **2** *v/i* disimular; **cover up for s.o.** encubrir a alguien

cov·er·age ['kʌvərɪdʒ] *by media* cobertura *f* informativa

cov·er·ing let·ter ['kʌvrɪŋ] carta *f*

cov·ert [koʊ'vɜːrt] *adj* encubierto

'**cov·er-up** encubrimiento *m*

cow [kaʊ] vaca *f*

cow·ard ['kauərd] cobarde *m/f*

cow·ard·ice ['kauərdıs] cobardía *f*

cow·ard·ly ['kauərdlı] *adj* cobarde

'cow·boy vaquero *m*

cow·er ['kauər] *v/i* agacharse, amilanarse

co-work·er ['kouwɜ:rkər] compañero(a) *m(f)* de trabajo

coy [kɔı] *adj* (*evasive*) evasivo; (*flirtatious*) coqueto

co·zy ['kouzı] *adj room* acogedor; *job* cómodo

CPU [si:pi:'ju:] *abbr* (= **central processing unit**) CPU *f* (= unidad *f* central de proceso)

crab [kræb] *n* cangrejo *m*

crack [kræk] **1** *n* grieta *f*; *in cup, glass* raja *f*; (*joke*) chiste *m* (malo) **2** *v/t cup, glass* rajar; *nut* cascar; *code* descifrar; F (*solve*) resolver; **~ a joke** contar un chiste **3** *v/i* rajarse; *get* **~ing** F poner manos a la obra F

♦ **crack down on** *v/t* castigar severamente

♦ **crack up** *v/i* sufrir una crisis nerviosa; F (*laugh*) desternillarse F

'crack·brained *adj* F chiflado F

'crack·down medidas *fpl* severas

cracked [krækt] *adj cup, glass* rajado; F (*crazy*) chiflado F

crack·er ['krækər] *to eat* galleta *f* salada

crack·le ['krækl] *v/i of fire* crepitar

cra·dle ['kreıdl] *n for baby* cuna *f*

craft[1] [kræft] NAUT embarcación *f*

craft[2] [kræft] (*skill*) arte *m*; (*trade*) oficio *m*

crafts·man ['kræftsmən] artesano *m*

craft·y ['kræftı] *adj* astuto

crag [kræg] *rock* peñasco *m*, risco *m*

cram [kræm] *v/t* (*pret & pp* **-med**) embutir

cramp [kræmp] *n* calambre *m*; *stomach* **~** retorcijón *m*

cramped [kræmpt] *adj room* pequeño

cramps [kræmps] *npl* calambre *m*; *stomach* **~** retorcijón *m*

cran·ber·ry ['krænberı] arándano *m* agrio

crane [kreın] **1** *n machine* grúa *f* **2** *v/t*:

~ one's neck estirar el cuello

crank [kræŋk] *n person* maniático(-a) *m(f)*, persona *f* rara

'crank·shaft cigüeñal *m*

crank·y ['kræŋkı] *adj* (*bad-tempered*) gruñón

crap [kræp] P **1** *n* (*excrement*) mierda *f* P; (*nonsense*) Span gilipolleces *fpl* P, *L.Am.* pendejadas *fpl* P, *Rpl* boludeces *fpl* P; (*poor quality item*) mierda *f* P **2** *v/i* (*defecate*) cagar V

crash [kræʃ] **1** *n noise* estruendo *m*, estrépito *m*; *accident* accidente *m*; COM quiebra *f*, crac *m*; COMPUT bloqueo *m*; *a* **~ of thunder** un trueno **2** *v/i of car, airplane* estrellarse (*into* con *or* contra); *of thunder* sonar; COM *of market* hundirse, desplomarse; COMPUT bloquearse, colgarse; F (*sleep*) dormir, *Span* sobar F; *the waves* **~ed onto the shore** las olas chocaban contra la orilla; *the vase* **~ed to the ground** el jarrón se cayó con estruendo **3** *v/t car* estrellar

♦ **crash out** *v/i* F (*fall asleep*) dormirse, *Span* quedarse sobado

'crash bar·ri·er quitamiedos *m inv*; 'crash course curso *m* intensivo; 'crash di·et dieta *f* drástica; 'crash hel·met casco *m* protector; 'crash-land *v/i* realizar un aterrizaje forzoso; 'crash 'land·ing aterrizaje *m* forzoso

crate [kreıt] (*packing case*) caja *f*

cra·ter ['kreıtər] *of volcano* cráter *m*

crave [kreıv] *v/t* ansiar

crav·ing ['kreıvıŋ] ansia *f*, deseo *m*; *of pregnant woman* antojo *m*; *I have a* **~ for ...** me apetece muchísimo ...

crawl [krɔ:l] **1** *n in swimming* crol *m*; *at a* **~** (*very slowly*) muy lentamente **2** *v/i on floor* arrastrarse; *of baby* andar a gatas; (*move slowly*) avanzar lentamente

♦ **crawl with** *v/t* estar abarrotado de

cray·fish ['kreıfıʃ] *freshwater* cangrejo *m* de río; *saltwater* langosta *f*

cray·on ['kreıɑ:n] *n* lápiz *m* de color

craze [kreız] locura *f* (**for** de); *the latest* **~** la última locura *or* moda

cra·zy ['kreɪzɪ] *adj* loco; *be ~ about* estar loco por

creak [kriːk] **1** *n of hinge, door* chirrido *m; of floor* crujido *m* **2** *v/i of hinge, door* chirriar; *of floor, shoes* crujir

creak·y ['kriːkɪ] *adj hinge, door* que chirria; *floor, shoes* que cruje

cream [kriːm] **1** *n for skin* crema *f; for coffee, cake* nata *f; (color)* crema *m* **2** *adj* crema

cream 'cheese queso *m* blanco para untar

cream·er ['kriːmər] *(pitcher)* jarra *f* para la nata; *for coffee* leche *f* en polvo

cream·y ['kriːmɪ] *adj (with lots of cream)* cremoso

crease [kriːs] **1** *n accidental* arruga *f; deliberate* raya *f* **2** *v/t accidentally* arrugar

cre·ate [krɪ'eɪt] *v/t & v/i* crear

cre·a·tion [krɪ'eɪʃn] *creación f*

cre·a·tive [krɪ'eɪtɪv] *adj* creativo

cre·a·tor [krɪ'eɪtər] creador(a) *m(f); (founder)* fundador(a) *m(f); the Creator* REL el Creador

crea·ture ['kriːtʃər] *animal, person* criatura *f*

crèche [kreʃ] *for children* guardería *f* (infantil); REL nacimiento *m*, belén *m*

cred·i·bil·i·ty [kredə'bɪlətɪ] credibilidad *f*

cred·i·ble ['kredəbl] *adj* creíble

cred·it ['kredɪt] **1** *n* FIN, *(honor)* crédito *m; be in ~* tener un saldo positivo; *get the ~ for sth* recibir reconocimiento por algo **2** *v/t (believe)* creer; *~ an amount to an account* abonar una cantidad en una cuenta

cred·i·ta·ble ['kredɪtəbl] *adj* estimable, honorable

'cred·it card tarjeta *f* de crédito

'cred·it lim·it límite *m* de crédito

cred·i·tor ['kredɪtər] acreedor(a) *m(f)*

'cred·it·wor·thy *adj* solvente

cred·u·lous ['kredjʊləs] *adj* crédulo

creed [kriːd] *(beliefs)* credo *m*

creek [kriːk] *(stream)* arroyo *m*

creep [kriːp] **1** *n pej* asqueroso(-a) *m(f)* **2** *v/i (pret & pp crept)* moverse sigilosamente

creep·er ['kriːpər] BOT enredadera *f*

creeps [kriːps] *npl* F: *the house / he gives me the ~* la casa / él me pone la piel de gallina F

creep·y ['kriːpɪ] *adj* F espeluznante F

cre·mate [krɪ'meɪt] *v/t* incinerar

cre·ma·tion [krɪ'meɪʃn] incineración *f*

cre·ma·to·ri·um [kremə'tɔːrɪəm] crematorio *m*

crept [krept] *pret & pp →* **creep**

cres·cent ['kresənt] *n shape* medialuna *f; ~ moon* cuarto *m* creciente

crest [krest] *of hill* cima *f; of bird* cresta *f*

crest·fal·len *adj* abatido

crev·ice ['krevɪs] grieta *f*

crew [kruː] *n of ship, airplane* tripulación *f; of repairmen etc* equipo *m; (crowd, group)* grupo *m*, pandilla *f*

'crew cut rapado *m*

'crew neck cuello *m* redondo

crib [krɪb] *n for baby* cuna *f*

crick [krɪk]: *have a ~ in the neck* tener tortícolis

crick·et ['krɪkɪt] *insect* grillo *m*

crime [kraɪm] *(offense)* delito *m; serious, also fig* crimen *m*

crim·i·nal ['krɪmɪnl] **1** *n* delincuente *m/f*, criminal *m/f* **2** *adj (relating to crime)* criminal; (LAW: *not civil)* penal; *(shameful)* vergonzoso; *act* delictivo; *it's ~ (shameful)* es un crimen

crim·son ['krɪmzn] *adj* carmesí

cringe [krɪndʒ] *v/i with embarrassment* sentir vergüenza

crip·ple ['krɪpl] **1** *n (disabled person)* inválido(-a) *m(f)* **2** *v/t person* dejar inválido; *fig: country, industry* paralizar

cri·sis ['kraɪsɪs] *(pl crises* ['kraɪsiːz]) crisis *f inv*

crisp [krɪsp] *adj weather, air* fresco; *lettuce, apple, bacon* crujiente; *new shirt, bills* flamante

cri·te·ri·on [kraɪ'tɪrɪən] *(standard)* criterio *m*

crit·ic ['krɪtɪk] crítico(-a) m(f)

crit·i·cal ['krɪtɪkl] adj (making criticisms, serious) crítico; moment etc decisivo

crit·i·cal·ly ['krɪtɪklɪ] adv speak etc en tono de crítica; ~ ill en estado crítico

crit·i·cism ['krɪtɪsɪzm] crítica f

crit·i·cize ['krɪtɪsaɪz] v/t criticar

croak [krəʊk] 1 n of frog croar m 2 v/i of frog croar

cro·chet ['krəʊʃeɪ] 1 n ganchillo m 2 v/t hacer a ganchillo

crock·e·ry ['krɑːkərɪ] vajilla f

croc·o·dile ['krɑːkədaɪl] cocodrilo m

cro·cus ['krəʊkəs] azafrán m

cro·ny ['krəʊnɪ] F amiguete m/f F

crook [krʊk] n ladrón (-ona) m(f); dishonest trader granuja m/f

crook·ed ['krʊkɪd] adj (not straight) torcido; (dishonest) deshonesto

crop [krɑːp] 1 n also fig cosecha f; plant grown cultivo m 2 v/t (pret & pp -ped) hair cortar; photo recortar
♦ crop up v/i salir

cross [krɑːs] 1 adj (angry) enfadado, enojado 2 n cruz f 3 v/t (go across) cruzar; ~ o.s. REL santiguarse; ~ one's legs cruzar las piernas; keep one's fingers ~ed cruzar los dedos; it never ~ed my mind no se me ocurrió 4 v/i (go across) cruzar; of lines cruzarse, cortarse
♦ cross off, cross out v/t tachar

'cross·bar of goal larguero m; of bicycle barra f; in high jump listón m; 'cross·check 1 n comprobación f 2 v/t comprobar; cross·coun·try ('ski·ing) esquí m de fondo

crossed 'check, Br crossed 'cheque [krɑːst] cheque m cruzado

cross·ex·am·i·na·tion LAW interrogatorio m; cross·ex'am·ine v/t LAW interrogar; cross-'eyed adj bizco

cross·ing ['krɑːsɪŋ] NAUT travesía f

'cross·roads nsg also fig encrucijada f; 'cross·sec·tion of people muestra f representativa; 'cross·walk paso m de peatones; 'cross·word (puz·zle) crucigrama m

crotch [krɑːtʃ] of person, pants entrepierna f

crouch [kraʊtʃ] v/i agacharse

crow [krəʊ] n bird corneja f; as the ~ flies en línea recta

'crow·bar palanca f

crowd [kraʊd] n multitud f, muchedumbre f; at sports event público m

crowd·ed ['kraʊdɪd] adj abarrotado (with de)

crown [kraʊn] 1 n on head, tooth corona f 2 v/t tooth poner una corona a

cru·cial ['kruːʃl] adj crucial

cru·ci·fix ['kruːsɪfɪks] crucifijo m

cru·ci·fix·ion [kruːsɪ'fɪkʃn] crucifixión f

cru·ci·fy ['kruːsɪfaɪ] v/t (pret & pp -ied) also fig crucificar

crude [kruːd] 1 adj (vulgar) grosero; (unsophisticated) primitivo 2 n: ~ (oil) crudo m

crude·ly ['kruːdlɪ] adv speak groseramente; made de manera primitiva

cru·el ['kruːəl] adj cruel (to con)

cru·el·ty ['kruːəltɪ] crueldad f (to con)

cruise [kruːz] 1 n crucero m; go on a ~ ir de crucero 2 v/i of people hacer un crucero; of car ir a velocidad de crucero; of plane volar

'cruise lin·er transatlántico m

cruis·ing speed ['kruːzɪŋ] of vehicle velocidad f de crucero; fig: of project etc ritmo m normal

crumb [krʌm] miga f

crum·ble ['krʌmbl] 1 v/t desmigajar 2 v/i of bread desmigajarse; of stonework desmenuzarse; fig: of opposition etc desmoronarse

crum·bly ['krʌmblɪ] adj cookie que se desmigaja; stonework que se desmenuza

crum·ple ['krʌmpl] 1 v/t (crease) arrugar 2 v/i (collapse) desplomarse

crunch [krʌntʃ] 1 n: when it comes to the ~ a la hora de la verdad 2 v/i of snow, gravel crujir

cru·sade [kruːˈseɪd] n also fig cruzada f

crush [krʌʃ] 1 n (crowd) muchedumbre f; **have a ~ on** estar loco por 2 *v/t* aplastar; (*crease*) arrugar; **they were ~ed to death** murieron aplastados 3 *v/i* (*crease*) arrugarse

crust [krʌst] *on bread* corteza f

crust·y ['krʌstɪ] *adj bread* crujiente

crutch [krʌtʃ] *walking aid* muleta f

cry [kraɪ] **1** *n* (*call*) grito m; **have a ~** llorar **2** *v/t* (*pret & pp **-ied**) (*call*) gritar **3** *v/i* (*pret & pp **-ied**) (*weep*) llorar

♦ **cry out** *v/t & v/i* gritar

♦ **cry out for** *v/t* (*need*) pedir a gritos

cryp·tic ['krɪptɪk] *adj* críptico

crys·tal ['krɪstl] cristal m

crys·tal·lize ['krɪstəlaɪz] **1** *v/t* cristalizar **2** *v/i* cristalizarse

cub [kʌb] cachorro m; *of bear* osezno m

Cu·ba ['kju:bə] Cuba

Cu·ban ['kju:bən] **1** *adj* cubano **2** *n* cubano(-a) m(f)

cube [kju:b] *shape* cubo m

cu·bic ['kju:bɪk] *adj* cúbico

cu·bic ca·pac·i·ty TECH cilindrada f

cu·bi·cle ['kju:bɪkl] (*changing room*) cubículo m

cu·cum·ber ['kju:kʌmbər] pepino m

cud·dle ['kʌdl] **1** *n* abrazo **2** *v/t* abrazar

cud·dly ['kʌdlɪ] *adj kitten etc* tierno

cue [kju:] *n for actor etc* pie m, entrada f; *for pool* taco m

cuff [kʌf] **1** *n of shirt* puño m; *of pants* vuelta f; (*blow*) cachete m; **off the ~** improvisado **2** *v/t* (*hit*) dar un cachete a

'**cuff link** gemelo m

cul-de-sac ['kʌldəsæk] callejón m sin salida

cu·li·nar·y ['kʌlɪnərɪ] *adj* culinario

cul·mi·nate ['kʌlmɪneɪt] *v/i* culminar (**in** en)

cul·mi·na·tion [kʌlmɪ'neɪʃn] culminación f

cul·prit ['kʌlprɪt] culpable m/f

cult [kʌlt] (*sect*) secta f

cul·ti·vate ['kʌltɪveɪt] *v/t also fig* cultivar

cul·ti·vat·ed ['kʌltɪveɪtɪd] *adj person* culto

cul·ti·va·tion [kʌltɪ'veɪʃn] *of land* cultivo m

cul·tu·ral ['kʌltʃərəl] *adj* cultural

cul·ture ['kʌltʃər] *artistic* cultura f

cul·tured ['kʌltʃərd] *adj* (*cultivated*) culto

'**cul·ture shock** choque m cultural

cum·ber·some ['kʌmbərsəm] *adj* engorroso

cu·mu·la·tive ['kju:mjʊlətɪv] *adj* acumulativo

cun·ning ['kʌnɪŋ] **1** *n* astucia f **2** *adj* astuto

cup [kʌp] *n* taza f; *trophy* copa f

cup·board ['kʌbərd] armario m

cup fi·nal final f de (la) copa

cu·po·la ['kju:pələ] cúpula f

cu·ra·ble ['kjʊrəbl] *adj* curable

cu·ra·tor [kjʊ'reɪtər] conservador(a) m(f)

curb [kɜ:rb] **1** *n of street* bordillo m; *on powers etc* freno m **2** *v/t* frenar

cur·dle ['kɜ:rdl] *v/i of milk* cortarse

cure [kjʊr] **1** *n* MED cura f **2** *v/t* MED, *meat* curar

cur·few ['kɜ:rfju:] toque m de queda

cu·ri·os·i·ty [kjʊrɪ'ɑ:sətɪ] (*inquisitiveness*) curiosidad f

cu·ri·ous ['kjʊrɪəs] *adj* (*inquisitive*, *strange*) curioso

cu·ri·ous·ly ['kjʊrɪəslɪ] *adv* (*inquisitively*) con curiosidad; (*strangely*) curiosamente; **~ enough** curiosamente

curl [kɜ:rl] **1** *n in hair* rizo m; *of smoke* voluta f **2** *v/t hair* rizar; (*wind*) enroscar **3** *v/i of hair* rizarse; *of leaf*, *paper etc* ondularse

♦ **curl up** *v/i* acurrucarse

curl·y ['kɜ:rlɪ] *adj hair* rizado; *tail* enroscado

cur·rant ['kʌrənt] (*dried fruit*) pasa f de Corinto

cur·ren·cy ['kʌrənsɪ] *money* moneda f; **foreign ~** divisas fpl

cur·rent ['kʌrənt] **1** *n in sea*, ELEC corriente f **2** *adj* (*present*) actual

'**cur·rent ac·count** *Br* cuenta f corriente; **cur·rent af'fairs** npl la actualidad; **cur·rent af'fairs pro·gram**, *Br* **cur·rent af'fairs pro-**

gramme programa *m* de actualidad; **cur·rent e'vents** *npl* la actualidad

cur·rent·ly ['kʌrəntlɪ] *adv* actualmente

cur·ric·u·lum [kə'rɪkjʊləm] plan *m* de estudios

cur·ric·u·lum vi·tae ['viːtaɪ] *Br* currículum *m* vitae

cur·ry ['kʌrɪ] curry *m*

curse [kɜːrs] **1** *n* (*spell*) maldición *f*; (*swearword*) palabrota *f* **2** *v/t* maldecir; (*swear at*) insultar **3** *v/i* (*swear*) decir palabrotas

cur·sor ['kɜːrsər] COMPUT cursor *m*

cur·so·ry ['kɜːrsərɪ] *adj* rápido, superficial

curt [kɜːrt] *adj* brusco, seco

cur·tail [kɜːr'teɪl] *v/t* acortar

cur·tain ['kɜːrtn] cortina *f*; THEA telón *m*

curve [kɜːrv] **1** *n* curva *f* **2** *v/i* (*bend*) curvarse

cush·ion ['kʊʃn] **1** *n for couch etc* cojín *m* **2** *v/t blow, fall* amortiguar

cus·tard ['kʌstərd] natillas *fpl*

cus·to·dy ['kʌstədɪ] *of children* custodia *f*; **in ~** *LAW* detenido

cus·tom ['kʌstəm] (*tradition*) costumbre *f*; COM clientela *f*; **it's the ~ in France** es costumbre en Francia; **as was his ~** como era costumbre en él

cus·tom·a·ry ['kʌstəmərɪ] *adj* acostumbrado, de costumbre; **it is ~ to ...** es costumbre ...

cus·tom-'built *adj* hecho de encargo

cus·tom·er ['kʌstəmər] cliente(-a) *m(f)*

cus·tom·er re'la·tions *npl* relaciones *fpl* con los clientes

cus·tom·er 'serv·ice atención *f* al cliente

cus·tom-'made *adj* hecho de encargo

cus·toms ['kʌstəmz] *npl* aduana *f*; **'cus·toms clear·ance** despacho *m* de aduanas; **'cus·toms in·spec·tion** inspección *f* aduanera; **'cus·toms of·fi·cer** funciona-

rio(-a) *m(f)* de aduanas

cut [kʌt] **1** *n with knife etc, of garment* corte *m*; (*reduction*) recorte *m* (**in** de) **2** *v/t* (*pret & pp* **cut**) cortar; (*reduce*) recortar; *hours* acortar; **get one's hair ~** cortarse el pelo; **I've ~ my finger** me he cortado el dedo

♦ **cut back 1** *v/i in costs* recortar gastos **2** *v/t staff numbers* recortar

♦ **cut down 1** *v/t tree* talar, cortar **2** *v/i in expenses* gastar menos; *in smoking / drinking* fumar / beber menos

♦ **cut down on** *v/t*: **cut down on the cigarettes** fumar menos; **cut down on chocolate** comer menos chocolate

♦ **cut off** *v/t with knife, scissors etc* cortar; (*isolate*) aislar; **I was cut off** se me ha cortado la comunicación

♦ **cut out** *v/t with scissors* recortar; (*eliminate*) eliminar; **cut that out!** F ¡ya está bien! F; **be cut out for sth** estar hecho para algo

♦ **cut up** *v/t meat etc* trocear

'cut·back recorte *m*

cute [kjuːt] *adj* (*pretty*) guapo, lindo; (*sexually attractive*) atractivo; (*smart, clever*) listo; **it looks really ~ on you** eso te queda muy mono

cu·ti·cle ['kjuːtɪkl] cutícula *f*

'cut-off date fecha *f* límite; **cut-'price** *adj goods* rebajado; *store* de productos rebajados; **'cut-throat** *adj competition* despiadado

cut·ting ['kʌtɪŋ] **1** *n from newspaper etc* recorte *m* **2** *adj remark* hiriente

cy·ber·space ['saɪbərspeɪs] ciberespacio *m*

cy·cle ['saɪkl] **1** *n* (*bicycle*) bicicleta *f*; (*series of events*) ciclo *m* **2** *v/i* ir en bicicleta

'cy·cle path vía *f* para bicicletas; *part of roadway* carril *m* bici

cy·cling ['saɪklɪŋ] ciclismo *m*

cy·clist ['saɪklɪst] ciclista *m/f*

cyl·in·der ['sɪlɪndər] cilindro *m*

cy·lin·dri·cal [sɪ'lɪndrɪkl] *adj* cilíndrico

cyn·ic ['sɪnɪk] escéptico(-a) *m(f)*, suspicaz *m/f*

cyn·i·cal ['sɪnɪkl] *adj* escéptico, suspicaz

cyn·i·cal·ly ['sɪnɪklɪ] *adv smile, say* con escepticismo *or* suspicacia

cyn·i·cism ['sɪnɪsɪzm] escepticismo *m*, suspicacia *f*

cy·press ['saɪprəs] ciprés *m*

cyst [sɪst] quiste *m*

Czech [tʃek] **1** *adj* checo; *the ~ Republic* la República Checa **2** *n person* checo(-a) *m(f)*; *language* checho *m*

D

DA *abbr* (= *district attorney*) fiscal *m/f* (del distrito)

dab [dæb] **1** *n small amount* pizca *f* **2** *v/t* (*pret & pp* **-bed**) (*remove*) quitar; (*apply*) poner

◆**dab·ble in** ['dæbl] *v/t* ser aficionado a

dad [dæd] *talking to him* papá *m*; *talking about him* padre *m*

dad·dy ['dædɪ] *talking to him* papi *m*; *talking about him* padre *m*

daf·fo·dil ['dæfədɪl] narciso *m*

dag·ger ['dægər] daga *f*

dai·ly ['deɪlɪ] **1** *n* (*paper*) diario *m* **2** *adj* diario

dain·ty ['deɪntɪ] *adj* grácil, delicado

dair·y ['derɪ] *on farm* vaquería *f*

'dair·y prod·ucts *npl* productos *mpl* lácteos

dais ['deɪɪs] tarima *f*

dai·sy ['deɪzɪ] margarita *f*

dam [dæm] **1** *n for water* presa *f* **2** *v/t* (*pret & pp* **-med**) *river* embalsar

dam·age ['dæmɪdʒ] **1** *n* daños *mpl*; *fig: to reputation etc* daño *m* **2** *v/t also fig* dañar; *you're damaging your health* estás perjudicando tu salud

dam·a·ges ['dæmɪdʒɪz] *npl* LAW daños *mpl* y perjuicios

dam·ag·ing ['dæmɪdʒɪŋ] *adj* perjudicial

dame [deɪm] F (*woman*) mujer *f*, *Span* tía *f* F

damn [dæm] **1** *int* F ¡mecachis! F **2** *n* F: *I don't give a ~!* ¡me importa

un pimiento! F **3** *adj* F maldito F **4** *adv* F muy; *a ~ stupid thing* una tontería monumental **5** *v/t* (*condemn*) condenar; *~ it!* F ¡maldita sea! F; *I'm ~ed if ...* F ya lo creo que ... F

damned [dæmd] → *damn* *adj*, *adv*

damn·ing ['dæmɪŋ] *adj evidence* condenatorio; *report* crítico

damp [dæmp] *adj* húmedo

damp·en ['dæmpən] *v/t* humedecer

dance [dæns] **1** *n* baile *m* **2** *v/i* bailar; *would you like to ~?* ¿le gustaría bailar?

danc·er ['dænsər] bailarín (-ina) *m(f)*

danc·ing ['dænsɪŋ] baile *m*

dan·de·li·on ['dændɪlaɪən] diente *m* de león

dan·druff ['dændrʌf] caspa *f*

dan·druff sham'poo champú *m* anticaspa

Dane [deɪn] danés(-esa) *m(f)*

dan·ger ['deɪndʒər] peligro *m*; *be in ~* estar en peligro; *be out of ~ of patient* estar fuera de peligro; *be in no ~* no estar en peligro

dan·ger·ous ['deɪndʒərəs] *adj* peligroso

dan·ger·ous 'driv·ing conducción *f* peligrosa

dan·ger·ous·ly ['deɪndʒərəslɪ] *adv drive* peligrosamente; *~ ill* gravemente enfermo

dan·gle ['dæŋgl] **1** *v/t* balancear **2** *v/i*

colgar

Da·nish ['deɪnɪʃ] **1** adj danés **2** n language danés m

'**Da·nish (pas·try)** pastel m de hojaldre (dulce)

dare [der] **1** v/i atreverse; **how ~ you!** ¡cómo te atreves! **2** v/t: ~ **to do sth** atreverse a hacer algo; ~ **s.o. to do sth** desafiar a alguien para que haga algo

dare·dev·il ['derdevɪl] temerario(-a) m(f)

dar·ing ['derɪŋ] adj atrevido

dark [dɑːrk] **1** n oscuridad f; **in the ~** en la oscuridad; **after ~** después de anochecer; **keep s.o. in the ~ about sth** fig no revelar algo a alguien **2** adj oscuro; hair oscuro, moreno; ~ **green / blue** verde / azul oscuro

dark·en ['dɑːrkn] v/i of sky oscurecerse

dark 'glass·es npl gafas fpl oscuras, L.Am. lentes fpl oscuras

dark·ness ['dɑːrknɪs] oscuridad f; **in ~** a oscuras

'**dark·room** PHOT cuarto m oscuro

dar·ling ['dɑːrlɪŋ] **1** n cielo m; **yes my ~** sí cariño **2** adj encantador; ~ **Ann, how are you?** querida Ann, ¿cómo estás?

darn¹ [dɑːrn] **1** n (mend) zurcido m **2** v/t (mend) zurcir

darn², **darned** [dɑːrn, dɑːrnd] → **damn** adj, adv

dart [dɑːrt] **1** n for throwing dardo m **2** v/i lanzarse, precipitarse

darts [dɑːrts] nsg dardos mpl

'**dart(s)·board** diana f

dash [dæʃ] **1** n punctuation raya f; (small amount) chorrito m; (MOT: ~board) salpicadero m; **make a ~ for** correr hacia **2** v/i correr; **he ~ed downstairs** bajó las escaleras corriendo **3** v/t hopes frustrar, truncar

♦**dash off 1** v/i irse **2** v/t (write quickly) escribir rápidamente

'**dash·board** salpicadero m

da·ta ['deɪtə] datos mpl

'**da·ta·base** base f de datos; **da·ta 'cap·ture** captura f de datos; **da·ta**

'**pro·cess·ing** proceso m or tratamiento m de datos; **da·ta pro'tec·tion** protección f de datos; **da·ta 'stor·age** almacenamiento m de datos

date¹ [deɪt] fruit dátil m

date² [deɪt] **1** n fecha f; (meeting) cita f; (person) pareja f; **what's the ~ today?** ¿qué fecha es hoy?, ¿a qué fecha estamos?; **out of ~** clothes pasado de moda; passport caducado; **up to ~** al día **2** v/t letter, check fechar; (go out with) salir con; **that ~s you** (shows your age) eso demuestra lo viejo que eres

dat·ed ['deɪtɪd] adj anticuado

daub [dɒːb] v/t embadurnar

daugh·ter ['dɒːtər] hija f

'**daugh·ter-in-law** (pl **daughters-in-law**) nuera f

daunt [dɒːnt] v/t acobardar, desalentar

daw·dle ['dɒːdl] v/i perder el tiempo

dawn [dɒːn] **1** n amanecer m, alba f; fig: of new age albores mpl **2** v/i amanecer; **it ~ed on me that ...** me di cuenta de que ...

day [deɪ] día m; **what ~ is it today?** ¿qué día es hoy?, ¿a qué día estamos?; ~ **off** día m de vacaciones; **by ~** durante el día; ~ **by ~** día tras día; **the ~ after** el día siguiente; **the ~ after tomorrow** pasado mañana; **the ~ before** el día anterior; **the ~ before yesterday** anteayer; ~ **in ~ out** un día sí y otro también; **in those ~s** en aquellos tiempos; **one ~** un día; **the other ~** (recently) el otro día; **let's call it a ~!** ¡dejémoslo!

'**day·break** amanecer m, alba f; '**day care** servicio m de guardería; '**day·dream 1** n fantasía f **2** v/i soñar despierto; '**day dream·er** soñador(a) m(f); '**day·light** luz f del día; '**day·light 'sav·ing time** horario m de verano; '**day·time**: **in the ~** durante el día; '**day trip** excursión f en el día

daze [deɪz] n: **in a ~** aturdido

dazed [deɪzd] adj aturdido

daz·zle ['dæzl] *v/t also fig* deslumbrar

DC [diː'siː] *abbr* (= *direct current*) cc (= corriente *f* continua); (= *District of Columbia*) Distrito *m* de Columbia

dead [ded] **1** *adj person, plant* muerto; *battery* agotado; *light bulb* fundido; F *place* muerto F; *the phone is ~* no hay línea **2** *adv* F (*very*) tela de F, la mar de F; *~ beat, ~ tired* hecho polvo; *that's ~ right* tienes toda la razón del mundo **3** *npl: the ~* (*~ people*) los muertos; *in the ~ of night* a altas horas de la madrugada

dead·en ['dedn] *v/t pain, sound* amortiguar

dead 'end *street* callejón *m* sin salida; **dead·'end job** trabajo *m* sin salidas; **dead 'heat** empate *m*; **'dead·line** fecha *f* tope; *for newspaper, magazine* hora *f* de cierre; *meet a ~* cumplir un plazo; **'dead·lock** *n in talks* punto *m* muerto

dead·ly ['dedlɪ] *adj* (*fatal*) mortal F, F (*boring*) mortal F

deaf [def] *adj* sordo

deaf·and-'dumb *adj* sordomudo

deaf·en ['defn] *v/t* ensordecer

deaf·en·ing ['defnɪŋ] *adj* ensordecedor

deaf·ness ['defnɪs] sordera *f*

deal [diːl] **1** *n* acuerdo *m*; *I thought we had a ~* creía que habíamos hecho un trato; *it's a ~!* ¡trato hecho!; *a good ~* (*bargain*) una ocasión; (*a lot*) mucho; *a great ~ of* (*lots*) mucho(s) **2** *v/t* (*pret & pp* **dealt**) *cards* repartir; *~ a blow to* asestar un golpe a
♦ **deal in** *v/t* (*trade in*) comerciar con; *deal in drugs* traficar con drogas
♦ **deal out** *v/t cards* repartir
♦ **deal with** *v/t* (*handle*) tratar; *situation* hacer frente a; *customer, applications* encargarse de; (*do business with*) hacer negocios con

deal·er ['diːlər] (*merchant*) comerciante *m/f*; (*drug ~*) traficante *m/f*

deal·ing ['diːlɪŋ] (*drug ~*) tráfico *m*

deal·ings ['diːlɪŋz] *npl* (*business*) tratos *mpl*

dealt [delt] *pret & pp* → **deal**

dean [diːn] *of college* decano(-a) *m(f)*

dear [dɪr] *adj* querido; (*expensive*) caro; *Dear Sir* Muy Sr. Mío; *Dear Richard / Margaret* Querido Richard / Querida Margaret; (*oh*) *~!, ~ me!* ¡oh, cielos!

dear·ly ['dɪrlɪ] *adv love* muchísimo

death [deθ] muerte *f*

'death cer·tif·i·cate certificado *m* de defunción; **'death pen·al·ty** pena *f* de muerte; **'death toll** saldo *m* de víctimas mortales

de·ba·ta·ble [dɪ'beɪtəbl] *adj* discutible

de·bate [dɪ'beɪt] **1** *n also* POL debate *m* **2** *v/i* debatir; *I ~d with myself whether to go* me debatía entre ir o no ir **3** *v/t* debatir

de·bauch·er·y [dɪ'bɒːtʃərɪ] libertinaje *m*

deb·it ['debɪt] **1** *n* cargo *m* **2** *v/t account* cargar en; *amount* cargar

'deb·it card tarjeta *f* de débito

deb·ris [də'briː] *nsg of building* escombros *mpl*; *of airplane* restos *mpl*

debt [det] deuda *f*; *be in ~ financially* estar endeudado

debt·or ['detər] deudor(-a) *m(f)*

de·bug [diː'bʌg] *v/t* (*pret & pp* **-ged**) *room* limpiar de micrófonos; COMPUT depurar

dé·but ['deɪbjuː] *n* debut *m*

dec·ade ['dekeɪd] década *f*

dec·a·dence ['dekədəns] decadencia *f*

dec·a·dent ['dekədənt] *adj* decadente

de·caf·fein·at·ed [dɪ'kæfɪneɪtɪd] *adj* descafeinado

de·cant·er [dɪ'kæntər] licorera *f*

de·cap·i·tate [dɪ'kæpɪteɪt] *v/t* decapitar

de·cay [dɪ'keɪ] **1** *n of wood, plant* putrefacción *f*; *of civilization* declive *m*; *in teeth* caries *f inv* **2** *v/i of wood, plant* pudrirse; *of civilization* decaer; *of teeth* cariarse de·ceased [dɪ'siːst]: *the ~* el difunto / la difunta

de·ceit [dɪ'siːt] engaño m, mentira f

de·ceit·ful [dɪ'siːtfəl] adj mentiroso

de·ceive [dɪ'siːv] v/t engañar

De·cem·ber [dɪ'sembər] diciembre m

de·cen·cy ['diːsənsɪ] decencia f; *he had the ~ to ...* tuvo la delicadeza de ...

de·cent ['diːsənt] adj decente; (*adequately dressed*) presentable

de·cen·tral·ize [diː'sentrəlaɪz] v/t descentralizar

de·cep·tion [dɪ'sepʃn] engaño m

de·cep·tive [dɪ'septɪv] adj engañoso

de·cep·tive·ly [dɪ'septɪvlɪ] adv: *it looks ~ simple* parece muy fácil

dec·i·bel ['desɪbel] decibelio m

de·cide [dɪ'saɪd] **1** v/t decidir **2** v/i decidir; *you ~ decide tú*

de·cid·ed [dɪ'saɪdɪd] adj (*definite*) tajante

de·cid·er [dɪ'saɪdər]: *this match will be the ~* este partido será el que decida

dec·i·du·ous [dɪ'sɪduəs] adj de hoja caduca

dec·i·mal ['desɪml] n decimal m

dec·i·mal 'point coma f (decimal)

dec·i·mate ['desɪmeɪt] v/t diezmar

de·ci·pher [dɪ'saɪfər] v/t descifrar

de·ci·sion [dɪ'sɪʒn] decisión f; *come to a ~* llegar a una decisión

de'ci·sion-mak·er: *who's the ~ here?* ¿quién toma aquí las decisiones?

de·ci·sive [dɪ'saɪsɪv] adj decidido; (*crucial*) decisivo

deck [dek] *of ship* cubierta f; *of cards* baraja f

'deck·chair tumbona f

dec·la·ra·tion [deklə'reɪʃn] (*statement*) declaración f

de·clare [dɪ'kler] v/t (*state*) declarar

de·cline [dɪ'klaɪn] **1** n (*fall*) descenso m; *in standards* caída f; *in health* empeoramiento m **2** v/t *invitation* declinar; *~ to comment* declinar hacer declaraciones **3** v/i (*refuse*) rehusar; (*decrease*) declinar; *of*

health empeorar

de·clutch [diː'klʌtʃ] v/i desembragar

de·code [diː'koʊd] v/t descodificar

de·com·pose [diːkəm'poʊz] v/i descomponerse

dé·cor ['deɪkɔːr] decoración f

dec·o·rate ['dekəreɪt] v/t *with paint* pintar; *with paper* empapelar; (*adorn*) decorar; *soldier* condecorar

dec·o·ra·tion [dekə'reɪʃn] *paint* pintado m; *paper* empapelado m; (*ornament*) decoración f

dec·o·ra·tive ['dekərətɪv] adj decorativo

dec·o·ra·tor ['dekəreɪtər] (*interior ~*) decorador(a) m(f); *with paint* pintor(a) m(f); *with wallpaper* empapelador(a) m(f)

de·co·rum [dɪ'kɔːrəm] decoro m

de·coy ['diːkɔɪ] n señuelo m

de·crease **1** n ['diːkriːs] disminución f, reducción f (*in* de) **2** v/t [dɪ'kriːs] disminuir, reducir **3** v/i [dɪ'kriːs] disminuir, reducirse

de·crep·it [dɪ'krepɪt] adj *car, coat, shoes* destartalado; *person* decrépito

ded·i·cate ['dedɪkeɪt] v/t *book etc* dedicar; *~ o.s. to.* dedicarse a

ded·i·cat·ed ['dedɪkeɪtɪd] adj dedicado

ded·i·ca·tion [dedɪ'keɪʃn] *in book* dedicatoria f; *to cause, work* dedicación f

de·duce [dɪ'duːs] v/t deducir

de·duct [dɪ'dʌkt] v/t descontar

de·duc·tion [dɪ'dʌkʃn] *from salary, (conclusion*) deduccción f

deed [diːd] n (*act*) acción f, obra f; LAW escritura f

dee·jay ['diːdʒeɪ] F disk jockey m/f, *Span* pincha m/f F

deem [diːm] v/t estimar

deep [diːp] adj *profundo; color* intenso; *be in ~ trouble* estar metido en serios apuros

deep·en ['diːpn] **1** v/t profundizar **2** v/i hacerse más profundo; *of crisis, mystery* agudizarse

'deep freeze n congelador m; '**deep-froz·en food** comida f congelada; **'deep-fry** v/t (*pret & pp* **-ied**) freír (*en mucho aceite*); **deep 'fry·er** freidora *f*

deer [dɪr] (*pl* **deer**) ciervo *m*

de·face [dɪ'feɪs] v/t desfigurar, dañar

def·a·ma·tion [defə'meɪʃn] difamación *f*

de·fam·a·to·ry [dɪ'fæmətərɪ] adj difamatorio

de·fault ['dɪ:fɔːlt] adj COMPUT por defecto

de·feat [dɪ'fiːt] **1** n derrota *f* **2** v/t derrotar; *of task, problem* derrotar, vencer

de·feat·ist [dɪ'fiːtɪst] adj attitude derrotista

de·fect ['dɪ:fekt] n defecto *m*

de·fec·tive [dɪ'fektɪv] adj defectuoso

de'fence etc Br → **defense** etc

de·fend [dɪ'fend] v/t defender

de·fend·ant [dɪ'fendənt] acusado(-a) *m(f)*; *in civil case* demandado(-a) *m(f)*

de·fense [dɪ'fens] defensa *f*; **come to s.o.'s ~** salir en defensa de alguien

de'fense budg·et POL presupuesto *m* de defensa

de'fense law·yer abogado(-a) *m(f)* defensor(a)

de·fense·less [dɪ'fenslɪs] adj indefenso

de'fense play·er SP defensa *m/f*; **De'fense Se·cre·ta·ry** POL ministro(-a) *m(f)* de Defensa; *in USA* secretario *m* de Defensa; **de'fense wit·ness** LAW testigo *m/f* de la defensa

de·fen·sive [dɪ'fensɪv] **1** n: **on the ~** a la defensiva; **go on the ~** ponerse a la defensiva **2** adj weaponry defensivo; **stop being so ~!** ¡no hace falta que te pongas tan a la defensiva!

de·fen·sive·ly [dɪ'fensɪvlɪ] adv a la defensiva

de·fer [dɪ'fɜːr] v/t (*pret & pp* **-red**) (*postpone*) aplazar, diferir

de·fer·ence ['defərəns] deferencia *f*

def·er·en·tial [defə'renʃl] adj deferente

de·fi·ance [dɪ'faɪəns] desafío *m*; **in ~ of** desafiando

de·fi·ant [dɪ'faɪənt] adj desafiante

de·fi·cien·cy [dɪ'fɪʃənsɪ] (*lack*) deficiencia *f*, carencia *f*

de·fi·cient [dɪ'fɪʃənt] adj deficiente, carente; **be ~ in ...** carecer de ...

def·i·cit ['defɪsɪt] déficit *m*

de·fine [dɪ'faɪn] v/t word, objective definir

def·i·nite ['defɪnɪt] adj date, time, answer definitivo; improvement claro; (*certain*) seguro; **nothing ~ has been arranged** no se ha acordado nada de forma definitiva

def·i·nite 'ar·ti·cle GRAM artículo *m* determinado or definido

def·i·nite·ly ['defɪnɪtlɪ] adv con certeza, sin lugar a dudas

def·i·ni·tion [defɪ'nɪʃn] definición *f*

def·i·ni·tive [dɪ'fɪnətɪv] adj definitivo

de·flect [dɪ'flekt] v/t desviar; criticism distraer; **be ~ed from** desviarse de

de·for·est·a·tion [dɪfɑːrɪ'steɪʃn] deforestación *f*

de·form [dɪ'fɔːrm] v/t deformar

de·for·mi·ty [dɪ'fɔːrmɪtɪ] deformidad *f*

de·fraud [dɪ'frɔːd] v/t defraudar

de·frost [dɪ:'frɔːst] v/t food, fridge descongelar

deft [deft] adj hábil, diestro

de·fuse [dɪ:'fjuːz] v/t bomb desactivar; situation calmar

de·fy [dɪ'faɪ] v/t (*pret & pp* **-ied**) desafiar

de·gen·e·rate [dɪ'dʒenəreɪt] v/i degenerar; ~ **into** degenerar en

de·grade [dɪ'greɪd] v/t degradar

de·grad·ing [dɪ'greɪdɪŋ] adj position, work degradante

de·gree [dɪ'griː] from university título *m*; of temperature, angle, latitude grado *m*; **there is a ~ of truth in that** hay algo de verdad en eso; **a ~ of compassion** algo de compasión; **by ~s** gradualmente; **get one's ~** graduarse, *L.Am.* egresar

de·hy·drat·ed [diːhaɪˈdreɪtɪd] *adj* deshidratado

de-ice [diːˈaɪs] *v/t* deshelar

de-ic·er [diːˈaɪsər] *spray* descongelador *m*, descongelante *m*

deign [deɪn] *v/i*: ~ **to** dignarse a

de·i·ty [ˈdiːɪtɪ] deidad *f*

de·jec·ted [dɪˈdʒektɪd] *adj* abatido, desanimado

de·lay [dɪˈleɪ] **1** *n* retraso *m* **2** *v/t* retrasar; *be ~ed* llevar retraso **3** *v/i* retrasarse

del·e·gate [ˈdelɪgət] **1** *n* delegado(-a) *m(f)* **2** [ˈdelɪgeɪt] *v/t task* delegar; *person* delegar en

del·e·ga·tion [delɪˈgeɪʃn] delegación *f*

de·lete [dɪˈliːt] *v/t* borrar; *(cross out)* tachar; ~ **where not applicable** táchese donde no corresponda

de·le·tion [dɪˈliːʃn] *act* borrado *m*; *that deleted* supresión *f*

deli [ˈdelɪ] → **delicatessen**

de·lib·e·rate 1 *adj* [dɪˈlɪbərət] deliberado, intencionado **2** *v/i* [dɪˈlɪbəreɪt] deliberar

de·lib·e·rate·ly [dɪˈlɪbərətlɪ] *adv* deliberadamente, a propósito

del·i·ca·cy [ˈdelɪkəsɪ] delicadeza *f*; *of health* fragilidad *f*; *food* exquisitez *f*, manjar *m*

del·i·cate [ˈdelɪkət] *adj fabric, problem* delicado; *health* frágil

del·i·ca·tes·sen [delɪkəˈtesn] *tienda de productos alimenticios de calidad*

del·i·cious [dɪˈlɪʃəs] *adj* delicioso

de·light [dɪˈlaɪt] *n* placer *m*

de·light·ed [dɪˈlaɪtɪd] *adj* encantado; *I'd be ~ to come* me encantaría venir

de·light·ful [dɪˈlaɪtfəl] *adj* encantador

de·lim·it [diːˈlɪmɪt] *v/t* delimitar

de·lir·i·ous [dɪˈlɪrɪəs] *adj* MED delirante; *(ecstatic)* entusiasmado; *she's ~ about the new job* está como loca con el nuevo trabajo

de·liv·er [dɪˈlɪvər] *v/t* entregar, repartir; *message* dar; *baby* dar a luz; *speech* pronunciar

de·liv·er·y [dɪˈlɪvərɪ] *of goods, mail* entrega *f*, reparto *m*; *of baby* parto *m*

de·liv·er·y charge gastos *mpl* de envío; **de·liv·er·y date** fecha *f* de entrega; **de·liv·er·y man** repartidor *m*; **de·liv·er·y note** nota *f* de entrega; **de·liv·er·y serv·ice** servicio *m* de reparto; **de·liv·er·y van** furgoneta *f* de reparto

de·lude [dɪˈluːd] *v/t* engañar; *you're deluding yourself* te estás engañando a ti mismo

de·luge [ˈdeljuːdʒ] **1** *n* diluvio *m*; *fig* avalancha *f* **2** *v/t fig* inundar (*with* de)

de·lu·sion [dɪˈluːʒn] engaño *m*; *you're under a ~ if you think …* te engañas si piensas que …

de luxe [dəˈlʊks] *adj* de lujo

♦ **delve into** [delv] *v/t* rebuscar en

de·mand [dɪˈmænd] **1** *n* exigencia *f*; *by union* reivindicación *f*; COM demanda *f*; *in ~* solicitado **2** *v/t* exigir; *(require)* requerir

de·mand·ing [dɪˈmændɪŋ] *adj job* que exige mucho; *person* exigente

de·mean·ing [dɪˈmiːnɪŋ] *adj* degradante

de·men·ted [dɪˈmentɪd] *adj* demente

de·mise [dɪˈmaɪz] fallecimiento *m*; *fig* desaparición *f*

dem·o [ˈdemoʊ] *protest* manifestación *f*; *of video etc* maqueta *f*

de·moc·ra·cy [dɪˈmɑːkrəsɪ] democracia *f*

dem·o·crat [ˈdeməkræt] demócrata *m/f*; *Democrat* POL Demócrata *m/f*

dem·o·crat·ic [deməˈkrætɪk] *adj* democrático

dem·o·crat·ic·al·ly [deməˈkrætɪklɪ] *adv* democráticamente

'dem·o disk disco *m* de demostración

dem·o·graph·ic [demoʊˈgræfɪk] *adj* demográfico

de·mol·ish [dɪˈmɑːlɪʃ] *v/t building* demoler; *argument* destruir, echar por tierra

dem·o·li·tion [demə'lɪʃn] *of building* demolición *f*; *of argument* destrucción *f*

de·mon ['diːmən] demonio *m*

dem·on·strate ['demənstreɪt] **1** *v/t* demostrar **2** *v/i politically* manifestarse

dem·on·stra·tion [demən'streɪʃn] demostración *f*; *protest* manifestación *f*

de·mon·stra·tive [dɪ'mɑːnstrətɪv] *adj person* extrovertido, efusivo; GRAM demostrativo

de·mon·stra·tor ['demənstreɪtər] *protester* manifestante *m/f*

de·mor·al·ized [dɪ'mɔːrəlaɪzd] *adj* desmoralizado

de·mor·al·iz·ing [dɪ'mɔːrəlaɪzɪŋ] *adj* desmoralizado

de·mote [diː'moʊt] *v/t* degradar

de·mure [dɪ'mjʊər] *adj* solemne, recatado

den [den] *(study)* estudio *m*

de·ni·al [dɪ'naɪəl] *of rumor, accusation* negación *f*; *of request* denegación *f*

den·im ['denɪm] tela *f* vaquera

den·ims ['denɪmz] *npl (jeans)* vaqueros *mpl*

Den·mark ['denmɑːrk] Dinamarca

de·nom·i·na·tion [dɪnɑːmɪ'neɪʃn] *of money* valor *m*; *religious* confesión *f*

de·nounce [dɪ'naʊns] *v/t* denunciar

dense [dens] *adj smoke, fog* denso; *foliage* espeso; *crowd* compacto; F *(stupid)* corto

dense·ly ['denslɪ] *adv*: ~ *populated* densamente poblado

den·si·ty ['densɪtɪ] *of population* densidad *f*

dent [dent] **1** *n* abolladura *f* **2** *v/t* abollar

den·tal ['dentl] *adj* dental; ~ *surgeon* odontólogo(-a) *m(f)*

den·ted ['dentɪd] *adj* abollado

den·tist ['dentɪst] dentista *m/f*

den·tist·ry ['dentɪstrɪ] odontología *f*

den·tures ['dentʃərz] *npl* dentadura *f* postiza

Den·ver boot ['denvər] cepo *m*

de·ny [dɪ'naɪ] *v/t (pret & pp -ied)* *charge, rumor* negar; *right, request* denegar

de·o·do·rant [diː'oʊdərənt] desodorante *m*

de·part [dɪ'pɑːrt] *v/i* salir; ~ *from (deviate from)* desviarse de

de·part·ment [dɪ'pɑːrtmənt] departamento *m*; *of government* ministerio *m*

De·part·ment of 'De·fense Ministerio *m* de Defensa; **De·part·ment of 'State** Ministerio *m* de Asuntos Exteriores; **De·part·ment of the In·te·ri·or** Ministerio *m* del Interior; **de'part·ment store** grandes almacenes *mpl*

de·par·ture [dɪ'pɑːrtʃər] salida *f*; *of person from job* marcha *f*; *(deviation)* desviación *f*; *a new ~ for government, organization* una innovación; *for company* un cambio; *for actor, artist, writer* una nueva experiencia

de'par·ture lounge sala *f* de embarque

de'par·ture time hora *f* de salida

de·pend [dɪ'pend] *v/i* depender; *that ~s* depende; *it ~s on the weather* depende del tiempo; *I ~ on you* dependo de ti

de·pen·da·ble [dɪ'pendəbl] *adj* fiable

de·pen·dant [dɪ'pendənt] → *dependent*

de·pen·dence, de·pen·den·cy [dɪ'pendəns, dɪ'pendənsɪ] dependencia *f*

de·pen·dent [dɪ'pendənt] **1** *n persona a cargo de otra*; *how many ~s do you have?* ¿cuántas personas tiene a su cargo? **2** *adj* dependiente (*on* de)

de·pict [dɪ'pɪkt] *v/t* describir

de·plete [dɪ'pliːt] *v/t* agotar, mermar

de·plor·a·ble [dɪ'plɔːrəbl] *adj* deplorable

de·plore [dɪ'plɔːr] *v/t* deplorar

de·ploy [dɪ'plɔɪ] *v/t (use)* utilizar; *(position)* desplegar

de·pop·u·la·tion [diːpɑːpjə'leɪʃn] despoblación *f*

de·port [dɪˈpɔːrt] v/t deportar

de·por·ta·tion [diːpɔːrˈteɪʃn] deportación f

de·por'ta·tion or·der orden f de deportación

de·pose [dɪˈpəʊz] v/t deponer

de·pos·it [dɪˈpɑːzɪt] **1** n in bank, of oil depósito m; of coal yacimiento m; on purchase señal f, depósito m **2** v/t money depositar, Span ingresar; (put down) depositar

de'pos·it ac·count Br cuenta f de ahorro or de depósito

dep·o·si·tion [diːpoʊˈzɪʃn] LAW declaración f

dep·ot [ˈdiːpoʊ] (train station) estación f de tren; (bus station) estación f de autobuses; for storage depósito m

de·praved [dɪˈpreɪvd] adj depravado

de·pre·ci·ate [dɪˈpriːʃieɪt] v/i FIN depreciarse

de·pre·ci·a·tion [dɪpriːʃiˈeɪʃn] FIN depreciación f

de·press [dɪˈpres] v/t person deprimir

de·pressed [dɪˈprest] adj person deprimido

de·press·ing [dɪˈpresɪŋ] adj deprimente

de·pres·sion [dɪˈpreʃn] MED, economic depresión f; meteorological borrasca f

dep·ri·va·tion [deprɪˈveɪʃn] privación f

de·prive [dɪˈpraɪv] v/t privar; ~ s.o. of sth privar a alguien de algo

de·prived [dɪˈpraɪvd] adj desfavorecido

depth [depθ] profundidad f; of color intensidad f; in ~ (thoroughly) en profundidad; in the ~s of winter en pleno invierno; be out of one's ~ in water no tocar el fondo; fig: in discussion etc saber muy poco

dep·u·ta·tion [depjuˈteɪʃn] delegación f

♦ **dep·u·tize for** [ˈdepjutaɪz] v/t sustituir

dep·u·ty [ˈdepjʊtɪ] segundo(-a) m(f)

'dep·u·ty lead·er vicelíder m/f

de·rail [dɪˈreɪl] v/t hacer descarrilar; **be ~ed** of train descarrilar

de·ranged [dɪˈreɪndʒd] adj perturbado, trastornado

de·reg·u·late [diːˈreɡjʊleɪt] v/t liberalizar, desregular

de·reg·u·la·tion [diːreɡjuˈleɪʃn] liberalización f, desregulación f

der·e·lict [ˈderəlɪkt] adj en ruinas

de·ride [dɪˈraɪd] v/t ridiculizar, mofarse de

de·ri·sion [dɪˈrɪʒn] burla f, mofa f

de·ri·sive [dɪˈraɪsɪv] adj burlón

de·ri·sive·ly [dɪˈraɪsɪvlɪ] adv burlonamente

de·ri·so·ry [dɪˈraɪsərɪ] adj amount, salary irrisorio

de·riv·a·tive [dɪˈrɪvətɪv] adj (not original) poco original

de·rive [dɪˈraɪv] v/t obtener, encontrar; **be ~d from** of word derivar(se) de

der·ma·tol·o·gist [dɜːrməˈtɑːlədʒɪst] dermatólogo(-a) m(f)

de·rog·a·to·ry [dɪˈrɑːɡətɔːrɪ] adj despectivo

de·scend [dɪˈsend] **1** v/t descender por; **be ~ed from** descender de **2** v/i descender; of mood, darkness caer

de·scen·dant [dɪˈsendənt] descendiente m/f

de·scent [dɪˈsent] descenso m; (ancestry) ascendencia f

de·scribe [dɪˈskraɪb] v/t describir; ~ **sth as sth** definir a algo como algo

de·scrip·tion [dɪˈskrɪpʃn] descripción f

des·e·crate [ˈdesɪkreɪt] v/t profanar

des·e·cra·tion [desɪˈkreɪʃn] profanación f

de·seg·re·gate [diːˈseɡrəɡeɪt] v/t acabar con la segregación racial en

des·ert¹ [ˈdezərt] n also fig desierto m

de·sert² [dɪˈzɜːrt] **1** v/t (abandon) abandonar **2** v/i of soldier desertar

des·ert·ed [dɪˈzɜːrtɪd] adj desierto

de·sert·er [dɪˈzɜːrtər] MIL desertor(a) m(f)

de·ser·ti·fi·ca·tion [dɪzɜːrtɪfɪˈkeɪʃn] desertización f

de·ser·tion [dɪˈzɜːrʃn] (*abandonment*) abandono m; MIL deserción f

des·ert 'is·land isla f desierta

de·serve [dɪˈzɜːrv] v/t merecer

de·sign [dɪˈzaɪn] **1** n diseño m; (*pattern*) motivo m **2** v/t diseñar

des·ig·nate [ˈdezɪgneɪt] v/t *person* designar; *area* declarar

de·sign·er [dɪˈzaɪnər] diseñador(a) m(f)

de'sign·er clothes npl ropa f de diseño

de'sign fault defecto m de diseño

de'sign school escuela f de diseño

de·sir·a·ble [dɪˈzaɪrəbl] adj deseable; *house* apetecible, atractivo

de·sire [dɪˈzaɪr] n deseo m; *I have no ~ to see him* no me apetece verle

desk [desk] *in classroom* pupitre m; *in home, office* mesa f; *in hotel* recepción f

'desk clerk recepcionista m/f; **'desk di·a·ry** agenda f; **'desk·top** *also on screen* escritorio m; *computer* Span ordenador m de escritorio, L.Am. computadora f de escritorio; **desk·top 'pub·lish·ing** autoedición f

des·o·late [ˈdesələt] adj *place* desolado

de·spair [dɪˈsper] **1** n desesperación f; *in ~* desesperado **2** v/i desesperarse; *I ~ of finding something to wear* he perdido la esperanza de encontrar algo para ponerme

des·per·ate [ˈdespərət] adj desesperado; *be ~* estar desesperado; *be ~ for a drink/cigarette* necesitar una bebida/un cigarrillo desesperadamente

des·per·a·tion [despəˈreɪʃn] desesperación f; *an act of ~* un acto desesperado

des·pic·a·ble [dɪsˈpɪkəbl] adj despreciable

de·spise [dɪˈspaɪz] v/t despreciar

de·spite [dɪˈspaɪt] prep a pesar de

de·spon·dent [dɪˈspɑːndənt] adj abatido, desanimado

des·pot [ˈdespɑːt] déspota m/f

des·sert [dɪˈzɜːrt] postre m

des·ti·na·tion [destɪˈneɪʃn] destino m

des·tined [ˈdestɪnd] adj: *be ~ for* fig estar destinado a

des·ti·ny [ˈdestɪnɪ] destino m

des·ti·tute [ˈdestɪtuːt] adj indigente; *be ~* estar en la miseria

de·stroy [dɪˈstrɔɪ] v/t destruir

de·stroy·er [dɪˈstrɔɪr] NAUT destructor m

de·struc·tion [dɪˈstrʌkʃn] destrucción f

de·struc·tive [dɪˈstrʌktɪv] adj destructivo; *child* revoltoso

de·tach [dɪˈtætʃ] v/t separar, soltar

de·tach·a·ble [dɪˈtætʃəbl] adj desmontable, separable

de·tached [dɪˈtætʃt] adj (*objective*) distanciado

de·tach·ment [dɪˈtætʃmənt] (*objectivity*) distancia f

de·tail [ˈdiːteɪl] n detalle m; *in ~* en detalle

de·tailed [ˈdiːteɪld] adj detallado

de·tain [dɪˈteɪn] v/t (*hold back*) entretener; *as prisoner* detener

de·tain·ee [diːteɪnˈiː] detenido(-a) m(f)

de·tect [dɪˈtekt] v/t percibir; *of device* detectar

de·tec·tion [dɪˈtekʃn] *of criminal, crime* descubrimiento m; *of smoke etc* detección f

de·tec·tive [dɪˈtektɪv] detective m/f

de'tec·tive nov·el novela f policiaca *or* de detectives

de·tec·tor [dɪˈtektər] detector m

dé·tente [ˈdeɪtɑːnt] POL distensión f

de·ten·tion [dɪˈtenʃn] (*imprisonment*) detención f

de·ter [dɪˈtɜːr] v/t (*pret & pp -red*) disuadir; *~ s.o. from doing sth* disuadir a alguien de hacer algo

de·ter·gent [dɪˈtɜːrdʒənt] detergente m

de·te·ri·o·rate [dɪˈtɪriəreɪt] v/i deteriorarse; *of weather* empeorar

de·te·ri·o·ra·tion [dɪtɪriəˈreɪʃn] deterioro m; *of weather* empeoramiento *m*

de·ter·mi·na·tion [dɪtɜːrmɪˈneɪʃn]
(*resolution*) determinación *f*

de·ter·mine [dɪˈtɜːrmɪn] *v/t* (*establish*) determinar

de·ter·mined [dɪˈtɜːrmɪnd] *adj* resuelto, decidido; *I'm ~ to succeed* estoy decidido a triunfar

de·ter·rent [dɪˈterənt] *n* elemento *m* disuasorio; *act as a ~* actuar como elemento disuasorio; *nuclear ~* disuasión *f* nuclear

de·test [dɪˈtest] *v/t* detestar

de·test·a·ble [dɪˈtestəbl] *adj* detestable

de·to·nate [ˈdetəneɪt] **1** *v/t* hacer detonar *or* explotar **2** *v/i* detonar, explotar

de·to·na·tion [detəˈneɪʃn] detonación *f*, explosión *f*

de·tour [ˈdiːtʊr] *n* rodeo *m*; (*diversion*) desvío *m*; *make a ~* dar un rodeo

♦**de·tract from** [dɪˈtrækt] *v/t* *achievement* quitar méritos a; *beauty* quitar atractivo a

de·tri·ment [ˈdetrɪmənt]: *to the ~ of* en detrimento de

de·tri·men·tal [detrɪˈmentl] *adj* perjudicial (*to* para)

deuce [duːs] *in tennis* deuce *m*

de·val·u·a·tion [diːvæljʊˈeɪʃn] *of currency* devaluación *f*

de·val·ue [diːˈvæljuː] *v/t* *currency* devaluar

dev·a·state [ˈdevəsteɪt] *v/t* *crops, countryside, city* devastar; *fig: person* asolar

dev·a·stat·ing [ˈdevəsteɪtɪŋ] *adj* devastador

de·vel·op [dɪˈveləp] **1** *v/t* *film* revelar; *land, site* urbanizar; *activity, business* desarrollar; (*originate*) desarrollar; (*improve on*) perfeccionar; *illness, cold* contraer **2** *v/i* (*grow*) desarrollarse; *~ into* convertirse en

de·vel·op·er [dɪˈveləpər] *of property* promotor(a) *m(f)* inmobiliario(-a)

de·vel·op·ing 'coun·try [dɪˈveləpɪŋ] país *m* en vías de desarrollo

de·vel·op·ment [dɪˈveləpmənt] *of*

film revelado *m*; *of land, site* urbanización *f*; *of business, country* desarrollo *m*; (*event*) acontecimiento *m*; (*origination*) desarrollo *m*; (*improving*) perfeccionamiento *m*

de·vice [dɪˈvaɪs] *tool* aparato *m*, dispositivo *m*

dev·il [ˈdevl] *also fig* diablo *m*, demonio *m*

de·vi·ous [ˈdiːvɪəs] *adj* (*sly*) retorcido

de·vise [dɪˈvaɪz] *v/t* idear

de·void [dɪˈvɔɪd] *adj*: *be ~ of* estar desprovisto de

dev·o·lu·tion [diːvəˈluːʃn] POL traspaso *m* de competencias

de·vote [dɪˈvoʊt] *v/t* dedicar (*to* a)

de·vot·ed [dɪˈvoʊtɪd] *adj* son etc afectuoso; *be ~ to s.o.* tener mucho cariño a alguien

dev·o·tee [dɪvoʊˈtiː] entusiasta *m/f*

de·vo·tion [dɪˈvoʊʃn] devoción *f*

de·vour [dɪˈvaʊər] *v/t* *food, book* devorar

de·vout [dɪˈvaʊt] *adj* devoto

dew [duː] rocío *m*

dex·ter·i·ty [dekˈsterətɪ] destreza *f*

di·a·be·tes [daɪəˈbiːtiːz] *nsg* diabetes *f*

di·a·bet·ic [daɪəˈbetɪk] **1** *n* diabético(-a) *m(f)* **2** *adj* diabético; *foods* para diabéticos

di·ag·nose [ˈdaɪəgnoʊz] *v/t* diagnosticar; *she has been ~d as having cancer* se le ha diagnosticado un cáncer

di·ag·no·sis [daɪəgˈnoʊsɪs] (*pl **di·agnoses** [daɪəgˈnoʊsiːz]) diagnóstico *m*

di·ag·o·nal [daɪˈægənl] *adj* diagonal

di·ag·o·nal·ly [daɪˈægənlɪ] *adv* diagonalmente, en diagonal

di·a·gram [ˈdaɪəgræm] diagrama *m*

di·al [ˈdaɪl] **1** *n of clock* esfera *f*; *of instrument* cuadrante *m*; TELEC disco *m* **2** *v/t & v/i* (*pret & pp **-ed**, Br **-led**) TELEC marcar

di·a·lect [ˈdaɪəlekt] dialecto *m*

di·al·ing tone *Br* → **dial tone**

di·a·log, *Br* **di·a·logue** [ˈdaɪəlɒg] diálogo *m*

di·a·log box COMPUT ventana *f* de diálogo

'di·al tone tono *m* de marcar

di·am·e·ter [daɪˈæmɪtər] diámetro *m*; *a circle 6 cms in ~* un círculo de 6 cms. de diámetro

di·a·met·ri·cal·ly [daɪəˈmetrɪkəlɪ] *adv*: *~ opposed* diametralmente opuesto

di·a·mond ['daɪmənd] *also in cards* diamante *m*; *shape* rombo *m*

di·a·per ['daɪpər] pañal *m*

di·a·phragm ['daɪəfræm] ANAT, *contraceptive* diafragma *m*

di·ar·rhe·a, *Br* **di·ar·rhoe·a** [daɪəˈriːə] diarrea *f*

di·a·ry ['daɪrɪ] *for thoughts* diario *m*; *for appointments* agenda *f*

dice [daɪs] **1** *n* dado *m*; *pl* dados *mpl* **2** *v/t food* cortar en dados

di·chot·o·my [daɪˈkɑːtəmɪ] dicotomía *f*

dic·tate [dɪkˈteɪt] *v/t* dictar

dic·ta·tion [dɪkˈteɪʃn] dictado *m*

dic·ta·tor [dɪkˈteɪtər] POL dictador(a) *m(f)*

dic·ta·to·ri·al [dɪktəˈtɔːrɪəl] *adj* dictatorial

dic·ta·tor·ship [dɪkˈteɪtərʃɪp] dictadura *f*

dic·tion·a·ry ['dɪkʃənerɪ] diccionario *m*

did [dɪd] *pret →* **do**

die [daɪ] *v/i* morir; *~ of cancer / Aids* morir de cáncer / sida; *I'm dying to know / leave* me muero de ganas de saber / marchar
♦ **die away** *v/i of noise* desaparecer
♦ **die down** *v/i of noise* irse apagando; *of storm* amainar; *of fire* irse extinguiendo; *of excitement* calmarse
♦ **die out** *v/i of custom, species* desaparecer

die·sel ['diːzl] *fuel* gasoil *m*, gasóleo *m*

di·et ['daɪət] **1** *n (regular food)* dieta *f*; *for losing weight, for health reasons* dieta *f*, régimen *m* **2** *v/i to lose weight* hacer dieta *or* régimen

di·e·ti·tian [daɪəˈtɪʃn] experto(-a) *m(f)* en dietética

dif·fer ['dɪfər] *v/i (be different)* ser distinto; *(disagree)* discrepar; *the male ~s from the female in …* el macho se diferencia de la hembra por …

dif·fe·rence ['dɪfrəns] diferencia *f*; *it doesn't make any ~ (doesn't change anything)* no cambia nada; *(doesn't matter)* da lo mismo

dif·fe·rent ['dɪfrənt] *adj* diferente, distinto *(from, than* de)

dif·fe·ren·ti·ate [dɪfəˈrenʃɪeɪt] *v/i* diferenciar, distinguir *(between* entre); *~ between treat differently* establecer diferencias entre

dif·fe·rent·ly ['dɪfrəntlɪ] *adv* de manera diferente

dif·fi·cult ['dɪfɪkəlt] *adj* difícil

dif·fi·cul·ty ['dɪfɪkəltɪ] dificultad *f*; *with ~* con dificultades

dif·fi·dence ['dɪfɪdəns] retraimiento *m*

dif·fi·dent ['dɪfɪdənt] *adj* retraído

dig [dɪg] *v/t & v/i (pret & pp* **dug***)* cavar
♦ **dig out** *v/t (find)* encontrar
♦ **dig up** *v/t* levantar, cavar; *information* desenterrar

di·gest [daɪˈdʒest] *v/t also fig* digerir

di·gest·i·ble [daɪˈdʒestəbl] *adj food* digerible

di·ges·tion [daɪˈdʒestʃn] digestión *f*

di·ges·tive [daɪˈdʒestɪv] *adj* digestivo

dig·ger ['dɪgər] *machine* excavadora *f*

dig·it ['dɪdʒɪt] *(number)* dígito *m*; *a 4 ~ number* un número de 4 dígitos

di·gi·tal ['dɪdʒɪtl] *adj* digital

dig·ni·fied ['dɪgnɪfaɪd] *adj* digno

dig·ni·ta·ry ['dɪgnɪterɪ] dignatario(-a) *m(f)*

dig·ni·ty ['dɪgnɪtɪ] dignidad *f*

di·gress [daɪˈgres] *v/i* divagar, apartarse del tema

di·gres·sion [daɪˈgreʃn] digresión *f*

dike [daɪk] *wall* dique *m*

di·lap·i·dat·ed [dɪˈlæpɪdeɪtɪd] *adj* destartalado

di·late [daɪˈleɪt] *v/i of pupils* dilatarse

di·lem·ma [dɪˈlemə] dilema *m*; *be in*

a ~ estar en un dilema

dil·et·tante [dɪlə'tæntɪ] diletante *m/f*

dil·i·gent ['dɪlɪdʒənt] *adj* diligente

di·lute [daɪ'luːt] *v/t* diluir

dim [dɪm] **1** *adj* *room* oscuro; *light* tenue; *outline* borroso, confuso; (*stupid*) tonto; *prospects* remoto **2** *v/t* (*pret & pp* **-med**): atenuar; ~ *the headlights* poner las luces cortas **3** *v/i* (*pret & pp* **-med**) *of lights* atenuarse

dime [daɪm] moneda de diez centavos

di·men·sion [daɪ'menʃn] dimensión *f*

di·min·ish [dɪ'mɪnɪʃ] *v/t & v/i* disminuir

di·min·u·tive [dɪ'mɪnʊtɪv] **1** *n* diminutivo *m* **2** *adj* diminuto

dim·ple ['dɪmpl] hoyuelo *m*

din [dɪn] *n* estruendo *m*

dine [daɪn] *v/i* *fml* cenar

din·er ['daɪnər] *person* comensal *m/f*; *restaurant* restaurante *m* barato

din·ghy ['dɪŋgɪ] (*small yacht*) bote *m* de vela; (*rubber boat*) lancha *f* neumática

din·gy ['dɪndʒɪ] *adj* sórdido; (*dirty*) sucio

din·ing car ['daɪnɪŋ] RAIL vagón *m* restaurante, coche *m* comedor; **'din·ing room** comedor *m*; **'din·ing ta·ble** mesa *f* de comedor

din·ner ['dɪnər] *in the evening* cena *f*; *at midday* comida *f*; (*formal gathering*) cena *f* de gala

'din·ner guest invitado(-a) *m(f)* a cenar; **'din·ner jack·et** esmoquin *m*; **'din·ner par·ty** cena *f*; **'din·ner serv·ice** vajilla *f*

di·no·saur ['daɪnəsɔːr] dinosaurio *m*

dip [dɪp] **1** *n* (*swim*) baño *m*, zambullida *f*; *for food* salsa *f*; (*slope*) inclinación *f*, pendiente *f*; (*depression*) hondonada *f* **2** *v/t* (*pret & pp* **-ped**) meter; ~ *the headlights* poner las luces cortas **3** *v/i* (*pret & pp* **-ped**) *of road* bajar

di·plo·ma [dɪ'ploʊmə] diploma *m*

di·plo·ma·cy [dɪ'ploʊməsɪ] *also fig* diplomacia *f*

di·plo·mat ['dɪpləmæt] diplomáti-

co(-a) *m(f)*

di·plo·mat·ic [dɪplə'mætɪk] *adj also fig* diplomático

dip·lo·mat·i·cal·ly [dɪplə'mætɪklɪ] *adv* de forma diplomática

dip·lo·mat·ic im·mu·ni·ty inmunidad *f* diplomática

di·rect [daɪ'rekt] **1** *adj* directo **2** *v/t* *play, movie, attention* dirigir; *can you ~ me to the museum?* ¿me podría indicar cómo se va al museo?

di·rect 'cur·rent ELEC corriente *f* continua

di·rec·tion [dɪ'rekʃn] dirección *f*; ~*s to get to a place* indicaciones *fpl*; (*instructions*) instrucciones *fpl*; *for medicine* posología *f*; *let's ask for* ~*s* preguntemos cómo se va; ~*s for use* modo *m* de empleo

di·rec·tion 'in·di·ca·tor MOT intermitente *m*

di·rec·tive [dɪ'rektɪv] directiva *f*

di·rect·ly [dɪ'rektlɪ] **1** *adv* (*straight*) directamente; (*soon*) pronto; (*immediately*) ahora mismo **2** *conj* en cuanto

di·rec·tor [dɪ'rektər] director(a) *m(f)*

di·rec·to·ry [dɪ'rektərɪ] directorio *m*; TELEC guía *f* telefónica

dirt [dɜːrt] suciedad *f*

'dirt cheap *adj* F tirado F

dirt·y ['dɜːrtɪ] **1** *adj* sucio; (*pornographic*) pornográfico, obsceno **2** *v/t* (*pret & pp* **-ied**) ensuciar

dirt·y 'trick jugarreta *f*; *play a ~ on s.o.* hacer una jugarreta a alguien

dis·a·bil·i·ty [dɪsə'bɪlətɪ] discapacidad *f*, minusvalía *f*

dis·a·bled [dɪs'eɪbld] **1** *n*: *the ~* los discapacitados *mpl* **2** *adj* discapacitado

dis·ad·van·tage [dɪsəd'væntɪdʒ] (*drawback*) desventaja *f*; *be at a ~* estar en desventaja

dis·ad·van·taged [dɪsəd'væntɪdʒd] *adj* desfavorecido

dis·ad·van·ta·geous [dɪsædvæn-

'teɪdʒəs] *adj* desventajoso, desfavorable

dis·a·gree [dɪsə'griː] *v/i of person* no estar de acuerdo, discrepar; *let's agree to* ~ aceptemos que no nos vamos a poner de acuerdo

♦ **disagree with** *v/t of person* no estar de acuerdo con, discrepar con; *of food* sentar mal; *lobster disagrees with me* la langosta me sienta mal

dis·a·gree·a·ble [dɪsə'griːəbl] *adj* desagradable

dis·a·gree·ment [dɪsə'griːmənt] desacuerdo *m*; (*argument*) discusión *f*

dis·ap·pear [dɪsə'pɪr] *v/i* desaparecer

dis·ap·pear·ance [dɪsə'pɪrəns] desaparición *f*

dis·ap·point [dɪsə'pɔɪnt] *v/t* desilusionar, decepcionar

dis·ap·point·ed [dɪsə'pɔɪntɪd] *adj* desilusionado, decepcionado

dis·ap·point·ing [dɪsə'pɔɪntɪŋ] *adj* decepcionante

dis·ap·point·ment [dɪsə'pɔɪntmənt] desilusión *f*, decepción *f*

dis·ap·prov·al [dɪsə'pruːvl] desaprobación *f*

dis·ap·prove [dɪsə'pruːv] *v/i* desaprobar, estar en contra; ~ *of* desaprobar, estar en contra de

dis·ap·prov·ing [dɪsə'pruːvɪŋ] *adj* desaprobatorio, de desaprobación

dis·ap·prov·ing·ly [dɪsə'pruːvɪŋlɪ] *adv* con desaprobación

dis·arm [dɪs'ɑːrm] **1** *v/t* desarmar **2** *v/i* desarmarse

dis·ar·ma·ment [dɪs'ɑːrməmənt] desarme *m*

dis·arm·ing [dɪs'ɑːrmɪŋ] *adj* cautivador

dis·as·ter [dɪ'zæstər] desastre *m*

di·sas·ter ar·e·a zona *f* catastrófica; *fig* (*person*) desastre *m*

di·sas·trous [dɪ'zæstrəs] *adj* desastroso

dis·band [dɪs'bænd] **1** *v/t* disolver **2** *v/i* disolverse

dis·be·lief [dɪsbə'liːf] incredulidad *f*;

in ~ con incredulidad

disc [dɪsk] (*CD*) compact *m* (disc)

dis·card [dɪ'skɑːrd] *v/t* desechar; *boyfriend* deshacerse de

di·scern [dɪ'sɜːrn] *v/t* distinguir, percibir

di·scern·i·ble [dɪ'sɜːrnəbl] *adj* perceptible

di·scern·ing [dɪ'sɜːrnɪŋ] *adj* entendido, exigente

dis·charge 1 *n* ['dɪstʃɑːrdʒ] *from hospital* alta *f*; *from army* licencia *f* **2** *v/t* [dɪs'tʃɑːrdʒ] *from hospital* dar el alta a; *from army* licenciar; *from job* despedir

di·sci·ple [dɪ'saɪpl] *religious* discípulo *m*

dis·ci·pli·nar·y [dɪsɪ'plɪnərɪ] *adj* disciplinario

dis·ci·pline ['dɪsɪplɪn] **1** *n* disciplina *f* **2** *v/t child, dog* castigar; *employee* sancionar

'disc jock·ey disc jockey *m/f*, *Span* pinchadiscos *m/f inv*

dis·claim [dɪs'kleɪm] *v/t* negar

dis·close [dɪs'klous] *v/t* revelar

dis·clo·sure [dɪs'klouʒər] revelación *f*

dis·co ['dɪskou] discoteca *f*

dis·col·or, *Br* **dis·col·our** [dɪs'kʌlər] *v/i* decolorar

dis·com·fort [dɪs'kʌmfərt] (*pain*) molestia *f*; (*embarrassment*) incomodidad *f*

dis·con·cert [dɪskən'sɜːrt] *v/t* desconcertar

dis·con·cert·ed [dɪskən'sɜːrtɪd] *adj* desconcertado

dis·con·nect [dɪskə'nekt] *v/t* desconectar

dis·con·so·late [dɪs'kɑːnsələt] *adj* desconsolado

dis·con·tent [dɪskən'tent] descontento *m*

dis·con·tent·ed [dɪskən'tentɪd] *adj* descontento

dis·con·tin·ue [dɪskən'tɪnjuː] *v/t product* dejar de producir; *bus, train service* suspender; *magazine* dejar de publicar

dis·cord ['dɪskɔːrd] MUS discordancia *f*; *in relations* discordia *f*

dis·co·theque ['dɪskətek] discoteca *f*

dis·count 1 *n* ['dɪskaʊnt] descuento *m* **2** *v/t* [dɪs'kaʊnt] *goods* descontar; *theory* descartar

dis·cour·age [dɪs'kʌrɪdʒ] *v/t* (*dissuade*) disuadir (*from* de); (*dishearten*) desanimar, desalentar

dis·cour·age·ment [dɪs'kʌrɪdʒmənt] disuasión *f*; (*being disheartened*) desánimo *m*, desaliento *m*

dis·cov·er [dɪ'skʌvər] *v/t* descubrir

dis·cov·er·er [dɪ'skʌvərər] descubridor(a) *m(f)*

dis·cov·er·y [dɪ'skʌvərɪ] descubrimiento *m*

dis·cred·it [dɪs'kredɪt] *v/t* desacreditar

dis·creet [dɪ'skriːt] *adj* discreto

dis·creet·ly [dɪ'skriːtlɪ] *adv* discretamente

dis·crep·an·cy [dɪ'skrepənsɪ] discrepancia *f*

dis·cre·tion [dɪ'skreʃn] discreción *f*; *at your ~* a discreción; *use your ~* usa tu criterio

dis·crim·i·nate [dɪ'skrɪmɪneɪt] *v/i* discriminar (*against* contra); *~ between* (*distinguish*) distinguir entre

dis·crim·i·nat·ing [dɪ'skrɪmɪneɪtɪŋ] *adj* entendido, exigente

dis·crim·i·na·tion [dɪ'skrɪmɪneɪʃn] *sexual, racial etc* discriminación *f*

dis·cus ['dɪskəs] SP *object* disco *m*; *event* lanzamiento *m* de disco

dis·cuss [dɪ'skʌs] *v/t* discutir; *of article* analizar

dis·cus·sion [dɪ'skʌʃn] discusión *f*

'dis·cus throw·er lanzador(a) *m(f)* de disco

dis·dain [dɪs'deɪn] *n* desdén *m*

dis·ease [dɪ'ziːz] enfermedad *f*

dis·em·bark [dɪsəm'baːrk] *v/i* desembarcar

dis·en·chant·ed [dɪsən'tʃæntɪd] *adj*: *~ with* desencantado con

dis·en·gage [dɪsən'geɪdʒ] *v/t* soltar

dis·en·tan·gle [dɪsən'tæŋgl] *v/t* desenredar

dis·fig·ure [dɪs'fɪgər] *v/t* desfigurar

dis·grace [dɪs'greɪs] **1** *n* vergüenza *f*; *it's a ~!* ¡qué vergüenza!; *in ~* desacreditado **2** *v/t* deshonrar

dis·grace·ful [dɪs'greɪsfəl] *adj* behavior, situation vergonzoso, lamentable

dis·grunt·led [dɪs'grʌntld] *adj* descontento

dis·guise [dɪs'gaɪz] **1** *n* disfraz *m*; *in ~* disfrazado **2** *v/t voice, handwriting* cambiar; *fear, anxiety* disfrazar; *~ o.s. as* disfrazarse de; *he was ~d as* iba disfrazado de

dis·gust [dɪs'gʌst] **1** *n* asco *m*, repugnancia *f*; *in ~* asqueado **2** *v/t* dar asco a, repugnar; *I'm ~ed by ...* me da asco *or* me repugna ...

dis·gust·ing [dɪs'gʌstɪŋ] *adj habit, smell, food* asqueroso, repugnante; *it is ~ that ...* da asco que ..., es repugnante que ...

dish [dɪʃ] (*part of meal, container*) plato *m*

'dish·cloth paño *m* de cocina

dis·heart·ened [dɪs'haːrtnd] *adj* desalentado, descorazonado

dis·heart·en·ing [dɪs'haːrtnɪŋ] *adj* descorazonador

dis·hev·eled [dɪ'ʃevld] *adj hair, clothes* desaliñado; *person* despeinado

dis·hon·est [dɪs'aːnɪst] *adj* deshonesto

dis·hon·es·ty [dɪs'aːnɪstɪ] deshonestidad *f*

dis·hon·or [dɪs'aːnər] *n* deshonra *f*; *bring ~ on* deshonrar a

dis·hon·o·ra·ble [dɪs'aːnərəbl] *adj* deshonroso

dis·hon·our *etc Br* → **dishonor** *etc*

'dish·wash·er *person* lavaplatos *m/f inv*; *machine* lavavajillas *m inv*, lavaplatos *m inv*; **'dish·wash·ing liq·uid** lavavajillas *m inv*; **'dish·wa·ter** agua *f* de lavar los platos

dis·il·lu·sion [dɪsɪ'luːʒn] *v/t* desilusionar

dis·il·lu·sion·ment [dɪsɪ'luːʒnmənt]

desilusión f

dis·in·clined [dısın'klaınd] *adj*: **she was ~ to believe him** no estaba inclinada a creerle

dis·in·fect [dısın'fekt] *v/t* desinfectar

dis·in·fec·tant [dısın'fektənt] desinfectante *m*

dis·in·her·it [dısın'herıt] *v/t* desheredar

dis·in·te·grate [dıs'ıntəgreıt] *v/i* desintegrarse; *of marriage* deshacerse

dis·in·terest·ed [dıs'ıntərestıd] *adj* (*unbiased*) desinteresado

dis·joint·ed [dıs'dʒɔıntıd] *adj* deshilvanado

disk [dısk] *also* COMPUT disco *m*; **on ~** en disco

'**disk drive** COMPUT unidad *f* de disco

disk·ette [dıs'ket] disquete *m*

dis·like [dıs'laık] **1** *n* antipatía *f* **2** *v/t*: **she ~s being kept waiting** no le gusta que la hagan esperar; **I ~ him** no me gusta

dis·lo·cate ['dısləkeıt] *v/t shoulder* dislocar

dis·lodge [dıs'lɑːdʒ] *v/t* desplazar, mover de su sitio

dis·loy·al [dıs'lɔıəl] *adj* desleal

dis·loy·al·ty [dıs'lɔıəltı] deslealtad *f*

dis·mal ['dızməl] *adj weather* horroroso, espantoso; *news, prospect* negro; *person* (*sad*) triste; *person* (*negative*) negativo; *failure* estrepitoso

dis·man·tle [dıs'mæntl] *v/t* desmantelar

dis·may [dıs'meı] **1** *n* (*alarm*) consternación *f*; (*disappointment*) desánimo *m* **2** *v/t* consternar

dis·miss [dıs'mıs] *v/t employee* despedir; *suggestion* rechazar; *idea, possibility* descartar

dis·miss·al [dıs'mısl] *of employee* despido *m*

dis·mount [dıs'maʊnt] *v/i* desmontar

dis·o·be·di·ence [dısə'biːdıəns] desobediencia *f*

dis·o·be·di·ent [dısə'biːdıənt] *adj* desobediente

dis·o·bey [dısə'beı] *v/t* desobedecer

dis·or·der [dıs'ɔːrdər] (*untidiness*) desorden *m*; (*unrest*) desórdenes *mpl*; MED dolencia *f*

dis·or·der·ly [dıs'ɔːrdərlı] *adj room, desk* desordenado; *mob* alborotado

dis·or·gan·ized [dıs'ɔːrgənaızd] *adj* desorganizado

dis·o·ri·ent·ed [dıs'ɔːrıəntıd] *adj* desorientado

dis·own [dıs'oʊn] *v/t* repudiar, renegar de

di·spar·ag·ing [dı'spærıdʒıŋ] *adj* despreciativo

di·spar·i·ty [dı'spærətı] disparidad *f*

dis·pas·sion·ate [dı'spæʃənət] *adj* (*objective*) desapasionado

di·spatch [dı'spætʃ] *v/t* (*send*) enviar

di·spen·sa·ry [dı'spensərı] *in pharmacy* dispensario *m*

◆ **di·spense with** [dı'spens] *v/t* prescindir de

di·sperse [dı'spɜːrs] **1** *v/t* dispersar **2** *v/i of crowd* dispersarse; *of mist* disiparse

di·spir·it·ed [dı'pırıtıd] *adj* desalentado, abatido

dis·place [dıs'pleıs] *v/t* (*supplant*) sustituir

di·splay [dı'spleı] **1** *n* muestra *f*; *in store window* objetos *mpl* expuestos; COMPUT pantalla *f*; **be on ~** estar expuesto **2** *v/t emotion* mostrar; *at exhibition, for sale* exponer; COMPUT visualizar

di·splay cab·i·net *in museum, shop* vitrina *f*

dis·please [dıs'pliːz] *v/t* desagradar, disgustar

dis·plea·sure [dıs'pleʒər] desagrado *m*, disgusto *m*

dis·po·sa·ble [dı'spoʊzəbl] *adj* desechable; **~ income** ingreso(s) *m(pl)* disponible(s)

dis·pos·al [dı'spoʊzl] eliminación *f*; **I am at your ~** estoy a su disposición; **put sth at s.o.'s ~** poner algo a disposición de alguien

◆ **dis·pose of** [dı'spoʊz] *v/t* (*get rid*

of) deshacerse de

dis·posed [dɪˈspoʊzd] *adj*: **be ~ to do sth** (*willing*) estar dispuesto a hacer algo; **be well ~ toward** estar bien dispuesto hacia

dis·po·si·tion [dɪspəˈzɪʃn] (*nature*) carácter *m*

dis·pro·por·tion·ate [dɪsprəˈpɔːrʃənət] *adj* desproporcionado

dis·prove [dɪsˈpruːv] *v/t* refutar

dis·pute [dɪˈspjuːt] **1** *n* disputa *f*; *industrial* conflicto *m* laboral **2** *v/t* discutir; (*fight over*) disputarse; **I don't ~ that** eso no lo discuto

dis·qual·i·fi·ca·tion [dɪskwɑːlɪfɪˈkeɪʃn] descalificación *f*

dis·qual·i·fy [dɪsˈkwɑːlɪfaɪ] *v/t* (*pret & pp* **-ied**) descalificar

dis·re·gard [dɪsrəˈɡɑːrd] **1** *n* indiferencia *f* **2** *v/t* no tener en cuenta

dis·re·pair [dɪsrəˈper]: **in a state of ~** deteriorado

dis·rep·u·ta·ble [dɪsˈrepjʊtəbl] *adj* poco respetable; *area* de mala reputación

dis·re·spect [dɪsrəˈspekt] falta *f* de respeto

dis·re·spect·ful [dɪsrəˈspektfəl] *adj* irrespetuoso

dis·rupt [dɪsˈrʌpt] *v/t train service* trastornar, alterar; *meeting, class* interrumpir

dis·rup·tion [dɪsˈrʌpʃn] *of train service* alteración *f*; *of meeting, class* interrupción *f*

dis·rup·tive [dɪsˈrʌptɪv] *adj* perjudicial; **he's very ~ in class** causa muchos problemas en clase

dis·sat·is·fac·tion [dɪssætɪsˈfækʃn] insatisfacción *f*

dis·sat·is·fied [dɪsˈsætɪsfaɪd] *adj* insatisfecho

dis·sen·sion [dɪˈsenʃn] disensión *f*

dis·sent [dɪˈsent] **1** *n* discrepancia *f* **2** *v/i*: **~ from** disentir de

dis·si·dent [ˈdɪsɪdənt] *n* disidente *m/f*

dis·sim·i·lar [dɪsˈsɪmɪlər] *adj* distinto

dis·so·ci·ate [dɪˈsoʊʃɪeɪt] *v/t* disociar; **~ o.s. from** disociarse de

dis·so·lute [ˈdɪsəluːt] *adj* disoluto

dis·so·lu·tion [dɪsəˈluːʃn] POL disolución *f*

dis·solve [dɪˈzɑːlv] **1** *v/t substance* disolver **2** *v/i of substance* disolverse

dis·suade [dɪˈsweɪd] *v/t* disuadir; **~ s.o. from doing sth** disuadir a alguien de hacer algo

dis·tance [ˈdɪstəns] **1** *n* distancia *f*; **in the ~** en la lejanía **2** *v/t* distanciar; **~ o.s. from** distanciarse de

dis·tant [ˈdɪstənt] *adj place, time, relative* distante, lejano; *fig* (*aloof*) distante

dis·taste [dɪsˈteɪst] desagrado *m*

dis·taste·ful [dɪsˈteɪstfəl] *adj* desagradable

dis·till·er·y [dɪsˈtɪləri] destilería *f*

dis·tinct [dɪˈstɪŋkt] *adj* (*clear*) claro; (*different*) distinto; **as ~ from** a diferencia de

dis·tinc·tion [dɪˈstɪŋkʃn] (*differentiation*) distinción *f*; *hotel* / *product of* **~** un hotel / producto destacado

dis·tinc·tive [dɪˈstɪŋktɪv] *adj* característico

dis·tinct·ly [dɪˈstɪŋktli] *adv* claramente, con claridad; (*decidedly*) verdaderamente

dis·tin·guish [dɪˈstɪŋɡwɪʃ] *v/t* distinguir (**between** entre)

dis·tin·guished [dɪˈstɪŋɡwɪʃt] *adj* distinguido

dis·tort [dɪˈstɔːrt] *v/t* distorsionar

dis·tract [dɪˈstrækt] *v/t* distraer

dis·trac·tion [dɪˈstrækʃn] distracción *f*; *drive s.o. to* **~** sacar a alguien de quicio

dis·traught [dɪˈstrɔːt] *adj* angustiado, consternado

dis·tress [dɪˈstres] **1** *n* sufrimiento *m*; **in ~** *of ship, aircraft* en peligro **2** *v/t* (*upset*) angustiar

dis·tress·ing [dɪˈstresɪŋ] *adj* angustiante

dis'tress sig·nal señal *m* de socorro

dis·trib·ute [dɪˈstrɪbjuːt] *v/t* distribuir, repartir; COM distribuir

dis·tri·bu·tion [dɪstrɪˈbjuːʃn] distribución *f*

dis·tri·bu·tion ar·range·ment COM

acuerdo *m* de distribución

dis·trib·u·tor [dɪsˈtrɪbjuːtər] COM distribuidor(a) *m(f)*

dis·trict [ˈdɪstrɪkt] *(area)* zona *f*; *(neighborhood)* barrio *m*

dis·trict at·tor·ney fiscal *m/f* del distrito

dis·trust [dɪsˈtrʌst] **1** *n* desconfianza *f* **2** *v/t* desconfiar de

dis·turb [dɪsˈtɜːrb] *v/t (interrupt)* molestar; *(upset)* preocupar; *do not ~* no molestar

dis·turb·ance [dɪsˈtɜːrbəns] *(interruption)* molestia *f*; *~s (civil unrest)* disturbios *mpl*

dis·turbed [dɪsˈtɜːrbd] *adj (concerned, worried)* preocupado, inquieto; *mentally* perturbado

dis·turb·ing [dɪsˈtɜːrbɪŋ] *adj (worrying)* inquietante; *you may find some scenes ~* algunas de las escenas pueden herir la sensibilidad del espectador

dis·used [dɪsˈjuːzd] *adj* abandonado

ditch [dɪtʃ] **1** *n* zanja *f* **2** *v/t* F *(get rid of)* deshacerse de; *boyfriend* plantar F; *plan* abandonar

dith·er [ˈdɪðər] *v/i* vacilar

dive [daɪv] **1** *n* salto *m* de cabeza; *underwater* inmersión *f*; *of plane* descenso *m* en picado; F *bar etc* antro *m* F; *take a ~* F *of dollar etc* desplomarse **2** *v/i (pret also dove)* tirarse de cabeza; *underwater* bucear; *of plane* descender en picado

div·er [ˈdaɪvər] *off board* saltador(a) *m(f)* de trampolín; *underwater* buceador(a) *m(f)*

di·verge [daɪˈvɜːrdʒ] *v/i* bifurcarse

di·verse [daɪˈvɜːrs] *adj* diverso

di·ver·si·fi·ca·tion [daɪvɜːrsɪfɪˈkeɪʃn] COM diversificación *f*

di·ver·si·fy [daɪˈvɜːrsɪfaɪ] *v/i (pret & pp -ied)* COM diversificarse

di·ver·sion [daɪˈvɜːrʃn] *for traffic* desvío *m*; *to distract attention* distracción *f*

di·ver·si·ty [daɪˈvɜːrsəti] diversidad *f*

di·vert [daɪˈvɜːrt] *v/t traffic, attention* desviar

di·vest [daɪˈvest] *v/t*: *~ s.o. of sth* despojar a alguien de algo

di·vide [dɪˈvaɪd] *v/t also fig* dividir; *~ 16 by 4* dividir 16 entre 4

div·i·dend [ˈdɪvɪdend] FIN dividendo *m*; *pay ~s fig* resultar beneficioso

di·vine [dɪˈvaɪn] *adj also* F divino

div·ing [ˈdaɪvɪŋ] *from board* salto *m* de trampolín; *(scuba ~)* buceo *m*, submarinismo *m*

'div·ing board trampolín *m*

di·vis·i·ble [dɪˈvɪzəbl] *adj* divisible

di·vi·sion [dɪˈvɪʒn] división *f*

di·vorce [dɪˈvɔːrs] **1** *n* divorcio *m*; *get a ~* divorciarse **2** *v/t* divorciarse de; *get ~d* divorciarse **3** *v/i* divorciarse

di·vorced [dɪˈvɔːrst] *adj* divorciado

di·vor·cee [dɪvɔːrˈsiː] divorciado(-a) *m(f)*

di·vulge [daɪˈvʌldʒ] *v/t* divulgar, dar a conocer

DIY [diːaɪˈwaɪ] *abbr (= do it yourself)* bricolaje *m*

DI'Y store tienda *f* de bricolaje

diz·zi·ness [ˈdɪzɪnɪs] mareo *m*

diz·zy [ˈdɪzɪ] *adj* mareado; *feel ~* estar mareado

DJ [ˈdiːdʒeɪ] *abbr (= disc jockey)* disc jockey *m/f*, Span pinchadiscos *m/f inv*; *(= dinner jacket)* esmoquin *m*

DNA [diːenˈeɪ] *abbr (= deoxyribonucleic acid)* AND *m (=* ácido *m* desoxirribonucleico)

do [duː] **1** *v/t (pret did, pp done)* hacer; *100 mph etc* ir a; *~ one's hair* arreglarse el pelo; *what are you ~ing tonight?* ¿qué vas a hacer esta noche?; *I don't know what to ~* no sé qué hacer; *~ it right now!* hazlo ahora mismo; *have one's hair done* ir al peluquero **2** *v/i (pret did, pp done) (be suitable, enough)*: *that'll ~ nicely* eso bastará; *that will ~!* ¡ya vale!; *~ well of business* ir bien; *he's ~ing well* le van bien las cosas; *well done! (congratulations!)* ¡bien hecho!; *how ~ you ~ ?* encantado de conocerle 3 v/aux: ~ *you know him?* ¿lo conoces?; *I don't know* no sé; ~ *you like Des Moines? – yes I ~* ¿te gusta Des Moines? – sí; *he works hard, doesn't he?* trabaja mucho, ¿verdad?; *don't you believe me?* ¿no me crees?; *you ~ believe me, don't you?* me crees, ¿verdad?; *you don't know the answer, ~ you? – no I don't* no sabes la respuesta, ¿no es así? – no, no la sé

♦ **do away with** v/t (abolish) abolir

♦ **do in** v/t F (exhaust) machacar F; *I'm done in* estoy hecho polvo F

♦ **do out of** v/t: *do s.o. out of sth* timar alguien a algo F

♦ **do up** v/t (renovate) renovar; *buttons, coat* abrocharse; *laces* atarse

♦ **do with** v/t: *I could do with ...* no me vendría mal ...; *he won't have anything to do with it* (won't get involved) no quiere saber nada de ello

♦ **do without 1** v/i: *you'll have to do without* te las tendrás que arreglar **2** v/t pasar sin

do·cile ['dəʊsəl] adj dócil

dock[1] [dɑːk] **1** n NAUT muelle m **2** v/i of ship atracar; of spaceship acoplarse

dock[2] [dɑːk] n LAW banquillo m (de los acusados)

'**dock·yard** Br astillero m

doc·tor ['dɑːktər] n MED médico m; form of address doctor m

doc·tor·ate ['dɑːktərət] doctorado m

doc·trine ['dɑːktrɪn] doctrina f

doc·u·dra·ma ['dɑːkjʊdrɑːmə] docudrama m

doc·u·ment ['dɑːkjʊmənt] n documento m

doc·u·men·ta·ry [dɑːkjʊ'mentərɪ] n program documental m

doc·u·men·ta·tion [dɑːkjʊmen'teɪʃn] documentación f

dodge [dɑːdʒ] v/t blow, person esquivar; issue, question eludir

doe [dəʊ] deer cierva f

dog [dɒːg] **1** n perro(-a) m(f) **2** v/t

(pret & pp -ged) of bad luck perseguir

'**dog catch·er** perrero(-a) m(f)

dog-eared ['dɒːgɪrd] adj book sobado, con las esquinas dobladas

dog·ged ['dɒːgɪd] adj tenaz

dog·gie ['dɒːgɪ] in children's language perrito m

dog·gy bag ['dɒːgɪbæg] bolsa para las sobras de la comida

'**dog·house**: *be in the ~* F haber caído en desgracia

dog·ma ['dɒːgmə] dogma m

dog·mat·ic [dɒːg'mætɪk] adj dogmático

do-good·er ['duːgʊdər] pej buen(a) samaritano(-a) m(f)

'**dog tag** MIL chapa f de identificación

'**dog-tired** adj F hecho polvo F

do-it-your·self [duːɪtjər'self] bricolaje m

dol·drums ['dəʊldrəmz]: *be in the ~* of economy estar en un bache; of person estar deprimido

♦ **dole out** v/t repartir

doll [dɑːl] toy muñeca f; F woman muñeca f F

♦ **doll up** v/t: *get dolled up* emperifollarse

dol·lar ['dɑːlər] dólar m

dol·lop ['dɑːləp] n F cucharada f

dol·phin ['dɑːlfɪn] delfín m

dome [dəʊm] of building cúpula f

do·mes·tic [də'mestɪk] **1** adj chores doméstico, del hogar; news, policy nacional **2** n empleado(-a) m(f) del hogar

do·mes·tic 'an·i·mal animal m doméstico

do·mes·ti·cate [də'mestɪkeɪt] v/t animal domesticar; *be ~d* of person estar domesticado

do'mes·tic flight vuelo m nacional

dom·i·nant ['dɑːmɪnənt] adj dominante

dom·i·nate ['dɑːmɪneɪt] v/t dominar

dom·i·na·tion [dɑːmɪ'neɪʃn] dominación f

dom·i·neer·ing [dɑːmɪ'nɪrɪŋ] adj dominante

dom·i·no ['dɑːmɪnou] ficha f de dominó; **play ~es** jugar al dominó

do·nate [dou'neɪt] v/t donar

do·na·tion [dou'neɪʃn] donación f, donativo m; MED donación f

done [dʌn] pp → **do**

don·key ['dɑːŋkɪ] burro m

do·nor ['dounər] of money, MED donante m/f

do·nut ['dounʌt] dónut m

doo·dle ['duːdl] v/i garabatear

doom [duːm] n (fate) destino m; (ruin) fatalidad f

doomed [duːmd] adj project condenado al fracaso; **we are ~** (bound to fail) estamos condenados al fracaso; (going to die) vamos a morir

door [dɔːr] puerta f; **there's someone at the ~** hay alguien en la puerta

'**door·bell** timbre m; '**door·knob** pomo m; '**door·man** portero m; '**door·mat** felpudo m; '**door·step** umbral m; '**door·way** puerta f

dope [doup] n **1** (drugs) droga f; F (idiot) lelo(-a) m(f); F (information) información f **2** v/t drogar

dor·mant ['dɔːrmənt] adj plant aletargado; volcano inactivo

dor·mi·to·ry ['dɔːrmɪtɔːrɪ] dormitorio m (colectivo); (hall of residence) residencia f de estudiantes

dos·age ['dousɪdʒ] dosis f inv

dose [dous] n dosis f inv

dot [dɑːt] n punto m; **on the ~** (exactly) en punto

♦ **dote on** [dout] v/t adorar a

dot.com (**com·pa·ny**) [dɑːt'kɑːm] empresa f punto.com

dot·ing ['doutɪŋ] adj: **my ~ aunt** mi tía, que tanto me adora

dot·ted line ['dɑːtɪd] línea f de puntos

dou·ble ['dʌbl] **1** n person doble m/f; room habitación f doble **2** adj doble; **inflation is now in ~ figures** la inflación ha superado ya el 10% **3** adv: **they offered me ~ what the others did** me ofrecieron el doble que la otra gente **4** v/t doblar, duplicar **5** v/i doblarse, duplicarse; **it ~s**

as ... hace también de ...

♦ **double back** v/i (go back) volver sobre sus pasos

♦ **double up** v/i in pain doblarse; (share) compartir habitación

doub·le-'bass contrabajo m; **doub·le-'bed** cama f de matrimonio; **doub·le-breast·ed** [dʌbl-'brestɪd] adj cruzado; **doub·le-'check** v/t & v/i volver a comprobar; **doub·le 'chin** papada f; **doub·le'cross** v/t engañar, traicionar; **doub·le 'glaz·ing** doble acristalamiento m; **doub·le'park** v/i aparcar en doble fila; '**doub·le-quick** adj: **in ~ time** muy rápidamente; '**doub·le room** habitación f doble

doub·les ['dʌblz] in tennis dobles mpl

doubt [daut] **1** n duda f; (uncertainty) dudas fpl; **be in ~** ser incierto; **not be in ~** estar claro; **no ~** (probably) sin duda **2** v/t dudar; **we never ~ed you** nunca dudamos de ti

doubt·ful ['dautfəl] adj remark, look dubitativo; **be ~ of person** tener dudas; **it is ~ whether ...** es dudoso que ...

doubt·ful·ly ['dautfəlɪ] adv lleno de dudas

doubt·less ['dautlɪs] adv sin duda, indudablemente

dough [dou] masa f; F (money) Span pasta f F, L.Am. plata f F

dove[1] [dʌv] also fig paloma f

dove[2] [douv] pret → **dive**

dow·dy ['daudɪ] adj poco elegante

Dow Jones Av·er·age [daudʒounz-'ævərɪdʒ] índice m Dow Jones

down[1] [daun] n (feathers) plumón m

down[2] [daun] **1** adv (downward) (hacia) abajo; **pull the shade ~** baja la persiana; **put it ~ on the table** ponlo en la mesa; **when the leaves come ~** cuando se caen las hojas; **cut ~ a tree** cortar un árbol; **she was ~ on her knees** estaba arrodillada; **the plane was shot ~** el avión fue abatido; **~ there** allá abajo; **fall ~** caerse; **die ~** amainar; **$200**

~ (*as deposit*) una entrada de 200 dólares; ~ *south* hacia el sur; *be ~ of price, rate* haber descendido; *of numbers, amount* haber descendido; (*not working*) no funcionar; F (*depressed*) estar deprimido *or* con la depre F **2** *prep*: *run ~ the stairs* bajar las escaleras corriendo; *the lava rolled ~ the hill* la lava descendía por la colina; *walk ~ the street* andar por la calle; *the store is halfway ~ Baker Street* la tienda está a mitad de Baker Street; *~ the corridor* por el pasillo **3** *v/t* (*swallow*) tragar; (*destroy*) derribar

'**down-and-out** *n* vagabundo(-a) *m(f)*; '**down·cast** *adj* deprimido; '**down·fall** caída *f*; *be s.o.'s ~ of alcohol etc* ser la perdición de alguien; '**downgrade** *v/t* degradar; *the hurricane has been ~d to a storm* el huracán ha sido reducido a la categoría de tormenta; **down·heart·ed** [daun'hɑːrtɪd] *adj* abatido; **down'hill** *adv* cuesta abajo; *go ~ fig* ir cuesta abajo; '**down·hill ski·ing** descenso *m*; '**down·load** *v/t* COMPUT descargar, bajar; '**down·mark·et** *adj* barato; '**down pay·ment** entrada *f*; *make a ~ on sth* pagar la entrada de algo; '**down·play** *v/t* quitar importancia a; '**down·pour** chaparrón *m*, aguacero *m*; '**down·right 1** *adj lie* evidente; *idiot* completo **2** *adv dangerous* extremadamente; *stupid* completamente; '**down·side** (*disadvantage*) desventaja *f*, inconveniente *m*; '**down·size 1** *v/t car* reducir el tamaño de; *company* reajustar la plantilla de **2** *v/i of company* reajustar la plantilla; '**down·stairs 1** *adj* del piso de abajo; *my ~ neighbors* los vecinos de abajo **2** *adv*: *the kitchen is ~* la cocina está en el piso de abajo; *I ran ~* bajé corriendo; **down-to-'earth** *adj approach*, *person* práctico, realista; '**down·town 1** *n* centro *m* **2** *adj* del centro **2** *adv*: *I'm going ~* voy al centro; *he lives ~* vive en el

centro; '**down·turn** *in economy* bajón *m*

'**down·ward** ['daunwərd] **1** *adj* descendente **2** *adv* a la baja

doze [douz] **1** *n* cabezada *f*, sueño *m* **2** *v/i* echar una cabezada

♦ **doze off** *v/i* quedarse dormido

doz·en ['dʌzn] docena *f*; *~s of* F montonadas de F

drab [dræb] *adj* gris

draft [dræft] **1** *n of air* corriente *f*; *of document* borrador *m*; MIL reclutamiento *m*; ~ (*beer*), *beer on ~* cerveza *f* de barril **2** *v/t document* redactar un borrador de; MIL reclutar

'**draft dodg·er** prófugo(-a) *m(f)*

draft·ee [dræft'iː] recluta *m/f*

drafts·man ['dræftsmən] delineante *m/f*

draft·y ['dræftɪ] *adj*: *it's ~ here* hace mucha corriente aquí

drag [dræg] **1** *n*: *it's a ~ having to ...* F es un latazo tener que ... F; *he's a ~* F es un peñazo F; *the main ~* F la calle principal; *in ~* vestido de mujer **2** *v/t* (*pret & pp -ged*) (*pull*) arrastrar; (*search*) dragar; *~ s.o. into sth* (*involve*) meter a alguien en algo; *~ sth out of s.o.* (*get information from*) arrancar algo de alguien **3** *v/i* (*pret & pp -ged*) *of time* pasar despacio; *of show, movie* ser pesado

♦ **drag away** *v/t*: *drag o.s. away from the TV* despegarse de la TV

♦ **drag in** *v/t into conversation* introducir

♦ **drag on** *v/i* (*last long time*) alargarse

♦ **drag out** *v/t* (*prolong*) alargar

♦ **drag up** *v/t* F (*mention*) sacar a relucir

drag·on ['drægn] dragón *m*; *fig* bruja *f*

drain [dreɪn] **1** *n pipe* sumidero *m*, desagüe *m*; *under street* alcantarilla *f*; *a ~ on resources* una sangría en los recursos **2** *v/t water, vegetables* escurrir; *land* drenar; *glass, tank, oil* vaciar; *person* agotar **3** *v/i of dishes* escurrir

♦ **drain away** v/i *of liquid* irse

♦ **drain off** v/t *water* escurrir

drain·age ['dreɪnɪdʒ] (*drains*) desagües *mpl*; *of water from soil* drenaje *m*

'**drain·pipe** tubo *m* de desagüe

dra·ma ['drɑːmə] (*art form*) drama *m*, teatro *m*; (*excitement*) dramatismo *m*; (*play: on TV*) drama *m*, obra *f* de teatro

dra·mat·ic [drə'mætɪk] *adj* dramático; *scenery* espectacular

dra·mat·i·cal·ly [drə'mætɪklɪ] *adv* *say* con dramatismo, de manera dramática; *decline, rise, change etc* espectacularmente

dram·a·tist ['dræmətɪst] dramaturgo(-a) *m(f)*

dram·a·ti·za·tion [dræmətaɪ'zeɪʃn] (*play*) dramatización *f*

dram·a·tize ['dræmətaɪz] v/t *also fig* dramatizar

drank [dræŋk] *pret* → **drink**

drape [dreɪp] v/t *cloth* cubrir; **~d in** (*covered with*) cubierto con

drap·er·y ['dreɪpərɪ] ropajes *mpl*

drapes [dreɪps] *npl* cortinas *fpl*

dras·tic ['dræstɪk] *adj* drástico

draught *Br* → **draft**

draw [drɔː] **1** *n in match, competition* empate *m*; *in lottery* sorteo *m*; (*attraction*) atracción *f* **2** v/t (*pret* **drew**, *pp* **drawn**) *picture, map* dibujar; *cart* tirar de; *curtain* correr; *in lottery* sortear; *gun, knife* sacar; (*attract*) atraer; (*lead*) llevar; *from bank account* sacar, retirar **3** v/i (*pret* **drew**, *pp* **drawn**) dibujar; *in match, competition* empatar; **~ near** acercarse

♦ **draw back 1** v/i (*recoil*) echarse atrás **2** v/t (*pull back*) retirar

♦ **draw on 1** v/i (*approach*) aproximarse **2** v/t (*make use of*) utilizar

♦ **draw out** v/t *wallet, money from bank* sacar

♦ **draw up 1** v/t *document* redactar; *chair* acercar **2** v/i *of vehicle* parar

'**draw·back** desventaja *f*, inconveniente *m*

draw·er[1] [drɔːr] *of desk etc* cajón *m*

draw·er[2] [drɔːr]: **she's a good ~** dibuja muy bien

draw·ing ['drɔːɪŋ] dibujo *m*

'**draw·ing board** tablero *m* de dibujo; **go back to the ~** *fig* volver a empezar otra vez

'**draw·ing pin** *Br* chincheta *f*

drawl [drɔːl] *n* acento *m* arrastrado

drawn [drɔːn] *pp* → **draw**

dread [dred] v/t tener pavor a; **I ~ him ever finding out** me da pavor pensar que lo pueda llegar a descubrir; **I ~ going to the dentist** me da pánico ir al dentista

dread·ful ['dredfəl] *adj* horrible, espantoso; **it's a ~ pity you won't be there** es una auténtica pena que no vayas a estar ahí

dread·ful·ly ['dredfəlɪ] *adv* F (*extremely*) terriblemente, espantosamente F; *behave* fatal

dream [driːm] **1** *n* sueño *m* **2** *adj:* **win your ~ house!** ¡gane la casa de sus sueños! **3** v/t soñar; (*day~*) soñar (despierto) **4** v/i soñar; (*day~*) soñar (despierto); **I ~t about you last night** anoche soñé contigo

♦ **dream up** v/t inventar

dream·er ['driːmər] (*day~*) soñador(a) *m(f)*

dream·y ['driːmɪ] *adj voice, look* soñador

drear·y ['drɪrɪ] *adj* triste, deprimente

dredge [dredʒ] v/t *harbor, canal* dragar

♦ **dredge up** v/t *fig* sacar a relucir

dregs [dregz] *npl of coffee* posos *mpl*; **the ~ of society** la escoria de la sociedad

drench [drentʃ] v/t empapar; **get ~ed** empaparse

dress [dres] **1** *n for woman* vestido *m*; (*clothing*) traje *m*; **he has no ~ sense** no sabe vestir(se); **the company has a ~ code** la compañía tiene unas normas sobre la ropa que deben llevar los empleados **2** v/t *person* vestir; *wound* vendar; **get ~ed** vestirse **3** v/i (*get ~ed*) vestirse; *well, in black etc* vestir(se) (**in** de)

♦ **dress up** *v/i* arreglarse, vestirse elegante; (*wear a disguise*) disfrazarse (*as* de)

'**dress cir·cle** piso *m* principal

dress·er ['dresər] (*dressing table*) tocador *f*; *in kitchen* aparador *m*

dress·ing ['dresɪŋ] *for salad* aliño *m*, *Span* arreglo *m*; *for wound* vendaje *m*

dress·ing 'down regaño *m*; *give s.o. a ~* regañar a alguien; '**dress·ing room** *in theater* camerino *m*; '**dress·ing ta·ble** tocador *f*

'**dress·mak·er** modisto(-a) *m(f)*

'**dress re·hears·al** ensayo *m* general

dress·y ['dresɪ] *adj* F elegante

drew [dru:] *pret* → *draw*

drib·ble ['drɪbl] *v/i of person, baby* babear; *of water* gotear; SP driblar

dried [draɪd] *adj fruit etc* seco

dri·er [draɪr] → *dryer*

drift [drɪft] **1** *n of snow* ventisquero *m* **2** *v/i of snow* amontonarse; *of ship* ir a la deriva; (*go off course*) desviarse del rumbo; *of person* vagar

♦ **drift apart** *v/i of couple* distanciarse

drift·er ['drɪftər] vagabundo(-a) *m(f)*

drill [drɪl] **1** *n tool* taladro *m*; *exercise* simulacro *m*; MIL instrucción *f* **2** *v/t hole* taladrar, perforar **3** *v/i for oil* hacer perforaciones; MIL entrenarse

dril·ling rig ['drɪlɪŋrɪg] (*platform*) plataforma *f* petrolífera

dri·ly ['draɪlɪ] *adv remark* secamente, lacónicamente

drink [drɪŋk] **1** *n* bebida *f*; *a ~ of ...* un vaso de ...; *go for a ~* ir a tomar algo **2** *v/t* (*pret drank, pp drunk*) beber **3** *v/i* (*pret drank, pp drunk*) beber, *L.Am.* tomar; *I don't ~* no bebo

♦ **drink up 1** *v/i* (*finish drink*) acabarse la bebida **2** *v/t* (*drink completely*) beberse todo

drink·a·ble ['drɪŋkəbl] *adj* potable

drink 'driv·ing conducción *f* bajo los efectos del alcohol

drink·er ['drɪŋkər] bebedor(a) *m(f)*

drink·ing ['drɪŋkɪŋ]: *I'm worried about his ~* me preocupa que beba tanto; *a ~ problem* un problema con la bebida

'**drink·ing wa·ter** agua *f* potable

'**drinks ma·chine** máquina *f* expendedora de bebidas

drip [drɪp] **1** *n* gota *f*; MED gotero *m*, suero *m* **2** *v/i* (*pret & pp -ped*) gotear

'**drip-dry** *adj* que no necesita planchado

'**drip·ping** ['drɪpɪŋ] *adv*: *~ wet* empapado

drive [draɪv] **1** *n outing* vuelta *f*, paseo *m* (en coche); (*energy*) energía *f*; COMPUT unidad *f*; (*campaign*) campaña *f*; *it's a short ~ from the station* está a poca distancia en coche de la estación; *with left-/ right-hand ~* MOT con el volante a la izquierda/a la derecha **2** *v/t* (*pret drove, pp driven*) *vehicle* conducir, *L.Am.* manejar; (*own*) tener; (*take in car*) llevar (*en coche*); TECH impulsar; *that noise/he is driving me mad* ese ruido/él me está volviendo loco **3** *v/i* (*pret drove, pp driven*) conducir, *L.Am.* manejar; *don't drink and ~* si bebes, no conduzcas; *I ~ to work* voy al trabajo en coche

♦ **drive at** *v/t*: *what are you driving at?* ¿qué insinúas?

♦ **drive away 1** *v/t* llevarse en un coche; (*chase off*) ahuyentar **2** *v/i* marcharse

♦ **drive in** *v/t nail* remachar

♦ **drive off** → *drive away*

'**drive-in** *n* (*movie theater*) autocine *m*

driv·el ['drɪvl] *n* tonterías *fpl*

driv·en ['drɪvn] *pp* → *drive*

driv·er ['draɪvər] conductor(a) *m(f)*; COMPUT controlador *m*

'**driv·er's li·cense** carné *m* de conducir

drive·thru ['draɪvθru:] *restaurante/*

banco etc en el que se atiende al cliente sin que salga del coche
'**drive·way** camino *m* de entrada
driv·ing ['draɪvɪŋ] **1** *n* conducción *f*; *his ~ is appalling* conduce *or L.Am.* maneja fatal **2** *adj rain* torrencial
driv·ing 'force fuerza *f* motriz; '**driv·ing in·struc·tor** profesor(a) *m(f)* de autoescuela; '**driv·ing les·son** clase *f* de conducir; '**driv·ing li·cence** *Br* carné *m* de conducir; '**driv·ing school** autoescuela *f*; '**driv·ing test** examen *m* de conducir *or L.Am.* manejar
driz·zle ['drɪzl] **1** *n* llovizna *f* **2** *v/i* lloviznar
drone [droʊn] *n noise* zumbido *m*
droop [druːp] *v/i of plant* marchitarse; *her shoulders ~ed* se encorvó
drop [drɑːp] **1** *n* gota *f*; *in price, temperature* caída *f* **2** *v/t* (*pret & pp -ped*) *object* dejar caer; *person from car* dejar; *person from team* excluir; *(stop seeing)* abandonar; *charges, demand etc* retirar; *(give up)* dejar; *~ a line to* mandar unas líneas a **3** *v/i* (*pret & pp -ped*) caer, caerse; *(decline)* caer; *of wind* amainar
♦ **drop in** *v/i (visit)* pasar a visitar
♦ **drop off 1** *v/t person* dejar; *(deliver)* llevar **2** *v/i (fall asleep)* dormirse; *(decline)* disminuir
♦ **drop out** *v/i (withdraw)* retirarse; *drop out of school* abandonar el colegio
'**drop·out** (*from school*) alumno *m* que ha abandonado los estudios; *from society* marginado(-a) *m(f)*
drops [drɑːps] *npl for eyes* gotas *fpl*
drought [draʊt] sequía *f*
drove [droʊv] *pret* → **drive**
drown [draʊn] **1** *v/i* ahogarse **2** *v/t person, sound* ahogar; *be ~ed* ahogarse
drow·sy ['draʊzɪ] *adj* soñoliento(-a)
drudg·e·ry ['drʌdʒərɪ] *the job is sheer ~* el trabajo es terriblemente pesado
drug [drʌg] **1** *n* MED, *illegal* droga *f*; *be on ~s* drogarse **2** *v/t* (*pret & pp*

-ged) drogar
'**drug ad·dict** drogadicto(-a) *m(f)*
'**drug deal·er** traficante *m/f* (de drogas)
drug·gist ['drʌgɪst] farmacéutico(-a) *m(f)*
'**drug·store** *tienda en la que se venden medicinas, cosméticos, periódicos y que a veces tiene un bar*
'**drug traf·fick·ing** tráfico *m* de drogas
drum [drʌm] *n* MUS tambor *m*; *container* barril *m*
♦ **drum into** *v/t* (*pret & pp -med*): *drum sth into s.o.* meter algo en la cabeza de alguien
♦ **drum up** *v/t*: *drum up support* buscar apoyos
drum·mer ['drʌmər] tambor *m*, tamborilero(-a) *m(f)*
'**drum·stick** MUS baqueta *f*; *of poultry* muslo *m*
drunk [drʌŋk] **1** *n* borracho(-a) *m(f)* **2** *adj* borracho; *get ~* emborracharse **3** *pp* → **drink**
drunk·en [drʌŋkn] *voices, laughter* borracho; *party* con mucho alcohol
dry [draɪ] **1** *adj* seco; *where alcohol is banned* donde está prohibido el consumo de alcohol **2** *v/t & v/i* (*pret & pp -ied*) secar
♦ **dry out** *v/i* secarse; *of alcoholic* desintoxicarse
♦ **dry up** *v/i of river* secarse; F *(be quiet)* cerrar el pico F
'**dry-clean** *v/t* limpiar en seco; '**dry clean·er** tintorería *f*; '**dryclean·ing** *(clothes)*: *would you pick up my ~ for me?* ¿te importaría recogerme la ropa de la tintorería?
dry·er [draɪr] *machine* secadora *f*
DTP [diːtiː'piː] *abbr* (= *desk-top publishing*) autoedición *f*
du·al ['duːəl] *adj* doble
dub [dʌb] *v/t* (*pret & pp -bed*) *movie* doblar
du·bi·ous ['duːbɪəs] *adj* dudoso; *(having doubts)* inseguro; *I'm still ~ about the idea* todavía tengo mis dudas sobre la idea
duch·ess ['dʌtʃɪs] duquesa *f*

duck [dʌk] **1** n pato m, pata f **2** v/i agacharse **3** v/t one's head agachar; question eludir

dud [dʌd] n F (false bill) billete m falso

due [duː] adj (proper) debido; **the money - me** el dinero que se me debe; **payment is now -** el pago se debe hacer efectivo ahora; **is there a train - soon?** ¿va a pasar un tren pronto?; **when is the baby -?** ¿cuando está previsto que nazca el bebé?; **he's - to meet him next month** tiene previsto reunirse con él el próximo mes; **- to** (because of) debido a; **be - to** (be caused by) ser debido a; **in - course** en su debido momento

dues [duːz] npl cuota f

du·et [duːˈet] MUS dúo m

dug [dʌg] pret & pp → **dig**

duke [duːk] duque m

dull [dʌl] adj weather gris; sound, pain sordo; (boring) aburrido, soso

du·ly [ˈduːlɪ] adv (as expected) tal y como se esperaba; (properly) debidamente

dumb [dʌm] adj (mute) mudo; F (stupid) estúpido; **a pretty - thing to do** una tontería

dumb·found·ed [dʌmˈfaʊndɪd] adj boquiabierto

dump [dʌmp] **1** n for garbage vertedero m, basurero m; (unpleasant place) lugar m de mala muerte **2** v/t (deposit) dejar; (dispose of) deshacerse de; toxic waste, nuclear waste verter

dump·ling [ˈdʌmplɪŋ] bola de masa dulce o salada

dune [duːn] duna f

dung [dʌŋ] estiércol m

dun·ga·rees [dʌŋgəˈriːz] npl pantalones mpl de trabajo

dunk [dʌŋk] v/t in coffee etc mojar

du·o [ˈduːoʊ] MUS dúo m

du·plex (a·part·ment) [ˈduːpleks] dúplex m

du·pli·cate 1 n [ˈduːplɪkət] duplicado m; **in -** por duplicado **2** v/t [ˈduːplɪkeɪt] (copy) duplicar, hacer

un duplicado de; (repeat) repetir

du·pli·cate 'key llave f duplicada

du·ra·ble [ˈdʊrəbl] adj material duradero, durable; relationship duradero

du·ra·tion [dʊˈreɪʃn] duración f; **for the - of her visit** mientras dure su visita

du·ress [dʊˈres]: **under -** bajo coacción

dur·ing [ˈdʊrɪŋ] prep durante

dusk [dʌsk] crepúsculo m, anochecer m

dust [dʌst] **1** n polvo m **2** v/t quitar el polvo a; **- sth with sth** (sprinkle) espolvorear algo con algo

dust·er [ˈdʌstər] (cloth) trapo m del polvo

'dust jack·et sobrecubierta f

'dust·pan recogedor m

dust·y [ˈdʌstɪ] adj polvoriento

Dutch [dʌtʃ] **1** adj holandés; **go -** F pagar a escote F **2** n (language) neerlandés m; **the -** los holandeses

du·ty [ˈduːtɪ] deber m; (task) obligación f, tarea f; on goods impuesto m; **be on -** estar de servicio; **be off -** estar fuera de servicio

du·ty-'free 1 adj libre de impuestos **2** n productos mpl libres de impuestos

du·ty-'free shop tienda f libre de impuestos

DVD [diːviːˈdiː] abbr (= **digital versatile disk**) DVD m

dwarf [dwɔːrf] **1** n enano m **2** v/t empequeñecer

♦ **dwell on** [dwel] v/t: **dwell on the past** pensar en el pasado; **don't dwell on what he said** no des demasiada importancia a lo que ha dicho

dwin·dle [ˈdwɪndl] v/i disminuir, menguar

dye [daɪ] **1** n tinte m **2** v/t teñir

dy·ing [ˈdaɪɪŋ] adj person moribundo; industry, tradition en vías de desaparición

dy·nam·ic [daɪˈnæmɪk] adj dinámico

dy·na·mism [ˈdaɪnəmɪzm] dinamismo m

dy·na·mite [ˈdaɪnəmaɪt] n dinamita f

dy·na·mo ['daɪnəmoʊ] TECH dinamo f, dínamo f

dy·nas·ty ['daɪnəstɪ] dinastía f

dys·lex·i·a [dɪs'leksɪə] dislexia f

dys·lex·ic [dɪs'leksɪk] **1** adj disléxico **2** n disléxico(-a) m(f)

E

each [iːtʃ] **1** adj cada **2** adv: **he gave us one ~** nos dio uno a cada uno; **they're $1.50 ~** valen 1.50 dólares cada uno **3** pron cada uno; **~ other** el uno al otro; **we love ~ other** nos queremos

ea·ger ['iːgər] adj ansioso; **she's always ~ to help** siempre está deseando ayudar

ea·ger bea·ver F entusiasta m/f

ea·ger·ly ['iːgərlɪ] adv ansiosamente

ea·ger·ness ['iːgərnɪs] entusiasmo m

ea·gle ['iːgl] águila f

ea·gle-eyed [iːgl'aɪd] adj con vista de lince

ear[1] [ɪr] of person, animal oreja f; for music oído m

ear[2] [ɪr] of corn espiga f

'ear·ache dolor m de oídos; **'ear·drum** tímpano m; **'ear·lobe** lóbulo m

ear·ly ['ɜːrlɪ] **1** adj (not late) temprano; (ahead of time) anticipado; (farther back in time) primero; (in the near future) pronto; music antiguo; **let's have an ~ supper** cenemos temprano; **in ~ October** a principios de octubre; **in the ~ hours of the morning** a primeras horas de la madrugada; **an ~ Picasso** un Picasso de su primera época; **I'm an ~ riser** soy madrugador **2** adv (not late) pronto, temprano; (ahead of time) antes de tiempo; **it's too ~ to say** es demasiado pronto como para poder decir nada; **earlier than** antes que

'ear·ly bird madrugador(a) m(f)

ear·mark ['ɪrmɑːrk] v/t destinar; **~ sth for sth** destinar algo a algo

earn [ɜːrn] v/t salary ganar; interest devengar; holiday, drink etc ganarse; **~ one's living** ganarse la vida

ear·nest ['ɜːrnɪst] adj serio; **in ~** en serio

earn·ings ['ɜːrnɪŋz] npl ganancias fpl

'ear·phones npl auriculares mpl; **'ear-pierc·ing** adj estrepitoso; **'ear·plug** tapón m para el oído; **'ear·ring** pendiente m; **'ear·shot**: **within ~** al alcance del oído; **out of ~** fuera del alcance del oído

earth [ɜːrθ] (soil) tierra f; (world, planet) Tierra f; **where on ~ ...?** F ¿dónde diablos ...? F

earth·en·ware ['ɜːrθnwer] n loza f

earth·ly ['ɜːrθlɪ] adj terrenal; **it's no ~ use** F no sirve para nada

earth·quake ['ɜːrθkweɪk] terremoto m

earth-shat·ter·ing ['ɜːrθʃætərɪŋ] adj extraordinario

ease [iːz] **1** n facilidad f; **be at (one's) ~** sentirse cómodo; **feel ill at ~** sentirse incómodo **2** v/t (relieve) aliviar **3** v/i of pain disminuir

♦ease off **1** v/t (remove) quitar con cuidado **2** v/i of pain disminuir; of rain amainar

ea·sel ['iːzl] caballete m

eas·i·ly ['iːzəlɪ] adv (with ease) fácilmente; (by far) con diferencia

east [iːst] **1** n este m **2** adj oriental, este; wind del este **3** adv travel hacia el este

Eas·ter ['iːstər] Pascua f; period Semana f Santa

Eas·ter 'Day Domingo m de Resurrección

'Eas·ter egg huevo m de pascua

eas·ter·ly ['i:stərlɪ] adj del este

Eas·ter 'Mon·day Lunes m Santo

east·ern ['i:stərn] adj del este; (oriental) oriental

east·er·ner ['i:stərnər] habitante de la costa este estadounidense

Eas·ter 'Sun·day Domingo m de Resurrección

east·ward ['i:stwərd] adv hacia el este

eas·y ['i:zɪ] adj fácil; (relaxed) tranquilo; (slow down) tomarse las cosas con tranquilidad; **take things ~!** (calm down) ¡tranquilízate!

'eas·y chair sillón m

eas·y-go·ing ['i:zɪɡoʊɪŋ] adj tratable

eat [i:t] v/t & v/i (pret **ate**, pp **eaten**) comer

♦ **eat out** v/i comer fuera

♦ **eat up** v/t comerse; fig: use up acabar con

eat·a·ble ['i:təbl] adj comestible

eat·en ['i:tn] pp → **eat**

eau de Co·logne [oʊdəkə'loʊn] agua f de colonia

eaves [i:vz] npl alero m

eaves·drop ['i:vzdrɑːp] v/i (pret & pp **-ped**) escuchar a escondidas (**on s.o.** alguien)

ebb [eb] v/i of tide bajar

♦ **ebb away** v/i fig of courage, strength desvanecerse

e-busi·ness ['i:bɪznɪs] comercio m electrónico

ec·cen·tric [ɪk'sentrɪk] **1** adj excéntrico **2** n excéntrico(-a) m(f)

ec·cen·tric·i·ty [ɪksen'trɪsɪtɪ] excentricidad f

ech·o ['ekoʊ] **1** n eco m **2** v/i resonar **3** v/t words repetir; views mostrar acuerdo con

e·clipse [ɪ'klɪps] **1** n eclipse m **2** v/t fig eclipsar

e·co·lo·gi·cal [i:kə'lɑːdʒɪkl] adj ecológico

e·co·lo·gi·cal·ly [i:kə'lɑːdʒɪklɪ] adv ecológicamente

e·co·lo·gi·cal·ly 'friend·ly adj ecológico

e·col·o·gist [i:'kɑːlədʒɪst] ecologista m/f

e·col·o·gy [i:'kɑːlədʒɪ] ecología f

ec·o·nom·ic [i:kə'nɑːmɪk] adj económico

ec·o·nom·i·cal [i:kə'nɑːmɪkl] adj (cheap) económico; (thrifty) cuidadoso

ec·o·nom·i·cal·ly [i:kə'nɑːmɪklɪ] adv (in terms of economics) económicamente; (thriftily) de manera económica

ec·o·nom·ics [i:kə'nɑːmɪks] nsg (science) economía f; (npl: financial aspects) aspecto m económico

e·con·o·mist [ɪ'kɑːnəmɪst] economista m/f

e·con·o·mize [ɪ'kɑːnəmaɪz] v/i economizar, ahorrar

♦ **economize on** v/t economizar, ahorrar

e·con·o·my [ɪ'kɑːnəmɪ] of a country economía f; (saving) ahorro m

e'con·o·my class clase f turista; **e'con·o·my drive** intento m de ahorrar; **e'con·o·my size** tamaño m económico

e·co·sys·tem ['i:koʊsɪstm] ecosistema m

e·co·tour·ism ['i:koʊtʊrɪzm] ecoturismo m

ec·sta·sy ['ekstəsɪ] éxtasis m

ec·sta·tic [ɪk'stætɪk] adj muy emocionado, extasiado

Ec·ua·dor ['ekwədɔːr] n Ecuador

Ec·ua·dore·an [ekwə'dɔːrən] **1** adj ecuatoriano **2** n ecuatoriano(-a) m(f)

ec·ze·ma ['eksmə] eczema f

edge [edʒ] **1** n of knife filo m; of table, seat, road, cliff borde m; in voice irritación f; **on ~** tenso **2** v/t ribetear **3** v/i (move slowly) acercarse despacio

edge·wise ['edʒwaɪz] adv de lado; **I couldn't get a word in ~** no me dejó decir una palabra

edg·y ['edʒɪ] *adj* tenso

ed·i·ble ['edɪbl] *adj* comestible

ed·it ['edɪt] *v/t text* corregir; *book* editar; *newspaper* dirigir; *TV program, movie* montar

e·di·tion [ɪ'dɪʃn] edición *f*

ed·i·tor ['edɪtər] *of text, book* editor(a) *m(f)*; *of newspaper* director(a) *m(f)*; *of TV program, movie* montador(a) *m(f)*; *sports/political ~* redactor(a) *m(f)* de deportes/política

ed·i·to·ri·al [edɪ'tɔːrɪəl] **1** *adj* editorial **2** *n in newspaper* editorial *m*

EDP [iːdiː'piː] *abbr* (= *electronic data processing*) procesamiento *m* electrónico de datos

ed·u·cate ['edʒəkeɪt] *v/t child* educar; *consumers* concienciar

ed·u·cat·ed ['edʒəkeɪtɪd] *adj person* culto

ed·u·ca·tion [edʒə'keɪʃn] educación *f*; *the ~ system* el sistema educativo

ed·u·ca·tion·al [edʒə'keɪʃnl] *adj* educativo; (*informative*) instructivo

eel [iːl] anguila *f*

ee·rie ['ɪrɪ] *adj* escalofriante

ef·fect [ɪ'fekt] efecto *m*; *take ~ of medicine, drug* hacer efecto; *come into ~ of law* entrar en vigor

ef·fec·tive [ɪ'fektɪv] *adj* (*efficient*) efectivo; (*striking*) impresionante; *~ May 1* a partir del 1 de mayo

ef·fem·i·nate [ɪ'femɪnət] *adj* afeminado

ef·fer·ves·cent [efər'vesnt] *adj* efervescente; *personality* chispeante

ef·fi·cien·cy [ɪ'fɪʃənsɪ] *of person* eficiencia *f*; *of machine* rendimiento *m*; *of system* eficacia *f*

ef·fi·cient [ɪ'fɪʃənt] *adj person* eficiente; *machine* de buen rendimiento; *method* eficaz

ef·fi·cient·ly [ɪ'fɪʃəntlɪ] *adv* eficientemente

ef·flu·ent ['efluənt] aguas *fpl* residuales

ef·fort ['efərt] (*struggle, attempt*) esfuerzo *m*

ef·fort·less ['efərtlɪs] *adj* fácil

ef·fron·te·ry [ɪ'frʌntərɪ] desvergüenza *f*

ef·fu·sive [ɪ'fjuːsɪv] *adj* efusivo

e.g. [iːˈdʒiː] p. ej.

e·gal·i·tar·i·an [ɪgælɪ'terɪən] *adj* igualitario

egg [eg] huevo *m*; *of woman* óvulo *m*

♦ **egg on** *v/t* incitar

'egg·cup huevera *f*; **'egg·head** F cerebrito(-a) *m(f)* F; **'egg·plant** berenjena *f*; **'egg·shell** cáscara *f* de huevo; **'egg tim·er** reloj *m* de arena

e·go ['iːgou] PSYCH ego *m*; (*self-esteem*) amor *m* propio

e·go·cen·tric [iːgou'sentrɪk] *adj* egocéntrico

e·go·ism ['iːgouɪzm] egoismo *m*

e·go·ist ['iːgouɪst] egoísta *m/f*

E·gypt ['iːdʒɪpt] Egipto

E·gyp·tian [ɪ'dʒɪpʃn] **1** *adj* egipcio **2** *n* egipcio(-a) *m(f)*

ei·der·down ['aɪdərdaun] *quilt* edredón *m*

eight [eɪt] ocho

eigh·teen [eɪ'tiːn] dieciocho

eigh·teenth [eɪ'tiːnθ] *n & adj* decimoctavo

eighth [eɪtθ] *n & adj* octavo

eigh·ti·eth ['eɪtɪɪθ] *n & adj* octogésimo

eigh·ty ['eɪtɪ] ochenta

ei·ther ['aɪðər] **1** *adj* cualquiera de los dos; *with negative constructions* ninguno de los dos; (*both*) cada, ambos; *he wouldn't accept ~ of the proposals* no quería aceptar ninguna de las dos propuestas **2** *pron* cualquiera de los dos; *with negative constructions* ninguno de los dos **3** *adv* tampoco; *I won't go ~* yo tampoco iré **4** *conj*: *~ ... or choice* o ... o; *with negative constructions* ni ... ni

e·ject [ɪ'dʒekt] **1** *v/t* expulsar **2** *v/i from plane* eyectarse

♦ **eke out** [iːk] *v/t* (*make last*) hacer durar

el [el] → *elevated railroad*

e·lab·o·rate 1 *adj* [ɪ'læbərət] elaborado 2 *v/t* [ɪˈlæbəreɪt] elaborar 3 *v/i* [ɪˈlæbəreɪt] dar detalles

e·lab·o·rate·ly [ɪˈlæbəreɪtlɪ] *adv* elaboradamente

e·lapse [ɪˈlæps] *v/i* pasar

e·las·tic [ɪˈlæstɪk] **1** *adj* elástico **2** *n* elástico *m*

e·las·ti·ca·ted [ɪˈlæstɪkeɪtɪd] *adj* elástico

e·las·ti·ci·ty [ɪlæsˈtɪsətɪ] elasticidad *f*

e·las·ti·cized [ɪˈlæstɪsaɪzd] *adj* elástico

e·lat·ed [ɪˈleɪtɪd] *adj* eufórico

e·la·tion [ɪˈleɪʃn] euforia *f*

el·bow [ˈelbou] **1** *n* codo *m* **2** *v/t* dar un codazo a; **~ out of the way** apartar a codazos

el·der [ˈeldər] **1** *adj* mayor **2** *n* mayor *m/f*; **she's two years my ~** es dos años mayor que yo

el·der·ly [ˈeldərlɪ] **1** *adj* mayor **2** *n*: **the ~** las personas mayores

el·dest [ˈeldəst] **1** *adj* mayor **2** *n* mayor *m/f*; **the ~** el mayor

e·lect [ɪˈlekt] *v/t* elegir; **~ to do sth** decidir hacer algo

e·lect·ed [ɪˈlektɪd] *adj* elegido

e·lec·tion [ɪˈlekʃn] elección *f*; **call an ~** convocar elecciones

e·lec·tion cam·paign campaña *f* electoral

e·lec·tion day día *m* de las elecciones

e·lec·tive [ɪˈlektɪv] *adj* opcional; *subject* optativo

e·lec·tor [ɪˈlektər] elector(a) *m(f)*, votante *m/f*

e·lec·to·ral sys·tem [ɪˈlektərəl] sistema *m* electoral

e·lec·to·rate [ɪˈlektərət] electorado *m*

e·lec·tric [ɪˈlektrɪk] *adj* eléctrico; *fig atmosphere* electrizado

e·lec·tri·cal [ɪˈlektrɪkl] *adj* eléctrico

e·lec·tri·cal en·gi·neer ingeniero(-a) *m(f)* electrónico

e·lec·tri·cal en·gi·neer·ing ingeniería *f* electrónica

e·lec·tric 'blan·ket manta *f* or *L.Am.* cobija *f* eléctrica

e·lec·tric 'chair silla *f* eléctrica

e·lec·tri·cian [ɪlekˈtrɪʃn] electricista *m/f*

e·lec·tri·ci·ty [ɪlekˈtrɪsətɪ] electricidad *f*

e·lec·tric 'ra·zor maquinilla *f* eléctrica

e·lec·tric 'shock descarga *f* eléctrica

e·lec·tri·fy [ɪˈlektrɪfaɪ] *v/t* (*pret & pp* **-ied**) electrificar; *fig* electrizar

e·lec·tro·cute [ɪˈlektrəkjuːt] *v/t* electrocutar

e·lec·trode [ɪˈlektroud] electrodo *m*

e·lec·tron [ɪˈlektrɑːn] electrón *m*

e·lec·tron·ic [ɪlekˈtrɑːnɪk] *adj* electrónico

e·lec·tron·ic da·ta 'pro·ces·sing procesamiento *m* electrónico de datos

e·lec·tron·ic 'mail correo *m* electrónico

e·lec·tron·ics [ɪlekˈtrɑːnɪks] electrónica *f*

el·e·gance [ˈelɪgəns] elegancia *f*

el·e·gant [ˈelɪgənt] *adj* elegante

el·e·gant·ly [ˈelɪgəntlɪ] *adv* elegantemente

el·e·ment [ˈelɪmənt] *also* CHEM elemento *m*

el·e·men·ta·ry [elɪˈmentərɪ] *adj* (*rudimentary*) elemental

el·e'men·ta·ry school escuela *f* primaria

el·e'men·ta·ry teacher maestro(-a) *m(f)*

el·e·phant [ˈelɪfənt] elefante *m*

el·e·vate [ˈelɪveɪt] *v/t* elevar

el·e·vat·ed 'rail·road [ˈelɪveɪtɪd] ferrocarril *m* elevado

el·e·va·tion [elɪˈveɪʃn] (*altitude*) altura *f*

el·e·va·tor [ˈelɪveɪtər] ascensor *m*

el·e·ven [ɪˈlevn] once

el·e·venth [ɪˈlevnθ] *n & adj* undécimo; **at the ~ hour** justo en el último minuto

el·i·gi·ble [ˈelɪdʒəbl] *adj* que reúne los requisitos; **~ to vote** con derecho al voto; **be ~ to do sth** tener derecho a hacer algo

E

el·i·gi·ble 'bach·e·lor buen partido *m*

e·lim·i·nate [ɪ'lɪmɪneɪt] *v/t* eliminar; *poverty* acabar con; (*rule out*) descartar

e·lim·i·na·tion [ɪ'lɪmɪneɪʃn] eliminación *f*

e·lite [eɪ'liːt] **1** *n* élite *f* **2** *adj* de élite

elk [elk] ciervo *m* canadiense

e·lipse [ɪ'lɪps] elipse *f*

elm [elm] olmo *m*

e·lope [ɪ'loʊp] *v/i* fugarse con un amante

el·o·quence ['eləkwəns] elocuencia *f*

el·o·quent ['eləkwənt] *adj* elocuente

el·o·quent·ly ['eləkwəntlɪ] *adv* elocuentemente

El Sal·va·dor [el'sælvədɔːr] *n* El Salvador

else [els] *adv*: *anything ~?* ¿algo más?; *if you have nothing ~ to do* si no tienes nada más que hacer; *no one ~* nadie más; *everyone ~ is going* todos (los demás) van, va todo el mundo; *who ~ was there?* ¿quién más estaba allí?; *someone ~* otra persona; *something ~* algo más; *let's go somewhere ~* vamos a otro sitio; *or ~* si no

else·where ['elswer] *adv* en otro sitio

e·lude [ɪ'luːd] *v/t* (*escape from*) escapar de; (*avoid*) evitar; *the name ~s me* no recuerdo el nombre

e·lu·sive [ɪ'luːsɪv] *adj* evasivo

e·ma·ci·ated [ɪ'meɪsɪeɪtɪd] *adj* demacrado

e-mail ['iːmeɪl] **1** *n* correo *m* electrónico **2** *v/t person* mandar un correo electrónico a

'e-mail ad·dress dirección *f* de correo electrónico, dirección *f* electrónica

e·man·ci·pat·ed [ɪ'mænsɪpeɪtɪd] *adj* emancipado

e·man·ci·pa·tion [ɪmænsɪ'peɪʃn] emancipación *f*

em·balm [ɪm'bɑːm] *v/t* embalsamar

em·bank·ment [ɪm'bæŋkmənt] *of river* dique *m*; RAIL terraplén *m*

em·bar·go [em'bɑːrgoʊ] embargo *m*

em·bark [ɪm'bɑːrk] *v/i* embarcar

♦ **embark on** *v/t* embarcarse en

em·bar·rass [ɪm'bærəs] *v/t* avergonzar; *he ~ed me in front of everyone* me hizo pasar vergüenza delante de todos

em·bar·rassed [ɪm'bærəst] *adj* avergonzado; *I was ~ to ask* me daba vergüenza preguntar

em·bar·rass·ing [ɪm'bærəsɪŋ] *adj* embarazoso

em·bar·rass·ment [ɪm'bærəsmənt] embarazo *m*, apuro *m*

em·bas·sy ['embəsɪ] embajada *f*

em·bel·lish [ɪm'belɪʃ] *v/t* adornar; *story* exagerar

em·bers ['embərz] *npl* ascuas *fpl*

em·bez·zle [ɪm'bezl] *v/t* malversar

em·bez·zle·ment [ɪm'bezlmənt] malversación *f*

em·bez·zler [ɪm'bezlər] malversador(a) *m(f)*

em·bit·ter [ɪm'bɪtər] *v/t* amargar

em·blem ['embləm] emblema *m*

em·bod·i·ment [ɪm'bɑːdɪmənt] personificación *f*

em·bod·y [ɪm'bɑːdɪ] *v/t* (*pret & pp -ied*) personificar

em·bo·lism ['embəlɪzm] embolia *f*

em·boss [ɪm'bɑːs] *v/t metal* repujar; *paper* grabar en relieve

em·brace [ɪm'breɪs] **1** *n* abrazo *m* **2** *v/t* (*hug*) abrazar; (*take in*) abarcar **3** *v/i of two people* abrazarse

em·broi·der [ɪm'brɔɪdər] *v/t* bordar; *fig* adornar

em·broi·der·y [ɪm'brɔɪdərɪ] bordado *m*

em·bry·o ['embrioʊ] embrión *m*

em·bry·on·ic [embrɪ'ɑːnɪk] *adj fig* embrionario

em·e·rald ['emərəld] esmeralda *f*

e·merge [ɪ'mɜːrdʒ] *v/i* (*appear*) emerger, salir; *of truth* aflorar; *it has ~d that* se ha descubierto que

e·mer·gen·cy [ɪ'mɜːrdʒənsɪ] emergencia *f*; *in an ~* en caso de emergencia

emer·gen·cy 'ex·it salida *f* de emergencia; **e'mer·gen·cy land·ing**

aterrizaje *m* forzoso; **e'mer·gen·cy ser·vi·ces** *npl* servicios *mpl* de urgencia

em·er·y board ['eməri] lima *f* de uñas

em·i·grant ['emigrənt] emigrante *m/f*

em·i·grate ['emigreit] *v/i* emigrar

em·i·gra·tion [emi'greiʃn] emigración *f*

Em·i·nence ['eminəns] REL: *His ~* Su Eminencia

em·i·nent ['eminənt] *adj* eminente

em·i·nent·ly ['eminəntli] *adv* sumamente

e·mis·sion [ɪ'mɪʃn] *of gases* emisión *f*

e·mit [ɪ'mɪt] *v/t* (*pret & pp -ted*) emitir; *heat, odor* desprender

e·mo·tion [ɪ'mouʃn] emoción *f*

e·mo·tion·al [ɪ'mouʃənl] *adj problems, development* sentimental; (*full of emotion*) emotivo

em·pa·thize ['empəθaiz] *v/i*: *~ with* identificarse con

em·per·or ['empərər] emperador *m*

em·pha·sis ['emfəsis] *in word* acento *m*; *fig* énfasis *m*

em·pha·size ['emfəsaiz] *v/t syllable* acentuar; *fig* hacer hincapié en

em·phat·ic [ɪm'fætɪk] *adj* enfático

em·pire ['empair] imperio *m*

em·ploy [ɪm'plɔɪ] *v/t* emplear; *he's ~ed as a ...* trabaja de ...

em·ploy·ee [emplɔɪ'iː] empleado(-a) *m(f)*

em·ploy·er [em'plɔɪər] empresario(-a) *m(f)*

em·ploy·ment [em'plɔɪmənt] empleo *m*; (*work*) trabajo *m*; *be looking for ~* buscar trabajo

em'ploy·ment a·gen·cy agencia *f* de colocaciones

em·press ['empris] emperatriz *f*

emp·ti·ness ['emptinis] vacío *m*

emp·ty ['empti] **1** *adj* vacío; *promise* vana **2** *v/t* (*pret & pp -ied*) *drawer, pockets* vaciar; *glass, bottle* acabar **3** *v/i* (*pret & pp -ied*) *of room, street* vaciarse

em·u·late ['emjuleit] *v/t* emular

e·mul·sion [ɪ'mʌlʃn] *paint* emulsión *f*

en·a·ble [ɪ'neibl] *v/t* permitir; *~ s.o. to do sth* permitir a alguien hacer algo

en·act [ɪ'nækt] *v/t law* promulgar; THEA representar

e·nam·el [ɪ'næml] *n* esmalte *m*

enc *abbr* (= *enclosure(s)*) documento(s) *m(pl)* adjunto(s)

en·chant·ing [ɪn'tʃæntɪŋ] *adj* encantador

en·cir·cle [ɪn'sɜːrkl] *v/t* rodear

encl *abbr* (= *enclosure(s)*) documento(s) *m(pl)* adjunto(s)

en·close [ɪn'klouz] *v/t in letter* adjuntar; *area* rodear; *please find ~d ...* remito adjunto ...

en·clo·sure [ɪn'klouʒər] *with letter* documento *m* adjunto

en·core ['ɑːŋkɔːr] bis *m*

en·coun·ter [ɪn'kauntər] **1** *n* encuentro *m* **2** *v/t person* encontrarse con; *problem, resistance* tropezar con

en·cour·age [ɪn'kʌrɪdʒ] *v/t* animar; *violence* fomentar

en·cour·age·ment [ɪn'kʌrɪdʒmənt] ánimo *m*

en·cour·ag·ing [ɪn'kʌrɪdʒɪŋ] *adj* alentador

♦**en·croach on** [ɪn'kroutʃ] *v/t land* invadir; *rights* usurpar; *time* quitar

en·cy·clo·pe·di·a [ɪnsaɪklə'piːdɪə] enciclopedia *f*

end [end] **1** *n of journey, month* final *m*; (*extremity*) extremo *m*; (*bottom*) fondo *m*; (*conclusion, purpose*) fin *m*; *at the other ~ of town* al otro lado de la ciudad; *in the ~* al final; *for hours on ~* durante horas y horas; *stand sth on ~* poner de pie algo; *at the ~ of July* a finales de julio; *in the ~* al final; *put an ~ to* poner fin a **2** *v/t* terminar, finalizar **3** *v/i* terminar

♦**end up** *v/i* acabar

en·dan·ger [ɪn'deɪndʒər] *v/t* poner en peligro

en'dan·gered spe·cies *nsg* especie *f* en peligro de extinción

E

en·dear·ing [ɪn'dɪrɪŋ] *adj* simpático

en·deav·or [ɪn'devər] **1** *n* esfuerzo *m* **2** *v/t* procurar

en·dem·ic [ɪn'demɪk] *adj* endémico

end·ing ['endɪŋ] final *m*; GRAM terminación *f*

end·less ['endlɪs] *adj* interminable

en·dorse [ɪn'dɔːrs] *v/t check* endosar; *candidacy* apoyar; *product* representar

en·dorse·ment [ɪn'dɔːrsmənt] *of check* endoso *m*; *of candidacy* apoyo *m*; *of product* representación *f*

end 'prod·uct producto *m* final

end re'sult resultado *m* final

en·dur·ance [ɪn'dʊrəns] resistencia *f*

en·dure [ɪn'dʊər] **1** *v/t* resistir **2** *v/i (last)* durar

en·dur·ing [ɪn'dʊrɪŋ] *adj* duradero

end-'us·er usuario(-a) *m(f)* final

en·e·my ['enəmɪ] enemigo(-a) *m(f)*

en·er·get·ic [enər'dʒetɪk] *adj* enérgico

en·er·get·ic·al·ly [enər'dʒetɪklɪ] *adv* enérgicamente

en·er·gy ['enərdʒɪ] energía *f*

'en·er·gy-sav·ing *adj device* que ahorra energía

'en·er·gy sup·ply suministro *m* de energía

en·force [ɪn'fɔːrs] *v/t* hacer cumplir

en·gage [ɪn'geɪdʒ] **1** *v/t (hire)* contratar **2** *v/i* TECH engranar

♦ **engage in** *v/t* dedicarse a

en·gaged [ɪn'geɪdʒd] *adj to be married* prometido; **get ~** prometerse

en·gage·ment [ɪn'geɪdʒmənt] *(appointment, to be married)* compromiso *m*; MIL combate *m*

en'gage·ment ring anillo *m* de compromiso

en·gag·ing [ɪn'geɪdʒɪŋ] *adj smile, person* atractivo

en·gine ['endʒɪn] motor *m*

en·gi·neer [endʒɪ'nɪr] **1** *n* ingeniero(-a) *m(f)*; NAUT, RAIL maquinista *m/f* **2** *v/t fig: meeting etc* tramar

en·gi·neer·ing [endʒɪ'nɪrɪŋ] ingeniería *f*

Eng·land ['ɪŋglənd] Inglaterra

Eng·lish ['ɪŋglɪʃ] **1** *adj* inglés(-esa) **2** *n language* inglés *m*; **the ~** los ingleses

Eng·lish 'Chan·nel Canal *m* de la Mancha; **'Eng·lish·man** inglés *m*; **'Eng·lish·wom·an** inglesa *f*

en·grave [ɪn'greɪv] *v/t* grabar

en·grav·ing [ɪn'greɪvɪŋ] grabado *m*

en·grossed [ɪn'groʊst] *adj* absorto *(in* en)

en·gulf [ɪn'gʌlf] *v/t* devorar

en·hance [ɪn'hæns] *v/t* realzar

e·nig·ma [ɪ'nɪgmə] enigma *m*

e·nig·mat·ic [enɪg'mætɪk] *adj* enigmático

en·joy [ɪn'dʒɔɪ] *v/t* disfrutar; **~ o.s.** divertirse; **~ (your meal)!** ¡que aproveche!

en·joy·a·ble [ɪn'dʒɔɪəbl] *adj* agradable

en·joy·ment [ɪn'dʒɔɪmənt] diversión *f*

en·large [ɪn'lɑːrdʒ] *v/t* ampliar

en·large·ment [ɪn'lɑːrdʒmənt] ampliación *f*

en·light·en [ɪn'laɪtn] *v/t* educar

en·list [ɪn'lɪst] **1** *v/i* MIL alistarse **2** *v/t*: **I ~ed his help** conseguí que me ayudara

en·liv·en [ɪn'laɪvn] *v/t* animar

en·mi·ty ['enmətɪ] enemistad *f*

e·nor·mi·ty [ɪ'nɔːrmətɪ] magnitud *f*

e·nor·mous [ɪ'nɔːrməs] *adj* enorme; *satisfaction, patience* inmenso

e·nor·mous·ly [ɪ'nɔːrməslɪ] *adv* enormemente

e·nough [ɪ'nʌf] **1** *adj pron* suficiente, bastante; **will $50 be ~?** ¿llegará con 50 dólares?; **I've had ~!** ¡estoy harto!; **that's ~, calm down!** ¡ya basta, tranquilízate! **2** *adv* suficientemente, bastante; **the bag isn't big ~** la bolsa no es lo suficientemente *or* bastante grande; **strangely ~** curiosamente

en·quire [ɪn'kwaɪr] → **inquire**

en·raged [ɪn'reɪdʒd] *adj* enfurecido

en·rich [ɪn'rɪtʃ] *v/t* enriquecer

en·roll [ɪn'roʊl] *v/i* matricularse

en·roll·ment [ɪn'roʊlmənt] matrícula *f*

en·sue [ɪnˈsuː] v/i sucederse

en suite [ˈɑːnswiːt] adj: ~ *bathroom* baño *m* privado

en·sure [ɪnˈʃʊər] v/t asegurar

en·tail [ɪnˈteɪl] v/t conllevar

en·tan·gle [ɪnˈtæŋgl] v/t *in rope* enredar; *become ~d in* enredarse en; *become ~d with in love affair* liarse con

en·ter [ˈentər] **1** v/t *room, house* entrar en; *competition* participar en; *person, horse in race* inscribir; (*write down*) escribir; COMPUT introducir **2** v/i entrar; THEA entrar en escena; *in competition* inscribirse **3** *n* COMPUT intro *m*

en·ter·prise [ˈentərpraɪz] (*initiative*) iniciativa *f*; (*venture*) empresa *f*

en·ter·pris·ing [ˈentərpraɪzɪŋ] adj con iniciativa

en·ter·tain [entərˈteɪn] **1** v/t (*amuse*) entretener; (*consider: idea*) considerar **2** v/i (*have guests*): *we ~ a lot* recibimos a mucha gente

en·ter·tain·er [entərˈteɪnər] artista *m/f*

en·ter·tain·ing [entərˈteɪnɪŋ] adj entretenido

en·ter·tain·ment [entərˈteɪnmənt] entretenimiento *m*

en·thrall [ɪnˈθrɔːl] v/t cautivar

en·thu·si·asm [ɪnˈθuːzɪæzm] entusiasmo *m*

en·thu·si·ast [ɪnˈθuːzɪˈæst] entusiasta *m/f*

en·thu·si·as·tic [ɪnθuːzɪˈæstɪk] adj entusiasta; *be ~ about sth* estar entusiasmado con algo

en·thu·si·as·tic·al·ly [ɪnθuːzɪˈæstɪklɪ] adv con entusiasmo

en·tice [ɪnˈtaɪs] v/t atraer

en·tire [ɪnˈtaɪr] adj entero; *the ~ school is going* va a ir todo el colegio

en·tire·ly [ɪnˈtaɪrlɪ] adv completamente

en·ti·tle [ɪnˈtaɪtl] v/t: ~ *s.o. to sth* dar derecho a alguien a algo; *be ~d to* tener derecho a

en·ti·tled [ɪnˈtaɪtld] adj *book* titulado

en·trance [ˈentrəns] entrada *f*; THEA entrada *f* en escena

en·tranced [ɪnˈtrænst] adj encantado

'en·trance ex·am(·i·na·tion) examen *m* de acceso

'en·trance fee (cuota *f* de) entrada *f*

en·trant [ˈentrənt] participante *m/f*

en·treat [ɪnˈtriːt] v/t suplicar; ~ *s.o. to do sth* suplicar a alguien que haga algo

en·trenched [ɪnˈtrentʃt] adj *attitudes* arraigado

en·tre·pre·neur [ɑːntrəprəˈnɜːr] empresario(-a) *m(f)*

en·tre·pre·neur·i·al [ɑːntrəprəˈnɜːrɪəl] adj empresarial

en·trust [ɪnˈtrʌst] v/t confiar; ~ *s.o. with sth*, ~ *sth to s.o.* confiar algo a alguien

en·try [ˈentrɪ] entrada *f*; *for competition* inscripción *f*; *in diary etc* entrada *f*; *no ~* prohibida la entrada; *the winning ~ was painted by ...* el cuadro ganador fue pintado por ...

'en·try form impreso *m* de inscripción; **'en·try·phone** portero *m* automático; **'en·try vi·sa** visado *m*

e·nu·me·rate [ɪˈnuːməreɪt] v/t enumerar

en·vel·op [ɪnˈveləp] v/t cubrir

en·ve·lope [ˈenvəloup] sobre *m*

en·vi·a·ble [ˈenvɪəbl] adj envidiable

en·vi·ous [ˈenvɪəs] adj envidioso; *be ~ of s.o.* tener envidia de alguien

en·vi·ron·ment [ɪnˈvaɪrənmənt] (*nature*) medio *m* ambiente; (*surroundings*) entorno *m*, ambiente *m*

en·vi·ron·men·tal [ɪnvaɪrənˈmentl] adj medioambiental

en·vi·ron·men·tal·ist [ɪnvaɪrənˈmentəlɪst] ecologista *m/f*

en·vi·ron·men·tal·ly 'friend·ly [ɪnvaɪrənˈmentəlɪ] adj ecológico, que no daña el medio ambiente

en·vi·ron·men·tal pol'lu·tion contaminación *f* medioambiental

en·vi·ron·men·tal pro'tec·tion protección *f* medioambiental

en·vi·rons [ɪnˈvaɪrənz] npl alrededores *mpl*

en·vis·age [ɪn'vɪzɪdʒ] *v/t* imaginar

en·voy ['envɔɪ] enviado(-a) *m(f)*

en·vy ['envɪ] **1** *n* envidia *f*; **be the ~ of** ser la envidia de **2** *v/t* (*pret & pp -ied*) envidiar; **~ s.o. sth** envidiar a alguien por algo

e·phem·er·al [ɪ'femərəl] *adj* efímero

ep·ic ['epɪk] **1** *n* epopeya *f* **2** *adj journey* épico; **a task of ~ proportions** una tarea monumental

ep·i·cen·ter, *Br* **ep·i·cen·tre** ['epɪsentər] epicentro *m*

ep·i·dem·ic [epɪ'demɪk] epidemia *f*

ep·i·lep·sy ['epɪlepsɪ] epilepsia *f*

ep·i·lep·tic [epɪ'leptɪk] epiléptico(-a) *m(f)*

ep·i·lep·tic '*fit* ataque *m* epiléptico

ep·i·log, *Br* **ep·i·logue** ['epɪlɑːg] epílogo *m*

ep·i·sode ['epɪsoʊd] *of story, soap opera* episodio *m*, capítulo *m*; (*happening*) episodio *m*; *let's forget the whole ~* olvidemos lo sucedido

ep·i·taph ['epɪtæf] epitafio *m*

e·poch ['iːpɑːk] época *f*

e·poch-mak·ing ['iːpɑːkmeɪkɪŋ] *adj* que hace época

e·qual ['iːkwl] **1** *adj* igual; **~ amounts of milk and water** la misma cantidad de leche y de agua; **~ opportunities** igualdad *f* de oportunidades; **be ~ to** *a task* estar capacitado para **2** *n* igual *m/f* **3** *v/t* (*pret & pp -ed*, *Br -led*) *with numbers* equivaler; (*be as good as*) igualar; *four times twelve ~s 48* cuatro por doce, (igual a) cuarenta y ocho

e·qual·i·ty [ɪ'kwɑːlətɪ] igualdad *f*

e·qual·ize ['iːkwəlaɪz] **1** *v/t* igualar **2** *v/i* SP empatar

e·qual·iz·er ['iːkwəlaɪzər] SP gol *m* del empate

e·qual·ly ['iːkwəlɪ] *adv* igualmente; *share, divide* en partes iguales

e·qual 'rights *npl* igualdad *f* de derechos

e·quate [ɪ'kweɪt] *v/t* equiparar

e·qua·tion [ɪ'kweɪʒn] MATH ecuación *f*

e·qua·tor [ɪ'kweɪtər] ecuador *m*

e·qui·lib·ri·um [iːkwɪ'lɪbrɪəm] equilibrio *m*

e·qui·nox ['iːkwɪnɑːks] equinoccio *m*

e·quip [ɪ'kwɪp] *v/t* (*pret & pp -ped*) equipar; *he's not ~ped to handle it fig* no está preparado para llevarlo

e·quip·ment [ɪ'kwɪpmənt] equipo *m*

eq·ui·ty ['ekwətɪ] FIN acciones *fpl* ordinarias

e·quiv·a·lent [ɪ'kwɪvələnt] **1** *adj* equivalente; *be ~ to* equivaler a **2** *n* equivalente *m*

e·ra ['ɪrə] era *f*

e·rad·i·cate [ɪ'rædɪkeɪt] *v/t* erradicar

e·rase [ɪ'reɪz] *v/t* borrar

e·ras·er [ɪ'reɪzər] *for pencil* goma *f* (de borrar); *for chalk* borrador *m*

e·rect [ɪ'rekt] **1** *adj* erguido **2** *v/t* levantar, erigir

e·rec·tion [ɪ'rekʃn] *of building etc* construcción *f*; *of penis* erección *f*

er·go·nom·ic [ɜːrgoʊ'nɑːmɪk] *adj furniture* ergonómico

e·rode [ɪ'roʊd] *v/t also fig* erosionar

e·ro·sion [ɪ'roʊʒn] *also fig* erosión *f*

e·rot·ic [ɪ'rɑːtɪk] *adj* erótico

e·rot·i·cism [ɪ'rɑːtɪsɪzm] erotismo *m*

er·rand ['erənd] recado *m*; *run ~s* hacer recados

er·rat·ic [ɪ'rætɪk] *adj* irregular; *course* errático

er·ror ['erər] error *m*

'er·ror mes·sage COMPUT mensaje *m* de error

e·rupt [ɪ'rʌpt] *v/i of volcano* entrar en erupción; *of violence* brotar; *of person* explotar

e·rup·tion [ɪ'rʌpʃn] *of volcano* erupción *f*; *of violence* brote *m*

es·ca·late ['eskəleɪt] *v/i* intensificarse

es·ca·la·tion [eskə'leɪʃn] intensificación *f*

es·ca·la·tor ['eskəleɪtər] escalera *f* mecánica

es·cape [ɪ'skeɪp] **1** *n of prisoner, animal* fuga *f*; *of gas* escape *m*, fuga *f*; *have a narrow ~* escaparse por los pelos **2** *v/i of prisoner, animal, gas*

es·cap·arse 3 *v/t:* **the word ~s me** no consigo recordar la palabra

es·cape chute AVIA tobogán *m* de emergencia

es·cort 1 *n* ['eskɔːrt] acompañante *m/f*; *(guard)* escolta *m/f*; **under ~** escoltado 2 *v/t* [ɪ'skɔːrt] escoltar; *socially* acompañar

es·pe·cial [ɪ'speʃl] → **special**

es·pe·cial·ly [ɪ'speʃlɪ] *adv* especialmente

es·pi·o·nage ['espɪənɑːʒ] espionaje *m*

es·pres·so (**cof·fee**) [es'presoʊ] café *m* exprés

es·say ['eseɪ] *n creative* redacción *f*; *factual* trabajo *m*

es·sen·tial [ɪ'senʃl] *adj* esencial; **the ~ thing is …** lo esencial es …

es·sen·tial·ly [ɪ'senʃlɪ] *adv* esencialmente

es·tab·lish [ɪ'stæblɪʃ] *v/t company* fundar; *(create, determine)* establecer; **~ o.s. as** establecerse como

es·tab·lish·ment [ɪ'stæblɪʃmənt] *firm, shop etc* establecimiento *m*; **the Establishment** el orden establecido

es·tate [ɪ'steɪt] *(area of land)* finca *f*; *(possessions of dead person)* patrimonio *m*

es·tate a·gen·cy *Br* agencia *f* inmobiliaria

es·thet·ic [ɪs'θetɪk] *adj* estético

es·ti·mate ['estɪmət] 1 *n* estimación *f*; *for job* presupuesto *m* 2 *v/t* estimar; **~d time of arrival** hora *f* estimada de llegada

es·ti·ma·tion [estɪ'meɪʃn] estima *f*; **he has gone up/down in my ~** le tengo en más/menos estima; **in my ~** *(opinion)* a mi parecer

es·tranged [ɪs'treɪndʒd] *adj wife, husband* separado

es·tu·a·ry ['estʃəwerɪ] estuario *m*

ETA [iːtiː'eɪ] *abbr* (= **estimated time of arrival**) hora *f* estimada de llegada

etc [et'setrə] *abbr* (= **et cetera**) etc (= etcétera)

etch·ing ['etʃɪŋ] aguafuerte *m*

e·ter·nal [ɪ'tɜːrnl] *adj* eterno

e·ter·ni·ty [ɪ'tɜːrnətɪ] eternidad *f*

eth·i·cal ['eθɪkl] *adj* ético

eth·ics ['eθɪks] ética *f*; **code of ~** código *m* ético

eth·nic ['eθnɪk] *adj* étnico

eth·nic 'group grupo *m* étnico

eth·nic mi'nor·i·ty minoría *f* étnica

EU [iː'juː] *abbr* (= **European Union**) UE *f* (=Unión *f* Europea)

eu·phe·mism ['juːfəmɪzm] eufemismo *m*

eu·pho·ri·a [juː'fɔːrɪə] euforia *f*

eu·ro ['jʊroʊ] euro *m*

Eu·rope ['jʊrəp] Europa

Eu·ro·pe·an [jʊrə'pɪən] 1 *adj* europeo 2 *n* europeo(-a) *m(f)*

Eu·ro·pe·an Com'mis·sion Comisión *f* Europea; **Eu·ro·pe·an 'Par·lia·ment** Parlamento *m* Europeo; **Eu·ro'pe·an plan** media pensión *f*; **Eu·ro·pe·an 'Un·ion** Unión *f* Europea

eu·tha·na·si·a [juːθə'neɪzɪə] eutanasia *f*

e·vac·u·ate [ɪ'vækjueɪt] *v/t* evacuar

e·vade [ɪ'veɪd] *v/t* evadir

e·val·u·ate [ɪ'væljueɪt] *v/t* evaluar

e·val·u·a·tion [ɪvæljuˈeɪʃn] evaluación *f*

e·van·gel·ist [ɪ'vændʒəlɪst] evangelista *m/f*

e·vap·o·rate [ɪ'væpəreɪt] *v/i of water* evaporarse; *of confidence* desvanecerse

e·vap·o·ra·tion [ɪvæpə'reɪʃn] *of water* evaporación *f*

e·va·sion [ɪ'veɪʒn] evasión *f*

e·va·sive [ɪ'veɪsɪv] *adj* evasivo

eve [iːv] víspera *f*

e·ven ['iːvn] 1 *adj* (*regular*) regular; (*level*) llano; *number* par; *distribution* igualado; **I'll get ~ with him** me las pagará 2 *adv* incluso; **~ bigger/better** incluso *or* aún mayor/mejor; **not ~** ni siquiera; **~ so** aun así; **~ if** aunque; **~ if he begged me** aunque me lo suplicara 3 *v/t:* **~ the score** empatar, igualar el marcador

eve·ning ['iːvnɪŋ] tarde *f*; *after dark*

noche f; **in** the ~ por la tarde / noche; **this** ~ esta tarde / noche; **yesterday** ~ anoche f; **good** ~ buenas noches

'eve·ning class clase f nocturna; 'eve·ning dress **for woman** traje f de noche; **for man** traje f de etiqueta; eve·ning 'pa·per periódico m de la tarde or vespertino

e·ven·ly ['i:vnlɪ] adv (**regularly**) regularmente

e·vent [ɪ'vent] acontecimiento m; SP prueba f; **at all ~s** en cualquier caso

e·vent·ful [ɪ'ventfəl] adj agitado, lleno de incidentes

e·ven·tu·al [ɪ'ventʃuəl] adj final

e·ven·tu·al·ly [ɪ'ventʃuəlɪ] adv finalmente

ev·er ['evər] adv: **if I ~ hear you ...** como te oiga ...; **have you ~ been to Colombia?** ¿has estado alguna vez en Colombia?; **for** ~ siempre; ~ **since** desde entonces; ~ **since she found out about it** desde que se enteró de ello; ~ **since I've known him** desde que lo conozco

ev·er·green ['evərgri:n] n árbol m de hoja perenne

ev·er·last·ing [evər'læstɪŋ] adj **love** eterno

ev·ery ['evrɪ] adj cada; **I see him ~ day** le veo todos los días; **you have ~ reason to ...** tienes toda la razón para ...; **one in ~ ten** uno de cada diez; ~ **other day** cada dos días; ~ **now and then** de vez en cuando

ev·ery·bod·y ['evrɪbɑːdɪ] → everyone

ev·ery·day ['evrɪdeɪ] adj cotidiano

ev·ery·one ['evrɪwʌn] pron todo el mundo

ev·ery·thing ['evrɪθɪŋ] pron todo

ev·ery·where ['evrɪwer] adv en or por todos sitios; (**wherever**) dondequiera que

e·vict [ɪ'vɪkt] v/t desahuciar

ev·i·dence ['evɪdəns] **also** LAW prueba(s) f(pl); **give** ~ prestar declaración

ev·i·dent ['evɪdənt] adj evidente

ev·i·dent·ly ['evɪdəntlɪ] adv (**clearly**)

evidentemente; (**apparently**) aparentemente, al parecer

e·vil ['i:vl] **1** adj malo **2** n mal m

e·voke [ɪ'vouk] v/t **image** evocar

ev·o·lu·tion [i:və'lu:ʃn] evolución f

e·volve [ɪ'vɑːlv] v/i evolucionar

ewe [ju:] oveja f

ex- [eks] pref ex-

ex [eks] F (**former wife, husband**) ex m/f F

ex·act [ɪg'zækt] adj exacto

ex·act·ing [ɪg'zæktɪŋ] adj exigente; **task** duro

ex·act·ly [ɪg'zæktlɪ] adv exactamente

ex·ag·ge·rate [ɪg'zædʒəreɪt] v/t & v/i exagerar

ex·ag·ge·ra·tion [ɪgzædʒə'reɪʃn] exageración f

ex·am [ɪg'zæm] examen m; **take an** ~ hacer un examen; **pass / fail an** ~ aprobar / suspender un examen

ex·am·i·na·tion [ɪgzæmɪ'neɪʃn] examen m; **of patient** reconocimiento m

ex·am·ine [ɪg'zæmɪn] v/t examinar; **patient** reconocer

ex·am·in·er [ɪg'zæmɪnər] EDU examinador(a) m(f)

ex·am·ple [ɪg'zæmpl] ejemplo m; **for** ~ por ejemplo; **set a good / bad** ~ dar buen / mal ejemplo

ex·as·pe·rat·ed [ɪg'zæspəreɪtɪd] adj exasperado

ex·as·pe·rat·ing [ɪg'zæspəreɪtɪŋ] adj exasperante

ex·ca·vate ['ekskəveɪt] v/t excavar

ex·ca·va·tion [ekskə'veɪʃn] excavación f

ex·ca·va·tor ['ekskəveɪtər] excavadora f

ex·ceed [ɪk'si:d] v/t (**be more than**) exceder; (**go beyond**) sobrepasar

ex·ceed·ing·ly [ɪk'si:dɪŋlɪ] adv sumamente

ex·cel [ɪk'sel] **1** v/i (**pret & pp -led**) sobresalir (**at** en) **2** v/t (**pret & pp -led**): ~ **o.s.** superarse a sí mismo

ex·cel·lence ['eksələns] excelencia f

ex·cel·lent ['eksələnt] adj excelente

ex·cept [ɪk'sept] prep excepto; ~ **for** a excepción de; ~ **that** sólo que ex·cep·tion [ɪk'sepʃn] excepción *f*; **with the ~ of** a excepción de; **take ~ to** molestarse por

ex·cep·tion·al [ɪk'sepʃnl] *adj* excepcional

ex·cep·tion·al·ly [ɪk'sepʃnlɪ] *adv* (*extremely*) excepcionalmente

ex·cerpt ['eksɜːrpt] extracto *m*

ex·cess [ɪk'ses] **1** *n* exceso *m*; **eat/drink to ~** comer/beber en exceso; **in ~ of** superior a **2** *adj* excedente

ex·cess 'bag·gage exceso *m* de equipaje

ex·cess 'fare suplemento *m*

ex·ces·sive [ɪk'sesɪv] *adj* excesivo

ex·change [iks'tʃeɪndʒ] **1** *n* intercambio *m*; **in ~** a cambio (**for** de) **2** *v/t* cambiar

ex'change rate FIN tipo *m* de cambio

ex·ci·ta·ble [ɪk'saɪtəbl] *adj* excitable

ex·cite [ɪk'saɪt] *v/t* (*make enthusiastic*) entusiasmar

ex·cit·ed [ɪk'saɪtɪd] *adj* emocionado, excitado; *sexually* excitado; **get ~** emocionarse; **get ~ about** emocionarse *or* excitarse con

ex·cite·ment [ɪk'saɪtmənt] emoción *f*, excitación *f*

ex·cit·ing [ɪk'saɪtɪŋ] *adj* emocionante, excitante

ex·claim [ɪk'skleɪm] *v/t* exclamar

ex·cla·ma·tion [eksklə'meɪʃn] exclamación *f*

ex·cla·ma·tion point signo *m* de admiración

ex·clude [ɪk'skluːd] *v/t* excluir; *possibility* descartar

ex·clud·ing [ɪk'skluːdɪŋ] *prep* excluyendo

ex·clu·sive [ɪk'skluːsɪv] *adj* exclusivo

ex·com·mu·ni·cate [ekskə'mjuːnɪkeɪt] *v/t* REL excomulgar

ex·cru·ci·a·ting [ɪk'skruːʃɪeɪtɪŋ] *adj* *pain* terrible

ex·cur·sion [ɪk'skɜːrʃn] excursión *f*

ex·cuse **1** *n* [ɪk'skjuːs] excusa *f* **2** *v/t* [ɪk'skjuːz] (*forgive*) excusar, perdonar; (*allow to leave*) disculpar; **~ s.o.**

from sth dispensar a alguien de algo; **~ me** *to get past, interrupting* perdone, disculpe; *to get attention* perdone, oiga

e·x·e·cute ['eksɪkjuːt] *v/t* *criminal, plan* ejecutar

ex·e·cu·tion [eksɪ'kjuːʃn] *of criminal, plan* ejecución *f*

ex·e·cu·tion·er [eksɪ'kjuːʃnər] verdugo *m*

ex·ec·u·tive [ɪg'zekjʊtɪv] ejecutivo(-a) *m(f)*

ex·ec·u·tive 'brief·case maletín *m* de ejecutivo

ex·ec·u·tive 'wash·room baño *m* para ejecutivos

ex·em·pla·ry [ɪg'zemplərɪ] *adj* ejemplar

ex·empt [ɪg'zempt] *adj* exento; **be ~ from** estar exento de

ex·er·cise ['eksərsaɪz] **1** *n* ejercicio *m*; **take ~** hacer ejercicio **2** *v/t* *muscle* ejercitar; *dog* pasear; *caution* proceder con; **~ restraint** controlarse **3** *v/i* hacer ejercicio

'ex·er·cise bike bicicleta *f* estática

'ex·er·cise book EDU cuaderno de ejercicios

ex·ert [ɪg'zɜːrt] *v/t* *authority* ejercer; **~ o.s.** esforzarse

ex·er·tion [ɪg'zɜːrʃn] esfuerzo *m*

ex·hale [eks'heɪl] *v/t* exhalar

ex·haust [ɪg'zɔːst] **1** *n* *fumes* gases *mpl* de la combustión; *pipe* tubo *m* de escape **2** *v/t* (*tire*) cansar; (*use up*) agotar

ex·haust·ed [ɪg'zɔːstɪd] *adj* (*tired*) agotado

ex'haust fumes *npl* gases *mpl* de la combustión

ex·haust·ing [ɪg'zɔːstɪŋ] *adj* agotador

ex·haus·tion [ɪg'zɔːstʃn] agotamiento *m*

ex·haus·tive [ɪg'zɔːstɪv] *adj* exhaustivo

ex'haust pipe tubo *m* de escape

ex·hib·it [ɪg'zɪbɪt] **1** *n* *in exhibition* objeto *m* expuesto **2** *v/t* *of gallery* exhibir; *of artist* exponer; (*give evidence of*) mostrar

ex·hi·bi·tion [eksı'bıʃn] exposición *f*; *of bad behavior, skill* exhibición *f*

ex·hi·bi·tion·ist [eksı'bıʃnıst] exhibicionista *m/f*

ex·hil·a·rat·ing [ıg'zıləreıtıŋ] *adj* estimulante

ex·ile ['eksaıl] **1** *n* exilio *m*; *person* exiliado(-a) *m(f)* **2** *v/t* exiliar

ex·ist [ıg'zıst] *v/i* existir; **~ on** subsistir a base de

ex·ist·ence [ıg'zıstəns] existencia *f*; **be in ~** existir; **come into ~** crearse, nacer

ex·ist·ing [ıg'zıstıŋ] *adj* existente

ex·it ['eksıt] **1** *n* salida *f*; THEA salida *f*, mutis *m* **2** *v/i* COMPUT salir

ex·on·e·rate [ıg'zɑːnəreıt] *v/t* exonerar de

ex·or·bi·tant [ıg'zɔːrbıtənt] *adj* exorbitante

ex·ot·ic [ıg'zɑːtık] *adj* exótico

ex·pand [ık'spænd] **1** *v/t* expandir **2** *v/i* expandirse; *of metal* dilatarse
♦ **expand on** *v/t* desarrollar

ex·panse [ık'spæns] extensión *f*

ex·pan·sion [ık'spænʃn] expansión *f*; *of metal* dilatación *f*

ex·pa·tri·ate [eks'pætrıət] **1** *adj* expatriado **2** *n* expatriado(-a) *m(f)*

ex·pect [ık'spekt] **1** *v/t* esperar; (*suppose*) suponer, imaginar(se); (*demand*) exigir **2** *v/i*: **be ~ing** (*be pregnant*) estar en estado; **I ~ so** eso espero, creo que sí

ex·pec·tant [ık'spektənt] *adj crowd* expectante

ex·pec·tant 'moth·er futura madre *f*

ex·pec·ta·tion [ekspek'teıʃn] expectativa *f*

ex·pe·di·ent [ık'spiːdıənt] *adj* oportuno, conveniente

ex·pe·di·tion [ekspı'dıʃn] expedición *f*

ex·pel [ık'spel] *v/t* (*pret & pp* **-led**) *person* expulsar

ex·pend [ık'spend] *v/t energy* gastar

ex·pend·a·ble [ık'spendəbl] *adj person* prescindible

ex·pen·di·ture [ık'spendıtʃər] gasto *m*

ex·pense [ık'spens] gasto *m*; **at great ~** gastando mucho dinero; **at the company's ~** a cargo de la empresa; **a joke at my ~** una broma a costa mía; **at the ~ of his health** a costa de su salud

ex'pense ac·count cuenta *f* de gastos

ex·pen·ses [ık'spensız] *npl* gastos *mpl*

ex·pen·sive [ık'spensıv] *adj* caro

ex·pe·ri·ence [ık'spırıəns] **1** *n* experiencia *f* **2** *v/t* experimentar

ex·pe·ri·enced [ık'spırıənst] *adj* experimentado

ex·per·i·ment [ık'sperımənt] **1** *n* experimento *m* **2** *v/i* experimentar; **~ on animals** experimentar con; **~ with** (*try out*) probar

ex·per·i·men·tal [ıksperı'mentl] *adj* experimental

ex·pert ['ekspɜːrt] **1** *adj* experto **2** *n* experto(-a) *m(f)*

ex·pert ad'vice la opinión de un experto

ex·per·tise [ekspɜːr'tiːz] destreza *f*, pericia *f*

ex·pire [ık'spaır] *v/i* caducar

ex·pi·ry [ık'spaırı] *of lease, contract* vencimiento *m*; *of passport* caducidad *f*

ex'pi·ry date *of food, passport* fecha *f* de caducidad; **be past its ~** haber caducado

ex·plain [ık'spleın] **1** *v/t* explicar **2** *v/i* explicarse

ex·pla·na·tion [eksplə'neıʃn] explicación *f*

ex·plan·a·to·ry [ık'splænətɔːrı] *adj* explicativo

ex·plic·it [ık'splısıt] *adj instructions* explícito

ex·plic·it·ly [ık'splısıtlı] *adv state* explícitamente; *forbid* terminantemente

ex·plode [ık'sploud] **1** *v/i of bomb* explotar **2** *v/t bomb* hacer explotar

ex·ploit¹ ['eksplɔıt] *n* hazaña *f*

ex·ploit² [ık'splɔıt] *v/t person, resources* explotar

ex·ploi·ta·tion [eksplɔɪˈteɪʃn] *of person* explotación *f*

ex·plo·ra·tion [ekspləˈreɪʃn] exploración *f*

ex·plor·a·to·ry [ɪkˈsplɑːrətɔrɪ] *adj surgery* exploratorio

ex·plore [ɪkˈsplɔːr] *v/t country etc* explorar; *possibility* estudiar

ex·plor·er [ɪkˈsplɔːrər] explorador(a) *m(f)*

ex·plo·sion [ɪkˈsploʊʒn] *of bomb, in population* explosión *f*

ex·plo·sive [ɪkˈsploʊsɪv] *n* explosivo *m*

ex·port [ˈekspɔːrt] **1** *n action* exportación *f*; *item* producto *m* de exportación; **~s** *npl* exportaciones *fpl* **2** *v/t also* COMPUT exportar

ˈex·port cam·paign campaña *f* de exportación

ex·port·er [ˈekspɔːrtər] exportador(a) *m(f)*

ex·pose [ɪkˈspoʊz] *v/t (uncover)* exponer; *scandal* sacar a la luz; **he's been ~d as a liar** ha quedado como un mentiroso

ex·po·sure [ɪkˈspoʊʒər] exposición *f*; PHOT foto(grafía) *f*

ex·press [ɪkˈspres] **1** *adj (fast)* rápido; *(explicit)* expreso **2** *n train* expreso *m*; *bus* autobús *m* directo **3** *v/t* expresar; **~ o.s. well / clearly** expresarse bien / con claridad

ex·press el·e·va·tor ascensor rápido que sólo para en algunos pisos

ex·pres·sion [ɪkˈspreʃn] *voiced* muestra *f*; *phrase, on face* expresión *f*; **read with ~** leer con sentimiento

ex·pres·sive [ɪkˈspresɪv] *adj* expresivo

ex·press·ly [ɪkˈspreslɪ] *adv state* expresamente; *forbid* terminantemente

ex·press·way [ɪkˈspreswei] autopista *f*

ex·pul·sion [ɪkˈspʌlʃn] *from school, of diplomat* expulsión *f*

ex·qui·site [ekˈskwɪzɪt] *adj (beautiful)* exquisito

ex·tend [ɪkˈstend] **1** *v/t house, investigation* ampliar; *(make wider)* ensanchar; *(make bigger)* agrandar; *runway, path* alargar; *contract, visa* prorrogar; *thanks, congratulations* extender **2** *v/i of garden etc* llegar

ex·ten·sion [ɪkˈstenʃn] *to house* ampliación *f*; *of contract, visa* prórroga *f*; TELEC extensión *f*

ex·ten·sion ca·ble cable *m* de extensión

ex·ten·sive [ɪkˈstensɪv] *adj damage* cuantioso; *knowledge* considerable; *search* extenso, amplio

ex·tent [ɪkˈstent] alcance *m*; **to such an ~ that** hasta el punto de que; **to a certain ~** hasta cierto punto

ex·ten·u·at·ing cir·cum·stan·ces [ɪkˈstenueitiŋ] *npl* circunstancias *fpl* atenuantes

ex·te·ri·or [ɪkˈstɪrɪər] **1** *adj* exterior **2** *n* exterior *m*

ex·ter·mi·nate [ɪkˈstɜːrmɪneɪt] *v/t* exterminar

ex·ter·nal [ɪkˈstɜːrnl] *adj (outside)* exterior, externo

ex·tinct [ɪkˈstɪŋkt] *adj species* extinguido

ex·tinc·tion [ɪkˈstɪŋkʃn] *of species* extinción *f*

ex·tin·guish [ɪkˈstɪŋgwɪʃ] *v/t fire* extinguir, apagar; *cigarette* apagar

ex·tin·guish·er [ɪkˈstɪŋgwɪʃər] extintor *m*

ex·tort [ɪkˈstɔːrt] *v/t* obtener mediante extorsión; **~ money from** extorsionar a

ex·tor·tion [ɪkˈstɔːrʃn] extorsión *f*

ex·tor·tion·ate [ɪkˈstɔːrʃənət] *adj prices* desorbitado

ex·tra [ˈekstrə] **1** *n* extra *m*; *in movie* extra *m/f* **2** *adj* extra; **meals are ~** las comidas se pagan aparte; **that's $1 ~** cuesta 1 dólar más **3** *adv* super; **~ strong** extrafuerte; **~ special** muy especial

ex·tra ˈcharge recargo *m*

ex·tract[1] [ˈekstrækt] *n* extracto *m*

ex·tract[2] [ɪkˈstrækt] *v/t* sacar; *coal, oil, tooth* extraer; *information* sonsacar

ex·trac·tion [ɪkˈstrækʃn] *of oil, coal, tooth* extracción *f*

ex·tra·dite ['ekstrədaɪt] v/t extraditar

ex·tra·di·tion [ekstrə'dɪʃn] extradición f

ex·tra·di·tion trea·ty tratado m de extradición

ex·tra·mar·i·tal [ekstrə'mærɪtl] adj extramarital

ex·tra·or·di·nar·i·ly [ekstrɔ:rdɪn'erɪlɪ] adv extraordinariamente

ex·tra·or·di·na·ry [ɪk'strɔ:rdɪnerɪ] adj extraordinario

ex·trav·a·gance [ɪk'strævəgəns] with money despilfarro m; of claim etc extravagancia f

ex·trav·a·gant [ɪk'strævəgənt] adj with money despilfarrador; claim etc extravagante

ex·treme [ɪk'stri:m] **1** n extremo m **2** adj extremo; views extremista

ex·treme·ly [ɪk'stri:mlɪ] adv extremadamente, sumamente

ex·trem·ist [ɪk'stri:mɪst] extremista

m/f

ex·tri·cate ['ekstrɪkeɪt] v/t liberar

ex·tro·vert ['ekstrəvɜ:rt] **1** adj extrovertido **2** n extrovertido(-a) m(f)

ex·u·be·rant [ɪg'zu:bərənt] adj exuberante

ex·ult [ɪg'zʌlt] v/i exultar

eye [aɪ] **1** n of person, needle ojo m; **keep an ~ on** (look after) estar pendiente de; (monitor) estar pendiente de, vigilar **2** v/t mirar

'**eye·ball** globo m ocular; '**eye·brow** ceja f; '**eye-catch·ing** adj llamativo; '**eye·glass·es** npl gafas fpl, L.Am. anteojos mpl, L.Am. lentes mpl; '**eye·lash** pestaña f; '**eye·lid** párpado m; '**eye·lin·er** lápiz m de ojos; '**eye·sha·dow** sombra f de ojos; '**eye·sight** vista f; '**eye·sore** engendro m, monstruosidad f; '**eye strain** vista f cansada; '**eye·wit·ness** testigo m/f ocular

F

F abbr (= **Fahrenheit**) F

fab·ric ['fæbrɪk] (material) tejido m

fab·u·lous ['fæbjʊləs] adj fabuloso, estupendo

fab·u·lous·ly ['fæbjʊləslɪ] adv · rich tremendamente; beautiful increíblemente

fa·çade [fə'sɑ:d] of building, person fachada f

face [feɪs] **1** n cara f; **~ to ~** cara a cara; **lose ~** padecer una humillación **2** v/t (be opposite) estar enfrente de; (confront) enfrentarse de

♦ **face up to** v/t hacer frente a

'**face·cloth** toallita f; '**face·lift** lifting m, estiramiento m de piel; '**face pack** mascarilla f (facial); **face 'val·ue: take sth at ~** tomarse algo literalmente

fa·cial ['feɪʃl] n limpieza f de cutis

fa·cil·i·tate [fə'sɪlɪteɪt] v/t facilitar

fa·cil·i·ties [fə'sɪlɪtɪz] npl instalaciones fpl

fact [fækt] hecho m; **in ~, as a matter of ~** de hecho

fac·tion ['fækʃn] facción f

fac·tor ['fæktər] factor m

fac·to·ry ['fæktərɪ] fábrica f

fac·ul·ty ['fækəltɪ] (hearing etc), at university facultad f

fad [fæd] moda f

fade [feɪd] v/i of colors desteñirse, perder color; of memories desvanecerse

fad·ed ['feɪdɪd] adj color, jeans desteñido, descolorido

fag¹ [fæg] F (homosexual) maricón m

fag² [fæg] *Br* F (*cigarette*) pitillo *m* F
Fahr·en·heit ['færənhaɪt] *adj* Fahrenheit
fail [feɪl] **1** *v/i* fracasar; *of plan* fracasar, fallar **2** *v/t exam* suspender **3** *n*: **without ~** sin falta
fail·ing ['feɪlɪŋ] *n* fallo *m*
fail·ure ['feɪljər] fracaso *m*; *in exam* suspenso *m*; **I feel such a ~** me siento un fracasado
faint [feɪnt] **1** *adj line, smile* tenue; *smell, noise* casi imperceptible **2** *v/i* desmayarse
faint·ly ['feɪntlɪ] *adv smile, smell* levemente
fair¹ [fer] *n* COM feria *f*
fair² [fer] *adj hair* rubio; *complexion* claro; (*just*) justo
fair·ly ['ferlɪ] *adv treat* justamente, con justicia; (*quite*) bastante
fair·ness ['fernɪs] *of treatment* imparcialidad *f*
fair·y ['ferɪ] hada *f*
'fair·y tale cuento *m* de hadas
faith [feɪθ] fe *f*, confianza *f*; REL fe *f*
faith·ful ['feɪθfəl] *adj* fiel; **be ~ to one's partner** ser fiel a la pareja
faith·ful·ly ['feɪθfəlɪ] *adv* religiosamente
fake [feɪk] **1** *n* falsificación *f* **2** *adj* falso **3** *v/t* (*forge*) falsificar; (*feign*) fingir
Falk·land Is·lands ['fɔːlklənd] *npl*: **the ~** las Islas Malvinas
fall¹ [fɔːl] *n season* otoño *m*
fall² [fɔːl] **1** *v/i* (*pret* **fell**, *pp* **fallen**) *of person* caerse; *of government, prices, temperature, night* caer; **it ~s on a Tuesday** cae en martes; **~ ill** enfermar, caer enfermo; **I fell off the wall** me caí del muro **2** *n* caída *f*
♦ **fall back on** *v/t* recurrir a
♦ **fall behind** *v/i with work, studies* retrasarse
♦ **fall down** *v/i* caerse
♦ **fall for** *v/t person* enamorarse de; (*be deceived by*) dejarse engañar por; **I'm amazed you fell for it** me sorprende mucho que picaras
♦ **fall out** *v/i of hair* caerse; (*argue*) pelearse

♦ **fall over** *v/i* caerse
♦ **fall through** *v/i of plans* venirse abajo
fal·len ['fɔːlən] *pp → **fall***
fal·li·ble ['fæləbl] *adj* falible
'fall·out lluvia *f* radiactiva
false [fɑːls] *adj* falso
false a'larm falsa alarma *f*
false·ly ['fɑːlslɪ] *adv*: **be ~ accused of sth** ser acusado falsamente de algo
false 'start *in race* salida *f* nula
false 'teeth *npl* dentadura *f* postiza
fal·si·fy ['fɑːlsɪfaɪ] *v/t* (*pret & pp* **-ied**) falsificar
fame [feɪm] fama *f*
fa·mil·i·ar [fə'mɪljər] *adj* familiar; **get ~** (*intimate*) tomarse demasiadas confianzas; **be ~ with sth** estar familiarizado con algo; **that looks ~** eso me resulta familiar; **that sounds ~** me suena
fa·mil·i·ar·i·ty [fəmɪlɪ'ærɪtɪ] *with subject etc* familiaridad *f*
fa·mil·i·ar·ize [fə'mɪljəraɪz] *v/t*: **~ o.s. with ...** familiarizarse con ...
fam·i·ly ['fæməlɪ] familia *f*
fam·i·ly 'doc·tor médico *m/f* de familia; **'fam·i·ly name** apellido *m*; **fam·i·ly 'plan·ning** planificación *f* familiar; **fam·i·ly 'plan·ning clin·ic** clínica *f* de planificación familiar; **fam·i·ly 'tree** árbol *m* genealógico
fam·ine ['fæmɪn] hambruna *f*
fam·ished ['fæmɪʃt] *adj* F: **I'm ~** estoy muerto de hambre F
fa·mous ['feɪməs] *adj* famoso; **be ~ for ...** ser famoso por ...
fan¹ [fæn] *n* (*supporter*) seguidor(a) *m(f)*; *of singer, band* admirador(a) *m(f)*, fan *m/f*
fan² [fæn] **1** *n electric* ventilador *m*; *handheld* abanico *m* **2** *v/t* (*pret & pp* **-ned**) abanicar; **~ o.s.** abanicarse
fa·nat·ic [fə'nætɪk] *n* fanático(-a) *m(f)*
fa·nat·i·cal [fə'nætɪkl] *adj* fanático
fa·nat·i·cism [fə'nætɪsɪzm] fanatismo *m*
'fan belt MOT correa *f* del ventilador

'**fan club** club *m* de fans

fan·cy '**dress** disfraz *m*

fan·cy-'dress par·ty fiesta *f* de disfraces

fang [fæŋ] colmillo *m*

'**fan mail** cartas *fpl* de los fans

'**fan·ny pack** ['fænɪ] riñonera *f*

fan·ta·size ['fæntəsaɪz] *v/i* fantasear (**about** sobre)

fan·tas·tic [fæn'tæstɪk] *adj* (*very good*) fantástico, excelente; (*very big*) inmenso

fan·tas·tic·al·ly [fæn'tæstɪklɪ] *adv* (*extremely*) sumamente, increíblemente

fan·ta·sy ['fæntəsɪ] fantasía *f*

far [fɑːr] *adv* lejos; (*much*) mucho; ~ **bigger**/ **faster** mucho más grande / rápido; ~ **away** lejos; **how ~ is it to ...?** ¿a cuánto está ...?; **as ~ as the corner**/ **hotel** hasta la esquina / el hotel; **as ~ as I can see** tal y como lo veo yo; **as ~ as I know** que yo sepa; **you've gone too ~** *in behavior* te has pasado; **so ~ so good** por ahora muy bien

farce [fɑːrs] farsa *f*

fare [fer] *n price* tarifa *f*; *actual money* dinero *m*

Far 'East Lejano Oriente *m*

fare·well [fer'wel] *n* despedida *f*

fare·well par·ty fiesta *f* de despedida

far-fetched [fɑːr'fetʃt] *adj* inverosímil, exagerado

farm [fɑːrm] *n* granja *f*

farm·er ['fɑːrmər] granjero(-a) *m(f)*

'**farm·house** granja *f*, alquería F

farm·ing ['fɑːrmɪŋ] *n* agricultura *f*

'**farm·work·er** trabajador(a) *m(f)* del campo

'**farm·yard** corral *m*

far-'off *adj* lejano

far·sight·ed [fɑːr'saɪtɪd] *adj* previsor; *optically* hipermétrope

fart [fɑːrt] **1** *n* F pedo *m* F **2** *v/i* F tirarse un pedo F

far·ther ['fɑːðər] *adv* más lejos; ~ **away** más allá, más lejos

far·thest ['fɑːðəst] *adv travel etc* más lejos

fas·ci·nate ['fæsɪneɪt] *v/t* fascinar; **be ~d by ...** estar fascinado por ...

fas·ci·nat·ing ['fæsɪneɪtɪŋ] *adj* fascinante

fas·ci·na·tion [fæsɪ'neɪʃn] fascinación *f*

fas·cism ['fæʃɪzm] fascismo *m*

fas·cist ['fæʃɪst] **1** *n* fascista *m/f* **2** *adj* fascista

fash·ion ['fæʃn] *n* moda *f*; (*manner*) modo *m*, manera *f*; **in** ~ de moda; **out of** ~ pasado de moda

fash·ion·a·ble ['fæʃnəbl] *adj* de moda

fash·ion·a·bly ['fæʃnəblɪ] *adv dressed* a la moda

'**fash·ion-con·scious** *adj* que sigue la moda; '**fash·ion de·sign·er** modisto(-a) *m(f)*; '**fash·ion mag·a·zine** revista *f* de modas; '**fash·ion show** desfile *f* de moda, pase *m* de modelos

fast[1] [fæst] **1** *adj* rápido; **be ~** *of clock* ir adelantado **2** *adv* rápido; **stuck** ~ atascado; ~ **asleep** profundamente dormido

fast[2] [fæst] *n not eating* ayuno *m*

fas·ten ['fæsn] **1** *v/t window, lid* cerrar (*poniendo el cierre*); *dress* abrochar; ~ **sth onto sth** asegurar algo a algo **2** *v/i of dress etc* abrocharse

fas·ten·er ['fæsnər] *for dress, lid* cierre *f*

fast 'food comida *f* rápida; **fast-food 'res·tau·rant** restaurante *f* de comida rápida; **fast 'for·ward 1** *n on video etc* avance *m* rápido **2** *v/i* avanzar; '**fast lane** *on road* carril *m* rápido; **in the** ~ *fig: of life* con un tren de vida acelerado; '**fast train** (tren *m*) rápido *m*

fat [fæt] **1** *adj* gordo **2** *n on meat, for baking* grasa *f*

fa·tal ['feɪtl] *adj illness* mortal; *error* fatal

fa·tal·i·ty [fə'tælətɪ] víctima *f* mortal

fa·tal·ly ['feɪtlɪ] *adv* mortalmente; ~ **injured** herido mortalmente

fate [feɪt] destino *m*

fat·ed ['feɪtɪd] *adj*: **be ~ to do sth** estar predestinado a hacer algo 'fat-free *adj* sin grasas

fa·ther ['fɑ:ðər] *n* padre *m*; *Father Martin* REL el Padre Martin

fa·ther·hood ['fɑ:ðərhʊd] paternidad *f*

'fa·ther-in-law (*pl* *fathers-in-law*) suegro *m*

fa·ther·ly ['fɑ:ðəlɪ] *adj* paternal

fath·om ['fæðəm] *n* NAUT braza *f*

♦fathom out *v/t fig* entender

fa·tigue [fə'ti:g] *n* cansancio *m*, fatiga *f*

fat·so ['fætsoʊ] F gordinflón (-ona) *m(f)* F

fat·ten ['fætn] *v/t animal* engordar

fat·ty ['fætɪ] **1** *adj* graso **2** *n* (*person*) gordinflón (-ona) *m(f)*

fau·cet ['fɒːsɪt] *Span* grifo *m*, *L.Am.* llave *f*

fault [fɒːlt] *n* (*defect*) fallo *m*; *it's your/my ~* es culpa tuya/mía; *find ~ with ...* encontrar defectos a ...

fault·less ['fɒːltlɪs] *adj* impecable

fault·y ['fɒːltɪ] *adj goods* defectuoso

fa·vor ['feɪvər] **1** *n* favor *m*; *do s.o. a ~* hacer un favor a alguien; *do me a ~!* (*don't be stupid*) ¡haz el favor!; *in ~ of ...* a favor de ...; *be in ~ of ...* estar a favor de ... **2** *v/t* (*prefer*) preferir

fa·vo·ra·ble ['feɪvərəbl] *adj reply etc* favorable

fa·vo·rite ['feɪvərɪt] **1** *n* favorito(-a) *m(f)*; *food* comida *f* favorita **2** *adj* favorito

fa·vor·it·ism ['feɪvrɪtɪzm] favoritismo *m*

fa·vour *etc Br* → *favor etc*

fax [fæks] **1** *n* fax *m*; *send sth by ~* enviar algo por fax **2** *v/t* enviar por fax: ~ *sth to s.o.* enviar algo por fax a alguien

FBI [efbiː'aɪ] *abbr* (= *Federal Bureau of Investigation*) FBI *m*

fear [fɪr] **1** *n* miedo *m*, temor *m* **2** *v/t* temer, tener miedo a

fear·less ['fɪrlɪs] *adj* valiente, audaz

fear·less·ly ['fɪrlɪslɪ] *adv* sin miedo

fea·si·bil·i·ty stud·y ['fiːzə'bɪlətɪ] estudio *m* de viabilidad

fea·si·ble ['fiːzəbl] *adj* factible,

viable

feast [fiːst] *n* banquete *m*, festín *m*

feat [fiːt] *n* hazaña *f*, proeza *f*

fea·ther ['feðər] pluma *f*

fea·ture ['fiːtʃər] **1** *n* *on face* rasgo *m*, facción *f*; *of city, building, plan, style* característica *f*; *article in paper* reportaje *m*; *movie* largometraje *f*; *make a ~ of ...* destacar ... **2** *v/t: a movie featuring ...* una película en la que aparece ...

'fea·ture film largometraje *m*

Feb·ru·a·ry ['februeri] febrero *m*

fed [fed] *pret & pp* → *feed*

fed·e·ral ['fedərəl] *adj* federal

fed·e·ra·tion [fedə'reɪʃn] federación *f*

fed 'up *adj* F harto, hasta las narices F; *be ~ with ...* estar harto *or* hasta las narices de ...

fee [fiː] *of lawyer, doctor, consultant* honorarios *mpl*; *for entrance* entrada *f*; *for membership* cuota *f*

fee·ble ['fiːbl] *adj person, laugh* débil; *attempt* flojo; *excuse* pobre

feed [fiːd] *v/t* (*pret & pp fed*) alimentar, dar de comer a

'feed·back *n* reacción *f*; *we'll give you some ~ as soon as possible* le daremos nuestra opinión *or* nuestras reacciones lo antes posible

feel [fiːl] **1** *v/t* (*pret & pp felt*) (*touch*) tocar; (*sense*) sentir; (*think*) creer, pensar; *you can ~ the difference* se nota la diferencia **2** *v/i* (*pret & pp felt*): *it ~s like silk/cotton* tiene la textura de la seda/algodón; *your hand ~s hot* tienes la mano caliente; *I ~ hungry* tengo hambre; *I ~ tired* estoy cansado; *how are you ~ing today?* ¿cómo te encuentras hoy?; *how does it ~ to be rich?* ¿qué se siente siendo rico?; *do you ~ like a drink/meal?* ¿te apetece una bebida/comida?; *I ~ like going/staying* me apetece ir/quedarme; *I don't ~ like it* no me apetece

♦feel up *v/t sexually* manosear

♦feel up to *v/t* sentirse con fuerzas

para

feel·er ['fiːlər] *of insect* antena *f*

'feel·good fac·tor sensación *f* positiva

feel·ing ['fiːlɪŋ] sentimiento *m*; *(sensation)* sensación *f*; **what are your ~s about it?** ¿qué piensas sobre ello?; **I have this ~ that ...** tengo el presentimiento de que ...

feet [fiːt] *pl →* **foot**

fe·line ['fiːlaɪn] *adj* felino

fell [fel] *pret →* **fall**

fel·low ['felou] *n (man)* tipo *m*

fel·low 'cit·i·zen conciudadano(-a) *m(f)*; **fel·low 'coun·try·man** compatriota *m/f*; **fel·low 'man** prójimo *m*

fel·o·ny ['felənɪ] delito *m* grave

felt [felt] **1** *n* fieltro *m* **2** *pret & pp →* **feel**

felt 'tip, felt-tip 'pen rotulador *m*

fe·male ['fiːmeɪl] **1** *adj animal, plant* hembra; *relating to people* femenino **2** *n of animals, plants* hembra *f*; *person* mujer *f*

fem·i·nine ['femɪnɪn] **1** *adj also* GRAM femenino **2** *n* GRAM femenino *m*

fem·i·nism ['femɪnɪzm] feminismo *m*

fem·i·nist ['femɪnɪst] **1** *n* feminista *m/f* **2** *adj* feminista

fence [fens] *n around garden etc* cerca *f*, valla *f*; F *criminal* perista *m/f*; **sit on the ~** nadar entre dos aguas

♦ **fence in** *v/t land* cercar, vallar

fenc·ing ['fensɪŋ] SP esgrima *f*

fend [fend] *v/i:* **- for o.s.** valerse por sí mismo

fend·er ['fendər] MOT aleta *f*

fer·ment[1] [fə'ment] *v/i of liquid* fermentar

fer·ment[2] ['fɜːrment] *n (unrest)* agitación *f*

fer·men·ta·tion [fɜːrmen'teɪʃn] fermentación *f*

fern [fɜːrn] helecho *m*

fe·ro·cious [fə'rouʃəs] *adj* feroz

fer·ry ['ferɪ] *n* ferry *m*, transbordador *m*

fer·tile ['fɜːrtəl] *adj* fértil

fer·til·i·ty [fɜːr'tɪlətɪ] fertilidad *f*

fer·til·i·ty drug medicamento *m* para el tratamiento de la infertilidad

fer·ti·lize ['fɜːrtəlaɪz] *v/t* fertilizar

fer·ti·liz·er ['fɜːrtəlaɪzər] *for soil* fertilizante *m*

fer·vent ['fɜːrvənt] *adj admirer* ferviente

fer·vent·ly ['fɜːrvəntlɪ] *adv* fervientemente

fes·ter ['festər] *v/i of wound* enconarse

fes·ti·val ['festɪvl] festival *m*

fes·tive ['festɪv] *adj* festivo; **the ~ season** la época navideña, las Navidades

fes·tiv·i·ties [fe'stɪvətɪz] *npl* celebraciones *fpl*

fe·tal ['fiːtl] *adj* fetal

fetch [fetʃ] *v/t person* recoger; *thing* traer, ir a buscar; *price* alcanzar

fe·tus ['fiːtəs] feto *m*

feud [fjuːd] **1** *n* enemistad *f* **2** *v/i* estar enemistado

fe·ver ['fiːvər] fiebre *f*

fe·ver·ish ['fiːvərɪʃ] *adj* con fiebre; *fig: excitement* febril

few [fjuː] **1** *adj (not many)* pocos; **a ~** unos pocos; **quite a ~, a good ~** *(a lot)* bastantes **2** *pron (not many)* pocos(-as); **a ~** *(some)* unos pocos; **quite a ~, a good ~** *(a lot)* bastantes; **~ of them could speak English** de ellos muy pocos hablaban inglés

few·er ['fjuːər] *adj* menos; **~ than** menos que; *with numbers* menos de

fi·an·cé [fɪ'ɑːnseɪ] prometido *m*, novio *m*

fi·an·cée [fɪ'ɑːnseɪ] prometida *f*, novia *f*

fi·as·co [fɪ'æskou] fiasco *m*

fib [fɪb] *n* F bola *f* F

fi·ber ['faɪbər] *n* fibra *f*

'fi·ber·glass *n* fibra *f* de vidrio; **fi·ber 'op·tic** *adj* de fibra óptica; **fi·ber 'op·tics** tecnología *f* de la fibra óptica

fi·bre *Br →* **fiber**

fick·le ['fɪkl] *adj* inconstante,

mudable

fic·tion ['fɪkʃn] n (novels) literatura f de ficción; (made-up story) ficción f

fic·tion·al ['fɪkʃnl] adj de ficción

fic·ti·tious [fɪk'tɪʃəs] adj ficticio

fid·dle ['fɪdl] **1** n (violin) violín m **2** v/i: **~ around with** enredar con **3** v/t accounts, result amañar

fi·del·i·ty [fɪ'delətɪ] fidelidad f

fid·get ['fɪdʒɪt] v/i moverse; **stop ~ing!** ¡estate quieto!

fid·get·y ['fɪdʒɪtɪ] adj inquieto

field [fiːld] n of documents expediente m; COMPUT campo m; for sport campo m, L.Am. cancha f; (competitors in race) participantes mpl

field·er ['fiːldər] in baseball fildeador(-a) m(f)

field e·vents npl pruebas fpl de salto y lanzamiento

fierce [fɪrs] adj animal feroz; wind, storm violento

fierce·ly ['fɪrslɪ] adv ferozmente

fi·er·y ['faɪrɪ] adj fogoso, ardiente

fif·teen [fɪf'tiːn] quince

fif·teenth [fɪf'tiːnθ] n & adj decimoquinto

fifth [fɪfθ] n & adj quinto

fif·ti·eth ['fɪftɪɪθ] n & adj quincuagésimo

fif·ty ['fɪftɪ] cincuenta

fif·ty-'fif·ty adv a medias

fig [fɪg] higo m

fight [faɪt] **1** n lucha f, pelea f; (argument) pelea f; fig: for survival, championship etc lucha f; in boxing combate m; **have a ~** (argue) pelearse **2** v/t (pret & pp **fought**) enemy, person luchar contra, pelear contra; in boxing pelear contra; disease, injustice luchar contra, combatir **3** v/i (pret & pp **fought**) luchar, pelear; (argue) pelearse

♦ **fight for** v/t one's rights, a cause luchar por

fight·er ['faɪtər] combatiente m/f; airplane caza m; (boxer) púgil m; **she's a ~** tiene espíritu combativo

fight·ing ['faɪtɪŋ] n physical, verbal peleas fpl; MIL luchas fpl, combates mpl

fig·u·ra·tive ['fɪgjərətɪv] adj figurado

fig·ure ['fɪgər] **1** n figura f; (digit) cifra f **2** v/t F (think) imaginarse, pensar

♦ **figure on** v/t F (plan) pensar

♦ **figure out** v/t (understand) entender; calculation resolver

'fig·ure skat·er patinador(a) m(f) artístico(-a)

'fig·ure skat·ing patinaje m artístico

file[1] [faɪl] **1** n of documents expediente m; COMPUT archivo m, fichero m **2** v/t documents archivar

♦ **file away** v/t documents archivar

file[2] [faɪl] n for wood, fingernails lima f

'file cab·i·net archivador m

'file man·ag·er COMPUT administrador m de archivos

fi·li·al ['fɪlɪəl] adj filial

fill [fɪl] **1** v/t llenar; tooth empastar, L.Am. emplomar **2** n: **eat one's ~** hincharse

♦ **fill in** v/t form, hole rellenar; **fill s.o. in** poner a alguien al tanto

♦ **fill in for** v/t sustituir a

♦ **fill out 1** v/t form rellenar **2** v/i (get fatter) engordar

♦ **fill up 1** v/t llenar (hasta arriba) **2** v/i of stadium, theater llenarse

fil·let ['fɪlɪt] n filete m

fill·ing ['fɪlɪŋ] **1** n in sandwich relleno m; in tooth empaste m, L.Am. emplomadura f **2** adj: **be ~** of food llenar mucho

'fill·ing sta·tion estación f de servicio, gasolinera f

film [fɪlm] **1** n for camera carrete m; (movie) película f **2** v/t person, event filmar

'film-mak·er cineasta m/f

'film star estrella f de cine

fil·ter ['fɪltər] **1** n filtro m **2** v/t coffee, liquid filtrar

♦ **filter through** v/i of news reports filtrarse

'fil·ter pa·per papel m de filtro

'fil·ter tip (cigarette) cigarrillo m con filtro

filth [fɪlθ] suciedad f, mugre f

filth·y ['fɪlθɪ] *adj* sucio, mugriento;
language etc obsceno

fin [fɪn] *of fish* aleta *f*

fi·nal ['faɪnl] **1** *adj* (*last*) último;
decision final, definitivo **2** *n* SP final
f

fi·na·le [fɪ'nælɪ] final *m*

fi·nal·ist ['faɪnəlɪst] finalista *m/f*

fi·nal·ize ['faɪnəlaɪz] *v/t plans, design*
ultimar

fi·nal·ly ['faɪnəlɪ] *adv* finalmente, por
último; (*at last*) finalmente, por fin

fi·nance ['faɪnæns] **1** *n* finanzas *fpl*
2 *v/t* financiar

fi·nan·ces ['faɪnænsɪz] *npl* finanzas
fpl

fi·nan·cial [faɪ'nænʃl] *adj* financiero

fi·nan·cial·ly [faɪ'nænʃəlɪ] *adv* económicamente

fi·nan·cial 'year *Br* ejercicio *m* económico

fi·nan·cier [faɪ'nænsɪr] financie-
ro(-a) *m(f)*

find [faɪnd] *v/t* (*pret & pp* **found**) encontrar, hallar; *if you ~ it too
hot/cold* si te parece demasiado
frío/caliente; *~ s.o. innocent/
guilty* LAW declarar a alguien
inocente/culpable; *I ~ it strange
that ...* me sorprende que ...; *how
did you ~ the hotel?* ¿qué te pareció el hotel?

♦ **find out 1** *v/t* descubrir, averiguar
2 *v/i* (*discover*) descubrir; *can you
try to find out?* ¿podrías enterar-
te?

find·ings ['faɪndɪŋz] *npl of report*
conclusiones *fpl*

fine¹ [faɪn] *adj day, weather* bueno;
wine, performance, city excelente;
distinction, line fino; *how's that?* –
that's ~ ¿qué tal está? – bien; *that's
~ by me* por mí no hay ningún problema; *how are you?* – *~* ¿cómo estás? – bien

fine² [faɪn] **1** *n* multa *f* **2** *v/t* multar,
poner una multa a

fine-'tooth comb: *go through sth
with a ~* revisar algo minuciosamente

fine-'tune *v/t engine, fig* afinar, hacer

los últimos ajustes a

fin·ger ['fɪŋgər] **1** *n* dedo *m* **2** *v/t* tocar

'fin·ger·nail *n* uña *f*; **'fin·ger·print**
1 *n* huella *f* digital *or* dactilar **2** *v/t*
tomar las huellas digitales *or*
dactilares a; **'fin·ger·tip** *n* punta *f*
del dedo; *have sth at one's ~s* saberse algo al dedillo

fin·i·cky ['fɪnɪkɪ] *adj person* quisquilloso; *design* enrevesado

fin·ish ['fɪnɪʃ] **1** *v/t* acabar, terminar;
~ doing sth acabar *or* terminar de
hacer algo **2** *v/i* acabar, terminar
3 *n of product* acabado *m*; *of race* final *f*

♦ **finish off** *v/t* acabar, terminar

♦ **finish up** *v/t food* acabar, terminar;
he finished up liking it acabó gus-
tándole

♦ **finish with** *v/t boyfriend etc* cortar
con

fin·ish·ing line ['fɪnɪʃɪŋ] línea *f* de
meta

Fin·land ['fɪnlənd] Finlandia

Finn [fɪn] finlandés (-esa) *m(f)*

Finn·ish ['fɪnɪʃ] **1** *adj* finlandés **2** *n
language* finés *m*

fir [fɜːr] abeto *m*

fire [faɪr] **1** *n* fuego *m*; *electric, gas* estufa *f*; (*blaze*) incendio *m*; (*bonfire,
campfire etc*) hoguera *f*; *be on ~* estar ardiendo; *catch ~* prender; *set
sth on ~*, *set ~ to sth* prender fuego a algo **2** *v/i* (*shoot*) disparar
(*on/at* sobre/a) **3** *v/t* F (*dismiss*)
despedir

'fire a·larm alarma *f* contra incendios; **'fire·arm** arma *f* de fuego;
'fire·crack·er petardo *m*; **'fire
de·part·ment** (cuerpo *m* de) bomberos *mpl*; **'fire door** puerta *f* contra incendios; **'fire drill** simulacro *m*
de incendio; **'fire en·gine** coche *m*
de bomberos; **'fire es·cape** salida *f*
de incendios; **'fire ex·tin·guish·er**
extintor *m*; **'fire fight·er** bombero
(-a) *m(f)*; **'fire·guard** pantalla *f*,
parachispas *m inv*; **'fire·man** bombero *m*; **'fire·place** chimenea *f*, hogar *m*; **'fire sta·tion** parque *m* de

bomberos; '**fire truck** coche *m* de bomberos; '**fire·wood** leña *f*; '**fire·works** *npl* fuegos *mpl* artificiales

firm[1] [fɜːrm] *adj* firme; *a ~ deal* un acuerdo en firme

firm[2] [fɜːrm] *n* COM empresa *f*

first [fɜːrst] **1** *adj* primero; *who's ~ please?* ¿quién es el primero, por favor? **2** *n* primero(-a) *m(f)* **3** *adv* primero; *~ of all (for one reason)* en primer lugar; *at ~* al principio

first 'aid primeros *mpl* auxilios; **first·'aid box**, **first·'aid kit** botiquín *m* de primeros auxilios; '**first·born** *adj* primogénito; '**first class 1** *adj* ticket, seat de primera (clase); (very good) excelente **2** *adv* travel en primera (clase); '**first 'floor** planta *f* baja, *Br* primer piso *m*; '**first'hand** *adj* de primera mano; **First 'La·dy** of US primera dama *f*

first·ly ['fɜːrstlɪ] *adv* en primer lugar

first 'name nombre *m* (de pila); **first 'night** estreno *m*; **first of'fend·er** delincuente *m/f* sin antecedentes; **first of'fense** primer delito *m*; **first-'rate** *adj* excelente

fis·cal ['fɪskl] *adj* fiscal

fis·cal 'year año *m* fiscal

fish [fɪʃ] **1** *n* (*pl* **fish**) pez *m*; to eat pescado *m*; *drink like a ~* F beber como un cosaco F; *feel like a ~ out of water* sentirse fuera de lugar **2** *v/i* pescar

'**fish·bone** espina *f* (de pescado)

fish·er·man ['fɪʃərmən] pescador *m*

fish·ing ['fɪʃɪŋ] pesca *f*

'**fish·ing boat** (barco *m*) pesquero *m*; '**fish·ing line** sedal *m*; '**fish·ing rod** caña *f* de pescar

'**fish stick** palito *m* de pescado

fish·y ['fɪʃɪ] *adj* F (suspicious) sospechoso

fist [fɪst] puño *m*

fit[1] [fɪt] *n* MED ataque *m*; *a ~ of rage/jealousy* un arrebato de cólera/un ataque de celos

fit[2] [fɪt] *adj* physically en forma; morally adecuado; *he's not ~ to be President* no está en condiciones

ser Presidente; *keep ~* mantenerse en forma

fit[3] [fɪt] **1** *v/t* (attach) colocar; *these pants don't ~ me any more* estos pantalones ya no me entran; *it ~s you perfectly* te queda perfectamente **2** *v/i* (pret & pp **-ted**) of clothes quedar bien; of piece of furniture etc caber **3** *n*: *it's a good ~* of jacket etc queda bien; of piece of furniture cabe bien; *it's a tight ~* no hay mucho espacio

♦ **fit in 1** *v/i* of person in group encajar; *it fits in with our plans* encaja con nuestros planes **2** *v/t*: *fit s.o. in* into schedule etc hacer un hueco a alguien

fit·ful ['fɪtfəl] *adj* sleep intermitente

fit·ness ['fɪtnɪs] physical buena forma *f*

'**fit·ness cen·ter**, *Br* '**fit·ness cen·tre** gimnasio *m*

fit·ted 'kitch·en ['fɪtɪd] cocina *f* a medida

fit·ted 'sheet sábana *f* ajustable

fit·ter ['fɪtər] *n* técnico(-a) *m(f)*

fit·ting ['fɪtɪŋ] *adj* apropiado

fit·tings ['fɪtɪŋz] *npl* equipamiento *m*

five [faɪv] cinco

fix [fɪks] **1** *n* (solution) solución *f*; *be in a ~* F estar en un lío F **2** *v/t* (attach) fijar; (repair) arreglar, reparar; (arrange: meeting etc) organizar; lunch preparar; dishonestly: match etc amañar; *~ sth onto sth* fijar algo a algo; *I'll ~ you a drink* te preparé una bebida

♦ **fix up** *v/t* meeting organizar

fixed [fɪkst] *adj* fijo

fix·ings ['fɪkɪŋz] *npl* guarnición *f*

fix·ture ['fɪkstʃər] (in room) parte fija del mobiliario o la decoración de una habitación

♦ **fiz·zle out** ['fɪzl] *v/i* F quedarse en nada

flab [flæb] on body grasa *f*

flab·ber·gast ['flæbərgæst] *v/t* F: *be ~ed* quedarse estupefacto *or Span* alucinado F

flab·by ['flæbɪ] *adj* muscles etc fofo

flag¹ [flæg] *n* bandera *f*

flag² [flæg] *v/i* (*pret & pp* **-ged**) (*tire*) desfallecer

'flag·pole asta *f* (de bandera)

fla·grant ['fleigrənt] *adj* flagrante

'flag·ship *fig* estandarte *m*; **'flag-staff** asta *f* (de bandera); **'flag·stone** losa *f*

flair [fler] (*talent*) don *m*; **have a na-tural ~ for** tener dotes para

flake [fleik] *n of snow* copo *m*; *of skin* escama *f*; *of plaster* desconchón *m*

♦ **flake off** *v/i of skin* descamarse; *of plaster, paint* desconcharse

flak·y ['fleiki] *adj skin* con escamas; *paint* desconchado

flak·y 'pas·try hojaldre *m*

flam·boy·ant [flæm'bɔiənt] *adj personality* extravagante

flam·boy·ant·ly [flæm'bɔiəntli] *adv dressed* extravagantemente

flame [fleim] llama *f*; **go up in ~s** ser pasto de las llamas

fla·men·co [flə'meŋkou] flamenco *m*

fla·men·co danc·er bailaor(a) *m(f)*

flam·ma·ble ['flæməbl] *adj* inflamable

flan [flæn] tarta *f*

flank [flæŋk] **1** *n of horse etc* costado *m*; MIL flanco *m* **2** *v/t* flanquear

flap [flæp] **1** *n of envelope, pocket* solapa *f*; *of table* hoja *f*; **be in a ~** F estar histérico **2** *v/t* (*pret & pp* **-ped**) *wings* batir **3** *v/i* (*pret & pp* **-ped**) *of flag etc* ondear

flare [fler] **1** *n* (*distress signal*) bengala *f*; *in dress* vuelo *m* **2** *v/t*: **~ one's nostrils** hinchar las narices resoplando

♦ **flare up** *v/i of violence* estallar; *of illness, rash* exacerbarse, empeorar; *of fire* llamear; (*get very angry*) estallar

flash [flæʃ] **1** *n of light* destello *m*; PHOT flash *m*; **in a ~** F en un abrir y cerrar de ojos; **have a ~ of inspiration** tener una inspiración repentina; **a ~ of lightning** un relámpago **2** *v/i of light* destellar **3** *v/t*: **~ one's headlights** echar las luces

'flash·back *in movie* flash-back *m*, escena *f* retrospectiva

flash·er ['flæʃər] MOT intermitente *m*

'flash·light linterna *f*; PHOT flash *m*

flash·y ['flæʃi] *adj pej* ostentoso, chillón

flask [flæsk] (*hip ~*) petaca *f*

flat¹ [flæt] **1** *adj surface, land* llano, plano; *beer* sin gas; *battery* descargado; *tire* desinflado; *shoes* bajo; MUS bemol; **and that's ~** F y sanseacabó F **2** *adv* **~ out** *work, run, drive* a tope **3** *n* (*~ tire*) pinchazo *m*

flat² [flæt] *n Br* apartamento *m*, *Span* piso *m*

flat-chest·ed [flæt'tʃestid] *adj* plana de pecho

flat·ly ['flætli] *adv refuse, deny* rotundamente

'flat rate tarifa *f* única

flat·ten ['flætn] *v/t land, road* allanar, aplanar; *by bombing, demolition* arrasar

flat·ter ['flætər] *v/t* halagar, adular

flat·ter·er ['flætərər] adulador(a) *m(f)*

flat·ter·ing ['flætəriŋ] *adj comments* halagador; *color, clothes* favorecedor

flat·ter·y ['flætəri] halagos *mpl*, adulación *f*

'flat·ware (*cutlery*) cubertería *f*

flaunt [flɔːnt] *v/t* hacer ostentación de, alardear de

flau·tist ['flɔːtist] flautista *m/f*

fla·vor ['fleivər] **1** *n* sabor *m* **2** *v/t food* condimentar

fla·vor·ing ['fleivəriŋ] *n* aromatizante *m*

fla·vour *etc Br* → **flavor** *etc*

flaw [flɔː] *n* defecto *m*, fallo *m*

flaw·less ['flɔːlis] *adj* impecable

flea [fliː] pulga *f*

fleck [flek] mota *f*

fled [fled] *pret & pp* → **flee**

flee [fliː] *v/i* (*pret & pp* **fled**) escapar, huir

fleece [fliːs] *v/t* F desplumar F

fleet [fliːt] *n* NAUT, *of vehicles* flota *f*

fleet·ing [ˈfliːtɪŋ] *adj visit etc* fugaz; **catch a ~ glimpse of** vislumbrar fugazmente a

flesh [fleʃ] *n* carne *f*; *of fruit* pulpa *f*; **meet/ see s.o. in the ~** conocer/ ver a alguien en persona

flew [fluː] *pret* → **fly**

flex [fleks] *v/t muscles* flexionar

flex·i·bil·i·ty [fleksəˈbɪlətɪ] flexibilidad *f*

flex·i·ble [ˈfleksəbl] *adj* flexible

'**flex·time** [ˈflekstaɪm] horario *m* flexible

flick [flɪk] *v/t tail* sacudir; **he ~ed a fly off his hand** espantó una mosca que tenía en la mano; **she ~ed her hair out of her eyes** se apartó el pelo de los ojos

♦ **flick through** *v/t book, magazine* hojear

flick·er [ˈflɪkər] *v/i of light, screen* parpadear

fli·er [flaɪr] *(circular)* folleto *m*

flies [flaɪz] *npl Br on pants* bragueta *f*

flight [flaɪt] *n in airplane* vuelo *m*; *(fleeing)* huida *f*; **not capable of ~** incapaz de volar; **~ (of stairs)** tramo *m* (de escaleras)

'**flight at·tend·ant** auxiliar *m/f* de vuelo; '**flight crew** tripulación *f*; '**flight deck** AVIA cabina *f* del piloto; '**flight num·ber** número *m* de vuelo; '**flight path** ruta *f* de vuelo; '**flight re·cord·er** caja *f* negra; '**flight time** *departure* hora *f* del vuelo; *duration* duración *f* del vuelo

flight·y [ˈflaɪtɪ] *adj* inconstante

flim·sy [ˈflɪmzɪ] *adj structure, furniture* endeble; *dress, material* débil; *excuse* pobre

flinch [flɪntʃ] *v/i* encogerse

fling [flɪŋ] **1** *v/t (pret & pp flung)* arrojar, lanzar; **~ o.s. into a chair** dejarse caer en una silla **2** *n* F *(affair)* aventura *f*

♦ **flip over** [flɪp] *v/i* volcar

♦ **flip through** *v/t (pret & pp -ped)* *magazine* hojear

flip·per [ˈflɪpər] *for swimming* aleta *f*

flirt [flɜːrt] **1** *v/i* flirtear, coquetear **2** *n* ligón (-ona) *m(f)*

flir·ta·tious [flɜːrˈteɪʃəs] *adj* coqueto

float [floʊt] *v/i also* FIN flotar

float·ing vot·er [ˈfloʊtɪŋ] votante *m/f* indeciso(-a)

flock [flɑːk] **1** *n of sheep* rebaño *m* **2** *v/i* acudir en masa

flog [flɑːg] *v/t (pret & pp -ged)* *(whip)* azotar

flood [flʌd] **1** *n* inundación *f* **2** *v/t of river* inundar

♦ **flood in** *v/i* llegar en grandes cantidades

flood·ing [ˈflʌdɪŋ] inundaciones *fpl*

'**flood·light** *n* foco *m*

flood·lit [ˈflʌdlɪt] *adj match* con luz artificial

'**flood wa·ters** *npl* crecida *f*

floor [flɔːr] *n* suelo *m*; *(story)* piso *m*

'**floor·board** *n* tabla *f* del suelo; '**floor cloth** trapo *m* del suelo; '**floor lamp** lámpara *f* de pie

flop [flɑːp] **1** *v/i (pret & pp -ped)* dejarse caer; F *(fail)* pinchar F **2** *n* F *(failure)* pinchazo *m* F

flop·py [ˈflɑːpɪ] *adj ears* caído; *hat* blando; *(weak)* flojo

flop·py ('**disk**) disquete *m*

flor·ist [ˈflɔːrɪst] florista *m/f*

floss [flɑːs] **1** *n for teeth* hilo *m* dental **2** *v/t*: **~ one's teeth** limpiarse los dientes con hilo dental

flour [flaʊr] harina *f*

flour·ish [ˈflʌrɪʃ] *v/i of plant* crecer rápidamente; *of business, civilization* florecer, prosperar

flour·ish·ing [ˈflʌrɪʃɪŋ] *adj business, trade* floreciente, próspero

flow [floʊ] **1** *v/i* fluir **2** *n* flujo *m*

'**flow-chart** diagrama *m* de flujo

flow·er [flaʊr] **1** *n* flor *f* **2** *v/i* florecer

'**flow·er·bed** parterre *m*; '**flow·er·pot** tiesto *m*, maceta *f*; '**flow·er show** exposición *f* floral

flow·er·y [ˈflaʊrɪ] *adj pattern* floreado; *style of writing* florido

flown [floʊn] *pp* → **fly**

flu [fluː] gripe *f*

fluc·tu·ate [ˈflʌktjʊeɪt] *v/i* fluctuar

fluc·tu·a·tion [flʌktjʊˈeɪʃn] fluctuación f

flu·en·cy ['flu:ənsɪ] *in a language* fluidez f

flu·ent ['flu:ənt] *adj:* **he speaks ~ Spanish** habla español con soltura

flu·ent·ly ['flu:əntlɪ] *adv speak, write* con soltura

fluff [flʌf] *material* pelusa f

fluff·y ['flʌfɪ] *adj* esponjoso; **~ toy** juguete m de peluche

fluid ['flu:ɪd] n fluido m

flung [flʌŋ] *pret & pp* → **fling**

flunk [flʌŋk] *v/t* F *subject* suspender, *Span* catear F

flu·o·res·cent [flu'resnt] *adj light* fluorescente

flur·ry ['flʌrɪ] *of snow* torbellino m

flush [flʌʃ] **1** *v/t:* **~ the toilet** tirar de la cadena; **~ sth down the toilet** tirar algo por el retrete **2** *v/i (go red in the face)* ruborizarse; **the toilet won't ~** la cisterna no funciona **3** *adj (level):* **be ~ with ...** estar a la misma altura que ...

♦ **flush away** *v/t:* **flush sth away down toilet** tirar algo por el retrete

♦ **flush out** *v/t rebels etc* hacer salir

flus·ter ['flʌstər] *v/t:* **get ~ed** ponerse nervioso

flute [flu:t] MUS flauta f; *glass* copa f de champán

flut·ist ['flu:tɪst] flautista m/f

flut·ter ['flʌtər] *v/i of bird, wings* aletear; *of flag* ondear; *of heart* latir con fuerza

fly[1] [flaɪ] *n insect* mosca f

fly[2] [flaɪ] *n on pants* bragueta f

fly[3] [flaɪ] *v/i (pret flew, pp flown) of bird, airplane* volar; *in airplane* volar, ir en avión; *of flag* ondear; **~ into a rage** enfurecerse; **she flew out of the room** salió a toda prisa de la habitación **2** *v/t (pret flew, pp flown) airplane* pilotar; *airline* volar con; *(transport by air)* enviar por avión

♦ **fly away** *v/i of bird* salir volando; *of airplane* alejarse

♦ **fly back** *v/i (travel back)* volver en avión

♦ **fly in 1** *v/i of airplane, passengers* llegar en avión **2** *v/t supplies etc* transportar en avión

♦ **fly off** *v/i of hat etc* salir volando

♦ **fly out** *v/i* irse *(en avión);* **when do you fly out?** ¿cuándo os vais?

♦ **fly past** *v/i in formation* pasar volando en formación; *of time* volar

fly·ing ['flaɪɪŋ] n volar m

fly·ing 'sau·cer platillo m volante

foam [foʊm] *on liquid* espuma f

foam 'rub·ber gomaespuma f

FOB [efoʊ'bi:] *abbr (= free on board)* fab (= franco a bordo)

fo·cus ['foʊkəs] **1** n *of attention,* PHOT foco m; **be in ~ / out of ~** PHOT estar enfocado / desenfocado **2** *v/t:* **~ one's attention on** concentrar la atención en **3** *v/i* enfocar

♦ **focus on** *v/t problem, issue* concentrarse en; PHOT enfocar

fod·der ['fɑ:dər] forraje m

fog [fɑ:g] niebla f

♦ **fog up** *v/i (pret & pp -ged)* empañarse

'fog·bound *adj* paralizado por la niebla

fog·gy ['fɑ:gɪ] *adj* neblinoso, con niebla; **it's ~** hay niebla; **I haven't the foggiest idea** no tengo la más remota idea

foi·ble ['fɔɪbl] manía f

foil[1] [fɔɪl] n papel m de aluminio

foil[2] [fɔɪl] *v/t (thwart)* frustrar

fold[1] [foʊld] **1** *v/t paper etc* doblar; **~ one's arms** cruzarse de brazos **2** *v/i of business* quebrar **3** n *in cloth etc* pliegue m

♦ **fold up 1** *v/t* plegar **2** *v/i of chair, table* plegarse

fold[2] [foʊld] n *for sheep etc* redil m

fold·er ['foʊldər] *for documents,* COMPUT carpeta f

fold·ing ['foʊldɪŋ] *adj* plegable; **~ chair** silla f plegable

fo·li·age ['foʊlɪdʒ] follaje m

folk [foʊk] *npl (people)* gente f; **my ~s** *(family)* mi familia; **evening ~s** F buenas noches, gente F

'folk dance baile m popular; **'folk mu·sic** música f folk *or* popular; **'folk sing·er** cantante m/f de folk;

'**folk song** canción *m/f* folk *or* popular

fol·low ['fɑːloʊ] **1** *v/t* seguir; (*understand*) entender; **~ me** sígueme **2** *v/i logically* deducirse; *it ~s from this that ...* de esto se deduce que ...; *you go first and I'll ~* tú ve primero que yo te sigo; *the requirements are as ~s* los requisitos son los siguientes

♦ **follow up** *v/t letter, inquiry* hacer el seguimiento de

fol·low·er ['fɑːloʊər] seguidor(a) *m(f)*

fol·low·ing ['fɑːloʊɪŋ] **1** *adj* siguiente **2** *n people* seguidores(-as) *mpl* (*fpl*); *the ~* lo siguiente

'**fol·low-up meet·ing** reunión *f* de seguimiento

'**fol·low-up vis·it** *to doctor etc* visita *f* de seguimiento

fol·ly ['fɑːlɪ] (*madness*) locura *f*

fond [fɑːnd] *adj* (*loving*) cariñoso; *memory* entrañable; *he's ~ of travel/music* le gusta viajar/la música; *I'm very ~ of him* le tengo mucho cariño

fon·dle ['fɑːndl] *v/t* acariciar

fond·ness ['fɑːndnɪs] *for s.o.* cariño *m* (*for* por); *for wine, food* afición *f* (*for* por)

font [fɑːnt] *for printing* tipo *m*; *in church* pila *f* bautismal

food [fuːd] comida *f*

'**food chain** cadena *f* alimentaria

food·ie ['fuːdɪ] F gourmet *m/f*

'**food mix·er** robot *m* de cocina

food poi·son·ing ['fuːdpɔɪznɪŋ] intoxicación *f* alimentaria

fool [fuːl] **1** *n* tonto(-a) *m(f)*, idiota *m/f*; *you stupid ~!* ¡estúpido!; *make a ~ of o.s.* ponerse en ridículo **2** *v/t* engañar

♦ **fool around** *v/i* hacer el tonto; *sexually* tener un lío

♦ **fool around with** *v/t knife, drill etc* enredar con algo; *sexually* tener un lío con

'**fool·har·dy** *adj* temerario

fool·ish ['fuːlɪʃ] *adj* tonto

fool·ish·ly ['fuːlɪʃlɪ] *adv*: *I ~ ...* come-

tí la tontería de ...

'**fool·proof** *adj* infalible

foot [fʊt] (*pl feet* [fiːt]) *also measurement* pie *m*; *of animal* pata *f*; *on ~ a* pie, caminando, andando; *I've been on my feet all day* llevo todo el día de pie; *be back on one's feet* estar recuperado; *at the ~ of the page/ hill* al pie de la página / de la colina; *put one's ~ in it* F meter la pata F

'**foot·age** ['fʊtɪdʒ] secuencias *fpl*, imágenes *fpl*

'**foot·ball** *Br* (*soccer*) fútbol *m*; *American style* fútbol *m* americano; *ball* balón *m or* pelota *f* (de fútbol)

'**foot·ball play·er** *American style* jugador(a) *m(f)* de fútbol americano; *Br in soccer* jugador(a) *m(f)* de fútbol, futbolista *m/f*

'**foot·bridge** puente *m* peatonal

foot·er ['fʊtər] *in document* pie *m* de página

'**foot·hills** ['fʊthɪlz] *npl* estribaciones *fpl*

'**foot·hold** *n in climbing* punto *m* de apoyo; *gain a ~ fig* introducirse

foot·ing ['fʊtɪŋ] (*basis*): *put the business back on a secure ~* volver a afianzar la empresa; *lose one's ~* perder el equilibrio; *be on the same/a different ~* estar/no estar en igualdad de condiciones; *be on a friendly ~ with ...* tener relaciones de amistad con ...

foot·lights ['fʊtlaɪts] *npl* candilejas *fpl*; '**foot·mark** pisada *f*; '**foot·note** nota *f* a pie de página; '**foot·path** sendero *m*; '**foot·print** pisada *f*; '**foot·step** paso *m*; *follow in s.o.'s ~s* seguir los pasos de alguien; '**foot·stool** escabel *m*; '**foot·wear** calzado *m*

for [fər, fɔːr] *prep* ◊ *purpose, destination etc* para; *a train ~ ...* un tren para *or* hacia ...; *clothes ~ children* ropa para niños; *it's too big/ small ~ you* te queda demasiado grande/pequeño; *this is ~ you* esto es para ti; *what's ~ lunch?* ¿qué hay para comer?; *the steak is ~ me* el filete es para mí; *what is this ~?*

¿para qué sirve esto?; **what ~?** ¿para qué? ◊ *time* durante; **~ three days / two hours** durante tres días / dos horas; **it lasts ~ two hours** dura dos horas; **please get it done ~ Monday** por favor tenlo listo (para) el lunes ◊ *distance*: **I walked ~ a mile** caminé una milla; **it stretches for 100 miles** se extiende 100 millas ◊ (*in favor of*): **I am ~ the idea** estoy a favor de la idea ◊ (*instead of, in behalf of*): **let me do that ~ you** déjame que te lo haga; **we are agents ~ ...** somos representantes de ... ◊ (*in exchange for*): **I bought it ~ $25** lo compré por 25 dólares: **how much did you sell it ~?** ¿por cuánto lo vendiste?

for·bade [fər'bæd] *pret* → **forbid**

for·bid [fər'bɪd] *v/t* (*pret* **forbade**, *pp* **forbidden**) prohibir; **~ s.o. to do sth** prohibir a alguien hacer algo

for·bid·den [fər'bɪdn] **1** *adj* prohibido; **smoking / parking ~** prohibido fumar / aparcar **2** *pp* → **forbid**

for·bid·ding [fər'bɪdɪŋ] *adj person, tone, look* amenazador; *rockface* imponente; *prospect* intimidador

force [fɔːrs] **1** *n* fuerza *f*; **come into ~ of law etc** entrar en vigor; **the ~s** MIL las fuerzas **2** *v/t door, lock* forzar; **~ s.o. to do sth** forzar a alguien a hacer algo; **~ sth open** forzar algo
♦ **force back** *v/t tears* contener

forced [fɔːrst] *adj* forzado

forced 'land·ing aterrizaje *m* forzoso

force·ful ['fɔːrsfəl] *adj argument* poderoso; *speaker* vigoroso; *character* enérgico

force·ful·ly ['fɔːrsfəlɪ] *adv* de manera convincente

for·ceps ['fɔːrseps] *npl* MED fórceps *m inv*

for·ci·ble ['fɔːrsəbl] *adj entry* por la fuerza

for·ci·bly ['fɔːrsəblɪ] *adv* por la fuerza

ford [fɔːrd] *n* vado *m*

fore [fɔːr] *n*: **come to the ~** salir a la palestra

'fore·arm antebrazo *m*; 'fore·bears ['fɔːrberz] *npl* antepasados *mpl*; fore·bod·ing [fər'boʊdɪŋ] premonición *f*; 'fore·cast **1** *n* pronóstico *m*; *of weather* pronóstico *m* (del tiempo) **2** *v/t* (*pret & pp* **forecast**) pronosticar; 'fore·court (*of garage*) explanada en la parte de delante; fore·fa·thers ['fɔːrfɑːðərz] *npl* ancestros *mpl*; 'fore·fin·ger (dedo *m*) índice *m*; 'fore·front: **be in the ~ of** estar a la vanguardia de; 'fore·gone *adj*: **that's a ~ conclusion** eso ya se sabe de antemano; 'fore·ground primer plano *m*; 'fore·hand *in tennis* derecha *f*; 'fore·head frente *f*

for·eign ['fɔːrən] *adj* extranjero; **a ~ holiday** unas vacaciones en el extranjero

for·eign af·fairs *npl* asuntos *mpl* exteriores; **for·eign 'aid** ayuda *f* al exterior; **for·eign 'bod·y** cuerpo *m* extraño; **for·eign 'cur·ren·cy** divisa *f* extranjera

for·eign·er ['fɔːrənər] extranjero(-a) *m(f)*

for·eign ex·change divisas *fpl*; for·eign 'lan·guage idioma *m* extranjero; 'For·eign Of·fice *in UK* Ministerio *m* de Asuntos Exteriores; **for·eign 'pol·i·cy** política *f* exterior; **For·eign 'Sec·re·ta·ry** *in UK* Ministro(-a) *m(f)* de Asuntos Exteriores

'fore·man capataz *m*

'fore·most *adj* principal

fo·ren·sic 'med·i·cine [fə'rensɪk] medicina *f* forense

fo·ren·sic 'sci·en·tist forense *m/f*

'fore·run·ner predecesor(a) *m(f)*; fore·see *v/t* (*pret* **foresaw**, *pp* **foreseen**) prever; fore·see·a·ble [fər'siːəbl] *adj* previsible; **in the ~ future** en un futuro próximo; fore·'seen *pp* → **foresee**; 'fore·sight previsión *f*

for·est ['fɑːrɪst] bosque *m*

for·est·ry ['fɑːrɪstrɪ] silvicultura *f*

'fore·taste anticipo *m*

fore·tell v/t (pret & pp **foretold**) predecir

for·ev·er [fə'revər] adv siempre; **I will remember this day ~** no me olvidaré nunca de ese día

fore·word ['fɔːrwɜːrd] prólogo m

for·feit ['fɔːrfət] v/t (lose) perder; (give up) renunciar a

for·gave [fər'geɪv] pret → **forgive**

forge [fɔːrdʒ] v/t falsificar

♦**forge ahead** v/i progresar rápidamente

forg·er ['fɔːrdʒər] falsificador(a) m(f)

forg·er·y ['fɔːrdʒərɪ] falsificación f

for·get [fər'get] v/t (pret **forgot**, pp **forgotten**) olvidar; **I forgot his name** se me olvidó su nombre; **~ to do sth** olvidarse de hacer algo

for·get·ful [fər'getfəl] adj olvidadizo

for'get-me-not flower nomeolvides m inv

for·give [fər'gɪv] v/t & v/i (pret **forgave**, pp **forgiven**) perdonar

for·gi·ven [fər'gɪvn] pp → **forgive**

for·give·ness [fər'gɪvnɪs] perdón m

for·got [fər'gɑːt] pret → **forget**

for·got·ten [fər'gɑːtn] pp → **forget**

fork [fɔːrk] n for eating tenedor m; for garden horca f; in road bifurcación f

♦**fork out** v/t & v/i F (pay) apoquinar F

forked adj tongue bífido; stick bifurcado

fork·lift 'truck carretilla f elevadora

form [fɔːrm] **1** n shape forma f; (document) formulario m, impreso m; **be on/off ~** estar/no estar en forma **2** v/t in clay etc moldear; friendship establecer; opinion formarse; past tense etc formar; (constitute) formar, constituir **3** v/i (take shape, develop) formarse

form·al ['fɔːrml] adj formal; recognition etc oficial; dress de etiqueta

for·mal·i·ty [fər'mælətɪ] formalidad f

for·mal·ly ['fɔːrməlɪ] adv speak, behave formalmente; accepted, recognized oficialmente

for·mat ['fɔːrmæt] **1** v/t (pret & pp

-**ted**) diskette, document formatear **2** n of paper, program etc formato m

for·ma·tion [fɔːr'meɪʃn] formación f; **~ flying** vuelo m en formación

for·ma·tive ['fɔːrmətɪv] adj formativo; **in his ~ years** en sus años de formación

for·mer ['fɔːrmər] adj antiguo; **the ~** el primero; **the ~ arrangement** la situación de antes

for·mer·ly ['fɔːrmərlɪ] adv antiguamente

for·mi·da·ble ['fɔːrmɪdəbl] adj personality formidable; opponent, task terrible

for·mu·la ['fɔːrmjulə] MATH, CHEM, fig fórmula f

for·mu·late ['fɔːrmjuleɪt] v/t (express) formular

for·ni·cate ['fɔːrnɪkeɪt] v/i fml fornicar

for·ni·ca·tion [fɔːrnɪ'keɪʃn] fml fornicación f

fort [fɔːrt] MIL fuerte m

forth [fɔːrθ] adv: **back and ~** de un lado para otro; **and so ~** y así sucesivamente; **from that day ~** desde ese día en adelante

forth·com·ing ['fɔːrθkʌmɪŋ] adj (future) próximo; personality comunicativo

'**forth·right** adj directo

for·ti·eth ['fɔːrtɪɪθ] n & adj cuadragésimo

fort·night ['fɔːrtnaɪt] Br quincena f

for·tress ['fɔːrtrɪs] MIL fortaleza f

for·tu·nate ['fɔːrtʃnət] adj afortunado

for·tu·nate·ly ['fɔːrtʃnətlɪ] adv afortunadamente

for·tune ['fɔːrtʃən] (fate, money) fortuna f; (luck) fortuna f, suerte f; **tell s.o.'s ~** decir a alguien la buenaventura

'**for·tune-tell·er** adivino(-a) m(f)

for·ty ['fɔːrtɪ] cuarenta; **have ~ winks** F echarse una siestecilla F

fo·rum ['fɔːrəm] fig foro m

for·ward ['fɔːrwərd] **1** adv hacia delante **2** adj pej: person atrevido **3** n SP delantero(-a) m(f) **4** v/t letter reexpedir

'for·ward·ing ad·dress ['fɔːrwərd-ɪŋ] dirección a la que reexpedir correspondencia

'for·ward·ing a·gent COM transitario(-a) m(f)

'for·ward-look·ing adj con visión de futuro, moderno

fos·sil ['fɑːsəl] fósil m

fos·sil·ized ['fɑːsəlaɪzd] adj fosilizado

fos·ter ['fɑːstər] v/t child acoger, adoptar (temporalmente); attitude, belief fomentar

'fos·ter child niño(-a) m(f) en régimen de acogida; **'fos·ter home** hogar m de acogida; **'fos·ter par·ents** npl familia f de acogida

fought [fɔːt] pret & pp → **fight**

foul [faʊl] **1** n SP falta f **2** adj smell, taste asqueroso; weather terrible **3** v/t SP hacer (una) falta a

found¹ [faʊnd] v/t school etc fundar

found² [faʊnd] pret & pp → **find**

foun·da·tion [faʊn'deɪʃn] of theory etc fundamento m; (organization) fundación f

foun·da·tions [faʊn'deɪʃnz] npl of building cimientos mpl

found·er ['faʊndər] n fundador(a) m(f)

found·ing ['faʊndɪŋ] n fundación f

foun·dry ['faʊndrɪ] fundición f

foun·tain ['faʊntɪn] fuente f

'foun·tain pen pluma f (estilográfica)

four [fɔːr] cuatro; **on all ~s** a gatas, a cuatro patas

four-let·ter 'word palabrota f; **four-post·er** ('bed) cama f de dosel; **'four-star** adj hotel etc de cuatro estrellas

four·teen [fɔːr'tiːn] catorce

four·teenth [fɔːr'tiːnθ] n & adj decimocuarto

fourth [fɔːrθ] n & adj cuarto

four-wheel 'drive MOT vehículo m con tracción a las cuatro ruedas; type of drive tracción f a las cuatro ruedas

fowl [faʊl] ave f de corral

fox [fɑːks] **1** n zorro m **2** v/t (puzzle) dejar perplejo

foy·er ['fɔɪər] vestíbulo m

frac·tion ['frækʃn] fracción f; MATH fracción f, quebrado m

frac·tion·al·ly ['frækʃnəlɪ] adv ligeramente

frac·ture ['fræktʃər] **1** n fractura f **2** v/t fracturar; **he ~d his arm** se fracturó el brazo

frag·ile ['frædʒəl] adj frágil

frag·ment ['frægmənt] n fragmento m

frag·men·tar·y [fræg'məntərɪ] adj fragmentario

fra·grance ['freɪgrəns] fragancia f

fra·grant ['freɪgrənt] adj fragante

frail [freɪl] adj frágil, delicado

frame [freɪm] **1** n of picture, window marco m; of eyeglasses montura f; of bicycle cuadro m; **~ of mind** estado m de ánimo **2** v/t picture enmarcar; F person tender una trampa a

'frame-up F trampa f

'frame·work estructura f; for agreement marco m

France [fræns] Francia

fran·chise ['fræntʃaɪz] n for business franquicia f

frank [fræŋk] adj franco

frank·furt·er ['fræŋkfɜːrtər] salchicha f de Fráncfort

frank·ly ['fræŋklɪ] adv francamente

frank·ness ['fræŋknɪs] franqueza f

fran·tic ['fræntɪk] adj frenético

fran·ti·cal·ly ['fræntɪklɪ] adv frenéticamente

fra·ter·nal [frə'tɜːrnl] adj fraternal

fraud [frɔːd] fraude m; person impostor(a) m(f)

fraud·u·lent ['frɔːdjʊlənt] adj fraudulento

fraud·u·lent·ly ['frɔːdjʊləntlɪ] adv fraudulentamente

frayed [freɪd] adj cuffs deshilachado

freak [friːk] **1** n unusual event fenómeno m anormal; two-headed person, animal etc monstruo m, monstruosidad f; F strange person bicho m raro F; **a movie / jazz ~** F un fanático del cine / jazz F **2** adj wind, storm etc anormal

freck·le ['frekl] peca f

free [friː] **1** adj libre; no cost gratis, gratuito; **are you ~ this afternoon?** ¿estás libre esta tarde?; **~ and easy** relajado; **for ~** travel, get sth gratis **2** v/t prisoners liberar

free·bie ['friːbɪ] F regalo m; **as a ~** de regalo

free·dom ['friːdəm] libertad f

free·dom of 'speech libertad f de expresión

free·dom of the 'press libertad f de prensa

free 'en·ter·prise empresa f libre; **free 'kick** in soccer falta f, golpe m franco; **free·lance** ['friːlæns] **1** adj autónomo, free-lance **2** adv: **work ~** trabajar como autónomo or free-lance; **free·lanc·er** ['friːlænsər] autónomo(-a) m(f), free-lance m/f; **free·load·er** ['friːloʊdər] F gorrón (-ona) m(f)

free·ly ['friːlɪ] adv admit libremente

free mar·ket 'e·con·o·my economía f de libre mercado; **free-range 'chick·en** pollo m de corral; **free-range 'eggs** npl huevos mpl de corral; **free 'sam·ple** muestra f gratuita; **free 'speech** libertad f de expresión; **'free·way** autopista f; **free'wheel** v/i of cyclist ir sin pedalear; **free 'will** libre albedrío m; **he did it of his own ~** lo hizo por propia iniciativa

freeze [friːz] **1** v/t (pret **froze**, pp **frozen**) food, wages, video congelar; river congelar, helar **2** v/i (pret **froze**, pp **frozen**) of water congelarse, helarse

◆**freeze over** v/i of river helarse

'freeze-dried adj liofilizado

freez·er ['friːzər] congelador m

freez·ing ['friːzɪŋ] **1** adj muy frío; **it's ~ (cold)** of weather hace mucho frío; of water está muy frío; **I'm ~ (cold)** tengo mucho frío **2** n: **10 degrees below ~** diez grados bajo cero

'freez·ing com·part·ment congelador m

'freez·ing point punto m de congelación

freight [freɪt] n transporte; costs flete m

'freight car on train vagón m de mercancías

freight·er ['freɪtər] ship carguero m; airplane avión m de carga

'freight train tren m de mercancías

French [frentʃ] **1** adj francés **2** n language francés m; **the ~** los franceses

French 'bread pan m de barra; **French 'doors** npl puerta f cristalera; **'French fries** npl Span patatas fpl or L.Am. papas fpl fritas; **'French·man** francés m; **'French·wom·an** francesa f

fren·zied ['frenzɪd] adj attack, activity frenético; mob desenfrenado

fren·zy ['frenzɪ] frenesí m; **whip s.o. into a ~** poner a alguien frenético

fre·quen·cy ['friːkwənsɪ] also RAD frecuencia f

fre·quent¹ ['friːkwənt] adj frecuente; **how ~ are the trains?** ¿con qué frecuencia pasan trenes?

fre·quent² [frɪ'kwent] v/t bar frecuentar

fre·quent·ly ['friːkwəntlɪ] adv con frecuencia

fres·co ['freskoʊ] fresco m

fresh [freʃ] adj fresco; start nuevo; **don't you get ~ with your mother!** ¡no seas descarado con tu madre!

fresh 'air aire m fresco

fresh·en ['freʃn] v/i of wind refrescar

◆**freshen up 1** v/i refrescarse **2** v/t room, paintwork renovar, revivir

fresh·ly ['freʃlɪ] adv recién

'fresh·man estudiante m/f de primer año

fresh·ness ['freʃnɪs] frescura f

'fresh·wa·ter adj de agua dulce

fret [fret] v/i (pret & pp **-ted**) ponerse nervioso, inquietarse

Freud·i·an ['frɔɪdɪən] adj freudiano

fric·tion ['frɪkʃn] PHYS rozamiento m; between people fricción f

'fric·tion tape cinta f aislante

Fri·day ['fraɪdeɪ] viernes m inv

fridge [frɪdʒ] nevera f, frigorífico m

fried 'egg [fraɪd] huevo *m* frito

fried po'ta·toes *npl Span* patatas *fpl* or *L.Am.* papas *fpl* fritas

friend [frend] amigo(-a) *m(f)*; **make ~s of one person** hacer amigos; *of two people* hacerse amigos; **make ~s with s.o.** hacerse amigo de alguien

friend·li·ness ['frendlɪnɪs] simpatía *f*

friend·ly ['frendlɪ] *adj atmosphere* agradable; *person* agradable, simpático; *(easy to use)* fácil de usar; *argument, match, relations* amistoso; **be ~ with s.o.** *(be friends)* ser amigo de alguien

'friend·ship ['frendʃɪp] amistad *f*

fries [fraɪz] *npl Span* patatas *fpl* or *L.Am.* papas *fpl* fritas

fright [fraɪt] susto *m*; **give s.o. a ~** dar un susto a alguien, asustar a alguien; **scream with ~** gritar asustado

fright·en ['fraɪtn] *v/t* asustar; **be ~ed** estar asustado, tener miedo; **don't be ~ed** no te asustes, no tengas miedo; **be ~ed of** tener miedo de

♦ **frighten away** *v/t* ahuyentar, espantar

fright·en·ing ['fraɪtnɪŋ] *adj noise, person, prospect* aterrador, espantoso

frig·id ['frɪdʒɪd] *adj sexually* frígido

frill [frɪl] *on dress etc* volante *m*; *(fancy extra)* extra *m*

frill·y ['frɪlɪ] *adj* de volantes

fringe [frɪndʒ] *on dress, curtains etc* flecos *mpl*; *Br in hair* flequillo *m*; *(edge)* margen *m*

'fringe ben·e·fits *npl* ventajas *fpl* adicionales

frisk [frɪsk] *v/t* cachear

frisk·y ['frɪskɪ] *adj puppy etc* juguetón

♦ **frit·ter away** ['frɪtər] *v/t time* desperdiciar; *fortune* despilfarrar

fri·vol·i·ty [frɪ'vɑːlətɪ] frivolidad *f*

friv·o·lous ['frɪvələs] *adj* frívolo

frizz·y ['frɪzɪ] *adj hair* crespo

frog [frɑːg] rana *f*

'frog·man hombre *m* rana

from [frɑːm] *prep* ◊ *in time* desde; **~ 9 to 5** (*o'clock*) de 9 a 5; **~ the 18th century** desde el siglo XVIII; **~ today on** a partir de hoy; **~ next Tuesday** a partir del próximo martes ◊ *in space* de, desde; **~ here to there** de *or* desde aquí hasta allí; **we drove here ~ Las Vegas** vinimos en coche desde Las Vegas ◊ *origin* de; **a letter ~ Jo** una carta de Jo; **it doesn't say who it's ~** no dice de quién es; **I am ~ New Jersey** soy de Nueva Jersey; **made ~ bananas** hecho con plátanos ◊ *(because of)*: **tired ~ the journey** cansado del viaje; **it's ~ overeating** es por comer demasiado

front [frʌnt] **1** *n of building, book* portada *f*; *(cover organization)* tapadera *f*; MIL, *of weather* frente *m*; **in ~** delante; *in a race* en cabeza; **the car in ~** el coche de delante; **in ~ of** delante de; **at the ~ of** en la parte de delante de **2** *adj wheel, seat* delantero **3** *v/t TV program* presentar

front 'cov·er portada *f*; **front 'door** puerta *f* principal; **front 'en·trance** entrada *f* principal

fron·tier ['frʌntɪr] frontera *f*; *fig: of knowledge, science* límite *m*

front 'line MIL línea *f* del frente; **front 'page** *of newspaper* portada *f*, primera *f* plana; **front page 'news** *nsg* noticia *f* de portada *or* de primera plana; **front 'row** primera fila *f*; **front seat 'pas·sen·ger** *in car* pasajero(-a) *m(f)* de delante; **front-wheel 'drive** tracción *f* delantera

frost [frɑːst] *n* escarcha *f*; **there was a ~ last night** anoche cayó una helada

'frost·bite congelación *f*

'frost·bit·ten *adj* congelado

frost·ed glass ['frɑːstɪd] vidrio *m* esmerilado

frost·ing ['frɑːstɪŋ] *on cake* glaseado *m*

frost·y ['frɑːstɪ] *adj weather* gélido; *fig: welcome* glacial

froth [frɑːθ] *n* espuma *f*

froth·y ['frɑːθɪ] *adj cream etc* espumoso

frown [fraʊn] **1** *n*: **what's that ~ for?** ¿por qué frunces el ceño? **2** *v/i* fruncir el ceño

froze [frəʊz] *pret* → **freeze**

fro·zen ['frəʊzn] **1** *adj ground, food* congelado; *wastes* helado; **I'm ~** F estoy helado *or* congelado F **2** *pp* → **freeze**

fro·zen 'food comida *f* congelada

fruit [fruːt] fruta *f*

'fruit cake bizcocho *m* de frutas

fruit·ful ['fruːtfəl] *adj discussions etc* fructífero

'fruit juice *Span* zumo *m or L.Am.* jugo *m* de fruta

fruit 'sal·ad macedonia *f*

frus·trate [frʌ'streɪt] *v/t person, plans* frustrar

frus·trat·ed [frʌ'streɪtɪd] *adj* frustrado

frus·trat·ing [frʌ'streɪtɪŋ] *adj* frustrante

frus·tra·tion [frʌ'streɪʃn] frustración *f*

fry [fraɪ] *v/t* (*pret & pp* **-ied**) freír

'fry·pan sartén *f*

fuck [fʌk] *v/t* V *Span* follar con V, *L.Am.* coger V; **~!** ¡joder! V; **~ him!** ¡que se joda! V

♦**fuck off** *v/i* V: **fuck off!** ¡vete a la mierda! V

fuck·ing ['fʌkɪŋ] **1** *adj* V puto V **2** *adv* V: **it's ~ crazy** es un estupidez ¡coño!; **it was ~ brilliant!** ¡estuvo de puta madre! V

fu·el ['fjʊəl] **1** *n* combustible *m* **2** *v/t fig* avivar

fu·gi·tive ['fjuːdʒətɪv] *n* fugitivo(-a) *m(f)*

ful·fil *Br*, **ful·fill** [fʊl'fɪl] *v/t dream* cumplir, realizar; *task* realizar; *contract* cumplir; **feel ~ed** *in job, life* sentirse realizado

ful·fill·ing [fʊl'fɪlɪŋ] *adj*: **I have a ~ job** mi trabajo me llena

ful·fil·ment *Br*, **ful·fill·ment** [fʊl'fɪlmənt] *of contract etc* cumplimiento *m*; *moral, spiritual* satisfacción *f*

full [fʊl] *adj* lleno; *account, schedule* completo; *life* pleno; **~ of** *of water etc* lleno de; **~ up** *hotel etc, with food* lleno; **pay in ~** pagar al contado

full-'cov·er·age (*insurance*) seguro *m* a todo riesgo; **'full-grown** *adj* completamente desarrollado; **'full-length** *adj dress* de cuerpo entero; **~ movie** largometraje *m*; **full 'moon** luna *f* llena; **full 'stop** *Br* punto *m*; **full 'time 1** *adj worker, job* a tiempo completo **2** *adv work* a tiempo completo

ful·ly ['fʊlɪ] *adv* completamente; *describe* en detalle

fum·ble ['fʌmbl] *v/t ball* dejar caer

♦**fumble around** *v/i* rebuscar

fume [fjuːm] *v/i*: **be fuming** F *with anger* echar humo F

fumes [fjuːmz] *npl* humos *mpl*

fun [fʌn] diversión *f*; **it was great ~** fue muy divertido; **bye, have ~!** ¡adiós, que lo paséis bien!; **for ~** para divertirse; **make ~ of** burlarse de

func·tion ['fʌŋkʃn] **1** *n* (*purpose*) función *f*; (*reception etc*) acto *m* **2** *v/i* funcionar; **~ as** hacer de

func·tion·al ['fʌŋkʃnl] *adj* funcional

fund [fʌnd] **1** *n* fondo *m* **2** *v/t project etc* financiar

fun·da·men·tal [fʌndə'mentl] *adj* fundamental; (*crucial*) esencial

fun·da·men·tal·ist [fʌndə'mentlɪst] *n* fundamentalista *m/f*

fun·da·men·tal·ly [fʌndə'mentlɪ] *adv* fundamentalmente

fund·ing ['fʌndɪŋ] (*money*) fondos *mpl*, financiación *f*

fu·ne·ral ['fjuːnərəl] funeral *m*

'fu·ne·ral di·rec·tor encargado(-a) *m(f)* de una funeraria

'fu·ne·ral home funeraria *f*

fun·gus ['fʌŋgəs] hongos *mpl*

fu·nic·u·lar ('rail·way) [fjuː'nɪkjʊlər] funicular *m*

fun·nel ['fʌnl] *n of ship* chimenea *f*

fun·nies ['fʌnɪz] *npl* F sección de humor

fun·ni·ly ['fʌnɪlɪ] *adv* (*oddly*) de modo extraño; (*comically*) de for-

F

ma divertida; **~ enough** curiosamente

fun·ny ['fʌni] *adj* (*comical*) divertido, gracioso; (*odd*) curioso, raro; **that's not ~** eso no tiene gracia

'**fun·ny bone** hueso *m* de la risa

fur [fɜːr] piel *f*

fu·ri·ous ['fjʊrɪəs] *adj* (*angry*) furioso; (*intense*) furioso, feroz; *effort* febril; **at a ~ pace** a un ritmo vertiginoso

fur·nace ['fɜːrnɪs] horno *m*

fur·nish ['fɜːrnɪʃ] *v/t room* amueblar; (*supply*) suministrar

fur·ni·ture ['fɜːrnɪtʃər] mobiliario *m*, muebles *mpl*; **a piece of ~** un mueble

fur·ry ['fɜːrɪ] *adj animal* peludo

fur·ther ['fɜːrðər] **1** *adj* (*additional*) adicional; (*more distant*) más lejano; **there's been a ~ development** ha pasado algo nuevo; **until ~ notice** hasta nuevo aviso; **have you anything ~ to say?** ¿tiene algo más que añadir? **2** *adv walk, drive* más lejos; **~, I want to say ...** además, quiero decir ...; **two miles ~** (*on*) dos millas más adelante **3** *v/t cause etc* promover

fur·ther'more *adv* es más

fur·thest ['fɜːrðɪst] **1** *adj*: **the ~ point north** el punto más al norte; **the ~ stars** las estrellas más lejanas **2** *adv* más lejos; **this is the ~ north I've ever been** nunca había estado tan al norte

fur·tive ['fɜːrtɪv] *adj glance* furtivo

fur·tive·ly ['fɜːrtɪvlɪ] *adv* furtivamente

fu·ry ['fjʊrɪ] (*anger*) furia *f*, ira *f*

fuse [fjuːz] **1** *n* ELEC fusible *m* **2** *v/i* ELEC fundirse; **the lights have ~d** se han fundido los plomos **3** *v/t* ELEC fundir

'**fuse·box** caja *f* de fusibles

fu·se·lage ['fjuːzəlɑːʒ] fuselaje *m*

'**fuse wire** fusible *m* (*hilo*)

fu·sion ['fjuːʒn] fusión *f*

fuss [fʌs] *n* escándalo *m*; **make a ~** armar un escándalo; **make a ~ of** (*be very attentive to*) deshacerse en atenciones con

fuss·y ['fʌsɪ] *adj person* quisquilloso; *design etc* recargado; **be a ~ eater** ser un quisquilloso a la hora de comer

fu·tile ['fjuːtl] *adj* inútil, vano

fu·til·i·ty [fjuː'tɪlətɪ] inutilidad *f*

fu·ture ['fjuːtʃər] **1** *n also* GRAM futuro *m*; **in ~** en el futuro **2** *adj* futuro

fu·tures ['fjuːtʃərz] *npl* FIN futuros *mpl*

'**fu·tures mar·ket** FIN mercado *m* de futuros

fu·tur·is·tic [fjuːtʃə'rɪstɪk] *adj design* futurista

fuze [fjuːz] → **fuse**

fuzz·y ['fʌzɪ] *adj hair* crespo; (*out of focus*) borroso

G

gab [gæb] *n*: **have the gift of the ~** F tener labia F

gab·ble ['gæbl] *v/i* farfullar

♦ **gad around** [gæd] *v/i* (*pret & pp* **-ded**) pendonear

gad·get ['gædʒɪt] artilugio *m*, chisme *m*

gaffe [gæf] metedura *f* de pata

gag [gæg] **1** *n over mouth* mordaza *f*; (*joke*) chiste *m* **2** *v/t* (*pret & pp* **-ged**) *also fig* amordazar

gain [geɪn] *v/t* (*acquire*) ganar; *victory* obtener; **~ speed** cobrar velocidad; **~ 10 pounds** engordar 10 libras

ga·la ['geɪlə] gala *f*

gal·ax·y ['gæləksɪ] AST galaxia *f*

gale [geɪl] vendaval *m*

gal·lant ['gælənt] *adj* galante

gall blad·der ['gɒːlblædər] vesícula *f* biliar

gal·le·ry ['gælərɪ] *for art* museo *m*; *in theater* galería *f*

gal·ley ['gælɪ] *on ship* cocina *f*

♦ **gal·li·vant around** ['gælɪvænt] *v/i* pendonear

gal·lon ['gælən] galón *m* (*en EE.UU. 3,785 litros, en GB 4,546*); *~s of tea* F toneladas de té F

gal·lop ['gæləp] *v/i* galopar

gal·lows ['gæləʊz] *npl* horca *f*

gall·stone ['gɒːlstəʊn] cálculo *m* biliar

ga·lore [gə'lɔːr] *adj*: *apples / novels ~* manzanas / novelas a montones

gal·va·nize ['gælvənaɪz] *v/t* TECH galvanizar; *~ s.o. into activity* hacer que alguien se vuelva más activo

gam·ble ['gæmbl] *v/i* jugar

gam·bler ['gæmblər] jugador(a) *m(f)*

gam·bling ['gæmblɪŋ] *n* juego *m*

game [geɪm] *n* (*sport*) partido *m*; *children's, in tennis* juego *m*

'game re·serve coto *m* de caza

gang [gæŋ] *of friends* cuadrilla *f*, pandilla *f*; *of criminals* banda *f*

♦ **gang up on** *v/t* compincharse contra

'gang rape 1 *n* violación *f* colectiva **2** *v/t* violar colectivamente

gan·grene ['gæŋgriːn] MED gangrena *f*

gang·ster ['gæŋstər] gángster *m*

'gang war·fare lucha *f* entre bandas

'gang·way pasarela *f*

gap [gæp] *in wall* hueco *m*; *for parking, in figures* espacio *m*; *in time* intervalo *m*; *in conversation* interrupción *f*; *between two people's characters* diferencia *f*

gape [geɪp] *v/i of person* mirar boquiabierto

♦ **gape at** *v/t* mirar boquiabierto a

gap·ing ['geɪpɪŋ] *adj hole* enorme

gar·age [gə'rɑːʒ] *n for parking* garaje *m*; *for repairs* taller *m*; *Br for gas* gasolinera *f*

gar·bage ['gɑːrbɪdʒ] basura *f*; *fig* (*nonsense*) tonterías *fpl*; (*poor quality goods*) basura *f*, porquería *f*

'gar·bage bag bolsa *f* de la basura; **'gar·bage can** cubo *m* de la basura; *in street* papelera *f*; **'gar·bage truck** camión *m* de la basura

gar·bled ['gɑːrbld] *adj message* confuso

gar·den ['gɑːrdn] jardín *m*

'gar·den cen·ter, *Br* **'gar·den cen·tre** vivero *m*, centro *m* de jardinería

gar·den·er ['gɑːrdnər] aficionado(-a) *m(f)* a la jardinería; *professional* jardinero(-a) *m(f)*

gar·den·ing ['gɑːrdnɪŋ] jardinería *f*

gar·gle ['gɑːrgl] *v/i* hacer gárgaras

gar·goyle ['gɑːrgɔɪl] ARCHI gárgola *f*

gar·ish ['gerɪʃ] *adj color* chillón; *design* estridente

gar·land ['gɑːrlənd] *n* guirnalda *f*

gar·lic ['gɑːrlɪk] ajo *m*

gar·lic 'bread pan *m* con ajo

gar·ment ['gɑːrmənt] prenda *f* (de vestir)

gar·nish ['gɑːrnɪʃ] *v/t* guarnecer (*with* con)

gar·ri·son ['gærɪsn] *n place* plaza *f*; *troops* guarnición *f*

gar·ter ['gɑːrtər] liga *f*

gas [gæs] *n* gas *m*; (*gasoline*) gasolina *f*, *Rpl* nafta *f*

gash [gæʃ] *n* corte *m* profundo

gas·ket ['gæskɪt] junta *f*

gas·o·line ['gæsəliːn] gasolina *f*, *Rpl* nafta *f*

gasp [gæsp] **1** *n* grito *m* apagado **2** *v/i* lanzar un grito apagado; *~ for breath* luchar por respirar

'gas ped·al acelerador *m*; **'gas pipe·line** gasoducto *m*; **'gas pump** surtidor *m* (de gasolina); **'gas sta·tion** gasolinera *f*, *S.Am.* bomba *f*; **'gas stove** cocina *f* de gas

gas·tric ['gæstrɪk] *adj* MED gástrico

gas·tric 'flu MED gripe *f* gastrointestinal; **gas·tric 'juic·es** *npl* jugos *mpl* gástricos; **gas·tric 'ul·cer** MED úlcera *f* gástrica

gate [geɪt] *of house, at airport* puerta *f*; *made of iron* verja *f*

'**gate-crash** *v/t*: **~ a party** colarse en una fiesta

'**gate-way** *also fig* entrada *f*

gath·er ['gæðər] **1** *v/t facts, information* reunir; **am I to ~ that ...?** ¿debo entender que ...?; **~ speed** ganar velocidad **2** *v/i of crowd* reunirse

◆ **gather up** *v/t possessions* recoger

gath·er·ing ['gæðərɪŋ] *n (group of people)* grupo *m* de personas

gau·dy ['gɒːdɪ] *adj* chillón, llamativo

gauge [geɪdʒ] **1** *n* indicador *m* **2** *v/t pressure* medir, calcular; *opinion* estimar, calcular

gaunt [gɒːnt] *adj* demacrado

gauze [gɒːz] gasa *f*

gave [geɪv] *pret →* **give**

gaw·ky ['gɒːkɪ] *adj* desgarbado

gawp [gɒːp] *v/i* F mirar boquiabierto; **don't just stand there ~ing!** ¡no te quedes ahí boquiabierto!

gay [geɪ] **1** *n (homosexual)* homosexual *m*, gay *m* **2** *adj* homosexual, gay

gaze [geɪz] **1** *n* mirada *f* **2** *v/i* mirar fijamente

◆ **gaze at** *v/t* mirar fijamente

GB [dʒiː'biː] *abbr (= Great Britain)* GB (= Gran Bretaña)

GDP [dʒiːdiː'piː] *abbr (= gross domestic product)* PIB *m* (= producto *m* interior bruto)

gear [gɪr] *n (equipment)* equipo *m*; *in vehicles* marcha *f*

'**gear·box** MOT caja *f* de cambios

'**gear le·ver**, '**gear shift** MOT palanca *f* de cambios

geese [giːs] *pl →* **goose**

gel [dʒel] *for hair* gomina *f*; *for shower* gel *m*

gel·a·tine ['dʒelətiːn] gelatina *f*

gel·ig·nite ['dʒelɪgnaɪt] gelignita *f*

gem [dʒem] gema *f*, *fig (book etc)* joya *f*; *(person)* cielo *m*

Gem·i·ni ['dʒemɪnaɪ] ASTR Géminis *m/f inv*

gen·der ['dʒendər] género *m*

gene [dʒiːn] gen *m*; **it's in his ~s** lo lleva en los genes

gen·e·ral ['dʒenrəl] **1** *n* MIL general *m*; **in ~** en general, por lo general **2** *adj* general

gen·er·al e'lec·tion elecciones *fpl* generales

gen·er·al·i·za·tion [dʒenrəlaɪ'zeɪʃn] generalización *f*; **that's a ~** eso es generalizar

◆ **gen·er·al·ize** ['dʒenrəlaɪz] *v/i* generalizar

gen·er·al·ly ['dʒenrəlɪ] *adv* generalmente, por lo general; **~ speaking** en términos generales

gen·er·ate ['dʒenəreɪt] *v/t* generar; *a feeling* provocar

gen·e·ra·tion [dʒenə'reɪʃn] generación *f*

gen·e'ra·tion gap conflicto *m* generacional

gen·e·ra·tor ['dʒenəreɪtər] generador *m*

ge·ner·ic drug [dʒə'nerɪk] MED medicamento *m* genérico

gen·e·ros·i·ty [dʒenə'rɑːsətɪ] generosidad *f*

gen·e·rous ['dʒenərəs] *adj* generoso

ge·net·ic [dʒɪ'netɪk] *adj* genético

ge·net·i·cal·ly [dʒɪ'netɪklɪ] *adv* genéticamente; **~ modified crops** transgénico; **be ~ modified** estar modificado genéticamente

ge·net·ic 'code código *m* genético; **ge·net·ic en·gi'neer·ing** ingeniería *f* genética; **ge·net·ic 'fin·ger·print** identificación *f* genética

ge·net·i·cist [dʒɪ'netɪsɪst] genetista *m/f*, especialista *m/f* en genética

ge·net·ics [dʒɪ'netɪks] genética *f*

ge·ni·al ['dʒiːnjəl] *adj* afable, cordial

gen·i·tals ['dʒenɪtlz] *npl* genitales *mpl*

ge·ni·us ['dʒiːnjəs] genio *m*

gen·o·cide ['dʒenəsaɪd] genocidio *m*

gen·tle ['dʒentl] *adj person* tierno, delicado; *touch, detergent* suave; *breeze* suave, ligero; *slope* poco inclinado; **be ~ with it, it's fragile** ten mucho cuidado con él, es frágil

gen·tle·man ['dʒentlmən] caballero *m*; **he's a real ~** es todo un caballero

gen·tle·ness ['dʒentlnɪs] *of person* ternura *f*, delicadeza; *of touch, detergent, breeze* suavidad *f*; *of slope* poca inclinación *f*

gen·tly ['dʒentlɪ] *adv* con delicadeza, poco a poco; *a breeze blew* ~ sopla una ligera *or* suave brisa

gents [dʒents] *nsg toilet* servicio *m* de caballeros

gen·u·ine ['dʒenuɪn] *adj antique* genuino, auténtico; (*sincere*) sincero

gen·u·ine·ly ['dʒenuɪnlɪ] *adv* realmente, de verdad

ge·o·graph·i·cal [dʒɪə'græfɪkl] *adj features* geográfico

ge·og·ra·phy [dʒɪ'ɑːgrəfɪ] geografía *f*

ge·o·log·i·cal [dʒɪə'lɑːdʒɪkl] *adj* geológico

ge·ol·o·gist [dʒɪ'ɑːlədʒɪst] geólogo(-a) *m(f)*

ge·ol·o·gy [dʒɪ'ɑːlədʒɪ] geología *f*

ge·o·met·ric, **ge·o·met·ri·cal** [dʒɪə'metrɪk(l)] *adj* geométrico

ge·om·e·try [dʒɪ'ɑːmətrɪ] geometría *f*

ge·ra·ni·um [dʒə'reɪnɪəm] geranio *m*

ger·i·at·ric [dʒerɪ'ætrɪk] **1** *adj* geriátrico **2** *n* anciano(-a) *m(f)*

germ [dʒɜːrm] *also fig* germen *m*

Ger·man ['dʒɜːrmən] **1** *adj* alemán **2** *n person* alemán (-ana) *m(f)*; *language* alemán *m*

Ger·man 'mea·sles *nsg* rubeola *f*

Ger·man 'shep·herd pastor *m* alemán

Ger·ma·ny ['dʒɜːrmənɪ] Alemania *f*

ger·mi·nate ['dʒɜːrmɪneɪt] *v/i of seed* germinar

germ 'war·fare guerra *f* bacteriológica

ges·tic·u·late [dʒe'stɪkjʊleɪt] *v/i* gesticular

ges·ture ['dʒestʃər] *n also fig* gesto *m*

get [get] **1** *v/t* (*pret* **got**, *pp* **got**, **gotten**) (*obtain*) conseguir; (*fetch*)

traer; (*receive: letter, knowledge, respect*) recibir; (*catch: bus, train etc*) tomar, *Span* coger; (*understand*) entender; **you can ~ them at the corner shop** los puedes comprar en la tienda de la esquina; **can I ~ you something to drink?** ¿quieres tomar algo?; **~ tired** cansarse; **~ drunk** emborracharse; **I'm ~ting old** me estoy haciendo mayor; **~ the TV fixed** hacer que arreglen la televisión; **~ s.o. to do sth** hacer que alguien haga algo; **~ to do sth** (*have opportunity*) llegar a hacer algo; **~ one's hair cut** cortarse el pelo; **~ sth ready** preparar algo; **~ going** (*leave*) marcharse, irse; **have got** tener; **he's got a lot of money** tiene mucho dinero; **I have got to study/see him** tengo que estudiar / verlo; **I don't want to, but I've got to** no quiero, pero tengo que hacerlo; **~ to know** llegar a conocer **2** *v/i* (*arrive*) llegar

◆ **get along** *v/i* (*come to party etc*) ir; *with s.o.* llevarse bien; **how are you getting along at school?** ¿cómo te van las cosas en el colegio?; **the patient is getting along nicely** el paciente está progresando satisfactoriamente

◆ **get around** *v/i* (*travel*) viajar; (*be mobile*) desplazarse

◆ **get at** *v/t* (*criticize*) meterse con; (*imply, mean*) querer decir

◆ **get away 1** *v/i* (*leave*) marcharse, irse **2** *v/t*: **get sth away from s.o.** quitar algo a alguien

◆ **get away with** *v/t* salir impune de; **get away with it** salirse con la suya; **she lets him get away with anything** le permite todo; **I'll let you get away with it this time** por esta vez te perdonaré

◆ **get back 1** *v/i* (*return*) volver; **I'll get back to you on that tomorrow** le responderé a eso mañana **2** *v/t* (*obtain again*) recuperar

◆ **get by** *v/i* (*pass*) pasar; *financially* arreglárselas

◆ **get down 1** *v/i from ladder etc*

G

bajarse (*from* de); (*duck etc*) agacharse **2** *v/t* (*depress*) desanimar, deprimir

◆ **get down to** *v/t* (*start: work*) ponerse a; **get down to the facts** ir a los hechos

◆ **get in 1** *v/i* (*arrive*) llegar; *to car* subir(se), meterse; **how did they get in?** *of thieves, mice etc* ¿cómo entraron? **2** *v/t to suitcase etc* meter

◆ **get into** *v/t house* entrar en, meterse en; *car* subir(se) a, meterse en; *computer system* introducirse en

◆ **get off 1** *v/i from bus etc* bajarse; (*finish work*) salir; (*not be punished*) librarse **2** *v/t* (*remove*) quitar; *clothes, hat, footgear* quitarse; **get off my bike!** ¡bájate de mi bici!; **get off the grass!** ¡no pises la hierba!

◆ **get off with** *v/t*: **get off with a small fine** tener que pagar sólo una pequeña multa

◆ **get on 1** *v/i to bike, bus, train* montarse, subirse; (*be friendly*) llevarse bien; (*advance: of time*) hacerse tarde; (*become old*) hacerse mayor; (*make progress*) progresar; **it's getting on** *getting late* se está haciendo tarde; **he's getting on** se está haciendo mayor; **he's getting on for 50** está a punto de cumplir 50 **2** *v/t*: **get on the bus** / **one's bike** montarse en el autobús / la bici; **get one's shoes on** ponerse los zapatos; **I can't get these pants on** estos pantalones no me entran

◆ **get out 1** *v/i of car, prison etc* salir; **get out!** ¡vete!, ¡fuera de aquí!; **let's get out of here** ¡salgamos de aquí!; **I don't get out much these days** últimamente no salgo mucho **2** *v/t nail, sth jammed* sacar, extraer; *stain* quitar; *gun, pen* sacar

◆ **get over** *v/t fence etc* franquear; *disappointment* superar; *lover etc* olvidar

◆ **get over with** *v/t* terminar con; **let's get it over with** quitémonoslo de encima

◆ **get through** *v/i on telephone* conectarse; **obviously I'm just not**

getting through está claro que no me estoy haciendo entender; **get through to s.o.** (*make self understood*) comunicarse con alguien

◆ **get up 1** *v/i* levantarse **2** *v/t* (*climb*) subir

'**get·a·way** *from robbery* fuga *f*, huida *f*

'**get·a·way car** coche *m* utilizado en la fuga

'**get-to·geth·er** reunión *f*

ghast·ly ['gæstlɪ] *adj* terrible

gher·kin ['gɜːrkɪn] pepinillo *m*

ghet·to ['getoʊ] gueto *m*

ghost [goʊst] fantasma *m*

ghost·ly ['goʊstlɪ] *adj* fantasmal

'**ghost town** ciudad *f* fantasma

ghoul [guːl] macabro(-a) *m(f)*, morboso(-a) *m(f)*

ghoul·ish ['guːlɪʃ] *adj* macabro, morboso

gi·ant ['dʒaɪənt] **1** *n* gigante *m* **2** *adj* gigantesco, gigante

gib·ber·ish ['dʒɪbərɪʃ] F memeces *fpl* F, majaderías *fpl* F

gibe [dʒaɪb] *n* pulla *f*

gib·lets ['dʒɪblɪts] *npl* menudillos *mpl*

gid·di·ness ['gɪdɪnɪs] mareo *m*

gid·dy ['gɪdɪ] *adj* mareado; **feel ~** estar mareado

gift [gɪft] regalo *m*

gift cer·ti·fi·cate vale *m* de regalo

gift·ed ['gɪftɪd] *adj* con talento

'**gift-wrap 1** *n* papel *m* de regalo **2** *v/t* (*pret & pp* **-ped**) envolver para regalo

gig [gɪg] F concierto *m*, actuación *f*

gi·ga·byte ['gɪgəbaɪt] COMPUT gigabyte *m*

gi·gan·tic [dʒaɪ'gæntɪk] *adj* gigantesco

gig·gle ['gɪgl] **1** *v/i* soltar risitas **2** *n* risita *f*

gig·gly ['gɪglɪ] *adj* que suelta risitas

gill [gɪl] *of fish* branquia *f*

gilt [gɪlt] *n* dorado *m*; **~s** FIN valores *mpl* del Estado

gim·mick ['gɪmɪk] truco *m*, reclamo *m*

gim·mick·y ['gɪmɪkɪ] *adj* superficial,

artificioso

gin [dʒɪn] ginebra f; ~ and tonic gin-tonic m

gin·ger ['dʒɪndʒər] n spice jengibre m

'gin·ger·bread pan m de jengibre

gin·ger·ly ['dʒɪndʒərlɪ] adv cuidadosamente, delicadamente

gip·sy ['dʒɪpsɪ] gitano(-a) m(f)

gi·raffe [dʒɪ'ræf] jirafa f

gir·der ['gɜ:rdər] viga f

girl [gɜ:rl] chica f; (young) ~ niña f, chica f

'girl·friend of boy novia f; of girl amiga f

girl·ie mag·a·zine ['gɜ:rlɪ] revista f porno

girl·ish ['gɜ:rlɪʃ] adj de niñas

girl 'scout escultista f, scout f

gist [dʒɪst] esencia f

give [gɪv] v/t (pret gave, pp given) dar; as present regalar; (supply: electricity etc) proporcionar; talk, lecture, dar, pronunciar; cry, groan soltar; ~ her my love dale recuerdos (de mi parte); ~ s.o. a present hacer un regalo a alguien

♦ give away v/t as present regalar; (betray) traicionar; give o.s. away descubrirse, traicionarse

♦ give back v/t devolver

♦ give in 1 v/i (surrender) rendirse 2 v/t (hand in) entregar

♦ give off v/t smell, fumes emitir, despedir

♦ give onto v/i (open onto) dar a

♦ give out 1 v/t leaflets etc repartir 2 v/i of supplies, strength agotarse

♦ give up 1 v/t smoking etc dejar de; give o.s. up to the police entregarse a la policía 2 v/i (stop making effort) rendirse; I find it hard to give up me cuesta mucho dejarlo

♦ give way v/i of bridge etc hundirse

give-and-'take toma m y daca

giv·en ['gɪvn] pp → give

'giv·en name nombre m de pila

gla·ci·er ['gleɪʃər] glaciar m

glad [glæd] adj contento, alegre; I was ~ to see you me alegré de verte

glad·ly ['glædlɪ] adv con mucho gusto

glam·or ['glæmər] atractivo m, glamour m

glam·or·ize ['glæməraɪz] v/t hacer atractivo, ensalzar

glam·or·ous ['glæmərəs] adj atractivo, glamoroso →

glam·our Br → glamor

glance [glæns] 1 n ojeada f, vistazo m 2 v/i echar una ojeada or vistazo

♦ glance at v/t echar una ojeada or vistazo a

gland [glænd] glándula f

glan·du·lar 'fe·ver ['glændʒələr] mononucleosis f inv infecciosa

glare [gler] 1 n of sun, headlights resplandor m 2 v/i of headlights resplandecer

♦ glare at v/t mirar con furia a

glar·ing ['glerɪŋ] adj mistake garrafal

glar·ing·ly ['glerɪŋlɪ] adv: it's ~ obvious está clarísimo

glass [glæs] material vidrio m; for drink vaso m

glass 'case vitrina f

glass·es npl gafas fpl, L.Am. lentes mpl, L.Am. anteojos mpl

glaze [gleɪz] n vidriado m

♦ glaze over v/i of eyes vidriarse

glazed [gleɪzd] adj expression vidrioso

gla·zi·er ['gleɪzɪr] cristalero(-a) m(f), vidriero(-a) m(f)

glaz·ing ['gleɪzɪŋ] cristales mpl, vidrios mpl

gleam [gli:m] 1 n resplandor m, brillo m 2 v/i resplandecer, brillar

glee [gli:] júbilo m, regocijo m

glee·ful ['gli:fəl] adj jubiloso

glib [glɪb] adj fácil

glib·ly ['glɪblɪ] adv con labia

glide [glaɪd] v/i of bird, plane planear; of piece of furniture deslizarse

glid·er ['glaɪdər] planeador m

glid·ing ['glaɪdɪŋ] n sport vuelo m sin motor

glim·mer ['glɪmər] 1 n of light brillo m tenue; ~ of hope rayo m de esperanza 2 v/i brillar tenuemente

glimpse [glɪmps] 1 n vistazo m;

catch a ~ of vislumbrar **2** *v/t* vislumbrar

glint [glɪnt] **1** *n* destello *m*; *in eyes* centelleo *m* **2** *v/i of light* destellar; *of eyes* centellear

glis·ten ['glɪsn] *v/i* relucir, centellear

glit·ter ['glɪtər] *v/i* resplandecer, destellar

glit·ter·ati [glɪtə'rɑːtɪ] *npl* famosos *mpl*

gloat [gloʊt] *v/i* regodearse

♦ **gloat over** *v/t* regodearse de

glo·bal ['gloʊbl] *adj* global

glo·bal e'con·o·my economía *f* global; **glo·bal 'mar·ket** mercado *m* global; **glo·bal 'war·ming** calentamiento *m* global

globe [gloʊb] (*the earth*) globo *m*; (*model of earth*) globo *m* terráqueo

gloom [gluːm] (*darkness*) tinieblas *fpl*, oscuridad *f*; *mood* abatimiento *m*, melancolía *f*

gloom·i·ly ['gluːmɪlɪ] *adv* con abatimiento, melancólicamente

gloom·y ['gluːmɪ] *adj room* tenebroso, oscuro; *mood, person* abatido, melancólico

glo·ri·ous ['glɔːrɪəs] *adj weather, day* espléndido, maravilloso; *victory* glorioso

glo·ry ['glɔːrɪ] *n* gloria *f*

gloss [glɑːs] *n* (*shine*) lustre *m*, brillo *m*; (*general explanation*) glosa *f*

♦ **gloss over** *v/t* pasar por alto

glos·sa·ry ['glɑːsərɪ] *n* glosario *m*

'gloss paint pintura *f* brillante

gloss·y ['glɑːsɪ] **1** *adj paper* cuché, satinado **2** *n magazine* revista *f* en color (en papel cuché *or* satinado)

glove [glʌv] guante *m*

'glove com·part·ment guantera *f*

'glove pup·pet marioneta *f* de guiñol (de guante)

glow [gloʊ] **1** *n of light, fire* resplandor *m*, brillo *m*; *in cheeks* rubor *m* **2** *v/i of light, fire* resplandecer, brillar; *of cheeks* ruborizarse

glow·er [glaʊr] *v/i* fruncir el ceño

glow·ing ['gloʊɪŋ] *adj description* entusiasta

glu·cose ['gluːkoʊs] glucosa *f*

glue [gluː] **1** *n* pegamento *m*, cola *f* **2** *v/t* pegar, encolar; **~ sth to sth** pegar *or* encolar algo a algo; **be ~d to the radio / TV** F estar pegado a la radio / televisión F

glum [glʌm] *adj* sombrío, triste

glum·ly ['glʌmlɪ] *adv* con tristeza

glut [glʌt] *n* exceso *m*, superabundancia *f*

glut·ton ['glʌtən] glotón(-ona) *m(f)*

glut·ton·y ['glʌtənɪ] gula *f*, glotonería *f*

GMT [dʒiːem'tiː] *abbr* (= ***Greenwich Mean Time***) hora *f* del meridiano de Greenwich

gnarled [nɑːrld] *adj* nudoso

gnat [næt] *tipo de mosquito*

gnaw [nɒː] *v/t bone* roer

GNP [dʒiːen'piː] *abbr* (= ***gross national product***) PNB *m* (= producto *m* nacional bruto)

go [goʊ] **1** *n:* **on the ~** en marcha **2** *v/i* (*pret* **went**, *pp* **gone**) ir (**to** a); (*leave*) irse, marcharse; (*work, function*) funcionar; (*come out: of stain etc*) irse; (*cease: of pain etc*) pasarse; (*match: of colors etc*) ir bien, pegar; **~ shopping / jogging** ir de compras / a correr footing; **I must be ~ing** me tengo que ir; **let's ~!** ¡vamos!; **~ for a walk** ir a pasear *or* a dar un paseo; **~ to bed** ir(se) a la cama; **~ to school** ir al colegio; **how's the work ~ing?** ¿cómo va el trabajo?; **they're ~ing for $50** (*being sold at*) se venden por 50 dólares; **hamburger to ~** hamburguesa para llevar; **be all gone** (*finished*) haberse acabado; **~ green** ponerse verde; **be ~ing to do sth** ir a hacer algo

♦ **go ahead** *v/i and do sth* seguir adelante; **can I? – sure, go ahead** ¿puedo? – por supuesto, adelante

♦ **go ahead with** *v/t plans etc* seguir adelante con

♦ **go along with** *v/t suggestion* aceptar

♦ **go at** *v/t* (*attack*) atacar

♦ **go away** *v/i of person* irse, marcharse; *of rain, pain, clouds* desaparecer

♦ **go back** v/i (*return*) volver; (*date back*) remontarse; **we go back a long way** nos conocemos desde hace tiempo; **go back to sleep** volver a dormirse

♦ **go by** v/i of car, time pasar

♦ **go down** v/i bajar; of sun ponerse; of ship hundirse; **go down well/badly** of suggestion etc sentar bien/mal

♦ **go for** v/t (*attack*) atacar; **I don't much go for gin** no me va mucho la ginebra

♦ **go in** v/i to room, house entrar; of sun ocultarse; (*fit: of part etc*) ir, encajar

♦ **go in for** v/t competition, race tomar parte en; **I used to go in for badminton quite a lot** antes jugaba mucho al bádminton

♦ **go off 1** v/i (*leave*) marcharse; of bomb explotar, estallar; of gun dispararse; of alarm saltar; of milk etc echarse a perder **2** v/t: **I've gone off whiskey** ya no me gusta el whisky

♦ **go on** v/i (*continue*) continuar; (*happen*) ocurrir, pasar; **go on, do it!** (*encouraging*) ¡venga, hazlo!; **what's going on?** ¿qué pasa?

♦ **go on at** v/t (*nag*) meterse con

♦ **go out** v/i of person salir; of light, fire apagarse

♦ **go out with** v/t romantically salir con

♦ **go over** v/t (*check*) examinar; (*do again*) repasar

♦ **go through** v/t illness, hard times atravesar; (*check*) revisar, examinar; (*read through*) estudiar

♦ **go under** v/i (*sink*) hundirse; of company ir a la quiebra

♦ **go up** v/i subir

♦ **go without 1** v/t food etc pasar sin **2** v/i pasar privaciones

goad [goʊd] v/t pinchar; **~ s.o. into doing sth** pinchar a alguien para que haga algo

'**go-a-head 1** n luz f verde; **when we get the ~** cuando nos den la luz verde **2** adj (*enterprising, dynamic*) di-

námico

goal [goʊl] SP target portería f, L.Am. arco m; SP point gol m; (*objective*) objetivo m, meta f

goal·ie ['goʊlɪ] F portero(-a) m(f), L.Am. arquero(-a) m(f)

'**goal·keep·er** portero(-a) m(f), guardameta m/f, L.Am. arquero(-a) m(f); '**goal kick** saque m de puerta; '**goal·mouth** portería f; '**goal·post** poste m

goat [goʊt] cabra f

gob·ble ['gɑːbl] v/t engullir

♦ **gobble up** v/t engullir

gob·ble·dy·gook ['gɑːbldɪguːk] F jerigonza f

'**go-be·tween** intermediario(-a) m(f)

god [gɑːd] dios m; **thank God!** ¡gracias a Dios!; **oh God!** ¡Dios mío!

'**god·child** ahijado(-a) m(f)

'**god·daugh·ter** ahijada f

'**god·dess** ['gɑːdɪs] diosa f

'**god·fa·ther** also in mafia padrino m; **god·for·sak·en** ['gɑːdfərseɪkən] adj place dejado de la mano de Dios; '**god·moth·er** madrina f; '**god·pa·rent** man padrino m; woman madrina f; '**god·send** regalo m del cielo; '**god·son** ahijado m

go·fer ['goʊfər] F recadero(-a) m(f)

gog·gles ['gɑːglz] npl gafas fpl

go·ing ['goʊɪŋ] adj price etc vigente; **~ concern** empresa f en marcha

go·ings-on [goʊɪŋz'ɑːn] npl actividades fpl

gold [goʊld] **1** n oro m **2** adj de oro

gold·en ['goʊldn] adj sky, hair dorado

gold·en 'hand·shake gratificación entregada tras la marcha de un directivo

gold·en 'wed·ding (an·ni·ver·sa·ry) bodas fpl de oro

'**gold·fish** pez m de colores; '**gold med·al** medalla f de oro; '**gold mine** fig mina f; '**gold·smith** orfebre m/f

golf [gɑːlf] golf m

'**golf ball** pelota f de golf; '**golf club** organization club m de golf; stick palo *m* de golf; '**golf course** campo *m* de golf

golf·er ['gɑːlfər] golfista *m/f*

gone [gɑːn] *pp* → **go**

gong [gɑːŋ] gong *m*

good [gʊd] *adj* bueno; *food* bueno, rico; *a ~ many* muchos; *he's ~ at chess* se le da muy bien el ajedrez; *be ~ for s.o.* ser bueno para alguien

good·bye [gʊd'baɪ] adiós *m*, despedida *f*; *say ~ to s.o., wish s.o. ~* decir adiós a alguien, despedirse de alguien

'**good-for-noth·ing** *n* inútil *m/f*; **Good 'Fri·day** Viernes *m inv* Santo; **good-hu·mored**, *Br* **good-hu·moured** [gʊd'hjuːmərd] *adj* jovial, afable; **good-look·ing** [gʊd'lʊkɪŋ] *adj* woman, man guapo; **good-na·tured** [gʊd'neɪtʃərd] bondadoso

good·ness ['gʊdnɪs] *moral* bondad *f*; *of fruit etc* propiedades *fpl*, valor *m* nutritivo; *thank ~!* ¡gracias a Dios!

goods [gʊdz] *npl* COM mercancías *fpl*, productos *mpl*

good'will buena voluntad *f*

good·y-good·y ['gʊdɪgʊdɪ] *n* F: *she's a real ~* es demasiado buenaza F

goo·ey ['guːɪ] *adj* pegajoso

goof [guːf] *v/i* F meter la pata F

goose [guːs] (*pl geese* [giːs]) ganso *m*, oca *f*

goose·ber·ry ['gʊzberɪ] grosella *f*; '**goose bumps** *npl* carne *f* de gallina; '**goose pim·ples** *npl* carne *f* de gallina

gorge [gɔːrdʒ] **1** *n* garganta *f*, desfiladero *m* **2** *v/t*: *~ o.s. on sth* comer algo hasta hartarse

gor·geous ['gɔːrdʒəs] *adj* weather maravilloso; *dress, hair* precioso; *woman, man* buenísimo; *smell* estupendo

go·ril·la [gə'rɪlə] gorila *m*

gosh [gɑːʃ] *int* ¡caramba!, ¡vaya!

go-'slow huelga *f* de celo

gos·pel ['gɑːspl] *in Bible* evangelio *m*; *it's the ~ truth* es la pura verdad

gos·sip ['gɑːsɪp] **1** *n* cotilleo *m*; *person* cotilla *m/f* **2** *v/i* cotillear

'**gos·sip col·umn** ecos *mpl* de sociedad

'**gos·sip col·um·nist** escritor(a) *m(f)* de los ecos de sociedad

gossipy ['gɑːsɪpɪ] *adj* letter lleno de cotilleos

got [gɑːt] *pret & pp* → **get**

got·ten ['gɑːtn] *pp* → **get**

gour·met ['gʊrmeɪ] *n* gastrónomo(-a) *m(f)*, gourmet *m/f*

gov·ern ['gʌvərn] *v/t* country gobernar

gov·ern·ment ['gʌvərnmənt] gobierno *m*

gov·er·nor ['gʌvərnər] gobernador(a) *m(f)*

gown [gaʊn] *long dress* vestido *m*; *wedding dress* traje *m*; *of academic, judge* toga *f*; *of surgeon* bata *f*

grab [græb] *v/t* (*pret & pp -bed*) agarrar; *food* tomar; *~ some sleep* dormir

grace [greɪs] *of dancer etc* gracia *f*, elegancia *f*; *say ~ at meal* bendecir la mesa

grace·ful ['greɪsfəl] *adj* elegante

grace·ful·ly ['greɪsfəlɪ] *adv* move con gracia *or* elegancia

gra·cious ['greɪʃəs] *adj* person amable; *style, living* elegante; *good ~!* ¡Dios mío!

grade [greɪd] **1** *n* quality grado *m*; EDU curso *m*; (*mark*) nota *f* **2** *v/t* clasificar

'**grade cross·ing** paso *m* a nivel

'**grade school** escuela *f* primaria

gra·di·ent ['greɪdɪənt] pendiente *f*

grad·u·al ['grædʒʊəl] *adj* gradual

grad·u·al·ly ['grædʒʊəlɪ] *adv* gradualmente, poco a poco

grad·u·ate ['grædʒʊət] **1** *n* licenciado (-a) *m(f)*; *from high school* bachiller *m/f* **2** *v/i* from university licenciarse, *L.Am.* egresarse; *from high school* sacar el bachillerato

grad·u·a·tion [grædʒʊ'eɪʃn] graduación *f*

graf·fi·ti [grə'fiːtiː] graffiti *m*

graft [græft] **1** *n* BOT, MED injerto *m*; *corruption* corrupción *f* **2** *v/t* BOT, MED injertar

grain [greɪn] grano *m*; *in wood* veta *f*;
  go against the ~ ir contra la naturaleza de alguien

gram [græm] gramo *m*

gram·mar ['græmər] gramática *f*

gram·mat·i·cal [grə'mætɪkl] *adj* gramatical

gram·mat·i·cal·ly [grə'mætɪklɪ] *adv* gramaticalmente

grand [grænd] **1** *adj* grandioso; F *(very good)* estupendo, genial **2** *n* F *($1000)* mil dólares

gran·dad ['grændæd] F abuelito *m*

'grand·child nieto(-a) *m(f)*

'grand·daugh·ter nieta *f*

gran·deur ['grændʒər] grandiosidad *f*

'grand·fa·ther abuelo *m*

'grand·fa·ther clock reloj *m* de pie

gran·di·ose ['grændɪous] *adj* grandioso

grand 'jur·y jurado *m* de acusación, gran jurado; **'grand·ma** F abuelita *f*, yaya *f* F; **'grand·moth·er** abuela *f*; **'grand·pa** F abuelo *m*, yayo *m* F; **'grand·par·ents** *npl* abuelos *mpl*; **grand pi'an·o** piano *m* de cola; **grand 'slam** gran slam *m*; **'grand·son** nieto *m*; **'grand·stand** tribuna *f*

gran·ite ['grænɪt] granito *m*

gran·ny ['grænɪ] F abuelita *f*, yaya *f* F

grant [grænt] **1** *n money* subvención *f* **2** *v/t* conceder; **take sth for ~ed** dar algo por sentado; **take s.o. for ~ed** no apreciar a alguien lo suficiente

gran·u·lat·ed sug·ar ['grænuleɪtɪd] azúcar *m or f* granulado(-a)

gran·ule ['grænjuːl] gránulo *m*

grape [greɪp] uva *f*

'grape·fruit pomelo *m*, *L.Am.* toronja *f*; **'grape·fruit juice** *Span* zumo *m* de pomelo, *L.Am.* jugo *m* de toronja; **'grape·vine: I've heard through the ~ that ...** me ha contado un pajarito que ...

graph [græf] gráfico *m*, gráfica *f*

graph·ic ['græfɪk] **1** *adj (vivid)* gráfico **2** *n* COMPUT gráfico *m*

graph·ic·al·ly ['græfɪklɪ] *adv* descri-

be gráficamente

graph·ic de'sign·er diseñador(a) *m(f)* gráfico(-a)

♦ **grap·ple with** ['græpl] *v/t attacker* forcejear con; *problem etc* enfrentarse a

grasp [græsp] **1** *n physical* asimiento *m*; *mental* comprensión *f* **2** *v/t physically* agarrar; *(understand)* comprender

grass [græs] *n* hierba *f*

'grass·hop·per saltamontes *m inv*; **grass 'roots** *npl people* bases *fpl*; **grass 'wid·ow** mujer cuyo marido está a menudo ausente durante largos periodos de tiempo; **grass 'wid·ow·er** hombre cuya mujer está a menudo ausente durante largos periodos de tiempo

gras·sy ['græsɪ] *adj* lleno de hierba

grate[1] [greɪt] *n metal* parrilla *f*, reja *f*

grate[2] [greɪt] **1** *v/t in cooking* rallar **2** *v/i of sound* rechinar

grate·ful ['greɪtfəl] *adj* agradecido; **we are ~ for your help** (le) agradecemos su ayuda; **I'm ~ to him** le estoy agradecido

grate·ful·ly ['greɪtfəlɪ] *adv* con agradecimiento

grat·er ['greɪtər] rallador *m*

grat·i·fy ['grætɪfaɪ] *v/t (pret & pp -ied)* satisfacer, complacer

grat·ing ['greɪtɪŋ] **1** *n* reja *f* **2** *adj sound, voice* chirriante

grat·i·tude ['grætɪtuːd] gratitud *f*

gra·tu·i·tous [grə'tuːɪtəs] *adj* gratuito

gra·tu·i·ty [grə'tuːətɪ] propina *f*, gratificación *f*

grave[1] [greɪv] *n* tumba *f*, sepultura *f*

grave[2] [greɪv] *adj* grave

grav·el ['grævl] *n* gravilla *f*

'grave·stone lápida *f*

'grave·yard cementerio *m*

♦ **grav·i·tate toward** ['grævɪteɪt] *v/t* verse atraído por

grav·i·ty ['grævətɪ] PHYS gravedad *f*

gra·vy ['greɪvɪ] jugo *m* (de la carne)

gray [greɪ] *adj* gris; **be going ~** encanecer

gray-haired [greɪ'herd] *adj* canoso

'gray·hound galgo *m*

graze[1] [greɪz] *v/i of cow etc* pastar, pacer

graze[2] [greɪz] **1** *v/t arm etc* rozar, arañar **2** *n* rozadura *f*, arañazo *m*

grease [griːs] *n* grasa *f*

grease·proof 'pa·per papel *m* de cera *or* parafinado

greas·y ['griːsɪ] *adj food, hands, plate* grasiento; *hair, skin* graso

great [greɪt] *adj* grande, *before singular noun* gran; F (*very good*) estupendo, genial F; *how was it? – ~!* ¿cómo fue? – ¡estupendo *or* genial!; *~ to see you again!* ¡me alegro de volver a verte!

Great 'Brit·ain Gran Bretaña; **great·'grand·child** bisnieto(-a) *m(f)*; **great·'grand·daugh·ter** bisnieta *f*; **great·'grand·fa·ther** bisabuelo *m*; **great·'grand·moth·er** bisabuela *f*; **great·'grand·par·ents** *npl* bisabuelos *mpl*; **great·'grand·son** bisnieto *m*

great·ly ['greɪtlɪ] *adv* muy

great·ness ['greɪtnɪs] grandeza *f*

Greece [griːs] Grecia

greed [griːd] *for money* codicia *f*; *for food* gula *f*, glotonería *f*

greed·i·ly ['griːdɪlɪ] *adv* con codicia; *eat* con gula *or* glotonería

greed·y ['griːdɪ] *adj for food* glotón; *for money* codicioso

Greek [griːk] **1** *adj* griego **2** *n person* griego(-a) *m(f)*; *language* griego *m*

green [griːn] *adj* verde; *environmentally* ecologista, verde

green 'beans *npl* judías *fpl* verdes, *L.Am.* porotos *mpl* verdes, *Mex* ejotes *mpl*; **'green belt** cinturón *m* verde; **'green card** (*work permit*) permiso *m* de trabajo; **'green·field site** terreno *m* edificable en el campo; **'green·horn** F novato(-a) *m(f)* F; **'green·house** invernadero *m*; **'green·house ef·fect** efecto *m* invernadero; **'green·house gas** gas *m* invernadero

greens [griːnz] *npl* verduras *f*

green 'thumb: *have a ~* tener buena mano con la jardinería

greet [griːt] *v/t* saludar

greet·ing ['griːtɪŋ] saludo *m*

'greet·ing card tarjeta *f* de felicitación

gre·gar·i·ous [grɪ'gerɪəs] *adj person* sociable

gre·nade [grɪ'neɪd] granada *f*

grew [gruː] *pret* → **grow**

grey *Br* → **gray**

grid [grɪd] reja *f*, rejilla *f*

'grid·iron SP *campo de fútbol americano*

'grid·lock *in traffic* paralización *f* del tráfico

grief [griːf] dolor *m*, aflicción *f*

grief-strick·en ['griːfstrɪkn] *adj* afligido

griev·ance ['griːvəns] queja *f*

grieve [griːv] *v/i* sufrir; *~ for s.o.* llorar por alguien

grill [grɪl] **1** *n on window* reja *f* **2** *v/t* (*interrogate*) interrogar

grille [grɪl] reja *f*

grim [grɪm] *adj face* severo; *prospects* desolador; *surroundings* lúgubre

gri·mace ['grɪməs] *n* gesto *m*, mueca *f*

grime [graɪm] mugre *f*

grim·ly ['grɪmlɪ] *adv speak* en tono grave

grim·y ['graɪmɪ] *adj* mugriento

grin [grɪn] **1** *n* sonrisa *f* (amplia) **2** *v/i* (*pret & pp* **-ned**) sonreír abiertamente

grind [graɪnd] *v/t* (*pret & pp* **ground**) *coffee* moler; *meat* picar; *~ one's teeth* hacer rechinar los dientes

grip [grɪp] **1** *n*: *he lost his ~ on the rope* se le escapó la cuerda; *be losing one's ~* (*losing one's skills*) estar perdiendo el control **2** *v/t* (*pret & pp* **-ped**) agarrar

gripe [graɪp] **1** *n* F queja *f* **2** *v/i* F quejarse

grip·ping ['grɪpɪŋ] *adj* apasionante

gris·tle ['grɪsl] cartílago *m*

grit [grɪt] **1** *n* (*dirt*) arenilla *f*; *for roads* gravilla *f* **2** *v/t* (*pret & pp* **-ted**): *~ one's teeth* apretar los dientes

grit·ty ['grɪtɪ] *adj* F *book, movie etc* duro F, descarnado

groan [groʊn] **1** *n* gemido *m* **2** *v/i* gemir

gro·cer ['groʊsər] tendero(-a) *m(f)*

gro·cer·ies ['groʊsərɪz] *npl* comestibles *mpl*

gro·cer·y store ['groʊsərɪ] tienda *f* de comestibles *or Mex* abarrotes

grog·gy ['grɑːgɪ] *adj* F grogui F

groin [grɔɪn] ANAT ingle *f*

groom [gruːm] **1** *n for bride* novio *m; for horse* mozo *m* de cuadra **2** *v/t horse* almohazar; *(train, prepare)* preparar; **well ~ed** *in appearance* bien arreglado

groove [gruːv] ranura *f*

grope [groʊp] **1** *v/i in the dark* caminar a tientas **2** *v/t sexually* manosear

♦ **grope for** *v/t door handle, the right word* intentar encontrar

gross [groʊs] *adj (coarse, vulgar)* grosero; *exaggeration* tremendo; *error* craso; FIN bruto

gross do·mes·tic 'prod·uct producto *m* interior bruto

gross na·tion·al 'prod·uct producto *m* nacional bruto

ground[1] [graʊnd] **1** *n* suelo *m*, tierra *f*; *(reason)* motivo *m*; ELEC tierra *f*; **on the ~** en el suelo **2** *v/t* ELEC conectar a tierra

ground[2] [graʊnd] *pret & pp* → **grind**

'ground con·trol control *m* de tierra

'ground crew personal *m* de tierra

ground·ing ['graʊndɪŋ] *in subject* fundamento *m*; **he's had a good ~ in electronics** tiene buenos fundamentos de electrónica

ground·less ['graʊndlɪs] *adj* infundado

ground 'meat carne *f* picada; **'ground·nut** cacahuete *m, L.Am.* maní *m, Mex* cacahuate *m*; **'ground plan** plano *m*; **'ground staff** SP personal *m* de mantenimiento; *at airport* personal *m* de tierra; **'ground·work** trabajos *mpl* preliminares

group [gruːp] **1** *n* grupo *m* **2** *v/t* agrupar

group·ie ['gruːpɪ] F grupi *f* F

group 'ther·a·py terapia *f* de grupo

grouse [graʊs] **1** *n* F queja *f* **2** *v/i* F quejarse, refunfuñar

grov·el ['grɑːvl] *v/i fig* arrastrarse

grow [groʊ] **1** *v/i (pret grew, pp grown)* crecer; *of number, amount* crecer, incrementarse; **~ old / tired** envejecer / cansarse **2** *v/t (pret grew, pp grown) flowers* cultivar

♦ **grow up** *v/i of person, city* crecer; **grow up!** ¡no seas crío!

growl [graʊl] **1** *n* gruñido *m* **2** *v/i* gruñir

grown [groʊn] *pp* → **grow**

grown-up ['groʊnʌp] **1** *n* adulto(-a) *m(f)* **2** *adj* maduro

growth [groʊθ] *of person, economy* crecimiento *m; (increase)* incremento *m*; MED bulto *m*

grub [grʌb] *of insect* larva *f*, gusano *m*

grub·by ['grʌbɪ] *adj* mugriento *m*

grudge [grʌdʒ] **1** *n* rencor *m*; **bear s.o. a ~** guardar rencor a alguien **2** *v/t:* **~ s.o. sth** *feel envy* envidiar algo a alguien

grudg·ing ['grʌdʒɪŋ] *adj* rencoroso

grudg·ing·ly ['grʌdʒɪŋlɪ] *adv* de mala gana

gru·el·ing, *Br* **gru·el·ling** ['gruːəlɪŋ] *adj* agotador

gruff [grʌf] *adj* seco, brusco

grum·ble ['grʌmbl] *v/i* murmurar, refunfuñar

grum·bler ['grʌmblər] quejica *m/f*

grump·y ['grʌmpɪ] *adj* cascarrabias

grunt [grʌnt] **1** *n* gruñido *m* **2** *v/i* gruñir

guar·an·tee [gærən'tiː] **1** *n* garantía *f*; **~ period** periodo *m* de garantía **2** *v/t* garantizar

guar·an·tor [gærən'tɔːr] garante *m/f*

guard [gɑːrd] **1** *n (security ~)* guardia *m/f*, guarda *m/f*; MIL guardia *f; in prison* guardián (-ana) *m(f)*; **be on one's ~ against** estar en guardia contra **2** *v/t* guardar, proteger

♦ **guard against** *v/t* evitar

'guard dog perro *m* guardián

guard·ed ['gɑːrdɪd] *adj reply* cauteloso

G

guard·i·an ['gɑːrdɪən] LAW tutor(a) m(f)

guard·i·an 'an·gel ángel m de la guardia

Gua·te·ma·la [gwætə'mɑːlə] n Guatemala

Gua·te·ma·lan [gwætə'mɑːlən] **1** adj guatemalteco **2** n guatemalteco(-a) m(f)

guer·ril·la [gə'rɪlə] guerrillero(-a) m(f)

guer·ril·la 'war·fare guerra f de guerrillas

guess [ges] **1** n conjetura f, suposición f **2** v/t the answer adivinar; **I ~ so** me imagino or supongo que sí; **I ~ not** me imagino or supongo que no **3** v/i adivinar

'guess·work conjeturas fpl

guest [gest] invitado(-a) m(f)

'guest·house casa f de huéspedes

'guest·room habitación f para invitados

guf·faw [gʌ'fɔː] **1** n carcajada f, risotada f **2** v/i carcajearse

guid·ance ['gaɪdəns] orientación f, consejo m

guide [gaɪd] **1** n person guía m/f; book guía f **2** v/t guiar

'guide·book guía f

guid·ed mis·sile ['gaɪdɪd] misil m teledirigido

'guide dog Br perro m lazarillo

guid·ed 'tour visita f guiada

guide·lines ['gaɪdlaɪnz] npl directrices fpl, normas fpl generales

guilt [gɪlt] culpa f, culpabilidad f; LAW culpabilidad f

guilt·y ['gɪltɪ] adj also LAW culpable; **be ~ of sth** ser culpable de algo; **have a ~ conscience** tener remordimientos de conciencia

guin·ea pig ['gɪnɪpɪg] conejillo m de Indias, cobaya f; fig conejillo m de Indias

guise [gaɪz] apariencia f; **under the ~ of** bajo la apariencia de

gui·tar [gɪ'tɑːr] guitarra f

gui·tar case estuche m de guitarra

gui·tar·ist [gɪ'tɑːrɪst] guitarrista m/f

gui·tar play·er guitarrista m/f

gulf [gʌlf] golfo m; fig abismo m; **the Gulf** el Golfo

Gulf of 'Mex·i·co Golfo m de México

gull [gʌl] bird gaviota f

gul·let ['gʌlɪt] ANAT esófago m

gul·li·ble ['gʌlɪbl] adj crédulo, ingenuo

gulp [gʌlp] **1** n of water etc trago m **2** v/i in surprise tragar saliva

◆ **gulp down** v/t drink tragar; food engullir

gum¹ [gʌm] in mouth encía f

gum² [gʌm] n (glue) pegamento m, cola f; (chewing ~) chicle m

gump·tion ['gʌmpʃn] sentido m común

gun [gʌn] pistol, revolver pistola f, rifle rifle m; cannon cañón m

◆ **gun down** v/t (pret & pp **-ned**) matar a tiros

'gun·fire disparos mpl; **'gun·man** hombre m armado; **'gun·point: at ~** a punta de pistola; **'gun·shot** disparo m, tiro m; **'gun·shot wound** herida f de bala

gur·gle ['gɜːrgl] v/i of baby gorjear; of drain gorgotear

gu·ru ['guːruː] fig gurú m

gush [gʌʃ] v/i of liquid manar, salir a chorros

gush·y ['gʌʃɪ] adj F (enthusiastic) efusivo, exagerado

gust [gʌst] ráfaga f

gus·to ['gʌstoʊ] entusiasmo m

gust·y ['gʌstɪ] adj weather ventoso, con viento racheado; **~ wind** viento m racheado

gut [gʌt] **1** n intestino m; F (stomach) tripa f F **2** v/t (pret & pp **-ted**) (destroy) destruir

guts [gʌts] npl F (courage) agallas fpl F

guts·y ['gʌtsɪ] adj F (brave) valiente, con muchas agallas F

gut·ter ['gʌtər] on sidewalk cuneta f; on roof canal m, canalón m

guy [gaɪ] F tipo m F, Span tío m F; **hey, you ~s** eh, gente

guz·zle ['gʌzl] v/t tragar, engullir

gym [dʒɪm] gimnasio m

gym·na·si·um [dʒɪm'neɪzɪəm] gimnasio *m*

gym·nast ['dʒɪmnæst] gimnasta *m/f*

gym·nas·tics [dʒɪm'næstɪks] gimnasia *f*

'gym shoes *npl Br* zapatillas *fpl* de gimnasia

gy·nae·col·o·gy *etc Br* → **gynecology** *etc*

gy·ne·col·o·gist [gaɪnɪ'kɑːlədʒɪst] ginecólogo(-a) *m(f)*

gy·ne·col·o·gy [gaɪnɪ'kɑːlədʒɪ] ginecología *f*

gyp·sy ['dʒɪpsɪ] gitano(-a) *m(f)*

H

hab·it ['hæbɪt] hábito *m*, costumbre *m*; **get into the ~ of doing sth** adquirir el hábito de hacer algo

hab·it·a·ble ['hæbɪtəbl] *adj* habitable

hab·i·tat ['hæbɪtæt] hábitat *m*

ha·bit·u·al [hə'bɪtʊəl] *adj* habitual

hack [hæk] *n poor writer* gacetillero(-a) *m(f)*

hack·er ['hækər] COMPUT pirata *m/f* informático(-a)

hack·neyed ['hæknɪd] *adj* manido

had [hæd] *pret & pp* → **have**

had·dock ['hædək] eglefino *m*

haem·or·rhage *Br* → **hemorrhage**

hag·gard ['hægərd] *adj* demacrado

hag·gle ['hægl] *v/i* regatear; **~ over sth** regatear algo

hail [heɪl] *n* granizo *m*

'hail·stone piedra *f* de granizo

'hail·storm granizada *f*

hair [her] *n*, cabello *m*; *single* pelo *m*; (*body* ~) vello *m*; **have short/long ~** tener el pelo corto/largo

'hair·brush cepillo *m*; 'hair·cut corte *m* de pelo; **have a ~** cortarse el pelo; 'hair·do peinado *m*; 'hair·dress·er peluquero(-a) *m(f)*; **at the ~** en la peluquería; 'hair·dry·er secador *m* (de pelo)

hair·less ['herlɪs] *adj* sin pelo

'hair·pin horquilla *f*; hair·pin 'curve curva *f* muy cerrada; hair-rais·ing ['hereɪzɪŋ] *adj* espeluznante; hair

re·mov·er [herɪ'muːvər] depilatorio *m*; 'hair's breadth *fig*: **by a ~** por un pelo; hair-split·ting ['hersplɪtɪŋ] *n* sutilezas *fpl*; 'hair spray laca *f*; 'hair·style peinado *m*; 'hair·styl·ist estilista *m/f*, peluquero(-a) *m(f)*

hair·y ['herɪ] *adj arm, animal* peludo; F (*frightening*) espeluznante

half [hæf] **1** *n* (*pl* **halves** [hævz]) mitad *f*; **~ past ten, ~ after ten** las diez y media; **~ an hour** media hora; **~ a pound** media libra; **go halves with s.o. on sth** ir a medias con alguien en algo **2** *adj* medio; **at ~ price** a mitad de precio **3** *adv* a medias; **~ finished** a medio acabar

half-heart·ed [hæf'hɑːrtɪd] *adj* desganado; 'half note MUS nota *f* blanca; half 'pay media paga *f*; half 'time **1** *n* SP descanso *m* **2** *adj* SP: **~ score** marcador *m* en el descanso; half'way **1** *adj stage, point* intermedio **2** *adv* a mitad de camino

hall [hɔːl] *large room* sala *f*; (*hallway in house*) vestíbulo *m*

Hal·low·e·en [hæləʊ'wiːn] *víspera de Todos los Santos*

halo ['heɪləʊ] halo *m*

halt [hɔːlt] **1** *v/i* detenerse **2** *v/t* detener **3** *n* alto *m*; **come to a ~** detenerse

halve [hæv] *v/t input, costs, effort* reducir a la mitad; *apple* partir por la mitad

ham [hæm] jamón *m*

ham·burg·er ['hæmbɜːrgər] hamburguesa f

ham·mer ['hæmər] **1** n martillo m **2** v/i: ~ *at the door* golpear la puerta

ham·mock ['hæmək] hamaca f

ham·per[1] ['hæmpər] n *for food* cesta f

ham·per[2] v/t (*obstruct*) estorbar, obstacular

ham·ster ['hæmstər] hámster m

hand [hænd] n mano f; *of clock* manecilla f; (*worker*) brazo m; *at* ~, *to* ~ a mano; *at first* ~ de primera mano, directamente; *by* ~ a mano; *on the one* ~ ..., *on the other* ~ por una parte ..., por otra parte; *the work is in* ~ el trabajo se está llevando a cabo; *on your right* ~ a mano derecha; ~*s off!* ¡fuera las manos!; ~*s up!* ¡arriba las manos!; *change* ~*s* cambiar de manos; *give s.o. a* ~ echar una mano a alguien

♦ **hand down** v/t transmitir

♦ **hand in** v/t entregar

♦ **hand on** v/t pasar

♦ **hand out** v/t repartir

♦ **hand over** v/t entregar

'**hand·bag** *Br* bolso m, *L.Am.* cartera f; '**hand·bag·gage** equipaje m de mano; '**hand·book** manual m; '**hand·cuff** v/t esposar; **hand·cuffs** ['hæn(d)kʌfs] npl esposas fpl

hand·i·cap ['hændɪkæp] n desventaja f

hand·i·capped ['hændɪkæpt] adj *physically* minusválido, disminuido; ~ *by lack of funds* en desventaja por carecer de fondos

hand·i·craft ['hændɪkræft] artesanía f

hand·i·work ['hændɪwɜːrk] manualidades fpl

hand·ker·chief ['hæŋkərtʃɪf] pañuelo m

han·dle ['hændl] **1** n *of door* manilla f; *of suitcase* asa f; *of pan, knife* mango m **2** v/t *goods, difficult person* manejar; *case, deal* llevar, encargarse de; *let me* ~ *this* deja que me ocupe yo de esto

han·dle·bars ['hændlbɑːrz] npl manillar m, *L.Am.* manubrio m

'**hand lug·gage** equipaje m de mano; **hand·made** [hæn(d)'meɪd] adj hecho a mano; '**hand·rail** barandilla f; '**hand·shake** apretón m de manos

hands-off [hændz'ɑːf] adj no intervencionista

hand·some ['hænsəm] adj guapo, atractivo

hands-on [hændz'ɑːn] adj práctico; *he has a* ~ *style of management* le gusta implicarse en todos los aspectos de la gestión

'**hand·writ·ing** caligrafía f

hand·writ·ten ['hændrɪtn] adj escrito a mano

hand·y ['hændɪ] adj *tool, device* práctico; *it might come in* ~ nos puede venir muy bien

hang [hæŋ] **1** v/t (*pret & pp hung*) *picture* colgar; *person* colgar, ahorcar (*pret & pp -ed*) **2** v/i (*pret & pp hung*) colgar; *of dress, hair* caer, colgar **3** n: *get the* ~ *of sth* F agarrarle el tranquillo a algo F

♦ **hang around** v/i: *he's always hanging around on the street corner* siempre está rondando por la esquina

♦ **hang on** v/i (*wait*) esperar

♦ **hang on to** v/t (*keep*) conservar; *do you mind if I hang on to it for a while?* ¿te importa si me lo quedo durante un tiempo?

♦ **hang up** v/i TELEC colgar

han·gar ['hæŋər] hangar m

hang·er ['hæŋər] *for clothes* percha f

hang glid·er ['hæŋglaɪdər] *person* piloto m de ala delta; *device* ala f delta

hang glid·ing ['hæŋglaɪdɪŋ] ala f delta

'**hang·o·ver** resaca f

♦ **han·ker after** ['hæŋkər] v/t anhelar

han·kie, han·ky ['hæŋkɪ] F pañuelo m

hap·haz·ard [hæp'hæzərd] adj descuidado

hap·pen ['hæpn] v/i ocurrir, pasar, suceder; *if you* ~ *to see him* si por casualidad lo vieras; *what has* ~*ed to you?* ¿qué te ha pasado?

♦ **happen across** v/t encontrar por

casualidad

hap·pen·ing ['hæpnɪŋ] suceso *m*

hap·pi·ly ['hæpɪlɪ] *adv* alegremente; (*luckily*) afortunadamente

hap·pi·ness ['hæpɪnɪs] felicidad *f*

hap·py ['hæpɪ] *adj* feliz, contento; *coincidence* afortunado

hap·py-go-luck·y *adj* despreocupado

'hap·py hour *franja horaria en la que las bebidas se venden más baratas*

har·ass [hə'ræs] *v/t* acosar; *enemy* asediar, hostigar

har·assed [hər'æst] *adj* agobiado

har·ass·ment [hə'ræsmənt] acoso *m*

har·bor, *Br* **har·bour** ['hɑːrbər] **1** *n* puerto *m* **2** *v/t criminal* proteger; *grudge* albergar

hard [hɑːrd] **1** *adj* duro; (*difficult*) difícil; *facts, evidence* real; **~ of hearing** duro de oído **2** *adv hit, rain* fuerte; *work* duro; **try ~ to do sth** esforzarse por hacer algo

'hard·back *n* libro *m* de tapas duras; **hard-boiled** *adj egg* duro; **'hard cop·y** copia *f* impresa; **'hard core** *n* (*pornography*) porno *m* duro; **hard 'cur·ren·cy** divisa *f* fuerte; **hard 'disk** disco *m* duro

hard·en ['hɑːrdn] **1** *v/t* endurecer **2** *v/i of glue, attitude* endurecerse

'hard hat casco *m*; (*construction worker*) obrero(-a) *m(f)* (de la construcción); **hard·head·ed** [hɑːrd'hedɪd] *adj* pragmático; **hard-heart·ed** [hɑːrd'hɑːrtɪd] *adj* insensible; **hard 'line** línea *f* dura; **take a ~ line on** adoptar una línea dura en cuanto a; **hard'lin·er** partidario(-a) *m(f)* de la línea dura

hard·ly ['hɑːrdlɪ] *adv* apenas; **did you agree? – ~!** ¿estuviste de acuerdo? – ¡en absoluto!

hard·ness ['hɑːrdnɪs] dureza *f*; (*difficulty*) dificultad *f*

hard'sell venta *f* agresiva

hard·ship ['hɑːrdʃɪp] penuria *f*, privación *f*

hard 'up *adj*: **be ~** andar mal de dinero; **'hard·ware** ferretería *f*; COMPUT hardware *m*; **'hard·ware store** fe-

rretería *f*; **hard-work·ing** [hɑːrd-'wɜːrkɪŋ] *adj* trabajador

har·dy ['hɑːrdɪ] *adj* resistente

hare [her] liebre *f*

hare·brained ['herbreɪnd] *adj* alocado

harm [hɑːrm] **1** *n* daño *m*; **it wouldn't do any ~ to buy two** por comprar dos no pasa nada **2** *v/t* hacer daño a, dañar

harm·ful ['hɑːrmfəl] *adj* dañino, perjudicial

harm·less ['hɑːrmlɪs] *adj* inofensivo; *fun* inocente

har·mo·ni·ous [hɑːr'moʊnɪəs] *adj* armonioso

har·mo·nize ['hɑːrmənaɪz] *v/i* armonizar

har·mo·ny ['hɑːrmənɪ] MUS, *fig* armonía *f*

harp [hɑːrp] *n* arpa *f*

♦ **harp on about** *v/t* F dar la lata con F

har·poon [hɑːr'puːn] *n* arpón *m*

harsh [hɑːʃ] *adj words* duro, severo; *color* chillón; *light* potente

harsh·ly ['hɑːrʃlɪ] *adv* con dureza *or* severidad

har·vest ['hɑːrvɪst] *n* cosecha *f*

hash [hæʃ] F: **make a ~ of** fastidiar

hash browns *npl Span* patatas *fpl or L.Am.* papas *fpl* fritas

hash·ish ['hæʃiːʃ] hachís *m*

'hash mark almohadilla *f*, *el signo '#'*

haste [heɪst] *n* prisa *f*

has·ten ['heɪsn] *v/i*: **~ to do sth** apresurarse en hacer algo

hast·i·ly ['heɪstɪlɪ] *adv* precipitadamente

hast·y ['heɪstɪ] *adj* precipitado

hat [hæt] *n* sombrero *m*

hatch [hætʃ] *n for serving food* trampilla *f*; *on ship* escotilla *f*

♦ **hatch out** *v/i of eggs* romperse; *of chicks* salir del cascarón

hatch·et ['hætʃɪt] hacha *f*; **bury the ~** enterrar el hacha de guerra

hate [heɪt] **1** *n* odio *m* **2** *v/t* odiar

ha·tred ['heɪtrɪd] odio *m*

haugh·ty ['hɒtɪ] *adj* altanero

haul [hɒl] **1** *n of fish* captura *f*; **from**

robbery botín *m* **2** *v/t* (*pull*) arrastrar

haul·age ['hɔːlɪdʒ] transporte *m*

haul·i·er ['hɔːlɪr] transportista *m*

haunch [hɔːntʃ] *of person* trasero *m*; *of animal* pierna *f*

haunt [hɔːnt] **1** *v/t*: **this place is ~ed** en este lugar hay fantasmas **2** *n* lugar *m* favorito

haunt·ing ['hɔːntɪŋ] *adj tune* fascinante

Ha·van·a [hə'vænə] *n* La Habana

have [hæv] **1** *v/t* (*pret & pp* **had**) (*own*) tener; **I don't ~ a TV** no tengo televisión ◊ *breakfast, lunch* tomar ◊: **can I ~ a coffee?** ¿me da un café?; **can I ~ more time?** ¿me puede dar más tiempo? ◊ *must*: **~ (got) to** tener que ◊ *causative*: **I'll ~ it faxed to you** te lo mandaré por fax; **I'll ~ it repaired** haré que lo arreglen; **I had my hair cut** me corté el pelo **2** *v/aux*: **I ~ eaten** he comido; **~ you seen her?** ¿la has visto?

♦ **have back** *v/t*: **when can I have it back?** ¿cuándo me lo devolverá?

♦ **have on** *v/t* (*wear*) llevar puesto; **do you have anything on for tonight?** *have planned* ¿tenéis algo planeado para esta noche?

ha·ven ['heɪvn] *fig* refugio *m*

hav·oc ['hævək] estragos *mpl*; **play ~ with** hacer estragos en

hawk [hɔːk] *n also fig* halcón *m*

hay [heɪ] heno *m*

'hay fe·ver fiebre *f* del heno

haz·ard ['hæzərd] *n* riesgo *m*, peligro *m*

'haz·ard lights *npl* MOT luces *fpl* de emergencia

haz·ard·ous ['hæzərdəs] *adj* peligroso, arriesgado; **~ waste** residuos *mpl* peligrosos

haze [heɪz] neblina *f*

ha·zel ['heɪzl] *n tree* avellano *m*

'ha·zel·nut avellana *f*

haz·y ['heɪzɪ] *adj image, memories* confuso, vago; **I'm a bit ~ about it** no lo tengo muy claro

he [hiː] *pron* él; **~ is French / a doctor** es francés / médico; **you're funny,**

~'s not tú tienes gracia, él no

head [hed] **1** *n* cabeza *f*; (*boss, leader*) jefe(-a) *m(f)*; *Br: of school* director(a) *m(f)*; *on beer* espuma *f*; *of nail, line* cabeza *f*; **$15 a ~** 15 dólares por cabeza; **~s or tails?** ¿cara o cruz?; **at the ~ of the list** encabezando la lista; **~ over heels** *fall* rodando; *fall in love* locamente **2** *v/t* (*lead*) estar a la cabeza de; *ball* cabecear

♦ **head for** *v/t* dirigirse a *or* hacia

'head·ache dolor *m* de cabeza

'head·band cinta *f* para la cabeza

head·er ['hedər] *in soccer* cabezazo *m*; *in document* encabezamiento *m*

'head·hunt *v/t* COM buscar, captar

'head·hunt·er COM cazatalentos *m/f inv*

head·ing ['hedɪŋ] *in list* encabezamiento *m*

'head·lamp faro *m*; **'head·light** faro *m*; **'head·line** *n in newspaper* titular *m*; **make the ~s** saltar a los titulares; **'head·long** *adv fall* de cabeza; **'head·mas·ter** director *m*; **'head·mis·tress** directora *f*; **head 'of·fice** *of company* central *f*; **head·'on 1** *adv crash* de frente **2** *adj crash* frontal; **'head·phones** *npl* auriculares *mpl*; **'head·quar·ters** *npl of party, organization* sede *f*; *of army* cuartel *m* general; **'head·rest** reposacabezas *f inv*; **'head·room** *under bridge* gálibo *m*; *in car* espacio *m* vertical; **'head·scarf** pañuelo *m* (para la cabeza); **'head·strong** *adj* cabezudo, testarudo; **head 'teach·er** *Br* director(a) *m(f)*; **'head wait·er** maître *m*; **'head·wind** viento *m* contrario

head·y ['hedɪ] *adj drink, wine etc* que se sube a la cabeza

heal [hiːl] *v/t* curar

♦ **heal up** *v/i* curarse

health [helθ] salud *f*; **your ~!** ¡a tu salud!

'health club gimnasio *m* (*con piscina, pista de tenis, sauna etc*); **'health food** comida *f* integral; **'health food store** tienda *f* de comida integral; **'health in·su·rance** seguro *m* de enfermedad; '**health re·sort** centro *m* de reposo

health·y ['helθɪ] *adj person* sano; *food, lifestyle* saludable; *economy* saneado

heap [hi:p] *n* montón *m*

♦ **heap up** *v/t* amontonar

hear [hɪr] *v/t & v/i (pret & pp* **heard**) oír

♦ **hear about** *v/t:* **have you heard about Mike?** ¿te has enterado de lo de Mike?; **they're bound to hear about it sooner or later** se van a enterar tarde o temprano

♦ **hear from** *v/t (have news from)* tener noticias de

hear·ing ['hɪrɪŋ] oído *m*; LAW vista *f*; **his ~ is not so good now** ahora ya no oye tan bien; **she was within ~ / out of ~** estaba / no estaba lo suficientemente cerca como para oírlo

'**hear·ing aid** audífono *m*

'**hear·say** rumores *mpl*; **by ~** de oídas

hearse [hɜːrs] coche *m* fúnebre

heart [hɑːrt] *also fig* corazón *m*; *of problem* meollo *m*; **know sth by ~** saber algo de memoria; **~s in cards** corazones *mpl*

'**heart at·tack** infarto *m*; '**heart·beat** latido *m*; **heart·break·ing** ['hɑːrtbreɪkɪŋ] *adj* desgarrador; '**heart·brok·en** *adj* descorazonado; '**heart·burn** acidez *f* (de estómago); '**heart fail·ure** paro *m* cardíaco; **heart·felt** ['hɑːrtfelt] *adj sympathy* sincero

hearth [hɑːrθ] chimenea *f*

heart·less ['hɑːrtlɪs] *adj* despiadado

heart·rend·ing ['hɑːrtrendɪŋ] *adj plea, sight* desgarrador; '**heart throb** F ídolo *m*; '**heart trans·plant** transplante *m* de corazón

heart·y ['hɑːrtɪ] *adj appetite* voraz; *meal* copioso; *person* cordial, campechano

heat [hi:t] *n* calor *m*

♦ **heat up** *v/t* calentar

heat·ed ['hi:tɪd] *adj swimming pool* climatizado; *discussion* acalorado

heat·er ['hi:tər] *in room* estufa *f*; **turn on the ~** *in car* enciende la calefac-

ción

hea·then ['hi:ðn] *n* pagano(-a) *m(f)*

heat·ing ['hi:tɪŋ] calefacción *f*

'**heat·proof**, '**heat-re·sis·tant** *adj* resistente al calor; '**heat·stroke** insolación *f*; '**heat·wave** ola *f* de calor

heave [hi:v] *v/t (lift)* subir

heav·en ['hevn] cielo *m*; **good ~s!** ¡Dios mío!

heav·en·ly ['hevnlɪ] *adj* F divino F

heav·y ['hevɪ] *adj* pesado; *cold, rain, accent, loss* fuerte; *smoker, drinker* empedernido; *loss of life* grande; *bleeding* abundante; **there's ~ traffic** hay mucho tráfico

heav·y-'du·ty *adj* resistente

'**heav·y·weight** *adj* SP de los pesos pesados

heck·le ['hekl] *v/t* interrumpir (*molestando*)

hec·tic ['hektɪk] *adj* vertiginoso, frenético

hedge [hedʒ] *n* seto *m*

hedge·hog ['hedʒhɑːg] erizo *m*

heed [hi:d] *n:* **pay ~ to ...** hacer caso de ...

heel [hi:l] *of foot* talón *m*; *of shoe* tacón *m*

'**heel bar** zapatería *f*

hef·ty ['heftɪ] *adj weight, suitcase* pesado; *person* robusto

height [haɪt] altura *f*; **at the ~ of the season** en plena temporada

height·en ['haɪtn] *v/t effect, tension* intensificar

heir [er] heredero *m*

heir·ess ['erɪs] heredera *f*

held [held] *pret & pp* → **hold**

hel·i·cop·ter ['helɪkɑːptər] helicóptero *m*

hell [hel] infierno *m*; **what the ~ are you doing / do you want?** F ¿qué demonios estás haciendo / quieres? F: **go to ~!** F ¡vete a paseo! F; **a ~ of a lot** F un montonazo F; **one ~ of a nice guy** F un tipo muy simpático *or* Span legal F

hel·lo [hə'lou] hola; TELEC ¿sí?, *Span* ¿diga?, *S. Am.* ¿alo?, *Rpl* ¿oigo?, *Mex* ¿bueno?; **say ~ to s.o.** saludar a alguien

helm [helm] NAUT timón *m*

hel·met ['helmɪt] casco *m*

help [help] **1** *n* ayuda *f*; **~!** ¡socorro! **2** *v/t* ayudar; *just ~ yourself to food* toma lo que quieras; *I can't ~ it* no puedo evitarlo; *I couldn't ~ laughing* no pude evitar reírme

help·er ['helpər] ayudante *m/f*

help·ful ['helpfəl] *adj advice* útil; *person* servicial

help·ing ['helpɪŋ] *of food* ración *f*

help·less ['helplɪs] *adj (unable to cope)* indefenso; *(powerless)* impotente

help·less·ly ['helplɪslɪ] *adv* impotentemente

help·less·ness ['helplɪsnɪs] impotencia *f*

'help screen COMPUT pantalla *f* de ayuda

hem [hem] *n of dress etc* dobladillo *m*

hem·i·sphere ['hemɪsfɪr] hemisferio *m*

'hem·line bajo *m*

hem·or·rhage ['hemərɪdʒ] **1** *n* hemorragia *f* **2** *v/i* sangrar

hen [hen] gallina *f*

hench·man ['hentʃmən] *pej* sicario *m*

'hen par·ty despedida *f* de soltera

hen·pecked ['henpekt] *adj*: **~ husband** calzonazos *mpl*

hep·a·ti·tis [hepə'taɪtɪs] hepatitis *f*

her [hɜːr] **1** *adj* su; **~ ticket** su entrada; **~ books** sus libros **2** *pron direct object* la; *indirect object* le; *after prep* ella; *I know ~* la conozco; *I gave ~ the keys* le di las llaves; *I sold it to ~* se lo vendí; *this is for ~* esto es para ella; *who do you mean? – ~* ¿a quién te refieres? – a ella

herb [ɜːrb] hierba *f*

herb(·al) 'tea ['ɜːrb(əl)] infusión *f*

herd [hɜːrd] *n* rebaño *m*; *of elephants* manada *f*

here [hɪr] *adv* aquí; *over ~* aquí; *~'s to you!* *as toast* ¡a tu salud!; *~ you are giving sth* ¡aquí tienes!; *~ we are! finding sth* ¡aquí está!

he·red·i·ta·ry [hə'redɪterɪ] *adj disease* hereditario

he·red·i·ty [hə'redɪtɪ] herencia *f*

her·i·tage ['herɪtɪdʒ] patrimonio *m*

her·mit ['hɜːrmɪt] ermitaño(-a) *m(f)*

her·ni·a ['hɜːrnɪə] MED hernia *f*

he·ro ['hɪroʊ] héroe *m*

he·ro·ic [hɪ'roʊɪk] *adj* heroico

he·ro·i·cal·ly [hɪ'roʊɪklɪ] *adv* heroicamente

her·o·in ['heroʊɪn] heroína *f*

'her·o·in ad·dict heroinómano(-a) *m(f)*

her·o·ine ['heroʊɪn] heroína *f*

her·o·ism ['heroʊɪzm] heroísmo *m*

her·on ['herən] garza *f*

her·pes ['hɜːrpiːz] MED herpes *m*

her·ring ['herɪŋ] arenque *m*

hers [hɜːrz] *pron* el suyo, la suya; **~ are red** los suyos son rojos; *that book is ~* ese libro es suyo; *a cousin of ~* un primo suyo

her·self [hɜːr'self] *pron reflexive* se; *emphatic* ella misma; *she hurt ~* se hizo daño; *when she saw ~ in the mirror* cuando se vio en el espejo; *she saw it ~* lo vio ella misma; *by ~ (alone)* sola; *(without help)* ella sola, ella misma

hes·i·tant ['hezɪtənt] *adj* indeciso

hes·i·tant·ly ['hezɪtəntlɪ] *adv* con indecisión

hes·i·tate ['hezɪteɪt] *v/i* dudar, vacilar

hes·i·ta·tion [hezɪ'teɪʃn] vacilación *f*

het·er·o·sex·u·al [hetəroʊ'sekʃʊəl] *adj* heterosexual

hey·day ['heɪdeɪ] apogeo *m*

hi [haɪ] *int* ¡hola!

hi·ber·nate ['haɪbərneɪt] *v/i* hibernar

hic·cup ['hɪkʌp] *n* hipo *m*; *(minor problem)* tropiezo *m*, traspié *m*; *have the ~s* tener hipo

hick [hɪk] *pej* F palurdo(-a) *m(f)* F, pueblerino(-a) *m(f)* F

'hick town *pej* F ciudad *f* provinciana

hid [hɪd] *pret* → **hide**

hid·den ['hɪdn] **1** *adj meaning, treasure* oculto **2** *pp* → **hide**

hid·den a·gen·da *fig* objetivo *m* secreto

hide¹ [haɪd] **1** *v/t (pret hid, pp hidden)* esconder **2** *v/i (pret hid, pp hidden)* esconderse

hide² n of animal piel f

hide-and-'seek escondite m

'hide·a·way escondite m

hid·e·ous ['hɪdɪəs] adj espantoso, horrendo; person repugnante

hid·ing¹ ['haɪdɪŋ] (beating) paliza f

hid·ing² ['haɪdɪŋ]: be in ~ estar escondido; go into ~ esconderse

'hid·ing place escondite m

hi·er·ar·chy ['haɪrɑːrkɪ] jerarquía f

hi-fi ['haɪfaɪ] equipo m de alta fidelidad

high [haɪ] **1** adj alto; wind fuerte; (on drugs) colocado P; **have a very ~ opinion of** tener muy buena opinión de; **it is ~ time you understood** ya va siendo hora de que entiendas **2** n MOT directa f; in statistics máximo m; EDU escuela f secundaria, Span instituto m **3** adv: **~ in the sky** en lo alto; **that's as ~ as we can go** eso es lo máximo que podemos ofrecer

'high·brow adj intelectual; **'high·chair** trona f; **high-'class** adj de categoría; **high 'div·ing** salto m de trampolín; **high-'fre·quen·cy** adj de alta frecuencia; **high-'grade** adj de calidad superior; **high-hand·ed** [haɪ'hændɪd] adj despótico; **high-heeled** [haɪ'hiːld] adj de tacón alto; **'high jump** salto m de altura; **high-'lev·el** adj de alto nivel; **'high life** buena vida f; **'high·light 1** n (main event) momento m cumbre; in hair reflejo m **2** v/t with pen resaltar; COMPUT seleccionar, resaltar; **'high·light·er** pen fluorescente m

high·ly ['haɪlɪ] adv desirable, likely muy; **be ~ paid** estar muy bien pagado; **think ~ of s.o.** tener una buena opinión de alguien

high per'form·ance adj drill, battery de alto rendimiento; **high-pitched** [haɪ'pɪtʃt] adj agudo; **'high point of** life, career punto m culminante; **high-pow·ered** [haɪ'pauərd] adj engine potente; intellectual de alto(s) vuelo(s); salesman enérgico; **high 'pres·sure 1** n weather altas presiones fpl **2** adj TECH a gran presión;

salesman agresivo; job, lifestyle muy estresante; **high 'priest** sumo sacerdote m; **'high school** escuela f secundaria, Span instituto m; **high so'ci·e·ty** alta sociedad f; **high-speed 'train** tren m de alta velocidad; **high-'strung** adj muy nervioso; **high 'tech 1** n alta f tecnología **2** adj de alta tecnología; **high 'tide** marea f alta; **high 'wa·ter: at ~** con la marea alta; **'high·way** autopista f; **'high wire** in circus cuerda f floja

hi·jack ['haɪdʒæk] **1** v/t plane, bus secuestrar **2** n of plane, bus secuestro m

hi·jack·er ['haɪdʒækər] of plane, bus secuestrador(a) m(f)

hike¹ [haɪk] **1** n caminata f **2** v/i caminar

hike² [haɪk] n in prices subida f

hik·er ['haɪkər] senderista m/f

hik·ing ['haɪkɪŋ] senderismo m

'hik·ing boots npl botas fpl de senderismo

hi·lar·i·ous [hɪ'lerɪəs] adj divertidísimo, graciosísimo

hill [hɪl] colina f; (slope) cuesta f

hill·bil·ly ['hɪlbɪlɪ] F rústico montañés; **'hill·side** ladera f; **'hill·top** cumbre f

hill·y ['hɪlɪ] adj con colinas

hilt [hɪlt] puño m

him [hɪm] pron direct object lo; indirect object le; after prep él; **I know ~** lo conozco; **I gave ~ the keys** le di las llaves; **I sold it to ~** se lo vendí; **this is for ~** esto es para él; **who do you mean? – ~** ¿a quién te refieres? – a él

him·self [hɪm'self] pron reflexive se; emphatic él mismo; **he hurt ~** se hizo daño; **when he saw ~ in the mirror** cuando se vio en el espejo; **he saw it ~** lo vio él mismo; **by ~** (alone) solo; (without help) él solo, él mismo

hind [haɪnd] adj trasero

hin·der ['haɪndər] v/t obstaculizar, entorpecer

hin·drance ['hɪndrəns] estorbo m, obstáculo m

hind·sight ['haɪndsaɪt]: **with ~** a posteriori

H

hinge [hɪndʒ] *n* bisagra *f*
♦ **hinge on** *v/t* depender de

hint [hɪnt] *n* (*clue*) pista *f*; (*piece of advice*) consejo *m*; (*implied suggestion*) indirecta *f*; *of red, sadness etc* rastro *m*

hip [hɪp] *n* cadera *f*

hip 'pock·et bolsillo *m* trasero

hip·po·pot·a·mus [hɪpə'pɑːtəməs] hipopótamo *m*

hire [haɪr] *v/t* alquilar

his [hɪz] **1** *adj* su; ~ **ticket** su entrada; ~ **books** sus libros **2** *pron* el suyo, la suya; ~ **are red** los suyos son rojos; *that ticket is* ~ esa entrada es suya; *a cousin of* ~ un primo suyo

His·pan·ic [hɪ'spænɪk] **1** *n* hispano(-a) *m(f)* **2** *adj* hispano, hispánico

hiss [hɪs] *v/i of snake, audience* silbar

his·to·ri·an [hɪ'stɔːrɪən] historiador(a) *m(f)*

his·tor·ic [hɪ'stɑːrɪk] *adj* histórico

his·tor·i·cal [hɪ'stɑːrɪkl] *adj* histórico

his·to·ry ['hɪstərɪ] historia *f*

hit [hɪt] **1** *v/t* (*pret & pp hit*) golpear; (*collide with*) chocar contra; *he was* ~ *by a bullet* le alcanzó una bala; *it suddenly* ~ *me* (*I realized*) de repente me di cuenta; ~ *town* (*arrive*) llegar a la ciudad **2** *n* (*blow*) golpe *m*; MUS, (*success*) éxito *m*
♦ **hit back** *v/i physically* devolver el golpe; *verbally, with actions* responder
♦ **hit on** *v/t idea* dar con; (*flirt with*) intentar ligar con
♦ **hit out at** *v/t* (*criticize*) atacar

hit-and-run *adj*: ~ *accident* accidente en el que el vehículo causante se da a la fuga

hitch [hɪtʃ] **1** *n* (*problem*) contratiempo *m*; *without a* ~ sin ningún contratiempo **2** *v/t* (*fix*) enganchar; ~ *a ride* hacer autoestop **3** *v/i* (*hitchhike*) hacer autoestop
♦ **hitch up** *v/t wagon, trailer* enganchar

'hitch·hike *v/i* hacer autoestop;
'hitch·hik·er autoestopista *m/f*;
'hitch·hik·ing autoestop *m*

hi-'tech 1 *n* alta tecnología *f* **2** *adj* de alta tecnología

'hit·list lista *f* de blancos; **'hit·man** asesino *m* a sueldo; **hit-or-'miss** *adj* a la buena ventura; **'hit squad** grupo *m* de intervención especial

HIV [eɪtʃaɪ'viː] *abbr* (= *human immunodeficiency virus*) VIH *m* (= virus *m inv* de la inmunodeficiencia humana)

hive [haɪv] *for bees* colmena *f*
♦ **hive off** *v/t* COM (*separate off*) desprenderse de

HIV-'pos·i·tive *adj* seropositivo

hoard [hɔːrd] **1** *n* reserva *f* **2** *v/t* hacer acopio de; *money* acumular

hoard·er ['hɔːrdər] acaparador(a) *m(f)*

hoarse [hɔːrs] *adj* ronco

hoax [hoʊks] *n* bulo *m*, engaño *m*; *bomb* ~ amenaza *f* falsa de bomba

hob·ble ['hɑːbl] *v/i* cojear

hob·by ['hɑːbɪ] hobby *m*, afición *f*

ho·bo ['hoʊboʊ] F vagabundo(-a) *m(f)*

hock·ey ['hɑːkɪ] (*ice* ~) hockey *m* sobre hielo

hog [hɑːg] *n* (*pig*) cerdo *m*, *L.Am.* chancho *m*

hoist [hɔɪst] **1** *n* montacargas *m inv*; *manual* elevador *m* **2** *v/t* (*lift*) levantar, subir; *flag* izar

ho·kum ['hoʊkəm] F (*nonsense*) tonterías *fpl*; (*sentimental stuff*) cursilería *f*

hold [hoʊld] **1** *v/t* (*pret & pp held*) *in hand* llevar; (*support, keep in place*) sostener; *passport, license* tener; *prisoner, suspect* retener; (*contain*) contener; *job, post* ocupar; *course* mantener; ~ *my hand* dame la mano; ~ *one's breath* aguantar la respiración; *he can* ~ *his drink* sabe beber; ~ *s.o. responsible* hacer a alguien responsable; ~ *that ...* (*believe, maintain*) mantener que ...; ~ *the line, please* TELEC espere, por favor **2** *n in ship, plane* bodega *f*; *take* ~ *of sth* agarrar algo; *lose one's* ~ *on sth on rope* soltar algo; *on reality* perder el contacto con algo

♦ **hold against** v/t: **hold sth against s.o.** tener algo contra alguien

♦ **hold back 1** v/t crowds contener; facts, information guardar **2** v/i (not tell all): **I'm sure he's holding back** estoy seguro de que no dice todo lo que sabe

♦ **hold on** v/i (wait) esperar; **now hold on a minute!** ¡un momento!

♦ **hold on to** v/t (keep) guardar; belief aferrarse a

♦ **hold out 1** v/t hand tender; prospect ofrecer **2** v/i of supplies durar; (survive) resistir, aguantar

♦ **hold up** v/t hand levantar; bank etc atracar; (make late) retrasar; **I was held up by the traffic** he llegado tarde por culpa del tráfico; **hold s.o. up as an example** poner a alguien como ejemplo

♦ **hold with** v/t (approve of): **I don't hold with that sort of behavior** no me parece bien ese tipo de comportamiento

hold·er ['hoʊldər] (container) receptáculo m; of passport, ticket etc titular m/f; of record poseedor(a) m(f)

'**hold·ing com·pa·ny** holding m

'**hold·up** (robbery) atraco m; (delay) retraso m

hole [hoʊl] in sleeve, wood, bag agujero m; in ground hoyo m

hol·i·day ['hɑːlədeɪ] single day día m de fiesta; Br: period vacaciones fpl; **take a ~** tomarse vacaciones

Hol·land ['hɑːlənd] Holanda

hol·low ['hɑːloʊ] adj object hueco; cheeks hundido; promise vacío

hol·ly ['hɑːlɪ] acebo m

hol·o·caust ['hɑːləkɔːst] holocausto m

hol·o·gram ['hɑːləgræm] holograma m

hol·ster ['hoʊlstər] pistolera f

ho·ly ['hoʊlɪ] adj santo

Ho·ly 'Spir·it Espíritu m Santo

'**Ho·ly Week** Semana f Santa

home [hoʊm] **1** n casa f; (native country) tierra f; for old people residencia f; **New York is my ~** Nueva

York es mi hogar; **at ~** also SP en casa; (in country) en mi/su/nuestra tierra; **make yourself at ~** ponte cómodo; **at ~ and abroad** en el país y en el extranjero; **work from ~** trabajar desde casa **2** adv a casa; **go ~** ir a casa; to country ir a mi/tu/su tierra; to town, part of country ir a mi/tu/su ciudad

'**home ad·dress** domicilio m; **home 'bank·ing** telebanca f, banca f electrónica; '**home·com·ing** vuelta f a casa; **home com'put·er** Span ordenador m, L.Am. computadora f doméstica; '**home game** partido m en casa

home·less ['hoʊmlɪs] **1** adj sin casa **2** npl: **the ~** los sin casa

'**home·lov·ing** adj hogareño

home·ly ['hoʊmlɪ] adj (homeloving) hogareño; (not good-looking) feúcho

home'made adj casero

home 'mov·ie película f casera

ho·me·op·a·thy [hoʊmɪ'ɑːpəθɪ] homeopatía f

'**home page** web site página f personal; on web site página f inicial; '**home·sick** adj nostálgico; **be ~** tener morriña; '**home town** ciudad f natal

home·ward ['hoʊmwərd] adv to own house a casa; to own country a mi/tu/su país

'**home·work** EDU deberes mpl

'**home·work·ing** COM teletrabajo m

hom·i·cide ['hɑːmɪsaɪd] crime homicidio m; police department brigada f de homicidios

hom·o·graph ['hɑːməgræf] homógrafo m

ho·mo·pho·bi·a [hɑːmə'foʊbɪə] homofobia f

ho·mo·sex·u·al [hɑːmə'sekʃʊəl] **1** adj homosexual **2** n homosexual m/f

Hon·du·ran [hɑːn'dʊrən] **1** adj hondureño **2** n hondureño(-a) m(f)

Hon·du·ras [hɑːn'dʊrəs] n Honduras

hon·est ['ɑːnɪst] adj honrado

hon·est·ly ['ɑːnɪstlɪ] adv honradamente; **~!** ¡desde luego!

hon·es·ty ['aːnɪstɪ] honradez f

hon·ey ['hʌnɪ] miel f; F (*darling*) cariño m, vida f mía

'hon·ey·comb panal m

'hon·ey·moon n luna f de miel

honk [haːŋk] v/t horn tocar

hon·or ['aːnər] **1** n honor m **2** v/t honrar

hon·or·a·ble ['aːnrəbl] adj honorable

hon·our etc Br → **honor** etc

hood [hʊd] over head capucha f; over cooker campana f extractora; MOT capó m; F (*gangster*) matón(-ona) m(f)

hood·lum ['huːdləm] matón(-ona) m(f)

hoof [huːf] casco m

hook [hʊk] gancho m; *to hang clothes on* colgador m; *for fishing* anzuelo m; **off the ~** TELEC descolgado

hooked [hʊkt] adj enganchado (**on** a)

hook·er ['hʊkər] F fulana f F

hook·y ['hʊkɪ] F: *play ~* hacer novillos, Mex irse de pinta, S.Am. hacerse la rabona

hoo·li·gan ['huːlɪɡən] gamberro(-a) m(f)

hoo·li·gan·ism ['huːlɪɡənɪzm] gamberrismo m

hoop [huːp] aro m

hoot [huːt] **1** v/t horn tocar **2** v/i of car dar bocinazos; *of owl* ulular

hop¹ [haːp] n plant lúpulo m

hop² [haːp] v/i (pret & pp **-ped**) saltar

hope [hoʊp] **1** n esperanza f **2** v/i esperar; **~ for sth** esperar algo; *we all ~ for peace* todos ansiamos la paz; *I ~ so* eso espero; *I ~ not* espero que no **3** v/t: *I ~ you like it* espero que te guste

hope·ful ['hoʊpfəl] adj prometedor; *I'm ~ that ...* espero que ...

hope·ful·ly ['hoʊpfəlɪ] adv say, wait esperanzadamente; **~ he hasn't forgotten** esperemos que no se haya olvidado

hope·less ['hoʊplɪs] adj position, prospect desesperado; (useless: per-son) inútil

ho·ri·zon [hə'raɪzn] horizonte m

hor·i·zon·tal [haːrɪ'zaːntl] adj horizontal

hor·mone ['hɔːrmoʊn] hormona f

horn [hɔːrn] of animal cuerno m; MOT bocina f, claxon m

hor·net ['hɔːrnɪt] avispón m

horn-rimmed 'spec·ta·cles ['hɔːrn-rɪmd] npl gafas fpl de concha

horn·y ['hɔːrnɪ] adj F sexually cachondo F

hor·o·scope ['haːrəskoʊp] horóscopo m

hor·ri·ble ['haːrɪbl] adj horrible; person muy antipático

hor·ri·fy ['haːrɪfaɪ] v/t (pret & pp **-ied**) horrorizar; *I was horrified* me quedé horrorizado

hor·ri·fy·ing ['haːrɪfaɪɪŋ] adj horroroso

hor·ror ['haːrər] horror m

'hor·ror mov·ie película f de terror

hors d'œu·vre [ɔːr'dɜːrv] entremés m

horse [hɔːrs] caballo m

'horse·back: on ~ a caballo; **horse 'chest·nut** castaño m de Indias; **'horse·pow·er** caballo m (de vapor); **'horse race** carrera f de caballos; **'horse·shoe** herradura f

hor·ti·cul·ture ['hɔːrtɪkʌltʃər] horticultura f

hose [hoʊz] n manguera f

hos·pice ['haːspɪs] hospital m para enfermos terminales

hos·pi·ta·ble [haː'spɪtəbl] adj hospitalario

hos·pi·tal ['haːspɪtl] hospital m; **go into the ~** ir al hospital

hos·pi·tal·i·ty [haːspɪ'tælətɪ] hospitalidad f

host [hoʊst] n at party, reception anfitrión m; of TV program presentador(a) m(f)

hos·tage ['haːstɪdʒ] rehén m; **take s.o. ~** tomar a alguien como rehén

'hos·tage tak·er persona que toma rehenes

hos·tel ['haːstl] for students residencia f; (youth ~) albergue m

hos·tess ['hoʊstɪs] *at party, reception* anfitriona *f; on airplane* azafata *f; in bar* cabaretera *f*

hos·tile ['hɑːstl] *adj* hostil

hos·til·i·ty [hɑːˈstɪlətɪ] *of attitude etc* hostilidad *f;* **hostilities** hostilidades *fpl*

hot [hɑːt] *adj weather* caluroso; *object, water, food* caliente; *(spicy)* picante; **it's ~** *of weather* hace calor; **I'm ~** tengo calor; **she's pretty ~ at math** F *(good)* es una fenómena con las matemáticas F

'**hot dog** perrito *m* caliente

ho·tel [hoʊˈtel] hotel *m*

'**hot·plate** placa *f*

'**hot spot** *military, political* punto *m* caliente

hour [aʊr] hora *f*

hour·ly ['aʊrlɪ] *adj:* **at ~ intervals** a intervalos de una hora; **an ~ bus** un autobús que pasa cada hora

house [haʊs] *n* casa *f;* **at your ~** en tu casa

'**house·boat** barco-vivienda *f;* '**house·break·ing** allanamiento *m* de morada; '**house·hold** hogar *m;* **house·hold 'name** nombre *m* conocido; '**house hus·band** amo *m* de casa; '**house·keep·er** ama *f* de llaves; '**house·keep·ing** *activity* tareas *fpl* domésticas; *money* dinero *m* para gastos domésticos; **House of Rep·re·sent·a·tives** Cámara *f* de Representantes; **house·warm·ing (par·ty)** ['haʊswɔːrmɪŋ] fiesta *f* de estreno de una casa; '**house·wife** ama *f* de casa; '**house·work** tareas *fpl* domésticas

hous·ing ['haʊzɪŋ] vivienda *f;* TECH cubierta *f*

'**hous·ing con·di·tions** *npl* condiciones *fpl* de la vivienda

hov·el ['hɑːvl] chabola *f*

hov·er ['hɑːvər] *v/i of bird* cernerse; *of helicopter* permanecer inmóvil en el aire

'**hov·er·craft** aerodeslizador *m*, hovercraft *m*

how [haʊ] *adv* cómo; **~ are you?** ¿cómo estás?; **~ about ...?** ¿qué te

parece ...?; **~ about a drink?** ¿te apetece tomar algo?; **~ much?** ¿cuánto?; **~ much is it?** *cost* ¿cuánto vale *or* cuesta?; **~ many?** ¿cuántos?; **~ often?** ¿con qué frecuencia?; **~ funny/sad!** ¡qué divertido/triste!

how·ev·er *adv* sin embargo; **~ big/ rich/small they are** independientemente de lo grandes/ricos/pequeños que sean

howl [haʊl] *of dog* aullido *m; of person in pain* alarido *m; with laughter* risotada *f*

hub [hʌb] *of wheel* cubo *m*

'**hub·cap** tapacubos *m inv*

♦ **hud·dle together** ['hʌdl] *v/i* apiñarse, acurrucarse

hue [hjuː] tonalidad *f*

huff [hʌf]: **be in a ~** estar enfurruñado

hug [hʌg] *v/t (pret & pp -ged)* abrazar

huge [hjuːdʒ] *adj* enorme

hull [hʌl] *of ship* casco *m*

hul·la·ba·loo [hʌləbəˈluː] alboroto *m*

hum [hʌm] *(pret & pp -med)* **1** *v/t song, tune* tararear **2** *v/i of person* tararear; *of machine* zumbar

hu·man ['hjuːmən] **1** *n* humano *m* **2** *adj* humano; **~ error** error *m or* fallo *m* humano

hu·man 'be·ing ser *m* humano

hu·mane [hjuːˈmeɪn] *adj* humano

hu·man·i·tar·i·an [hjuːmænɪˈterɪən] *adj* humanitario

hu·man·i·ty [hjuːˈmænətɪ] humanidad *f*

hu·man 'race raza *f* humana

hu·man re'sources *npl* recursos *mpl* humanos

hum·ble ['hʌmbl] *adj* humilde

hum·drum ['hʌmdrʌm] *adj* monótono, anodino

hu·mid ['hjuːmɪd] *adj* húmedo

hu·mid·i·fi·er [hjuːˈmɪdɪfaɪr] humidificador *m*

hu·mid·i·ty [hjuːˈmɪdətɪ] humedad *f*

hu·mil·i·ate [hjuːˈmɪlɪeɪt] *v/t* humillar

hu·mil·i·at·ing [hjuːˈmɪlɪeɪtɪŋ] *adj*

H

humillante
hu·mil·i·a·tion [hju:mɪlɪ'eɪʃn] humillación *f*
hu·mil·i·ty [hju:'mɪlɪtɪ] humildad *f*
hu·mor ['hju:mər] humor *m*; *sense of* ~ sentido *m* del humor
hu·mor·ous ['hju:mərəs] *adj* gracioso
hu·mour *Br* → **humor**
hump [hʌmp] **1** *n of camel, person* joroba *f*; *on road* bache *m* **2** *v/t* F (*carry*) acarrear
hunch [hʌntʃ] *n* (*idea*) presentimiento *m*, corazonada *f*
hun·dred ['hʌndrəd] cien *m*; *a* ~ *dollars* cien dólares; *~s of birds* cientos *or* centenares de aves; *a* ~ *and one* ciento uno; *two* ~ doscientos
hun·dredth ['hʌndrədθ] *n & adj* centésimo
'hun·dred·weight 43 *kilogramos*
hung [hʌŋ] *pret & pp* → **hang**
Hun·gar·i·an [hʌŋ'gerɪən] **1** *adj* húngaro **2** *n person* húngaro(-a) *m(f)*; *language* húngaro *m*
Hun·ga·ry ['hʌŋgərɪ] Hungría
hun·ger ['hʌŋgər] *n* hambre *f*
hung·o·ver *adj*: *be* ~ tener resaca
hun·gry ['hʌŋgrɪ] *adj* hambriento; *I'm* ~ tengo hambre
hunk [hʌŋk] cacho *m*, pedazo *m*; F *man* cachas *m inv* F
hun·ky-dor·y [hʌŋkɪ'dɔːrɪ] *adj* F: *everything's* ~ todo va de perlas
hunt [hʌnt] **1** *n* caza *f*, búsqueda *f* **2** *v/t animal* cazar
♦ **hunt for** *v/t* buscar
hunt·er ['hʌntər] cazador(a) *m(f)*
hunt·ing ['hʌntɪŋ] caza *f*
hur·dle ['hɜːrdl] SP valla *f*; *fig* obstáculo *m*
hur·dler ['hɜːrdlər] SP vallista *m/f*
hur·dles *npl* SP vallas *fpl*
hurl [hɜːrl] *v/t* lanzar
hur·ray [huˈreɪ] *int* ¡hurra!
hur·ri·cane ['hʌrɪkən] huracán *m*
hur·ried ['hʌrɪd] *adj* apresurado
hur·ry ['hʌrɪ] **1** *n* prisa *f*; *be in a* ~ tener prisa **2** *v/i* (*pret & pp* -*ied*) darse prisa
♦ **hurry up 1** *v/i* darse prisa; *hurry up!*

¡date prisa! **2** *v/t* meter prisa a
hurt [hɜːrt] **1** *v/i* (*pret & pp* **hurt**) doler; *does it* ~? ¿te duele? **2** *v/t* (*pret & pp* **hurt**) *physically* hacer daño a; *emotionally* herir; *I've* ~ *my* ,*hand* me he hecho daño en la mano; *did he* ~ *you?* ¿te hizo daño?
hus·band ['hʌzbənd] marido *m*
hush [hʌʃ] *n* silencio *m*; ~! ¡silencio!
♦ **hush up** *v/t scandal etc* acallar
husk [hʌsk] *of peanuts etc* cáscara *f*
hus·ky ['hʌskɪ] *adj voice* áspero
hus·tle ['hʌsl] **1** *n* agitación *f*; ~ *and bustle* ajetreo *m* **2** *v/t person* empujar
hut [hʌt] cabaña *f*, refugio *m*; *workman's* cobertizo *m*
hy·a·cinth ['haɪəsɪnθ] jacinto *m*
hy·brid ['haɪbrɪd] *n* híbrido *m*
hy·drant ['haɪdrənt] boca *f* de riego *or* de incendios
hy·draul·ic [haɪ'drɔːlɪk] *adj* hidráulico
hy·dro·e·lec·tric [haɪdrouɪ'lektrɪk] *adj* hidroeléctrico
'hy·dro·foil ['haɪdrəfɔɪl] *boat* hidroplaneador *m*
hy·dro·gen ['haɪdrədʒən] hidrógeno *m*
'hy·dro·gen bomb bomba *f* de hidrógeno
hy·giene ['haɪdʒiːn] higiene *f*
hy·gien·ic [haɪ'dʒiːnɪk] *adj* higiénico
hymn [hɪm] himno *m*
hype [haɪp] *n* bombo *m*
hy·per·ac·tive [haɪpər'æktɪv] *adj* hiperactivo
hy·per·sen·si·tive [haɪpər'sensɪtɪv] *adj* hipersensible
hy·per·ten·sion [haɪpər'tenʃn] hipertensión *f*
hy·per·text ['haɪpərtekst] COMPUT hipertexto *m*
hy·phen ['haɪfn] guión *m*
hyp·no·sis [hɪp'nousɪs] hipnosis *f*
hyp·no·ther·a·py [hɪpnou'θerəpɪ] hipnoterapia *f*
hyp·no·tize ['hɪpnətaɪz] *v/t* hipnotizar
hy·po·chon·dri·ac [haɪpə'kɑːndrɪæk] *n* hipocondríaco(-a) *m(f)*

hy·poc·ri·sy [hɪˈpɑːkrəsɪ] hipocresía f

hyp·o·crite [ˈhɪpəkrɪt] hipócrita m/f

hyp·o·crit·i·cal [hɪpəˈkrɪtɪkl] adj hipócrita

hy·po·ther·mi·a [haɪpouˈθɜːrmɪə] hipotermia f

hy·poth·e·sis [haɪˈpɑːθəsɪs] (pl **hypotheses** [haɪˈpɑːθəsiːz]) hipótesis f inv

hy·po·thet·i·cal [haɪpəˈθetɪkl] adj hipotético

hys·ter·ec·to·my [hɪstəˈrektəmɪ] histerectomía f

hys·te·ri·a [hɪˈstɪrɪə] histeria f

hys·ter·i·cal [hɪˈsterɪkl] adj person, laugh histérico; F (very funny) tronchante F; **become ~** ponerse histérico

hys·ter·ics [hɪˈsterɪks] npl ataque f de histeria; (laughter) ataque f de risa

I

I [aɪ] pron yo; **~ am English / a student** soy inglés / estudiante; **you're crazy, ~'m not** tú estás loco, yo no

ice [aɪs] in drink, on road hielo m; **break the ~** fig romper el hielo
♦ **ice up** v/i of engine, wings helarse

ice·berg [ˈaɪsbɜːrg] iceberg m; **'ice·box** nevera f, Rpl heladera f; **'ice·break·er** ship rompehielos m inv; **'ice cream** helado m; **'ice cream par·lor**, Br **'ice cream par·lour** heladería f; **'ice cube** cubito m de hielo

iced [aɪst] adj drink helado

iced 'cof·fee café m helado

'ice hock·ey hockey m sobre hielo; **'ice rink** pista f de hielo; **'ice skate** patín m de cuchilla; **'ice skat·ing** patinaje m sobre hielo

i·ci·cle [ˈaɪsɪkl] carámbano m

i·con [ˈaɪkɑːn] also COMPUT icono m

i·cy [ˈaɪsɪ] adj road con hielo; surface helado; welcome frío

ID [aɪˈdiː] abbr (= **identity**) documentación f; **you got any ~ on you?** ¿lleva algún tipo de documentación?

i·dea [aɪˈdiːə] idea f; **good ~!** ¡buena idea!; **I have no ~** no tengo ni idea; **it's not a good ~ to ...** no es buena idea ...

i·deal [aɪˈdiːəl] adj (perfect) ideal

i·deal·is·tic [aɪdiːəˈlɪstɪk] adj idealista

i·deal·ly [aɪˈdiːəlɪ] adv: **~ situated** en una posición ideal; **~, we would do it like this** lo ideal sería que lo hiciéramos así

i·den·ti·cal [aɪˈdentɪkl] adj idéntico

i·den·ti·fi·ca·tion [aɪdentɪfɪˈkeɪʃn] identificación f; papers etc documentación f

i·den·ti·fy [aɪˈdentɪfaɪ] v/t (pret & pp **-ied**) identificar

i·den·ti·ty [aɪˈdentətɪ] identidad f; **~ card** carné m de identidad

i·de·o·log·i·cal [aɪdɪəˈlɑːdʒɪkl] adj ideológico

i·de·ol·o·gy [aɪdɪˈɑːlədʒɪ] ideología f

id·i·om [ˈɪdɪəm] (saying) modismo m

id·i·o·mat·ic [ɪdɪəˈmætɪk] adj natural

id·i·o·syn·cra·sy [ɪdɪəˈsɪŋkrəsɪ] peculiaridad f, rareza f

id·i·ot [ˈɪdɪət] idiota m/f, estúpido(-a) m/f

id·i·ot·ic [ɪdɪˈɑːtɪk] adj idiota, estúpido

i·dle [ˈaɪdl] **1** adj not working desocupado; (lazy) vago; threat vano; machinery inactivo **2** v/i of engine funcionar al ralentí

♦ **idle away** *v/t the time etc* pasar ociosamente

i·dol ['aɪdl] ídolo *m*

i·dol·ize ['aɪdəlaɪz] *v/t* idolatrar

i·dyl·lic [ɪ'dɪlɪk] *adj* idílico

if [ɪf] *conj* si; **– only I hadn't shouted at her** ojalá no le hubiera gritado

ig·nite [ɪg'naɪt] *v/t* inflamar

ig·ni·tion [ɪg'nɪʃn] *in car* encendido *m*; **– key** llave *m* de contacto

ig·no·rance ['ɪgnərəns] ignorancia *f*

ig·no·rant ['ɪgnərənt] *adj* ignorante; *(rude)* maleducado; **be – of sth** desconocer *or* ignorar algo

ig·nore [ɪg'nɔːr] *v/t* ignorar; COMPUT omitir

ill [ɪl] *adj* enfermo; **fall –, be taken –** caer enfermo; **feel – at ease** no sentirse a gusto, sentirse incómodo

il·le·gal [ɪ'liːgl] *adj* ilegal

il·le·gi·ble [ɪ'ledʒəbl] *adj* ilegible

il·le·git·i·mate [ɪlɪ'dʒɪtɪmət] *adj child* ilegítimo

ill-fat·ed [ɪl'feɪtɪd] *adj* infortunado

il·li·cit [ɪ'lɪsɪt] *adj* ilícito

il·lit·e·rate [ɪ'lɪtərət] *adj* analfabeto

ill-man·nered [ɪl'mænərd] *adj* maleducado

ill-na·tured [ɪl'neɪtʃərd] *adj* malhumorado

ill·ness ['ɪlnɪs] enfermedad *f*

il·log·i·cal [ɪ'lɑːdʒɪkl] *adj* ilógico

ill-tem·pered [ɪl'tempərd] *adj* malhumorado

ill'treat *v/t* maltratar

il·lu·mi·nate [ɪ'luːmɪneɪt] *v/t building etc* iluminar

il·lu·mi·nat·ing [ɪ'luːmɪneɪtɪŋ] *adj remarks etc* iluminador, esclarecedor

il·lu·sion [ɪ'luːʒn] ilusión *f*

il·lus·trate ['ɪləstreɪt] *v/t* ilustrar

il·lus·tra·tion [ɪlə'streɪʃn] ilustración *f*

il·lus·tra·tor [ɪlə'streɪtər] ilustrador(a) *m(f)*

ill 'will rencor *m*

im·age ['ɪmɪdʒ] imagen *f*; **he's the – of his father** es la viva imagen de su padre

'im·age-con·scious *adj* preocupado por la imagen

i·ma·gi·na·ble [ɪ'mædʒɪnəbl] *adj* imaginable; **the smallest size –** la talla más pequeña que se pueda imaginar

i·ma·gi·na·ry [ɪ'mædʒɪnəri] *adj* imaginario

i·ma·gi·na·tion [ɪmædʒɪ'neɪʃn] imaginación *f*; **it's all in your –** son imaginaciones tuyas

i·ma·gi·na·tive [ɪ'mædʒɪnətɪv] *adj* imaginativo

i·ma·gine [ɪ'mædʒɪn] *v/t* imaginar, imaginarse; **I can just – it** me lo imagino; **you're imagining things** son imaginaciones tuyas

im·be·cile ['ɪmbəsiːl] imbécil *m/f*

IMF [aɪem'ef] *abbr (= International Monetary Fund)* FMI *m* (= Fondo *m* Monetario Internacional)

im·i·tate ['ɪmɪteɪt] *v/t* imitar

im·i·ta·tion [ɪmɪ'teɪʃn] imitación *f*; **learn by –** aprender imitando

im·mac·u·late [ɪ'mækjʊlət] *adj* inmaculado

im·ma·te·ri·al [ɪmə'tɪriəl] *adj (not relevant)* irrelevante

im·ma·ture [ɪmə'ʃʊər] *adj* inmaduro

im·me·di·ate [ɪ'miːdɪət] *adj* inmediato; **the – family** los familiares más cercanos; **in the – neighborhood** en las inmediaciones

im·me·di·ate·ly [ɪ'miːdɪətlɪ] *adv* inmediatamente; **– after the bank/ church** justo después del banco/la iglesia

im·mense [ɪ'mens] *adj* inmenso

im·merse [ɪ'mɜːrs] *v/t* sumergir; **– o.s. in** sumergirse en

im·mer·sion heat·er [ɪ'mɜːrʃn] calentador *m* de agua eléctrico

im·mi·grant ['ɪmɪgrənt] *n* inmigrante *m/f*

im·mi·grate ['ɪmɪgreɪt] *v/i* inmigrar

im·mi·gra·tion [ɪmɪ'greɪʃn] inmigración *f*; **Immigration** *government department* (Departamento *m* de) Inmigración *f*

im·mi·nent ['ɪmɪnənt] *adj* inminente

im·mo·bi·lize [ɪ'moʊbɪlaɪz] *v/t factory* paralizar; *person, car* inmovi-

lizar
im·mo·bi·liz·er [ɪˈmoubɪlaɪzər] *on car* inmovilizador *m*

im·mod·e·rate [ɪˈmɑːdərət] *adj* desmedido, exagerado

im·mor·al [ɪˈmɔːrəl] *adj* inmoral

im·mor·al·i·ty [ɪmɔːˈrælɪtɪ] inmoralidad *f*

im·mor·tal [ɪˈmɔːrtl] *adj* inmortal

im·mor·tal·i·ty [ɪmɔːrˈtælɪtɪ] inmortalidad *f*

im·mune [ɪˈmjuːn] *adj to illness, infection* inmune; *from ruling, requirement* con inmunidad

im·mune sys·tem MED sistema *m* inmunológico

im·mu·ni·ty [ɪˈmjuːnətɪ] inmunidad *f*

im·pact [ˈɪmpækt] *n* impacto *m*; *the warning had no ~ on him* el aviso no le hizo cambiar lo más mínimo

im·pair [ɪmˈper] *v/t* dañar

im·paired [ɪmˈperd] *adj*: *with ~ hearing / sight* con problemas auditivos / visuales

im·par·tial [ɪmˈpɑːrʃl] *adj* imparcial

im·pass·a·ble [ɪmˈpæsəbl] *adj road* intransitable

im·passe [ˈɪmpæs] *in negotations etc* punto *m* muerto

im·pas·sioned [ɪmˈpæʃnd] *adj speech, plea* apasionado

im·pas·sive [ɪmˈpæsɪv] *adj* impasible

im·pa·tience [ɪmˈpeɪʃəns] impaciencia *f*

im·pa·tient [ɪmˈpeɪʃənt] *adj* impaciente

im·pa·tient·ly [ɪmˈpeɪʃəntlɪ] *adv* impacientemente

im·peach [ɪmˈpiːtʃ] *v/t President* iniciar un proceso de destitución contra

im·pec·ca·ble [ɪmˈpekəbl] *adj* impecable

im·pec·ca·bly [ɪmˈpekəblɪ] *adv* impecablemente

im·pede [ɪmˈpiːd] *v/t* dificultar

im·ped·i·ment [ɪmˈpedɪmənt] *in speech* defecto *m* del habla

im·pend·ing [ɪmˈpendɪŋ] *adj* inminente

im·pen·e·tra·ble [ɪmˈpenɪtrəbl] *adj* impenetrable

im·per·a·tive [ɪmˈperətɪv] **1** *adj* imprescindible **2** *n* GRAM imperativo *m*

im·per·cep·ti·ble [ɪmpəˈseptɪbl] *adj* imperceptible

im·per·fect [ɪmˈpɜːrfekt] **1** *adj* imperfecto **2** *n* GRAM imperfecto *m*

im·pe·ri·al [ɪmˈpɪrɪəl] *adj* imperial

im·per·son·al [ɪmˈpɜːrsənl] *adj* impersonal

im·per·so·nate [ɪmˈpɜːrsəneɪt] *v/t as a joke* imitar; *illegally* hacerse pasar por

im·per·ti·nence [ɪmˈpɜːrtɪnəns] impertinencia *f*

im·per·ti·nent [ɪmˈpɜːrtɪnənt] *adj* impertinente

im·per·tur·ba·ble [ɪmpərˈtɜːrbəbl] *adj* imperturbable

im·per·vi·ous [ɪmˈpɜːrvɪəs] *adj*: *~ to* inmune a

im·pe·tu·ous [ɪmˈpetʃuəs] *adj* impetuoso

im·pe·tus [ˈɪmpɪtəs] *of campaign etc* ímpetu *m*

im·ple·ment **1** *n* [ˈɪmplɪmənt] utensilio *m* **2** *v/t* [ˈɪmplɪment] *measures etc* poner en práctica

im·pli·cate [ˈɪmplɪkeɪt] *v/t* implicar; *~ s.o. in sth* implicar a alguien en algo

im·pli·ca·tion [ɪmplɪˈkeɪʃn] consecuencia *f*; *the ~ is that ...* implica que ...

im·pli·cit [ɪmˈplɪsɪt] *adj* implícito; *trust* inquebrantable

im·plore [ɪmˈplɔːr] *v/t* implorar

im·ply [ɪmˈplaɪ] *v/t* (*pret & pp -ied*) implicar; *are you ~ing I lied?* ¿insinúas que mentí?

im·po·lite [ɪmpəˈlaɪt] *adj* maleducado

im·port [ˈɪmpɔːrt] **1** *n* importación *f* **2** *v/t* importar

im·por·tance [ɪmˈpɔːrtəns] importancia *f*

im·por·tant [ɪmˈpɔːrtənt] *adj* importante

im·por·ter [ɪmˈpɔːrtər] importador(a) *m(f)*

im·pose [ɪmˈpouz] *v/t tax* imponer; ~ **o.s. on s.o.** molestar a alguien

im·pos·ing [ɪmˈpouzɪŋ] *adj* imponente

im·pos·si·bil·i·ty [ɪmpɑːsɪˈbɪlɪti] imposibilidad *f*

im·pos·si·ble [ɪmˈpɑːsɪbəl] *adj* imposible

im·pos·tor [ɪmˈpɑːstər] impostor(a) *m(f)*

im·po·tence [ˈɪmpətəns] impotencia *f*

im·po·tent [ˈɪmpətənt] *adj* impotente

im·pov·e·rished [ɪmˈpɑːvərɪʃt] *adj* empobrecido

im·prac·ti·cal [ɪmˈpræktɪkəl] *adj* poco práctico

im·press [ɪmˈpres] *v/t* impresionar; **be ~ed by s.o. / sth** quedar impresionado por alguien / algo; **I'm not ~ed** no me parece nada extraordinario

im·pres·sion [ɪmˈpreʃn] impresión *f*; (*impersonation*) imitación *f*; **make a good / bad ~ on s.o.** causar a alguien buena / mala impresión; **I get the ~ that ...** me da la impresión de que ...

im·pres·sion·a·ble [ɪmˈpreʃənəbl] *adj* influenciable

im·pres·sive [ɪmˈpresɪv] *adj* impresionante

im·print [ˈɪmprɪnt] *n of credit card* impresión *f*

im·pris·on [ɪmˈprɪzn] *v/t* encarcelar

im·pris·on·ment [ɪmˈprɪznmənt] encarcelamiento *m*

im·prob·a·ble [ɪmˈprɑːbəbl] *adj* improbable

im·prop·er [ɪmˈprɑːpər] *adj behavior* incorrecto

im·prove [ɪmˈpruːv] *v/t & v/i* mejorar

im·prove·ment [ɪmˈpruːvmənt] mejora *f*, mejoría *f*

im·pro·vise [ˈɪmprəvaɪz] *v/i* improvisar

im·pu·dent [ˈɪmpjʊdənt] *adj* insolente, desvergonzado

im·pulse [ˈɪmpʌls] impulso *m*; **do sth on an ~** hacer algo impulsivamente

'im·pulse buy compra *f* impulsiva

im·pul·sive [ɪmˈpʌlsɪv] *adj* impulsivo

im·pu·ni·ty [ɪmˈpjuːnəti] impunidad *f*; **with ~** impunemente

im·pure [ɪmˈpjʊr] *adj* impuro

in [ɪn] **1** *prep* ◇ en; ~ **Washington** en Washington; ~ **the street** en la calle; **put it ~ your pocket** métetelo en el bolsillo; **wounded ~ the leg / arm** herido en la pierna / el brazo ◇ ~ **1999** en 1999; ~ **two hours from now** dentro de dos horas; (*over period of*) en dos horas; ~ **the morning** por la mañana; ~ **the summer** en verano; ~ **August** en agosto ◇ ~ **English / Spanish** en inglés / español; ~ **a loud voice** en voz alta; ~ **his style** en su estilo; ~ **yellow** de amarillo ◇ ~ **crossing the road** (*while*) al cruzar la calle; ~ **agreeing to this** (*by virtue of*) al expresar acuerdo con esto ◇ ~ **his novel** en su novela; ~ **Faulkner** en Faulkner ◇ **three ~ all** tres en total; **one ~ ten** uno de cada diez **2** *adv*: **is he ~?** *at home* ¿está en casa?; **is the express ~ yet?** ¿ha llegado ya el expreso?; **when the diskette is ~** cuando el disquete está dentro; ~ **here** aquí dentro **3** *adj* (*fashionable, popular*) de moda

in·a·bil·i·ty [ɪnəˈbɪlɪti] incapacidad *f*

in·ac·ces·si·ble [ɪnəkˈsesɪbl] *adj* inaccesible

in·ac·cu·rate [ɪnˈækjʊrət] *adj* inexacto

in·ac·tive [ɪnˈæktɪv] *adj* inactivo

in·ad·e·quate [ɪnˈædɪkwət] *adj* insuficiente

in·ad·vis·a·ble [ɪnədˈvaɪzəbl] *adj* poco aconsejable

in·an·i·mate [ɪnˈænɪmət] *adj* inanimado

in·ap·pro·pri·ate [ɪnəˈproupriət] *adj remark, thing to do* inadecuado, improcedente; *choice* inapropiado

in·ar·tic·u·late [ɪnɑːrˈtɪkjʊlət] *adj*: **be ~** expresarse mal

in·au·di·ble [ɪnˈɔːdəbl] *adj* inaudible

in·au·gu·ral [ɪˈnɒːgjʊrəl] *adj speech* inaugural

in·au·gu·rate [ɪˈnɔːgjʊreɪt] *v/t* inaugurar

in·born [ˈɪnbɔːrn] *adj* innato

in·breed·ing [ˈɪnbriːdɪŋ] endogamia *f*

Inc. *abbr* (= *Incorporated*) S.A. (= sociedad *f* anónima)

in·cal·cu·la·ble [ɪnˈkælkjʊləbl] *adj damage* incalculable

in·ca·pa·ble [ɪnˈkeɪpəbl] *adj* incapaz; *be ~ of doing sth* ser incapaz de hacer algo

in·cen·di·a·ry de·vice [ɪnˈsendɪrɪ] artefacto *m* incendiario

in·cense¹ [ˈɪnsens] *n* incienso *m*

in·cense² [ɪnˈsens] *v/t* encolerizar

in·cen·tive [ɪnˈsentɪv] incentivo *m*

in·ces·sant [ɪnˈsesnt] *adj* incesante

in·ces·sant·ly [ɪnˈsesntlɪ] *adv* incesantemente

in·cest [ˈɪnsest] incesto *m*

inch [ɪntʃ] *n* pulgada *f*

in·ci·dent [ˈɪnsɪdənt] incidente *m*

in·ci·den·tal [ɪnsɪˈdentl] *adj* sin importancia; *~ expenses* gastos *mpl* varios

in·ci·den·tal·ly [ɪnsɪˈdentlɪ] *adv* a propósito

in·cin·e·ra·tor [ɪnˈsɪnəreɪtər] incinerador *m*

in·ci·sion [ɪnˈsɪʒn] incisión *f*

in·ci·sive [ɪnˈsaɪsɪv] *adj* incisivo

in·cite [ɪnˈsaɪt] *v/t* incitar; *~ s.o. to do sth* incitar a alguien a que haga algo

in·clem·ent [ɪnˈklemənt] *adj* inclemente

in·cli·na·tion [ɪnklɪˈneɪʃn] (*tendency, liking*) inclinación *f*

in·cline [ɪnˈklaɪn] *v/t*: *be ~d to do sth* tender a hacer algo

in·close, in·clos·ure → *enclose, enclosure*

in·clude [ɪnˈkluːd] *v/t* incluir

in·clud·ing [ɪnˈkluːdɪŋ] *prep* incluyendo

in·clu·sive [ɪnˈkluːsɪv] **1** *adj price* total, global **2** *prep*: *~ of* incluyendo, incluido **3** *adv*: *from Monday to Thursday* ~ de lunes a jueves, ambos inclusive; *it costs $1000* ~ cuesta 1.000 dólares todo incluido

in·co·her·ent [ɪnkoˈhɪərənt] *adj* incoherente

in·come [ˈɪnkəm] ingresos *mpl*

ˈin·come tax impuesto *m* sobre la renta

in·com·ing [ˈɪnkʌmɪŋ] *adj tide* que sube; *~ flight* vuelo *m* que llega; *~ mail* correo *m* recibido; *~ calls* llamadas *fpl* recibidas

in·com·pa·ra·ble [ɪnˈkɑːmpərəbl] *adj* incomparable

in·com·pat·i·bil·i·ty [ɪnkəmpætɪˈbɪlɪtɪ] incompatibilidad *f*

in·com·pat·i·ble [ɪnkəmˈpætɪbl] *adj* incompatible

in·com·pe·tence [ɪnˈkɑːmpɪtəns] incompetencia *f*

in·com·pe·tent [ɪnˈkɑːmpɪtənt] *adj* incompetente

in·com·plete [ɪnkəmˈpliːt] *adj* incompleto

in·com·pre·hen·si·ble [ɪnkɑːmprɪˈhensɪbl] *adj* incomprensible

in·con·cei·va·ble [ɪnkənˈsiːvəbl] *adj* inconcebible

in·con·clu·sive [ɪnkənˈkluːsɪv] *adj* no concluyente

in·con·gru·ous [ɪnˈkɑːŋgrʊəs] *adj* incongruente

in·con·sid·er·ate [ɪnkənˈsɪdərət] *adj* desconsiderado

in·con·sis·tent [ɪnkənˈsɪstənt] *adj argument, behavior* incoherente, inconsecuente; *player* irregular; *be ~ with sth* no ser consecuente con algo

in·con·so·la·ble [ɪnkənˈsoʊləbl] *adj* inconsolable, desconsolado

in·con·spic·u·ous [ɪnkənˈspɪkjʊəs] *adj* discreto

in·con·ve·ni·ence [ɪnkənˈviːnɪəns] *n* inconveniencia *f*

in·con·ve·ni·ent [ɪnkənˈviːnɪənt] *adj* inconveniente, inoportuno

in·cor·po·rate [ɪnˈkɔːrpəreɪt] *v/t* incorporar

in·cor·po·rat·ed [ɪnˈkɔːrpəreɪtɪd] *adj* COM: *ABC Incorporated* ABC, sociedad *f* anónima

in·cor·rect [ɪnkəˈrekt] *adj* incorrecto

in·cor·rect·ly [ɪnkəˈrektlɪ] *adv* incorrectamente

in·cor·ri·gi·ble [ɪnˈkɑːrɪdʒəbl] *adj* incorregible

in·crease 1 *v/t & v/i* [ɪnˈkriːs] aumentar 2 *n* [ˈɪnkriːs] aumento *m*

in·creas·ing [ɪnˈkriːsɪŋ] *adj* creciente

in·creas·ing·ly [ɪnˈkriːsɪŋli] *adv* cada vez más; *we're getting ~ concerned* cada vez estamos más preocupados

in·cred·i·ble [ɪnˈkredɪbl] *adj* (*amazing, very good*) increíble

in·crim·i·nate [ɪnˈkrɪmɪneɪt] *v/t* incriminar; *~ o.s.* incriminarse

in·cu·ba·tor [ˈɪŋkjubeɪtər] incubadora *f*

in·cur [ɪnˈkɜːr] *v/t* (*pret & pp -red*) *costs* incurrir en; *debts* contraer; *s.o.'s anger* provocar

in·cu·ra·ble [ɪnˈkjurəbl] *adj* incurable

in·debt·ed [ɪnˈdetɪd] *adj*: *be ~ to s.o.* estar en deuda con alguien

in·de·cent [ɪnˈdiːsnt] *adj* indecente

in·de·ci·sive [ɪndɪˈsaɪsɪv] *adj* indeciso

in·de·ci·sive·ness [ɪndɪˈsaɪsɪvnɪs] indecisión *f*

in·deed [ɪnˈdiːd] *adv* (*in fact*) ciertamente, efectivamente; *yes, agreeing* ciertamente, en efecto; *very much ~* muchísimo; *thank you very much ~* muchísimas gracias

in·de·fi·na·ble [ɪndɪˈfaɪnəbl] *adj* indefinible

in·def·i·nite [ɪnˈdefɪnɪt] *adj* indefinido; *~ article* GRAM artículo *m* indefinido

in·def·i·nite·ly [ɪnˈdefɪnɪtli] *adv* indefinidamente

in·del·i·cate [ɪnˈdelɪkət] *adj* poco delicado

in·dent 1 *n* [ˈɪndent] *in text* sangrado *m* 2 *v/t* [ɪnˈdent] *line* sangrar

in·de·pen·dence [ɪndɪˈpendəns] independencia *f*

In·de·pen·dence Day Día *m* de la Independencia

in·de·pen·dent [ɪndɪˈpendənt] *adj* independiente

in·de·pen·dent·ly [ɪndɪˈpendəntli] *adv deal with* por separado; *~ of* al margen de

in·de·scri·ba·ble [ɪndɪˈskraɪbəbl] *adj* indescriptible

in·de·scrib·a·bly [ɪndɪˈskraɪbəbli] *adv* indescriptiblemente

in·de·struc·ti·ble [ɪndɪˈstrʌktəbl] *adj* indestructible

in·de·ter·mi·nate [ɪndɪˈtɜːrmɪnət] *adj* indeterminado

in·dex [ˈɪndeks] *n for book* índice *m*

'in·dex card ficha *f*; 'in·dex fin·ger (dedo *m*) índice *m*; in·dex-'linked *adj Br* indexado

In·di·a [ˈɪndɪə] (la) India

In·di·an [ˈɪndɪən] 1 *adj* indio 2 *n from India* indio(-a) *m(f)*, hindú *m/f*; *American* indio(-a) *m(f)*

In·di·an 'sum·mer *in northern hemisphere* veranillo *m* de San Martín; *in southern hemisphere* veranillo *m* de San Juan

in·di·cate [ˈɪndɪkeɪt] 1 *v/t* indicar 2 *v/i when driving* poner el intermitente

in·di·ca·tion [ɪndɪˈkeɪʃn] indicio *m*

in·di·ca·tor [ˈɪndɪkeɪtər] *Br on car* intermitente *m*

in·dict [ɪnˈdaɪt] *v/t* acusar

in·dif·fer·ence [ɪnˈdɪfrəns] indiferencia *f*

in·dif·fer·ent [ɪnˈdɪfrənt] *adj* indiferente; (*mediocre*) mediocre; *are you totally ~ to the way I feel?* ¿no te importa lo más mínimo lo que sienta yo?

in·di·ges·ti·ble [ɪndɪˈdʒestɪbl] *adj* indigesto

in·di·ges·tion [ɪndɪˈdʒestʃn] indigestión *f*

in·dig·nant [ɪnˈdɪgnənt] *adj* indignado

in·dig·na·tion [ɪndɪgˈneɪʃn] indignación *f*

in·di·rect [ɪndɪˈrekt] *adj* indirecto

in·di·rect·ly [ɪndɪˈrektli] *adv* indirectamente

in·dis·creet [ɪndɪˈskriːt] *adj* indiscreto

in·dis·cre·tion [ɪndɪˈskreʃn] indiscreción *f*

in·dis·crim·i·nate [ɪndɪˈskrɪmɪnət]

adj indiscriminado

in·dis·pen·sa·ble [ɪndɪ'spensəbl] *adj* indispensable, imprescindible

in·dis·posed [ɪndɪ'spoʊzd] *adj (not well)* indispuesto; *be ~* hallarse indispuesto

in·dis·pu·ta·ble [ɪndɪ'spjuːtəbl] *adj* indiscutible

in·dis·pu·ta·bly [ɪndɪ'spjuːtəblɪ] *adv* indiscutiblemente

in·dis·tinct [ɪndɪ'stɪŋkt] *adj* indistinto, impreciso

in·dis·tin·guish·a·ble [ɪndɪ'stɪŋgwɪʃəbl] *adj* indistinguible

in·di·vid·u·al [ɪndɪ'vɪdʒʊəl] **1** *n* individuo *m* **2** *adj* individual

in·di·vid·u·a·list [ɪndɪ'vɪdʒʊəlɪst] *adj* individualista

in·di·vid·u·al·ly [ɪndɪ'vɪdʒʊəlɪ] *adv* individualmente

in·di·vis·i·ble [ɪndɪ'vɪzɪbl] *adj* indivisible

in·doc·tri·nate [ɪn'dɑːktrɪneɪt] *v/t* adoctrinar

in·do·lence ['ɪndələns] indolencia *f*

in·do·lent ['ɪndələnt] *adj* indolente

In·do·ne·sia [ɪndə'niːʒə] Indonesia

In·do·ne·sian [ɪndə'niːʒən] **1** *adj* indonesio **2** *n person* indonesio(-a) *m(f)*

in·door ['ɪndɔːr] *adj activities* de interior; *sport* de pista cubierta; *arena* cubierto; *athletics* en pista cubierta

in·doors [ɪn'dɔːrz] *adv* dentro

in·dorse → **endorse**

in·dulge [ɪn'dʌldʒ] **1** *v/t o.s., one's tastes* satisfacer **2** *v/i: ~ in a pleasure* entregarse a un placer; *if I might ~ in a little joke* si se me permite contar un chiste

in·dul·gent [ɪn'dʌldʒənt] *adj* indulgente

in·dus·tri·al [ɪn'dʌstrɪəl] *adj* industrial; *~ action* acciones *fpl* reivindicativas

in·dus·tri·al dis'pute conflicto *m* laboral

in·dus·tri·al·ist [ɪn'dʌstrɪəlɪst] industrial *m/f*

in·dus·tri·al·ize [ɪn'dʌstrɪəlaɪz] **1** *v/t* industrializar **2** *v/i* industrializarse

in·dus·tri·al 'waste residuos *mpl* industriales

in·dus·tri·ous [ɪn'dʌstrɪəs] *adj* trabajador, aplicado

in·dus·try ['ɪndəstrɪ] industria *f*

in·ef·fec·tive [ɪnɪ'fektɪv] *adj* ineficaz

in·ef·fec·tu·al [ɪnɪ'fektʃʊəl] *adj person* inepto, incapaz

in·ef·fi·cient [ɪnɪ'fɪʃənt] *adj* ineficiente

in·el·i·gi·ble [ɪn'elɪdʒɪbl] *adj: be ~* no reunir las condiciones

in·ept [ɪ'nept] *adj* inepto

in·e·qual·i·ty [ɪnɪ'kwɑːlɪtɪ] desigualdad *f*

in·es·ca·pa·ble [ɪnɪ'skeɪpəbl] *adj* inevitable

in·es·ti·ma·ble [ɪn'estɪməbl] *adj* inestimable

in·ev·i·ta·ble [ɪn'evɪtəbl] *adj* inevitable

in·ev·i·ta·bly [ɪn'evɪtəblɪ] *adv* inevitablemente

in·ex·cu·sa·ble [ɪnɪk'skjuːzəbl] *adj* inexcusable, injustificable

in·ex·haus·ti·ble [ɪnɪg'zɔːstəbl] *adj supply* inagotable

in·ex·pen·sive [ɪnɪk'spensɪv] *adj* barato, económico

in·ex·pe·ri·enced [ɪnɪk'spɪrɪənst] *adj* inexperto

in·ex·plic·a·ble [ɪnɪk'splɪkəbl] *adj* inexplicable

in·ex·pres·si·ble [ɪnɪk'spresɪbl] *adj joy* indescriptible

in·fal·li·ble [ɪn'fælɪbl] *adj* infalible

in·fa·mous ['ɪnfəməs] *adj* infame

in·fan·cy ['ɪnfənsɪ] infancia *f*

in·fant ['ɪnfənt] *adj* bebé *m*

in·fan·tile ['ɪnfəntaɪl] *adj pej* infantil, pueril

in·fan·try ['ɪnfəntrɪ] infantería *f*

in·fan·try 'sol·dier soldado *m/f* de infantería, infante *m/f*

in·fat·u·at·ed [ɪn'fætʃʊeɪtɪd] *adj: be ~ with s.o.* estar encaprichado de alguien

in·fect [ɪn'fekt] *v/t* infectar; *he ~ed everyone with his cold* contagió el resfriado a todo el mundo; *become ~ed of wound* infectarse; *of person*

contagiarse
in·fec·tion [ɪnˈfekʃn] infección *f*
in·fec·tious [ɪnˈfekʃəs] *adj disease* infeccioso; *laughter* contagioso
in·fer [ɪnˈfɜːr] *v/t* (*pret & pp* **-red**) inferir, deducir (**from** de)
in·fe·ri·or [ɪnˈfɪrɪər] *adj* inferior (**to** a)
in·fe·ri·or·i·ty [ɪnfɪrɪˈɑːrətɪ] *in quality* inferioridad *f*
in·fe·ri·or·i·ty com·plex complejo *m* de inferioridad
in·fer·tile [ɪnˈfɜːrtl] *adj woman, plant* estéril; *soil* estéril, yermo
in·fer·til·i·ty [ɪnfərˈtɪlɪtɪ] esterilidad *f*
in·fi·del·i·ty [ɪnfɪˈdelɪtɪ] infidelidad *f*
in·fil·trate [ˈɪnfɪltreɪt] *v/t* infiltrarse en
in·fi·nite [ˈɪnfɪnət] *adj* infinito
in·fin·i·tive [ɪnˈfɪnətɪv] infinitivo *m*
in·fin·i·ty [ɪnˈfɪnətɪ] infinidad *f*
in·firm [ɪnˈfɜːrm] *adj* enfermo, achacoso
in·fir·ma·ry [ɪnˈfɜːrmərɪ] enfermería *f*
in·fir·mi·ty [ɪnˈfɜːrmətɪ] debilidad *f*
in·flame [ɪnˈfleɪm] *v/t* despertar
in·flam·ma·ble [ɪnˈflæməbl] *adj* inflamable
in·flam·ma·tion [ɪnfləˈmeɪʃn] MED inflamación *f*
in·flat·a·ble [ɪnˈfleɪtəbl] *adj dinghy* hinchable, inflable
in·flate [ɪnˈfleɪt] *v/t* tire, *dinghy* hinchar, inflar; *economy* inflar
in·fla·tion [ɪnˈfleɪʃən] inflación *f*
in·fla·tion·a·ry [ɪnˈfleɪʃənərɪ] *adj* inflacionario, inflacionista
in·flec·tion [ɪnˈflekʃn] inflexión *f*
in·flex·i·ble [ɪnˈfleksɪbl] *adj* inflexible
in·flict [ɪnˈflɪkt] *v/t* infligir (**on** a)
'in-flight *adj*: ~ **entertainment** entretenimiento *m* durante el vuelo
in·flu·ence [ˈɪnfluəns] **1** *n* influencia *f*; **be a good/ bad ~ on s.o.** tener una buena / mala influencia en alguien **2** *v/t* influir en, influenciar
in·flu·en·tial [ɪnfluˈenʃl] *adj* influ...
...**za** [ɪnfluˈenzə] gripe *f*
...[ɪnˈfɔːrm] **1** *v/t* informar; ~

s.o. about sth informar a alguien de algo; **please keep me ~ed** por favor manténme informado **2** *v/i*: ~ **on s.o.** delatar a alguien
in·for·mal [ɪnˈfɔːrml] *adj* informal
in·for·mal·i·ty [ɪnfɔːrˈmælɪtɪ] informalidad *f*
in·form·ant [ɪnˈfɔːrmənt] confidente *m/f*
in·for·ma·tion [ɪnfərˈmeɪʃn] información *f*; **a piece of ~** una información
in·for·ma·tion 'sci·ence informática *f*; **in·for·ma·tion 'sci·en·tist** informático(-a) *m(f)*; **in·for·ma·tion tech'nol·o·gy** tecnologías *fpl* de la información
in·for·ma·tive [ɪnˈfɔːrmətɪv] *adj* informativo; **you're not being very ~** no estás dando mucha información
in·form·er [ɪnˈfɔːrmər] confidente *m/f*
in·fra·red [ɪnfrəˈred] *adj* infrarrojo
in·fra·struc·ture [ˈɪnfrəstrʌktʃər] infraestructura *f*
in·fre·quent [ɪnˈfriːkwənt] *adj* poco frecuente
in·fu·ri·ate [ɪnˈfjʊrɪeɪt] *v/t* enfurecer, exasperar
in·fu·ri·at·ing [ɪnˈfjʊrɪeɪtɪŋ] *adj* exasperante
in·fuse [ɪnˈfjuːz] *v/i of tea* infundir
in·fu·sion [ɪnˈfjuːʒn] (*herb tea*) infusión *f*
in·ge·ni·ous [ɪnˈdʒiːnɪəs] *adj* ingenioso
in·ge·nu·i·ty [ɪndʒɪˈnuːətɪ] lo ingenioso
in·got [ˈɪŋgət] lingote *m*
in·gra·ti·ate [ɪnˈgreɪʃɪeɪt] *v/t*: ~ **o.s. with s.o.** congraciarse con alguien
in·grat·i·tude [ɪnˈgrætɪtuːd] ingratitud *f*
in·gre·di·ent [ɪnˈgriːdɪənt] *also fig* ingrediente *m*
in·hab·it [ɪnˈhæbɪt] *v/t* habitar
in·hab·it·a·ble [ɪnˈhæbɪtəbl] *adj* habitable
in·hab·i·tant [ɪnˈhæbɪtənt] habitante *m/f*
in·hale [ɪnˈheɪl] **1** *v/t* inhalar **2** *v/i*

when smoking tragarse el humo
in·ha·ler [ɪn'heɪlər] inhalador *m*
in·her·it [ɪn'herɪt] *v/t* heredar
in·her·i·tance [ɪn'herɪtəns] herencia *f*
in·hib·it [ɪn'hɪbɪt] *v/t growth* impedir; *conversation* inhibir, cohibir
in·hib·it·ed [ɪn'hɪbɪtɪd] *adj* inhibido, cohibido
in·hi·bi·tion [ɪnhɪ'bɪʃn] inhibición *f*
in·hos·pi·ta·ble [ɪnha:'spɪtəbl] *adj person* inhospitalario; *city, climate* inhóspito
'in-house 1 *adj facilities* en el lugar de trabajo; **~ team** equipo *m* en plantilla **2** *adv work* en la empresa
in·hu·man [ɪn'hju:mən] *adj* inhumano
i·ni·tial [ɪ'nɪʃl] **1** *adj* inicial **2** *n* inicial *f* **3** *v/t (write ~s on)* poner las iniciales en
i·ni·tial·ly [ɪ'nɪʃlɪ] *adv* inicialmente, al principio
i·ni·ti·ate [ɪ'nɪʃɪeɪt] *v/t* iniciar
i·ni·ti·a·tion [ɪnɪʃɪ'eɪʃn] iniciación *f*, inicio *m*
i·ni·ti·a·tive [ɪ'nɪʃətɪv] iniciativa *f*; **do sth on one's own ~** hacer algo por iniciativa propia
in·ject [ɪn'dʒekt] *v/t drug, fuel, capital* inyectar
in·jec·tion [ɪn'dʒekʃn] *of drug, fuel, capital* inyección *f*
'in-joke: *it's an ~* es un chiste que entendemos nosotros
in·jure ['ɪndʒər] *v/t* lesionar; **he ~d his leg** se lesionó la pierna
in·jured ['ɪndʒərd] **1** *adj leg* lesionado; *feelings* herido **2** *npl:* **the ~** los heridos
in·ju·ry ['ɪndʒərɪ] lesión *f*; *wound* herida *f*
'in·ju·ry time SP tiempo *m* de descuento
in·jus·tice [ɪn'dʒʌstɪs] injusticia *f*
ink [ɪŋk] tinta *f*
ink·jet ('**prin·ter**) impresora *f* de chorro de tinta
in·land ['ɪnlənd] *adj* interior; *mail* nacional
in-laws ['ɪnlɒːz] *npl* familia *f* política

in·lay ['ɪnleɪ] *n* incrustación *f*
in·let ['ɪnlet] *of sea* ensenada *f*; *in machine* entrada *f*
in·mate ['ɪnmeɪt] *of prison* recluso(-a) *m(f)*; *of mental hospital* paciente *m/f*
inn [ɪn] posada *f*, mesón *m*
in·nate [ɪ'neɪt] *adj* innato
in·ner ['ɪnər] *adj* interior; **the ~ ear** el oído interno
in·ner 'cit·y barrios degradados del centro de la ciudad; **~ decay** degradación *f* del centro de la ciudad
'in·ner·most *adj feelings* más íntimo; *recess* más recóndito
in·ner 'tube cámara *f* (de aire)
in·no·cence ['ɪnəsəns] inocencia *f*
in·no·cent ['ɪnəsənt] *adj* inocente
in·noc·u·ous [ɪ'na:kjuəs] *adj* inocuo
in·no·va·tion [ɪnə'veɪʃn] innovación *f*
in·no·va·tive [ɪnə'veɪtɪv] *adj* innovador
in·no·va·tor ['ɪnəveɪtər] innovador(a) *m(f)*
in·nu·me·ra·ble [ɪ'nu:mərəbl] *adj* innumerable
i·noc·u·late [ɪ'na:kjuleɪt] *v/t* inocular
i·noc·u·la·tion [ɪna:kju'leɪʃn] inoculación *f*
in·of·fen·sive [ɪnə'fensɪv] *adj* inofensivo
in·or·gan·ic [ɪnɔːr'gænɪk] *adj* inorgánico
'in-pa·tient paciente *m/f* interno(-a)
in·put ['ɪnput] **1** *n into project etc* contribución *f*, aportación *f*; COMPUT entrada *f* **2** *v/t (pret & pp* **-ted** *or* **input)** *into project* contribuir, aportar; COMPUT introducir
in·quest ['ɪnkwest] investigación *f* (*into* sobre)
in·quire [ɪn'kwaɪr] *v/i* preguntar; **~ into sth** investigar algo
in·quir·y [ɪn'kwaɪrɪ] consulta *f*, pregunta *f*; *into rail crash etc* investigación *f*
in·quis·i·tive [ɪn'kwɪzətɪv] *adj* curioso, inquisitivo
in·sane [ɪn'seɪn] *adj person* loco, de-

mente; *idea* descabellado

in·san·i·ta·ry [ɪn'sænɪterɪ] *adj* antihigiénico

in·san·i·ty [ɪn'sænɪtɪ] locura *f*, demencia *f*

in·sa·ti·a·ble [ɪn'seɪʃəbl] *adj* insaciable

in·scrip·tion [ɪn'skrɪpʃn] inscripción *f*

in·scru·ta·ble [ɪn'skruːtəbl] *adj* inescrutable

in·sect ['ɪnsekt] insecto *m*

in·sec·ti·cide [ɪn'sektɪsaɪd] insecticida *f*

'in·sect re·pel·lent repelente *m* contra insectos

in·se·cure [ɪnsɪ'kjʊr] *adj* inseguro

in·se·cu·ri·ty [ɪnsɪ'kjʊrɪtɪ] inseguridad *f*

in·sen·si·tive [ɪn'sensɪtɪv] *adj* insensible

in·sen·si·tiv·i·ty [ɪnsensɪ'tɪvɪtɪ] insensibilidad *f*

in·sep·a·ra·ble [ɪn'sepərəbl] *adj* inseparable

in·sert 1 *n* ['ɪnsɜːrt] *in magazine etc* encarte *m* **2** *v/t* [ɪn'sɜːrt] *coin, finger, diskette* introducir, meter; *extra text* insertar

in·ser·tion [ɪn'sɜːrʃn] *act* introducción *f*, inserción *f*; *of text* inserción *f*

in·side [ɪn'saɪd] **1** *n of house, box* interior *m*; **somebody on the ~** algún de dentro; **~ out** del revés; **turn sth ~ out** dar la vuelta a algo (*de dentro a fuera*); **know sth ~ out** saberse algo al dedillo **2** *prep* dentro de; **~ the house** dentro de la casa; **~ of 2 hours** dentro de 2 horas **3** *adv stay, remain* dentro; *go, carry* adentro; **we went ~** entramos **4** *adj*: **~ information** información *f* confidencial; **~ lane** SP calle *f* de dentro; *on road* carril *m* de la derecha; **~ pocket** bolsillo *m* interior

in·sid·er [ɪn'saɪdər] *persona con acceso a información confidencial*

in·sid·er 'trad·ing FIN uso *m* de información privilegiada

in·sides [ɪn'saɪdz] *npl* tripas *fpl*

in·sid·i·ous [ɪn'sɪdɪəs] *adj* insidioso

in·sight ['ɪnsaɪt]: **this film offers an ~ into local customs** esta película permite hacerse una idea de las costumbres locales; **full of ~** muy perspicaz

in·sig·nif·i·cant [ɪnsɪg'nɪfɪkənt] *adj* insignificante

in·sin·cere [ɪnsɪn'sɪr] *adj* poco sincero, falso

in·sin·cer·i·ty [ɪnsɪn'serɪtɪ] falta *f* de sinceridad

in·sin·u·ate [ɪn'sɪnueɪt] *v/t* (*imply*) insinuar

in·sist [ɪn'sɪst] *v/i* insistir; **please keep it, I ~** por favor, insisto en que te lo quedes

♦ insist on *v/t* insistir en

in·sis·tent [ɪn'sɪstənt] *adj* insistente

in·so·lent ['ɪnsələnt] *adj* insolente

in·sol·u·ble [ɪn'sɑːljubl] *adj problem* irresoluble; *substance* insoluble

in·sol·vent [ɪn'sɑːlvənt] *adj* insolvente

in·som·ni·a [ɪn'sɑːmnɪə] insomnio *m*

in·spect [ɪn'spekt] *v/t* inspeccionar

in·spec·tion [ɪn'spekʃn] inspección *f*

in·spec·tor [ɪn'spektər] *in factory, police* inspector(a) *m(f)*; *on buses* revisor(a) *m(f)*

in·spi·ra·tion [ɪnspə'reɪʃn] inspiración *f*

in·spire [ɪn'spaɪr] *v/t respect etc* inspirar; **be ~d by s.o. / sth** estar inspirado por alguien / algo

in·sta·bil·i·ty [ɪnstə'bɪlɪtɪ] *of character, economy* inestabilidad *f*

in·stall [ɪn'stɔːl] *v/t* instalar

in·stal·la·tion [ɪnstə'leɪʃn] instalación *f*; *military* ~ instalación *f* militar

in·stal·ment *Br*, **in·stall·ment** [ɪn'stɔːlmənt] *of story, TV drama etc* episodio *m*; *payment* plazo *m*

in'stall·ment plan compra *f* a plazos

in·stance ['ɪnstəns] (*example*) ejemplo *m*; **for ~** por ejemplo

in·stant ['ɪnstənt] **1** *adj* instantáneo **2** *n* instante *m*; **in an ~** en un instante

in·stan·ta·ne·ous [ɪnstən'teɪnɪəs] *adj* instantáneo

in·stant 'cof·fee café *m* instantáneo

in·stant·ly ['ɪnstəntlɪ] *adv* al instante

in·stead [ɪnˈsted] adv: *I'll take that one ~* me llevaré mejor ese otro; *would you like coffee ~?* ¿preferiría mejor café?; *I'll have coffee ~ of tea* tomaré café en vez de té; *he went ~ of me* fue en mi lugar

in·step [ˈɪnstep] empeine m

in·stinct [ˈɪnstɪŋkt] instinto m

in·stinc·tive [ɪnˈstɪŋktɪv] adj instintivo

in·sti·tute [ˈɪnstɪtuːt] 1 n instituto m; *for elderly* residencia f de ancianos; *for mentally ill* psiquiátrico m 2 v/t *new law* establecer; *inquiry* iniciar

in·sti·tu·tion [ɪnstɪˈtuːʃn] institución f; (*setting up*) iniciación f

in·struct [ɪnˈstrʌkt] v/t (*order*) dar instrucciones a; (*teach*) instruir; *~ s.o. to do sth* (*order*) ordenar a alguien que haga algo

in·struc·tion [ɪnˈstrʌkʃn] instrucción f; *~s for use* instrucciones fpl de uso

in·struc·tion man·u·al manual m de instrucciones

in·struc·tive [ɪnˈstrʌktɪv] adj instructivo

in·struc·tor [ɪnˈstrʌktər] instructor(a) m(f)

in·stru·ment [ˈɪnstrʊmənt] MUS, *tool* instrumento m

in·sub·or·di·nate [ɪnsəˈbɔːrdɪnət] adj insubordinado

in·suf·fi·cient [ɪnsəˈfɪʃnt] adj insuficiente

in·su·late [ˈɪnsəleɪt] v/t also ELEC aislar

in·su·la·tion [ɪnsəˈleɪʃn] ELEC aislamiento m; *against cold* aislamiento m (térmico)

in·su·lin [ˈɪnsəlɪn] insulina f

in·sult 1 n [ˈɪnsʌlt] insulto m 2 v/t [ɪnˈsʌlt] insultar

in·sur·ance [ɪnˈʃʊrəns] seguro m

in·sur·ance com·pa·ny compañía f de seguros, aseguradora f; *in·surance pol·i·cy* póliza f de seguros; *in·surance pre·mi·um* prima f (del seguro)

in·sure [ɪnˈʃʊr] v/t asegurar

in·sured [ɪnˈʃʊrd] 1 adj asegurado

2 n: *the ~* el asegurado, la asegurada

in·sur·moun·ta·ble [ɪnsərˈmaʊntəbl] adj insuperable

in·tact [ɪnˈtækt] adj (*not damaged*) intacto

in·take [ˈɪnteɪk] *of college etc* remesa f; *we have an annual ~ of 300 students* cada año admitimos a 300 alumnos

in·te·grate [ˈɪntɪgreɪt] v/t integrar (*into* en)

in·te·grat·ed 'cir·cuit [ˈɪntɪgreɪtɪd] circuito m integrado

in·teg·ri·ty [ɪnˈtegrətɪ] (*honesty*) integridad f; *a man of ~* un hombre íntegro

in·tel·lect [ˈɪntəlekt] intelecto m

in·tel·lec·tual [ɪntəˈlektʃʊəl] 1 adj intelectual 2 n intelectual m/f

in·tel·li·gence [ɪnˈtelɪdʒəns] inteligencia f; (*information*) información f secreta

in·tel·li·gence of·fi·cer agente m/f del servicio de inteligencia

in·tel·li·gence ser·vice servicio m de inteligencia

in·tel·li·gent [ɪnˈtelɪdʒənt] adj inteligente

in·tel·li·gi·ble [ɪnˈtelɪdʒəbl] adj inteligible

in·tend [ɪnˈtend] v/t: *~ to do sth* tener la intención de hacer algo; *that's not what I ~ed* esa no era mi intención

in·tense [ɪnˈtens] adj *sensation, pleasure, heat, pressure* intenso; *personality* serio

in·ten·si·fy [ɪnˈtensɪfaɪ] (*pret & pp -ied*) 1 v/t *effect, pressure* intensificar 2 v/i intensificarse

in·ten·si·ty [ɪnˈtensətɪ] intensidad f

in·ten·sive [ɪnˈtensɪv] adj *study, training, treatment* intensivo

in·ten·sive 'care (u·nit) MED (unidad f de) cuidados mpl intensivos

in·ten·sive 'course *of language study* curso m intensivo

in·tent [ɪnˈtent] adj: *be ~ on doing sth* (*determined to do*) estar decidido a hacer algo; *be ~ on sth* (*concentrating on*) estar concentrado haciendo algo

in·ten·tion [ɪnˈtenʃn] intención *f*; *I have no ~ of ...* (*refuse to*) no tengo intención de ...

in·ten·tion·al [ɪnˈtenʃənl] *adj* intencionado

in·ten·tion·al·ly [ɪnˈtenʃnlɪ] *adv* a propósito, adrede

in·ter·ac·tion [ɪntərˈækʃn] interacción *f*

in·ter·ac·tive [ɪntərˈæktɪv] *adj* interactivo

in·ter·cede [ɪntərˈsiːd] *v/i* interceder

in·ter·cept [ɪntərˈsept] *v/t* interceptar

in·ter·change [ˈɪntərtʃeɪndʒ] *n of highways* nudo *m* vial

in·ter·change·a·ble [ɪntərˈtʃeɪndʒəbl] *adj* intercambiable

in·ter·com [ˈɪntərkɑːm] *in office, ship* interfono *m*; *for front door* portero *m* automático

in·ter·course [ˈɪntərkɔːrs] *sexual* coito *m*

in·ter·de·pend·ent [ɪntərdɪˈpendənt] *adj* interdependiente

in·ter·est [ˈɪntrəst] **1** *n also* FIN interés *m*; *take an ~ in sth* interesarse por algo **2** *v/t* interesar

in·ter·est·ed [ˈɪntrəstɪd] *adj* interesado; *be ~ in sth* estar interesado en algo; *thanks, but I'm not ~* gracias, pero no me interesa

in·ter·est-free 'loan préstamo *m* sin intereses

in·ter·est·ing [ˈɪntrəstɪŋ] *adj* interesante

'in·ter·est rate tipo *m* de interés

in·ter·face [ˈɪntərfeɪs] **1** *n* interface *m*, interfaz *f* **2** *v/i* relacionarse

in·ter·fere [ɪntərˈfɪr] *v/i* interferir, entrometerse

♦ **interfere with** *v/t* afectar a; *the lock had been interfered with* alguien había manipulado la cerradura

in·ter·fer·ence [ɪntərˈfɪrəns] intromisión *f*; *on radio* interferencia *f*

in·te·ri·or [ɪnˈtɪrɪər] **1** *adj* interior **2** *n* interior *m*; *Department of the Interior* Ministerio *m* del Interior

in·te·ri·or 'dec·o·ra·tor interiorista *m/f*, decorador(a) *m(f)* de interiores; **in·te·ri·or de'sign** interiorismo *m*; **in·te·ri·or de'sign·er** interiorista *m/f*

in·ter·lude [ˈɪntərluːd] *at theater* entreacto *m*, intermedio *m*; *at concert* intermedio *m*; (*period*) intervalo *m*

in·ter·mar·ry [ɪntərˈmærɪ] *v/i* (*pret & pp -ied*) casarse (*con miembros de otra raza, religión o grupo*); *the two tribes intermarried* los dos tribus se casaron entre sí

in·ter·me·di·a·ry [ɪntərˈmiːdɪərɪ] *n* intermediario

in·ter·me·di·ate [ɪntərˈmiːdɪət] *adj* intermedio *m*

in·ter·mis·sion [ɪntərˈmɪʃn] *in theater* entreacto *m*, intermedio *m*; *in movie theater* intermedio *m*, descanso *m*

in·tern [ɪnˈtɜːrn] *v/t* recluir

in·ter·nal [ɪnˈtɜːrnl] *adj* interno

in·ter·nal com'bus·tion en·gine motor *m* de combustión interna

in·ter·nal·ly [ɪnˈtɜːrnəlɪ] *adv* internamente

In·ter·nal 'Rev·e·nue (Ser·vice) Hacienda *f*, *Span* Agencia *f* Tributaria

in·ter·na·tion·al [ɪntərˈnæʃnl] *adj* internacional

In·ter·na·tion·al Court of 'Jus·tice Tribunal *m* Internacional de Justicia

in·ter·na·tion·al·ly [ɪntərˈnæʃnəlɪ] *adv* internacionalmente

In·ter·na·tion·al 'Mon·e·tar·y Fund Fondo *m* Monetario Internacional

In·ter·net [ˈɪntərnet] Internet *f*; *on the ~* en Internet

in·ter·nist [ɪnˈtɜːrnɪst] internista *m/f*

in·ter·pret [ɪnˈtɜːrprɪt] *v/t & v/i* interpretar

in·ter·pre·ta·tion [ɪntɜːrprɪˈteɪʃn] interpretación *f*

in·ter·pret·er [ɪnˈtɜːrprɪtər] intérprete *m/f*

in·ter·re·lat·ed [ɪntərrɪˈleɪtɪd] *adj facts* interrelacionado

in·ter·ro·gate [ɪnˈterəgeɪt] *v/t* inte-

rro·gar

in·ter·ro·ga·tion [ɪnterə'geɪʃn] interrogatorio *m*

in·ter·rog·a·tive [ɪntər'rɑːgətɪv] *n* GRAM (forma *f*) interrogativa *f*

in·ter·ro·ga·tor [ɪnterə'geɪtər] interrogador(a) *m(f)*

in·ter·rupt [ɪntər'rʌpt] *v/t & v/i* interrumpir

in·ter·rup·tion [ɪntər'rʌpʃn] interrupción *f*

in·ter·sect [ɪntər'sekt] **1** *v/t* cruzar **2** *v/i* cruzarse

in·ter·sec·tion ['ɪntərsekʃn] (*crossroads*) intersección *f*

in·ter·state ['ɪntərsteɪt] *n* autopista *f* interestatal

in·ter·val ['ɪntərvl] intervalo *m*; *in theater* entreacto *m*, intermedio *m*; *at concert* intermedio *m*

in·ter·vene [ɪntər'viːn] *v/i of person, police etc* intervenir

in·ter·ven·tion [ɪntər'venʃn] intervención *f*

in·ter·view ['ɪntərvjuː] **1** *n* entrevista *f* **2** *v/t* entrevistar

in·ter·view·ee [ɪntərvjuː'iː] *on TV* entrevistado(-a) *m(f)*; *for job* candidato(-a) *m(f)*

in·ter·view·er ['ɪntərvjuːər] entrevistador(a) *m(f)*

in·tes·tine [ɪn'testɪn] intestino *m*

in·ti·ma·cy ['ɪntɪməsɪ] *of friendship* intimidad *f*; *sexual* relaciones *fpl* íntimas

in·ti·mate ['ɪntɪmət] *adj* íntimo

in·tim·i·date [ɪn'tɪmɪdeɪt] *v/t* intimidar

in·tim·i·da·tion [ɪntɪmɪ'deɪʃn] intimidación *f*

in·to ['ɪntʊ] *prep* en; *he put it ~ his suitcase* lo puso en su maleta; *translate ~ English* traducir al inglés; *he's ~ classical music* F (*likes*) le gusta *or Span* le va mucho la música clásica; *he's ~ local politics* F (*is involved with*) está muy metido en el mundillo de la política local; *when you're ~ the job* cuando te hayas metido en el trabajo

in·tol·e·ra·ble [ɪn'tɑːlərəbl] *adj* intolerable

in·tol·e·rant [ɪn'tɑːlərənt] *adj* intolerante

in·tox·i·cat·ed [ɪn'tɑːksɪkeɪtɪd] *adj* ebrio, embriagado

in·tran·si·tive [ɪn'trænsɪtɪv] *adj* intransitivo

in·tra·ve·nous [ɪntrə'viːnəs] *adj* intravenoso

in·trep·id [ɪn'trepɪd] *adj* intrépido

in·tri·cate ['ɪntrɪkət] *adj* intrincado, complicado

in·trigue 1 *n* ['ɪntriːg] intriga *f* **2** *v/t* [ɪn'triːg] intrigar; *I would be ~d to know ...* tendría curiosidad por saber ...

in·tri·guing [ɪn'triːgɪŋ] *adj* intrigante

in·tro·duce [ɪntrə'duːs] *v/t* presentar; *new technique etc* introducir; *may I ~ ...?* permítame presentarle a ...; *~ s.o. to a new sport* iniciar a alguien en un deporte nuevo

in·tro·duc·tion [ɪntrə'dʌkʃn] *to person* presentación *f*; *to a new food, sport etc* iniciación *f*; *in book, of new techniques et* introducción *f*

in·tro·vert ['ɪntrəvɜːrt] *n* introvertido(-a) *m(f)*

in·trude [ɪn'truːd] *v/i* molestar

in·trud·er [ɪn'truːdər] intruso(-a) *m(f)*

in·tru·sion [ɪn'truːʒn] intromisión *f*

in·tu·i·tion [ɪntuː'ɪʃn] intuición *f*

in·vade [ɪn'veɪd] *v/t* invadir

in·val·id¹ [ɪn'vælɪd] *adj* nulo

in·va·lid² ['ɪnvəlɪd] *n* MED minusválido(-a) *m(f)*

in·val·i·date [ɪn'vælɪdeɪt] *v/t claim, theory* invalidar

in·val·u·a·ble [ɪn'væljʊbl] *adj help, contributor* inestimable

in·var·i·a·bly [ɪn'veɪrɪəblɪ] *adv* (*always*) invariablemente, siempre

in·va·sion [ɪn'veɪʒn] invasión *f*

in·vent [ɪn'vent] *v/t* inventar

in·ven·tion [ɪn'venʃn] *action* invención *f*; *thing invented* invento *m*

in·ven·tive [ɪn'ventɪv] *adj* inventivo, imaginativo

in·ven·tor [ɪn'ventər] inventor(-a) *m(f)*

in·ven·to·ry ['ɪnvəntɔːrɪ] inventario *m*

in·verse [ɪn'vɜːrs] *adj order* inverso

in·vert [ɪn'vɜːrt] *v/t* invertir

in·ver·te·brate [ɪn'vɜːrtɪbrət] *n* invertebrado *m*

in·vert·ed 'com·mas [ɪn'vɜːrtɪd] *npl* comillas *fpl*

in·vest [ɪn'vest] *v/t & v/i* invertir (*in* en)

in·ves·ti·gate [ɪn'vestɪgeɪt] *v/t* investigar

in·ves·ti·ga·tion [ɪnvestɪ'geɪʃn] investigación *f*

in·ves·ti·ga·tive 'jour·nal·ism [ɪn'vestɪgətɪv] periodismo *m* de investigación

in·vest·ment [ɪn'vestmənt] inversión *f*

in'vest·ment bank banco *m* de inversiones

in·ves·tor [ɪn'vestər] inversor(a) *m(f)*

in·vig·or·at·ing [ɪn'vɪgəreɪtɪŋ] *adj climate* vigorizante

in·vin·ci·ble [ɪn'vɪnsəbl] invencible

in·vis·i·ble [ɪn'vɪzɪbl] *adj* invisible

in·vi·ta·tion [ɪnvɪ'teɪʃn] invitación *f*

in·vite [ɪn'vaɪt] *v/t* invitar
♦ **invite in** *v/t*: *invite s.o. in* invitar a alguien a que entre

in·voice ['ɪnvɔɪs] **1** *n* factura *f* **2** *v/t customer* enviar la factura a

in·vol·un·ta·ry [ɪn'vɑːlənterɪ] *adj* involuntario

in·volve [ɪn'vɑːlv] *v/t hard work, expense* involucrar, entrañar; *it would ~ emigrating* supondría emigrar; *this doesn't ~ you* esto no tiene nada que ver contigo; *what does it ~?* ¿en qué consiste?; *get ~d with sth* involucrarse *or* meterse en algo; *the police didn't want to get ~d* la policía no quería intervenir; *get ~d with s.o.* emotionally, romantically tener una relación sentimental con alguien

in·volved [ɪn'vɑːlvd] *adj* (*complex*) complicado

in·volve·ment [ɪn'vɑːlvmənt] *in a*

project, crime etc participación *f*, intervención *f*

in·vul·ne·ra·ble [ɪn'vʌlnərəbl] *adj* invulnerable

in·ward ['ɪnwərd] **1** *adj feeling, smile* interior **2** *adv* hacia dentro

in·ward·ly ['ɪnwərdlɪ] *adv* por dentro

i·o·dine ['aɪoʊdiːn] yodo *m*

IOU [aɪoʊ'juː] *abbr* (= *I owe you*) pagaré *m*

IQ [aɪ'kjuː] *abbr* (= *intelligence quotient*) cociente *m* intelectual

I·ran [ɪ'rɑːn] Irán

I·ra·ni·an [ɪ'reɪnɪən] **1** *adj* iraní **2** *n* iraní *m/f*

I·raq [ɪ'ræk] Iraq, Irak

I·ra·qi [ɪ'rækɪ] **1** *adj* iraquí **2** *n* iraquí *m/f*

Ire·land ['aɪrlənd] Irlanda

i·ris ['aɪrɪs] *of eye* iris *m inv*; *flower* lirio *m*

I·rish ['aɪrɪʃ] *adj* irlandés

'I·rish·man irlandés *m*

'I·rish·wom·an irlandesa *f*

i·ron ['aɪərn] **1** *n substance* hierro *m*; *for clothes* plancha *f* **2** *v/t shirts etc* planchar

i·ron·ic(·al) [aɪ'rɑːnɪk(l)] *adj* irónico

i·ron·ing ['aɪərnɪŋ] planchado *m*; *do the ~* planchar

'i·ron·ing board tabla *f* de planchar

'i·ron·works fundición *f*

i·ron·y ['aɪrənɪ] ironía *f*; *the ~ of it all is that ...* lo irónico del tema es que ...

ir·ra·tion·al [ɪ'ræʃənl] *adj* irracional

ir·rec·on·ci·la·ble [ɪrekən'saɪləbl] *adj* irreconciliable

ir·re·cov·e·ra·ble [ɪrɪ'kʌvərəbl] *adj* irrecuperable

ir·re·gu·lar [ɪ'regjʊlər] *adj* irregular

ir·rel·e·vant [ɪ'reləvənt] *adj* irrelevante

ir·rep·a·ra·ble [ɪ'repərəbl] *adj* irreparable

ir·re·place·a·ble [ɪrɪ'pleɪsəbl] *adj object, person* irreemplazable

ir·re·pres·si·ble [ɪrɪ'presəbl] *adj sense of humor* incontenible; *person* irreprimible

ir·re·proach·a·ble [ɪrɪ'proʊtʃəbl] *adj*

irreprochable

ir·re·sis·ti·ble [ɪrɪ'zɪstəbl] *adj* irresistible

ir·re·spec·tive [ɪrɪ'spektɪv] *adv*: ~ *of* independientemente de

ir·re·spon·si·ble [ɪrɪ'spɑːnsɪbl] *adj* irresponsable

ir·re·trie·va·ble [ɪrɪ'triːvəbl] *adj* irrecuperable

ir·rev·e·rent [ɪ'revərənt] *adj* irreverente

ir·rev·o·ca·ble [ɪ'revəkəbl] *adj* irrevocable

ir·ri·gate ['ɪrɪgeɪt] *v/t* regar

ir·ri·ga·tion [ɪrɪ'geɪʃn] riego *m*

ir·ri·ga·tion ca'nal acequia *f*

ir·ri·ta·ble ['ɪrɪtəbl] *adj* irritable

ir·ri·tate ['ɪrɪteɪt] *v/t* irritar

ir·ri·tat·ing ['ɪrɪteɪtɪŋ] *adj* irritante

ir·ri·ta·tion [ɪrɪ'teɪʃn] irritación *f*

Is·lam ['ɪzlɑːm] (el) Islam

Is·lam·ic [ɪz'læmɪk] *adj* islámico

is·land ['aɪlənd] isla *f*

is·land·er ['aɪləndər] isleño(-a) *m(f)*

i·so·late ['aɪsəleɪt] *v/t* aislar

i·so·lat·ed ['aɪsəleɪtɪd] *adj* aislado

i·so·la·tion [aɪsə'leɪʃn] *of a region* aislamiento *m*; *in* ~ aisladamente

i·so·la·tion ward pabellón *m* de enfermedades infecciosas

ISP [aɪes'piː] *abbr* (= *Internet service provider*) proveedor *m* de (acceso a) Internet

Is·rael ['ɪzreɪl] Israel

Is·rae·li [ɪz'reɪli] **1** *adj* israelí **2** *n person* israelí *m/f*

is·sue ['ɪʃuː] **1** *n* (*matter*) tema *m*, asunto *m*; *of magazine* número *m*; *the point at* ~ el tema que se debate; *take* ~ *with s.o. / sth* discrepar de algo / alguien **2** *v/t* *coins* emitir; *passport, visa etc* expedir; *warning* dar; ~ *s.o. with sth* entregar algo a alguien

IT [aɪ'tiː] *abbr* (= *information technology*) tecnologías *fpl* de la información; ~ *department* departamento *m* de informática

it [ɪt] *pron as object* lo *m*, la *f*; *what color is* ~? – ~ *is red* ¿de qué color es? – es rojo; ~*'s raining* llueve; ~*'s me / him* soy yo / es él; ~*'s Charlie here* TELEC soy Charlie; ~*'s your turn* te toca; *that's* ~*!* (*that's right*) ¡eso es!; (*finished*) ¡ya está!

I·tal·ian [ɪ'tæljən] **1** *adj* italiano **2** *n person* italiano(-a) *m(f)*; *language* italiano *m*

i·tal·ic [ɪ'tælɪk] *adj* cursiva

i·tal·ics [ɪ'tælɪks] *npl* cursiva *f*

I·ta·ly ['ɪtəlɪ] Italia

itch [ɪtʃ] **1** *n* picor *m* **2** *v/i* picar

i·tem ['aɪtəm] *in list, accounts,* (*article*) artículo *m*; *on agenda* punto *m*; *of news* noticia *f*

i·tem·ize ['aɪtəmaɪz] *v/t* invoice detallar

i·tin·e·ra·ry [aɪ'tɪnərerɪ] itinerario *m*

its [ɪts] *poss adj* su; *where is* ~ *box?* ¿dónde está su caja?; *the dog has hurt* ~ *leg* el perro se ha hecho daño en la pata

it's [ɪts] → *it is, it has*

it·self [ɪt'self] *pron reflexive* se; *the dog hurt* ~ el perro se hizo daño; *the hotel* ~ *is fine* el hotel en sí (mismo) está bien; *by* ~ (*alone*) aislado, solo; (*automatically*) solo

i·vo·ry ['aɪvərɪ] marfil *m*

i·vy ['aɪvɪ] hiedra *f*

J

jab [dʒæb] *v/t* (*pret & pp* **-bed**) clavar
jab·ber ['dʒæbər] *v/i* parlotear
jack [dʒæk] MOT gato *m*; *in cards* jota *f*
- ◆**jack up** *v/t* MOT levantar con el gato
jack·et ['dʒækɪt] (*coat*) chaqueta *f*; *of book* sobrecubierta *f*
jack·et po'ta·to *Span* patata *f* or *L.Am.* papa *f* asada (*con piel*)
'**jack-knife** *v/i* derrapar (*por la parte del remolque*)
'**jack·pot** gordo *m*; *he hit the ~* le tocó el gordo
ja·cuz·zi® [dʒə'kuːzɪ] jacuzzi *m*
jade [dʒeɪd] *n* jade *m*
jad·ed ['dʒeɪdɪd] *adj* harto; *appetite* hastiado
jag·ged ['dʒægɪd] *adj* accidentado
jag·u·ar ['dʒægʊər] jaguar *m*
jail [dʒeɪl] *n* cárcel *f*; *he's in ~* está en la cárcel
jam¹ [dʒæm] *n for bread* mermelada *f*
jam² [dʒæm] **1** *n* MOT atasco *m*; F (*difficulty*) aprieto *m*; *be in a ~* estar en un aprieto **2** *v/t* (*pret & pp* **-med**) (*ram*) meter, embutir; (*cause to stick*) atascar; *broadcast* provocar interferencias en; *be ~med of roads* estar colapsado; *of door, window* estar atascado; *~ on the brakes* dar un frenazo **3** *v/i* (*pret & pp* **-med**) (*stick*) atascarse; *all ten of us managed to ~ into the car* nos las arreglamos para meternos los diez en el coche
jam-'packed *adj* F abarrotado (*with* de)
jan·i·tor ['dʒænɪtər] portero(-a) *m(f)*
Jan·u·a·ry ['dʒænʊerɪ] enero *m*
Ja·pan [dʒə'pæn] Japón
Jap·a·nese [dʒæpə'niːz] **1** *adj* japonés **2** *n person* japonés(-esa) *m(f)*; *language* japonés *m*; *the ~* los japoneses

jar¹ [dʒɑːr] *n container* tarro *m*
jar² [dʒɑːr] *v/i* (*pret & pp* **-red**) *of noise* rechinar; *~ on* rechinar en
jar·gon ['dʒɑːrgən] jerga *f*
jaun·dice ['dʒɔːndɪs] *n* ictericia *f*
jaun·diced ['dʒɔːndɪst] *adj fig* resentido
jaunt [dʒɔːnt] *n* excursión *f*; *go on a ~* ir de excursión
jaunt·y ['dʒɔːntɪ] *adj* desenfadado
jav·e·lin ['dʒævlɪn] (*spear*) jabalina *f*; *event* (lanzamiento *m* de) jabalina *f*
jaw [dʒɔː] *n* mandíbula *f*
jay·walk·er ['dʒeɪwɒːkər] peatón(-ona) *m(f)* imprudente
'**jay·walk·ing** *cruzar la calle de manera imprudente*
jazz [dʒæz] *n* jazz *m*
- ◆**jazz up** *v/t* F animar
jeal·ous ['dʒeləs] *adj* celoso; *be ~ of in love* tener celos de; *of riches etc* tener envidia de
jeal·ous·ly ['dʒeləslɪ] *adv* celosamente; *relating to possessions* con envidia
jeal·ous·y ['dʒeləsɪ] celos *mpl*; *of possessions* envidia *f*
jeans [dʒiːnz] *npl* vaqueros *mpl*, jeans *mpl*
jeep [dʒiːp] jeep *m*
jeer [dʒɪr] **1** *n* abucheo *m* **2** *v/i* abuchear; *~ at* burlarse de
Jel·lo® ['dʒeloʊ] gelatina *f*
jel·ly ['dʒelɪ] mermelada *f*
'**jel·ly bean** gominola *f*
'**jel·ly·fish** medusa *f*
jeop·ar·dize ['dʒepərdaɪz] *v/t* poner en peligro
jeop·ar·dy ['dʒepərdɪ]: *be in ~* estar en peligro
jerk¹ [dʒɜːrk] **1** *n* sacudida *f* **2** *v/t* dar un tirón a
jerk² [dʒɜːrk] *n* F imbécil *m/f*, *Span*

gilipollas *m/f inv* F

jerk·y ['dʒɜːrkɪ] *adj movement* brusco

jer·sey ['dʒɜːrzɪ] (*sweater*) suéter *m*, *Span* jersey *m*

jest [dʒest] **1** *n* broma *f*; **in ~** en broma **2** *v/i* bromear

Je·sus ['dʒiːzəs] Jesús

jet [dʒet] **1** *n of water* chorro *m*; (*nozzle*) boquilla *f*; (*airplane*) reactor *m*, avión *m* a reacción **2** *v/i* (*pret & pp* **-ted**) *travel* viajar en avión

jet-'black *adj* azabache; **'jet en·gine** reactor *m*; **'jet·lag** desfase *m* horario, jet lag *m*

jet·ti·son ['dʒetɪsn] *v/t also fig* tirar por la borda

jet·ty ['dʒetɪ] malecón *m*

Jew [dʒuː] judío(-a) *m(f)*

jew·el ['dʒuːəl] joya *f*, alhaja *f*; *fig: person* joya *f*

jew·el·er, *Br* **jew·el·ler** ['dʒuːlər] joyero(-a) *m(f)*

jew·el·lery *Br*, **jew·el·ry** ['dʒuːlrɪ] joyas *fpl*, alhajas *fpl*

Jew·ish ['dʒuːɪʃ] *adj* judío

jif·fy ['dʒɪfɪ] F: **in a ~** en un periquete F

jig·saw (puz·zle) ['dʒɪɡsɔː] rompecabezas *m inv*, puzzle *m*

jilt [dʒɪlt] *v/t* dejar plantado

jin·gle ['dʒɪŋɡl] **1** *n* (*song*) melodía *f* publicitaria **2** *v/i of keys, coins* tintinear

jinx [dʒɪŋks] *n* gafe *m*; **there's a ~ on this project** este proyecto está gafado

jit·ters ['dʒɪtərz] *npl* F: **I got the ~** me entró el pánico *or Span* canguelo F

jit·ter·y ['dʒɪtərɪ] *adj* F nervioso

job [dʒɒb] (*employment*) trabajo *m*, empleo *m*; (*task*) tarea *f*, trabajo *m*; **it's not my ~ to answer the phone** no me corresponde a mí contestar el teléfono; **I have a few ~s to do around the house** tengo que hacer unas cuantas cosas en la casa; **out of a ~** sin trabajo *or* empleo; **it's a good ~ you warned me** menos mal que me aviaste; **you'll have a ~** (*it'll be difficult*) te va a costar Dios y ayuda

'job de·scrip·tion (descripción *f* de las) responsabilidades *fpl* del puesto

'job hunt *v/i*: **be ~ing** buscar trabajo

job·less ['dʒɒblɪs] *adj* desempleado, *Span* parado

job sat·is·fac·tion satisfacción *f* con el trabajo

jock·ey ['dʒɒkɪ] *n* jockey *m/f*

jog [dʒɒɡ] **1** *n*: **go for a ~** ir a hacer jogging *or* footing **2** *v/i* (*pret & pp* **-ged**) *as exercise* hacer jogging *or* footing **3** *v/t* (*pret & pp* **-ged**) **~ s.o.'s memory** refrescar la memoria de alguien; **somebody ~ged my elbow** alguien me dio en el codo

♦ **jog along** *v/i* F ir tirando P

jog·ger ['dʒɒɡər] *person* persona *f* que hace jogging *or* footing; *shoe* zapatilla *f* de jogging *or* footing

jog·ging ['dʒɒɡɪŋ] jogging *m*, footing *m*; **go ~** ir a hacer jogging *or* footing

'jog·ging suit chándal *m*

john [dʒɒn] P (*toilet*) baño *m*, váter *m*

join [dʒɒɪn] *n* juntura *f* **2** *v/i of roads, rivers* juntarse; (*become a member*) hacerse socio **3** *v/t* (*connect*) unir; *person* unirse a; *club* hacerse socio de; (*go to work for*) entrar en; *of road* desembocar en; **I'll ~ you at the theater** me runiré contigo en el teatro

♦ **join in** *v/i* participar

♦ **join up** *v/i Br* MIL alistarse

join·er ['dʒɒɪnər] carpintero(-a) *m(f)*

joint [dʒɒɪnt] **1** *n* ANAT articulación *f*; *in woodwork* junta *f*; *of meat* pieza *f*; F (*place*) garito *m* F; *of cannabis* porro *m* F, canuto *m* F **2** *adj* (*shared*) conjunto

joint ac·count cuenta *f* conjunta

joint ven·ture empresa *f* conjunta

joke [dʒəʊk] **1** *n story* chiste *m*; (*practical ~*) broma *f*; **play a ~ on** gastar una broma a; **it's no ~** no tiene ninguna gracia **2** *v/i* bromear

jok·er ['dʒəʊkər] *person* bromista *m/f*; F *pej* payaso(-a) *m(f)*; *in cards* comodín *m*

J

jok·ing ['dʒoʊkɪŋ]: **~ apart** bromas aparte

jok·ing·ly ['dʒoʊkɪŋlɪ] adv en broma

jol·ly ['dʒɑːlɪ] adj alegre

jolt [dʒoʊlt] **1** n (jerk) sacudida f **2** v/t (push) **somebody ~ed my elbow** alguien me dio en el codo

jos·tle ['dʒɑːsl] v/t empujar

◆ **jot down** [dʒɑːt] v/t (pret & pp **-ted**) apuntar, anotar

jour·nal ['dʒɜːrnl] (magazine) revista f; (diary) diario m

jour·nal·ism ['dʒɜːrnəlɪzm] periodismo m

jour·nal·ist ['dʒɜːrnəlɪst] periodista m/f

jour·ney ['dʒɜːrnɪ] n viaje m

jo·vi·al ['dʒoʊvɪəl] adj jovial

joy [dʒɔɪ] alegría f, gozo m

'joy·stick COMPUT joystick m

ju·bi·lant ['dʒuːbɪlənt] adj jubiloso

ju·bi·la·tion [dʒuːbɪ'leɪʃn] júbilo m

judge [dʒʌdʒ] **1** n LAW juez m/f, jueza f; in competition juez m/f, miembro m del jurado **2** v/t juzgar; (estimate) calcular **3** v/i juzgar; **~ for yourself** júzgalo por ti mismo

judg(e)·ment ['dʒʌdʒmənt] LAW fallo m; (opinion) juicio m; **an error of ~** una equivocación; **he showed good ~** mostró tener criterio; **against my better ~** a pesar de no estar convencido; **the Last Judgment** REL el Juicio Final

'Judg(e)·ment Day Día m del Juicio Final

ju·di·cial [dʒuː'dɪʃl] adj judicial

ju·di·cious [dʒuː'dɪʃəs] adj juicioso

ju·do ['dʒuːdoʊ] judo m

jug·gle ['dʒʌgl] v/t also fig hacer malabarismos con

jug·gler ['dʒʌglər] malabarista m/f

juice [dʒuːs] n Span zumo m, L.Am. jugo m

juic·y ['dʒuːsɪ] adj jugoso; news, gossip jugoso, sabroso

juke·box ['dʒuːkbɑːks] máquina f de discos

Ju·ly [dʒʊ'laɪ] julio m

jum·ble ['dʒʌmbl] n revoltijo m

◆ **jumble up** v/t revolver

jum·bo (jet) ['dʒʌmboʊ] jumbo m

'jum·bo(-sized) adj gigante

jump [dʒʌmp] **1** n salto m; (increase) incremento m, subida f; **give a ~ of surprise** dar un salto **2** v/i saltar; (increase) dispararse; **you made me ~!** ¡me diste un susto!; **~ to one's feet** ponerse de pie de un salto; **~ to conclusions** sacar conclusiones precipitadas **3** v/t fence etc saltar; F (attack) asaltar; **~ the lights** saltarse el semáforo, pasarse un semáforo en rojo

◆ **jump at** v/t opportunity no dejar escapar

jump·er[1] ['dʒʌmpər] dress pichi m

jump·er[2] ['dʒʌmpər] SP saltador(a) m(f); horse caballo m de saltos

jump·y ['dʒʌmpɪ] adj nervioso; **get ~** ponerse nervioso

junc·tion ['dʒʌŋkʃn] of roads cruce m

junc·ture ['dʒʌŋktʃər] fml: **at this ~** en esta coyuntura

June [dʒuːn] junio m

jun·gle ['dʒʌŋgl] selva f, jungla f

ju·ni·or ['dʒuːnjər] **1** adj (subordinate) de rango inferior; (younger) más joven **2** n in rank subalterno(-a) m(f); **she is ten years my ~** es diez años más joven que yo

ju·ni·or 'high escuela f secundaria (para alumnos de entre 12 y 14 años)

junk [dʒʌŋk] n trastos mpl

'junk food comida f basura

junk·ie ['dʒʌŋkɪ] F drogota m/f F

'junk mail propaganda f postal; **'junk shop** cacharrería f; **'junk·yard** depósito m de chatarra

jur·is·dic·tion [dʒʊrɪs'dɪkʃn] LAW jurisdicción f

ju·ror ['dʒʊrər] miembro m del jurado

ju·ry ['dʒʊrɪ] jurado m

just [dʒʌst] **1** adj law, cause justo **2** adv (barely) justo; (exactly) justo, justamente; (only) sólo, solamente; **have ~ done sth** acabar de hacer algo; **I've ~ seen her** la acabo de ver; **~ about** (almost) casi; **I was ~ about to leave when ...** estaba a punto de salir cuando ...; **~ like that**

(*abruptly*) de repente; **~ now** (*at the moment*) ahora mismo; **I saw her ~ now** (*a few moments ago*) la acabo de ver; **~ you wait!** ¡ya verás!; **~ be quiet!** ¡cállate de una vez!

jus·tice ['dʒʌstɪs] justicia *f*

jus·ti·fi·a·ble [dʒʌstɪ'faɪəbl] *adj* justificable

jus·ti·fi·a·bly [dʒʌstɪ'faɪəblɪ] *adv* justificadamente

jus·ti·fi·ca·tion [dʒʌstɪfɪ'keɪʃn] justificación *f*; **there's no ~ for behavior like that** ese comportamiento es injustificable *or* no tiene

justificación

jus·ti·fy ['dʒʌstɪfaɪ] *v/t* (*pret & pp -ied*) *also text* justificar

just·ly ['dʒʌstlɪ] *adv* (*fairly*) con justicia; (*rightly*) con razón

♦ **jut out** [dʒʌt] *v/i* (*pret & pp -ted*) sobresalir

ju·ve·nile ['dʒuːvənl] **1** *adj crime* juvenil; *court* de menores; *pej* infantil **2** *n fml* menor *m/f*

ju·ve·nile de·lin·quen·cy delincuencia *f* juvenil

ju·ve·nile de·lin·quent delincuente *m/f* juvenil

K

k [keɪ] *abbr* (= **kilobyte**) k (= kilobyte *m*); (= **thousand**) mil

kan·ga·roo [kæŋɡə'ruː] canguro *m*

ka·ra·te [kə'rɑːtɪ] kárate *m*

ka·ra·te chop golpe *m* de kárate

ke·bab [kɪ'bæb] pincho *m*, brocheta *f*

keel [kiːl] NAUT quilla *f*

♦ **keel over** *v/i of structure* desplomarse; *of person* desmayarse

keen [kiːn] *adj interest* gran; *competition* reñido

keep [kiːp] **1** *n* (*maintenance*) manutención *f*; **for ~s** F para siempre **2** *v/t* (*pret & pp* **kept**) guardar; (*not lose*) conservar; (*detain*) entretener; *family* mantener; *animals* tener; **you can ~ it** (*it's for you*) te lo puedes quedar; **~ trying!** ¡sigue intentándolo!; **don't ~ interrupting!** ¡deja de interrumpirme!; **~ a promise** cumplir una promesa; **~ s.o. company** hacer compañía a alguien; **~ s.o. waiting** hacer esperar a alguien; **he can't ~ anything to himself** no sabe guardar un secreto; **I kept the news of the accident to myself** no dije nada sobre el accidente; **~ sth from s.o.** ocultar algo a

alguien; **we kept the news from him** no le contamos la noticia **3** *v/i* (*pret & pp* **kept**) *of food, milk* aguantar, conservarse; **~ calm!** ¡tranquilízate!; **~ quiet!** ¡cállate!

♦ **keep away 1** *v/i*: **keep away from that building** no te acerques a ese edificio **2** *v/t*: **keep the children away from the stove** no dejes que los niños se acerquen a la cocina

♦ **keep back** *v/t* (*hold in check*) contener; *information* ocultar

♦ **keep down** *v/t voice* bajar; *costs, inflation etc* reducir; *food* retener; **tell the kids to keep the noise down** diles a los niños que no hagan tanto ruido; **I can't keep anything down** devuelvo todo lo que como

♦ **keep in** *v/t in school* castigar (*a quedarse en clase*); **the hospital's keeping her in** la tienen en observación

♦ **keep off 1** *v/t* (*avoid*) evitar; **keep off the grass!** ¡prohibido pisar el césped! **2** *v/i*: **if the rain keeps off** si no llueve

♦ **keep on 1** *v/i* continuar; **if you keep on interrupting me** si no dejas de interrumpirme; **keep on trying** sigue intentándolo **2** v/t: **the company kept them on** la empresa los mantuvo en el puesto; **keep your coat on!** ¡no te quites el abrigo!

♦ **keep on at** v/t (nag): **my parents keep on at me to get a job** mis padres no dejan de decirme que busque un trabajo

♦ **keep out 1** v/t: **it keeps the cold out** protege del frío; **they must be kept out** no pueden entrar **2** v/i: **I told you to keep out!** ¡te dije que no entraras!; **I would keep out of it if I were you** of discussion etc yo en tu lugar no me metería; **keep out** as sign prohibida la entrada, prohibido el paso

♦ **keep over** v/t path seguir; rules cumplir, respetar

♦ **keep up 1** v/i when walking, running etc seguir or mantener el ritmo (**with** de); **keep up with s.o.** (stay in touch with) mantener contacto con alguien **2** v/t pace seguir, mantener; payments estar al corriente de; bridge, pants sujetar

keep·ing ['kiːpɪŋ] n: **be in ~ with** decor combinar con; **in ~ with** promises de acuerdo con

'**keep·sake** recuerdo m

keg [keg] barril m

ken·nel ['kenl] n caseta f del perro

ken·nels ['kenlz] npl residencia f canina

kept [kept] pret & pp → **keep**

ker·nel ['kɜːrnl] almendra f

ker·o·sene ['kerəsiːn] queroseno m

ketch·up ['ketʃʌp] ketchup m

ket·tle ['ketl] hervidor m

key [kiː] **1** n to door, drawer llave f, on keyboard, piano tecla f, of piece of music clave f; on map leyenda f **2** adj (vital) clave, crucial **3** v/t & v/i COMPUT teclear

♦ **key in** v/t data introducir, teclear

'**key·board** COMPUT, MUS teclado m; **key·board·er** COMPUT operador(a) m(f), persona que introduce datos en el ordenador; '**key·card** tarjeta f (de hotel)

keyed-up [kiːd'ʌp] adj nervioso

'**key·hole** ojo m de la cerradura; **key·note** '**speech** discurso m central; '**key·ring** llavero m

kha·ki ['kækɪ] adj caqui

kick [kɪk] **1** n patada f; **he got a ~ out of watching them suffer** disfrutó viéndoles sufrir; (just) **for ~s** F por diversión **2** v/t dar una patada a; F habit dejar **3** v/i of person patalear; of horse, mule cocear

♦ **kick around** v/t ball dar patadas a; F (discuss) comentar

♦ **kick in** v/t P money apoquinar F

♦ **kick off** v/i comenzar, sacar de centro; F (start) empezar

♦ **kick out** v/t of bar, company echar; of country, organization expulsar

♦ **kick up** v/t: **kick up a fuss** montar un numerito

'**kick·back** F (bribe) soborno m

'**kick-off** SP saque m

kid [kɪd] **1** n F (child) crío m F, niño m; **when I was a ~** cuando era pequeño; **~ brother** hermano m pequeño; **~ sister** hermana f pequeña **2** v/t (pret & pp **-ded**) F tomar el pelo a F **3** v/i (pret & pp **-ded**) F bromear; **I was only ~ding** estaba bromeando

kid·der ['kɪdər] F vacilón m F

kid 'gloves: **handle s.o. with ~** tratar a alguien con guante de seda

kid·nap ['kɪdnæp] v/t (pret & pp **-ped**) secuestrar

kid·nap·(p)er ['kɪdnæpər] secuestrador m

'**kid·nap·(p)ing** ['kɪdnæpɪŋ] secuestro m

kid·ney ['kɪdnɪ] ANAT riñón m; in cooking riñones mpl

'**kid·ney bean** alubia f roja de riñón

'**kid·ney ma·chine** MED riñón m artificial, máquina f de diálisis

kill [kɪl] v/t matar; **the drought ~ed all the plants** las plantas murieron como resultado de la sequía; **I had six hours to ~** tenía seis horas sin nada que hacer; **be ~ed in an accident** matarse en un accidente, morirse en un accidente; **~ o.s.** suici-

darse; **~ o.s. laughing** F morirse de
risa F

kil·ler ['kɪlər] (*murderer*) asesino *m*;
be a ~ of disease ser mortal

kil·ling ['kɪlɪŋ] *n* asesinato *m*; **make a
~** F (*lots of money*) forrarse F

kil·ling·ly ['kɪlɪŋlɪ] *adv* F: **~ funny**
para morirse de risa F

kiln [kɪln] horno *m*

ki·lo ['kiːloʊ] kilo *m*

ki·lo·byte ['kɪloʊbaɪt] COMPUT kilobyte *m*

ki·lo·gram ['kɪloʊɡræm] kilogramo
m

ki·lo·me·ter, *Br* **ki·lo·me·tre**
[kɪ'lɑːmɪtər] kilómetro *m*

kind[1] [kaɪnd] *adj* agradable, amable

kind[2] [kaɪnd] *n* (*sort*) tipo *m*; (*make*,
brand) marca *f*; **all ~s of people**
toda clase de personas; **I did
nothing of the ~!** ¡no hice nada parecido!; **~ of ...** *sad, lonely, etc* un
poco ...; **that's very ~ of you** gracias
por tu amabilidad

kin·der·gar·ten ['kɪndərɡɑːrtn]
guardería *f*, jardín *m* de infancia

kind-heart·ed [kaɪnd'hɑːrtɪd] *adj*
agradable, amable

kind·ly ['kaɪndlɪ] **1** *adj* amable, agradable **2** *adv* con amabilidad; **~ don't
interrupt** por favor, no me inte-
rrumpa; **~ lower your voice** ¿le importaría hablar más bajo?

kind·ness ['kaɪndnɪs] amabilidad *f*

king [kɪŋ] rey *m*

king·dom ['kɪŋdəm] reino *m*

king-size(d) *adj* F *cigarettes* extra-
largo; **~ bed** cama *f* de matrimonio
grande

kink [kɪŋk] *n in hose etc* doblez *f*

kink·y ['kɪŋkɪ] *adj* F vicioso

ki·osk ['kiːɑːsk] quiosco *m*

kiss [kɪs] **1** *n* beso *m* **2** *v/t* besar **3** *v/i*
besarse

kiss of 'life boca *f* a boca, respiración
f artificial; **give s.o. the ~** hacer a alguien el boca a boca

kit [kɪt] (*equipment*) equipo *m*; **tool ~**
caja *f* de herramientas

kitch·en ['kɪtʃɪn] cocina *f*

kitch·en·ette [kɪtʃɪ'net] *cocina pequeña*

**kitch·en 'sink: you've got every-
thing but the ~** F llevas la casa a
cuestas F

kite [kaɪt] *for flying* cometa *f*

kit·ten ['kɪtn] gatito *m*

kit·ty ['kɪtɪ] *money* fondo *m*

klutz [klʌts] F (*clumsy person*) mana-
zas *m* F

knack [næk] habilidad *f*; **he has a ~
of upsetting people** tiene la habilidad de disgustar a la gente; **I soon
got the ~ of the new machine** le
pillé el truco a la nueva máquina rápidamente

knead [niːd] *v/t dough* amasar

knee [niː] *n* rodilla *f*

'knee·cap *n* rótula *f*

kneel [niːl] *v/i* (*pret & pp* **knelt**) arrodillarse

'knee-length *adj* hasta la rodilla

knelt [nelt] *pret & pp* → **kneel**

knew [nuː] *pret* → **know**

knick-knacks ['nɪknæks] *npl* F bara-
tijas *fpl*

knife [naɪf] **1** *n* (*pl* **knives** [naɪvz]) *for
food* cuchillo *m*; *carried outside* na-
vaja *f* **2** *v/t* acuchillar, apuñalar

knight [naɪt] *n* caballero *m*

knit [nɪt] **1** *v/t* (*pret & pp* **-ted**) tejer
2 *v/i* (*pret & pp* **-ted**) tricotar

♦ **knit together** *v/i of broken bone*
soldarse

knit·ting ['nɪtɪŋ] punto *m*

'knit·ting nee·dle aguja *f* para hacer
punto

'knit·wear prendas *fpl* de punto

knob [nɑːb] *on door* pomo *m*; *on
drawer* tirador *m*; *of butter* nuez *f*,
trocito *m*

knock [nɑːk] **1** *n on door*, (*blow*) golpe *m*; **there was a ~ on the door** llamaron a la puerta **2** *v/t* (*hit*) golpear;
F (*criticize*) criticar, meterse con
F; **he was ~ed to the ground** le
tiraron al suelo **3** *v/i on the door* llamar

♦ **knock around 1** *v/t* F (*beat*) pegar a
2 *v/i* F (*travel*) viajar

♦ **knock down** *v/t of car* atropellar;
building tirar; *object* tirar al suelo; F

(*reduce the price of*) rebajar
♦ **knock off 1** v/t P (*steal*) mangar P **2** v/i F (*stop work for the day*) acabar, *Span* plegar F
♦ **knock out** v/t (*make unconscious*) dejar K.O.; *of medicine* dejar para el arrastre F; *power lines etc* destruir; (*eliminate*) eliminar
♦ **knock over** v/t tirar; *of car* atropellar
'**knock·down** *adj*: **at a ~ price** tirado; **knock-kneed** [naːkˈniːd] *adj* patizambo; '**knock·out** *n in boxing* K.O. *m*
knot [naːt] **1** *n* nudo *m* **2** v/t (*pret & pp* **-ted**) anudar
knot·ty ['naːtɪ] *adj problem* complicado
know [nou] **1** v/t (*pret* **knew**, *pp* **known**) *fact, language, how to do sth* saber; *person, place* conocer; (*recognize*) reconocer; **will you let him ~ that ...?** ¿puedes decirle que ...? **2** v/i (*pret* **knew**, *pp* **known**) saber; *I don't ~* no (lo) sé; **yes, I ~** sí, lo sé **3** *n*: **people in the ~** los enterados
'**know·how** pericia *f*

know·ing ['nouɪŋ] *adj* cómplice
know·ing·ly ['nouɪŋlɪ] *adv* (*wittingly*) deliberadamente; *smile etc* con complicidad
'**know-it-all** F sabiondo F
knowl·edge ['naːlɪdʒ] conocimiento *m*; **to the best of my ~** por lo que sé; **have a good ~ of ...** tener buenos conocimientos de ...
knowl·edge·a·ble ['naːlɪdʒəbl] *adj*: **she's very ~ about music** sabe mucho de música
known [noun] *pp* → **know**
knuck·le ['nʌkl] nudillo *m*
♦ **knuckle down** v/i F aplicarse F
♦ **knuckle under** v/i F pasar por el aro F
KO [keɪˈou] (*knockout*) K.O.
Ko·ran [kəˈræn] Corán *m*
Ko·re·a [kəˈriːə] Corea
Ko·re·an [kəˈriːən] **1** *adj* coreano **2** *n* coreano(a) *m(f)*; *language* coreano *m*
ko·sher ['kouʃər] *adj* REL kosher; F legal F
kow·tow ['kautau] v/i F reverenciar
ku·dos ['kjuːdɑːs] reconocimiento *m*, prestigio *m*

K

L

lab [læb] laboratorio *m*
la·bel ['leɪbl] **1** *n* etiqueta *f* **2** v/t (*pret & pp* **-ed**, *Br* **-led**) *bags* etiquetar
la·bor ['leɪbər] *n* (*work*) trabajo *m*; *in pregnancy* parto *m*; **be in ~** estar de parto
la·bor·a·to·ry ['læbrətourɪ] laboratorio *m*
la·bor·a·to·ry tech'ni·cian técnico(-a) *m(f)* de laboratorio
la·bored ['leɪbərd] *adj style, speech* elaborado
la·bor·er ['leɪbərər] obrero(-a) *m(f)*
la·bo·ri·ous [ləˈbɔːrɪəs] *adj* laborioso

'**la·bor u·nion** sindicato *m*
'**la·bor ward** MED sala *f* de partos
la·bour *etc Br* → **labor** *etc*
lace [leɪs] *n material* encaje *m*; *for shoe* cordón *m*
♦ **lace up** v/t *shoes* atar
lack [læk] **1** *n* falta *f*, carencia *f* **2** v/t carecer de; *he ~s confidence* le falta confianza **3** v/i: *be ~ing* faltar
lac·quer ['lækər] *n for hair* laca *f*
lad [læd] muchacho *m*, chico *m*
lad·der ['lædər] *n* escalera *f* (*de mano*)
la·den ['leɪdn] *adj* cargado (**with** de)

la·dies room ['leɪdiːz] servicio *m* de señoras

la·dle ['leɪdl] *n* cucharón *m*, cazo *m*

la·dy ['leɪdɪ] señora *f*

'**la·dy·bug** mariquita *f*

'**la·dy·like** *adj* femenino

lag [læg] *v/t* (*pret & pp* -**ged**) *pipes* revestir con aislante

♦ **lag behind** *v/i* quedarse atrás

la·ger ['lɑːgər] cerveza *f* rubia

la·goon [lə'guːn] laguna *f*

laid [leɪd] *pret & pp* → **lay**

laid-back [leɪd'bæk] *adj* tranquilo, despreocupado

lain [leɪn] *pp* → **lie**

lake [leɪk] lago *m*

lamb [læm] *animal, meat* cordero *m*

lame [leɪm] *adj person* cojo; *excuse* pobre

la·ment [lə'ment] **1** *n* lamento *m* **2** *v/t* lamentar

lam·en·ta·ble ['læməntəbl] *adj* lamentable

lam·i·nat·ed ['læmɪneɪtɪd] *adj surface* laminado; *paper* plastificado

lam·i·nat·ed 'glass cristal *m* laminado

lamp [læmp] lámpara *f*

'**lamp·post** farola *f*

'**lamp·shade** pantalla *f* (*de lámpara*)

land [lænd] **1** *n* tierra *f*; **by ~** por tierra; **on ~** en tierra; **work on the ~** *as farmer* trabajar la tierra **2** *v/t airplane* aterrizar; *job* conseguir **3** *v/i of airplane* aterrizar; *of capsule on the moon* alunizar; *of ball, sth thrown* caer; *it ~ed right on top of his head* le cayó justo en la cabeza

'**land·ing** ['lændɪŋ] *n of airplane* aterrizaje *m*; *on moon* alunizaje *m*; *of staircase* rellano *m*

'**land·ing field** pista *f* de aterrizaje; '**land·ing gear** tren *m* de aterrizaje; '**land·ing strip** pista *f* de aterrizaje

'**land·la·dy** *of hostel etc* dueña *f*; *of rented room* casera *f*; *Br: of bar* patrona *f*; '**land·lord** *of hostel etc* dueño *m*; *of rented room* casero *m*; *Br: of bar* patrón *m*; '**land·mark** punto *m* de referencia; *fig* hito *m*; '**land own·er** terrateniente *m*/*f*; **land·scape**

['lændskeɪp] **1** *n* (*also painting*) paisaje *m* **2** *adv print* en formato apaisado; '**land·slide** corrimiento *m* de tierras; **land·slide 'vic·to·ry** victoria *f* arrolladora

lane [leɪn] *in country* camino *m*, vereda *f*; *(alley)* callejón *m*; MOT carril *m*

lan·guage ['læŋgwɪdʒ] lenguaje *m*; *of nation* idioma *f*, lengua *f*

'**lan·guage lab** laboratorio *m* de idiomas

lank [læŋk] *adj hair* lacio

lank·y ['læŋkɪ] *adj person* larguirucho

lan·tern ['læntərn] farol *m*

lap¹ [læp] *n of track* vuelta *f*

lap² [læp] *n of water* chapoteo *m*

♦ **lap up** *v/t* (*pret & pp* -**ped**) *drink, milk* beber a lengüetadas; *flattery* deleitarse con

lap³ [læp] *n of person* regazo *m*

la·pel [lə'pel] solapa *f*

lapse [læps] **1** *n* (*mistake, slip*) desliz *m*; *of time* lapso *m*; *a ~ of attention* un momento de distracción; *a ~ of memory* un olvido **2** *v/i of membership* vencer; *~ into silence / despair* sumirse en el silencio / la desesperación; *she ~d into English* empezó a hablar en inglés

lap·top ['læptɑːp] COMPUT ordenador *m* portátil, *L.Am.* computadora *f* portátil

lar·ce·ny ['lɑːrsənɪ] latrocinio *m*

lard [lɑːrd] manteca *f* de cerdo

lard·er ['lɑːrdər] despensa *f*

large [lɑːrdʒ] *adj* grande; **be at ~ of** *criminal, wild animal* andar suelto

large·ly ['lɑːrdʒlɪ] *adv* (*mainly*) en gran parte, principalmente

lark [lɑːrk] *bird* alondra *f*

lar·va ['lɑːrvə] larva *f*

lar·yn·gi·tis [lærɪn'dʒaɪtɪs] laringitis *f*

lar·ynx ['lærɪŋks] laringe *f*

la·ser ['leɪzər] láser *m*

'**la·ser beam** rayo *m* láser

'**la·ser print·er** impresora *f* láser

lash¹ [læʃ] *v/t with whip* azotar

♦ **lash down** *v/t with rope* amarrar

♦ **lash out** *v/i with fists, words* atacar (*at* a), arremeter (*at* contra)

L

lash² [læʃ] *n* (*eyelash*) pestaña *f*

last¹ [læst] **1** *adj in series* último; (*preceding*) anterior; **~ Friday** el viernes pasado; **~ but one** penúltimo; **~ night** anoche; **~ but not least** por último, pero no por ello menos importante **2** *adv* **at ~** por fin, al fin

last² [læst] *v/i* durar

last·ing ['læstɪŋ] *adj* duradero

last·ly ['læstlɪ] *adv* por último, finalmente

latch [lætʃ] *n* pestillo *m*

late [leɪt] **1** *adj*: **the bus is ~ again** el autobús vuelve a llegar tarde; **it's ~** es tarde; **it's getting ~** se está haciendo tarde; **of ~** últimamente, recientemente; **the ~ 19th century** la última parte del siglo XIX; **in the ~ 19th century** a finales del siglo XIX **2** *adv arrive, leave* tarde

late·ly ['leɪtlɪ] *adv* últimamente, recientemente

lat·er ['leɪtər] *adv* más tarde; **see you ~!** ¡hasta luego!; **~ on** más tarde

lat·est ['leɪtɪst] *adj news, girlfriend* último

lathe [leɪð] *n* torno *m*

la·ther ['lɑːðər] *n from soap* espuma *f*; **in a ~** (*sweaty*) empapado de sudor

Lat·in ['lætɪn] **1** *adj* latino **2** *n* latín *m*

Lat·in A·mer·i·ca Latinoamérica, América Latina

Lat·in A·mer·i·can 1 *n* latinoamericano(-a) *m(f)* **2** *adj* latinoamericano

La·ti·no [læˈtiːnou] **1** *adj* latino **2** *n* latino(-a)

lat·i·tude ['lætɪtuːd] *geographical* latitud *f*; (*freedom to act*) libertad *f*

lat·ter ['lætər] **1** *adj* último **2** *n*: **Mr Brown and Mr White, of whom the ~ was ...** el Señor Brown y el Señor White, de quien el segundo *or* este último era ...

laugh [læf] **1** *n* risa *f*; **it was a ~** F fue genial **2** *v/i* reírse

♦ **laugh at** *v/t* reírse de

'laugh·ing stock: **make o.s. a ~** ponerse en ridículo; **become a ~** ser el hazmerreír

laugh·ter ['læftər] risas *fpl*

launch [lɔːntʃ] **1** *n small boat* lancha *f*; *of ship* botadura *f*; *of rocket, new product* lanzamiento *m* **2** *v/t rocket, new product* lanzar; *ship* botar

'launch cer·e·mo·ny ceremonia *f* de lanzamiento

'launch(·ing) pad plataforma *f* de lanzamiento

laun·der ['lɔːndər] *v/t clothes* lavar (y planchar); *money* blanquear

laun·dro·mat ['lɔːndrəmæt] lavandería *f*

laun·dry ['lɔːndrɪ] *place* lavadero *m*; *dirty clothes* ropa *f* sucia; *clean clothes* ropa *f* lavada; **do the ~** lavar la ropa, *Span* hacer la colada

lau·rel ['lɑːrəl] laurel *m*

lav·a·to·ry ['lævətɔːrɪ] *place* cuarto *m* de baño, lavabo *m*; *equipment* retrete *m*

lav·en·der ['lævəndər] espliego *m*, lavanda *f*

lav·ish ['lævɪʃ] *adj* espléndido

law [lɔː] ley *f*, *subject* derecho *m*; **be against the ~** estar prohibido, ser ilegal

law-a·bid·ing ['lɔːəbaɪdɪŋ] *adj* respetuoso con la ley

'law court juzgado *m*

law·ful ['lɔːfəl] *adj* legal; *wife* legítimo

law·less ['lɔːlɪs] *adj* sin ley

lawn [lɔːn] césped *m*

'lawn mow·er cortacésped *m*

'law·suit pleito *m*

law·yer ['lɔːjər] abogado(-a) *m(f)*

lax [læks] *adj* poco estricto

lax·a·tive ['læksətɪv] *n* laxante *m*

lay¹ [leɪ] *v/t* (*pret & pp* **laid**) (*put down*) dejar, poner; *eggs* poner; V *sexually* tirarse a V

lay² [leɪ] *pret* → **lie**

♦ **lay into** *v/t* (*attack*) arremeter contra

♦ **lay off** *v/t workers* despedir

♦ **lay on** *v/t* (*provide*) organizar

♦ **lay out** *v/t objects* colocar, disponer; *page* diseñar, maquetar

'lay-by *Br: on road* área *f* de descanso

lay·er ['leɪər] estrato *m*; *of soil, paint* capa *f*

'lay·man laico *m*

L

leave

'**lay-off** despido *m*
'**lay-out** diseño *m*
♦ **laze around** [leɪz] *v/i* holgazanear
la·zy ['leɪzɪ] *adj person* holgazán, perezoso; *day* ocioso
lb *abbr* (= *pound*) libra *f* (*de peso*)
LCD [elsi:'di:] *abbr* (= *liquid crystal display*) LCD, pantalla *f* de cristal líquido
lead¹ [li:d] **1** *v/t* (*pret & pp led*) *procession, race* ir al frente de; *company, team* dirigir; (*guide, take*) conducir **2** *v/i* (*pret & pp led*) *in race, competition* ir en cabeza; (*provide leadership*) tener el mando; *a street ~ing of the square* una calle que sale de la plaza; *where is this ~ing?* ¿adónde nos lleva esto? **3** *n in race* ventaja *f*; *be in the ~* estar en cabeza; *take the ~* ponerse en cabeza; *lose the ~* perder la cabeza
♦ **lead on** *v/i* (*go in front*) ir delante
♦ **lead up to** *v/t* preceder a; *I wonder what she's leading up to* me pregunto a dónde quiere ir a parar
lead² [li:d] *for dog* correa *f*
lead³ [led] *substance* plomo *m*
lead·ed ['ledɪd] *adj gas* con plomo
lead·er ['li:dər] líder *m*
lead·er·ship ['li:dərʃɪp] *of party etc* liderazgo *m*
'**lead·er·ship con·test** pugna *f* por el liderazgo
lead-free ['ledfri:] *adj gas* sin plomo
lead·ing ['li:dɪŋ] *adj runner* en cabeza; *company, product* puntero
'**lead·ing-edge** *adj company* en la vanguardia; *technology* de vanguardia
leaf [li:f] (*pl leaves* [li:vz]) hoja *f*
♦ **leaf through** *v/t* hojear
leaf·let ['li:flət] folleto *m*
league [li:g] liga *f*
leak [li:k] **1** *n in roof* gotera *f*; *in pipe* agujero *m*; *of air, gas* fuga *f*, escape *m*; *of information* filtración *f* **2** *v/i of boat* hacer agua; *of pipe* tener un agujero; *of liquid, gas* fugarse, escaparse
♦ **leak out** *v/i of air, gas* fugarse, escaparse; *of news* filtrarse

leak·y ['li:kɪ] *adj pipe* con agujeros; *boat* que hace agua
lean¹ [li:n] **1** *v/i* (*be at an angle*) estar inclinado; *~ against sth* apoyarse en algo **2** *v/t* apoyar
lean² [li:n] *adj meat* magro; *style, prose* pobre, escueto
leap [li:p] **1** *n* salto *m*; *a great ~ forward* un gran salto adelante **2** *v/i* (*pret & pp -ed or leapt*) saltar; *he ~t over the fence* saltó la valla; *they ~t into the river* se tiraron al río
leapt [lept] *pret & pp* → **leap**
'**leap year** año *m* bisiesto
learn [lɜrn] **1** *v/t* aprender; (*hear*) enterarse de; *~ how to do sth* aprender a hacer algo **2** *v/i* aprender
learn·er ['lɜrnər] estudiante *m/f*
learn·ing ['lɜrnɪŋ] *n* (*knowledge*) conocimientos *mpl*; *act* aprendizaje *m*
'**learn·ing curve** curva *f* de aprendizaje; *be on the ~* tener que aprender cosas nuevas
lease [li:s] **1** *n* (*contrato m de*) arrendamiento *m* **2** *v/t apartment, equipment* arrendar
♦ **lease out** *v/t apartment, equipment* arrendar
lease 'pur·chase arrendamiento *m* con opción de compra
leash [li:ʃ] *for dog* correa *f*
least [li:st] **1** *adj* (*slightest*) menor; *the ~ amount, money, baggage* menos; *there's not the ~ reason to ...* no hay la más mínima razón para que ...* **2** *adv* menos **3** *n* lo menos; *he drank the ~* fue el que menos bebió; *not in the ~ surprised* en absoluto sorprendido; *at ~* por lo menos
leath·er ['leðər] **1** *n* piel *f*, cuero **2** *adj* de piel, de cuero
leave [li:v] **1** *n* (*vacation*) permiso *m*; *on ~* de permiso **2** *v/t* (*pret & pp left*) *city, place* marcharse de, irse de; *person, food, memory,* (*forget*) dejar; *let's ~ things as they are* dejemos las cosas tal y como están; *how did you ~ things with him?* ¿cómo quedaron las cosas con él?; *~ s.o. / sth alone* (*not touch, not interfere with*) dejar a alguien / algo en paz; *be left*

quedar; **there is nothing left** no queda nada; **I only have one left** sólo me queda uno **3** v/i (*pret & pp* **left**) *of person* marcharse, irse; *of plane, train, bus* salir

♦ **leave behind** v/t *intentionally* dejar; (*forget*) dejarse

♦ **leave on** v/t *hat, coat* dejar puesto; *TV, computer* dejar encendido

♦ **leave out** v/t *word, figure* omitir; (*not put away*) no guardar; **leave me out of this** a mí no me metas en esto

leav·ing par·ty fiesta *f* de despedida

lec·ture ['lektʃər] **1** *n* clase *f*; *to general public* conferencia *f* **2** v/i *at university* dar clases (**in** de); *to general public* dar una conferencia

'lec·ture hall sala *f* de conferencias

lec·tur·er ['lektʃərər] profesor(a) *m(f)*

LED [eli:'di:] *abbr* (= **light-emitting diode**) LED *m* (= diodo *m* emisor de luz)

led [led] *pret & pp* → **lead**

ledge [ledʒ] *of window* alféizar *f*; *on rock face* saliente *m*

ledg·er ['ledʒər] COM libro *m* mayor

leek [li:k] puerro *m*

leer [lɪr] *n sexual* mirada *f* impúdica; *evil* mirada *f* maligna

left¹ [left] **1** *adj* izquierdo **2** *n also* POL izquierda *f*; **on the** ~ a la izquierda; **to the** ~ *turn, look* a la izquierda **3** *adv turn, look* a la izquierda

left² [left] *pret & pp* → **leave**

'left-hand *adj* de la izquierda; **on your** ~ **side** a tu izquierda; **left-hand 'drive: this car is** ~ este coche tiene el volante a la izquierda; **left-'hand·ed** *adj* zurdo; **left 'lug·gage (of·fice)** *Br* consigna *f*; **'left-o·vers** *npl food* sobras *fpl*; **'left-wing** *adj* POL izquierdista, de izquierdas

leg [leg] *of person* pierna *f*; *of animal* pata *f*; **pull s.o.'s** ~ tomar el pelo a alguien

leg·a·cy ['legəsɪ] legado *m*

le·gal ['li:gl] *adj* legal

le·gal ad·vis·er asesor(a) *m(f)* jurídico(-a)

le·gal·i·ty [lɪ'gælətɪ] legalidad *f*

le·gal·ize ['li:gəlaɪz] v/t legalizar

le·gend ['ledʒənd] leyenda *f*

le·gen·da·ry ['ledʒəndrɪ] *adj* legendario

le·gi·ble ['ledʒəbl] *adj* legible

le·gis·late ['ledʒɪsleɪt] v/i legislar

le·gis·la·tion [ledʒɪs'leɪʃn] legislación *f*

le·gis·la·tive ['ledʒɪslətɪv] *adj* legislativo

le·gis·la·ture ['ledʒɪsləʧər] POL legislativo *m*

le·git·i·mate [lɪ'dʒɪtɪmət] *adj* legítimo

leg room espacio *m* para las piernas

lei·sure ['li:ʒər] ocio *m*; **I look forward to having more** ~ estoy deseando tener más tiempo libre; **do it at your** ~ tómate tu tiempo para hacerlo

lei·sure·ly ['li:ʒəlɪ] *adj pace, lifestyle* tranquilo, relajado

'lei·sure time tiempo *m* libre

le·mon ['lemən] limón *m*

le·mon·ade [lemə'neɪd] limonada *f*

'le·mon juice zumo *m* de limón, *L.Am.* jugo *m* de limón

le·mon 'tea té *m* con limón

lend [lend] v/t (*pret & pp* **lent**) prestar

length [leŋθ] longitud *f*; (*piece: of material etc*) pedazo *m*; **at** ~ *describe, explain* detalladamente; (*finally*) finalmente

length·en ['leŋθən] v/t alargar

length·y ['leŋθɪ] *adj speech, stay* largo

le·ni·ent ['li:nɪənt] *adj* indulgente, poco severo

lens [lenz] *of camera* objetivo *m*, lente *f*; *of eyeglasses* cristal *m*; *of eye* cristalino *m*; (*contact* ~) lente *m* de contacto, *Span* lentilla *f*

'lens cov·er *of camera* tapa *f* del objetivo

Lent [lent] REL Cuaresma *f*

lent [lent] *pret & pp* → **lend**

len·til ['lentl] lenteja *f*

len·til 'soup sopa *f* de lentejas

Le·o ['li:oʊ] ASTR Leo *m/f inv*

leop·ard ['lepərd] leopardo *m*

le·o·tard ['li:oʊtɑːrd] malla *f*

les·bi·an ['lezbɪən] **1** *n* lesbiana *f*

2 *adj* lésbico, lesbiano

less [les] *adv* menos; *it costs* ~ cuesta menos; ~ *than $200* menos de 200 dólares

les·sen ['lesn] **1** *v/t* disminuir **2** *v/i* reducirse, disminuir

les·son ['lesn] lección *f*

let [let] *v/t* (*pret & pp* **let**) (*allow*) dejar, permitir; ~ *s.o. do sth* dejar a alguien hacer algo; ~ *me go!* ¡déjame!; ~ *him come in!* ¡déjale entrar!; ~*'s go/ stay* vamos / quedémonos; ~*'s not argue* no discutamos; ~ *alone* mucho menos; ~ *go of sth* of *rope, handle* soltar algo; ~ *go of me!* ¡suéltame!

◆ **let down** *v/t hair* soltarse; *blinds* bajar; (*disappoint*) decepcionar, defraudar; *dress, pants* alargar

◆ **let in** *v/t to house* dejar pasar

◆ **let off** *v/t* (*not punish*) perdonar; *from car* dejar; *the court let him off with a small fine* el tribunal sólo le impuso una pequeña multa

◆ **let out** *v/t of room, building* alquilar, *Mex* rentar; *jacket etc* agrandar; *groan, yell* soltar

◆ **let up** *v/i* (*stop*) amainar

le·thal ['li:θl] *adj* letal

le·thar·gic [lɪ'θɑːrdʒɪk] *adj* aletargado, apático

leth·ar·gy ['leθərdʒɪ] sopor *m*, apatía *f*

let·ter ['letər] *of alphabet* letra *f*; *in mail* carta *f*

'let·ter·box *Br* buzón *m*; **'let·ter·head** (*heading*) membrete *m*; (*headed paper*) papel *m* con membrete; **let·ter of 'cred·it** COM carta *f* de crédito

let·tuce ['letɪs] lechuga *f*

'let·up: *without a* ~ sin interrupción

leu·ke·mia [luːˈkiːmɪə] leucemia *f*

lev·el ['levl] **1** *adj field, surface* nivelado, llano; *in competition, scores* igualado; *draw* ~ *with s.o.* *in race* ponerse a la altura de alguien **2** *n on scale, in hierarchy*, (*amount*) nivel *m*; *on the* ~ F (*honest*) honrado

lev·el-head·ed [levl'hedɪd] *adj* ecuánime, sensato

le·ver ['levər] **1** *n* palanca *f* **2** *v/t*: ~ *sth open* abrir algo haciendo palanca

lev·er·age ['levrɪdʒ] apalancamiento *m*; (*influence*) influencia *f*

lev·y ['levɪ] *v/t* (*pret & pp* **-ied**) *taxes* imponer

lewd [luːd] *adj* obsceno

li·a·bil·i·ty [laɪə'bɪlətɪ] (*responsibility*) responsabilidad *f*; (*likeliness*) propensión *f*

li·a·bil·i·ty in·sur·ance seguro *m* a terceros

li·a·ble ['laɪəbl] *adj* (*responsible*) responsable (*for* de); *be* ~ *to* (*likely*) ser propenso a

◆ **li·aise with** [lɪ'eɪz] *v/t* actuar de enlace con

li·ai·son [lɪ'eɪzɑːn] (*contacts*) contacto *m*, enlace *m*

li·ar [laɪr] mentiroso(-a) *m(f)*

li·bel ['laɪbl] **1** *n* calumnia *f*, difamación *f* **2** *v/t* calumniar, difamar

lib·e·ral ['lɪbərəl] *adj* (*broadminded*), POL liberal; (*generous*: *portion etc*) abundante

lib·e·rate ['lɪbəreɪt] *v/t* liberar

lib·e·rat·ed ['lɪbəreɪtɪd] *adj* liberado

lib·e·ra·tion [lɪbə'reɪʃn] liberación *f*

lib·er·ty ['lɪbərtɪ] libertad *f*; *at* ~ *of prisoner etc* en libertad; *be at* ~ *to do sth* tener libertad para hacer algo

Li·bra ['liːbrə] ASTR Libra *m/f inv*

li·brar·i·an [laɪˈbreɪrɪən] bibliotecario(-a) *m(f)*

li·bra·ry ['laɪbrerɪ] biblioteca *f*

Lib·y·a ['lɪbɪə] Libia

Lib·y·an ['lɪbɪən] **1** *adj* libio **2** *n* libio(-a) *m(f)*

lice [laɪs] *pl* → **louse**

li·cence *Br* → **license 1** *n*

li·cense ['laɪsns] **1** *n* permiso *m*, licencia *f* **2** *v/t* autorizar; *be* ~*d* tener permiso *or* licencia

'li·cense num·ber (número *m* de) matrícula *f*

'li·cense plate *of car* (placa *f* de) matrícula *f*

lick [lɪk] **1** *n* lamedura *f* **2** *v/t* lamer; ~ *one's lips* relamerse

lick·ing ['lɪkɪŋ] F (*defeat*): *we got a* ~ nos dieron una paliza F

L

li·co·rice ['lɪkərɪs] regaliz *m*

lid [lɪd] (*top*) tapa *f*

lie¹ [laɪ] **1** *n* (*untruth*) mentira *f* **2** *v/i* mentir

lie² [laɪ] *v/i* (*pret* **lay**, *pp* **lain**) *of person* estar tumbado; *of object* estar; (*be situated*) estar, encontrarse; **~ on your stomach** túmbate boca abajo

♦ **lie down** *v/i* tumbarse

lie-in: *Br* **have a ~** quedarse un rato más en la cama

lieu [luː]: *in* **~** *of* en lugar de

lieu·ten·ant [luˈtenənt] teniente *m/f*

life [laɪf] (*pl* **lives** [laɪvz]) vida *f*; *of machine* vida *f*, duración *f*; *that's* **~!** ¡así es la vida!

'life belt salvavidas *m inv*; **'life·boat** *from ship* bote *m* salvavidas; *from land* lancha *f* de salvamento; **'life ex·pect·an·cy** esperanza *f* de vida; **'life·guard** socorrista *m/f*; **'life his·to·ry** historia *f* de la vida; **life im·pris·on·ment** cadena *f* perpetua; **'life in·sur·ance** seguro *m* de vida; **'life jack·et** chaleco *m* salvavidas

life·less ['laɪflɪs] *adj* sin vida

life·like ['laɪflaɪk] *adj* realista

'life·long *adj* de toda la vida; **'life pre·serv·er** salvavidas *m inv*; **'life-sav·ing** *adj medical equipment, drug* que salva vidas; **'life-sized** *adj* de tamaño natural; **'life-threat·en·ing** *adj* que puede ser mortal; **'life·time** vida *f*; *in my* **~** durante mi vida

lift [lɪft] **1** *v/t* levantar **2** *v/i of fog* disiparse **3** *n Br* (*elevator*) ascensor *m*; *give s.o. a* **~** llevar a alguien (en coche)

♦ **lift off** *v/i of rocket* despegar

'lift-off *of rocket* despegue *m*

lig·a·ment ['lɪgəmənt] ligamento *m*

light¹ [laɪt] **1** *n* luz *f*; *in the* **~** *of* a la luz de; *have you got a* **~?** ¿tienes fuego? **2** *v/t* (*pret & pp* **-ed** *or* **lit**) *fire, cigarette* encender; (*illuminate*) iluminar **3** *adj color, sky* claro; *room* luminoso

light² [laɪt] **1** *adj* (*not heavy*) ligero **2** *adv*: *travel* **~** viajar ligero de equipaje

♦ **light up 1** *v/t* (*illuminate*) iluminar **2** *v/i* (*start to smoke*) encender un cigarrillo

'light bulb bombilla *f*

light·en¹ ['laɪtn] *v/t color* aclarar

light·en² ['laɪtn] *v/t load* aligerar

♦ **lighten up** *v/i of person* alegrarse; *come on, lighten up* venga, no te tomes las cosas en serio

light·er ['laɪtər] *for cigarettes* encendedor *m*, *Span* mechero *m*

light-head·ed [laɪtˈhedɪd] *adj* (*dizzy*) mareado; **light-'heart·ed** [laɪtˈhɑːrtɪd] *adj* alegre; **'light·house** faro *m*

light·ing ['laɪtɪŋ] iluminación *f*

light·ly ['laɪtlɪ] *adv touch* ligeramente; *get off* **~** salir bien parado

light·ness¹ ['laɪtnɪs] *of room, color* claridad *f*

light·ness² ['laɪtnɪs] *in weight* ligereza *f*

light·ning ['laɪtnɪŋ]: *a flash of* **~** relámpago; *they were struck by* **~** les cayó un rayo

'light·ning con·duc·tor pararrayos *m inv*

'light pen lápiz *m* óptico; **'light·weight** *n in boxing* peso *m* ligero; **'light year** año *m* luz

like¹ [laɪk] **1** *prep* como; *be* **~** *s.o.* ser como alguien; *what is she* **~?** ¿cómo es?; *it's not* **~** *him* (*not his character*) no es su estilo **2** *conj* F (*as*) como; **~** *I said* como dije

like² [laɪk] *v/t*: *I* **~** *it/ her* me gusta; *I would* **~** *...* querría ...; *I would* **~** *to ...* me gustaría ...; *would you* **~** *...?* ¿querrías ...?; *would you* **~** *to ...?* ¿querrías ...?; *she* **~s** *to swim* le gusta nadar; *if you* **~** si quieres

like·a·ble ['laɪkəbl] *adj* simpático

like·li·hood ['laɪklɪhʊd] probabilidad *f*; *in all* **~** con toda probabilidad

like·ly ['laɪklɪ] *adj* (*probable*) probable; *not* **~!** ¡ni hablar!

like·ness ['laɪknɪs] (*resemblance*) parecido *m*

'like·wise ['laɪkwaɪz] *adv* igualmente; *pleased to meet you* **– ~!** encantado de conocerle – ¡lo mismo digo!

lik·ing ['laɪkɪŋ] afición f (**for** a); **to your ~** a su gusto; **take a ~ to s.o.** tomar cariño a alguien

li·lac ['laɪlək] *flower* lila f; *color* lila m

li·ly ['lɪlɪ] lirio m

li·ly of the 'val·ley lirio m de los valles

limb [lɪm] miembro m

lime¹ [laɪm] *fruit, tree* lima f

lime² [laɪm] *substance* cal f

lime'green *adj* verde lima

'lime·light: **be in the ~** estar en el candelero

lim·it ['lɪmɪt] **1** n límite m; **within ~s** dentro de un límite; **be off ~s** *of place* ser zona prohibida; **that's the ~!** ¡es el colmo! **F 2** v/t limitar

lim·i·ta·tion [lɪmɪ'teɪʃn] limitación f

lim·it·ed 'com·pa·ny Br sociedad f limitada

lim·o ['lɪmoʊ] F limusina f

lim·ou·sine ['lɪməzi:n] limusina f

limp¹ [lɪmp] *adj* flojo

limp² [lɪmp] *n*: **he has a ~** cojea

line¹ [laɪn] *n of text, on road,* TELEC línea f; *of trees* fila f, hilera f; *of people* fila f, cola f; *of business* especialidad f; **what ~ are you in?** ¿a qué te dedicas?; **the ~ is busy** está ocupado, Span está comunicando; **hold the ~** no cuelgue; **draw the ~ at sth** no estar dispuesto a hacer algo; **~ of inquiry** línea f de investigación; **~ of reasoning** argumentación f; **stand in ~** hacer cola; **in ~ with ...** (*conforming with*) en las mismas líneas que

line² [laɪn] v/t *with lining* forrar

♦ **line up** v/i hacer cola

lin·e·ar ['lɪnɪər] *adj* lineal

lin·en ['lɪnɪn] *material* lino m; (*sheets etc*) ropa f blanca

lin·er ['laɪnər] *ship* transatlántico m

lines·man ['laɪnzmən] SP juez m de línea, linier m

lin·ger ['lɪŋgər] v/i *of person* entretenerse; *of pain* persistir

lin·ge·rie ['lænʒəri:] lencería f

lin·guist ['lɪŋgwɪst] lingüista m/f; **she's a good ~** se le dan bien los idiomas

lin·guis·tic [lɪŋ'gwɪstɪk] *adj* lingüístico

lin·ing ['laɪnɪŋ] *of clothes* forro m; *of brakes,* pipe revestimiento m

link [lɪŋk] **1** n (*connection*) conexión f; *between countries* vínculo m; *in chain* eslabón m **2** v/t conectar

♦ **link up** v/i encontrarse; TV conectar

li·on ['laɪən] león m

lip [lɪp] labio m

'lip·read v/i (*pret & pp* **-read** [red]) leer los labios

'lip·stick barra f de labios

li·queur [lɪ'kjʊr] licor m

liq·uid ['lɪkwɪd] **1** n líquido m **2** *adj* líquido

liq·ui·date ['lɪkwɪdeɪt] v/t *assets* liquidar; F (*kill*) cepillarse a F

liq·ui·da·tion [lɪkwɪ'deɪʃn] liquidación f; **go into ~** ir a la quiebra

liq·ui·di·ty [lɪ'kwɪdɪtɪ] FIN liquidez f

liq·uid·ize ['lɪkwɪdaɪz] v/t licuar

liq·uid·iz·er ['lɪkwɪdaɪzər] licuadora f

liq·uor ['lɪkər] bebida f alcohólica

'liq·uor store tienda f de bebidas alcohólicas

lisp [lɪsp] **1** n ceceo m **2** v/i cecear

list [lɪst] **1** n lista f **2** v/t enumerar; COMPUT listar

lis·ten ['lɪsn] v/i escuchar; **I tried to persuade him, but he wouldn't ~** intenté convencerle, pero no me hizo ningún caso

♦ **listen in** v/i escuchar

♦ **listen to** v/t *radio, person* escuchar

lis·ten·er ['lɪsnər] *to radio* oyente m/f; **he's a good ~** sabe escuchar

list·ings mag·a·zine ['lɪstɪŋz] guía f de espectáculos

list·less ['lɪstlɪs] *adj* apático, lánguido

lit [lɪt] *pret & pp* → **light**

li·ter ['li:tər] litro m

lit·e·ral ['lɪtərəl] *adj* literal

lit·e·ral·ly ['lɪtərəlɪ] *adv* literalmente

lit·e·ra·ry ['lɪtərerɪ] *adj* literario

lit·e·rate ['lɪtərət] *adj* culto; **be ~** saber leer y escribir

lit·e·ra·ture ['lɪtrətʃər] literatura f; *about a product* folletos mpl, pros-

L

pectos *mpl*

li·tre *Br* → **liter**

lit·ter ['lɪtər] basura *f*; *of animal* camada *f*

'lit·ter bas·ket *Br* papelera *f*

lit·tle ['lɪtl] **1** *adj* pequeño; *the ~ ones* los pequeños **2** *n* poco *m*; *the ~ I know* lo poco que sé; *a ~* un poco; *a ~ bread / wine* un poco de pan / vino; *a ~ is better than nothing* más vale poco que nada **3** *adv* poco; *~ by ~* poco a poco; *a ~ better / bigger* un poco mejor / más grande; *a ~ before 6* un poco antes de las 6

live¹ [lɪv] *v/i* vivir

♦ **live on 1** *v/t rice, bread* sobrevivir a base de **2** *v/i* (*continue living*) sobrevivir, vivir

♦ **live it up**: *live it up* pasarlo bien

♦ **live up to** *v/t* responder a

♦ **live with** *v/t person* vivir con

live² [laɪv] *adj broadcast* en directo; *ammunition* real; *wire* con corriente

live·li·hood ['laɪvlɪhʊd] vida *f*, sustento *m*; *earn one's ~* ganarse la vida

live·li·ness ['laɪvlɪnɪs] *of person, music* vivacidad *f*; *of debate* lo animado

live·ly ['laɪvlɪ] *adj* animado

liv·er ['lɪvər] MED, *food* hígado *m*

live·stock ['laɪvstɑːk] ganado *m*

liv·id ['lɪvɪd] *adj* (*angry*) enfurecido, furioso

liv·ing ['lɪvɪŋ] **1** *adj* vivo **2** *n* vida *f*; *what do you do for a ~?* ¿en qué trabajas?; *earn one's ~* ganarse la vida; *standard of ~* estándar *m* de vida

'liv·ing room sala *f* de estar, salón *m*

liz·ard ['lɪzərd] lagarto *m*

load [loʊd] **1** *n* also ELEC carga *f*; *~s of* F montones de F **2** *v/t car, truck, gun* cargar; *camera* poner el carrete a; COMPUT: *software* cargar (en memoria)

load·ed ['loʊdɪd] F *adj* (*very rich*) forrado F; (*drunk*) como una cuba

loaf [loʊf] *n* (*pl* **loaves** [loʊvz]) pan *m*; *a ~ of bread* una barra de pan, un pan

♦ **loaf around** *v/i* F gandulear F

loaf·er ['loʊfər] *shoe* mocasín *m*

loan [loʊn] **1** *n* préstamo *m*; *on ~* prestado **2** *v/t* prestar; *~ s.o. sth* prestar algo a alguien

loathe [loʊð] *v/t* detestar, aborrecer

loath·ing ['loʊðɪŋ] odio *m*, aborrecimiento *m*

lob·by ['lɑːbɪ] *n in hotel, theater* vestíbulo *m*; POL lobby *m*, grupo *m* de presión

lobe [loʊb] *of ear* lóbulo *m*

lob·ster ['lɑːbstər] langosta *f*

lo·cal ['loʊkl] **1** *adj* local; *the ~ people* la gente del lugar; *I'm not ~* no soy de aquí **2** *n*: *the ~s* los del lugar; *are you a ~?* ¿eres de aquí?

'lo·cal call TELEC llamada *f* local; **lo·cal e'lec·tions** *npl* elecciones *fpl* municipales; **lo·cal 'gov·ern·ment** administración *f* municipal

lo·cal·i·ty [loʊ'kælətɪ] localidad *f*

lo·cal·ly ['loʊkəlɪ] *adv* live, work cerca, en la zona; *it's well known ~* es muy conocido en la zona; *they are grown ~* son cultivados en la región

lo·cal 'pro·duce productos *mpl* del lugar

'lo·cal time hora *f* local

lo·cate [loʊ'keɪt] *v/t new factory etc* emplazar, ubicar; (*identify position of*) situar; *be ~d* encontrarse

lo·ca·tion [loʊ'keɪʃn] (*siting*) emplazamiento *m*; (*identifying position of*) localización *f*; *on ~ movie* en exteriores

lock¹ [lɑːk] *of hair* mechón *m*

lock² [lɑːk] **1** *n on door* cerradura *f* **2** *v/t door* cerrar (con llave)

♦ **lock away** *v/t* guardar bajo llave

♦ **lock in** *v/t person* encerrar

♦ **lock out** *v/t of house* dejar fuera; *I locked myself out* me dejé las llaves dentro

♦ **lock up** *v/t in prison* encerrar

lock·er ['lɑːkər] taquilla *f*

'lock·er room vestuario *m*

lock·et ['lɑːkɪt] guardapelo *m*

lock·smith ['lɑːksmɪθ] cerrajero(-a) *m(f)*

lo·cust ['loʊkəst] langosta *f*

lodge [lɑːdʒ] **1** *v/t complaint* presentar **2** *v/i of bullet* alojarse

lodg·er [ˈlɑːdʒər] huésped *m/f*

loft [lɑːft] buhardilla *f*, desván *m*

loft·y [ˈlɑːftɪ] *adj heights, ideals* elevado

log [lɑːg] *n wood* tronco *m*; *written record* registro *m*

♦ **log off** *v/i* (*pret & pp* **-ged**) salir

♦ **log on** *v/i* entrar

♦ **log on to** *v/t* entrar a

log·book *captain's* cuaderno *m* de bitácora; *driver's* documentación *f* del vehículo

log 'cab·in cabaña *f*

log·ger·heads [ˈlɑːgərhedz]: **be at ~** estar enfrentado

lo·gic [ˈlɑːdʒɪk] lógica *f*

lo·gic·al [ˈlɑːdʒɪkl] *adj* lógico

lo·gic·al·ly [ˈlɑːdʒɪklɪ] *adv* lógicamente

lo·gis·tics [ləˈdʒɪstɪks] logística *f*

lo·go [ˈlougou] logotipo *m*

loi·ter [ˈlɔɪtər] *v/i* holgazanear

lol·li·pop [ˈlɑːlɪpɑːp] piruleta *f*

Lon·don [ˈlʌndən] Londres

lone·li·ness [ˈlounlɪnɪs] *of person, place* soledad *f*

lone·ly [ˈlounlɪ] *adj person* solo; *place* solitario

lon·er [ˈlounər] solitario(-a) *m(f)*

long¹ [lɔːŋ] **1** *adj* largo; *it's a ~ way* hay un largo camino; *it's two feet ~* mide dos pies de largo; *the movie is three hours ~* la película dura tres horas **2** *adv* mucho tiempo; *don't be ~* no tardes mucho; *5 weeks is too ~* 5 semanas son mucho tiempo; *will it take ~?* ¿llevará mucho tiempo?; *that was ~ ago* eso fue hace mucho tiempo; *~ before then* mucho antes; *before ~* al poco tiempo; *we can't wait any ~er* no podemos esperar más tiempo; *she no ~er works here* ya no trabaja aquí; *so ~ as* (*provided*) siempre que; *so ~!* ¡hasta la vista!

long² [lɔːŋ] *v/i*: *~ for sth* home echar en falta algo; *change* anhelar *or* desear algo; *be ~ing to do sth* anhelar *or* desear hacer algo

long-'dis·tance *adj race* de fondo; *flight* de larga distancia; *a ~ phone-call* una llamada de larga distancia, una conferencia interurbana

lon·gev·i·ty [lɑːnˈdʒevɪtɪ] longevidad *f*

long·ing [ˈlɔːŋɪŋ] *n* anhelo *m*, deseo *m*

lon·gi·tude [ˈlɑːŋgɪtuːd] longitud *f*

'long jump salto *m* de longitud; **'long-range** *adj missile* de largo alcance; *forecast* a largo plazo; **long-sight·ed** [lɔːŋˈsaɪtɪd] *adj* hipermétrope; **long-sleeved** [lɔːŋˈsliːvd] *adj* de manga larga; **long-'stand·ing** *adj* antiguo; **'long-term** *adj* a largo plazo; **' long wave** RAD onda *f* larga; **long-wind·ed** [lɔːŋˈwɪndɪd] *adj* prolijo

look [lʊk] **1** *n* (*appearance*) aspecto *m*; (*glance*) mirada *f*; *give s.o. / sth a ~* mirar a alguien / mirar algo; *have a ~ at sth* (*examine*) echar un vistazo a algo; *can I have a ~?* ¿puedo echarle un vistazo?; *can I have a ~ around?* in store etc ¿puedo echar un vistazo?; *~s* (*beauty*) atractivo *m*, guapura *f* **2** *v/i* mirar; (*search*) buscar; (*seem*) parecer; *you ~ tired / different* pareces cansado / diferente; *he ~s about 25* aparenta 25 años; *how do things ~ to you?* ¿qué te parece cómo están las cosas?; *that ~s good* tiene buena pinta

♦ **look after** *v/t children* cuidar (de); *property, interests* proteger

♦ **look ahead** *v/i fig* mirar hacia el futuro

♦ **look around 1** *v/i* mirar **2** *v/t museum, city* dar una vuelta por

♦ **look at** *v/t* mirar; (*examine*) estudiar; (*consider*) considerar; *it depends how you look at it* depende de cómo lo mires

♦ **look back** *v/i* mirar atrás

♦ **look down on** *v/t* mirar por encima del hombro a

♦ **look for** *v/t* buscar

♦ **look forward to** *v/t* estar deseando; *I'm looking forward to the vacation* tengo muchas ganas de empezar las vacaciones

♦ **look in on** v/t (*visit*) hacer una visita a

♦ **look into** v/t (*investigate*) investigar

♦ **look on 1** v/i (*watch*) quedarse mirando **2** v/t: **look on s.o./sth as** (*consider*) considerar a alguien/algo como

♦ **look onto** v/t *garden, street* dar a

♦ **look out** v/i *through, from window etc* mirar; (*pay attention*) tener cuidado; **look out!** ¡cuidado!

♦ **look out for** v/t buscar; (*be on guard against*) tener cuidado con

♦ **look out of** v/t *window* mirar por

♦ **look over** v/t *translation* revisar, repasar; *house* inspeccionar

♦ **look through** v/t *magazine, notes* echar un vistazo a, hojear

♦ **look to** v/t (*rely on*): **we look to you for help** acudimos a usted en busca de ayuda

♦ **look up 1** v/i *from paper etc* levantar la mirada; (*improve*) mejorar **2** v/t *word, phone number* buscar; (*visit*) visitar

♦ **look up to** v/t (*respect*) admirar

'**look‧out** *person* centinela *m*, vigía *m*; **be on the ~ for** estar buscando

♦ **loom up** v/i aparecer (**out of** de entre)

loon‧y ['lu:nɪ] **1** *n* F chalado(-a) *m(f)* F **2** *adj* F chalado F

loop [lu:p] *n* bucle *m*

'**loop‧hole** *in law etc* resquicio *m* or vacío *m* legal

loose [lu:s] *adj connection, button* suelto; *clothes* suelto, holgado; *morals* disoluto, relajado; *wording* impreciso; **~ change** suelto *m*, *L.Am.* sencillo *m*; **~ ends** *of problem, discussion* cabos *mpl* sueltos

loose‧ly ['lu:slɪ] *adv worded* vagamente

loos‧en ['lu:sn] v/t *collar, knot* aflojar

loot [lu:t] **1** *n* botín *m* **2** v/i saquear

loot‧er ['lu:tər] saqueador(a) *m(f)*

♦ **lop off** [lɑ:p] v/t (*pret & pp* **-ped**) *branch* cortar; podar

lop-sid‧ed [lɑ:p'saɪdɪd] *adj* torcido; *balance of committee etc* desigual

Lord [lɔ:rd] (*God*) Señor *m*

Lord's 'Prayer padrenuestro *m*

lor‧ry ['lɑ:rɪ] *Br* camión *m*

lose [lu:z] **1** v/t (*pret & pp* **lost**) *object, match* perder **2** v/i (*pret & pp* **lost**) SP perder; *of clock* retrasarse; **I'm lost** me he perdido; **get lost!** F ¡vete al paseo!

♦ **lose out** v/i salir perdiendo

los‧er ['lu:zər] perdedor(a) *m(f)*; F *in life* fracasado(-a) *m(f)*

loss [lɑ:s] pérdida *f*; **make a ~** tener pérdidas; **I'm at a ~ what to say** no sé qué decir

lost [lɑ:st] **1** *adj* perdido **2** *pret & pp* → **lose**

lost-and-'found, *Br* **lost 'prop‧er‧ty (of‧fice)** oficina *f* de objetos perdidos

lot [lɑ:t]: **a ~ (of)**, **~s (of)** mucho, muchos; **a ~ of books**, **~s of books** muchos libros; **a ~ of butter**, **~s of butter** mucha mantequilla; **a ~ better/easier** mucho mejor/más fácil

lo‧tion ['loʊʃn] loción *f*

lot‧te‧ry ['lɑ:tərɪ] lotería *f*

loud [laʊd] *adj voice, noise* fuerte; *music* fuerte, alto; *color* chillón

loud'speak‧er altavoz *m*, *L.Am.* altoparlante *m*

lounge [laʊndʒ] *in house* salón *m*

♦ **lounge around** v/i holgazanear

'**lounge suit** *Br* traje *m* de calle

louse [laʊs] (*pl* **lice** [laɪs]) piojo *m*

lous‧y ['laʊzɪ] *adj* F asqueroso F; **I feel ~** me siento de pena F

lout [laʊt] gamberro *m*

lov‧a‧ble ['lʌvəbl] *adj* adorable, encantador

love [lʌv] **1** *n* amor *m*; *in tennis* nada *f*; **be in ~** estar enamorado (**with** de); **fall in ~** enamorarse (**with** de); **make ~** hacer el amor; **make ~ to ...** hacer el amor con; **yes, my ~** sí, amor **2** v/t *person, country, wine* amar; **she ~s to watch tennis** le encanta ver tenis

'**love af‧fair** aventura *f* amorosa; '**love let‧ter** carta *f* de amor; '**love-life** vida *f* amorosa

love·ly ['lʌvlɪ] *adj face, hair, color, tune* precioso, lindo; *person, character* encantador; *holiday, weather, meal* estupendo; **we had a ~ time** nos lo pasamos de maravilla

lov·er ['lʌvər] amante *m/f*

lov·ing ['lʌvɪŋ] *adj* cariñoso

lov·ing·ly ['lʌvɪŋlɪ] *adv* con cariño

low [loʊ] **1** *adj bridge, salary, price, voice, quality* bajo; **be feeling ~** estar deprimido; **we're ~ on gas/ tea** nos queda poca gasolina/ té **2** *n in weather* zona *f* de bajas presiones, borrasca *f; in sales, statistics* mínimo *m*

low·brow ['loʊbraʊ] *adj* poco intelectual, popular; **low-'cal·o·rie** *adj* bajo en calorías; **'low-cut** *adj dress* escotado

low·er ['loʊər] *v/t to the ground, hemline, price* bajar; *flag* arriar; *pressure* reducir

'low-fat *adj* de bajo contenido graso; **'low-key** *adj* discreto, mesurado; **'low·lands** *npl* tierras *fpl* bajas; **low-'pres·sure ar·e·a** zona *f* de bajas presiones, borrasca *f;* **'low sea·son** temporada *f* baja; **'low tide** marea *f* baja

loy·al ['lɔɪəl] *adj* leal, fiel (**to** a)

loy·al·ly ['lɔɪəlɪ] *adv* lealmente, fielmente

loy·al·ty ['lɔɪəltɪ] lealtad *f* (**to** a)

loz·enge ['lɑːzɪndʒ] *shape* rombo *m; tablet* pastilla *f*

Ltd *abbr* (= **limited**) S.L. (= sociedad *f* limitada)

lu·bri·cant ['luːbrɪkənt] lubricante *m*

lu·bri·cate ['luːbrɪkeɪt] *v/t* lubricar

lu·bri·ca·tion [luːbrɪ'keɪʃn] lubricación *f*

lu·cid ['luːsɪd] *adj (clear, sane)* lúcido

luck [lʌk] suerte *f; bad ~* mala suerte; **good ~!** ¡buena suerte!

♦ **luck out** *v/i* F tener mucha suerte

luck·i·ly ['lʌkɪlɪ] *adv* afortunadamente, por suerte

luck·y ['lʌkɪ] *adj person, coincidence* afortunado; *day, number* de la suerte; **you were ~** tuviste suerte; **she's**

~ to be alive tiene suerte de estar con vida; **that's ~!** ¡qué suerte!

lu·cra·tive ['luːkrətɪv] *adj* lucrativo

lu·di·crous ['luːdɪkrəs] *adj* ridículo

lug [lʌg] *v/t (pret & pp -ged)* arrastrar

lug·gage ['lʌgɪdʒ] equipaje *m*

luke·warm ['luːkwɔːrm] *adj water* tibio, templado; *reception* indiferente

lull [lʌl] **1** *n in storm, fighting* tregua *f; in conversation* pausa *f* **2** *v/t:* **~ s.o. into a false sense of security** dar a alguien una falsa sensación de seguridad

lul·la·by ['lʌləbaɪ] canción *f* de cuna, nana *f*

lum·ba·go [lʌm'beɪgoʊ] lumbago *m*

lum·ber ['lʌmbər] *n (timber)* madera *f*

lu·mi·nous ['luːmɪnəs] *adj* luminoso

lump [lʌmp] *n of sugar, earth* terrón *m; (swelling)* bulto *m*

♦ **lump together** *v/t* agrupar

lump 'sum pago *m* único

lump·y ['lʌmpɪ] *adj liquid, sauce* grumoso; *mattress* lleno de bultos

lu·na·cy ['luːnəsɪ] locura *f*

lu·nar ['luːnər] *adj* lunar

lu·na·tic ['luːnətɪk] *n* lunático(-a) *m(f)*, loco(-a) *m(f)*

lunch [lʌntʃ] *n* almuerzo *m*, comida *f; have ~* almorzar, comer

'lunch box fiambrera *f;* **'lunch break** pausa *f* para el almuerzo; **'lunch hour** hora *f* del almuerzo; **'lunch-time** hora *f* del almuerzo

lung [lʌŋ] pulmón *m*

'lung can·cer cáncer *m* de pulmón

♦ **lunge at** [lʌndʒ] *v/t* arremeter contra

lurch [lɜːrtʃ] *v/i of drunk* tambalearse; *of ship* dar sacudidas

lure [lʊr] **1** *n* atractivo *m* **2** *v/t* atraer

lu·rid ['lʊrɪd] *adj color* chillón; *details* espeluznante

lurk [lɜːrk] *v/i of person* estar oculto, estar al acecho

lus·cious ['lʌʃəs] *adj fruit, dessert* jugoso, exquisito; F *woman, man* cautivador

lush [lʌʃ] *adj vegetation* exuberante

lust [lʌst] *n* lujuria *f*

lux·u·ri·ous [lʌɡ'ʒʊrɪəs] *adj* lujoso

lux·u·ri·ous·ly [lʌɡ'ʒʊrɪəslɪ] *adv* lujosamente

lux·u·ry ['lʌkʃərɪ] **1** *n* lujo *m* **2** *adj* de lujo

lymph gland ['lɪmfɡlænd] ganglio *m* linfático

lynch [lɪntʃ] *v/t* linchar

lyr·i·cist ['lɪrɪsɪst] letrista *m/f*

lyr·ics ['lɪrɪks] *npl* letra *f*

M

MA [em'eɪ] *abbr* (= *Master of Arts*) Máster *m* en Humanidades

ma'am [mæm] señora *f*

ma·chine [mə'ʃiːn] **1** *n* máquina *f* **2** *v/t with sewing machine* coser a máquina; TECH trabajar a máquina

ma'chine gun *n* ametralladora *f*

ma·chine-'read·a·ble *adj* legible por *Span* el ordenador *or L.Am.* la computadora

ma·chin·e·ry [mə'ʃiːnərɪ] (*machines*) maquinaria *f*

ma·chine trans'la·tion traducción *f* automática

ma·chis·mo [mə'kɪzmoʊ] machismo *m*

mach·o ['mætʃoʊ] *adj* macho

mack·in·tosh ['mækɪntɑːʃ] impermeable *m*

mac·ro ['mækroʊ] COMPUT macro *m*

mad [mæd] *adj* (*insane*) loco; F (*angry*) enfadado; *a ~ idea* una idea disparatada; *be ~ about* F estar loco por; *drive s.o. ~* volver loco a alguien; *go ~* (*become insane, with enthusiasm*) volverse loco; *like ~* F *run, work* como un loco F; *Pa got real ~ when I told him* papá se puso hecho una furia cuando se lo conté

mad·den ['mædən] *v/t* (*infuriate*) sacar de quicio

mad·den·ing ['mædnɪŋ] *adj* exasperante

made [meɪd] *pret & pp* → *make*

'mad·house *fig* casa *f* de locos

mad·ly ['mædlɪ] *adv* como loco; *~ in love* locamente enamorado

'mad·man loco *m*

mad·ness ['mædnɪs] locura *f*

Ma·don·na [mə'dɑːnə] madona *f*

Ma·fi·a ['mɑːfɪə]: *the ~* la mafia

mag·a·zine [mæɡə'ziːn] *printed* revista *f*

mag·got ['mæɡət] gusano *m*

Ma·gi ['meɪdʒaɪ] REL: *the ~* los Reyes Magos

ma·gic ['mædʒɪk] **1** *n* magia *f*; *as if by ~*, *like ~* como por arte de magia **2** *adj* mágico; *there's nothing ~ about it* no tiene nada de mágico

mag·i·cal ['mædʒɪkl] *adj* mágico

ma·gi·cian [mə'dʒɪʃn] *performer* mago(-a) *m(f)*

ma·gic 'spell hechizo *m*; **ma·gic 'trick** truco *m* de magia; **mag·ic 'wand** varita *f* mágica

mag·nan·i·mous [mæɡ'nænɪməs] *adj* magnánimo

mag·net ['mæɡnɪt] imán *m*

mag·net·ic [mæɡ'netɪk] *adj* magnético; *fig: personality* cautivador

mag·net·ic 'stripe banda *f* magnética

mag·net·ism [mæɡ'netɪzm] *of person* magnetismo *m*

mag·nif·i·cence [mæɡ'nɪfɪsəns] magnificencia *f*

mag·nif·i·cent [mæɡ'nɪfɪsənt] *adj* magnífico

mag·ni·fy ['mæɡnɪfaɪ] *v/t* (*pret & pp -ied*) aumentar; *difficulties* magnificar

'mag·ni·fy·ing glass lupa *f*

mag·ni·tude ['mægnɪtu:d] magnitud f

ma·hog·a·ny [mə'hɑːgənɪ] caoba f

maid [meɪd] (*servant*) criada f; *in hotel* camarera f

'maid·en name ['meɪdn] apellido m de soltera

maid·en 'voy·age viaje m inaugural

mail [meɪl] **1** n correo m; *put sth in the* ~ echar algo al correo **2** v/t *letter* enviar (por correo)

'mail·box *also* COMPUT buzón m

'mail·ing list lista f de direcciones

'mail·man cartero m; **mail·'or·der cat·a·log**, *Br* **mail·'or·der cat·a·logue** catálogo m de venta por correo; **mail·'or·der firm** empresa f de venta por correo; **'mail·shot** mailing m

maim [meɪm] v/t mutilar

main [meɪn] *adj* principal; *she's alive, that's the* ~ *thing* está viva, que es lo principal

'main course plato m principal; **main 'en·trance** entrada f principal; **'main·frame** *Span* ordenador m central, *L.Am.* computadora f central; **'main·land** tierra f firme; *on the* ~ en el continente

main·ly ['meɪnlɪ] *adv* principalmente

main 'road carretera f general

'main street calle f principal

main·tain [meɪn'teɪn] v/t mantener

main·te·nance ['meɪntənəns] mantenimiento m; *pay* ~ pagar una pensión alimenticia

'main·te·nance costs *npl* gastos *mpl* de mantenimiento

'main·te·nance staff personal m de mantenimiento

ma·jes·tic [mə'dʒestɪk] *adj* majestuoso

ma·jes·ty ['mædʒestɪ] majestuosidad f; *Her Majesty* Su Majestad

ma·jor ['meɪdʒər] **1** *adj* (*significant*) importante, principal; *in C* ~ MUS en C mayor **2** n MIL comandante m

♦ **major in** v/t especializarse en

ma·jor·i·ty [mə'dʒɑːrətɪ] *also* POL mayoría f; *be in the* ~ ser mayoría

make [meɪk] **1** n (*brand*) marca f **2** v/t (*pret & pp* **made**) hacer; *cars* fabricar, producir; *movie* rodar; *speech* pronunciar; (*earn*) ganar; MATH hacer; *two and two* ~ *four* dos y dos son cuatro; ~ *s.o. do sth* (*force to*) obligar a alguien a hacer algo; (*cause to*) hacer que alguien haga algo; *you can't* ~ *me do it!* ¡no puedes obligarme a hacerlo!; ~ *s.o. happy/angry* hacer feliz/enfadar a alguien; ~ *a decision* tomar una decisión; *made in Japan* hecho en Japón; ~ *it* (*catch bus, train*) llegar a tiempo; (*come*) ir; (*succeed*) tener éxito; (*survive*) sobrevivir; *what time do you* ~ *it?* ¿qué hora llevas?; ~ *believe* imaginarse; ~ *do with* conformarse con; *what do you* ~ *of it?* ¿qué piensas?

♦ **make for** v/t (*go toward*) dirigirse hacia

♦ **make off** v/i escaparse

♦ **make off with** v/t (*steal*) llevarse

♦ **make out** v/t *list* hacer, elaborar; *check* extender; (*see*) distinguir; (*imply*) pretender

♦ **make over** v/t (*transfer*) ceder

♦ **make up 1** v/i *of woman, actor* maquillarse; *after quarrel* reconciliarse **2** v/t *story, excuse* inventar; *face* maquillar; (*constitute*) suponer, formar; *be made up of* estar compuesto de; *make up one's mind* decidirse; *make it up after quarrel* reconciliarse

♦ **make up for** v/t compensar por

'make-be·lieve n ficción f, fantasía f

mak·er ['meɪkər] (*manufacturer*) fabricante m

make·shift ['meɪkʃɪft] *adj* improvisado

make-up ['meɪkʌp] (*cosmetics*) maquillaje m

'make-up bag bolsa f del maquillaje

mal·ad·just·ed [mæləd'dʒʌstɪd] *adj* inadaptado

male [meɪl] **1** *adj* (*masculine*) masculino; *animal, bird, fish* macho; ~ *bosses* los jefes varones; *a* ~ *teacher* un profesor **2** n *man* hombre m, varón m; *animal, bird, fish* macho m

male 'chau·vin·ism machismo m; **male chau·vin·ist 'pig** machista m; **male 'nurse** enfermero m

ma·lev·o·lent [məˈlevələnt] *adj* malévolo

mal·func·tion [mælˈfʌŋkʃn] **1** n fallo m (**in** de) **2** v/i fallar

mal·ice [ˈmælɪs] malicia f

ma·li·cious [məˈlɪʃəs] *adj* malicioso

ma·lig·nant [məˈlɪgnənt] *adj tumor* maligno

mall [mɔːl] (*shopping ~*) centro m comercial

mal·nu·tri·tion [mælnuːˈtrɪʃn] desnutrición f

mal·treat [mælˈtriːt] v/t maltratar

mal·treat·ment [mælˈtriːtmənt] maltrato m

mam·mal [ˈmæml] mamífero m

man [mæn] **1** n (*pl* **men** [men]) hombre m; (*humanity*) el hombre; *in checkers* ficha f **2** v/t (*pret & pp* **-ned**) *telephones, front desk* atender; *spacecraft* tripular

man·age [ˈmænɪdʒ] **1** v/t *business* dirigir; *money* gestionar; *suitcase* poder con; **~ to ...** conseguir ... **2** v/i (*cope*) arreglárselas

man·age·a·ble [ˈmænɪdʒəbl] *adj* (*easy to handle*) manejable; (*feasible*) factible

man·age·ment [ˈmænɪdʒmənt] (*managing*) gestión f, administración f; (*managers*) dirección f

man·age·ment 'buy·out compra de una empresa por sus directivos; **man·age·ment con'sult·ant** consultor(a) m(f) en administración de empresas; **'man·age·ment stud·ies** estudios *mpl* de administración de empresas; **'man·age·ment team** equipo m directivo

man·ag·er [ˈmænɪdʒər] *of hotel, company* director(a) m(f); *of shop, restaurant* encargado(a) m(f)

man·a·ge·ri·al [mænɪˈdʒɪrɪəl] *adj* de gestión; **a ~ post** un puesto directivo

man·ag·ing di'rec·tor director(a) m(f) gerente

man·da·rin (**or·ange**) [ˈmændərɪn(ˈɔːrɪndʒ)] mandarina f

man·date [ˈmændeɪt] (*authority*) mandato m; (*task*) tarea f

man·da·to·ry [ˈmændətɔːrɪ] *adj* obligatorio

mane [meɪn] *of horse* crines *fpl*

ma·neu·ver [məˈnuːvər] **1** n maniobra f **2** v/t maniobrar; **she ~ed him into giving her the assignment** consiguió convencerle para que le diera el trabajo

man·gle [ˈmæŋgl] v/t (*crush*) destrozar

man·han·dle [ˈmænhændl] v/t mover a la fuerza

man·hood [ˈmænhʊd] (*maturity*) madurez f; (*virility*) virilidad f

'man-hour hora-hombre f

'man·hunt persecución f

ma·ni·a [ˈmeɪnɪə] (*craze*) pasión f

ma·ni·ac [ˈmeɪnɪæk] F chiflado(-a) m(f) F

man·i·cure [ˈmænɪkjʊr] manicura f

man·i·fest [ˈmænɪfest] **1** *adj* manifiesto **2** v/t manifestar; **~ itself** manifestarse

ma·nip·u·late [məˈnɪpjəleɪt] v/t *person, bones* manipular

ma·nip·u·la·tion [mənɪpjəˈleɪʃn] *of person, bones* manipulación f

ma·nip·u·la·tive [məˈnɪpjələtɪv] *adj* manipulador

man'kind la humanidad

man·ly [ˈmænlɪ] *adj* (*brave*) de hombres; (*strong*) varonil

'man-made *adj fibers, materials* sintético; *crater, structure* artificial

man·ner [ˈmænər] *of doing sth* manera f, modo m; (*attitude*) actitud f

man·ners [ˈmænərz] *npl* modales *mpl*; **good/ bad ~** buena/mala educación; **have no ~** ser un maleducado

ma·noeu·vre *Br* → **maneuver**

'man·pow·er (*workers*) mano f de obra; *for other tasks* recursos *mpl* humanos

man·sion [ˈmænʃn] mansión f

'man·slaugh·ter *Br* homicidio m sin premeditación

man·tel·piece ['mæntlpi:s] repisa *f* de chimenea

man·u·al ['mænjuəl] **1** *adj* manual **2** *n* manual *m*

man·u·al·ly ['mænjuəli] *adv* a mano

man·u·fac·ture [mænjuˈfæktʃər] **1** *n* fabricación *f* **2** *v/t equipment* fabricar

man·u·fac·tur·er [mænjuˈfæktʃərər] fabricante *m*

man·u·fac·tur·ing [mænjuˈfæktʃərɪŋ] *adj industry* manufacturero

ma·nure [məˈnʊr] estiércol *m*

man·u·script ['mænjuskrɪpt] manuscrito *m*

man·y ['meni] **1** *adj* muchos; *take as ~ apples as you like* toma las manzanas que quieras; *not ~ people / taxis* no mucha gente / muchos taxis; *too ~ problems / beers* demasiados problemas / demasiadas cervezas **2** *pron* muchos; *a great ~, a good ~* muchos; *how ~ do you need?* ¿cuántos necesitas?; *as ~ as 200 are still missing* hay hasta 200 desaparecidos

'**man-year** año-hombre *m*

map [mæp] mapa *m*

♦ **map out** *v/t* (*pret & pp* **-ped**) proyectar

ma·ple ['meɪpl] arce *m*

mar [mɑ:r] *v/t* (*pret & pp* **-red**) empañar

mar·a·thon ['mærəθɑ:n] *race* maratón *m or f*

mar·ble ['mɑ:rbl] *material* mármol *m*

March [mɑ:rtʃ] marzo *m*

march [mɑ:rtʃ] **1** *n* marcha *f* **2** *v/i* marchar

march·er ['mɑ:rtʃər] manifestante *m/f*

Mar·di Gras ['mɑ:rdɪgrɑ:] martes *m inv* de Carnaval

mare [mer] yegua *f*

mar·ga·rine [mɑ:rdʒəˈri:n] margarina *f*

mar·gin ['mɑ:rdʒɪn] *also* COM margen *m*

mar·gin·al ['mɑ:rdʒɪnl] *adj* (*slight*) marginal

mar·gin·al·ly ['mɑ:rdʒɪnli] *adv*

(*slightly*) ligeramente

mar·i·hua·na, mar·i·jua·na [mærɪˈhwɑ:nə] marihuana *f*

ma·ri·na [məˈri:nə] puerto *m* deportivo

mar·i·nade [mærɪˈneɪd] *n* adobo *m*

mar·i·nate ['mærɪneɪt] *v/t* adobar, marinar

ma·rine [məˈri:n] **1** *adj* marino **2** *n* MIL marine *m/f*, infante *m/f* de marina

mar·i·tal ['mærɪtl] *adj* marital

mar·i·tal 'sta·tus estado *m* civil

mar·i·time ['mærɪtaɪm] *adj* marítimo

mar·jo·ram ['mɑ:rdʒərəm] mejorana *f*

mark [mɑ:rk] **1** *n* señal *f*, marca *f*; (*stain*) marca *f*, mancha *f*; (*sign, token*) signo *m*, señal *f*; (*trace*) señal *f*; EDU nota *f*; *leave one's ~* dejar huella **2** *v/t* (*stain*) manchar; EDU calificar; (*indicate, commemorate*) marcar **3** *v/i of fabric* mancharse

♦ **mark down** *v/t goods* rebajar

♦ **mark out** *v/t with a line etc* marcar; *fig* (*set apart*) distinguir

♦ **mark up** *v/t price* subir; *goods* subir de precio

marked [mɑ:rkt] *adj* (*definite*) marcado, notable

mark·er ['mɑ:rkər] (*highlighter*) rotulador *m*

mar·ket ['mɑ:rkɪt] **1** *n* mercado *m*; (*stock ~*) bolsa *f*; *on the ~* en el mercado **2** *v/t* comercializar

mar·ket·a·ble ['mɑ:rkɪtəbl] *adj* comercializable

mar·ket e'con·o·my economía *f* de mercado

mar·ket 'for·ces *npl* fuerzas *fpl* del mercado

mar·ket·ing ['mɑ:rkɪtɪŋ] marketing *m*

'**mar·ket·ing cam·paign** campaña *f* de marketing; '**mar·ket·ing de·part·ment** departamento *m* de marketing; '**mar·ket·ing mix** marketing mix *m*, el producto, el precio, la distribución y la promoción; '**mar·ket·ing strat·e·gy** estrategia *f* de marketing

M

mar·ket 'lead·er líder *m* del mercado; **'mar·ket·place** *in town* plaza *f* del mercado; *for commodities* mercado *m*; **mar·ket re'search** investigación *f* de mercado; **mar·ket 'share** cuota *f* de mercado

mark-up ['mɑːrkʌp] margen *m*

mar·ma·lade ['mɑːrməleɪd] mermelada *f* de naranja

mar·quee [mɑːr'kiː] carpa *f*

mar·riage ['mærɪdʒ] matrimonio *m*; *event* boda *f*

'mar·riage cer·tif·i·cate certificado *m* de matrimonio

marriage 'guid·ance coun·se·lor consejero(-a) *m(f)* matrimonial

mar·ried ['mærɪd] *adj* casado; **be ~ to ...** estar casado con ...

married 'life vida *f* matrimonial

mar·ry ['mæri] *v/t (pret & pp -ied)* casarse con; *of priest* casar; **get married** casarse

marsh [mɑːrʃ] pantano *m*, ciénaga *f*

mar·shal ['mɑːrʃl] *n in police* jefe(-a) *m(f)* de policía; *in security service* miembro *m* del servicio de seguridad

marsh·mal·low [mɑːrʃ'mæloʊ] *dulce de consistencia blanda*

marsh·y ['mɑːrʃi] *adj* pantanoso

mar·tial arts [mɑːrʃl'ɑːrts] *npl* artes *fpl* marciales

mar·tial 'law ley *f* marcial

mar·tyr ['mɑːrtər] mártir *m/f*

mar·tyred ['mɑːrtərd] *adj fig* de mártir

mar·vel ['mɑːrvl] maravilla *f*
♦ **marvel at** *v/t* maravillarse de

mar·ve·lous, *Br* **mar·vel·lous** ['mɑːrvələs] *adj* maravilloso

Marx·ism ['mɑːrksɪzm] marxismo *m*

Marx·ist ['mɑːrksɪst] **1** *adj* marxista **2** *n* marxista *m/f*

mar·zi·pan ['mɑːrzɪpæn] mazapán *m*

mas·ca·ra [mæ'skærə] rímel *m*

mas·cot ['mæskət] mascota *f*

mas·cu·line ['mæskjʊlɪn] *adj* masculino

mas·cu·lin·i·ty [mæskjʊ'lɪnɪti] *(virility)* masculinidad *f*

mash [mæʃ] *v/t* hacer puré de, majar

mashed po·ta·toes [mæʃt] *npl* puré *m* de patatas *or L.Am.* papas

mask [mæsk] **1** *n* máscara *f*; *to cover mouth, nose* mascarilla *f* **2** *v/t feelings* enmascarar

'mask·ing tape cinta *f* adhesiva de pintor

mas·o·chism ['mæsəkɪzm] masoquismo *m*

mas·o·chist ['mæsəkɪst] masoquista *m/f*

ma·son ['meɪsn] cantero *m*

ma·son·ry ['meɪsnri] albañilería *f*

mas·que·rade [mæskə'reɪd] **1** *n fig* mascarada *f* **2** *v/i*: **~ as** hacerse pasar por

mass¹ [mæs] **1** *n (great amount)* gran cantidad *f*; *(body)* masa *f*; **the ~es** las masas; **~es of** F un montón de F **2** *v/i* concentrarse

mass² [mæs] REL misa *f*

mas·sa·cre ['mæsəkər] **1** *n* masacre *f*, matanza *f*; F *in sport* paliza *f* **2** *v/t* masacrar; F *in sport* dar una paliza a

mas·sage ['mæsɑːʒ] **1** *n* masaje *m* **2** *v/t* dar un masaje en; *figures* maquillar

'mas·sage par·lor, *Br* **'mas·sage par·lour** salón *m* de masajes

mas·sa·cre ['mæsəkər] masajista *m*

mas·seuse [mæ'sɜːrz] masajista *f*

mas·sive ['mæsɪv] *adj* enorme; *heart attack* muy grave

mass 'me·di·a *npl* medios *mpl* de comunicación; **mass-pro'duce** *v/t* fabricar en serie; **mass pro'duc·tion** fabricación *f* en serie

mast [mæst] *of ship* mástil *m*; *for radio signal* torre *f*

mas·ter ['mæstər] **1** *n of dog* dueño *m*, amo *m*; *of ship* patrón *m*; **be a ~ of** ser un maestro de **2** *v/t skill, language, situation* dominar

'mas·ter bed·room dormitorio *m* principal

'mas·ter key llave *f* maestra

mas·ter·ly ['mæstəli] *adj* magistral

'mas·ter·mind 1 *n* cerebro *m* **2** *v/t* dirigir, organizar; **Mas·ter of 'Arts** Máster *m* en Humanidades; **mas·ter of 'cer·e·mo·nies** maestro *m* de ceremonias; **'mas·ter·piece** obra *f* maestra

'mas·ter's (de·gree) máster *m*

mas·ter·y ['mæstərɪ] dominio *m*

mas·tur·bate ['mæstərbeɪt] *v/i* masturbarse

mat [mæt] *for floor* estera *f*; *for table* salvamanteles *m inv*

match¹ [mætʃ] *for cigarette* cerilla *f*, fósforo *m*

match² [mætʃ] **1** *n* SP partido *m*; *in chess* partida *f*; **be no ~ for s.o.** no estar a la altura de alguien; **meet one's ~** encontrar la horma de su zapato **2** *v/t (be the same as)* coincidir con; *(be in harmony with)* hacer juego con; *(equal)* igualar **3** *v/i of colors, patterns* hacer juego

'match·box caja *f* de cerillas

match·ing ['mætʃɪŋ] *adj* a juego

'match stick cerilla *f*, fósforo *m*

mate [meɪt] **1** *n of animal* pareja *f*; NAUT oficial *m/f* **2** *v/i* aparearse; **these birds ~ for life** estas aves viven con la misma pareja toda la vida

ma·te·ri·al [mə'tɪrɪəl] **1** *n (fabric)* tejido *m*; *(substance)* material *m*; *~s* materiales *mpl* **2** *adj* material

ma·te·ri·al·ism [mə'tɪrɪəlɪzm] materialismo *m*

ma·te·ri·al·ist [mətɪrɪə'lɪst] materialista *m/f*

ma·te·ri·al·is·tic [mətɪrɪə'lɪstɪk] *adj* materialista

ma·te·ri·al·ize [mə'tɪrɪəlaɪz] *v/i (appear)* aparecer; *(come into existence)* hacerse realidad

ma·ter·nal [mə'tɜːrnl] *adj* maternal

ma·ter·ni·ty [mə'tɜːrnətɪ] maternidad *f*

ma'ter·ni·ty dress vestido *m* premamá; **ma'ter·ni·ty leave** baja *f* por maternidad; **ma'ter·ni·ty ward** pabellón *m* de maternidad

math [mæθ] matemáticas *fpl*

math·e·mat·i·cal [mæθə'mætɪkl] *adj* matemático

math·e·ma·ti·cian [mæθəmə'tɪʃn] matemático(-a) *m(f)*

math·e·mat·ics [mæθ'mætɪks] matemáticas *fpl*

maths *Br* → **math**

mat·i·née ['mætɪneɪ] sesión *f* de tarde

ma·tri·arch ['meɪtrɪɑːrk] matriarca *f*

mat·ri·mo·ny ['mætrəmoʊnɪ] matrimonio *m*

matt [mæt] *adj* mate

mat·ter ['mætər] **1** *n (affair)* asunto *m*; PHYS materia *f*; **you're only making ~s worse** sólo estás empeorando las cosas; **as a ~ of course** automáticamente; **as a ~ of fact** de hecho; **what's the ~?** ¿qué pasa?; **no ~ what she says** diga lo que diga **2** *v/i* importar; **it doesn't ~** no importa

mat·ter-of-'fact *adj* tranquilo

mat·tress ['mætrɪs] colchón *m*

ma·ture [mə'tʃʊr] **1** *adj* maduro **2** *v/i of person* madurar; *of insurance policy etc* vencer

ma·tu·ri·ty [mə'tʃʊrətɪ] madurez *f*

maul [mɔːl] *v/t of lion, tiger* atacar; *of critics* destrozar

max·i·mize ['mæksɪmaɪz] *v/t* maximizar

max·i·mum ['mæksɪməm] **1** *adj* máximo; **it will cost $500 ~** costará 500 dólares como máximo **2** *n* máximo *m*

May [meɪ] mayo *m*

may [meɪ] *v/aux ◇ possibility*: **it ~ rain** puede que llueva; **you ~ be right** puede que tengas razón; **it ~ not happen** puede que no ocurra *◇ permission* poder; **~ I help / smoke?** ¿puedo ayudar / fumar?

may·be ['meɪbɪ] *adv* quizás, tal vez

'May Day el Primero de Mayo

may·o, may·on·naise ['meɪoʊ, meɪə'neɪz] mayonesa *f*

may·or [mer] alcalde *m*

maze [meɪz] laberinto *m*

MB *abbr (= megabyte)* MB (= megabyte *m*)

MBA [embiː'eɪ] *abbr (= Master of Business Administration)* MBA *m* (= Máster *m* en Administración de Empresas)

MBO [embiː'oʊ] *abbr (= management buyout)* compra de una em-

M

presa por sus directivos

MC [em'siː] *abbr* (= *master of ceremonies*) maestro *m* de ceremonias

MD [em'diː] *abbr* (= *Doctor of Medicine*) Doctor(a) *m(f)* en Medicina; (= *managing director*) director(a) *m(f)* gerente

me [miː] *pron direct & indirect object* me; *after prep* mí; *he knows* ~ me conoce; *he gave* ~ *the keys* me dio las llaves; *he sold it to* ~ me lo vendió; *this is for* ~ esto es para mí; *who do you mean,* ~? ¿a quién te refieres?, ¿a mí?; *with* ~ conmigo; *it's* ~ soy yo; *taller than* ~ más alto que yo

mead·ow ['medoʊ] prado *m*

mea·ger, *Br* **mea·gre** ['miːgər] *adj* escaso, exiguo

meal [miːl] comida *f*; *enjoy your* ~ ¡que aproveche!

'meal·time hora *f* de comer

mean¹ [miːn] *adj with money* tacaño; (*nasty*) malo, cruel; *that was a* ~ *thing to say* ha estado fatal que dijeras eso

mean² [miːn] **1** *v/t* (*pret & pp* **meant**) (*intend to say*) querer decir; (*signify*) querer decir, significar; *you weren't* ~*t to hear that* no era mi intención que oyeras eso; ~ *to do sth* tener la intención de hacer algo; *be* ~*t for* ser para; *of remark* ir dirigido a; *doesn't it* ~ *anything to you?* (*doesn't it matter?*) ¿no te importa para nada? **2** *v/i* (*pret & pp* **meant**): ~ *well* tener buena intención

mean·ing ['miːnɪŋ] *of word* significado *m*

mean·ing·ful ['miːnɪŋfʊl] *adj* (*comprehensible*) con sentido; (*constructive*), *glance* significativo

mean·ing·less ['miːnɪŋlɪs] *adj* sin sentido

means [miːnz] *npl financial* medios *mpl*; (*nsg: way*) medio *m*; *a* ~ *of transport* un medio de transporte; *by all* ~ (*certainly*) por supuesto; *by all* ~ *check my figures* comprueba mis cifras, faltaría más; *by no* ~ *rich/poor* ni mucho menos rico/pobre; *by* ~ *of* mediante

meant [ment] *pret & pp* → **mean²**

mean·time ['miːntaɪm] **1** *adv* mientras tanto **2** *n*: *in the* ~ mientras tanto

mea·sles ['miːzlz] *nsg* sarampión *m*

mea·sure ['meʒər] **1** *n* (*step*) medida *f*; *we've had a* ~ *of success* (*certain amount*) hemos tenido cierto éxito **2** *v/t & v/i* medir

♦ **measure out** *v/t area, drink, medicine* medir; *sugar, flour, ingredients* pesar

♦ **measure up** *v/i* estar a la altura (*to* de)

mea·sure·ment ['meʒərmənt] medida *f*; *system of* ~ sistema *m* de medidas

'mea·sur·ing tape cinta *f* métrica

meat [miːt] carne *f*

'meat·ball albóndiga *f*

'meat·loaf masa de carne cocinada en forma de barra de pan

me·chan·ic [mɪ'kænɪk] mecánico(-a) *m(f)*

me·chan·i·cal [mɪ'kænɪkl] *adj also fig* mecánico

me·chan·i·cal en·gi·neer ingeniero(-a) *m(f)* industrial

me·chan·i·cal en·gi·neer·ing ingeniería *f* industrial

me·chan·i·cal·ly [mɪ'kænɪklɪ] *adv also fig* mecánicamente

mech·a·nism ['mekənɪzm] mecanismo *m*

mech·a·nize ['mekənaɪz] *v/t* mecanizar

med·al ['medl] medalla *f*

med·a·list, *Br* **med·al·list** ['medəlɪst] medallista *m/f*

med·dle ['medl] *v/i* entrometerse; *don't* ~ *with the TV* no enredes con la televisión

me·di·a ['miːdɪə] *npl*: *the* ~ los medios de comunicación

'me·di·a cov·er·age cobertura *f* informativa; **'me·di·a e·vent** acontecimiento *m* informativo; **me·di·a 'hype** revuelo *m* informativo

me·di·an strip [miːdɪən'strɪp] mediana *f*

'me·di·a stud·ies ciencias *fpl* de la

información

me·di·ate ['miːdɪeɪt] v/i mediar

me·di·a·tion [miːdɪ'eɪʃn] mediación f

me·di·a·tor ['miːdɪeɪtər] mediador(a) m(f)

med·i·cal ['medɪkl] **1** adj médico **2** n reconocimiento m médico

'**med·i·cal cer·tif·i·cate** certificado m médico; '**med·i·cal ex·am·i·na·tion** reconocimiento m médico; '**med·i·cal his·to·ry** historial m médico; '**med·i·cal pro·fes·sion** profesión f médica; (doctors) médicos mpl; '**med·i·cal rec·ord** ficha f médica

Med·i·care ['medɪker] seguro de enfermedad para los ancianos en Estados Unidos

med·i·cat·ed ['medɪkeɪtɪd] adj medicinal

med·i·ca·tion [medɪ'keɪʃn] medicamento m, medicina f

me·dic·i·nal [mɪ'dɪsɪnl] adj medicinal

med·i·cine ['medsən] science medicina f; (medication) medicina f, medicamento m

'**med·i·cine cab·i·net** botiquín m

med·i·e·val [medɪ'iːvl] adj medieval

me·di·o·cre [miːdɪ'oʊkər] adj mediocre

me·di·oc·ri·ty [miːdɪ'ɑːkrətɪ] of work etc, person mediocridad f

med·i·tate ['medɪteɪt] v/i meditar

med·i·ta·tion [medɪ'teɪʃn] meditación f

Med·i·ter·ra·ne·an [medɪtə'reɪnɪən] **1** adj mediterráneo **2** n: **the ~** el Mediterráneo

me·di·um ['miːdɪəm] **1** adj (average) medio; steak a punto **2** n size talla f media; (means) medio m; (spiritualist) médium m/f

me·di·um-sized ['miːdɪəmsaɪzd] adj de tamaño medio; **me·di·um 'term**: **in the ~** a medio plazo; '**me·di·um wave** RAD onda f media

med·ley ['medlɪ] (assortment) mezcla f

meek [miːk] adj manso, dócil

meet [miːt] **1** v/t (pret & pp **met**) by appointment encontrarse con, reunirse con; by chance, of eyes encontrarse con; (get to know) conocer; (collect) ir a buscar; in competition enfrentarse con; (satisfy) satisfacer; **~ a deadline** cumplir un plazo **2** v/i (pret & pp **met**) encontrarse; in competition enfrentarse; of committee etc reunirse; **have you two met?** ¿os conocíais? **3** n SP reunión f

♦ **meet with** v/t person, opposition, approval encontrarse con; **my attempts met with failure** mis intentos fracasaron

meet·ing ['miːtɪŋ] by chance encuentro m; of committee, in business reunión f; **he's in a ~** está reunido

'**meet·ing place** lugar m de encuentro

meg·a·byte ['megəbaɪt] COMPUT megabyte m

mel·an·chol·y ['melənkəlɪ] adj melancólico

mel·low ['meloʊ] **1** adj suave **2** v/i of person suavizarse, sosegarse

me·lo·di·ous [mɪ'loʊdɪəs] adj melodioso

mel·o·dra·mat·ic [melədrə'mætɪk] adj melodramático

mel·o·dy ['melədɪ] melodía f

mel·on ['melən] melón m

melt [melt] **1** v/i fundirse, derretirse **2** v/t fundir, derretir

♦ **melt away** v/i fig desvanecerse

♦ **melt down** v/t metal fundir

melt·ing pot ['meltɪŋpɑːt] fig crisol m

mem·ber ['membər] miembro m

Mem·ber of 'Con·gress diputado(-a) m(f)

Mem·ber of 'Par·lia·ment Br diputado(-a) m(f)

mem·ber·ship ['membərʃɪp] afiliación f; (number of members) número m de miembros; **he applied for ~ of the club** solicitó ser admitido en el club

'**mem·ber·ship card** tarjeta f de socio

mem·brane ['membreɪn] membrana f

me·men·to [me'mentou] recuerdo *m*

mem·o ['memou] nota *f*

mem·oirs ['memwɑːrz] *npl* memorias *fpl*

'mem·o pad bloc *m* de notas

mem·o·ra·ble ['memərəbl] *adj* memorable

me·mo·ri·al [mɪ'mɔːrɪəl] **1** *adj* conmemorativo **2** *n* monumento *m* conmemorativo

Me'mo·ri·al Day Día *f* de los Caídos

mem·o·rize ['meməraɪz] *v/t* memorizar

mem·o·ry ['memərɪ] (*recollection*) recuerdo *m*; (*power of recollection*), COMPUT memoria *f*; **I have no ~ of the accident** no recuerdo el accidente; **have a good/bad ~** tener buena/mala memoria; **in ~ of** en memoria de

men [men] *pl* → **man**

men·ace ['menɪs] **1** *n* amenaza *f*; *person* peligro *m* **2** *v/t* amenazar

men·ac·ing ['menɪsɪŋ] *adj* amenazador

mend [mend] **1** *v/t* reparar; *clothes* coser, remendar; *shoes* remendar **2** *n*: **be on the ~** *after illness* estar recuperándose

me·ni·al ['miːnɪəl] *adj* ingrato, penoso

men·in·gi·tis [menɪn'dʒaɪtɪs] meningitis *f*

men·o·pause ['menəpɔːz] menopausia *f*

'men's room servicio *m* de caballeros

men·stru·ate ['menstrʊeɪt] *v/i* menstruar

men·stru·a·tion [menstrʊ'eɪʃn] menstruación *f*

men·tal ['mentl] *adj* mental; F (*crazy*) chiflado F, pirado F

men·tal a'rith·me·tic cálculo *m* mental; **men·tal 'cru·el·ty** crueldad *f* mental; **'men·tal hos·pi·tal** hospital *m* psiquiátrico; **men·tal 'ill·ness** enfermedad *f* mental

men·tal·i·ty [men'tælətɪ] mentalidad *f*

men·tal·ly ['mentəlɪ] *adv* (*inwardly*)

mentalmente

men·tal·ly 'hand·i·capped *adj* con minusvalía psíquica

men·tal·ly 'ill *adj*: **be ~** sufrir una enfermedad mental

men·tion ['menʃn] **1** *n* mención *f*; **she made no ~ of it** no lo mencionó **2** *v/t* mencionar; **don't ~ it** (*you're welcome*) no hay de qué

men·tor ['mentɔːr] mentor(a) *m(f)*

men·u ['menuː] *for food*, COMPUT menú *m*

mer·ce·na·ry ['mɜːrsɪnərɪ] **1** *adj* mercenario **2** *n* MIL mercenario(-a) *m(f)*

mer·chan·dise ['mɜːrtʃəndaɪz] mercancías *fpl*, *L.Am.* mercadería *f*

mer·chant ['mɜːrtʃənt] comerciante *m/f*

mer·chant 'bank *Br* banco *m* mercantil

mer·ci·ful ['mɜːrsɪfəl] *adj* compasivo, piadoso

mer·ci·ful·ly ['mɜːrsɪfəlɪ] *adv* (*thankfully*) afortunadamente

mer·ci·less ['mɜːrsɪlɪs] *adj* despiadado

mer·cu·ry ['mɜːrkjʊrɪ] mercurio *m*

mer·cy ['mɜːrsɪ] clemencia *f*, compasión *f*; **be at s.o.'s ~** estar a merced de alguien

mere [mɪr] *adj* mero, simple

mere·ly ['mɪrlɪ] *adv* meramente, simplemente

merge [mɜːrdʒ] *v/i* *of two lines etc* juntarse, unirse; *of companies* fusionarse

merg·er ['mɜːrdʒər] COM fusión *f*

mer·it ['merɪt] **1** *n* (*worth*) mérito *m*; (*advantage*) ventaja *f*; **she got the job on ~** consiguió el trabajo por méritos propios **2** *v/t* merecer

mer·ry ['merɪ] *adj* alegre; **Merry Christmas!** ¡Feliz Navidad!

'mer·ry-go-round tiovivo *m*

mesh [meʃ] malla *f*

mess [mes] (*untidiness*) desorden *m*; (*trouble*) lío *m*; **I'm in a bit of a ~** estoy metido en un lío; **be a ~** *of room, desk* estar desordenado; *of hair* estar revuelto; *of situation, s.o.'s life* ser un desastre

♦**mess around 1** *v/i* enredar **2** *v/t person* jugar con

♦**mess around with** *v/t* enredar con; *s.o.'s wife* tener un lío con

♦**mess up** *v/t room, papers* desordenar; *task* convertir en una chapuza; *plans, marriage* estropear, arruinar

mes·sage ['mesɪdʒ] *also of movie etc* mensaje *m*

mes·sen·ger ['mesɪndʒər] (*courier*) mensajero(-a) *m(f)*

mess·y ['mesɪ] *adj room, person* desordenado; *job* sucio; *divorce, situation* desagradable

met [met] *pret & pp →* **meet**

me·tab·o·lism [mə'tæbəlɪzm] metabolismo *m*

met·al ['metl] **1** *n* metal *m* **2** *adj* metálico

me·tal·lic [mɪ'tælɪk] *adj* metálico

met·a·phor ['metəfər] metáfora *f*

me·te·or ['miːtɪər] meteoro *m*

me·te·or·ic [miːtɪ'ɑːrɪk] *adj fig* meteórico

me·te·or·ite ['miːtɪəraɪt] meteorito *m*

me·te·or·o·log·i·cal [miːtɪrə'lɑːdʒɪkl] *adj* meteorológico

me·te·or·ol·o·gist [miːtɪə'rɑːlədʒɪst] meteorólogo(-a) *m(f)*

me·te·or·ol·o·gy [miːtɪə'rɑːlədʒɪ] meteorología *f*

me·ter[1] ['miːtər] *for gas, electricity* contador *m*; (*parking ~*) parquímetro *m*

me·ter[2] ['miːtər] *unit of length* metro *m*

'me·ter read·ing lectura *f* del contador

meth·od ['meθəd] método *m*

me·thod·i·cal [mɪ'θɑːdɪkl] *adj* metódico

me·thod·i·cal·ly [mɪ'θɑːdɪklɪ] *adv* metódicamente

me·tic·u·lous [mə'tɪkjʊləs] *adj* meticuloso, minucioso

me·tre *Br →* **meter**[2]

met·ric ['metrɪk] *adj* métrico

me·trop·o·lis [mɪ'trɑːpəlɪs] metrópolis *f inv*

met·ro·pol·i·tan [metrə'pɑːlɪtən] *adj* metropolitano

mew [mjuː] *→* **miaow**

Mex·i·can ['meksɪkən] **1** *adj* mexicano, mejicano **2** *n* mexicano(-a) *m(f)*, mejicano(-a) *m(f)*

Mex·i·co ['meksɪkou] México, Méjico

Mex·i·co 'Cit·y *n* Ciudad *f* de México, *Mex* México, *Mex* el Distrito Federal, *Mex* el D.F.

mez·za·nine (floor) ['mezəniːn] entresuelo *m*

mi·aow [mɪau] **1** *n* maullido *m* **2** *v/i* maullar

mice [maɪs] *pl →* **mouse**

mick·ey mouse [mɪkɪ'maus] *adj pej* P *course, qualification* de tres al cuarto P

mi·cro·bi·ol·o·gy [maɪkroubaɪ'ɑːlədʒɪ] microbiología *f*; **'mi·cro·chip** microchip *m*; **'mi·cro·cli·mate** microclima *m*; **mi·cro·cosm** ['maɪkroukɑːzm] microcosmos *m inv*; **'mi·cro·e·lec·tron·ics** microelectrónica *f*; **'mi·cro·film** microfilm *m*; **'mi·cro·or·gan·ism** microorganismo *m*; **'mi·cro·phone** micrófono *m*; **mi·cro·proc·es·sor** microprocesador *m*; **'mi·cro·scope** microscopio *m*; **mi·cro·scop·ic** [maɪkrə'skɑːpɪk] *adj* microscópico; **'mi·cro·wave** oven microondas *m inv*

mid·air [mɪd'er]: **in ~** pleno vuelo

mid·day [mɪd'deɪ] mediodía *m*

mid·dle ['mɪdl] **1** *adj* del medio; *the ~ child of five* el tercero de cinco hermanos **2** *n* medio *m*; *it's the ~ of the night!* ¡estamos en plena noche!; *in the ~ of* of floor, room en medio de; of period of time a mitad *or* mediados de; *in the ~ of winter* en pleno invierno; *be in the ~ of doing sth* estar ocupado haciendo algo

'mid·dle-aged *adj* de mediana edad; **'Mid·dle Ag·es** *npl* Edad *f* Media; **mid·dle-'class** *adj* de clase media; **'mid·dle class(es)** clases *fpl* medias; **Mid·dle 'East** Oriente *m* Medio; **'mid·dle·man** intermediario *m*;

mid·dle 'man·age·ment mandos *mpl* intermedios; **mid·dle 'name** segundo nombre *m*; **'mid·dle-weight** *boxer* peso *m* medio

mid·dling ['mɪdlɪŋ] *adj* regular

mid·field·er [mɪd'fiːldər] centrocampista *m/f*

midg·et ['mɪdʒɪt] *adj* en miniatura

'mid·night ['mɪdnaɪt] medianoche *f*; **at ~** a medianoche; **'mid·sum·mer** pleno verano *m*; **'mid·way** *adv*: **we'll stop for lunch ~** pararemos para comer a mitad de camino; **~ through the meeting** a mitad de la reunión; **'mid·week** *adv* a mitad de semana; **'Mid·west** Medio Oeste *m* (de Estados Unidos); **'mid·wife** comadrona *f*; **'mid·win·ter** pleno invierno *m*

might[1] [maɪt] *v/aux* poder, ser posible que; **I ~ be late** puede *or* es posible que llegue tarde; **it ~ never happen** puede *or* es posible que no ocurra nunca; **he ~ have left** a lo mejor se ha ido; **you ~ have told me!** ¡me lo podías haber dicho!

might[2] [maɪt] (*power*) poder *m*, fuerza *f*

might·y ['maɪtɪ] **1** *adj* poderoso **2** *adv* F (*extremely*) muy, cantidad de F

mi·graine ['miːɡreɪn] migraña *f*

mi·grant 'work·er ['maɪɡrənt] trabajador(a) *m(f)* itinerante

mi·grate [maɪ'ɡreɪt] *v/i* emigrar

mi·gra·tion [maɪ'ɡreɪʃn] emigración *f*

mike [maɪk] F micro *m* F

mild [maɪld] *adj weather, climate* apacible; *cheese, voice* suave; *curry etc* no muy picante; *person* afable, apacible

mil·dew ['mɪlduː] moho *m*

mild·ly ['maɪldlɪ] *adv say sth* con suavidad; *spicy* ligeramente; **to put it ~** por no decir algo peor

mild·ness ['maɪldnɪs] *of weather, voice* suavidad *f*; *of person* afabilidad *f*

mile [maɪl] milla *f*; **be ~s better/easier** F ser mil veces mejor / más fácil F

mile·age ['maɪlɪdʒ] millas *fpl* recorridas; **unlimited ~** kilometraje *m* ilimitado

'mile·stone *fig* hito *m*

mil·i·tant ['mɪlɪtənt] **1** *adj* militante **2** *n* militante *m/f*

mil·i·ta·ry ['mɪlɪterɪ] **1** *adj* militar **2** *n*: **the ~** el ejército, las fuerzas armadas

mil·i·ta·ry a'cad·e·my academia *f* militar; **mil·i·ta·ry po'lice** policía *f* militar; **mil·i·tar·y 'serv·ice** servicio *m* militar

mi·li·tia [mɪ'lɪʃə] milicia *f*

milk [mɪlk] **1** *n* leche *f* **2** *v/t* ordeñar

milk 'choc·o·late chocolate *m* con leche; **milk of mag'ne·sia** leche *f* de magnesia; **'milk·shake** batido *m*

'milk·y ['mɪlkɪ] *adj with lots of milk* con mucha leche; *made with milk* con leche

Milk·y 'Way Vía *f* Láctea

mill [mɪl] *for grain* molino *m*; *for textiles* fábrica *f* de tejidos

♦ **mill around** *v/i* pulular

mil·len·ni·um [mɪ'lenɪəm] milenio *m*

mil·li·gram, *Br* **mil·li·gramme** ['mɪlɪɡræm] miligramo *m*

mil·li·me·ter, *Br* **mil·li·me·tre** ['mɪlɪmiːtər] milímetro *m*

mil·lion ['mɪljən] millón *m*

mil·lion·aire [mɪljə'ner] millonario(-a) *m(f)*

mime [maɪm] *v/t* representar con gestos

mim·ic ['mɪmɪk] **1** *n* imitador(a) *m(f)* **2** *v/t* (*pret & pp* **-ked**) imitar

mince [mɪns] *v/t* picar

'mince·meat carne *f* picada

mince 'pie empanada *f* de carne picada

mind [maɪnd] **1** *n* mente *f*; **it's uppermost in my ~** es lo que más me preocupa; **it's all in your ~** son imaginaciones tuyas; **be out of one's ~** haber perdido el juicio; **bear** *o* **keep sth in ~** recordar; **I've a good ~ to …** estoy considerando seriamente …; **change one's ~** cambiar de opinión; **it didn't enter my ~** no se me ocurrió; **give s.o. a piece of one's ~** cantarle a alguien las cuarenta; **make up one's ~** decidirse; **have something on one's ~** tener algo en la cabeza; **keep one's ~ on sth** concentrarse en algo **2** v/t (*look after*) cuidar (de); (*heed*) prestar atención a; **I don't ~ what we do** no me importa lo que hagamos; **do you ~ if I smoke?, do you ~ my smoking?** ¿le importa que fume?; **would you ~ opening the window?** ¿le importaría abrir la ventana?; **~ the step!** ¡cuidado con el escalón!; **~ your own business!** ¡métete en tus asuntos! **3** v/i: **~!** ¡ten cuidado!; **never ~!** ¡no importa!; **I don't ~** no me importa, me da igual

mind-bog·gling ['maɪndbɒglɪŋ] adj increíble

mind·less ['maɪndlɪs] adj violence gratuito

mine[1] [maɪn] pron el mío, la mía; **~ are red** los míos son rojos; **that book is ~** eso libro es mío; **a cousin of ~** un primo mío

mine[2] [maɪn] **1** n for coal etc mina f **2** v/i: **~ for** extraer

mine[3] [maɪn] **1** n (*explosive*) mina f **2** v/t minar

'mine·field MIL campo m de minas; fig campo m minado

min·er ['maɪnər] minero(-a) m(f)

min·e·ral ['mɪnərəl] n mineral m

'min·e·ral wa·ter agua f mineral

'mine·sweep·er NAUT dragaminas m inv

min·gle ['mɪŋgl] v/i of sounds, smells mezclarse; at party alternar

min·i ['mɪni] skirt minifalda f

min·i·a·ture ['mɪnɪtʃər] adj en miniatura

'min·i·bus microbús m

min·i·mal ['mɪnɪməl] adj mínimo

min·i·mal·ism ['mɪnɪməlɪzm] minimalismo m

min·i·mize ['mɪnɪmaɪz] v/t risk, delay minimizar, reducir al mínimo; (*downplay*) minimizar, quitar importancia a

min·i·mum ['mɪnɪməm] **1** adj mínimo **2** n mínimo m

min·i·mum 'wage salario m mínimo

min·ing ['maɪnɪŋ] minería f

'min·i·se·ries nsg TV miniserie f

'min·i·skirt minifalda f

min·is·ter ['mɪnɪstər] POL ministro(-a) m(f); REL ministro(-a) m(f), pastor(a) m(f)

min·is·te·ri·al [mɪnɪ'stɪrɪəl] adj ministerial

min·is·try ['mɪnɪstri] POL ministerio m

mink [mɪŋk] animal, fur visón m; coat abrigo m de visón

mi·nor ['maɪnər] **1** adj problem, setback menor, pequeño; operation, argument de poca importancia; aches and pains leve; **in D ~** MUS en D menor **2** n LAW menor m/f de edad

mi·nor·i·ty [maɪ'nɒrətɪ] minoría f, **be in the ~** ser minoría

mint [mɪnt] n herb menta f; chocolate pastilla f de chocolate con sabor a menta; hard candy caramelo m de menta

mi·nus ['maɪnəs] **1** n (~ sign) (signo m de) menos **2** prep menos; **temperatures of ~ 18** temperaturas de 18 grados bajo cero

mi·nus·cule ['mɪnəskjuːl] adj minúsculo

mi·nute[1] ['mɪnɪt] of time minuto m; **in a ~** (*soon*) en un momento; **just a ~** un momento

mi·nute[2] [maɪ'nuːt] adj (*tiny*) diminuto, minúsculo; (*detailed*) minucioso; **in ~ detail** minuciosamente

'mi·nute hand ['mɪnɪt] minutero m

mi·nute·ly [maɪ'nuːtlɪ] adv in detail minuciosamente; (*very slightly*) mínimamente

min·utes ['mɪnɪts] npl of meeting acta(s) f(pl)

mir·a·cle ['mɪrəkl] milagro m

mi·rac·u·lous [mɪ'rækjʊləs] adj milagroso

mi·rac·u·lous·ly [mɪ'rækjʊləslɪ] adv milagrosamente

mi·rage ['mɪrɑːʒ] espejismo m

mir·ror ['mɪrər] **1** n espejo m; MOT (espejo m) retrovisor m **2** v/t reflejar

mis·an·thro·pist [mɪ'zænθrəpɪst] misántropo(-a) m(f)

mis·ap·pre·hen·sion [mɪsæprɪ'hen-

M

[n]: **be under a ~** estar equivocado

mis·be·have [mɪsbə'heɪv] v/i portarse mal

mis·be·hav·ior, Br **mis·be·hav·iour** [mɪsbə'heɪvɪər] mal comportamiento m

mis·cal·cu·late [mɪs'kælkjʊleɪt] v/t & v/i calcular mal

mis·cal·cu·la·tion [mɪs'kælkjʊleɪʃn] error m de cálculo

mis·car·riage ['mɪskærɪdʒ] MED aborto m (espontáneo); **~ of justice** error m judicial

mis·car·ry ['mɪskærɪ] v/i (pret & pp **-ied**) of plan fracasar

mis·cel·la·ne·ous [mɪsə'leɪnɪəs] adj diverso; **put it in the file marked "~"** ponlo en la carpeta de "varios"

mis·chief ['mɪstʃɪf] (naughtiness) travesura f, trastada f

mis·chie·vous ['mɪstʃɪvəs] adj (naughty) travieso; (malicious) malicioso

mis·con·cep·tion [mɪskən'sepʃn] idea f equivocada

mis·con·duct [mɪs'kɑːndʌkt] mala conducta f

mis·con·strue [mɪskən'struː] v/t malinterpretar

mis·de·mea·nor, Br **mis·de·mea·nour** [mɪsdə'miːnər] falta f, delito m menor

mi·ser ['maɪzər] avaro(-a) m(f)

mis·e·ra·ble ['mɪzrəbl] adj (unhappy) triste, infeliz; weather, performance horroroso

mi·ser·ly ['maɪzərlɪ] adj person avaro; **a ~ \$150** 150 míseros dólares

mi·se·ry ['mɪzərɪ] (unhappiness) tristeza f, infelicidad f; (wretchedness) miseria f

mis·fire [mɪs'faɪr] v/i of joke, scheme salir mal

mis·fit ['mɪsfɪt] in society inadaptado(-a) m(f)

mis·for·tune [mɪs'fɔːrtʃən] desgracia f

mis·giv·ings [mɪs'gɪvɪŋz] npl recelo m, duda f

mis·guid·ed [mɪs'gaɪdɪd] adj person equivocado; attempt, plan desacer-

tado

mis·han·dle [mɪs'hændl] v/t situation llevar mal

mis·hap ['mɪshæp] contratiempo m

mis·in·form [mɪsɪn'fɔːrm] v/t informar mal

mis·in·ter·pret [mɪsɪn'tɜːrprɪt] v/t malinterpretar

mis·in·ter·pre·ta·tion [mɪsɪntɜːrprɪ-'teɪʃn] mala interpretación f

mis·judge [mɪs'dʒʌdʒ] v/t person, situation juzgar mal

mis·lay [mɪs'leɪ] v/t (pret & pp **-laid**) perder

mis·lead [mɪs'liːd] v/t (pret & pp **-led**) engañar

mis·lead·ing [mɪs'liːdɪŋ] adj engañoso

mis·man·age [mɪs'mænɪdʒ] v/t gestionar mal

mis·man·age·ment [mɪs'mænɪdʒmənt] mala gestión f

mis·match ['mɪsmætʃ]: **there's a ~ between the two sets of figures** los dos grupos de cifras no se corresponden

mis·placed ['mɪspleɪst] adj loyalty inmerecido; enthusiasm inoportuno

mis·print ['mɪsprɪnt] errata f

mis·pro·nounce [mɪsprə'naʊns] v/t pronunciar mal

mis·pro·nun·ci·a·tion [mɪsprənʌnsɪ'eɪʃn] pronunciación f incorrecta

mis·read [mɪs'riːd] v/t (pret & pp **-read** [red]) word, figures leer mal; situation malinterpretar

mis·rep·re·sent [mɪsreprɪ'zent] v/t deformar, tergiversar

miss¹ [mɪs]: **Miss Smith** la señorita Smith; **~!** ¡señorita!

miss² [mɪs] **1** n SP fallo m; **give sth a ~** meeting, party etc no ir a algo **2** v/t target no dar en; emotionally echar de menos; bus, train, airplane perder; (not notice) pasar por alto; (not be present at) perderse; **I ducked and he ~ed me** me agaché y no me dio; **you just ~ed her** (she's just left) se acaba de marchar; **we must have ~ed the turnoff** nos hemos debido pasar el desvío; **you don't ~ much!**

¡no se te escapa una!; **~ a class** faltar a una clase **3** v/i fallar

mis·shap·en [mɪsˈʃeɪpən] adj deforme

mis·sile [ˈmɪsəl] misil m; (sth thrown) arma f arrojadiza

miss·ing [ˈmɪsɪŋ] adj desaparecido; **be ~** of person, plane haber desaparecido; **the ~ money** el dinero que falta

mis·sion [ˈmɪʃn] task misión f; people delegación f

mis·sion·a·ry [ˈmɪʃənrɪ] REL misionero(-a) m(f)

mis·spell [mɪsˈspel] v/t escribir incorrectamente

mist [mɪst] neblina f

♦ **mist over** v/i of eyes empañarse

♦ **mist up** v/i of mirror, window empañarse

mis·take [mɪˈsteɪk] **1** n error m, equivocación f; **make a ~** cometer un error or una equivocación, equivocarse; **by ~** por error or equivocación **2** v/t (pret **mistook**, pp **mistaken**) confundir; **~ X for Y** confundir X con Y

mis·tak·en [mɪˈsteɪkən] **1** adj erróneo, equivocado; **be ~** estar equivocado **2** pp → **mistake**

mis·ter [ˈmɪstər] → **Mr**

mis·took [mɪˈstʊk] pret → **mistake**

mis·tress [ˈmɪstrɪs] lover amante f, querida f; of servant ama f; of dog dueña f, ama f

mis·trust [mɪsˈtrʌst] **1** n desconfianza f (**of** en) **2** v/t desconfiar de

mist·y [ˈmɪstɪ] adj weather neblinoso; eyes empañado; color borroso

mis·un·der·stand [mɪsʌndərˈstænd] v/t (pret & pp **-stood**) entender mal

mis·un·der·stand·ing [mɪsʌndərˈstændɪŋ] (mistake) malentendido m; (argument) desacuerdo m

mis·use n [mɪsˈjuːs] uso m indebido **2** v/t [mɪsˈjuːz] usar indebidamente

miti·ga·ting cir·cum·stan·ces [ˈmɪtɪgeɪtɪŋ] npl circunstancias fpl atenuantes

mitt [mɪt] in baseball guante m de

béisbol

mit·ten [ˈmɪtən] mitón m

mix [mɪks] **1** n (mixture) mezcla f; cooking: ready to use preparado m **2** v/t mezclar; cement preparar; **~ the flour in well** mezclar la harina bien **3** v/i socially relacionarse

♦ **mix up** v/t (confuse) confundir (**with** con); (put in wrong order) revolver, desordenar; **be mixed up** emotionally tener problemas emocionales; of figures estar confundido; of papers estar revuelto or desordenado; **be mixed up in** estar metido en; **get mixed up with** verse liado con

♦ **mix with** v/t (associate with) relacionarse con

mixed [mɪkst] adj feelings contradictorio; reactions, reviews variado

mixed 'mar·riage matrimonio m mixto

mix·er [ˈmɪksər] for food batidora f; drink refresco m (para mezclar con bebida alcohólica); **she's a good ~** es muy sociable

mix·ture [ˈmɪkstʃər] mezcla f; medicine preparado m

mix-up [ˈmɪksʌp] confusión f

moan [moʊn] **1** n of pain gemido m **2** v/i in pain gemir

mob [mɑːb] **1** n muchedumbre f **2** v/t (pret & pp **-bed**) asediar, acosar

mo·bile [ˈmoʊbəl] **1** adj person con movilidad; (that can be moved) móvil; **she's a lot less ~ now** ahora tiene mucha menos movilidad **2** n móvil m

mo·bile 'home casa f caravana

mo·bile 'phone Br teléfono m móvil

mo·bil·i·ty [məˈbɪlətɪ] movilidad f

mob·ster [ˈmɑːbstər] gángster m

mock [mɑːk] **1** adj fingido, simulado; **~ exams/elections** exámenes mpl/elecciones fpl de prueba **2** v/t burlarse de

mock·er·y [ˈmɑːkərɪ] (derision) burlas fpl; (travesty) farsa f

mock-up [ˈmɑːkʌp] (model) maqueta f, modelo m

mode [moʊd] (form), COMPUT modo

m; **~ of transportation** medio *m* de transporte

mod·el ['mɑːdl] **1** *adj employee, husband* modélico, modelo; **~ boat / plane** maqueta *f* de un barco / avión **2** *n miniature* maqueta *f,* modelo *m;* (*pattern*) modelo *m;* (*fashion ~*) modelo *m/f;* **male ~** modelo *m* **3** *v/t* (*pret & pp* **-ed,** *Br* **-led**): **~ clothes** trabajar de modelo; **she ~s swimsuits** trabaja de modelo de bañadores **4** *v/i* (*pret & pp* **-ed,** *Br* **-led**) *for designer* trabajar de modelo; *for artist, photographer* posar

mo·dem ['moʊdem] módem *m*

mod·e·rate 1 *adj* ['mɑːdərət] moderado **2** *n* ['mɑːdərət] POL moderado(-a) *m(f)* **3** *v/t* ['mɑːdəreit] moderar

mod·e·rate·ly ['mɑːdərətlɪ] *adv* medianamente, razonablemente

mod·e·ra·tion [mɑːdə'reɪʃn] moderación *f;* **in ~** con moderación

mod·ern ['mɑːdn] *adj* moderno; **in the ~ world** en el mundo contemporáneo

mod·ern·i·za·tion [mɑːdənaɪ'zeɪʃn] modernización *f*

mod·ern·ize ['mɑːdənaɪz] **1** *v/t* modernizar **2** *v/i of business, country* modernizarse

mod·ern 'lan·gua·ges *npl* lenguas *fpl* modernas

mod·est ['mɑːdɪst] *adj* modesto

mod·es·ty ['mɑːdɪstɪ] modestia *f*

mod·i·fi·ca·tion [mɑːdɪfɪ'keɪʃn] modificación *f*

mod·i·fy ['mɑːdɪfaɪ] *v/t* (*pret & pp* **-ied**) modificar

mod·u·lar ['mɑːdʊlər] *adj furniture* por módulos

mod·ule ['mɑːduːl] módulo *m*

moist [mɔɪst] *adj* húmedo

moist·en ['mɔɪsn] *v/t* humedecer

mois·ture ['mɔɪstʃər] humedad *f*

mois·tur·iz·er ['mɔɪstʃəraɪzər] *for skin* crema *f* hidratante

mo·lar ['moʊlər] muela *f,* molar *m*

mo·las·ses [mə'læsɪz] *nsg* melaza *f*

mold¹ [moʊld] *on food* moho *m*

mold² [moʊld] **1** *n* molde *m* **2** *v/t clay,*

character moldear

mold·y ['moʊldɪ] *adj food* mohoso

mole [moʊl] *on skin* lunar *m*

mo·lec·u·lar [mə'lekjʊlər] *adj* molecular

mol·e·cule ['mɑːlɪkjuːl] molécula *f*

mo·lest [mə'lest] *v/t child, woman* abusar sexualmente de

mol·ly·cod·dle ['mɑːlɪkɑːdl] *v/t* F mimar, consentir

mol·ten ['moʊltən] *adj* fundido

mom [mɑːm] F mamá *f*

mo·ment ['moʊmənt] momento *m;* **at the ~** en estos momentos, ahora mismo; **for the ~** por el momento, por ahora

mo·men·tar·i·ly [moʊmən'terɪlɪ] *adv* (*for a moment*) momentáneamente; (*in a moment*) de un momento a otro

mo·men·ta·ry ['moʊməntərɪ] *adj* momentáneo

mo·men·tous [mə'mentəs] *adj* trascendental, muy importante

mo·men·tum [mə'mentəm] impulso *m*

mon·arch ['mɑːnərk] monarca *m/f*

mon·ar·chy ['mɑːnərkɪ] monarquía *f*

mon·as·te·ry ['mɑːnəsterɪ] monasterio *m*

mo·nas·tic [mə'næstɪk] *adj* monástico

Mon·day ['mʌndeɪ] lunes *m inv*

mon·e·ta·ry ['mɑːnɪterɪ] *adj* monetario

mon·ey ['mʌnɪ] dinero *m*

'mon·ey belt faltriquera *f;* **'mon·ey·lend·er** prestamista *m/f;* **'mon·ey mar·ket** mercado *m* monetario; **'mon·ey or·der** giro *m* postal

mon·grel ['mʌŋgrəl] perro *m* cruzado

mon·i·tor [mɑː'niːtər] **1** *n* COMPUT monitor *m* **2** *v/t* controlar

monk [mʌŋk] monje *m*

mon·key ['mʌŋkɪ] mono *m;* F *child* diablillo *m* F

♦ **monkey around with** *v/t* F enredar con

'mon·key wrench llave *f* inglesa

mon·o·gram ['mɑːnəgræm] monograma *m*

mon·o·grammed ['mɑːnəgræmd] *adj* con monograma

mon·o·log, *Br* **mon·o·logue** ['mɑːnəlɑːg] monólogo *m*

mo·nop·o·lize [mə'nɑːpəlaız] *v/t* monopolizar

mo·nop·o·ly [mə'nɑːpəlɪ] monopolio *m*

mo·not·o·nous [mə'nɑːtənəs] *adj* monótono

mo·not·o·ny [mə'nɑːtənɪ] monotonía *f*

mon·soon [mɑːn'suːn] monzón *m*

mon·ster ['mɑːnstər] *n* monstruo *m*

mon·stros·i·ty [mɑːn'strɑːsətɪ] monstruosidad *f*

mon·strous ['mɑːnstrəs] *adj* (*frightening, huge*) monstruoso; (*shocking*) escandaloso

month [mʌnθ] mes *m*; *how much do you pay a ~?* ¿cuánto pagas al mes?

month·ly ['mʌnθlɪ] **1** *adj* mensual **2** *adv* mensualmente **3** *n magazine* revista *f* mensual

mon·u·ment ['mɑːnʊmənt] monumento *m*

mon·u·ment·al [mɑːnʊ'mentl] *adj fig* monumental

mood [muːd] (*frame of mind*) humor *m*; (*bad ~*) mal humor *m*; *of meeting, country* atmósfera *f*; *be in a good / bad ~* estar de buen / mal humor; *I'm in the ~ for a pizza* me apetece una pizza

mood·y ['muːdɪ] *adj* temperamental; (*bad-tempered*) malhumorado

moon [muːn] *n* luna *f*

'moon·light 1 *n* luz *f* de luna **2** *v/i* F estar pluriempleado irregularmente; *he's ~ing as a barman* tiene un segundo empleo de camarero

'moon·lit *adj* iluminado por la luna

moor [mʊr] *v/t boat* atracar

moor·ing ['mʊrɪŋ] atracadero *m*

moose [muːs] alce *m* americano

mop [mɑːp] **1** *n for floor* fregona *f*; *for dishes* estropajo *m* (*con mango*) **2** *v/t* (*pret & pp -ped*) *floor* fregar; *eyes, face* limpiar

♦ **mop up** *v/t* limpiar; MIL acabar con

mope [moʊp] *v/i* estar abatido

mor·al ['mɔːrəl] **1** *adj* moral; *person, behavior* moralista **2** *n of story* moraleja *f*; **~s** moral *f*, moralidad *f*

mo·rale [mə'ræl] moral *f*

mo·ral·i·ty [mə'rælətɪ] moralidad *f*

mor·bid ['mɔːrbɪd] *adj* morboso

more [mɔːr] **1** *adj* más; *there are no eggs* no quedan huevos; *some tea?* ¿más té?; *~ and ~ students / time* cada vez más estudiantes / tiempo **2** *adv* más; *~ important* más importante; *~ often* más a menudo; *~ and ~* cada vez más; *~ or less* más o menos; *once ~* una vez más; *he paid ~ than $100 for it* pagó más de 100 dólares por él; *he earns ~ than I do* gana más que yo; *I don't live there any ~* ya no vivo allí **3** *pron* más; *do you want some ~?* ¿quieres más?; *a little ~* un poco más

more·o·ver [mɔːr'roʊvər] *adv* además, lo que es más

morgue [mɔːrg] depósito *m* de cadáveres

morn·ing ['mɔːrnɪŋ] mañana *f*; *in the ~* por la mañana; *this ~* esta mañana; *tomorrow ~* mañana por la mañana; *good ~* buenos días

morn·ing 'sick·ness náuseas *fpl* matutinas (*típicas del embarazo*)

mo·ron ['mɔːrɑːn] F imbécil *m/f* F, subnormal *m/f* F

mo·rose [mə'roʊs] *adj* hosco, malhumorado

mor·phine ['mɔːrfiːn] morfina *f*

mor·sel ['mɔːrsl] pedacito *m*

mor·tal ['mɔːrtl] **1** *adj* mortal **2** *n* mortal *m/f*

mor·tal·i·ty [mɔːr'tælətɪ] mortalidad *f*

mor·tar¹ ['mɔːrtər] MIL mortero *m*

mor·tar² ['mɔːrtər] (*cement*) mortero *m*, argamasa *f*

mort·gage ['mɔːrgɪdʒ] **1** *n* hipoteca *f*, préstamo *m* hipotecario **2** *v/t* hipotecar

mor·ti·cian [mɔːr'tɪʃn] encargado(-a) *m(f)* de una funeraria

mor·tu·a·ry ['mɔːrtʊerɪ] depósito *m* de cadáveres

mo·sa·ic [moʊ'zeɪɪk] mosaico *m*

M

Mos·cow ['mɑːskaʊ] Moscú
Mos·lem ['mʊzlɪm] **1** *adj* musulmán **2** *n* musulmán(-ana) *m(f)*
mosque [mɑːsk] mezquita *f*
mos·qui·to [mɑːs'kiːtoʊ] mosquito *m*
moss [mɑːs] musgo *m*
moss·y ['mɑːsɪ] *adj* cubierto de musgo
most [moʊst] **1** *adj* la mayoría de **2** *adv* (*very*) muy, sumamente; *the ~ beautiful/interesting* el más hermoso/interesante; *that's the one I like ~* ése es el que más me gusta; *~ of all* sobre todo **3** *pron* la mayoría de; *I've read ~ of her novels* he leído la mayoría de sus novelas; *at* (*the*) *~* como mucho; *make the ~ of* aprovechar al máximo
most·ly ['moʊstlɪ] *adv* principalmente, sobre todo
mo·tel [moʊ'tel] motel *m*
moth [mɑːθ] mariposa *f* nocturna; (*clothes ~*) polilla *f*
'moth·ball bola *f* de naftalina
moth·er ['mʌðər] **1** *n* madre *f* **2** *v/t* mimar
'moth·er·board COMPUT placa *f* madre
'moth·er·hood maternidad *f*
Moth·er·ing 'Sun·day → *Mother's Day*
'moth·er-in-law (*pl* **mothers-in-law**) suegra *f*
moth·er·ly ['mʌðərlɪ] *adj* maternal
moth·er-of-'pearl nácar *m*;
'Moth·er's Day Día *f* de la Madre;
'moth·er tongue lengua *f* materna
mo·tif [moʊ'tiːf] motivo *m*
mo·tion ['moʊʃn] **1** *n* (*movement*) movimiento *m*; (*proposal*) moción *f*; *put o set things in ~* poner las cosas en marcha **2** *v/t*: *he ~ed me forward* me indicó con un gesto que avanzara
mo·tion·less ['moʊʃnlɪs] *adj* inmóvil
mo·ti·vate ['moʊtɪveɪt] *v/t person* motivar
mo·ti·va·tion [moʊtɪ'veɪʃn] motivación *f*
mo·tive ['moʊtɪv] motivo *m*

mo·tor ['moʊtər] motor *m*
'mo·tor·bike moto *f*; **'mo·tor·boat** lancha *f* motora; **mo·tor·cade** ['moʊtəkeɪd] caravana *f* de coches; **'mo·tor·cy·cle** motocicleta *f*; **'mo·tor·cy·clist** motociclista *m/f*; **'mo·tor home** autocaravana *f*
mo·tor·ist ['moʊtərɪst] conductor(a) *m(f)*, automovilista *m/f*
'mo·tor me·chan·ic mecánico(-a) *m(f)* (de automóviles); **'mo·tor rac·ing** carreras *fpl* de coches; **'mo·tor·scoot·er** vespa® *f*; **'mo·tor ve·hi·cle** vehículo *m* de motor; **'mo·tor·way** *Br* autopista *f*
mot·to ['mɑːtoʊ] lema *m*
mould *etc Br* → **mold** *etc*
mound [maʊnd] montículo *m*
mount [maʊnt] **1** *n* (*mountain*) monte *m*; (*horse*) montura *f*; *Mount McKinley* el Monte McKinley **2** *v/t steps* subir; *horse, bicycle* montar en; *campaign, photo* montar **3** *v/i* aumentar, crecer
♦ mount up *v/i* acumularse
moun·tain ['maʊntɪn] montaña *f*
'moun·tain bike bicicleta *f* de montaña
moun·tain·eer [maʊntɪ'nɪr] montañero(-a) *m(f)*, alpinista *m/f*, *L.Am.* andinista *m/f*
moun·tain·eer·ing [maʊntɪ'nɪrɪŋ] montañismo *m*, alpinismo *m*, *L.Am.* andinismo *m*
moun·tain·ous ['maʊntɪnəs] *adj* montañoso
mount·ed po·lice ['maʊntɪd] policía *f* montada
mourn [mɔːrn] **1** *v/t* llorar **2** *v/i*: *~ for s.o.* llorar la muerte de alguien
mourn·er ['mɔːrnər] doliente *m/f*
mourn·ful ['mɔːrnfəl] *adj voice, face* triste
mourn·ing ['mɔːrnɪŋ] luto *m*, duelo *m*; *be in ~* estar de luto; *wear ~* vestir de luto
mouse [maʊs] (*pl* **mice** [maɪs]) *also* COMPUT ratón *m*
'mouse mat COMPUT alfombrilla *f*
mous·tache → **mustache**

mouth [mauθ] of person boca f; of river desembocadura f

mouth·ful ['mauθfəl] of food bocado m; of drink trago m

'**mouth·or·gan** armónica f;
'**mouth·piece** of instrument boquilla f; (spokesperson) portavoz m/f;
'**mouth·wash** enjuague m bucal, elixir m bucal; '**mouth·wa·ter·ing** adj apetitoso

move [mu:v] **1** n in chess, checkers movimiento m; (step, action) paso m; (change of house) mudanza f; **make the first** ~ dar el primer paso; **get a ~ on!** F ¡espabílate! F; **don't make a ~!** ¡ni te muevas! **2** v/t object mover; (transfer) trasladar; emotionally conmover; ~ **those papers out of your way** aparta esos papeles; ~ **house** mudarse de casa **3** v/i moverse; (transfer) trasladarse

♦**move around** v/i in room andar; from place to place trasladarse, mudarse

♦**move away** v/i alejarse, apartarse; (move house) mudarse

♦**move in** v/i to house, neighborhood mudarse; to office trasladarse

♦**move on** v/i to another town mudarse; to another job cambiarse; to another subject pasar a hablar de

♦**move out** v/i of house mudarse; of area marcharse

♦**move up** v/i in league ascender, subir; (make room) correrse

move·ment ['mu:vmənt] also organization, MUS movimiento m

mov·ers ['mu:vərz] npl firm empresa f de mudanzas; (men) empleados mpl de una empresa de mudanzas

mov·ie ['mu:vɪ] película f; **go to a ~ o the ~s** ir al cine

mov·ie·go·er ['mu:vɪgouər] aficionado(a) m/f al cine

'**mov·ie the·a·ter** cine m, sala f de cine

mov·ing ['mu:vɪŋ] adj that can move movible; emotionally conmovedor

mow [mou] v/t grass cortar

♦**mow down** v/t segar la vida de

mow·er ['mouər] cortacésped m

MP [em'pi:] abbr (= **Member of Parliament**) Br diputado(-a) m(f); abbr (= **Military Policeman**) policía m militar

mph [empi:'eɪtʃ] abbr (= **miles per hour**) millas fpl por hora

Mr ['mɪstər] Sr.

Mrs ['mɪsɪz] Sra.

Ms [mɪz] Sra. (casada o no casada)

much [mʌtʃ] **1** adj mucho; **so money** tanto dinero; **as ~ ... as ...** tanto ... como **2** adv mucho; **I don't like him ~** no me gusta mucho; **he's ~ more intelligent than ...** es mucho más inteligente que ...; **the house is ~ too large for one person** la casa es demasiado grande para una sola persona; **very ~** mucho; **thank you very ~** muchas gracias; **I love you very ~** te quiero muchísimo; **too ~** demasiado **3** pron mucho; **what did she say? – nothing ~** ¿qué dijo? – nada importante; **as ~ as ...** tanto ... como; **it may cost as ~ as half a million dollars** puede que haya malversado hasta medio millón de dólares; **I thought as ~** eso es lo que pensaba

muck [mʌk] (dirt) suciedad f

mu·cus ['mju:kəs] mocos mpl, mucosidad f

mud [mʌd] barro m

mud·dle ['mʌdl] **1** n lío m **2** v/t person liar; **you've gotten the story all ~d** te has hecho un lío con la historia

♦**muddle up** v/t desordenar; (confuse) liar

mud·dy ['mʌdɪ] adj embarrado

mues·li ['mju:zlɪ] muesli m

muf·fin ['mʌfɪn] magdalena f

muf·fle ['mʌfl] v/t ahogar, amortiguar

♦**muffle up** v/i abrigarse

muf·fler ['mʌflər] MOT silenciador m

mug¹ [mʌg] for tea, coffee taza f; F (face) jeta f F, Span careto m F

mug² [mʌg] v/t (pret & pp **-ged**) (attack) atracar

mug·ger ['mʌgər] atracador(a) m(f)

mug·ging ['mʌgɪŋ] atraco m

mug·gy ['mʌgɪ] adj bochornoso

M

mule [mju:l] *animal* mulo(-a) *m(f)*; (*slipper*) pantufla *f*

♦ **mull over** [mʌl] *v/t* reflexionar sobre

mul·ti·lat·e·ral [mʌltɪ'lætərəl] *adj* POL multilateral

mul·ti·lin·gual [mʌltɪ'lɪŋgwəl] *adj* multilingüe

mul·ti·me·di·a [mʌltɪ'mi:dɪə] **1** *n* multimedia *f* **2** *adj* multimedia

mul·ti·na·tion·al [mʌltɪ'næʃnl] **1** *adj* multinacional **2** *n* COM multinacional *f*

mul·ti·ple ['mʌltɪpl] *adj* múltiple

mul·ti·ple 'choice ques·tion pregunta *f* tipo test

mul·ti·ple scle·ro·sis [skle'roʊsɪs] esclerosis *f* múltiple

mul·ti·pli·ca·tion [mʌltɪplɪ'keɪʃn] multiplicación *f*

mul·ti·ply ['mʌltɪplaɪ] **1** *v/t* (*pret & pp* **-ied**) multiplicar **2** *v/i* (*pret & pp* **-ied**) multiplicarse

mum·my ['mʌmɪ] *Br* mamá *f*

mum·ble ['mʌmbl] **1** *n* murmullo *m* **2** *v/t* farfullar **3** *v/i* hablar entre dientes

mumps [mʌmps] *nsg* paperas *fpl*

munch [mʌntʃ] *v/t & v/i* mascar

mu·ni·ci·pal [mju:'nɪsɪpl] *adj* municipal

mu·ral ['mjʊrəl] mural *m*

mur·der ['mɜ:rdər] **1** *n* asesinato *m* **2** *v/t person* asesinar, matar; *song* destrozar

mur·der·er ['mɜ:rdərər] asesino(-a) *m(f)*

mur·der·ous ['mɜ:rdrəs] *adj rage, look* asesino

murk·y ['mɜ:rkɪ] *adj water* turbio, oscuro; *fig* turbio

mur·mur ['mɜ:rmər] **1** *n* murmullo *m* **2** *v/t* murmurar

mus·cle ['mʌsl] músculo *m*

mus·cu·lar ['mʌskjʊlər] *adj pain, strain* muscular; *person* musculoso

muse [mju:z] *v/i* meditar, reflexionar (*on* sobre)

mu·se·um [mju:'zɪəm] museo *m*

mush·room ['mʌʃrʊm] **1** *n* seta *f*, hongo *m*; (*button ~*) champiñón *m*

2 *v/i* crecer rápidamente

mu·sic ['mju:zɪk] música *f*; *in written form* partitura *f*

mu·sic·al ['mju:zɪkl] **1** *adj* musical; *person* con talento para la música **2** *n* musical *m*

'mu·sic·(·al) box caja *f* de música

mu·sic·al 'in·stru·ment instrumento *m* musical

mu·si·cian [mju:'zɪʃn] músico(-a) *m(f)*

mus·sel ['mʌsl] mejillón *m*

must [mʌst] *v/aux* ◊ *necessity* tener que, deber; *I ~ be on time* tengo que or debo llegar a la hora; *do you have to leave now? yes, I ~* ¿tienes que marcharte ahora? – sí, debo marcharme; *I ~n't be late* no tengo que llegar tarde, no debo llegar tarde ◊ *probability* deber de; *it ~ be about 6 o'clock* deben de ser las seis; *they ~ have arrived by now* ya deben de haber llegado

mus·tache [mə'stæʃ] bigote *m*

mus·tard ['mʌstərd] mostaza *f*

must·y ['mʌstɪ] *adj room* que huele a humedad; *smell* a humedad

mute [mju:t] *adj animal* mudo

mut·ed ['mju:tɪd] *adj color* apagado; *criticism* débil

mu·ti·late ['mju:tɪleɪt] *v/t* mutilar

mu·ti·ny ['mju:tɪnɪ] **1** *n* motín *m* **2** *v/i* (*pret & pp* **-ied**) amotinarse

mut·ter ['mʌtər] *v/t & v/i* murmurar

mut·ton ['mʌtn] carnero *m*

mu·tu·al ['mju:tʃʊəl] *adj* mutuo

muz·zle ['mʌzl] **1** *n of animal* hocico *m*; *for dog* bozal *m* **2** *v/t* poner un bozal a; *~ the press* amordazar a la prensa

my [maɪ] *adj* mi; *~ house* mi casa; *~ parents* mis padres

my·op·ic [maɪ'ɑ:pɪk] *adj* miope

my·self [maɪ'self] *pron reflexive* me; *emphatic* yo mismo(-a); *when I saw ~ in the mirror* cuando me vi en el espejo; *I saw it ~* lo vi yo mismo; *by ~* (*alone*) solo; (*without help*) yo solo, yo mismo

mys·te·ri·ous [mɪ'stɪrɪəs] *adj* misterioso

mys·te·ri·ous·ly [mɪˈstɪrɪəslɪ] *adv* misteriosamente

mys·te·ry [ˈmɪstərɪ] misterio *m*; ~ *(story)* relato *m* de misterio

mys·ti·fy [ˈmɪstɪfaɪ] *v/t* (*pret & pp -ied*) dejar perplejo

myth [mɪθ] *also fig* mito *m*

myth·i·cal [ˈmɪθɪkl] *adj* mítico

my·thol·o·gy [mɪˈθɑːlədʒɪ] mitología *f*

N

nab [næb] *v/t* (*pret & pp -bed*) F (*take for o.s.*) pescar F, agarrar

nag [næg] **1** *v/i* (*pret & pp -ged*) *of person* dar la lata **2** *v/t* (*pret & pp -ged*): ~ *s.o. to do sth* dar la lata a alguien para que haga algo

nag·ging [ˈnægɪŋ] *adj person* quejica; *doubt* persistente; *pain* continuo

nail [neɪl] *for wood* clavo *m*; *on finger, toe* uña *f*

'nail clip·pers *npl* cortaúñas *m inv*; **'nail file** lima *f* de uñas; **'nail pol·ish** esmalte *m* de uñas; **'nail pol·ish re·mov·er** quitaesmaltes *m inv*; **'nail scis·sors** *npl* tijeras *fpl* de manicura; **'nail var·nish** esmalte *m* de uñas

na·ive [naɪˈiːv] *adj* ingenuo

na·ked [ˈneɪkɪd] *adj* desnudo; *to the ~ eye* a simple vista

name [neɪm] **1** *n* nombre *m*; *what's your ~?* ¿cómo te llamas?; *call s.o. ~s* insultar a alguien; *make a ~ for o.s.* hacerse un nombre **2** *v/t*: *they ~d him Ben* le llamaron Ben

♦ **name for** *v/t*: *name s.o. for s.o.* poner a alguien el nombre de alguien

name·ly [ˈneɪmlɪ] *adv* a saber

'name·sake tocayo(-a) *m(f)*, homónimo(-a) *m(f)*

'name·tag *on clothing etc* etiqueta *f*

nan·ny [ˈnænɪ] niñera *f*

nap [næp] *n* cabezada *f*; *have a ~* echar una cabezada

nape [neɪp]: ~ *of the neck* nuca *f*

nap·kin [ˈnæpkɪn] (*table ~*) servilleta *f*; (*sanitary ~*) compresa *f*

nar·cot·ic [nɑːrˈkɑːtɪk] *n* narcótico *m*, estupefaciente *m*

nar·cot·ics a·gent agente *m/f* de la brigada de estupefacientes

nar·rate [nəˈreɪt] *v/t* narrar

nar·ra·tion [nəˈreɪʃn] (*telling*) narración *f*

nar·ra·tive [ˈnærətɪv] **1** *n* (*story*) narración *f* **2** *adj poem, style* narrativo

nar·ra·tor [nəˈreɪtər] narrador(a) *m(f)*

nar·row [ˈnæroʊ] *adj street, bed, victory* estrecho; *views, mind* cerrado

nar·row·ly [ˈnæroʊlɪ] *adv win* por poco; ~ *escape sth* escapar por poco de algo

nar·row-mind·ed [næroʊˈmaɪndɪd] *adj* cerrado

na·sal [ˈneɪzl] *adj voice* nasal

nas·ty [ˈnæstɪ] *adj person, smell* desagradable, asqueroso; *thing to say* malintencionado; *weather* horrible; *cut, wound* feo; *disease* serio

na·tion [ˈneɪʃn] nación *f*

na·tion·al [ˈnæʃənl] **1** *adj* nacional **2** *n* ciudadano(-a) *m(f)*

na·tion·al 'an·them himno *m* nacional

na·tion·al 'debt deuda *f* pública

na·tion·al·ism [ˈnæʃənəlɪzm] nacionalismo *m*

na·tion·al·i·ty [næʃəˈnælətɪ] nacionalidad *f*

na·tion·al·ize [ˈnæʃənəlaɪz] *v/t industry etc* nacionalizar

na·tion·al 'park parque *m* nacional

na·tive [ˈneɪtɪv] **1** *adj* nativo; ~

tongue lengua *f* materna **2** *n* nativo(-a) *m(f)*, natural *m/f*; *tribesman* nativo(-a) *m(f)*, indígena *m/f*; *he's a ~ of New York* es natural de Nueva York

na·tive 'coun·try país *m* natal

na·tive 'speak·er hablante *m/f* nativo(-a)

NATO ['neɪtoʊ] *abbr* (= *North Atlantic Treaty Organization*) OTAN *f* (= Organización *f* del Tratado del Atlántico Norte)

nat·u·ral ['nætʃrəl] *adj* natural

nat·u·ral 'gas gas *m* natural

nat·u·ral·ist ['nætʃrəlɪst] naturalista *m/f*

nat·u·ral·ize ['nætʃrəlaɪz] *v/t*: *become ~d* naturalizarse, nacionalizarse

nat·u·ral·ly ['nætʃərəli] *adv* (*of course*) naturalmente; *behave, speak* con naturalidad; (*by nature*) por naturaleza

nat·u·ral 'sci·ence ciencias *fpl* naturales

nat·u·ral 'sci·en·tist experto(-a) *m(f)* en ciencias naturales

na·ture ['neɪtʃər] naturaleza *f*

na·ture re'serve reserva *f* natural

naugh·ty ['nɒːti] *adj* travieso, malo; *photograph, word etc* picante

nau·se·a ['nɒːzɪə] náusea *f*

nau·se·ate ['nɒːzɪeɪt] *v/t* (*disgust*) dar náuseas a

nau·se·at·ing ['nɒːzɪeɪtɪŋ] *adj smell, taste* nauseabundo; *person* repugnante

nau·seous ['nɒːʃəs] *adj* nauseabundo; *feel ~* tener náuseas

nau·ti·cal ['nɒːtɪkl] *adj* náutico

'nau·ti·cal mile milla *f* náutica

na·val ['neɪvl] *adj* naval

'na·val base base *f* naval

na·vel ['neɪvl] ombligo *m*

nav·i·ga·ble ['nævɪgəbl] *adj river* navegable

nav·i·gate ['nævɪgeɪt] *v/i in ship, airplane*, COMPUT navegar; *in car* hacer de copiloto

nav·i·ga·tion [nævɪ'geɪʃn] navegación *f*; *in car* direcciónes *fpl*

nav·i·ga·tor ['nævɪgeɪtər] *on ship* oficial *m* de derrota; *in airplane* navegante *m/f*; *in car* copiloto *m/f*

na·vy ['neɪvɪ] armada *f*, marina *f* (de guerra)

na·vy 'blue 1 *n* azul *m* marino **2** *adj* azul marino

near [nɪr] **1** *adv* cerca; *come a bit ~er* acércate un poco más **2** *prep* cerca de; *~ the bank* cerca del banco; *do you go ~ the bank?* ¿pasa cerca del banco? **3** *adj* cercano, próximo; *the ~est bus stop* la parada de autobús más cercana *or* próxima; *in the ~ future* en un futuro próximo

near·by [nɪr'baɪ] *adv live* cerca

near·ly ['nɪrlɪ] *adv* casi

near-sight·ed [nɪr'saɪtɪd] *adj* miope

neat [niːt] *adj* ordenado; *whiskey* solo, seco; *solution* ingenioso; F (*terrific*) genial F, estupendo F

ne·ces·sar·i·ly ['nesəserəli] *adv* necesariamente

ne·ces·sa·ry ['nesəserɪ] *adj* necesario, preciso; *it is ~ to ...* es necesario ..., hay que ...

ne·ces·si·tate [nɪ'sesɪteɪt] *v/t* exigir, hacer necesario

ne·ces·si·ty [nɪ'sesɪtɪ] (*being necessary*) necesidad *f*; (*something necessary*) necesidad *f*, requisito *m* imprescindible

neck [nek] *n* cuello *m*

neck·lace ['neklɪs] collar *m*; **'neck·line** *of dress* escote *m*; **'neck·tie** corbata *f*

née [neɪ] *adj* de soltera

need [niːd] **1** *n* necesidad *f*; *if ~ be* si fuera necesario; *in ~* necesitado; *be in ~ of sth* necesitar algo; *there's no ~ to be rude/upset* no hace falta ser grosero/que te enfades **2** *v/t* necesitar; *you'll ~ to buy one* tendrás que comprar uno; *you don't ~ to wait* no hace falta que esperes; *I ~ to talk to you* tengo que *or* necesito hablar contigo; *~ I say more?* ¿hace falta que añada algo?

nee·dle ['niːdl] *for sewing, injection, on dial* aguja *f*

'nee·dle·work costura *f*

need·y ['niːdɪ] adj necesitado

neg·a·tive ['negətɪv] adj negativo; **answer in the ~** dar una respuesta negativa

ne·glect [nɪ'glekt] **1** n abandono m, descuido m **2** v/t garden, one's health descuidar, desatender; **~ to do sth** no hacer algo

ne·glect·ed [nɪ'glektɪd] adj garden abandonado, descuidado; author olvidado; **feel ~** sentirse abandonado

neg·li·gence ['neglɪdʒəns] negligencia f

neg·li·gent ['neglɪdʒənt] adj negligente

neg·li·gi·ble ['neglɪdʒəbl] adj quantity, amount insignificante

ne·go·ti·a·ble [nɪ'ɡouʃəbl] adj salary, contract negociable

ne·go·ti·ate [nɪ'ɡouʃɪeɪt] **1** v/i negociar **2** v/t deal, settlement negociar; obstacles franquear, salvar; **bend in road** tomar

ne·go·ti·a·tion [nɪɡouʃɪ'eɪʃn] negociación f; **be under ~** estar siendo negociado

ne·go·ti·a·tor [nɪ'ɡouʃɪeɪtər] negociador(a) m(f)

Ne·gro ['niːɡrou] negro(-a) m(f)

neigh [neɪ] v/i relinchar

neigh·bor ['neɪbər] vecino(-a) m(f)

neigh·bor·hood ['neɪbərhʊd] in town vecindario m, barrio m; **in the ~ of ...** fig alrededor de ...

neigh·bor·ing ['neɪbərɪŋ] adj house, state vecino, colindante

neigh·bor·ly ['neɪbərlɪ] adj amable

neigh·bour etc Br → **neighbor** etc

nei·ther ['niːðər] **1** adj ninguno; **~ applicant was any good** ninguno de los candidatos era bueno **2** pron ninguno(-a) m(f) **3** adv: **~ ... nor ...** ni ... ni ... **4** conj: **~ do I** yo tampoco; **~ can I** yo tampoco

ne·on light ['niːɑːn] luz f de neón

neph·ew ['nefjuː] sobrino m

nerd [nɜːrd] F petardo(-a) m(f) F

nerve [nɜːrv] nervio m; (courage) valor m; (impudence) descaro m; **it's bad for my ~s** me pone de los nervios; **get on s.o.'s ~s** sacar de quicio

a alguien

nerve-rack·ing ['nɜːrvrækɪŋ] adj angustioso, exasperante

ner·vous ['nɜːrvəs] adj person nervioso, inquieto; twitch nervioso; **I'm ~ about meeting them** la reunión con ellos me pone muy nervioso

ner·vous 'break·down crisis f inv nerviosa

ner·vous 'en·er·gy energía f

ner·vous·ness ['nɜːrvəsnɪs] nerviosismo m

ner·vous 'wreck manojo m de nervios

nerv·y ['nɜːrvɪ] adj (fresh) descarado

nest [nest] n nido m

nes·tle ['nesl] v/i acomodarse

net[1] [net] for fishing, tennis red f

net[2] [net] adj price, weight neto

net 'cur·tain visillo m

net 'pro·fit beneficio m neto

net·tle ['netl] n ortiga f

'net·work of contacts, cells, COMPUT red f

neu·rol·o·gist [nuː'rɑːlədʒɪst] neurólogo(-a) m(f)

neu·ro·sis [nuː'rousɪs] neurosis f inv

neu·rot·ic [nuː'rɑːtɪk] adj neurótico

neu·ter ['nuːtər] v/t animal castrar

neu·tral ['nuːtrl] **1** adj country neutral; color neutro **2** n gear punto m muerto; **in ~** en punto muerto

neu·tral·i·ty [nuː'trælətɪ] neutralidad f

neu·tral·ize ['nuːtrəlaɪz] v/t neutralizar

nev·er ['nevər] adv nunca; **you're ~ going to believe this** no te vas a creer esto; **you ~ promised, did you?** no lo llegaste a prometer, ¿verdad?

nev·er-'end·ing adj interminable

nev·er·the·less [nevərðə'les] adv sin embargo, no obstante

new [nuː] adj nuevo; **this system is still ~ to me** todavía no me he hecho con este sistema; **I'm ~ to the job** soy nuevo en el trabajo; **that's nothing ~** no es nada nuevo

'new·born adj recién nacido

new·com·er ['nuːkʌmər] recién

N

llegado(-a) *m(f)*
new·ly ['nu:lɪ] *adv* (*recently*) recientemente, recién
new·ly·weds [wedz] *npl* recién casados *mpl*
new 'moon luna *f* nueva
news [nu:z] *nsg also* RAD noticias *fpl;*
on TV noticias *fpl,* telediario *m;*
that's ~ to me no sabía eso
'news·a·gen·cy agencia *f* de noticias;
'news·cast TV noticias *fpl,* telediario *m; on radio* noticias *fpl;*
'news·cast·er TV presentador(a) *m(f)* de informativos; **'news·deal·er** quiosquero(-a) *m(f);*
'news flash flash *m* informativo, noticia *f* de última hora;
'news·pa·per periódico *m;* **'news·read·er** TV *etc* presentador(a) *m(f)* de informativos; **'news re·port** reportaje *m;* **'news·stand** quiosco *m;*
'news·ven·dor vendedor(a) *m(f)* de periódicos
'New Year año *m* nuevo; *Happy ~!* ¡Feliz Año Nuevo!; **New Year's 'Day** Día *m* de Año Nuevo; **New Year's 'Eve** Nochevieja *f;* **New York** [jɔ:rk] **1** *adj* neoyorquino **2** *n:* *~ (City)* Nueva York; **New York·er** ['jɔ:rkər] *n* neoyorquino(-a) *m(f);*
New Zea·land ['zi:lənd] Nueva Zelanda; **New Zea·land·er** ['zi:ləndər] neozelandés(-esa) *m(f),* neocelandés(-esa) *m(f)*
next [nekst] **1** *adj in time* próximo, siguiente; *in space* siguiente, de al lado; *~ week* la próxima semana, la semana que viene; *the ~ week he came back again* volvió a la semana siguiente; *who's ~?* ¿quién es el siguiente? **2** *adv* luego, después; *~, we're going to study ...* a continuación, vamos a estudiar ...; *~ to* (*beside*) al lado de; (*in comparison with*) en comparación con
next-'door 1 *adj neighbor* de al lado **2** *adv live* al lado
next of 'kin pariente *m* más cercano
nib·ble ['nɪbl] *v/t* mordisquear
Nic·a·ra·gua [nɪkəˈrɑːgwə] Nicaragua

Nic·a·ra·guan [nɪkəˈrɑːgwən] **1** *adj* nicaragüense **2** *n* nicaragüense *m/f*
nice [naɪs] *adj trip, house, hair* bonito, *L.Am.* lindo; *person* agradable, simpático; *weather* bueno, agradable; *meal, food* bueno, rico; *be ~ to your sister!* ¡trata bien a tu hermana!; *that's very ~ of you* es muy amable de tu parte
nice·ly ['naɪslɪ] *adv written, presented* bien; (*pleasantly*) amablemente
ni·ce·ties ['naɪsətɪz] *npl* sutilezas *fpl,* refinamientos *mpl;* *social ~* cumplidos *mpl*
niche [ni:ʃ] *in market* hueco *m,* nicho *m;* (*special position*) hueco *m*
nick [nɪk] *n* (*cut*) muesca *f,* mella *f; in the ~ of time* justo a tiempo
nick·el ['nɪkl] níquel *m;* (*coin*) moneda de cinco centavos
'nick·name *n* apodo *m,* mote *m*
niece [ni:s] sobrina *f*
nig·gard·ly ['nɪgərdlɪ] *adj amount, person* mísero
night [naɪt] noche *f; tomorrow ~* mañana por la noche; *11 o'clock at ~* las 11 de la noche; *travel by ~* viajar de noche; *during the ~* por la noche; *stay the ~* quedarse a dormir; *a room for 2 ~s* una habitación para 2 noches; *work ~s* trabajar de noche; *good ~* buenas noches; *in the middle of the ~* en mitad de la noche
'night·cap *drink* copa *f* (*tomada antes de ir a dormir*); **'night·club** club *m* nocturno, discoteca *f;* **'night·dress** camisón *m;* **'night·fall**: *at ~* al anochecer; **'night flight** vuelo *m* nocturno; **'night·gown** camisón *m*
nigh·tin·gale ['naɪtɪŋgeɪl] ruiseñor *m*
'night·life vida *f* nocturna
night·ly ['naɪtlɪ] **1** *adj: a ~ event* algo que sucede todas las noches **2** *adv* todas las noches
'night·mare *also fig* pesadilla *f;* **'night por·ter** portero *m* de noche; **'night school** escuela *f* nocturna; **'night shift** turno *m* de noche; **'night·shirt** camisa *f* de dormir;

'night·spot local *m* nocturno;
'night·time: *at ~*, *in the ~* por la noche

nil [nɪl] *Br* cero

nim·ble ['nɪmbl] *adj* ágil

nine [naɪn] nueve

nine·teen [naɪn'tiːn] diecinueve

nine·teenth [naɪn'tiːnθ] *n & adj* decimonoveno

nine·ti·eth ['naɪntɪɪθ] *n & adj* nonagésimo

nine·ty ['naɪntɪ] noventa

ninth [naɪnθ] *n & adj* noveno

nip [nɪp] *n* (*pinch*) pellizco *m*; (*bite*) mordisco *m*

nip·ple ['nɪpl] pezón *m*

ni·tro·gen ['naɪtrədʒn] nitrógeno *m*

no [noʊ] **1** *adv* no **2** *adj*: *there's ~ coffee/ tea left* no queda café / té; *I have ~ family/ money* no tengo familia / dinero; *I'm ~ linguist/ expert* no soy un lingüista / experto; *~ smoking/ parking* prohibido fumar / aparcar

no·bil·i·ty [noʊ'bɪlətɪ] nobleza *f*

no·ble ['noʊbl] *adj* noble

no·bod·y ['noʊbədɪ] *pron* nadie; *~ knows* nadie lo sabe; *there was ~ at home* no había nadie en casa

nod [nɑːd] **1** *n* movimiento *m* de la cabeza **2** *v/i* (*pret & pp* **-ded**) asentir con la cabeza

♦ **nod off** *v/i* (*fall asleep*) quedarse dormido

no·hop·er [noʊ'hoʊpər] F inútil *m/f* F

noise [nɔɪz] ruido *m*

nois·y ['nɔɪzɪ] *adj* ruidoso

nom·i·nal ['nɑːmɪnl] *adj amount* simbólico

nom·i·nate ['nɑːmɪneɪt] *v/t* (*appoint*) nombrar; *~ s.o. for a post* (*propose*) proponer a alguien para un puesto

nom·i·na·tion [nɑːmɪ'neɪʃn] (*appointment*) nombramiento *m*; (*proposal*) nominación *f*; *who was your ~?* ¿a quién propusiste?

nom·i·nee [nɑːmɪ'niː] candidato(-a) *m*(*f*)

non ... [nɑːn] no ...

non·al·co·hol·ic *adj* sin alcohol

non·a·ligned *adj* no alineado

non·cha·lant ['nɑːnʃələnt] *adj* despreocupado

non·com·mis·sioned 'of·fi·cer suboficial *m/f*

non·com'mit·tal *adj person, response* evasivo

non·de·script ['nɑːndɪskrɪpt] *adj* anodino

none [nʌn] *pron*: *~ of the students* ninguno de los estudiantes; *~ of the water* nada del agua; *there are ~ left* no queda ninguno; *there is ~ left* no queda nada

non·en·ti·ty nulidad *f*

none·the·less [nʌnðə'les] *adv* sin embargo, no obstante

non·ex'ist·ent *adj* inexistente

non'fic·tion no ficción *f*

non(·in)'flam·ma·ble *adj* incombustible, no inflamable

non·in·ter'fer·ence, non·in·ter·'ven·tion no intervención *f*

non·'i·ron *adj shirt* que no necesita plancha

'no-no: *that's a ~* F de eso nada

no·'non·sense *approach* directo

non'pay·ment impago *m*

non·pol'lut·ing *adj* que no contamina

non'res·i·dent *n* no residente *m/f*

non·re·turn·a·ble [nɑːnrɪ'tɜːrnəbl] *adj* no retornable

non·sense ['nɑːnsəns] disparate *m*, tontería *f*; *don't talk ~* no digas disparates *or* tonterías; *~, it's easy!* ¡tonterías, ¡es fácil!

non'skid *adj tires* antideslizante

non'slip *adj surface* antideslizante

non'smok·er *person* no fumador(a) *m*(*f*)

non'stand·ard *adj* no estándar

non'stick *adj pans* antiadherente

non'stop 1 *adj flight, train* directo, sin escalas; *chatter* ininterrumpido **2** *adv fly, travel* directamente; *chatter, argue* sin parar

non'swim·mer: *be a ~* no saber nadar

non'u·nion *adj* no sindicado

non·vi·o·lence no violencia *f*

non·vi·o·lent *adj* no violento

N

noo·dles ['nuːdlz] *npl* tallarines *mpl* (chinos)

nook [nʊk] rincón *m*

noon [nuːn] mediodía *m*; **at** ~ al mediodía

'no-one → **nobody**

noose [nuːs] lazo *m* corredizo

nor [nɔːr] *conj* ni; ~ **do I** yo tampoco, ni yo

norm [nɔːrm] norma *f*

nor·mal ['nɔːrml] *adj* normal

nor·mal·i·ty [nɔːr'mælətɪ] normalidad *f*

nor·mal·ize ['nɔːrməlaɪz] *v/t relationships* normalizar

nor·mal·ly ['nɔːrməlɪ] *adv (usually)* normalmente; *(in a normal way)* normalmente, con normalidad

north [nɔːrθ] **1** *n* norte *m*; **to the** ~ **of** al norte de **2** *adj* norte **3** *adv travel* al norte; ~ **of** al norte de

North Am·er·i·ca América del Norte, Norteamérica; **North Am·er·i·can 1** *n* norteamericano(-a) *m(f)* **2** *adj* norteamericano; **north'east** *n* nordeste *m*, noreste *m*

nor·ther·ly ['nɔːrðəlɪ] *adj* norte, del norte

nor·thern ['nɔːrðən] norteño, del norte

nor·thern·er ['nɔːrðənər] norteño(-a) *m(f)*

North Ko·re·a Corea del Norte; **North Ko·re·an 1** *adj* norcoreano **2** *n* norcoreano(-a) *m(f)*; **North 'Pole** Polo *m* Norte

north·ward ['nɔːrðwərd] *adv travel* hacia el norte

north·west [nɔːrð'west] *n* noroeste *m*

Nor·way ['nɔːrweɪ] Noruega

Nor·we·gian [nɔːr'wiːdʒn] **1** *adj* noruego **2** *n person* noruego(-a) *m(f)*; *language* noruego *m*

nose [nəʊz] nariz *m*; *of animal* hocico *m*; *it was right under my* ~*!* ¡lo tenía delante de mis narices!

♦ **nose around** *v/i* F husmear

'nose·bleed: have a ~ sangrar por la nariz

nos·tal·gia [nɑ'stældʒə] nostalgia *f*

nos·tal·gic [nɑ'stældʒɪk] *adj* nostálgico

nos·tril ['nɑːstrəl] ventana *f* de la nariz

nos·y ['nəʊzɪ] *adj* F entrometido

not [nɑːt] *adv* no; ~ **this one, that one** éste no, ése; ~ **now** ahora no; ~ **like that** así no; ~ **before Tuesday** / **next week** no antes del martes / de la próxima semana; ~ **for me, thanks** para mí no, gracias; ~ **a lot** no mucho; *it's* ~ **ready** / **allowed** no está listo / permitido; **I don't know** no lo sé; **he didn't help** no ayudó

no·ta·ble ['nəʊtəbl] *adj* notable

no·ta·ry ['nəʊtərɪ] notario(-a) *m(f)*

notch [nɑːtʃ] *n* muesca *f*, mella *f*

note [nəʊt] *n written*, MUS nota *f*; **take** ~**s** tomar notas; **take** ~ **of sth** prestar atención a algo

♦ **note down** *v/t* anotar

'note·book cuaderno *m*, libreta *f*; COMPUT *Span* ordenador *m* portátil, *L.Am.* computadora *f* portátil

not·ed ['nəʊtɪd] *adj* destacado

'note·pad bloc *m* de notas

'note·pa·per papel *m* de carta

noth·ing ['nʌθɪŋ] *pron* nada; ~ **but** sólo; ~ **much** no mucho; **for** ~ *(for free)* gratis; *(for no reason)* por nada; **I'd like** ~ **better** me encantaría

no·tice ['nəʊtɪs] **1** *n on bulletin board, in street* cartel *m*, letrero *m*; *(advance warning)* aviso *m*; *in newspaper* anuncio *m*; **at short** ~ con poca antelación; **until further** ~ hasta nuevo aviso; **give s.o. his** / **her** ~ *to quit job* despedir a alguien; *to leave house* comunicar a alguien que tiene que abandonar la casa; **hand in one's** ~ *to employer* presentar la dimisión; **four weeks'** ~ cuatro semanas de preaviso; **take** ~ **of sth** observar algo, prestar atención a algo; **take no** ~ **of s.o.** / **sth** no hacer caso de alguien / algo **2** *v/t* notar, fijarse en

no·tice·a·ble ['nəʊtɪsəbl] *adj* apreciable, evidente

no·ti·fy ['nəʊtɪfaɪ] *v/t* (*pret & pp* **-ied**) notificar, informar

no·tion ['nəʊʃn] noción *f*, idea *f*

no·tions ['noʊsnz] *npl* artículos *mpl* de costura

no·to·ri·ous [noʊ'tɔːrɪəs] *adj* de mala fama

nou·gat ['nuːgət] *especie de turrón*

noun [naʊn] nombre *m*, sustantivo *m*

nour·ish·ing ['nʌrɪʃɪŋ] *adj* nutritivo

nour·ish·ment ['nʌrɪʃmənt] alimento *m*, alimentación *f*

nov·el ['nɑːvl] *n* novela *f*

nov·el·ist ['nɑːvlɪst] novelista *m/f*

nov·el·ty ['nɑːvəltɪ] (*being new*) lo novedoso; (*sth new*) novedad *f*

No·vem·ber [noʊ'vembər] noviembre *m*

nov·ice ['nɑːvɪs] principiante *m/f*

now [naʊ] *adv* ahora; ~ *and again*, *and then* de vez en cuando; *by ~* ya; *from ~ on* de ahora en adelante; *right ~* ahora mismo; *just ~* (*at this moment*) en este momento; (*a little while ago*) hace un momento; ~, *~!* ¡vamos!, ¡venga!; ~, *where did I put it?* ¿y ahora dónde lo he puesto?

now·a·days ['naʊədeɪz] *adv* hoy en día

no·where ['noʊwer] *adv* en ningún lugar; *it's ~ near finished* no está acabado ni mucho menos; *he was ~ to be seen* no se le veía en ninguna parte

noz·zle ['nɑːzl] boquilla *f*

nu·cle·ar ['nuːklɪər] *adj* nuclear

nu·cle·ar 'en·er·gy energía *f* nuclear; **nu·cle·ar fis·sion** ['fɪʃn] fisión *f* nuclear; **'nu·cle·ar-free** *adj* desnuclearizado; **nu·cle·ar 'phys·ics** física *f* nuclear; **nu·cle·ar 'pow·er** energía *f* nuclear; POL potencia *f* nuclear; **nu·cle·ar 'pow·er sta·tion** central *f* nuclear; **nu·cle·ar re'ac·tor** reactor *m* nuclear; **nu·cle·ar 'waste** residuos *mpl* nucleares; **nu·cle·ar 'weap·on** arma *f* nuclear

nude [nuːd] **1** *adj* desnudo **2** *n* *painting* desnudo *m*; *in the ~* desnudo

nudge [nʌdʒ] *v/t* dar un toque con el codo a

nud·ist ['nuːdɪst] *n* nudista *m/f*

nui·sance ['nuːsns] incordio *m*, molestia *f*; *make a ~ of o.s.* dar la lata; *what a ~!* ¡qué incordio!

nuke [nuːk] *v/t* F atacar con armas nucleares

null and 'void [nʌl] *adj* nulo y sin efecto

numb [nʌm] *adj* entumecido; *emotionally* insensible

num·ber ['nʌmbər] **1** *n* número *m*; *a ~ of people* un cierto número de personas **2** *v/t* (*put a ~ on*) numerar

nu·mer·al ['nuːmərəl] número *m*

nu·me·rate ['nuːmərət] *adj* que sabe sumar y restar

nu·me·rous ['nuːmərəs] *adj* numeroso

nun [nʌn] monja *f*

nurse [nɜːrs] enfermero(-a) *m(f)*

nur·se·ry ['nɜːrsərɪ] guardería *f*; *for plants* vivero *m*

'nur·se·ry rhyme canción *f* infantil; **'nur·se·ry school** parvulario *m*, jardín *m* de infancia; **'nur·se·ry school teach·er** profesor(a) *m(f)* de parvulario

nurs·ing ['nɜːrsɪŋ] enfermería *f*

'nurs·ing home *for old people* residencia *f*

nut [nʌt] nuez *f*; *for bolt* tuerca *f*; ~*s* F (*testicles*) pelotas *fpl* F

'nut·crack·ers *npl* cascanueces *m inv*

nu·tri·ent ['nuːtrɪənt] nutriente *m*

nu·tri·tion [nuː'trɪʃn] nutrición *f*

nu·tri·tious [nuː'trɪʃəs] *adj* nutritivo

nuts [nʌts] *adj* F (*crazy*) chalado F, pirado F; *be ~ about s.o.* estar coladito por alguien F

'nut·shell: *in a ~* en una palabra

nut·ty ['nʌtɪ] *adj taste* a nuez; F (*crazy*) chalado F, pirado F

ny·lon ['naɪlɑːn] **1** *n* nylon *m* **2** *adj* de nylon

N

O

oak [ouk] *tree, wood* roble *m*

oar [ɔːr] remo *m*

o·a·sis [ou'eɪsɪs] (*pl* **oases** [ou'eɪsiːz]) *also fig* oasis *m inv*

oath [ouθ] LAW, (*swearword*) juramento *m*; **on ~** bajo juramento

'oat·meal harina *f* de avena

oats [outs] *npl* copos *mpl* de avena

o·be·di·ence [ou'biːdɪəns] obediencia *f*

o·be·di·ent [ou'biːdɪənt] *adj* obediente

o·be·di·ent·ly [ou'biːdɪəntlɪ] *adv* obedientemente

o·bese [ou'biːs] *adj* obeso

o·bes·i·ty [ou'biːsɪtɪ] obesidad *f*

o·bey [ou'beɪ] *v/t* obedecer

o·bit·u·a·ry [ə'bɪtʊərɪ] *n* necrología *f*, obituario *m*

ob·ject¹ ['ɑːbdʒɪkt] *n also* GRAM objeto *m*; (*aim*) objetivo *m*

ob·ject² [əb'dʒekt] *v/i* oponerse
♦ **object to** *v/t* oponerse a

ob·jec·tion [əb'dʒekʃn] objeción *f*

ob·jec·tio·na·ble [əb'dʒekʃnəbl] *adj* (*unpleasant*) desagradable

ob·jec·tive [əb'dʒektɪv] **1** *adj* objetivo **2** *n* objetivo *m*

ob·jec·tive·ly [əb'dʒektɪvlɪ] *adv* objetivamente

ob·jec·tiv·i·ty [əbdʒek'tɪvətɪ] objetividad *f*

ob·li·ga·tion [ɑːblɪ'geɪʃn] obligación *f*; **be under an ~ to s.o.** tener una obligación para con alguien

ob·lig·a·to·ry [ə'blɪgətɔːrɪ] *adj* obligatorio

o·blige [ə'blaɪdʒ] *v/t* obligar; **much ~d!** muy agradecido

o·blig·ing [ə'blaɪdʒɪŋ] *adj* atento, servicial

o·blique [ə'bliːk] **1** *adj reference* indirecto **2** *n in punctuation* barra *f* inclinada

o·blit·er·ate [ə'blɪtəreɪt] *v/t city* destruir, arrasar; *memory* borrar

o·bliv·i·on [ə'blɪvɪən] olvido *m*; **fall into ~** caer en el olvido

o·bliv·i·ous [ə'blɪvɪəs] *adj*: **be ~ of sth** no ser consciente de algo

ob·long ['ɑːblɒŋ] *adj* rectangular

ob·nox·ious [əb'nɑːkʃəs] *adj person* detestable, odioso; *smell* repugnante

ob·scene [ɑːb'siːn] *adj* obsceno; *salary, poverty* escandaloso

ob·scen·i·ty [əb'senətɪ] obscenidad *f*

ob·scure [əb'skjʊr] *adj* oscuro

ob·scu·ri·ty [əb'skjʊrətɪ] oscuridad *f*

ob·ser·vance [əb'zɜːrvns] *of festival* práctica *f*

ob·ser·vant [əb'zɜːrvnt] *adj* observador

ob·ser·va·tion [ɑːbzə'veɪʃn] *of nature, stars* observación *f*; (*comment*) observación *f*, comentario *m*

ob·ser·va·to·ry [əb'zɜːrvətɔːrɪ] observatorio *m*

ob·serve [əb'zɜːrv] *v/t* observar

ob·serv·er [əb'zɜːrvər] observador(a) *m(f)*

ob·sess [ɑːb'ses] *v/t* obsesionar; **be ~ed by/with** estar obsesionado con/por

ob·ses·sion [ɑːb'seʃn] obsesión *f*

ob·ses·sive [ɑːb'sesɪv] *adj* obsesivo

ob·so·lete ['ɑːbsəliːt] *adj* obsoleto

ob·sta·cle ['ɑːbstəkl] obstáculo *m*

ob·ste·tri·cian [ɑːbstə'trɪʃn] obstetra *m/f*, tocólogo(-a) *m(f)*

ob·stet·rics [ɑːb'stetrɪks] obstetricia *f*, tocología *f*

ob·sti·na·cy ['ɑːbstɪnəsɪ] obstinación *f*

ob·sti·nate ['ɑːbstɪnət] *adj* obstinado

ob·sti·nate·ly ['ɑːbstɪnətlɪ] *adv* obstinadamente

ob·struct [əb'strʌkt] v/t road obstruir; *investigation, police* obstaculizar

ob·struc·tion [əb'strʌkʃn] *on road etc* obstrucción f

ob·struc·tive [əb'strʌktɪv] adj *behavior, tactics* obstruccionista

ob·tain [əb'teɪn] v/t obtener, lograr

ob·tain·a·ble [əb'teɪnəbl] adj *products* disponible

ob·tru·sive [əb'truːsɪv] adj molesto; *the plastic chairs are rather ~* las sillas de plástico desentonan por completo

ob·tuse [əb'tuːs] adj fig duro de mollera

ob·vi·ous ['ɑːbvɪəs] adj obvio, evidente

ob·vi·ous·ly ['ɑːbvɪəslɪ] adv obviamente; *~!* ¡por supuesto!

oc·ca·sion [ə'keɪʒn] ocasión f

oc·ca·sion·al [ə'keɪʒənl] adj ocasional, esporádico; *I like the ~ Scotch* me gusta tomarme un whisky de vez en cuando

oc·ca·sion·al·ly [ə'keɪʒnlɪ] adv ocasionalmente, de vez en cuando

oc·cult [ə'kʌlt] **1** adj oculto **2** n: *the ~* lo oculto

oc·cu·pant ['ɑːkjupənt] ocupante m/f

oc·cu·pa·tion [ɑːkju'peɪʃn] ocupación f

oc·cu·pa·tion·al 'ther·a·pist [ɑːkju'peɪʃnl] terapeuta m/f ocupacional

oc·cu·pa·tion·al 'ther·a·py terapia f ocupacional

oc·cu·py ['ɑːkjupaɪ] v/t (*pret & pp -ied*) ocupar

oc·cur [ə'kɜːr] v/i (*pret & pp -red*) ocurrir, suceder; *it ~red to me that ...* se me ocurrió que ...

oc·cur·rence [ə'kʌrəns] acontecimiento m

o·cean ['oʊʃn] océano m

o·ce·a·nog·ra·phy [oʊʃn'ɑːɡrəfɪ] oceanografía f

o'clock [ə'klɑːk]: *at five/ six ~* a las cinco/ seis

Oc·to·ber [ɑːk'toʊbər] octubre m

oc·to·pus ['ɑːktəpəs] pulpo m

OD [oʊ'diː] v/i F: *~ on drug* tomar una sobredosis de

odd [ɑːd] adj (*strange*) raro, extraño; (*not even*) impar; *the ~ one out* el bicho raro; *50 ~* cerca de 50

'odd·ball F bicho m raro F

odds [ɑːdz] npl: *be at ~ with sth/ s.o.* no concordar con algo/ estar peleado con alguien; *the ~ are 10 to one* las apuestas están en 10 a 1; *the ~ are that ...* lo más probable es que ...; *against all the ~* contra lo que se esperaba

odds and 'ends npl objects cacharros mpl; *things to do* cosillas fpl

'odds-on adj favorite indiscutible

o·di·ous ['oʊdɪəs] adj odioso

o·dom·e·ter [oʊ'dɑːmətər] cuentakilómetros m inv

o·dor, Br **o·dour** ['oʊdər] olor m

of [ɑːv], [əv] prep possession de; *the name ~ the street/ hotel* el nombre de la calle/ del hotel; *the color ~ the car* el color del coche; *five minutes ~ twelve* las doce menos cinco, *L.Am* cinco para las doce; *die ~ cancer* morir de cáncer; *love ~ money/ adventure* amor por el dinero/ la aventura; *~ the three this is ...* de los tres éste es ...

off [ɑːf] **1** prep: *~ the main road* (*away from*) apartado de la carretera principal; (*leading off*) saliendo de la carretera principal; *$20 ~ the price* una rebaja en el precio de 20 dólares; *he's ~ his food* no come nada, está desganado **2** adv: *be ~ of light, TV, machine* estar apagado; *of brake, lid, top* no estar puesto; *not at work* faltar; *on vacation* estar de vacaciones; (*canceled*) estar cancelado; *we're ~ tomorrow* (*leaving*) nos vamos mañana; *I'm ~ to New York* me voy a Nueva York; *with his pants/ hat ~* sin los pantalones/ el sombrero; *take a day ~* tomarse un día de fiesta *or* un día libre; *it's 3 miles ~* está a tres millas de distancia; *it's a long way ~ in distance* está muy lejos; *in future* todavía queda mucho tiempo; **he got into his car and drove** ~ se subió al coche y se marchó; **~ and on** de vez en cuando **3** *adj*: **the ~ switch** el interruptor de apagado

of·fence *Br* → **offense**

of·fend [ə'fend] *v/t* (*insult*) ofender

of·fend·er [ə'fendər] LAW delincuente *m/f*

of·fense [ə'fens] LAW delito *m*; **take ~ at sth** ofenderse por algo

of·fen·sive [ə'fensiv] **1** *adj behavior, remark* ofensivo; *smell* repugnante **2** *n* (MIL: *attack*) ofensiva *f*; **go on(to) the ~** pasar a la ofensiva

of·fer ['ɒfər] **1** *n* oferta *f* **2** *v/t* ofrecer; **~ s.o. sth** ofrecer algo a alguien

off'hand *adj attitude* brusco

of·fice ['ɒfɪs] *building* oficina *f*; *room* oficina *f*, despacho *m*; *position* cargo *m*

'**of·fice block** bloque *m* de oficinas

'**of·fice hours** *npl* horas *fpl* de oficina

of·fi·cer ['ɒfɪsər] MIL oficial *m/f*; *in police* agente *m/f*

of·fi·cial [ə'fɪʃl] **1** *adj* oficial *m* funcionario(-a) *m(f)*

of·fi·cial·ly [ə'fɪʃlɪ] *adv* oficialmente

of·fi·ci·ate [ə'fɪʃieɪt] *v/i*: **with X officiating** con X celebrando la ceremonia

of·fi·cious [ə'fɪʃəs] *adj* entrometido

'**off-line** *adv work* fuera de línea; **be ~** *of printer etc* estar desconectado; **go ~** desconectarse

'**off-peak** *adj rates* en horas valle, fuera de las horas punta

'**off-sea·son 1** *adj rates, vacation* de temporada baja **2** *n* temporada *f* baja

'**off·set** *v/t* (*pret & pp* **-set**) *losses, disadvantage* compensar

'**off·shore** *adj drilling rig* cercano a la costa; *investment* en el exterior

'**off·side 1** *adj wheel etc* del lado del conductor **2** *adv* SP fuera de juego

'**off·spring** *of person* vástagos *mpl*, hijos *mpl*; *of animal* crías *fpl*

off-the-'rec·ord *adj* confidencial

'**off-white** *adj* blancuzco

of·ten ['ɒfn] *adv* a menudo, frecuen-

temente *m*

oil [ɔɪl] **1** *n for machine, food, skin* aceite *m*; *petroleum* petróleo *m* **2** *v/t hinges, bearings* engrasar

'**oil change** cambio *m* del aceite; '**oil com·pa·ny** compañía *f* petrolera; '**oil-field** *n* yacimiento *m* petrolífero; '**oil-fired** *adj central heating* de gasóleo *or* fuel; '**oil paint·ing** óleo *m*; '**oil-pro·duc·ing coun·try** país *m* productor de petróleo; '**oil re·fin·e·ry** refinería *f* de petróleo; '**oil rig** plataforma *f* petrolífera; '**oil·skins** *npl* ropa *f* impermeable; '**oil slick** marea *f* negra; '**oil tank·er** petrolero *m*; '**oil well** pozo *m* petrolífero

oil·y ['ɔɪlɪ] *adj* grasiento

oint·ment ['ɔɪntmənt] ungüento *m*, pomada *f*

ok [oʊ'keɪ] *adj, adv* F: **can I? – ~** ¿puedo? – de acuerdo *or Span* vale; **is it ~ with you if …?** ¿te parecería bien si …?; **does that look ~?** ¿queda bien?; **that's ~ by me** por mí, ningún problema; **are you ~?** (*well, not hurt*) ¿estás bien?; **are you ~ for Friday?** ¿te va bien el viernes?; **he's ~** (*is a good guy*) es buena persona; **is this bus ~ for …?** ¿este autobús va a …?

old [oʊld] *adj* viejo; (*previous*) anterior, antiguo; **an ~ man/ woman** un anciano/una anciana, un viejo/una vieja; **how ~ are you/ is he?** ¿cuántos años tienes/tiene?; **he's getting ~** está haciéndose mayor

old 'age vejez *f*

old-'fash·ioned *adj clothes, style, ideas* anticuado, pasado de moda; *word* anticuado

ol·ive ['ɒlɪv] aceituna *f*, oliva *f*

'**ol·ive oil** aceite *m* de oliva

O·lym·pic 'Games [ə'lɪmpɪk] *npl* Juegos *mpl* Olímpicos

om·e·let, *Br* **om·e·lette** ['ɒmlɪt] tortilla *f* (francesa)

om·i·nous ['ɒmɪnəs] *adj* siniestro

o·mis·sion [oʊ'mɪʃn] omisión *f*

o·mit [ə'mɪt] *v/t* (*pret & pp* **-ted**) omitir; **~ to do sth** no hacer algo

om·nip·o·tent [ɑːm'nɪpətənt] *adj*

omnipotente

om·nis·ci·ent [ɑːmˈnɪsɪənt] *adj* omnisciente

on [ɑːn] **1** *prep* en; **~ the table/wall** en la mesa/la pared; **~ the bus/train** en el autobús/el tren; **~ TV/the radio** en la televisión/la radio; **~ Sunday** el domingo; **~ the 1st of ...** el uno de ...; **this is ~ me** (*I'm paying*) invito yo; **have you any money ~ you?** ¿llevas dinero encima?; **~ his arrival/departure** cuando llegue/se marche; **~ hearing this** al escuchar esto **2** *adv*: **be ~** *of light, TV, computer etc* estar encendido *or* L.Am. prendido; *of brake, lid, top* estar puesto; *of meeting etc*: *be scheduled to happen* haber sido acordado; **it's ~ at 5 am** *of TV program* lo dan *or Span* ponen a las cinco; **what's ~ tonight?** *on TV etc* ¿qué dan *or Span* ponen esta noche?; (*what's planned?*) ¿qué planes hay para esta noche?; **with his hat ~** con el sombrero puesto; **you're ~** (*I accept your offer etc*) trato hecho; **~ you go** (*go ahead*) adelante; **walk/talk ~** seguir caminando/hablando; **and so ~** etcétera; **~ and ~** *talk etc* sin parar **3** *adj*: **the ~ switch** el interruptor de encendido

once [wʌns] **1** *adv* (*one time, formerly*) una vez; **~ again, ~ more** una vez más; **at ~** (*immediately*) de inmediato, inmediatamente; **all at ~** (*suddenly*) de repente; (*all*) **at ~** (*together*) al mismo tiempo; **~ upon a time there was ...** érase una vez ...; **in a while** de vez en cuando; **~ and for all** de una vez por todas; **for ~** por una vez **2** *conj* una vez que; **~ you have finished** una vez que hayas acabado

one [wʌn] **1** *number* uno *m* **2** *adj* un(a); **~ day** un día **3** *pron* uno(-a); **which ~?** ¿cuál?; **~ by ~** *enter, deal with* uno por uno; **we help ~ another** nos ayudamos mutuamente; **what can ~ say/do?** ¿qué puede uno decir/hacer?; **the little ~s** los pequeños; **I for ~** yo personalmente

one-'off *n* (*unique event, person*) hecho *m* aislado; (*exception*) excepción *f*

one-par·ent 'fam·i·ly familia *f* monoparental

one'self *pron* uno(-a) mismo(-a) *m(f)*; **do sth by ~** hacer algo sin ayuda; **look after ~** cuidarse; **be by ~** estar solo

one-sid·ed [wʌnˈsaɪdɪd] *adj discussion, fight* desigual; **one-track 'mind** *hum*: **have a ~** ser un obseso; **'one-way street** calle *f* de sentido único; **'one-way tick·et** billete *m* de ida

on·ion [ˈʌnjən] cebolla *f*

'on-line *adv* en línea; **go ~ to** conectarse a

'on-line serv·ice COMPUT servicio *m* en línea

on·look·er [ˈɑːnlʊkər] espectador(a) *m(f)*, curioso(-a) *m(f)*

on·ly [ˈəʊnlɪ] **1** *adv* sólo, solamente; **he was here ~ yesterday** estuvo aquí ayer mismo; **not ~ ... but ... also ...** no sólo *or* solamente ... sino también ...; **~ just** por poco **2** *adj* único; **~ son** hijo único

'on·set comienzo *m*

'on·side *adv* SP en posición reglamentaria

on-the-job 'train·ing formación *f* continua

on·to [ˈɑːntuː] *prep*: **put sth ~ sth** (*on top of*) poner algo encima de algo

on·ward [ˈɑːnwərd] *adv* hacia adelante; **from ... ~** de ... en adelante

ooze [uːz] **1** *v/i of liquid, mud* rezumar **2** *v/t* rezumar; **he ~s charm** rezuma *or* rebosa encanto

o·paque [əʊˈpeɪk] *adj glass* opaco

OPEC [ˈəʊpek] *abbr* (= *Organization of Petroleum Exporting Countries*) OPEP *f* (= Organización *f* de Países Exportadores de Petróleo)

o·pen [ˈəʊpən] **1** *adj also honest* abierto; **in the ~ air** al aire libre **2** *v/t* abrir **3** *v/i of door, shop* abrir; *of flower* abrirse

♦ **open up** *v/i of person* abrirse

o·pen-'air *adj meeting, concert* al aire libre; *pool* descubierto; 'o·pen day jornada *f* de puertas abiertas; o·pen-'end·ed *adj contract etc* abierto

o·pen·ing ['oʊpənɪŋ] *in wall etc* abertura *f*; *(beginning: of film, novel etc)* comienzo *m*; *(job)* puesto *m* vacante

'o·pen·ing hours *npl* horario *m* de apertura

o·pen·ly ['oʊpənlɪ] *adv (honestly, frankly)* abiertamente

o·pen-mind·ed *adj* de mentalidad abierta; o·pen 'plan of·fice oficina *f* de planta abierta; 'o·pen tick·et billete *m* abierto

op·e·ra ['ɑːpərə] ópera *f*

'op·e·ra glass·es *npl* gemelos *mpl*, prismáticos *mpl*; 'op·e·ra house (teatro *m* de la) ópera *f*; 'op·e·ra sing·er cantante *m/f* de ópera

op·e·rate ['ɑːpəreɪt] **1** *v/i of company* operar, actuar; *of airline, bus service,* MED operar; *of machine* funcionar (**on** con) **2** *v/t machine* manejar

♦ operate on *v/t* MED operar; *they operated on his leg* le operaron de la pierna

'op·e·rat·ing in·struc·tions *npl* instrucciones *fpl* de funcionamiento; 'op·e·rat·ing room MED quirófano *m*; 'op·e·rat·ing sys·tem COMPUT sistema *m* operativo

op·e·ra·tion [ɑːpə'reɪʃn] MED operación *f*; *of machine* manejo *m*; ~**s** *of company* operaciones *fpl*, actividades *fpl*; *have an ~* MED ser operado

op·e·ra·tor ['ɑːpəreɪtər] TELEC operador(a) *m(f)*; *of machine* operario(-a) *m(f)*; *(tour ~)* operador *m* turístico

oph·thal·mol·o·gist [ɑːfθæl'mɑːlədʒɪst] oftalmólogo(-a) *m(f)*

o·pin·ion [ə'pɪnjən] opinión *f*; *in my ~* en mi opinión

o'pin·ion poll encuesta *f* de opinión

op·po·nent [ə'poʊnənt] oponente *m/f*, adversario(-a) *m(f)*

op·por·tune ['ɑːpərtuːn] *adj fml* oportuno

op·por·tun·ist [ɑːpər'tuːnɪst] oportunista *m/f*

op·por·tu·ni·ty [ɑːpər'tuːnətɪ] oportunidad *f*

op·pose [ə'poʊz] *v/t* oponerse a; *be ~d to ...* estar en contra de ...; *John, as ~d to George ...* John, al contrario que George ...

op·po·site ['ɑːpəzɪt] **1** *adj* contrario; *views, characters, meaning* opuesto; *the ~ side of town / end of the road* el otro lado de la ciudad / el otro extremo de la calle; *the ~ sex* el sexo opuesto **2** *n: the ~ of* lo contrario de

op·po·site 'num·ber homólogo(-a) *m(f)*

op·po·si·tion [ɑːpə'zɪʃn] *to plan,* POL oposición *f*

op·press [ə'pres] *v/t the people* oprimir

op·pres·sive [ə'presɪv] *adj rule, dictator* opresor; *weather* agobiante

opt [ɑːpt] *v/t: ~ to do sth* optar por hacer algo

op·ti·cal il·lu·sion ['ɑːptɪkl] ilusión *f* óptica

op·ti·cian [ɑːp'tɪʃn] óptico(-a) *m(f)*

op·ti·mism ['ɑːptɪmɪzm] optimismo *m*

op·ti·mist ['ɑːptɪmɪst] optimista *m/f*

op·ti·mist·ic [ɑːptɪ'mɪstɪk] *adj* optimista

op·ti·mist·ic·al·ly [ɑːptɪ'mɪstɪklɪ] *adv* con optimismo

op·ti·mum ['ɑːptɪməm] **1** *adj* óptimo **2** *n: the ~* lo ideal

op·tion ['ɑːpʃn] opción *f*

op·tion·al ['ɑːpʃnl] *adj* optativo

op·tion·al 'ex·tras *npl* accesorios *mpl* opcionales

or [ɔːr] *conj* o; *before a word beginning with the letter o* u

o·ral ['ɔːrəl] *adj exam, sex* oral; *hygiene* bucal

or·ange ['ɔːrɪndʒ] **1** *adj* naranja **2** *n fruit* naranja *f*; *color* naranja *m*

or·ange·ade ['ɔːrɪndʒeɪd] naranjada *f*

'or·ange juice *Span* zumo *m or L.Am.* jugo *m* de naranja

or·a·tor ['ɔːrətər] orador(a) *m(f)*

or·bit ['ɔːrbɪt] **1** *n of earth* órbita *f* **2** *v/t the earth* girar alrededor de

or·chard ['ɔːrtʃərd] huerta *f* (de frutales)

or·ches·tra ['ɔːrkɪstrə] orquesta *f*

or·chid ['ɔːrkɪd] orquídea *f*

or·dain [ɔːr'deɪn] *v/t* ordenar

or·deal [ɔːr'diːl] calvario *m*, experiencia *f* penosa

or·der ['ɔːrdər] **1** *n* (*command*) orden *f*; (*sequence, being well arranged*) orden *m*; *for goods* pedido *m*; **take s.o.'s ~** *in restaurant* preguntar a alguien lo que va a tomar; *in ~ to* para; **out of ~** (*not functioning*) estropeado; (*not in sequence*) desordenado **2** *v/t* (*put in sequence, proper layout*) ordenar; *goods* pedir, encargar; *meal* pedir; **~ s.o. to do sth** ordenar a alguien hacer algo *or* que haga algo **3** *v/i in restaurant* pedir

or·der·ly ['ɔːrdəlɪ] **1** *adj lifestyle* ordenado, metódico **2** *n in hospital* celador(a) *m(f)*

or·di·nal (**num·ber**) ['ɔːrdɪnl] (número *m*) ordinal *m*

or·di·nar·i·ly [ɔːrdɪ'nerɪlɪ] *adv* (*as a rule*) normalmente

or·di·nar·y ['ɔːrdɪnerɪ] *adj* común, normal

ore [ɔːr] mineral, mena *f*

or·gan ['ɔːrɡən] ANAT, MUS órgano *m*

or·gan·ic [ɔːr'ɡænɪk] *adj food* ecológico, biológico; *fertilizer* orgánico

or·gan·i·cal·ly [ɔːr'ɡænɪklɪ] *adv grown* ecológicamente, biológicamente

or·gan·ism ['ɔːrɡənɪzm] organismo *m*

or·gan·i·za·tion [ɔːrɡənaɪ'zeɪʃn] organización *f*

or·gan·ize ['ɔːrɡənaɪz] *v/t* organizar

or·gan·ized 'crime crimen *m* organizado

or·gan·iz·er ['ɔːrɡənaɪzər] *person* organizador(a) *m(f)*

or·gasm ['ɔːrɡæzm] orgasmo *m*

O·ri·ent ['ɔːrɪent] Oriente *m*

o·ri·ent ['ɔːrɪənt] *v/t* (*direct*) orientar; **~ o.s.** (*get bearings*) orientarse

O·ri·en·tal [ɔːrɪ'entl] **1** *adj* oriental **2** *n* oriental *m/f*

or·i·gin ['ɑːrɪdʒɪn] origen *m*

o·rig·i·nal [ə'rɪdʒənl] **1** *adj* (*not copied, first*) original **2** *n painting etc* original *m*

o·rig·i·nal·i·ty [ərɪdʒən'ælətɪ] originalidad *f*

o·rig·i·nal·ly [ə'rɪdʒənəlɪ] *adv* originalmente; (*at first*) originalmente, en un principio

o·rig·i·nate [ə'rɪdʒɪneɪt] **1** *v/t scheme, idea* crear **2** *v/i of idea, belief* originarse; *of family* proceder

o·rig·i·na·tor [ə'rɪdʒɪneɪtər] *of scheme etc* creador(a) *m(f)*; **he's not an ~** no es un creador nato

or·na·ment ['ɔːrnəmənt] *n* adorno *m*

or·na·men·tal [ɔːrnə'mentl] *adj* ornamental

or·nate [ɔːr'neɪt] *adj style, architecture* recargado

or·phan ['ɔːrfn] *n* huérfano(-a) *m(f)*

or·phan·age ['ɔːrfənɪdʒ] orfanato *m*

or·tho·dox ['ɔːrθədɑːks] *adj* REL, *fig* ortodoxo

or·tho·pe·dic [ɔːrθə'piːdɪk] *adj* ortopédico

os·ten·si·bly [ɑː'stensəblɪ] *adv* aparentemente

os·ten·ta·tion [ɑːsten'teɪʃn] ostentación *f*

os·ten·ta·tious [ɑːsten'teɪʃəs] *adj* ostentoso

os·ten·ta·tious·ly [ɑːsten'teɪʃəslɪ] *adv* de forma ostentosa

os·tra·cize ['ɑːstrəsaɪz] *v/t* condenar al ostracismo

oth·er ['ʌðər] **1** *adj* otro; **~ people might not agree** puede que otros no estén de acuerdo; **the ~ day** (*recently*) el otro día; **every ~ day / person** cada dos días / personas **2** *n*: **the ~** el otro; **the ~s** los otros

oth·er·wise ['ʌðərwaɪz] **1** *conj* de lo contrario, si no **2** *adv* (*differently*) de manera diferente

ot·ter ['ɑːtər] nutria *f*

ought [ɒːt] *v/aux*: **I / you ~ to know** debo / debes saberlo; **you ~ to have done it** deberías haberlo hecho

O

ounce [aʊns] onza f

our [aʊr] adj nuestro m, nuestra f; ~ **brother** nuestro hermano; ~ **books** nuestros libros

ours [aʊrz] pron el nuestro, la nuestra; ~ **are red** los nuestros son rojos; **that book is** ~ ese libro es nuestro; **a friend of** ~ un amigo nuestro

our·selves [aʊr'selvz] pron reflexive nos; emphatic nosotros mismos mpl, nosotras mismas fpl; **we hurt** ~ nos hicimos daño; **when we saw** ~ **in the mirror** cuando nos vimos en el espejo; **we saw it** ~ lo vimos nosotros mismos; **by** ~ (alone) solos; (without help) nosotros solos, nosotras mismos

oust [aʊst] v/t from office derrocar

out [aʊt] adv: **be** ~ of light, fire estar apagado; of flower estar en flor; (not at home, not in building), of sun haber salido; of calculations estar equivocado; (be published) haber sido publicado; (no longer in competition) estar eliminado; (no longer in fashion) estar pasado de moda; **the secret is** ~ el secreto ha sido revelado; ~ **here in Dallas** aquí en Dallas; **he's** ~ **in the garden** está en el jardín; (get) ~! ¡vete!; (get) ~ **of my room!** ¡fuera de mi habitación!; **that's** ~! (out of the question) ¡eso es imposible!; **he's** ~ **to win** (fully intends to) va a por la victoria

out·board 'mo·tor motor m de fueraborda

'out·break of violence, war estallido m

'out·build·ing edificio m anexo

'out·burst emotional arrebato m, arranque m

'out·cast paria m/f

'out·come resultado m

'out·cry protesta f

out'dat·ed adj anticuado

out'do v/t (pret **-did**, pp **-done**) superar

out'door adj toilet, activities, life al aire libre

out'doors adv fuera

out·er ['aʊtər] adj wall etc exterior

out·er 'space espacio m exterior

'out·fit (clothes) traje m, conjunto m; (company, organization) grupo m

'out·go·ing adj flight saliente; personality extrovertido

out'grow v/t (pret **-grew**, pp **-grown**) old ideas dejar atrás

out·ing ['aʊtɪŋ] (trip) excursión f

out'last v/t durar más que

'out·let of pipe desagüe m; for sales punto m de venta; ELEC enchufe m

'out·line 1 n of person, building etc perfil m, contorno m; of plan, novel resumen m **2** v/t plans etc resumir

out'live v/t sobrevivir a

'out·look (prospects) perspectivas fpl

'out·ly·ing adj areas periférico

out'num·ber v/t superar en número

out of prep ◊ motion fuera de; **run** ~ **the house** salir corriendo de la casa; **it fell** ~ **the window** se cayó por la ventana ◊ position: **20 miles** ~ **Detroit** a 20 millas de Detroit ◊ cause por; ~ **jealousy / curiosity** por celos / curiosidad ◊ without: **we're** ~ **gas / beer** no nos queda gasolina / cerveza ◊ from a group de cada; **5** ~ **10** 5 de cada 10

out-of-'date adj anticuado, desfasado

out-of-the-'way adj apartado

'out·pa·tient paciente m/f externo(-a)

'out·pa·tients' (clin·ic) clínica f ambulatoria

'out·per·form v/t superar a

'out·put 1 n of factory producción f; COMPUT salida f **2** v/t (pret & pp **-ted** or **output**) (produce) producir

'out·rage 1 n feeling indignación f; act ultraje m, atrocidad f **2** v/t indignar, ultrajar; **I was** ~**d to hear ...** me indignó escuchar que ...

out·ra·geous [aʊt'reɪdʒəs] adj acts atroz; prices escandaloso

'out·right 1 adj winner absoluto **2** adv win completamente; kill en el acto

out'run v/t (pret **-ran**, pp **-run**) correr más que

'**out·set** principio *m*, comienzo *m*; *from the* ~ desde el principio *or* comienzo

out'shine *v/t* (*pret & pp* **-shone**) eclipsar

'**out·side 1** *adj surface, wall* exterior; *lane de fuera* **2** *adv sit*, *go* fuera **3** *prep* fuera de; (*apart from*) aparte de **4** *n of building*, *case etc* exterior *m*; *at the* ~ a lo sumo

out·side 'broad·cast emisión *f* desde exteriores

out·sid·er [aʊt'saɪdər] *in life* forastero(-a) *m(f)*; *be an* ~ *in election*, *race* no ser uno de los favoritos

'**out·size** *adj clothing* de talla especial

'**out·skirts** *npl* afueras *fpl*

out'smart → **outwit**

out'stand·ing *adj success*, *quality* destacado, sobresaliente; *writer*, *athlete* excepcional; FIN: *invoice*, *sums* pendiente

out·stretched ['aʊtstretʃt] *adj hands* extendido

out'vote *v/t*: *be ~d* perder la votación

out·ward ['aʊtwərd] *adj appearance* externo; ~ *journey* viaje *m* de ida

out·ward·ly ['aʊtwərdlɪ] *adv* aparentemente

out'weigh *v/t* pesar más que

out'wit *v/t* (*pret & pp* **-ted**) mostrarse más listo que

o·val ['oʊvl] *adj* oval, ovalado

o·va·ry ['oʊvərɪ] ovario *m*

o·va·tion [oʊ'veɪʃn] ovación *f*; *give s.o. a standing* ~ aplaudir a alguien de pie

ov·en ['ʌvn] horno *m*

'**ov·en glove**, '**ov·en mitt** manopla *f* para el horno; '**ov·en-proof** *adj* refractario; '**ov·en-read·y** *adj* listo para el horno

o·ver ['oʊvər] **1** *prep* (*above*) sobre, encima de; (*across*) al otro lado de; (*more than*) más de; (*during*) durante; *she walked* ~ *the street* cruzó la calle; *travel all* ~ *Brazil* viajar por todo Brasil; *let's talk* ~ *a drink / meal* hablemos mientras tomamos una bebida / comemos; *we're* ~ *the worst* lo peor ya ha

pasado; ~ *and above* además de **2** *adv*: *be* ~ (*finished*) haber acabado; *there were just 6* ~ sólo quedaban seis; ~ *to you* (*your turn*) te toca a ti; ~ *in Japan* allá en Japón; ~ *here* / *there* por aquí / allá; *it hurts all* ~ me duele por todas partes; *painted white all* ~ pintado todo de blanco; *it's all* ~ se ha acabado; ~ *and* ~ *again* una y otra vez; *do sth* ~ (*again*) volver a hacer algo

o·ver·all ['oʊvərɔːl] **1** *adj length* total **2** *adv* (*in general*) en general; *it measures six feet* ~ mide en total seis pies

o·ver·alls ['oʊvərɔːlz] *npl* Span mono *m*, *L.Am.* overol *m*

o·ver'awe *v/t* intimidar; *be ~d by s.o.* / *sth* sentirse intimidado por alguien / algo

o·ver'bal·ance *v/i* perder el equilibrio

o·ver'bear·ing *adj* dominante, despótico

'**o·ver·board** *adv* por la borda; *man* ~! ¡hombre al agua!; *go* ~ *for s.o.* / *sth* entusiasmarse muchísimo con alguien / algo

'**o·ver·cast** *adj day* nublado; *sky* cubierto

o·ver'charge *v/t customer* cobrar de más a

'**o·ver·coat** abrigo *m*

o·ver'come *v/t* (*pret* **-came**, *pp* **-come**) *difficulties*, *shyness* superar, vencer; *be* ~ *by emotion* estar embargado por la emoción

o·ver'crowd·ed *adj train* atestado; *city* superpoblado

o·ver'do *v/t* (*pret* **-did**, *pp* **-done**) (*exaggerate*) exagerar; *in cooking* recocer, cocinar demasiado; *you're* ~*ing things* te estás excediendo

o·ver'done *adj meat* demasiado hecho

'**o·ver·dose** *n* sobredosis *f inv*

'**o·ver·draft** descubierto *m*; *have an* ~ tener un descubierto

o·ver'draw *v/t* (*pret* **-drew**, *pp* **-drawn**) *account* dejar al descubierto; *be $800* ~*n* tener un descubierto de 800 dólares

o·ver'dressed *adj* demasiado trajeado

'o·ver'drive MOT superdirecta *f*

o·ver'due *adj*: *his apology was long ~* se debía haber disculpado hace tiempo

o·ver·es·ti·mate *v/t abilities*, *value* sobreestimar

o·ver·ex·pose *v/t photograph* sobreexponer

'o·ver·flow[1] *n pipe* desagüe *m*, rebosadero *m*

o·ver'flow[2] *v/i of water* desbordarse

o·ver'grown *adj garden* abandonado, cubierto de vegetación; *he's an ~ baby* es como un niño

o·ver'haul *v/t engine*, *plans* revisar

'o·ver·head **1** *adj lights*, *railway* elevado **2** *n* FIN gastos *mpl* generales

o·ver'hear *v/t* (*pret & pp* ***-heard***) oír por casualidad

o·ver'heat·ed *adj* recalentado

o·ver'joyed [ouvər'dʒɔɪd] *adj* contentísimo, encantado

'o·ver·kill: *that's ~* eso es exagerar

'o·ver·land **1** *adj route* terrestre **2** *adv travel* por tierra

o·ver'lap *v/i* (*pret & pp* ***-ped***) *of tiles etc* solaparse; *of periods of time* coincidir; *of theories* tener puntos en común

o·ver'leaf *adv*: *see ~* véase al dorso

o·ver'load *v/t vehicle*, ELEC sobrecargar

o·ver'look *v/t of tall building etc* dominar; (*not see*) pasar por alto

'o·ver·ly ['ouvərlɪ] *adv* excesivamente, demasiado

'o·ver·night *adv travel* por la noche; *stay ~* quedarse a pasar la noche

o·ver·night 'bag bolso *m* de viaje

o·ver'paid: *be ~* cobrar demasiado

'o·ver·pass paso *m* elevado

o·ver·pop·u·lat·ed [ouvər'pɑːpjuleɪtɪd] *adj* superpoblado

o·ver'pow·er *v/t physically* dominar

o·ver·pow·er·ing [ouvər'pauriŋ] *adj smell* fortísimo; *sense of guilt* insoportable

o·ver'priced [ouvər'praɪst] *adj* demasiado caro

o·ver·rat·ed [ouvə'reɪtɪd] *adj* sobrevalorado

o·ver·re'act *v/i* reaccionar exageradamente

o·ver'ride *v/t* (*pret* ***-rode***, *pp* ***-ridden***) anular

o·ver'rid·ing *adj concern* primordial

o·ver'rule *v/t decision* anular

o·ver'run *v/t* (*pret* ***-ran***, *pp* ***-run***) *country* invadir; *time* superar; *be ~ with* estar plagado de

o·ver'seas **1** *adv live*, *work* en el extranjero; *go* al extranjero **2** *adj* extranjero

o·ver'see *v/t* (*pret* ***-saw***, *pp* ***-seen***) supervisar

o·ver'shad·ow *v/t fig* eclipsar

'o·ver·sight descuido *m*

o·ver·sim·pli·fi·ca·tion simplificación *f* excesiva

o·ver·sim·pli·fy *v/t* (*pret & pp* ***-ied***) simplificar en exceso

o·ver'sleep *v/i* (*pret & pp* ***-slept***) quedarse dormido

o·ver'state *v/t* exagerar

o·ver'state·ment exageración *f*

o·ver'step *v/t* (*pret & pp* ***-ped***) *fig* traspasar; *~ the mark* propasarse, pasarse de la raya

o·ver'take *v/t* (*pret* ***-took***, *pp* ***-taken***) *in work*, *development* adelantarse a; *Br* MOT adelantar

o·ver'throw[1] *v/t* (*pret* ***-threw***, *pp* ***-thrown***) derrocar

'o·ver·throw[2] *n* derrocamiento *m*

'o·ver·time **1** *n* SP: *in ~* en la prórroga **2** *adv*: *work ~* hacer horas extras

'o·ver·ture ['ouvərtʃur] MUS obertura *f*; *make ~s to* establecer contactos con

o·ver'turn **1** *v/t vehicle* volcar; *object* dar la vuelta a; *government* derribar **2** *v/i of vehicle* volcar

'o·ver·view visión *f* general

'o·ver·weight *adj* con sobrepeso; *be ~* estar demasiado gordo

o·ver'whelm [ouvər'welm] *v/t with work* abrumar, inundar; *with emotion* abrumar; *be ~ed by* by *response* estar abrumado por

o·ver·whelm·ing [oʊvər'welmɪŋ] *adj feeling* abrumador; *majority* aplastante

o·ver'work 1 *n* exceso *m* de trabajo **2** *v/i* trabajar en exceso **3** *v/t* hacer trabajar en exceso

owe [oʊ] *v/t* deber; ~ *s.o. $500* deber a alguien 500 dólares; *how much do I ~ you?* ¿cuánto te debo?

ow·ing to ['oʊɪŋ] *prep* debido a

owl [aʊl] búho *m*

own¹ [oʊn] *v/t* poseer; *who ~s the restaurant?* ¿de quién es el restaurante?, ¿quién es el propietario del restaurante?

own² [oʊn] **1** *adj* propio **2** *pron*: *a car/ an apartment of my* ~ mi propio coche/apartamento; *on my/ his* ~ yo/él solo

♦ **own up** *v/i* confesar

own·er ['oʊnər] dueño(-a) *m(f)*, propietario(-a) *m(f)*

own·er·ship ['oʊnərʃɪp] propiedad *f*

ox [ɑːks] (*pl* **oxen** ['ɑːksn]) buey *m*

ox·ide ['ɑːksaɪd] óxido *m*

ox·y·gen ['ɑːksɪdʒən] oxígeno *m*

oy·ster ['ɔɪstər] ostra *f*

oz *abbr* (= *ounce(s)*) onza(s) *f(pl)*

o·zone ['oʊzoʊn] ozono *m*

'o·zone lay·er capa *f* de ozono

P

PA [piːˈeɪ] *abbr* (= *personal assistant*) secretario(-a) *m(f)* personal

pace [peɪs] **1** *n* (*step*) paso *m*; (*speed*) ritmo *m* **2** *v/i*: ~ *up and down* pasear de un lado a otro

'pace·mak·er MED marcapasos *m inv*; SP liebre *f*

Pa·cif·ic [pəˈsɪfɪk]: *the* ~ (*Ocean*) el (Océano) Pacífico

pac·i·fi·er ['pæsɪfaɪər] chupete *m*

pac·i·fism ['pæsɪfɪzm] pacifismo *m*

pac·i·fist ['pæsɪfɪst] *n* pacifista *m/f*

pac·i·fy ['pæsɪfaɪ] *v/t* (*pret & pp* **-ied**) tranquilizar; *country* pacificar

pack [pæk] **1** *n* (*back*~) mochila *f*; *of cereal, food, cigarettes* paquete *m*; *of cards* baraja *f* **2** *v/t item of clothing etc* meter en la maleta; *goods* empaquetar; *groceries* meter en una bolsa; ~ *one's bag/ suitcase* hacer la bolsa/ la maleta **3** *v/i* hacer la maleta

pack·age ['pækɪdʒ] **1** *n* paquete *m* **2** *v/t in packs* embalar; *idea, project* presentar

'pack·age deal *for holiday* paquete *m*

'pack·age tour viaje *m* organizado

pack·ag·ing ['pækɪdʒɪŋ] *of product* embalaje *m*; *of idea, project* presentación *f*; *it's all* ~ *fig* es sólo imagen

packed [pækt] *adj* (*crowded*) abarrotado

pack·et ['pækɪt] paquete *m*

pact [pækt] pacto *m*

pad¹ [pæd] **1** *n for protection* almohadilla *f*; *for absorbing liquid* compresa *f*; *for writing* bloc *m* **2** *v/t* (*pret & pp* **-ded**) *with material* acolchar; *speech, report* meter paja en

pad² *v/i* (*pret & pp* **-ded**) (*move quietly*) caminar silenciosamente

pad·ded shoulders ['pædɪd] hombreras *fpl*

pad·ding ['pædɪŋ] *material* relleno *m*; *in speech etc* paja *f*

pad·dle ['pædəl] **1** *n for canoe* canalete *m*, remo *m* **2** *v/i in canoe* remar; *in water* chapotear

pad·dock ['pædək] potrero *m*

pad·lock ['pædlɑːk] **1** *n* candado *m* **2** *v/t gate* cerrar con candado; *I ~ed*

my bike to the railings até mi bicicleta a la verja con candado

page¹ [peɪdʒ] *n of book etc* página *f*; **~ number** número *m* de página

page² [peɪdʒ] *v/t (call)* llamar; *by PA* llamar por megafonía; *by beeper* llamar por el buscapersonas *or Span* busca

pag·er ['peɪdʒər] buscapersonas *m inv*, *Span* busca *m*

paid [peɪd] *pret & pp* → **pay**

paid em·ploy·ment empleo *m* remunerado

pail [peɪl] cubo *m*

pain [peɪn] dolor *m*; **be in ~** sentir dolor; **take ~s to ...** tomarse muchas molestias por ...; **a ~ in the neck** una lata F, un tostón F

pain·ful ['peɪnfəl] *adj* dolorido; *blow, condition, subject* doloroso; *(laborious)* difícil; **my arm is still very ~** me sigue doliendo mucho el brazo

pain·ful·ly ['peɪnfəlɪ] *adv (extremely, acutely)* extremadamente

pain·kill·er ['peɪnkɪlər] analgésico *m*

pain·less ['peɪnlɪs] *adj* indoloro; **be completely ~** doler nada

pains·tak·ing ['peɪnzteɪkɪŋ] *adj* meticuloso

paint [peɪnt] **1** *n* pintura *f* **2** *v/t* pintar

paint·brush ['peɪntbrʌʃ] *large* brocha *f*; *small* pincel *m*

paint·er ['peɪntər] *decorator* pintor(a) *m(f)* (de brocha gorda); *artist* pintor(a) *m(f)*

paint·ing ['peɪntɪŋ] *activity* pintura *f*; *picture* cuadro *m*

paint·work ['peɪntwɜːrk] pintura *f*

pair [per] *of shoes, gloves, objects* par *m*; *of people, animals* pareja *f*

pa·ja·ma 'jack·et camisa *f* de pijama

pa·ja·ma 'pants *npl* pantalón *m* de pijama

pa·ja·mas [pəˈdʒɑːməz] *npl* pijama *m*

Pa·ki·stan [pɑːkɪˈstɑːn] Paquistán, Pakistán

Pa·ki·sta·ni [pɑːkɪˈstɑːnɪ] **1** *n* paquistaní *m/f*, pakistaní *m/f* **2** *adj* paquistaní, pakistaní

pal [pæl] F *(friend)* amigo(-a) *m(f)*,

Span colega *m/f* F; **hey ~, got a light?** oye amigo *or Span* tío, ¿tienes fuego?

pal·ace ['pælɪs] palacio *m*

pal·ate ['pælət] paladar *m*

pa·la·tial [pəˈleɪʃl] *adj* palaciego

pale [peɪl] *of person* pálido; **she went ~** palideció; **~ pink / blue** rosa / azul claro

Pal·e·stine ['pæləstaɪn] Palestina

Pal·e·stin·i·an [pæləˈstɪnɪən] **1** *n* palestino(-a) *m(f)* **2** *adj* palestino

pal·let ['pælɪt] palé *m*

pal·lor ['pælər] palidez *f*

palm [pɑːm] *of hand* palma *f*; *tree* palmera *f*

pal·pi·ta·tions [pælpɪˈteɪʃnz] *npl* MED palpitaciones *fpl*

pal·try ['pɒltrɪ] *adj* miserable

pam·per ['pæmpər] *v/t* mimar

pam·phlet ['pæmflɪt] *for information* folleto *m*; *political* panfleto *m*

pan [pæn] **1** *n for cooking* cacerola *f*; *for frying* sartén *f* **2** *v/t* (*pret & pp* **-ned**) F *(criticize)* poner por los suelos F

♦ **pan out** *v/i (develop)* salir

Pan·a·ma ['pænəmɑː] Panamá

Pan·a·ma Ca'nal: the ~ el Canal de Panamá

Pan·a·ma 'Cit·y Ciudad *f* de Panamá

Pan·a·ma·ni·an [pænəˈmeɪnɪən] **1** *adj* panameño **2** *n* panameño(-a) *m(f)*

pan·cake ['pænkeɪk] crepe *m*, *L.Am.* panqueque *m*

pan·da ['pændə] (oso *m*) panda *m*

pan·de·mo·ni·um [pændɪˈmoʊnɪəm] pandemónium *m*, pandemonio *m*

♦ **pan·der to** ['pændər] *v/t* complacer

pane [peɪn] *of glass* hoja *f*

pan·el ['pænl] panel *m*; *people* grupo *m*, panel *m*

pan·el·ing, *Br* **pan·el·ling** ['pænəlɪŋ] paneles *mpl*; *of ceiling* artesonado *m*

pang [pæŋ]: **~s of hunger** retortijones *mpl*; **~s of remorse** remordimientos *mpl*

'pan·han·dle *v/i* F mendigar

pan·ic ['pænɪk] **1** *n* pánico *m* **2** *v/i*

(*pret & pp* **-ked**) ser preso del pánico; ***don't ~*** ¡que no cunda el pánico!

'**pan·ic buy·ing** FIN compra *f* provocada por el pánico; '**pan·ic sel·ling** FIN venta *f* provocada por el pánico; '**pan·ic-strick·en** preso del pánico

pan·o·ra·ma [pænə'rɑːmə] panorama *m*

pa·no·ram·ic [pænə'ræmɪk] *adj view* panorámico

pan·sy ['pænzɪ] *flower* pensamiento *m*

pant [pænt] *v/i* jadear

pan·ties ['pæntɪz] *npl Span* bragas *fpl*, *L.Am.* calzones *mpl*

pan·ti·hose → **pantyhose**

pants [pænts] *npl* pantalones *mpl*

pan·ty·hose ['pæntɪhouz] medias *fpl*, pantis *mpl*

pa·pal ['peɪpl] *adj* papal

pa·per ['peɪpər] **1** *n* papel *m*; (*news~*) periódico *m*; *academic* estudio *m*; *at conference* ponencia *f*; (*examination ~*) examen *m*; **~s** (*documents*) documentos *mpl*; *of vehicle*, (*identity ~s*) papeles *mpl*, documentación *f*; **a piece of ~** un trozo de papel **2** *adj* de papel **3** *v/t room, walls* empapelar

'**pa·per·back** libro *m* en rústica; '**pa·per 'bag** bolsa *f* de papel; '**pa·per boy** repartidor *m* de periódicos; '**pa·per clip** clip *m*; '**pa·per cup** vaso *m* de papel; '**pa·per·work** papeleo *m*

par [pɑːr] *in golf* par *m*; **be on a ~ with** ser comparable a; **feel below ~** sentirse en baja forma

par·a·chute ['pærəʃuːt] **1** *n* paracaídas *m inv* **2** *v/i* saltar en paracaídas **3** *v/t troops, supplies* lanzar en paracaídas

par·a·chut·ist ['pærəʃuːtɪst] paracaidista *m/f*

pa·rade [pə'reɪd] **1** *n procession* desfile *m* **2** *v/i* desfilar; (*walk about*) pasearse **3** *v/t knowledge, new car* hacer ostentación de

par·a·dise ['pærədaɪs] paraíso *m*

par·a·dox ['pærədɑːks] paradoja *f*

par·a·dox·i·cal [pærə'dɑːksɪkl] *adj* paradójico

par·a·dox·i·cal·ly [pærə'dɑːksɪklɪ]

adv paradójicamente

par·a·graph ['pærəgræf] párrafo *m*

Par·a·guay ['pærəgwaɪ] Paraguay

Par·a·guay·an [pærə'gwaɪən] **1** *adj* paraguayo **2** *n* paraguayo(-a) *m(f)*

par·al·lel ['pærəlel] **1** *n* GEOM paralela *f*; GEOG paralelo *m*; *fig* paralelismo *m*; **draw a ~** establecer un paralelismo; **do two things in ~** hacer dos cosas al mismo tiempo **2** *adj also fig* paralelo **3** *v/t* (*match*) equipararse a

pa·ral·y·sis [pə'ræləsɪs] parálisis *f*

par·a·lyze ['pærəlaɪz] *v/t also fig* paralizar

par·a·med·ic [pærə'medɪk] *n* auxiliar *m/f* sanitario(-a)

pa·ram·e·ter [pə'ræmɪtər] parámetro *m*

par·a·mil·i·tar·y [pærə'mɪlɪterɪ] **1** *adj* paramilitar **2** *n* paramilitar *m/f*

par·a·mount ['pærəmaunt] *adj* supremo, extremo; **be ~** ser de importancia capital

par·a·noi·a [pærə'nɔɪə] paranoia *f*

par·a·noid [pærə'nɔɪd] *adj* paranoico

par·a·pher·na·li·a [pærəfər'neɪlɪə] parafernalia *f*

par·a·phrase ['pærəfreɪz] *v/t* parafrasear

par·a·pleg·ic [pærə'pliːdʒɪk] *n* parapléjico(-a) *m(f)*

par·a·site ['pærəsaɪt] *also fig* parásito *m*

par·a·sol ['pærəsɑːl] sombrilla *f*

par·a·troop·er ['pærətruːpər] paracaidista *m/f* (*militar*)

par·cel ['pɑːrsl] *n* paquete *m*

♦ **parcel up** *v/t* empaquetar

parch [pɑːrtʃ] *v/t* secar; **be ~ed** F *of person* estar muerto de sed F

par·don ['pɑːrdn] **1** *n* LAW indulto *m*; **I beg your ~?** (*what did you say?*) ¿cómo ha dicho?; **I beg your ~** (*I'm sorry*) discúlpeme **2** *v/t* perdonar; LAW indultar; **~ me?** ¿perdón?, ¿qué?

pare [per] *v/t* (*peel*) pelar

par·ent ['perənt] *father* padre *m*; *mother* madre *f*; **my ~s** mis padres

pa·ren·tal [pə'rentl] *adj* de los padres

'par·ent com·pa·ny empresa *f* matriz

pa·ren·the·sis [pə'renθəsɪs] (*pl* **parentheses** [pə'renθəsi:z]) paréntesis *m inv*

par·ent-'teach·er as·so·ci·a·tion asociación *f* de padres y profesores

par·ish ['pærɪʃ] parroquia *f*

park¹ [pɑːrk] *n* parque *m*

park² [pɑːrk] *v/t & v/i* MOT estacionar, *Span* aparcar

par·ka ['pɑːrkə] parka *f*

par·king ['pɑːrkɪŋ] MOT estacionamiento *m*, *Span* aparcamiento *m*; **no ~** prohibido aparcar

'par·king brake freno *m* de mano; 'par·king disc disco *m* (de aparcamiento); 'par·king ga·rage párking *m*, *Span* aparcamiento *m*; 'par·king lot estacionamiento *m*, *Span* aparcamiento *m* (al aire libre); 'par·king me·ter parquímetro *m*; 'par·king place (plaza *f* de) estacionamiento *or Span* aparcamiento, sitio *m* para estacionar *or Span* aparcar; 'par·king tick·et multa *f* de estacionamiento

par·lia·ment ['pɑːrləmənt] parlamento *m*

par·lia·men·ta·ry [pɑːrlə'mentərɪ] *adj* parlamentario

pa·role [pə'roʊl] **1** *n* libertad *f* condicional; **be on ~** estar en libertad condicional **2** *v/t* poner en libertad condicional; **be ~d** salir en libertad condicional

par·rot ['pærət] *n* loro *m*

pars·ley ['pɑːrslɪ] perejil *m*

part [pɑːrt] **1** *n* (*portion, area*) parte *f*; (*episode*) parte *f*, episodio *m*; *of machine* pieza *f* (de repuesto); *in play, film* papel *m*; *in hair* raya *f*; **take ~ in** tomar parte en **2** *adv* (*partly*) en parte; **~ American, ~ Spanish** medio americano medio español; **~ fact, ~ fiction** con una parte de realidad y una parte de ficción **3** *v/i* separarse **4** *v/t*: **~ one's hair** hacerse la raya

♦ **part with** *v/t* desprenderse de

'part ex·change: **take sth in ~** llevarse algo como parte del pago

par·tial ['pɑːrʃl] *adj* (*incomplete*) parcial; **be ~ to** tener debilidad por

par·tial·ly ['pɑːrʃəlɪ] *adv* parcialmente

par·ti·ci·pant [pɑːr'tɪsɪpənt] participante *m/f*

par·ti·ci·pate [pɑːr'tɪsɪpeɪt] *v/i* participar

par·ti·ci·pa·tion [pɑːrtɪsɪ'peɪʃn] participación *f*

par·ti·cle ['pɑːrtɪkl] PHYS partícula *f*; (*small amount*) pizca *f*

par·tic·u·lar [pər'tɪkjələr] *adj* (*specific*) particular, concreto; (*demanding*) exigente; *about friends, employees* selectivo; *pej* especial, quisquilloso; *you know how ~ she is* ya sabes lo especial que es; *this ~ morning* precisamente esta mañana; *in ~* en particular; *it's a ~ favorite of mine* es uno de mis preferidos

par·tic·u·lar·ly [pər'tɪkjələrlɪ] *adv* particularmente, especialmente

par·ti·tion [pɑːr'tɪʃn] **1** *n* (*screen*) tabique *m*; *of country* partición *f*, división *f* **2** *v/t country* dividir

♦ **partition off** *v/t* dividir con tabiques

part·ly ['pɑːrtlɪ] *adv* en parte

part·ner ['pɑːrtnər] COM socio(-a) *m(f)*; *in relationship* compañero(-a) *m(f)*; *in tennis, dancing* pareja *f*

part·ner·ship ['pɑːrtnərʃɪp] COM sociedad *f*; *in particular activity* colaboración *f*

part of 'speech parte *f* de la oración; 'part own·er copropietario(-a) *m(f)*; 'part-time **1** *adj* a tiempo parcial **2** *adv work* a tiempo parcial; part-'tim·er: **be a ~** trabajar a tiempo parcial

par·ty ['pɑːrtɪ] **1** *n* (*celebration*) fiesta *f*; POL partido *m*; (*group of people*) grupo *m*; **be a ~ to** tomar parte en **2** *v/i* (*pret & pp -ied*) F salir de marcha F

pass [pæs] **1** *n for entry, in mountains* desfiladero *m*; **make a ~ at** tirarle los tejos a **2** *v/t* (*hand*) pasar; (*go past*) pasar por delante de;

(*overtake*) adelantar; (*go beyond*) sobrepasar; (*approve*) aprobar; ~ **an exam** aprobar un examen; ~ **sentence** LAW dictar sentencia; ~ **the time** pasar el tiempo **3** v/i of time pasar; in exam aprobar; (*go away*) pasarse

♦ **pass around** v/t repartir

♦ **pass away** v/i euph fallecer, pasar a mejor vida

♦ **pass by 1** v/t (*go past*) pasar por **2** v/i (*go past*) pasarse

♦ **pass on 1** v/t information, book pasar; ~ **the savings to ...** of supermarket etc revertir el ahorro en ... **2** v/i (*euph: die*) fallecer, pasar a mejor vida

♦ **pass out** v/i (*faint*) desmayarse

♦ **pass through** v/t town pasar por

♦ **pass up** v/t opportunity dejar pasar

pass·a·ble ['pæsəbl] adj road transitable; (*acceptable*) aceptable

pas·sage ['pæsɪdʒ] (*corridor*) pasillo m; from poem, book pasaje m; of time paso m

pas·sage·way ['pæsɪdʒweɪ] pasillo m

pas·sen·ger ['pæsɪndʒər] pasajero(-a) m(f)

'**pas·sen·ger seat** asiento m de pasajero

pas·ser·by [pæsər'baɪ] (*pl* **passersby**) transeúnte m/f

pas·sion ['pæʃn] pasión f; **a crime of** ~ un crimen pasional

pas·sion·ate ['pæʃnət] adj lover apasionado; (*fervent*) fervoroso

pas·sive ['pæsɪv] **1** adj pasivo **2** n GRAM (voz f) pasiva f; **in the** ~ en pasiva

'**pass mark** EDU nota f mínima para aprobar; **Pass·o·ver** ['pæsoʊvər] REL Pascua f de los hebreos; **pass·port** ['pæspɔrt] pasaporte m; '**pass·port con·trol** control m de pasaportes; '**pass·word** contraseña f

past [pæst] **1** adj (*former*) pasado; **his** ~ **life** su pasado; **the** ~ **few days** los últimos días; **that's all** ~ **now** todo eso es agua pasada **2** n pasado m; **in the** ~ antiguamente **3** prep in

position después de; **it's half** ~ **two** son las dos y media; **it's** ~ **seven o'clock** pasan de las siete; **it's** ~ **your bedtime** hace rato que tenías que haberte ido a la cama **4** adv: **run/walk** ~ pasar

pas·ta ['pæstə] pasta f

paste [peɪst] **1** n (*adhesive*) cola f **2** v/t (*stick*) pegar

pas·tel ['pæstl] **1** n color pastel m **2** adj pastel

pas·time ['pæstaɪm] pasatiempo m

pas·tor ['pæstər] vicario m

past par·ti·ci·ple GRAM participio m pasado

pas·tra·mi [pə'strɑːmɪ] pastrami m, carne de vaca ahumada con especias

pas·try ['peɪstrɪ] for pie masa f; small cake pastel m

'**past tense** GRAM (tiempo m) pasado m

pas·ty ['peɪstɪ] adj complexion pálido

pat [pæt] **1** n palmadita f; **give s.o. a** ~ **on the back** fig dar una palmadita a alguien en la espalda **2** v/t (*pret & pp* **-ted**) dar palmaditas a

patch [pætʃ] **1** n on clothing parche m; (*area*) mancha f; **a bad** ~ (*period of time*) un mal momento, una mala racha; ~**es of fog** zonas de niebla; **not be a** ~ **on** fig no tener ni punto de comparación con **2** v/t clothing remendar

♦ **patch up** v/t (*repair temporarily*) hacer un remiendo a, arreglar a medias; quarrel solucionar

patch·work ['pætʃwɜrk] **1** n needlework labor f de retazo **2** adj hecho de remiendos

patch·y ['pætʃɪ] quality desigual; work, performance irregular

pâ·té [pɑː'teɪ] paté m

pa·tent ['peɪtnt] **1** adj patente, evidente **2** n for invention patente f **3** v/t invention patentar

pa·tent 'leath·er charol m

pa·tent·ly ['peɪtntlɪ] (*clearly*) evidentemente, claramente

pa·ter·nal [pə'tɜːrnl] relative paterno; pride, love paternal

pa·ter·nal·ism [pə'tɜːrnlɪzm] pater-

P

nalismo *m*

pa·ter·nal·is·tic [pətɜːrnl'ɪstɪk] *adj* paternalista

pa·ter·ni·ty [pə'tɜːrnɪtɪ] paternidad *f*

path [pæθ] *also fig* camino *m*

pa·thet·ic [pə'θetɪk] *adj invoking pity* patético; F (*very bad*) lamentable F

path·o·log·i·cal [pæθə'lɑːdʒɪkl] *adj* patológico

pa·thol·o·gist [pə'θɑːlədʒɪst] patólogo(-a) *m(f)*

pa·thol·o·gy [pə'θɑːlədʒɪ] patología *f*

pa·tience ['peɪʃns] paciencia *f*

pa·tient ['peɪʃnt] **1** *n* paciente *m/f* **2** *adj* paciente; *just be ~!* ¡ten paciencia!

pa·tient·ly ['peɪʃntlɪ] *adv* pacientemente

pat·i·o ['pætɪou] patio *m*

pat·ri·ot ['peɪtrɪət] patriota *m/f*

pat·ri·ot·ic [peɪtrɪ'ɑːtɪk] *adj* patriótico

pa·tri·ot·ism ['peɪtrɪətɪzm] patriotismo *m*

pa·trol [pə'troul] **1** *n* patrulla *f*; *be on ~* estar de patrulla **2** *v/t* (*pret & pp -led*) *streets, border* patrullar

pa·trol car coche *m* patrulla; **pa·trol·man** policía *m*, patrullero *m*; **pa·trol wag·on** furgón *m* policial

pa·tron ['peɪtrən] *of store, movie theater* cliente *m/f; of artist, charity etc* patrocinador(a) *m(f)*

pa·tron·ize ['pætrənaɪz] *v/t person* tratar con condescendencia *or* como a un niño

pa·tron·iz·ing ['pætrənaɪzɪŋ] condescendiente

pa·tron 'saint santo(-a) *m(f)* patrón(-ona), patrón(-ona) *m(f)*

pat·ter ['pætər] **1** *n of rain etc* repiqueteo *m*; F *of salesman* parloteo *m* F **2** *v/i* repiquetear

pat·tern ['pætərn] *n on wallpaper, fabric* estampado *m; for knitting, sewing* diseño *m*; (*model*) modelo *m; in behavior, events* pauta *f*

pat·terned ['pætərnd] *adj* estampado

paunch [pɔːntʃ] barriga *f*

pause [pɔːz] **1** *n* pausa *f* **2** *v/i* parar; *when speaking* hacer una pausa **3** *v/t tape* poner en pausa

pave [peɪv] *with concrete* pavimentar; *with slabs* adoquinar; *~ the way for fig* preparar el terreno para

pave·ment ['peɪvmənt] (*roadway*) calzada *f*; Br (*sidewalk*) acera *f*

pav·ing stone ['peɪvɪŋ] losa *f*

paw [pɔː] **1** *n of animal* pata *f*; F (*hand*) pezuña *f* F **2** *v/t* F sobar F

pawn¹ [pɔːn] *n in chess* peón *m; fig* títere *m*

pawn² [pɔːn] *v/t* empeñar

'pawn·bro·ker prestamista *m/f*

'pawn·shop casa *f* de empeños

pay [peɪ] **1** *n* paga *f*, sueldo *m; in the ~ of* a sueldo de **2** *v/t* (*pret & pp paid*) *employee, sum, bill* pagar; *~ attention* prestar atención; *~ s.o. a compliment* hacer un cumplido a alguien **3** *v/i* (*pret & pp paid*) pagar; (*be profitable*) ser rentable; *it doesn't ~ to ...* no conviene ...; *~ for purchase* pagar; *you'll ~ for this! fig* ¡me las pagarás!

♦ **pay back** *v/t person* devolver el dinero a; *loan* devolver

♦ **pay in** *v/t to bank* ingresar

♦ **pay off 1** *v/t debt* liquidar; (*bribe*) sobornar **2** *v/i* (*be profitable*) valer la pena

♦ **pay up** *v/i* pagar

pay·a·ble ['peɪəbl] *adj* pagadero

'pay check, Br 'pay cheque cheque *m* del sueldo

'pay·day día *m* de paga

pay·ee [peɪ'iː] beneficiario(-a) *m(f)*

'pay en·ve·lope sobre *m* con la paga

pay·er ['peɪər] pagador(a) *m(f) they are good ~s* pagan puntualmente

pay·ment ['peɪmənt] pago *m*

'pay phone teléfono *m* público; 'pay·roll salarios *mpl; employees* nómina *f*; *be on the ~* estar en nómina; 'pay·slip nómina *f* (*papel*)

PC [piː'siː] *abbr* (= *personal computer*) PC *m*, Span ordenador *m or* L.Am. computadora personal; (= *politically correct*) políticamente correcto

pea [piː] *Span* guisante *m*, *L.Am.* arveja *f*, *Mex* chícharo *m*

peace [piːs] paz *f*; (*quietness*) tranquilidad

peace·a·ble ['piːsəbl] *adj person* pacífico

'**Peace Corps** organización gubernamental estadounidense de ayuda al desarrollo

peace·ful ['piːsfəl] *adj* tranquilo; *demonstration* pacífico

peace·ful·ly ['piːsfəlɪ] *adv* pacíficamente

peach [piːtʃ] *fruit* melocotón *m*, *L.Am.* durazno *m*; *tree* melocotonero *m*, *L.Am.* duraznero *m*

pea·cock ['piːkɑːk] pavo *m* real

peak [piːk] **1** *n of mountain* cima *f*; *mountain* pico *m*; *fig* clímax *m* **2** *v/i* alcanzar el máximo

'**peak hours** *npl* horas *fpl* punta

pea·nut ['piːnʌt] cacahuete *m*, *L.Am.* maní *m*, *Mex* cacahuate *m*; **get paid ~s** F cobrar una miseria F; **that's ~s to him** F eso es calderilla para él F

pea·nut 'but·ter crema *f* de cacahuete

pear [per] pera *f*

pearl [pɜːrl] perla *f*

peas·ant ['peznt] campesino(-a) *m(f)*

peb·ble ['pebl] guijarro *m*

pe·can ['piːkən] pacana *f*

peck [pek] **1** *n bite* picotazo *m*; *kiss* besito *m* **2** *v/t bite* picotear; *kiss* dar un besito a

pe·cu·li·ar [pɪ'kjuːljər] *adj* (*strange*) raro; **~ to** (*special*) característico de

pe·cu·li·ar·i·ty [pɪkjuːlɪ'ærətɪ] (*strangeness*) rareza *f*; (*special feature*) peculiaridad *f*, característica *f*

ped·al ['pedl] **1** *n of bike* pedal *m* **2** *v/i* (*turn ~s*) pedalear; (*cycle*) recorrer en bicicleta

pe·dan·tic [pɪ'dæntɪk] *adj* puntilloso

ped·dle ['pedl] *v/t drugs* traficar *or* trapichear con

ped·es·tal ['pedəstl] *for statue* pedestal *m*

pe·des·tri·an [pɪ'destrɪən] *n* peatón(-ona) *m(f)*

pe·des·tri·an 'cros·sing paso *m* de peatones

pe·di·at·ric [piːdɪ'ætrɪk] *adj* pediátrico

pe·di·a·tri·cian [piːdɪə'trɪʃn] pediatra *m/f*

pe·di·at·rics [piːdɪ'ætrɪks] pediatría *f*

ped·i·cure ['pedɪkjʊr] pedicura *f*

ped·i·gree ['pedɪgriː] **1** *n of animal* pedigrí; *of person* linaje *m* **2** *adj* con pedigrí

pee [piː] *v/i* F hacer pis F, mear F

peek [piːk] **1** *n* ojeada *f*, vistazo *m* **2** *v/i* echar una ojeada *or* vistazo

peel [piːl] **1** *n* piel *f* **2** *v/t fruit, vegetables* pelar **3** *v/i of nose, shoulders* pelarse; *of paint* levantarse

♦ **peel off 1** *v/t wrapper etc* quitar; *jacket etc* quitarse **2** *v/i of wrapper* quitarse

peep [piːp] → **peek**

peep·hole ['piːphoʊl] mirilla *f*

peer¹ [pɪr] *n* (*equal*) igual *m*

peer² [pɪr] *v/i* mirar; **~ through the mist** buscar con la mirada entre la niebla; **~ at** forzar la mirada para ver

peeved [piːvd] F mosqueado F

peg [peg] *n for hat, coat* percha *f*; *for tent* clavija *f*; **off the ~** de confección

pe·jo·ra·tive [pɪ'dʒɑːrətɪv] *adj* peyorativo

pel·let ['pelɪt] pelotita *f*; (*bullet*) perdigón *m*

pelt [pelt] **1** *v/t*: **~ s.o. with sth** tirar algo a alguien **2** *v/i*: **they ~ed along the road** F fueron a toda mecha por la carretera F; **it's ~ing down** F está diluviando F

pel·vis ['pelvɪs] pelvis *f*

pen¹ [pen] *n* (*ballpoint ~*) bolígrafo *m*; (*fountain ~*) pluma *f* (estilográfica)

pen² [pen] (*enclosure*) corral *m*

pen³ [pen] → **penitentiary**

pe·nal·ize ['piːnəlaɪz] *v/t* penalizar

pen·al·ty ['penltɪ] sanción *f*; SP penalti *m*; **take the ~** *in soccer* lanzar el penalti 'pen·al·ty ar·e·a SP área f de castigo; 'pen·al·ty clause LAW cláusula f de penalización; 'pen·al·ty kick (lanzamiento m de) penalti m; pen·al·ty 'shoot-out tanda f de penaltis; 'pen·al·ty spot punto m de penalti

pen·cil ['pensıl] lápiz m

pen·cil sharp·en·er sacapuntas m inv

pen·dant ['pendənt] necklace colgante m

pend·ing ['pendıŋ] 1 prep en espera de 2 adj pendiente; be ~ awaiting a decision estar pendiente; about to happen ser inminente

pen·e·trate ['penıtreıt] v/t (pierce) penetrar; market penetrar en

pen·e·trat·ing ['penıtreıtıŋ] adj stare, scream penetrante; analysis exhaustivo

pen·e·tra·tion [penı'treıʃn] penetración f; of defences incursión f; of market entrada f

'pen friend amigo(-a) m(f) por correspondencia

pen·guin ['peŋgwın] pingüino m

pen·i·cil·lin [penı'sılın] penicilina f

pe·nin·su·la [pə'nınsʊlə] península f

pe·nis ['piːnıs] pene m

pen·i·tence ['penıtəns] (remorse) arrepentimiento m

pen·i·tent ['penıtənt] adj arrepentido

pen·i·ten·ia·ry [penı'tenʃərı] prisión f, cárcel f

'pen name seudónimo m

pen·nant ['penənt] banderín f

pen·ni·less ['penılıs] adj sin un centavo

pen·ny ['penı] penique m

'pen pal amigo(-a) m(f) por correspondencia

pen·sion ['penʃn] pensión f

♦ pension off v/t jubilar

'pen·sion fund fondo m de pensiones

'pen·sion scheme plan m de jubilación

pen·sive ['pensıv] adj pensativo

Pen·ta·gon ['pentəgaːn]: the ~ el Pentágono

pen·tath·lon [pen'tæθlən] pentatlón m

Pen·te·cost ['pentıkaːst] Pentecostés m

pent·house ['penthaʊs] ático m (de lujo)

pent-up ['pentʌp] adj reprimido

pe·nul·ti·mate [pe'nʌltımət] adj penúltimo

peo·ple ['piːpl] npl gente f; (individuals) personas fpl; (nsg: race, tribe) pueblo m; the ~ (citizens) el pueblo, los ciudadanos; the Spanish ~ los españoles; a lot of ~ think ... muchos piensan que ...; ~ say ... se dice que ..., dicen que ...

pep·per ['pepər] spice pimienta f; vegetable pimiento m

pep·per·mint candy caramelo m de menta

'pep talk ['peptɔːk]: give a ~ decir unas palabras de aliento

per [pɜːr] prep por; ~ annum al año, por año

per·ceive [pər'siːv] v/t with senses percibir; (view, interpret) interpretar

per·cent [pər'sent] adv por ciento

per·cent·age [pər'sentıdʒ] porcentaje m, tanto m por ciento

per·cep·ti·ble [pər'septəbl] adj perceptible

per·cep·ti·bly [pər'septəblı] adv visiblemente

per·cep·tion [pər'sepʃn] through senses percepción f; of situation apreciación f; (insight) perspicacia f

per·cep·tive [pər'septıv] adj perceptivo

perch [pɜːrtʃ] 1 n for bird percha f 2 v/i of bird posarse; of person sentarse

per·co·late ['pɜːrkəleıt] v/i of coffee filtrarse

per·co·la·tor ['pɜːrkəleıtər] cafetera f de filtro

per·cus·sion [pər'kʌʃn] percusión f

per·cus·sion in·stru·ment instrumento m de percusión

pe·ren·ni·al [pə'renıəl] n BOT árbol m de hoja perenne

per·fect 1 n ['pɜːrfıkt] GRAM pretérito *m* perfecto **2** *adj* perfecto **3** *v/t* [pərˈfekt] perfeccionar

per·fec·tion [pərˈfekʃn] perfección *f*; **do sth to ~** hacer algo a la perfección

per·fec·tion·ist [pərˈfekʃnɪst] *n* perfeccionista *m/f*

per·fect·ly [ˈpɜːrfɪktlɪ] perfectamente; (*totally*) completamente

per·fo·rat·ed [ˈpɜːrfəreɪtɪd] *adj line* perforado

per·fo·ra·tions [pɜːrfəˈreɪʃnz] *npl* perforaciones *fpl*

per·form [pərˈfɔːrm] **1** *v/t* (*carry out*) realizar, llevar a cabo; *of actors, musician etc* interpretar, representar **2** *v/i of actor, musician, dancer* actuar; *of machine* funcionar

per·form·ance [pərˈfɔːrməns] *by actor, musician etc* actuación *f*, interpretación *f*; *of play* representación *f*; *of employee* rendimiento *m*; *of official, company, in sport* actuación *f*; *of machine* rendimiento *m*

per'form·ance car coche *m* de gran rendimiento

per·form·er [pərˈfɔːrmər] intérprete *m/f*

per·fume [ˈpɜːrfjuːm] perfume *m*

per·func·to·ry [pərˈfʌŋktərɪ] *adj* superficial

per·haps [pərˈhæps] *adv* quizá(s), tal vez; *~* **it's not too late** puede que no sea demasiado tarde

per·il [ˈperəl] peligro *m*

per·il·ous [ˈperələs] *adj* peligroso

pe·rim·e·ter [pəˈrɪmɪtər] perímetro *m*

pe·rim·e·ter fence cerca *f*

pe·ri·od [ˈpɪrɪəd] periodo *m*, período *m*; (*menstruation*) periodo *m*, regla *f*; *punctuation mark* punto *m*; **I don't want to, ~!** F ¡no me da la gana y punto! F

pe·ri·od·ic [pɪrɪˈɑːdɪk] *adj* periódico

pe·ri·od·i·cal [pɪrɪˈɑːdɪkl] *n* publicación *f* periódica

pe·ri·od·i·cal·ly [pɪrɪˈɑːdɪklɪ] *adv* periódicamente, con periodicidad

pe·riph·e·ral [pəˈrɪfərəl] **1** *adj* (*not crucial*) secundario **2** *n* COMPUT pe-

riférico *m*

pe·riph·e·ry [pəˈrɪfərɪ] periferia *f*

per·ish [ˈperɪʃ] *v/i of rubber* estropearse, picarse; *of person* perecer

per·ish·a·ble [ˈperɪʃəbl] *adj food* perecedero

per·jure [ˈpɜːrdʒər] *v/t:* **~ o.s.** perjurar

per·ju·ry [ˈpɜːrdʒərɪ] perjurio *m*

perk [pɜːrk] *n of job* ventaja *f*

♦ **perk up 1** *v/t* animar **2** *v/i* animarse

perk·y [ˈpɜːrkɪ] (*cheerful*) animado

perm [pɜːrm] **1** *n* permanente *f* **2** *v/t* hacer la permanente; **she had her hair ~ed** se hizo la permanente

per·ma·nent [ˈpɜːrmənənt] *adj* permanente

per·ma·nent·ly [ˈpɜːrmənəntlɪ] *adv* permanentemente

per·me·a·ble [ˈpɜːrmɪəbl] *adj* permeable

per·me·ate [ˈpɜːrmɪeɪt] *v/t* impregnar

per·mis·si·ble [pərˈmɪsəbl] *adj* permisible

per·mis·sion [pərˈmɪʃn] permiso *m*; **ask s.o.'s ~ to ...** pedir permiso a alguien para ...

per·mis·sive [pərˈmɪsɪv] *adj* permisivo

per·mit [ˈpɜːrmɪt] **1** *n* licencia *f* **2** *v/t* (*pret & pp* **-ted**) [pərˈmɪt] permitir; **~ s.o. to do sth** permitir a alguien que haga algo

per·pen·dic·u·lar [pɜːrpənˈdɪkjələr] *adj* perpendicular

per·pet·u·al [pərˈpetʃʊəl] *adj* perpetuo; *interruptions* continuo

per·pet·u·al·ly [pərˈpetʃʊəlɪ] *adv* constantemente

per·pet·u·ate [pərˈpetʃʊeɪt] *v/t* perpetuar

per·plex [pərˈpleks] *v/t* dejar perplejo

per·plexed [pərˈplekst] *adj* perplejo

per·plex·i·ty [pərˈpleksɪtɪ] perplejidad *f*

per·se·cute [ˈpɜːrsɪkjuːt] *v/t* perseguir; (*hound*) acosar

per·se·cu·tion [pɜːrsɪˈkjuːʃn] persecución *f*; (*harassment*) acoso *m*

per·se·cu·tor [pɜːrsɪˈkjuːtər] perseguidor(a) m(f)

per·se·ver·ance [pɜːrsɪ'vɪrəns] perseverancia f

per·se·vere [pɜːrsɪ'vɪr] v/i perseverar

per·sist [pər'sɪst] v/i persistir; **~ in** persistir en

per·sis·tence [pər'sɪstəns] (*perseverance*) perseverancia f; (*continuation*) persistencia f

per·sis·tent [pər'sɪstənt] adj person, questions perseverante; rain, unemployment etc persistente

per·sis·tent·ly [pər'sɪstəntlɪ] adv (*continually*) constantemente

per·son ['pɜːrsn] persona f; **in ~** en persona

per·son·al ['pɜːrsənl] adj (*private*) personal; *life* privado; **don't make ~ remarks** no hagas comentarios personales

per·son·al as·sist·ant secretario(-a) m(f) personal; **'per·son·al col·umn** sección f de anuncios personales; **per·son·al com·put·er** Span ordenador m personal, L.Am. computadora f personal; **per·son·al 'hy·giene** higiene f personal

per·son·al·i·ty [pɜːrsə'nælətɪ] personalidad f; (*celebrity*) personalidad f, personaje m

per·son·al·ly ['pɜːrsənəlɪ] adv (*for my part*) personalmente; (*in person*) en persona; **don't take it ~** no te lo tomes como algo personal

per·son·al 'or·gan·iz·er organizador m personal; **per·son·al 'pro·noun** pronombre m personal; **per·son·al 'ster·e·o** walkman m ®

per·son·i·fy [pɜːr'sɑːnɪfaɪ] v/t (*pret & pp **-ied***) of person personificar

per·son·nel [pɜːrsə'nel] employees, department personal m

per·son·nel man·a·ger director(a) m(f) de personal

per·spec·tive [pər'spektɪv] PAINT perspectiva f; **get sth into ~** poner algo en perspectiva

per·spi·ra·tion [pɜːrspɪ'reɪʃn] sudor m, transpiración f

per·spire [pɜːr'spaɪr] v/i sudar, transpirar

per·suade [pər'sweɪd] v/t person persuadir; **~ s.o. to do sth** persuadir a alguien para que haga algo

per·sua·sion [pər'sweɪʒn] persuasión f

per·sua·sive [pər'sweɪsɪv] adj persuasivo

per·ti·nent ['pɜːrtɪnənt] adj fml pertinente

per·turb [pər'tɜːrb] v/t perturbar

per·turb·ing [pər'tɜːrbɪŋ] adj perturbador

Pe·ru [pə'ruː] n Perú

pe·ruse [pə'ruːz] v/t fml leer atentamente

Pe·ru·vi·an [pə'ruːvɪən] **1** adj peruano **2** n peruano(-a) m(f)

per·va·sive [pər'veɪsɪv] adj influence, ideas dominante

per·verse [pər'vɜːrs] adj (*awkward*) terco; **just to be ~** sólo para llevar la contraria

per·ver·sion [pər'vɜːrʃn] sexual perversión f

per·vert ['pɜːrvɜːrt] n sexual pervertido(-a) m(f)

pes·si·mism ['pesɪmɪzm] pesimismo m

pes·si·mist ['pesɪmɪst] pesimista m/f

pes·si·mist·ic [pesɪ'mɪstɪk] adj pesimista

pest [pest] plaga f; F person tostón m F

pes·ter ['pestər] v/t acosar; **~ s.o. to do sth** molestar or dar la lata a alguien para que haga algo

pes·ti·cide ['pestɪsaɪd] pesticida f

pet [pet] **1** n animal animal m doméstico or de compañía; (*favorite*) preferido(-a) m(f) **2** adj preferido, favorito **3** v/t (*pret & pp **-ted***) animal acariciar **4** v/i (*pret & pp **-ted***) of couple magrearse F

pet·al ['petl] pétalo m

♦**pe·ter out** ['piːtər] v/i of rain amainar; of rebellion irse extinguiendo; of path ir desapareciendo

pe·tite [pə'tiːt] adj chiquito(-a); size menudo

pe·ti·tion [pə'tɪʃn] n petición f

'pet name nombre m cariñoso

pet·ri·fied ['petrɪfaɪd] adj person petrificado; scream, voice aterrorizado

pet·ri·fy ['petrɪfaɪ] v/t (pret & pp -ied) dejar petrificado

pet·ro·chem·i·cal [petroʊ'kemɪkl] adj petroquímico

pet·rol ['petrl] Br gasolina f, Arg nafta f

pe·tro·le·um [pɪ'troʊlɪəm] petróleo m

pet·ting ['petɪŋ] magreo m F

pet·ty ['petɪ] adj person, behavior mezquino; details, problem sin importancia

pet·ty 'cash dinero m para gastos menores

pet·u·lant ['petʃələnt] adj caprichoso

pew [pjuː] banco m (de iglesia)

pew·ter ['pjuːtər] peltre m

phar·ma·ceu·ti·cal [fɑːrmə'suːtɪkl] adj farmacéutico

phar·ma·ceu·ti·cals [fɑːmə'suːtɪklz] npl fármacos mpl

phar·ma·cist ['fɑːrməsɪst] in store farmacéutico(-a) m(f)

phar·ma·cy ['fɑːrməsɪ] store farmacia f

phase [feɪz] fase f; go through a difficult ~ atravesar una mala etapa
♦ phase in v/t introducir gradualmente
♦ phase out v/t eliminar gradualmente

PhD [piːeɪtʃ'diː] abbr (= Doctor of Philosophy) Doctorado m

phe·nom·e·nal [fɪ'nɑːmɪnl] adj fenomenal

phe·nom·e·nal·ly [fɪ'nɑːmɪnlɪ] adv extraordinariamente; stupid increíblemente

phe·nom·e·non [fɪ'nɑːmɪnɑːn] fenómeno m

phil·an·throp·ic [fɪlən'θrɑːpɪk] adj filantrópico

phi·lan·thro·pist [fɪ'lænθrəpɪst] filántropo(-a) m(f)

phi·lan·thro·py [fɪ'lænθrəpɪ] filantropía f

Phil·ip·pines ['fɪlɪpiːnz] npl: the ~ las Filipinas

phil·is·tine ['fɪlɪstaɪn] n filisteo(-a) m(f)

phi·los·o·pher [fɪ'lɑːsəfər] filósofo(-a) m(f)

phil·o·soph·i·cal [fɪlə'sɑːfɪkl] adj filosófico

phi·los·o·phy [fɪ'lɑːsəfɪ] filosofía f

pho·bi·a ['foʊbɪə] fobia f

phone [foʊn] **1** n teléfono m; be on the ~ (have a ~) tener teléfono; be talking estar hablando por teléfono **2** v/t llamar (por teléfono) a **3** v/i llamar (por teléfono)

'phone book guía f (de teléfonos); 'phone booth cabina f (de teléfonos); 'phone-call llamada f (telefónica); 'phone card tarjeta f telefónica; 'phone num·ber número m de teléfono

pho·net·ics [fə'netɪks] fonética f

pho·n(e)y ['foʊnɪ] adj F falso

pho·to ['foʊtoʊ] foto f

'pho·to al·bum álbum m de fotos; 'pho·to·cop·i·er fotocopiadora f; 'pho·to·cop·y **1** n fotocopia f **2** v/t (pret & pp -ied) fotocopiar

pho·to·gen·ic [foʊtoʊ'dʒenɪk] adj fotogénico

pho·to·graph ['foʊtəgræf] **1** n fotografía f **2** v/t fotografiar

pho·tog·ra·pher [fə'tɑːgrəfər] fotógrafo(-a) m(f)

pho·tog·ra·phy [fə'tɑːgrəfɪ] fotografía f

phrase [freɪz] **1** n frase f **2** v/t expresar

'phrase-book guía f de conversación

phys·i·cal ['fɪzɪkl] **1** adj físico **2** n MED reconocimiento m médico

phys·i·cal 'hand·i·cap minusvalía f física

phys·i·cal·ly ['fɪzɪklɪ] adv físicamente

phys·i·cal·ly hand·i·cap·ped disminuido(-a) m(f) físico

phy·si·cian [fɪ'zɪʃn] médico(-a) m(f)

phys·i·cist ['fɪzɪsɪst] físico(-a) m(f)

phys·ics ['fɪzɪks] física f

phys·i·o·ther·a·pist [fɪzɪoʊ'θerəpıst] fisioterapeuta *m/f*

phys·i·o·ther·a·py [fızıou'θerəpı] fisioterapia *f*

phy·sique [fı'zi:k] físico *m*

pi·a·nist ['pıənıst] pianista *m/f*

pi·an·o [pı'ænou] piano *m*

pick [pık] **1** *n:* **take your ~** elige el que prefieras **2** *v/t* (*choose*) escoger, elegir; *flowers, fruit* recoger; **~ one's nose** meterse el dedo en la nariz **3** *v/i:* **~ and choose** ser muy exigente

♦ **pick at** *v/t:* **pick at one's food** comer como un pajarito

♦ **pick on** *v/t* (*treat unfairly*) meterse con; (*select*) elegir

♦ **pick out** *v/t* (*identify*) identificar

♦ **pick up 1** *v/t object* recoger, *Span* coger; *habit* adquirir, *Span* coger; *illness* contraer, *Span* coger; *in car, from ground, from airport etc* recoger; *telephone* descolgar; *language, skill* aprender; (*buy*) comprar; *criminal* detener; **pick s.o. up** *sexually* ligar con alguien **2** *v/i* (*improve*) mejorar

pick·et ['pıkıt] **1** *n of strikers* piquete *m* **2** *v/t* hacer piquete delante de

'pick·et fence valla *f* de estacas

'pick·et line piquete *m*

pick·le ['pıkl] *v/t* encurtir; *fish* poner en escabeche; *meat* poner en adobo

pick·les ['pıklz] *npl* (*dill ~*) encurtidos *mpl*

'pick·pock·et carterista *m/f*

pick·up (truck) ['pıkʌp] camioneta *f*

pick·y ['pıkı] *adj* F tiquismiquis F

pic·nic ['pıknık] **1** *n* picnic *m* **2** *v/i* (*pret & pp* **-ked**) ir de picnic

pic·ture ['pıktʃər] **1** *n* (*photo*) fotografía *f*; (*painting*) cuadro *m*; (*illustration*) dibujo *m*; (*movie*) película *f*, *on TV* imagen *f*; **keep s.o. in the ~** mantener a alguien al día **2** *v/t* imaginar

'pic·ture book libro *m* ilustrado

pic·ture 'post·card postal *f*

pic·tur·esque [pıktʃə'resk] *adj* pintoresco

pie [paı] pastel *m*

piece [pi:s] (*fragment*) fragmento *m*; *component, in board game* pieza *f*; **a ~ of pie/bread** un trozo de pastel / una rebanada de pan; **a ~ of advice** un consejo; **go to ~s** derrumbarse; **take to ~s** desmontar

♦ **piece together** *v/t broken plate* recomponer; *facts, evidence* reconstruir

piece·meal ['pi:smi:l] *adv* poco a poco

piece·work ['pi:swɜ:rk] trabajo *m* a destajo

pier [pır] *at seaside* malecón *m*

pierce [pırs] *v/t* (*penetrate*) perforar; *ears* agujerear

pierc·ing ['pırsıŋ] *adj scream* desgarrador; *gaze* penetrante; *wind* cortante

pig [pıg] *also fig* cerdo *m*; *greedy* glotón(-a) *m(f)*

pi·geon ['pıdʒın] paloma *f*

'pi·geon·hole 1 *n* casillero *m* **2** *v/t person* encasillar; *proposal* archivar

pig·gy·bank ['pıgıbæŋk] hucha *f*

pig·head·ed [pıg'hedıd] *adj* F cabezota F

'pig·pen *also fig* pocilga *f*

'pig·skin piel *f* de cerdo; **'pig·tail** coleta *f*

pile [paıl] montón *m*, pila *f*; **a ~ of work** F un montón de trabajo F

♦ **pile up 1** *v/i of work, bills* acumularse **2** *v/t* amontonar

piles [paılz] *nsg* MED hemorroides *fpl*

pile-up ['paılʌp] MOT choque *m* múltiple

pil·fer·ing ['pılfərıŋ] hurtos *mpl*

pil·grim ['pılgrım] peregrino(-a) *m(f)*

pil·grim·age ['pılgrımıdʒ] peregrinación *f*

pill [pıl] pastilla *f*; **be on the ~** tomar la píldora

pil·lar ['pılər] pilar *m*

pil·lion ['pıljən] *of motor bike* asiento *m* trasero

pil·low ['pılou] *n* almohada *f*

'pill·ow·case, 'pil·low·slip funda *f* de almohada

pi·lot ['paılət] **1** *n of airplane* piloto *m/f; for ship* práctico *m* **2** *v/t airplane* pilotar '**pi·lot scheme** plan *m* piloto

pimp [pɪmp] *n* proxeneta *m*, *Span* chulo *m* F

pim·ple ['pɪmpl] grano *m*

PIN [pɪn] (= *personal identification number*) PIN *m* (= número *m* de identificación personal)

pin [pɪn] **1** *n for sewing* alfiler *m*; *in bowling* bolo *m*; (*badge*) pin *m*; ELEC clavija *f*; *safety ~* imperdible *m* **2** *v/t* (*pret & pp -ned*) (*hold down*) mantener; (*attach*) sujetar

♦ **pin down** *v/t*: *pin s.o. down to a date* forzar a alguien a concretar una fecha

♦ **pin up** *v/t notice* sujetar con chinchetas

pin·cers ['pɪnsərz] *npl of crab* pinzas *fpl*; *tool* tenazas *fpl*; *a pair of ~* unas tenazas *fpl*

pinch [pɪntʃ] **1** *n* pellizco *m*; *of salt, sugar etc* pizca *f*; *at a ~* si no queda otro remedio; *with numbers* como máximo **2** *v/t* pellizcar **3** *v/i of shoes* apretar

pine[1] [paɪn] *n tree* pino *m*; *wood* (madera *f* de) pino *m*

pine[2] [paɪn] *v/i*: *~ for* echar de menos

pine·ap·ple ['paɪnæpl] piña *f*, *L.Am.* ananá(s) *f*

ping [pɪŋ] **1** *n* sonido *m* metálico **2** *v/i* hacer un sonido metálico

ping-pong ['pɪŋpɑːŋ] pimpón *m*, ping-pong *m*

pink [pɪŋk] *adj* rosa

pin·na·cle ['pɪnəkl] *fig* cima *f*

'**pin·point** *v/t* determinar

pins and 'nee·dles *npl* hormigueo *m*

'**pin·stripe** *adj* a rayas

pint [paɪnt] pinta *f, medida equivalente a 0,473 litros en Estados Unidos o a 0,568 litros en Gran Bretaña*

'**pin-up** modelo *m/f* de revista

pi·o·neer [paɪə'nɪr] **1** *n* pionero(-a) *m*(*f*) **2** *v/t* ser pionero en

pi·o·neer·ing [paɪə'nɪrɪŋ] *adj work* pionero

pi·ous ['paɪəs] piadoso

pip [pɪp] *n of fruit* pepita *f*

pipe [paɪp] **1** *n for smoking* pipa *f*; *for water, gas, sewage* tubería *f* **2** *v/t* conducir por tuberías

♦ **pipe down** *v/i* F cerrar el pico F

piped mu·sic [paɪpt'mjuːzɪk] hilo *m* musical

'**pipe·line** *for oil* oleoducto *m*; *for gas* gasoducto *m*; *in the ~ fig* en trámite

pip·ing hot [paɪpɪŋ'hɑːt] *adj* muy caliente

pi·rate ['paɪrət] **1** *n* pirata *m/f* **2** *v/t software* piratear

Pis·ces ['paɪsiːz] ASTR Piscis *m/f inv*

piss [pɪs] **1** *v/i* P (*urinate*) mear P **2** *n* P (*urine*) meada *f* P

pissed [pɪst] *adj* P (*annoyed*) cabreado P; *Br* P (*drunk*) borracho, pedo F

pis·tol ['pɪstl] pistola *f*

pis·ton ['pɪstən] pistón *m*

pit[1] [pɪt] *n* (*hole*) hoyo *m*; (*coal mine*) mina *f*; *in fruit* hueso *m*

pitch[1] [pɪtʃ] *n* MUS tono *m*

pitch[2] [pɪtʃ] **1** *v/i in baseball* lanzar la pelota **2** *v/t tent* montar; *ball* lanzar

'**pitch black** *adj* negro como el carbón

pitch·er[1] ['pɪtʃər] *baseball player* lanzador(a) *m*(*f*), pítcher *m/f*

pitch·er[2] ['pɪtʃər] *container* jarra *f*

pith [pɪθ] *n of citrus fruit* piel *f* blanca

pit·i·ful ['pɪtɪfəl] *adj sight* lastimoso; *excuse, attempt* lamentable

pit·i·less ['pɪtɪləs] *adj* despiadado

pits [pɪts] *npl in motor racing* boxes *mpl*

'**pit stop** *in motor racing* parada *f* en boxes

pit·tance ['pɪtns] miseria *f*

pit·y ['pɪtɪ] **1** *n* pena *f*, lástima *f*; *it's a ~ that* es una pena *or* lástima que; *what a ~!* ¡qué pena!; *take ~ on* compadecerse de **2** *v/t* (*pret & pp -ied*) *person* compadecerse de

piv·ot ['pɪvət] *v/i* pivotar

piz·za ['piːtsə] pizza *f*

plac·ard ['plækɑːrd] pancarta *f*

place [pleɪs] **1** *n* sitio *m*, lugar *m*; *in race, competition* puesto *m*; (*seat*) sitio *m*, asiento *m*; *I've lost my ~ in book* no sé por dónde iba; *at my/his ~* en mi/su casa; *in ~ of* en lugar de;

feel out of ~ sentirse fuera de lugar; *take* ~ tener lugar, llevarse a cabo; *in the first* ~ (*firstly*) en primer lugar; (*in the beginning*) en principio **2** *v/t* (*put*) poner, colocar; *I know you but I can't quite* ~ *you* te conozco pero no recuerdo de qué; ~ *an order* hacer un pedido

'place mat mantel *m* individual

plac·id ['plæsɪd] *adj* apacible

pla·gia·rism ['pleɪdʒərɪzm] plagio *m*

pla·gia·rize ['pleɪdʒəraɪz] *v/t* plagiar

plague [pleɪg] **1** *n* plaga *f* **2** *v/t* (*bother*) molestar

plain¹ [pleɪn] *n* llanura *f*

plain² [pleɪn] **1** *adj* (*clear, obvious*) claro; (*not fancy*) simple; (*not pretty*) feíllo; (*not patterned*) liso; (*blunt*) directo; ~ *chocolate* chocolate amargo **2** *adv* verdaderamente; *it's* ~ *crazy* es una verdadera locura

'plain-clothes: *in* ~ de paisano

plain·ly ['pleɪnlɪ] *adv* (*clearly*) evidentemente; (*bluntly*) directamente; (*simply*) con sencillez; *he's* ~ *upset* está claro que está enfadado

plain 'spo·ken *adj* directo

plain·tiff ['pleɪntɪf] demandante *m/f*

plain·tive ['pleɪntɪv] *adj* quejumbroso

plan [plæn] **1** *n* (*project, intention*) plan *m*; (*drawing*) plano *m*; *wedding* ~*s* preparaciones *fpl* para la boda **2** *v/t* (*pret & pp* -*ned*) (*prepare*) planear; (*design*) hacer los planos de; ~ *to do sth,* ~ *on doing sth* planear hacer algo **3** *v/i* (*pret & pp* -*ned*) hacer planes

plane¹ [pleɪn] *n* (*airplane*) avión *m*

plane² [pleɪn] *tool* cepillo *m*

plan·et ['plænɪt] planeta *f*

plank [plæŋk] *of wood* tablón *m*; *fig: of policy* punto *m*

plan·ning ['plænɪŋ] planificación *f*; *at the* ~ *stage* en fase de estudio

plant¹ [plænt] **1** *n* planta *f* **2** *v/t* plantar

plant² [plænt] *n* (*factory*) fábrica *f*, planta *f*; (*equipment*) maquinaria *f*

plan·ta·tion [plæn'teɪʃn] plantación *f*

plaque [plæk] *on wall, teeth* placa *f*

plas·ter ['plæstər] **1** *n* *on wall, ceiling* yeso *m* **2** *v/t wall, ceiling* enyesar; *be* ~*ed with* estar recubierto de

'plas·ter cast escayola *f*

plas·tic ['plæstɪk] **1** *n* plástico *m* **2** *adj* (*made of* ~) de plástico

plas·tic 'bag bolsa *f* de plástico; **plas·tic (mon·ey)** plástico *m*, tarjetas *fpl* de pago; **plas·tic 'sur·geon** cirujano(-a) *m(f)* plástico(-a); **plas·tic 'sur·ge·ry** cirugía *f* estética

plate [pleɪt] *n for food* plato *m*; (*sheet of metal*) chapa *f*; PHOT placa *f*

pla·teau ['plætou] *n* meseta *f*

plat·form ['plætfɔːrm] (*stage*) plataforma *f*; *of railroad station* andén *m*; *fig: political* programa *m*

plat·i·num ['plætɪnəm] **1** *n* platino *m* **2** *adj* de platino

plat·i·tude ['plætɪtuːd] tópico *m*

pla·ton·ic [plə'tɑːnɪk] *adj relationship* platónico

pla·toon [plə'tuːn] *of soldiers* sección *f*

plat·ter ['plætər] *for meat, fish* fuente *f*

plau·si·ble ['plɔːzəbl] *adj* plausible

play [pleɪ] **1** *n in theater, on TV* obra *f* (de teatro); *of children, in match*, TECH juego *m* **2** *v/i* jugar; *of musician* tocar **3** *v/t musical instrument* tocar; *piece of music* intepretar, tocar; *game* jugar; *tennis, football* jugar a; *opponent* jugar contra; (*perform: Macbeth etc*) representar; *particular role* interpretar, hacer el papel de; ~ *a joke on* gastar una broma a

♦ **play around** *v/i* F (*be unfaithful*) acostarse con otras personas

♦ **play down** *v/t* quitar importancia a

♦ **play up** *v/i of machine* dar problemas; *of child* dar guerra

play·act ['pleɪækt] *v/i* (*pretend*) fingir

play·boy ['pleɪbɔɪ] playboy *m*

play·er ['pleɪr] SP jugador(a) *m(f)*; (*musician*) intérprete *m/f*; (*actor*) actor *m*, actriz *f*

play·ful ['pleɪfəl] *adj punch etc* de broma

play·ground ['pleɪgraʊnd] zona *f* de juegos

'**play·group** guardería *f*

play·ing card ['pleɪŋkɑːrd] carta *f*

play·ing field ['pleɪŋfiːld] campo *m* de deportes

play·mate ['pleɪmeɪt] compañero(-a) *m(f)* de juego

play·wright ['pleɪraɪt] autor(a) *m(f)*

pla·za ['plɑːzə] *for shopping* centro *m* comercial

plc [piːel'siː] *Br abbr* (= **public limited company**) S.A. *f* (= sociedad *f* anónima)

plea [pliː] *n* súplica *f*

plead [pliːd] *v/i:* ~ **for mercy** pedir clemencia; ~ **guilty / not guilty** declararse culpable / inocente; **she ~ed with me not to go** me suplicó que no fuera

pleas·ant ['pleznt] *adj* agradable

please [pliːz] **1** *adv* por favor; **more tea? – yes,** ~ ¿más té? – sí, por favor; ~ **do** claro que sí, por supuesto **2** *v/t* complacer; ~ **yourself!** ¡haz lo que quieras!

pleased [pliːzd] *adj* contento; (*satisfied*) satisfecho; ~ **to meet you** encantado de conocerle; **I'm very ~ to be here** estoy muy contento de estar aquí

pleas·ing ['pliːzɪŋ] *adj* agradable

pleas·ure ['pleʒər] (*happiness, satisfaction, delight*) satisfacción *f*; *as opposed to work* placer *m*; **it's a ~** (*you're welcome*) no hay de qué; **with ~** faltaría más

pleat [pliːt] *n in skirt* tabla *f*

pleat·ed skirt ['pliːtɪd] falda *f* de tablas

pledge [pledʒ] **1** *n* (*promise*) promesa *f*; (*guarantee*) compromiso *m*; (*money*) donación *f*; **Pledge of Allegiance** juramento de lealtad a la bandera estadounidense **2** *v/t* (*promise*) prometer; (*guarantee*) comprometerse; *money* donar

plen·ti·ful ['plentɪfəl] *adj* abundante

plen·ty ['plentɪ] (*abundance*) abundancia *f*; ~ **of books / food** muchos libros / mucha comida; **we have ~ of**

room tenemos espacio más que suficiente; **that's** ~ es suficiente; **there's ~ for everyone** hay (suficiente) para todos

pli·a·ble ['plaɪəbl] *adj* flexible

pli·ers ['plaɪərz] *npl* alicates *mpl*; **a pair of** ~ unos alicates

plight [plaɪt] situación *f* difícil

plod [plɑːd] *v/i* (*pret & pp* **-ded**) (*walk*) arrastrarse

♦ **plod on** *v/i with a job* avanzar laboriosamente

plod·der ['plɑːdər] (*at work, school*) *persona no especialmente lista pero muy trabajadora*

plot[1] [plɑːt] *n* (*land*) terreno *m*

plot[2] [plɑːt] **1** *n* (*conspiracy*) complot *m*; *of novel* argumento *m* **2** *v/t* (*pret & pp* **-ted**) tramar **3** *v/i* (*pret & pp* **-ted**) conspirar

plot·ter ['plɑːtər] conspirador(a) *m(f)*; COMPUT plóter *m*

plough *Br*, **plow** [plaʊ] **1** *n* arado *m* **2** *v/t & v/i* arar

♦ **plow back** *v/t profits* reinvertir

pluck [plʌk] *v/t eyebrows* depilar; *chicken* desplumar

♦ **pluck up** *v/t:* **pluck up courage to** … reunir el valor para …

plug [plʌg] **1** *n for sink, bath* tapón *m*; *electrical* enchufe *m*; (*spark* ~) bujía *f*; **give a book a** ~ dar publicidad a un libro **2** *v/t* (*pret & pp* **-ged**) *hole* tapar; *new book etc* hacer publicidad de

♦ **plug away at** *v/t* F trabajar con esfuerzo en

♦ **plug in** *v/t* enchufar

plum[1] [plʌm] *n fruit* ciruela *f*; *tree* ciruelo *m* **2** *adj* F: **a ~ job** un chollo de trabajo

plum·age ['pluːmɪdʒ] plumaje *m*

plumb [plʌm] *adj* vertical

♦ **plumb in** *v/t washing machine* conectar a la red del agua

plumb·er ['plʌmər] *Span* fontanero(-a) *m(f)*, *L.Am.* plomero(-a) *m(f)*

plumb·ing ['plʌmɪŋ] *pipes* tuberías *fpl*

plume [pluːm] (*feather*) pluma *f*; *of*

smoke nube *f*

plum·met ['plʌmɪt] *v/i of airplane, prices* caer en picado

plump [plʌmp] *adj* rellenito

♦ **plump for** *v/t* F decidirse por

plunge [plʌndʒ] **1** *n* salto *m*; *in prices* caída *f*; **take the ~** dar el paso **2** *v/i* precipitarse; *of prices* caer en picado **3** *v/t* hundir; (*into water*) sumergir; *the city was ~d into darkness* la ciudad quedó inmersa en la oscuridad; *the news ~d him into despair* la noticia lo hundió en la desesperación

plung·ing ['plʌndʒɪŋ] *adj neckline* escotado

plu·per·fect ['pluːpɜːrfɪkt] *n* GRAM pluscuamperfecto *m*

plu·ral ['plʊərəl] **1** *n* plural *m* **2** *adj* plural

plus [plʌs] **1** *prep* más; *I want John ~ two other volunteers ...* quiero a John y a otros dos voluntarios **2** *adj* más de; *$500 ~* más de 500 dólares **3** *n symbol* signo *m* más; (*advantage*) ventaja *f* **4** *conj* (*moreover, in addition*) además

plush [plʌʃ] *adj* lujoso

'plus sign signo *m* más

ply·wood ['plaɪwʊd] madera *f* contrachapada

PM [piː'em] *Br abbr* (= *Prime Minister*) Primer(a) *m* (*f*) Ministro(-a)

p.m. [piː'em] *abbr* (= *post meridiem*) p.m.; *at 3* ~ a las 3 de la tarde; *at 11* ~ a las 11 de la noche

pneu·mat·ic [nuː'mætɪk] *adj* neumático

pneu·mat·ic 'drill martillo *m* neumático

pneu·mo·ni·a [nuː'moʊnɪə] pulmonía *f*, neumonía *f*

poach[1] [poʊtʃ] *v/t cook* hervir

poach[2] [poʊtʃ] *v/t & v/i* (*hunt*) cazar furtivamente; *fish* pescar furtivamente

poached egg [poʊtʃt'eg] huevo *m* escalfado

poach·er ['poʊtʃər] *of game* cazador(a) *m* (*f*) furtivo(-a); *of fish* pescador(a) *m* (*f*) furtivo(-a)

P.O. Box [piː'oʊbɑːks] apartado *m* de correos

pock·et ['pɑːkɪt] **1** *n* bolsillo *m*; *line one's own ~s* llenarse los bolsillos; *be $10 out of ~* salir perdiendo 10 dólares **2** *adj* radio, dictionary de bolsillo **3** *v/t* meter en el bolsillo

'pock·et·book (*purse*) bolso *m*; (*billfold*) cartera *f*; *book* libro *m* de bolsillo; **pock·et** '**cal·cu·la·tor** calculadora *f* de bolsillo; '**pock·et·knife** navaja *f*

po·di·um ['poʊdɪəm] podio *m*

po·em ['poʊɪm] poema *m*

po·et ['poʊɪt] poeta *m/f*, poetisa *f*

po·et·ic [poʊ'etɪk] *adj* poético

po·et·ic 'jus·tice justicia *f* divina

po·et·ry ['poʊɪtrɪ] poesía *f*

poign·ant ['pɔɪnjənt] *adj* conmovedor

point [pɔɪnt] **1** *n of pencil, knife* punta *f*; *in competition, argument* punto *m*; (*purpose*) objetivo *m*; (*moment*) momento *m*; *in decimals* coma *f*; *what's the ~ of telling him?* ¿qué se consigue diciéndoselo?; *the ~ I'm trying to make ...* lo que estoy intentando decir ...; *at one ~* en un momento dado; *that's beside the ~* eso no viene a cuento; *be on the ~ of* estar a punto de; *get to the ~* ir al grano; *the ~ is ...* la cuestión es que ...; *there's no ~ in waiting / trying* no vale la pena esperar / intentarlo **2** *v/i* señalar con el dedo **3** *v/t*: *he ~ed the gun at me* me apuntó con la pistola

♦ **point out** *v/t sights* indicar; *advantages etc* destacar

♦ **point to** *v/t with finger* señalar con el dedo; *fig* (*indicate*) indicar

'point-blank 1 *adj refusal, denial* categórico; *at ~ range* a quemarropa **2** *adv refuse, deny* categóricamente

point·ed ['pɔɪntɪd] *adj remark* mordaz

point·er ['pɔɪntər] *for teacher* puntero *m*; (*hint*) consejo *m*; (*sign, indication*) indicador *m*

point·less ['pɔɪntləs] *adj* inútil; *it's ~ trying* no sirve de nada intentarlo

'point of sale *place* punto *m* de venta; *promotional material* material *m* promocional

'point of view punto *m* de vista

poise [pɔɪz] confianza *f*

poised [pɔɪzd] *adj person* con aplomo

poi·son ['pɔɪzn] **1** *n* veneno *m* **2** *v/t* envenenar

poi·son·ous ['pɔɪznəs] *adj* venenoso

poke [pəʊk] **1** *n* empujón *m* **2** *v/t* (*prod*) empujar; (*stick*) clavar; **he ~d his head out of the window** asomó la cabeza por la ventana; **~ fun at** reírse de; **~ one's nose into** F meter las narices en F

♦ poke around *v/i* F husmear

pok·er ['pəʊkər] *card game* póquer *m*

pok·y ['pəʊkɪ] *adj* F (*cramped*) enano, minúsculo

Po·land ['pəʊlənd] Polonia

po·lar ['pəʊlər] *adj* polar

po·lar 'bear oso *m* polar *or* blanco

po·lar·ize ['pəʊləraɪz] *v/t* polarizar

Pole [pəʊl] polaco(-a) *m(f)*

pole[1] [pəʊl] *for support* poste *m*; *for tent, pushing things* palo *m*

pole[2] [pəʊl] *of earth* polo *m*

'pole star estrella *f* polar; 'pole-vault salto *m* con pértiga; 'pole-vault·er saltador(a) *m(f)* de pértiga

po·lice [pə'liːs] *n* policía *f*

po·lice car coche *m* de policía; po·lice·man policía *m*; po·lice state estado *m* policial; po·lice sta·tion comisaría *f* (de policía); po·lice·wo·man (mujer *f*) policía *f*

pol·i·cy[1] ['pɑːlɪsɪ] política *f*

pol·i·cy[2] ['pɑːlɪsɪ] (*insurance ~*) póliza *f*

po·li·o ['pəʊlɪəʊ] polio *f*

Pol·ish ['pəʊlɪʃ] **1** *adj* polaco **2** *n* polaco *m*

pol·ish ['pɑːlɪʃ] **1** *n* abrillantador *m*; (*nail ~*) esmalte *m* de uñas **2** *v/t* dar brillo a; *speech* pulir

♦ polish off *v/t food* acabar, comerse

♦ polish up *v/t skill* perfeccionar

pol·ished ['pɑːlɪʃt] *adj performance* brillante

po·lite [pə'laɪt] *adj* educado

po·lite·ly [pə'laɪtlɪ] *adv* educadamente

po·lite·ness [pə'laɪtnɪs] educación *f*

po·lit·i·cal [pə'lɪtɪkl] *adj* político

po·lit·i·cal·ly cor·rect [pə'lɪtɪklɪ kə'rekt] políticamente correcto

pol·i·ti·cian [pɑːlɪ'tɪʃn] político(-a) *m(f)*

pol·i·tics ['pɑːlətɪks] política *f*; **I'm not interested in ~** no me interesa la política; **what are his ~?** ¿cuáles son sus ideas políticas?

poll [pəʊl] **1** *n* (*survey*) encuesta *f*, sondeo *m*; **the ~s** (*election*) las elecciones; **go to the ~s** (*vote*) acudir a las urnas **2** *v/t people* sondear; *votes* obtener

pol·len ['pɑːlən] polen *m*

'pol·len count concentración *f* de polen en el aire

poll·ing booth ['pəʊlɪŋ] cabina *f* electoral

'poll·ing day día *m* de las elecciones

poll·ster ['pəʊlstər] encuestador(a) *m(f)*

pol·lu·tant [pə'luːtənt] contaminante *m*

pol·lute [pə'luːt] *v/t* contaminar

pol·lu·tion [pə'luːʃn] contaminación *f*

po·lo ['pəʊləʊ] SP polo *m*

'po·lo neck *sweater* suéter *m* de cuello alto

'po·lo shirt polo *m*

pol·y·es·ter [pɑːlɪ'estər] poliéster *m*

pol·y·eth·yl·ene [pɑːlɪ'eθɪliːn] polietileno *m*

pol·y·sty·rene [pɑːlɪ'staɪriːn] poliestireno *m*

pol·y·un·sat·u·rat·ed [pɑːlɪʌn'sætjəreɪtɪd] *adj* poliinsaturado

pom·pous ['pɑːmpəs] *adj* pomposo

pond [pɑːnd] estanque *m*

pon·der ['pɑːndər] *v/i* reflexionar

pon·tiff ['pɑːntɪf] pontífice *m*

pon·y ['pəʊnɪ] poni *m*

'pon·y·tail coleta *f*

poo·dle ['puːdl] caniche *m*

pool[1] [puːl] (*swimming ~*) piscina *f*, *L.Am.* pileta *f*, *Mex* alberca *f*; *of*

P

water, blood charco *m*

pool² [puːl] *game* billar *m* americano

pool³ [puːl] **1** *n (common fund)* bote *m*, fondo *m* común **2** *v/t resources* juntar

'**pool hall** sala *f* de billares

'**pool table** mesa *f* de billar americano

poop [puːp] *n* F caca *f* F

pooped [puːpt] *adj* F hecho polvo F

poor [pʊr] **1** *adj* pobre; *(not good)* mediocre, malo; *be in ~ health* estar enfermo; *~ old Tony!* ¡pobre(cito) Tony! **2** *npl: the ~* los pobres

poor·ly ['pʊlɪ] **1** *adv* mal **2** *adj (unwell): feel ~* encontrarse mal

pop¹ [paːp] **1** *n noise* pequeño ruido *m* **2** *v/i (pret & pp -ped) of balloon etc* estallar **3** *v/t (pret & pp -ped) cork* hacer saltar; *balloon* pinchar

pop² [paːp] **1** *n* MUS pop *m* **2** *adj* pop

pop³ [paːp] F *(father)* papá *m* F

pop⁴ [paːp] *v/t (pret & pp -ped)* F *(put)* meter

♦ **pop up** *v/i* F *(appear)* aparecer

'**pop con·cert** concierto *m* (de música) pop

pop·corn ['paːpkɔːrn] palomitas *fpl* de maíz

pope [poʊp] *n* papa *m*

pop group grupo *m* (de música) pop

pop·py ['paːpɪ] amapola *f*

Pop·sicle® ['paːpsɪkl] polo *m* *(helado)*

'**pop song** canción *f* pop

pop·u·lar ['paːpjʊlər] *adj* popular; *contrary to ~ belief* contrariamente a lo que se piensa

pop·u·lar·i·ty [paːpjʊ'lærətɪ] popularidad *f*

pop·u·late ['paːpjʊleɪt] *v/t* poblar

pop·u·la·tion [paːpjʊ'leɪʃn] población *f*

porce·lain ['pɔːrsəlɪn] **1** *n* porcelana *f* **2** *adj* de porcelana

porch [pɔːrtʃ] porche *m*

por·cu·pine ['pɔːrkjʊpaɪn] puercoespín *m*

pore [pɔːr] *of skin* poro *m*

♦ **pore over** *v/t* estudiar detenidamente

pork [pɔːrk] cerdo *m*

porn [pɔːrn] *n* F porno *m* F

porn(o) [pɔːrn, 'pɔːrnoʊ] *adj* F porno F

por·no·graph·ic [pɔːrnə'græfɪk] *adj* pornográfico

porn·og·ra·phy [pɔːr'naːgrəfɪ] pornografía *f*

po·rous ['pɔːrəs] *adj* poroso

port¹ [pɔːrt] *n town, area* puerto *m*

port² [pɔːrt] *adj (left-hand)* a babor

por·ta·ble ['pɔːrtəbl] **1** *adj* portátil **2** *n* COMPUT portátil *m*; *TV* televisión *f* portátil

por·ter ['pɔːrtər] *for luggage* mozo(-a) *m(f)*

port·hole ['pɔːrthoʊl] NAUT portilla *f*

por·tion ['pɔːrʃn] parte *f*; *of food* ración *f*

por·trait ['pɔːrtreɪt] **1** *n* retrato *m* **2** *adv print* en formato vertical

por·tray [pɔːr'treɪ] *of artist, photographer* retratar; *of actor* interpretar; *of author* describir

por·tray·al [pɔːr'treɪəl] *by actor* interpretación *f*, representación *f*; *by author* descripción *f*

Por·tu·gal ['pɔːrtʃʊgl] Portugal

Por·tu·guese [pɔːrtʃʊ'giːz] **1** *adj* portugués **2** *person* portugués(-esa) *m(f)*; *language* portugués *m*

pose [poʊz] **1** *n (pretense)* pose *f*; *it's all a ~* no es más que una pose **2** *v/i for artist, photographer* posar; *~ as* hacerse pasar por **3** *v/t: ~ a problem/a threat* representar un problema/una amenaza

posh [paːʃ] *adj Br* F elegante, *pej* pijo

po·si·tion [pə'zɪʃn] **1** *n* posición *f*; *(stance, point of view)* postura *f*; *(job)* puesto *m*, empleo *m*; *(status)* posición *f* (social) **2** *v/t* situar, colocar

pos·i·tive ['paːzətɪv] *adj* positivo; *be ~ (sure)* estar seguro

pos·i·tive·ly ['paːzətɪvlɪ] *adv (decidedly)* verdaderamente, sin lugar a dudas; *(definitely)* claramente

pos·sess [pə'zes] *v/t* poseer

pos·ses·sion [pə'zeʃn] posesión *f*; *~s* posesiones *fpl*

pos·ses·sive [pə'zesɪv] *adj person,* GRAM posesivo

pos·si·bil·i·ty [pɑːsəˈbɪlətɪ] posibilidad f; **there is a ~ that ...** cabe la posibilidad de que ...

pos·si·ble [ˈpɑːsəbl] adj posible; **the shortest/quickest route ~** la ruta más corto/rápido posible; **the best ~ ...** el mejor ...

possibly [ˈpɑːsəblɪ] adv (perhaps) puede ser, quizás; **that can't ~ be right** no puede ser; **they're doing everything they ~ can** están haciendo todo lo que pueden; **could you ~ tell me ...?** ¿tendría la amabilidad de decirme ...?

post¹ [poʊst] **1** n of wood, metal poste m **2** v/t notice pegar; on notice board poner; profits presentar; **keep s.o. ~ed** mantener a alguien al corriente

post² [poʊst] **1** n (place of duty) puesto m **2** v/t soldier, employee destinar; guards apostar

post³ [poʊst] Br **1** n (mail) correo m **2** v/t letter echar al correo

post·age [ˈpoʊstɪdʒ] franqueo m

post·age stamp fml sello m, L.Am. estampilla f, Mex timbre m

post·al [ˈpoʊstl] adj postal

post·card (tarjeta f) postal f;
post·code Br código m postal;
post·date v/t posfechar

post·er [ˈpoʊstər] póster m, L.Am. afiche m

pos·te·ri·or [pɑːˈstɪrɪər] n (hum: buttocks) trasero m

pos·ter·i·ty [pɑːˈsterɑtɪ] posteridad f; **for ~** para la posteridad

post·grad·u·ate [ˈpoʊstgrædʒʊət] **1** n posgraduado(-a) m(f) **2** adj de posgrado

post·hu·mous [ˈpɑːstʊməs] adj póstumo

post·hu·mous·ly [ˈpɑːstʊməslɪ] adv póstumamente

post·ing [ˈpoʊstɪŋ] (assignment) destino m

post·mark [ˈpoʊstmɑːrk] n matasellos m inv

post·mor·tem [poʊstˈmɔːrtəm] n autopsia f

post of·fice oficina f de correos

post·pone [poʊstˈpoʊn] v/t pospo-ner, aplazar

post·pone·ment [poʊstˈpoʊnmənt] aplazamiento m

pos·ture [ˈpɑːstʃər] postura f

post·war adj de posguerra

pot¹ [pɑːt] for cooking olla f; for coffee cafetera f; for tea tetera f; for plant maceta f

pot² [pɑːt] F (marijuana) maría f F

po·ta·to [pəˈteɪtoʊ] Span patata f, L.Am. papa f

po·ta·to chips, Br **po·ta·to crisps** npl Span patatas fpl fritas, L.Am. papas fpl fritas

pot·bel·ly [ˈpɑːtbelɪ] barriga f

po·tent [ˈpoʊtənt] adj potente

po·ten·tial [pəˈtenʃl] **1** adj potencial **2** n potencial m

po·ten·tial·ly [pəˈtenʃəlɪ] adv potencialmente

pot·hole [ˈpɑːthoʊl] in road bache m

pot·ter [ˈpɑːtər] n alfarero(-a) m(f)

pot·ter·y [ˈpɑːtərɪ] n alfarería f

pot·ty [ˈpɑːtɪ] n for baby orinal m

pouch [paʊtʃ] bag bolsa f; for tobacco petaca f; for amunition cartuchera f; for mail saca f

poul·try [ˈpoʊltrɪ] birds aves fpl de corral; meat carne f de ave

pounce [paʊns] v/i of animal saltar; fig echarse encima

pound¹ [paʊnd] n weight libra f (453,6 gr)

pound² [paʊnd] n for strays perrera f; for cars depósito m

pound³ [paʊnd] v/i of heart palpitar con fuerza; **~ on** (hammer on) golpear en

pound ster·ling libra f esterlina

pour [pɔːr] **1** v/t into a container ver-ter; (spill) derramar; **~ s.o. some coffee** servir café a alguien **2** v/i: **it's ~ing (with rain)** está lloviendo a cántaros

◆pour out v/t liquid servir; troubles contar

pout [paʊt] v/i hacer un mohín

pov·er·ty [ˈpɑːvərtɪ] pobreza f

pov·er·ty-strick·en [ˈpɑːvərtɪstrɪkn] depauperado

pow·der [ˈpaʊdər] **1** n polvo m; for

face polvos *mpl*, colorete *m* **2** *v/t face* empolvarse

pow·er ['pauər] **1** *n* (*strength*) fuerza *f*; *of engine* potencia; (*authority*) poder *m*; (*energy*) energía *f*; (*electricity*) electricidad *f*; *in ~* POL en el poder; *fall from ~* POL perder el poder **2** *v/t*: *be ~ed by* estar impulsado por

'**pow·er·as·sist·ed steering** dirección *f* asistida; '**pow·er cut** apagón *m*; '**pow·er fail·ure** apagón *m*

pow·er·ful ['pauərfəl] *adj* poderoso; *car* potente; *drug* fuerte

pow·er·less ['pauərlɪs] *adj* impotente; *be ~ to …* ser incapaz de …

'**pow·er line** línea *f* de conducción eléctrica; '**pow·er out·age** apagón *m*; '**pow·er sta·tion** central *f* eléctrica; '**pow·er steer·ing** dirección *f* asistida; '**pow·er u·nit** fuente *f* de alimentación

PR [piː'ɑːr] *abbr* (= *public relations*) relaciones *fpl* públicas

prac·ti·cal ['præktɪkl] *adj* práctico; *layout* funcional

prac·ti·cal 'joke broma *f* (*que se gasta*)

prac·tic·al·ly ['præktɪklɪ] *adv behave*, *think* de manera práctica; (*almost*) prácticamente, casi

prac·tice [præktɪs] **1** *n* práctica *f*; (*rehearsal*) ensayo *m*; (*custom*) costumbre *f*; *in ~* (*in reality*) en la práctica; *be out of ~* estar desentrenado; *~ makes perfect* a base de práctica se aprende **2** *v/i* practicar; *of musician* ensayar; *of footballer* entrenarse **3** *v/t* practicar; *law, medicine* ejercer

prac·tise *Br* → *practice v/i & v/t*

prag·mat·ic [præg'mætɪk] *adj* pragmático

prag·ma·tism ['prægmətɪzm] pragmatismo *m*

prai·rie ['prerɪ] pradera *f*

praise [preɪz] **1** *n* elogio *m*, alabanza *f* **2** *v/t* elogiar

'**praise·wor·thy** *adj* elogiable

prank [præŋk] travesura *f*

prat·tle ['prætl] *v/i* F parlotear F

pray [preɪ] *v/i* rezar

prayer [prer] oración *f*

preach [priːtʃ] **1** *v/i in church* predicar; (*moralize*) sermonear **2** *v/t sermon* predicar

preach·er ['priːtʃər] predicador(a) *m(f)*

pre·am·ble [priː'æmbl] preámbulo *m*

pre·car·i·ous [prɪ'kerɪəs] *adj* precario

pre·car·i·ous·ly [prɪ'kerɪəslɪ] *adv* precariamente

pre·cau·tion [prɪ'kɒːʃn] precaución *f*; *as a ~* como precaución

pre·cau·tion·a·ry [prɪ'kɒːʃnrɪ] *adj measure* preventivo

pre·cede [prɪ'siːd] *v/t in time* preceder; (*walk in front of*) ir delante de

prec·e·dent ['presɪdənt] precedente *m*

pre·ced·ing [prɪ'siːdɪŋ] *adj week*, *chapter* anterior

pre·cinct ['priːsɪŋkt] (*district*) distrito *m*

pre·cious ['preʃəs] *adj* preciado; *gem* precioso

pre·cip·i·tate [prɪ'sɪpɪteɪt] *v/t crisis* precipitar

pré·cis ['preɪsiː] *n* resumen *m*

pre·cise [prɪ'saɪs] *adj* preciso

pre·cise·ly [prɪ'saɪslɪ] *adv* exactamente

pre·ci·sion [prɪ'sɪʒn] precisión *f*

pre·co·cious [prɪ'kouʃəs] *adj child* precoz

pre·con·ceived ['priːkənsiːvd] *adj idea* preconcebido

pre·con·di·tion [priːkən'dɪʃn] condición *f* previa

pred·a·tor ['predətər] *animal* depredador(a) *m(f)*

pred·a·to·ry ['predətɔːrɪ] *adj* depredador

pre·de·ces·sor ['priːdɪsesər] *in job* predecesor(a) *m(f)*; *machine* modelo *m* anterior

pre·des·ti·na·tion [priːdestɪ'neɪʃn] predestinación *f*

pre·des·tined [priː'destɪnd] *adj*: *be ~ to* estar predestinado a

pre·dic·a·ment [prɪ'dɪkəmənt] apuro *m*

pre·dict [prɪ'dɪkt] v/t predecir, pronosticar

pre·dict·a·ble [prɪ'dɪktəbl] adj predecible

pre·dic·tion [prɪ'dɪkʃn] predicción f, pronóstico m

pre·dom·i·nant [prɪ'dɑ:mɪnənt] adj predominante

pre·dom·i·nant·ly [prɪ'dɑ:mɪnəntlɪ] adv predominantemente

pre·dom·i·nate [prɪ'dɑ:mɪneɪt] v/i predominar

pre·fab·ri·cat·ed [pri:'fæbrɪkeɪtɪd] adj prefabricado

pref·ace ['prefɪs] n prólogo m, prefacio m

pre·fer [prɪ'fɜ:r] v/t (pret & pp **-red**) preferir; ~ **X to Y** preferir X a Y; ~ **to do** preferir hacer

pref·e·ra·ble ['prefərəbl] adj preferible; **anywhere is ~ to this** cualquier sitio es mejor que éste

pref·e·ra·bly ['prefərəblɪ] adv preferentemente

pref·e·rence ['prefərəns] preferencia f

pref·er·en·tial [prefə'renʃl] adj preferente

pre·fix ['pri:fɪks] n prefijo m

preg·nan·cy ['pregnənsɪ] embarazo m

preg·nant ['pregnənt] adj woman embarazada; animal preñada

pre·heat ['pri:hi:t] v/t oven precalentar

pre·his·tor·ic [pri:hɪs'tɑ:rɪk] adj prehistórico

pre·judge [pri:'dʒʌdʒ] v/t prejuzgar, juzgar de antemano

prej·u·dice ['predʒʊdɪs] **1** n prejuicio m **2** v/t person predisponer, influir; chances perjudicar

prej·u·diced ['predʒʊdɪst] adj parcial, predispuesto

pre·lim·i·na·ry [prɪ'lɪmɪnerɪ] adj preliminar

pre·mar·i·tal [pri:'mærɪtl] adj prematrimonial

pre·ma·ture ['pri:mətʊr] adj prematuro

pre·med·i·tat·ed [pri:'medɪteɪtɪd] adj premeditado

prem·i·er ['premɪr] n (Prime Minister) primer(a) ministro(-a) m(f)

prem·i·ère ['premɪr] n estreno m

prem·is·es ['premɪsɪz] npl local m

pre·mi·um ['pri:mɪəm] n in insurance prima f

pre·mo·ni·tion [premə'nɪʃn] premonición f, presentimiento m

pre·na·tal [pri:'neɪtl] adj prenatal

pre·oc·cu·pied [prɪ'ɑ:kjʊpaɪd] adj preocupado

prep·a·ra·tion [prepə'reɪʃn] preparación f; in preparation **for** como preparación a; **~s** preparativos mpl

pre·pare [prɪ'per] **1** v/t preparar; **be ~d to do sth** be willing estar dispuesto a hacer algo; **be ~d for sth** be expecting, ready estar preparado para algo **2** v/i prepararse

prep·o·si·tion [prepə'zɪʃn] preposición f

pre·pos·ter·ous [prɪ'pɑ:stərəs] adj ridículo, absurdo

pre·req·ui·site [pri:'rekwɪzɪt] requisito m previo

pre·scribe [prɪ'skraɪb] v/t of doctor recetar

pre·scrip·tion [prɪ'skrɪpʃn] MED receta f

pres·ence ['prezns] presencia f; in **the ~ of** en presencia de, delante de

pres·ence of 'mind presencia f de ánimo

pres·ent¹ ['preznt] **1** adj (current) actual; **be** = estar presente **2** n: **the ~** also GRAM el presente; **at ~** en este momento

pres·ent² ['preznt] n (gift) regalo m

pres·ent³ [prɪ'zent] v/t presentar; award entregar; ~ **s.o. with sth**, ~ **sth to s.o.** entregar algo a alguien

pre·sen·ta·tion [preznˈteɪʃn] to audience presentación f

pres·ent-day [preznt'deɪ] adj actual

pre·sent·er [prɪ'zentər] presentador(a) m(f)

pres·ent·ly ['prezntlɪ] adv (at the moment) actualmente; (soon) pronto

'pres·ent tense tiempo m presente

pres·er·va·tion [prezər'veɪʃn] conservación *f; of standards, peace* mantenimiento *m*

pre·ser·va·tive [prɪˈzɜːrvətɪv] *n* conservante *m*

pre·serve [prɪˈzɜːrv] **1** *n* (*domain*) dominio *m* **2** *v/t standards, peace etc* mantener; *food, wood* conservar

pre·side [prɪˈzaɪd] *v/i at meeting* presidir; ~ *over meeting* presidir

pres·i·den·cy [ˈprezɪdənsɪ] presidencia *f*

pres·i·dent [ˈprezɪdnt] POL, *of company* presidente(-a) *m(f)*

pres·i·den·tial [prezɪˈdenʃl] *adj* presidencial

press [pres] **1** *n:* **the** ~ la prensa **2** *v/t button* pulsar, presionar; (*urge*) presionar; (*squeeze*) apretar; *clothes* planchar **3** *v/i:* ~ *for* presionar para obtener

'**press a·gen·cy** agencia *f* de prensa

'**press con·fer·ence** rueda *f* or conferencia *f* de prensa

press·ing [ˈpresɪŋ] *adj* urgente

pres·sure [ˈpreʃər] **1** *n* presión *f*; *be under* ~ estar sometido a presión; *he is under* ~ *to resign* lo están presionando para que dimita **2** *v/t* presionar

pres·tige [preˈstiːʒ] prestigio *m*

pres·ti·gious [preˈstɪdʒəs] *adj* prestigioso

pre·su·ma·bly [prɪˈzuːməblɪ] *adv* presumiblemente, probablemente

pre·sume [prɪˈzuːm] *v/t* suponer; *they were* ~*d dead* los dieron por muertos; ~ *to do sth fml* tomarse la libertad de hacer algo

pre·sump·tion [prɪˈzʌmpʃn] *of innocence, guilt* presunción *f*

pre·sump·tu·ous [prɪˈzʌmptʊəs] *adj* presuntuoso

pre·sup·pose [priːsəˈpoʊs] *v/t* presuponer

pre-tax [ˈpriːtæks] *adj* antes de impuestos

pre·tence *Br →* **pretense**

pre·tend [prɪˈtend] **1** *v/t* fingir, hacer como si; *claim* pretender; ~ *to be s.o.* hacerse pasar por alguien; *the children are ~ing to be spacemen*

los niños están jugando a que son astronautas **2** *v/i* fingir

pre·tense [prɪˈtens] farsa *f*

pre·ten·tious [prɪˈtenʃəs] *adj* pretencioso

pre·text [ˈpriːtekst] pretexto *m*

pret·ty [ˈprɪtɪ] **1** *adj village, house, fabric etc* bonito, lindo; *child, woman* guapo, lindo **2** *adv* (*quite*) bastante

pre·vail [prɪˈveɪl] *v/i* (*triumph*) prevalecer

pre·vail·ing [prɪˈveɪlɪŋ] *adj* predominante

pre·vent [prɪˈvent] *v/t* impedir, evitar; ~ *s.o.* (*from*) *doing sth* impedir que alguien haga algo

pre·ven·tion [prɪˈvenʃn] prevención *f*

pre·ven·tive [prɪˈventɪv] *adj* preventivo

pre·view [ˈpriːvjuː] **1** *n of movie, exhibition* preestreno *m* **2** *v/t* hacer la presentación previa de

pre·vi·ous [ˈpriːvɪəs] *adj* anterior, previo

pre·vi·ous·ly [ˈpriːvɪəslɪ] *adv* anteriormente, antes

pre-war [ˈpriːwɔːr] *adj* de preguerra, de antes de la guerra

prey [preɪ] *n* presa *f*; ~ *to* presa de

♦ **prey on** *v/t* atacar; *fig: of con man etc* aprovecharse de

price [praɪs] **1** *n* precio *m* **2** *v/t* COM poner precio a

price·less [ˈpraɪslɪs] *adj* que no tiene precio

'**price tag** etiqueta *f* del precio

'**price war** guerra *f* de precios

price·y [ˈpraɪsɪ] *adj* F carillo F

prick[1] [prɪk] **1** *n pain* punzada *f* **2** *v/t* (*jab*) pinchar

prick[2] [prɪk] *n* ∨ (*penis*) polla *f* ∨, carajo *m* ∨; ∨ *person Span* gilipollas *m inv* ∨, *L.Am.* pendejo *m* ∨

♦ **prick up** *v/t: prick up one's ears* *of dog* aguzar las orejas; *of person* prestar atención

prick·le [ˈprɪkl] *on plant* espina *f*

prick·ly [ˈprɪklɪ] *adj beard, plant* que pincha; (*irritable*) irritable

pride [praɪd] **1** *n in person, achieve-*

ment orgullo m; (self-respect) amor m propio **2** v/t: **~ o.s. on** enorgullecerse de

priest [priːst] n sacerdote m; (parish ~) cura m

pri·ma·ri·ly [praɪˈmerɪlɪ] adv principalmente

pri·ma·ry [ˈpraɪmərɪ] **1** adj principal **2** n POL elecciones fpl primarias

prime [praɪm] **1** n: **be in one's ~** estar en la flor de la vida **2** adj example, reason primordial; **of ~ importance** de suprema importancia

prime 'min·is·ter primer(a) ministro m(f)

'prime time n TV horario m de mayor audiencia

prim·i·tive [ˈprɪmɪtɪv] adj primitivo

prince [prɪns] príncipe m

prin·cess [prɪnˈses] princesa f

prin·ci·pal [ˈprɪnsəpl] **1** adj principal **2** n of school director(a) m(f); of university rector(a) m(f)

prin·ci·pal·ly [ˈprɪnsəplɪ] adv principalmente

prin·ci·ple [ˈprɪnsəpl] principio m; **on ~** por principios; **in ~** en principio

print [prɪnt] **1** n in book, newspaper etc letra f; (photograph) grabado m; **out of ~** agotado **2** v/t imprimir; (use block capitals) escribir en mayúsculas

♦ print out v/t imprimir

print·ed mat·ter [ˈprɪntɪd] impresos mpl

print·er [ˈprɪntər] person impresor(a) m(f); machine impresora f; company imprenta f

print·ing press [ˈprɪntɪŋpres] imprenta f

'print·out copia f impresa

pri·or [ˈpraɪr] **1** adj previo **2** prep: **~ to** antes de

pri·or·i·tize [praɪˈɔːrətaɪz] v/t (put in order of priority) ordenar atendiendo a las prioridades; (give priority to) dar prioridad a

pri·or·i·ty [praɪˈɑːrətɪ] prioridad f; **have ~** tener prioridad

pris·on [ˈprɪzn] prisión f, cárcel f

pris·on·er [ˈprɪznər] prisionero(-a)

m(f); **take s.o. ~** hacer prisionero a alguien

pris·on·er of 'war prisionero(-a) m(f) de guerra

pri·va·cy [ˈprɪvəsɪ] intimidad f

pri·vate [ˈpraɪvət] **1** adj privado **2** n MIL soldado m/f raso; **in ~** en privado

pri·vate·ly [ˈpraɪvətlɪ] adv (in private) en privado; with one other a solas; (inwardly) para sí; **~ owned** en manos privadas

'pri·vate sec·tor sector m privado

pri·va·tize [ˈpraɪvətaɪz] v/t Br privatizar

priv·i·lege [ˈprɪvəlɪdʒ] (special treatment) privilegio m; (honor) honor m

priv·i·leged [ˈprɪvəlɪdʒd] adj privilegiado

prize [praɪz] **1** n premio m **2** v/t apreciar, valorar

prize·win·ner [ˈpraɪzwɪnər] premiado(-a) m(f)

prize·win·ning [ˈpraɪzwɪnɪŋ] premiado

pro¹ [prou] n: **the ~s and cons** los pros y los contras

pro² [prou] → **professional**

pro³ [prou]: **be ~ ...** (in favor of) estar a favor de; **the ~ Clinton Democrats** los demócratas partidarios de Clinton

prob·a·bil·i·ty [prɑːbəˈbɪlətɪ] probabilidad f

prob·a·ble [ˈprɑːbəbl] adj probable

prob·a·bly [ˈprɑːbəblɪ] adv probablemente

pro·ba·tion [prəˈbeɪʃn] in job período m de prueba; LAW libertad f condicional; **be given ~** ser puesto en libertad condicional

pro'ba·tion of·fi·cer oficial encargado de la vigilancia de los que están en libertad condicional

pro'ba·tion pe·ri·od in job período m de prueba

probe [proub] **1** n (investigation) investigación f; scientific sonda f **2** v/t examinar; (investigate) investigar

prob·lem [ˈprɑːbləm] problema m; **no ~!** ¡claro!

P

pro·ce·dure [prə'siːdʒər] procedimiento *m*

pro·ceed [prə'siːd] *v/i* (*go: of people*) dirigirse; *of work etc* proseguir, avanzar; ~ *to do sth* pasar a hacer algo

pro·ceed·ings [prə'siːdɪŋz] *npl* (*events*) actos *mpl*

pro·ceeds ['prəʊsiːdz] *npl* recaudación *f*

pro·cess ['prɑːses] **1** *n* proceso *m*; *in the ~* (*while doing it*) al hacerlo **2** *v/t food* tratar; *raw materials, data* procesar; *application* tramitar

pro·ces·sion [prə'seʃn] desfile *m*; *religious* procesión *f*

pro·ces·sor ['prɑːsesər] procesador *m*

pro·claim [prə'kleɪm] *v/t* declarar, proclamar

prod [prɑːd] **1** *n* empujoncito *m* **2** *v/t* (*pret & pp* **-ded**) dar un empujoncito a; *with elbow* dar un codazo a

prod·i·gy ['prɑːdɪdʒɪ]: (*child*) ~ niño(-a) *m(f)* prodigio

prod·uce¹ ['prɑːduːs] *n* productos *mpl* del campo

pro·duce² [prə'duːs] *v/t* producir; (*manufacture*) fabricar; (*bring out*) sacar

pro·duc·er [prə'duːsər] productor(a) *m(f)*; (*manufacturer*) fabricante *m/f*

prod·uct ['prɑːdʌkt] producto *m*

pro·duc·tion [prə'dʌkʃn] producción *f*

pro·duc·tion ca·pac·i·ty capacidad *f* de producción

pro·duc·tion costs *npl* costos *mpl* de producción

pro·duc·tive [prə'dʌktɪv] *adj* productivo

pro·duc·tiv·i·ty [prɑːdʌk'tɪvətɪ] productividad *f*

pro·fane [prə'feɪn] *adj language* profano

pro·fess [prə'fes] *v/t* manifestar

pro·fes·sion [prə'feʃn] profesión *f*; *what's your ~?* ¿a qué se dedica?

pro·fes·sion·al [prə'feʃnl] **1** *adj* profesional; *turn ~* hacerse profesional

2 *n* profesional *m/f*

pro·fes·sion·al·ly [prə'feʃnlɪ] *adv play sport* profesionalmente; (*well, skillfully*) con profesionalidad

pro·fes·sor [prə'fesər] catedrático(-a) *m(f)*

pro·fi·cien·cy [prə'fɪʃnsɪ] competencia *f*

pro·fi·cient [prə'fɪʃnt] competente; (*skillful*) hábil

pro·file ['prəʊfaɪl] *of face* perfil *m*

prof·it ['prɑːfɪt] **1** *n* beneficio *m* **2** *v/i*: ~ *by*, ~ *from* beneficiarse de

prof·it·a·bil·i·ty [prɑːfɪtə'bɪlətɪ] rentabilidad *f*

prof·it·a·ble ['prɑːfɪtəbl] *adj* rentable

'prof·it mar·gin margen *m* de beneficios

pro·found [prə'faʊnd] *adj* profundo

pro·found·ly [prə'faʊndlɪ] *adv* profundamente, enormemente

prog·no·sis [prɑːg'nəʊsɪs] pronóstico *m*

pro·gram ['prəʊgræm] **1** *n* programa *m* **2** *v/t* (*pret & pp* **-med**) COMPUT programar

pro·gramme *Br →* **program**

pro·gram·mer ['prəʊgræmər] programador(a) *m(f)*

pro·gress 1 *n* ['prɑːgres] progreso *m*; *make ~* hacer progresos; *in ~* en curso **2** *v/i* [prə'gres] (*advance in time*) avanzar; (*move on*) pasar; (*make ~*) progresar; *how is the work ~ing?* ¿cómo avanza el trabajo?

pro·gres·sive [prə'gresɪv] *adj* (*enlightened*) progresista; (*which progresses*) progresivo

pro·gres·sive·ly [prə'gresɪvlɪ] *adv* progresivamente

pro·hib·it [prə'hɪbɪt] *v/t* prohibir

pro·hi·bi·tion [prəʊɪ'bɪʃn] prohibición *f*; *during Prohibition* durante la ley seca

pro·hib·i·tive [prə'hɪbɪtɪv] *adj prices* prohibitivo

proj·ect¹ ['prɑːdʒekt] *n* (*plan, undertaking*) proyecto *m*; EDU trabajo *m*; (*housing area*) barriada *f* de viviendas sociales

pro·ject² [prə'dʒekt] **1** v/t *movie* proyectar; *figures, sales* calcular **2** v/i (*stick out*) sobresalir

pro·jec·tion [prə'dʒekʃn] (*forecast*) previsión f

pro·jec·tor [prə'dʒektər] *for slides* proyector m

pro·lif·ic [prə'lɪfɪk] adj *writer, artist* prolífico

pro·log, *Br* **pro·logue** ['prəʊlɑːg] prólogo m

pro·long [prə'lɔːŋ] v/t prolongar

prom [prɑːm] (*school dance*) baile de fin de curso

prom·i·nent ['prɑːmɪnənt] adj *nose, chin* prominente; (*significant*) destacado

prom·is·cu·i·ty [prɑːmɪ'skjuːətɪ] promiscuidad f

pro·mis·cu·ous [prə'mɪskjʊəs] adj promiscuo

prom·ise ['prɑːmɪs] **1** n promesa f **2** v/t prometer; *she ~d to help* prometió ayudar; *~ sth to s.o.* prometer algo a alguien **3** v/i: *do you ~?* ¿lo prometes?

prom·is·ing ['prɑːmɪsɪŋ] adj prometedor

pro·mote [prə'məʊt] v/t *employee* ascender; (*encourage, foster*) promover; COM promocionar

pro·mot·er [prə'məʊtər] *of sports event* promotor(a) m(f)

pro·mo·tion [prə'məʊʃn] *of employee* ascenso m; *of scheme, idea*, COM promoción f

prompt [prɑːmpt] **1** adj (*on time*) puntual; (*speedy*) rápido **2** adv: *at two o'clock ~* a las dos en punto **3** v/t (*cause*) provocar; *actor* apuntar **4** n COMPUT mensaje m; *go to the c ~ ir a c:*

prompt·ly ['prɑːmptlɪ] adv (*on time*) puntualmente; (*immediately*) inmediatamente

prone [prəʊn] adj: *be ~ to* ser propenso a

pro·noun ['prəʊnaʊn] pronombre m

pro·nounce [prə'naʊns] v/t *word* pronunciar; (*declare*) declarar

pro·nounced [prə'naʊnst] adj *accent* marcado; *views* fuerte

pron·to ['prɑːntəʊ] adv F ya, en seguida

pro·nun·ci·a·tion [prənʌnsɪ'eɪʃn] pronunciación f

proof [pruːf] n prueba(s) f(pl); *of book* prueba f

prop [prɑːp] **1** v/t (*pret & pp -ped*) apoyar **2** n THEA accesorio m
♦ **prop up** v/t apoyar

prop·a·gan·da [prɑːpə'gændə] propaganda f

pro·pel [prə'pel] v/t (*pret & pp -led*) propulsar

pro·pel·lant [prə'pelənt] *in aerosol* propelente m

pro·pel·ler [prə'pelər] *of boat* hélice f

prop·er ['prɑːpər] adj (*real*) de verdad; (*fitting*) adecuado; *it's not ~* no está bien; *put it back in its ~ place* vuelve a ponerlo en su sitio

prop·er·ly ['prɑːpərlɪ] adv (*correctly*) bien; (*fittingly*) adecuadamente

prop·er·ty ['prɑːpərtɪ] propiedad f; (*land*) propiedad(es) f(pl)

'prop·er·ty de·vel·op·er promotor(-a) m(f) inmobiliario(a)

proph·e·cy ['prɑːfəsɪ] profecía f

proph·e·sy ['prɑːfəsaɪ] v/t (*pret & pp -ied*) profetizar

pro·por·tion [prə'pɔːrʃn] proporción f; *a large ~ of North Americans* gran parte de los norteamericanos; *~s* (*dimensions*) proporciones fpl

pro·por·tion·al [prə'pɔːrʃnl] adj proporcional

pro·por·tion·al rep·re·sen·ta·tion POL representación f proporcional

pro·pos·al [prə'pəʊzl] (*suggestion*) propuesta f; *of marriage* proposición f

pro·pose [prə'pəʊz] **1** v/t (*suggest*) sugerir, proponer; (*plan*) proponerse **2** v/i (*make offer of marriage*) pedir la mano (*to* a)

prop·o·si·tion [prɑːpə'zɪʃn] **1** n propuesta f **2** v/t *woman* hacer proposiciones a

pro·pri·e·tor [prə'praɪətər] propietario(-a) m(f)

pro·pri·e·tress [prə'praɪətrɪs] propietaria *f*

prose [prouz] prosa *f*

pros·e·cute ['prɑːsɪkjuːt] *v/t* LAW procesar

pros·e·cu·tion [prɑːsɪ'kjuːʃn] LAW procesamiento *m*; *lawyers* acusación *f*; **he's facing ~** lo van a procesar

pros·e·cu·tor → **public prosecutor**

pros·pect ['prɑːspekt] **1** *n* (*chance, likelihood*) probabilidad *f*; (*thought of something in the future*) perspectiva *f*; **~s** perspectivas *fpl* (de futuro) **2** *v/i*: **~ for** gold buscar

pro·spec·tive [prə'spektɪv] *adj* potencial

pros·per ['prɑːspər] *v/i* prosperar

pros·per·i·ty [prɑː'sperətɪ] prosperidad *f*

pros·per·ous ['prɑːspərəs] *adj* próspero

pros·ti·tute ['prɑːstɪtuːt] *n* prostituta *f*; **male ~** prostituto *m*

pros·ti·tu·tion [prɑːstɪ'tuːʃn] prostitución *f*

pros·trate ['prɑːstreɪt] *adj* postrado; **be ~ with grief** estar postrado por el dolor

pro·tect [prə'tekt] *v/t* proteger

pro·tec·tion [prə'tekʃn] protección *f*

pro·tec·tion mon·ey *dinero pagado a delincuentes a cambio de obtener protección*; *paid to terrorists* impuesto *m* revolucionario

pro·tec·tive [prə'tektɪv] *adj* protector

pro·tec·tive 'cloth·ing ropa *f* protectora

pro·tec·tor [prə'tektər] protector(a) *m(f)*

pro·tein ['proutiːn] proteína *f*

pro·test 1 *n* ['proutest] protesta *f* **2** *v/t* [prə'test] protestar, quejarse de; (*object to*) protestar contra **3** *v/i* [prə'test] protestar

Prot·es·tant ['prɑːtɪstənt] **1** *n* protestante *m/f* **2** *adj* protestante

pro·test·er [prə'testər] manifestante *m/f*

pro·to·col ['proutəkɑːl] protocolo *m*

pro·to·type ['proutətaɪp] prototipo *m*

pro·tract·ed [prə'træktɪd] *adj* prolongado, largo

pro·trude [prə'truːd] *v/i* sobresalir

pro·trud·ing [prə'truːdɪŋ] *adj* saliente; *ears, teeth* prominente

proud [praud] *adj* orgulloso; **be ~ of** estar orgulloso de

proud·ly ['praudlɪ] *adv* con orgullo, orgullosamente

prove [pruːv] *v/t* demostrar, probar

prov·erb ['prɑːvɜːrb] proverbio *m*, refrán *m*

pro·vide [prə'vaɪd] *v/t* proporcionar; **~ sth to s.o., ~ s.o. with sth** proporcionar algo a alguien; **~d (that)** (*on condition that*) con la condición de que, siempre que

♦ **provide for** *v/t family* mantener; *of law etc* prever

prov·ince ['prɑːvɪns] provincia *f*

pro·vin·cial [prə'vɪnʃl] *adj city* provincial; *pej: attitude* de pueblo, provinciano

pro·vi·sion [prə'vɪʒn] (*supply*) suministro *m*; *of law, contract* disposición *f*

pro·vi·sion·al [prə'vɪʒnl] *adj* provisional

pro·vi·so [prə'vaɪzou] condición *f*

prov·o·ca·tion [prɑːvə'keɪʃn] provocación *f*

pro·voc·a·tive [prə'vɑːkətɪv] *adj* provocador(a); *sexually* provocativo

pro·voke [prə'vouk] *v/t* (*cause, annoy*) provocar

prow [prau] NAUT proa *f*

prow·ess ['prauɪs] proezas *fpl*

prowl [praul] *v/i of tiger, burglar* merodear

prowl·er ['praulər] merodeador(a) *m(f)*

prox·im·i·ty [prɑːk'sɪmətɪ] proximidad *f*

prox·y ['prɑːksɪ] (*authority*) poder *m*; *person* apoderado(-a) *m(f)*

prude [pruːd] mojigato(-a) *m(f)*

pru·dence ['pruːdns] prudencia *f*

pru·dent ['pruːdnt] *adj* prudente

prud·ish ['pruːdɪʃ] *adj* mojigato

prune¹ [pruːn] *n* ciruela *f* pasa

prune² [pruːn] *v/t plant* podar; *fig* reducir

pry [praɪ] v/i (pret & pp **-ied**) entrometerse

♦ **pry into** v/t entrometerse en

PS ['pi:es] abbr (= **postscript**) PD (= posdata f)

pseu·do·nym ['su:dənɪm] pseudónimo m

psy·chi·at·ric [saɪkɪ'ætrɪk] adj psiquiátrico

psy·chi·a·trist [saɪ'kaɪətrɪst] psiquiatra m/f

psy·chi·a·try [saɪ'kaɪətrɪ] psiquiatría f

psy·chic ['saɪkɪk] adj research paranormal; **I'm not** ~ no soy vidente

psy·cho·a·nal·y·sis [saɪkouən'æləsɪs] psicoanálisis m

psy·cho·an·a·lyst [saɪkou'ænəlɪst] psicoanalista m/f

psy·cho·an·a·lyze [saɪkou'ænəlaɪz] v/t psicoanalizar

psy·cho·log·i·cal [saɪkə'lɑːdʒɪkl] adj psicológico

psy·cho·log·i·cal·ly [saɪkə'lɑːdʒɪklɪ] adv psicológicamente

psy·chol·o·gist [saɪ'kɑːlədʒɪst] psicólogo(-a) m(f)

psy·chol·o·gy [saɪ'kɑːlədʒɪ] psicología f

psy·cho·path ['saɪkoupæθ] psicópata m/f

psy·cho·so·mat·ic [saɪkousə'mætɪk] adj psicosomático

PTO [pi:ti:'ou] abbr (= **please turn over**) véase al dorso

pub [pʌb] Br bar m

pu·ber·ty ['pju:bərtɪ] pubertad f

pu·bic hair ['pju:bɪk] vello m púbico

pub·lic ['pʌblɪk] **1** adj público **2** n: **the** ~ el público; **in** ~ en público

pub·li·ca·tion [pʌblɪ'keɪʃn] publicación f

pub·lic 'hol·i·day día m festivo

pub·lic·i·ty [pʌb'lɪsətɪ] publicidad f

pub·li·cize ['pʌblɪsaɪz] v/t (make known) publicar, hacer público; COM dar publicidad a

pub·lic 'li·bra·ry biblioteca f pública

pub·lic·ly ['pʌblɪklɪ] adv públicamente

pub·lic 'pros·e·cu·tor fiscal m/f;
pub·lic re'la·tions npl relaciones públicas fpl; **'pub·lic school** colegio m público; Br colegio m privado;
'pub·lic sec·tor sector m público

pub·lish ['pʌblɪʃ] v/t publicar

pub·lish·er ['pʌblɪʃər] person editor(a) m(f); company editorial f

pub·lish·ing ['pʌblɪʃɪŋ] industria f editorial

'pub·lish·ing com·pa·ny editorial f

pud·dle ['pʌdl] charco m

Puer·to Ri·can [pwertou'ri:kən] **1** adj portorriqueño, puertorriqueño **2** n portorriqueño(-a) m(f), puertorriqueño(-a) m(f)

Puer·to Ri·co [pwertou'ri:kou] Puerto Rico

puff [pʌf] **1** n of wind racha f; from cigarette calada f; of smoke bocanada f **2** v/i (pant) resoplar; ~ **on a cigarette** dar una calada a un cigarrillo

puff·y ['pʌfɪ] adj eyes, face hinchado

puke [pju:k] **1** n P substance vomitona f P **2** v/i P echar la pota P

pull [pul] **1** n on rope tirón m; F (appeal) gancho m F; F (influence) enchufe m F **2** v/t (drag) arrastrar; (tug) tirar de; tooth sacar; ~ **a muscle** sufrir un tirón en un músculo **3** v/i tirar

♦ **pull ahead** v/i in race, competition adelantarse

♦ **pull apart** v/t (separate) separar

♦ **pull away** v/t apartar

♦ **pull down** v/t (lower) bajar; (demolish) derribar

♦ **pull in** v/i of bus, train llegar

♦ **pull off** v/t quitar; item of clothing quitarse; F conseguir

♦ **pull out 1** v/t sacar; troops retirar;
2 v/i retirarse; of ship salir

♦ **pull over** v/i parar en el arcén

♦ **pull through** v/i from an illness recuperarse

♦ **pull together 1** v/i (cooperate) cooperar **2** v/t: **pull o.s. together** tranquilizarse

♦ **pull up 1** v/t (raise) subir; item of clothing subirse; plant, weeds arrancar **2** v/i of car etc parar

pul·ley ['pʊlɪ] polea f

pull·o·ver ['pʊloʊvər] suéter m, *Span* jersey m

pulp [pʌlp] *of fruit* pulpa f; *for paper-making* pasta f

pul·pit ['pʊlpɪt] púlpito m

pul·sate [pʌl'seɪt] v/i *of heart, blood* palpitar; *of music* vibrar

pulse [pʌls] pulso m

pul·ver·ize ['pʌlvəraɪz] v/t pulverizar

pump [pʌmp] **1** n bomba f; (*gas ~*) surtidor m **2** v/t bombear

♦ **pump up** v/t inflar

pump·kin ['pʌmpkɪn] calabaza f

pun [pʌn] juego m de palabras

punch [pʌnʃ] **1** n *blow* puñetazo m; *implement* perforadora f **2** v/t *with fist* dar un puñetazo a; *hole, ticket* agujerear

'**punch line** golpe m, punto m culminante

punc·tu·al ['pʌŋktʊəl] adj puntual

punc·tu·al·i·ty [pʌŋktʊ'ælətɪ] puntualidad f

punc·tu·al·ly ['pʌŋktʊəlɪ] adv puntualmente

punc·tu·ate ['pʌŋktʊeɪt] v/t puntuar

punc·tu·a·tion ['pʌŋktʊ'eɪʃn] puntuación f

punc·tu·a·tion mark signo m de puntuación

punc·ture ['pʌŋktʃər] **1** n perforación f **2** v/t perforar

pun·gent ['pʌndʒənt] adj fuerte

pun·ish ['pʌnɪʃ] v/t *person* castigar

pun·ish·ing ['pʌnɪʃɪŋ] adj *schedule* exigente; *pace* fuerte

pun·ish·ment ['pʌnɪʃmənt] castigo m

punk (rock) ['pʌŋk(rɑːk)] MUS (música f) punk m

pu·ny ['pjuːnɪ] adj *person* enclenque

pup [pʌp] cachorro m

pu·pil[1] ['pjuːpl] *of eye* pupila f

pu·pil[2] ['pjuːpl] (*student*) alumno(-a) m(f)

pup·pet ['pʌpɪt] *also fig* marioneta f

'**pup·pet gov·ern·ment** gobierno m títere

pup·py ['pʌpɪ] cachorro m

pur·chase[1] ['pɜːrtʃəs] **1** n adquisición f, compra f **2** v/t adquirir, comprar

pur·chase[2] ['pɜːrtʃəs] (*grip*) agarre m

pur·chas·er ['pɜːrtʃəsər] comprador(a) m(f)

pure [pjʊr] adj puro; **~ new wool** pura lana f virgen

pure·ly ['pjʊrlɪ] adv puramente

pur·ga·to·ry ['pɜːrɡətɔːrɪ] purgatorio m

purge [pɜːrdʒ] **1** n *of political party* purga f **2** v/t purgar f

pu·ri·fy ['pjʊrɪfaɪ] v/t (*pret & pp -ied*) *water* depurar

pu·ri·tan ['pjʊrɪtən] puritano(-a) m(f)

pu·ri·tan·i·cal [pjʊrɪ'tænɪkl] adj puritano

pu·ri·ty ['pjʊrɪtɪ] pureza f

pur·ple ['pɜːrpl] adj morado

Pur·ple 'Heart MIL. medalla concedida a los soldados heridos en combate

pur·pose ['pɜːrpəs] (*aim, object*) propósito m, objeto m; **on ~** a propósito; **what is the ~ of your visit?** ¿cuál es el objeto de su visita?

pur·pose·ful ['pɜːrpəsfəl] adj decidido

pur·pose·ly ['pɜːrpəslɪ] adv decidamente

purr [pɜːr] v/i *of cat* ronronear

purse [pɜːrs] n (*pocket book*) bolso m; *Br for money* monedero m

pur·sue [pər'suː] v/t *person* perseguir; *career* ejercer; *course of action* proseguir

pur·su·er [pər'suːər] perseguidor(a) m(f)

pur·suit [pər'suːt] (*chase*) persecución f; *of happiness etc* búsqueda f; (*activity*) actividad f; **those in ~** los perseguidores

pus [pʌs] pus m

push [pʊʃ] **1** n (*shove*) empujón m; **at the ~ of a button** apretando un botón **2** v/t (*shove*) empujar; *button* apretar, pulsar; (*pressurize*) presionar; F *drugs* pasar F, mercadear con; **be ~ed for cash** F estar pelado F, estar sin un centavo; **be ~ed for time** F ir mal de tiempo F; **be ~ing 40** F rondar los 40 **3** v/i empujar

♦ **push ahead** v/i seguir adelante

♦ **push along** v/t cart etc empujar

♦ **push away** v/t apartar

♦ **push off** v/t lid destapar

♦ **push on** v/i (continue) continuar

♦ **push up** v/t prices hacer subir

push·er ['puʃər] F of drugs camello m
F

push-up ['puʃʌp] flexión f (de brazos)

push·y ['puʃɪ] adj F avasallador, agresivo

puss, pus·sy (cat) [pus, 'pusɪ (kæt)]
F minino m F

♦ **pussyfoot around** ['pusɪfut] v/i F andarse con rodeos

put [put] v/t (pret & pp put): poner;
question hacer; ~ the cost at ... estimar el costo en ...

♦ **put across** v/t idea etc hacer llegar

♦ **put aside** v/t money apartar, ahorrar; work dejar a un lado

♦ **put away** v/t in closet etc guardar; in
institution encerrar; F (consume)
consumir, cepillarse F; money apartar, ahorrar; animal sacrificar

♦ **put back** v/t (replace) volver a poner

♦ **put by** v/t money apartar, ahorrar

♦ **put down** v/t dejar; deposit entregar; rebellion reprimir; (belittle) dejar en mal lugar; **put down in
writing** poner por escrito; **put one's
foot down** in car apretar el acelerador; (be firm) plantarse; **put sth
down to sth** (attribute) atribuir algo
a algo

♦ **put forward** v/t idea etc proponer,
presentar

♦ **put in** v/t meter; time dedicar;
request, claim presentar

♦ **put in for** v/t (apply for) solicitar

♦ **put off** v/t light, radio, TV apagar;
(postpone) posponer, aplazar;
(deter) desalentar; (repel) desagradar; **I was put off by the smell** el
olor me quitó las ganas; **that put me
off shellfish for life** me quitó las
ganas de volver a comer marisco

♦ **put on** v/t light, radio, TV encender,
L.Am. prender; tape, music poner;
jacket, shoes, eye glasses ponerse;
(perform) representar; (assume) fingir; **put on make-up** maquillarse;
put on the brake frenar; **put on
weight** engordar; **she's just
putting it on** está fingiendo

♦ **put out** v/t hand extender; fire, light
apagar

♦ **put through** v/t: **put s.o. through
to s.o.** on phone poner a alguien con
alguien

♦ **put together** v/t (assemble, organize) montar

♦ **put up** v/t hand, fence, building levantar; person alojar; prices subir;
poster, notice colocar; money aportar; **put your hands up!** ¡arriba las
manos!; **put up for sale** poner en
venta

♦ **put up with** v/t (tolerate) aguantar

putt [pʌt] v/i SP golpear con el putter

put·ty ['pʌtɪ] masilla f

puz·zle ['pʌzl] **1** n (mystery) enigma
m; game pasatiempos mpl; (jigsaw)
puzzle m; (crossword) crucigrama m
2 v/t desconcertar; **one thing ~s me**
hay algo que no acabo de entender

puz·zling ['pʌzlɪŋ] adj desconcertante

PVC [pi:vi:'si:] abbr (= **polyvinyl
chloride**) PVC m (= cloruro m de
polivinilo)

py·ja·mas Br → **pajamas**

py·lon ['paɪlən] torre f de alta tensión

P

Q

quack[1] [kwæk] **1** *n of duck* graznido *m* **2** *v/i* graznar

quack[2] [kwæk] *n* F (*bad doctor*) matasanos *m/f inv* F

quad·ran·gle ['kwɑːdræŋgl] *figure* cuadrángulo *m*; *courtyard* patio *m*

quad·ru·ped ['kwɑːdruped] cuadrúpedo *m*

quad·ru·ple ['kwɑːdrupl] *v/i* cuadruplicarse

quad·ru·plets ['kwɑːdruplɪts] *npl* cuatrillizos(-as) *mpl* (*fpl*)

quads [kwɑːdz] *npl* F cuatrillizos(-as) *mpl* (*fpl*)

quag·mire ['kwɑːgmaɪr] *fig* atolladero *m*

quail [kweɪl] *v/i* temblar (*at* ante)

quaint [kweɪnt] *adj cottage* pintoresco; (*eccentric: ideas etc*) extraño

quake [kweɪk] **1** *n* (*earthquake*) terremoto *m* **2** *v/i of earth, with fear* temblar

qual·i·fi·ca·tion [kwɑːlɪfɪˈkeɪʃn] *from university etc* título *m*; **have the right ~s for a job** estar bien cualificado para un trabajo

qual·i·fied ['kwɑːlɪfaɪd] *adj doctor, engineer, plumber etc* titulado; (*restricted*) limitado; *I am not ~ to judge* no estoy en condiciones de poder juzgar

qual·i·fy ['kwɑːlɪfaɪ] **1** *v/t* (*pret & pp -ied*) *of degree, course etc* habilitar; *remark etc* matizar **2** *v/i* (*pret & pp -ied*) (*get degree etc*) titularse, *L.Am.* egresar; *in competition* calificarse; *that doesn't ~ as ...* eso no cuenta como ...

qual·i·ty ['kwɑːlətɪ] calidad *f*; (*characteristic*) cualidad *f*

qual·i·ty con'trol control *m* de calidad

qualm [kwɑːm]: *have no ~s about ...* no tener reparos en ...

quan·da·ry ['kwɑːndərɪ] dilema *m*

quan·ti·fy ['kwɑːntɪfaɪ] *v/t* (*pret & pp -ied*) cuantificar

quan·ti·ty ['kwɑːntətɪ] cantidad *f*

quan·tum 'phys·ics ['kwɑːntəm] física *f* cuántica

quar·an·tine ['kwɑːrəntiːn] cuarentena *f*

quar·rel ['kwɑːrəl] **1** *n* pelea *f* **2** *v/i* (*pret & pp -ed*, *Br -led*) pelearse

quar·rel·some ['kwɑːrəlsʌm] *adj* peleón

quar·ry[1] ['kwɑːrɪ] *in hunt* presa *f*

quar·ry[2] ['kwɑːrɪ] *for mining* cantera *f*

quart [kwɔːrt] cuarto *m* de galón

quar·ter ['kwɔːrtər] cuarto *m*; *25 cents* cuarto *m* de dólar; *part of town* barrio *m*; *a ~ of an hour* un cuarto de hora; *a ~ of 5* las cinco menos cuarto, *L.Am.* un cuarto para las cinco; *a ~ after 5* las cinco y cuarto

'quar·ter·back SP quarterback *m*, en fútbol americano, jugador que dirige el juego de ataque; **quar·ter·'fi·nal** cuarto *m* de final; **quar·ter·'fi·nal·ist** cuartofinalista *m/f*

quar·ter·ly ['kwɔːrtərlɪ] **1** *adj* trimestral **2** *adv* trimestralmente

'quar·ter·note MUS negra *f*

quar·ters ['kwɔːrtərz] *npl* MIL alojamiento *m*

quar·tet [kwɔːr'tet] MUS cuarteto *m*

quartz [kwɔːrts] cuarzo *m*

quash [kwɑːʃ] *v/t rebellion* aplastar, sofocar; *court decision* revocar

qua·ver ['kweɪvər] **1** *n in voice* temblor *m* **2** *v/i of voice* temblar

quea·sy ['kwiːzɪ] *adj* mareado; *get ~* marearse

queen [kwiːn] reina *f*

queen 'bee abeja *f* reina

queer [kwɪr] *adj* (*peculiar*) raro, extraño

queer·ly ['kwɪrlɪ] *adv* de manera extraña

quell [kwel] *v/t protest* acallar; *riot* aplastar, sofocar

quench [kwentʃ] *v/t thirst* apagar, saciar; *flames* apagar

que·ry ['kwɪrɪ] **1** *n* duda *f*, pregunta *f* **2** *v/t (pret & pp -ied) (express doubt about)* cuestionar; *(check)* comprobar; ~ *sth with s.o.* preguntar algo a alguien

quest [kwest] busca *f*

ques·tion ['kwestʃn] **1** *n* pregunta *f*; *(matter)* cuestión *f*, asunto *m*; *in ~ (being talked about)* en cuestión; *(in doubt)* en duda; *it's a ~ of money/ time* es una cuestión de dinero/ tiempo; *that's out of the ~* eso es imposible **2** *v/t person* preguntar a; LAW interrogar; *(doubt)* cuestionar, poner en duda

ques·tion·a·ble ['kwestʃnəbl] *adj* cuestionable, dudoso

ques·tion·ing ['kwestʃnɪŋ] **1** *adj look, tone* inquisitivo **2** *n* interrogatorio *m*

'ques·tion mark signo *m* de interrogación

ques·tion·naire [kwestʃə'ner] cuestionario *m*

queue [kjuː] *n Br* cola *f*

quib·ble ['kwɪbl] *v/i* discutir *(por algo insignificante)*

quick [kwɪk] *adj* rápido; *be ~!* ¡date prisa!; *let's have a ~ drink* vamos a tomarnos algo rápidamente; *can I have a ~ look?* ¿me dejas echarle un vistazo?; *that was ~!* ¡qué rápido!

quick·ly ['kwɪklɪ] *adv* rápidamente, rápido, deprisa

'quick·sand arenas *fpl* movedizas

'quick·sil·ver azogue *m*; **quick-wit·ted** [kwɪk'wɪtɪd] *adj* agudo

qui·et ['kwaɪət] *adj* tranquilo; *engine* silencioso; *keep ~ about sth* guardar silencio sobre algo; ~*!* ¡silencio!

♦ **qui·et·en down** ['kwaɪətn] **1** *v/t children, class* tranquilizar, hacer callar **2** *v/i of children* tranquilizarse, callarse; *of political situation* calmarse

qui·et·ly ['kwaɪətlɪ] *adv (not loudly)* silenciosamente; *(without fuss)* discretamente; *(peacefully)* tranquilamente; *speak ~* hablar en voz baja

qui·et·ness ['kwaɪətnɪs] *of voice* suavidad *f*; *of night, street* silencio *m*, calma *f*

quilt [kwɪlt] *on bed* edredón *m*

quilt·ed ['kwɪltɪd] *adj* acolchado

quin·ine ['kwɪniːn] quinina *f*

quin·tet [kwɪn'tet] MUS quinteto *m*

quip [kwɪp] **1** *n joke* broma *f*; *remark* salida *f* **2** *v/i (pret & pp -ped)* bromear

quirk [kwɜːrk] peculiaridad *f*, rareza *f*

quirk·y ['kwɜːrkɪ] *adj* peculiar, raro

quit [kwɪt] **1** *v/t (pret & pp quit) job* dejar, abandonar; ~ *doing sth* dejar de hacer algo **2** *v/i (pret & pp quit) (leave job)* dimitir; COMPUT salir

quite [kwaɪt] *adv - (fairly)* bastante; *(completely)* completamente; *not ~ ready* no listo del todo; *I didn't ~ understand* no entendí bien; *is that right? - not ~* ¿es verdad? - no exactamente; ~*!* ¡exactamente!; ~ *a lot* bastante; ~ *a few* bastantes; *it was ~ a surprise* fue toda una sorpresa

quits [kwɪts] *adj: be ~ with s.o.* estar en paz con alguien

quit·ter ['kwɪtər] F *persona que abandona fácilmente*

quiv·er ['kwɪvər] *v/i* estremecerse

quiz [kwɪz] **1** *n concurso m (de preguntas y respuestas)* **2** *v/t (pret & pp -zed)* interrogar *(about* sobre)

'quiz mas·ter *presentador de un concurso de preguntas y respuestas*

'quiz pro·gram, *Br* **'quiz pro·gramme** programa *m* concurso *(de preguntas y respuestas)*

quo·ta ['kwoʊtə] cuota *f*

quo·ta·tion [kwoʊ'teɪʃn] *from author* cita *f*; *(price)* presupuesto *m*

quo'ta·tion marks *npl* comillas *fpl*

quote [kwoʊt] **1** *n from author* cita *f*; *(price)* presupuesto *m*; *(quotation mark)* comilla *f*; *in ~s* entre comillas **2** *v/t text* citar; *price* dar **3** *v/i:* ~ *from an author* citar de un autor

Q

R

rab·bi ['ræbaɪ] rabino *m*

rab·bit ['ræbɪt] conejo *m*

rab·ble ['ræbl] chusma *f*, multitud *f*

rab·ble-rous·er ['ræblrauzər] agitador(a) *m(f)*

ra·bies ['reɪbiːz] *nsg* rabia *f*

rac·coon [rə'kuːn] mapache *m*

race¹ [reɪs] *n of people* raza *f*

race² [reɪs] **1** *n* SP carrera *f*; *the ~s horse races* las carreras **2** *v/i (run fast)* correr; *he ~d through his meal/work* acabó su comida/trabajo a toda velocidad **3** *v/t* correr contra; *I'll ~ you* te echo una carrera

'race·course hipódromo *m*;
'race·horse caballo *m* de carreras;
'race riot disturbios *mpl* raciales;
'race·track circuito *m*; *for horses* hipódromo *m*

ra·cial ['reɪʃl] *adj* racial; *~ equality* igualdad *f* racial

rac·ing ['reɪsɪŋ] carreras *fpl*

rac·ism ['reɪsɪzm] racismo *m*

ra·cist ['reɪsɪst] **1** *n* racista *m/f* **2** *adj* racista

rack [ræk] **1** *n (for bikes)* barras para aparcar bicicletas; *for bags on train* portaequipajes *m inv*; *for CDs* mueble *m* **2** *v/t:* ~ *one's brains* devanarse los sesos

rack·et¹ ['rækɪt] SP raqueta *f*

rack·et² ['rækɪt] *(noise)* jaleo *m*; *(criminal activity)* negocio *m* sucio

ra·dar ['reɪdɑːr] radar *m*

'ra·dar screen pantalla *f* de radar

'ra·dar trap control *m* de velocidad por radar

ra·di·al 'tire, *Br* **ra·di·al 'tyre** ['reɪdɪəl] neumático *m* radial

ra·di·ance ['reɪdɪəns] esplendor *m*, brillantez *f*

ra·di·ant ['reɪdɪənt] *adj smile, appearance* resplandeciente, brillante

ra·di·ate ['reɪdɪeɪt] *v/i of heat, light* irradiar

ra·di·a·tion [reɪdɪ'eɪʃn] PHYS radiación *f*

ra·di·a·tor ['reɪdɪeɪtər] *in room, car* radiador *m*

rad·i·cal ['rædɪkl] **1** *adj* radical **2** *n* POL radical *m/f*

rad·i·cal·ism ['rædɪkəlɪzm] POL radicalismo *m*

rad·i·cal·ly ['rædɪklɪ] *adv* radicalmente

ra·di·o ['reɪdɪoʊ] radio *f*; *on the ~* en la radio; *by ~* por radio

ra·di·o·ac·tive [reɪdɪoʊ'æktɪv] *adj* radiactivo; **ra·di·o·ac·tive 'waste** residuos *mpl* radiactivos; **ra·di·o·ac·tiv·i·ty** [reɪdɪoʊæk'tɪvətɪ] radiactividad *f*; **ra·di·o a'larm** radio *m* despertador

ra·di·og·ra·pher [reɪdɪ'ɑːgrəfər] técnico(-a) *m(f)* de rayos X

ra·di·og·ra·phy [reɪdɪ'ɑːgrəfɪ] radiografía *f*

'ra·di·o sta·tion emisora *f* de radio;
'ra·di·o tax·i radiotaxi *m*; **ra·di·o·'ther·a·py** radioterapia *f*

rad·ish ['rædɪʃ] rábano *m*

ra·di·us ['reɪdɪəs] radio *m*

raf·fle ['ræfl] *n* rifa *f*

raft [ræft] balsa *f*

raf·ter ['ræftər] viga *f*

rag [ræg] *n for cleaning etc* trapo *m*; *in ~s* con harapos

rage [reɪdʒ] **1** *n* ira *f*, cólera *f*; *be in a ~* estar encolerizado; *be all the ~* F estar arrasando **F 2** *v/i of storm* bramar

rag·ged ['rægɪd] *adj* andrajoso

raid [reɪd] **1** *n by troops* incursión *f*; *by police* redada *f*; *by robbers* atraco *m*; FIN ataque *m*, incursión *f* **2** *v/t of troops* realizar una incursión en; *of police* realizar una redada en; *of robbers* atracar; *fridge, orchard* saquear

raid·er ['reɪdər] *on bank etc* atracador(a) *m(f)*

rail [reɪl] *n on track* riel *m*, carril *m*; *(hand~)* pasamanos *m inv*, baranda *f*; *for towel* barra *f*; **by ~** en tren

rail·ings ['reɪlɪŋz] *npl around park etc* verja *f*

'**rail·road** ferrocarril *m*; '**rail·road sta·tion** estación *f* de ferrocarril or de tren; '**rail·way** *Br* ferrocarril *m*

rain [reɪn] **1** *n* lluvia *f*; **in the ~** bajo la lluvia **2** *v/i* llover; **it's ~ing** llueve

'**rain·bow** arco *m* iris; '**rain·check**: **can I take a ~ on that?** F ¿lo podríamos aplazar para algún otro momento?; '**rain·coat** impermeable *m*; '**rain·drop** gota *f* de lluvia; '**rain·fall** pluviosidad *f*, precipitaciones *fpl*; '**rain for·est** selva *f*; '**rain·proof** *fabric* impermeable; '**rain·storm** tormenta *f*, aguacero *m*

rain·y ['reɪnɪ] *adj* lluvioso; **it's ~** llueve mucho

rain·y sea·son estación *f* de las lluvias

raise [reɪz] **1** *n in salary* aumento *m* de sueldo **2** *v/t shelf etc* levantar; *offer* incrementar; *children* criar; *question* plantear; *money* reunir

rai·sin ['reɪzn] pasa *f*

rake [reɪk] *n for garden* rastrillo *m*
♦ **rake up** *v/t leaves* rastrillar; *fig* sacar a la luz

ral·ly ['rælɪ] *n (meeting, reunion)* concentración *f*; *political* mitin *m*; MOT rally *m*; *in tennis* peloteo *m*
♦ **rally round** **1** *v/i (pret & pp -ied)* acudir a ayudar **2** *v/t (pret & pp -ied)*: **rally round s.o.** acudir a ayudar a alguien

RAM [ræm] COMPUT *abbr (= **random access memory**)* RAM *f (=* memoria *f* de acceso aleatorio)

ram [ræm] **1** *n* carnero *m* **2** *v/t (pret & pp -med) ship, car* embestir

ram·ble ['ræmbl] **1** *n walk* caminata *f*, excursión *f* **2** *v/i walk* caminar; *in speaking* divagar; *(talk incoherently)* hablar sin decir nada coherente

ram·bler ['ræmblər] *walker*

ram·bling ['ræmblɪŋ] **1** *n walking* senderismo *m*; *in speech* divagaciones *fpl* **2** *adj speech* inconexo

ramp [ræmp] rampa *f*; *for raising vehicle* elevador *m*

ram·page ['ræmpeɪdʒ] **1** *v/i* pasar arrasando con todo **2** *n*: **go on the ~** pasar arrasando con todo

ram·pant ['ræmpənt] *adj inflation* galopante

ram·part ['ræmpɑːrt] muralla *f*

ram·shack·le ['ræmʃækl] *adj* destartalado, desvencijado

ran [ræn] *pret* → **run**

ranch [ræntʃ] rancho *m*

ranch·er ['ræntʃər] ranchero(-a) *m(f)*

ran·cid ['rænsɪd] *adj* rancio

ran·cor ['ræŋkər] rencor *m*

R & D [ɑːrən'diː] *abbr (= **research and development**)* I+D *f (=* investigación *f* y desarrollo)

ran·dom ['rændəm] **1** *adj* al azar; **~ sample** muestra *f* aleatoria **2** *n*: **at ~** al azar

ran·dy ['rændɪ] *adj Br* F cachondo F; **it makes me ~** me pone cachondo

rang [ræŋ] *pret* → **ring**

range [reɪndʒ] **1** *n of products* gama *f*; *of gun, airplane* alcance *m*; *of voice* registro *m*; *of mountains* cordillera *f*; **at close ~** de cerca **2** *v/i*: **~ from X to Y** ir desde X a Y

rang·er ['reɪndʒər] guardabosques *m/f inv*

rank [ræŋk] **1** *n* MIL, *in society* rango *m*; **the ~s** MIL la tropa **2** *v/t* clasificar
♦ **rank among** *v/t* figurar entre

ran·kle ['ræŋkl] *v/i* doler; **it still ~s (with him)** todavía le duele

ran·sack ['rænsæk] *v/t* saquear

ran·som ['rænsəm] *n* rescate *m*; **hold s.o. to ~** pedir un rescate por alguien

'**ran·som mon·ey** (dinero *m* del) rescate *m*

rant [rænt] *v/i*: **~ and rave** despotricar

rap [ræp] **1** *n at door etc* golpe *m*; MUS rap *m* **2** *v/t (pret & pp -ped) table etc* golpear

♦ **rap at** v/t window etc golpear

rape¹[reɪp] **1** n violación f **2** v/t violar

rape²[reɪp] n BOT colza f

'rape vic·tim víctima m/f de una violación

rap·id['ræpɪd] adj rápido

ra·pid·i·ty[rə'pɪdətɪ] rapidez f

rap·id·ly['ræpɪdlɪ] adv rápidamente

rap·ids['ræpɪdz] npl rápidos mpl

rap·ist['reɪpɪst] violador(a) m(f)

rap·port[ræ'pɔːr] relación f; **we have a good ~** nos entendemos muy bien

rap·ture['ræptʃər]: **go into ~s over** extasiarse con

rap·tur·ous['ræptʃərəs] adj clamoroso

rare [rer] adj raro; steak poco hecho

rare·ly['rerlɪ] adv raramente, raras veces

rar·i·ty['rerətɪ] rareza f

ras·cal['ræskl] pícaro(-a) m(f)

rash¹[ræʃ] n MED sarpullido m, erupción f cutánea

rash²[ræʃ] adj action, behavior precipitado

rash·ly['ræʃlɪ] adv precipitadamente

rasp·ber·ry['ræzberɪ] frambuesa f

rat[ræt] n rata f

rate[reɪt] **1** n of exchange tipo m; of pay tarifa f; (price) tarifa f, precio m; (speed) ritmo m; **~ of interest** FIN tipo m de interés; **at this ~** (at this speed) a este ritmo; (if we carry on like this) si seguimos así; **at any ~** (anyway) en todo caso; (at least) por lo menos **2** v/t: **~ s.o. as ...** considerar a alguien (como) ...; **~ s.o. highly** tener buena opinión de alguien

rather['ræðər] adv (fairly, quite) bastante; **I would ~ stay here** preferiría quedarme aquí; **or would you ~ ...?** ¿o preferiría ...?

rat·i·fi·ca·tion[rætɪfɪ'keɪʃn] ratificación f

rat·i·fy['rætɪfaɪ] v/t (pret & pp **-ied**) ratificar

rat·ings['reɪtɪŋz] npl índice m de audiencia

ra·ti·o['reɪʃɪou] proporción f

ra·tion['ræʃn] **1** n ración f **2** v/t supplies racionar

ra·tion·al['ræʃənl] adj racional

ra·tion·al·i·ty[ræʃə'nælɪtɪ] racionalidad f

ra·tion·al·i·za·tion[ræʃənəlaɪ'zeɪʃn] racionalización f

ra·tion·al·ize['ræʃənəlaɪz] **1** v/t racionalizar **2** v/i buscar una explicación racional

ra·tion·al·ly['ræʃənlɪ] adv racionalmente

'rat race vida frenética y competitiva

rat·tle['rætl] **1** n noise traqueteo m, golpeteo m; toy sonajero m **2** v/t chains etc entrechocar **3** v/i of chains etc entrechocarse; of crates traquetear

♦ **rattle off** v/t poem, list of names decir rápidamente

♦ **rattle through** v/t hacer rápidamente

'rat·tle·snake serpiente f de cascabel

rau·cous['rɔːkəs] adj laughter, party estridente

rav·age['rævɪdʒ] **1** n: **the ~s of time** los estragos del tiempo **2** v/t arrasar; **~d by war** arrasado por la guerra

rave[reɪv] **1** v/i (talk deliriously) delirar; (talk wildly) desvariar; **~ about sth** (be very enthusiastic) estar muy entusiasmado con algo **2** n party fiesta f tecno

ra·ven['reɪvn] cuervo m

rav·e·nous['rævənəs] adj (very hungry) famélico; **have a ~ appetite** tener un hambre canina

rav·e·nous·ly['rævənəslɪ] adv con voracidad

rave re'view crítica f muy entusiasta

ra·vine[rə'viːn] barranco m

rav·ing['reɪvɪŋ] adv: **~ mad** chalado

rav·ish·ing['rævɪʃɪŋ] adj encantador, cautivador

raw[rɔː] adj meat, vegetable crudo; sugar sin refinar; iron sin tratar

raw ma'te·ri·als npl materias fpl primas

ray[reɪ] rayo m; **a ~ of hope** un rayo de esperanza

raze[reɪz] v/t: **~ to the ground** arrasar *or* asolar por completo

ra·zor ['reɪzər] maquinilla *f* de afeitar

'**ra·zor blade** cuchilla *f* de afeitar

re [riː] *prep* COM con referencia a

reach [riːtʃ] **1** *n*: **within** ~ al alcance; **out of** ~ fuera del alcance **2** *v/t* llegar a; *decision, agreement, conclusion* alcanzar, llegar a; **can you ~ it?** ¿alcanzas?, ¿llegas?

♦ **reach out** *v/i* extender el brazo

re·act [rɪ'ækt] *v/i* reaccionar

re·ac·tion [rɪ'ækʃn] reacción *f*

re·ac·tion·ar·y [rɪ'ækʃnrɪ] **1** *n* POL reaccionario(-a) *m(f)* **2** *adj* POL reaccionario

re·ac·tor [rɪ'æktər] *nuclear reactor m*

read [riːd] (*pret & pp* **read** [red]) **1** *v/t also* COMPUT leer **2** *v/i* leer; ~ **to s.o.** leer a alguien

♦ **read out** *v/t aloud* leer en voz alta

♦ **read up on** *v/t* leer mucho sobre, estudiar

rea·da·ble ['riːdəbl] *adj handwriting* legible; *book* ameno

read·er ['riːdər] *person* lector(a) *m(f)*

read·i·ly ['redɪlɪ] *adv admit, agree* de buena gana

read·i·ness ['redɪnɪs]: **in a state of** ~ preparado par actuar; **their** ~ **to help** la facilidad con la que ayudaron

read·ing ['riːdɪŋ] *activity* lectura *f*; **take a** ~ **from the meter** leer el contador

'**read·ing mat·ter** lectura *f*

re·ad·just [riːə'dʒʌst] **1** *v/t equipment, controls* reajustar **2** *v/i to conditions* volver a adaptarse

read-'on·ly file COMPUT archivo *m* sólo de lectura

read-'on·ly mem·o·ry COMPUT memoria *f* sólo de lectura

read·y ['redɪ] *adj (prepared)* listo, preparado; *(willing)* dispuesto; **get (o.s.)** ~ prepararse; **get sth ready** preparar algo

read·y 'cash dinero *m* contante y sonante; **read·y-made** *adj stew etc* precocinado; *solution* ya hecho; **read·y-to-wear** *adj* de confección

re·al [riːl] *adj* real; *surprise, genius* auténtico; **he's a** ~ **idiot** es un auténtico idiota

'**re·al es·tate** bienes *mpl* inmuebles

'**re·al es·tate a·gent** agente *m/f* inmobiliario(-a)

re·al·ism ['rɪəlɪzəm] realismo *m*

re·al·ist ['rɪəlɪst] realista *m/f*

re·al·is·tic [rɪə'lɪstɪk] *adj* realista

re·al·is·tic·al·ly [rɪə'lɪstɪklɪ] *adv* realísticamente

re·al·i·ty [rɪ'ælətɪ] realidad *f*

re·al·i·za·tion [rɪəlaɪ'zeɪʃn]: **the** ~ **dawned on me that ...** me di cuenta de que ...

re·al·ize ['rɪəlaɪz] *v/t* darse cuenta de; FIN (*yield*) producir; *(sell)* realizar, liquidar; **I** ~ **now that ...** ahora me doy cuenta de que ...

re·al·ly ['rɪəlɪ] *adv in truth* de verdad; *big, small* muy; **I am** ~ ~ **sorry** lo siento en el alma; **~?** ¿de verdad?; **not** ~ *as reply* la verdad es que no

re·al time *n* COMPUT tiempo *m* real

'**re·al-time** *adj* COMPUT en tiempo real

re·al·tor ['riːltər] agente *m/f* inmobiliario(-a)

re·al·ty ['riːltɪ] bienes *mpl* inmuebles

reap [riːp] *v/t* cosechar

re·ap·pear [riːə'pɪr] *v/i* reaparecer

re·ap·pear·ance [riːə'pɪrəns] reaparición *f*

rear [rɪr] **1** *n* parte *f* de atrás **2** *adj legs* de atrás; *seats, wheels, lights* trasero

rear 'end 1 *n* F *of person* trasero *m* **2** *v/t* MOT F dar un golpe por atrás a

rear 'light *of car* luz *f* trasera

re·arm [riː'ɑːrm] **1** *v/t* rearmar **2** *v/i* rearmarse

'**rear·most** *adj* último

re·ar·range [riːə'reɪndʒ] *v/t flowers* volver a colocar; *furniture* reordenar; *schedule, meetings* cambiar

rear-view 'mir·ror espejo *m* retrovisor

rea·son ['riːzn] **1** *n faculty* razón *f*; *(cause)* razón *f*, motivo *m*; **see/ listen to** ~ atender a razones **2** *v/i*: ~ **with s.o.** razonar con alguien

rea·so·na·ble ['riːznəbl] *adj person*

razonable; *a ~ number of people* un buen número de personas

rea·son·a·bly ['riːznəblɪ] *adv act, behave* razonablemente; *(quite)* bastante

rea·son·ing ['riːznɪŋ] razonamiento *m*

re·as·sure [riːə'ʃʊr] *v/t* tranquilizar; *she ~d us of her continued support* nos aseguró que continuábamos contando con su apoyo

re·as·sur·ing [riːə'ʃʊrɪŋ] *adj* tranquilizador

re·bate ['riːbeɪt] *money back* reembolso *m*

reb·el[1] ['rebl] *n* rebelde *m/f*; *~ troops* tropas *fpl* rebeldes

re·bel[2] [rɪ'bel] *v/i (pret & pp -led)* rebelarse

reb·el·lion [rɪ'beljən] rebelión *f*

reb·el·lious [rɪ'beljəs] *adj* rebelde

reb·el·lious·ly [rɪ'beljəslɪ] *adv* con rebeldía

reb·el·lious·ness [rɪ'beljəsnɪs] rebeldía *f*

re·bound [rɪ'baʊnd] *v/i of ball etc* rebotar

re·buff [rɪ'bʌf] *n* desaire *m*, rechazo *m*

re·build ['riːbɪld] *v/t (pret & pp -built)* reconstruir

re·buke [rɪ'bjuːk] *v/t* reprender

re·call [rɪ'kɔːl] *v/t goods* retirar del mercado; *(remember)* recordar

re·cap ['riːkæp] *v/i (pret & pp -ped)* recapitular

re·cap·ture [riː'kæptʃər] *v/t* MIL reconquistar; *criminal* volver a detener

re·cede [rɪ'siːd] *v/i of flood waters* retroceder

re·ced·ing [rɪ'siːdɪŋ] *adj forehead, chin* hundido; *have a ~ hairline* tener entradas

re·ceipt [rɪ'siːt] *for purchase* recibo *m*; *acknowledge ~ of sth* acusar recibo de algo; *~s* FIN ingresos *mpl*

re·ceive [rɪ'siːv] *v/t* recibir

re·ceiv·er [rɪ'siːvər] *of letter* destinatario(-a) *m(f)*; TELEC auricular *m*; *for radio* receptor *m*

re·ceiv·er·ship [rɪ'siːvərʃɪp]: *be in ~* estar en suspensión de pagos

re·cent ['riːsnt] *adj* reciente

re·cent·ly ['riːsntlɪ] *adv* recientemente

re·cep·tion [rɪ'sepʃn] recepción *f*; *(welcome)* recibimiento *m*

re·cep·tion desk recepción *f*

re·cep·tion·ist [rɪ'sepʃnɪst] recepcionista *m/f*

re·cep·tive [rɪ'septɪv] *adj*: *be ~ to sth* ser receptivo a algo

re·cess ['riːses] *n in wall etc* hueco *m*; EDU recreo *m*; *of legislature* periodo *m* vacacional

re·ces·sion [rɪ'seʃn] *economic* recesión *f*

re·charge [riː'tʃɑːrdʒ] *v/t battery* recargar

re·ci·pe ['resəpɪ] receta *f*

're·ci·pe book libro *m* de cocina, recetario *m*

re·cip·i·ent [rɪ'sɪpɪənt] *of parcel etc* destinatario(-a) *m(f)*; *of payment* receptor(a) *m(f)*

re·cip·ro·cal [rɪ'sɪprəkl] *adj* recíproco

re·cit·al [rɪ'saɪtl] MUS recital *m*

re·cite [rɪ'saɪt] *v/t poem* recitar; *details, facts* enumerar

reck·less ['reklɪs] *adj* imprudente; *driving* temerario

reck·less·ly ['reklɪslɪ] *adv* con imprudencia; *drive* con temeridad

reck·on ['rekən] *v/t (think, consider)* estimar, considerar; *I ~ it won't happen* creo que no va a pasar
- **reckon on** *v/t* contar con
- **reckon with** *v/t*: *have s.o. / sth to reckon with* tener que vérselas con alguien / algo

reck·on·ing ['rekənɪŋ] estimaciones *fpl*, cálculos *mpl*; *by my ~* según mis cálculos

re·claim [rɪ'kleɪm] *v/t land from sea* ganar, recuperar; *lost property, rights* reclamar

re·cline [rɪ'klaɪn] *v/i* reclinarse

re·clin·er [rɪ'klaɪnər] *chair* sillón *m* reclinable

re·cluse [rɪ'kluːs] solitario(-a) *m(f)*

rec·og·ni·tion [rekəg'nɪʃn] *of state, s.o.'s achievements* reconocimiento *m*; **in ~ of** en reconocimiento a; **be changed beyond ~** estar irreconocible

rec·og·niz·a·ble [rekəg'naɪzəbl] *adj* reconocible

rec·og·nize ['rekəgnaɪz] *v/t* reconocer

re·coil [rɪ'kɔɪl] *v/i* echarse atrás, retroceder

rec·ol·lect [rekə'lekt] *v/t* recordar

rec·ol·lec·tion [rekə'lekʃn] recuerdo *m*; **I have no ~ of the accident** no me acuerdo del accidente

rec·om·mend [rekə'mend] *v/t* recomendar

rec·om·men·da·tion [rekəmen'deɪʃn] recomendación *f*

rec·om·pense ['rekəmpens] *n* recompensa *f*

rec·on·cile ['rekənsaɪl] *v/t people* reconciliar; *differences, facts* conciliar; **~ o.s. to …** hacerse a la idea de …; **be ~d** *of two people* haberse reconciliado

rec·on·cil·i·a·tion [rekənsɪlɪ'eɪʃn] *of people* reconciliación *f*; *of differences, facts* conciliación *f*

re·con·di·tion [riːkən'dɪʃn] *v/t* reacondicionar

re·con·nais·sance [rɪ'kɑːnɪsns] MIL reconocimiento *m*

re·con·sid·er [riːkən'sɪdər] **1** *v/t offer, one's position* reconsiderar **2** *v/i*: **won't you please ~?** ¿por qué no lo reconsideras, por favor?

re·con·struct [riːkən'strʌkt] *v/t* reconstruir

rec·ord[1] ['rekɔːrd] *n* MUS disco *m*; SP *etc* récord *m*; *written document etc* registro *m*, documento *m*; *in database* registro *m*; **~s** archivos *mpl*; **say sth off the ~** decir algo oficiosamente; **have a criminal ~** tener antecedentes penales; **have a good ~ for sth** tener un buen historial en materia de algo

re·cord[2] [rɪ'kɔːrd] *v/t electronically* grabar; *in writing* anotar

'rec·ord-break·ing *adj* récord

re·cord·er [rɪ'kɔːrdər] MUS flauta *f* dulce

'rec·ord hold·er plusmarquista *m/f*

re·cord·ing [rɪ'kɔːrdɪŋ] grabación *f*

re·cord·ing stu·di·o estudio *m* de grabación

'rec·ord play·er tocadiscos *m inv*

re·count [rɪ'kaʊnt] *v/t (tell)* relatar

re·count ['riːkaʊnt] **1** *n of votes* segundo recuento *m* **2** *v/t (count again)* volver a contar

re·coup [rɪ'kuːp] *v/t financial losses* resarcirse de

re·cov·er [rɪ'kʌvər] **1** *v/t sth lost, stolen goods* recuperar; *composure* recobrar **2** *v/i from illness* recuperarse

re·cov·er·y [rɪ'kʌvərɪ] recuperación *f*; **he has made a good ~** se ha recuperado muy bien

rec·re·a·tion [rekrɪ'eɪʃn] ocio *m*

rec·re·a·tion·al [rekrɪ'eɪʃnl] *adj done for pleasure* recreativo

re·cruit [rɪ'kruːt] **1** *n* MIL recluta *m/f*; *to company* nuevo(-a) trabajador(a) **2** *v/t new staff* contratar

re·cruit·ment [rɪ'kruːtmənt] MIL reclutamiento *m*; *to company* contratación *f*

re'cruit·ment drive MIL campaña *f* de reclutamiento; *to company* campaña *f* de contratación

rec·tan·gle ['rektæŋgl] rectángulo *m*

rec·tan·gu·lar [rek'tæŋgjʊlər] *adj* rectangular

rec·ti·fy ['rektɪfaɪ] *v/t (pret & pp -ied)* rectificar

re·cu·pe·rate [rɪ'kuːpəreɪt] *v/i* recuperarse

re·cur [rɪ'kɜːr] *v/i (pret & pp -red) of error, event* repetirse; *of symptoms* reaparecer

re·cur·rent [rɪ'kʌrənt] *adj* recurrente

re·cy·cla·ble [riː'saɪkləbl] *adj* reciclable

re·cy·cle [riː'saɪkl] *v/t* reciclar

re·cy·cling [riː'saɪklɪŋ] reciclado *m*

red [red] **1** *adj* rojo **2** *n*: **in the ~** FIN en números rojos

Red 'Cross Cruz *f* Roja

red·den ['redn] *v/i (blush)* ponerse

colorado

re·dec·o·rate [riːˈdekəreɪt] *v/t with paint* volver a pintar; *with paper* volver a empapelar

re·deem [rɪˈdiːm] *v/t debt* amortizar; REL redimir

re·deem·ing fea·ture [rɪˈdiːmɪŋ]: *his one - is that …* lo único que lo salva es que …

re·demp·tion [rɪˈdempʃn] REL redención *f*

re·de·vel·op [riːdɪˈveləp] *v/t part of town* reedificar

red-hand·ed [red'hændɪd] *adj:* **catch s.o.** - coger a alguien con las manos en la masa; **'red·head** pelirrojo(-a) *m(f)*; **red·'hot** *adj* al rojo vivo; **red·'let·ter day** día *m* señalado; **red 'light** *at traffic lights* semáforo *m* (en) rojo; **red 'light dis·trict** zona *f* de prostitución; **red 'meat** carne *f* roja; **'red·neck** F *individuo racista y reaccionario, normalmente de clase trabajadora*

re·dou·ble [riːˈdʌbl] *v/t:* - **one's efforts** redoblar los esfuerzos

red 'pep·per *vegetable* pimiento *m* rojo

red 'tape F burocracia *f*, papeleo *m*

re·duce [rɪˈduːs] *v/t* reducir; *price* rebajar

re·duc·tion [rɪˈdʌkʃn] reducción *f*; *in price* rebaja *f*

re·dun·dant [rɪˈdʌndənt] *adj (unnecessary)* innecesario; **be made - Br** *at work* ser despedido

reed [riːd] BOT junco *m*

reef [riːf] *in sea* arrecife *m*

'reef knot nudo *m* de rizos

reek [riːk] *v/i* apestar (**of** a)

reel [riːl] *n of film* rollo *m*; *of thread* carrete *m*

♦ **reel off** *v/t* soltar

re·e·lect *v/t* reelegir

re·e·lec·tion reelección *f*

re·'en·try *of spacecraft* reentrada *f*

ref [ref] F árbitro(-a) *m(f)*

re·fer [rɪˈfɜːr] *v/t (pret & pp -red):* - **a decision / problem to s.o.** remitir una decisión / un problema a alguien

♦ **refer to** *v/t (allude to)* referirse a; *dictionary etc* consultar

ref·er·ee [refəˈriː] SP árbitro(-a) *m(f)*; *(for job)* persona que pueda dar referencias

ref·er·ence [ˈrefərəns] referencia *f*; **with - to** con referencia a

'ref·er·ence book libro *m* de consulta; **'ref·er·ence li·bra·ry** biblioteca *f* de consulta; **'ref·er·ence num·ber** número *m* de referencia

ref·e·ren·dum [refəˈrendəm] referéndum *m*

re·fill [ˈriːfɪl] *v/t tank, glass* volver a llenar

re·fine [rɪˈfaɪn] *v/t oil, sugar* refinar; *technique* perfeccionar

re·fined [rɪˈfaɪnd] *adj manners, language* refinado

re·fine·ment [rɪˈfaɪnmənt] *to process, machine* mejora *f*

re·fin·e·ry [rɪˈfaɪnərɪ] refinería *f*

re·fla·tion [ˈriːfleɪʃn] reflación *f*

re·flect [rɪˈflekt] **1** *v/t light* reflejar; **be -ed in** reflejarse en **2** *v/i (think)* reflexionar

re·flec·tion [rɪˈflekʃn] *in water, glass etc* reflejo *m*; *(consideration)* reflexión *f*

re·flex [ˈriːfleks] *in body* reflejo *m*

re·flex re·'ac·tion acto *m* reflejo

re·form [rɪˈfɔːrm] **1** *n* reforma *f* **2** *v/t* reformar

re·form·er [rɪˈfɔːrmər] reformador(a) *m(f)*

re·frain[1] [rɪˈfreɪn] *v/i fml* abstenerse; **please - from smoking** se ruega no fumar

re·frain[2] [rɪˈfreɪn] *in song, poem* estribillo *m*

re·fresh [rɪˈfreʃ] *v/t person* refrescar; **feel -ed** sentirse fresco

re·fresh·er course [rɪˈfreʃər] curso *m* de actualización *or* reciclaje

re·fresh·ing [rɪˈfreʃɪŋ] *adj drink* refrescante; *experience* reconfortante

re·fresh·ments [rɪˈfreʃmənts] *npl* refrigerio *m*

re·fri·ge·rate [rɪˈfrɪdʒəreɪt] *v/t* refrigerar; **keep -d** conservar refrigerado

re·fri·ge·ra·tor [rɪˈfrɪdʒəreɪtər] frigorífico *m*, refrigerador *m*

re·fu·el [riːˈfjuəl] **1** *v/i airplane* reabastecer de combustible a **2** *v/i of airplane* repostar

ref·uge [ˈrefjuːdʒ] refugio *m*; **take ~** *from storm etc* refugiarse

ref·u·gee [refjuˈdʒiː] refugiado(-a) *m(f)*

ref·u·gee camp campo *m* de refugiados

re·fund [ˈriːfʌnd] **1** *n* [ˈriːfʌnd] reembolso *m*; **give s.o. a ~** devolver el dinero a alguien **2** *v/t* [rɪˈfʌnd] reembolsar

re·fus·al [rɪˈfjuːzl] negativa *f*

re·fuse [rɪˈfjuːz] **1** *v/i* negarse **2** *v/t* *help, food* rechazar; **~ s.o. sth** negar algo a alguien; **~ to do sth** negarse a hacer algo

re·gain [rɪˈgeɪn] *v/t* recuperar

re·gal [ˈriːgl] *adj* regio

re·gard [rɪˈgɑːrd] **1** *n*: **have great ~ for s.o.** sentir gran estima por alguien; **in this ~** en este sentido; **with ~ to** con respecto a; *(kind)* **~s** saludos; **give my ~s to Paula** dale saludos *or* recuerdos a Paula de mi parte; **with no ~ for** sin tener en cuenta **2** *v/t*: **~ s.o. / sth as sth** considerar a alguien / algo como algo; **I ~ it as an honor** para mí es un honor; **as ~s** con respecto a

re·gard·ing [rɪˈgɑːrdɪŋ] *prep* con respecto a

re·gard·less [rɪˈgɑːrdlɪs] *adv* a pesar de todo; **~ of** sin tener en cuenta

re·gime [reɪˈʒiːm] *(government)* régimen *m*

re·gi·ment [ˈredʒɪmənt] *n* regimiento *m*

re·gion [ˈriːdʒən] región *f*; **in the ~ of** del orden de

re·gion·al [ˈriːdʒənl] *adj* regional

re·gis·ter [ˈredʒɪstər] **1** *n* registro *m*; *at school* lista *f* **2** *v/t birth, death* registrar; *vehicle* matricular; *letter* certificar; *emotion* mostrar; **send a letter ~ed** enviar una carta por correo certificado **3** *v/i at university, for a course* matricularse; *with police* registrarse

re·gis·tered let·ter [ˈredʒɪstərd] carta *f* certificada

re·gis·tra·tion [redʒɪˈstreɪʃn] registro *m*; *at university, for course* matriculación *f*

re·gis·tra·tion num·ber *Br* MOT (número *m* de) matrícula *f*

re·gret [rɪˈgret] **1** *v/t (pret & pp -ted)* lamentar, sentir **2** *n* arrepentimiento *m*, pesar *m*

re·gret·ful [rɪˈgretfəl] *adj* arrepentido

re·gret·ful·ly [rɪˈgretfəlɪ] *adv* lamentablemente

re·gret·ta·ble [rɪˈgretəbl] *adj* lamentable

re·gret·ta·bly [rɪˈgretəblɪ] *adv* lamentablemente

reg·u·lar [ˈregjʊlər] **1** *adj* regular; *(normal, ordinary)* normal **2** *n at bar etc* habitual *m/f*

reg·u·lar·i·ty [regjʊˈlærətɪ] regularidad *f*

reg·u·lar·ly [ˈregjʊlərlɪ] *adv* regularmente

reg·u·late [ˈregʊleɪt] *v/t* regular

reg·u·la·tion [regʊˈleɪʃn] *(rule)* regla *f*, norma *f*

re·hab [ˈriːhæb] F rehabilitación *f*

re·ha·bil·i·tate [riːhəˈbɪlɪteɪt] *v/t* *ex-criminal* rehabilitar

re·hears·al [rɪˈhɜːrsl] ensayo *m*

re·hearse [rɪˈhɜːrs] *v/t & v/i* ensayar

reign [reɪn] **1** *n* reinado *m* **2** *v/i* reinar

re·im·burse [riːɪmˈbɜːrs] *v/t* reembolsar

rein [reɪn] rienda *f*

re·in·car·na·tion [riːɪnkɑːrˈneɪʃn] reencarnación *f*

re·in·force [riːɪnˈfɔːrs] *v/t* *structure* reforzar; *beliefs* reafirmar

re·in·forced con·crete [riːɪnˈfɔːrst] hormigón *m* armado

re·in·force·ments [riːɪnˈfɔːrsmənts] *npl* MIL refuerzos *mpl*

re·in·state [riːɪnˈsteɪt] *v/t* *person in office* reincorporar; *paragraph in text* volver a colocar

re·it·e·rate [riːˈɪtəreɪt] *v/t fml* reiterar

re·ject [rɪˈdʒekt] *v/t* rechazar

R

re·jec·tion [rɪ'dʒekʃn] rechazo *m*; *he felt a sense of ~* se sintió rechazado

re·lapse [rɪ'læps] *n* MED recaída *f*; *have a ~* sufrir una recaída

re·late [rɪ'leɪt] 1 *v/t story* relatar, narrar; *~ sth to sth connect* relacionar algo con algo 2 *v/i*: *~ to be connected with* estar relacionado con; *he doesn't ~ to people* no se relaciona fácilmente con la gente

re·lat·ed [rɪ'leɪtɪd] *adj by family* emparentado; *events, ideas etc* relacionado; *are you two ~?* ¿sois parientes?

re·la·tion [rɪ'leɪʃn] *in family* pariente *m/f*; (*connection*) relación *f*; *business/diplomatic ~s* relaciones *fpl* comerciales/diplomáticas

re·la·tion·ship [rɪ'leɪʃnʃɪp] relación *f*

rel·a·tive ['relətɪv] 1 *n* pariente *m/f* 2 *adj* relativo; *X is ~ to Y* X está relacionado con Y

rel·a·tive·ly ['relətɪvlɪ] *adv* relativamente

re·lax [rɪ'læks] 1 *v/i* relajarse; *~!, don't get angry* ¡tranquilízate!, no te enfades 2 *v/t muscle, pace* relajar

re·lax·a·tion [riːlæk'seɪʃn] relajación *f*; *what do you do for ~?* ¿qué haces para relajarte?

re·laxed [rɪ'lækst] *adj* relajado

re·lax·ing [rɪ'læksɪŋ] *adj* relajante

re·lay [riː'leɪ] 1 *v/t message* pasar; *radio, TV signals* retransmitir 2 *n*: *~* (*race*) carrera *f* de relevos

re·lease [rɪ'liːs] 1 *n from prison* liberación *f*, puesta *f* en libertad; *of CD etc* lanzamiento *m*; *CD, record* trabajo *m* 2 *v/t prisoner* liberar, poner en libertad; *parking brake* soltar; *information* hacer público

rel·e·gate ['relɪgeɪt] *v/t* relegar

re·lent [rɪ'lent] *v/i* ablandarse, ceder

re·lent·less [rɪ'lentlɪs] *adj* (*determined*) implacable; *rain etc* que no cesa

re·lent·less·ly [rɪ'lentlɪslɪ] *adv* implacablemente; *rain* sin cesar

rel·e·vance ['reləvəns] pertinencia *f*

rel·e·vant ['reləvənt] *adj* pertinente

re·li·a·bil·i·ty [rɪlaɪə'bɪlətɪ] fiabilidad *f*

re·li·a·ble [rɪ'laɪəbl] *adj* fiable; *information* fiable, fidedigna

re·li·a·bly [rɪ'laɪəblɪ] *adv*: *I am ~ informed that* sé de buena fuente que

re·li·ance [rɪ'laɪəns] confianza *f*, dependencia *f*; *~ on s.o./sth* confianza en alguien/algo, dependencia de alguien/algo

re·li·ant [rɪ'laɪənt] *adj*: *be ~ on* depender de

rel·ic ['relɪk] reliquia *f*

re·lief [rɪ'liːf] alivio *m*; *that's a ~* qué alivio; *in ~ in art* en relieve

re·lieve [rɪ'liːv] *v/t pressure, pain* aliviar; (*take over from*) relevar; *be ~d at news etc* sentirse aliviado

re·li·gion [rɪ'lɪdʒən] religión *f*

re·li·gious [rɪ'lɪdʒəs] *adj* religioso

re·li·gious·ly [rɪ'lɪdʒəslɪ] *adv* (*conscientiously*) religiosamente

re·lin·quish [rɪ'lɪŋkwɪʃ] *v/t* renunciar a

rel·ish ['relɪʃ] 1 *n sauce* salsa *f*; (*enjoyment*) goce *m* 2 *v/t idea, prospect* gozar con; *I don't ~ the idea* la idea no me entusiasma

re·live [riː'lɪv] *v/t the past, an event* revivir

re·lo·cate [riːlə'keɪt] *v/i of business, employee* trasladarse

re·lo·ca·tion [riːlə'keɪʃn] *of business, employee* traslado *m*

re·luc·tance [rɪ'lʌktəns] reticencia *f*

re·luc·tant [rɪ'lʌktənt] *adj* reticente, reacio; *be ~ to do sth* ser reacio a hacer algo

re·luc·tant·ly [rɪ'lʌktəntlɪ] *adv* con reticencia

♦**re·ly on** [rɪ'laɪ] *v/t* (*pret & pp -ied*) depender de; *rely on s.o. to do sth* contar con alguien para hacer algo

re·main [rɪ'meɪn] *v/i* (*be left*) quedar; (*stay*) permanecer

re·main·der [rɪ'meɪndər] 1 *n also* MATH resto *m* 2 *v/t* vender como saldo

re·main·ing [rɪ'meɪnɪŋ] *adj* restante

re·mains [rɪ'meɪnz] *npl of body* restos *mpl* (mortales)

re·make ['riːmeɪk] *n of movie* nueva versión *f*

re·mand [rɪ'mænd] **1** *v/t:* ~ *s.o. in custody* poner a alguien en prisión preventiva **2** *n: be on* ~ *in prison* estar en prisión preventiva; *on bail* estar en libertad bajo fianza

re·mark [rɪ'mɑːrk] **1** *n* comentario *m*, observación *f* **2** *v/t* comentar, observar

re·mar·ka·ble [rɪ'mɑːrkəbl] *adj* notable, extraordinario

re·mark·a·bly [rɪ'mɑːrkəblɪ] *adv* extraordinariamente

re·mar·ry [riː'mærɪ] *v/i* (*pret & pp* **-ied**) volver a casarse

rem·e·dy ['remədɪ] *n* MED, *fig* remedio *m*

re·mem·ber [rɪ'membər] **1** *v/t s.o., sth* recordar, acordarse de; ~ *to lock the door* acuérdate de cerrar la puerta; ~ *me to her* dale recuerdos de mi parte **2** *v/i* recordar, acordarse; *I don't* ~ no recuerdo, no me acuerdo

re·mind [rɪ'maɪnd] *v/t:* ~ *s.o. of sth* recordar algo a alguien; ~ *s.o. of s.o.* recordar alguien a alguien; *you* ~ *me of your father* me recuerdas a tu padre

re·mind·er [rɪ'maɪndər] recordatorio *m*; *for payment* recordatorio *m* de pago

rem·i·nisce [remɪ'nɪs] *v/i* contar recuerdos

rem·i·nis·cent [remɪ'nɪsənt] *adj:* *be* ~ *of sth* recordar a algo, tener reminiscencias de algo

re·miss [rɪ'mɪs] *adj fml* negligente, descuidado

re·mis·sion [rɪ'mɪʃn] remisión *f*; *go into* ~ MED remitir

rem·nant ['remnənt] resto *m*

re·morse [rɪ'mɔːrs] remordimientos *mpl*

re·morse·less [rɪ'mɔːrslɪs] *adj person* despiadado; *pace, demands* implacable

re·mote [rɪ'moʊt] *adj village, possibility* remoto; (*aloof*) distante; *ancestor* lejano

re·mote 'ac·cess COMPUT acceso *m* remoto

re·mote con'trol control *m* remoto; *for TV* mando *m* a distancia

re·mote·ly [rɪ'moʊtlɪ] *adv related, connected* remotamente; *it's just* ~ *possible* es una posibilidad muy remota

re·mote·ness [rɪ'moʊtnəs]: *the* ~ *of the house* la lejanía *or* lo aislado de la casa

re·mov·a·ble [rɪ'muːvəbl] *adj* de quita y pon

re·mov·al [rɪ'muːvl] eliminación *f*

re·move [rɪ'muːv] *v/t* eliminar; *top, lid* quitar; *coat etc* quitarse; *doubt, suspicion* despejar; *growth, organ* extirpar

re·mu·ner·a·tion [rɪmjuːnə'reɪʃn] remuneración *f*

re·mu·ner·a·tive [rɪ'mjuːnərətɪv] *adj* bien remunerado

re·name [riː'neɪm] *v/t* cambiar el nombre a

ren·der ['rendər] *v/t service* prestar; ~ *s.o. helpless / unconscious* dejar a alguien indefenso / inconsciente

ren·der·ing ['rendərɪŋ] *of piece of music* interpretación *f*

ren·dez·vous ['rɑːndeɪvuː] *romantic* cita *f*; MIL encuentro *m*

re·new [rɪ'nuː] *v/t contract, license* renovar; *discussions* reanudar; *feel* ~*ed* sentirse como nuevo

re·new·al [rɪ'nuːəl] *of contract etc* renovación *f*; *of discussions* reanudación *f*

re·nounce [rɪ'naʊns] *v/t title, rights* renunciar a

ren·o·vate ['renəveɪt] *v/t* renovar

ren·o·va·tion [renə'veɪʃn] renovación *f*

re·nown [rɪ'naʊn] renombre *m*

re·nowned [rɪ'naʊnd] *adj* renombrado; *be* ~ *for sth* ser célebre por algo

rent [rent] **1** *n* alquiler *m*; *for* ~ se alquila **2** *v/t apartment, car, equipment* alquilar, *Mex* rentar

rent·al ['rentl] *for apartment, TV* alquiler *m*, *Mex* renta *f*

'rent·al a·gree·ment acuerdo *m* de alquiler

R

'rent·al car coche *m* de alquiler

rent-'free *adv* sin pagar alquiler

re·o·pen [riː'oʊpn] **1** *v/t* reabrir; *negotiations* reanudar **2** *v/i of theater etc* volver a abrir

re·or·gan·i·za·tion [riːɔːrgənaɪz'eɪʃn] reorganización *f*

re·or·gan·ize [riː'ɔːrgənaɪz] *v/t* reorganizar

rep [rep] COM representante *m/f*, comercial *m/f*

re·paint [riː'peɪnt] *v/t* repintar

re·pair [rɪ'per] **1** *v/t fence, TV* reparar; *shoes* arreglar **2** *n to fence, TV* reparación *f*; *of shoes* arreglo *m*; **in a good/bad state of ~** en buen/mal estado

re'pair·man técnico *m*

re·pa·tri·ate [riː'pætrieɪt] *v/t* repatriar

re·pa·tri·a·tion [riː'pætri'eɪʃn] repatriación *f*

re·pay [riː'peɪ] *v/t* (*pret & pp* **-paid**) *money* devolver; *person* pagar

re·pay·ment [riː'peɪmənt] devolución *f*; *installment* plazo *m*

re·peal [rɪ'piːl] *v/t law* revocar

re·peat [rɪ'piːt] **1** *v/t* repetir; **am I ~ing myself?** ¿me estoy repitiendo? **2** *n TV program etc* repetición *f*

re·peat 'busi·ness COM negocio *m* que se repite

re·peat·ed [rɪ'piːtɪd] *adj* repetido

re·peat·ed·ly [rɪ'piːtɪdlɪ] *adv* repetidamente, repetidas veces

re·peat 'or·der COM pedido *m* repetido

re·pel [rɪ'pel] *v/t* (*pret & pp* **-led**) *invaders, attack* rechazar; *insects* repeler, ahuyentar; (*disgust*) repeler, repugnar

re·pel·lent [rɪ'pelənt] **1** *n* (*insect ~*) repelente *m* **2** *adj* repelente, repugnante

re·pent [rɪ'pent] *v/i* arrepentirse

re·per·cus·sions [riːpər'kʌʃnz] *npl* repercusiones *fpl*

rep·er·toire ['repərtwɑːr] repertorio *m*

rep·e·ti·tion [repɪ'tɪʃn] repetición *f*

re·pet·i·tive [rɪ'petɪtɪv] *adj* repetiti-

vo

re·place [rɪ'pleɪs] *v/t* (*put back*) volver a poner; (*take the place of*) reemplazar, sustituir

re·place·ment [rɪ'pleɪsmənt] *person* sustituto(-a) *m(f)*; *thing* recambio *m*, reemplazo *m*

re·place·ment 'part (pieza *f* de) recambio *m*

re·play ['riːpleɪ] **1** *n recording* repetición *f* (de la jugada); *match* repetición *f* (del partido) **2** *v/t match* repetir

re·plen·ish [rɪ'plenɪʃ] *v/t container* rellenar; *supplies* reaprovisionar

rep·li·ca ['replɪkə] réplica *f*

re·ply [rɪ'plaɪ] **1** *n* respuesta *f*, contestación *f* **2** *v/t & v/i* (*pret & pp* **-ied**) responder, contestar

re·port [rɪ'pɔːrt] **1** *n* (*account*) informe *m*; *by journalist* reportaje *m* **2** *v/t facts* informar; *to authorities* informar de, dar parte de; **~ s.o. to the police** denunciar a alguien a la policía; **he is ~ed to be in Washington** se dice que está en Washington **3** *v/i of journalist* informar; (*present o.s.*) presentarse (**to** ante)

♦ **report to** *v/t in business* trabajar a las órdenes de

re'port card boletín *m* de evaluación

re·port·er [rɪ'pɔːrtər] reportero(-a) *m(f)*

re·pos·sess [riːpə'zes] *v/t* COM embargar

rep·re·hen·si·ble [reprɪ'hensəbl] *adj* recriminable

rep·re·sent [reprɪ'zent] *v/t* representar

rep·re·sen·ta·tive [reprɪ'zentətɪv] **1** *n* representante *m/f*; POL representante *m/f*, diputado(-a) *m(f)* **2** *adj* (*typical*) representativo

re·press [rɪ'pres] *v/t revolt* reprimir; *feelings, laughter* reprimir, controlar

re·pres·sion [rɪ'preʃn] POL represión *f*

re·pres·sive [rɪ'presɪv] *adj* POL represivo

re·prieve [rɪ'priːv] **1** *n* LAW indulto *m*; *fig* aplazamiento *m* **2** *v/t prisoner* indultar

rep·ri·mand ['reprɪmænd] *v/t* reprender

re·print ['riːprɪnt] **1** *n* reimpresión *f* **2** *v/t* reimprimir

re·pri·sal [rɪ'praɪzl] represalia *f*; **take ~s** tomar represalias; **in ~ for** en represalia por

re·proach [rɪ'prouʧ] **1** *n* reproche *m*; **be beyond ~** ser irreprochable **2** *v/t*: **~ s.o. for sth** reprochar algo a alguien

re·proach·ful [rɪ'prouʧfəl] *adj* de reproche

re·proach·ful·ly [rɪ'prouʧfəlɪ] *adv* **look** con una mirada de reproche; **say** con tono de reproche

re·pro·duce [riːprə'duːs] **1** *v/t atmosphere, mood* reproducir **2** *v/i* BIO reproducirse

re·pro·duc·tion [riːprə'dʌkʃn] reproducción *f*

re·pro·duc·tive [rɪprə'dʌktɪv] *adj* reproductivo

rep·tile ['reptaɪl] reptil *m*

re·pub·lic [rɪ'pʌblɪk] república *f*

re·pub·li·can [rɪ'pʌblɪkn] **1** *n* republicano(-a) *m(f)*; **Republican** POL Republicano(-a) *m(f)* **2** *adj* republicano

re·pu·di·ate [rɪ'pjuːdɪeɪt] *v/t* (*deny*) rechazar

re·pul·sive [rɪ'pʌlsɪv] *adj* repulsivo

rep·u·ta·ble ['repjutəbl] *adj* reputado, acreditado

rep·u·ta·tion [repjʊ'teɪʃn] reputación *f*; **have a good/ bad ~** tener una buena / mala reputación

re·put·ed [rep'jutəd] *adj*: **be ~ to be** tener fama de ser

re·put·ed·ly [rep'jutədlɪ] *adv* según se dice

re·quest [rɪ'kwest] **1** *n* petición *f*, solicitud *f*; **on ~** por encargo **2** *v/t* pedir, solicitar

re·qui·em ['rekwɪəm] MUS réquiem *m*

re·quire [rɪ'kwaɪr] *v/t* (*need*) requerir, necesitar; **it ~s great care** se requiere mucho cuidado; **as ~d by law** como estipula la ley; **guests are ~d to …** se ruega a los invitados que …

re·quired [rɪ'kwaɪrd] *adj* (*necessary*) necesario

re·quire·ment [rɪ'kwaɪrmənt] (*need*) necesidad *f*, (*condition*) requisito *m*

req·ui·si·tion [rekwɪ'zɪʃn] *v/t* requisar

re·route [riː'ruːt] *v/t airplane etc* desviar

re·run ['riːrʌn] **1** *n of TV program* reposición *f* **2** *v/t* (*pret* **-ran**, *pp* **-run**) *tape* volver a poner

re·sched·ule [riː'ʃeduːl] *v/t* volver a programar

res·cue ['reskjuː] **1** *n* rescate *m*; **come to s.o.'s ~** acudir al rescate de alguien **2** *v/t* rescatar

'res·cue par·ty equipo *m* de rescate

re·search [rɪ'sɜːrʧ] *n* investigación *f* ♦ **research into** *v/t* investigar

re·search and de'vel·op·ment investigación *f* y desarrollo

re'search as·sis·tant ayudante *m/f* de investigación

re·search·er [rɪ'sɜːrʧər] investigador(a) *m(f)*

re'search proj·ect proyecto *m* de investigación

re·sem·blance [rɪ'zembləns] parecido *m*, semejanza *f*

re·sem·ble [rɪ'zembl] *v/t* parecerse a

re·sent [rɪ'zent] *v/t* estar molesto por

re·sent·ful [rɪ'zentfəl] *adj* resentido

re·sent·ful·ly [rɪ'zentfəlɪ] *adv* con resentimiento

re·sent·ment [rɪ'zentmənt] resentimiento *m*

res·er·va·tion [rezər'veɪʃn] reserva *f*; **I have a ~** *in hotel, restaurant* tengo una reserva

re·serve [rɪ'zɜːrv] **1** *n* reserva *f*; SP reserva *m/f*; **~s** FIN reservas *fpl*; **keep sth in ~** tener algo en la reserva **2** *v/t seat, table* reservar; *judgment* reservarse

re·served [rɪ'zɜːrvd] *adj table, manner* reservado

res·er·voir ['rezərvwɑːr] *for water* embalse *m*, pantano *m*

re·shuf·fle ['riːʃʌfl] **1** *n* POL remodelación *f* **2** *v/t* POL remodelar

R

re·side [rɪ'zaɪd] *v/i fml* residir

res·i·dence ['rezɪdəns] *fml: house etc* residencia *f*; *(stay)* estancia *f*

'res·i·dence per·mit permiso *m* de residencia

'res·i·dent ['rezɪdənt] **1** *n* residente *m/f* **2** *adj (living in a building)* residente

res·i·den·tial [rezɪ'denʃl] *adj district* residencial

res·i·due ['rezɪdu:] residuo *m*

re·sign [rɪ'zaɪn] **1** *v/t position* dimitir de; **~ o.s. to** resignarse a **2** *v/i from job* dimitir

res·ig·na·tion [rezɪg'neɪʃn] *from job* dimisión *f; mental* resignación *f*

re·signed [re'zaɪnd] *adj* resignado; *we have become ~ to the fact that ...* nos hemos resignado a aceptar que ...

re·sil·i·ent [rɪ'zɪlɪənt] *adj personality* fuerte; *material* resistente

res·in ['rezɪn] resina *f*

re·sist [rɪ'zɪst] **1** *v/t* resistir; *new measures* oponer resistencia a **2** *v/i* resistir

re·sist·ance [rɪ'zɪstəns] resistencia *f*

re·sist·ant [rɪ'zɪstənt] *adj material* resistente; *~ to heat/ rust* resistente al calor / a la oxidación

res·o·lute ['rezəlu:t] *adj* resuelto

res·o·lu·tion [rezə'lu:ʃn] resolución *f; made at New Year etc* propósito *m*

re·solve [rɪ'zɑːlv] *v/t problem, mystery* resolver; *~ to do sth* resolver hacer algo

re·sort [rɪ'zɔːrt] *n place* centro *m* turístico; *as a last ~* como último recurso

♦ **resort to** *v/t violence, threats* recurrir a

♦ **re·sound with** [rɪ'zaʊnd] *v/t* resonar con

re·sound·ing [rɪ'zaʊndɪŋ] *adj success, victory* clamoroso

re·source [rɪ'sɔːrs] recurso *m*

re·source·ful [rɪ'sɔːrsfəl] *adj person* lleno de recursos; *attitude, approach* ingenioso

re·spect [rɪ'spekt] **1** *n* respeto *m*; *show ~ to* mostrar respeto hacia;

with ~ to con respecto a; *in this/ that ~* en cuanto a esto / eso; *in many ~s* en muchos aspectos; *pay one's last ~s to s.o.* decir el último adiós a alguien **2** *v/t* respetar

re·spect·a·bil·i·ty [rɪspektə'bɪlətɪ] respetabilidad *f*

re·spec·ta·ble [rɪ'spektəbl] *adj* respetable

re·spec·ta·bly [rɪ'spektəblɪ] *adv* respetablemente

re·spect·ful [rɪ'spektfəl] *adj* respetuoso

re·spect·ful·ly [rɪ'spektfəlɪ] *adv* respetuosamente, con respeto

re·spec·tive [rɪ'spektɪv] *adj* respectivo

re·spec·tive·ly [rɪ'spektɪvlɪ] *adv* respectivamente

res·pi·ra·tion [respɪ'reɪʃn] respiración *f*

res·pi·ra·tor [respɪ'reɪtər] MED respirador *m*

re·spite ['respaɪt] respiro *m; without ~* sin respiro

re·spond [rɪ'spɑːnd] *v/i* responder

re·sponse [rɪ'spɑːns] respuesta *f*

re·spon·si·bil·i·ty [rɪspɑːnsɪ'bɪlətɪ] responsabilidad *f; accept ~ for* aceptar responsabilidad de; *a job with more ~* un trabajo con más responsabilidad

re·spon·si·ble [rɪ'spɑːnsəbl] *adj* reponsable (*for* de); *job* de responsabilidad

re·spon·sive [rɪ'spɑːnsɪv] *adj brakes* que responde bien; *a ~ audience* una audiencia que muestra interés

rest¹ [rest] **1** *n* descanso *m; he needs a ~* necesita descansar; *set s.o.'s mind at ~* tranquilizar a alguien **2** *v/i* descansar; *~ on of theory, box* apoyarse en; *it all ~s with him* todo depende de él **3** *v/t (lean, balance)* apoyar

rest² [rest]: *the ~* el resto

res·tau·rant ['restrɑːnt] restaurante *m*

'res·tau·rant car vagón *m or* coche *m* restaurante

'rest cure cura *f* de reposo *or* descanso

rest·ful ['restfəl] *adj* tranquilo, relajante

'**rest home** residencia *f* de ancianos

rest·less ['restlıs] *adj* inquieto; *have a ~ night* pasar una mala noche

rest·less·ly ['restlıslı] *adv* sin descanso

res·to·ra·tion [restə'reıʃn] restauración *f*

re·store [rı'stɔːr] *v/t building etc* restaurar; (*bring back*) devolver

re·strain [rı'streın] *v/t* contener; *~ o.s.* contenerse

re·straint [rı'streınt] (*moderation*) moderación *f*, comedimiento *m*

re·strict [rı'strıkt] *v/t* restringir, limitar; *I'll ~ myself to …* me limitaré a …

re·strict·ed [rı'strıktıd] *adj view* limitado

re·strict·ed 'ar·e·a MIL zona *f* de acceso restringido

re·stric·tion [rı'strıkʃn] restricción *f*, limitación *f*; *place ~s upon s.o.* imponer restricciones *or* limitaciones a alguien

'**rest room** aseo *m*, servicios *mpl*

re·sult [rı'zʌlt] *n* resultado *m*; *as a ~ of this* como resultado de esto
♦ **result from** *v/t* resultar de
♦ **result in** *v/t* tener como resultado

re·sume [rı'zjuːm] **1** *v/t* reanudar **2** *v/i* continuar

ré·su·mé ['rezumeı] currículum *m* (vitae)

re·sump·tion [rı'zʌmpʃn] reanudación *f*

re·sur·face [riː'sɜːfıs] **1** *v/t roads* volver a asfaltar **2** *v/i* (*reappear*) reaparecer

res·ur·rec·tion [rezə'rekʃn] REL resurrección *f*

re·sus·ci·tate [rı'sʌsıteıt] *v/t* resucitar, revivir

re·sus·ci·ta·tion [rısʌsı'teıʃn] resucitación *f*

re·tail ['riːteıl] **1** *adv: sell sth ~* vender algo al por menor **2** *v/i: it ~s at …* su precio de venta al público es de …

re·tail·er ['riːteılər] minorista *m/f*

'**re·tail out·let** punto *m* de venta

'**re·tail price** precio *m* de venta al público

re·tain [rı'teın] *v/t* conservar; *heat* retener

re·tain·er [rı'teınər] FIN anticipo *m*

re·tal·i·ate [rı'tælıeıt] *v/i* tomar represalias

re·tal·i·a·tion [rıtælı'eıʃn] represalias *fpl*; *in ~ for* como represalia por

re·tard·ed [rı'tɑːrdıd] *adj mentally* retrasado mental

re·think [riː'θıŋk] *v/t* (*pret & pp -thought*) replantear

re·ti·cence ['retısns] reserva *f*

re·ti·cent ['retısnt] *adj* reservado

re·tire [rı'taır] *v/i from work* jubilarse

re·tired [rı'taırd] *adj* jubilado

re·tire·ment [rı'taırmənt] jubilación *f*

re'tire·ment age edad *f* de jubilación

re·tir·ing [rı'taırıŋ] *adj* retraído, reservado

re·tort [rı'tɔːrt] **1** *n* réplica *f* **2** *v/t* replicar

re·trace [rı'treıs] *v/t: they ~d their footsteps* volvieron sobre sus pasos

re·tract [rı'trækt] *v/t claws* retraer; *undercarriage* replegar; *statement* retirar

re·train [riː'treın] *v/i* reciclarse

re·treat [rı'triːt] **1** *v/i* retirarse **2** *n* MIL retirada *f*; *place* retiro *m*

re·trieve [rı'triːv] *v/t* recuperar

re·triev·er [rı'triːvər] *dog* perro *m* cobrador

ret·ro·ac·tive [retroʊ'æktıv] *adj law etc* retroactivo

ret·ro·ac·tive·ly [retroʊ'æktıvlı] *adv* con retroactividad

ret·ro·grade ['retrəgreıd] *adj move, decision* retrógrado

ret·ro·spect ['retrəspekt]: *in ~* en retrospectiva

ret·ro·spec·tive [retrə'spektıv] *n* retrospectiva *f*

re·turn [rı'tɜːrn] **1** *n to a place* vuelta *f*, regreso *m*; (*giving back*) devolución *f*; COMPUT retorno *m*; *in tennis* resto *m*

R

m; (*profit*) rendimiento *m; Br ticket* billete *m or L.Am.* boleto *m* de ida y vuelta; **by ~** (*of post*) a vuelta de correo; **many happy ~s** (**of the day**) feliz cumpleaños; **in ~ for** a cambio de **2** *v/t* devolver; (*put back*) volver a colocar **3** *v/i* (*go back, come back*) volver, regresar; *of good times, doubts etc* volver

re·turn 'flight vuelo *m* de vuelta

re·turn 'jour·ney viaje *m* de vuelta

re·u·ni·fi·ca·tion [riːjuːnɪfɪˈkeɪʃn] reunificación *f*

re·u·nion [riːˈjuːnjən] reunión *f*

re·u·nite [riːjuːˈnaɪt] *v/t* reunir

re·us·a·ble [riːˈjuːzəbl] *adj* reutilizable

re·use [riːˈjuːz] *v/t* reutilizar

rev [rev] *n* revolución *f;* **~s per minute** revoluciones por minuto

♦ **rev up** *v/t* (*pret & pp* **-ved**) *engine* revolucionar

re·val·u·a·tion [riːvæljʊˈeɪʃn] revaluación *f*

re·veal [rɪˈviːl] *v/t* (*make visible*) revelar; (*make known*) revelar, desvelar

re·veal·ing [rɪˈviːlɪŋ] *adj remark* revelador; *dress* insinuante, atrevido

♦ **rev·el in** [ˈrevl] *v/t* (*pret & pp* **-ed**, *Br* **-led**) deleitarse con

rev·e·la·tion [revəˈleɪʃn] revelación *f*

re·venge [rɪˈvendʒ] *n* venganza *f;* **take one's ~** vengarse; **in ~ for** como venganza por

rev·e·nue [ˈrevənuː] ingresos *mpl*

re·ver·be·rate [rɪˈvɜːrbəreɪt] *v/i of sound* reverberar

re·vere [rɪˈvɪr] *v/t* reverenciar

rev·e·rence [ˈrevərəns] reverencia *f*

Rev·e·rend [ˈrevərənd] REL Reverendo *m*

rev·e·rent [ˈrevərənt] *adj* reverente

re·verse [rɪˈvɜːrs] **1** *adj sequence* inverso; **in ~ order** en orden inverso **2** *n* (*back*) dorso *m;* MOT marcha *f* atrás; **the ~** (*the opposite*) lo contrario **3** *v/t sequence* invertir; **~ a vehicle** dar marcha atrás con un vehículo **4** *v/i* MOT hacer marcha atrás

re·vert [rɪˈvɜːrt] *v/i:* **~ to** volver a

re·view [rɪˈvjuː] **1** *n of book, movie* reseña *f*, crítica *f; of troops* revista *f; of situation etc* revisión *f* **2** *v/t book, movie* reseñar, hacer una crítica de; *troops* pasar revista a; *situation etc* revisar; EDU repasar

re·view·er [rɪˈvjuːər] *of book, movie* crítico(-a) *m(f)*

re·vise [rɪˈvaɪz] *v/t opinion, text* revisar

re·vi·sion [rɪˈvɪʒn] *of opinion, text* revisión *f*

re·viv·al [rɪˈvaɪvl] *of custom, old style etc* resurgimiento *m; of patient* reanimación *f*

re·vive [rɪˈvaɪv] **1** *v/t custom, old style etc* hacer resurgir; *patient* reanimar **2** *v/i of business, exchange rate etc* reactivarse

re·voke [rɪˈvoʊk] *v/t law* derogar; *license* revocar

re·volt [rɪˈvoʊlt] **1** *n* rebelión *f* **2** *v/i* rebelarse

re·volt·ing [rɪˈvoʊltɪŋ] *adj* (*disgusting*) repugnante

rev·o·lu·tion [revəˈluːʃn] POL revolución *f;* (*turn*) vuelta *f*, revolución *f*

rev·o·lu·tion·ar·y [revəˈluːʃn ərɪ] **1** *n* POL revolucionario(-a) *m(f)* **2** *adj* revolucionario

rev·o·lu·tion·ize [revəˈluːʃnaɪz] *v/t* revolucionar

re·volve [rɪˈvɑːlv] *v/i* girar (**around** en torno a)

re·volv·er [rɪˈvɑːlvər] revólver *m*

re·volv·ing 'door [rɪˈvɑːlvɪŋ] puerta *f* giratoria

re·vue [rɪˈvjuː] THEA revista *f*

re·vul·sion [rɪˈvʌlʃn] repugnancia *f*

re·ward [rɪˈwɔːrd] **1** *n* recompensa *f* **2** *v/t financially* recompensar

re·ward·ing [rɪˈwɔːrdɪŋ] *adj experience* gratificante

re·wind [riːˈwaɪnd] *v/t* (*pret & pp* **-wound**) *film, tape* rebobinar

re·write [riːˈraɪt] *v/t* (*pret* **-wrote**, *pp* **-written**) reescribir

rhe·to·ric [ˈretərɪk] retórica *f*

rhe·to·ric·al 'ques·tion [rɪˈtɑːrɪkl] pregunta *f* retórica

rheu·ma·tism [ˈruːmətɪzm] reumatismo *m*

rhi·no·ce·ros [raɪˈnɑːsərəs] rinoceronte *m*

rhu·barb [ˈruːbɑːrb] ruibarbo *m*

rhyme [raɪm] **1** *n* rima *f* **2** *v/i* rimar

rhythm [ˈrɪðm] ritmo *m*

rib [rɪb] ANAT costilla *f*

rib·bon [ˈrɪbən] cinta *f*

rice [raɪs] arroz *m*

rich [rɪtʃ] **1** *adj* (*wealthy*) rico; *food* sabroso; *it's too ~* es muy pesado **2** *npl*: *the ~* los ricos

rich·ly [ˈrɪtʃlɪ] *adv*: *be ~ deserved* ser muy merecido

rick·et·y [ˈrɪkətɪ] *adj* desvencijado

ric·o·chet [ˈrɪkəʃeɪ] *v/i* rebotar

rid [rɪd]: *get ~ of* deshacerse de

rid·dance [ˈrɪdns] F: *good ~ to her!* ¡espero no volver a verla nunca!

rid·den [ˈrɪdn] *pp* → *ride*

rid·dle [ˈrɪdl] **1** *n* acertijo *m* **2** *v/t*: *be ~d with* estar lleno de

ride [raɪd] **1** *n* *on horse, in vehicle* paseo *m*, vuelta *f*; (*journey*) viaje *m*; *do you want a ~ into town?* ¿quieres que te lleve al centro? **2** *v/t* (*pret rode, pp ridden*) *horse* montar a; *bike* montar en **3** *v/i* (*pret rode, pp ridden*) *on horse* montar; *can you ~?* ¿sabes montar?; *those who were riding at the back of the bus* los que iban en la parte de atrás del autobús

rid·er [ˈraɪdər] *on horse* jinete *m*, amazona *f*; *on bicycle* ciclista *m/f*; *on motorbike* motorista *m/f*

ridge [rɪdʒ] *raised strip* borde *m*; *of mountain* cresta *f*; *of roof* caballete *m*

rid·i·cule [ˈrɪdɪkjuːl] **1** *n* burlas *fpl* **2** *v/t* ridiculizar, poner en ridículo

ri·dic·u·lous [rɪˈdɪkjələs] *adj* ridículo

ri·dic·u·lous·ly [rɪˈdɪkjələslɪ] *adv* *expensive, difficult* terriblemente; *it's ~ easy* es facilísimo

rid·ing [ˈraɪdɪŋ] *on horseback* equitación *f*

ri·fle [ˈraɪfl] *n* rifle *m*

rift [rɪft] *in earth* grieta *f*; *in party etc* escisión *f*

rig [rɪg] **1** *n* (*oil ~*) plataforma *f* petro-

lífera; (*truck*) camión *m* **2** *v/t* (*pret & pp -ged*) *elections* amañar

right [raɪt] **1** *adj* (*correct*) correcto; (*suitable*) adecuado, apropiado; (*not left*) derecho; *it's not ~ to treat people like that* no está bien tratar así a la gente; *it's the ~ thing to do* es lo que hay que hacer; *be ~ of answer* ser correcto; *of person* tener razón; *of clock* ir bien; *put things ~* arreglar las cosas; *that's ~!* ¡eso es!; *that's all ~ doesn't matter* no te preocupes; *when s.o. says thank you* de nada; *is quite good* está bastante bien; *I'm all ~ not hurt* estoy bien; *have got enough* no, gracias; *all ~, that's enough!* ¡ahora sí que ya está bien! **2** *adv* (*directly*) justo; (*correctly*) correctamente; (*not left*) a la derecha; *he broke it ~ off* lo rompió por completo; *~ back in 1982* allá en 1982; *~ now* ahora mismo **3** *n civil, legal etc* derecho *m*; *not left,* POL derecha *f*; *on the ~ also* POL a la derecha; *turn to the ~, take a ~* gira a la derecha; *be in the ~* tener razón; *know ~ from wrong* distinguir lo que está bien de lo que está mal

right-'an·gle ángulo *m* recto; *at ~s to* en o formando ángulo recto con

right·ful [ˈraɪtfəl] *adj heir, owner etc* legítimo

'right-hand *adj*: *on the ~ side* a mano derecha; **right-hand 'drive** *n* MOT vehículo *m* con el volante a la derecha; **right-hand·ed** [raɪtˈhændɪd] *adj person* diestro; **right-hand 'man** mano *f* derecha; **right of 'way** *in traffic* preferencia *f*; *across land* derecho *m* de paso; **right 'wing** *n* POL derecha *f*; SP banda *f* derecha; **right-'wing** *adj* POL de derechas; **right-'wing·er** POL derechista *m/f*; **right-wing ex'trem·ism** POL extremismo *m* de derechas

rig·id [ˈrɪdʒɪd] *adj* rígido

rig·or [ˈrɪgər] *of discipline* rigor *m*; *the ~s of the winter* los rigores del invierno

rig·or·ous [ˈrɪgərəs] *adj* riguroso

R

rig·or·ous·ly ['rɪgərəslɪ] *adv* check, *examine* rigurosamente

rig·our *Br* → **rigor**

rile [raɪl] *v/t* F fastidiar, *Span* mosquear F

rim [rɪm] *of wheel* llanta *f*; *of cup* borde *m*; *of eye glasses* montura *f*

ring[1] [rɪŋ] *n* (*circle*) círculo *m*; *on finger* anillo *m*; *in boxing* cuadrilátero *m*, ring *m*; *at circus* pista *f*

ring[2] [rɪŋ] **1** *n of bell* timbrazo *m*; *of voice* tono *m*; *give s.o. a ~* Br TELEC dar un telefonazo a alguien **2** *v/t* (*pret* **rang**, *pp* **rung**) *bell* hacer sonar **3** *v/i* (*pret* **rang**, *pp* **rung**) *of bell* sonar; *please ~ for attention* toque el timbre para que lo atiendan

'**ring·lead·er** cabecilla *m/f*

'**ring-pull** anilla *f*

rink [rɪŋk] pista *f* de patinaje

rinse [rɪns] **1** *n for hair color* reflejo *m* **2** *v/t* aclarar

ri·ot ['raɪət] **1** *n* disturbio *m* **2** *v/i* causar disturbios

ri·ot·er ['raɪətər] alborotador(a) *m(f)*

'**ri·ot po·lice** policía *f* antidisturbios

rip [rɪp] **1** *n in cloth etc* rasgadura *f* **2** *v/t* (*pret* & *pp* **-ped**) *cloth* rasgar; *~ sth open* romper algo rasgándolo

♦ **rip off** *v/t* F *customers* robar F, clavar F; (*cheat*) timar

♦ **rip up** *v/t letter, sheet* hacer pedazos

ripe [raɪp] *adj fruit* maduro

rip·en ['raɪpn] *v/i of fruit* madurar

ripe·ness ['raɪpnɪs] *of fruit* madurez *f*

'**rip-off** *n* F robo *m* F

rip·ple ['rɪpl] *on water* onda *f*

rise [raɪz] **1** *v/i* (*pret* **rose**, *pp* **risen**) *from chair etc* levantarse; *of sun* salir; *of rocket* ascender, subir; *of price, temperature, water* subir **2** *n in price, temperature* subida *f*, aumento *m*; *in water level* subida *f*; *in salary* aumento *m*; *give ~ to* dar pie a

ris·en ['rɪzn] *pp* → **rise**

ris·er ['raɪzər]: *be an early ~* ser un madrugador; *be a late ~* levantarse tarde

risk [rɪsk] **1** *n* riesgo *m*, peligro *m*; *take a ~* arriesgarse **2** *v/t* arriesgar;

let's ~ it arriesguémonos

risk·y ['rɪskɪ] *adj* arriesgado

ris·qué [rɪ'skeɪ] *adj* subido de tono

rit·u·al ['rɪtʊəl] **1** *n* ritual *m* **2** *adj* ritual

ri·val ['raɪvl] **1** *n* rival *m/f* **2** *v/t* (*pret* & *pp* **-ed**, *Br* **-led**) rivalizar con; *I can't ~ that* no puedo rivalizar con eso

ri·val·ry ['raɪvlrɪ] rivalidad *f*

riv·er ['rɪvər] río *m*

'**riv·er·bank** ribera *f*; '**riv·er·bed** lecho *m*; **Riv·er 'Plate** *n*: *the ~* el Río de la Plata; '**riv·er·side 1** *adj* a la orilla del río **2** *n* ribera *f*, orilla *f* del río

riv·et ['rɪvɪt] **1** *n* remache *m* **2** *v/t* remachar; *~ sth to sth* unir algo a algo con remaches

riv·et·ing ['rɪvɪtɪŋ] *adj* fascinante

road [roʊd] *in country* carretera *f*; *in city* calle *f*; *it's just down the ~* está muy cerca

'**road·block** control *m* de carretera; '**road hog** conductor(a) temerario(-a); '**road-hold·ing** *of vehicle* adherencia *f*, agarre *m*; '**road map** mapa *m* de carreteras; **road 'safe·ty** seguridad *f* vial; '**road·side**: *at the ~* al borde de la carretera; '**road·sign** señal *f* de tráfico; '**road·way** calzada *f*; '**road·wor·thy** *adj* en condiciones de circular

roam [roʊm] *v/i* vagar

roar [rɔːr] **1** *n of traffic, engine* estruendo *m*; *of lion* rugido *m*; *of person* grito *m*, bramido *m* **2** *v/i of engine, lion* rugir; *of person* gritar, bramar; *~ with laughter* reírse a carcajadas

roast [roʊst] **1** *n of beef etc* asado *m* **2** *v/t* asar **3** *v/i of food* asarse; *we're ~ing* nos estamos asando

roast 'beef rosbif *m*

roast 'pork cerdo *m* asado

rob [rɑːb] *v/t* (*pret* & *pp* **-bed**) *person* robar a; *bank* atracar, robar; *I've been ~bed* me han robado

rob·ber ['rɑːbər] atracador(a) *m(f)*

rob·ber·y ['rɑːbərɪ] atraco *m*, robo *m*

robe [roʊb] *of judge* toga *f*; *of priest* sotana *f*; (*bath~*) bata *f*

rob·in ['rɑːbɪn] petirrojo *m*

ro·bot ['roʊbɑːt] robot *m*

ro·bust [roʊ'bʌst] *adj person, structure* robusto; *material* resistente; *be in ~ health* tener una salud de hierro

rock [rɑːk] **1** *n* roca *f*; MUS rock *m*; *on the ~s of drink* con hielo; *their marriage is on the ~s* su matrimonio está en crisis **2** *v/t baby* acunar; *cradle* mecer; (*surprise*) sorprender, impactar **3** *v/i on chair* mecerse; *of boat* balancearse

'**rock band** grupo *m* de rock; **rock 'bot·tom**: *reach ~* tocar fondo; '**rock-bot·tom** *adj prices* mínimo; '**rock climb·er** escalador(a) *m(f)*; '**rock climb·ing** escalada *f* (en roca)

rock·et ['rɑːkɪt] **1** *n* cohete *m* **2** *v/i of prices etc* dispararse

rock·ing chair ['rɑːkɪŋ] mecedora *f*

'**rock·ing horse** caballito *m* de juguete

rock 'n' roll [rɑːkn'roʊl] rock and roll *m*

'**rock star** estrella *f* del rock

rock·y ['rɑːkɪ] *adj beach, path* pedregoso

rod [rɑːd] vara *f*; *for fishing* caña *f*

rode [roʊd] *pret* → **ride**

ro·dent ['roʊdnt] roedor *m*

rogue [roʊg] granuja *m/f*, bribón(-ona) *m(f)*

role [roʊl] papel *m*

'**role mod·el** ejemplo *m*

roll [roʊl] **1** *n* (*bread ~*) panecillo *m*; *of film* rollo *m*; *of thunder* retumbo *m*; (*list, register*) lista *f* **2** *v/i of ball etc* rodar; *of boat* balancearse **3** *v/t*: *~ sth into a ball* hacer una bola con algo; *~ sth along the ground* hacer rodar algo por el suelo

♦ **roll over 1** *v/i* darse la vuelta **2** *v/t person, object* dar la vuelta a; (*renew*) renovar; (*extend*) refinanciar

♦ **roll up 1** *v/t sleeves* remangar **2** *v/i* F (*arrive*) llegar

'**roll-call** lista *f*

roll·er ['roʊlər] *for hair* rulo *m*

'**roll·er blade**® *n* patín *m* en línea; '**roll·er blind** *Br* persiana *f*; **roll·er coast·er** ['roʊlərkoʊstər] montaña *f* rusa; '**roll·er skate** *n* patín *m* (de ruedas)

roll·ing pin ['roʊlɪŋ] rodillo *m* de cocina

ROM [rɑːm] COMPUT *abbr* (= **read only memory**) ROM *f* (= memoria *f* de sólo lectura)

Ro·man ['roʊmən] **1** *adj* romano **2** *n* romano(-a) *m(f)*

Ro·man 'Cath·o·lic 1 *n* REL católico(-a) *m(f)* romano(-a) *m(f)* **2** *adj* católico romano

ro·mance [rə'mæns] *n* (*affair*) aventura *f* (amorosa); *novel* novela *f* rosa; *movie* película *f* romántica

ro·man·tic [roʊ'mæntɪk] *adj* romántico

ro·man·tic·al·ly [roʊ'mæntɪklɪ] *adv*: *be ~ involved with s.o.* tener un romance con alguien

roof [ruːf] techo *m*, tejado *m*; *have a ~ over one's head* tener un techo donde dormir

'**roof-rack** MOT baca *f*

rook·ie ['rʊkɪ] F novato(-a) *m(f)*

room [ruːm] habitación *f*; (*space*) espacio *m*, sitio *m*; *there's no ~ for ...* no hay sitio para ..., no cabe ...

'**room clerk** recepcionista *m/f*; '**room·mate** *sharing room* compañero(-a) *m(f)* de habitación; *sharing apartment* compañero(-a) *m(f)* de apartamento; '**room ser·vice** servicio *m* de habitaciones; **room 'tem·per·a·ture** temperatura *f* ambiente

room·y ['ruːmɪ] *adj house, car etc* espacioso; *clothes* holgado

root [ruːt] *n* raíz *f*; *~s of person* raíces *fpl*

♦ **root for** *v/t* F apoyar

♦ **root out** *v/t* (*get rid of*) cortar de raíz; (*find*) encontrar

rope [roʊp] cuerda *f*; *thick* soga *f*; *show s.o. the ~s* F poner a alguien al tanto

♦ **rope off** *v/t* acordonar

R

ro·sa·ry ['rouzərɪ] REL rosario m

rose[1] [rouz] BOT rosa f

rose[2] [rouz] pret → *rise*

rose·ma·ry ['rouzmerɪ] romero m

ros·ter ['rɑːstər] turnos mpl; *actual document* calendario m con los turnos

ros·trum ['rɑːstrəm] estrado m

ros·y ['rouzɪ] adj cheeks sonrosado; *future* de color de rosa

rot [rɑːt] **1** n *in wood* putrefacción f **2** v/i (pret & pp **-ted**) *of food, wood* pudrirse; *of teeth* cariarse

ro·tate [rou'teɪt] **1** v/i *of blades, earth* girar **2** v/t hacer girar; *crops* rotar

ro·ta·tion [rou'teɪʃn] *around the sun etc* rotación f; **do sth in ~** hacer algo por turnos rotatorios

rot·ten ['rɑːtn] adj food, wood etc podrido; F weather, luck horrible; **that was a ~ trick** F ¡qué mala idea!

rough [rʌf] **1** adj surface, ground accidentado; hands, skin áspero; voice ronco; (violent) bruto; crossing movido; seas bravo; (approximate) aproximado; **~ draft** borrador m **2** adv: **sleep ~** dormir a la intemperie **3** n *in golf* rough m **4** v/t: **~ it** apañárselas

♦ rough up v/t F dar una paliza a

rough·age ['rʌfɪdʒ] *in food* fibra f

rough·ly ['rʌflɪ] adv (approximately) aproximadamente; (harshly) brutalmente; **~ speaking** aproximadamente

rou·lette [ruː'let] ruleta f

round [raund] **1** adj redondo; **in ~ figures** en números redondos **2** n *of mailman, doctor, drinks, competition* ronda f; *of toast* rebanada f; *in boxing match* round m, asalto m **3** v/t *corner* doblar **4** adv, prep → *around*

♦ round off v/t edges redondear; meeting, night out concluir

♦ round up v/t figure redondear (hacia la cifra más alta); suspects, criminals detener

round·a·bout ['raundəbaut] **1** adj route, way of saying sth indirecto **2** n Br on road rotonda f, Span glorieta f; 'round-the-world adj alrededor

del mundo; **round 'trip** viaje m de ida y vuelta; **round trip 'tick·et** billete m or L.Am. boleto m de ida y vuelta; 'round-up *of cattle* rodeo m; *of suspects, criminals* redada f; *of news* resumen m

rouse [rauz] v/t from sleep despertar; interest, emotions excitar, provocar

rous·ing ['rauzɪŋ] adj speech, finale emocionante

route [ruːt] n ruta f, recorrido m

rou·tine [ruː'tiːn] **1** adj habitual **2** n rutina f; **as a matter of ~** como rutina

row[1] [rou] n (line) hilera f; **5 days in a ~** 5 días seguidos

row[2] [rou] **1** v/t boat llevar remando **2** v/i remar

row·boat ['roubout] bote m de remos

row·dy ['raudɪ] adj alborotador, Span follonero

roy·al ['rɔɪəl] adj real

roy·al·ty ['rɔɪəltɪ] royal persons realeza f; on book, recording derechos mpl de autor

rub [rʌb] v/t (pret & pp **-bed**) frotar

♦ rub down v/t to clean lijar

♦ rub in v/t cream, ointment extender, frotar; **don't rub it in!** fig ¡no me lo restriegues por las narices!

♦ rub off **1** v/t dirt limpiar frotando; paint etc borrar **2** v/i: **it rubs off on you** se te contagia

rub·ber ['rʌbər] **1** n material goma f, caucho m; P (condom) goma f P **2** adj de goma or caucho

rub·ber 'band goma f elástica

rub·ber 'gloves npl guantes mpl de goma

rub·ble ['rʌbl] escombros mpl

ru·by ['ruːbɪ] jewel rubí m

ruck·sack ['rʌksæk] mochila f

rud·der ['rʌdər] timón m

rud·dy ['rʌdɪ] adj complexion rubicundo

rude [ruːd] adj person, behavior maleducado, grosero; language grosero; **it is ~ to ...** es de mala educación ...; **I didn't mean to be ~** no pretendía faltar al respeto

rude·ly ['ruːdlɪ] adv (impolitely) groseramente

rude·ness ['ru:dnɪs] mala f educación, grosería f

ru·di·men·ta·ry [ru:dɪ'mentərɪ] adj rudimentario

ru·di·ments ['ru:dɪmənts] npl rudimentos mpl

rue·ful ['ru:fəl] adj arrepentido, compungido

rue·ful·ly ['ru:fəlɪ] adv con arrepentimiento

ruf·fi·an ['rʌfɪən] rufián m

ruf·fle ['rʌfl] **1** n on dress volante m **2** v/t hair despeinar; clothes arrugar; person alterar; **get ~d** alterarse

rug [rʌg] alfombra f; (blanket) manta f (de viaje)

rug·by ['rʌgbɪ] rugby m

'**rug·by match** partido m de rugby

'**rug·by play·er** jugador(a) m(f) de rugby

rug·ged ['rʌgɪd] adj scenery, cliffs escabroso, accidentado; face de rasgos duros; resistance decidido

ru·in ['ru:ɪn] **1** n ruina f; ~**s** ruinas fpl; **in** ~**s** city, building en ruinas; plans, marriage arruinado **2** v/t arruinar; **be** ~**ed** financially estar arruinado or en la ruina

rule [ru:l] **1** n of club, game regla f, norma f; of monarch reinado m; for measuring regla f; **as a** ~ por regla general **2** v/t country gobernar; **the judge** ~**d that ...** el juez dictaminó que ... **3** v/i of monarch reinar

♦ **rule out** v/t descartar

rul·er ['ru:lər] for measuring regla f; of state gobernante m/f

rul·ing ['ru:lɪŋ] **1** n fallo m, decisión f **2** adj party gobernante, en el poder

rum [rʌm] n drink ron m

rum·ble ['rʌmbl] v/i of stomach gruñir; of thunder retumbar

♦ **rum·mage around** ['rʌmɪdʒ] v/i buscar revolviendo

'**rum·mage sale** rastrillo m benéfico

ru·mor, Br **ru·mour** ['ru:mər] **1** n rumor m **2** v/t: **it is ~ed that ...** se rumorea que ...

rump [rʌmp] of animal cuartos mpl traseros

rum·ple ['rʌmpl] v/t clothes, paper arrugar

rump'steak filete m de lomo

run [rʌn] **1** n on foot, in pantyhose carrera f; Br: in car viaje m; carrera f; THEA: of play temporada f; **it has had a three year** ~ of play lleva tres años en cartel; **go for a** ~ ir a correr; **make a** ~ **for it** salir corriendo; **a criminal on the** ~ un criminal fugado; **in the short / long** ~ a corto / largo plazo; **a** ~ **on the dollar** un movimiento especulativo contra el dólar **2** v/i (pret **ran**, pp **run**) of person, animal correr; of river correr, discurrir; of paint, make-up correrse; of play estar en cartel; of engine, machine, software funcionar; in election presentarse; ~ **for President** presentarse a las elecciones presidenciales; **the trains** ~ **every ten minutes** pasan trenes cada diez minutos; **it doesn't** ~ **on Saturdays** of bus, train no funciona los sábados; **don't leave the water** ~**ning** no dejes el grifo abierto; **his nose is** ~**ning** le moquea la nariz; **her eyes are** ~**ning** le lloran los ojos **3** v/t (pret **ran**, pp **run**) race correr; business, hotel, project etc dirigir; software usar; car tener; (use) usar; **can I** ~ **you to the station?** ¿te puedo llevar hasta la estación?; **he ran his eye down the page** echó una ojeada a la página

♦ **run across** v/t (meet) encontrarse con; (find) encontrar

♦ **run away** v/i salir corriendo, huir; from home escaparse

♦ **run down 1** v/t (knock down) atropellar; (criticize) criticar; stocks reducir **2** v/i of battery agotarse

♦ **run into** v/t (meet) encontrarse con; difficulties tropezar con

♦ **run off 1** v/i salir corriendo **2** v/t (print off) tirar

♦ **run out** v/i of contract vencer; of supplies agotarse; **time has run out** se ha acabado el tiempo

♦ **run out of** v/t time, supplies quedarse sin; **I ran out of gas** me quedé sin gasolina; **I'm running out of patience** se me está acabando la paciencia

♦ **run over 1** v/t *(knock down)* atropellar; **can we run over the details again?** ¿podríamos repasar los detalles otra vez? **2** v/i *of water etc* desbordarse

♦ **run through** v/t *(rehearse, go over)* repasar

♦ **run up** v/t *debts, large bill* acumular; *clothes* coser

run·a·way ['rʌnəweɪ] n persona que se ha fugado de casa

run-'down adj *person* débil, apagado; *part of town, building* ruinoso

rung[1] [rʌŋ] *of ladder* peldaño m

rung[2] [rʌŋ] pp → **ring**

run·ner ['rʌnər] *athlete* corredor(a) m(f)

run·ner 'beans npl judías fpl verdes, *L.Am.* porotos mpl verdes, *Mex* ejotes mpl

run·ner-'up subcampeón(-ona) m(f)

run·ning ['rʌnɪŋ] **1** n SP el correr; *(jogging)* footing m; *of business* gestión f **2** adj: **for two days ~** durante dos días seguidos

run·ning 'wa·ter agua f corriente

run·ny ['rʌnɪ] adj *mixture* fluido, líquido; *nose* que moquea

'run-up SP carrerilla f; **in the ~ to** en el periodo previo a

'run·way pista f (de aterrizaje / despegue)

R

rup·ture ['rʌptʃər] **1** n ruptura f **2** v/i *of pipe etc* romperse

ru·ral ['rʊrəl] adj rural

ruse [ruːz] artimaña f

rush [rʌʃ] **1** n prisa f; **do sth in a ~** hacer algo con prisas; **be in a ~** tener prisa; **what's the big ~?** ¿qué prisa tenemos? **2** v/t *person* meter prisa a; *meal* comer a toda prisa; **~ s.o. to the hospital** llevar a alguien al hospital a toda prisa **3** v/i darse prisa

'rush hour hora f punta

Rus·sia ['rʌʃə] Rusia

Rus·sian ['rʌʃən] **1** adj ruso **2** n ruso(-a) m(f); *language* ruso m

rust [rʌst] **1** n óxido m **2** v/i oxidarse

rus·tle ['rʌsl] **1** n *of silk, leaves* susurro m **2** v/i *of silk, leaves* susurrar

♦ **rustle up** v/t F *meal* improvisar

'rust-proof adj inoxidable

rust re·mov·er ['rʌstrɪmuːvər] desoxidante m

rust·y ['rʌstɪ] adj oxidado; **my French is pretty ~** tengo el francés muy abandonado; **I'm a little ~** estoy un poco falto de forma

rut [rʌt] *in road* rodada f; **be in a ~** *fig* estar estancado

ruth·less ['ruːθlɪs] adj implacable, despiadado

ruth·less·ly ['ruːθlɪslɪ] adv sin compasión, despiadadamente

ruth·less·ness ['ruːθlɪsnɪs] falta f de compasión

rye [raɪ] centeno m

'rye bread pan m de centeno

S

sab·bat·i·cal [sə'bætɪkl] n *year* año m sabático; **a 6 month ~** 6 meses de excedencia

sab·o·tage ['sæbətɑːʒ] **1** n sabotaje m **2** v/t sabotear

sab·o·teur [sæbə'tɜːr] sabotea-

dor(a) m(f)

sac·cha·rin ['sækərɪn] n sacarina f

sa·chet ['sæʃeɪ] *of shampoo, cream etc* sobrecito m

sack [sæk] **1** n *bag* saco m; *for groceries* bolsa f **2** v/t F echar sa·cred ['seıkrıd] adj sagrado

sac·ri·fice ['sækrıfaıs] 1 n sacrificio m; make ~s fig hacer sacrificios 2 v/t sacrificar

sac·ri·lege ['sækrılıdʒ] sacrilegio m

sad [sæd] adj person, face, song triste; state of affairs lamentable, desgraciado

sad·dle ['sædl] 1 n silla f de montar 2 v/t horse ensillar; ~ s.o. with sth fig endilgar algo a alguien

sa·dism ['seıdızm] sadismo m

sa·dist ['seıdıst] sádico(-a) m(f)

sa·dis·tic [sə'dıstık] adj sádico

sad·ly ['sædlı] adv look, say etc con tristeza; (regrettably) lamentablemente

sad·ness ['sædnıs] tristeza f

safe [seıf] 1 adj seguro; driver prudente; (not in danger) a salvo; is it to walk here? ¿se puede andar por aquí sin peligro? 2 n caja f fuerte

safe·guard 1 n garantía f; as a ~ against como garantía contra 2 v/t salvaguardar

safe·keep·ing: give sth to s.o. for ~ dar algo a alguien para que lo custodie

safe·ly ['seıflı] adv arrive sin percances; (successfully) sin problemas; drive prudentemente; assume con certeza

safe·ty ['seıftı] seguridad f

'safe·ty belt cinturón m de seguridad; 'safe·ty-con·scious adj: be ~ tener en cuenta la seguridad; safe·ty 'first prevención f de accidentes; 'safe·ty pin imperdible m

sag [sæg] 1 n of ceiling etc combadura f 2 v/i (pret & pp -ged) of ceiling combarse; of rope destensarse; of tempo disminuir

sa·ga ['sɑːgə] saga f

sage [seıdʒ] n herb salvia f

Sa·git·tar·i·us [sædʒı'terıəs] ASTR Sagitario m/f inv

said [sed] pret & pp → say

sail [seıl] 1 n of boat vela f; trip viaje m (en barco); go for a ~ salir a navegar 2 v/t yacht manejar 3 v/i navegar; (depart) zarpar, hacerse a la mar

'sail·board 1 n tabla f de windsurf 2 v/i hacer windsurf; 'sail·board·ing windsurf m; 'sail·boat barco m de vela, velero m

sail·ing ['seılıŋ] SP vela f

'sail·ing ship barco de vela, velero m

sail·or ['seılər] in the navy marino m/f; in the merchant navy, SP marinero(-a) m(f); I'm a good/bad ~ no me mareo/me mareo con facilidad

saint [seınt] santo m

sake [seık]: for my ~ por mí; for the ~ of peace por la paz

sal·ad ['sæləd] ensalada f

sal·ad 'dress·ing aliño m or aderezo m para ensalada

sal·a·ry ['sælərı] sueldo m, salario m

'sal·a·ry scale escala f salarial

sale [seıl] venta f; reduced prices rebajas fpl; for ~ sign se vende; is this for ~? ¿está a la venta?; be on ~ estar a la venta; at reduced prices estar de rebajas

sales [seılz] npl department ventas fpl

'sales clerk in store vendedor(a) m(f), dependiente(-a) m(f); 'sales fig·ures npl cifras fpl de ventas; 'sales·man vendedor m; sales 'man·ag·er jefe(-a) m(f) de ventas; 'sales meet·ing reunión f del departamento de ventas; 'sales·wo·man vendedora f

sa·lient ['seılıənt] adj sobresaliente, destacado

sa·li·va [sə'laıvə] saliva f

salm·on ['sæmən] (pl salmon) salmón m

sa·loon [sə'luːn] Br MOT turismo m; (bar) bar m

salt [sɒlt] 1 n sal f 2 v/t food salar

'salt·cel·lar salero m; salt 'wa·ter agua f salada; 'salt-wa·ter fish pez m de agua salada

salt·y ['sɒltı] adj salado

sa·lu·tar·y ['sæljʊterı] adj experience beneficioso

sa·lute [sə'luːt] 1 n MIL saludo m; take the ~ presidir un desfile 2 v/t saludar; fig (hail) elogiar 3 v/i MIL saludar

Sal·va·dor(e)·an [sælvə'dɔːrən]

1 *adj* salvadoreño **2** *n* salvadoreño(-a) *m(f)*

sal·vage ['sælvɪdʒ] *v/t from wreck* rescatar

sal·va·tion [sæl'veɪʃn] *also fig* salvación *f*

Sal·va·tion 'Ar·my Ejército *m* de Salvación

same [seɪm] **1** *adj* mismo **2** *pron*: **the** ~ lo mismo; **Happy New Year – the** ~ **to you** Feliz Año Nuevo – igualmente; **he's not the** ~ **any more** ya no es el mismo; **life isn't the** ~ **without you** la vida es distinta sin ti; **all the** ~ (*even so*) aun así; **men are all the** ~ todos los hombres son iguales; **it's all the** ~ **to me** me da lo mismo, me da igual **3** *adv*: **the** ~ igual

sam·ple ['sæmpl] *n* muestra *f*

sanc·ti·mo·ni·ous [sæŋktɪ'moʊnɪəs] *adj* mojigato

sanc·tion ['sæŋkʃn] **1** *n* (*approval*) consentimiento *m*, aprobación *f*; (*penalty*) sanción *f* **2** *v/t* (*approve*) sancionar

sanc·ti·ty ['sæŋktətɪ] carácter *m* sagrado

sanc·tu·a·ry ['sæŋktʃʊerɪ] santuario *m*

sand [sænd] **1** *n* arena *f* **2** *v/t with sandpaper* lijar

san·dal ['sændl] sandalia *f*

'sand·bag saco *m* de arena; 'sand·blast *v/t* arenar; 'sand dune duna *f*

sand·er ['sændər] *tool* lijadora *f*

'sand·pa·per **1** *n* lija *f* **2** *v/t* lijar

'sand·stone arenisca *f*

sand·wich ['sænwɪtʃ] **1** *n* *Span* bocadillo *m*, *L.Am.* sandwich *m* **2** *v/t*: **be ~ed between two …** estar encajonado entre dos …

sand·y ['sændɪ] *adj soil* arenoso; *feet, towel etc* lleno de arena; *hair* rubio oscuro; ~ **beach** playa *f* de arena

sane [seɪn] *adj* cuerdo

sang [sæŋ] *pret* → **sing**

san·i·tar·i·um [sænɪ'terɪəm] sanatorio *m*

san·i·tar·y ['sænɪterɪ] *adj conditions* salubre, higiénico; ~ **installations** instalaciones *fpl* sanitarias

'san·i·ta·ry nap·kin compresa *f*

san·i·ta·tion [sænɪ'teɪʃn] (*sanitary installations*) instalaciones *fpl* sanitarias; (*removal of waste*) saneamiento *m*

san·i·ta·tion de·part·ment servicio *m* de limpieza

san·i·ty ['sænətɪ] razón *f*, juicio *m*

sank [sæŋk] *pret* → **sink**

San·ta Claus ['sæntəklɔːz] Papá Noel *m*, Santa Claus *m*

sap [sæp] **1** *n in tree* savia *f* **2** *v/t* (*pret & pp* **-ped**) *s.o.'s energy* consumir

sap·phire ['sæfaɪr] *n jewel* zafiro *m*

sar·casm ['sɑːrkæzm] sarcasmo *m*

sar·cas·tic [sɑːr'kæstɪk] *adj* sarcástico

sar·cas·ti·cal·ly [sɑːr'kæstɪklɪ] *adv* sarcásticamente

sar·dine [sɑːr'diːn] sardina *f*

sar·don·ic [sɑːr'dɑːnɪk] *adj* sardónico

sar·don·i·cal·ly [sɑːr'dɑːnɪklɪ] *adv* sardónicamente

sash [sæʃ] *on dress* faja *f*; *on uniform* fajín *m*

sat [sæt] *pret & pp* → **sit**

Sa·tan ['seɪtn] Satán, Satanás

sat·el·lite ['sætəlaɪt] satélite *m*

'sat·el·lite dish antena *f* parabólica

sat·el·lite T'V televisión *f* por satélite

sat·in ['sætɪn] **1** *adj* satinado **2** *n* satín *m*

sat·ire ['sætaɪr] sátira *f*

sa·tir·i·cal [sə'tɪrɪkl] *adj* satírico

sat·i·rist ['sætərɪst] escritor(a) *m(f)* de sátiras

sat·i·rize ['sætəraɪz] *v/t* satirizar

sat·is·fac·tion [sætɪs'fækʃn] satisfacción *f*

sat·is·fac·to·ry [sætɪs'fæktərɪ] *adj* satisfactorio; (*just good enough*) suficiente

sat·is·fy ['sætɪsfaɪ] *v/t* (*pret & pp* **-ied**) satisfacer; *conditions* cumplir; **I am satisfied** (*had enough to eat*) estoy lleno; **I am satisfied that …** (*convinced*) estoy convencido *or* satisfecho de que …; **I hope you're** *satisfied!* ¡estarás contento!

Sat·ur·day ['sætərdeɪ] sábado *m*

sauce [sɒːs] salsa *f*

'**sauce·pan** cacerola *f*

sau·cer ['sɒːsər] plato *m* (*de taza*)

sauc·y ['sɒːsɪ] *adj person, dress* descarado

Sa·u·di A·ra·bi·a [saʊdɪəˈreɪbɪə] Arabia Saudí *or* Saudita

Sa·u·di A·ra·bi·an [saʊdɪəˈreɪbɪən] **1** *adj* saudita, saudí **2** *n* saudita *m/f*, saudí *m/f*

sau·na ['sɒːnə] sauna *f*

saun·ter ['sɒːntər] *v/i* andar sin prisas

saus·age ['sɒːsɪdʒ] salchicha *f*

sav·age ['sævɪdʒ] **1** *adj animal, attack* salvaje; *criticism* feroz **2** *n* salvaje *m/f*

sav·age·ry ['sævɪdʒrɪ] crueldad *f*

save [seɪv] **1** *v/t* (*rescue*) rescatar, salvar; *money, time, effort* ahorrar; (*collect*), COMPUT guardar; *goal* parar; REL salvar **2** *v/i* (*put money aside*) ahorrar; SP hacer una parada **3** *n* SP parada *f*

♦ **save up for** *v/t* ahorrar para

sav·er ['seɪvər] *person* ahorrador(a) *m(f)*

sav·ing ['seɪvɪŋ] *amount saved, activity* ahorro *m*

sav·ings ['seɪvɪŋz] *npl* ahorros *mpl*

'**sav·ings ac·count** cuenta *f* de ahorros; '**sav·ings and** '**loan** caja *f* de ahorros; '**sav·ings bank** caja *f* de ahorros

sa·vior, *Br* **sa·viour** ['seɪvjər] REL salvador *m*

sa·vor ['seɪvər] *v/t* saborear

sa·vor·y ['seɪvərɪ] *adj not sweet* salado

sa·vour *etc Br → savor etc*

saw[1] [sɒː] **1** *n tool* serrucho *m*, sierra *f* **2** *v/t* aserrar

saw[2] [sɒː] *pret → see*

♦ **saw off** *v/t* cortar (con un serrucho)

'**saw·dust** serrín *m*, aserrín *m*

sax·o·phone ['sæksəfoʊn] saxofón *m*

say [seɪ] **1** *v/t* (*pret & pp* **said**) decir; *poem* recitar; *that is to* ~ es decir;

what do you ~ *to that?* ¿qué opinas de eso?; *what does the note* ~? ¿qué dice la nota?, ¿qué pone en la nota? **2** *n*: *have one's* ~ expresar una opinión

say·ing ['seɪɪŋ] dicho *m*

scab [skæb] *on skin* costra *f*

scaf·fold·ing ['skæfəldɪŋ] *on building* andamiaje *m*

scald [skɒːld] *v/t* escaldar

scale[1] [skeɪl] *on fish, reptile* escama *f*

scale[2] [skeɪl] **1** *n* (*size*) escala *f*, tamaño *m*; *on thermometer, map*, MUS escala *f*; *on a larger* ~ a gran escala; *on a smaller* ~ a pequeña escala **2** *v/t cliffs etc* escalar

♦ **scale down** *v/t* disminuir, reducir

scale '**draw·ing** dibujo *m* a escala

scales [skeɪlz] *npl for weighing* báscula *f*, peso *m*

scal·lop ['skæləp] *n shellfish* vieira *f*

scalp [skælp] *n* cuero *m* cabelludo

scal·pel ['skælpl] bisturí *m*

scal·per ['skælpər] revendedor *m*

scam [skæm] F chanchullo *m* F

scam·pi ['skæmpɪ] gambas *fpl* rebozadas

scan [skæn] **1** *v/t* (*pret & pp* **-ned**) *horizon* otear; *page* ojear; COMPUT escanear **2** *n of brain* escáner *m*; *of fetus* ecografía *f*

♦ **scan in** COMPUT escanear

scan·dal ['skændl] escándalo *m*

scan·dal·ize ['skændəlaɪz] *v/t* escandalizar

scan·dal·ous ['skændələs] *adj affair, prices* escandaloso

scan·ner ['skænər] MED, COMPUT escáner *m*; *for foetus* ecógrafo *m*

scant [skænt] *adj* escaso

scant·i·ly ['skæntɪlɪ] *adv*: *be* ~ *clad* andar ligero de ropa

scant·y ['skæntɪ] *adj skirt* cortísimo; *bikini* mínimo

scape·goat ['skeɪpgoʊt] cabeza *f* de turco, chivo *m* expiatorio

scar [skɑːr] **1** *n* cicatriz *f* **2** *v/t* (*pret & pp* **-red**) cicatrizar

scarce [skers] *adj in short supply* escaso; *make o.s.* ~ desaparecer

scarce·ly ['skerslɪ] *adv*: *he had* ~

said it when ... apenas lo había dicho cuando ...; *there was ~ anything left* no quedaba casi nada; *I ~ know her* apenas la conozco

scar·ci·ty ['skersɪtɪ] escasez f

scare [sker] **1** v/t asustar, atemorizar; *be ~d of* tener miedo de **2** n (*panic, alarm*) miedo m, temor m; *give s.o. a ~* dar a alguien un susto

♦ **scare away** v/t ahuyentar

'scare·crow espantapájaros m inv

scare·mon·ger ['skermʌŋgər] alarmista m/f

scarf [skɑːrf] *around neck, over head* pañuelo m; *woollen* bufanda f

scar·let ['skɑːrlət] adj escarlata

scar·let 'fe·ver escarlatina f

scar·y ['skerɪ] adj *sight* espeluznante; *~ music* música de miedo

scath·ing ['skeɪðɪŋ] adj feroz

scat·ter ['skætər] **1** v/t *leaflets* esparcir; *seeds* diseminar; *be ~ed all over the room* estar esparcido por toda la habitación **2** v/i *of people* dispersarse

scat·ter·brained ['skætərbreɪnd] adj despistado

scat·tered ['skætərd] adj *showers, family, villages* disperso

scav·enge ['skævɪndʒ] v/i rebuscar; *~ for sth* rebuscar en busca de algo

scav·en·ger ['skævɪndʒər] *animal, bird* carroñero m; (*person*) persona que busca comida entre la basura

sce·na·ri·o [sɪ'nɑːrɪoʊ] situación f

scene [siːn] *of accident, crime etc* lugar m; (*argument*) escena f, número m; *make a ~* hacer una escena, montar un número; *~s* THEA decorados mpl; *jazz/rock ~* mundo del jazz/rock; *behind the ~s* entre bastidores

sce·ne·ry ['siːnərɪ] THEA escenario m

scent [sent] n olor m; (*perfume*) perfume m, fragancia f

scep·tic etc Br → **skeptic** etc

sched·ule ['skedjuːl] **1** n *of events, work* programa m; *of exams* calendario m; *for train, work, of lessons* horario m; *be on ~ of work* ir según lo

previsto; *of train* ir a la hora prevista; *be behind ~ of work, train etc* ir con retraso **2** v/t (*put on ~*) programar; *it's ~d for completion next month* está previsto que se complete el próximo mes

sched·uled 'flight ['ʃeduːld] vuelo m regular

scheme [skiːm] **1** n (*plan*) plan m, proyecto m; (*plot*) confabulación f **2** v/i (*plot*) confabularse

schem·ing ['skiːmɪŋ] adj maquinador

schiz·o·phre·ni·a [skɪtsə'friːnɪə] esquizofrenia f

schiz·o·phren·ic [skɪtsə'frenɪk] **1** n esquizofrénico(-a) m(f) **2** adj esquizofrénico

schol·ar ['skɑːlər] erudito(-a) m(f)

schol·ar·ly ['skɑːlərlɪ] adj erudito

schol·ar·ship ['skɑːlərʃɪp] (*scholarly work*) estudios mpl; *financial award* beca f

school [skuːl] n escuela f, colegio m; (*university*) universidad f

'school bag (*satchel*) cartera f; **'school·boy** escolar m; **'school-child·ren** npl escolares mpl; **'school days** npl; *do you remember your ~?* ¿te acuerdas de cuándo ibas al colegio?; **'school·girl** escolar f; **'school·mate** Br compañero m de colegio; **'school·teach·er** maestro(-a) m(f), profesor(a) m(f)

sci·at·i·ca [saɪ'ætɪkə] ciática f

sci·ence ['saɪəns] ciencia f

sci·ence 'fic·tion ciencia f ficción

sci·en·tif·ic [saɪən'tɪfɪk] adj científico

sci·en·tist ['saɪəntɪst] científico(-a) m(f)

scis·sors ['sɪzərz] npl tijeras fpl

scoff¹ [skɑːf] v/t F (*eat fast*) zamparse F

scoff² [skɑːf] v/i (*mock*) burlarse, mofarse

♦ **scoff at** v/t burlarse de, mofarse de

scold [skoʊld] v/t *child, husband* regañar

scoop [skuːp] **1** n *implement* cuchara f; *of dredger* pala f; *story* exclusiva f

2 *v/t:* **~ sth into sth** recoger algo para meterlo en algo

♦ **scoop up** *v/t* recoger

scoot·er ['sku:tər] *with motor* escúter *m*; *child's* patinete *m*

scope [skoʊp] *alcance m*; (*freedom, opportunity*) oportunidad *f*; **he wants more ~ to do his own thing** quiere más libertad para hacer lo que quiere

scorch [skɔːrʃ] *v/t* quemar

scorch·ing ['skɔːrʃɪŋ] *adj* abrasador

score [skɔːr] **1** *n* SP resultado *m*; *in competition* puntuación *f*; (*written music*) partitura *f*; *of movie etc* banda *f* sonora, música *f*; **what's the ~?** SP ¿cómo van?; **have a ~ to settle with s.o.** tener una cuenta pendiente con alguien; **keep (the) ~** llevar el tanteo **2** *v/t goal* marcar; *point* anotar; (*cut: line*) marcar **3** *v/i* marcar; (*keep the ~*) llevar el tanteo; **that's where he ~s** ése es su punto fuerte

'**score·board** marcador *m*

scor·er ['skɔːrər] *of goal* goleador(a) *m(f)*; *of point* anotador(a) *m(f)*; (*official score-keeper*) encargado del marcador

scorn [skɔːrn] **1** *n* desprecio *m*; **pour ~ on sth** despreciar algo, menospreciar algo **2** *v/t idea, suggestion* despreciar

scorn·ful ['skɔːrnfəl] *adj* despreciativo

scorn·ful·ly ['skɔːrnfəlɪ] *adv* con desprecio

Scor·pi·o ['skɔːrpioʊ] ASTR Escorpio *m/f inv*

Scot [skɑːt] escocés(-esa) *m(f)*

Scotch [skɑːtʃ] (*whiskey*) whisky *m* escocés

Scotch 'tape® celo *m*, *L.Am.* Durex® *m*

scot-'free *adv:* **get off ~** salir impune

Scot·land ['skɑːtlənd] Escocia

Scots·man ['skɑːtsmən] escocés *m*

Scots·wom·an ['skɑːtswʊmən] escocesa *f*

Scot·tish ['skɑːtɪʃ] *adj* escocés

scoun·drel ['skaʊndrəl] canalla *m/f*

scour[1] ['skaʊər] *v/t* (*search*) rastrear,

peinar

scour[2] ['skaʊər] *v/t pans* fregar

scout [skaʊt] *n* (*boy ~*) boy-scout *m*

scowl [skaʊl] **1** *n* ceño *m* **2** *v/i* fruncir el ceño

scram [skræm] *v/i* (*pret & pp -med*) F largarse F; **~!** ¡largo!

scram·ble ['skræmbl] **1** *n* (*rush*) prisa *f* **2** *v/t message* cifrar, codificar **3** *v/i* (*climb*) trepar; **he ~d to his feet** se levantó de un salto

scram·bled 'eggs ['skræmbld] *npl* huevos *mpl* revueltos

scrap [skræp] **1** *n metal* chatarra *f*; (*fight*) pelea *f*; *of food* trocito *m*; *of evidence* indicio *m*; *of common sense* pizca *f* **2** *v/t* (*pret & pp -ped*) *plan, project* abandonar; *paragraph* borrar

'**scrap·book** álbum *m* de recortes

scrape [skreɪp] **1** *n on paintwork etc* arañazo *m* **2** *v/t paintwork* rayar; **~ a living** apañarse

♦ **scrape through** *v/i in exam* aprobar por los pelos

'**scrap heap:** **be good for the ~** *of person* estar para el arrastre; *of object* estar para tirar; **scrap 'met·al** chatarra *f*; **scrap 'pa·per** papel *m* usado

scrap·py ['skræpɪ] *adj work, play* desorganizado

scratch [skrætʃ] **1** *n mark* marca *f*; **have a ~** *to stop itching* rascarse; **start from ~** empezar desde cero; **your work isn't up to ~** tu trabajo es insuficiente **2** *v/t* (*mark: skin*) arañar; (*mark: paint*) rayar; *because of itch* rascar **3** *v/i of cat etc* arañar; *because of itch* rascarse

scrawl [skrɔːl] **1** *n* garabato *m* **2** *v/t* garabatear

scraw·ny ['skrɔːnɪ] *adj* escuálido

scream [skriːm] **1** *n* grito *m*; **~s of laughter** carcajadas *fpl* **2** *v/i* gritar

screech [skriːtʃ] **1** *n of tires* chirrido *m*; (*scream*) chillido *m* **2** *v/i of tires* chirriar; (*scream*) chillar

screen [skriːn] **1** *n in room, hospital* mampara *f*; *protective* cortina *f*; *in movie theater* pantalla *f*; COMPUT monitor *m*, pantalla *f* **2** *v/t* (*protect, hide*) ocultar; *movie* proyectar; *for security reasons* investigar

'screen·play guión *m*; 'screen sav·er COMPUT salvapantallas *m inv*; 'screen test *for movie* prueba *f*

screw [skru:] **1** *n* tornillo *m*; V (*sex*) polvo *m* V **2** *v/t with a screwdriver* atornillar (**to** a); V (*have sex with*) echar un polvo con V; F (*cheat*) timar F

♦ screw up **1** *v/t eyes* cerrar; *piece of paper* arrugar; F (*make a mess of*) fastidiar F **2** *v/i* F (*make a bad mistake*) meter la pata F

'screw·driv·er destornillador *m*

screwed 'up [skru:d'ʌp] *adj* F *psychologically* acomplejado

'screw top *on bottle* tapón *m* de rosca

screw·y ['skru:ɪ] *adj* F chiflado F; *idea, film* descabellado F

scrib·ble ['skrɪbl] **1** *n* garabato *m* **2** *v/t & v/i* garabatear

scrimp [skrɪmp] *v/i*: **~ and scrape** pasar apuros, pasar estrecheces

script [skrɪpt] *for movie, play* guión *m*; *form of writing* caligrafía *f*

scrip·ture ['skrɪptʃər] escritura *f*; **the (Holy) Scriptures** las Sagradas Escrituras

'script·writ·er guionista *m / f*

scroll [skroʊl] *n* (*manuscript*) manuscrito *m*

♦ scroll down *v/i* COMPUT avanzar

♦ scroll up *v/i* COMPUT retroceder

scrounge [skraʊndʒ] *v/t* gorronear

scroung·er ['skraʊndʒər] gorrón(-ona) *m(f)*

scrub [skrʌb] *v/t* (*pret & pp* **-bed**) *floors* fregar; *hands* frotar

scrub·bing brush ['skrʌbɪŋ] *for floor* cepillo *m* para fregar

scruff·y ['skrʌfɪ] *adj* andrajoso, desaliñado

scrum [skrʌm] *in rugby* melé *f*

♦ scrunch up [skrʌntʃ] *v/t plastic cup etc* estrujar

scru·ples ['skru:plz] *npl* escrúpulos *mpl*

scru·pu·lous ['skru:pjələs] *adj with moral principles* escrupuloso;

(*thorough*) meticuloso; *attention to detail* minucioso

scru·pu·lous·ly ['skru:pjələslɪ] *adv* (*meticulously*) minuciosamente

scru·ti·nize ['skru:tɪnaɪz] *v/t* (*examine closely*) estudiar, examinar

scru·ti·ny ['skru:tɪnɪ] escrutinio *m*; **come under ~** ser objeto de investigación

scu·ba div·ing ['sku:bə] submarinismo *m*

scuf·fle ['skʌfl] *n* riña *f*

sculp·tor ['skʌlptər] escultor(a) *m(f)*

sculp·ture ['skʌlptʃər] escultura *f*

scum [skʌm] *on liquid* película *f* de suciedad; *pej: people* escoria *f*

sea [si:] mar *m*; **by the ~** junto al mar

'sea·bed fondo *m* marino; 'sea·bird ave *f* marina; sea·far·ing ['si:feriŋ] *adj nation* marinero; 'sea·food marisco *m*; 'sea·front paseo *m* marítimo; 'sea·go·ing *adj vessel* de altura; 'sea·gull gaviota *f*

seal[1] [si:l] *n animal* foca *f*

seal[2] [si:l] **1** *n on document* sello *m*; TECH junta *f*, sello *m* **2** *v/t container* sellar

♦ seal off *v/t area* aislar

'sea lev·el: **above ~** sobre el nivel del mar; **below ~** bajo el nivel del mar

seam [si:m] *n on garment* costura *f*; *of ore* filón *m*

'sea·man marinero *m*

seam·stress ['si:mstrɪs] modista *f*

'sea·port puerto *m* marítimo

'sea pow·er *nation* potencia *f* marítima

search [sɜ:rtʃ] **1** *n* búsqueda *f*; **be in ~ of** estar en busca de **2** *v/t baggage, person* registrar; **~ a place for s.o.** buscar a alguien en un lugar

♦ search for *v/t* buscar

search·ing ['sɜ:rtʃɪŋ] *adj look* escrutador; *question* difícil

'search·light reflector *m*; 'search par·ty grupo *m* de rescate; 'search war·rant orden *f* de registro

'sea·shore orilla *f*; 'sea·sick *adj* mareado; **get ~** marearse; 'sea·side costa *f*, playa *f*; **~ resort** centro *m* de veraneo costero

sea·son ['si:zn] *n* (*winter, spring etc*) estación *f*; *for tourism etc* temporada *f*; **plums aren't in ~ at the moment** ahora no es temporada de ciruelas

sea·son·al ['si:znl] *adj fruit, vegetables* del tiempo; *employment* temporal

sea·soned ['si:znd] *adj wood* seco; *traveler, campaigner* experimentado

sea·son·ing ['si:zniŋ] condimento *m*

'**sea·son tick·et** abono *m*

seat [si:t] **1** *n in room, bus, plane* asiento *m*; *in theater* butaca *f*; *of pants* culera *f*; **please take a ~** por favor, siéntese **2** *v/t* (*have seating for*): **the hall can ~ 200 people** la sala tiene capacidad para 200 personas; **please remain ~ed** por favor, permanezcan sentados

'**seat belt** cinturón *m* de seguridad

'**sea ur·chin** erizo *m* de mar

'**sea·weed** alga(s) *f* (*pl*)

se·clud·ed [sɪ'klu:dɪd] *adj* apartado

se·clu·sion [sɪ'klu:ʒn] aislamiento *m*

sec·ond¹ ['sekənd] **1** *n of time* segundo *m* **2** *adj* segundo **3** *adv come in* en segundo lugar **4** *v/t motion* apoyar

se·cond² [sɪ'kɑ:nd] *v/t*: **be ~ed to ser** asignado a

sec·ond·a·ry ['sekənderɪ] *adj* secundario; **of ~ importance** de menor importancia

sec·ond·a·ry ed·u·ca·tion educación *f* secundaria

se·cond 'best *adj*: **be ~** ser el segundo mejor; *inferior* ser un segundón; **sec·ond 'big·gest** *adj*: **it is the ~ company in the area** es la segunda empresa más grande de la zona; **sec·ond 'class** *adj ticket* de segunda clase; **sec·ond 'floor** primer piso *m*, *Br* segundo piso *m*; '**sec·ond hand** *n on clock* segundero *m*; **sec·ond-'hand 1** *adj* de segunda mano **2** *adv buy* de segunda mano

sec·ond·ly ['sekəndlɪ] *adv* en segundo lugar

sec·ond-'rate *adj* inferior

sec·ond 'thoughts: **I've had ~** he cambiado de idea

se·cre·cy ['si:krəsɪ] secretismo *m*

se·cret ['si:krət] **1** *n* secreto *m*; **in ~** en secreto **2** *adj* secreto

se·cret 'a·gent agente *m* / *f* secreto

sec·re·tar·i·al [sekrə'terɪəl] *adj tasks, job* de secretario

sec·re·ta·ry ['sekrəterɪ] secretario(-a) *m* (*f*); POL ministro(-a) *m* (*f*)

Sec·re·tar·y of 'State *in USA* Secretario(-a) *m* (*f*) de Estado

se·crete [sɪ'kri:t] *v/t* (*give off*) segregar; (*hide away*) esconder

se·cre·tion [sɪ'kri:ʃn] secreción *f*

se·cre·tive ['si:krətɪv] *adj* reservado

se·cret·ly ['si:krətlɪ] *adv* en secreto

se·cret po'lice policía *f* secreta

se·cret 'ser·vice servicio *m* secreto

sect [sekt] secta *f*

sec·tion ['sekʃn] *of book, company, text* sección *f*; *of building* zona *f*; *of apple* parte *f*

sec·tor ['sektər] sector *m*

sec·u·lar ['sekjələr] *adj* laico

se·cure [sɪ'kjʊr] **1** *adj shelf etc* seguro; *job, contract* fijo **2** *v/t shelf etc* asegurar; *help* conseguir

se·cu·ri·ties mar·ket FIN mercado *m* de valores

se·cu·ri·ty [sɪ'kjʊrətɪ] seguridad *f*; *for investment* garantía *f*

se·cu·ri·ty a·lert alerta *f*; **se·cu·ri·ty check** control *m* de seguridad; **se·cu·ri·ty-con·scious** *adj* consciente de la seguridad; **se·cu·ri·ty for·ces** *npl* fuerzas *fpl* de seguridad; **se·cu·ri·ty guard** guardia *m* / *f* de seguridad; **se·cu·ri·ty risk** *person* peligro *m* (para la seguridad)

se·dan [sɪ'dæn] MOT turismo *m*

se·date [sɪ'deɪt] *v/t* sedar

se·da·tion [sɪ'deɪʃn]: **be under ~** estar sedado

sed·a·tive ['sedətɪv] *n* sedante *m*

sed·en·ta·ry ['sedənterɪ] *adj job* sedentario

sed·i·ment ['sedɪmənt] sedimento *m*

se·duce [sɪ'du:s] *v/t* seducir

se·duc·tion [sɪ'dʌkʃn] seducción *f*

se·duc·tive [sɪ'dʌktɪv] *adj dress* seductor; *offer* tentador

see [si:] *v/t* (*pret saw*, *pp seen*) ver;

S

(*understand*) entender, ver; *romantically* ver, salir con; *I ~* ya veo; *can I ~ the manager?* ¿puedo ver al encargado?; *you should ~ a doctor* deberías ir a que te viera un médico; *~ s.o. home* acompañar a alguien a casa; *~ you!* F ¡hasta la vista!, ¡chao! F

♦ see about *v/t* (*look into*): *I'll see about getting it repaired* me encargaré de que lo arreglen

♦ see off *v/t at airport etc* despedir; (*chase away*) espantar

♦ see out *v/t: see s.o. out* acompañar a alguien a la puerta

♦ see to *v/t: see to sth* ocuparse de algo; *see to it that sth gets done* asegurarse de que algo se haga

seed [si:d] semilla *f*; *in tennis* cabeza *f* de serie; *go to ~ of person* descuidarse; *of district* empeorarse

seed·ling ['si:dlɪŋ] planta *f* de semillero

seed·y ['si:dɪ] *adj bar, district* de mala calaña

see·ing 'eye dog ['si:ɪŋ] perro *m* lazarillo

see·ing (that) ['si:ɪŋ] *conj* dado que, ya que

seek [si:k] *v/t* (*pret & pp* sought) buscar

seem [si:m] *v/i* parecer; *it ~s that ...* parece que ...

seem·ing·ly ['si:mɪŋlɪ] *adv* aparentemente

seen [si:n] *pp* → see

seep [si:p] *v/i of liquid* filtrarse

♦ seep out *v/i of liquid* filtrarse

see·saw ['si:sɔ:] *n* subibaja *m*

seethe [si:ð] *v/i: be seething with anger* estar a punto de estallar (de cólera)

'see-through *adj dress, material* transparente

seg·ment ['segmənt] segmento *m*

seg·ment·ed [seg'məntɪd] *adj* segmentado, dividido

seg·re·gate ['segrɪgeɪt] *v/t* segregar

seg·re·ga·tion [segrɪ'geɪʃn] segregación *f*

seis·mol·o·gy [saɪz'mɑːlədʒɪ] sismología *f*

seize [si:z] *v/t s.o., s.o.'s arm* agarrar; *opportunity* aprovechar; *of Customs, police etc* incautarse de

♦ seize up *v/i of engine* atascarse

sei·zure ['si:ʒər] MED ataque *m*; *of drugs etc* incautación *f*; *amount seized* alijo *m*

sel·dom ['seldəm] *adv* raramente, casi nunca

se·lect [sɪ'lekt] 1 *v/t* seleccionar 2 *adj* (*exclusive*) selecto

se·lec·tion [sɪ'lekʃn] selección *f*; (*choosing*) elección *f*

se·lec·tion pro·cess proceso *m* de selección

se·lec·tive [sɪ'lektɪv] *adj* selectivo

self [self] (*pl* selves [selvz]) ego *m*; *my other ~* mi otro yo

self-ad·dressed 'en·ve·lope [selfə'drest]: *send us a ~* envíenos un sobre con sus datos; self-as·sur·ance confianza *f* en sí mismo; self-as·sured [selfə'ʃurd] *adj* seguro de sí mismo; self-ca·ter·ing a·part·ment [self'keɪtərɪŋ] *Br* apartamento *m or Span* piso *m* sin servicio de comidas; self-'cen·tered, *Br* self-'cen·tred [self'sentərd] *adj* egoísta; self-'clean·ing *adj oven* con autolimpieza; self-con·fessed [selfkən'fest] *adj*: *he's a ~ megalomaniac* se confiesa megalómano; self-'con·fi·dence confianza *f* en sí mismo; self-'con·fi·dent *adj* seguro de sí mismo; self-'con·scious *adj* tímido; self-'con·scious·ness timidez *f*; self-con·tained [selfkən'teɪnd] *adj apartment* independiente; self-con·trol autocontrol *m*; self-de·fence *Br*, self-de·fense autodefensa *f*; *in ~* en defensa propia; self-'dis·ci·pline autodisciplina *f*; self-'doubt inseguridad *f*; self-em·ployed [selfɪm'plɔɪd] *adj* autónomo; self-es·teem autoestima *f*; self-'ev·i·dent *adj* obvio; self-ex·pres·sion autoexpresión *f*; self-'gov·ern·ment autogobierno *m*; self-'in·terest interés *m* propio

self·ish ['selfɪʃ] *adj* egoísta
self·less ['selflɪs] *adj* desinteresado
self-made 'man [self'meɪd] hombre *m* hecho a sí mismo; **self-'pit·y** autocompasión *f*; **self-'por·trait** autorretrato *m*; **self-pos·sessed** [selfpə'zest] *adj* sereno; **self-re'li·ant** *adj* autosuficiente; **self-re'spect** amor *m* propio; **self-'right·eous** [self'raɪtʃəs] *adj pej* santurrón, intolerante; **self-sat·is·fied** [self'sætɪzfaɪd] *adj pej* pagado de sí mismo; **self-'ser·vice** *adj* de autoservicio; **self-ser·vice 'res·tau·rant** (restaurante *m*) autoservicio *m*; **self-taught** [self'tɔːt] *adj* autodidacta
sell [sel] *v/t & v/i* (*pret & pp* **sold**) vender
♦ **sell out** *v/i of product* agotarse; **we've sold out** se nos ha(n) agotado
♦ **sell out of** *v/t* agotar las existencias de
♦ **sell up** *v/i* vender todo
'sell-by date fecha *f* límite de venta; **be past its ~** haber pasado la fecha límite de venta
sell·er ['selər] vendedor(a) *m(f)*
sell·ing ['selɪŋ] COM ventas *fpl*
'sell·ing point COM ventaja *f*
Sel·lo·tape® ['seləteɪp] *Br* celo *m*, *L.Am.* Durex® *m*
se·men ['siːmən] semen *m*
se·mes·ter [sɪ'mestər] semestre *m*
sem·i ['semɪ] *n* truck camión *m* semirremolque
'sem·i·cir·cle semicírculo *m*; **sem·i·'cir·cu·lar** *adj* semicircular; **sem·i·'co·lon** punto *m* y coma; **sem·i·con'duc·tor** ELEC semiconductor *m*; **sem·i'fi·nal** semifinal *f*; **sem·i'fi·nal·ist** semifinalista *m/f*; **sem·i·nar** ['semɪnɑːr] seminario *m*; **sem·i'skilled** *adj* semicualificado
sen·ate ['senət] senado *m*
sen·a·tor ['senətər] senador(a) *m(f)*; **Senator George Schwarz** el Senador George Schwarz
send [send] *v/t* (*pret & pp* **sent**) enviar, mandar; **~ her my best wishes** dale recuerdos de mi parte
♦ **send back** *v/t* devolver
♦ **send for** *v/t* mandar buscar
♦ **send in** *v/t troops, application* enviar, mandar; *next interviewee* hacer pasar
♦ **send off** *v/t letter, fax etc* enviar, mandar
send·er ['sendər] *of letter* remitente *m/f*
se·nile ['siːnaɪl] *adj* senil
se·nil·i·ty [sɪ'nɪlətɪ] senilidad *f*
se·ni·or ['siːnjər] *adj* (*older*) mayor; *in rank* superior
se·ni·or 'cit·i·zen persona *f* de la tercera edad
se·ni·or·i·ty [siːnj'ɑːrətɪ] *in job* antigüedad *f*
sen·sa·tion [sen'seɪʃn] sensación *f*
sen·sa·tion·al [sen'seɪʃnl] *adj news, discovery* sensacional
sense [sens] **1** *n* (*meaning, point, hearing etc*) sentido *m*; (*feeling*) sentimiento *m*; (*common sense*) sentido *m* común, sensatez *f*; *in a ~* en cierto sentido; *talk ~, man!* ¡no digas tonterías!; *come to one's ~s* entrar en razón; *it doesn't make ~* no tiene sentido; *there's no ~ in waiting* no tiene sentido que esperemos **2** *v/t s.o.'s presence* sentir, notar; *I could ~ that something was wrong* tenía la sensación de que algo no iba bien
sense·less ['senslɪs] *adj* (*pointless*) absurdo
sen·si·ble ['sensəbl] *adj* sensato; *clothes, shoes* práctico, apropiado
sen·si·bly ['sensəblɪ] *adv* con sensatez; *she wasn't ~ dressed* no llevaba ropa apropiada
sen·si·tive ['sensətɪv] *adj skin, person* sensible
sen·si·tiv·i·ty [sensə'tɪvətɪ] *of skin, person* sensibilidad *f*
sen·sor ['sensər] sensor *m*
sen·su·al ['senʃʊəl] *adj* sensual
sen·su·al·i·ty [senʃʊ'ælətɪ] sensualidad *f*
sen·su·ous ['senʃʊəs] *adj* sensual
sent [sent] *pret & pp* → **send**

sen·tence ['sentəns] **1** n GRAM oración f; LAW sentencia f **2** v/t LAW sentenciar, condenar

sen·ti·ment ['sentɪmənt] (*sentimentality*) sentimentalismo m; (*opinion*) opinión f

sen·ti·men·tal [sentɪ'mentl] adj sentimental

sen·ti·men·tal·i·ty [sentɪmen'tælətɪ] sentimentalismo m

sen·try ['sentrɪ] centinela m

sep·a·rate¹ ['sepərət] adj separado; **keep sth ~ from sth** guardar algo separado de algo

sep·a·rate² ['sepəreɪt] **1** v/t separar; **~ sth from sth** separar algo de algo **2** v/i of couple separarse

sep·a·rat·ed ['sepəreɪtɪd] adj couple separado

sep·a·rate·ly ['sepərətlɪ] adv pay, treat por separado

sep·a·ra·tion [sepə'reɪʃn] separación f

Sep·tem·ber [sep'tembər] septiembre m

sep·tic ['septɪk] adj séptico; **go ~ of wound** infectarse

se·quel ['siːkwəl] continuación f

se·quence ['siːkwəns] n secuencia f; **in ~** en orden; **out of ~** en desorden; **the ~ of events** la secuencia de hechos

se·rene [sɪ'riːn] adj sereno

ser·geant ['sɑːrdʒənt] sargento m/f

se·ri·al ['sɪrɪəl] n on TV, radio serie f, serial m; in magazine novela f por entregas

se·ri·al·ize ['sɪrɪəlaɪz] v/t novel on TV emitir en forma de serie; in newspaper publicar por entregas

'se·ri·al kill·er asesino(-a) m(f) en serie; **'se·ri·al num·ber** of product número m de serie; **'se·ri·al port** COMPUT puerto m (en) serie

se·ries ['sɪriːz] nsg serie f

se·ri·ous ['sɪrɪəs] adj situation, damage, illness grave; (person: earnest) serio; company serio; **I'm ~** lo digo en serio; **we'd better take a ~ look at it** deberíamos examinarlo seriamente

se·ri·ous·ly ['sɪrɪəslɪ] adv injured gravemente; **~ intend to ...** tener intenciones firmes de ...; **~?** ¿en serio?; **take s.o. ~** tomar a alguien en serio

se·ri·ous·ness ['sɪrɪəsnɪs] of person seriedad f; of situation seriedad f, gravedad f; of illness gravedad f

ser·mon ['sɜːrmən] sermón m

ser·vant ['sɜːrvənt] sirviente(-a) m(f)

serve [sɜːrv] **1** n in tennis servicio m, saque m **2** v/t food, meal servir; customer in shop atender; one's country, the people servir a; **it ~s you right** ¡te lo mereces! **3** v/i servir; in tennis servir, sacar

♦ **serve up** v/t meal servir

serv·er ['sɜːrvər] in tennis jugador(a) m(f) al servicio; COMPUT servidor m

ser·vice ['sɜːrvɪs] **1** n to customers, community servicio m; for vehicle, machine revisión f; in tennis servicio m, saque m; **~s** (~ sector) el sector servicios; **the ~s** MIL las fuerzas armadas **2** v/t vehicle, machine revisar

'ser·vice ar·e·a área f de servicio; **'ser·vice charge** in restaurant servicio m (tarifa); **'ser·vice in·dus·try** industria f de servicios; **'ser·vice·man** MIL militar m; **'ser·vice pro·vid·er** COMPUT proveedor m de servicios; **'ser·vice sec·tor** sector m servicios; **'ser·vice sta·tion** estación f de servicio

ser·vile ['sɜːrvəl] adj pej servil

serv·ing ['sɜːrvɪŋ] n of food ración f

ses·sion ['seʃn] sesión f; with boss reunión f

set [set] **1** n of tools juego m; of books colección f; (group of people) grupo m; MATH conjunto m; (THEA: scenery) decorado m; where a movie is made plató m; in tennis set m; **television ~** televisor m; **a ~ of dishes** una vajilla; **a ~ of glasses** una cristalería **2** v/t (pret & pp **set**) (place) colocar; movie, novel etc ambientar; date, time, limit fijar; mechanism, alarm poner; clock poner en hora; broken limb recomponer; jewel engastar; (type~) componer; ~ *the table* poner la mesa **3** *v/i* (*pret & pp* **set**) *of sun* ponerse; *of glue* solidificarse **4** *adj views, ideas* fijo; (*ready*) preparado; *be dead ~ on sth* estar empeñado en hacer algo; *be very ~ in one's ways* ser de ideas fijas; ~ *meal* menú *m* (del día)

♦ **set apart** *v/t* distinguir

♦ **set aside** *v/t material, food* apartar; *money* ahorrar

♦ **set back** *v/t in plans etc* retrasar; *it set me back $400* me salió por 400 dólares

♦ **set off 1** *v/i on journey* salir **2** *v/t explosion* provocar; *bomb* hacer explotar; *chain reaction* desencadenar; *alarm* activar

♦ **set out 1** *v/i on journey* salir (*for* hacia) **2** *v/t ideas, goods* exponer; *set out to do sth* (*intend*) tener la intención de hacer algo

♦ **set to** *v/i* (*start on a task*) empezar a trabajar

♦ **set up 1** *v/t new company* establecer; *equipment, machine* instalar; *market stall* montar; *meeting* organizar; F (*frame*) tender una trampa a **2** *v/i in business* emprender un negocio

'**set·back** contratiempo *m*

set·tee [se'ti:] (*couch, sofa*) sofá *m*

set·ting ['setɪŋ] *n of novel etc* escenario *m*; *of house* ubicación *f*

set·tle ['setl] **1** *v/i of bird, dust* posarse; *of building* hundirse; *to live* establecerse **2** *v/t dispute, uncertainty* resolver, solucionar; *debts* saldar; *nerves, stomach* calmar; *that ~s it!* ¡está decidido!

♦ **settle down** *v/i* (*stop being noisy*) tranquilizarse; (*stop wild living*) sentar la cabeza; *in an area* establecerse

♦ **settle for** *v/t* (*take, accept*) conformarse con

♦ **settle up with** *v/t* (*pay*) ajustar cuentas con

set·tled ['setld] *adj weather* estable

set·tle·ment ['setlmənt] *of claim* resolución *f*; *of debt* liquidación *f*; *of dispute* acuerdo *m*; (*payment*) suma *f*; *of building* hundimiento *m*

set·tler ['setlər] *in new country* colono *m*

'**set-up** (*structure*) estructura *f*; (*relationship*) relación *f*; F (*frame-up*) trampa *f*

sev·en ['sevn] siete

sev·en·teen [sevn'ti:n] diecisiete

sev·en·teenth [sevn'ti:nθ] *n & adj* décimoséptimo

sev·enth ['sevnθ] *n & adj* séptimo

sev·en·ti·eth ['sevntɪɪθ] *n & adj* septuagésimo

sev·en·ty ['sevntɪ] setenta

sev·er ['sevər] *v/t* cortar; *relations* romper

sev·er·al ['sevrl] **1** *adj* varios **2** *pron* varios(-as) *mpl* (*fpl*)

se·vere [sɪ'vɪr] *adj illness* grave; *penalty, winter, weather* severo; *teacher* estricto

se·vere·ly [sɪ'vɪrlɪ] *adv punish, speak* con severidad; *injured, disrupted* gravemente

se·ver·i·ty [sɪ'verətɪ] severidad *f*; *of illness* gravedad *f*

Se·ville [sə'vɪl] *n* Sevilla

sew [soʊ] *v/t & v/i* (*pret* **-ed**, *pp* **sewn**) coser

♦ **sew on** *v/t button* coser

sew·age ['su:ɪdʒ] aguas *fpl* residuales

'**sew·age plant** planta *f* de tratamiento de aguas residuales, depuradora *f*

sew·er ['su:ər] alcantarilla *f*, cloaca *f*

sew·ing ['soʊɪŋ] *skill* costura *f*; *that being sewn* labor *f*

'**sew·ing ma·chine** máquina *f* de coser

sewn [soʊn] *pp* → **sew**

sex [seks] (*act, gender*) sexo *m*; *have ~ with* tener relaciones sexuales con, acostarse con

sex·ist ['seksɪst] **1** *adj* sexista **2** *n* sexista *m/f*

sex·u·al ['sekʃʊəl] *adj* sexual

sex·u·al as'sault agresión *f* sexual; **sex·u·al ha'rass·ment** acoso *m* sexual; **sex·u·al 'in·ter·course** relaciones *fpl* sexuales

sex·u·al·i·ty [sekʃʊˈælətɪ] sexualidad f

sex·u·al·ly ['sekʃʊlɪ] adv sexualmente; **~ transmitted disease** enfermedad f de transmisión sexual

sex·y ['seksɪ] adj sexy inv

shab·bi·ly ['ʃæbɪlɪ] adv dressed con desaliño; treat muy mal, de manera muy injusta

shab·by ['ʃæbɪ] adj coat etc desgastado, raído; treatment malo, muy injusto

shack [ʃæk] choza f

shade [ʃeɪd] 1 n for lamp pantalla f; of color tonalidad f; on window persiana f; **in the ~** a la sombra 2 v/t from sun, light proteger de la luz

shad·ow ['ʃædoʊ] n sombra f

shad·y ['ʃeɪdɪ] adj spot umbrío; character, dealings sospechoso

shaft [ʃæft] TECH eje m, árbol m; of mine pozo m

shag·gy ['ʃægɪ] adj hair, dog greñudo

shake [ʃeɪk] 1 n sacudida f; **give sth a good ~** agitar algo bien 2 v/t (pret **shook**, pp **shaken**) agitar; emotionally conmocionar; **he shook his head** negó con la cabeza; **~ hands** estrechar or darse la mano; **~ hands with s.o.** estrechar or dar la mano a alguien 3 v/i (pret **shook**, pp **shaken**) of voice, building, person temblar

shak·en ['ʃeɪkən] 1 adj emotionally conmocionado 2 pp → **shake**

'**shake-up** reestructuración f

'**shak·y** ['ʃeɪkɪ] adj table etc inestable; after illness débil; after shock conmocionado; grasp of sth, grammar etc flojo; voice, hand tembloroso

shall [ʃæl] v/aux ◊ future: **I - do my best** haré todo lo que pueda ◊ suggesting: **~ we go?** ¿nos vamos?

shal·low ['ʃæloʊ] adj water poco profundo; person superficial

sham·bles ['ʃæmblz] nsg caos m

shame [ʃeɪm] 1 n vergüenza f, Col, Mex,Ven pena f; **bring ~ on** avergonzar a, Col, Mex, Ven apenar a; **~ on you!** ¡debería darte vergüenza!; **what a ~!** ¡qué pena or lástima! 2 v/t

avergonzar, Col, Mex,Ven apenar; **~ s.o. into doing sth** avergonzar a alguien para que haga algo

shame·ful ['ʃeɪmfəl] adj vergonzoso

shame·ful·ly ['ʃeɪmfəlɪ] adv vergonzosamente

shame·less ['ʃeɪmlɪs] adj desvergonzado

sham·poo [ʃæm'puː] 1 n champú m 2 v/t customer lavar la cabeza a; hair lavar

shan·ty town ['ʃæntɪ] Span barrio m de chabolas, L.Am. barriada f, Arg villa f miseria, Chi callampa f, Mex ciudad f perdida, Urug cantegril m

shape [ʃeɪp] 1 n forma f 2 v/t clay modelar; person's life, character determinar; **the future** dar forma a

shape·less ['ʃeɪplɪs] adj dress etc amorfo

shape·ly ['ʃeɪplɪ] adv figure esbelto

share [ʃer] 1 n parte f; FIN acción f; **I did my ~ of the work** hice la parte del trabajo que me correspondía 2 v/t & v/i compartir

♦**share out** v/t repartir

'**share·hold·er** accionista m/f

shark [ʃɑːrk] fish tiburón m

sharp [ʃɑːrp] 1 adj knife afilado; mind vivo; pain agudo; taste ácido 2 adv MUS demasiado alto; **at 3 o'clock ~** a las tres en punto

sharp·en ['ʃɑːrpn] v/t knife afilar; pencil sacar punta a; skills perfeccionar

sharp 'prac·tice triquiñuelas fpl, tejemanejes mpl

shat [ʃæt] pret & pp → **shit**

shat·ter ['ʃætər] 1 v/t glass hacer añicos; illusions destrozar 2 v/i of glass hacerse añicos

shat·tered ['ʃætərd] adj F (exhausted) destrozado F, hecho polvo F; (very upset) destrozado F

shat·ter·ing ['ʃætərɪŋ] adj news, experience demoledor, sorprendente

shave [ʃeɪv] 1 v/t afeitar 2 v/i afeitarse 3 n afeitado m; **have a ~** afeitarse; **that was a close ~!** ¡le faltó un pelo!

♦**shave off** v/t beard afeitar; *from piece of wood* rebajar

shav·en ['ʃeɪvn] *adj head* afeitado

shav·er ['ʃeɪvər] *electric* máquinilla *f* de afeitar (eléctrica)

shav·ing brush ['ʃeɪvɪŋ] brocha *f* de afeitar

'**shav·ing soap** jabón *m* de afeitar

shawl [ʃɔːl] chal *m*

she [ʃiː] *pron* ella; **~ is German** / **a student** es alemana / estudiante; **you're funny, ~'s not** tú tienes gracia, ella no

shears [ʃɪrz] *npl for gardening* tijeras *fpl* (de podar); *for sewing* tijeras *fpl* (grandes)

sheath [ʃiːθ] *for knife* funda *f*; *contraceptive* condón *m*

shed[1] [ʃed] *v/t* (*pret & pp* **shed**) *blood, tears* derramar; *leaves* perder; **~ light on** *fig* arrojar luz sobre

shed[2] [ʃed] *n* cobertizo *m*

sheep [ʃiːp] (*pl* **sheep**) oveja *f*

'**sheep·dog** perro *m* pastor

sheep-herd·er ['ʃiːpɜːrdər] pastor *m*

sheep·ish ['ʃiːpɪʃ] *adj* avergonzado

'**sheep·skin** *adj lining* (de piel) de borrego

sheer [ʃɪr] *adj madness, luxury* puro, verdadero; *hell* verdadero; *drop, cliffs* escarpado

sheet [ʃiːt] *for bed* sábana *f*; *of paper* hoja *f*; *of metal* chapa *f*, plancha *f*; *of glass* hoja *f*, lámina *f*

shelf [ʃelf] (*pl* **shelves** [ʃelvz]) estante *m*; **shelves** estanterías *fpl*

shell [ʃel] *n 1 of mussel etc* concha *f*; *of egg* cáscara *f*; *of tortoise* caparazón *m*; MIL proyectil *m*; **come out of one's ~** *fig* salir del caparazón *2 v/t peas* pelar; MIL bombardear (*con artillería*)

'**shell·fire** fuego *m* de artillería

'**shell·fish** marisco *m*

shel·ter ['ʃeltər] **1** *n* refugio *m*; (*bus ~*) marquesina *f* **2** *v/i from rain, bombing etc* refugiarse **3** *v/t* (*protect*) proteger

shel·tered ['ʃeltərd] *adj place* resguardado; **lead a ~ life** llevar una vida protegida

shelve [ʃelv] *v/t fig* posponer

shep·herd ['ʃepərd] *n* pastor *m*

sher·iff ['ʃerɪf] sheriff *m/f*

sher·ry ['ʃeri] jerez *m*

shield [ʃiːld] **1** *n* escudo *m*; *sports trophy* trofeo *m* (*en forma de escudo*); TECH placa *f* protectora; *of policeman* placa *f* **2** *v/t* (*protect*) proteger

shift [ʃɪft] **1** *n* cambio *m*; *period of work* turno *m* **2** *v/t* (*move*) mover; *stains etc* eliminar **3** *v/i* (*move*) moverse; (*change*) trasladarse, desplazarse; *of wind* cambiar; **he was ~ing!** F iba a toda mecha F

'**shift key** COMPUT tecla *f* de mayúsculas; '**shift work** trabajo *m* por turnos; '**shift work·er** trabajador(a) *m(f)* por turnos

shift·y ['ʃɪfti] *adj pej* sospechoso

shim·mer ['ʃɪmər] *v/i* brillar; *of roads in heat* reverberar

shin [ʃɪn] *n* espinilla *f*

shine [ʃaɪn] **1** *v/i* (*pret & pp* **shone**) brillar; *fig: of student etc* destacar (**at** en) **2** *v/t* (*pret & pp* **shone**): **could you ~ a light in here?** ¿podrías alumbrar aquí? **3** *n on shoes etc* brillo *m*

shin·gle ['ʃɪŋgl] *on beach* guijarros *mpl*

shin·gles ['ʃɪŋglz] *nsg* MED herpes *m*

shin·y ['ʃaɪni] *adj surface* brillante

ship [ʃɪp] **1** *n* barco *m*, buque *m* **2** *v/t* (*pret & pp* **-ped**) (*send*) enviar; *by sea* enviar por barco

ship·ment ['ʃɪpmənt] (*consignment*) envío *m*

'**ship·own·er** naviero(-a) *m(f)*, armador(a) *m(f)*

ship·ping ['ʃɪpɪŋ] (*sea traffic*) navíos *mpl*, buques *mpl*; (*sending, dispatch*) envío *m*; (*sending by sea*) envío *m* por barco

'**ship·ping com·pa·ny** (*compañía f*) naviera *f*

ship·ping costs *npl* gastos *mpl* de envío

ship'shape *adj* ordenado, organizado; **'ship·wreck 1** n naufragio m **2** v/t: **be ~ed** naufragar; **'ship·yard** astillero m

shirk [ʃɜːrk] v/t eludir

shirk·er [ˈʃɜːrkər] vago(-a) m(f)

shirt [ʃɜːrt] camisa f; **in his ~ sleeves** en mangas de camisa

shit [ʃɪt] **1** n P mierda f P; **I need a ~** tengo que cagar P **2** v/i (pret & pp **shat**) P cagar **3** int P mierda P

shit·ty [ˈʃɪtɪ] adj F asqueroso F; **I feel ~** me encuentro de pena F

shiv·er [ˈʃɪvər] v/i tiritar

shock [ʃɑːk] **1** n shock m, impresión f; ELEC descarga f; **be in ~** MED estar en estado de shock **2** v/t impresionar, dejar boquiabierto; **I was ~ed by the news** la noticia me impresionó or dejó boquiabierto; **an artist who tries to ~ his public** un artista que intenta escandalizar a su público

'shock ab·sorb·er [əbˈsɔːrbər] MOT amortiguador m

shock·ing [ˈʃɑːkɪŋ] adj behavior, poverty impresionante, escandaloso; F prices escandaloso; F weather, spelling terrible

shock·ing·ly [ˈʃɑːkɪŋlɪ] adv behave escandalosamente

shod·dy [ˈʃɑːdɪ] adj goods de mala calidad; behavior vergonzoso

shoe [ʃuː] zapato m

'shoe·horn calzador m; **'shoe·lace** cordón m; **'shoe·mak·er** zapatero(-a) m(f); **'shoe mend·er** zapatero(-a) m(f) remendón(-ona); **'shoe·store** zapatería f; **'shoe·string: do sth on a ~** hacer algo con cuatro duros

shone [ʃɑːn] pret & pp → **shine**

♦ **shoo away** [ʃuː] v/t children, chicken espantar

shook [ʃʊk] pret → **shake**

shoot [ʃuːt] **1** n BOT brote m **2** v/t (pret & pp **shot**) disparar; and kill matar de un tiro; movie rodar; **~ s.o. in the leg** disparar a alguien en la pierna

♦ **shoot down** v/t airplane derribar; fig: suggestion echar por tierra

♦ **shoot off** v/i (rush off) irse deprisa

♦ **shoot up** v/i of prices dispararse; of children crecer mucho; of new suburbs, buildings etc aparecer de repente; F of drug addict chutarse F

shoot·ing star [ˈʃuːtɪŋ] estrella f fugaz

shop [ʃɑːp] **1** n tienda f; **talk ~** hablar del trabajo **2** v/i (pret & pp **-ped**) comprar; **go ~ping** ir de compras

shop·keep·er [ˈʃɑːkiːpər] tendero(-a) m(f); **shop·lift·er** [ˈʃɑːplɪftər] ladrón(-ona) m(f) (en tienda); **shop·lift·ing** [ˈʃɑːplɪftɪŋ] n hurtos mpl (en tiendas)

shop·per [ˈʃɑːpər] person comprador(a) m(f)

shop·ping [ˈʃɑːpɪŋ] items compra f; **I hate ~** odio hacer la compra; **do one's ~** hacer la compra

'shop·ping bag bolsa f de la compra; **'shop·ping cen·ter**, Br **'shop·ping cen·tre** centro m comercial; **'shop·ping list** lista f de la compra; **'shop·ping mall** centro m comercial

shop 'stew·ard representant m/f sindical

shore [ʃɔːr] orilla f; **on ~** (not at sea) en tierra

short [ʃɔːrt] **1** adj corto; in height bajo; **it's just a ~ walk** está a poca distancia a pie; **we're ~ of fuel** nos queda poco combustible; **he's not ~ of ideas** no le faltan ideas; **time is ~** hay poco tiempo **2** adv: **cut ~** vacation, meeting interrumpir; **stop a person ~** hacer pararse a una persona; **go ~ of** pasar sin; **in ~** en resumen

short·age [ˈʃɔːrtɪdʒ] escasez f, falta f

short 'cir·cuit n cortocircuito m; **short·com·ing** [ˈʃɔːrtkʌmɪŋ] defecto m; **'short·cut** atajo m

short·en [ˈʃɔːrtn] v/t dress, hair, vacation acortar; chapter, article abreviar; working week day reducir

short·en·ing [ˈʃɔːrtnɪŋ] grasa utilizada para hacer masa de pastelería

'short·fall déficit m; **'short·hand** n taquigrafía f; **short·hand·ed**

short·hand·ed [ʃɔːrtˈhændɪd] adj falto de personal; **short-lived** [ʃɔːrtˈlɪvd] adj efímero

short·ly [ˈʃɔːrtlɪ] adv (soon) pronto; ~ **before / after** justo antes / después

short·ness [ˈʃɔːrtnɪs] of visit brevedad f; in height baja f estatura

shorts [ʃɔːrts] npl pantalones mpl cortos, shorts mpl; underwear calzoncillos mpl

short·sight·ed [ʃɔːrtˈsaɪtɪd] adj miope; fig corto de miras; **short-sleeved** [ˈʃɔːrtsliːvd] adj de manga corta; **short-staffed** [ʃɔːrtˈstæft] adj falto de personal; **short 'sto·ry** relato m or cuento corto; **short-tem·pered** [ʃɔːrtˈtempərd] adj irascible; **'short-term** adj a corto plazo; **'short time**: be on ~ of workers trabajar a jornada reducida; **'short wave** onda f corta

shot¹ [ʃɑːt] from gun disparo m; (photograph) fotografía f; (injection) inyección f; be a good / poor ~ tirar bien / mal; he accepted like a ~ aceptó al instante; he ran off like a ~ se fue como una bala

shot² [ʃɑːt] pret & pp → **shoot**

'shot·gun escopeta f

should [ʃʊd] v/aux: **what** ~ **I do?** ¿qué debería hacer?; **you** ~**n't do that** no deberías hacer eso; **that** ~ **be long enough** debería ser lo suficientemente largo; **you** ~ **have heard him!** ¡tendrías que haberle oído!

shoul·der [ˈʃoʊldər] n ANAT hombro m

'shoul·der bag bolso m (de bandolera); **'shoul·der blade** omóplato m, omoplato; **'shoul·der strap** of brassiere, dress tirante m; of bag correa f

shout [ʃaʊt] **1** n grito m **2** v/t & v/i gritar
♦ shout at v/t gritar a

shout·ing [ˈʃaʊtɪŋ] griterío m

shove [ʃʌv] **1** n empujón m **2** v/t & v/i empujar
♦ shove in v/i in line meterse empujando
♦ shove off v/i F (go away) largarse F

shov·el [ˈʃʌvl] **1** n pala f **2** v/t (pret & pp **-ed**, Br **-led**): ~ **snow off the path** retirar a paladas la nieve del camino

show [ʃoʊ] **1** n THEA espectáculo m; TV programa m; of emotion muestra f; **on** ~ at exhibition expuesto, en exposición **2** v/t (pret **-ed**, pp **shown**) passport, ticket enseñar, mostrar; interest, emotion mostrar; at exhibition exponer; movie proyectar; ~ **s.o. sth**, ~ **sth to s.o.** enseñar or mostrar algo a alguien **3** v/i (pret **-ed**, pp **shown**) (be visible) verse; **what's** ~**ing at ...?** at movie theater qué ponen en el ...?
♦ show around v/t enseñar; **he showed us around** nos enseñó la casa / el edificio etc
♦ show in v/t hacer pasar a
♦ show off **1** v/t skills mostrar **2** v/i pej presumir, alardear
♦ show up **1** v/t shortcomings etc poner de manifiesto; **don't show me up in public** (embarrass) no me avergüences en público **2** v/i (be visible) verse; F (arrive) aparecer

'show busi·ness el mundo del espectáculo; **'show·case** n vitrina f; fig escaparate m; **'show·down** enfrentamiento m

show·er [ˈʃaʊər] **1** n of rain chaparrón m, chubasco m; to wash ducha f, Mex regadera f; (party) fiesta con motivo de un bautizo, una boda etc, en la que los invitados llevan obsequios; **take a** ~ ducharse **2** v/i ducharse **3** v/t: ~ **s.o. with compliments / praise** colmar a alguien de cumplidos / alabanzas

'show·er cap gorro m de baño; **'show·er cur·tain** cortina f de ducha; **'show·er·proof** adj impermeable

'show·jump·ing concurso m de saltos

shown [ʃoʊn] pp → **show**

'show-off n pej fanfarrón(-ona) m(f)

'show·room sala f de exposición f; **in** ~ **condition** como nuevo

show·y ['ʃoʊɪ] *adj* llamativo

shrank [ʃræŋk] *pret* → **shrink**

shred [ʃred] **1** *n of paper etc* trozo *m*; *of fabric* jirón *m*; **there isn't a ~ of evidence** no hay prueba alguna **2** *v/t* (*pret & pp* **-ded**) *paper* hacer trizas; *in cooking* cortar en tiras

shred·der ['ʃredər] *for documents* trituradora *f* (de documentos)

shrewd [ʃruːd] *adj person* astuto; *judgement, investment* inteligente

shrewd·ness ['ʃruːdnɪs] *of person* astucia *f*; *of decision* inteligencia *f*

shriek [ʃriːk] **1** *n* alarido *m*, chillido *m* **2** *v/i* chillar

shrill [ʃrɪl] *adj* estridente, agudo

shrimp [ʃrɪmp] gamba *f*; *larger Span* langostino *m*, *L.Am.* camarón *m*

shrine [ʃraɪn] santuario *m*

shrink¹ [ʃrɪŋk] *v/i* (*pret* **shrank**, *pp* **shrunk**) *of material* encoger(se); *of level of support etc* reducirse

shrink² [ʃrɪŋk] *n* F (*psychiatrist*) psiquiatra *m/f*

'shrink-wrap *v/t* (*pret & pp* **-ped**) envolver en plástico adherente

'shrink-wrap·ping *material plástico adherente para envolver*

shriv·el ['ʃrɪvl] *v/i* (*pret & pp* **-ed**, *Br* **-led**) *of skin* arrugarse; *of leaves* marchitarse

shrub [ʃrʌb] arbusto *m*

shrub·ber·y ['ʃrʌbərɪ] arbustos *mpl*

shrug [ʃrʌg] **1** *n*: **... he said with a ~** ... dijo encogiendo los hombros **2** *v/i* (*pret & pp* **-ged**) encoger los hombros **3** *v/t* (*pret & pp* **-ged**): **~ one's shoulders** encoger los hombros

shrunk [ʃrʌŋk] *pp* → **shrink**

shud·der ['ʃʌdər] **1** *n of fear, disgust* escalofrío *m*; *of earth, building* temblor *m* **2** *v/i with fear, disgust* estremecerse; *of earth, building* temblar

shuf·fle ['ʃʌfl] **1** *v/t cards* barajar **2** *v/i in walking* arrastrar los pies

shun [ʃʌn] *v/t* (*pret & pp* **-ned**) rechazar

shut [ʃʌt] *v/t & v/i* (*pret & pp* **shut**) cerrar

♦ **shut down 1** *v/t business* cerrar; *computer* apagar **2** *v/i of business* cerrarse; *of computer* apagarse

♦ **shut off** *v/t* cortar

♦ **shut up** *v/i* F (*be quiet*) callarse; **shut up!** ¡cállate!

shut·ter ['ʃʌtər] *on window* contraventana *f*; PHOT obturador *m*

'shut·ter speed PHOT tiempo *m* de exposición

shut·tle ['ʃʌtl] *v/i*: **~ between** *of bus* conectar; *of airplane* hacer el puente aéreo entre

'shut·tle·bus *at airport* autobús *m* de conexión; **'shut·tle·cock** SP volante *m*; **'shut·tle ser·vice** servicio *m* de conexión

shy [ʃaɪ] *adj* tímido

shy·ness ['ʃaɪnɪs] timidez *f*

Si·a·mese 'twins [saɪə'miːz] *npl* siameses *mpl* (*fpl*)

sick [sɪk] *adj* enfermo; *sense of humor* morboso, macabro; *society* enfermo; **be ~** (*vomit*) vomitar; **be ~ of** (*fed up with*) estar harto de

sick·en ['sɪkn] **1** *v/t* (*disgust*) poner enfermo **2** *v/i*: **be ~ing for sth** estar incubando algo

sick·en·ing ['sɪknɪŋ] *adj stench* nauseabundo; *behavior, crime* repugnante

'sick leave baja *f* (por enfermedad); **be on ~** estar de baja

sick·ly ['sɪklɪ] *adj person* enfermizo; *color* pálido

sick·ness ['sɪknɪs] enfermedad *f*; (*vomiting*) vómitos *mpl*

side [saɪd] *n of box, house, field* lado *m*; *of mountain* ladera *f*, vertiente *f*; *of person* costado *m*; SP equipo *m*; **take ~s** (*favor one ~*) tomar partido (**with** por); **I'm on your ~** estoy de parte tuya; **~ by ~** uno al lado del otro; **at the ~ of the road** al lado de la carretera; **on the big/small ~** un poco grande/pequeño

♦ **side with** *v/t* tomar partido por

'side·board aparador *m*; **'side·burns** *npl* patillas *fpl*; **'side dish** plato *m* de acompañamiento; **'side ef·fect** efecto *m* secundario; **'side·light** MOT luz *f* de posición;

'**side·line 1** *n* actividad *f* complementaria **2** *v/t*: *feel ~d* sentirse marginado; '**side·step** *v/t* (*pret & pp -ped*) *fig* evadir; '**side street** bocacalle *f*; '**side·track** *v/t* distraer; *get ~ed* distraerse; '**side·walk** acera *f*, *Rpl* vereda *f*, *Mex* banqueta *f*; **side·walk 'caf·é** terraza *f*; **side·ways** ['saɪdweɪz] *adv* de lado

siege [siːdʒ] *n* sitio *m*; *lay ~ to* sitiar
sieve [sɪv] *n* tamiz *m*
sift [sɪft] *v/t flour* tamizar; *data* examinar a fondo
♦ **sift through** *v/t details, data* pasar por el tamiz

sigh [saɪ] **1** *n* suspiro *m*; *heave a ~ of relief* suspirar de alivio **2** *v/i* suspirar

sight [saɪt] *n* vista *f*; (*power of seeing*) vista *f*, visión *f*; *~s of city* lugares *mpl* de interés; *he can't stand the ~ of blood* no aguanta ver sangre; *I caught ~ of him just as …* lo vi justo cuando …; *know by ~* conocer de vista; *within ~ of* a la vista de; *as soon as the car was out of ~* en cuanto se dejó de ver el coche; *what a ~ you look!* ¡qué pintas llevas!; *lose ~ of objective etc* olvidarse de
sight·see·ing ['saɪtsiːɪŋ]: *we like ~* nos gusta hacer turismo; *go ~* hacer turismo
'**sight·see·ing tour** visita *f* turística
sight·seer ['saɪtsiːər] *n* turista *m/f*
sign [saɪn] **1** *n* señal *f*; *outside shop, on building* cartel *m*, letrero *m*; *it's a ~ of the times* es un signo de los tiempos que corren **2** *v/t & v/i* firmar
♦ **sign in** *v/i* registrarse
♦ **sign up** *v/i* (*join the army*) alistarse
sig·nal ['sɪgnl] **1** *n* señal *f*; *send out all the wrong ~s* dar a una impresión equivocada **2** *v/i* (*pret & pp -ed*, *Br -led*) *of driver* poner el intermitente
sig·na·to·ry ['sɪgnətɔːrɪ] *n* signatario(-a) *m(f)*, firmante *m/f*
sig·na·ture ['sɪgnətʃər] firma *f*
sig·na·ture 'tune sintonía *f*
sig·net ring ['sɪgnɪt] sello *m* (*anillo*)
sig·nif·i·cance [sɪg'nɪfɪkəns] impor-

tancia *f*, relevancia *f*
sig·nif·i·cant [sɪg'nɪfɪkənt] *adj event etc* importante, relevante; (*quite large*) considerable
sig·nif·i·cant·ly [sɪg'nɪfɪkəntlɪ] *adv larger, more expensive* considerablemente
sig·ni·fy ['sɪgnɪfaɪ] *v/t* (*pret & pp -ied*) significar, suponer
'**sign lan·guage** lenguaje *m* por señas
'**sign·post** señal *f*
si·lence ['saɪləns] **1** *n* silencio *m*; *in ~* en silencio **2** *v/t* hacer callar
si·lenc·er ['saɪlənsər] *on gun* silenciador *m*
si·lent ['saɪlənt] *adj* silencioso; *movie* mudo; *stay ~* (*not comment*) permanecer callado
sil·hou·ette [sɪluː'et] *n* silueta *f*
sil·i·con ['sɪlɪkən] silicio *m*
sil·i·con 'chip chip *m* de silicio
sil·i·cone ['sɪlɪkoʊn] silicona *f*
silk [sɪlk] **1** *n* seda *f* **2** *adj shirt etc* de seda
silk·y ['sɪlkɪ] *adj hair, texture* sedoso
sil·li·ness ['sɪlɪnɪs] tontería *f*, estupidez *f*
sil·ly ['sɪlɪ] *adj* tonto, estúpido
si·lo ['saɪloʊ] silo *m*
sil·ver ['sɪlvər] **1** *n metal, medal* plata *f*; (*~ objects*) (objetos *mpl* de) plata *f* **2** *adj ring* de plata; *hair* canoso
sil·ver med·al medalla *f* de plata;
sil·ver-plat·ed [sɪlvər'pleɪtɪd] *adj* plateado; **sil·ver·ware** ['sɪlvərwer] plata *f*; **sil·ver 'wed·ding** bodas *fpl* de plata
sim·i·lar ['sɪmɪlər] *adj* parecido, similar; *be ~ to* ser parecido a, parecerse a
sim·i·lar·i·ty [sɪmɪ'lærətɪ] parecido *m*, similitud *f*
sim·i·lar·ly ['sɪmɪlərlɪ] *adv* de la misma manera
sim·mer ['sɪmər] *v/i in cooking* cocer a fuego lento; *be ~ing* (*with rage*) estar a punto de explotar
♦ **simmer down** *v/i* tranquilizarse
sim·ple ['sɪmpl] *adj* (*easy, not fancy*) sencillo; *person* simple

sim·ple-mind·ed [sɪmpl'maɪndɪd] *adj pej* simplón

sim·pli·ci·ty [sɪm'plɪsətɪ] *of task, design* sencillez *f*, simplicidad *f*

sim·pli·fy ['sɪmplɪfaɪ] *v/t* (*pret & pp -ied*) simplificar

sim·plis·tic [sɪm'plɪstɪk] *adj* simplista

sim·ply ['sɪmplɪ] *adv* sencillamente; *it is ~ the best* es sin lugar a dudas el mejor

sim·u·late ['sɪmjuleɪt] *v/t* simular

sim·ul·ta·ne·ous [saɪml'teɪnɪəs] *adj* simultáneo

sim·ul·ta·ne·ous·ly [saɪml'teɪnɪəslɪ] *adv* simultáneamente

sin [sɪn] **1** *n* pecado *m* **2** *v/i* (*pret & pp -ned*) pecar

since [sɪns] **1** *prep* desde; *~ last week* desde la semana pasada **2** *adv* desde entonces; *I haven't seen him ~* no lo he visto desde entonces **3** *conj in expressions of time* desde que; (*seeing that*) ya que, dado que; *~ you left* desde que te marchaste; *~ I have been living here* desde que vivo aquí; *~ you don't like it* ya que *or* dado que no te gusta

sin·cere [sɪn'sɪr] *adj* sincero

sin·cere·ly [sɪn'sɪrlɪ] *adv* sinceramente; *I ~ hope he appreciates it* espero de verdad que lo aprecie; *Yours ~* atentamente

sin·cer·i·ty [sɪn'serətɪ] sinceridad *f*

sin·ful ['sɪnfəl] *adj person* pecador; *things* pecaminoso; *it is ~ to ...* es pecado ...

sing [sɪŋ] *v/t & v/i* (*pret* **sang**, *pp* **sung**) cantar

singe [sɪndʒ] *v/t* chamuscar

sing·er ['sɪŋər] cantante *m/f*

sin·gle ['sɪŋgl] **1** *adj* (*sole*) único, solo; (*not double*) único; (*not married*) soltero(-a); *there wasn't a ~ mistake* no había ni un solo error; *in ~ file* en fila india **2** *n* MUS sencillo *m*; (*~ room*) habitación *f* individual; *person* soltero(-a) *m(f)*; *Br ticket* billete *m or L.Am.* boleto *m* de ida; *holidays for ~s* vacaciones para gente sin pareja; *~s in tennis* individuales *mpl*

♦ **single out** *v/t* (*choose*) seleccionar; (*distinguish*) distinguir

sin·gle-breast·ed [sɪŋgl'brestɪd] *adj* recto, con una fila de botones; **sin·gle-'hand·ed** [sɪŋgl'hændɪd] *adj & adv* en solitario; **sin·gle-mind·ed** [sɪŋgl'maɪndɪd] *adj* determinado, resuelto; **Sin·gle 'Mar·ket** (*in Europe*) Mercado *m* Único; **sin·gle 'moth·er** madre *f* soltera; **sin·gle 'pa·rent** padre *m*/madre *f* soltero(-a); **sin·gle pa·rent 'fam·i·ly** familia *f* monoparental; **sin·gle 'room** habitación *f* individual

sin·gu·lar ['sɪŋgjulər] **1** *adj* GRAM singular **2** *n* GRAM singular *m*; *in the ~* en singular

sin·is·ter ['sɪnɪstər] *adj* siniestro; *sky* amenazador

sink [sɪŋk] **1** *n in kitchen* fregadero *m*; *in bathroom* lavabo *m* **2** *v/i* (*pret* **sank**, *pp* **sunk**) *of ship, object* hundirse; *of sun* ponerse; *of interest rates, pressure etc* bajar; *he sank onto the bed* se tiró a la cama **3** *v/t* (*pret* **sank**, *pp* **sunk**) *ship* hundir; *funds* invertir

♦ **sink in** *v/i of liquid* penetrar; *it still hasn't really sunk in of realization* todavía no lo he asumido

sin·ner ['sɪnər] pecador(a) *m(f)*

si·nus ['saɪnəs] seno *m* (*nasal*)

si·nus·i·tis [saɪnə'saɪtɪs] MED sinusitis *f*

sip [sɪp] **1** *n* sorbo *m* **2** *v/t* (*pret & pp -ped*) sorber

sir [sɜːr] señor *m*; *excuse me, ~* perdone, caballero

si·ren ['saɪrən] sirena *f*

sir·loin ['sɜːrlɔɪn] solomillo *m*

sis·ter ['sɪstər] hermana *f*

'sis·ter-in-law (*pl* **sisters-in-law**) cuñada *f*

sit [sɪt] *v/i* (*pret & pp* **sat**) estar sentado; (*~ down*) sentarse

♦ **sit down** *v/i* sentarse

♦ **sit up** *v/i in bed* incorporarse; (*straighten one's back*) sentarse derecho; (*wait up at night*) esperar levantado

sit·com ['sɪtkɑːm] telecomedia f, comedia f de situación

site [saɪt] **1** n emplazamiento m; of battle lugar m **2** v/t new offices etc situar

sit·ting ['sɪtɪŋ] n of committee, court, for artist sesión f; for meals turno m

'sit·ting room sala f de estar, salón m

sit·u·at·ed ['sɪtueɪtɪd] adj situado

sit·u·a·tion [sɪtu'eɪʃn] situación f

six [sɪks] seis

six·teen [sɪks'tiːn] dieciséis

six·teenth [sɪks'tiːnθ] n & adj decimosexto

sixth [sɪksθ] n & adj sexto

six·ti·eth ['sɪkstɪɪθ] n & adj sexagésimo

six·ty ['sɪkstɪ] sesenta

size [saɪz] tamaño m; of loan importe m; of jacket talla f; of shoes número m
♦ **size up** v/t evaluar, examinar

size·a·ble ['saɪzəbl] adj house, order considerable; meal copioso

siz·zle ['sɪzl] v/i chisporrotear

skate [skeɪt] **1** n patín m **2** v/i patinar

skate·board ['skeɪtbɔːrd] n monopatín m

skate·board·er ['skeɪtbɔːrdər] persona que patina en monopatín

skate·board·ing ['skeɪtbɔːrdɪŋ] patinaje m en monopatín

skat·er ['skeɪtər] patinador(a) m(f)

skat·ing ['skeɪtɪŋ] patinaje m

'skat·ing rink pista f de patinaje

skel·e·ton ['skelɪtn] esqueleto m

'skel·e·ton key llave f maestra

skep·tic ['skeptɪk] escéptico(-a) m(f)

skep·ti·cal ['skeptɪkl] adj escéptico

skep·ti·cism ['skeptɪsɪzm] escepticismo m

sketch [sketʃ] **1** n boceto m, esbozo m; THEA sketch m **2** v/t bosquejar

'sketch·book cuaderno m de dibujo

sketch·y ['sketʃɪ] adj knowledge etc básico, superficial

skew·er ['skjuər] n brocheta f

ski [skiː] **1** n esquí m **2** v/i esquiar

'ski boots npl botas fpl de esquí

skid [skɪd] **1** n of car patinazo m; of person resbalón m **2** v/i (pret & pp

-ded) of car patinar; of person resbalar

ski·er ['skiːər] esquiador(a) m(f)

ski·ing ['skiːɪŋ] esquí m

'ski in·struc·tor monitor(a) m(f) de esquí

skil·ful etc Br → **skillful** etc

'ski lift remonte m

skill [skɪl] destreza f, habilidad f

skilled [skɪld] adj capacitado, preparado

skilled 'work·er trabajador(a) m(f) cualificado

'skill·ful ['skɪlfəl] adj hábil, habilidoso

skill·ful·ly ['skɪlfəlɪ] adv con habilidad or destreza

skim [skɪm] v/t (pret & pp **-med**) surface rozar; milk desnatar, descremar
♦ **skim off** v/t the best escoger
♦ **skim through** v/t text leer por encima

skimmed 'milk [skɪmd] leche f desnatada or descremada

skimp·y ['skɪmpɪ] adj account etc superficial; dress cortísimo; bikini mínimo

skin [skɪn] **1** n piel f **2** v/t (pret & pp **-ned**) despellejar, desollar

'skin div·ing buceo m (en bañador)

skin·flint ['skɪnflɪnt] F agarrado(a) m(f) F, roñoso(-a) m(f)

'skin graft injerto m de piel

skin·ny ['skɪnɪ] adj escuálido

'skin-tight adj ajustado

skip [skɪp] **1** n (little jump) brinco m, saltito m **2** v/i (pret & pp **-ped**) brincar **3** v/t (pret & pp **-ped**) (omit) pasar por alto

'ski pole bastón m de esquí

skip·per ['skɪpər] NAUT patrón (-ona) m(f), capitán (-ana) m(f); of team capitán(-ana) m(f)

'ski re·sort estación f de esquí

skirt [skɜːrt] n falda f

'ski run pista f de esquí

'ski tow telesquí m

skull [skʌl] cráneo m

skunk [skʌŋk] mofeta f

sky [skaɪ] cielo m

'sky·light claraboya f; **'sky·line** horizonte *m*; **sky·scrap·er** ['skaɪskreɪpər] rascacielos *m inv*

slab [slæb] *of stone* losa *f*; *of cake etc* trozo *m* grande

slack [slæk] *adj rope* flojo; *work* descuidado; *period* tranquilo; **disciplíne is very ~** no hay disciplina

slack·en ['slækn] *v/t rope, pace* aflojar

♦ **slacken off** *v/i of trading, pace* disminuir

slacks [slæks] *npl* pantalones *mpl*

slain [sleɪn] *pp → slay*

slam [slæm] **1** *v/t (pret & pp -med) door* cerrar de un golpe **2** *v/i (pret & pp -med) of door* cerrarse de golpe

♦ **slam down** *v/t* estampar

slan·der ['slændər] **1** *n* difamación *f* **2** *v/t* difamar

slan·der·ous ['slændərəs] *adj* difamatorio

slang [slæŋ] argot *m*, jerga *f*; *of a specific group* jerga *f*

slant [slænt] **1** *v/i* inclinarse **2** *n* inclinación *f*; *given to a story* enfoque *m*

slant·ing ['slæntɪŋ] *adj roof* inclinado; *eyes* rasgado

slap [slæp] **1** *n* (*blow*) bofetada *f*, cachete *m* **2** *v/t (pret & pp -ped)* dar una bofetada *or* un cachete a; **~ s.o. in the face** dar una bofetada a alguien **3** *adv* F de plano F

'slap·dash *adj* chapucero

slash [slæʃ] **1** *n cut* corte *m*, raja *f*; *in punctuation* barra *f* **2** *v/t skin etc* cortar; *prices, costs* recortar drásticamente; **~ one's wrists** cortarse las venas

slate [sleɪt] *n* pizarra *f*

slaugh·ter ['slɔːtər] **1** *n of animals* sacrificio *m*; *of people, troops* matanza *f* **2** *v/t animals* sacrificar; *people, troops* masacrar

'slaugh·ter·house *for animals* matadero *m*

Slav [slɑːv] *adj* eslavo

slave [sleɪv] *n* esclavo(-a) *m(f)*

'slave-driv·er F negrero(-a) *m(f)* F

slay [sleɪ] *v/t (pret slew, pp slain)* asesinar

slay·ing ['sleɪɪŋ] (*murder*) asesinato

sleaze [sliːz] POL corrupción *f*

slea·zy ['sliːzɪ] *adj bar* sórdido; *person* de mala calaña

sled, sledge [sled, sledʒ] *n* trineo *m*

'sledge ham·mer mazo *m*

sleep [sliːp] **1** *n* sueño *m*; **go to ~** dormirse; **I need a good ~** necesito dormir bien; **I couldn't get to ~** no pude dormirme **2** *v/i (pret & pp slept)* dormir; **~ late** dormir hasta tarde

♦ **sleep on** *v/t*: **sleep on sth** *decision* consultar algo con la almohada

♦ **sleep with** *v/t* (*have sex with*) acostarse con

sleep·i·ly ['sliːpɪlɪ] *adv*: **say sth ~** decir algo medio dormido

'sleep·ing bag ['sliːpɪŋ] saco *m* de dormir; **'sleep·ing car** RAIL coche *m* cama; **'sleep·ing pill** somnífero *m*, pastilla *f* para dormir

sleep·less ['sliːplɪs] *adj*: **have a ~ night** pasar la noche en blanco

'sleep·walk·er sonámbulo(-a) *m(f)*

'sleep·walk·ing sonambulismo *m*

sleep·y ['sliːpɪ] *adj* adormilado, somnoliento; *town* tranquilo; **I'm ~** tengo sueño

sleet [sliːt] *n* aguanieve *f*

sleeve [sliːv] *of jacket etc* manga *f*

sleeve·less ['sliːvlɪs] *adj* sin mangas

sleigh [sleɪ] *n* trineo *m*

sleight of 'hand [slaɪt] juegos *mpl* de manos

slen·der ['slendər] *adj figure, arms* esbelto; *income, margin* escaso; *chance* remoto

slept [slept] *pret & pp → sleep*

slew [sluː] *pret → slay*

slice [slaɪs] **1** *n of bread* rebanada *f*; *of cake* trozo *m*; *of salami, cheese* loncha *f*; *fig: of profits etc* parte *f* **2** *v/t loaf etc* cortar (en rebanadas)

sliced 'bread [slaɪst] pan *m* de molde en rebanadas

slick [slɪk] **1** *adj performance* muy logrado; (*pej: cunning*) con mucha labia **2** *n of oil* marea *f* negra

slid [slɪd] *pret & pp → slide*

slide [slaɪd] **1** *n for kids* tobogán *m*; PHOT diapositiva *f* **2** *v/i (pret & pp* slid) deslizarse; *of exchange rate etc* descender **3** *v/t (pret & pp* **slid**) deslizar

slid·ing 'door ['slaɪdɪŋ] puerta *f* corredera

slight [slaɪt] *adj* delgado, *figure* menudo; *(small)* pequeño; *accent* ligero; *I have a ~ headache* me duele un poco la cabeza; *no, not in the ~est* no, en absoluto

slight·ly ['slaɪtlɪ] *adv* un poco

slim [slɪm] **1** *adj* delgado; *chance* remoto **2** *v/i (pret & pp* **-med**): *I'm ~ming* estoy a dieta

slime [slaɪm] *(mud)* lodo *m*; *of slug etc* baba *f*

slim·y ['slaɪmɪ] *adj liquid* viscoso; *river bed* lleno de lodo

sling [slɪŋ] **1** *n for arm* cabestrillo *m* **2** *v/t (pret & pp* **slung**) F *(throw)* tirar

slip [slɪp] **1** *n on ice etc* resbalón *m*; *(mistake)* desliz *m*; *a ~ of paper* un trozo de papel; *a ~ of the tongue* un lapsus; *give s.o. the ~* dar esquinazo a alguien **2** *v/i (pret & pp* **-ped**) *on ice etc* resbalar; *of quality etc* empeorar; *he ~ped out of the room* se fue de la habitación sigilosamente **3** *v/t (pret & pp* **-ped**) *(put)*: *he ~ped it into his briefcase* lo metió en su maletín sigilosamente; *it ~ped my mind* se me olvidó

♦ **slip away** *v/i of time* pasar; *of opportunity* esfumarse; *(die quietly)* morir tranquilamente

♦ **slip off** *v/t jacket etc* quitarse

♦ **slip on** *v/t jacket etc* ponerse

♦ **slip out** *v/i (go out)* salir (sigilosamente)

♦ **slip up** *v/i (make mistake)* equivocarse

slipped 'disc [slɪpt] hernia *f* discal

slip·per ['slɪpər] zapatilla *f (de estar por casa)*

slip·per·y ['slɪpərɪ] *adj surface, road* resbaladizo; *fish* escurridizo

slip·shod ['slɪpʃɑːd] *adj* chapucero

'slip-up *(mistake)* error *m*

slit [slɪt] **1** *n (tear)* raja *f*; *(hole)* rendija *f*; *in skirt* corte *m* **2** *v/t (pret & pp*

slit) abrir; *~ s.o.'s throat* degollar a alguien

slith·er ['slɪðər] *v/i* deslizarse

sliv·er ['slɪvər] trocito *m*; *of wood, glass* astilla *f*

slob [slɑːb] *pej* dejado(-a) *m/f*, guarro(-a) *m/f*

slob·ber ['slɑːbər] *v/i* babear

slog [slɑːg] *n* paliza *f*

slo·gan ['slougən] eslogan *m*

slop [slɑːp] *v/t (pret & pp* **-ped**) derramar

slope [sloup] **1** *n of roof, handwriting* inclinación *f*; *of mountain* ladera *f*; *built on a ~* construido en una pendiente **2** *v/i* inclinarse; *the road ~s down to the sea* la carretera baja hasta el mar

slop·py ['slɑːpɪ] *adj* descuidado; *too sentimental* sensiblero

slot [slɑːt] *n* ranura *f*; *in schedule* hueco *m*

♦ **slot in 1** *v/t (pret & pp* **-ted**) introducir **2** *v/i (pret & pp* **-ted**) encajar

'slot ma·chine *for cigarettes, food* máquina *f* expendedora; *for gambling* máquina *f* tragaperras

slouch [slautʃ] *v/i*: *don't ~* ponte derecho

slov·en·ly ['slʌvnlɪ] *adj* descuidado

slow [slou] *adj* lento; *be ~ of clock* ir retrasado

♦ **slow down 1** *v/t work, progress* restrasar; *traffic, production* ralentizar **2** *v/i in walking, driving* reducir la velocidad; *of production etc* relantizarse; *you need to slow down in lifestyle* tienes que tomarte las cosas con calma

'slow·down *in production* ralentización *f*

slow·ly ['slouslɪ] *adv* despacio, lentamente

slow 'mo·tion: *in ~* a cámara lenta

slow·ness ['slounɪs] lentitud *f*

'slow·poke F tortuga *f* F

slug [slʌg] *n animal* babosa *f*

slug·gish ['slʌgɪʃ] *adj* lento

slum [slʌm] *n* suburbio *m*, arrabal

slump [slʌmp] **1** *n in trade* desplome *m* **2** *v/i economically* desplomarse,

S

hundirse; (*collapse: of person*) desplomarse

slung [slʌŋ] *pret & pp →* **sling**

slur [slɜːr] **1** *n on s.o.'s character* difamación *f* **2** *v/t* (*pret & pp* **-red**) *words* arrastrar

slurp [slɜːrp] *v/t* sorber

slurred [slɜːrd] *adj:* **his speech was ~** habló arrastrando las palabras

slush [slʌʃ] *n* nieve *f* derretida; (*pej: sentimental stuff*) sensiblería *f*

'slush fund fondo *m* para corruptelas

slush·y [ˈslʌʃɪ] *adj snow* derretido; *movie, novel* sensiblero

slut [slʌt] *pej* fulana *f*

sly [slaɪ] *adj* ladino; **on the ~** a escondidas

smack [smæk] **1** *n:* **a ~ on the bottom** un azote; **a ~ in the face** una bofetada **2** *v/t child* pegar; *bottom* dar un azote en

small [smɔːl] *adj* pequeño, *L.Am.* chico

small 'change cambio *m*, suelto *m*, *L.Am.* sencillo *m*; **small 'hours** *npl* madrugada *f*; **small·pox** [ˈsmɔːlpɑːks] viruela *f*; **small print** letra *f* pequeña; **'small talk: make ~** hablar de banalidades *or* trivialidades

smart¹ [smɑːrt] *adj* (*elegant*) elegante; (*intelligent*) inteligente; *pace* rápido; **get ~ with** hacerse el listillo con

smart² [smɑːrt] *v/i* (*hurt*) escocer

'smart ass F sabelotodo *m/f* F

'smart card tarjeta *f* inteligente

♦ **smart·en up** [ˈsmɑːrtn] *v/t appearance* mejorar; *room* arreglar

smart·ly [ˈsmɑːrtlɪ] *adv dressed* con elegancia

smash [smæʃ] **1** *n noise* estruendo *m*; (*car crash*) choque *m*; *in tennis* smash *m*, mate *m* **2** *v/t break* hacer pedazos *or* añicos; **he ~ed the toys against the wall** estrelló los juguetes contra la pared; **~ sth to pieces** hacer algo añicos **3** *v/i break* romperse; **the driver ~ed into ...** el conductor se estrelló contra ...

♦ **smash up** *v/t place* destrozar

smash 'hit F exitazo *m* F

smat·ter·ing [ˈsmætərɪŋ] *of a language* nociones *fpl*

smear [smɪr] **1** *n of ink* borrón *m*; *of paint* mancha *f*; MED citología *f*; *on character* difamación *f* **2** *v/t character* difamar; **~ X over Y** untar *or* embadurnar Y de X

'smear cam·paign campaña *f* de difamación

smell [smel] **1** *n* olor *m*; **it has no ~** no huele a nada; **sense of ~** sentido *m* del olfato **2** *v/t oler* **3** *v/i unpleasantly* oler (mal); (*sniff*) olfatear; **you ~ of beer** hueles a cerveza; **it ~s good** huele bien

smell·y [ˈsmelɪ] *adj* apestoso; **she had ~ feet** le olían los pies

smile [smaɪl] **1** *n* sonrisa *f* **2** *v/i* sonreír

♦ **smile at** *v/t* sonreír a

smirk [smɜːrk] **1** *n* sonrisa *f* maligna **2** *v/i* sonreír malignamente

smog [smɑːg] niebla *f* tóxica

smoke [smoʊk] **1** *n* humo *m*; **have a ~** fumarse un cigarrillo **2** *v/t cigarettes* fumar; *bacon* ahumar **3** *v/i of person* fumar

smok·er [ˈsmoʊkər] *person* fumador(-a) *m(f)*

smok·ing [ˈsmoʊkɪŋ]: **~ is bad for you** fumar es malo; **no ~** prohibido fumar

'smok·ing car RAIL compartimento *m* de fumadores

smok·y [ˈsmoʊkɪ] *adj room, air* lleno de humo

smol·der, *Br* **smoul·der** [ˈsmoʊldər] *v/i with anger* arder de rabia; *with desire* arder en deseos; **the fire was still ~ing** todavía ardían los rescoldos

smooth [smuːð] **1** *adj surface, skin* liso, suave; *sea* en calma; (*peaceful*) tranquilo; *ride, flight* sin vibraciones; *transition* sin problemas; *pej: person* meloso **2** *v/t hair* alisar

♦ **smooth down** *v/t with sandpaper etc* alisar

♦ **smooth out** *v/t paper, cloth* alisar

♦ **smooth over** *v/t:* **smooth things over** suavizar las cosas

smooth·ly ['smuːðlɪ] *adv without any problems* sin incidentes

smoth·er ['smʌðər] *v/t flames* apagar, sofocar; *person* asfixiar; **~ s.o. with kisses** comerse a alguien a besos

smoul·der ['smoʊldər] *v/i Br* → **smolder**

smudge [smʌdʒ] **1** *n of paint* mancha *f*; *of ink* borrón *m* **2** *v/t ink* emborronar; *paint* difuminar

smug [smʌg] *adj* engreído

smug·gle ['smʌgl] *v/t* pasar de contrabando

smug·gler ['smʌglər] contrabandista *m/f*

smug·gling ['smʌglɪŋ] contrabando *m*

smug·ly ['smʌglɪ] *adv* con engreimiento *or* suficiencia

smut·ty ['smʌtɪ] *adj joke* obsceno

snack [snæk] *n* tentempié *m*, aperitivo *m*

'**snack bar** cafetería *f*

snag [snæg] *n* (*problem*) inconveniente *m*, pega *f*

snail [sneɪl] *n* caracol *m*

snake [sneɪk] *n* serpiente *f*

snap [snæp] **1** *n* chasquido *m*; PHOT foto *f* **2** *v/t* (*pret & pp* **-ped**) *break* romper; ***none of your business, she ~ped*** no es asunto tuyo, saltó **3** *v/i* (*pret & pp* **-ped**) *break* romperse **4** *adj decision*, *judgement* rápido, súbito

♦ **snap up** *v/t bargains* llevarse

snap fast·en·er ['snæpfæsnər] automático *m*, corchete *m*

snap·py ['snæpɪ] *adj person, mood* irascible; *decision, response* rápido; (*elegant*) elegante

'**snap·shot** foto *f*

snarl [snɑːrl] **1** *n of dog* gruñido *m* **2** *v/i* gruñir

snatch [snætʃ] **1** *v/t* arrebatar; (*steal*) robar; (*kidnap*) secuestrar; **~ sth from s.o.** arrebatar algo a alguien **2** *v/i*: ***don't ~*** no lo agarres

♦ **snatch at** *v/t* intentar agarrar

snaz·zy ['snæzɪ] *adj* F vistoso, *Span* chulo F

sneak [sniːk] *v/t* (*remove, steal*) llevarse; **~ a glance at** mirar con disimulo a **2** *v/i*: **~ into the room** entrar a la habitación a hurtadillas

sneak·ers ['sniːkərz] *npl* zapatillas *fpl* de deporte

sneak·ing ['sniːkɪŋ] *adj*: **have a ~ suspicion that …** sospechar que …

sneak·y ['sniːkɪ] *adj* F (*crafty*) ladino, cuco F

sneer [snɪr] **1** *n* mueca *f* desdeñosa **2** *v/i* burlarse (***at*** de)

sneeze [sniːz] **1** *n* estornudo *m* **2** *v/i* estornudar

snick·er ['snɪkər] *n* risita *f* **2** *v/i* reírse (*en voz baja*)

sniff [snɪf] **1** *v/i to clear nose* sorberse los mocos; *of dog* olfatear **2** *v/t* (*smell*) oler; *of dog* olfatear

snip [snɪp] *n* F (*bargain*) ganga *f*

snip·er ['snaɪpər] francotirador(a) *m(f)*

snitch [snɪtʃ] **1** *n* (*telltale*) chivato(-a) *m(f)* **2** *v/i* chivarse

sniv·el ['snɪvl] *v/i* gimotear

snob [snɑːb] presuntuoso(-a) *m(f)*

snob·ber·y ['snɑːbərɪ] presuntuosidad *f*

snob·bish ['snɑːbɪʃ] *adj* presuntuoso

snoop [snuːp] *n* fisgón(-ona) *m(f)*

♦ **snoop around** *v/i* fisgonear

snoot·y ['snuːtɪ] *adj* presuntuoso

snooze [snuːz] **1** *n* cabezada *f*; **have a ~** echar una cabezada **2** *v/i* echar una cabezada

snore [snɔːr] *v/i* roncar

snor·ing ['snɔːrɪŋ] ronquidos *mpl*

snor·kel ['snɔːrkl] *n* snorkel *m*, tubo *m* para buceo

snort [snɔːrt] *v/i of bull, person* bufar, resoplar

snout [snaʊt] *of pig, dog* hocico *m*

snow [snoʊ] **1** *n* nieve *f* **2** *v/i* nevar

♦ **snow under** *v/t*: **be snowed under** estar desbordado

'**snow·ball** bola *f* de nieve; '**snow·bound** *adj* aislado por la nieve; '**snow chains** *npl* MOT cadenas *fpl* para la nieve; '**snow·drift** nevero *m*; '**snow·drop** campanilla *f* de invierno; '**snow·flake** copo *m* de nieve; '**snow·man** muñeco *m* de nieve; '**snow·plow** quitanieves *f inv*; '**snow·storm** tormenta *f* de nieve

snow·y ['snoʊɪ] *adj weather* de nieve; *roads, hills* nevado

snub [snʌb] **1** *n* desaire **2** *v/t* (*pret & pp* **-bed**) desairar

snub-nosed ['snʌbnoʊzd] *adj* con la nariz respingona

snug [snʌg] *adj* (*tight-fitting*) ajustado; *we are nice and ~ in here* aquí se está muy a gusto

♦ **snug·gle down** ['snʌgl] *v/i* acurrucarse

♦ **snug·gle up to** *v/t* acurrucarse contra

so [soʊ] **1** *adv* tan; *it was ~ easy* fue tan fácil; *I'm ~ cold* tengo tanto frío; *that was ~ kind of you* fue muy amable de tu parte; *not ~ much* no tanto; *~ much easier* mucho más fácil; *you shouldn't eat / drink ~ much* no deberías comer / beber tanto; *I miss you ~* te echo tanto de menos; *~ am / do I* yo también; *~ is she / does she* ella también; *and ~ on* etcétera **2** *pron*: *I hope / think ~* eso espero / creo; *you didn't tell me – I did* – sí que lo hice; *50 or ~* unos 50 **3** *conj for that reason* así que; *in order that* para que; *I got up late and ~ I missed the train* me levanté tarde y por eso perdí el tren; *~ (that) I could come too* para que yo también pudiera venir; *~ what?* F ¿y qué? F

soak [soʊk] *v/t* (*steep*) poner en remojo; *of water, rain* empapar

♦ **soak up** *v/t liquid* absorber; *soak up the sun* tostarse al sol

soaked [soʊkt] *adj* empapado; *be ~ to the skin* estar calado hasta los huesos

soak·ing (wet) ['soʊkɪŋ] *adj* empapado

so-and-so ['soʊənsoʊ] F (*unknown person*) fulanito *m*; (*euph: annoying person*) canalla *m/f*

soap [soʊp] *for washing* jabón *m*

'**soap** (**op·e·ra**) telenovela *f*

soap·y ['soʊpɪ] *adj water* jabonoso

soar [sɔːr] *v/i of rocket etc* elevarse; *of prices* dispararse

sob [sɑːb] **1** *n* sollozo *m* **2** *v/i* (*pret & pp* **-bed**) sollozar

so·ber ['soʊbər] *adj* (*not drunk*) sobrio; (*serious*) serio

♦ **sober up** *v/i*: *he sobered up* se le pasó la borrachera

so-'called *adj* (*referred to as*) así llamado; (*incorrectly referred to as*) mal llamado

soc·cer ['sɑːkər] fútbol *m*

'**soc·cer hoo·li·gan** hincha *m* violento

so·cia·ble ['soʊʃəbl] *adj* sociable

so·cial ['soʊʃl] *adj* social

so·cial 'dem·o·crat socialdemócrata *m/f*

so·cial·ism ['soʊʃəlɪzm] socialismo *m*

so·cial·ist ['soʊʃəlɪst] **1** *adj* socialista **2** *n* socialista *m/f*

so·cial·ize ['soʊʃəlaɪz] *v/i* socializar (**with** con)

'**so·cial life** vida *f* social; **so·cial 'sci·ence** ciencia *f* social; '**so·cial work** trabajo *m* social; '**so·cial work·er** asistente(-a) *m(f)* social

so·ci·e·ty [sə'saɪətɪ] sociedad *f*

so·ci·ol·o·gist [soʊsɪ'ɑːlədʒɪst] sociólogo(-a) *m(f)*

so·ci·ol·o·gy [soʊsɪ'ɑːlədʒɪ] sociología *f*

sock¹ [sɑːk] *for wearing* calcetín *m*

sock² [sɑːk] **1** *n* (*punch*) puñetazo *m* **2** *v/t* (*punch*) dar un puñetazo a

sock·et ['sɑːkɪt] *for light bulb* casquillo *m*; *of arm* cavidad *f*; *of eye* cuenca *f*; ELEC enchufe *m*

so·da ['soʊdə] (*~ water*) soda *f*; (*soft drink*) refresco *m*; (*ice-cream ~*) refresco de soda con helado

sod·den ['sɑːdn] *adj* empapado

so·fa ['soʊfə] sofá *m*

'**so·fa-bed** sofá cama *m*

soft [sɑːft] *adj voice, light, color, skin* suave; *pillow, attitude* blando; *have a ~ spot for* tener una debilidad por

'**soft drink** refresco *m*

'**soft drug** droga *f* blanda

soft·en ['sɑːfn] **1** *v/t position* ablandar; *impact, blow* amortiguar **2** *v/i of butter, ice cream* ablandarse, reblandecerse

soft·ly ['sɑ:ftlɪ] *adv* suavemente

soft 'toy peluche *m*

soft·ware ['sɑ:ftwer] software *m*

sog·gy ['sɑ:gɪ] *adj* empapado

soil [sɔɪl] **1** *n* (*earth*) tierra *f* **2** *v/t* ensuciar

so·lar 'en·er·gy ['soʊlər] energía *f* solar; 'so·lar pan·el panel *m* solar; 'solar sys·tem sistema *m* solar

sold [soʊld] *pret & pp* → **sell**

sol·dier ['soʊldʒər] soldado *m*

♦ soldier on *v/i* seguir adelante; *we'll have to soldier on without her* nos las tendremos que arreglar sin ella

sole¹ [soʊl] *n of foot* planta *f*; *of shoe* suela *f*

sole² [soʊl] *adj* único

sole·ly ['soʊlɪ] *adv* únicamente

sol·emn ['sɑ:ləm] *adj* solemne

so·lem·ni·ty [sə'lemnətɪ] solemnidad *f*

sol·emn·ly ['sɑ:ləmlɪ] *adv* solemnemente

so·lic·it [sə'lɪsɪt] *v/i of prostitute* abordar clientes

so·lic·i·tor [sə'lɪsɪtər] *Br* abogado(-a) *m(f)* (*que no aparece en tribunales*)

sol·id ['sɑ:lɪd] *adj* sólido; (*without holes*) compacto; *gold, silver* macizo; *a ~ hour* una hora seguida

sol·i·dar·i·ty [sɑ:lɪ'dærətɪ] solidaridad *f*

so·lid·i·fy [sə'lɪdɪfaɪ] *v/i* (*pret & pp -ied*) solidificarse

sol·id·ly ['sɑ:lɪdlɪ] *adv built* sólidamente; *in favor of sth* unánimente

so·lil·o·quy [sə'lɪləkwɪ] soliloquio *m*

sol·i·taire [sɑ:lɪ'ter] *card game* solitario *m*

sol·i·ta·ry ['sɑ:lɪterɪ] *adj life, activity* solitario; (*single*) único

sol·i·ta·ry con'fine·ment prisión *f* incomunicada

sol·i·tude ['sɑ:lɪtu:d] soledad *f*

so·lo ['soʊloʊ] **1** *n* MUS solo *m* **2** *adj* en solitario

so·lo·ist ['soʊloʊɪst] solista *m/f*

sol·u·ble ['sɑ:ljʊbl] *adj substance, problem* soluble

so·lu·tion [sə'lu:ʃn] (*also mixture*) solución *f*

solve [sɑ:lv] *v/t problem* solucionar, resolver; *mystery* resolver; *crossword* resolver, sacar

sol·vent ['sɑ:lvənt] *adj financially* solvente

som·ber, *Br* som·bre ['sɑ:mbər] *adj* (*dark*) oscuro; (*serious*) sombrío

some [sʌm] **1** *adj*: *would you like ~ water/ cookies?* ¿quieres agua/ galletas?; *~ countries* algunos países; *I gave him ~ money* le di (algo de) dinero; *~ people say that …* hay quien dice … **2** *pron*: *~ of the group* parte del grupo; *would you like ~?* ¿quieres?; *milk? – no thanks, I already have ~* ¿leche? – gracias, ya tengo **3** *adv* (*a bit*): *we'll have to wait ~* tendremos que esperar algo *or* un poco

some·bod·y ['sʌmbədɪ] *pron* alguien; 'some·day *adv* algún día; 'some·how *adv* (*by one means or another*) de alguna manera; (*for some unknown reason*) por alguna razón; *I've never liked him ~* por alguna razón u otra nunca me cayó bien

'some·one *pron* → **somebody**

'some·place *adv* → **somewhere**

som·er·sault ['sʌmərsɒlt] **1** *n* salto mortal **2** *v/i* dar un salto mortal

'some·thing *pron* algo; *would you like ~ to drink/ eat?* ¿te gustaría beber/comer algo?; *is ~ wrong?* ¿pasa algo?

'some·time *adv*: *let's have lunch ~* quedemos para comer un día de éstos; *~ last year* en algún momento del año pasado

'some·times ['sʌmtaɪmz] *adv* a veces

'some·what *adv* un tanto

'some·where **1** *adv* en alguna parte *or* algún lugar **2** *pron*: *let's go to ~ quiet* vamos a algún sitio tranquilo; *I was looking for ~ to park* buscaba un sitio donde aparcar

S

son [sʌn] hijo *m*

so·na·ta [sə'nɑːtə] MUS sonata *f*

song [sɒŋ] canción *f*

'song·bird pájaro *m* cantor

'song·writ·er cantautor(a) *m(f)*

'son-in-law (*pl* **sons-in-law**) yerno *m*

'son·net ['sɑːnɪt] soneto *m*

son of a 'bitch *n* V hijo *m* de puta P

soon [suːn] *adv* pronto; ***how ~ can you be ready to leave?*** ¿cuándo estarás listo para salir?; ***he left ~ after I arrived*** se marchó al poco de llegar yo; ***can't you get here any ~er?*** ¿no podrías llegar antes?; ***as ~ as*** tan pronto como; ***as ~ as possible*** lo antes posible; ***~er or later*** tarde o temprano; ***the ~er the better*** cuanto antes mejor

soot [sʊt] hollín *m*

soothe [suːð] *v/t* calmar

so·phis·ti·cat·ed [sə'fɪstɪkeɪtɪd] *adj* sofisticado

so·phis·ti·ca·tion [sə'fɪstɪkeɪʃn] sofisticación *f*

soph·o·more ['sɑːfəmɔːr] estudiante *m/f* de segundo año

sop·py ['sɑːpɪ] *adj* F sensiblero

so·pra·no [sə'prænoʊ] *n singer* soprano *m/f*; *voice* voz *f* de soprano

sor·did ['sɔːrdɪd] *adj affair, business* sórdido

sore [sɔːr] **1** *adj* (*painful*) dolorido; F (*angry*) enojado, *Span* mosqueado F; ***is it ~?*** ¿duele?; ***I'm ~ all over*** me duele todo el cuerpo **2** *n* llaga *f*

sor·row ['sɑːroʊ] *n* pena *f*

sor·ry ['sɑːrɪ] *adj day, sight,* (*sad*) triste; (***I'm***) ***~!*** *apologizing* ¡lo siento!; ***I'm ~ that I didn't tell you sooner*** lamento no habértelo dicho antes; ***I was so ~ to hear of her death*** me dio mucha pena oír lo de su muerte; (***I'm***) ***~ but I can't help*** lo siento pero no puedo ayudar; ***I won't be ~ to leave here*** no me arrepentiré de irme de aquí; ***I feel ~ for her*** siento pena *or* lástima por ella; ***be a ~ sight*** ofrecer un espectáculo lamentable

sort [sɔːrt] **1** *n* clase *f*, tipo *m*; ***~ of*** F un poco, algo; ***is it finished?*** – ***~ of*** F

¿está acabado? – más o menos **2** *v/t* ordenar, clasificar; COMPUT ordenar

♦ **sort out** *v/t papers* ordenar, clasificar; *problem* resolver, arreglar

SOS [esoʊ'es] SOS *m*; *fig* llamada *f* de auxilio

so-'so *adv* F así así F

sought [sɔːt] *pret & pp* → **seek**

soul [soʊl] REL, *fig: of a nation etc* alma *f*; *character* personalidad *f*; ***the poor ~*** el pobrecillo

sound[1] [saʊnd] **1** *adj* (*sensible*) sensato; (*healthy*) sano; *sleep* profundo **2** *adv*: ***be ~ asleep*** estar profundamente dormido

sound[2] [saʊnd] **1** *n* sonido *m*; (*noise*) ruido *m* **2** *v/t* (*pronounce*) pronunciar; MED auscultar; ***~ one's horn*** tocar la bocina **3** *v/i*: ***that ~s interesting*** parece interesante; ***she ~ed unhappy*** parecía triste

♦ **sound out** *v/t* sondear; ***I sounded her out about the idea*** sondeé a ver qué le parecía la idea

'sound card COMPUT tarjeta *f* de sonido

'sound ef·fects *npl* efectos *mpl* sonoros

sound·ly ['saʊndlɪ] *adv sleep* profundamente; *beaten* rotundamente

'sound·proof *adj* insonorizado

'sound·track banda *f* sonora

soup [suːp] sopa *f*

'soup bowl cuenco *m*; **souped-up** [suːpt'ʌp] *adj* F trucado; **'soup plate** plato *m* sopero; **'soup spoon** cuchara *f* sopera

sour [saʊr] *adj apple, orange* ácido, agrio; *milk* cortado; *comment* agrio

source [sɔːrs] *n* fuente *f*; *of river* nacimiento *m*

'sour cream nata *f* agria

south [saʊθ] **1** *adj* sur, del sur **2** *n* sur *m*; ***to the ~ of*** al sur de **3** *adv* al sur; ***~ of*** al sur de

South 'Af·ric·a Sudáfrica; **South 'Af·ri·can** *adj* sudafricano **2** *n* sudafricano(-a) *m(f)*; **South A'mer·i·ca** Sudamérica, América del Sur; **South A'mer·i·can 1** *adj* sudamericano **2** *n* sudamerica-

no(-a) *m(f)*; **south-'east 1** *n* sudeste *m*, sureste *m* **2** *adj* sudeste, sureste
3 *adv* al sudeste *or* sureste; **~ of** al
sudeste de; **south'·east·ern** *adj* del
sudeste

south·er·ly ['sʌðərlɪ] *adj wind* sur, del
sur; *direction* sur

south·ern ['sʌðərn] *adj* sureño

south·ern·er ['sʌðərnər] sureño(-a)
m(f)

south·ern·most ['sʌðərnmoust] *adj*
más al sur

South 'Pole Polo *m* Sur

south·ward ['sauθwərd] *adv* hacia el
sur

south'west 1 *n* sudoeste *m*, suroeste
m **2** *adj* sudoeste, suroeste **3** *adv* al
sudoeste *or* suroeste; **~ of** al sudoeste *or* suroeste de

south'west·ern *adj* del sudoeste *or*
suroeste

sou·ve·nir [su:və'nɪr] recuerdo *m*

sove·reign ['sɑːvrɪn] *adj state* soberano

sove·reign·ty ['sɑːvrɪntɪ] *of state* soberanía *f*

So·vi·et ['souvɪət] *adj* soviético

So·vi·et 'U·nion Unión *f* Soviética

sow[1] [sau] *n (female pig)* cerda *f*,
puerca *f*

sow[2] [sou] *v/t (pret* **sowed***, pp* **sown***)
seeds* sembrar

sown [soun] *pp* → **sow**[2]

'soy bean [sɔɪ] semilla *f* de soja

soy 'sauce salsa *f* de soja

space [speɪs] *n* espacio *m*
  ♦ **space out** *v/t* espaciar

'space-bar COMPUT barra *f*
espaciadora; **'space-craft** nave *f*
espacial; **'space-ship** nave *f* espacial; **'space shut·tle** transbordador
m espacial; **'space sta·tion** estación *f* espacial; **'space-suit** traje *m*
espacial

spa·cious ['speɪʃəs] *adj* espacioso

spade [speɪd] *for digging* pala *f*; **~s** in
card game picas *fpl*

'spade-work *fig* trabajo *m* preliminar

spa·ghet·ti [spə'getɪ] *nsg* espaguetis
mpl

Spain [speɪn] España

span [spæn] *v/t (pret & pp* **-ned***)*
abarcar; *of bridge* cruzar

Span·iard ['spænjərd] español(a)
m(f)

Span·ish ['spænɪʃ] **1** *adj* español **2** *n
language* español *m*; **the ~** los españoles

spank [spæŋk] *v/t* azotar

spank·ing ['spæŋkɪŋ] *n* azotaina *f*

span·ner ['spænər] *Br* llave *f*

spare [sper] **1** *v/t:* **can you ~ me $50?**
¿me podrías dejar 50 dólares?; **we
can't ~ a single employee** no podemos prescindir ni de un solo trabajador; **can you ~ the time?** ¿tienes tiempo?; **I have time to ~** me
sobra el tiempo; **there were 5 to ~**
sobraban cinco **2** *adj pair of glasses,
set of keys* de repuesto; **do you have
any ~ cash?** ¿no te sobrará algo de
dinero? **3** *n* recambio *m*, repuesto *m*

spare 'part pieza *f* de recambio *or* repuesto; **spare 'ribs** *npl* costillas *fpl*
de cerdo; **spare 'room** habitación *f*
de invitados; **spare 'time** tiempo *m*
libre; **spare 'tire**, *Br* **spare 'tyre**
MOT rueda *f* de recambio *or* repuesto

spar·ing ['sperɪŋ] *adj* moderado; *be
~ with* no derrochar

spa·ring·ly ['sperɪŋlɪ] *adv* con moderación

spark [spɑːrk] *n* chispa *f*

spar·kle ['spɑːrkl] *v/i* destellar

spar·kling 'wine ['spɑːrklɪŋ] vino *m*
espumoso

'spark plug bujía *f*

spar·row ['spærou] gorrión *m*

sparse [spɑːrs] *adj vegetation* escaso

sparse·ly ['spɑːrslɪ] *adv:* **~ populated** poco poblado

spar·tan ['spɑːrtn] *adj room*
espartano

spas·mod·ic [spæz'mɑːdɪk] *adj* intermitente

spat [spæt] *pret & pp* → **spit**

spate [speɪt] *fig* oleada *f*

spa·tial ['speɪʃl] *adj* espacial

spat·ter ['spætər] *v/t:* **the car ~ed
mud all over me** el coche me salpi-
có de barro

S

speak [spiːk] **1** v/i (pret **spoke**, pp **spoken**) hablar (**to**, **with** con); (make a speech) dar una charla; **we're not ~ing** (**to each other**) (we've quarreled) no nos hablamos; **~ing** TELEC al habla **2** v/t (pret **spoke**, pp **spoken**) foreign language hablar; **she spoke her mind** dijo lo que pensaba

♦ **speak for** v/t hablar en nombre de

♦ **speak out** v/i: **speak out against injustice** denunciar la injusticia

♦ **speak up** v/i (speak louder) hablar más alto

speak·er [ˈspiːkər] at conference conferenciante m/f; (orator) orador(a) m(f); of sound system altavoz m, L.Am. altoparlante m; of language hablante m/f

spear [spɪr] lanza f

spear·mint [ˈspɪrmɪnt] hierbabuena f

spe·cial [ˈspeʃl] adj especial; **be on ~** estar de oferta

spe·cial ef·fects npl efectos mpl especiales

spe·cial·ist [ˈspeʃlɪst] especialista m/f

spe·cial·ize [ˈspeʃəlaɪz] v/i especializarse (**in** en)

spe·cial·ly [ˈspeʃlɪ] adv → **especially**

spe·cial·ty [ˈspeʃəltɪ] especialidad f

spe·cies [ˈspiːʃiːz] nsg especie f

spe·cif·ic [spəˈsɪfɪk] adj específico

spe·cif·i·cal·ly [spəˈsɪfɪklɪ] adv específicamente

spec·i·fi·ca·tions [spesɪfɪˈkeɪʃnz] npl of machine etc especificaciones fpl

spe·ci·fy [ˈspesɪfaɪ] v/t (pret & pp **-ied**) especificar

spe·ci·men [ˈspesɪmən] muestra f

speck [spek] of dust, soot mota f

specs [speks] npl Br F (**spectacles**) gafas fpl, L.Am. lentes mpl

spec·ta·cle [ˈspektəkl] (impressive sight) espectáculo m

spec·tac·u·lar [spekˈtækjʊlər] adj espectacular

spec·ta·tor [spekˈteɪtər] espectador(a) m(f)

spec·ta·tor sport deporte m espectáculo

spec·trum [ˈspektrəm] fig espectro m

spec·u·late [ˈspekjʊleɪt] v/i also FIN especular

spec·u·la·tion [spekjʊˈleɪʃn] also FIN especulación f

spec·u·la·tor [ˈspekjʊleɪtər] FIN especulador(a) m(f)

sped [sped] pret & pp → **speed**

speech [spiːtʃ] (address) discurso m; in play parlamento m; (ability to speak) habla f, dicción f; (way of speaking) forma f de hablar

speech de·fect defecto m del habla

speech·less [ˈspiːtʃlɪs] adj with shock, surprise sin habla; **I was left ~** me quedé sin habla

speech ther·a·pist logopeda m/f;
speech ther·a·py logopedia f;
speech writ·er redactor(a) m(f) de discursos

speed [spiːd] **1** n velocidad f; (promptness) rapidez f; **at a ~ of 150 mph** a una velocidad de 150 millas por hora **2** v/i (pret & pp **sped**) run correr; drive too quickly sobrepasar el límite de velocidad; **we were ~ing along** íbamos a toda velocidad

♦ **speed by** v/i pasar a toda velocidad

♦ **speed up 1** v/i of car, driver acelerar; when working apresurarse **2** v/t process acelerar

speed·boat motora f, planeadora f

speed bump resalto m (para reducir la velocidad del tráfico), Arg despertador m, Mex tope m

speed·i·ly [ˈspiːdɪlɪ] adv con rapidez

speed·ing [ˈspiːdɪŋ] n: **fined for ~** multado por exceso de velocidad

speed·ing fine multa f por exceso de velocidad

speed lim·it on roads límite m de velocidad

speed·om·e·ter [spiːˈdɑːmɪtər] velocímetro m

speed trap control m de velocidad por radar

speed·y [ˈspiːdɪ] adj rápido

spell [spel] **1** v/t word deletrear; **how**

do you ~ ...? ¿cómo se escribe ... ?
2 v/i deletrear

spell[2] [spel] *n* (*period of time*) periodo *m*, temporada *f*; **I'll take a ~ at the wheel** te relevaré un rato al volante

'**spell·bound** *adj* hechizado;
'**spell·check** COMPUT: **do a ~ on** pasar el corrector ortográfico a;
'**spell·check·er** COMPUT corrector *m* ortográfico

spell·ing ['spelɪŋ] ortografía *f*

spend [spend] v/t (*pret & pp* **spent**) *money* gastar; *time* pasar

'**spend·thrift** *n pej* derrochador(a) *m*(*f*)

spent [spent] *pret & pp* → **spend**

sperm [spɜːrm] espermatozoide *m*; (*semen*) esperma *f*

'**sperm bank** banco *m* de esperma

'**sperm count** recuento *m* espermático

sphere [sfɪr] *also fig* esfera *f*; **~ of influence** ámbito *m* de influencia

spice [spaɪs] *n* (*seasoning*) especia *f*

spic·y ['spaɪsɪ] *adj food* con especias; (*hot*) picante

spi·der ['spaɪdər] araña *f*

'**spi·der·web** telaraña *f*, tela *f* de araña

spike [spaɪk] *n* pincho *m*; *on running shoe* clavo *m*

spill [spɪl] **1** v/t derramar **2** v/i derramarse **3** *n* derrame *m*

spin[1] [spɪn] **1** *n* (*turn*) giro *m* **2** v/t (*pret & pp* **spun**) hacer girar **3** v/i (*pret & pp* **spun**) *of wheel* girar, dar vueltas; **my head is ~ning** me da vueltas la cabeza

spin[2] [spɪn] v/t *wool, cotton* hilar; *web* tejer

♦ **spin around** v/i *of person, car* darse la vuelta

♦ **spin out** v/t alargar

spin·ach ['spɪnɪdʒ] espinacas *fpl*

spin·al ['spaɪnl] *adj* de la columna vertebral

spin·al 'col·umn columna *f* vertebral

spin·al 'cord médula *f* espinal

'**spin doc·tor** F asesor encargado de

dar la mejor prensa posible a un político o asunto; '**spin-dry** v/t centrifugar; **spin-'dry·er** centrifugadora *f*

spine [spaɪn] *of person, animal* columna *f* vertebral; *of book* lomo *m*; *on plant, hedgehog* espina *f*

'**spin·less** ['spaɪnlɪs] *adj* (*cowardly*) débil

'**spin-off** producto *m* derivado

spin·ster ['spɪnstər] solterona *f*

spin·y ['spaɪnɪ] *adj* espinoso

spi·ral ['spaɪrəl] **1** *n* espiral *f* **2** v/i (*rise quickly*) subir vertiginosamente

spi·ral 'stair·case escalera *f* de caracol

spire [spaɪr] aguja *f*

spir·it ['spɪrɪt] *n* espíritu *m*; (*courage*) valor *m*; **in a ~ of cooperation** con espíritu de cooperación

spir·it·ed ['spɪrɪtɪd] *adj* (*energetic*) enérgico

'**spir·it lev·el** nivel *m* de burbuja

spir·its ['spɪrɪts] *npl* (*morale*) la moral; **be in good/poor ~** tener la moral alta/baja

spir·i·tu·al ['spɪrɪtʃʊəl] *adj* espiritual

spir·it·u·al·ism ['spɪrɪtʃəlɪzm] espiritismo *m*

spir·it·u·al·ist ['spɪrɪtʃəlɪst] *n* espiritista *m/f*

spit [spɪt] v/i (*pret & pp* **spat**) *of person* escupir; **it's ~ting with rain** está chispeando

♦ **spit out** v/t *food, liquid* escupir

spite [spaɪt] *n* rencor *m*; **in ~ of** a pesar de

spite·ful ['spaɪtfəl] *adj* malo, malicioso

spite·ful·ly ['spaɪtfəlɪ] *adv* con maldad *or* malicia

spit·ting 'im·age ['spɪtɪŋ]: **be the ~ of s.o.** ser el vivo retrato de alguien

splash [splæʃ] **1** *n small amount of liquid* chorrito *m*; *of color* mancha *f* **2** v/t *person* salpicar **3** v/i chapotear; *of water* salpicar

♦ **splash down** v/i *of spacecraft* amerizar

♦ **splash out** v/i *in spending* gastarse una fortuna

splen·did ['splendɪd] *adj* espléndido

S

splen·dor, Br **splen·dour** ['splendər]
esplendor m

splint [splɪnt] n MED tablilla f

splin·ter ['splɪntər] **1** n astilla f **2** v/i
astillarse

'splin·ter group grupo m escindido

split [splɪt] **1** n damage raja f;
(disagreement) escisión f; (division,
share) reparto m **2** v/t (pret & pp
split) damage rajar; logs partir en
dos; (cause disagreement in) escindir;
(share) repartir **3** v/i (pret & pp
split) (tear) rajarse; (disagree)
escindirse
♦ **split up** v/i of couple separarse

split per·son·al·i·ty PSYCH doble
personalidad f

split·ting ['splɪtɪŋ] adj: ~ **headache**
dolor m de cabeza atroz

splut·ter ['splʌtər] v/i farfullar

spoil [spɔɪl] v/t estropear, arruinar

'spoil·sport F aguafiestas m/f inv F

spoilt [spɔɪlt] adj child consentido,
mimado; **be ~ for choice** tener mucho donde elegir

spoke[1] [spouk] of wheel radio m

spoke[2] [spouk] pret → **speak**

spo·ken ['spoukən] pp → **speak**

spokes·man ['spouksmən] portavoz
m

spokes·per·son ['spoukspɜːrsən]
portavoz m/f

spokes·wom·an ['spoukswumən]
portavoz f

sponge [spʌndʒ] n esponja f
♦ **sponge off**, **sponge on** v/t F vivir a
costa de

'sponge cake bizcocho m

spong·er ['spʌndʒər] F gorrón(-ona)
m(f) F

spon·sor ['spɑːnsər] **1** n patrocinador m **2** v/t patrocinar

spon·sor·ship ['spɑːnsərʃɪp] patrocinio m

spon·ta·ne·ous [spɑːn'teɪnɪəs] adj
espontáneo

spon·ta·ne·ous·ly [spɑːn'teɪnɪəslɪ]
adv espontáneamente

spook·y ['spuːkɪ] adj F espeluznante,
terrorífico

spool [spuːl] n carrete m

spoon [spuːn] n cuchara f

'spoon-feed v/t (pret & pp **-fed**) fig
dar todo mascado a

spoon·ful ['spuːnful] cucharada f

spo·rad·ic [spə'rædɪk] adj esporádico

sport [spɔːrt] n deporte m

sport·ing ['spɔːrtɪŋ] adj deportivo; **a
~ gesture** un gesto deportivo

'sports car [spɔːrts] (coche m) deportivo m; **'sports·coat** chaqueta f
de sport; **sports 'jour·nal·ist** periodista m/f deportivo(-a); **'sportsman** deportista m; **'sports
med·i·cine** medicina f deportiva;
'sports news nsg noticias fpl deportivas; **'sports page** página f de
deportes; **'sports·wear** ropa f de
deporte; **'sports·wom·an** deportista f

sport·y ['spɔːrtɪ] adj person deportista; clothes deportivo

spot[1] [spɑːt] (pimple etc) grano m;
(part of pattern) lunar m; **a ~ of ...** (a
little) algo de …, un poco de …

spot[2] [spɑːt] (place) lugar m, sitio m;
on the ~ (in the place in question) en
el lugar; (immediately) en ese momento; **put s.o. on the ~** poner a alguien en un aprieto

spot[3] [spɑːt] v/t (pret & pp **-ted**)
(notice) ver; (identify) ver, darse
cuenta de

spot 'check n control m al azar; **carry out spot checks** llevar a cabo
controles al azar

spot·less ['spɑːtlɪs] adj inmaculado,
impecable

'spot·light n foco m

spot·ted ['spɑːtɪd] adj fabric de luna-
res

spot·ty ['spɑːtɪ] adj with pimples con
granos

spouse [spaʊs] fml cónyuge m/f

spout [spaʊt] **1** n pitorro m **2** v/i of
liquid chorrear **3** v/t F soltar F

sprain [spreɪn] **1** n esguince m **2** v/t
hacerse un esguince en

sprang [spræŋ] pret → **spring**

sprawl [sprɔːl] v/i despatarrarse; of
city expandirse; **send s.o. ~ing** of

punch derribar de un golpe

sprawl·ing ['sprɔːlɪŋ] adj city, suburbs en expansión

spray [spreɪ] **1** n of sea water, from fountain rociada f; for hair spray m; container aerosol m, spray m **2** v/t rociar; ~ **sth with sth** rociar algo con algo

'**spray·gun** pistola f pulverizadora

spread [spred] **1** n of disease, religion etc propagación f; F (big meal) comilona f F **2** v/t (pret & pp **spread**) (lay) extender; butter, jelly untar; news, rumor difundir; disease propagar; arms, legs extender **3** v/i (pret & pp **spread**) of disease, fire propagarse; of rumor, news difundirse; of butter extenderse, untarse

'**spread·sheet** COMPUT hoja f de cálculo

spree [spriː] F: **go (out) on a** ~ ir de juerga; **go on a shopping** ~ salir a comprar a lo loco

sprig [sprɪg] ramita f

spright·ly ['spraɪtlɪ] adj lleno de energía

spring[1] [sprɪŋ] n season primavera f

spring[2] [sprɪŋ] n device muelle m

spring[3] [sprɪŋ] **1** n (jump) brinco m, salto m; (stream) manantial m **2** v/i (pret **sprang**, pp **sprung**) brincar, saltar; ~ **from** proceder de; **he sprang to his feet** se levantó de un salto

'**spring·board** trampolín m; **spring 'chick·en** hum: **she's no** ~ no es ninguna niña; **spring-'clean·ing** limpieza f a fondo; '**spring·time** primavera f

spring·y ['sprɪŋɪ] adj mattress, ground mullido; walk ligero; piece of elastic elástico

sprin·kle ['sprɪŋkl] v/t espolvorear; ~ **sth with sth** espolvorear algo con algo

sprin·kler ['sprɪŋklər] for garden aspersor m; in ceiling rociador m contra incendios

sprint [sprɪnt] **1** n esprint m; SP carrera f de velocidad **2** v/i (run fast) correr a toda velocidad; of runner esprintar

sprint·er ['sprɪntər] SP esprínter m/f, velocista m/f

sprout [spraʊt] **1** v/i of seed brotar **2** n: (**Brussels**) ~**s** coles fpl de Bruselas

spruce [spruːs] adj pulcro

sprung [sprʌŋ] pp → **spring**

spry [spraɪ] adj lleno de energía

spun [spʌn] pret & pp → **spin**

spur [spɜːr] n espuela f; fig incentivo; **on the** ~ **of the moment** sin pararse a pensar

♦ **spur on** v/t (pret & pp **-red**) (encourage) espolear

spurt [spɜːrt] **1** n in race arrancada f; **put on a** ~ acelerar **2** v/i of liquid chorrear

sput·ter ['spʌtər] v/i of engine chisporrotear

spy [spaɪ] **1** n espía m/f **2** v/i (pret & pp **-ied**) espiar **3** v/t (pret & pp **-ied**) (see) ver

♦ **spy on** v/t espiar

squab·ble ['skwaːbl] **1** n riña f **2** v/i reñir

squal·id ['skwaːlɪd] adj inmundo, miserable

squal·or ['skwaːlər] inmundicia f

squan·der ['skwaːndər] v/t money despilfarrar

square [skwer] **1** adj in shape cuadrado; ~ **miles** millas cuadradas **2** n also MATH cuadrado m; in town plaza f; in board game casilla f; **we're back to** ~ **one** volvemos al punto de partida

♦ **square up** v/i hacer cuentas

square 'root raíz f cuadrada

squash[1] [skwaːʃ] n vegetable calabacera f

squash[2] [skwaːʃ] n game squash m

squash[3] [skwaːʃ] v/t (crush) aplastar

squat [skwaːt] **1** adj person, build chaparro; figure, buildings bajo **2** v/i (pret & pp **-ted**) sit agacharse; ~ **in a building** ocupar ilegalmente un edificio

squat·ter ['skwaːtər] ocupante m/f ilegal, Span okupa m/f F

squeak [skwiːk] **1** n of mouse chillido m; of hinge chirrido m **2** v/i of mouse chillar; *of hinge* chirriar; *of shoes* crujir

squeak·y ['skwi:kɪ] *adj hinge* chirriante; *shoes* que crujen; *voice* chillón

'**squeak·y clean** *adj* F bien limpio

squeal [skwi:l] **1** *n* chillido; *there was a ~ of brakes* se oyó una frenada estruendosa **2** *v/i* chillar; *of brakes* armar un estruendo

squeam·ish ['skwi:mɪʃ] *adj* aprensivo

squeeze [skwi:z] **1** *n of hand, shoulder* apretón *m* **2** *v/t* (*press*) apretar; (*remove juice from*) exprimir

♦ **squeeze in 1** *v/i to a car etc* meterse a duras penas **2** *v/t* hacer hueco para

♦ **squeeze up** *v/i to make space* apretarse

squid [skwɪd] *n* calamar *m*

squint [skwɪnt] *n: she has a ~* es estrábica, tiene estrabismo

squirm [skwɜːrm] *v/t* retorcerse

squir·rel ['skwɪrl] *n* ardilla *f*

squirt [skwɜːrt] **1** *v/t* lanzar un chorro de **2** *n* F *pej* canijo(-a) *m(f)* F, mequetrefe *m/f* F

St *abbr* (= *saint*) Sto; Sta (= santo *m*; santa *f*); (= *street*) c/ (= calle *f*)

stab [stæb] **1** *n* F intento *m*; *have a ~ at sth* intentar algo **2** *v/t* (*pret & pp* **-bed**) *person* apuñalar

sta·bil·i·ty [stəˈbɪlətɪ] estabilidad *f*

sta·bil·ize ['steɪbɪlaɪz] **1** *v/t prices, boat* estabilizar **2** *v/i of prices etc* estabilizarse

sta·ble[1] ['steɪbl] *n for horses* establo *m*

sta·ble[2] ['steɪbl] *adj* estable; *patient's condition* estacionario

stack [stæk] **1** *n* (*pile*) pila *f*; (*smokestack*) chimenea *f*; *~s of* F montones de F **2** *v/t* apilar

sta·di·um ['steɪdɪəm] *n* estadio *m*

staff [stæf] *npl* (*employees*) personal *m*; (*teachers*) profesorado *m*; *~ are not allowed to …* los empleados no tienen permitido …

staf·fer ['stæfər] empleado(-a) *m(f)*

'**staff·room** *in school* sala *f* de profesores

stag [stæg] ciervo *m*

stage[1] [steɪdʒ] *in life, project etc* etapa *f*

stage[2] [steɪdʒ] **1** *n* THEA escenario *m*; *go on the ~* hacerse actor / actriz **2** *v/t play* escenificar, llevar a escena; *demonstration* llevar a cabo

stage 'door entrada *f* de artistas;

'**stage fright** miedo *m* escénico;

'**stage hand** tramoyista *m/f*

stag·ger ['stægər] **1** *v/i* tambalearse **2** *v/i* (*amaze*) dejar anonadado; *coffee breaks etc* escalonar

stag·ger·ing ['stægərɪŋ] *adj* asombroso

stag·nant ['stægnənt] *adj also fig* estancado

stag·nate [stægˈneɪt] *v/i fig* estancarse

stag·na·tion [stægˈneɪʃn] estancamiento *m*

'**stag par·ty** despedida *f* de soltero

stain [steɪn] **1** *n* (*dirty mark*) mancha *f*; *for wood* tinte *m* **2** *v/t* (*dirty*) manchar; *wood* teñir **3** *v/i of wine etc* manchar, dejar mancha; *of fabric* mancharse

stained-glass 'win·dow [steɪnd] vidriera *f*

stain·less 'steel ['steɪnlɪs] *n* acero *m* inoxidable

'**stain re·mov·er** [rɪˈmuːvər] quitamanchas *m inv*

stair [ster] *n* escalón *m*; *the ~s* la(s) escalera(s)

'**stair·case** escalera(s) *f(/ pl)*

stake [steɪk] **1** *n of wood* estaca *f*; *when gambling* apuesta *f*; (*investment*) participación *f*; *be at ~* estar en juego **2** *v/t tree* arrodrigar; *money* apostar; *reputation* jugarse; *person* ayudar (*económicamente*)

stale [steɪl] *adj bread* rancio; *air* viciado; *fig: news* viejo

'**stale·mate** *in chess* tablas *fpl* (*por rey ahogado*); *fig* punto *m* muerto

stalk[1] [stɒːk] *n of fruit, plant* tallo *m*

stalk[2] [stɒːk] *v/t* (*follow*) acechar; *person* seguir

stalk·er ['stɒːkər] *persona que sigue a*

otra obsesivamente

stall¹ [stɔːl] *n at market* puesto *m; for cow, horse* casilla *f*

stall² [stɔːl] **1** *v/i of vehicle, engine* calarse; *of plane* entrar en pérdida; (*play for time*) intentar ganar tiempo **2** *v/t engine* calar; *person* retener

stal·li·on ['stæljən] semental *m*

stalls [stɔːlz] *npl* patio *m* de butacas

stal·wart ['stɔːlwərt] *adj support, supporter* incondicional

stam·i·na ['stæmɪnə] resistencia *f*

stam·mer ['stæmər] **1** *n* tartamudeo *m* **2** *v/i* tartamudear

stamp¹ [stæmp] **1** *n for letter* sello *m,* L.Am. estampilla *f,* Mex timbre *m; device* tampón *m; mark made with device* sello *m* **2** *v/t* sellar; **~ed addressed envelope** sobre *m* franqueado con la dirección

stamp² [stæmp] *v/t:* **~ one's feet** patear

♦**stamp out** *v/t* (*eradicate*) terminar con

'**stamp collec·ting** filatelia *f;* '**stamp col·lec·tion** collección *f* de sellos *or* L.Am. estampillas *or* Mex timbres; '**stamp col·lec·tor** coleccionista *m/f* de sellos *or* L.Am. estampillas *or* Mex timbres

stam·pede [stæm'piːd] **1** *n of cattle etc* estampida *f; of people* desbandada *f* **2** *v/i of cattle etc* salir de estampida; *of people* salir en desbandada

stance [stæns] (*position*) postura *f*

stand [stænd] **1** *n at exhibition* puesto *m,* stand *m;* (*witness ~*) estrado *m;* (*support, base*) soporte *m;* **take the ~** LAW subir al estrado **2** *v/i* (*pret & pp* **stood**) *of building* encontrarse, hallarse; *as opposed to sit* estar de pie; (*rise*) ponerse de pie; **did you notice two men ~ing near the window?** ¿viste a dos hombres al lado de la ventana?; **there was a large box ~ing in the middle of the floor** había una caja muy grande en mitad del suelo; **the house ~s at the corner of ...** la casa se encuentra en la esquina de ...; **~ still** quedarse quieto; **where do you ~ with Liz?**

¿cual es tu situación con Liz? **3** *v/t* (*pret & pp* **stood**) (*tolerate*) aguantar, soportar; (*put*) colocar; **you don't ~ a chance** no tienes ninguna posibilidad; **~ one's ground** mantenerse firme

♦**stand back** *v/i* echarse atrás

♦**stand by 1** *v/i* (*not take action*) quedarse sin hacer nada; (*be ready*) estar preparado **2** *v/t person* apoyar; *decision* atenerse a

♦**stand down** *v/i* (*withdraw*) retirarse

♦**stand for** *v/t* (*tolerate*) aguantar, (*represent*) significar

♦**stand in for** *v/t* sustituir

♦**stand out** *v/i* destacar

♦**stand up 1** *v/i* levantarse **2** *v/t* F plantar F

♦**stand up for** *v/t* defender; **stand up for yourself!** ¡defiéndete!

♦**stand up to** *v/t* hacer frente a

stan·dard ['stændərd] **1** *adj* (*usual*) habitual **2** *n* (*level of excellence*) nivel *m;* TECH estándar *m;* **be up to ~** cumplir el nivel exigido; **not be up to ~** estar por debajo del nivel exigido; **my parents set very high ~s** mis padres exigen mucho

stan·dard·ize ['stændərdaɪz] *v/t* normalizar

stan·dard of 'li·ving nivel *m* de vida

'**stand·by 1** *n ticket* billete *m* stand-by; **be on ~** estar en stand-by *or* en lista de espera **2** *adv fly* con un billete stand-by

'**stand·by pas·sen·ger** pasajero(-a) *m(f)* en stand-by *or* en lista de espera

stand·ing ['stændɪŋ] *n in society etc* posición *f;* (*repute*) reputación *f;* **a musician/ politician of some ~** un reputado músico/ político; **a relationship of long ~** una relación establecida hace mucho tiempo

'**stand·ing room:** **~ only** no quedan asientos

stand·off·ish [stænd'ɑːfɪʃ] *adj* distante; '**stand·point** punto *m* de vista; '**stand·still:** **be at a ~** estar paralizado; **bring to a ~** paralizar

S

stank [stæŋk] *pret* → **stink**

stan·za ['stænzə] estrofa *f*

sta·ple¹ ['steɪpl] *n foodstuff* alimento *m* básico

sta·ple² ['steɪpl] **1** *n* (*fastener*) grapa *f* **2** *v/t* grapar

sta·ple 'di·et dieta *f* básica

'sta·ple gun grapadora *f* industrial

sta·pler ['steɪplər] grapadora *f*

star [stɑːr] **1** *n also person* estrella *f* **2** *v/t* (*pret & pp* **-red**) *of movie* estar protagonizado por **3** *v/i* (*pret & pp* **-red**) *in movie*: *Depardieu* **~red in** ... Depardieu protagonizó ...

'star·board *adj* de estribor

starch [stɑːrtʃ] *in foodstuff* fécula *f*

stare [ster] **1** *n* mirada *f* fija **2** *v/i* mirar fijamente; **~ at** mirar fijamente

'star·fish estrella *f* de mar

stark [stɑːrk] **1** *adj landscape* desolado; *reminder, picture etc* desolador; *in* **~ contrast to** en marcado contraste con **2** *adv*: **~ naked** completamente desnudo

star·ling ['stɑːrlɪŋ] estornino *m*

star·ry ['stɑːrɪ] *adj night* estrellado

star·ry-eyed [stɑːrɪ'aɪd]] *adj person* cándido, ingenuo

Stars and 'Stripes la bandera estadounidense

start [stɑːrt] **1** *n* (*beginning*) comienzo *m*, principio *m*; *of race* salida *f*; *get off to a good/bad* **~** empezar bien/mal; *from the* **~** desde el principio; *well, it's a* **~!** bueno, ¡algo es algo! **2** *v/i* empezar, comenzar; *of engine, car* arrancar; **~ing from tomorrow** a partir de mañana **3** *v/t* empezar, comenzar; *engine, car* arrancar; *business* montar; **~ to do sth**, **~ doing sth** empezar *or* comenzar a hacer algo; *he* **~ed to cry** se puso a llorar

start·er ['stɑːrtər] (*part of meal*) entrada *f*, entrante *m*; *of car* motor *m* de arranque

'start·ing point punto *m* de partida

'start·ing sal·a·ry sueldo *m* inicial

start·le ['stɑːrtl] *v/t* sobresaltar

start·ling ['stɑːrtlɪŋ] *adj* sorprendente, asombroso

starv·a·tion [stɑːr'veɪʃn] inanición *f*, hambre *f*

starve [stɑːrv] *v/i* pasar hambre; **~ to death** morir de inanición *or* hambre; *I'm starving* F me muero de hambre F

state¹ [steɪt] **1** *n* (*condition, country*) estado *m*; *the States* (los) Estados Unidos **2** *adj capital etc* estatal, del estado; *banquet etc* de estado

state² [steɪt] *v/t* declarar

'State De·part·ment Departamento *m* de Estado, *Ministerio de Asuntos Exteriores*

state·ment ['steɪtmənt] declaración *f*; (*bank* **~**) extracto *m*

state of e'mer·gen·cy estado *m* de emergencia

state-of-the-'art *adj* modernísimo

states·man ['steɪtsmən] hombre *m* de estado

state 'troop·er policía *m/f* estatal

state 'vis·it visita *f* de estado

stat·ic (**e·lec·'tric·i·ty**) ['stætɪk] electricidad *f* estática

sta·tion ['steɪʃn] **1** *n* RAIL estación *f*; RAD emisora *f*, TV canal *m* **2** *v/t guard etc* apostar; *be* **~ed in** *of soldier* estar destinado en

sta·tion·a·ry ['steɪʃnərɪ] *adj* parado

sta·tion·er ['steɪʃənər] papelería *f*

sta·tion·er·y ['steɪʃənerɪ] artículos *mpl* de papelería

sta·tion 'man·ag·er RAIL jefe *m* de estación

'sta·tion wag·on ranchera *f*

sta·tis·ti·cal [stə'tɪstɪkl] *adj* estadístico

sta·tis·ti·cal·ly [stə'tɪstɪklɪ] *adv* estadísticamente

sta·tis·ti·cian [stætɪs'tɪʃn] estadístico(-a) *m(f)*

sta·tis·tics [stə'tɪstɪks] (*nsg: science*) estadística *f*; (*npl: figures*) estadísticas *fpl*

stat·ue ['stætʃuː] estatua *f*

Stat·ue of 'Lib·er·ty Estatua *f* de la Libertad

sta·tus ['steɪtəs] categoría *f*, posición *f*; *women want equal* **~ with men** las mujeres quieren igualdad con los hombres

'**sta·tus bar** COMPUT barra *f* de estado

'**sta·tus sym·bol** símbolo *m* de estatus

stat·ute ['stætu:t] estatuto *m*

staunch [stɔ:ntʃ] *adj supporter* incondicional; *friend* fiel

stay [steɪ] **1** *n* estancia *f*, *L.Am.* estadía *f* **2** *v/i in a place* quedarse; *in a condition* permanecer; ~ **in a hotel** alojarse en un hotel; ~ **right there!** ¡quédate ahí!; ~ **put** no moverse

♦ **stay away** *v/i*: **tell the children to stay away** diles a los niños que no se acerquen

♦ **stay away from** *v/t* no acercarse a

♦ **stay behind** *v/i* quedarse

♦ **stay up** *v/i (not go to bed)* quedarse levantado

stead·i·ly ['stedɪlɪ] *adv improve etc* constantemente

stead·y ['stedɪ] **1** *adj (not shaking)* firme; *(continuous)* continuo; *beat* regular; *boyfriend* estable **2** *adv*: **they've been going ~ for two years** llevan saliendo dos años; ~ **on!** ¡un momento! **3** *v/t (pret & pp -ied)* afianzar; *voice* calmar

steak [steɪk] filete *m*

steal [sti:l] **1** *v/t (pret stole, pp stolen) money etc* robar **2** *v/i (pret stole, pp stolen) (be a thief)* robar; **he stole into the bedroom** entró furtivamente en la habitación

'**stealth bomb·er** [stelθ] bombardero *m* invisible

stealth·y ['stelθɪ] *adj* sigiloso

steam [sti:m] **1** *n* vapor *m* **2** *v/t food* cocinar al vapor

♦ **steam up** *v/i of window* empañarse

steamed up [sti:md'ʌp] *adj* F *(angry)* enojado, *Span* mosqueado F

steam·er ['sti:mər] *for cooking* olla *f* para cocinar al vapor

'**steam i·ron** plancha *f* de vapor

steel [sti:l] **1** *n* acero *m* **2** *adj (made of ~)* de acero

'**steel·work·er** trabajador(a) *m(f)* del acero

'**steel·works** acería *f*

steep[1] [sti:p] *adj hill etc* empinado; F: *prices* caro

steep[2] [sti:p] *v/t (soak)* poner en remojo

stee·ple ['sti:pl] torre *f*

'**stee·ple·chase** *in athletics* carrera *f* de obstáculos

steep·ly ['sti:plɪ] *adv*: **climb** ~ *of path* subir pronunciadamente; *of prices* dispararse

steer[1] [stɪr] *n animal* buey *m*

steer[2] [stɪr] *v/t car* conducir, *L.Am.* manejar; *boat* gobernar; *person* guiar; *conversation* llevar

steer·ing ['stɪrɪŋ] *n* MOT dirección *f*

'**steer·ing wheel** volante *m*, *S.Am.* timón *m*

stem[1] [stem] *n of plant* tallo *m*; *of glass* pie *m*; *of pipe* tubo *m*; *of word* raíz *f*

♦ **stem from** *v/t (pret & pp -med)* derivarse de

stem[2] [stem] *v/t (block)* contener

'**stem·ware** ['stemwer] cristalería *f*

stench [stentʃ] peste *f*, hedor *m*

sten·cil ['stensɪl] **1** *n* plantilla *f* **2** *v/t (pret & pp -ed*, *Br -led) pattern* estarcir

step [step] **1** *n (pace)* paso *m*; *(stair)* escalón *m*; *(measure)* medida *f*; ~ **by** ~ paso a paso **2** *v/i (pret & pp -ped)*: ~ **on sth** pisar algo; ~ **into a puddle** pisar un charco; *I* ~**ped back** di un paso atrás; ~ **forward** dar un paso adelante

♦ **step down** *v/i from post etc* dimitir

♦ **step out** *v/i (go out for a short time)* salir un momento

♦ **step up** *v/t (increase)* incrementar

'**step·broth·er** hermanastro *m*; '**step·daugh·ter** hijastra *f*; '**step·fa·ther** padrastro *m*; '**step·lad·der** escalera *f* de tijera; '**step·moth·er** madrastra *f*

step·ping stone ['stepɪŋ] pasadera *f*; *fig* trampolín *m*

'**step·sis·ter** hermanastra *f*

'**step·son** hijastro *m*

ster·e·o ['sterɪoʊ] *n (sound system)* equipo *m* de música

ster·e·o·type ['sterɪoʊtaɪp] *n* estereotipo *m*

S

ster·ile ['sterəl] *adj* estéril

ster·il·ize ['sterəlaɪz] *v/t woman, equipment* esterilizar

ster·ling ['stɜːrlɪŋ] *n* FIN libra *f* esterlina

stern[1] [stɜːrn] *adj* severo

stern[2] [stɜːrn] *n* NAUT popa *f*

stern·ly ['stɜːrnlɪ] *adv* con severidad

ster·oids ['sterɔɪdz] *npl* esteroides *mpl*

steth·o·scope ['steθəskoup] *n* fonendoscopio *m*, estetoscopio *m*

Stet·son® ['stetsn] *n* sombrero *m* de vaquero

ste·ve·dore ['stiːvədɔːr] estibador *m*

stew [stuː] *n* guiso *m*

stew·ard ['stuːərd] *n on plane* auxiliar *m* de vuelo; *on ship* camarero *m*; *at demonstration, meeting* miembro *m* de la organización

stew·ard·ess [stuːər'des] *on plane* auxiliar *f* de vuelo; *on ship* camarera *f*

stewed [stuːd] *adj apples, plums* en compota

stick[1] [stɪk] *n palo m; of policeman* porra *f*, *(walking ~)* bastón *m*; **live out in the ~s** F vivir en el quinto pino F, vivir en el campo

stick[2] [stɪk] **1** *v/t (pret & pp stuck) with adhesive* pegar; F *(put)* meter **2** *v/i (pret & pp stuck) (jam)* atascarse; *(adhere)* pegarse

♦ **stick around** *v/i* F quedarse

♦ **stick by** *v/t* F apoyar, no abandonar

♦ **stick out** *v/i (protrude)* sobresalir; *(be noticeable)* destacar; *his ears stick out* tiene las orejas salidas

♦ **stick to** *v/t of sth sticky* pegarse a; F *plan etc* seguir; F *(trail, follow)* pegarse a F

♦ **stick together** *v/i* mantenerse unidos

♦ **stick up** *v/t poster, leaflet* pegar

♦ **stick up for** *v/t* F defender

stick·er ['stɪkər] pegatina *f*

'stick-in-the-mud F aburrido(-a) *m(f)* F, soso(-a) *m(f)* F

stick·y ['stɪkɪ] *adj hands, surface* pegajoso; *label* adhesivo

stiff [stɪf] **1** *adj cardboard, manner* rígido; *brush, penalty, competition* duro; *muscle, body* agarrotado; *mixture, paste* consistente; *drink* cargado **2** *adv:* **be scared ~** F estar muerto de miedo F; **be bored ~** F aburrirse como una ostra F

stiff·en ['stɪfn] *v/i of person* agarrotarse

♦ **stiffen up** *v/i of muscle* agarrotarse

stiff·ly ['stɪflɪ] *adv* con rigidez; *fig* forzadamente

stiff·ness ['stɪfnəs] *of muscles* agarrotamiento *m; fig: of manner* rigidez *f*

sti·fle ['staɪfl] *v/t yawn, laugh* reprimir, contener; *criticism, debate* reprimir

sti·fling ['staɪflɪŋ] *adj* sofocante; *it's ~ in here* hace un calor sofocante aquí dentro

stig·ma ['stɪgmə] estigma *m*

sti·let·tos [stɪ'letouz] *npl shoes* zapatos *mpl* de tacón de aguja

still[1] [stɪl] **1** *adj (not moving)* quieto; *with no wind* sin viento; *it was very ~ no wind* no soplaba nada de viento **2** *adv:* **keep ~!** ¡estáte quieto!; **stand ~!** ¡no te muevas!

still[2] [stɪl] *adv (yet)* todavía, aún; *(nevertheless)* de todas formas; *do you ~ want it?* ¿todavía *or* aún lo quieres?; *she ~ hasn't finished* todavía *or* aún no ha acabado; *I ~ don't understand* sigo sin entenderlo; *she might ~ come* puede que aún venga; *they are ~ my parents* siguen siendo mis padres; *~ more (even more)* todavía más

'still·born *adj:* **be ~** nacer muerto

still 'life naturaleza *f* muerta, bodegón *m*

stilt·ed ['stɪltɪd] *adj* forzado

stim·u·lant ['stɪmjʊlənt] estimulante *m*

stim·u·late ['stɪmjʊleɪt] *v/t person* estimular; *growth, demand* estimular, provocar

stim·u·lat·ing ['stɪmjʊleɪtɪŋ] *adj* estimulante

stim·u·la·tion [stɪmjʊ'leɪʃn] estimulación *f*

S

stim·u·lus ['stɪmjʊləs] (*incentive*) estímulo *m*

sting [stɪŋ] **1** *n from bee, jellyfish* picadura *f* **2** *v/t* (*pret & pp* **stung**) *of bee, jellyfish* picar **3** *v/i* (*pret & pp* **stung**) *of eyes, scratch* escocer

sting·ing ['stɪŋɪŋ] *adj remark, criticism* punzante

stin·gy ['stɪndʒɪ] *adj* F agarrado F, rácano F

stink [stɪŋk] **1** *n* (*bad smell*) peste *f*, hedor *m*; F (*fuss*) escándalo F; **make a ~** F armar un escándalo F **2** *v/i* (*pret* **stank**, *pp* **stunk**) (*smell bad*) apestar; F (*be very bad*) dar asco

stint [stɪnt] *n* temporada *f*; **do a ~ in the army** pasar una temporada en el ejército

♦ **stint on** *v/t* F racanear F

stip·u·late ['stɪpjʊleɪt] *v/t* estipular

stip·u·la·tion [stɪpjʊ'leɪʃn] estipulación *f*

stir [stɜːr] **1** *n*: **give the soup a ~** darle vueltas a la sopa; **cause a ~** causar revuelo **2** *v/t* (*pret & pp* **-red**) remover, dar vueltas a **3** *v/i* (*pret & pp* **-red**) *of sleeping person* moverse

♦ **stir up** *v/t crowd* agitar; *bad memories* traer a la memoria

stir-'cra·zy *adj* F majareta F

'stir-fry *v/t* (*pret & pp* **-ied**) freír rápidamente y dando vueltas

stir·ring ['stɜːrɪŋ] *adj music, speech* conmovedor

stir·rup ['stɪrəp] estribo *m*

stitch [stɪtʃ] **1** *n in sewing* puntada *f*; *in knitting* punto *m*; **-es** MED puntos *mpl*; **be in ~es** *laughing* partirse de risa; **have a ~** tener flato **2** *v/t sew* coser

♦ **stitch up** *v/t wound* coser, suturar

stitch·ing ['stɪtʃɪŋ] (*stitches*) cosido *m*

stock [stɑːk] **1** *n* (*reserves*) reservas *fpl*; COM *of store* existencias *fpl*; (*animals*) ganado *m*; FIN acciones *fpl*; *for soup etc* caldo *m*; **in ~** en existencias; **out of ~** agotado; **take ~** hacer balance **2** *v/t* COM (*have*) tener en existencias; COM (*sell*) vender

♦ **stock up on** *v/t* aprovisionarse de

'stock·breed·er ganadero(-a) *m(f)*; **'stock·brok·er** corredor(a) *m(f)* de bolsa; **'stock cube** pastilla *f* de caldo concentrado; **'stock ex·change** bolsa *f* (de valores); **'stock·hold·er** accionista *m/f*

stock·ing ['stɑːkɪŋ] media *f*

stock·ist ['stɑːkɪst] distribuidor(a) *m(f)*

'stock mar·ket mercado *m* de valores; **'stock·mar·ket crash** crack *m* bursátil; **'stock·pile 1** *n of food, weapons* reservas *fpl* **2** *v/t* acumular; **'stock·room** almacén *m*; **stock·still** *adv*: **stand ~** quedarse inmóvil; **'stock·tak·ing** inventario *m*

'stock·y ['stɑːkɪ] *adj* bajo y robusto

stodg·y ['stɑːdʒɪ] *adj food* pesado

sto·i·cal ['stoʊɪkl] *adj* estoico

sto·i·cism ['stoʊɪsɪzm] estoicismo *m*

stole [stoʊl] *pret* → **steal**

stol·en ['stoʊlən] *pp* → **steal**

stom·ach ['stʌmək] **1** *n* estómago *m*, tripa *f* **2** *v/t* (*tolerate*) soportar

'stom·ach·ache dolor *m* de estómago

stone [stoʊn] *n* piedra *f*

stoned [stoʊnd] *adj* F (*on drugs*) colocado F

stone-'deaf *adj*: **be ~** estar más sordo que una tapia

'stone·wall *v/i* F andarse con evasivas

ston·y ['stoʊnɪ] *adj ground, path* pedregoso

stood [stʊd] *pret & pp* → **stand**

stool [stuːl] (*seat*) taburete *m*

stoop¹ [stuːp] **1** *n*: **have a ~** estar encorvado **2** *v/i* (*bend down*) agacharse

stoop² [stuːp] *n* (*porch*) porche *m*

stop [stɑːp] **1** *n for train, bus* parada *f*; **come to a ~** detenerse; **put a ~ to** poner fin a **2** *v/t* (*pret & pp* **-ped**) (*put an end to*) poner fin a; (*prevent*) impedir; (*cease*), *person in street* parar; *car, bus, train, etc*: *of driver* detener; *check* bloquear; **~ doing sth** dejar de hacer algo; **it has ~ped raining** ha parado *or* dejado de llover; **I ~ped her from leaving** impedí

que se fuera **3** *v/i* (*pret & pp* **-ped**)
(*come to a halt*) pararse, detenerse;
in a particular place: *of bus, train* parar
♦ **stop by** *v/i* (*visit*) pasarse
♦ **stop off** *v/i* hacer una parada
♦ **stop over** *v/i* hacer escala
♦ **stop up** *v/t sink* atascar
'**stop·gap** solución *f* intermedia;
'**stop·light** (*traffic light*) semáforo
m; (*brake light*) luz *m* de freno;
'**stop·o·ver** *n* parada *f*; *in air travel*
escala *f*
stop·per ['stɑːpər] *for bath, bottle* tapón *m*
stop·ping ['stɑːpɪŋ]: *no* ~ *sign* prohibido estacionar
'**stop sign** (señal *f* de) stop *m*
'**stop·watch** cronómetro *m*
stor·age ['stɔːrɪdʒ] almacenamiento
m; *put sth in* ~ almacenar algo; *be in*
~ estar almacenado
'**stor·age ca·pac·i·ty** COMPUT capacidad *f* de almacenamiento
'**stor·age space** espacio *m* para
guardar cosas
store [stɔːr] **1** *n* tienda *f*; (*stock*) reserva *f*; (*storehouse*) almacén *m* **2** *v/t* almacenar; COMPUT guardar
'**store·front** fachada *f* de tienda;
'**store·house** almacén *m*; '**store·
keep·er** tendero(-a) *m(f)*;
'**store·room** almacén *m*; **store
'win·dow** escaparate *m*, *L.Am.* vidriera *f*, *Mex* aparador *m*
sto·rey *Br* → **story²**
stork [stɔːrk] cigüeña *f*
storm [stɔːrm] *n* tormenta *f*
'**storm drain** canal *m* de desagüe;
'**storm warn·ing** aviso *m* de tormenta; **storm 'win·dow** contraventana *f*
storm·y ['stɔːrmɪ] *adj weather*,
relationship tormentoso
sto·ry¹ ['stɔːrɪ] (*tale*) cuento *m*;
(*account*) historia *f*; (*newspaper
article*) artículo *m*; F (*lie*) cuento *m*
sto·ry² ['stɔːrɪ] *of building* piso *m*,
planta *f*
stout [staʊt] *adj person* relleno, corpulento; *boots* resistente; *defender*

valiente
stove [stoʊv] *for cooking* cocina *f*,
Col, Mex, Ven estufa *f*; *for heating* estufa *f*
stow [stoʊ] *v/t* guardar
♦ **stow away** *v/i* viajar de polizón
'**stow·a·way** *n* polizón *m*
strag·gler ['stræglər] rezagado(-a)
m(f)
straight [streɪt] **1** *adj line, back* recto;
hair liso; (*honest, direct*) franco;
whiskey solo; (*tidy*) en orden;
(*conservative*) serio; (*not homosexual*) heterosexual; *be a* ~ *A
student* sacar sobresaliente en todas las asignaturas; *keep a* ~ *face*
contener la risa **2** *adv* (*in a straight
line*) recto; (*directly, immediately*) directamente; (*clearly*) con claridad;
stand up ~! ¡ponte recto!; *look s.o.*
~ *in the eye* mirar a los ojos de alguien; *go* ~ F *of criminal* reformarse;
give it to me ~ F dímelo sin rodeos;
~ *ahead be situated* todo derecho;
walk, drive todo recto; *look* hacia delante; *carry* ~ *on of driver etc* seguir
recto; ~*away*, ~ *off* en seguida; ~ *out*
directamente; ~ *up without ice* solo
straight·en ['streɪtn] *v/t* enderezar
♦ **straighten out 1** *v/t situation* resolver; F *person* poner por el buen camino **2** *v/i of road* hacerse recto
♦ **straighten up** *v/i* ponerse derecho
straight'for·ward *adj* (*honest, direct*)
franco; (*simple*) simple
strain¹ [streɪn] **1** *n on rope* tensión *f*;
on engine, heart esfuerzo *m*; *on
person* agobio *m* **2** *v/t fig*: *finances,
budget* crear presión en; ~ *one's
back* hacerse daño en la espalda; ~
one's eyes forzar la vista
strain² [streɪn] *v/t vegetables* escurrir;
oil, fat etc colar
strain³ [streɪn] *n of virus* cepa *f*
strained [streɪnd] *adj relations* tirante
strain·er ['streɪnər] *for vegetables etc*
colador *m*
strait [streɪt] estrecho *m*
strait·laced [streɪt'leɪst] *adj* mojigato
strand¹ [strænd] *n of wool, thread* he-

bra *f*; *a* ~ *of hair* un pelo

strand² [strænd] *v/t* abandonar; *be* ~*ed* quedarse atrapado *or* tirado

strange [streɪndʒ] *adj* (*odd, curious*) extraño, raro; (*unknown, foreign*) extraño

strange·ly ['streɪndʒlɪ] *adv* (*oddly*) de manera extraña; ~ *enough* aunque parezca extraño

strang·er ['streɪndʒər] (*person you don't know*) extraño(-a) *m(f)*, desconocido(-a) *m(f)*; *I'm a ~ here myself* yo tampoco soy de aquí

stran·gle ['stræŋgl] *v/t person* estrangular

strap [stræp] *n of purse, watch* correa *f*; *of brassiere, dress* tirante *m*; *of shoe* tira *f*

◆ **strap in** *v/t* (*pret & pp* **-ped**) poner el cinturón de seguridad a

◆ **strap on** *v/t* ponerse

strap·less ['stræplɪs] *adj* sin tirantes

stra·te·gic [strə'tiːdʒɪk] *adj* estratégico

strat·e·gy ['strætədʒɪ] estrategia *f*

straw¹ [strɔː] *material* paja *f*; *that's the last ~!* ¡es la gota que colma el vaso!

straw² [strɔː] *for drink* pajita *f*

straw·ber·ry ['strɔːberɪ] *fruit* fresa *f*, *S.Am.* frutilla *f*

stray [streɪ] **1** *adj animal* callejero; *bullet* perdido **2** *n dog* perro *m* callejero; *cat* gato *m* callejero **3** *v/i of animal, child* extraviarse, perderse; *fig: of eyes, thoughts* desviarse

streak [striːk] **1** *n of dirt, paint* raya *f*; *in hair* mechón *m*; *fig: of nastiness etc* vena *f* **2** *v/i move quickly* pasar disparado

streak·y ['striːkɪ] *adj* veteado

stream [striːm] **1** *n* riachuelo *m*; *fig: of people, complaints* oleada *f*; *come on* ~ entrar en funcionamiento **2** *v/i: there were tears ~ing down my face* me bajaban ríos de lágrimas por la cara; *people ~ed out of the building* la gente salía en masa

stream·er ['striːmər] serpentina *f*

'**stream·line** *v/t fig* racionalizar

'**stream·lined** *adj car, plane* aerodi-

námico; *fig: organization* racionalizado

street [striːt] calle *f*

'**street·car** tranvía *f*; '**street·light** farola *f*; '**street peo·ple** *npl* los sin techo; '**street val·ue** *of drugs* valor *m* en la calle; '**street·walk·er** F prostituta *f*; '**street·wise** *adj* espabilado

strength [streŋθ] fuerza *f*; *fig* (*strong point*) punto *m* fuerte; *of friendship etc* solidez *f*; *of emotion* intensidad *f*; *of currency* fortaleza *f*

strength·en ['streŋθn] **1** *v/t muscles, currency* fortalecer; *bridge* reforzar; *country, ties, relationship* consolidar **2** *v/i of bonds, ties* consolidarse; *of currency* fortalecerse

stren·u·ous ['strenjʊəs] *adj* agotador

stren·u·ous·ly ['strenjʊəslɪ] *adv* deny tajantemente

stress [stres] **1** *n* (*emphasis*) énfasis *m*; (*tension*) estrés *m*; *on syllable* acento *m*; *be under* ~ estar estresado **2** *v/t* (*emphasize: syllable*) acentuar; *importance etc* hacer hincapié en; *I must* ~ *that ...* quiero hacer hincapié en que ...

stressed 'out [strest] *adj* F estresado

stress·ful ['stresfəl] *adj* estresante

stretch [stretʃ] **1** *n of land, water* extensión *f*; *of road* tramo *m*; *at a* ~ (*non-stop*) de un tirón **2** *adj fabric* elástico **3** *v/t material, income* estirar; F *rules* ser flexible con; *he* ~*ed out his hand* estiró la mano; *my job* ~*es me* mi trabajo me obliga a esforzarme **4** *v/i to relax muscles, reach sth* estirarse; (*spread*) extenderse; *of fabric* estirarse, dar de sí

stretch·er ['stretʃər] camilla *f*

strict [strɪkt] *adj* estricto

strict·ly ['strɪktlɪ] *adv* con rigor; *it is* ~ *forbidden* está terminantemente prohibido

strid·den ['strɪdn] *pp* → **stride**

stride [straɪd] **1** *n* zancada *f*; *take sth in one's* ~ tomarse algo con tranquilidad; *make great* ~*s fig* avanzar a pasos agigantados **2** *v/i* (*pret*

strode, *pp* **stridden**) caminar dando zancadas

stri·dent ['straɪdnt] *adj also fig* estridente

strike [straɪk] **1** *n of workers* huelga *f*; *in baseball* strike *m*; *of oil* descubrimiento *m*; **be on ~** estar en huelga; **go on ~** ir a la huelga **2** *v/i* (*pret & pp* **struck**) *of workers* hacer huelga; (*attack*) atacar; *of disaster* sobrevenir; *of clock* dar las horas; **the clock struck three** el reloj dio las tres **3** *v/t* (*pret & pp* **struck**) (*hit*) golpear; *fig*: *of disaster* sacudir; *match* encender; *oil* descubrir; **didn't it ever ~ you that …?** ¿no se te ocurrió que …?; **she struck me as being …** me dio la impresión de ser …

♦ **strike out 1** *v/t* (*delete*) tachar; *in baseball* eliminar a, *L.Am.* ponchar **2** *v/i in baseball* quedar eliminado, *L.Am.* poncharse

'**strike·break·er** esquirol(a) *m(f)*

strik·er ['straɪkər] (*person on strike*) huelguista *m/f*; *in soccer* delantero(-a) *m(f)*

strik·ing ['straɪkɪŋ] *adj* (*marked*) sorprendente, llamativo; (*eye-catching*) deslumbrante

string [strɪŋ] *n also of violin, racket etc* cuerda *f*; **~s** *musicians* la sección de cuerda; **pull ~s** mover hilos; **a ~ of** (*series*) una serie de

♦ **string along 1** *v/i* (*pret & pp* **strung**) F apuntarse F **2** *v/t* (*pret & pp* **strung**) F: **string s.o. along** dar falsas esperanzas a alguien

♦ **string up** *v/t* F colgar

stringed '**in·stru·ment** [strɪŋd] instrumento *m* de cuerda

strin·gent ['strɪndʒnt] *adj* riguroso

'**string play·er** instrumentista *m/f* de cuerda

strip [strɪp] **1** *n of land* franja *f*; *of cloth* tira *f*; (*comic ~*) tira *f* cómica **2** *v/t* (*pret & pp* **-ped**) (*remove*) quitar; (*undress*) desnudar; **~ s.o. of sth** despojar a alguien de algo **3** *v/i* (*pret & pp* **-ped**) (*undress*) desnudarse; *of stripper* hacer striptease

'**strip club** club *m* de striptease

stripe [straɪp] raya *f*; *indicating rank* galón *m*

striped [straɪpt] *adj* a rayas

'**strip joint** F → **strip club**

strip·per ['strɪpər] artista *m/f* de striptease

'**strip show** espectáculo *m* de striptease

strip'tease striptease *m*

strive [straɪv] *v/i* (*pret* **strove**, *pp* **striven**) esforzarse; **~ to do sth** esforzarse por hacer algo; **~ for** luchar por

striv·en ['strɪvn] *pp* → **strive**

strobe (**light**) [stroʊb] luz *f* estroboscópica

strode [stroʊd] *pret* → **stride**

stroke [stroʊk] **1** *n* MED derrame *m* cerebral; *when writing* trazo *m*; *when painting* pincelada *f*; (*style of swimming*) estilo *m*; **~ of luck** golpe de suerte; **she never does a ~** (*of work*) no pega ni golpe **2** *v/t* acariciar

stroll [stroʊl] **1** *n* paseo *m* **2** *v/i* caminar

stroll·er ['stroʊlər] *for baby* silla *f* de paseo

strong [strɒːŋ] *adj* fuerte; *structure* resistente; *candidate* claro, con muchas posibilidades; *support, supporter, views, objection* firme; *tea, coffee* cargado, fuerte

'**strong·hold** *fig* baluarte *m*

strong·ly ['strɒːŋlɪ] *adv* fuertemente, rotundamente

strong-mind·ed [strɒːŋ'maɪndɪd] *adj* decidido; '**strong point** (*punto m*) fuerte *m*; '**strong·room** cámara *f* acorazada; **strong-willed** [strɒːŋ'wɪld] *adj* tenaz

strove [stroʊv] *pret* → **strive**

struck [strʌk] *pret & pp* → **strike**

struc·tur·al ['strʌktʃərəl] *adj* estructural

struc·ture ['strʌktʃər] **1** *n* (*something built*) construcción *f*; *of novel, society etc* estructura *f* **2** *v/t* estructurar

strug·gle ['strʌgl] **1** *n* lucha *f* **2** *v/i with a person* forcejear; (*have a hard time*) luchar; **he was struggling**

with the door tenía problemas para abrir la puerta; **~ to do sth** luchar por hacer algo

strum [strʌm] v/t (pret & pp **-med**) guitar rasguear

strung [strʌŋ] pret & pp → **string**

strut [strʌt] v/i (pret & pp **-ted**) pavonearse

stub [stʌb] **1** n of cigarette colilla f; of check matriz f; of ticket resguardo m **2** v/t (pret & pp **-bed**): **~ one's toe** darse un golpe en el dedo (del pie)
♦ **stub out** v/t apagar (apretando)

stub·ble ['stʌbl] on man's face barba f incipiente

stub·born ['stʌbərn] adj person testarudo, terco; defense, refusal, denial tenaz, pertinaz

stub·by ['stʌbɪ] adj regordete

stuck [stʌk] **1** pret & pp → **stick 2** adj F: **be ~ on s.o.** estar colado por alguien F

stuck-'up adj F engreído

stu·dent ['stuːdnt] at high school alumno(-a) m(f); at college, university estudiante m/f

stu·dent 'nurse estudiante m/f de enfermería

stu·dent 'teach·er profesor(a) m(f) en prácticas

stu·di·o ['stuːdɪoʊ] of artist, sculptor estudio m; (film ~, TV ~) estudio m, plató m

stu·di·ous ['stuːdɪəs] adj estudioso

stud·y ['stʌdɪ] **1** n estudio m **2** v/t & v/i (pret & pp **-ied**) estudiar

stuff [stʌf] **1** n (things) cosas fpl **2** v/t turkey rellenar; **~ sth into sth** meter algo dentro de algo

stuffed 'toy [stʌft] muñeco m de peluche

stuff·ing ['stʌfɪŋ] relleno m

stuff·y ['stʌfɪ] adj room cargado; person anticuado, estirado

stum·ble ['stʌmbl] v/i tropezar
♦ **stumble across** v/t toparse con
♦ **stumble over** v/t tropezar con; words trastabillarse con

stum·bling-block ['stʌmblɪŋ] escollo m

stump [stʌmp] **1** n of tree tocón m

2 v/t of question, questioner dejar perplejo
♦ **stump up** v/t F aflojar, Span apoquinar F

stun [stʌn] v/t (pret & pp **-ned**) of blow dejar sin sentido; of news dejar atónito or de piedra

stung [stʌŋ] pret & pp → **sting**

stunk [stʌŋk] pp → **stink**

stun·ning ['stʌnɪŋ] adj (amazing) increíble, sorprendente; (very beautiful) imponente

stunt [stʌnt] n for publicity truco m; in movie escena f peligrosa

'**stunt·man** in movie doble m, especialista m

stu·pe·fy ['stuːpɪfaɪ] v/t (pret & pp **-ied**) dejar perplejo

stu·pen·dous [stuː'pendəs] adj extraordinario

stu·pid ['stuːpɪd] adj estúpido; **what a ~ thing to say / do!** ¡qué estupidez!

stu·pid·i·ty [stuː'pɪdətɪ] estupidez f

stu·por ['stuːpər] aturdimiento m

stur·dy ['stɜːrdɪ] adj person robusto; table, plant resistente

stut·ter ['stʌtər] v/i tartamudear

sty [staɪ] for pig pocilga f

style [staɪl] n estilo m; (fashion) moda f; **go out of ~** pasarse de moda

styl·ish ['staɪlɪʃ] adj elegante

styl·ist ['staɪlɪst] (hair ~) estilista m/f

sub·com·mit·tee ['sʌbkəmɪtɪ] subcomité m

sub·com·pact (**car**) [sʌb'kɑːmpækt] utilitario de pequeño tamaño

sub·con·scious [sʌb'kɑːnʃəs] adj subconsciente; **the ~ (mind)** el subconsciente

sub·con·scious·ly [sʌb'kɑːnʃəslɪ] adv inconscientemente

sub·con·tract [sʌbkɑːn'trækt] v/t subcontratar

sub·con·trac·tor [sʌbkɑːn'træktər] subcontratista m/f

sub·di·vide [sʌbdɪ'vaɪd] v/t subdividir

sub·due [səb'duː] v/t rebellion, mob someter, contener

sub·dued [səb'duːd] adj apagado

sub·head·ing [ˈsʌbhedɪŋ] subtítulo *m*

sub·hu·man [sʌbˈhjuːmən] *adj* inhumano

sub·ject 1 *n* [ˈsʌbdʒɪkt] (*topic*) tema *m*; (*branch of learning*) asignatura *f*, materia *f*; GRAM sujeto *m*; *of monarch* súbdito(-a) *m(f)*; ***change the*** ~ cambiar de tema 2 *adj* [ˈsʌbdʒɪkt]: ***be*** ~ ***to*** *have tendency to* ser propenso a; *be regulated by* estar sujeto a; ~ ***to availability*** *goods* promoción válida hasta fin de existencias 3 *v/t* [səbˈdʒekt] someter

sub·jec·tive [səbˈdʒektɪv] *adj* subjetivo

sub·junc·tive [səbˈdʒʌŋktɪv] *n* GRAM subjuntivo *m*

sub·let [ˈsʌblet] *v/t* (*pret & pp* ***-let***) realquilar

sub·ma·chine gun metralleta *f*

sub·ma·rine [ˈsʌbməriːn] submarino *m*

sub·merge [səbˈmɜːrdʒ] 1 *v/t* sumergir 2 *v/i* *of submarine* sumergirse

sub·mis·sion [səbˈmɪʃn] (*surrender*) sumisión *f*; *to committee etc* propuesta *f*

sub·mis·sive [səbˈmɪsɪv] *adj* sumiso

sub·mit [səbˈmɪt] 1 *v/t* (*pret & pp* ***-ted***) *plan, proposal* presentar 2 *v/i* (*pret & pp* ***-ted***) someterse

sub·or·di·nate [səˈbɔːrdɪneɪt] 1 *adj* *employee, position* subordinado 2 *n* subordinado(-a) *m(f)*

sub·poe·na [səˈpiːnə] 1 *n* citación *f* 2 *v/t* *person* citar

♦ **sub·scribe to** [səbˈskraɪb] *v/t* *magazine etc* suscribirse a; *theory* suscribir

sub·scrib·er [səbˈskraɪbər] *to magazine* suscriptor(a) *m(f)*

sub·scrip·tion [səbˈskrɪpʃn] suscripción *f*

sub·se·quent [ˈsʌbsɪkwənt] *adj* posterior

sub·se·quent·ly [ˈsʌbsɪkwəntlɪ] *adv* posteriormente

sub·side [səbˈsaɪd] *v/i* *of flood waters* bajar; *of high winds* amainar; *of building* hundirse; *of fears, panic* calmarse

sub·sid·i·a·ry [səbˈsɪdɪerɪ] *n* filial *f*

sub·si·dize [ˈsʌbsɪdaɪz] *v/t* subvencionar

sub·si·dy [ˈsʌbsɪdɪ] subvención *f*

♦ **sub·sist on** *v/t* subsistir a base de

sub·sis·tence 'farm·er [səbˈsɪstəns] agricultor(a) *m(f)* de subsistencia

sub·sis·tence lev·el nivel *m* mínimo de subsistencia

sub·stance [ˈsʌbstəns] (*matter*) sustancia *f*

sub·stan·dard [sʌbˈstændərd] *adj* *performance* deficiente; *shoes, clothes* con tara

sub·stan·tial [səbˈstænʃl] *adj* sustancial, considerable

sub·stan·tial·ly [səbˈstænʃlɪ] *adv* (*considerably*) considerablemente; (*in essence*) sustancialmente, esencialmente

sub·stan·ti·ate [səbˈstænʃɪeɪt] *v/t* probar

sub·stan·tive [səbˈstæntɪv] *adj* significativo

sub·sti·tute [ˈsʌbstɪtuːt] 1 *n* *for person* sustituto(-a) *m(f)*; *for commodity* sustituto *m*; SP suplente *m/f* 2 *v/t* sustituir, reemplazar; ~ ***X for Y*** sustituir Y por X 3 *v/i*: ~ ***for s.o.*** sustituir a alguien

sub·sti·tu·tion [sʌbs tɪˈtuːʃn] (*act*) sustitución *f*; ***make a*** ~ SP hacer un cambio *or* sustitución

sub·ti·tle [ˈsʌbtaɪtl] *n* subtítulo *m*

sub·tle [ˈsʌtl] *adj* sutil

sub·tract [səbˈtrækt] *v/t* *number* restar

sub·urb [ˈsʌbɜːrb] zona *f* residencial de la periferia

sub·ur·ban [səˈbɜːrbən] *adj* *housing* de la periferia; *attitudes, lifestyle* aburguesado

sub·ver·sive [səbˈvɜːrsɪv] 1 *adj* subversivo 2 *n* subversivo(-a) *m(f)*

sub·way [ˈsʌbweɪ] metro *m*

sub 'ze·ro *adj* bajo cero

suc·ceed [səkˈsiːd] 1 *v/i* (*be successful*) tener éxito; *to throne* suceder en el trono; ~ ***in doing sth*** conseguir hacer algo 2 *v/t* (*come* *after*) suceder

suc·ceed·ing [sək'si:dɪŋ] *adj* siguiente

suc·cess [sək'ses] éxito *m*; **be a ~ of** *book, play, idea* ser un éxito; *of person* tener éxito

suc·cess·ful [sək'sesfəl] *adj person* con éxito; **be ~ in business** tener éxito en los negocios; **be ~ in doing sth** lograr hacer algo

suc·cess·ful·ly [sək'sesfəlɪ] *adv* con éxito

suc·ces·sion [sək'seʃn] sucesión *f*; **three days in ~** tres días seguidos

suc·ces·sive [sək'sesɪv] *adj* sucesivo

suc·ces·sor [sək'sesər] sucesor(a) *m(f)*

suc·cinct [sək'sɪŋkt] *adj* sucinto

suc·cu·lent ['sʌkjʊlənt] *meat, fruit* suculento

suc·cumb [sə'kʌm] *v/i* (*give in*) sucumbir

such [sʌtʃ] **1** *adj* (*of that kind*) tal; **~ men are dangerous** los hombres así son peligrosos; **I know of many ~ cases** conozco muchos casos así; **don't make ~ a fuss** no armes tanto alboroto; **I never thought it would be ~ a success** nunca imaginé que sería un éxito tal; **~ as** como; **there is no ~ word as ...** no existe la palabra ... **2** *adv* tan; **as ~** como tal

suck [sʌk] **1** *v/t candy etc* chupar; **~ one's thumb** chuparse el dedo **2** *v/i* P: **it ~s** (*is awful*) es una mierda P
  ♦ **suck up 1** *v/t* absorber **2** *v/i* F: **suck up to s.o.** hacer la pelota a alguien

suck·er ['sʌkər] F (*person*) primo(-a) *m/f* F, ingenuo(-a) *m/f*; F (*lollipop*) piruleta *f*

suc·tion ['sʌkʃn] succión *f*

sud·den ['sʌdn] *adj* repentino; **all of a ~** de repente

sud·den·ly ['sʌdnlɪ] *adv* de repente

suds [sʌdz] *npl* (*soap ~*) espuma *f*

sue [su:] *v/t* demandar

suede [sweɪd] *n* ante *m*

suf·fer ['sʌfər] **1** *v/i* (*be in great pain*) sufrir; (*deteriorate*) deteriorarse; **be ~ing from** sufrir **2** *v/t loss, setback, heart attack* sufrir

suf·fer·ing ['sʌfərɪŋ] *n* sufrimiento *m*

suf·fi·cient [sə'fɪʃnt] *adj* suficiente

suf·fi·cient·ly [sə'fɪʃntlɪ] *adv* suficientemente

suf·fo·cate ['sʌfəkeɪt] **1** *v/i* asfixiarse **2** *v/t* asfixiar

suf·fo·ca·tion [sʌfə'keɪʃn] asfixia *f*

sug·ar ['ʃʊgər] **1** *n* azúcar *m or f*; **how many ~s?** ¿cuántas cucharadas de azúcar? **2** *v/t* echar azúcar a; **is it ~ed?** ¿lleva azúcar?

'sug·ar bowl azucarero *m*

'sug·ar cane caña *f* de azúcar

sug·gest [sə'dʒest] *v/t* sugerir

sug·ges·tion [sə'dʒestʃən] sugerencia *f*

su·i·cide ['su:ɪsaɪd] suicidio *m*; **commit ~** suicidarse

suit [su:t] **1** *n* traje *m*; *in cards* palo *m* **2** *v/t of clothes, color* sentar bien a; **~ yourself!** F ¡haz lo que quieras!; **be ~ed for sth** estar hecho para algo

sui·ta·ble ['su:təbl] *adj partner, words, clothing* apropiado, adecuado; *time* apropiado

sui·ta·bly ['su:təblɪ] *adv* apropiadamente, adecuadamente

'suit·case maleta *f*, *L.Am.* valija *f*

suite [swi:t] *of rooms*, MUS suite *f*; *furniture* tresillo *m*

sul·fur ['sʌlfər] azufre *m*

sul·fur·ic ac·id [sʌl'fjuːrɪk] ácido *m* sulfúrico

sulk [sʌlk] *v/i* enfurruñarse; **be ~ing** estar enfurruñado

sulk·y ['sʌlkɪ] *adj* enfurruñado

sul·len ['sʌlən] *adj* malhumorado, huraño

sul·phur *etc Br* → **sulfur** *etc*

sul·try ['sʌltrɪ] *adj climate* sofocante, bochornoso; *sexually* sensual

sum [sʌm] (*total*) total *m*, suma *f*; (*amount*) cantidad *f*; *in arithmetic* suma *f*; **a large ~ of money** una gran cantidad de dinero; **~ insured** suma *f* asegurada; **the ~ total of his efforts** la suma de sus esfuerzos
  ♦ **sum up 1** *v/t* (*pret & pp* **-med**) (*summarize*) resumir; (*assess*) catalogar **2** *v/i* (*pret & pp* **-med**) LAW recapitular

sum·mar·ize ['sʌməraiz] v/t resumir

sum·ma·ry ['sʌməri] n resumen m

sum·mer ['sʌmər] verano m

sum·mit ['sʌmɪt] of mountain cumbre f, cima f; POL cumbre f

'**sum·mit meet·ing → summit**

sum·mon ['sʌmən] v/t staff, ministers llamar; meeting convocar

♦ **summon up** v/t: **he summoned up his strength** hizo acopio de fuerzas

sum·mons ['sʌmənz] nsg LAW citación f

sump [sʌmp] for oil cárter m

sun [sʌn] sol m; **in the ~** al sol; **out of the ~** a la sombra; **he has had too much ~** le ha dado demasiado el sol

'**sun·bathe** v/i tomar el sol; '**sun·bed** cama f de rayos UVA; '**sun·block** crema f solar de alta protección; '**sun·burn** quemadura f (del sol); '**sun·burnt** adj quemado (por el sol)

Sun·day ['sʌndei] domingo m

'**sun·dial** reloj m de sol

sun·dries ['sʌndriz] npl varios mpl

sung [sʌŋ] pp → **sing**

'**sun·glass·es** npl gafas fpl or L.Am. anteojos mpl de sol

sunk [sʌŋk] pp → **sink**

sunk·en ['sʌŋkn] adj ship, cheeks hundido

sun·ny ['sʌni] adj day soleado; disposition radiante; **it is ~** hace sol

'**sun·rise** amanecer m; '**sun·set** atardecer m, puesta f de sol; '**sun·shade** sombrilla f; '**sun·shine** sol m; '**sun·stroke** insolación f; '**sun·tan** bronceado m; **get a ~** broncearse

su·per ['su:pər] **1** adj F genial F, estupendo F **2** n (janitor) portero(-a) m(f)

su·perb [sʊ'pɜːrb] adj excelente

su·per·fi·cial [su:pər'fɪʃl] adj superficial

su·per·flu·ous [sʊ'pɜːrfluəs] adj superfluo

su·per·hu·man [su:pər'hjuːmən] adj efforts sobrehumano

su·per·in·tend·ent [su:pərɪn'tendənt] of apartment block portero(-a) m(f)

su·pe·ri·or [su:'pɪriər] **1** adj (better) superior; pej: attitude arrogante **2** n in organization superior m

su·per·la·tive [su:'pɜːrlətɪv] **1** adj superb excelente **2** n GRAM superlativo m

'**su·per·mar·ket** supermercado m

su·per'nat·u·ral 1 adj powers sobrenatural **2** n: **the ~** lo sobrenatural

'**su·per·pow·er** POL superpotencia f

su·per·son·ic [su:pər'sɑːnɪk] adj flight, aircraft supersónico

su·per·sti·tion [su:pər'stɪʃn] superstición f

su·per·sti·tious [su:pər'stɪʃəs] adj person supersticioso

su·per·vise ['su:pərvaɪz] v/t class vigilar; workers supervisar; activities dirigir

su·per·vi·sor ['su:pərvaɪzər] at work supervisor(a) m(f)

sup·per ['sʌpər] cena f, L.Am. comida f

sup·ple ['sʌpl] adj person ágil; limbs, material flexible

sup·ple·ment ['sʌplɪmənt] (extra payment) suplemento m

sup·pli·er [sə'plaɪər] COM proveedor m

sup·ply [sə'plaɪ] **1** n suministro m, abastecimiento m; **~ and demand** la oferta y la demanda; **supplies of food** provisiones fpl; **office supplies** material f de oficina **2** v/t (pret & pp **-ied**) goods suministrar; **~ s.o. with sth** suministrar algo a alguien; **be supplied with ...** venir con ...

sup·port [sə'pɔːrt] **1** n for structure soporte m; (backing) apoyo m **2** v/t building, structure soportar, sostener; financially mantener; (back) apoyar

sup·port·er [sə'pɔːrtər] partidario(-a) m(f); of football team etc seguidor(a) m(f)

sup·port·ive [sə'pɔːrtɪv] adj comprensivo; **be ~** apoyar (**toward**, **of** a)

sup·pose [sə'pouz] v/t (imagine) suponer; **I ~ so** supongo (que sí); **you**

are not ~d to ... (*not allowed to*) no deberías ...; *it is ~d to be delivered today* se supone que lo van a entregar hoy; *it's ~d to be very beautiful* se supone que es hermosísimo

sup·pos·ed·ly [sə'pouzɪdlɪ] *adv* supuestamente

sup·pos·i·to·ry [sə'pɑːzɪtɔːrɪ] MED supositorio *m*

sup·press [sə'pres] *v/t rebellion etc* reprimir, sofocar

sup·pres·sion [sə'preʃn] represión *f*

su·prem·a·cy [suː'preməsɪ] supremacía *f*

su·preme [suː'priːm] *adj* supremo

Su·preme Court Tribunal *m* Supremo, *L.Am.* Corte *f* Suprema

sur·charge ['sɜːrtʃɑːrdʒ] *n* recargo *m*

sure [ʃur] **1** *adj* seguro; *I'm not ~* no estoy seguro; *be ~ about sth* estar seguro de algo; *make ~ that ...* asegurarse de que ... **2** *adv*: *~ enough* efectivamente; *it ~ is hot today* F vaya calor que hace F; *~!* F ¡claro!

sure·ly ['ʃurlɪ] *adv* (*gladly*) claro que sí; *~ you don't mean that!* ¡ no lo dirás en serio!; *~ somebody knows* alguien tiene que saberlo

sur·e·ty ['ʃurətɪ] *for loan* fianza *f*, depósito *m*

surf [sɜːrf] **1** *n on sea* surf *m* **2** *v/t*: *the Net* navegar por Internet

sur·face ['sɜːrfɪs] **1** *n of table, object, water* superficie *f*; *on the ~* fig a primera vista **2** *v/i of swimmer, submarine* salir a la superficie; (*appear*) aparecer

'sur·face mail correo *m* terrestre

'surf·board tabla *f* de surf

surf·er ['sɜːrfər] *on sea* surfista *m/f*

surf·ing ['sɜːrfɪŋ] surf *m*; *go ~* ir a hacer surf

surge [sɜːrdʒ] *n in electric current* sobrecarga *f*; *in demand etc* incremento *m* repentino

♦ **surge forward** *v/i of crowd* avanzar atropelladamente

sur·geon ['sɜːrdʒən] cirujano(-a) *m(f)*

sur·ge·ry ['sɜːrdʒərɪ] cirugía *f*; *undergo ~* ser intervenido quirúr-

gicamente

sur·gi·cal ['sɜːrdʒɪkl] *adj* quirúrgico

sur·gi·cal·ly ['sɜːrdʒɪklɪ] *adv* quirúrgicamente

sur·ly ['sɜːrlɪ] *adj* arisco, hosco

sur·mount [sər'maunt] *v/t difficulties* superar

sur·name ['sɜːrneɪm] apellido *m*

sur·pass [sər'pæs] *v/t* superar

sur·plus ['sɜːrpləs] **1** *n* excedente *m* **2** *adj* excedente

sur·prise [sər'praɪz] **1** *n* sorpresa *f*; *it came as no ~* no me sorprendió **2** *v/t* sorprender; *be / look ~d* estar / parecer sorprendido

sur·pris·ing [sər'praɪzɪŋ] *adj* sorprendente; *it's not ~ that ...* no me sorprende que ...

sur·pris·ing·ly [sər'praɪzɪŋlɪ] *adv* sorprendentemente

sur·ren·der [sə'rendər] **1** *v/i of army* rendirse **2** *v/t weapons etc* entregar **3** *n* rendición *f*; (*handing in*) entrega *f*

sur·ro·gate 'moth·er ['sʌrəgət] madre *f* de alquiler

sur·round [sə'raund] **1** *v/t* rodear; *~ed by* rodeado de *or* por **2** *n of picture etc* marco *m*

sur·round·ing [sə'raundɪŋ] *adj* circundante

sur·round·ings [sə'raundɪŋz] *npl of village* alrededores *mpl*; (*environment*) entorno *m*

sur·vey ['sɜːrveɪ] **1** *n* ['sɜːrveɪ] *of modern literature etc* estudio *m*; *of building* tasación *f*, peritaje; *poll* encuesta *f* **2** *v/t* [sər'veɪ] (*look at*) contemplar; *building* tasar, peritar

sur·vey·or [sɜːr'veɪr] tasador(a) *m(f)* *or* perito (-a) *m(f)* de la propiedad

sur·viv·al [sər'vaɪvl] supervivencia *f*

sur·vive [sər'vaɪv] **1** *v/i* sobrevivir; *how are you? – I'm surviving* ¿cómo estás? – voy tirando; *his two surviving daughters* las dos hijas que aún viven **2** *v/t accident, operation* sobrevivir a; (*outlive*) sobrevivir

sur·vi·vor [sər'vaɪvər] superviviente

m/f; **he's a ~** *fig* es incombustible

sus·cep·ti·ble [səˈseptəbl] *adj emotionally* sensible, susceptible; **be ~ to the cold/heat** ser sensible al frío/calor

sus·pect 1 *n* [ˈsʌspekt] sospechoso(-a) *m(f)* **2** *v/t* [səˈspekt] *person* sospechar de; (*suppose*) sospechar

sus·pect·ed [səˈspektɪd] *adj murderer* presunto; *cause, heart attack etc* supuesto

sus·pend [səˈspend] *v/t* (*hang*) colgar; *from office, duties* suspender

sus·pend·ers [səˈspendərz] *npl for pants* tirantes *mpl*, *S.Am.* suspensores *mpl*

sus·pense [səˈspens] *Span* suspense *m*, *L.Am.* suspenso *m*

sus·pen·sion [səˈspenʃn] MOT, *from duty* suspensión *f*

sus·pen·sion bridge puente *m* colgante

sus·pi·cion [səˈspɪʃn] sospecha *f*

sus·pi·cious [səˈspɪʃəs] *adj* (*causing suspicion*) sospechoso; (*feeling suspicion*) receloso, desconfiado; **be ~ of** sospechar de

sus·pi·cious·ly [səˈspɪʃəslɪ] *adv behave* de manera sospechosa; *ask* con recelo *or* desconfianza

sus·tain [səˈsteɪn] *v/t* sostener

sus·tain·a·ble [səˈsteɪnəbl] *adj* sostenible

swab [swɑːb] *material* torunda *f*; *test* muestra *f*

swag·ger [ˈswægər] *n*: **walk with a ~** caminar pavoneándose

swal·low[1] [ˈswɑːloʊ] **1** *v/t liquid, food* tragar, tragarse **2** *v/i* tragar

swal·low[2] [ˈswɑːloʊ] *n bird* golondrina *f*

swam [swæm] *pret* → **swim**

swamp [swɑːmp] **1** *n* pantano *m* **2** *v/t*: **be ~ed with** estar inundado de

swamp·y [ˈswɑːmpɪ] *adj* pantanoso

swan [swɑːn] cisne *m*

swap [swɑːp] **1** *v/t* (*pret & pp* **-ped**) cambiar; **~ sth for sth** cambiar algo por algo **2** *v/i* (*pret & pp* **-ped**) hacer un cambio

swarm [swɔːrm] **1** *n of bees* enjambre

m **2** *v/i*: **the town was ~ing with ...** la ciudad estaba abarrotada de ...

swar·thy [ˈswɔːrðɪ] *adj face, complexion* moreno

swat [swɑːt] *v/t* (*pret & pp* **-ted**) *insect, fly* aplastar, matar

sway [sweɪ] **1** *n* (*influence, power*) dominio *m* **2** *v/i* tambalearse

swear [swer] *v/t* (*pret* **swore**, *pp* **sworn**) (*use swearword*) decir palabrotas *or* tacos; **~ at s.o.** insultar a alguien; **I ~** lo juro **2** *v/t* (*pret* **swore**, *pp* **sworn**) (*promise*), LAW jurar

♦ **swear in** *v/t witnesses etc* tomar juramento a

'**swear·word** palabrota *f*, taco *m*

sweat [swet] **1** *n* sudor *m*; **covered in ~** empapado de sudor **2** *v/i* sudar

'**sweat·band** banda *f* (en la frente); *on wrist* muñequera *f*

sweat·er [ˈswetər] suéter *m*, *Span* jersey *m*

'**sweat·shirt** sudadera *f*

sweat·y [ˈswetɪ] *adj hands* sudoroso

Swede [swiːd] sueco(-a) *m(f)*

Swe·den [ˈswiːdn] Suecia *f*

Swe·dish [ˈswiːdɪʃ] **1** *adj* sueco **2** *n* sueco *m*

sweep [swiːp] **1** *v/t* (*pret & pp* **swept**) *floor, leaves* barrer **2** *n* (*long curve*) curva *f*

♦ **sweep up** *v/t mess, crumbs* barrer

sweep·ing [ˈswiːpɪŋ] *adj statement* demasiado generalizado; *changes* radical

sweet [swiːt] *adj taste, tea* dulce; F (*kind*) amable; F (*cute*) mono

sweet and 'sour *adj* agridulce

'**sweet·corn** maíz *m*, *S.Am.* choclo *m*

sweet·en [ˈswiːtn] *v/t drink, food* endulzar

sweet·en·er [ˈswiːtnər] *for drink* edulcorante *m*

'**sweet·heart** novio(-a) *m(f)*

swell [swel] **1** *v/i* (*pp* **swollen**) *of wound, limb* hincharse **2** *adj* F (*good*) genial F, fenomenal F **3** *n of the sea* oleaje *m*

swell·ing [ˈswelɪŋ] *n* MED hinchazón *f*

swel·ter·ing [ˈsweltərɪŋ] *adj heat, day*

sofocante

swept [swept] *pret & pp* → **sweep**

swerve [swɜːrv] *v/i of driver, car* girar bruscamente, dar un volantazo

swift [swɪft] *adj* rápido

swim [swɪm] **1** *v/i* (*pret* **swam**, *pp* **swum**) nadar; **go ~ming** ir a nadar; *my head is ~ming* me da vueltas la cabeza **2** *n* baño *m*; **go for a ~** ir a darse un baño

swim·mer ['swɪmər] nadador(a) *m(f)*

swim·ming ['swɪmɪŋ] natación *f*

'**swim·ming pool** piscina *f*, *Mex* alberca *f*, *Rpl* pileta *f*

'**swim·suit** traje *m* de baño, bañador *m*

swin·dle ['swɪndl] **1** *n* timo *m*, estafa *f* **2** *v/t* timar, estafar; **~ s.o. out of sth** estafar algo a alguien

swine [swaɪn] F (*person*) cerdo(-a) *m(f)* F

swing [swɪŋ] **1** *n* oscilación *f*; *for child* columpio *m*; **~ to the Democrats** giro favorable a los Demócratas **2** *v/t* (*pret & pp* **swung**) balancear; *hips* menear **3** *v/i* (*pret & pp* **swung**) balancearse; (*turn*) girar; *of public opinion etc* cambiar

swing-'door puerta *f* basculante *or* de vaivén

Swiss [swɪs] **1** *adj* suizo **2** *n person* suizo(-a) *m(f)*; **the ~** los suizos

switch [swɪtʃ] **1** *n for light* interruptor *m*; (*change*) cambio *m* **2** *v/t* (*change*) cambiar de **3** *v/i* (*change*) cambiar

♦ **switch off** *v/t lights, engine, PC, TV* apagar

♦ **switch on** *v/t lights, engine, PC, TV* encender, *L.Am.* prender

'**switch·board** centralita *f*, *L.Am.* conmutador *m*

'**switch·o·ver** cambio *m* (**to** a)

Swit·zer·land ['swɪtsərlənd] Suiza

swiv·el ['swɪvl] *v/i* (*pret & pp* **-ed**, *Br* **-led**) *of chair, monitor* girar

swol·len ['swoʊlən] **1** *pp* → **swell** **2** *adj* hinchado

swoop [swuːp] *v/i of bird* volar en picado

♦ **swoop down on** *v/t prey* caer en pi-

cado sobre

♦ **swoop on** *v/t of police etc* hacer una redada contra

sword [sɔːrd] espada *f*

'**sword·fish** pez *f* espada

swore [swɔːr] *pret* → **swear**

sworn [swɔːrn] *pp* → **swear**

swum [swʌm] *pp* → **swim**

swung [swʌŋ] *pret & pp* → **swing**

syc·a·more ['sɪkəmɔːr] plátano *m* (árbol)

syl·la·ble ['sɪləbl] sílaba *f*

syl·la·bus ['sɪləbəs] plan *m* de estudios

sym·bol ['sɪmbəl] símbolo *m*

sym·bol·ic [sɪm'bɑːlɪk] *adj* simbólico

sym·bol·ism ['sɪmbəlɪzm] simbolismo *m*

sym·bol·ist ['sɪmbəlɪst] simbolista *m/f*

sym·bol·ize ['sɪmbəlaɪz] *v/t* simbolizar

sym·met·ri·cal [sɪ'metrɪkl] *adj* simétrico

sym·me·try ['sɪmətrɪ] simetría *f*

sym·pa·thet·ic [sɪmpə'θetɪk] *adj* (*showing pity*) compasivo; (*understanding*) comprensivo; **be ~ toward a person/an idea** simpatizar con una persona/idea

♦ **sym·pa·thize with** ['sɪmpəθaɪz] *v/t person, views* comprender

sym·pa·thiz·er ['sɪmpəθaɪzər] POL simpatizante *m/f*

sym·pa·thy ['sɪmpəθɪ] (*pity*) compasión *f*; (*understanding*) comprensión *f*; **don't expect any ~ from me!** no esperes que te compadezca

sym·pho·ny ['sɪmfənɪ] sinfonía *f*

'**sym·pho·ny or·ches·tra** orquesta *f* sinfónica

symp·tom ['sɪmptəm] *also fig* síntoma *f*

symp·to·mat·ic [sɪmptə'mætɪk] *adj*: **be ~ of** *fig* ser sintomático de

syn·chro·nize ['sɪŋkrənaɪz] *v/t* sincronizar

syn·o·nym ['sɪnənɪm] sinónimo *m*

sy·non·y·mous [sɪ'nɑːnɪməs] *adj* sinónimo; **be ~ with** *fig* ser sinónimo de

S

syn·tax ['sɪntæks] sintaxis *f inv*

syn·the·siz·er ['sɪnθəsaɪzər] MUS sintetizador *m*

syn·thet·ic [sɪn'θetɪk] *adj* sintético

syph·i·lis ['sɪfɪlɪs] sífilis *f*

Syr·i·a ['sɪrɪə] Siria

Syr·i·an ['sɪrɪən] **1** *adj* sirio sirio(-a) *m(f)* **2** *n*

sy·ringe [sɪ'rɪndʒ] *n* jeringuilla *f*

syr·up ['sɪrəp] almíbar *m*

sys·tem ['sɪstəm] *also* COMPUT sistema *m*; ***the braking* ~** el sistema de frenado; ***the digestive* ~** el aparato digestivo

sys·te·mat·ic [sɪstə'mætɪk] *adj* sistemático

sys·tem·at·i·cal·ly [sɪstə'mætɪklɪ] *adv* sistemáticamente

sys·tems 'an·a·lyst ['sɪstəmz] COMPUT analista *m/f* de sistemas

T

tab [tæb] *n for pulling* lengüeta *f*; *in text* tabulador *m*; *bill* cuenta *f*; ***pick up the* ~** pagar (la cuenta)

ta·ble ['teɪbl] *n* mesa *f*; *of figures* cuadro *m*

'ta·ble·cloth mantel *m*; **'ta·ble lamp** lámpara *f* de mesa; **ta·ble of 'contents** índice *m* (de contenidos); **'ta·ble·spoon** *object* cuchara *f* grande; *quantity* cucharada *f* grande

ta·blet ['tæblɪt] MED pastilla *f*

'ta·ble ten·nis tenis *m* de mesa

tab·loid ['tæblɔɪd] *n newspaper* periódico *m* sensacionalista (*de tamaño tabloide*)

ta·boo [tə'buː] *adj* tabú *inv*

ta·cit ['tæsɪt] *adj* tácito

ta·ci·turn ['tæsɪtɜːrn] *adj* taciturno

tack [tæk] **1** *n* (*nail*) tachuela *f* **2** *v/t* (*sew*) hilvanar **3** *v/i of yacht* dar bordadas

tack·le ['tækl] **1** *n* (*equipment*) equipo *m*; SP entrada *f*; ***fishing* ~** aparejos *mpl* de pesca **2** *v/t* SP entrar a; *problem* abordar; *intruder* hacer frente a

tack·y ['tækɪ] *adj paint, glue* pegajoso; F (*cheap, poor quality*) chabacano, *Span* hortera F; *behavior* impresentable

tact [tækt] tacto *m*

tact·ful ['tæktfəl] *adj* diplomático

tact·ful·ly ['tæktfəlɪ] *adv* diplomáticamente

tac·tic·al ['tæktɪkl] *adj* táctico

tac·tics ['tæktɪks] *npl* táctica *f*

tact·less ['tæktlɪs] *adj* indiscreto

tad·pole ['tædpoul] renacuajo *m*

tag [tæg] *n* (*label*) etiqueta *f*

♦ **tag along** *v/i* (*pret & pp* **-ged**) pegarse

tail [teɪl] *n of bird, fish* cola *f*; *of mammal* cola *f*, rabo *m*

'tail light luz *f* trasera

tai·lor ['teɪlər] *n* sastre *m*

tai·lor-made [teɪlər'meɪd] *adj suit, solution* hecho a medida

'tail·pipe *of car* tubo *m* de escape

'tail·wind viento *m* de cola

taint·ed ['teɪntɪd] *adj food* contaminado; *reputation* empañado

Tai·wan [taɪ'wɑːn] Taiwán

Tai·wan·ese [taɪwɑːn'iːz] **1** *adj* taiwanés(-esa) *m(f)*; *dialect* taiwanés *m* **2** *n* taiwanés

take [teɪk] *v/t* (*pret* **took**, *pp* **taken**) (*remove*) llevarse, *Span* coger; (*steal*) llevarse; (*transport, accompany*) llevar; (*accept: money, gift, credit cards*) aceptar; (*study: maths, French*) hacer, estudiar; *photograph, photocopy* hacer, sacar; *exam, degree* hacer; *shower* darse; *stroll* dar; *medicine, s.o.'s temperature, taxi* tomar;

(*endure*) aguantar; **how long does it ~?** ¿cuánto tiempo lleva?; **I'll ~ it** *when shopping* me lo llevo; **it ~s a lot of courage** se necesita mucho valor

♦ **take after** *v/t* parecerse a

♦ **take apart** *v/t* (*dismantle*) desmontar; F (*criticize*) hacer pedazos; F (*reprimand*) echar una bronca a F; F *in physical fight* machacar F

♦ **take away** *v/t pain* hacer desaparecer; *object* quitar; MATH restar; **take sth away from s.o.** quitar algo a alguien

♦ **take back** *v/t* (*return: object*) devolver; *person* llevar de vuelta; (*accept back*) dejar volver; **that takes me back** *of music, thought etc* me trae recuerdos

♦ **take down** *v/t from shelf* bajar; *scaffolding* desmontar; *trousers* bajarse; (*write down*) anotar, apuntar

♦ **take in** *v/t* (*take indoors*) recoger; (*give accommodation to*) acoger; (*make narrower*) meter; (*deceive*) engañar; (*include*) incluir

♦ **take off 1** *v/t clothes, hat* quitarse; *10% etc* descontar; (*mimic*) imitar; (*cut off*) cortar; **take a day / week off** tomarse un día / una semana de vacaciones **2** *v/i of airplane* despegar, *L.Am.* decolar; (*become popular*) empezar a cuajar

♦ **take on** *v/t job* aceptar; *staff* contratar

♦ **take out** *v/t from bag, money from bank* sacar; *tooth* sacar, extraer; *word from text* quitar, borrar; sacar; *insurance policy* suscribir; **he took her out to dinner** la llevó a cenar; **take the dog out** sacar al perro a pasear; **take the kids out to the park** llevar a los niños al parque; **don't take it out on me!** ¡no la pagues conmigo!

♦ **take over 1** *v/t company etc* absorber, adquirir; **tourists took over the town** los turistas invadieron la ciudad **2** *v/i of new management etc* asumir el cargo; *of new government* asumir el poder; (*do sth in s.o.'s place*) tomar el relevo

♦ **take to** *v/t* (*like*): **how did they take to the new idea?** ¿qué les pareció la nueva idea?; **I immediately took to him** me cayó bien de inmediato; **he has taken to getting up early** le ha dado por levantarse temprano; **she took to drink** se dio a la bebida

♦ **take up** *v/t carpet etc* levantar; (*carry up*) subir; (*shorten: dress etc*) acortar; *hobby* empezar a hacer; *subject* empezar a estudiar; *offer* aceptar; *new job* comenzar; *space, time* ocupar; **I'll take you up on your offer** aceptaré tu oferta

'**take-home pay** salario *m* neto

tak·en ['teɪkən] *pp* → **take**

'**take-off** *of airplane* despegue *m*, *L.Am.* decolaje *m*; (*impersonation*) imitación *f*; '**take-o·ver** COM absorción *f*, adquisición *f*; '**take-o·ver bid** oferta *f* pública de adquisición, OPA *f*

ta·kings ['teɪkɪŋz] *npl* recaudación *f*

tal·cum pow·der ['tælkəmpaʊdər] polvos *mpl* de talco

tale [teɪl] cuento *m*, historia *f*

tal·ent ['tælənt] talento *m*

tal·ent·ed ['tæləntɪd] *adj* con talento; **she's very ~** tiene mucho talento

'**tal·ent scout** cazatalentos *m inv*

talk [tɔːk] **1** *v/i* hablar; **can I talk to …?** ¿podría hablar con …?; **I'll ~ to him about it** hablaré del tema con él **2** *v/t English etc* hablar; **~ business / politics** hablar de negocios / de política; **~ s.o. into sth** persuadir a alguien para que haga algo **3** *n* (*conversation*) charla *f*, *C.Am.*, *Mex* plática *f*; (*lecture*) conferencia *f*, **give a ~ on sth** dar una conferencia sobre algo; **~s** negociaciones *fpl*; **he's all ~** *pej* habla mucho y no hace nada

♦ **talk back** *v/i* responder, contestar

♦ **talk down to** *v/t* hablar con aires de superioridad a

♦ **talk over** *v/t* hablar de, discutir

talk·a·tive ['tɔːkətɪv] *adj* hablador

talk·ing-to ['tɔːkɪŋtuː] sermón *m*, rapapolvo *m*; **give s.o. a good ~** echar a alguien un buen sermón *or* rapapolvo 'talk show programa *m* de entrevistas

tall [tɔːl] *adj* alto; *it is ten meters ~* mide diez metros de alto

tall 'or·der: *that's a ~* eso es muy difícil

tall 'sto·ry cuento *m* chino

tal·ly ['tælɪ] **1** *n* cuenta *f* **2** *v/i* (*pret & pp* **-ied**) cuadrar, encajar
♦ tally with *v/t* cuadrar con, encajar con

tame [teɪm] *adj animal* manso, domesticado; *joke etc* soso
♦ tam·per with ['tæmpər] *v/t lock* intentar forzar; *brakes* tocar

tam·pon ['tæmpɑːn] tampón *m*

tan [tæn] **1** *n from sun* bronceado *m*; *(color)* marrón *m* claro; *get a ~* ponerse moreno **2** *v/i* (*pret & pp* **-ned**) *in sun* broncearse **3** *v/t* (*pret & pp* **-ned**) *leather* curtir

tan·dem ['tændəm] *(bike)* tándem *m*

tan·gent ['tændʒənt] MATH tangente *f*

tan·ge·rine [tændʒə'riːn] mandarina *f*

tan·gi·ble ['tændʒɪbl] *adj* tangible

tan·gle ['tæŋgl] *n* lío *m*, maraña *f*
♦ tangle up: *get tangled up of string etc* quedarse enredado

tan·go ['tæŋgou] *n* tango *m*

tank [tæŋk] *for water* depósito *m*, tanque *m*; *for fish* pecera *f*; MOT depósito *m*; MIL, *for skin diver* tanque *m*

tank·er ['tæŋkər] *truck* camión *m* cisterna; *ship* buque *m* cisterna; *for oil* petrolero *m*

'tank top camisa *f* sin mangas

tanned [tænd] *adj* moreno, bronceado

Tan·noy® ['tænɔɪ] megafonía *f*

tan·ta·liz·ing ['tæntəlaɪzɪŋ] *adj* sugerente

tan·ta·mount ['tæntəmaunt] *adj*: *be ~ to* equivaler a

tan·trum ['tæntrəm] rabieta *f*

tap [tæp] **1** *n (faucet)* grifo *m*, *L.Am.* llave *f* **2** *v/t* (*pret & pp* **-ped**) *(knock)* dar un golpecito en; *phone* intervenir
♦ tap into *v/t resources* explotar

'tap dance *n* claqué *m*

tape [teɪp] **1** *n* cinta *f* **2** *v/t conversation etc* grabar; *with sticky tape* pegar con cinta adhesiva

'tape deck pletina *f*; 'tape drive COMPUT unidad *f* de cinta; 'tape meas·ure cinta *f* métrica

tap·er ['teɪpər] *v/i* estrecharse
♦ taper off *v/i of production, figures* disminuir

'tape re·cor·der magnetofón *m*, *L.Am.* grabador *m*

'tape re·cor·ding grabación *f* (magnetofónica)

ta·pes·try ['tæpɪstrɪ] *cloth* tapiz *m*; *art* tapicería *f*

'tape·worm tenia *f*, solitaria *f*

tar [tɑːr] *n* alquitrán *m*

tar·dy ['tɑːrdɪ] *adj* tardío

tar·get ['tɑːrgɪt] **1** *n in shooting* blanco *m*; *for sales, production* objetivo *m* **2** *v/t market* apuntar a

'tar·get 'au·di·ence audiencia *f* a la que está orientado el programa; 'tar·get date fecha *f* fijada; 'tar·get 'fig·ure cifra *f* objetivo; 'tar·get group COM grupo *m* estratégico; 'tar·get mar·ket mercado *m* objetivo

tar·iff ['tærɪf] *(price)* tarifa *f*; *(tax)* arancel *m*

tar·mac ['tɑːrmæk] *for road surface* asfalto *m*; *at airport* pista *f*

tar·nish ['tɑːrnɪʃ] *v/t metal* deslucir, deslustrar; *reputation* empañar

tar·pau·lin [tɑːr'pɔːlɪn] lona *f* *(impermeable)*

tart [tɑːrt] *n* tarta *f*, pastel *m*

tar·tan ['tɑːrtn] tartán *m*

task [tæsk] tarea *f*

'task force *for a special job* equipo *m* de trabajo; MIL destacamento *m*

tas·sel ['tæsl] borla *f*

taste [teɪst] **1** *n* gusto *m*; *of food etc* sabor *m*; *he has no ~* tiene mal gusto **2** *v/t also fig* probar

taste·ful ['teɪstfəl] *adj* de buen gusto

taste·ful·ly ['teɪstfəlɪ] *adv* con buen gusto

taste·less ['teɪstlɪs] *adj food* insípido; *remark* de mal gusto

tast·ing ['teɪstɪŋ] *of wine* cata *f*, degustación *f*

tast·y ['teɪstɪ] *adj* sabroso, rico

tat·tered ['tætərd] *adj clothes* andrajoso; *book* destrozado

tat·ters ['tætərz]: **in ~** *clothes* hecho jirones; *reputation, career* arruinado

tat·too [tə'tu:] *n* tatuaje *m*

tat·ty ['tætɪ] *adj* F sobado, gastado

taught [tɔ:t] *pret & pp* → **teach**

taunt [tɔ:nt] **1** *n* pulla *f* **2** *v/t* mofarse de

Taur·us ['tɔ:rəs] ASTR Tauro *m/f inv*

taut [tɔ:t] *adj* tenso

taw·dry ['tɔ:drɪ] *adj* barato, cursi

tax [tæks] **1** *n* impuesto *m*; *before/ after ~* sin descontar / descontando impuestos **2** *v/t people* cobrar impuestos a; *product* gravar

tax·a·ble '**in·come** ingresos *mpl* gravables

ta·x·a·tion [tæk'seɪʃn] (*act of taxing*) imposición *f* de impuestos; (*taxes*) fiscalidad *f*, impuestos *mpl*

'**tax avoid·ance** elusión *f* legal de impuestos; '**tax brack·et** banda *f* impositiva; '**tax-de·duct·i·ble** *adj* desgravable; '**tax eva·sion** evasión *f* fiscal; '**tax-free** *adj* libre de impuestos; '**tax ha·ven** paraíso *m* fiscal

tax·i ['tæksɪ] *n* taxi *m*

'**tax·i driv·er** taxista *m/f*

tax·ing ['tæksɪŋ] *adj* difícil, arduo

'**tax in·spec·tor** inspector(a) *m(f)* de Hacienda

'**tax·i rank** parada *f* de taxis

'**tax·pay·er** contribuyente *m/f*; '**tax re·turn** *form* declaración *f* de la renta; '**tax year** año *m* fiscal

TB [ti:'bi:] *abbr* (= *tuberculosis*) tuberculosis *f*

tea [ti:] *drink* té *m*; *meal* merienda *f*

tea·bag ['ti:bæg] bolsita *f* de té

teach [ti:tʃ] **1** *v/t* (*pret & pp* **taught**) *person, subject* enseñar; *~ s.o. to do sth* enseñar a alguien a hacer algo **2** *v/i* (*pret & pp* **taught**): *I taught at that school* di clases en ese colegio; *he always wanted to ~* siempre quiso ser profesor

tea·cher ['ti:tʃər] *at primary school*

maestro(-a) *m(f)*; *at secondary school, university* profesor(a) *m(f)*

tea·cher 'train·ing formación *f* pedagógica, magisterio *m*

tea·ching ['ti:tʃɪŋ] *profession* enseñanza *f*, docencia *f*

'**tea·ching aid** material *m* didáctico

'**tea cloth** paño *m* de cocina; '**tea·cup** taza *f* de té; '**tea 'drink·er** bebedor(a) *m(f)* de té

'**tea leaf** hoja *f* de té

team [ti:m] equipo *m*

'**team·mate** compañero(-a) *m(f)* de equipo

team 'spir·it espíritu *m* de equipo

team·ster ['ti:mstər] camionero(-a) *m(f)*

'**team·work** trabajo *m* en equipo

'**tea·pot** tetera *f*

tear[1] [ter] **1** *n in cloth etc* desgarrón *m*, rotura *f* **2** *v/t* (*pret* **tore**, *pp* **torn**) *paper, cloth* rasgar; *be torn between two alternatives* debatirse entre dos alternativas **3** *v/i* (*run fast, drive fast*) (*pret* **tore**, *pp* **torn**) (*run fast, drive fast*) ir a toda velocidad

♦ **tear down** *v/t poster* arrancar; *building* derribar

♦ **tear out** *v/t* arrancar

♦ **tear up** *v/t paper* romper, rasgar; *agreement* romper

tear[2] [tɪr] *in eye* lágrima *f*; *burst into ~s* echarse a llorar; *be in ~s* estar llorando

tear·drop ['tɪrdrɑ:p] lágrima *f*

tear·ful ['tɪrfəl] *adj* lloroso

'**tear gas** gas *m* lacrimógeno

tease [ti:z] *v/t person* tomar el pelo a, burlarse de; *animal* hacer rabiar

'**tea·spoon** *object* cucharilla *f*; *quantity* cucharadita *f*

teat [ti:t] teta *f*

tech·ni·cal ['teknɪkl] *adj* técnico

tech·ni·cal·i·ty [teknɪ'kælətɪ] (*technical nature*) tecnicismo *m*; LAW detalle *m* técnico

tech·ni·cal·ly ['teknɪklɪ] *adv* técnicamente

tech·ni·cian [tek'nɪʃn] técnico(-a) *m(f)*

T

tech·nique [tek'niːk] técnica *f*

tech·no·log·i·cal [teknə'lɑːdʒɪkl] *adj* tecnológico

tech·nol·o·gy [tek'nɑːlədʒɪ] tecnología *f*

tech·no·phob·i·a [teknə'foʊbɪə] rechazo *m* de las nuevas tecnologías

ted·dy bear ['tedɪbər] osito *m* de peluche

te·di·ous ['tiːdɪəs] *adj* tedioso

tee [tiː] *n* in golf tee *m*

teem [tiːm] *v/i*: *be ~ing with rain* llover a cántaros; *be ~ing with tourists/ants* estar abarrotado de turistas/lleno de hormigas

teen·age ['tiːneɪdʒ] *adj fashions* adolescente, juvenil; *a ~ boy/girl* un adolescente/una adolescente

teen·ag·er ['tiːneɪdʒər] adolescente *m/f*

teens [tiːnz] *npl* adolescencia *f*; *be in one's ~* ser un adolescente; *reach one's ~* alcanzar la adolescencia

tee·ny ['tiːnɪ] *adj* F chiquitín F

teeth [tiːθ] *pl → tooth*

teethe [tiːð] *v/i* echar los dientes

'teeth·ing prob·lems *npl* problemas *mpl* iniciales

tel·e·com·mu·ni·ca·tions [telɪkəmjuːnɪ'keɪʃnz] telecomunicaciones *fpl*

tel·e·gram ['telɪɡræm] telegrama *m*

tel·e·graph pole ['telɪɡræf] poste *m* telegráfico

tel·e·path·ic [telɪ'pæθɪk] *adj* telepático; *you must be ~!* ¡debes tener telepatía!

te·lep·a·thy [tɪ'lepəθɪ] telepatía *f*

tel·e·phone ['telɪfoʊn] **1** *n* teléfono *m*; *be on the ~* (*be speaking*) estar hablando por teléfono; (*possess a phone*) tener teléfono **2** *v/t person* telefonear, llamar por teléfono a **3** *v/i* telefonear, llamar por teléfono

'tel·e·phone bill factura *f* del teléfono; **'tel·e·phone book** guía *f* telefónica, listín *m* telefónico; **'tel·e·phone booth** cabina *f* telefónica; **'tel·e·phone call** llamada *f* telefónica; **'tel·e·phone con·ver·sa·tion** conversación *f* por teléfono *or* telefónica; **'tel·e·phone di·rec·to·ry** guía *f* telefónica, listín *m* telefónico; **'tel·e·phone ex·change** central *f* telefónica, centralita *f*; **'tel·e·phone mes·sage** mensaje *m* telefónico; **'tel·e·phone num·ber** número *m* de teléfono

tel·e·pho·to lens [telɪ'foʊtoʊlenz] teleobjetivo *m*

tel·e·sales ['telɪseɪlz] televentas *fpl*

tel·e·scope ['telɪskoʊp] telescopio *m*

tel·e·thon ['telɪθaːn] maratón *m* benéfico televisivo

tel·e·vise ['telɪvaɪz] *v/t* televisar

tel·e·vi·sion ['telɪvɪʒn] televisión *f*; *set* televisión *f*, televisor *m*; *on ~* en *or* por (la) televisión; *watch ~* ver la televisión

'tel·e·vi·sion au·di·ence audiencia *f* televisiva; **'tel·e·vi·sion pro·gram**, *Br* **'tel·e·vi·sion pro·gramme** programa *m* televisivo; **'tel·e·vision set** televisión *f*, televisor *m*; **'tel·e·vi·sion stu·di·o** estudio *m* de televisión

tell [tel] **1** *v/t* (*pret & pp told*) *story* contar; *lie* decir, contar; *I can't ~ the difference* no veo la diferencia; *s.o. sth* decir algo a alguien; *don't ~ Mom* no se lo digas a mamá; *could you ~ me the way to ...?* ¿me podría decir por dónde se va a ...?; *~ s.o. to do sth* decir a alguien que haga algo; *you're ~ing me!* F ¡a mí me lo vas a contar! **2** *v/i* (*pret & pp told*) (*have effect*) hacerse notar; *the heat is ~ing on him* el calor está empezando a afectarle; *time will ~* el tiempo lo dirá

tell·er ['telər] cajero(-a) *m(f)*

tell·ing ['telɪŋ] *adj* contundente

tell·ing 'off regañina *f*

tell·tale ['telteɪl] **1** *adj signs* revelador **2** *n* chivato(-a) *m(f)*

temp [temp] **1** *n employee* trabajador(a) *m(f)* temporal **2** *v/i* hacer trabajo temporal

tem·per ['tempər] (*bad ~*) mal humor *m*; *be in a ~* estar de mal humor; *keep one's ~* mantener la calma; *lose one's ~* perder los estribos

tem·pe·ra·ment ['temprəmənt] temperamento *m*

tem·pe·ra·men·tal [temprə'mentl] *adj* (*moody*) temperamental

tem·pe·rate ['tempərət] *adj* templado

tem·pe·ra·ture ['temprətʃər] temperatura *f*; (*fever*) fiebre *f*; **have a ~** tener fiebre

tem·ple¹ ['templ] REL templo *m*

tem·ple² ['templ] ANAT sien *f*

tem·po ['tempou] tempo *m*

tem·po·rar·i·ly [tempə'rerılı] *adv* temporalmente

tem·po·ra·ry ['tempəreri] *adj* temporal

tempt [tempt] *v/t* tentar

temp·ta·tion [temp'teıʃn] tentación *f*

tempt·ing ['temptıŋ] *adj* tentador

ten [ten] diez

te·na·cious [tı'neıʃəs] *adj* tenaz

te·nac·i·ty [tı'næsıtı] tenacidad *f*

ten·ant ['tenənt] *of building* inquilino(-a) *m(f)*; *of farm, land* arrendatario(-a) *m(f)*

tend¹ [tend] *v/t* (*look after*) cuidar (de)

tend² [tend]: **~ to do sth** soler hacer algo; **~ toward sth** tender hacia algo

ten·den·cy ['tendənsı] tendencia *f*

ten·der¹ ['tendər] *adj* (*sore*) sensible, delicado; (*affectionate*) cariñoso, tierno; *steak* tierno

ten·der² ['tendər] *n* COM oferta *f*

ten·der·ness ['tendərnıs] (*soreness*) dolor *m*; *of kiss etc* cariño *m*, ternura *f*

ten·don ['tendən] tendón *m*

ten·nis ['tenıs] tenis *m*

'**ten·nis ball** pelota *f* de tenis; '**ten·nis court** pista *f* de tenis, cancha *f* de tenis; '**ten·nis pla·yer** tenista *m/f*; '**ten·nis rack·et** raqueta *f* de tenis

ten·or ['tenər] MUS tenor *m*

tense¹ [tens] *n* GRAM tiempo *m*

tense² [tens] *adj muscle, moment* tenso; *voice, person* tenso, nervioso

♦ **tense up** *v/i* ponerse tenso

ten·sion ['tenʃn] *of rope, in movie, novel* tensión *f*; *in atmosphere, voice* tensión *f*, tirantez *f*

tent [tent] tienda *f*

ten·ta·cle ['tentəkl] tentáculo *m*

ten·ta·tive ['tentətıv] *adj move, offer* provisional

ten·ter·hooks ['tentərhuks]: **be on ~** estar sobre ascuas

tenth [tenθ] **1** *adj* décimo **2** *n* décimo *m*, décima parte *f*; *of second, degree* décima *f*

tep·id ['tepıd] *adj water, reaction* tibio

term [tɜːrm] *in office etc* mandato *m*; *Br* EDU trimestre *m*; (*condition*) término *m*, condición *f*; (*word*) término *m*; **be on good/bad ~s with s.o.** llevarse bien/mal con alguien; **in the long/short ~** a largo/corto plazo; **come to ~s with sth** llegar a aceptar algo

ter·mi·nal ['tɜːrmınl] **1** *n at airport, for buses, containers* terminal *f*; ELEC, COMPUT terminal *m*; *of battery* polo *m* **2** *adj illness* terminal

ter·mi·nal·ly ['tɜːrmınəlı] *adv*: **~ ill** en la fase terminal de una enfermedad

ter·mi·nate ['tɜːrmıneıt] **1** *v/t contract* rescindir; *pregnancy* interrumpir **2** *v/i* finalizar

ter·mi·na·tion [tɜːrmı'neıʃn] *of contract* rescisión *f*; *of pregnancy* interrupción *f*

ter·mi·nol·o·gy [tɜːrmı'nɑːlədʒı] terminología *f*

ter·mi·nus ['tɜːrmınəs] *for buses* final *m* de trayecto; *for trains* estación *f* terminal

ter·race ['terəs] terraza *f*

ter·ra cot·ta [terə'kɑːtə] *adj* de terracota

ter·rain [te'reın] terreno *m*

ter·res·tri·al [te'restrıəl] **1** *n* terrestre *m* **2** *adj television* por vía terrestre

ter·ri·ble ['terəbl] *adj* terrible, horrible

ter·ri·bly ['terəblı] *adv* (*very*) tremendamente

ter·rif·ic [tə'rıfık] *adj* estupendo

ter·rif·i·cal·ly [tə'rıfıklı] *adv* (*very*)

tremendamente

ter·ri·fy ['terɪfaɪ] *v/t* (*pret & pp* **-ied**) aterrorizar; *be terrified* estar aterrorizado

ter·ri·fy·ing ['terɪfaɪɪŋ] *adj* aterrador

ter·ri·to·ri·al [terɪ'tɔːrɪəl] *adj* territorial

ter·ri·to·ri·al 'wa·ters *npl* aguas *fpl* territoriales

ter·ri·to·ry ['terɪtɔːrɪ] territorio *m*; *fig* ámbito *m*, territorio *m*

ter·ror ['terər] terror *m*

ter·ror·ism ['terərɪzm] terrorismo *m*

ter·ror·ist ['terərɪst] terrorista *m/f*

'ter·ror·ist at·tack atentado *m* terrorista

'ter·ror·ist or·gan·i·za·tion organización *f* terrorista

ter·ror·ize ['terəraɪz] *v/t* aterrorizar

terse [tɜːrs] *adj* tajante, seco

test [test] **1** *n* prueba *f*; *academic, for driving* examen *m* **2** *v/t* probar, poner a prueba

tes·ta·ment ['testəmənt] *to s.o.'s life etc* testimonio *m*; *Old/New Testament* REL Viejo/Nuevo Testamento *m*

'test-drive *v/t* (*pret* **-drove**, *pp* **-driven**) *car* probar en carretera

tes·ti·cle ['testɪkl] testículo *m*

tes·ti·fy ['testɪfaɪ] *v/i* (*pret & pp* **-ied**) LAW testificar, prestar declaración

tes·ti·mo·ni·al [testɪ'mounɪəl] *n* referencias *fpl*

tes·ti·mo·ny ['testɪmənɪ] LAW testimonio *m*

'test tube tubo *m* de ensayo, probeta *f*

'test-tube ba·by niño(-a) *m(f)* probeta

tes·ty ['testɪ] *adj* irritable

te·ta·nus ['tetənəs] tétanos *m*

teth·er ['teðər] **1** *v/t horse* atar **2** *n* correa *f*; *be at the end of one's ~* estar al punto de perder la paciencia

text [tekst] texto *m*

'text·book libro *m* de texto

tex·tile ['tekstaɪl] *n* textil *m*

tex·ture ['tekstʃər] textura *f*

Thai [taɪ] **1** *adj* tailandés **2** *n person*

tailandés(-esa) *m(f)*; *language* tailandés *m*

Thai·land ['taɪlænd] Tailandia

than [ðæn] *adv* que; *bigger/faster ~ me* más grande/más rápido que yo; *more than 50* más de 50

thank [θæŋk] *v/t* dar las gracias a; *~ you* gracias; *no ~ you* no, gracias

thank·ful ['θæŋkfəl] *adj* agradecido; *we have to be ~ that ...* tenemos que dar gracias de que ...

thank·ful·ly ['θæŋkfəlɪ] *adv* (*luckily*) afortunadamente

thank·less ['θæŋklɪs] *adj task* ingrato

thanks [θæŋks] *npl* gracias *fpl*; *~!* ¡gracias!; *~ to* gracias a

Thanks·giv·ing (Day) [θæŋks'gɪvɪndeɪ] Día *m* de Acción de Gracias

that [ðæt] **1** *adj* ese *m*, esa *f*; *more remote* aquel *m*, aquella; *~ one* ése **2** *pron* ése *m*, ésa; *more remote* aquél *m*, aquella *f*; *what is ~?* ¿qué es eso?; *who is ~?* ¿quién es ése?; *~'s mine* ése es mío; *~'s tea* es té; *~'s very kind* qué amable **3** *rel pron* que; *the person/car ~ you see* el coche/la persona que ves **4** *conj* que; *I think ~ ...* creo que ... **5** *adv* (*so*) tan; *~ big/expensive* tan grande/caro

thaw [θɔː] *v/i of snow* derretirse, fundirse; *of frozen food* descongelarse

the [ðə] el, la; *plural* los, las; *~ sooner ~ better* cuanto antes, mejor

the·a·ter ['θɪətər] teatro *m*

'the·a·ter crit·ic crítico *m* teatral

the·a·tre Br → **theater**

the·at·ri·cal [θɪ'ætrɪkl] *adj also fig* teatral

theft [θeft] robo *m*

their [ðer] *adj* su; (*his or her*) su; *~ brother* su hermano; *~ books* sus libros

theirs [ðerz] *pron* el suyo, la suya; *~ are red* los suyos son rojos; *that book is ~* ese libro es suyo; *a friend of ~* un amigo suyo

them [ðem] *pron direct object* los *mpl*, las *fpl*; *indirect object* les; *after prep* ellos *mpl*, ellas *fpl*; *I know ~* los/las conozco; *I gave ~ the keys* les di las llaves; *I sold it to* ~ se lo vendí; *he lives with* ~ vive con ellos / ellas; *if a person asks for help, you should help* ~ si una persona pide ayuda, hay que ayudarla

theme [θi:m] tema *m*

'**theme park** parque *m* temático

'**theme song** tema *m* musical

them·selves [ðem'selvz] *pron reflexive* se; *emphatic* ellos mismos *mpl*, ellas mismas *fpl*; **they hurt** ~ se hicieron daño; *when they saw* ~ *in the mirror* cuando se vieron en el espejo; *they saw it* ~ lo vieron ellos mismos; *by* ~ (*alone*) solos; (*without help*) ellos solos, ellos mismos

then [ðen] *adv* (*at that time*) entonces; (*after that*) luego, después; *deducing* entonces; *by* ~ para entonces

the·o·lo·gian [θɪə'loʊdʒɪən] teólogo *m*

the·ol·o·gy [θɪ'ɑːlədʒɪ] teología *f*

the·o·ret·i·cal [θɪə'retɪkl] *adj* teórico

the·o·ret·i·cal·ly [θɪə'retɪklɪ] *adv* en teoría

the·o·ry ['θɪrɪ] teoría *f*; *in* ~ en teoría

ther·a·peu·tic [θerə'pjuːtɪk] *adj* terapéutico

ther·a·pist ['θerəpɪst] terapeuta *m/f*

ther·a·py ['θerəpɪ] terapia *f*

there [ðer] *adv* allí, ahí, allá; *over* ~ allí, ahí, allá; *down* ~ allí *or* ahí *or* allá abajo; ~ *is / are* ... hay ...; ~ *is / are not* ... no hay ...; ~ *you are giving sth* aquí tienes; *finding sth* aquí está; *completing sth* ya está; ~ *and back* ida y vuelta; *it's 5 miles* ~ *and back* entre ida y vuelta hay cinco millas; ~ *he is!* ¡ahí está!; ~, ~! ¡venga!

there·a·bouts [ðerə'baʊts] *adv* aproximadamente

there·fore ['ðerfɔːr] *adv* por (lo) tanto

ther·mom·e·ter [θər'mɑːmɪtər] termómetro *m*

ther·mos flask ['θɜːrməs] termo *m*

ther·mo·stat ['θɜːrməstæt] termostato *m*

these [ðiːz] **1** *adj* estos(-as) **2** *pron* éstos *mpl*, éstas *fpl*

the·sis ['θiːsɪs] (*pl* **theses** ['θiːsiːz])

tesis *f inv*

they [ðeɪ] *pron* ellos *mpl*, ellas *fpl*; ~ *are Mexican* son mexicanos; ~*'re going, but we're not* ellos van, pero nosotros no; *if anyone looks at this*, ~ *will see that* ... si alguien mira esto, verá que ...; ~ *say that* ... dicen que ...; ~ *are going to change the law* van a cambiar la ley

thick [θɪk] *adj soup* espeso; *fog* denso; *wall, book* grueso; *hair* poblado; F (*stupid*) corto; *it's 3 cm* ~ tiene 3 cm de grosor

thick·en ['θɪkən] *v/t sauce* espesar

thick·set [θɪkset] *adj* fornido

thick-skinned [θɪk'skɪnd] *adj fig* insensible

thief [θiːf] (*pl* **thieves** [θiːvz]) ladrón(-ona) *m(f)*

thigh [θaɪ] muslo *m*

thim·ble ['θɪmbl] dedal *m*

thin [θɪn] *adj person* delgado; *hair* ralo, escaso; *soup* claro; *coat, line* fino

thing [θɪŋ] cosa *f*; ~*s* (*belongings*) cosas *fpl*; *how are* ~*s*? ¿cómo te va?; *it's a good* ~ *you told me* menos mal que me lo dijiste; *what a* ~ *to do / say!* ¡qué barbaridad!

thing·um·a·jig ['θɪŋʌmədʒɪg] F *object* chisme *m*; *person* fulanito *m*

think [θɪŋk] *v/t & v/i* (*pret & pp* **thought**) pensar; *hold an opinion* pensar, creer; *I* ~ *so* creo que sí; *I don't* ~ *so* creo que no; *I* ~ *so too* pienso lo mismo; *what do you* ~? ¿qué piensas *or* crees?; *what do you* ~ *of it?* ¿qué te parece?; *I can't* ~ *of anything more* no se me ocurre nada más; ~ *hard!* ¡piensa más!; *I'm* ~*ing about emigrating* estoy pensando en emigrar

◆ **think over** *v/t* reflexionar sobre

◆ **think through** *v/t* pensar bien

◆ **think up** *v/t plan* idear

'**think tank** grupo *m* de expertos

thin-skinned [θɪn'skɪnd] *adj* sensible

third [θɜːrd] **1** *adj* tercero **2** *n* tercero(a) *m(f)*; *fraction* tercio *m*, tercera parte *f*

third·ly ['θɜːrdlɪ] *adv* en tercer lugar

third 'par·ty tercero *m*; **third-par·ty**

in·sur·ance seguro *m* a terceros;
third 'per·son GRAM tercera persona *f*; **'third-rate** *adj* de tercera, de
pacotilla F; **Third 'World** Tercer
Mundo *m*

thirst [θɜːrst] sed *f*

thirst·y ['θɜːrstɪ] *adj* sediento; **be ~**
tener sed

thir·teen [θɜːr'tiːn] trece

thir·teenth [θɜːr'tiːnθ] *n & adj* deci-
motercero

thir·ti·eth ['θɜːrtɪɪθ] *n & adj* trigésimo

thir·ty ['θɜːrtɪ] treinta

this [ðɪs] **1** *adj* este *m*, esta *f*; **~ one**
éste **2** *pron* esto *m*, esta *f*; **~ is good**
esto es bueno; **~ is ... introducing s.o.**
éste / ésta es ...; TELEC soy ... **3** *adv*: **~**
big / high así de grande / de alto

thorn [θɔːrn] espina *f*

thorn·y ['θɔːrnɪ] *adj also fig* espinoso

thor·ough ['θɜːrou] *adj search* minucioso; *knowledge* profundo; *person*
concienzudo

thor·ough·bred ['θɜːroubred] *horse*
purasangre *m*

thor·ough·ly ['θɜːroulɪ] *adv* completamente; *clean up* a fondo; *search* minuciosamente; *I'm ~ ashamed* estoy avergonzadísimo

those [ðouz] **1** *adj* esos *mpl*, esas *fpl*;
more remote aquellos *mpl*, aquellas
fpl **2** *pron* ésos *mpl*, ésas *fpl*; *more*
remote aquéllos *mpl*, aquéllas *mpl*

though [ðou] **1** *conj* (*although*) aunque; *as ~* como si **2** *adv* sin embargo;
it's not finished ~ pero no está acabado

thought[1] [θɔːt] *single* idea *f*; *collective*
pensamiento *m*

thought[2] [θɔːt] *pret & pp* → **think**

thought·ful ['θɔːtfəl] *adj* pensativo;
book serio; (*considerate*) atento

thought·less ['θɔːtlɪs] *adj* desconsiderado

thou·sand ['θauznd] mil *m*; **~s of** miles de; *a ~ and ten* mil diez

thou·sandth ['θauzndθ] *n & adj* milé-
simo

thrash [θræʃ] *v/t* golpear, dar una paliza a; SP dar una paliza a

♦ **thrash around** *v/i with arms etc* re-

volverse

♦ **thrash out** *v/t solution* alcanzar

thrash·ing ['θræʃɪŋ] *also* SP paliza *f*

thread [θred] **1** *n* hilo *m*; *of screw* rosca *f* **2** *v/t needle* enhebrar; *beads* ensartar

thread·bare ['θredber] *adj* raído

threat [θret] amenaza *f*

threat·en ['θretn] *v/t* amenazar

threat·en·ing ['θretnɪŋ] *adj* amenazador

three [θriː] tres

three-'quart·ers tres cuartos *mpl*

thresh [θreʃ] *v/t corn* trillar

thresh·old ['θreʃhould] *of house, new*
age umbral *m*; *on the ~ of* en el umbral *or* en puertas de

threw [θruː] *pret* → **throw**

thrift [θrɪft] ahorro *m*

thrift·y ['θrɪftɪ] *adj* ahorrativo

thrill [θrɪl] **1** *n* emoción *f*, estremeci-
miento *m* **2** *v/t*: *be ~ed* estar entusiasmado

thrill·er ['θrɪlər] *movie* película *f* de
Span suspense *or L.Am.* suspenso;
novel novela *f* de *Span* suspense *or*
L.Am. suspenso

thrill·ing ['θrɪlɪŋ] *adj* emocionante

thrive [θraɪv] *v/i of plant* medrar, crecer bien; *of business, economy* prosperar

throat [θrout] garganta *f*

'throat loz·enge pastilla *f* para la
garganta

throb [θrɑːb] **1** *n of heart* latido *m*; *of*
music zumbido *m* **2** *v/i* (*pret & pp*
-bed) *of heart* latir; *of music* zumbar

throm·bo·sis [θrɑːm'bousɪs] trombosis *f*

throne [θroun] trono *m*

throng [θrɑːŋ] *n* muchedumbre *f*

throt·tle ['θrɑːtl] **1** *n on motorbike*
acelerador *m*; *on boat* palanca *f* del
gas; *on motorbike* mango *m* del gas
2 *v/t* (*strangle*) estrangular

♦ **throttle back** *v/i* desacelerar

through [θruː] **1** *prep* ◊ (*across*) a través de; *go ~ the city* atravesar la
ciudad ◊ (*during*) durante; **~ the**
winter / summer durante el invierno / verano; *Monday ~ Friday* de lu-

nes a viernes ◊ (*by means of*) a través de, por medio de; **arranged ~ him** acordado por él **2** *adv*: **wet ~** completamente mojado; **watch a movie ~** ver una película de principio a fin **3** *adj*: **be ~ of couple** haber terminado; (*have arrived: of news etc*) haber llegado; **you're ~** TELEC ya puede hablar; **I'm ~ with ...** (*finished with*) he terminado con ...

'**through flight** vuelo *m* directo

through-out[θruː'aʊt] **1** *prep* durante, a lo largo de **2** *adv* (*in all parts*) en su totalidad

'**through train** tren *m* directo

throw [θroʊ] **1** *v/t* (*pret* **threw**, *pp* **thrown**) tirar; *of horse* tirar, desmontar; (*disconcert*) desconcertar; *party* dar **2** *n* lanzamiento *m*; **it's your ~** te toca tirar

◆ **throw away** *v/t* tirar, *L.Am.* botar

◆ **throw off** *v/t jacket etc* quitarse rápidamente; *cold etc* deshacerse de

◆ **throw on** *v/t clothes* ponerse rápidamente

◆ **throw out** *v/t old things* tirar, *L.Am.* botar; *from bar, job, home* echar; *from country* expulsar; *plan* rechazar

◆ **throw up 1** *v/t ball* lanzar hacia arriba; **throw up one's hands** echarse las manos a la cabeza **2** *v/i* (*vomit*) vomitar

'**throw-a-way** *adj remark* insustancial, pasajero; (*disposable*) desechable

'**throw-in** SP saque *m* de banda

thrown [θroʊn] *pp* → **throw**

thru [θruː] → **through**

thrush [θrʌʃ] *bird* zorzal *m*

thrust [θrʌst] *v/t* (*pret* & *pp* **thrust**) (*push hard*) empujar; *knife* hundir; **~ sth into s.o.'s hands** poner algo en las manos de alguien; **~ one's way through the crowd** abrirse paso a empujones entre la multitud

thud [θʌd] *n* golpe *m* sordo

thug [θʌg] matón *m*

thumb [θʌm] **1** *n* pulgar *m* **2** *v/t*: **~ a ride** hacer autoestop

thumb-tack ['θʌmtæk] chincheta *f*

thump [θʌmp] **1** *n blow* porrazo *m*;

noise golpe *m* sordo **2** *v/t person* dar un porrazo a; **~ one's fist on the table** pegar un puñetazo en la mesa **3** *v/i of heart* latir con fuerza; **~ on the door** aporrear la puerta

thun-der ['θʌndər] *n* truenos *mpl*

thun-der-ous ['θʌndərəs] *adj applause* tormenta *f*

thun-der-storm ['θʌndərstɔːrm] tormenta *f* (*con truenos*)

'**thun-der-struck** *adj* atónito

thun-der-y ['θʌndərɪ] *adj weather* tormentoso

Thurs-day ['θɜːrzdeɪ] jueves *m inv*

thus [ðʌs] *adv* (*in this way*) así

thwart [θwɔːrt] *v/t person, plans* frustrar

thyme [taɪm] tomillo *m*

thy-roid gland ['θaɪrɔɪdglænd] (glándula *f*) tiroides *m inv*

tick [tɪk] **1** *n of clock* tictac *m*; (*checkmark*) señal *f* de visto bueno **2** *v/i of clock* hacer tictac

tick-et ['tɪkɪt] *for bus, train, lottery* billete *m*, *L.Am.* boleto *m*; *for airplane* billete *m*, *L.Am.* pasaje *m*; *for theater, concert, museum* entrada *f*, *L.Am.* boleto *m*; *for speeding etc* multa *f*

'**tick-et col-lec-tor** revisor(a) *m(f)*; '**tick-et in-spec-tor** revisor(a) *m(f)*; '**tick-et ma-chine** máquina *f* expendedora de billetes; '**tick-et of-fice** *at station* mostrador *m* de venta de billetes; THEA taquilla *f*, *L.Am.* boletería *f*

tick-ing ['tɪkɪŋ] *noise* tictac *m*

tick-le ['tɪkl] **1** *v/t person* hacer cosquillas a **2** *v/i of material* hacer cosquillas; **stop that, you're tickling!** ¡para ya, me haces cosquillas!

tick-lish ['tɪklɪʃ] *adj*: **be ~ of person** tener cosquillas

ti-dal wave ['taɪdlweɪv] maremoto *m* (*ola*)

tide [taɪd] marea *f*; **high ~** marea alta; **low ~** marea baja; **the ~ is in/out** la marea está alta/baja

◆ **tide over** *v/t*: **20 dollars will tide me over** 20 dólares me bastarán

ti-di-ness ['taɪdɪnɪs] orden *m*

ti-dy ['taɪdɪ] *adj* ordenado

♦ **tidy away** v/t (pret & pp **-ied**) guardar

♦ **tidy up 1** v/t room, shelves ordenar; **tidy o.s. up** arreglarse **2** v/i recoger

tie [taɪ] **1** n (necktie) corbata f; SP (even result) empate m; **he doesn't have any ~s** no está atado a nada **2** v/t knot hacer, atar; hands atar; ~ **two ropes together** atar dos cuerdas **3** v/i SP empatar

♦ **tie down** v/t also fig atar

♦ **tie up** v/t person, laces atar; boat amarrar; hair recoger; **I'm tied up tomorrow** (busy) mañana estaré muy ocupado

tier [tɪr] of hierarchy nivel m; in stadium grada f

ti·ger ['taɪgər] tigre m

tight [taɪt] **1** adj clothes ajustado, estrecho; security estricto; (hard to move) apretado; (properly shut) cerrado; (not leaving much time) justo de tiempo; F (drunk) como una cuba F **2** adv hold fuerte; shut bien

tight·en ['taɪtn] v/t screw apretar; control endurecer; security intensificar; ~ **one's grip on sth** on rope etc asir algo con más fuerza; on power etc incrementar el control sobre algo

♦ **tighten up** v/i in discipline, security ser más estricto

tight-fist·ed [taɪt'fɪstɪd] adj agarrado

tight·ly ['taɪtlɪ] adv → **tight**

tight·rope ['taɪtroʊp] cuerda f floja

tights [taɪts] npl Br medias fpl, pantis mpl

tile [taɪl] on floor baldosa f; on wall azulejo m; on roof teja f

till[1] [tɪl] → **until**

till[2] [tɪl] n (cash register) caja f (registradora)

till[3] [tɪl] v/t soil labrar

tilt [tɪlt] **1** v/t inclinar **2** v/i inclinarse

tim·ber ['tɪmbər] madera f (de construcción)

time [taɪm] tiempo m; (occasion) vez f; ~ **is up** se acabó (el tiempo); **for the ~ being** por ahora, por el momento; **have a good ~** pasarlo bien; **have a good ~!** ¡que lo paséis bien!;

what's the ~?, do you have the ~? ¿qué hora es?; **the first ~** la primera vez; **four ~s** cuatro veces; ~ **and again** una y otra vez; **all the ~** todo el rato; **two / three at a ~** de dos en dos / de tres en tres; **at the same ~** speak, reply etc a la vez; (however) al mismo tiempo; **in ~** con tiempo; **on ~** puntual; **in no ~** en un santiamén

'**time bomb** bomba f de relojería; '**time clock** in factory reloj m registrador; '**time-con·sum·ing** adj que lleva mucho tiempo; '**time dif·fer·ence** diferencia f horaria; '**time-lag** intervalo m; '**time lim·it** plazo m

time·ly ['taɪmlɪ] adj oportuno

'**time out** SP tiempo m muerto

tim·er ['taɪmər] device temporizador m; person cronometrador m

'**time-sav·ing** n ahorro m de tiempo; '**time-scale** of project plazo m (de tiempo); '**time switch** temporizador m; '**time-warp** salto m en el tiempo; '**time zone** huso m horario

tim·id ['tɪmɪd] adj tímido

tim·ing ['taɪmɪŋ] of dancer sincronización f; of actor utilización f de las pausas y del ritmo; **the ~ of the announcement was perfect** el anuncio fue realizado en el momento perfecto

tin [tɪn] metal estaño m; Br (can) lata f

tin·foil ['tɪnfɔɪl] papel m de aluminio

tinge [tɪndʒ] n of color, sadness matiz m

tin·gle ['tɪŋgl] n hormigueo m

♦ **tin·ker with** ['tɪŋkər] v/t enredar con

tin·kle ['tɪŋkl] n of bell tintineo m

tin·sel ['tɪnsl] espumillón m

tint [tɪnt] **1** n of color matiz m; in hair tinte m **2** v/t hair teñir

tint·ed ['tɪntɪd] glasses con un tinte; paper coloreado

ti·ny ['taɪnɪ] adj diminuto, minúsculo

tip[1] [tɪp] n of stick, finger punta f; of mountain cumbre f; of cigarette filtro m

tip[2] [tɪp] **1** n advice consejo m; money propina f **2** v/t (pret & pp **-ped**) *waiter etc* dar propina a

♦ **tip off** *v/t* avisar

♦ **tip over** *v/t* jug volcar; *liquid* derramar; *he tipped water all over me* derramó agua encima mío

'**tip-off** soplo *m*

tipped [tɪpt] *adj cigarettes* con filtro

tip·py·toe ['tɪpɪtoʊ]: *on* ~ de puntillas

tip·sy ['tɪpsɪ] *adj* achispado

tire[1] [taɪr] *n* neumático *m*, *L.Am.* llanta *f*

tire[2] [taɪr] **1** *v/t* cansar, fatigar **2** *v/i* cansarse, fatigarse; *he never* ~*s of telling the story* nunca se cansa de contar la historia

tired [taɪrd] *adj* cansado, fatigado; *be* ~ *of s.o.* / *sth* estar cansado de algo / alguien

tired·ness ['taɪrdnɪs] cansancio *m*, fatiga *f*

tire·less ['taɪrlɪs] *adj efforts* incansable, infatigable

tire·some ['taɪrsəm] *adj (annoying)* pesado

tir·ing ['taɪrɪŋ] *adj* agotador

tis·sue ['tɪʃuː] ANAT tejido *m*; *(handkerchief)* pañuelo *m* de papel, Kleenex® *m*

'**tis·sue pa·per** papel *m* de seda

tit[1] [tɪt] *bird* herrerillo *m*

tit[2] [tɪt]: *give s.o.* ~ *for tat* pagar a alguien con la misma moneda

tit[3] [tɪt] V *(breast)* teta *f* V

ti·tle ['taɪtl] *of novel, person etc* título *m*; LAW título *m* de propiedad

'**ti·tle·hold·er** SP campeón(-ona) *m(f)*

tit·ter ['tɪtər] *v/i* reírse tontamente

to [tuː] *unstressed* [tə] **1** *prep* a; ~ *Japan* / *Chicago* a Japón / Chicago; *let's go* ~ *my place* vamos a mi casa; *walk* ~ *the station* caminar a la estación; ~ *the north* / *south of* ... al norte / sur de ...; *give sth* ~ *s.o.* dar algo a alguien; *from Monday* ~ *Wednesday* de lunes a miércoles; *from 10* ~ *15 people* de 10 a 15 personas **2** *with verbs:* ~ *speak* hablar; *learn* ~ *swim* aprender a nadar; *nice* ~ *eat* sabroso; *too heavy* ~

carry demasiado pesado para llevarlo; ~ *be honest with you* ... para ser sincero ... **3** *adv:* ~ *and fro* de un lado para otro

toad [toʊd] sapo *m*

toad·stool ['toʊdstuːl] seta *f* venenosa

toast [toʊst] **1** *n* pan *m* tostado; *when drinking* brindis *m inv*; *propose a* ~ *to s.o.* proponer un brindis en honor de alguien **2** *v/t when drinking* brindar por

toast·er ['toʊstər] tostador(a) *m(f)*

to·bac·co [tə'bækoʊ] tabaco *m*

to·bog·gan [tə'bɑːgən] *n* tobogán *m*

to·day [tə'deɪ] *adv* hoy

tod·dle ['tɑːdl] *v/i of child* dar los primeros pasos

tod·dler ['tɑːdlər] niño *m* pequeño

to·do [tə'duː] F revuelo *m*

toe [toʊ] **1** *n* dedo *m* del pie; *of shoe* puntera *f* **2** *v/t:* ~ *the line* acatar la disciplina

toe·nail ['toʊneɪl] uña *f* del pie

to·geth·er [tə'geðər] *adv* juntos(-as); *mix two drinks* ~ mezclar dos bebidas; *don't all talk* ~ no hablen todos a la vez

toil [tɔɪl] *n* esfuerzo *m*

toi·let ['tɔɪlɪt] *place* cuarto *m* de baño, servicio *m*; *equipment* retrete *m*; *go to the* ~ ir al baño

'**toi·let pa·per** papel *m* higiénico

toi·let·ries ['tɔɪlɪtrɪz] *npl* artículos *mpl* de tocador

'**toi·let roll** rollo *m* de papel higiénico

to·ken ['toʊkən] *(sign)* muestra *f*; *(gift* ~*)* vale *m*; *(disk)* ficha *f*

told [toʊld] *pret & pp* → **tell**

tol·e·ra·ble ['tɑːlərəbl] *adj pain etc* soportable; *(quite good)* aceptable

tol·e·rance ['tɑːlərəns] tolerancia *f*

tol·e·rant ['tɑːlərənt] *adj* tolerante

tol·e·rate ['tɑːləreɪt] *v/t noise, person* tolerar; *I won't* ~ *it!* ¡no lo toleraré!

toll[1] [toʊl] *v/i of bell* tañer

toll[2] [toʊl] *n (deaths)* mortandad *f*, número *m* de víctimas

toll[3] [toʊl] *n for bridge, road* peaje *m*; TELEC tarifa *f*

'toll booth cabina *f* de peaje; **'toll-free** *adj* TELEC gratuito; **'toll road** carretera *f* de peaje

to·ma·to [təˈmeɪtoʊ] tomate *m*, *Mex* jitomate *m*

to·ma·to **'ketch·up** ketchup *m*

to·ma·to **'sauce** *for pasta etc* salsa *f* de tomate

tomb [tuːm] tumba *f*

tom·boy [ˈtɑːmbɔɪ] niña *f* poco femenina

tomb·stone [ˈtuːmstoʊn] lápida *f*

tom·cat [ˈtɑːmkæt] gato *m*

to·mor·row [təˈmɔːroʊ] *adv* mañana; **the day after ~** pasado mañana; **~ morning** mañana por la mañana

ton [tʌn] tonelada *f* (907 *kg*)

tone [toʊn] *of color, conversation* tono *m*; *of musical instrument* timbre *m*; *of neighborhood* nivel *m*; **~ of voice** tono *m* de voz

◆ **tone down** *v/t demands, criticism* bajar el tono de

ton·er [ˈtoʊnər] tóner *m*

tongs [tɑːŋz] *npl* tenazas *fpl*; *for hair* tenacillas *fpl* de rizar

tongue [tʌŋ] *n* lengua *f*

ton·ic [ˈtɑːnɪk] MED tónico *m*

'ton·ic (**wa·ter**) (agua *f*) tónica *f*

to·night [təˈnaɪt] *adv* esta noche

ton·sil [ˈtɑːnsɪl] amígdala *f*

ton·sil·li·tis [tɑːnsəˈlaɪtɪs] amigdalitis *f*

too [tuː] *adv* (*also*) también; (*excessively*) demasiado; **me ~** yo también; **~ big / hot** demasiado grande / caliente; **~ much rice** demasiado arroz; **eat ~ much** comer demasiado

took [tuːk] *pret* → **take**

tool [tuːl] herramienta *f*

toot [tuːt] *v/t* F tocar

tooth [tuːθ] (*pl* **teeth** [tiːθ]) diente *m*

'tooth·ache dolor *m* de muelas

'tooth·brush cepillo *m* de dientes

tooth·less [ˈtuːθlɪs] *adj* desdentado

'tooth·paste pasta *f* de dientes, dentífrico *m*

'tooth·pick palillo *m*

top [tɑːp] **1** *n of mountain* cima *f*; *of tree* copa *f*; *of wall, screen, page* parte *f* superior; (*lid: of bottle etc*) tapón *m*; *of pen* capucha *f*; *clothing* camiseta *f*, top *m*; (MOT: *gear*) directa *f*; **on ~ of** encima de, sobre; **at the ~ of the page** en la parte superior de la página; **at the ~ of the mountain** en la cumbre; **be ~ of the class / league** ser el primero de la clase / de la liga; **get to the ~** *of company, mountain* llegar a la cumbre; **be over the ~** (*exaggerated*) ser una exageración **2** *adj branches* superior; *floor* de arriba, último; *management, official* alto; *player* mejor; *speed, note* máximo **3** *v/t* (*pret & pp* **-ped**): **~ped with** ... *of cake* con una capa de ... por encima

◆ **top up** *v/t glass, tank* llenar

top 'hat sombrero *m* de copa

top 'heav·y *adj* sobrecargado en la parte superior

top·ic [ˈtɑːpɪk] tema *m*

top·i·cal [ˈtɑːpɪkl] *adj* de actualidad

top·less [ˈtɑːplɪs] *adj* en topless

top·most [ˈtɑːpmoʊst] *adj branches, floor* superior

top·ping [ˈtɑːpɪŋ] *on pizza* ingrediente *m*

top·ple [ˈtɑːpl] **1** *v/i* derrumbarse **2** *v/t government* derrocar

top 'se·cret *adj* altamente confidencial

top·sy-tur·vy [tɑːpsɪˈtɜːrvɪ] *adj* (*in disorder*) desordenado; *world* al revés

torch [tɔːrtʃ] *with flame* antorcha *f*

tore [tɔːr] *pret* → **tear**

tor·ment 1 *n* [ˈtɔːrment] tormento *m* **2** *v/t* [tɔːrˈment] *person, animal* atormentar; **~ed by doubt** atormentado por la duda

torn [tɔːrn] *pp* → **tear**

tor·na·do [tɔːrˈneɪdoʊ] tornado *m*

tor·pe·do [tɔːrˈpiːdoʊ] **1** *n* torpedo *m* **2** *v/t also fig* torpedear

tor·rent [ˈtɑːrənt] *also fig* torrente *m*; *of lava* colada *f*

tor·ren·tial [təˈrenʃl] *adj rain* torrencial

tor·toise [ˈtɔːrtəs] tortuga *f*

tor·ture [ˈtɔːrtʃər] **1** *n* tortura *f* **2** *v/t*

torturar

toss [tɑːs] **1** v/t ball lanzar, echar; rider desmontar; salad remover; **~ a coin** echar a cara o cruz **2** v/i: **~ and turn** dar vueltas

to·tal [ˈtoʊtl] **1** n total m **2** adj sum, amount total; disaster rotundo, completo; idiot de tomo y lomo; stranger completo **3** v/t F car cargarse F; **the truck was ~ed** el camión quedó destrozado

to·tal·i·tar·i·an [toʊtælɪˈterɪən] adj totalitario

to·tal·ly [ˈtoʊtəlɪ] adv totalmente

tote bag [ˈtoʊtbæg] bolsa f grande

tot·ter [ˈtɑːtər] v/i of person tambalearse

touch [tʌtʃ] **1** n toque m; sense tacto m; **lose ~ with s.o.** perder el contacto con alguien; **keep in ~ with s.o.** mantenerse en contacto con alguien; **we kept in ~** seguimos en contacto; **be out of ~** no estar al corriente; **the leader was out of ~ with the people** el líder estaba desconectado de lo que pensaba la gente; **in ~** SP fuera **2** v/t tocar; emotionally conmover **3** v/i tocar; of two lines etc tocarse

♦ **touch down** v/i of airplane aterrizar; SP marcar un ensayo

♦ **touch on** v/t (mention) tocar, mencionar

♦ **touch up** v/t photo retocar; Br: sexually manosear

touch·down [ˈtʌtʃdaʊn] of airplane aterrizaje m; SP touchdown m, ensayo m

touch·ing [ˈtʌtʃɪŋ] adj conmovedor

touch·line [ˈtʌtʃlaɪn] SP línea f de banda

touch screen pantalla f táctil

touch·y [ˈtʌtʃɪ] adj person susceptible

tough [tʌf] adj person, meat, punishment duro; question, exam difícil; material resistente, fuerte

♦ **tough·en up** [ˈtʌfn] v/t person hacer más fuerte

tough guy F tipo m duro F

tour [tʊr] **1** n of museum etc recorrido m; of area viaje m (**of** por); of band etc

gira f **2** v/t area recorrer **3** v/i of band etc estar de gira

tour guide guía m/f turístico(-a)

tour·i·sm [ˈtʊrɪzm] turismo m

tour·ist [ˈtʊrɪst] turista m/f

tour·ist at·trac·tion atracción f turística; **tour·ist in·dus·try** industria f turística; **tour·ist (in·for·'ma·tion) of·fice** oficina f de turismo; **tour·ist sea·son** temporada f turística

tour·na·ment [ˈtɜrnəmənt] torneo m

tour op·er·a·tor operador m turístico

tous·led [ˈtaʊzld] adj hair revuelto

tow [toʊ] **1** v/t car, boat remolcar **2** n: **give s.o. a ~** remolcar a alguien

♦ **tow away** v/t car llevarse

to·ward [tɔːrd] prep hacia; **we are working ~ a solution** estamos intentando encontrar una solución

tow·el [ˈtaʊəl] toalla f

tow·er [ˈtaʊər] n torre m

♦ **tower over** v/t of building elevarse por encima de; of person ser mucho más alto que

town [taʊn] ciudad f; small pueblo m

town 'cen·ter, Br **town 'cen·tre** centro m de la ciudad / del pueblo; **town 'coun·cil** ayuntamiento m; **town 'hall** ayuntamiento m

'tow·rope cuerda f para remolcar

tox·ic [ˈtɑːksɪk] adj tóxico

tox·ic 'waste residuos mpl tóxicos

tox·in [ˈtɑːksɪn] BIO toxina f

toy [tɔɪ] juguete m

'toy store juguetería f, tienda f de juguetes

♦ **toy with** v/t object juguetear con; idea darle vueltas a

trace [treɪs] **1** n of substance resto m **2** v/t (find) localizar; (follow: footsteps of) seguir el rastro a; (draw) trazar

track [træk] n (path) senda f, camino m; for horses hipódromo m; for dogs canódromo m; for cars circuito m; for athletics pista f; on CD canción f, corte m; RAIL vía f; **~ 10** RAIL vía 10; **keep ~ of sth** llevar la cuenta de algo

◆ **track down** v/t localizar

'**track·suit** chándal m

trac·tor ['træktər] tractor m

trade [treɪd] **1** n (commerce) comercio m; (profession, craft) oficio m **2** v/i (do business) comerciar; **~ in sth** comerciar en algo **3** v/t (exchange) intercambiar; **~ sth for sth** intercambiar algo por algo

◆ **trade in** v/t when buying entregar como parte del pago

'**trade fair** feria f de muestras; '**trade·mark** marca f registrada; '**trade mis·sion** misión f comercial

trad·er ['treɪdər] comerciante m

trade 'se·cret secreto m de la casa, secreto m comercial

trades·man ['treɪdzmən] (plumber etc) electricista, fontanero / plomero etc

tra·di·tion [trə'dɪʃn] tradición f

tra·di·tion·al [trə'dɪʃnl] adj tradicional

tra·di·tion·al·ly [trə'dɪʃnlɪ] adv tradicionalmente

traf·fic ['træfɪk] n on roads, in drugs tráfico m

◆ **traffic in** v/t (pret & pp **-ked**) drugs traficar con

'**traf·fic cir·cle** rotonda f, Span glorieta; '**traf·fic cop** F poli m de tráfico F; '**traf·fic is·land** isleta f; '**traf·fic jam** atasco m; '**traf·fic light** semáforo m; '**traf·fic po·lice** policía f de tráfico; '**traf·fic sign** señal f de tráfico

tra·ge·dy ['trædʒədɪ] tragedia f

tra·gic ['trædʒɪk] adj trágico

trail [treɪl] **1** n (path) camino m, senda f; of blood rastro m **2** v/t (follow) seguir la pista de; (tow) arrastrar **3** v/i (lag behind) ir a la zaga

trail·er ['treɪlər] pulled by vehicle remolque m; (mobile home) caravana f; of film avance m, tráiler m

train[1] [treɪn] n tren m; **go by ~** ir en tren

train[2] [treɪn] **1** v/t team, athlete entrenar; employee formar; dog adiestrar **2** v/i of team, athlete entrenarse; of teacher etc formarse

train·ee [treɪ'niː] aprendiz(a) m(f)

train·er ['treɪnər] SP entrenador(a) m(f); of dog adiestrador(a) m(f)

train·ers ['treɪnərz] npl Br shoes zapatillas fpl de deporte

train·ing ['treɪnɪŋ] of new staff formación f; SP entrenamiento m; **be in ~** SP estar entrenándose; **be out of ~** SP estar desentrenado

'**train·ing course** cursillo m de formación

'**train·ing scheme** plan m de formación

'**train sta·tion** estación f de tren

trait [treɪt] rasgo m

trai·tor ['treɪtər] traidor(a) m(f)

tram·ple ['træmpl] v/t pisotear; **be ~d to death** morir pisoteado; **be ~d underfoot** ser pisoteado

◆ **trample on** v/t person, object pisotear

tram·po·line ['træmpəliːn] cama f elástica

trance [træns] trance m; **go into a ~** entrar en trance

tran·quil ['træŋkwɪl] adj tranquilo

tran·quil·i·ty [træŋ'kwɪlətɪ] tranquilidad f

tran·quil·iz·er ['træŋkwɪlaɪzər] tranquilizante m

trans·act [træn'zækt] v/t deal negociar

trans·ac·tion [træn'zækʃn] action transacción f; deal negociación f

trans·at·lan·tic [trænzət'læntɪk] adj transatlántico

tran·scen·den·tal [trænsen'dentl] adj trascendental

tran·script ['trænskrɪpt] transcripción f

trans·fer 1 v/t [træns'fɜːr] (pret & pp **-red**) transferir **2** v/i (pret & pp **-red**) in traveling hacer transbordo; from one language to another etc pasar **3** n ['trænsfɜːr] also of money transferencia f; in travel transbordo m

trans·fer·a·ble [træns'fɜːrəbl] adj ticket transferible

'**trans·fer fee** for football player traspaso m

trans·form [trænsˈfɔːrm] *v/t* transformar

trans·form·a·tion [trænsfərˈmeɪʃn] transformación *f*

trans·form·er [trænsˈfɔːrmər] ELEC transformador *m*

trans·fu·sion [trænsˈfjuːʒn] transfusión *f*

tran·sis·tor [trænˈzɪstər] transistor *m*; (*radio*) transistor *m*, radio *m* transistor

tran·sit [ˈtrænzɪt]: **in ~** en tránsito

tran·si·tion [trænˈsɪʒn] transición *f*

tran·si·tion·al [trænˈsɪʒnl] *adj* de transición

'tran·sit lounge *at airport* sala *f* de tránsito

'trans·it pas·sen·ger pasajero *m* en tránsito

trans·late [trænsˈleɪt] *v/t & v/i* traducir

trans·la·tion [trænsˈleɪʃn] traducción *f*

trans·la·tor [trænsˈleɪtər] traductor(a) *m(f)*

trans·mis·sion [trænzˈmɪʃn] *of news, program* emisión *f*; *of disease,* MOT transmisión *f*

trans·mit [trænzˈmɪt] *v/t* (*pret & pp -ted*) *news, program* emitir; *disease* transmitir

trans·mit·ter [trænzˈmɪtər] *for radio, TV* emisora *f*

trans·par·en·cy [trænsˈpærənsɪ] PHOT diapositiva *f*

trans·par·ent [trænsˈpærənt] *adj* transparente; (*obvious*) obvio

trans·plant MED **1** *v/t* [trænsˈplænt] transplantar **2** *n* [ˈtrænsplænt] transplante *m*

trans·port 1 *v/t* [trænsˈpɔːrt] *goods, people* transportar **2** *n* [ˈtrænspɔːrt] *of goods, people* transporte *m*

trans·por·ta·tion [trænspɔːrˈteɪʃn] *of goods, people* transporte *m*; **means of ~** medio *m* de transporte; **public ~** transporte *m* público; **Department of Transportation** Ministerio *m* de Transporte

trans·ves·tite [trænsˈvestaɪt] travestí *m*, travestido *m*

trap [træp] **1** *n* trampa *f*; **set a ~ for s.o.** tender una trampa a alguien **2** *v/t* (*pret & pp -ped*) atrapar; **be ~ped** *by enemy, flames, landslide etc* quedar atrapado

'trap·door [ˈtræpdɔːr] trampilla *f*

tra·peze [trəˈpiːz] trapecio *m*

trap·pings [ˈtræpɪŋz] *npl of power* parafernalia *f*

trash [træʃ] (*garbage*) basura *f*; (*poor product*) bazofia *f*; (*despicable person*) escoria *f*

'trash·can [ˈtræʃkæn] cubo *m* de la basura

trash·y [ˈtræʃɪ] *adj goods* barato

trau·mat·ic [trəˈmætɪk] *adj* traumático

trau·ma·tize [ˈtraʊmətaɪz] *v/t* traumatizar

trav·el [ˈtrævl] **1** *n* viajes *mpl*; **do you like ~?** ¿te gusta viajar?; **on my ~s** en mis viajes **2** *v/i* (*pret & pp -ed, Br -led*) viajar **3** *v/t miles* viajar, recorrer

'trav·el a·gen·cy agencia *f* de viajes; **'trav·el a·gent** agente *m* de viajes; **'trav·el bag** bolsa *f* de viaje

trav·el·er, *Br* **trav·el·ler** [ˈtrævələr] viajero(-a) *m(f)*

'trav·el·er's check, *Br* **'trav·el·ler's cheque** cheque *m* de viaje

'trav·el ex·pens·es *npl* gastos *mpl* de viaje; **'trav·el in·sur·ance** seguro *m* de asistencia en viajes; **'trav·el pro·gram,** *Br* **'trav·el pro·gramme** *on TV etc* programa *m* de viajes; **'trav·el·sick** *adj* mareado

trawl·er [ˈtrɔːlər] (*barco m*) arrastrero *m*

tray [treɪ] bandeja *f*

treach·er·ous [ˈtretʃərəs] *adj* traicionero

treach·er·y [ˈtretʃərɪ] traición *f*

tread [tred] **1** *n* pasos *mpl*; *of staircase* huella *f* (del peldaño); *of tire* dibujo *m* **2** *v/i* (*pret* **trod**, *pp* **trodden**) andar; **mind where you ~** cuida dónde pisas

♦ **tread on** *v/t s.o.'s foot* pisar

trea·son [ˈtriːzn] traición *f*

trea·sure [ˈtreʒər] **1** *n also person* tesoro *m* **2** *v/t gift etc* apreciar mucho

trea·sur·er ['treʒərər] tesorero(-a) *m(f)*

Trea·sur·y De·part·ment ['treʒərı] Ministerio *m* de Hacienda

treat [tri:t] **1** *n* placer *m*; *it was a real ~* fue un auténtico placer; *I have a ~ for you* tengo una sorpresa agradable para ti; *it's my ~* (*I'm paying*) yo invito **2** *v/t* tratar; *~ s.o. to sth* invitar a alguien a algo

treat·ment ['tri:tmənt] tratamiento *m*

treat·y ['tri:tı] tratado *m*

tre·ble¹ ['trebl] *n* MUS soprano *m*

tre·ble² ['trebl] **1** *adv*: *~ the price* el triple del precio **2** *v/i* triplicarse

tree [tri:] árbol *m*

trem·ble ['trembl] *v/i* temblar

tre·men·dous [trı'mendəs] *adj* (*very good*) estupendo; (*enormous*) enorme '

tre·men·dous·ly [trı'mendəslı] *adv* (*very*) tremendamente; (*a lot*) enormemente

trem·or ['tremər] *of earth* temblor *m*

trench [trentʃ] trinchera *f*

trend [trend] tendencia *f*; (*fashion*) moda *f*

trend·y ['trendı] *adj* de moda; *views* moderno

tres·pass ['trespæs] *v/i* entrar sin autorización; *no ~ing* prohibido el paso

♦ **trespass on** *v/t land* entrar sin autorización en; *privacy* entrometerse en

tres·pass·er ['trespæsər] intruso(-a) *m(f)*

tri·al ['traɪəl] LAW juicio *m*; *of equipment* prueba *f*; *be on ~* LAW estar siendo juzgado; *have sth on ~ equipment* tener algo a prueba

tri·al 'pe·ri·od periodo *m* de prueba

tri·an·gle ['traɪæŋgl] triángulo *m*

tri·an·gu·lar [traɪ'æŋgjʊlər] *adj* triangular

tribe [traɪb] tribu *f*

tri·bu·nal [traɪ'bju:nl] tribunal *m*

tri·bu·ta·ry ['trɪbjətərı] *of river* afluente *m*

trick [trık] **1** *n* (*to deceive, knack*) truco *m*; *play a ~ on s.o.* gastar una broma a alguien **2** *v/t* engañar; *~ s.o. into doing sth* engañar a alguien para que haga algo

trick·e·ry ['trıkərı] engaños *mpl*

trick·le ['trıkl] **1** *n* hilo *m*, reguero *m*; *fig: of money* goteo *m* **2** *v/i* gotear, escurrir

trick·ster ['trıkstər] embaucador(a) *m(f)*

trick·y ['trıkı] *adj* (*difficult*) difícil

tri·cy·cle ['traısıkl] triciclo *m*

tri·fle ['traıfl] *n* (*triviality*) nadería *f*

tri·fling ['traıflıŋ] *adj* insignificante

trig·ger ['trıgər] *n on gun* gatillo *m*; *on camcorder* disparador *m*

♦ **trigger off** *v/t* desencadenar

trim [trım] **1** *adj* (*neat*) muy cuidado; *figure* delgado **2** *v/t* (*pret & pp -med*) *hair, hedge* recortar; *budget, costs* recortar, reducir; (*decorate: dress*) adornar **3** *n* (*light cut*) recorte *m*; *just a ~, please* to hairdresser corte sólo las puntas, por favor; *in good ~* en buenas condiciones

trim·ming ['trımıŋ] *on clothes* adorno *m*; *with all the ~s* dish con la guarnición clásica; *car* con todos los extras

trin·ket ['trıŋkıt] baratija *f*

tri·o ['tri:oʊ] MUS trío *m*

trip [trıp] **1** *n* (*journey*) viaje *m* **2** *v/i* (*pret & pp -ped*) (*stumble*) tropezar **3** *v/t* (*pret & pp -ped*) (*make fall*) poner la zancadilla a

♦ **trip up 1** *v/t* (*make fall*) poner la zancadilla a; (*cause to go wrong*) confundir **2** *v/i* (*stumble*) tropezar; (*make a mistake*) equivocarse

tripe [traıp] *to eat* mondongo *m*, *Span* callos *mpl*

trip·le ['trıpl] → **treble**

trip·lets ['trıplıts] *npl* trillizos *mpl*

tri·pod ['traıpa:d] PHOT trípode *m*

trite [traıt] *adj* manido

tri·umph ['traıʌmf] *n* triunfo *m*

triv·i·al ['trıvıəl] *adj* trivial

triv·i·al·i·ty [trıvı'ælətı] trivialidad *f*

trod [tra:d] *pret* → **tread**

trod·den ['tra:dn] *pp* → **tread**

trol·ley ['tra:lı] (*streetcar*) tranvía *f*

trom·bone [trɑ:m'boʊn] trombón *m*

troops [tru:ps] *npl* tropas *fpl*

tro·phy ['troʊfɪ] trofeo *m*

tro·pic ['trɑ:pɪk] trópico *m*

trop·i·cal ['trɑ:pɪkl] *adj* tropical

trop·ics ['trɑ:pɪks] *npl* trópicos *mpl*

trot [trɑ:t] *v/i* (*pret & pp* **-ted**) trotar

trou·ble ['trʌbl] **1** *n* (*difficulties*) problema *m*, problemas *mpl*; (*inconvenience*) molestia *f*; (*disturbance*) conflicto *m*, desorden *m*; **go to a lot of ~ to do sth** complicarse mucho la vida para hacer algo; **no ~!** no es molestia; **get into ~** meterse en líos **2** *v/t* (*worry*) preocupar, inquietar; (*bother, disturb*) molestar

'**trou·ble-free** *adj* sin complicaciones; '**trou·ble·mak·er** *m*(*f*); '**trou·ble·shoot·er** *persona encargada de resolver problemas*; '**trou·bleshoot·ing** resolución *f* de problemas

trou·ble·some ['trʌblsəm] *adj* problemático

trou·sers ['traʊzərz] *npl Br* pantalones *mpl*

trout [traʊt] (*pl* **trout**) trucha *f*

tru·ant ['tru:ənt]: **play ~** hacer novillos, *Mex* irse de pinta, *S. Am.* hacerse la rabona

truce [tru:s] tregua *f*

truck [trʌk] camión *m*

'**truck driv·er** camionero(-a) *m*(*f*); '**truck farm** huerta *f*; '**truck farm·er** horticultor(a) *m*(*f*); '**truck stop** restaurante *m* de carretera

trudge [trʌdʒ] **1** *v/i* caminar fatigosamente **2** *n* caminata *f*

true [tru:] *adj* verdadero, cierto; *friend, American* auténtico; **come ~** *of hopes, dream* hacerse realidad

trul·y ['tru:lɪ] *adv* verdaderamente, realmente; **Yours ~** le saluda muy atentamente

trum·pet ['trʌmpɪt] *n* trompeta *f*

trum·pet·er ['trʌmpɪtər] trompetista *m*/*f*

trunk [trʌŋk] *of tree, body* tronco *m*; *of elephant* trompa *f*; (*large case*) baúl *m*; *of car* maletero *m*, *C.Am.*, *Mex* cajuela *f*, *Rpl* baúl *m*

trust [trʌst] **1** *n* confianza *f*; FIN fondo *m* de inversión **2** *v/t* confiar en

trust·ed ['trʌstɪd] *adj* de confianza

trust·ee [trʌs'ti:] fideicomisario(-a) *m*(*f*)

trust·ful, trust·ing ['trʌstfʊl, 'trʌstɪŋ] *adj* confiado

trust·wor·thy ['trʌstwɜ:rðɪ] *adj* de confianza

truth [tru:θ] verdad *f*

truth·ful ['tru:θfəl] *adj person* sincero; *account* verdadero

try [traɪ] **1** *v/t* (*pret & pp* **-ied**) probar; LAW juzgar; **~ to do sth** intentar hacer algo, tratar de hacer algo **2** *v/i* (*pret & pp* **-ied**): **he didn't even ~** ni siquiera lo intentó; **you must ~ harder** debes esforzarte más **3** *n* intento *m*; **can I have a ~?** *of food* ¿puedo probar?; *at doing sth* ¿puedo intentarlo?

♦ **try on** *v/t clothes* probar

♦ **try out** *v/t new machine, new method* probar

try·ing ['traɪɪŋ] *adj* (*annoying*) molesto, duro

T-shirt ['ti:ʃɜ:rt] camiseta *f*

tub [tʌb] (*bath*) bañera *f*, *L. Am.* tina *f*; *for liquid* cuba *f*; *for yoghurt, ice cream* envase *m*

tub·by ['tʌbɪ] *adj* rechoncho

tube [tu:b] tubo *m*

tube·less ['tu:blɪs] *adj tire* sin cámara de aire

tu·ber·cu·lo·sis [tu:bɜ:rkjə'loʊsɪs] tuberculosis *f*

tuck [tʌk] **1** *n in dress* pinza *f* **2** *v/t* (*put*) meter

♦ **tuck away** *v/t* (*put away*) guardar; F (*eat quickly*) zamparse F

♦ **tuck in 1** *v/t children* arropar; *sheets* remeter **2** *v/i* (*start eating*) ponerse a comer

♦ **tuck up** *v/t sleeves etc* remangar; **tuck s.o. up in bed** meter a alguien en la cama

Tues·day ['tu:zdeɪ] martes *m inv*

tuft [tʌft] *of hair* mechón *m*; *of grass* mata *f*

tug [tʌg] **1** *n* (*pull*) tirón *m*; NAUT remolcador *m* **2** *v/t* (*pret & pp* **-ged**)

(*pull*) tirar de

tu·i·tion [tuː'ɪʃn] clases *fpl*

tu·lip ['tuːlɪp] tulipán *m*

tum·ble ['tʌmbl] *v/i* caer, caerse

tum·ble-down ['tʌmbldaʊn] *adj* destartalado

tum·bler ['tʌmblər] *for drink* vaso *m*; *in circus* acróbata *m/f*

tum·my ['tʌmɪ] F tripa *f* F, barriga *f* F

'**tum·my ache** dolor *m* de tripa *or* barriga

tu·mor, *Br* **tu·mour** ['tuːmər] tumor *m*

tu·mult ['tuːmʌlt] tumulto *m*

tu·mul·tu·ous [tuː'mʌlʃʊəs] *adj* tumultuoso

tu·na ['tuːnə] atún *m*

tune [tuːn] **1** *n* melodía *f*; *be in ~ of instrument* estar afinado; *sing in ~* cantar sin desafinar; *be out of ~ of singer* desafinar; *of instrument* estar desafinado **2** *v/t instrument* afinar

◆ **tune in** *v/i Radio, TV* sintonizar

◆ **tune in to** *v/t Radio, TV* sintonizar (con)

◆ **tune up 1** *v/i of orchestra, players* afinar **2** *v/t engine* poner a punto

tune·ful ['tuːnfəl] *adj* melodioso

tun·er ['tuːnər] *hi-fi* sintonizador *m*

tune-up ['tuːnʌp] *of engine* puesta *f* a punto

tun·nel ['tʌnl] *n* túnel *m*

tur·bine ['tɜːrbaɪn] turbina *f*

tur·bu·lence ['tɜːrbjələns] *in air travel* turbulencia *f*

tur·bu·lent ['tɜːrbjələnt] *adj* turbulento

turf [tɜːrf] césped *m*; *piece* tepe *m*

Turk [tɜːrk] turco(-a) *m(f)*

Tur·key ['tɜːrkɪ] Turquía *f*

tur·key ['tɜːrkɪ] pavo *m*

Turk·ish ['tɜːrkɪʃ] **1** *adj* turco **2** *n language* turco *m*

tur·moil ['tɜːrmɔɪl] desorden *m*, agitación *f*

turn [tɜːrn] **1** *n* (*rotation*) vuelta *f*; *in road* curva *f*; *junction* giro *m*; *in vaudeville* número *m*; *take ~s in doing sth* turnarse para hacer algo; *it's my ~* me toca a mí; *it's not your ~ yet* no te toca todavía; *take a ~ at*

the wheel turnarse para conducir *or L.Am.* manejar; *do s.o. a good ~* hacer un favor a alguien **2** *v/t wheel* girar; *corner* dar la vuelta a; *~ one's back on s.o.* dar la espalda a alguien **3** *v/i of driver, car, wheel* girar; *of person: turn around* volverse; *~ left/right here* gira aquí a la izquierda/a la derecha; *it has ~ed sour/cold* se ha cortado/enfriado; *it ~ed blue* se volvió *or* puso azul; *he has ~ed 40* ha cumplido cuarenta años

◆ **turn around 1** *v/t object* dar la vuelta a; *company* dar un vuelco a; COM (*deal with*) procesar, preparar **2** *v/i of person* volverse, darse la vuelta; *of driver* dar la vuelta

◆ **turn away 1** *v/t* (*send away*) rechazar; *the doorman turned us away* el portero no nos dejó entrar **2** *v/i* (*walk away*) marcharse; (*look away*) desviar la mirada

◆ **turn back 1** *v/t edges, sheets* doblar **2** *v/i of walkers etc* volver; *in course of action* echarse atrás

◆ **turn down** *v/t offer, invitation* rechazar; *volume, TV, heating* bajar; *edge, collar* doblar

◆ **turn in 1** *v/i* (*go to bed*) irse a dormir **2** *v/t to police* entregar

◆ **turn off 1** *v/t TV, engine* apagar; *faucet* cerrar; *heater* apagar; *it turns me off* F *sexually* me quita las ganas F **2** *v/i of car, driver* doblar

◆ **turn on 1** *v/t TV, engine, heating* encender, *L.Am.* prender; *faucet* abrir; F *sexually* excitar F **2** *v/i of machine* encenderse, *L.Am.* prenderse

◆ **turn out 1** *v/t lights* apagar **2** *v/i: it turned out well* salió bien; *as it turned out* al final; *he turned out to be ...* resultó ser ...

◆ **turn over 1** *v/i in bed* darse la vuelta; *of vehicle* volcar, dar una vuelta de campana **2** *v/t* (*put upside down*) dar la vuelta a; *page* pasar; FIN facturar

◆ **turn up 1** *v/t collar* subirse; *volume, heating* subir **2** *v/i* (*arrive*) aparecer

turn·ing ['tɜːrnɪŋ] giro *m*

'**turn·ing point** punto *m* de inflexión

tur·nip ['tɜːrnɪp] nabo *m*

'**turn·out** *of people* asistencia *f*; '**turn·o·ver** FIN facturación *f*; **staff ~** rotación *f* de personal; '**turn·pike** autopista *f* de peaje; '**turn sig·nal** *on car* intermitente *m*; '**turn·stile** torniquete *m* (*de entrada*); '**turn·ta·ble** *of record player* plato *m*, visión

tur·quoise ['tɜːrkwɔɪz] *adj* turquesa

tur·ret ['tʌrɪt] *of castle* torrecilla *f*; *of tank* torreta *f*

tur·tle ['tɜːrtl] tortuga *f* (marina)

tur·tle·neck '**sweat·er** suéter *m* de cuello alto

tusk [tʌsk] colmillo *m*

tu·tor ['tuːtər] *at university* tutor *m*; (*private*) ~ profesor(a) *m(f)* particular

tu·xe·do [tʌkˈsiːdou] esmoquin *m*

TV [tiːˈviː] televisión *f*; **on ~** en la televisión

T'V din·ner menú *m* precocinado; **T'V guide** guía *f* televisiva; **T'V pro·gram**, *Br* **T'V pro·gramme** programa *m* de televisión

twad·dle ['twɑːdl] F tonterías *fpl*

twang [twæŋ] **1** *n in voice* entonación *f* nasal **2** *v/t guitar string* puntear

tweez·ers ['twiːzərz] *npl* pinzas *fpl*

twelfth [twelfθ] *n & adj* duodécimo

twelve [twelv] doce

twen·ti·eth ['twentɪɪθ] *n & adj* vigésimo

twen·ty ['twentɪ] veinte

twice [twaɪs] *adv* dos veces; ~ **as much** el doble

twid·dle ['twɪdl] *v/t* dar vueltas a; ~ **one's thumbs** holgazanear

twig [twɪg] *n* ramita *f*

twi·light ['twaɪlaɪt] crepúsculo *m*

twin [twɪn] gemelo *m*

'**twin beds** *npl* camas *fpl* gemelas

twinge [twɪndʒ] *of pain* punzada *f*

twin·kle ['twɪŋkl] *v/i of stars* parpa-

twin 'room habitación *f* con camas gemelas

'**twin town** ciudad *f* hermana

twirl [twɜːrl] **1** *v/t* hacer girar **2** *n of cream etc* voluta *f*

twist [twɪst] **1** *v/t* retorcer; ~ **one's ankle** torcerse el tobillo **2** *v/i of road, river* serpentear **3** *n in rope, road* vuelta *f*; *in plot, story* giro *m* inesperado

twist·y ['twɪstɪ] *adj road* serpenteante

twit [twɪt] F memo(-a) *m(f)* F

twitch [twɪtʃ] **1** *n nervous* tic *m* **2** *v/i* (*jerk*) moverse (ligeramente)

twit·ter ['twɪtər] *v/i of birds* gorjear

two [tuː] dos; **the ~ of them** los dos, ambos

two-faced ['tuːfeɪst] *adj* falso; '**two-stroke** *adj engine* de dos tiempos; **two-way** '**traf·fic** tráfico *m* en dos direcciones

ty·coon [taɪˈkuːn] magnate *m*

type [taɪp] **1** *n* (*sort*) tipo *m*, clase *f*; **what ~ of ...?** ¿qué tipo *or* clase de ...? **2** *v/i* (*use a keyboard*) escribir a máquina **3** *v/t with a typewriter* mecanografiar, escribir a máquina

'**type·set** *v/t* componer

'**type·writ·er** máquina *f* de escribir

ty·phoid ['taɪfɔɪd] fiebre *f* tifoidea

ty·phoon [taɪˈfuːn] tifón *m*

ty·phus ['taɪfəs] tifus *m*

typ·i·cal ['tɪpɪkl] *adj* típico; **that's ~ of you/ him!** ¡típico tuyo/de él!

typ·i·cal·ly ['tɪpɪklɪ] *adv* típicamente; ~ **American** típicamente americano

typ·ist ['taɪpɪst] mecanógrafo(-a) *m(f)*

ty·ran·ni·cal [tɪˈrænɪkl] *adj* tiránico

ty·ran·nize ['tɪrənaɪz] *v/t* tiranizar

ty·ran·ny ['tɪrənɪ] tiranía *f*

ty·rant ['taɪrənt] tirano(-a) *m(f)*

tyre *Br* → **tire**[1]

T

U

ug·ly ['ʌglɪ] *adj* feo

UK [juː'keɪ] *abbr* (= **United Kingdom**) RU *m* (= Reino *m* Unido)

ul·cer ['ʌlsər] úlcera *f*; *in mouth* llaga *f*

ul·ti·mate ['ʌltɪmət] *adj* (*final*) final; (*fundamental*) esencial; *the ~ car* (*best, definitive*) lo último en coches

ul·ti·mate·ly ['ʌltɪmətlɪ] *adv* (*in the end*) en última instancia

ul·ti·ma·tum [ʌltɪ'meɪtəm] ultimátum *m*

ul·tra·sound ['ʌltrəsaʊnd] MED ultrasonido *m*; (*scan*) ecografía *f*

ul·tra·vi·o·let [ʌltrə'vaɪələt] *adj* ultravioleta

um·bil·i·cal cord [ʌm'bɪlɪkl] cordón *m* umbilical

um·brel·la [ʌm'brelə] paraguas *m inv*

um·pire ['ʌmpaɪr] *n* árbitro *m*; *in tennis* juez *m/f* de silla

ump·teen [ʌmp'tiːn] *adj* F miles de F

UN [juː'en] *abbr* (= **United Nations**) ONU *f* (= Organización *f* de las Naciones Unidas)

un·a·ble [ʌn'eɪbl] *adj*: *be ~ to do sth* (*not know how to*) no saber hacer algo; (*not be in a position to*) no poder hacer algo

un·ac·cept·a·ble [ʌnək'septəbl] *adj* inaceptable; *it is ~ that* es inaceptable que

un·ac·count·a·ble [ʌnə'kaʊntəbl] *adj* inexplicable

un·ac·cus·tomed [ʌnə'kʌstəmd] *adj*: *be ~ to sth* no estar acostumbrado a algo

un·a·dul·ter·at·ed [ʌnə'dʌltəreɪtɪd] *adj fig* (*absolute*) absoluto

un·A·mer·i·can [ʌnə'merɪkən] *adj* poco americano; *activities* antiamericano

u·nan·i·mous [juː'nænɪməs] *adj verdict* unánime; *be ~ on* ser unánime

respecto a

u·nan·i·mous·ly [juː'nænɪməslɪ] *adv vote, decide* unánimemente

un·ap·proach·a·ble [ʌnə'proʊtʃəbl] *adj person* inaccesible

un·armed [ʌn'ɑːrmd] *adj person* desarmado; *~ combat* combate *m* sin armas

un·as·sum·ing [ʌnə'suːmɪŋ] *adj* sin pretensiones

un·at·tached [ʌnə'tætʃt] *adj* (*without a partner*) sin compromiso, sin pareja

un·at·tend·ed [ʌnə'tendɪd] *adj* desatendido; *leave sth ~* dejar algo desatendido

un·au·thor·ized [ʌn'ɒːθəraɪzd] *adj* no autorizado

un·a·void·a·ble [ʌnə'vɔɪdəbl] *adj* inevitable

un·a·void·a·bly [ʌnə'vɔɪdəblɪ] *adv*: *be ~ detained* entretenerse sin poder evitarlo

un·a·ware [ʌnə'wer] *adj*: *be ~ of* no ser consciente de

un·a·wares [ʌnə'werz] *adv* desprevenido; *catch s.o. ~* agarrar *or Span* coger a alguien desprevenido

un·bal·anced [ʌn'bælənst] *adj also* PSYCH desequilibrado

un·bear·a·ble [ʌn'berəbl] *adj* insoportable

un·beat·a·ble [ʌn'biːtəbl] *adj team* invencible; *quality* insuperable

un·beat·en [ʌn'biːtn] *adj team* invicto

un·be·knownst: [ʌnbɪ'noʊnst] *adj*: *~ to her* sin que ella lo supiera

un·be·lie·va·ble [ʌnbɪ'liːvəbl] *adj also* F increíble; *he's ~* F (*very good / bad*) es increíble

un·bi·as(s)ed [ʌn'baɪəst] *adj* imparcial

un·block [ʌn'blɑːk] *v/t pipe* desatascar

un·born [ʌnˈbɔːrn] *adj* no nacido

un·break·a·ble [ʌnˈbreɪkəbl] *adj plates* irrompible; *world record* inalcanzable

un·but·ton [ʌnˈbʌtn] *v/t* desabotonar

un·called-for [ʌnˈkɒːldfɔːr] *adj*: **be ~** estar fuera de lugar

un·can·ny [ʌnˈkænɪ] *adj resemblance* increíble, asombroso; *skill* inexplicable; *(worrying: feeling)* extraño, raro

un·ceas·ing [ʌnˈsiːsɪŋ] *adj* incesante

un·cer·tain [ʌnˈsɜːrtn] *adj future, origins* incierto; **be ~ about sth** no estar seguro de algo; *what will happen? – it's ~* ¿qué ocurrirá? – no se sabe

un·cer·tain·ty [ʌnˈsɜːrtntɪ] incertidumbre *f*; *there is still ~ about his health* todavía hay incertidumbre en torno a su estado de salud

un·checked [ʌnˈtʃekt] *adj*: *let sth go ~* no controlar algo

un·cle [ˈʌŋkl] tío *m*

un·com·for·ta·ble [ʌnˈkʌmftəbl] *adj chair* incómodo; *feel ~ about sth about decision etc* sentirse incómodo con algo; *I feel ~ with him* me siento incómodo con él

un·com·mon [ʌnˈkɑːmən] *adj* poco corriente, raro; *it's not ~* no es raro *or* extraño

un·com·pro·mis·ing [ʌnˈkɑːprəmaɪzɪŋ] *adj* inflexible

un·con·cerned [ʌnˈkɑːsɜːrnd] *adj* indiferente; *be ~ about s.o. / sth* no preocuparse por alguien / algo

un·con·di·tion·al [ʌnkənˈdɪʃnl] *adj* incondicional

un·con·scious [ʌnˈkɑːnʃəs] *adj* MED, PSYCH inconsciente; *knock ~* dejar inconsciente; *be ~ of sth* (*not aware*) no ser consciente de algo

un·con·trol·la·ble [ʌnkənˈtroʊləbl] *adj anger, children* incontrolable; *desire* incontrolable, irresistible

un·con·ven·tion·al [ʌnkənˈvenʃnl] *adj* poco convencional

un·co·op·er·a·tive [ʌnkoʊˈɑːpərətɪv] *adj*: **be ~** no estar dispuesto a colaborar

un·cork [ʌnˈkɔːrk] *v/t bottle* descorchar

un·cov·er [ʌnˈkʌvər] *v/t remove cover from* destapar; *plot, ancient remains* descubrir

un·dam·aged [ʌnˈdæmɪdʒd] *adj* intacto

un·daunt·ed [ʌnˈdɒːntɪd] *adj* impertérrito; *carry on ~* seguir impertérrito

un·de·cid·ed [ʌndɪˈsaɪdɪd] *adj question* sin resolver; *be ~ about s.o. / sth* estar indeciso sobre alguien / algo

un·de·ni·a·ble [ʌndɪˈnaɪəbl] *adj* innegable

un·de·ni·a·bly [ʌndɪˈnaɪəblɪ] *adv* innegablemente

un·der [ˈʌndər] **1** *prep* (*beneath*) debajo de, bajo; (*less than*) menos de; *~ the water* bajo el agua; *it is ~ review / investigation* está siendo revisado / investigado **2** *adv* (*anesthetized*) anestesiado

un·der·age *adj*: *~ drinking* el consumo de alcohol por menores de edad

un·der·arm *adv*: *throw a ball ~* lanzar una pelota soltándola por debajo de la altura del hombro

un·der·car·riage tren *m* de aterrizaje

un·der·cov·er *adj agent* secreto

un·der·cut *v/t* (*pret & pp -cut*) COM vender más barato que

un·der·dog *n*: *support the ~* apoyar al más débil

un·der·done *adj meat* poco hecho

un·der·es·ti·mate *v/t* subestimar

un·der·ex·posed *adj* PHOT subexpuesto

un·der·fed *adj* malnutrido

un·der·go *v/t* (*pret -went, pp -gone*) *surgery, treatment* ser sometido a; *experiences* sufrir; *the hotel is ~ing refurbishment* se están efectuando renovaciones en el hotel

un·der·grad·u·ate estudiante *m/f* universitario(-a) (*todavía no licenciado(a)*)

un·der·ground 1 *adj passages etc*

subterráneo; POL *resistance, newspaper etc* clandestino **2** *adv work* bajo tierra; **go ~** POL pasar a la clandestinidad

'**un·der·growth** maleza *f*

un·der'hand *adj* (*devious*) poco honrado

un·der'lie *v/t* (*pret* **-lay**, *pp* **-lain**) (*form basis of*) sostener

un·der'line *v/t text* subrayar

un·der'ly·ing *adj causes, problems* subyacente

un·der'mine *v/t s.o.'s position, theory* minar, socavar

un·der·neath [ʌndər'niːθ] **1** *prep* debajo de, bajo **2** *adv* debajo

'**un·der·pants** *npl* calzoncillos *mpl*

'**un·der·pass** *for pedestrians* paso *m* subterráneo

un·der·priv·i·leged [ʌndər'prɪvɪlɪdʒd] *adj* desfavorecido

un·der'rate *v/t* subestimar, infravalorar

'**un·der·shirt** camiseta *f*

un·der·sized [ʌndər'saɪzd] *adj* demasiado pequeño

'**un·der·skirt** enaguas *fpl*

un·der·staffed [ʌndər'stæft] *adj* sin suficiente personal

un·der·stand [ʌndər'stænd] **1** *v/t* (*pret & pp* **-stood**) entender, comprender; *language* entender; *I ~ that you ...* tengo entendido que ...; *they are understood to be in Canada* se cree que están en Canadá **2** *v/i* (*pret & pp* **-stood**) entender, comprender

un·der·stand·a·ble [ʌndər'stændəbl] *adj* comprensible

un·der·stand·a·bly [ʌndər'stændəblɪ] *adv* comprensiblemente

un·der·stand·ing [ʌndər'stændɪŋ] **1** *adj person* comprensivo **2** *n of problem, situation* interpretación *f*; (*agreement*) acuerdo *m*; **on the ~ that ...** (*condition*) a condición de que ...

'**un·der·state·ment** *n*: *that's an ~* ¡y te quedas corto!

un·der'take *v/t* (*pret* **-took**, *pp* **-taken**) *task* emprender; *~ to do sth*

(*agree to*) encargarse de hacer algo

un·der·tak·er ['ʌndərteɪkər] *Br* encargado *m* de una funeraria

'**un·der·tak·ing** (*enterprise*) proyecto *m*, empresa *f*; *give an ~ to do sth* comprometerse a hacer algo

un·der'val·ue *v/t* infravalorar

'**un·der·wear** ropa *f* interior

un·der'weight *adj*: *be ~* pesar menos de lo normal

'**un·der·world** *criminal* hampa *f*; *in mythology* Hades *m*

un·der'write *v/t* (*pret* **-wrote**, *pp* **-written**) FIN asegurar, garantizar

un·de·served [ʌndɪ'zɜːrvd] *adj* inmerecido

un·de·sir·a·ble [ʌndɪ'zaɪrəbl] *adj features, changes* no deseado; *person* indeseable; *~ element person* persona *f* problemática

un·dis·put·ed [ʌndɪ'spjuːtɪd] *adj champion, leader* indiscutible

un·do [ʌn'duː] *v/t* (*pret* **-did**, *pp* **-done**) *parcel, wrapping* abrir; *buttons, shirt* desabrochar; *shoelaces* desatar; *s.o. else's work* deshacer

un·doubt·ed·ly [ʌn'daʊtɪdlɪ] *adv* indudablemente

un·dreamt-of [ʌn'dremtəv] *adj riches* inimaginable

un·dress [ʌn'dres] **1** *v/t* desvestir, desnudar; *get ~ed* desvestirse, desnudarse **2** *v/i* desvestirse, desnudarse

un·due [ʌn'duː] *adj* (*excessive*) excesivo

un·du·ly [ʌn'duːlɪ] *adv punished, blamed* injustamente; (*excessively*) excesivamente

un·earth [ʌn'ɜːrθ] *v/t* descubrir; *ancient remains* desenterrar

un·earth·ly [ʌn'ɜːrθlɪ] *adv*: *at this ~ hour* a esta hora intempestiva

un·eas·y [ʌn'iːzɪ] *adj relationship, peace* tenso; *feel ~ about* estar inquieto por

un·eat·a·ble [ʌn'iːtəbl] *adj* incomible

un·e·co·nom·ic [ʌniːkə'nɑːmɪk] *adj* antieconómico, no rentable

un·ed·u·cat·ed [ʌn'edʒəkeɪtɪd] *adj*

inculto, sin educación

un·em·ployed [ʌnɪmˈplɔɪd] adj desempleado, Span parado

un·em·ploy·ment [ʌnɪmˈplɔɪmənt] desempleo m, Span paro m

un·end·ing [ʌnˈendɪŋ] adj interminable

un·e·qual [ʌnˈiːkwəl] adj desigual; be ~ to the task no estar a la altura de lo que requiere el trabajo

un·er·ring [ʌnˈerɪŋ] adj judgement, instinct infalible

un·e·ven [ʌnˈiːvn] adj quality desigual; surface, ground irregular

un·e·ven·ly [ʌnˈiːvnlɪ] adv distributed, applied de forma desigual; be matched of two contestants no estar en igualdad de condiciones

un·e·vent·ful [ʌnɪˈventfəl] adj day, journey sin incidentes

un·ex·pec·ted [ʌnɪkˈspektɪd] adj inesperado

un·ex·pec·ted·ly [ʌnɪkˈspektɪdlɪ] adv inesperadamente, de forma inesperada

un·fair [ʌnˈfer] adj injusto; that's ~ eso no es justo

un·faith·ful [ʌnˈfeɪθfəl] adj husband, wife infiel; be ~ to s.o. ser infiel a alguien

un·fa·mil·i·ar [ʌnfəˈmɪljər] adj desconocido, extraño; be ~ with sth desconocer algo

un·fas·ten [ʌnˈfæsn] v/t belt desabrochar

un·fa·vo·ra·ble, Br un·fa·vou·ra·ble [ʌnˈfeɪvərəbl] adj desfavorable

un·feel·ing [ʌnˈfiːlɪŋ] adj person insensible

un·fin·ished [ʌnˈfɪnɪʃt] adj inacabado; leave sth ~ dejar algo sin acabar

un·fit [ʌnˈfɪt] adj: be ~ physically estar en baja forma; be ~ to eat no ser apto para el consumo; be ~ to drink no ser potable; he's ~ to be a parent no tiene lo que se necesita para ser padre

un·fix [ʌnˈfɪks] v/t part soltar, desmontar

un·flap·pa·ble [ʌnˈflæpəbl] adj impasible

un·fold [ʌnˈfoʊld] 1 v/t sheets, letter desdoblar; one's arms descruzar 2 v/i of story etc desarrollarse; of view abrirse

un·fore·seen [ʌnfɔːrˈsiːn] adj imprevisto

un·for·get·ta·ble [ʌnfərˈgetəbl] adj inolvidable

un·for·giv·a·ble [ʌnfərˈgɪvəbl] adj imperdonable; that was ~ of you eso ha sido imperdonable

un·for·tu·nate [ʌnˈfɔːrtʃənət] adj people desafortunado; event desgraciado; choice of words desafortunado, desacertado; that's ~ for you has tenido muy mala suerte

un·for·tu·nate·ly [ʌnˈfɔːrtʃənətlɪ] adv desgraciadamente

un·found·ed [ʌnˈfaʊndɪd] adj infundado

un·friend·ly [ʌnˈfrendlɪ] adj person antipático; place desagradable; welcome hostil; software de difícil manejo

un·fur·nished [ʌnˈfɜːrnɪʃt] adj sin amueblar

un·god·ly [ʌnˈgɑːdlɪ] adj: at this ~ hour a esta hora intempestiva

un·grate·ful [ʌnˈgreɪtfəl] adj desagradecido

un·hap·pi·ness [ʌnˈhæpɪnɪs] infelicidad f

un·hap·py [ʌnˈhæpɪ] adj person, look infeliz; day triste; customer etc descontento

un·harmed [ʌnˈhɑːrmd] adj ileso; be ~ salir ileso

un·health·y [ʌnˈhelθɪ] adj person enfermizo; conditions, food, economy poco saludable

un·heard-of [ʌnˈhɜːrdɒv] adj inaudito

un·hurt [ʌnˈhɜːrt] adj: be ~ salir ileso

un·hy·gien·ic [ʌnhaɪˈdʒiːnɪk] adj antihigiénico

u·ni·fi·ca·tion [juːnɪfɪˈkeɪʃn] unificación f

u·ni·form [ˈjuːnɪfɔːrm] 1 n uniforme m 2 adj uniforme

u·ni·fy [ˈjuːnɪfaɪ] v/t (pret & pp -ied) unificar

U

u·ni·lat·e·ral [juːnɪˈlætərəl] *adj* unilateral

un·i·ma·gi·na·ble [ʌnɪˈmædʒɪnəbl] *adj* inimaginable

un·i·ma·gi·na·tive [ʌnɪˈmædʒɪnətɪv] *adj* sin imaginación

un·im·por·tant [ʌnɪmˈpɔːrtənt] *adj* poco importante

un·in·hab·i·ta·ble [ʌnɪnˈhæbɪtəbl] *adj* inhabitable

un·in·hab·it·ed [ʌnɪnˈhæbɪtɪd] *adj building* deshabitado; *region* desierto

un·in·jured [ʌnˈɪndʒərd] *adj*: **be ~** salir ileso

un·in·tel·li·gi·ble [ʌnɪnˈtelɪdʒəbl] *adj* ininteligible

un·in·ten·tion·al [ʌnɪnˈtenʃnl] *adj* no intencionado; *sorry, that was ~* lo siento, ha sido sin querer

un·in·ten·tion·al·ly [ʌnɪnˈtenʃnli] *adv* sin querer

un·in·te·rest·ing [ʌnˈɪntrəstɪŋ] *adj* sin interés

un·in·ter·rupt·ed [ʌnɪntəˈrʌptɪd] *adj sleep, two hours' work* ininterrumpido

u·nion [ˈjuːnjən] POL unión *f*; (*labor ~*) sindicato *m*

u·nique [juːˈniːk] *adj* único

u·nit [ˈjuːnɪt] unidad *f*; **~ of measurement** unidad *f* de medida; **power ~** fuente *f* de alimentación

u·nit 'cost COM costo *m* or Span coste *m* unitario *or* por unidad

u·nite [juːˈnaɪt] **1** *v/t* unir **2** *v/i* unirse

u·nit·ed [juːˈnaɪtɪd] *adj* unido

U·nit·ed 'King·dom Reino *m* Unido; **U·nit·ed 'Na·tions** Naciones *fpl* Unidas; **U·nit·ed 'States (of A·mer·i·ca)** Estados *mpl* Unidos (de América)

u·ni·ty [ˈjuːnətɪ] unidad *f*

u·ni·ver·sal [juːnɪˈvɜːrsl] *adj* universal

u·ni·ver·sal·ly [juːnɪˈvɜːrsəlɪ] *adv* universalmente

u·ni·verse [ˈjuːnɪvɜːrs] universo *m*

u·ni·ver·si·ty [juːnɪˈvɜːrsətɪ] **1** *n* universidad *f*; **he is at ~** está en la universidad **2** *adj* universitario

un·just [ʌnˈdʒʌst] *adj* injusto

un·kempt [ʌnˈkempt] *adj appearance* descuidado; *hair* revuelto

un·kind [ʌnˈkaɪnd] *adj* desgradable, cruel

un·known [ʌnˈnoʊn] **1** *adj* desconocido **2** *n*: *a journey into the ~* un viaje hacia lo desconocido

un·lead·ed [ʌnˈledɪd] *adj* sin plomo

un·less [ənˈles] *conj* a menos que, a no ser que; *don't say anything ~ you're sure* no digas nada a menos que *or* a no ser que estés seguro

un·like [ʌnˈlaɪk] *prep* (*not similar to*) diferente de; *it's ~ him to drink so much* él no suele beber tanto; *that photograph is so ~ you* has salido completamente diferente en esa fotografía

un·like·ly [ʌnˈlaɪklɪ] *adj* (*improbable*) improbable; *explanation* inverosímil; *he is ~ to win* es improbable *or* poco probable que gane

un·lim·it·ed [ʌnˈlɪmɪtɪd] *adj* ilimitado

un·list·ed [ʌnˈlɪstɪd] *adj*: **be ~** no aparecer en la guía telefónica

un·load [ʌnˈloʊd] *v/t* descargar

un·lock [ʌnˈlɑːk] *v/t* abrir

un·luck·i·ly [ʌnˈlʌkɪlɪ] *adv* desgraciadamente, por desgracia

un·luck·y [ʌnˈlʌkɪ] *adj day, choice* aciago, funesto; *person* sin suerte; *that was so ~ for you!* ¡qué mala suerte tuviste!

un·manned [ʌnˈmænd] *adj spacecraft* no tripulado

un·mar·ried [ʌnˈmærɪd] *adj* soltero

un·mis·ta·ka·ble [ʌnmɪˈsteɪkəbl] *adj* inconfundible

un·moved [ʌnˈmuːvd] *adj*: *he was ~ by her tears* sus lágrimas no lo conmovieron

un·mu·si·cal [ʌnˈmjuːzɪkl] *adj person* sin talento musical; *sounds* estridente

un·nat·u·ral [ʌnˈnætʃrəl] *adj* anormal; *it's not ~ to be annoyed* es normal estar enfadado

un·ne·ces·sa·ry [ʌnˈnesəserɪ] *adj* innecesario

un·nerv·ing [ʌn'nɜːrvɪŋ] *adj* desconcertante

un·no·ticed [ʌn'noʊtɪst] *adj*: **it went ~** pasó desapercibido

un·ob·tain·a·ble [ʌnəb'teɪnəbl] *adj* goods no disponible; TELEC desconectado

un·ob·tru·sive [ʌnəb'truːsɪv] *adj* discreto

un·oc·cu·pied [ʌn'ɒkjʊpaɪd] *adj* building, house desocupado; post vacante

un·of·fi·cial [ʌnə'fɪʃl] *adj* no oficial; **this is still ~ but …** esto todavía no es oficial, pero …

un·of·fi·cial·ly [ʌnə'fɪʃlɪ] *adv* extraoficialmente

un·or·tho·dox [ʌn'ɔːrθədɑːks] *adj* poco ortodoxo

un·pack [ʌn'pæk] **1** *v/t* deshacer **2** *v/i* deshacer el equipaje

un·paid [ʌn'peɪd] *adj* work no remunerado

un·pleas·ant [ʌn'pleznt] *adj* desagradable; **he was very ~ to her** fue muy desagradable con ella

un·plug [ʌn'plʌg] *v/t* (*pret & pp* **-ged**) TV, computer desenchufar

un·pop·u·lar [ʌn'pɑːpjələr] *adj* impopular

un·pre·ce·dent·ed [ʌn'presɪdntɪd] *adj* sin precedentes; **it was ~ for a woman to …** no tenía precedentes que una mujer …

un·pre·dict·a·ble [ʌnprɪ'dɪktəbl] *adj* person, weather imprevisible, impredecible

un·pre·ten·tious [ʌnprɪ'tenʃəs] *adj* person, style, hotel modesto, sin pretensiones

un·prin·ci·pled [ʌn'prɪnsɪpld] *adj* sin principios

un·pro·duc·tive [ʌnprə'dʌktɪv] *adj* meeting, discussion infructuoso; soil improductivo

un·pro·fes·sion·al [ʌnprə'feʃnl] *adj* poco profesional

un·prof·it·a·ble [ʌn'prɑːfɪtəbl] *adj* no rentable

un·pro·nounce·a·ble [ʌnprə'naʊnsəbl] *adj* impronunciable

un·pro·tect·ed [ʌnprə'tektɪd] *adj* borders desprotegido, sin protección; **~ sex** sexo *m* sin preservativos

un·pro·voked [ʌnprə'voʊkt] *adj* attack no provocado

un·qual·i·fied [ʌn'kwɑːlɪfaɪd] *adj* worker, doctor etc sin titulación

un·ques·tio·na·bly [ʌn'kwestʃnəblɪ] *adv* (without doubt) indiscutiblemente

un·ques·tion·ing [ʌn'kwestʃnɪŋ] *adj* attitude, loyalty incondicional

un·rav·el [ʌn'rævl] *v/t* (*pret & pp* **-ed**, Br **-led**) string, knitting desenredar; mystery, complexities desentrañar

un·rea·da·ble [ʌn'riːdəbl] *adj* book ilegible

un·re·al [ʌn'rɪəl] *adj* irreal; **this is ~!** ¡esto es increíble! F

un·re·al·is·tic [ʌnrɪə'lɪstɪk] *adj* poco realista

un·rea·so·na·ble [ʌn'riːznəbl] *adj* person poco razonable, irrazonable; demand, expectation excesivo, irrazonable; **you're being ~** no estás siendo razonable

un·re·lat·ed [ʌnrɪ'leɪtɪd] *adj* issues no relacionado; people no emparentado

un·re·lent·ing [ʌnrɪ'lentɪŋ] *adj* implacable

un·rel·i·a·ble [ʌnrɪ'laɪəbl] *adj* car, machine poco fiable; person informal

un·rest [ʌn'rest] malestar *m*; (rioting) disturbios *mpl*

un·re·strained [ʌnrɪ'streɪnd] *adj* emotions incontrolado

un·road·wor·thy [ʌn'roʊdwɜːrðɪ] *adj* que no está en condiciones de circular

un·roll [ʌn'roʊl] *v/t* carpet, scroll desenrollar

un·ru·ly [ʌn'ruːlɪ] *adj* revoltoso

un·safe [ʌn'seɪf] *adj* peligroso; **it's ~ to drink / eat** no se puede beber / comer

un·san·i·tar·y [ʌn'sænɪterɪ] *adj* conditions, drains insalubre

un·sat·is·fac·to·ry [ʌnsætɪs'fæktərɪ] *adj* insatisfactorio

U

un·sa·vo·ry [ʌn'seɪvərɪ] *adj person, reputation* indeseable; *district* desagradable

un·scathed [ʌn'skeɪðd] *adj (not injured)* ileso; *(not damaged)* intacto

un·screw [ʌn'skru:] *v/t top* desenroscar; *shelves, hooks* desatornillar

un·scru·pu·lous [ʌn'skru:pjələs] *adj* sin escrúpulos

un·self·ish [ʌn'selfɪʃ] *adj* generoso

un·set·tled [ʌn'setld] *adj issue* sin decidir; *weather, stock market, lifestyle* inestable; *bills* sin pagar

un·shav·en [ʌn'ʃeɪvn] *adj* sin afeitar

un·sight·ly [ʌn'saɪtlɪ] *adj* horrible, feo

un·skilled [ʌn'skɪld] *adj* no cualificado

un·so·cia·ble [ʌn'souʃəbl] *adj* insociable

un·so·phis·ti·cat·ed [ʌnsə'fɪstɪkeɪtɪd] *adj person, beliefs* sencillo; *equipment* simple

un·sta·ble [ʌn'steɪbl] *adj* inestable

un·stead·y [ʌn'stedɪ] *adj hand* tembloroso; *ladder* inestable; *be ~ on one's feet* tambalearse

un·stint·ing [ʌn'stɪntɪŋ] *adj* generoso; *be ~ in one's efforts/ generosity* no escatimar esfuerzos / generosidad

un·suc·cess·ful [ʌnsək'sesfəl] *adj writer etc* fracasado; *candidate* perdedor; *party, attempt* fallido; *he tried but was ~* lo intentó sin éxito

un·suc·cess·ful·ly [ʌnsək'sesfəlɪ] *adv try, apply* sin éxito

un·suit·a·ble [ʌn'su:təbl] *adj partner, film, clothing* inadecuado; *thing to say* inoportuno

un·sus·pect·ing [ʌnsəs'pektɪŋ] *adj* confiado

un·swerv·ing [ʌn'swɜːrvɪŋ] *adj loyalty, devotion* inquebrantable

un·think·a·ble [ʌn'θɪŋkəbl] *adj* impensable

un·ti·dy [ʌn'taɪdɪ] *adj room, desk* desordenado; *hair* revuelto

un·tie [ʌn'taɪ] *v/t knot, laces, prisoner* desatar

un·til [ən'tɪl] **1** *prep* hasta; *from*

Monday ~ Friday desde el lunes hasta el viernes; *I can wait ~ tomorrow* puedo esperar hasta mañana; *not ~ Friday* no antes del viernes; *it won't be finished ~ July* no estará acabado hasta julio **2** *conj* hasta que; *can you wait ~ I'm ready?* ¿puedes esperar hasta que esté listo?; *they won't do anything ~ you say so* no harán nada hasta que (no) se lo digas

un·time·ly [ʌn'taɪmlɪ] *adj death* prematuro

un·tir·ing [ʌn'taɪrɪŋ] *adj efforts* incansable

un·told [ʌn'tould] *adj suffering* indecible; *riches* inconmensurable; *story* nunca contado

un·trans·lat·a·ble [ʌntræns'leɪtəbl] *adj* intraducible

un·true [ʌn'tru:] *adj* falso

un·used[1] [ʌn'ju:zd] *adj goods* sin usar

un·used[2] [ʌn'ju:st] *adj*: *be ~ to sth* no estar acostumbrado a algo; *be ~ to doing sth* no estar acostumbrado a hacer algo

un·u·su·al [ʌn'ju:ʒl] *adj* poco corriente; *it is ~ ...* es raro *or* extraño ...

un·u·su·al·ly [ʌn'ju:ʒəlɪ] *adv* inusitadamente; *the weather's ~ cold* hace un frío inusual

un·veil [ʌn'veɪl] *v/t memorial, statue etc* desvelar

un·well [ʌn'wel] *adj* indispuesto, mal; *be ~* sentirse indispuesto *or* mal

un·will·ing [ʌn'wɪlɪŋ] *adj* poco dispuesto, reacio; *be ~ to do sth* no estar dispuesto a hacer algo, ser reacio a hacer algo

un·will·ing·ly [ʌn'wɪlɪŋlɪ] *adv* de mala gana, a regañadientes

un·wind [ʌn'waɪnd] **1** *v/t (pret & pp -wound) tape* desenrollar **2** *v/i (pret & pp -wound) of tape* desenrollarse; *of story* irse desarrollando; *(relax)* relajarse

un·wise [ʌn'waɪz] *adj* imprudente

un·wrap [ʌn'ræp] *v/t (pret & pp -ped) gift* desenvolver

un·writ·ten [ʌnˈrɪtn] *adj law*, *rule* no escrito

un·zip [ʌnˈzɪp] *v/t* (*pret & pp* **-ped**) *dress etc* abrir la cremallera de; COMPUT descomprimir

up [ʌp] **1** *adv position* arriba; *movement* hacia arriba; **~ *in the sky/ ~ on the roof*** (arriba) en el cielo/tejado; **~ *here/ there*** aquí/ allí arriba; **be ~** (*out of bed*) estar levantado; *of sun* haber salido; (*be built*) haber sido construido, estar acabado; *of shelves* estar montado; *of prices, temperature* haber subido; (*have expired*) haberse acabado; **what's ~?** F ¿qué pasa?; **~ *to the year 1989*** hasta el año 1989; **he came ~ to me** se me acercó; **what are you ~ to these days?** ¿qué es de tu vida?; **what are those kids ~ to?** ¿qué están tramando esos niños?; **be ~ to something** (*bad*) estar tramando algo; **I don't feel ~ to it** no me siento en condiciones de hacerlo; **it's ~ to you** tú decides; **it is ~ to them to solve it** (*their duty*) les corresponde a ellos resolverlo; **be ~ and about** *after illness* estar recuperado **2** *prep:* **further ~ the mountain** más arriba de la montaña; **he climbed ~ a tree** se subió a un árbol; **they ran ~ the street** corrieron por la calle; **the water goes ~ this pipe** el agua sube por esta tubería; **we traveled ~ to Chicago** subimos hasta Chicago **3** *n:* **~s and downs** altibajos *mpl*

'up·bring·ing educación *f*

'up·com·ing *adj* (*forthcoming*) próximo

up·date¹ *v/t file, records* actualizar; **~ *s.o. on sth*** poner a alguien al corriente de algo

'up·date² *n* actualización *f*; **can you give me an ~ on the situation?** ¿me puedes poner al corriente de la situación?

up'grade *v/t computers etc* actualizar; (*replace with new versions*) modernizar; *product* modernizar; **~ *s.o. to business class*** cambiar a alguien a clase ejecutiva

up·heav·al [ʌpˈhiːvl] *emotional* conmoción *f*; *physical* trastorno *m*; *political, social* sacudida *f*

up·hill 1 *adv walk* cuesta arriba **2** *adj* [ˈʌphɪl] *struggle* arduo, difícil

up'hold *v/t* (*pret & pp* **-held**) *traditions, rights* defender, conservar; (*vindicate*) confirmar

up·hol·ster·y [ʌpˈhoʊlstərɪ] (*coverings*) tapicería *f*; (*padding*) relleno *m*

'up·keep *of buildings, parks etc* mantenimiento *m*

'up·load *v/t* COMPUT cargar

up'mar·ket *adj restaurant, hotel* de categoría

up·on [əˈpɑːn] *prep →* **on**

up·per [ˈʌpər] *adj part of sth* superior; *stretches of a river* alto; *deck* superior, de arriba

up·per 'class *adj accent, family* de clase alta

up·per 'clas·ses *npl* clases *fpl* altas

'up·right 1 *adj citizen* honrado **2** *adv sit* derecho

'up·right (ˈpi·an·o) piano *m* vertical

'up·ris·ing levantamiento *m*

'up·roar (*loud noise*) alboroto *m*; (*protest*) tumulto *m*

up·set 1 *v/t* (*pret & pp* **-set**) *drink, glass* tirar; *emotionally* disgustar **2** *adj emotionally* disgustado; **get ~ about sth** disgustarse por algo; **have an ~ stomach** tener el estómago mal

up'set·ting *adj* triste

'up·shot (*result, outcome*) resultado *m*

up·side 'down *adv* boca abajo; **turn sth ~** *box etc* poner algo al revés *or* boca abajo

up·stairs 1 *adv* arriba **2** *adj room* de arriba

'up·start advenedizo(-a) *m(f)*

'up·stream *adv* río arriba

'up·take FIN respuesta *f* (*of* a); **be quick/ slow on the ~** F ser/no ser muy espabilado F

up'tight *adj* F (*nervous*) tenso; (*inhib-*

ited) estrecho

up-to-'date *adj information* actualizado; *fashions* moderno

'up·turn *in economy* mejora *f*

up·ward ['ʌpwərd] *adv fly, move* hacia arriba; **~ of 10,000** más de 10.000

u·ra·ni·um [juˈreɪnɪəm] uranio *m*

ur·ban ['ɜːrbən] *adj* urbano

ur·ban·i·za·tion [ɜːrbənaɪˈzeɪʃn] urbanización *f*

ur·chin ['ɜːrtʃɪn] golfillo(-a) *m(f)*

urge [ɜːrdʒ] **1** *n* impulso *m*; *I felt an ~ to hit her* me entraron ganas de pegarle; *I have an ~ to do something new* siento la necesidad de hacer algo nuevo **2** *v/t:* **~ s.o. to do sth** rogar a alguien que haga algo

♦ **urge on** *v/t (encourage)* animar

ur·gen·cy ['ɜːrdʒənsɪ] *of situation* urgencia *f*

ur·gent ['ɜːrdʒənt] *adj job, letter* urgente; *be in ~ need of sth* necesitar algo urgentemente; *is it ~?* ¿es urgente?

u·ri·nate ['jʊrəneɪt] *v/i* orinar

u·rine ['jʊrɪn] orina *f*

urn [ɜːrn] urna *f*

U·ru·guay ['jʊrəgwaɪ] Uruguay

U·ru·guay·an [jʊrəˈgwaɪən] **1** *adj* uruguayo **2** *n* uruguayo(-a) *m(f)*

US [juːˈes] *abbr* (= **United States**) EE.UU. *mpl* (= Estados *mpl* Unidos)

us [ʌs] *pron* nos; *after prep* nosotros(-as); *they love ~* nos quieren; *she gave ~ the keys* nos dio las llaves; *he sold it to ~* eso se nos vendió; *that's for ~* eso es para nosotros; *who's that? – it's ~* ¿quién es? – ¡somos nosotros!

USA [juːesˈeɪ] *abbr* (= **United States of America**) EE.UU. *mpl* (= Estados *mpl* Unidos)

us·a·ble ['juːzəbl] *adj* utilizable; *it's not ~* no se puede utilizar

us·age ['juːzɪdʒ] uso *m*

use 1 *v/t tool, word* utilizar, usar; *skills, knowledge, car* usar; *a lot of gas* consumir; *pej: person* utilizar; *I could ~ a drink* F no me vendría mal una copa **2** *n* [juːs] uso *m*, utilización

f; *be of great ~ to s.o.* ser de gran utilidad para alguien; *it's of no ~ to me* no me sirve; *is that of any ~?* ¿eso sirve para algo?; *it's no ~* no sirve de nada; *it's no ~ trying/ waiting* no sirve de nada intentarlo/esperar

♦ **use up** *v/t* agotar

used¹ [juːzd] *adj car etc* de segunda mano

used² [juːst] *adj:* **be ~ to s.o./sth** estar acostumbrado a alguien/algo; *get ~ to s.o./sth* acostumbrarse a alguien/algo; *be ~ to doing sth* estar acostumbrado a hacer algo; *get ~ to doing sth* acostumbrarse a hacer algo

used³ [juːst]: *I ~ to like him* antes me gustaba; *they ~ to meet every Saturday* solían verse todos los sábados

use·ful ['juːsfəl] *adj* útil

use·ful·ness ['juːsfʊlnɪs] utilidad *f*

use·less ['juːslɪs] *adj* inútil; *machine, computer* inservible; *be ~ person* ser un inútil F; *it's ~ trying (there's no point)* no vale la pena intentarlo

us·er ['juːzər] *of product* usuario(-a) *m(f)*

us·er-'friend·ly *adj* de fácil manejo

ush·er ['ʌʃər] *n (at wedding)* persona que se encarga de indicar a los asistentes dónde se deben sentar

♦ **usher in** *v/t new era* anunciar

u·su·al ['juːʒl] *adj* habitual, acostumbrado; *as ~* como de costumbre; *the ~, please* lo de siempre, por favor

u·su·al·ly ['juːʒəlɪ] *adv* normalmente; *I ~ start at 9* suelo empezar a las 9

u·ten·sil [juːˈtensl] utensilio *m*

u·te·rus ['juːtərəs] útero *m*

u·til·i·ty [juːˈtɪlətɪ] *(usefulness)* utilidad *f*; *public utilities* servicios *mpl* públicos

u·til·ize ['juːtɪlaɪz] *v/t* utilizar

ut·most ['ʌtmoʊst] **1** *adj* sumo **2** *n:* **do one's ~** hacer todo lo posible

ut·ter ['ʌtər] **1** *adj* completo, total **2** *v/t sound* decir, pronunciar

ut·ter·ly ['ʌtərlɪ] *adv* completamente,

totalmente
U-turn ['juːtɜːrn] cambio *m* de senti-

do; *do a ~ fig: in policy etc* dar un giro de 180 grados

V

va·cant ['veɪkənt] *adj building* vacío; *position* vacante; *look, expression* vago, distraído
va·cant·ly ['veɪkəntlɪ] *adv* distraídamente
va·cate [veɪ'keɪt] *v/t room* desalojar
va·ca·tion [veɪ'keɪʃn] *n* vacaciones *fpl*; *be on ~* estar de vacaciones; *go to ... on ~* ir de vacaciones a ...
va·ca·tion·er [veɪ'keɪʃənər] turista *m/f; in summer* veraneante *m/f*
vac·cin·ate ['væksɪneɪt] *v/t* vacunar; *be ~d against ...* estar vacunado contra ...
vac·cin·a·tion [væksɪ'neɪʃn] *action* vacunación *f*; *(vaccine)* vacuna *f*
vac·cine ['væksiːn] vacuna *f*
vac·u·um ['vækjʊəm] **1** *n* PHYS, *fig* vacío *m* **2** *v/t floors* pasar el aspirador por, aspirar
'**vac·u·um clean·er** aspirador *m*, aspiradora *f*; '**vac·u·um flask** termo *m*; **vac·u·um-'packed** *adj* envasado al vacío
vag·a·bond ['vægəbɑːnd] vagabundo(-a) *m(f)*
va·gi·na [və'dʒaɪnə] vagina *f*
va·gi·nal ['vædʒɪnl] *adj* vaginal
va·grant ['veɪɡrənt] vagabundo(-a) *m(f)*
vague [veɪɡ] *adj* vago; *he was very ~ about it* no fue muy preciso
vague·ly ['veɪɡlɪ] *adv answer,* *(slightly)* vagamente; *possible* muy poco
vain [veɪn] **1** *adj person* vanidoso; *hope* vano **2** *n: in ~* en vano
val·en·tine ['væləntaɪn] *card* tarjeta *f* del día de San Valentín; *Valentine's Day* día de San Valentín *or* de los

enamorados
val·et 1 *n* ['væleɪ] *person* mozo *m* **2** *v/t* ['vælət] *car* lavar y limpiar
'**val·et ser·vice** *for clothes* servicio *m* de planchado; *for cars* servicio *m* de lavado y limpiado
val·iant ['væljənt] *adj* valiente, valeroso
val·iant·ly ['væljəntlɪ] *adv* valientemente, valerosamente
val·id ['vælɪd] *adj* válido
val·i·date ['vælɪdeɪt] *v/t with official stamp* sellar; *s.o.'s alibi* dar validez a
va·lid·i·ty [və'lɪdətɪ] validez *f*
val·ley ['vælɪ] valle *m*
val·u·a·ble ['væljʊbl] **1** *adj* valioso **2** *n: ~s* objetos *mpl* de valor
val·u·a·tion [væljʊ'eɪʃn] tasación *f*, valoración *f*
val·ue ['væljuː] **1** *n* valor *m*; *be good ~* ofrecer buena relación calidad-precio; *get ~ for money* recibir una buena relación calidad-precio; *rise/fall in ~* aumentar / disminuir de valor **2** *v/t s.o.'s friendship, one's freedom* valorar; *I ~ your advice* valoro tus consejos; *have an object ~d* pedir la valoración *or* tasación de un objeto
valve [vælv] válvula *f*
van [væn] camioneta *f*, furgoneta *f*
van·dal ['vændl] vándalo *m*, gamberro(-a) *m(f)*
van·dal·ism ['vændəlɪzm] vandalismo *m*
van·dal·ize ['vændəlaɪz] *v/t* destrozar *(intencionadamente)*
van·guard ['væŋɡɑːrd] vanguardia *f*; *be in the ~ of fig* estar a la vanguardia de

va·nil·la [və'nɪlə] **1** *n* vainilla *f* **2** *adj* de vainilla

van·ish ['vænɪʃ] *v/i* desaparecer

van·i·ty ['vænətɪ] *of person* vanidad *f*

'van·i·ty case neceser *m*

van·tage point ['væntɪdʒ] *on hill etc* posición *f* aventajada

va·por ['veɪpər] vapor *m*

va·por·ize ['veɪpəraɪz] *v/t of atomic bomb, explosion* vaporizar

'va·por trail *of airplane* estela *f*

va·pour *Br* → **vapor**

var·i·a·ble ['verɪəbl] **1** *adj* variable **2** *n* MATH, COMPUT variable *f*

var·i·ant ['verɪənt] *n* variante *f*

var·i·a·tion [verɪ'eɪʃn] variación *f*

var·i·cose vein ['værɪkous] variz *f*

var·ied ['verɪd] *adj* variado

va·ri·e·ty [və'raɪətɪ] (*variedness, type*) variedad *f*; *a ~ of things to do* (*range, mixture*) muchas cosas para hacer

var·i·ous ['verɪəs] *adj* (*several*) varios; (*different*) diversos

var·nish ['vɑːrnɪʃ] **1** *n for wood* barniz *m*; *for fingernails* esmalte *m* **2** *v/t wood* barnizar; *fingernails* poner esmalte a, pintar

var·y ['verɪ] **1** *v/i* (*pret & pp* **-ied**) variar; *it varies* depende **2** *v/t* (*pret & pp* **-ied**) variar

vase [veɪz] jarrón *m*

vas·ec·to·my [və'sektəmɪ] vasectomía *f*

vast [væst] *adj desert, knowledge* vasto; *number, improvement* enorme

vast·ly ['væstlɪ] *adv* enormemente

VAT [viːeɪ'tiː, væt] *Br abbr* (= **value-added tax**) IVA *m* (= impuesto *m* sobre el valor añadido)

Vat·i·can ['vætɪkən]: *the ~* el Vaticano

vau·de·ville ['vɒːdvɪl] vodevil *m*

vault¹ [vɒːlt] *n in roof* bóveda *f*; *~s* (*cellar*) sótano *m*; *of bank* cámara *f* acorazada

vault² [vɒːlt] **1** *n* SP salto *m* **2** *v/t beam etc* saltar

VCR [viːsiː'ɑːr] *abbr* (= **video cassette recorder**) aparato *m* de *Span* vídeo *or L.Am.* video

VDU [viːdiː'juː] *abbr* (= **visual display unit**) monitor *m*

veal [viːl] ternera *f*

veer [vɪr] *v/i* girar, torcer

ve·gan ['viːgn] **1** *n* vegetariano(-a) *m(f)* estricto (-a) (*que no come ningún producto de origen animal*) **2** *adj* vegetariano estricto

vege·ta·ble ['vedʒtəbl] hortaliza *f*; *~s* verduras *fpl*

ve·ge·tar·i·an [vedʒɪ'terɪən] **1** *n* vegetariano(-a) *m(f)* **2** *adj* vegetariano

ve·ge·tar·i·an·ism [vedʒɪ'terɪənɪzm] vegetarianismo *m*

veg·e·ta·tion [vedʒɪ'teɪʃn] vegetación *f*

ve·he·mence ['viːəməns] vehemencia *f*

ve·he·ment ['viːəmənt] *adj* vehemente

ve·he·ment·ly ['viːəməntlɪ] *adv* vehementemente

ve·hi·cle ['viːɪkl] *also fig* vehículo *m*

veil [veɪl] **1** *n* velo *m* **2** *v/t* cubrir con un velo

vein [veɪn] ANAT vena *f*; *in this ~ fig* en este tono

Vel·cro® ['velkrou] velcro *m*

ve·loc·i·ty [vɪ'lɑːsətɪ] velocidad *f*

vel·vet ['velvɪt] *n* terciopelo *m*

vel·vet·y ['velvɪtɪ] *adj* aterciopelado

ven·det·ta [ven'detə] vendetta *f*

vend·ing ma·chine ['vendɪŋ] máquina *f* expendedora

vend·or ['vendər] LAW parte *f* vendedora

ve·neer [və'nɪr] *on wood* chapa *f*; *of politeness etc* apariencia *f*, fachada *f*

ven·e·ra·ble ['venərəbl] *adj* venerable

ven·e·rate ['venəreɪt] *v/t* venerar

ven·e·ra·tion [venə'reɪʃn] veneración *f*

ven·e·re·al dis·ease [vɪ'nɪrɪəl] enfermedad *f* venérea

ve·ne·tian 'blind persiana *f* veneciana

Ven·e·zue·la [venɪz'weɪlə] Venezuela

Ven·e·zue·lan [venɪz'weɪlən] **1** *adj*

venezolano 2 *n* venezolano(-a) *m(f)*

ven·geance ['vendʒəns] venganza *f*; **with a ~** con ganas

ven·i·son ['venɪsn] venado *m*

ven·om ['venəm] *also fig* veneno *m*

ven·om·ous ['venəməs] *adj snake* venenoso; *fig* envenenado

vent [vent] *n for air* respiradero *m*; **give ~ to** *feelings* dar rienda suelta a

ven·ti·late ['ventɪleɪt] *v/t* ventilar

ven·ti·la·tion [ventɪ'leɪʃn] ventilación *f*

ven·ti·la·tion shaft pozo *m* de ventilación

ven·ti·la·tor ['ventɪleɪtər] ventilador *m*; MED respirador *m*

ven·tril·o·quist [ven'trɪləkwɪst] ventrilocuo(-a) *m(f)*

ven·ture ['ventʃər] **1** *n (undertaking)* iniciativa *f*; COM empresa *f* **2** *v/i* aventurarse

ven·ue ['venjuː] *for meeting* lugar *m*; *for concert* local *m*, sala *f*

ve·ran·da [və'rændə] porche *m*

verb [vɜːrb] verbo *m*

verb·al ['vɜːrbl] *adj (spoken)* verbal

verb·al·ly ['vɜːrbəlɪ] *adv* de palabra

ver·ba·tim [vɜːr'beɪtɪm] *adv* literalmente

ver·dict ['vɜːrdɪkt] LAW veredicto *m*; **what's your ~?** ¿qué te parece?, ¿qué opinas?

verge [vɜːrdʒ] *n of road* arcén *m*; **be on the ~ of** *ruin* estar al borde de; *tears* estar a punto de

♦ verge on *v/t* rayar en

ver·i·fi·ca·tion [verɪfɪ'keɪʃn] *(checking)* verificación *f*; *(confirmation)* confirmación *f*

ver·i·fy ['verɪfaɪ] *v/t (pret & pp -ied) (check)* verificar; *(confirm)* confirmar

ver·mi·cel·li [vɜːrmɪ'tʃelɪ] *nsg* fideos *mpl*

ver·min ['vɜːrmɪn] *npl* bichos *mpl*, alimañas *fpl*

ver·mouth [vɜːr'muːθ] vermut *m*

ver·nac·u·lar [vər'nækjələr] *n* lenguaje *m* de la calle

ver·sa·tile ['vɜːrsətl] *adj* polifacético, versátil

ver·sa·til·i·ty [vɜːrsə'tɪlətɪ] polivalencia *f*, versatilidad *f*

verse [vɜːrs] verso *m*

versed [vɜːrst] *adj:* **be well ~ in a subject** estar muy versado en una materia

ver·sion ['vɜːrʃn] versión *f*

ver·sus ['vɜːrsəs] *prep* SP, LAW contra

ver·te·bra ['vɜːrtɪbrə] vértebra *f*

ver·te·brate ['vɜːrtɪbreɪt] *n* vertebrado(-a) *m(f)*

ver·ti·cal ['vɜːrtɪkl] *adj* vertical

ver·ti·go ['vɜːrtɪɡoʊ] vértigo *m*

ver·y ['verɪ] **1** *adv* muy; **was it cold? – not ~** ¿hizo frío? – no mucho; **the ~ best** el mejor de todos **2** *adj:* **at that ~ moment** en ese mismo momento; **that's the ~ thing I need** *(exact)* eso es precisamente lo que necesito; **the ~ thought of** sólo de pensar en; **right at the ~ top/ bottom** arriba/al fondo del todo

ves·sel ['vesl] NAUT buque *m*

vest [vest] chaleco *m*

ves·tige ['vestɪdʒ] vestigio *m*

vet¹ [vet] *n (veterinary surgeon)* veterinario(-a) *m(f)*

vet² [vet] *v/t (pret & pp -ted) applicants etc* examinar, investigar

vet³ [vet] MIL veterano(-a) *m(f)*

vet·e·ran ['vetərən] **1** *n* veterano(-a) *m(f)* **2** *adj* veterano

vet·e·ri·nar·i·an [vetərə'nerɪən] veterinario(-a) *m(f)*

ve·to ['viːtoʊ] **1** *n* veto *m* **2** *v/t* vetar

vex [veks] *v/t (concern, worry)* molestar, irritar

vexed [vekst] *adj (worried)* molesto, irritado; **the ~ question of** la polémica cuestión de

vi·a ['vaɪə] *prep* vía

vi·a·ble ['vaɪəbl] *adj* viable

vi·brate [vaɪ'breɪt] *v/i* vibrar

vi·bra·tion [vaɪ'breɪʃn] vibración *f*

vic·ar ['vɪkər] *Br* vicario *m*

vice¹ [vaɪs] vicio *m*; **the problem of ~** el problema del vicio

vice² *Br* → **vise**

V

vice 'pres·i·dent vicepresidente(-a) *m(f)*

'vice squad brigada *f* antivicio

vi·ce ver·sa [vaɪs'vɜːrsə] *adv* viceversa

vi·cin·i·ty [vɪ'sɪnətɪ] zona *f*; *in the ~ of ...* the church etc en las cercanías de ...; *$500 etc* rondando ...

vi·cious ['vɪʃəs] *adj* dog fiero; *attack, temper, criticism* feroz

vi·cious 'cir·cle círculo *m* vicioso

vi·cious·ly ['vɪʃəslɪ] *adv* con brutalidad

vic·tim ['vɪktɪm] víctima *f*

vic·tim·ize ['vɪktɪmaɪz] *v/t* tratar injustamente

vic·tor ['vɪktər] vencedor(a) *m(f)*

vic·to·ri·ous [vɪk'tɔːrɪəs] *adj* victorioso

vic·to·ry ['vɪktərɪ] victoria *f*; *win a ~ over ...* obtener una victoria sobre ...

vid·e·o ['vɪdɪoʊ] **1** *n* Span vídeo *m*, L.Am. video *m*; *have X on ~* tener a X en Span vídeo *or* L.Am. video **2** *v/t* grabar en Span vídeo *or* L.Am. video

'vid·e·o cam·e·ra videocámara *f*; **vid·e·o cas'sette** videocasete *m*; **'vid·e·o con·fer·ence** TELEC videoconferencia *f*; **'vid·e·o game** videojuego *m*; **'vid·e·o·phone** videoteléfono *m*; **'vid·e·o re·cord·er** aparato *m* de Span vídeo *or* L.Am. video; **'vid·e·o re·cord·ing** grabación *f* en Span vídeo *or* L.Am. video; **'vid·e·o·tape** cinta *f* de Span vídeo *or* L.Am. video

vie [vaɪ] *v/i* competir

Vi·et·nam [vɪet'nɑːm] Vietnam

Vi·et·nam·ese [vɪetnə'miːz] **1** *adj* vietnamita **2** *n* vietnamita *m/f*; *language* vietnamita *m*

view [vjuː] **1** *n* vista *f*; *of situation* opinión *f*; *in ~ of* teniendo en cuenta; *be on ~ of paintings* estar expuesto al público; *with a ~ to* con vistas a **2** *v/t* events, situation ver, considerar; *TV program, house* ver **3** *v/i* (watch TV) ver la televisión

view·er ['vjuːər] *TV* telespectador(a) *m(f)*

'view·find·er PHOT visor *m*

'view·point punto *m* de vista

vig·or ['vɪgər] (*energy*) vigor *m*

vig·or·ous ['vɪgərəs] *adj* shake vigoroso; *person* enérgico; *denial* rotundo

vig·or·ous·ly ['vɪgərəslɪ] *adv* shake con vigor; *deny, defend* rotundamente

vig·our *Br* → *vigor*

vile [vaɪl] *adj* smell asqueroso; *thing to do* vil

vil·la ['vɪlə] chalet *m*; *in the country* villa *f*

vil·lage ['vɪlɪdʒ] pueblo *m*

vil·lag·er ['vɪlɪdʒər] aldeano(-a) *m(f)*

vil·lain ['vɪlən] malo(a) *m(f)*

vin·di·cate ['vɪndɪkeɪt] *v/t* (*show to be correct*) dar la razón a; (*show to be innocent*) vindicar; *I feel ~d* los hechos me dan ahora la razón

vin·dic·tive [vɪn'dɪktɪv] *adj* vengativo

vin·dic·tive·ly [vɪn'dɪktɪvlɪ] *adv* vengativamente

vine [vaɪn] vid *f*

vin·e·gar ['vɪnɪgər] vinagre *m*

vine·yard ['vɪnjɑːrd] viñedo *m*

vin·tage ['vɪntɪdʒ] **1** *n of wine* cosecha *f* **2** *adj* (*classic*) clásico *m*

vi·o·la [vɪ'oʊlə] MUS viola *f*

vi·o·late ['vaɪəleɪt] *v/t* violar

vi·o·la·tion [vaɪə'leɪʃn] violación *f*; (*traffic ~*) infracción *f*

vi·o·lence ['vaɪələns] violencia *f*; *outbreak of ~* estallido de violencia

vi·o·lent ['vaɪələnt] *adj* violento; *have a ~ temper* tener muy mal genio

vi·o·lent·ly ['vaɪələntlɪ] *adv* react violentamente; *object* rotundamente; *fall ~ in love with s.o.* enamorarse perdidamente de alguien

vi·o·let ['vaɪələt] *n color* violeta *m*; *plant* violeta *f*

vi·o·lin [vaɪə'lɪn] violín *m*

vi·o·lin·ist [vaɪə'lɪnɪst] violinista *m/f*

VIP [viːaɪ'piː] *abbr* (= *very important person*) VIP *m*

vi·per ['vaɪpər] *snake* víbora *f*

vi·ral ['vaɪrəl] *adj infection* vírico, viral

vir·gin ['vɜːrdʒɪn] virgen *m/f*

vir·gin·i·ty [vɜːr'dʒɪnətɪ] virginidad *f*; **lose one's ~** perder la virginidad

Vir·go ['vɜːrgoʊ] ASTR Virgo *m/f inv*

vir·ile ['vɪrəl] *adj man* viril; *prose* vigoroso

vi·ril·i·ty [vɪ'rɪlətɪ] virilidad *f*

vir·tu·al ['vɜːrtʃʊəl] *adj* virtual

vir·tu·al·ly ['vɜːrtʃʊəlɪ] *adv* (*almost*) virtualmente, casi

vir·tu·al re'al·i·ty realidad *f* virtual

vir·tue ['vɜːrtʃuː] virtud *f*; **in ~ of** en virtud de

vir·tu·o·so [vɜːrtʃuː'oʊzoʊ] MUS virtuoso(-a) *m(f)*

vir·tu·ous ['vɜːrtʃʊəs] *adj* virtuoso

vir·u·lent ['vɪrʊlənt] *adj* virulento

vi·rus ['vaɪrəs] MED, COMPUT virus *m inv*

vi·sa ['viːzə] visa *f*, visado *m*

vise [vaɪs] torno *m* de banco

vis·i·bil·i·ty [vɪzə'bɪlətɪ] visibilidad *f*

vis·i·ble ['vɪzəbl] *adj object, difference* visible; *anger* evidente; **not be ~ to the naked eye** no ser visible a simple vista

vis·i·bly ['vɪzəblɪ] *adv different* visiblemente; **he was ~ moved** estaba visiblemente conmovido

vi·sion ['vɪʒn] *also* REL visión *f*

vis·it ['vɪzɪt] **1** *n* visita *f*; **pay a ~ to the doctor/dentist** visitar al doctor/dentista; **pay s.o. a ~** hacer una visita a alguien **2** *v/t* visitar

vis·it·ing card ['vɪzɪtɪŋ] tarjeta *f* de visita

'vis·it·ing hours *npl at hospital* horas *fpl* de visita

vis·it·or ['vɪzɪtər] (*guest*) visita *f*; (*tourist*), *to museum etc* visitante *m/f*

vi·sor ['vaɪzər] visera *f*

vis·u·al ['vɪʒʊəl] *adj* visual

vis·u·al 'aid medio *m* visuale

vis·u·al dis'play u·nit monitor *m*

vis·u·al·ize ['vɪʒʊəlaɪz] *v/t* visualizar; (*foresee*) prever

vis·u·al·ly ['vɪʒʊlɪ] *adv* visualmente

vis·u·al·ly im'paired *adj* con discapacidad visual

vi·tal ['vaɪtl] *adj* (*essential*) vital; **it is ~ that …** es vital que …

vi·tal·i·ty [vaɪ'tælətɪ] *of person, city etc* vitalidad *f*

vi·tal·ly ['vaɪtəlɪ] *adv*: **~ important** de importancia vital

vi·tal 'or·gans *npl* órganos *mpl* vitales

vi·tal sta'tis·tics *npl of woman* medidas *fpl*

vit·a·min ['vaɪtəmɪn] vitamina *f*

'vit·a·min pill pastilla *f* vitamínica

vit·ri·ol·ic [vɪtrɪ'ɑːlɪk] *adj* virulento

vi·va·cious [vɪ'veɪʃəs] *adj* vivaz

vi·vac·i·ty [vɪ'væsətɪ] vivacidad *f*

viv·id ['vɪvɪd] *adj color* vivo; *memory, imagination* vívido

viv·id·ly ['vɪvɪdlɪ] *adv* (*brightly*) vivamente; (*clearly*) vívidamente

V-neck ['viːnek] cuello *m* de pico

vo·cab·u·la·ry [voʊ'kæbjʊlərɪ] vocabulario *m*

vo·cal ['voʊkl] *adj to do with the voice* vocal; *expressing opinions* ruidoso; **a ~ opponent** un declarado adversario

'vo·cal cords *npl* cuerdas *fpl* vocales

'vo·cal group MUS grupo *m* vocal

vo·cal·ist ['voʊkəlɪst] MUS vocalista *m/f*

vo·ca·tion [və'keɪʃn] (*calling*) vocación *f*; (*profession*) profesión *f*

vo·ca·tion·al [və'keɪʃnl] *adj guidance* profesional

vod·ka ['vɑːdkə] vodka *m*

vogue [voʊg] moda *f*; **be in ~** estar en boga

voice [vɔɪs] **1** *n* voz *f* **2** *v/t opinions* expresar

'voice·mail correo *m* de voz

void [vɔɪd] **1** *n* vacío *m* **2** *adj*: **~ of** carente de

vol·a·tile ['vɑːlətəl] *adj personality, moods* cambiante; *markets* inestable

vol·ca·no [vɑːl'keɪnoʊ] volcán *m*

vol·ley ['vɑːlɪ] *n of shots* ráfaga *f*; *in tennis* volea *f*

'vol·ley·ball voleibol *m*

volt [voʊlt] voltio *m*

volt·age ['voʊltɪdʒ] voltaje *m*

vol·ume ['vɑːljəm] volumen *m*; *of*

container capacidad *f*; *of book* volumen *m*, tomo *m*

vol·ume con'trol control *m* del volumen

vol·un·tar·i·ly [vɑːlənˈterɪlɪ] *adv* voluntariamente

vol·un·ta·ry [ˈvɑːləntərɪ] *adj* voluntario

vol·un·teer [vɑːlənˈtɪr] **1** *n* voluntario(-a) *m(f)* **2** *v/i* ofrecerse voluntariamente

vo·lup·tu·ous [vəˈlʌptʃuəs] *adj figure* voluptuoso

vom·it [ˈvɑːmət] **1** *n* vómito *m* **2** *v/i* vomitar

♦ **vomit up** *v/t* vomitar

vo·ra·cious [vəˈreɪʃəs] *adj appetite* voraz

vo·ra·cious·ly [vəˈreɪʃəslɪ] *also fig* vorazmente

vote [voʊt] **1** *n* voto *m*; **have the ~** (*be entitled to vote*) tener el derecho al voto **2** *v/i* POL votar; **~ for/ against** votar a favor/ en contra **3** *v/t*: **they**

~d him President lo votaron presidente; **they ~d to stay behind** votaron (a favor de) quedarse atrás

♦ **vote in** *v/t new member* elegir en votación

♦ **vote on** *v/t issue* someter a votación

♦ **vote out** *v/t of office* rechazar en votación

vot·er [ˈvoʊtər] POL votante *m/f*

vot·ing [ˈvoʊtɪŋ] POL votación *f*

'vot·ing booth cabina *f* electoral

vouch for [vaʊtʃ] *v/t truth of sth* dar fe de; *person* responder por

vouch·er [ˈvaʊtʃər] vale *m*

vow [vaʊ] **1** *n* voto *m* **2** *v/t*: **~ to do sth** prometer hacer algo

vow·el [vaʊl] vocal *f*

voy·age [ˈvɔɪɪdʒ] *n* viaje *m*

vul·gar [ˈvʌlgər] *adj person, language* vulgar, grosero

vul·ne·ra·ble [ˈvʌlnərəbl] *adj to attack, criticism* vulnerable

vul·ture [ˈvʌltʃər] buitre *m*

W

wad [wɑːd] *n of paper, absorbent cotton etc* bola *f*; **a ~ of $100 bills** un fajo de billetes de 100 dólares

wad·dle [ˈwɑːdl] *v/i of duck* caminar; *of person* anadear

wade [weɪd] *v/i* caminar en el agua

♦ **wade through** *v/t book, documents* leerse

wa·fer [ˈweɪfər] *cookie* barquillo *m*; REL hostia *f*

'wa·fer-thin *adj* muy fino

waf·fle¹ [ˈwɑːfl] *n to eat* gofre *m*

waf·fle² [ˈwɑːfl] *v/i* andarse con rodeos

wag [wæg] **1** *v/t* (*pret & pp* **-ged**) *tail, finger* menear **2** *v/i* (*pret & pp* **-ged**) *of tail* menearse

wage¹ [weɪdʒ] *v/t*: **~ war** hacer la guerra

wage² [weɪdʒ] *n* salario *m*, sueldo *m*; **~s** salario *m*, sueldo *m*

'wage earn·er asalariado(-a) *m(f)*;

'wage freeze congelación *f* salarial; **'wage ne·go·ti·a·tions** *npl* negociación *f* salarial; **'wage pack·et** *fig* salario *m*, sueldo *m*

wag·gle [ˈwægl] *v/t hips* menear; *ears, loose screw etc* mover

wag·on [ˈwægən] *Br* RAIL vagón *m*; **be on the ~** F haber dejado la bebida

wail [weɪl] **1** *n of person, baby* gemido *m*; *of siren* sonido *m*, aullido *m* **2** *v/i of person, baby* gemir; *of siren* sonar, aullar

waist [weɪst] cintura f

'waist·coat Br chaleco m

'waist·line cintura f

wait [weɪt] 1 n espera f; *I had a long ~ for a train* esperé mucho rato el tren 2 v/i esperar; *have you been ~ing long?* ¿llevan mucho rato esperando? 3 v/t: *don't ~ supper for me* no me esperéis a cenar; *~ table* trabajar de camarero(-a)

♦ **wait for** v/t esperar; *wait for me!* ¡esperame!

♦ **wait on** v/t (*serve*) servir; (*wait for*) esperar

♦ **wait up** v/i esperar levantando

wait·er ['weɪtər] camarero m

wait·ing ['weɪtɪŋ] n espera f; *no ~ sign* señal f de prohibido estacionar

'wait·ing list lista f de espera

'wait·ing room sala f de espera

wait·ress ['weɪtrɪs] camarera f

waive [weɪv] v/t *right* renunciar; *requirement* no aplicar

wake¹ [weɪk] 1 v/i (*pret* woke, *pp* woken): *~ (up)* despertarse 2 v/t (*pret* woke, *pp* woken): *~ (up)* despertar

wake² [weɪk] n *of ship* estela f; *in the ~ of* fig tras; *missionaries followed in the ~ of the explorers* a los exploradores siguieron los misioneros

'wake-up call: *could I have a ~ at 6.30?* ¿me podrían despertar a las 6.30?

Wales [weɪlz] Gales

walk [wɔːk] 1 n paseo m; *longer* caminata f; (*path*) camino m; *it's a long/ short ~ to the office* hay una caminata / un paseo hasta la oficina; *go for a ~* salir a dar un paseo, salir de paseo; *it's a five-minute ~* está a cinco minutos a pie 2 v/i caminar, andar; *as opposed to driving* ir a pie; *she ~ed over to the window* se acercó a la ventana 3 v/t *dog* sacar a pasear; *~ the streets* (*walk around*) caminar por las calles

♦ **walk out** v/i *of spouse* marcharse; *from theater etc* salir; (*go on strike*) declararse en huelga

♦ **walk out on** v/t: *walk out on s.o.* abandonar a alguien

walk·er ['wɔːkər] (*hiker*) excursionista m/f; *for baby, old person* andador m; *be a slow/ fast ~* caminar or andar despacio / rápido

walk-in 'clos·et vestidor m, armario m empotrado

walk·ing ['wɔːkɪŋ] n (*hiking*) excursionismo m; *~ is one of the best forms of exercise* caminar es uno de los mejores ejercicios; *it's within ~ distance* se puede ir caminando or andando

'walk·ing stick bastón m

'walk·ing tour visita f a pie

'Walk·man® walkman m; 'walk·out (*strike*) huelga f; 'walk·over (*easy win*) paseo m; 'walk·up n apartamento en un edificio sin ascensor

wall [wɔːl] external, fig muro m; of room pared f; *go to the ~ of company* quebrar; *drive s.o. up the ~* F hacer que alguien se suba por las paredes

wal·let ['wɑːlɪt] (*billfold*) cartera f

wal·lop ['wɑːləp] 1 n F *blow* tortazo m F, galletazo m F 2 v/t F dar un golpetazo a F; *opponent* dar una paliza a F

'wall·pa·per 1 n papel m pintado 2 v/t empapelar

wall-to-wall 'car·pet Span moqueta f, L.Am. alfombra f

wal·nut ['wɔːlnʌt] nuez f; *tree, wood* nogal m

waltz [wɔːlts] n vals m

wan [wɑːn] adj face pálido m

wan·der ['wɑːndər] v/i (*roam*) vagar, deambular; (*stray*) extraviarse; *my attention began to ~* empecé a distraerme

♦ **wander around** v/i deambular, pasear

wane [weɪn] v/i of interest, enthusiasm decaer, menguar

wan·gle ['wæŋgl] v/t F agenciarse F

want [wɑːnt] 1 n: *for ~ of* por falta de 2 v/t querer; (*need*) necesitar; *~ to do sth* querer hacer algo; *I ~ to stay here* quiero quedarme aquí; *do you ~ to come too? – no, I don't ~ to*

¿quieres venir tú también? – no, no quiero; *you can have whatever you ~* toma lo que quieras; *it's not what I ~ed* no es lo que quería; *she ~s you to go back* quiere que vuelvas; *he ~s a haircut* necesita un corte de pelo 3 *v/i: he ~s for nothing* no le falta nada

'**want ad** anuncio *m* por palabras (*buscando algo*)

want·ed ['wɑːntɪd] *adj by police* buscado por la policía

want·ing ['wɑːntɪŋ] *adj:* *the team is ~ in experience* al equipo le falta experiencia

wan·ton ['wɑːntən] *adj* gratuito

war [wɔːr] *n also fig* guerra *f*; *be at ~* estar en guerra

war·ble ['wɔːrbl] *v/i of bird* trinar

ward [wɔːrd] *n in hospital* sala *f*; *child* pupilo(-a) *m(f)*

♦ **ward off** *v/t blow* parar; *attacker* rechazar; *cold* evitar

war·den ['wɔːrdn] *of prison* director(-a) *m(f)*, alcaide(sa) *m(f)*; *Br of hostel* vigilante *m/f*

'**ward·robe** *for clothes* armario *m*; (*clothes*) guardarropa *m*

ware·house ['werhaus] almacén *m*

'**war·fare** guerra *f*

'**war·head** ojiva *f*

war·i·ly ['werɪlɪ] *adv* cautelosamente

warm [wɔːrm] *adj hands, room, water* caliente; *weather, welcome* cálido; *coat* de abrigo; *it's ~er than yesterday* hace más calor que ayer

♦ **warm up** 1 *v/t* calentar 2 *v/i* calentarse; *of athlete etc* calentar

warm-heart·ed ['wɔːrmhɑːrtɪd] *adj* cariñoso, simpático

warm·ly ['wɔːrmlɪ] *adv welcome, smile* calurosamente; *~ dressed* abrigado

warmth [wɔːrmθ] calor *m*; *of welcome, smile* calor *m*, calidez *m*

'**warm-up** SP calentamiento *m*

warn [wɔːrn] *v/t* advertir, avisar

warn·ing ['wɔːrnɪŋ] *n* advertencia *f*, aviso *m*; *without ~* sin previo aviso

warp [wɔːrp] 1 *v/t wood* combar; *character* corromper 2 *v/i of wood* combarse

warped [wɔːrpt] *adj fig* retorcido

'**war·plane** avión *m* de guerra

war·rant ['wɔːrənt] 1 *n* orden *f* judicial 2 *v/t* (*deserve, call for*) justificar

war·ran·ty ['wɔːrəntɪ] (*guarantee*) garantía *f*; *be under ~* estar en garantía

war·ri·or ['wɔːrɪər] guerrero(-a) *m(f)*

'**war·ship** buque *m* de guerra

wart [wɔːrt] verruga *f*

'**war·time** tiempos *mpl* de guerra

war·y ['werɪ] *adj* cauto, precavido; *be ~ of* desconfiar de

was [wʌz] *pret* → **be**

wash [wɑːʃ] 1 *n* lavado *m*; *have a ~* lavarse; *that shirt needs a ~* hay que lavar esa camisa 2 *v/t* lavar 3 *v/i* lavarse

♦ **wash up** *v/i* (*wash one's hands and face*) lavarse

wash·a·ble ['wɑːʃəbl] *adj* lavable

'**wash·ba·sin**, '**wash·bowl** lavabo *m*

'**wash·cloth** toallita *f*

washed out [wɑːʃt'aut] *adj* agotado

wash·er ['wɑːʃər] *for faucet etc* arandela *f*; → **washing machine**

wash·ing ['wɑːʃɪŋ] (*clothes washed*) ropa *f* limpia; (*dirty clothes*) ropa *f* sucia; *do the ~* lavar la ropa, hacer la colada

'**wash·ing ma·chine** lavadora *f*

'**wash·room** lavabo *m*, aseo *m*

wasp [wɑːsp] *insect* avispa *f*

waste [weist] 1 *n* desperdicio *m*; *from industrial process* desechos *mpl*; *it's a ~ of time / money* es una pérdida de tiempo / dinero 2 *adj* residual 3 *v/t* derrochar; *money* gastar; *time* perder

♦ **waste away** *v/i* consumirse

'**waste dis·pos·al** (*unit*) trituradora *f* de basuras

waste·ful ['weɪstfəl] *adj* despilfarrador, derrochador

'**waste·land** erial *m*; **waste·pa·per** papel *m* usado; '**waste·pa·per bas·ket** papelera *f*; '**waste pipe** tubería *f* de desagüe; '**waste**

prod·uct desecho *m*

watch [wɑːtʃ] **1** *n timepiece* reloj *m*; **keep ~** hacer la guardia, vigilar **2** *v/t film, TV* ver; (*look after*) vigilar **3** *v/i* mirar, observar

◆ **watch for** *v/t* esperar

◆ **watch out** *v/i* (*be wary of*) tener cuidado; **watch out!** ¡cuidado!

◆ **watch out for** *v/t* tener cuidado con

watch·ful [ˈwɑːtʃfəl] *adj* vigilante

'**watch·mak·er** relojero(-a) *m(f)*

wa·ter [ˈwɔːtər] **1** *n* agua *f*; **~s** NAUT aguas *fpl* **2** *v/t plant* regar **3** *v/i*: **my eyes are ~ing** me lloran los ojos; **my mouth is ~ing** se me hace la boca agua

◆ **water down** *v/t drink* aguar, diluir

'**wa·ter can·non** cañón *m* de agua;'**wa·ter·col·or**, *Br* '**wa·ter·col·our** acuarela *f*; '**wa·ter·cress** berro *m*

wa·tered down [ˈwɔːtərd] *adj fig* dulcificado

'**wa·ter·fall** cascada *f*, catarata *f*

'**wa·ter·ing can** [ˈwɔːtərɪŋ] regadera *f*

'**wa·ter·ing hole** *hum* bar *m*

'**wa·ter lev·el** nivel *m* del agua; '**wa·ter lil·y** nenúfar *m*; '**wa·ter·line** línea *f* de flotación; **wa·ter·logged** [ˈwɔːtərlɑːgd] *adj earth, field* anegado; *boat* lleno de agua; '**wa·ter main** tubería *f* principal; '**wa·ter·mark** filigrana *f*; '**wa·ter·mel·on** sandía *f*; '**wa·ter pol·lu·tion** contaminación *f* del agua; '**wa·ter po·lo** waterpolo *m*; '**wa·ter·proof** *adj* impermeable; '**wa·ter·shed** *fig* momento *m* clave; '**wa·ter·side** *n* orilla *f*; **at the ~** en la orilla; '**wa·ter·ski·ing** esquí *m* acuático; '**wa·ter·tight** *adj compartment* estanco; *fig* irrefutable; '**wa·ter·way** curso *m* de agua navegable; '**wa·ter·wings** *npl* flotadores *mpl* (*para los brazos*); **wa·ter·works** F: **turn on the ~** ponerse a llorar como una magdalena F

wa·ter·y [ˈwɔːtərɪ] *adj* aguado

watt [wɑːt] *n* vatio *m*

wave[1] [weɪv] *n in sea* ola *f*

wave[2] [weɪv] **1** *n of hand* saludo *m*

2 *v/i with hand* saludar con la mano; **~ to s.o.** saludar con la mano a alguien **3** *v/t flag etc* agitar

'**wave·length** RAD longitud *f* de onda; **be on the same ~** *fig* estar en la misma onda

wa·ver [ˈweɪvər] *v/i* vacilar, titubear

wav·y [ˈweɪvɪ] *adj hair, line* ondulado

wax [wæks] *n for floor, furniture* cera *f*; *in ear* cera *f*, cerumen

way [weɪ] **1** *n* (*method*) manera *f*, forma *f*; (*manner*) manera *f*, modo *m*; (*route*) camino *m*; **I don't like the ~ he behaves** no me gusta cómo se comporta; **can you tell me the ~ to …?** ¿me podría decir cómo se va a …?; **this ~** (*like this*) así; (*in this direction*) por aquí; **by the ~** (*incidentally*) por cierto, a propósito; **by ~ of** (*via*) por; (*in the form of*) a modo de; **in a ~** (*in certain respects*) en cierto sentido; **be under ~** haber comenzado, estar en marcha; **give ~** MOT ceder el paso; (*collapse*) ceder; **give ~ to** (*be replaced by*) ser reemplazado por; **have one's** (**own**) **~** salirse con la suya; **OK, we'll do it your ~** de acuerdo, la haremos a tu manera; **lead the ~** abrir el (el) camino; *fig* marcar la pauta; **lose one's ~** perderse; **be in the ~** (*be an obstruction*) estar en medio; **it's on the ~ to the station** está camino de la estación; **I was on my ~ to the station** iba camino de la estación; **no ~!** ¡ni hablar!, ¡de ninguna manera!; **there's no ~ he can do it** es imposible que lo haga **2** *adv* F (*much*): **it's ~ too soon to decide** es demasiado pronto como para decidir; **they are ~ behind with their work** van atrasadísimos en el trabajo

way 'in entrada *f*; **way of 'life** modo *m* de vida; **way 'out** *n also fig: from situation* salida *f*

we [wiː] *pron* nosotros *mpl*, nosotras *fpl*; **~ are the best** somos los mejores; **they're going, but ~'re not** ellos van, pero nosotros no

weak [wiːk] *adj* débil; *tea, coffee* poco cargado

weak·en ['wiːkən] **1** v/t debilitar **2** v/i debilitarse

weak·ling ['wiːklɪŋ] morally cobarde m/f, physically enclenque m/f

weak·ness ['wiːknɪs] debilidad f; **have a ~ for sth** (liking) sentir debilidad por algo

wealth [welθ] riqueza f; **a ~ of** abundancia de

wealth·y ['welθɪ] adj rico

wean [wiːn] v/t destetar

weap·on ['wepən] arma f

wear [wer] **1** n: **~ (and tear)** desgaste m; **clothes for everyday/evening ~** ropa f de diario/de noche **2** v/t (pret **wore**, pp **worn**) (have on) llevar; (damage) desgastar **3** v/i (pret **wore**, pp **worn**) (wear out) desgastarse; (last) durar

♦ **wear away 1** v/i desgastarse **2** v/t desgastar

♦ **wear down** v/t agotar

♦ **wear off** v/i of effect, feeling pasar

♦ **wear out 1** v/t (tire) agotar; shoes desgastar **2** v/i of shoes, carpet desgastarse

wea·ri·ly ['wɪrɪlɪ] adv cansinamente

wear·ing ['werɪŋ] adj (tiring) agotador

wear·y ['wɪrɪ] adj cansado

weath·er ['weðər] **1** n tiempo m; **what's the ~ like?** ¿qué tiempo hace?; **be feeling under the ~** estar pachucho **2** v/t crisis capear, superar

'weath·er-beat·en adj curtido; **'weath·er chart** mapa m del tiempo; **'weath·er fore·cast** pronóstico m del tiempo; **'weath·er·man** hombre m del tiempo

weave [wiːv] **1** v/t (pret **wove**, pp **woven**) **2** v/i (pret **wove**, pp **woven**) move zigzaguear

web [web] of spider tela f; **the Web** COMPUT la Web

webbed 'feet patas fpl palmeadas

'web page página f web

'web site sitio m web

wed·ding ['wedɪŋ] boda f

'wed·ding an·ni·ver·sa·ry aniversario m de boda; **'wed·ding cake** pastel m or tarta f de boda; **'wed·ding day** día f de la boda; **'wed·ding dress** vestido m de boda or novia; **'wed·ding ring** anillo m de boda

wedge [wedʒ] **1** n to hold sth in place cuña f, of cheese etc trozo m **2** v/t: **~ a door open** calzar una puerta para que se quede abierta

Wed·nes·day ['wenzdeɪ] miércoles m inv

weed [wiːd] **1** n mala hierba **2** v/t escardar

♦ **weed out** v/t (remove) eliminar; candidates descartar

'weed-kill·er herbicida m

weed·y ['wiːdɪ] adj F esmirriado, enclenque

week [wiːk] semana f; **a ~ tomorrow** dentro de una semana

'week·day día m de la semana

week·end fin m de semana; **on the ~** el fin de semana

week·ly ['wiːklɪ] **1** adj semanal **2** n magazine semanario m **3** adv semanalmente

weep [wiːp] v/i (pret & pp **wept**) llorar

'weep·ing wil·low sauce m llorón

weep·y ['wiːpɪ] adj: **be ~** estar lloroso

wee-wee 1 n F pipí m; **do a ~** hacer pipí **2** v/i F hacer pipí

weigh[1] [weɪ] **1** v/t pesar **2** v/i pesar; **how much do you ~?** ¿cuánto pesas?

weigh[2] [weɪ] v/t: **~ anchor** levar anclas

♦ **weigh down** v/t cargar; **be weighed down with** bags ir cargado con; worries estar abrumado por

♦ **weigh on** v/t preocupar

♦ **weigh up** v/t (assess) sopesar

weight [weɪt] peso m; **put on ~** engordar, ganar peso; **lose ~** adelgazar, perder peso

♦ weight down v/t sujetar (con pesos)

weight·less ['weɪtləs] adj ingrávido

weight·less·ness ['weɪtləsnəs] ingravidez f

'weight-lift·er levantador(a) m(f) de pesas

'weight-lift·ing halterofilia f, levantamiento m de pesas

weight·y ['weɪtɪ] *adj fig (important)* serio

weir [wɪr] *presa f (rebasadero)*

weird [wɪrd] *adj* extraño, raro

weird·ly ['wɪrdlɪ] *adv* extrañamente

weird·o ['wɪrdoʊ] *n* F bicho *m* raro F

wel·come ['welkəm] **1** *adj* bienvenido; *you're ~!* ¡de nada!; *you're ~ to try some* prueba algunos, por favor **2** *n* bienvenida *f* **3** *v/t guests etc* dar la bienvenida a; *fig: decision etc* acoger positivamente

weld [weld] *v/t* soldar

weld·er ['weldər] soldador(a) *m(f)*

wel·fare ['welfer] bienestar *m; financial assistance* subsidio *m* estatal; *be on ~* estar recibiendo subsidios del Estado

'wel·fare check *cheque con el importe del subsidio estatal;* **wel·fare 'state** estado *m* del bienestar; **'wel·fare work** trabajo *m* social; **'wel·fare work·er** asistente *m/f* social

well¹ [wel] *n for water, oil* pozo *m*

well² **1** *adv* bien; *as ~ (too)* también; *as ~ as (in addition to)* así como; *it's just as ~ you told me* menos mal que me lo dijiste; *very ~* muy bien; *~, ~!* surprise ¡caramba!; *~ ... uncertainty, thinking* bueno ...; *you might as ~ spend the night here* ya puestos quédate a pasar la noche aquí; *you might as ~ throw it out* yo de ti lo tiraría **2** *adj: be ~* estar bien; *how are you? – I'm very ~* ¿cómo estás? – muy bien; *feel ~* sentirse bien; *get ~ soon!* ¡ponte bueno!, ¡que te mejores!

well-'bal·anced *adj person, diet* equilibrado; **well-be'haved** *adj* educado; **well-'be·ing** bienestar *m;* **well-'built** *adj also euph* fornido; **well-'done** *adj meat* muy hecho; **well-'dressed** *adj* bien vestido; **well-'earned** *adj* merecido; **well-'heeled** *adj* F adinerado, *Span* con pasta F; **well-in'formed** *adj* bien informado; **well-'known** *adj fact* conocido; *person* conocido, famoso; **well-'made** *adj* bien hecho; **well-'man·nered** *adj* educado; **well-**

'mean·ing *adj* bienintencionado; **well-'off** *adj* acomodado; **well-'paid** *adj* bien pagado; **well-'read** *adj: be ~* haber leído mucho; **well-'timed** *adj* oportuno; **well-to-'do** *adj* acomodado; **'well-wish·er** admirador(a) *m(f);* **well-'worn** *adj* gastado

Welsh [welʃ] **1** *adj* galés **2** *n language* galés; *the ~* los galeses

went [went] *pret →* **go**

wept [wept] *pret & pp →* **weep**

were [wer] *pret →* **be**

west [west] **1** *n* oeste *m; the West (Western nations)* el Occidente; *(western part of a country)* el oeste **2** *adj* del oeste; *~ Africa* África occidental **3** *adv travel* hacia el oeste; *~ of* al oeste de

West 'Coast *of USA* Costa *f* Oeste

west·er·ly ['westərlɪ] *adj wind* del oeste; *direction* hacia el oeste

west·ern ['westərn] **1** *adj* occidental; *Western* occidental **2** *n movie* western *m,* película *f* del oeste

West·ern·er ['westərnər] occidental *m/f*

west·ern·ized ['westərnaɪzd] *adj* occidentalizado

West 'In·di·an 1 *adj* antillano **2** *n* antillano(-a) *m(f)*

West In·dies ['ɪndɪz] *npl: the ~* las Antillas

west·ward ['westwərd] *adv* hacia el oeste

wet [wet] *adj* mojado; *(damp)* húmedo; *(rainy)* lluvioso; *get ~* mojarse; *~ paint as sign* recién pintado; *be ~ through* estar empapado

wet 'blan·ket F aguafiestas *m/f inv*

'wet suit *for diving* traje *m* de neopreno

whack [wæk] **1** *n* F *(blow)* porrazo *m* F; F *(share)* parte *f* **2** *v/t* F dar un porrazo a F

whacked [wækt] *adj* F hecho polvo F

whale [weɪl] ballena *f*

whal·ing ['weɪlɪŋ] caza *f* de ballenas

wharf [wɔːrf] *n* embarcadero *m*

what [wɑːt] **1** *pron* qué; *~ is that?* ¿qué es eso?; *~ is it? (what do you*

W

want) ¿qué quieres?; **~?** (*what do you want*) ¿qué?; (*what did you say*) ¿qué?, ¿cómo?; *astonishment* ¿qué?; **~ about some dinner?** ¿os apetece cenar?; **~ about heading home?** ¿y si nos fuéramos a casa?; **~ for?** (*why*) ¿para qué?; **so ~?** ¿y qué?; **~ is the book about?** ¿de qué trata el libro?; *take ~ you need* toma lo que te haga falta **2** *adj* qué; **~ university are you at?** ¿en qué universidad estás?; **~ color is the car?** ¿de qué color es el coche?

what·ev·er [wɑːt'evər] **1** *pron*: *I'll do ~ you want* haré lo que quieras; **~ gave you that idea?** ¿se puede saber qué te ha dado esa idea?; **~ the season** en cualquier estación; **~ people say** diga lo que diga la gente **2** *adj* cualquier; *you have no reason ~ to worry* no tienes por qué preocuparte en absoluto

wheat [wiːt] trigo *m*

whee·dle ['wiːdl] *v/t*: **~ sth out of s.o.** camelar algo a alguien

wheel [wiːl] **1** *n* rueda *f*; (*steering ~*) volante *m* **2** *v/t bicycle* empujar **3** *v/i of birds* volar en círculo

♦ **wheel around** *v/i* darse la vuelta

'**wheel·bar·row** carretilla *f*; '**wheel·chair** silla *f* de ruedas; '**wheel clamp** cepo *m*

wheeze [wiːz] *n* resoplido *m*

when [wen] **1** *adv* cuándo; **~ do you open?** ¿a qué hora abren? **2** *conj* cuando; **~ I was a child** cuando era niño

when·ev·er [wen'evər] *adv* (*each time*) cada vez que; *call me ~ you like* llámame cuando quieras; *I go to Paris ~ I can afford it* voy a París siempre que me lo puedo permitir

where [wer] **1** *adv* dónde; **~ from?** ¿de dónde?; **~ to?** ¿a dónde? **2** *conj* donde; *this is ~ I used to live* aquí es donde vivía antes

where·a·bouts [werə'bauts] **1** *adv* dónde **2** *npl*: *nothing is known of his ~* está en paradero desconocido

where·as *conj* mientras que

wher·ev·er [wer'evər] **1** *conj* donde-

quiera que; *sit ~ you like* siéntate donde prefieras **2** *adv* dónde

whet [wet] *v/t* (*pret & pp* **-ted**) *appetite* abrir

wheth·er ['weðər] *conj* si; *I don't know ~ to tell him or not* no sé si decírselo o no; **~ you approve or not** te parezca bien o no

which [wɪtʃ] **1** *adj* qué; **~ one is yours?** ¿cuál es tuyo? **2** *pron interrogative* cuál; *relative* que; *take one, it doesn't matter ~* toma uno, no importa cuál

which·ev·er [wɪtʃ'evər] **1** *adj*: **~ color you choose** elijas el color que elijas **2** *pron*: **~ you like** el que quieras; *use ~ of the methods you prefer* utiliza el método que prefieras

whiff [wɪf] (*smell*) olorcillo *m*

while [waɪl] **1** *conj* mientras; (*although*) si bien **2** *n* rato *m*; *a long ~* un rato largo; *for a ~* durante un tiempo; *I lived in Tokyo for a ~* viví en Tokio una temporada; *I'll wait a ~ longer* esperaré un rato más

♦ **while away** *v/t* pasar

whim [wɪm] capricho *m*

whim·per ['wɪmpər] **1** *n* gimoteo *m* **2** *v/i* gimotear

whine [waɪn] *v/i of dog* gimotear; F (*complain*) quejarse

whip [wɪp] **1** *n* látigo *m* **2** *v/t* (*pret & pp* **-ped**) (*beat*) azotar; *cream* batir, montar; F (*defeat*) dar una paliza a F

♦ **whip up** *v/t* (*arouse*) agitar

'**whipped cream** [wɪpt] nata *f* montada

whip·ping ['wɪpɪŋ] (*beating*) azotes *mpl*; F (*defeat*) paliza *f* F

'**whip·round** F colecta *f*; *have a ~* hacer una colecta

whirl [wɜːrl] **1** *n*: *my mind is in a ~* me da vueltas la cabeza **2** *v/i* dar vueltas

'**whirl·pool** *in river* remolino *m*; *for relaxation* bañera *f* de hidromasaje

whirr [wɜːr] *v/i* zumbar

whisk [wɪsk] **1** *n kitchen implement* **2** *v/t eggs* batir

♦ **whisk away** *v/t* retirar rápidamente

whis·kers ['wɪskərz] *npl of man* pati-

llas *fpl; of animal* bigotes *mpl*
whis·key ['wɪskɪ] whisky *m*
whis·per ['wɪspər] **1** *n* susurro *m*; (*rumor*) rumor *m* **2** *v/i* susurrar **3** *v/t* susurrar
whis·tle ['wɪsl] **1** *n sound* silbido *m*; *device* silbato *m* **2** *v/t & v/i* silbar
white [waɪt] **1** *n color* blanco *m*; *of egg* clara *f; person* blanco(-a) *m(f)* **2** *adj* blanco; *her face went* ~ se puso blanca
white 'Christ·mas Navidades *fpl* blancas; **white 'cof·fee** *Br* café *m* con leche; **white-col·lar 'work·er** persona que trabaja en una oficina; **'White House** Casa *f* Blanca; **white 'lie** mentira *f* piadosa; **white 'meat** carne *f* blanca; **'white-out** (*for text*) Tipp-Ex® *m*; **'white·wash 1** *n* cal *f; fig* encubrimiento *m* **2** *v/t* encalar; **white 'wine** vino *m* blanco
whit·tle ['wɪtl] *v/t wood* tallar
♦ **whittle down** *v/t* reducir
whiz(z) [wɪz] *n:* **be a ~ at** F ser un genio de
♦ **whizz by, whizz past** *v/i of time, car* pasar zumbando
'whizz·kid F joven *m/f* prodigio
who [huː] *pron interrogative* ¿quién?; *relative* que; ~ *do you want to speak to* ¿con quién quieres hablar?; *I don't know* ~ *to believe* no sé a quién creer
who·dun·(n)it [huː'dʌnɪt] *libro o película centrados en la resolución de un caso*
who·ev·er [huː'evər] *pron* quienquiera; ~ *can that be calling at this time of night?* ¿pero quién llama a estas horas de la noche?
whole [hoʊl] **1** *adj* entero; *the* ~ *town/ country* toda la ciudad / todo el país; *it's a* ~ *lot easier/ better* es mucho más fácil / mucho mejor **2** *n* totalidad *f; the* ~ *of the United States* la totalidad de los Estados Unidos; *on the* ~ en general
whole-heart·ed [hoʊl'hɑːrtɪd] *adj* incondicional; **whole-heart·ed·ly** [hoʊl'hɑːrtɪdlɪ] *adv* incondicionalmente; **whole·meal 'bread** pan *m*

integral; **'whole·sale 1** *adj* al por mayor; *fig* indiscriminado **2** *adv* al por mayor; **whole·sal·er** ['hoʊlseɪlər] mayorista *m/f*; **whole·some** ['hoʊlsəm] *adj* saludable, sano
whol·ly ['hoʊlɪ] *adv* completamente
whol·ly owned 'sub·sid·i·ar·y subsidiaria *f* en propiedad absoluta
whom [huːm] *pron fml* quién; ~ *did you see?* ¿a quién vio?; *the person to* ~ *I was speaking* la persona con la que estaba hablando
whoop·ing cough ['huːpɪŋ] tos *f* ferina
whop·ping ['wɑːpɪŋ] *adj* F enorme
whore [hɔːr] *n* prostituta *f*
whose [huːz] **1** *pron interrogative* de quién; *relative* cuyo(-a); ~ *is this?* ¿de quién es esto?; *a country* ~ *economy is booming* un país cuya economía está experimentando un boom **2** *adj* de quién; ~ *bike is that?* ¿de quién es esa bici?
why [waɪ] *adv interrogative, relative* por qué; *that's* ~ por eso; ~ *not?* ¿por qué no?
wick [wɪk] pabilo *m*
wick·ed ['wɪkɪd] *adj* malvado, perverso
wick·er ['wɪkər] *adj* de mimbre
wick·er 'chair silla *f* de mimbre
wick·et ['wɪkɪt] *in station, bank etc* ventanilla *f*
wide [waɪd] *adj* ancho; *experience, range* amplio; *be 12 feet* ~ tener 12 pies de ancho
wide a'wake *adj* completamente despierto
wide·ly ['waɪdlɪ] *adv used, known* ampliamente
wid·en ['waɪdn] **1** *v/t* ensanchar **2** *v/i* ensancharse
wide-'o·pen *adj* abierto de par en par; **wide-'rang·ing** *adj* amplio; **'wide·spread** *adj* extendido, muy difundido
wid·ow ['wɪdoʊ] *n* viuda *f*
wid·ow·er ['wɪdoʊər] viudo *m*
width [wɪdθ] anchura *f*, ancho *m*
wield [wiːld] *v/t weapon* empuñar; *power* detentar

W

wife [waɪf] (*pl* **wives** [waɪvz]) mujer *f*, esposa *f*

wig [wɪg] peluca *f*

wig·gle ['wɪgl] *v/t* menear

wild [waɪld] **1** *adj animal* salvaje; *flower* silvestre; *teenager*, *party* descontrolado; (*crazy: scheme*) descabellado; *applause* arrebatado; *be ~ about ...* (*enthusiastic*) estar loco por ...; *go ~* (*express enthusiasm*) volverse loco; (*become angry*) ponerse hecho una furia; *run ~ of children* desahogarse **2** *n*: *the ~s* los parajes remotos

wil·der·ness ['wɪldərnɪs] desierto *m*, yermo *m*

'wild·fire: *spread like ~* extenderse como un reguero de pólvora; **wild·'goose chase** búsqueda *f* infructuosa; **'wild·life** flora *f* y fauna; *~ program* TV documental *f* sobre la naturaleza

wild·ly ['waɪldlɪ] *adv applaud* enfervorizadamente; *I'm not ~ enthusiastic about the idea* la idea no me emociona demasiado

wil·ful *Br* → **willful**

will¹ [wɪl] *n* LAW testamento *m*

will² [wɪl] *n* (*willpower*) voluntad *f*

will³ [wɪl] *v/aux*: *I ~ let you know tomorrow* te lo diré mañana; *~ you be there?* ¿estarás allí?; *I won't be back until late* volveré tarde; *you ~ call me, won't you?* me llamarás, ¿verdad?; *I'll pay for this – no you won't* esto lo pago yo – no, ni hablar; *the car won't start* el coche no arranca; *~ you tell her that ...?* ¿le quieres decir que ...?; *~ you have some more tea?* ¿quiere más té?; *~ you stop that!* ¡basta ya!

will·ful ['wɪlfəl] *adj person* tozudo, obstinado; *action* deliberado, intencionado

will·ing ['wɪlɪŋ] *adj* dispuesto

will·ing·ly ['wɪlɪŋlɪ] *adv* gustosamente

will·ing·ness ['wɪlɪŋnɪs] buena disposición *f*

wil·low ['wɪlou] sauce *m*

'will·pow·er fuerza *f* de voluntad

wil·ly-nil·ly [wɪlɪ'nɪlɪ] *adv* (*at random*) a la buena de Dios

wilt [wɪlt] *v/i of plant* marchitarse

wi·ly ['waɪlɪ] *adj* astuto

wimp [wɪmp] F enclenque *m/f* F, blandengue *m/f* F

win [wɪn] **1** *n* victoria *f*, triunfo *m* **2** *v/t & v/i* (*pret & pp* **won**) ganar

♦ **win back** *v/t* recuperar

wince [wɪns] *v/i* hacer una mueca de dolor

winch [wɪntʃ] *n* torno *m*, cabestrante *m*

wind¹ [wɪnd] **1** *n* viento *m*; (*flatulence*) gases *mpl*; *get ~ of ...* enterarse de ... **2** *v/t*: *be ~ed* quedarse sin respiración

wind² [waɪnd] **1** *v/i* (*pret & pp* **wound**) zigzaguear, serpentear; *~ around* enrollarse en **2** *v/t* (*pret & pp* **wound**) enrollar

♦ **wind down 1** *v/i of party etc* ir finalizando **2** *v/t car window* bajar, abrir; *business* ir reduciendo

♦ **wind up 1** *v/t clock* dar cuerda a; *car window* subir, cerrar; *speech, presentation* finalizar; *business, affairs* concluir; *company* cerrar **2** *v/i* (*finish*) concluir; *wind up in hospital* acabar en el hospital

'wind·bag F cotorra *f* F

'wind·fall *fig* dinero *m* inesperado

wind·ing ['waɪndɪŋ] *adj* zigzagueante, serpenteante

'wind in·stru·ment instrumento *m* de viento

'wind·mill molino *m* de viento

win·dow ['wɪndou] *also* COMPUT ventana *f*; *of car* ventana *f*, ventanilla *f*; *in the ~ of store* en el escaparate *or* L.Am. la vidriera

'win·dow box jardinera *f*; **'win·dow clean·er** *person* limpiacristales *m/f inv*; **'win·dow·pane** cristal *f* (*de una ventana*); **'win·dow seat** *on plane, train* asiento *m* de ventana; **'win·dow-shop** *v/i* (*pret & pp -ped*): *go ~ping* ir de escaparates *or* L.Am. vidrieras; **win·dow·sill** ['wɪndousɪl] alféizar *m*

'wind·pipe tráquea *f*; **'wind·screen**

Br, '**wind·shield** parabrisas *m inv;* '**wind·shield wip·er** limpiaparabrisas *m inv;* '**wind·surf·er** *person* windsurfista *m/f; board* tabla *f* de windsurf; '**wind·surf·ing** el windsurf

wind·y ['wɪndɪ] *adj* ventoso; *a ~ day* un día de mucho viento; *it's very ~ today* hoy hace mucho viento; *it's getting ~* está empezando a soplar el viento

wine [waɪn] vino *m*

'**wine bar** *bar especializado en vinos;* '**wine cel·lar** bodega *f;* '**wine glass** copa *f* de vino; '**wine list** lista *f* de vinos; '**wine mak·er** viticultor(a) *m(f);* '**wine mer·chant** comerciante *m/f* de vinos

win·ery ['waɪnərɪ] bodega *f*

wing [wɪŋ] *n* ala *f;* SP lateral *m/f,* extremo *m/f*

'**wing·span** envergadura *f*

wink [wɪŋk] **1** *n* guiño *m; I didn't sleep a ~* F no pegué ojo **2** *v/i of person* guiñar, hacer un guiño; *~ at s.o.* guiñar *or* hacer un guiño a alguien

win·ner ['wɪnər] ganador(a) *m(f),* vencedor(a) *m(f); of lottery* acertante *m/f*

win·ning ['wɪnɪŋ] *adj* ganador

'**win·ning post** meta *f*

win·nings ['wɪnɪŋz] *npl* ganancias *fpl*

win·ter ['wɪntər] *n* invierno *m*

win·ter 'sports *npl* deportes *mpl* de invierno

win·try ['wɪntrɪ] *adj* invernal

wipe [waɪp] *v/t* limpiar; *tape* borrar

♦ **wipe out** *v/t (kill, destroy)* eliminar; *debt* saldar

wip·er ['waɪpər] → **windshield wiper**

wire [waɪr] *n* alambre *m;* ELEC cable *m*

wire·less ['waɪrlɪs] radio *f*

wire 'net·ting tela *f* metálica

wir·ing ['waɪrɪŋ] *n* ELEC cableado *m*

wir·y ['waɪrɪ] *adj person* fibroso

wis·dom ['wɪzdəm] *of person* sabiduría *f; of action* prudencia *f,* sensatez *f*

'**wis·dom tooth** muela *f* del juicio

wise [waɪz] *adj* sabio; *action, decision* prudente, sensato

'**wise·crack** *n* F chiste *m,* comentario *m* gracioso

'**wise guy** *pej* sabelotodo *m*

wise·ly ['waɪzlɪ] *adv act* prudentemente, sensatamente

wish [wɪʃ] **1** *n* deseo *m; best ~es* un saludo cordial; *make a ~* pedir un deseo **2** *v/t* desear; *I ~ that you could stay* ojalá te pudieras quedar; *~ s.o. well* desear a alguien lo mejor; *I ~ed him good luck* le deseé buena suerte **3** *v/i: ~ for* desear

'**wish·bone** espoleta *f*

wish·ful 'think·ing ['wɪʃfəl] ilusiones *fpl; that's ~ on her part* que no se haga ilusiones

wish·y-wash·y ['wɪʃɪwɑːʃɪ] *adj person* anodino; *color* pálido

wisp [wɪsp] *of hair* mechón *m; of smoke* voluta *f*

wist·ful ['wɪstfəl] *adj* nostálgico

wist·ful·ly ['wɪstfəlɪ] *adv* con nostalgia

wit [wɪt] *(humor)* ingenio *m; person* ingenioso(-a) *m(f); be at one's ~s' end* estar desesperado; *keep one's ~s about one* mantener la calma; *be scared out of one's ~s* estar aterrorizado

witch [wɪtʃ] bruja *f*

'**witch·hunt** *fig* caza *f* de brujas

with [wɪð] *prep* con; *shivering ~ fear* temblando de miedo; *a girl ~ brown eyes* una chica de ojos castaños; *are you ~ me? (do you understand)* ¿me sigues?; *~ no money* sin dinero

with·draw [wɪð'drɔː] **1** *v/t (pret -drew,* pp *-drawn) complaint, money, troops* retirar **2** *v/i (pret -drew,* pp *-drawn) of competitor, troops* retirarse

with·draw·al [wɪð'drɔːəl] *of complaint, application, troops* retirada *f; of money* reintegro *m*

with·draw·al symp·toms *npl* síndrome *m* de abstinencia

with·drawn [wɪð'drɔːn] *adj person* retraído

with·er ['wɪðər] *v/i* marchitarse

W

with·hold v/t (pret & pp **-held**) *information* ocultar; *payment* retener; *consent* negar

with·in prep (*inside*) dentro de; *in expressions of time* en menos de; **~ five miles of home** a cinco millas de casa; **we kept ~ the budget** no superamos el presupuesto; **it is well ~ your capabilities** lo puedes conseguir perfectamente; **~ reach** al alcance de la mano

with·out prep sin; **~ looking / asking** sin mirar / preguntar

with·stand v/t (pret & pp **-stood**) resistir, soportar

wit·ness ['wɪtnɪs] **1** n testigo m/f **2** v/t ser testigo de; **I ~ed his signature** firmé en calidad de testigo

'wit·ness stand estrado m del testigo

wit·ti·cism ['wɪtɪsɪzm] comentario m gracioso or agudo

wit·ty ['wɪtɪ] adj ingenioso, agudo

wob·ble ['wɑːbl] v/i tambalearse

wob·bly ['wɑːblɪ] adj tambaleante

wok [wɑːk] wok m, *sartén típica de la cocina china*

woke [woʊk] pret → **wake**

wok·en ['woʊkn] pp → **wake**

wolf [wʊlf] **1** n (pl **wolves** [wʊlvz]) *animal* lobo m; fig (*womanizer*) don juan m **2** v/t: **~** (**down**) engullir

'wolf whis·tle n silbido m

'wolf-whis·tle v/i: **~ at s.o.** silbar a alguien (*como piropo*)

wom·an ['wʊmən] (pl **women** ['wɪmɪn]) mujer f

wom·an 'doc·tor médica f

wom·an 'driv·er conductora f

wom·an·iz·er ['wʊmənaɪzər] mujeriego(-a) m(f)

wom·an·ly ['wʊmənlɪ] adj femenino

wom·an 'priest mujer f sacerdote

womb [wuːm] matriz f, útero m

wom·en ['wɪmɪn] pl → **woman**

wom·en's lib [wɪmɪnz'lɪb] la liberación de la mujer

wom·en's lib·ber [wɪmɪnz'lɪbər] partidario(-a) m(f) de la liberación de la mujer

won [wʌn] pret & pp → **win**

won·der ['wʌndər] **1** n (*amazement*) asombro m; **no ~!** ¡no me sorprende!; **it's a ~ that ...** es increíble que ... **2** v/i preguntarse; **I've often ~ed about that** me he preguntado eso a menudo **3** v/t preguntarse; **I ~ if you could help** ¿le importaría ayudarme?

won·der·ful ['wʌndərfəl] adj maravilloso

won·der·ful·ly ['wʌndərfəlɪ] adv (*extremely*) maravillosamente

won't [woʊnt] → **will⁰**

wood [wʊd] n madera f; *for fire* leña f; (*forest*) bosque m

wood·ed ['wʊdɪd] adj arbolado

wood·en ['wʊdn] adj (*made of wood*) de madera

wood·peck·er ['wʊdpekər] pájaro m carpintero

'wood·wind MUS sección f de viento de madera

'wood·work carpintería f

wool [wʊl] n lana f

wool·en, Br **wool·len** ['wʊlən] **1** adj de lana **2** n prenda f de lana

word [wɜːrd] **1** n palabra f; **I didn't understand a ~ of what she said** no entendí nada de lo que dijo; **is there any ~ from ...?** ¿se sabe algo de ...?; **I've had ~ from my daughter** (*news*) he recibido noticias de mi hija; **you have my ~** tienes mi palabra; **have ~s** (*argue*) discutir; **have a ~ with** hablar con alguien; **the ~s of song** la letra **2** v/t *article, letter* redactar

word·ing ['wɜːrdɪŋ]: **the ~ of a letter** la redacción de una carta

word 'pro·cess·ing procesamiento m de textos

word 'pro·ces·sor *software* procesador m de textos

wore [wɔːr] pret → **wear**

work [wɜːrk] **1** n (job) trabajo m; (*employment*) trabajo m, empleo m; **out of ~** desempleado, Span en el paro; **be at ~** estar en el trabajo; **I go to ~ by bus** voy al trabajo en autobús **2** v/i *of person* trabajar; *of machine*, (*succeed*) funcionar; **how**

does it ~? *of device* ¿cómo funciona? **3** *v/t employee* hacer trabajar; *machine* hacer funcionar, utilizar

♦ **work off** *v/t bad mood, anger* desahogarse de; *flab* perder haciendo ejercicio

♦ **work out 1** *v/t problem, puzzle* resolver; *solution* encontrar, hallar **2** *v/i at gym* hacer ejercicios; *of relationship etc* funcionar, ir bien

♦ **work out to** *v/t (add up to)* sumar

♦ **work up** *v/t appetite* abrir; **work up enthusiasm** entusiasmarse; **get worked up** *(get angry)* alterarse; *(get nervous)* ponerse nervioso

work·a·ble ['wɜːrkəbl] *adj solution* viable

work·a·hol·ic [wɜːrkə'hɑːlɪk] *n* F *persona adicta al trabajo*

'**work·day** *(hours of work)* jornada *f* laboral; *(not a holiday)* día *m* de trabajo

work·er ['wɜːrkər] trabajador(a) *m(f)*; **she's a good ~** trabaja bien

'**work·force** trabajadores *mpl*

'**work hours** *npl* horas *fpl* de trabajo

work·ing ['wɜːrkɪŋ] *n* funcionamiento *m*

'**work·ing class** clase *f* trabajadora; '**work·ing-class** *adj* de clase trabajadora; '**work·ing con·di·tions** *npl* condiciones *fpl* de trabajo; **work·ing 'day** → **workday**; '**work·ing hours** → **workhours**; **work·ing 'know·ledge** conocimientos *mpl* básicos; **work·ing 'moth·er** madre *f* que trabaja

'**work·load** cantidad *f* de trabajo; '**work·man** obrero *m*; '**work·man·like** *adj* competente; '**work·man·ship** factura *f*, confección *f*; **work of 'art** obra *f* de arte; '**work·out** sesión *f* de ejercicios; '**work per·mit** permiso *m* de trabajo; '**work·shop** *also seminar* taller *m*; '**work sta·tion** estación *f* de trabajo; '**work·top** encimera *f*

world [wɜːrld] mundo *m*; **the ~ of computers / the theater** el mundo de la informática / del teatro; **out of this ~** F sensacional

world-'class *adj* de categoría mundial; **World 'Cup** Mundial *m*, Copa *f* del Mundo; **world-'fa·mous** *adj* mundialmente famoso

world·ly ['wɜːrldlɪ] *adj* mundano

world 'pow·er potencia *f* mundial; **world 're·cord** récord *m* mundial *or* del mundo; **world 'war** guerra *f* mundial; '**world·wide 1** *adj* mundial **2** *adv* en todo el mundo

worm [wɜːrm] *n* gusano *m*

worn [wɔːrn] *pp* → **wear**

worn-'out *adj shoes, carpet, part* gastado; *person* agotado

wor·ried ['wʌrɪd] *adj* preocupado

wor·ried·ly ['wʌrɪdlɪ] *adv* con preocupación

wor·ry ['wʌrɪ] **1** *n* preocupación *f* **2** *v/t (pret & pp -ied)* preocupar **3** *v/i (pret & pp -ied)* preocuparse; **don't ~, I'll get it!** ¡no te molestes, ya respondo yo!

wor·ry·ing ['wʌrɪɪŋ] *adj* preocupante

worse [wɜːrs] **1** *adj* peor; **get ~** empeorar **2** *adv* peor

wors·en ['wɜːrsn] *v/i* empeorar

wor·ship ['wɜːrʃɪp] **1** *n* culto *m* **2** *v/t (pret & pp -ped)* adorar, rendir culto a; *fig* adorar

worst [wɜːrst] **1** *adj & adv* peor **2** *n:* **the ~** lo peor; **if the ~ comes to ~** en el peor de los casos

worst-case scen'a·ri·o el peor de los casos

worth [wɜːrθ] *adj:* **$20 ~ of gas** 20 dólares de gasolina; **be ~ ... in** *monetary terms* valer ...; **the book's ~ reading** vale la pena leer el libro; **be ~ it** valer la pena

worth·less ['wɜːrθlɪs] *adj person* inútil; **be ~** *of object* no valer nada

worth'while *adj* que vale la pena; **be ~** valer la pena

worth·y ['wɜːrðɪ] *adj* digno; *cause* justo; **be ~ of** *(deserve)* merecer

would [wʊd] *v/aux:* **I ~ help if I could** te ayudaría si pudiera; **I said that I ~ go** dije que iría; **I told him I ~ not leave unless ....** le dije que no me iría a no ser que ...; **~ you like to go to the movies?** ¿te gustaría ir al cine?; **~ you mind if I smoked?** ¿le importa si fumo?; **~ you tell her that ...?** ¿le podrías decir que ...?; **~ you close the door?** ¿podrías cerrar la puerta?; **I ~ have told you but ...** te lo habría dicho pero ...; **I ~ not have been so angry if ...** no me habría enfadado tanto si ...

wound[1] [wu:nd] **1** *n* herida *f* **2** *v/t with weapon, remark* herir

wound[2] [waund] *pret & pp* → **wind**[2]

wove [wouv] *pret* → **weave**

wov·en [ˈwouvn] *pp* → **weave**

wow [wau] *int* ¡hala!

wrap [ræp] *v/t* (*pret & pp* **-ped**) *parcel, gift* envolver; **he ~ped a scarf around his neck** se puso una bufanda al cuello

♦ **wrap up** *v/i against the cold* abrigarse

wrap·per [ˈræpər] *for candy etc* envoltorio *m*

wrap·ping [ˈræpɪŋ] envoltorio *m*

'wrap·ping pa·per papel *m* de envolver

wrath [ræθ] ira *f*

wreath [ri:θ] corona *f* de flores

wreck [rek] **1** *n* restos *mpl*; **be a nervous ~** ser un manojo de nervios **2** *v/t ship* hundir; *car* destrozar; *plans, marriage* arruinar

wreck·age [ˈrekɪdʒ] *of car, plane* restos *mpl*; *of marriage, career* ruina *f*

wreck·er [ˈrekər] grúa *f*

wreck·ing com·pa·ny [ˈrekɪŋ] empresa *f* de auxilio en carretera

wrench [rentʃ] **1** *n tool* llave *f* **2** *v/t* (*pull*) arrebatar; **~ one's wrist** hacerse un esguince en la muñeca

wres·tle [ˈresl] *v/i* luchar

♦ **wrestle with** *v/t problems* combatir

wres·tler [ˈreslər] luchador(a) *m(f)* (de lucha libre)

wres·tling [ˈreslɪŋ] lucha *f* libre

'wres·tling con·test combate *m* de lucha libre

wrig·gle [ˈrɪgl] *v/i* (*squirm*) menearse; *along the ground* arrastrarse; *into small space* escurrirse

♦ **wriggle out of** *v/t* librarse de

♦ **wring out** *v/t* (*pret & pp* **wrung**) *cloth* escurrir

wrin·kle [ˈrɪŋkl] **1** *n* arruga *f* **2** *v/t clothes* arrugar **3** *v/i of clothes* arrugarse

wrist [rɪst] muñeca *f*

'wrist·watch reloj *m* de pulsera

writ [rɪt] LAW mandato *m* judicial

write [raɪt] **1** *v/t* (*pret* **wrote**, *pp* **written**) escribir; *check* extender **2** *v/i* (*pret* **wrote**, *pp* **written**) escribir

♦ **write down** *v/t* escribir, tomar nota de

♦ **write off** *v/t debt* cancelar, anular; *car* destrozar

writ·er [ˈraɪtər] escritor(a) *m(f)*; *of book, song* autor(a) *m(f)*

'write-up reseña *f*

writhe [raɪð] *v/i* retorcerse

writ·ing [ˈraɪtɪŋ] *words, text* escritura *f*; (*hand-~*) letra *f*; **in ~** por escrito

'writ·ing desk escritorio *m*

'writ·ing pa·per papel *m* de escribir

writ·ten [ˈrɪtn] *pp* → **write**

wrong [rɒːŋ] **1** *adj answer, information* equivocado; *decision, choice* erróneo; **be ~** *of person* estar equivocado; *of answer* ser incorrecto; *morally* ser injusto; **what's ~?** ¿qué pasa?; **there is something ~ with the car** al coche le pasa algo; **you have the ~ number** TELEC se ha equivocado **2** *adv* mal; **go ~** *of person* equivocarse; *of marriage, plan etc* fallar **3** *n* mal *m*; **right a ~** deshacer un entuerto; **he knows right from ~** sabe distinguir entre el bien y el mal; **be in the ~** tener la culpa

wrong·ful [ˈrɒːŋfəl] *adj* ilegal

wrong·ly [ˈrɒːŋlɪ] *adv* erróneamente

wrote [rout] *pret* → **write**

wrought 'i·ron [rɔːt] hierro *m* forjado

wrung [rʌŋ] *pret & pp* → **wring**

wry [raɪ] *adj* socarrón

xen·o·pho·bi·a [zenouˈfoubɪə] xenofobia *f*

X

X-ray ['eksreɪ] **1** n rayo m X; picture radiografía f **2** v/t radiografiar, sacar un radiografía de

xy·lo·phone [zaɪlə'fəʊn] xilofón m

Y

yacht [jɑːt] yate m

yacht·ing ['jɑːtɪŋ] vela f

yachts·man ['jɑːtsmən] navegante m/f (en embarcación de vela)

Yank [jæŋk] F yanqui m/f

yank [jæŋk] v/t tirar de

yap [jæp] v/i (pret & pp **-ped**) of small dog ladrar (con ladridos agudos); F (talk a lot) parlotear F, largar F

yard¹ [jɑːrd] of prison, institution etc patio m; behind house jardín m; for storage almacén m (al aire libre)

yard² [jɑːrd] measurement yarda f

'yard·stick patrón m

yarn [jɑːrn] n (thread) hilo m; F (story) batallita f F

yawn [jɔːn] **1** n bostezo m **2** v/i bostezar

year [jɪr] año m; **I've known her for ~s** la conozco desde hace años; **be six ~s old** tener seis años (de edad)

year·ly ['jɪrlɪ] **1** adj anual **2** adv anualmente

yearn [jɜːrn] v/i anhelar

♦ **yearn for** v/t ansiar

yearn·ing ['jɜːrnɪŋ] n anhelo m

yeast [jiːst] levadura f

yell [jel] **1** n grito m **2** v/t & v/i gritar

yel·low ['jeləʊ] **1** n amarillo m **2** adj amarillo

yel·low 'pag·es npl páginas fpl amarillas

yelp [jelp] **1** n aullido m **2** v/i aullar

yes [jes] int sí; **she said ~** dijo que sí

'yes·man pej pelotillero m

yes·ter·day ['jestərdeɪ] **1** adv ayer; **the day before ~** anteayer; **~ afternoon** ayer por la tarde **2** n ayer m

yet [jet] **1** adv todavía, aún; **as ~** aún, todavía; **have you finished ~?** ¿has acabado ya?; **he hasn't arrived ~** todavía or aún no ha llegado; **is he here ~? – not ~** ¿ha llegado ya? – todavía or aún no; **~ bigger / longer** aún más grande / largo; **the fastest one ~** el más rápido hasta el momento **2** conj sin embargo; **I'm not sure** sin embargo no estoy seguro

yield [jiːld] **1** n from fields etc cosecha f; from investment rendimiento m **2** v/t fruit, good harvest proporcionar; interest rendir, devengar **3** v/i (give way) ceder; of driver ceder el paso

yo·ga ['jəʊgə] yoga m

yog·hurt ['jəʊgərt] yogur m

yolk [jəʊk] yema f

you [juː] pron singular tú, L.Am. usted, Rpl, C.Am. vos; formal usted; plural: Span vosotros, vosotras, L.Am. ustedes; formal ustedes; **~ are clever** eres / es inteligente; **do ~ know him?** ¿lo conoces / conoce?; **~**

go, I'll stay tú ve / usted vaya, yo me quedo; **~ *never know*** nunca se sabe; **~ *have to pay*** hay que pagar; ***exercise is good for* ~** es bueno hacer ejercicio

young [jʌŋ] *adj* joven

young·ster ['jʌŋstər] joven *m/f*

your [jʊr] *adj singular* tu, *L.Am.* su; *formal* su; *plural: Span* vuestro, *L.Am.* su; *formal* su; **~ *house*** tu / su casa; **~ *books*** tus / sus libros

yours [jʊrz] *pron singular* la tuyo, la tuya, *L.Am.* el suyo, la suya; *formal* el suyo, la suya; *plural* el vuestro, la vuestra, *L.Am.* el suyo, la suya; *formal* el suyo, la suya; ***a friend of* ~** un amigo tuyo / suyo / vuestro; **~ *... at end of letter*** un saludo

your·self [jʊr'self] *pron reflexive* te, *L.Am.* se; *formal* se; *emphatic* tú mismo *m*, tú misma *f*, *L.Am.* usted mismo, usted misma; *Rpl, C.Am.* vos mismo, vos misma; *formal* usted mismo, usted misma; ***did you hurt* ~?** ¿te hiciste / se hizo daño?; ***when you see* ~ *in the mirror*** cuando te ves / se ve en el espejo; ***by* ~** *(alone)* solo; *(without help)* tú solo, tú mis-

mo, *Rpl, C.Am.* vos solo, vos mismo, *L.Am.* usted solo, usted mismo; *formal* usted solo, usted mismo

your·selves [jʊr'selvz] *pron reflexive* os, *L.Am.* se; *formal* se; *emphatic* vosotros mismos *mpl*, vosotras mismas *fpl*, *L.Am.* ustedes mismos, ustedes mismas; *formal* ustedes mismos, ustedes mismas; ***did you hurt* ~?** ¿os hicisteis / se hicieron daño?; ***when you see* ~ *in the mirror*** cuando os veis / se ven en el espejo; ***by* ~** *(alone)* solos; *(without help)* vosotros solos, *L.Am.* ustedes solos, ustedes mismos; *formal* ustedes solos, ustedes mismos

youth [juːθ] *n* juventud *f*; *(young man)* joven *m/f*

youth club club *m* juvenil

'youth·ful ['juːθfəl] *adj* joven; *fashion, idealism* juvenil

'youth hos·tel albergue *m* juvenil

Yu·go·sla·vi·a [juːgə'slɑːvɪə] Yugoslavia

Yu·go·sla·vi·an [juːgə'slɑːvɪən] **1** *adj* yugoslavo **2** *n* yugoslavo(-a) *m(f)*

yup·pie ['jʌpɪ] F yupi *m/f*

Z

zap [zæp] *v/t* (*pret & pp* **-ped**) F (COMPUT: *delete*) borrar; *(kill)* liquidar F; *(hit)* golpear; *(send)* enviar

♦ **zap along** *v/i* F *(move fast)* volar F

zapped [zæpt] *adj* F *(exhausted)* hecho polvo F

zap·per ['zæpər] *for changing TV channels* telemando *m*, mando *m* a distancia

zap·py ['zæpɪ] *adj* F *car, pace* rápido; *(lively, energetic)* vivo

zeal [ziːl] celo *m*

ze·bra ['zebrə] cebra *f*

ze·ro ['zɪroʊ] cero *m*; ***10 degrees***

below **~** 10 bajo cero

♦ **zero in on** *v/t (identify)* centrarse en

ze·ro 'growth crecimiento *m* cero

zest [zest] *(zest)* entusiasmo *m*

zig·zag ['zɪgzæg] **1** *n* zigzag *m* **2** *v/i* (*pret & pp* **-ged**) zigzaguear

zilch [zɪltʃ] F nada de nada

zinc [zɪŋk] cinc *m*

zip [zɪp] *Br* cremallera *f*

♦ **zip up** *v/t* (*pret & pp* **-ped**) *dress, jacket* cerrar la cremallera de; COMPUT compactar

'zip code código *m* postal

zip·per ['zɪpər] cremallera *f*

zit [zɪt] F *on face* grano *m*

zo·di·ac ['zoʊdɪæk] zodiaco *m*; *signs of the* ~ signos *mpl* del zodiaco

zom·bie ['zɑːmbɪ] F (*idiot*) estúpido(-a) *m(f)* F; *feel like a* ~ (*exhausted*) sentirse como un zombi

zone [zoʊn] zona *f*

zonked [zɑːŋkt] *adj* P (*exhausted*) molido P

zoo [zuː] zoo *m*

zo·o·log·i·cal [zuːə'lɑːdʒɪkl] *adj* zoológico

zo·ol·o·gist [zuː'ɑːlədʒɪst] zoólogo(-a) *m(f)*

zo·ol·o·gy [zuː'ɑːlədʒɪ] zoología *f*

zoom [zuːm] *v/i* F (*move fast*) ir zumbando F

♦ **zoom in on** *v/t* PHOT hacer un zoom sobre

zoom 'lens zoom *m*

zuc·chi·ni [zuː'kiːnɪ] calabacín *m*

Spanish verb conjugations

In the following conjugation patterns verb stems are shown in normal type and verb endings in *italic* type. Irregular forms are indicated by **bold** type.

Notes on the formation of tenses.

The following stems can be used to generate derived forms.

Stem forms	Derived forms
I. From the **Present indicative**, *3rd pers sg* (mand*a*, vend*e*, recib*e*)	**Imperative** *2nd pers. sg* (¡mand*a*! ¡vend*e*! ¡recib*e*!)
II. From the **Present subjunctive**, *2nd* and *3rd pers sg* and all plural forms (mand*es*, mand*e*, mand*emos*, mand*éis*, mand*en* – vend*as*, vend*a*, vend*amos*, vend*áis*, vend*an* – recib*as*, recib*a*, recib*amos*, recib*áis*, recib*an*)	**Imperative** *1st pers pl, 3rd pers sg* and *pl* as well as the negative imperative of the *2nd pers sg* and *pl* (no mand*es*, mand*e* Vd., mand*emos*, no mand*éis*, mand*en* Vds. – no vend*as*, vend*a* Vd., vend*amos*, no vend*áis*, vend*an* Vds. – no recib*as etc*)
III. From the **Preterite**, *3rd pers pl* (mand*aron*, vend*ieron*, recib*ieron*)	a) **Imperfect Subjunctive I** by changing ...ron to ...*ra* (mand*ara*, vend*iera*, recib*iera*) b) **Imperfect Subjunctive II** by changing ...ron to ...*se* (mand*ase*, vend*iese*, recib*iese*) c) **Future Subjunctive** by changing ...ron to ...*re* (mand*are*, vend*iere*, recib*iere*)
IV. From the **Infinitive** (mand*ar*, vend*er*, recib*ir*)	a) **Imperative** *2nd pers pl* by changing ...r to ...*d* (mand*ad*, vend*ed*, recib*id*) b) **Present participle** by changing ...ar to ...*ando*, ...er and ...ir to ...*iendo* (or sometimes ...*yendo*) (mand*ando*, vend*iendo*, recib*iendo*) c) **Future** by adding the *Present* tense endings of **haber** (mand*aré*, vend*eré*, recib*iré*) d) **Conditional** by adding the *Imperfect* endings of **haber** (mand*aría*, vend*ería*, recib*iría*)
V. From the **Past participle** (mand*ado*, vend*ido*, recib*ido*)	all **compound tenses** by placing a form of **haber** or **ser** in front of the participle.

First Conjugation

<1a> **mandar.** No change to the written or spoken form of the stem.

Simple tenses

Indicative

	Present	Imperfect	Preterite
sg	mando	mandaba	mandé
	mandas	mandabas	mandaste
	manda	mandaba	mandó
pl	mandamos	mandábamos	mandamos
	mandáis	mandabais	mandasteis
	mandan	mandaban	mandaron

	Future	Conditional
sg	mandaré	mandaría
	mandarás	mandarías
	mandará	mandaría
pl	mandaremos	mandaríamos
	mandaréis	mandaríais
	mandarán	mandarían

Subjunctive

	Present	Imperfect I	Imperfect II
sg	mande	mandara	mandase
	mandes	mandaras	mandases
	mande	mandara	mandase
pl	mandemos	mandáramos	mandásemos
	mandéis	mandarais	mandaseis
	manden	mandaran	mandasen

	Future	Imperative
sg	mandare	—
	mandares	manda (no mandes)
	mandare	mande Vd.
pl	mandáremos	mandemos
	mandareis	mandad (no mandéis)
	mandaren	manden Vds.

Infinitive: mandar
Present participle: mandando
Past participle: mandado

Compound tenses

1. **Active forms:** the conjugated form of **haber** is placed before the *Past participle* (which does not change):

Indicative

Perfect	*he* mand*ado*	**Future perfect**	*habré* mand*ado*
Pluperfect	*había* mand*ado*	**Past conditional**	*habría* mand*ado*
Past anterior	*hube* mand*ado*		
Past infinitive	*haber* mand*ado*	**Past gerundive**	*habiendo* mand*ado*

Subjunctive

Perfect	*haya* mand*ado*	**Future perfect**	*hubiere* mand*ado*
Pluperfect	*hubiera* mand*ado*		
	hubiese mand*ado*		

2. **Passive forms:** the conjugated form of **ser** (or **haber**) is placed before the *Past participle* (which does not change):

Indicative

Present	*soy* mand*ado*	**Past anterior**	*hube sido* mand*ado*
Imperfect	*era* mand*ado*	**Future**	*seré* mand*ado*
Preterite	*fui* mand*ado*	**Future perfect**	*habré sido* mand*ado*
Perfect	*he sido* mand*ado*	**Conditional**	*sería* mand*ado*
Pluperfect	*había sido* mand*ado*	**Past conditional**	*habría sido* mand*ado*

Infinitive		Gerundive	
Present	*ser* mand*ado* etc	**Present**	*siendo* mand*ado*
Past	*haber sido* mand*ado*	**Past**	*habiendo sido* mand*ado*

Subjunctive

Present	*sea* mand*ado*	**Pluperfect**	*hubiera sido* mand*ado*
			hubiese sido mand*ado*
Imperfect	*fuera* mand*ado*		
	fuese mand*ado*		
Future	*fuere* mand*ado*	**Future perfect**	*hubiere sido* mand*ado*
Past	*haya sido* mand*ado*		

	Infinitive	Present Indicative	Present Subjunctive	Preterite
<1b>	cambiar. Model for all ...*iar* verbs, unless formed like *variar* <1c>.			
		cambio	cambie	cambié
		cambias	cambies	cambiaste
		cambia	cambie	cambió
		cambiamos	cambiemos	cambiamos
		cambiáis	cambiéis	cambiasteis
		cambian	cambien	cambiaron

	Infinitive	Present Indicative	Present Subjunctive	Preterite

\<1c\> **variar.** *i* becomes *í* when the stem is stressed.

		varío	varíe	varié
		varías	varíes	variaste
		varía	varíe	varió
		variamos	variemos	variamos
		variáis	variéis	variasteis
		varían	varíen	variaron

\<1d\> **evacuar.** Model for all *...uar* verbs, unless formed like *acentuar* \<1e\>.

		evacuo	evacue	evacué
		evacuas	evacues	evacuaste
		evacua	evacue	evacuó
		evacuamos	evacuemos	evacuamos
		evacuáis	evacuéis	evacuasteis
		evacuan	evacuen	evacuaron

\<1e\> **acentuar.** *u* becomes *ú* when the stem is stressed.

		acentúo	acentúe	acentué
		acentúas	acentúes	acentuaste
		acentúa	acentúe	acentuó
		acentuamos	acentuemos	acentuamos
		acentuáis	acentuéis	acentuasteis
		acentúan	acentúen	acentuaron

\<1f\> **cruzar.** Final *z* in the stem becomes *c* before *e*. Model for all *...zar* verbs.

		cruzo	cruce	crucé
		cruzas	cruces	cruzaste
		cruza	cruce	cruzó
		cruzamos	crucemos	cruzamos
		cruzáis	crucéis	cruzasteis
		cruzan	crucen	cruzaron

\<1g\> **tocar.** Final *c* in the stem becomes *qu* before *e*. Model for all *...car* verbs.

		toco	toque	toqué
		tocas	toques	tocaste
		toca	toque	tocó
		tocamos	toquemos	tocamos
		tocáis	toquéis	tocasteis
		tocan	toquen	tocaron

	Infinitive	Present Indicative	Present Subjunctive	Preterite

\<1h\> pagar. Final *g* in the stem becomes *gu* (*u* is silent) before *e*. Model for all ...*gar* verbs.

pago	pague	pagué
pagas	pagues	pagaste
paga	pague	pagó
pagamos	paguemos	pagamos
pagáis	paguéis	pagasteis
pagan	paguen	pagaron

\<1i\> fraguar. Final *gu* in the stem becomes *gü* before *e* (*u* with dieresis is pronounced). Model for all ...*guar* verbs.

fraguo	fragüe	fragüé
fraguas	fragües	fraguaste
fragua	fragüe	fraguó
fraguamos	fragüemos	fraguamos
fraguáis	fragüéis	fraguasteis
fraguan	fragüen	fraguaron

\<1k\> pensar. Stressed *e* in the stem becomes *ie*.

pienso	piense	pensé
piensas	pienses	pensaste
piensa	piense	pensó
pensamos	pensemos	pensamos
pensáis	penséis	pensasteis
piensan	piensen	pensaron

\<1l\> errar. Stressed *e* in the stem becomes *ye* (because it comes at the beginning of the word).

yerro	yerre	erré
yerras	yerres	erraste
yerra	yerre	erró
erramos	erremos	erramos
erráis	erréis	errasteis
yerran	yerren	erraron

\<1m\> contar. Stressed *o* of the stem becomes *ue* (*u* is pronounced).

cuento	cuente	conté
cuentas	cuentes	contaste
cuenta	cuente	contó
contamos	contemos	contamos
contáis	contéis	contasteis
cuentan	cuenten	contaron

	Infinitive	Present Indicative	Present Subjunctive	Preterite

<1n> **agorar.** Stressed *o* of the stem becomes *üe* (*u* with dieresis is pronounced).

	agüero	agüere	agoré
	agüeras	agüeres	agoraste
	agüera	agüere	agoró
	agoramos	agoremos	agoramos
	agoráis	agoréis	agorasteis
	agüeran	agüeren	agoraron

<1o> **jugar.** Stressed *u* in the stem becomes *ue*; final *g* of the stem becomes *gu* before *e*: (*see* <1h>); *conjugar*, *enjugar* and *enjugarse* are regular.

	juego	juegue	jugué
	juegas	juegues	jugaste
	juega	juegue	jugó
	jugamos	juguemos	jugamos
	jugáis	juguéis	jugasteis
	juegan	jueguen	jugaron

<1p> **estar.** *Present indicative 1st pers sg* in *...oy*, otherwise regular, but note the stressed *a*; the *Present subjunctive* has a stress on the *e* in the endings (apart from *1st pers pl*); *Preterite etc* as <21>. Otherwise regular.

	estoy	esté	estuve
	estás	estés	estuviste
	está	esté	estuvo
	estamos	estemos	estuvimos
	estáis	estéis	estuvisteis
	están	estén	estuvieron

<1q> **andar.** *Preterite* and derived forms like *estar* as in <21>. Otherwise regular.

	ando	ande	anduve
	andas	andes	anduviste
	anda	ande	anduvo
	andamos	andemos	anduvimos
	andáis	andéis	anduvisteis
	andan	anden	anduvieron

<1r> **dar.** *Present indicative 1st pers sg* in *...oy*, otherwise regular. *Present subjunctive 1st* and *3rd pers sg* takes an accent. *Preterite etc* follow the regular second conjugation. Otherwise regular.

	doy	dé	di
	das	des	diste
	da	dé	dio
	damos	demos	dimos
	dáis	deis	disteis
	dan	den	dieron

Second Conjugation

<2a> vender. No change to the written or spoken form of the stem.

Simple tenses

Indicative

	Present	**Imperfect**	**Preterite**
sg	vendo	vendía	vendí
	vendes	vendías	vendiste
	vende	vendía	vendió
pl	vendemos	vendíamos	vendimos
	vendéis	vendíais	vendisteis
	venden	vendían	vendieron

	Future	**Conditional**
sg	venderé	vendería
	venderás	venderías
	venderá	vendería
pl	venderemos	venderíamos
	venderéis	venderíais
	venderán	venderían

Subjunctive

	Present	**Imperfect I**	**Imperfect II**
sg	venda	vendiera	vendiese
	vendas	vendieras	vendieses
	venda	vendiera	vendiese
pl	vendamos	vendiéramos	vendiésemos
	vendáis	vendierais	vendieseis
	vendan	vendieran	vendiesen

	Future	**Imperative**
sg	vendiere	—
	vendieres	vende (no vendas)
	vendiere	venda Vd.
pl	vendiéremos	vendamos
	vendiereis	vended (no vendáis)
	vendieren	vendan Vds.

Infinitive: vender
Present participle: vendiendo
Past participle: vendido

Compound tenses

Formed with the *Past participle* together with **haber** and **ser**; see <1a>.

Infinitive	Present Indicative	Present Subjunctive	Preterite

<2b> vencer. Final *c* of the stem becomes *z* before *a* and *o*. Model for all ...*cer* verbs where the ...*cer* is preceded by a consonant.

	venzo	venza	vencí
	vences	venzas	venciste
	vence	venza	venció
	vencemos	venzamos	vencimos
	vencéis	venzáis	vencisteis
	vencen	venzan	vencieron

<2c> coger. Final *g* of the stem becomes *j* before *a* and *o*. Model for all ...*ger* verbs.

	cojo	coja	cogí
	coges	cojas	cogiste
	coge	coja	cogió
	cogemos	cojamos	cogimos
	cogéis	cojáis	cogisteis
	cogen	cojan	cogieron

<2d> merecer. Final *c* of the stem becomes *zc* before *a* and *o*.

	merezco	merezca	merecí
	mereces	merezcas	mereciste
	merece	merezca	mereció
	merecemos	merezcamos	merecimos
	merecéis	merezcáis	merecisteis
	merecen	merezcan	merecieron

<2e> creer. Unstressed *i* between two vowels becomes *y*. Past participle: *creído*. Present participle: *creyendo*.

	creo	crea	creí
	crees	creas	creíste
	cree	crea	creyó
	creemos	creamos	creímos
	creéis	creáis	creísteis
	creen	crean	creyeron

<2f> tañer. Unstressed *i* is omitted after *ñ* and *ll*; compare <3h> Present participle: *tañendo*.

	taño	taña	tañí
	tañes	tañas	tañiste
	tañe	taña	**tañó**
	tañemos	tañamos	tañimos
	tañéis	tañáis	tañisteis
	tañen	tañan	**tañeron**

	Infinitive	Present Indicative	Present Subjunctive	Preterite

\<2g\> **perder.** Stressed *e* in the stem becomes *ie*; model for many other verbs.

		pierdo	pierda	perdí
		pierdes	pierdas	perdiste
		pierde	pierda	perdió
		perdemos	perdamos	perdimos
		perdéis	perdáis	perdisteis
		pierden	pierdan	perdieron

\<2h\> **mover.** Stressed *o* in the stem becomes *ue*. ...*olver* verbs form their *Past participle* with ...*uelto*.

		muevo	mueva	moví
		mueves	muevas	moviste
		mueve	mueva	movió
		movemos	movamos	movimos
		movéis	mováis	movisteis
		mueven	muevan	movieron

\<2i\> **oler.** Stressed *o* in the stem becomes *hue*... (when it comes at the beginning of the word).

		huelo	huela	olí
		hueles	huelas	oliste
		huele	huela	olió
		olemos	olamos	olimos
		oléis	oláis	olisteis
		huelen	huelan	olieron

\<2k\> **haber.** Many irregular forms. In the *Future* and *Conditional* the *e* after the stem *hab*... is dropped. Future: *habré*. Imperative *2nd pers sg*: *he*.

		he	haya	hube
		has	hayas	hubiste
		ha	haya	hubo
		hemos	hayamos	hubimos
		habéis	hayáis	hubisteis
		han	hayan	hubieron

\<2l\> **tener.** Irregular in most forms. In the *Future* and *Conditional* the *e* coming after the stem is dropped and a *d* is inserted. Future: *tendré*. Imperative *2nd pers sg*: *ten*.

		tengo	tenga	tuve
		tienes	tengas	tuviste
		tiene	tenga	tuvo
		tenemos	tengamos	tuvimos
		tenéis	tengáis	tuvisteis
		tienen	tengan	tuvieron

	Infinitive	Present Indicative	Present Subjunctive	Preterite

<2m> caber. Irregular in many forms. In the *Future* and *Conditional* the *e* coming after the stem is dropped. Future: *cabré*.

		quep*o*	quep*a*	cupe
		cab*es*	quep*as*	cup*iste*
		cab*e*	quep*a*	cup*o*
		cab*emos*	quep*amos*	cup*imos*
		cab*éis*	quep*áis*	cup*isteis*
		cab*en*	quep*an*	cup*ieron*

<2n> saber. Irregular in many forms. In the *Future* and *Conditional* the *e* coming after the stem is dropped. Future: *sabré*.

		s**é**	sep*a*	supe
		sab*es*	sep*as*	sup*iste*
		sab*e*	sep*a*	sup*o*
		sab*emos*	sep*amos*	sup*imos*
		sab*éis*	sep*áis*	sup*isteis*
		sab*en*	sep*an*	sup*ieron*

<2o> caer. In the *Present* ...*ig*... is inserted after the stem. Unstressed *i* between vowels changes to *y* as with <2e>. Past participle: *caído*. Present participle: *cayendo*.

		cai**g***o*	cai**g***a*	caí
		cae*s*	cai**g***as*	caíste
		cae	cai**g***a*	cayó
		cae*mos*	cai**g***amos*	caímos
		caé*is*	cai**g***áis*	caísteis
		cae*n*	cai**g***an*	cayeron

<2p> traer. In the *Present* ...*ig*... is inserted after the stem. The *Preterite* ends in ...*je*. In the *Present participle i* changes to *y*. Past participle: *traído*. Present participle: *trayendo*.

		trai**g***o*	trai**g***a*	traje
		trae*s*	trai**g***as*	traj*iste*
		trae	trai**g***a*	traj*o*
		trae*mos*	trai**g***amos*	traj*imos*
		traé*is*	trai**g***áis*	traj*isteis*
		trae*n*	trai**g***an*	traj*eron*

<2q> valer. In the *Present* ...*g*... is inserted after the stem. In the *Future* and *Conditional* the *e* coming after the stem is dropped and a ...*d*... inserted. Future: *valdré*.

		val**g***o*	val**g***a*	valí
		val*es*	val**g***as*	val*iste*
		val*e*	val**g***a*	val*ió*
		val*emos*	val**g***amos*	val*imos*
		val*éis*	val**g***áis*	val*isteis*
		val*en*	val**g***an*	val*ieron*

	Infinitive	Present Indicative	Present Subjunctive	Preterite

\<2r\> **poner.** ...*g*... is inserted in the *Present*. Irregular in the *Preterite* and *Past participle*. In the *Future* and *Conditional* the *e* coming after the stem is dropped and a ...*d*... inserted. Future: *pondré*. Past participle: *puesto*. Imperative *2nd pers sg*: *pon*.

pon*go*	pong*a*	puse
pon*es*	pong*as*	pus*iste*
pone	pong*a*	puso
pon*emos*	pong*amos*	pus*imos*
pon*éis*	pong*áis*	pus*isteis*
pon*en*	pong*an*	pus*ieron*

\<2s\> **hacer.** In the *1st* person of the *Present Indicative* and *Subjunctive* *g* replaces *c*. Irregular in the *Preterite* and *Past participle*. In the *Future* and *Conditional* the *ce* is dropped. In the *Imperative sg* just the stem is used with ...*c* changing to ...*z*. Future: *haré*. Imperative *2nd pers sg*: *haz*. Past participle: *hecho*.

ha*go*	hag*a*	hice
hac*es*	hag*as*	hic*iste*
hace	hag*a*	hizo
hac*emos*	hag*amos*	hic*imos*
hac*éis*	hag*áis*	hic*isteis*
hac*en*	hag*an*	hic*ieron*

\<2t\> **poder.** Stressed *o* in the stem changes to ...*ue*... in the *Present* and the *Imperative*. Irregular in the *Preterite* and *Present participle*. In the *Future* and *Conditional* the *e* coming after the stem is dropped. Future: *podré*. Present participle: *pudiendo*.

pued*o*	pued*a*	pude
pued*es*	pued*as*	pud*iste*
pued*e*	pued*a*	pudo
pod*emos*	pod*amos*	pud*imos*
pod*éis*	pod*áis*	pud*isteis*
pued*en*	pued*an*	pud*ieron*

\<2u\> **querer.** Stressed *e* in the stem changes to *ie* in the *Present* and *Imperative*. Irregular in the *Preterite*. In the *Future* and *Conditional* the *e* coming after the stem is dropped. Future: *querré*.

quier*o*	quier*a*	quise
quier*es*	quier*as*	quis*iste*
quier*e*	quier*a*	quiso
quer*emos*	quer*amos*	quis*imos*
quer*éis*	quer*áis*	quis*isteis*
quier*en*	quier*an*	quis*ieron*

	Infinitive	Present Indicative	Present Subjunctive	Preterite

<2v> **ver.** *Present indicative 1st pers sg*, *Present subjunctive* and *Imperfect* are formed on the stem *ve...*, otherwise formation is regular using the shortened stem *v...* Irregular in the *Past participle*. Past participle: *visto*.

ve*o*	ve*a*	v*i*
ve*s*	ve*as*	v*iste*
ve	ve*a*	v*io*
ve*mos*	ve*amos*	v*imos*
ve*is*	ve*áis*	v*isteis*
ve*n*	ve*an*	v*ieron*

Infinitive	Present Indicative	Present Subjunctive	Imperfect Indicative	Preterite

<2w> **ser.** Totally irregular with several different stems being used. Past participle: *sido*. Imperative *2nd pers sg*: *sé*. *2nd pers pl*: *sed*.

so*y*	se*a*	er*a*	fu*i*
er*es*	se*as*	er*as*	fu*iste*
es	se*a*	er*a*	fu*e*
so*mos*	se*amos*	ér*amos*	fu*imos*
so*is*	se*áis*	er*ais*	fu*isteis*
so*n*	se*an*	er*an*	fu*eron*

<2x> **placer.** Used almost exclusively in the *3rd pers sg*. Irregular forms: *Present subjunctive* pl*ega* and pl*egue* as well as *plazca*; *Preterite* pl*ugo* (or *plació*), pl*ugieron* (or *placieron*); *Imperfect subjunctive* pl*uguiera*, pl*uguiese* (or *placiera*, *placiese*); *Future subjunctive* pl*uguiere* (or *placiere*).

<2y> **yacer.** Used mainly on gravestones and so used primarily in the *3rd pers*. The *Present indicative 1st pers sg* and *Present subjunctive* have three forms. The *Imperative* is regular; just the stem with *c* changing to *z*. *Present indicative*: ya*zco*, ya*zgo*, ya*go*, ya*ces* etc; *Present subjunctive*: ya*zca*, ya*zga*, ya*ga* etc; *Imperative* ya*ce* and ya*z*.

<2z> **raer.** The regular forms of the *Present indicative 1st pers sg* and *Present subjunctive* are less common that the forms with inserted *...ig...* as in <2o>: ra*igo*, ra*iga*; but also ra*yo*, ra*ya* (less common). Otherwise regular.

<2za> **roer.** As well as their regular forms the *Present indicative 1st pers sg* and *Present subjunctive* have the less common forms: ro*igo*, ro*iga*, ro*yo*, ro*ya*.

Third Conjugation

\<3a\> recibir. No change to the written or spoken form of the stem.

Simple tenses

Indicative

	Present	**Imperfect**	**Preterite**
sg	recib*o*	recib*ía*	recib*í*
	recib*es*	recib*ías*	recib*iste*
	recib*e*	recib*ía*	recib*ió*
pl	recib*imos*	recib*íamos*	recib*imos*
	recib*ís*	recib*íais*	recib*isteis*
	recib*en*	recib*ían*	recib*ieron*

	Future	**Conditional**
sg	recib*iré*	recib*iría*
	recib*irás*	recib*irías*
	recib*irá*	recib*iría*
pl	recib*iremos*	recib*iríamos*
	recib*iréis*	recib*iríais*
	recib*irán*	recib*irían*

Subjunctive

	Present	**Imperfect I**	**Imperfect II**
sg	recib*a*	recib*iera*	recib*iese*
	recib*as*	recib*ieras*	recib*ieses*
	recib*a*	recib*iera*	recib*iese*
pl	recib*amos*	recib*iéramos*	recib*iésemos*
	recib*áis*	recib*ierais*	recib*ieseis*
	recib*an*	recib*ieran*	recib*iesen*

	Future	**Imperative**
sg	recib*iere*	—
	recib*ieres*	recib*e* (no recib*as*)
	recib*iere*	recib*a* Vd.
pl	recib*iéremos*	recib*amos*
	recib*iereis*	recib*id* (no recib*áis*)
	recib*ieren*	recib*an* Vds.

Infinitive : recib*ir*
Present participle : recib*iendo*
Past participle : recib*ido*

Compound tenses

Formed with the *Past participle* together with **haber** and **ser**, see \<1a\>.

	Infinitive	Present Indicative	Present Subjunctive	Preterite

\<3b\> **esparcir.** Final *c* of the stem becomes *z* before *a* and *o*.

		esparz*o*	esparz*a*	esparcí
		esparc*es*	esparz*as*	esparc*iste*
		esparc*e*	esparz*a*	esparc*ió*
		esparc*imos*	esparz*amos*	esparc*imos*
		esparc*ís*	esparz*áis*	esparc*isteis*
		esparc*en*	esparz*an*	esparc*ieron*

\<3c\> **dirigir.** Final *g* of the stem becomes *j* before *a* and *o*.

		dirij*o*	dirij*a*	dirigí
		dirig*es*	dirij*as*	dirig*iste*
		dirig*e*	dirij*a*	dirig*ió*
		dirig*imos*	dirij*amos*	dirig*imos*
		dirig*ís*	dirij*áis*	dirig*isteis*
		dirig*en*	dirij*an*	dirig*ieron*

\<3d\> **distinguir.** Final *gu* of the stem becomes *g* before *a* and *o*.

		disting*o*	disting*a*	distinguí
		distingu*es*	disting*as*	distingu*iste*
		distingu*e*	disting*a*	distingu*ió*
		distingu*imos*	disting*amos*	distingu*imos*
		distingu*ís*	disting*áis*	distingu*isteis*
		distingu*en*	disting*an*	distingu*ieron*

\<3e\> **delinquir.** Final *qu* of the stem becomes *c* before *a* and *o*.

		delinc*o*	delinc*a*	delinquí
		delinqu*es*	delinc*as*	delinqu*iste*
		delinqu*e*	delinc*a*	delinqu*ió*
		delinqu*imos*	delinc*amos*	delinqu*imos*
		delinqu*ís*	delinc*áis*	delinqu*isteis*
		delinqu*en*	delinc*an*	delinqu*ieron*

\<3f\> **lucir.** Final *c* of the stem becomes *zc* before *a* and *o*.

		luzc*o*	luzc*a*	lucí
		luc*es*	luzc*as*	luc*iste*
		luc*e*	luzc*a*	luc*ió*
		luc*imos*	luzc*amos*	luc*imos*
		luc*ís*	luzc*áis*	luc*isteis*
		luc*en*	luzc*an*	luc*ieron*

\<3g\> **concluir.** A *y* is inserted after the stem unless the ending begins with *i*. Past participle: *concluido*. Present participle: *concluyendo*.

		concluy*o*	concluy*a*	concluí
		concluy*es*	concluy*as*	conclu*iste*
		concluy*e*	concluy*a*	conclu*yó*
		conclu*imos*	concluy*amos*	conclu*imos*
		conclu*ís*	concluy*áis*	conclu*isteis*
		concluy*en*	concluy*an*	conclu*yeron*

	Infinitive	Present Indicative	Present Subjunctive	Preterite

<3h> gruñir. Unstressed *i* is dropped after *ñ*, *ll* and *ch*. Likewise *mullir*: *mulló*, *mulleron*, *mullendo*; *henchir*: *hinchó*, *hincheron*, *hinchendo*. Present participle: *gruñendo*.

gruño	gruña	gruñí
gruñes	gruñas	gruñiste
gruñe	gruña	**gruñó**
gruñimos	gruñamos	gruñimos
gruñís	gruñáis	gruñisteis
gruñen	gruñan	**gruñeron**

<3i> sentir. Stressed *e* of the stem becomes *ie*; unstressed *e* remains unchanged before endings starting with *i*, but before other endings it changes to ...*i*...; likewise *adquirir*: stressed *i* of the stem becomes *ie*; unstressed *i* remains unchanged in all forms. Present participle: *sintiendo*.

siento	sienta	sentí
sientes	sientas	sentiste
siente	sienta	sintió
sentimos	sintamos	sentimos
sentís	sintáis	sentisteis
sienten	sientan	sintieron

<3k> dormir. Stressed *o* of the stem becomes *ue*; unstressed *o* is unchanged when the ending starts with *i*; otherwise it changes to ...*u*... Present participle: *durmiendo*.

duermo	duerma	dormí
duermes	duermas	dormiste
duerme	duerma	*durmió*
dormimos	durmamos	dormimos
dormís	durmáis	dormisteis
duermen	duerman	*durmieron*

<3l> medir. The *e* of the stem is kept if the ending contains an *i*. Otherwise it changes to ...*i*... whether stressed or unstressed. Present participle: *midiendo*.

mido	mida	medí
mides	midas	mediste
mide	mida	midió
medimos	midamos	medimos
medís	midáis	medisteis
miden	midan	midieron

	Infinitive	Present Indicative	Present Subjunctive	Preterite

<3m> reír. As *medir* <3l>; when *e* changes to *i* any second *i* belonging to the ending is dropped. Past participle: *reído*. Present participle: *riendo*.

río	ría	reí
ríes	rías	reíste
ríe	ría	rió
reímos	riamos	reímos
reís	riáis	reísteis
ríen	rían	rieron

<3n> erguir. As *medir* in the *Present indicative*, *Subjunctive* and *Imperative*. Other forms follow *sentir* with initial *ie...* changing to *ye...* Present participle: *irguiendo*. Imperative: *irgue*, *yergue*.

irgo, yergo	irga, yerga	erguí
irgues, yergues	irgas, yergas	erguiste
irgue, yergue	irga, yerga	irguió
erguimos	irgamos, yergamos	erguimos
erguís	irgáis, yergáis	erguisteis
irguen, yerguen	irgan, yergan	irguieron

<3o> conducir. Final *c* of the stem, as with *lucir* (3f), becomes *zc* before *a* and *o*. *Preterite* is irregular with *...je*.

conduzco	conduzca	conduje
conduces	conduzcas	condujiste
conduce	conduzca	condujo
conducimos	conduzcamos	condujimos
conducís	conduzcáis	condujisteis
conducen	conduzcan	condujeron

<3p> decir. In the *Present* and *Imperative e* and *i* are changed, as with *medir*; in the *Present indicative 1st pers sg* and in the *Present subjunctive c* becomes *g*. Irregular *Future* and *Conditional* based on a shortened *Infinitive*. *Preterite* has *je*. Future: *diré*. Past participle: *dicho*. Present participle: *diciendo*. Imperative *2nd pers sg*: *di*.

digo	diga	dije
dices	digas	dijiste
dice	diga	dijo
decimos	digamos	dijimos
decís	digáis	dijisteis
dicen	digan	dijeron

	Infinitive	Present Indicative	Present Subjunctive	Preterite

<3q> oír. In the *Present indicative 1st pers sg* and *Present subjunctive ...ig...* is inserted after the *o...* of the stem. Unstressed *...i...* changes to *...y...* when coming between two vowels. Past participle: *oído.* Present participle: *oyendo.*

oigo	oiga	oí
oyes	oigas	oíste
oye	oiga	oyó
oímos	oigamos	oímos
oís	oigáis	oísteis
oyen	oigan	oyeron

<3r> salir. In the *Present indicative 1st pers sg* and the *Present subjunctive* a *...g...* is inserted after the stem. In the *Future* and *Conditional* the *i* is replaced by *d*. Future: *saldré.* Imperative: *2nd pers sg*: *sal.*

salgo	salga	salí
sales	salgas	saliste
sale	salga	salió
salimos	salgamos	salimos
salís	salgáis	salisteis
salen	salgan	salieron

	Infinitive	Present Indicative	Present Subjunctive	Imperfect Indicative	Preterite

<3s> venir. In the *Present* two changes: either a *...g...* is inserted after the stem or *e,ie* and *i* follow the same changes as *sentir*. In the *Future* and *Conditional* the *i* is dropped and replaced by *d*. Future: *vendré.* Present participle: *viniendo.* Imperative *2nd pers sg*: *ven.*

vengo	venga	venía	vine
vienes	vengas	venías	viniste
viene	venga	venía	vino
venimos	vengamos	veníamos	vinimos
venís	vengáis	veníais	vinisteis
vienen	vengan	venían	vinieron

<3t> ir. Totally irregular with several different stems being used. Present participle: *yendo*

voy	vaya	iba	fui
vas	vayas	ibas	fuiste
va	vaya	iba	fue
vamos	vayamos	íbamos	fuimos
vais	vayáis	ibais	fuisteis
van	vayan	iban	fueron

Imperative: **ve** (no **vayas**), **vaya** Vd, **vamos**, *id* (no **vayáis**), **vayan** Vds.

Notas sobre el verbo inglés

a) Conjugación

1. **El tiempo presente** tiene la misma forma que el infinitivo en todas las personas menos la 3ª del singular; en ésta, se añade una -*s* al infinitivo, p.ej. *he brings*, o se añade -*es* si el infinitivo termina en sibilante (ch, sh, ss, zz), p.ej. *he passes*. Esta *s* tiene dos pronunciaciones distintas: tras consonante sorda se pronuncia sorda, p.ej. *he paints* [peɪnts]; tras consonante sonora se pronuncia sonora, *he sends* [sendz]; -*es* se pronuncia también sonora, sea la *e* parte de la desinencia o letra final del infinitivo, p.ej. *he washes* ['wɑːʃɪz], *he urges* ['ɜːrdʒɪz]. Los verbos que terminan en -*y* la cambian en -*ies* en la tercera persona, p.ej. *he worries, he tries*, pero son regulares los verbos que en el infinitivo tienen una vocal delante de la -*y*, p.ej. *he plays*. El verbo *to be* es irregular en todas las personas: *I am, you are, he is, we are, you are, they are*. Tres verbos más tienen forma especial para la tercera persona del singular: *do-he does, go-he goes, have-he has*.

   En los demás tiempos, todas las personas son iguales. **El pretérito** y **el participio del pasado** se forman añadiendo -*ed* al infinitivo, p.ej. *I passed, passed*, o añadiendo -*d* a los infinitivos que terminan en -*e*, p.ej. *I faced, faced*. (Hay muchos verbos irregulares: v. abajo). Esta -*(e)d* se pronuncia generalmente como [t]: *passed* [pæst], *faced* [feɪst]; pero cuando se añade a un infinitivo que termina en consonante sonora o en un sonido consonántico sonoro o en *r*, se pronuncia como [d]: *warmed* [wɔːrmd], *moved* [muːvd], *feared* [fɪrd]. Si el infinitivo termina en -*d* o -*t*, la desinencia -*ed* se pronuncia [ɪd]. Si el infinitivo termina en -*y*, ésta se cambia en -*ie*, antes de añadirse la -*d*: *try-tried* [traɪd], *pity-pitied* ['pɪtiːd]. **Los tiempos compuestos del pasado** se forman con el verbo auxiliar *have* y el participio del pasado, como en español: **perfecto** *I have faced*, **pluscuamperfecto** *I had faced*. Con el verbo auxiliar *will* (*shall*) y el infinitivo se forma **el futuro**, p.ej. *I shall face*; y con el verbo auxiliar *would* (*should*) y el infinitivo se forma **el condicional**, p.ej. *I should face*. En cada tiempo existe además una forma continua que se forma con el verbo *be* (= estar) y el participio del presente (v. abajo): *I am going, I was writing, I had been staying, I shall be waiting*, etc.

2. **El subjuntivo** ha dejado casi de existir en inglés, salvo en algún caso especial (*if I were you, so be it, it is proposed that a vote be taken*, etc.). En el presente, tiene en todas las personas la misma forma que el infinitivo, *that I go, that he go*, etc.

3. **El participio del presente** y **el gerundio** tienen la misma forma en inglés, añadiéndose al infinitivo la desinencia -*ing*: *painting, sending*. Pero 1) Los verbos cuyo infinitivo termina en -*e* mudan la pierden al añadir -*ing*, p.ej. *love-loving, write-writing* (excepciones que conservan la -*e*: *dye-dyeing, singe-singeing*); 2) El participio del presente de los verbos *die, lie, vie*, etc. se escribe *dying, lying, vying*, etc.

4. Existe una clase de verbos ligeramente irregulares, que terminan en consonante simple precedida de vocal simple acentuada; en éstos, antes de añadir la desinencia *-ing* o *-ed*, se dobla la consonante:

lob	lob*bed*	lob*bing*	compel	compel*led*	compel*ling*
wed	wed*ded*	wed*ding*	control	control*led*	control*ling*
beg	beg*ged*	beg*ging*	bar	bar*red*	bar*ring*
step	step*ped*	step*ping*	stir	stir*red*	stir*ring*
quit	quit*ted*	quit*ting*			

Los verbos que terminan en *-l*, *-p*, aunque precedida de vocal átona, tienen doblada la consonante en los dos participios en el inglés escrito en Gran Bretaña, aunque no en el de Estados Unidos:

travel	trave*l*ed,	trave*l*ing,
	Br travel*led*,	*Br* travel*ling*

Los verbos que terminan en *-c* la cambian en *-ck* al añadirse las desinencias *-ed*, *-ing*:

traffic	traffi*ck*ed	traffi*ck*ing

5. **La voz pasiva** se forma exactamente como en español, con el verbo *be* y el participio del pasado: *I am obliged*, *he was fined*, *they will be moved*, etc.

6. Cuando se dirige uno directamente a otra(s) persona(s) en inglés se emplea únicamente el pronombre *you*. *You* se traduce por el *tú*, *vosotros*, *usted* y *ustedes* del español.

b) Los verbos irregulares ingleses

Se citan las tres partes principales de cada verbo: infinitivo, pretérito, participio del pasado.

alight - alighted, alit - alighted, alit
arise - arose - arisen
awake - awoke - awoken, awaked
be (am, is, are) - was (were) - been
bear - bore - borne
beat - beat - beaten
become - became - become
begin - began - begun
behold - beheld - beheld
bend - bent - bent
beseech - besought, beseeched - besought, beseeched
bet - bet, betted - bet, betted
bid - bid - bid

bind - bound - bound
bite - bit - bitten
bleed - bled - bled
blow - blew - blown
break - broke - broken
breed - bred - bred
bring - brought - brought
broadcast - broadcast - broadcast
build - built - built
burn - burnt, burned - burnt, burned
burst - burst - burst
bust - bust(ed) - bust(ed)
buy - bought - bought
cast - cast - cast
catch - caught - caught

choose - chose - chosen
cleave (*cut*) - clove, cleft - cloven, cleft
cleave (*adhere*) - cleaved - cleaved
cling - clung - clung
come - came - come
cost (*v/i*) - cost - cost
creep - crept - crept
crow - crowed, crew - crowed
cut - cut - cut
deal - dealt - dealt
dig - dug - dug
do - did - done
draw - drew - drawn
dream - dreamt, dreamed - dreamt, dreamed
drink - drank - drunk
drive - drove - driven
dwell - dwelt, dwelled - dwelt, dwelled
eat - ate - eaten
fall - fell - fallen
feed - fed - fed
feel - felt - felt
fight - fought - fought
find - found - found
flee - fled - fled
fling - flung - flung
fly - flew - flown
forbear - forbore - forborne
forbid - forbad(e) - forbidden
forecast - forecast(ed) - forecast(ed)
forget - forgot - forgotten
forgive - forgave - forgiven
forsake - forsook - forsaken
freeze - froze - frozen
get - got - got, gotten
give - gave - given
go - went - gone
grind - ground - ground
grow - grew - grown
hang - hung, (*v/t*) hanged - hung, (*v/t*) hanged
have - had - had
hear - heard - heard

heave - heaved, NAUT hove - heaved, NAUT hove
hew - hewed - hewed, hewn
hide - hid - hidden
hit - hit - hit
hold - held - held
hurt - hurt - hurt
keep - kept - kept
kneel - knelt, kneeled - knelt, kneeled
know - knew - known
lay - laid - laid
lead - led - led
lean - leaned, leant - leaned, leant
leap - leaped, leapt - leaped, leapt
learn - learned, learnt - learned, learnt
leave - left - left
lend - lent - lent
let - let - let
lie - lay - lain
light - lighted, lit - lighted, lit
lose - lost - lost
make - made - made
mean - meant - meant
meet - met - met
mow - mowed - mowed, mown
pay - paid - paid
plead - pleaded, pled - pleaded, pled
prove - proved - proved, proven
put - put - put
quit - quit(ted) - quit(ted)
read - read [red] - read [red]
rend - rent - rent
rid - rid - rid
ride - rode - ridden
ring - rang - rung
rise - rose - risen
run - ran - run
saw - sawed - sawn, sawed
say - said - said
see - saw - seen
seek - sought - sought
sell - sold - sold
send - sent - sent
set - set - set

sew - sewed - sewed, sewn
shake - shook - shaken
shear - sheared - sheared, shorn
shed - shed - shed
shine - shone - shone
shit - shit(ted), shat - shit(ted), shat
shoe - shod - shod
shoot - shot - shot
show - showed - shown
shrink - shrank - shrunk
shut - shut - shut
sing - sang - sung
sink - sank - sunk
sit - sat - sat
slay - slew - slain
sleep - slept - slept
slide - slid - slid
sling - slung - slung
slink - slunk - slunk
slit - slit - slit
smell - smelt, smelled - smelt, smelled
smite - smote - smitten
sow - sowed - sown, sowed
speak - spoke - spoken
speed - sped, speeded - sped, speeded
spell - spelt, spelled - spelt, spelled
spend - spent - spent
spill - spilt, spilled - spilt, spilled
spin - spun, span - spun
spit - spat - spat
split - split - split
spoil - spoiled, spoilt - spoiled, spoilt
spread - spread - spread
spring - sprang, sprung - sprung

stand - stood - stood
stave - staved, stove - staved, stove
steal - stole - stolen
stick - stuck - stuck
sting - stung - stung
stink - stunk, stank - stunk
strew - strewed - strewed, strewn
stride - strode - stridden
strike - struck - struck
string - strung - strung
strive - strove - striven
swear - swore - sworn
sweep - swept - swept
swell - swelled - swollen
swim - swam - swum
swing - swung - swung
take - took - taken
teach - taught - taught
tear - tore - torn
tell - told - told
think - thought - thought
thrive - throve - thriven
throw - threw - thrown
thrust - thrust - thrust
tread - trod - trodden
understand - understood - understood
wake - woke, waked - woken, waked
wear - wore - worn
weave - wove - woven
wed - wed(ded) - wed(ded)
weep - wept - wept
wet - wet(ted) - wet(ted)
win - won - won
wind - wound - wound
wring - wrung - wrung
write - wrote - written

Numerales – Numbers

Números cardinales – Cardinal Numbers

0	zero, *Br tb* nought *cero*	90	ninety *noventa*
1	one *uno, una*	100	a hundred, one hundred *cien(to)*
2	two *dos*	101	a hundred and one *ciento uno*
3	three *tres*	110	a hundred and ten *ciento diez*
4	four *cuatro*	200	two hundred *doscientos, -as*
5	five *cinco*	300	three hundred *trescientos, -as*
6	six *seis*	400	four hundred *cuatrocientos, -as*
7	seven *siete*	500	five hundred *quinientos, -as*
8	eight *ocho*	600	six hundred *seiscientos, -as*
9	nine *nueve*	700	seven hundred *setecientos, -as*
10	ten *diez*	800	eight hundred *ochocientos, -as*
11	eleven *once*	900	nine hundred *novecientos, -as*
12	twelve *doce*	1000	a thousand, one thousand *mil*
13	thirteen *trece*	1959	one thousand nine hundred and fifty-nine *mil novecientos cincuenta y nueve*
14	fourteen *catorce*		
15	fifteen *quince*		
16	sixteen *dieciséis*		
17	seventeen *diecisiete*		
18	eighteen *dieciocho*		
19	nineteen *diecinueve*		
20	twenty *veinte*		
21	twenty-one *veintiuno*		
22	twenty-two *veintidós*	2000	two thousand *dos mil*
30	thirty *treinta*	1 000 000	a million, one million *un millón*
31	thirty-one *treinta y uno*		
40	forty *cuarenta*		
50	fifty *cincuenta*		
60	sixty *sesenta*	2 000 000	two million *dos millones*
70	seventy *setenta*		
80	eighty *ochenta*		

Notas:

i) En los números ingleses se utiliza un punto para separar los decimales:

1.25   **uno coma veinticinco**   one point two five

ii) Se usa una coma en los lugares en los que en español utilizaríamos un punto:

1,000,000 = 1.000.000 o 1 000 000

Números ordinales – Ordinal Numbers

1st	first	1°	primero
2nd	second	2°	segundo
3rd	third	3°	tercero
4th	fourth	4°	cuarto
5th	fifth	5°	quinto
6th	sixth	6°	sexto
7th	seventh	7°	séptimo
8th	eighth	8°	octavo
9th	ninth	9°	noveno, nono
10th	tenth	10°	décimo
11th	eleventh	11°	undécimo
12th	twelfth	12°	duodécimo
13th	thirteenth	13°	decimotercero
14th	fourteenth	14°	decimocuarto
15th	fifteenth	15°	decimoquinto
16th	sixteenth	16°	decimosexto
17th	seventeenth	17°	decimoséptimo
18th	eighteenth	18°	decimoctavo
19th	nineteenth	19°	decimonoveno, decimonono
20th	twentieth	20°	vigésimo
21st	twenty-first	21°	vigésimo prim(er)o
22nd	twenty-second	22°	vigésimo segundo
30th	thirtieth	30°	trigésimo
31st	thirty-first	31°	trigésimo prim(er)o
40th	fortieth	40°	cuadragésimo
50th	fiftieth	50°	quincuagésimo
60th	sixtieth	60°	sexagésimo
70th	seventieth	70°	septuagésimo
80th	eightieth	80°	octogésimo
90th	ninetieth	90°	nonagésimo
100th	hundredth	10°	centésimo
101st	hundred and first	101°	centésimo primero
110th	hundred and tenth	110°	centésimo décimo
200th	two hundredth	200°	ducentésimo
300th	three hundredth	300°	trecentésimo
400th	four hundredth	400°	cuadringentésimo
500th	five hundredth	500°	quingentésimo
600th	six hundredth	600°	sexcentésimo
700th	seven hundredth	700°	septingentésimo
800th	eight hundredth	800°	octingentésimo
900th	nine hundredth	900°	noningentésimo
1000th	thousandth	1000°	milésimo
2000th	two thousandth	2000°	dos milésimo
1,000,100th	millionth	1 000 100°	millonésimo
2,000,000th	two millionth	2 000 000°	dos millonésimo

Números quebrados y otros – Fractions and other Numerals

½	one half, a half	*medio, media*
1½	one and a half	*uno y medio*
2½	two and a half	*dos y medio*
⅓	one third, a third	*un tercio, la tercera parte*
⅔	two thirds	*dos tercios, las dos terceras partes*
¼	one quarter, a quarter	*un cuarto, la cuarta parte*
¾	three quarters	*tres cuartos, las tres cuartas partes*
⅕	one fifth, a fifth	*un quinto*
3⅘	three and four fifths	*tres y cuatro quintos*
1/11	one eleventh, an eleventh	*un onzavo*
5/12	five twelfths	*cinco dozavos*
1/1000	one thousandth, a thousandth	*un milésimo*
	seven times as big, seven times bigger	*siete veces más grande*
	twelve times more	*doce veces más*
	first(ly)	*en primer lugar*
	second(ly) etc	*en segundo lugar*
7 + 8 = 15	seven and (*or* plus) eight are (*or* is) fifteen	*siete y (or más) ocho son quince*
10 – 3 = 7	ten minus three is seven, three from ten leaves seven	*diez menos tres resta siete, de tres a diez van siete*
2 x 3 = 6	two times three is six	*dos por tres son seis*
20 ÷ 4 = 5	twenty divided by four is five	*veinte dividido por cuatro es cinco*

Fechas – Dates

1996	nineteen ninety-six	*mil novecientos noventa y seis*
2005	two thousand (and) five	*dos mil cinco*

the 10th of November, November 10 (ten)
el diez de noviembre, el 10 de noviembre

the 1st of March, March 1 (first)
el uno de marzo, *L.Am.* el primero de marzo, el 1° de marzo

Headword in **bold** Lema en **negrita**	**A•mer•i•ca** [əˈmerɪkə] *continent* América; *USA* Estados *mpl* Unidos
International Phonetic Alphabet Transcripción fonética	**in•sult 1** *n* [ˈɪnsʌlt] insulto *m* **2** *v/t* [ɪnˈsʌlt] insultar
Translation in normal characters with gender shown in *italics* Traducción en caracteres normales con el género en *cursiva*	**'break•down** *of vehicle, machine* avería *f*; *of talks* ruptura *f*; (*nervous ~*) crisis *f inv* nerviosa; *of figures* desglose *m*
Hyphenation points Indicación de división silábica	**con•sum•er** **con•fi•dence** confianza *f* de los consumidores; **con'sum•er goods** *npl* bienes *mpl* de consumo; **con'sum•er so•ci•e•ty** sociedad *f* de consumo
Stress shown in headwords ' identifica la sílaba acentuada	**'mov•ie thea•ter** cine *m*, sala *f* de cine
Examples and phrases in **bold italics** Ejemplos y frases en **negrita y cursiva**	**i•deal•ly** [aɪˈdɪəlɪ] *adv*: **~ situated** en una posición ideal; **~, we would do it like this** lo ideal sería que lo hiciéramos así
Indicating words in *italics* Indicadores semánticos en *cursiva*	**stub•born** [ˈstʌbən] *adj person* testarudo, terco; *defense, refusal, denial* tenaz, pertinaz
	busi•ness [ˈbɪznɪs] negocios *mpl*; (*company*) empresa *f*; (*sector*) sector *m*; (*affair, matter*) asunto *m*; *as subject of study* empresariales *fpl*; **on ~** de negocios
Swung dash replaces the entire headword La tilde reemplaza al lema	**by•gones** [ˈbaɪgɑːnz]: **let ~ be ~** lo pasado, pasado está **tran•sit** [ˈtrænzɪt]: **in ~** en tránsito